GEOFFREY CHAUCER was born in London about 1340, the son of a well-to-do and well-connected wine merchant. As a boy, he served as a page to the countess of Ulster, and later as a valet in the royal household. In 1360, after his capture while fighting in the French wars, Edward III paid his ransom, and later Chaucer married Philippa de Roet, a maid of honor to the queen and sister-in-law to John of Gaunt, Chaucer's patron.

Chaucer spent many years in royal employment, as comptroller of customs for the port of London, as justice of the peace for Kent, and as a member of Parliament. His appointments took him on various missions to France and Italy, where he encountered the works of Boccaccio, Petrarch, and the poetry of Dante—influences that are manifest in his own writing.

Chaucer's *oeuvre* is commonly divided into three periods: the French (to 1372), consisting of such works as a translation of the *Roman de la Rose* and *The Book of the Duchess;* the Italian (1372–1385), including *The House of Fame, The Parliament of Fowls,* and *Troilus and Criseyde;* and the English (1385–1400), culminating in *The Canterbury Tales*. In 1400, he died, leaving twenty-four of the apparently one hundred and twenty tales he had planned for his final masterpiece. Not all of the twenty-four were completed. Those he completed, however, were sufficient to ensure his enduring reputation. Chaucer became the first of England's great men to be buried in what came to be called the Poet's Corner of Westminster Abbey.

# Geoffrey Chaucer

# THE CANTERBURY TALES

Selected, with translations,
critical introductions, and notes

Edited, introduced, and translated by

*Peter G. Beidler*

building on the earlier edition of
A. Kent Hieatt
and Constance Hieatt

BANTAM CLASSICS

THE CANTERBURY TALES
A Bantam Book

PUBLISHING HISTORY
First Bantam edition published May 1964
Bantam Classic edition / March 1981
Bantam Classic reissue / May 2006

Published by Bantam Dell
A Division of Random House, Inc.
New York, New York

This is a work of fiction. Names, characters, places, and incidents either are the product of the author's imagination or are used fictitiously. Any resemblance to actual persons, living or dead, events, or locales is entirely coincidental.

ISBN-10: 0-553-21082-3
ISBN-13: 978-0-553-21082-8

Printed in the United States of America
Published simultaneously in Canada

www.bantamdell.com

OPM   45

# THE
# CANTERBURY TALES

❦

# PREFACE

## ❦

THIS EDITION builds on the excellent work that A. Kent Hieatt and his wife, Constance Hieatt, did for the first Bantam edition more than four decades ago. It shares their broad goals as expressed in the preface to that edition:

> What we offer here speeds comprehension, so that more can be read, and provides flexibility, so that parts can be read in the original and parts in translation if necessary. We think that a facing-page translation will bring understanding of the original faster than do marginal glossing and notes at the bottom of the page, because these latter aids often do not clarify some of the syntactical relationships that leave most beginners at sea.

Although I have made a few small changes in the edition and the translations that the Hieatts provided to *The Canterbury Tales,* six main new features stand out in this second edition:

• "The Reeve's Tale," newly edited and translated. This tale will be of particular interest because it carries forward the quarrel between the Miller and the Reeve and because it continues the sequence of pieces in the first fragment: the General Prologue, "The Knight's Tale," "The Miller's Tale," and "The Reeve's Tale." This tale will especially appeal to students because two of its central characters are Cambridge University students who, like many college boys eternally, think they can trick a local

tradesman and who view sex as a commodity to be
used for all the wrong reasons, such as revenge and
bragging rights back in the college residence hall.

• "The Shipman's Tale," newly edited and translated.
This tale gives us a different kind of fabliau, which
is a term for a short comic verse tale, of which the
Miller's and Reeve's tales are earlier examples. It
offers a nice contrast to those other two fabliaux in
the quality of its humor, its tone, and its implied
attitude to husbands, wives, and clerics. "The
Shipman's Tale" will be of particular interest to those
who enjoy the wonderful performance of the Wife of
Bath, since this tale was almost surely composed
originally for her. Readers will want to compare the
Wife's possible motives for telling this tale with her
motives for telling her Arthurian romance, also
included in this collection.

• A comprehensive new introduction that summarizes
some of the important historical events and
movements that defined the world for Chaucer and his
pilgrims: the murder of Thomas Becket in his own
cathedral in Canterbury in 1170; the Black Death of
1349; the English Rising of 1381; the chivalric life
and early death of Edward the Black Prince, followed
almost immediately by the ascension to the English
throne of his son, the hapless Richard II;
and the troubled times for the medieval papacy.

• Introductions to each of the tales designed to
prepare readers for a better understanding and
enjoyment of the tale to follow. There were no
such introductions in the original edition.

• Newly written and more conveniently placed notes
to individual words, phrases, and concepts in the
various tales. Instead of being gathered at the end of

the book and mixed into one long alphabetical list,
the notes are here conveniently gathered in line-order
at the end of the brief introduction to each new
section or tale, just before the tale itself begins. In
composing the notes I have tried not to interfere with
matters of interpretation that are better left to
individual teachers and readers. Rather, I identify
technical terms whose meanings are not clear from
the context and the translation, the authorities,
authors, and biblical texts Chaucer refers to, the
geographical place names, and some other matters
that will seem unfamiliar to modern readers.

• A new and more easily understood system for
learning to pronounce Chaucerian Middle English,
one that does not require the use of confusing
phonetic symbols.

For the parts of *The Canterbury Tales* that the Hieatts
worked on, I have kept most of their editing decisions and
the wording of their translation. The first edition, after all, is
their work and has stood the test of time for many, many teach-
ers, students, and general readers. I have occasionally changed
a bit of punctuation in the left-page edition, based on W. W.
Skeat's 1900 Clarendon edition. I have made a greater num-
ber of small changes in the wording to their right-page trans-
lations to smooth out the flow of the language and to reflect
more accurately their rendering of certain Chaucerian words
and phrases.

My own editing of the added pieces—"The Reeve's
Prologue," "The Reeve's Tale," and "The Shipman's Tale"—
differs somewhat from that of the Hieatts. For example, I
tend to use fewer semicolons than, following Skeat, they
used. I generally prefer periods. Readers who realize that vir-
tually all punctuation in Chaucer is added by modern editors
will scarcely be bothered by my decisions any more than they
were by the Hieatts'. Chaucer did not have access to periods,
commas, dashes, semicolons, question marks, exclamation

marks, or quotation marks, so all modern decisions to use such pointing are attempts to have modern editions approximate Chaucer's original meanings, emphases, and language flow. In my translations of the materials of the Reeve and the Shipman, I have tried, as the Hieatts did in their translations, to reflect both the grace and the bluntness of Chaucer's own language. Where my right-page prose translations lack stylistic grace, that is mostly the result of my attempts to keep the translations more or less parallel with Chaucer's left-page verse so that readers can most easily read across the pages to find roughly equivalent expressions. Chaucer's language patterns are so close to those of modern English that often my task was to do little more than modernize Chaucer's spelling.

I am sure that the Hieatts were aware of the flatness, as compared with the liveliness of Chaucer's own verse, of all translations of *The Canterbury Tales*. I am sure that they would join me in hoping that most readers will use the full resources of this volume as they work to experience directly the wondrous gracefulness of the Chaucerian original. My enduring hope in building on and reissuing the work of the Hieatts is, like theirs, that most readers will use the accessibility of our translations as an impetus to reading more of the Canterbury stories than the selections we present here, and that they will have gained here both the desire and the confidence to read them in Chaucer's original Middle English verse.

—PGB

# CONTENTS

# INTRODUCTION

AT THE START of *The Canterbury Tales* Geoffrey Chaucer tells us that on a certain day in April, in the mid-1380s, he spent the night in the Tabard Inn in Southwark, on the south bank of the Thames. He went there so that he could get an early start the next morning on a pilgrimage to Canterbury, some sixty miles to the southeast, where he would pay homage at the tomb of the martyred Thomas Becket. That evening some twenty-nine other pilgrims came into the Tabard in preparation for a similar journey. Chaucer was impressed with this socially, occupationally, and morally varied array of men and women. This congenial and fun-loving group also impressed the jolly innkeeper, who offered to join the pilgrimage. The innkeeper proposed that to entertain and instruct each other, the pilgrims should tell each other a series of tales on the trip down to Canterbury and back. He offered, moreover, to act as master of ceremonies by selecting the order in which the tale-tellers would speak and to act as judge of the tales. The best teller, he said, would get a free dinner at the Tabard back in London.

That pilgrimage was certainly fiction, but such pilgrimages did take place in Chaucer's time, and it is entirely likely that Chaucer himself made at least one such journey to Canterbury. He almost certainly knew some people very like the pilgrims he describes—the worthy Knight, the quarrelsome Miller, the debonaire Prioress, the busy Man of Law, the Christ-like Parson, and even the sexually ambiguous Pardoner—but there is no question that the pilgrims are Chaucer's creations, drawn more from his fertile imagination than from life. And there is no doubt whatever that each of the tales he puts into the mouths of these pilgrims was written by Chaucer.

Even though he almost always takes his plots from earlier tales, Chaucer always puts his own distinctive stamp on them, either to fit them to the personality of the teller or, more often, just to make them better or more dramatic stories. By "dramatic," I mean several things. First, I mean that his tales are more like drama than most of his sources were. There is narrative summary, yes, but Chaucer also gives us a series of scenes in which the characters speak in realistic dialogue. Second, by dramatic, I mean that we can consider the pilgrimage itself a kind of dramatic performance in which the pilgrims are themselves actors on a shifting stage that starts in London and moves toward Canterbury. There is dramatic dialogue among the pilgrims. The drunken Miller shows his contempt for the sedate and aristocratic "Knight's Tale" set in ancient Athens by retelling some elements of its plot as a raunchy tale set in contemporary Oxford, and then the angry Reeve, having taken personal offense at "The Miller's Tale," gets his revenge by telling a tale in which a proud miller gets bopped on the head by his wife. And, third, by dramatic, I mean that Chaucer strives to assign to each tale a teller appropriate to it, so that the tale and the pilgrim characterize each other. "The Wife of Bath's Tale" is a different tale in the mouth of Alison than it would be if another teller told it, and our understanding of the Wife of Bath is enriched by our knowing that she tells this tale rather than another.

Although Chaucer died before this particular fictional pilgrimage to Canterbury was completed—indeed, before he completed more than a fifth of the projected 120 tales—what Chaucer did finish was enough to give him a revered place among the great writers of the world, and even to give him the title of "the father of English literature." Although that term sounds a bit sexist these days—no one speaks of "the mother of English literature"—it does convey the important place that many generations of readers of literature have accorded to him. What do we know about this great man named Geoffrey Chaucer?

## CHAUCER'S LIFE

Geoffrey Chaucer was England's first great poet and, except perhaps for Shakespeare, England's most accomplished and influential one. Chaucer was born around 1340, more than two centuries before Shakespeare, and his works suggested several plots and literary techniques that helped to make Shakespeare the great dramatist that he became.

Chaucer was the son of a prosperous London wine merchant who made use of his connections to secure for young Geoffrey a place as page to the countess of Ulster and later as valet in the royal household. When he was around twenty, Chaucer was captured while in military service in France, but King Edward III paid his ransom. Not so long after that, Chaucer married Philippa de Roet, a maid of honor to the queen of England and sister-in-law to John of Gaunt, Chaucer's patron.

Chaucer spent many years as a civil servant. He was comptroller of customs for the port of London, a justice of the peace for Kent, and even for a time a member of Parliament. He went on several trade and diplomatic journeys to the Continent—to France, to the Low Countries, and at least twice to Italy. On those journeys he encountered some of the gems of Continental literature that were to have such a strong influence on his own developing genius.

Although he wrote other fine works, most notably the tragic love story *Troilus and Criseyde* (also available in a Random House translation), Chaucer's most enduring masterpiece is *The Canterbury Tales,* the subject of the current volume. This work, which serves as the centerpiece for his enduring reputation, is an amazing compendium of genres: the romances or courtly tales of love and adventure of high-class men and women; the fabliaux, or comic tales often involving middle-class folk engaged in raunchy misconduct; saints' legends; moral exempla; religious tales and sermons; confessional narratives; tragedies; allegories; meditations; and even parodies.

The twenty or so tales that Chaucer did complete are not

consecutive, except for the first four (those of the Knight, the Miller, the Reeve, and the Cook, which breaks off after only a few lines, never to be completed). The others come in a series of nine fragments in which certain tales are linked together but are not clearly linked with the other fragments. After the first four, we can only speculate on what Chaucer's intended ordering of the tales might have been, if indeed he ever had a fully worked-out plan. Chaucer's death prevented him from completing the 120 tales he had envisioned. What we call *The Canterbury Tales*—the title is ours, not Chaucer's—is little more than an ambitious beginning. Still, the tales that Chaucer did complete are so rich, varied, and skillfully wrought that they provide the basis for his towering reputation as a poet and storyteller.

We have only a vague idea of what Chaucer looked like. There are no fully reliable portraits of him that survive from when he was alive, but several drawings made later, often derived from each other, show him to have a kindly face and a forked beard. His own self-description in *The Canterbury Tales* suggests that he was not a large man, except perhaps in his girth. Of his love life, marriage, and financial situation we know little, and that little is often ambiguous and circumstantial. We don't even know for certain when he died, though 1400 is a reasonable and conveniently round estimate.

Chaucer is buried in Westminster Abbey in London. Many later English poets so admired Chaucer's work that they asked to be buried near him. That crowded area of the abbey later came to be called the Poet's Corner. Chaucer was the first poet to occupy it. Although he wrote other fine literary works, Chaucer's most varied and delightful work is *The Canterbury Tales*. To understand the nature of the pilgrimage that is its fictional impetus, we need to understand something of the life of Thomas Becket, the man whose elaborate tomb in Canterbury was the destination of Chaucer and his twenty-nine fellow pilgrims.

## THOMAS BECKET

Thomas Becket was born in London in 1118. He was educated there, but he eventually went abroad to study the law. He worked for a merchant for a time, then through his father's influence was assigned to the cathedral at Canterbury as an administrative assistant to Theobald, the archbishop. It was an important post for Thomas because the cathedral there was the home of the mother church of England, its archbishop the most powerful church man in the British Isles.

In 1154, at the death of his father, the twenty-one-year-old Henry became king of England. Henry II asked Theobald to recommend someone to be his chancellor. Theobald recommended Becket, then in his midthirties, and Henry took the recommendation. Becket and Henry hit it off so well that when Theobald died in 1161, Henry took the bold move of naming Becket to be Archbishop of Canterbury, and thus the head of the Christian church in England. His choice was ratified by the pope and by the monks at Canterbury, and Becket took up his new duties.

Henry's goal in naming Becket to be archbishop was clear enough: he wanted the powerful medieval Christian church to be under his control. Who but his trusted friend could better assure the new king of the sure and strong leadership of both church and state? Becket had his own loyalties, however, and soon found that he could not always serve both his king and his pope, not to mention follow the teachings of Christ. Disagreements between the king and the archbishop were initially managed diplomatically enough, but both men dug their heels in on the question of who had jurisdiction over the infractions of clergymen. Henry thought that such infractions should be tried in civil courts, but Becket insisted that as clergy they were under the sole jurisdiction of the ecclesiastical courts. The two former friends became fierce opponents over this issue and after a time Becket, fearing the power of Henry, went into exile in France.

When Henry invited the lesser Archbishop of York to preside officially over the precoronation of his son as king-elect of England, thus bypassing the Archbishop of Canterbury, Becket returned to England, bringing with him from the pope documents suspending the Archbishop of York and excommunicating two bishops. When Becket put those into effect after his return, Henry was so frustrated that he muttered, in the presence of four of his knights, something like, "Will no one rid me of this troublesome priest?" The four knights took him at his word and rode to Canterbury. They entered the cathedral, where Becket awaited them. They attacked him with their swords and murdered him as he prayed.

Henry was deeply upset when he heard the news of Becket's death, apparently not entirely sure that he had wanted his question of the knights to be taken as a literal command to murder the archbishop, but the deed had been done. Almost immediately after Becket's death certain miraculous cures were said to have been effected on sick people who came to Canterbury to be near garments, body fluids, or artifacts associated with the fallen archbishop. Henry ultimately did penance for his words by making his own pilgrimage to Canterbury. He walked the last mile barefoot and then allowed the monks to whip him.

These dramatic events soon made Canterbury the most frequent pilgrim destination in England. The location of Canterbury just sixty miles from London and on the usual land route to France helped assure its popularity as a pilgrim or traveler stopover, but the main reason was Becket himself. Becket was soon deemed a saint. Two centuries later Chaucer did not even need to give St. Thomas's name in the famous General Prologue to *The Canterbury Tales*. Everyone knew who he meant by the "holy, blissful martyr" who helped people "when they were sick."

We do not know whether in the mid-1380s Chaucer actually went on a pilgrimage to Canterbury. It may all have been just a flight of his imagination, a literary device to give a framework to a series of tales he wanted to bring together. But none of it would have happened, in life or in literature, if a certain Thomas Becket had not stood up to his king and been willing to pay, in December 1170, the supreme penalty.

Becket's confrontation with his king came two centuries before Chaucer, a court poet who had his own dealings—not all of them smooth—with the British royalty.

## THE BLACK PRINCE

The Black Prince was never king of England, except perhaps in the hearts of his countrymen. He was the oldest son of Edward III, a powerful king who became embroiled in what came to be known as the Hundred Years' War—that series of diplomatic and military conflicts between England and France that consumed the energies and funds of both nations for around a century as both strove to carve out and maintain their holdings and their identities as nations. After the successful Norman invasion of England in 1066, the French considered the foggy island across the channel to be their own property and imposed their language, rulers, and customs on it. As the power of individual kings and princes rose and fell, however, the foggy island grew to think of itself as the dog that should wag the tail of the sometimes less powerful lands across the channel to the south and west.

When Charles IV of France died in 1328, Edward III of England, a nephew of the previous French king, advanced his claim to the throne of France. The barons of France, however, had other ideas and named Philip of Valois, a cousin to the previous king, as the new king of France. Edward at the time had other matters to attend to at home and lacked the power to make his own claim stick. A decade later Edward III fought a series of decisive battles against the French navy and then mounted a serious invasion of French soil. Taking his teenage son Edward the Prince of Wales with him, he scored an important military victory in 1346 at Crécy. Although the young prince did not play a large part in the battle, he witnessed the decisive elements in that victory: the strong military leadership of his father and the superior speed and range of the English longbow against the slower and heavier crossbows of the French.

A decade after that, in 1356, the Prince of Wales became

a military commander in his own right at the battle at Poitiers, where the English managed to score a major victory against a much larger French army on their own turf. The English forces even captured the French king, John, and carried him back to England as a royal prisoner while the terms of ransom could be worked out. The battle at Poitiers was a stunning victory for England and for its handsome young prince, whose instant fame made him the most eligible bachelor in Europe. Although he is known to have had a number of love affairs, when it came to marriage, he selected his own cousin, the lovely Joan of Kent. Edward III thought it a stupid match, hoping that his son would make a marriage that would bring political advantage with a nation on the Continent, but young Edward put love above politics, and by doing so endeared himself to his countrymen. How could they not, after all, admire their chivalrous Prince of Wales for falling in love with one of their own and who boldly proclaimed, by making such a match, "an English girl is the girl for me!" They were happy enough to overlook the fact that Joan was, at age thirty-three, two years his senior and a widow.

Young Edward went with his bride to set up his court in Bordeaux as prince of Aquitaine, that vast region in what is now southwestern France. Although he managed his new holdings with some skill, he found it increasingly difficult to be a foreign ruler of the region he had conquered in battle. In the end a number of difficulties made his life miserable. He ran out of money, he went on a fruitless expedition to claim holdings in Spain, and he contracted an illness that cannot now be identified for sure. Was it a venereal disease, a liver disease brought on by too much drinking, or some sort of flu or dysentery? Whatever it was, he never quite recovered from it, even after he returned with his wife and second son to England, where he died several years later in 1376.

The name that the French later bestowed on their enemy, *Le Prins Noire,* has come to suggest to the English their pride in the romance and military brilliance of their global ambitions. The Black Prince's body now lies in the cathedral in Canterbury, complete with an effigy in full armor and the fleur-de-lis, the lily that now symbolizes the French national spirit. It is possible that Geoffrey Chaucer, then a member of the royal court, was a member of the procession that carried his body from London, along the pilgrims' way, to Canterbury.

Though he never became king, the Black Prince was the father of Richard, the young lad who became King Richard II at the death of Edward III.

## RICHARD II

Richard II came to the throne at the tender age of eleven, a year after the death of his father, Edward the Black Prince, in 1376 and upon the death of his grandfather, Edward III, in 1377. Because of the circumstances of his kingship, his youth, and plain old bad luck, Richard was deposed by his cousin after only twenty-two years as king. His most memorable accomplishment in those years came in 1381 when, at age fourteen, he stood up to the peasants who stormed London (more on that confrontation below).

Because of his youth, Richard had trouble establishing his authority, even when he was old enough to begin to understand why it was important that he do so. His advisers and his uncles kept him on the defensive during most of his reign. One uncle, Gloucester, was strong enough to imprison the young king in the Tower of London, to dismiss his chancellor and other key advisers, and to replace them with his own appointees. In that purge of the palace went none other than Geoffrey Chaucer, who found himself dismissed from the minor office he held there.

Richard's other uncle, John of Gaunt, brother to the Black Prince, was kindlier and even more powerful than Gloucester. Gaunt could probably with relative ease have usurped the throne and named himself king. He had the power to do so, but not the desire, and his forbearance paid off for his posterity. His descendants by various wives were to become kings of England, Portugal, and Spain. Gaunt's eldest son, Henry Bolingbroke, more ambitious than his father, had joined in

Gloucester's attempt to challenge Richard's authority and had even headed up the army that opposed the young king.

When he reached twenty-one, Richard successfully declared himself king in fact and not just in name. With that declaration he began to receive the support of the various factions that were a part of political life in medieval England. In doing so the experience and advice of his uncle John of Gaunt was helpful—so helpful that Richard was reluctant to punish his cousin Henry, Gaunt's son, for his earlier actions against the throne. After he took charge of his nation for real, Richard was reluctant to alienate the powerful Gaunt by killing his son, so he arranged a comfortable exile for Henry in France.

That turned out to be a bad mistake on Richard's part. In 1399, John of Gaunt died and Richard claimed Gaunt's lands for the crown. Then he went off to Ireland to consolidate his holdings there. When Henry, still in exile across the channel, learned that he was to lose the inheritance he considered to be his own property, he came back across the channel, garnered support among the barons, and proclaimed himself king. By the time Richard heard what was going on and came home to put down the rebellion, the rebellion had already succeeded. Richard had no choice but to abdicate. Within a year Richard had died in prison, victim to his youth, inexperience, and bad judgment.

Richard II was the king whom Chaucer served under for his most productive final quarter-century. At Richard's deposition in 1399, Chaucer appealed to the new king, Henry IV, the son of his former patron, for financial support. Henry granted it, but Chaucer did not live long enough to enjoy it for more than a few months. He apparently died in 1400, the same year as Richard. The century, the era, was over. Richard, the last of the Plantagenet kings, was dead, and Henry, the first of the Lancastrian kings, was on the throne.

Richard II has not been treated well by history. He was overshadowed politically by the more illustrious kingships of his grandfather Edward III and his cousin Henry IV. He was overshadowed militarily both by his namesake, Richard I, the

Lion-Hearted, and by his father, the gallant Edward the Black Prince. Richard II was an unfortunate king. He was a young king. He was a weak king. But he was not the evil king he was portrayed to be in Shakespeare's play *Richard II*. He peaked early. There is no way he could have known that his triumphant moment was to come when, at age fourteen, he played an uncharacteristically bold role in the quelling of the English Rising in 1381.

## THE ENGLISH RISING

The English Rising, the first major revolt of the commoners against a member of the British royalty, was made possible by a number of social and economic forces. The immediate cause of the rising was a spring 1381 per-capita tax on the English people by their king—under the advice of his advisers and aristocratic friends. Angry at the imposition of the third such tax in four years, and even angrier that the tax collectors seemed to have inaccurate records about who had already paid up, the men of Essex flat out refused to pay. They confronted the tax collector with their angry complaints and sent him running back to London. The authorities there sent a judge and some jurors back to try the recalcitrant taxpayers, but meanwhile word of the resistance spread to villagers in other towns in Essex and in nearby Kent, virtually all of whom applauded the courage of their neighbors. When the representatives of justice came back to try them, the brave men of Essex seized the judges, the jurors, and the clerks and beheaded them.

Word of their actions spread to others, and soon an angry mob of men, armed with primitive weapons designed more for hunting and agriculture than for military operations, headed for London to talk with their king, young Richard II. Led by the men of Essex and Kent, they swept into London, opened the prisons and freed the prisoners, killed whoever resisted them, set fire to several buildings, and isolated the young Richard and his frightened advisers in the Tower of London. Richard had nothing that could be called a police or militia or standing army—at least not one large enough to control so large a group. What troops the king could command were far away in Portugal tending to the interests of the crown there. Besides, armies were for invading other nations or for keeping other nations from invading yours. It never occurred to the king or his advisers that they would have to deal with an internal revolt, and especially one not from an upstart baron but from—of all things!—the common people.

Though historians once referred to this rebellion as the Peasants' Revolt of 1381, most historians, made aware that the support for it came not merely from farmworkers but also from England's growing class of businessmen, townspeople, artisans, and even clerics, now refer to it as the English Rising of 1381. These people from so many walks of life shared the peasants' frustration with the continual demands of the king and his aristocratic supporters for financial support for wars and projects they had no particular interest in and from which they could see no benefit to themselves. No one had enough power or courage to organize such a rising, but once the rising was in progress, they were happy enough to let the rebels come into the city and even to join them—though sometimes from a cautious distance.

Young Richard had little idea what to do. Nor did his advisers, some of whom the angry crowds outside the Tower of London demanded that the king turn over to them for immediate execution. The spokesmen for the rebellion made it clear right from the start that it was not their boy-king that they were angry with but the members of his high-handed aristocracy. They wanted to talk to the king, not to harm him. Richard, acting probably on the advice of one or more of his advisers, decided to ride out among the people, listen to their demands, promise them anything they wanted, and send them home. We don't know whose idea it was, but it was Richard himself who had to put the plan into effect. Still in only his third year as crowned king and not used to taking charge of much of anything, he bravely mounted his horse and rode outside the gates of the tower to confront the noisy rebels.

He did listen to the demands of the leaders of the rebellion. They told him, for example, that they wanted him to abolish the system of villeinage whereby the peasants were bound to the land they did not own, forced to work for someone else who did. They demanded not to have to pay any more feudal dues to their lords. The king hastily agreed to all of their demands. Calmed by his ready acquiescence to what they knew were pretty unreasonable demands, many of the rebels took his advice and, grateful that he promised amnesty to all who took part in the rebellion if they went home, many of them left London. Some stayed behind to await written documents signed by the king granting them their demands. While they waited, some of them broke into the tower and executed several of Richard's most hated administrators.

The next day Richard came out again to hear more of the rebels' demands. A man named Wat Tyler repeated the demands of the day before and added a few more: the end to all lordship except that of the king himself, the freedom and social equality of all citizens, the confiscation of church property and its use for the welfare of the people, and so on. The king said that if the rebels would all go on home, he would grant their demands.

Then Wat Tyler apparently said something insulting and one of the king's retainers, emboldened by the reduced numbers of the rebels, insulted Tyler back. The king ordered the mayor of London to arrest Tyler, but Tyler struck the mayor with his sword. The mayor struck back, badly wounding Tyler, who then fell back. The king set off in pursuit but stopped when he saw the arrows pointed at him by other rebels. Richard then called out to them, "Let me be your leader!" The rebels, impressed at his bravery, lowered their arrows and meekly followed him to the edge of town. The king's men then killed Tyler and set his head on a pole for all to see, then arrested those of the rebels still in town. The king pardoned them, however, and they gladly left for home.

Now that the revolt was over and the rebels were home again, the king declared that his promises had been made under duress, and he refused to honor them. Because things went on pretty much as they had before the rebellion, it is easy to conclude that the English Rising was a colossal failure. In a sense it was, because the commoners of England would have to wait many generations for their demands to be met in reality. Still, the aristocracy of England cannot have failed to hear, in the noisy rumblings from Essex and Kent, that their world had changed. After 1381, they could no longer treat the people in quite the same way. From now on they had to listen, or at least pretend to listen, to those rumblings.

King Richard must have known as he made his promises to the people shouting outside the Tower of London that he would not keep those promises. Even if he wanted to, he probably felt that he did not have the power to make such sweeping changes to the social fabric of the nation. He would not have had the historical perspective that we now have, a perspective that suggests that the Black Death three decades earlier, followed by continuing recurrences of the plague, had already made a permanent change in that social fabric. Without that change no peasants' rebellion would have been possible in the first place.

## THE BLACK DEATH

The Black Death was a particularly virulent and deadly onslaught of the bubonic plague in Europe in the middle of the fourteenth century. It was brought to southeastern Europe around 1347–48 and quickly spread along the shipping and overland trade routes to the north and west, ultimately causing the deaths of hundreds, then thousands, then millions of men, women, and children. The terrible disease takes its name from the appearance of dark "buboes" or boils that typically started in the armpits and the groin, then spread to the rest of the body, and finally caused death.

It was not known until the turn of the twentieth century that the plague was spread by infected fleas that inhabited the fur of rats before it killed them. Then the fleas jumped to the bodies of other rats, which they also killed. When the rat population was thinned out, the infected fleas jumped to less-preferred hosts, human beings, and by biting them brought about their infection and death. In Chaucer's time various other assumptions were made about the cause of the great mortality at midcentury: that the stars were in certain unpropitious alignments, that God used this method to punish sinners, that Jews were poisoning Christian wells, and so on. Such explanations were against all logic. No one could identify a convincing astrological alignment of stars, many people known to be virtuous died while others known to be corrupt lived, and Jews died in at least equal numbers to Christians. Still, medieval physicians and philosophers had no better explanations, though they did notice that the plague tended to arrive in a community not long after a sick sailor or trader visited, and that one way that sometimes helped people to avoid the plague was to shun contact with those who already had it.

How many died in the Black Death that ravaged Europe in the half-dozen years at midcentury? We can never know for sure. The plague leaves no traces in the bones of those it kills, and medieval demographic records are few, irregular, and unreliable. The records that we do have, even when they are fairly reliable, are sometimes incomplete owing to the fact that those who kept them died of the plague while keeping them. Earlier estimates based on what records there were suggested that a quarter to a third of the population died in that period. Those estimates are almost surely low. After an extensive study of the records, Ole J. Benedictow published at the end of a four-hundred-page book his own estimate: "over half of the populations in the regions and countries for which there are data of useful quality and numbers died in the Black Death, probably around 60 percent. Most of the mortality was due to the plague disease, and a significant or substantial amount was due to secondary catastrophic effects." By "secondary catastrophic effects" Benedictow meant, for example, the deaths of family members caused not by the plague itself but by exposure or starvation after other members of their families died. Benedictow goes on: "If these data are representative of the Black Death's ravages elsewhere in Europe, and Europe's population at the time was around 80 million persons, as commonly believed, 50 million of them died in the Black Death" (*The Black Death, 1346–1353,* Boydell Press, 2004, p. 382).

In modern times of relatively small catastrophes involving only a tiny percentage of the total population, it is almost impossible to imagine one of such scope or what its effects might be on the people of, say, modern Europe or North America. What might this country be like if in a five-year period more than half of all Americans died? But let's consider some of the actual effects in medieval Europe.

One effect was a greater attention to one's own pleasures. Those who survived the Black Death were painfully aware of the fragility and brevity of human life. Many of them devoted themselves more fully to fun than they might once have—to drinking, for example, and to promiscuity. After all, if the good and the bad were to die without warning in equal numbers, why not have a little bad fun while still alive? Besides, who was left alive to tell the carousers not to carouse? And if a man could once only covet his neighbor's wife, now he found her suddenly available to him—even eager to join him—because her husband and her brothers were dead.

One of the most enduring effects of the Black Death was economic. In medieval Europe some 90 percent of the population lived in the countryside, where the Black Death hit with particular virulence. The men and women who worked the lord's fields and pastures suffered before they died, of course, but those who did survive found themselves suddenly in a much stronger bargaining position. They could, if they wanted, stay and continue to work his fields, but the implications of that phrase "if they wanted" were profound. Whereas before they had no alternative but to work the land they were born on and to spend most of their time working their lord's fields rather than the smaller ones he assigned for their own use, they now found themselves courted by neighboring landowners who desperately offered them more or better fields of their own or even offered to let them work for wages rather than for the use of certain fields. Suddenly these workers were in demand. Suddenly they had a choice. Suddenly they were able to bargain about whom they worked for, where they worked, what kind of work they did, and on what terms they did it. Suddenly they were no longer serfs but incipient capitalists. They quickly grew accustomed to demanding the right to serve whom they wanted and on what terms they would serve him. Is it any wonder, then, that three decades later, when their young king Richard sent his men down to levy still another tax on them, they had the confidence to tell him, quite thunderously, *no*?

Another important effect of the Black Death was that the clerical population was reduced greatly. One of the horrid ironies of the Black Death was that the most devoted of the clerics, those who stayed closest to their parishioners, administered to them in their suffering, and offered them the last rites, placed themselves in the greatest danger and died in the greatest numbers. Their deaths left large gaps in the clerical populations of Europe, gaps that sometimes were filled by greedier or less-qualified churchmen, like pardoners. The result was a shift away from the standard that the men of the cloth were seriously devoted to helping the poor and to saving souls. Trends toward a more secular and self-centered clergy were already well in place before the onslaught of the plague, but there is no question that the disease tended further to lower the moral levels of clergymen who served the Christian church.

## THE MEDIEVAL CHRISTIAN CHURCH

The medieval Christian church was an institution increasingly divided. The fourteenth-century church was in some ways a comfortingly uniform institution. The Protestant Reformation was still a century off, so to be a Christian was to be a Catholic. All Christians, at least in theory, took their direction from the pope, whose interpretations and edicts came down to people by way of the archbishops, bishops, priests, deacons, and so on. There was, indeed, a separate chain of command for the "regular" clergy, so called because they lived apart and according to a rule (French *regle*). These were the clerics who lived in monasteries, nunneries, and friaries. They took their directions from the pope, yes, but not through the archbishops or bishops or priests, but from their chapter leaders. In a sense, then, the secular clergy (priests) often found themselves in direct competition with the regular clergy (monks and, especially, friars) for the souls and purses of the people. Already, then, there were divisions in the church and frictions among the various clergymen.

But there were other divisions. The most obvious was what has come to be called the Great Schism. That strange phenomenon, which took place at about the time that the young Richard II became king, came about when the French cardinals were dissatisfied with the newly appointed pope, Urban VI, in Rome. They boldly named their own rival pope and set him up in Avignon. The English tended to support the Italian pope, if only to show dissatisfaction with the upstart French, with whom they had been in conflict for years over ownership of lands on both sides of the English Channel, but the fact was that for the last quarter of the fourteenth century, when Chaucer was in his most productive mode, there were two Catholic popes, each proclaiming himself to be the rightly appointed and anointed head of Christianity. Each purported to speak for God and so to have the right to denounce the other pope. How could ordinary Christians not be puzzled and confused? How could they not begin to wonder whether, since both of these men purported to speak for God, either of them really did—especially when many local clergymen were proving to be so self-serving, greedy, and even lustful?

Even further dividing the English church was an Englishman named John Wyclif. Wyclif was an ordained priest who early in his career criticized the excesses of the clergy and the tendency of popes to think they had the right to interfere with the civil authority of the kings of England.

Wyclif is most famous, however, for instigating the translation of the Bible into English. He wanted the English people to be able to read for themselves or hear the scriptures read in their own language, rather than in the Latin language that they did not understand. To most Christians today it seems natural to make the word of God as revealed in the holy scriptures available to Christians in their own language, but in Chaucer's time it was considered to be a heretical act. It was, after all, in the interests of the pope, who claimed to speak for God, to select the scriptures that other Christians heard and to interpret those scriptures for them. The pope had no interest in giving the people, English or other, direct access to the Bible, if only because that would get them thinking that they could interpret it for themselves. Wyclif died before the English Bible was finished, but others carried on and some copies were available to people who could read and who could afford them. The invention of the printing press that would put the Bible in many hands was still a century away.

A small but increasingly influential group of Wyclif's follower-priests, called Lollards, went about reading the scriptures in English to English men and women. That was an important start, and Wyclif's Bible later formed the basis for the earliest printed Bibles in the next century. Wyclif never thought of himself as part of a Protestant reformation, but he helped to make the Reformation possible by helping to plant the desire in Christians to read the word of God directly rather than have it selected and interpreted for them by the church hierarchy.

It is not clear what Chaucer thought of Wyclif and the Lollards, though surely he knew about them and shared some of their criticism of corrupt clerics. And he must have applauded Wyclif's desire to write in the English vernacular so that the men and women of England could understand what was written. After all, Chaucer was at the same time engaged in a project to make imaginative literature available to his countrymen in their own language. Both Wyclif and Chaucer helped to raise the status of English by letting the people know that their mother tongue was no longer a mongrel bark spoken only by the lower classes in the streets and fields, but a language that was fine enough to be written down, worthy for recording not only vernacular poetry but also sophisticated religious sentiments and, indeed, the very words of God.

How were those Middle English words pronounced? This

is not the place to attempt to give full training in how to pronounce Chaucerian Middle English, but readers of this volume might like to know some basic principles.

## PRONOUNCING CHAUCERIAN MIDDLE ENGLISH

Chaucer's English is called Middle English to distinguish it both from the Old English of the *Beowulf*-poet and other early Anglo-Saxon writers and from the Modern English of Shakespeare and later writers up to the present day. You all know Modern English. In this section we will attempt to use your knowledge of the pronunciation of Modern English to coach you in your correct pronunciation of Middle English. You can learn to pronounce Chaucer's verse pretty well if you master a dozen basic rules. Many of them are simple enough, others are more complicated or confusing. You may want to pay particular attention to rules number *1, 3, 4, 7, 8, 10, 15, 16, 18, 21, 23, 24,* and *25.*

Keep in mind that for Chaucer there was no one "correct" way to spell a word. What we now think of as spelling rules did not become established until the eighteenth century. Although you may find Chaucer's spelling variations frustrating, in some ways those variations help you to know how to pronounce his words because you can generally assume that virtually all of the letters that Chaucer used were pronounced. He was, after all, writing phonetically—that is, writing the spellings that to him yielded the pronunciation he had in mind.

To apply the various pronunciation rules below, you will want to start with the letter or letters that Chaucer used and seek that letter in the numbered rules. The consonants will give you little trouble, but see rules *1–3.* The vowels will be more difficult because in some words Modern English has shifted away from Chaucer's pronunciation. That is why, until a century or so ago, many readers of Chaucer assumed that he was a sloppy rhymester. In fact, however, once we understood that the problem was ours, not his, and once we understood the principles reflected in rules *4–23* below, we learned that he was amazingly careful in his rhymes. As you use these rules for pronouncing his vowels, remember that for many of the letters—*e, o,* and *i,* for example—you will have to decide which of several rules applies in that case. Keep in mind, also, that a vowel-cluster, like *ou,* is to be treated as one sound, and so should be looked up under the rule for *ou,* not the rules for *o* and *u* separately.

You will need also to remember that according to his own poetic principles, which we have come to understand only in the past century, Chaucer was careful in writing meters. All of the poetry in this book is in iambic pentameter. To understand how his meters sounded, then, you will need to apply rules *24* and *25* as you read his lines. The reward for learning all these rules is an appreciation of the musical beauty of Chaucerian verse and the delight of reading England's first important poet in his own language. He could not learn our variety of English because he died too soon, but we can learn his.

## Chaucer's Consonants

Few of Chaucer's consonants have changed in the six hundred years since he wrote. The letter *g,* for example, was for Chaucer much the same letter it was for us. That is, sometimes it was given a hard sound as in *good,* sometimes a softer sound, as in *gentil.* Similarly, the letter *c* could have a hard sound as in *cat* or a soft one as in *citee.* Modern pronunciation is a good guide for these two letters, with the vowels *i* and *e* after the letter producing the soft sound. To pronounce Chaucerian consonants as he did, however, you need to keep three rules in mind.

1. *k, g, l, r*—Pronounce these letters, even if they have become silent in Modern English. Chaucer wrote in a time before there were considered to be "correct" spellings of words, so don't expect great consistency as you read Middle English. He often spelled words differently within a couple of lines of each other. He tended

to spell phonetically, the way the word "sounded" to him at the time. Generally, if he put a consonant there, he wanted it pronounced. Thus, he pronounced the *k* in *knyght,* the *g* in *gnaw,* the *l* in *folk.* As for the letter *r,* which has become almost silent in Modern English, Chaucer would have trilled it, as does modern Irish, Scottish, and Spanish. Here are some examples in which now near-silent consonants would have been pronounced:

*palmer, know, March, root, inspired, yonge, halfe* (half), *bring* (bring), *knokke* (knock)

**2. *y*—**The letter *y* is usually a vowel (generally interchangeable with the letter *i*) but sometimes was a consonant (as in *yellow*). When it was a consonant, it was pronounced as it still is. For the pronunciation of the vowels *i* and *y,* see rules *15* and *16* below. Here are some examples of the use of *y* as a consonant:

*yonge, yeman* (yeoman), *yate* (gate), *yis* (yes), *yit* (yet), *yore, ye* (yes, you), *you*

**3. *gh*—**The consonant-cluster *gh,* now silent as in "though" or pronounced "f" as in "enough," would have been given a Germanic guttural sound, something like our modern "k" but deeper in the throat, as in the German "ich." The Middle English *knyght,* then, would have sounded something like "caneect." For the sound of the *y* in *knyght,* see rule *16* below. Examples:

*droghte* (dryness), *foughten* (fought), *draughte* (draft, as in drawn from a barrel), *caught, noght* (not), *y-taught* (taught), *raught* (reached), *ynogh* (enough)

## Chaucer's Vowels

Chaucer's vowels are more troublesome than his consonants, mostly because of what linguists now call the Great

Vowel Shift, which occurred gradually but in a fairly regular way in the two hundred years after Chaucer's death at the end of the fourteenth century. To pronounce Middle English we need to leap back through the Great Vowel Shift to his way of speaking those vowels. Fortunately, the modern pronunciation and spelling of a word are almost always—more than 90 percent of the time—a good guide to its pre-Shift pronunciation. The key is to start with the Middle English spelling of the word and then find the vowel in the list below. Note that for some letters, the *e* and the *o* and the *i* in particular, there is more than one possible pronunciation. For these you will need to decide which choice fits the case.

Note also that some of the Chaucerian vowels are now technically diphthongs, or vowel glides—vowels that involve a glide from one sound to another. For example, the first vowel in Chaucer's word *whyte* (white) was not a glide. It was pronounced "wheet." Our modern "white," however, is actually a two-sound vowel: "wha-eet." That glide from the "a" to the "ee" is called a diphthong. Note that in Chaucer's time our diphthong "ou" was not one, so the vowel in Chaucer's *house,* which in our Modern English is pronounced "hahoose," would in Middle English have rhymed with our Modern English "goose."

**4. *a, aa***—Pronounced "ah" always, like the *a* in Modern English "father." One of the fortunate features of Middle English is that the letter *a* was always pronounced like the *a* in "father"—unless it was followed by the *i, y, u,* or *w* (see the next two rules). Examples:

*Aprill, bathed, that, than, hath, al* (all), *halfe, Tabard* (name of inn), *pilgrimage, take, tale, aventure* (chance), *pace, lady, grace, nat* (not)

**5. *ai, ay***—Pronounced "ah-ee," like the *ai*-diphthong in the Modern English "aisle." See also rule *12* below. Examples:

*day, lay, array, ay* (always), *mayde* (maid), *sayde* (said), *verray* (true), *slayn, faire*

**6. au, aw**—Pronounced "ah-oo," like the *ou*-diphthong in Modern English "house" and "sour." Examples:

*straunge* (strange, distant), *caught, Caunterbury, fel-awshipe, caught, acordaunt, y-taught* (taught), *Austin* (Augustine), *bawdrik* (baldrick), *sauce*

**7. e, ee**—Pronounced "eh," as in Modern English "men" and "bed," if the word has the short-*e* sound today. In other words, these short-*e* words have not changed the vowel pronunciation in six hundred years. Examples:

*gentil, ende, engendred, wende* (go), *wente* (went), *hem* (them), *wel, weren, yet, beste, reste, breeth* (breath)

**8. e, ee**—Pronounced "ay" as in Modern English "hay" and "play" if the word is pronounced "ee" now. But see rule *9* below for an important exception. Examples:

*he, she, we, me, seken, swete, slepen, fredom, be, fiftene*

**9. e, ee**—Pronounced like the "a" in Modern English "math" and "at," if the word is pronounced "ee" or "ay" now and spelled *ea*. Examples:

*heeth* (heath), *erly* (early), *greet* (great), *seson* (season), *esed* (eased), *beeste* (beast, animal)

**10. e**—Pronounced "uh," like the unaccented *a* at the end of Modern English "sofa," if the letter *e* appears at the end of a line or if Chaucer's iambic pentameter seems to require it elsewhere in the line. Sometimes, though, these *e*'s can be left unpronounced, depending on the metrical requirements of the line (see rules *24* and *25* below). Examples:

*chapeleyne, rote, sonne, melodye, ende, nyne, felaweshipe, ryse, take*

**11.** *e*—Pronounced "ah" in certain words in which it precedes the letter *r*. You can see from the list of examples that the Middle English pronunciation of the *er* was often identical with the Modern English, though we have often changed the spelling to *ar*. Examples:

*berne* (barn), *clerk* (clark), *derk* (dark), *ers* (arse), *ferre* (far), *ferther* (farther), *herke* (hark), *hert* (hart, stag), *herte* (heart), *person* (parson), *sterre* (star), *sterte* (start), *werre* (war), *werte* (wart), *yerde* (yard, staff)

**12.** *ei, ey*—Pronounced "ah-ee," like the *ai*-diphthong in the Modern English "aisle." See also rule *5* above. The *ai, ay, ei,* and *ey* spellings all yielded the same sound. Examples:

*veyne, feith, they, wey, reysed* (campaigned), *vileinye, leyd* (layed), *deyntee* (dainty, delicate), *curteisye* (courtesy)

**13.** *eu, ew*—Pronounced "ee-oo," like *ew* in Modern English "few" and "mew" in most words except the seven listed in rule *14* next. Examples:

*reule* (rule, regulation), *reuled* (ruled), *newe, stewe* (small coop or room), *mewe* (fishpond)

**14.** *eau, ew*—Pronounced "eh-oo"—a diphthong vowelglide sound not duplicated in a Modern English word, but a little like the vowel sounds of "pay you." This sound is found only in the following seven Middle English words. Examples:

*fewe, lewed* (lewd, ignorant), *dew, shewe* (show), *shrewe, beaute, hewe*

**15. *i, y*—**Pronounced "ih" like the short *i* in "him," "thin," "wistful" if the vowel in that word today has the short-*i* sound. Thus, words with the short-*i* sound in Modern English had the same sound for Chaucer. Examples:

*priketh, skille, offring, Aprill, with, his, in, it, is, swich* (such), *pilgrimage, blisful, martir, bifel, riden* (ridden), *ilke* (same), *thinges*

**16. *i, y*—**Pronounced "ee" like the *ee* in Modern English "sheet" and "free" in words where the vowel is pronounced like the diphthong "eye" ("ah-ee") today, as in "bright" and "sigh," and "fly." It is also the sound of the participial marker *y-* that appears as prefix to some past-tense verbs like *y-falle* (had fallen) and *y-ronne* (had run). Examples:

*night, knyght, I, my, by, nyne* (nine), *twenty, melodye, ryse, devyse* (devise), *whyl* (while), *wyde* (wide, spacious), *tyme, worthy, ryden, wys* (wise), *wyped* (wiped), *yë* (eye), *y-ronne* (had run), *y-come* (had come), *y-wroght* (had made)

**17. *oi, oy*—**Pronounced "oh-ee," like the *oy* in Modern English "boy" and "decoy." This sound has not changed since Chaucer's time. Examples:

*coy, floytinge* (playing on the flute), *Seinte Loy, cloystre* (cloister), *oistre* (oyster), *point* (spear tip)

**18.** *o, oo*—Often pronounced "aw," as in Modern English "claw" and "hawk." The word is pronounced with that sound frequently—for example, if the Middle English *o* or *oo* appears in a word that is now pronounced like the vowel sound in "stone," "hot," "would," or "ought." Examples:

*ofte* (often), *hooly* (holy), *folk, spoken, fo* (foe), *so, also, no, hote* (hotly), *smoot* (smote)

**19.** *o, oo*—Pronounced like the vowel in Modern English "look" and "full" if the word in which *o* or *oo* appears is now pronounced like the vowel in Modern English "monk," "nun," and "shove." Examples:

*sondry* (sundry, varied), *love, above, of, yonge, sunne, fredom, month*

**20.** *o, oo*—Pronounced "oh" like the long *o* in Modern English "most" and "stone" if the word is now spelled *oo* or pronounced like the *oo* in Modern English "food." Examples:

*rote* (root), *good, to, blood*

**21.** *ou, ow*—Usually pronounced "oo," like the vowel in Modern English "ooze" and "shoe." For the exception, see rule *22* below. Examples:

*shoures* (showers), *licour* (liquid, moisture), *cours* (course), *fowles* (fowls, birds), *flour* (flower), *you, yow* (you), *oure, your, resoun* (reason), *aboute* (around)

**22.** *ou, ow*—Pronounced "aw-uh," like a two-syllable *aw* in Modern English "crawl" or *au* in the name Paul. This pronunciation is used when the Modern English equivalent of the word has a long *o* or "oh" sound as in "know." Examples:

*knowen* (know), *soule* (soul), *unknowe* (unknown), *lowe*

**23. *u***—Pronounced like the vowel sound in Modern English "look" and "full." Because there is only one alternative in this list of rules for the single *u*, you can always assume that when the letter appears without another vowel, it rhymes with the vowel sound of "book." Examples:

*ful, fustian* (coarse cloth), *muchel* (much), *crulle* (curly), *lusty*

## Iambic Pentameter

The right-page translations that accompany the left-page Chaucerian texts are in prose. Our goal in doing the translations was not to be poetic in rendering Chaucer's verse but to be accurate in conveying, line by line, his meanings. The right-page translations do not rhyme and are not in any regular poetic meter. They are inevitably, then, somewhat flat and inelegant. We cannot read Chaucer's own *Canterbury Tales* in his own language, however, without understanding something about early English iambic pentameter. Chaucer cannot be said to be the first English poet to write in iambic pentameter, but there is no question that by using it almost exclusively in this work, Chaucer established it as the gold standard of English poetic meters and set the pattern for much of the English poetry—including Shakespeare's—that followed.

An iamb is a two-syllable poetic unit in which the first syllable is unaccented, the second accented. Some examples of iambic words in Modern English are "alone," "return," and "pretend." That is, we say "a**lone**," not "**a**lone," "re**turn**," not "**re**turn," and "pre**tend**" not "**pre**tend." Some two-syllable words can be iambic, as these are, but two separate words can also form a natural iamb when said together: "the cow," "in tune," "on top." An iambic pentameter line is a line joining together five iambic units in such a way that we end up with a ten-syllable line in which the first is unaccented, the second accented, the third unaccented, and so on until the tenth syllable, which is accented. Here are examples of four Modern English iambic pentameter lines:

When Spike was young he ate a lot of junk.
He ate up all my aphrodisiacs.
That stupid dog is on the roof asleep,
And now he barely has the strength to leap.

Note that the rhyming of the last two lines make them a "couplet," but the main point here is that the first line has ten words, the second six, and the third eight, yet each has ten syllables and each is made up of five iambic units. The key to their being in iambic pentameter is not the number of words or merely the number of syllables, but that each line can be scanned without a great deal of forcing into five repeating units, each of which has an unstressed syllable followed by a stressed one. To fully appreciate Chaucer's poetry in *The Canterbury Tales,* we need to be able to read his lines in more-or-less regular iambic pentameter. Two important final rules, then, have to do with Chaucer's way of putting his English into iambic pentameter.

**24. Final *e***—When an *e* appears at the end of a word that comes at the end of a line of Chaucer's poetry, it should be read as an unstressed eleventh syllable. Although that eleventh syllable technically makes the line not precisely an iambic pentameter line, most scholars believe that Chaucer expected us to read that final *e* as a weak "uh" sounding syllable. After all, Chaucer almost always rhymes one final-e word with another, and there would be no point in doing that if they were not both to be said aloud. See rule *10* above.

**25. Internal *e***—Sometimes an *e* within the line can be dropped if the pentameter requirements of the line are such that the line scans better with the *e* left silent.

Chaucer had flexibility in that he could choose whether to pronounce certain unaccented internal *e*'s. To approximate Chaucer's reading of the lines, then, we need to determine which *e*'s need to be pronounced to make the lines most gracefully iambic. For example, in lines 35–36 of the General Prologue, we have Chaucer speaking this couplet:

But natheles, whyl I have tyme and space,
Er that I ferther in this tale pace ...

First off, notice the final *e*'s at the end of the two lines. They would need to be pronounced because of rule *24* above. But what about the other *e*'s? Well, it turns out that in the first line both *e*'s in *natheles* would be pronounced because the word is actually a Chaucerian contraction of "none the less" and because the iambic requires them to be. But the *e*'s at the end of *have* and *tyme* (time) would not be pronounced because that would give the line too many syllables. For *tyme* the following *and* supplies the unaccented part of the final iamb. In the second line the *e*'s in *Er* (ere, before) and *ferther* (farther) all need to be pronounced because they are necessary both to convey the meaning of the words and to fill out the iambic pentameter. But what about the final *e* in *tale* (meaning here story, account)? Unlike the *e* in *tyme,* which was silent, the *e* in *tale* must be spoken to provide the unaccented part of the closing iamb. The lines, therefore, would be pronounced thus, with the accented syllables in bold:

But **na**theles, whyl **I** hav **tym** and **space**,
Er **that** I **fer**ther **in** this **tale pace** ...

Different readers might scan these lines slightly differently, but the point is that Chaucer has given himself—and us—at least one way to scan his lines as iambic pentameter. Not all of his lines can be made to scan perfectly, any more than all of the end-rhymes in his couplets sound identical. Indeed, there is considerable evidence that he was more interested in meaning than in scansion or rhyming. But his verse is without question far more regular than scholars a century ago thought it was, and we now have the means, with a little time and effort, to hear him correctly.

## Chaucer's Personal Pronouns

Chaucer's personal pronouns are a good general guide to his pronunciation of other words. One of the best ways to read Chaucer correctly is to learn to pronounce his personal pronouns, since these come by so often:

> *I, my,* and *mine* were pronounced "ee," "mee," and "meen."

> *he, she, me,* and *we* were pronounced "hay," "shay," "may," and "way."

> *you, yow, youre, his, her,* and *it* were pronounced as they still are, "you," "your," "his," "her," and "it." The possessive pronoun *its* did not exist yet, and Chaucer uses *his* instead, pronounced like the Modern English "his."

> *our* rhymed with Modern English "sure" and "lure"; *they* was pronounced as a diphthong "thy-ee." The plural pronoun "them" did not exist yet; Chaucer used the pronoun *hem* instead, pronounced like the Modern English "hem."

Middle English is a lovely language. To hear some excellent Chaucer professors read it aloud as it was meant to sound, buy some tapes from The Chaucer Studio in care of the English Department at Brigham Young University, Provo, UT 84602-6218, or go online to http://academics.vmi.edu/english/audio/audio_index.html and give a listen. You'll see how graceful it sounds. Learning to pronounce Chaucerian English is not an easy task, but it is doable, and once you start to get the hang of it you will better appreciate not only the stories Chaucer told but also the musical beauty of the language in which he told them.

# THE
# CANTERBURY TALES

# THE
# GENERAL PROLOGUE

# INTRODUCTION

❦

THE GENERAL PROLOGUE to *The Canterbury Tales* is a stunning piece of work. In it Chaucer describes the gathering of thirty men and women at the Tabard Inn on London's south bank. They have little in common except that they are all on their way to pay homage at the tomb of Thomas Becket in the great cathedral in Canterbury where he had been murdered two centuries earlier by men eager to please the king of England. In the course of that evening, they discover a common interest: to be entertained and edified on their journey by tales told by their fellow pilgrims. In the owner of the Tabard Inn, they find a willing leader, a gregarious man later identified by name as Harry Bailey. The Host decides to join them and act as master of the storytelling.

The General Prologue is 860 lines long and is rightly famous for its vivid descriptions of the individual pilgrims. But it is more than that, as this brief outline of the structure of the Prologue shows:

1. *Introductory description* (lines 1–18). These lines celebrate the coming of sweet April showers after the dry deadness of March. The sun shines, the earth awakens, the buds poke through the ground, the birds sing. This physical renewal in nature is matched by a spiritual renewal in men and women who feel the need to make a pilgrimage to Canterbury in quest of help from the holy martyr Thomas Becket.

2. *Gathering of the pilgrims* (19–43). Chaucer tells how, while he was at the Tabard Inn in Southwark

ready to go on a pilgrimage, twenty-nine others came
in, heading in the same direction and for the same
purpose. He tells us that he will describe them—
who they were, their rank, their clothing.

3. *Descriptions of the pilgrims* (44–716). In this
large centerpiece of the General Prologue, Chaucer
describes most (but not all) of the pilgrims. We have
no way of knowing whether he meant to revisit the
General Prologue and fill out the missing or partial
portraits or whether he expected to describe them
more fully when he got to know them better on the
pilgrimage and before they told their tales. I shall
have more to say about the descriptions, and the
order of the descriptions, below.

4. *Chaucer's apology* (717–48). Chaucer dodges the
blame for the "villainous" tales that some of the
churlish pilgrims tell. He is only, he says, doing his
job as witness and reporter, and he has no authority
to change the words they actually said. He also
apologizes (clearly with tongue in cheek) for not
knowing how to list the pilgrims according to their
rank or "degree."

5. *Introduction of the Host* (749–823). Chaucer
describes the innkeeper, usually referred to as the
Host, who enjoys the merry pilgrims so much that
he offers to go along with them to Canterbury. He
proposes a tale-telling contest—each person to tell
two tales on the way, two on the way back—in which
the person who tells the best tales shall get a free
dinner when they all return to the Tabard. The pilgrims
are all to chip in to pay for the meal.

6. *The next day* (824–860). After a night's sleep, at
first light the pilgrims are roused by the Host and
start their journey. They draw straws and the Knight
cheerfully agrees to tell the first tale.

In the long centerpiece of the prologue, Chaucer describes
the pilgrims in the following order, with square brackets

indicating pilgrims he mentions but does not describe. Read down in the three columns:

| Knight | Merchant | Parson |
|---|---|---|
| Squire | Clerk | Plowman |
| Yeoman | Sergeant of Law | |
| | Franklin | Miller |
| Prioress | [Five Guildsmen] | Manciple |
| [Nun] | Cook | Reeve |
| [Nun's Priest] | Shipman | |
| Monk | Doctor | Summoner |
| Friar | Wife of Bath | Pardoner |

I have put them in three columns to suggest some possible ways to group them. In the first column we have the Knight, his son, and his yeoman and the members of the regular clergy (that is, clergy who are supposedly governed by an official code of rules). In the second column we have the large middle class. And in the third column we have the good Parson and his brother the Plowman and then the five who are generally thought of as the lowlifes or rascals on the pilgrimage. The ordering, however, is by no means rigid, and Chaucer seems to have wanted to describe the pilgrims more or less as he encountered them, not according to any prearranged logical or categorical plan. To be sure, there is perhaps a very general movement from high class to lower class, and perhaps also a very general movement from moral superiority to moral inferiority, but those patterns are violated frequently.

One of Chaucer's most likely sources for the idea of a group of wandering storytellers was Boccaccio's midfourteenth-century *Decameron,* which Chaucer almost certainly knew. Chaucer, however, made the framing device his own. In the *Decameron* the ten tale-tellers are all young men and women of the nobility. Chaucer's gathering of pilgrims is not only larger and more varied, but also more democratic and more dramatic. They represent virtually every segment of British society—those who worked, those who fought, and

those who prayed—and they interact together in more inter-
esting ways than do Boccaccio's. Unlike Boccaccio's tellers,
who are gathered together to escape the onslaught of the
bubonic plague that was killing their fellow citizens in Flor-
ence, Chaucer's pilgrims are joined by a desire to move
toward something positive: the shrine of a Christian martyr.
We should also note that whereas there are no religious tale-
tellers in the *Decameron,* Chaucer was especially interested
in the religious pilgrims. They by no means outnumber the
secular pilgrims, but their portraits are on average about
twice as long as those of the secular pilgrims. There is, to be
sure, criticism of the clergy in the *Decameron,* but the criti-
cism there is conveyed *by* the storytellers. In *The Canterbury
Tales* much of the criticism is *of* the storytellers.

There is much to say about the individual pilgrims, but I
leave the pleasures of discovering them to individual readers,
and perhaps to their teachers. Some readers will not want to
read through all of the descriptions at once, but may prefer to
read them in conjunction with their tales. After all, one of the
innovations in *The Canterbury Tales* is that, unlike Boccaccio
before him, Chaucer went to considerable lengths to assign
to the various tellers tales that at least generally suit their
class, their education, their marital situation, their personal
interests, and in some cases their annoyance with a fellow
pilgrim.

## NOTES

**Zephirus** (line 5). The west wind.

**Ram** (8). A reference to the zodiacal sign of the Ram in
Aries, where the "young" sun would be passing in mid- to
late April. In the introduction to "The Man of Law's Tale"
(not included in this book), the specific date of April 18 is
mentioned.

**holy blisful martir** (17). The tomb of Thomas Becket, who
was murdered in Canterbury Cathedral in December 1170,

was the most frequent pilgrim destination in medieval England.

**gentil** (72). Refers more to the Knight's gentle birth than to his gentle treatment of others, though for this man, both senses of the word applied. He is both a gentleman and a gentle man.

**Stratford atte Bowe** (125). That is, not the pure French of France, but French learned in England. The reference is probably to the Prioress's accent.

*Amor vincit omnia* (162). Latin for "Love conquers everything."

**venerye** (166). Hunting. As the rest of the description makes clear, the Monk loves to hunt. The term probably did not yet have its more modern connotation of "the things of Venus," though hints of the Monk's sexual interests lurk in this portrait.

**Seint Maure, Seint Beneit** (173). Saint Maurus was an early follower of Saint Benedict, the founder of the Benedictine order of monasteries and the writer of its original strict set of rules. Saint Maurus introduced the Benedictine rule into France.

**Austin** (187). Saint Augustine, who wrote a monastic rule urging monks to do hard physical labor.

**frankeleyns** (216). Landowners, usually indicating wealth. See the portrait of the Franklin starting at line 333 below.

*"In principio"* (256). Latin for "In the beginning," the opening lines of both Genesis and the gospel according to John.

**Middelburgh, Orewelle** (279). Middleburg was a Dutch port, Orwell an English one. Their locations, and the fact that the Merchant wears a Flemish beaver hat and deals in Flemish currency, suggests that his main commerce was with the Low Countries.

**Parvys** (312). Probably the porch of St. Paul's Cathedral in London, a customary place in Chaucer's time for clients to consult lawyers.

**complexioun, sangwyn** (335). An individual's temperament or disposition was thought to be determined by the proportions of the four humors in his or her constitution. The four humors were blood, phlegm, choler (yellow bile), and melancholy (black bile). In the sanguine humor, which might be indicated by a flushed face, the blood was thought to be hot and moist. See notes to lines 422 and 423 below.

**hote somer** (396). The reference to the hot summer sun is curious since the time of the year is April. It might be a Chaucerian oversight or inconsistency, or it might simply mean that the Shipman's tan from the previous summer is still with him. It is unlikely that we are to imagine the Shipman's voyages taking him below the equator (as it is currently located) where the seasons are reversed, since his usual routes seemed to confine him to the European seas and the Mediterranean. Chaucer mentions the Shipman's having visited in the *Magdalen* Bordeaux (southern France), Dartmouth (southwest England), Hull (Yorkshire), Carthage (either Tunisia or Spain), Gotland (Sweden), Cape Finistere (western Spain), and Brittany (northwestern France).

**hoot, cold, moiste, drye** (422). The four conditions that influenced the humors. There is no need here to go into the complexities of medieval medical theory and its connections to astrology, but it does seem that the Doctor was well versed in those theories and, for his time, a reasonably reliable physician, though perhaps a greedy one.

**humour** (423). The humors were bodily fluids that were supposed to influence human health and spirits: the blood, the phlegm, choler, and bile. Ailments were thought to have been caused by an imbalance in these fluids brought about in part by the warmth and dryness referred to in the previous line.

**Esculapius, Deiscorides, Rufus, Ypocras, Haly, Galien, Serapion, Razis, Avicen, Averrois, Damascien, Constantyn, Bernard, Gatesden, Gilbertyn** (431–36). This catalogue of medical writers shows some sophistication in the Doctor's learning.

**the Bible** (440). It is difficult to know what to make of the statement that the Doctor spent little time studying the Bible. For one thing, it was generally considered improper for laypeople to attempt to read or interpret the Bible for themselves, since they were supposed to learn about religious matters from official members of the church hierarchy. On the other hand, it might be that the Doctor placed more trust in medical writers, many of whom were pagan, than on the grace of God to cure human illness.

**Ypres, Gaunt** (450). The Flemish towns of Ypres and Ghent were famous for the quality of their weavers in Chaucer's time.

**at chirche-dore** (462). The official or legal part of a marriage took place outside the church door in front of witnesses. Then the wedding party went inside for a nuptial mass.

**withouten** (463). The phrase "withouten oother companye in youthe" suggests that Alisoun of Bath was a virgin at her first wedding at age twelve (not an unusual age for a first marriage in Chaucer's time), and remained faithful, even to her old husbands. Some readers, however, have chosen to read "withouten" to mean "not to mention" or "in addition to," thus hinting that Alisoun may have had many lovers in her young days.

**Jerusalem, Rome, Boloigne, Galice, Coloigne** (465–68). These were traditional destinations for Christian pilgrims in medieval times. It is particularly impressive that the Wife would have made three pilgrimages to Jerusalem in the Holy Lands—a long, expensive, and dangerous journey. Rome was the seat of the Catholic church and home to one of the two contending popes in Chaucer's time. It is telling that she visits there and not Avignon, in a part of Europe controlled by France, where the other pope resided. At Boulogne-sur-Mer, in northern France, was an image, supposedly delivered in a rudderless boat, of the Virgin Mary. At Galicia, in northwestern Spain, was a shrine to St. James. At Cologne, in what is now Germany, were several shrines, including a shrine to the eleven thousand virgins supposed to have been massacred there.

**foot-mantel** (474). Literally, a "foot-cloak," by which Chaucer means a set of chaps or leggings designed to protect the Wife's dress from being soiled by the sweat of her horse and the splashed mud of a medieval pathway. The use of the foot-mantle and the mention of her spurs suggests that she rode the horse astride rather than sidesaddle.

**"Questio quid iuris"** (648). Latin for "The question is, what part of the law?" The point here is that the Summoner knows almost no Latin but keeps parroting the same phrase over and over, hoping that his auditors will know even less and be impressed by his supposed learning.

**significavit** (664). Latin for "this signifies" or "be it known that"—the first word of a writ that authorized civil authorities to seize and imprison a person who had violated an ecclesiastical law. The offense in such cases was typically failure to pay one's tithes, but other violations might also result in such a transfer of penalizing authority: adultery, fornication, perjury, and so on.

**Rouncival** (672). There was a St. Mary Rouncevale hospital in Charing Cross, London, that was perhaps connected to the convent of Our Lady of Roncevalles in Spain. Perhaps the Pardoner was a fund-raiser who sold indulgences, or pardons for sins, to raise money for that hospital.

**"Com hider, love"** (674). "Come to me, my love." The song that the Pardoner and his friend the Summoner sing as a duet has sometimes been supposed to indicate a homosexual connection between the two men.

**vernicle** (687). A cloth badge, indicating a pilgrimage to Rome, showing the image of Christ on the veil of St. Veronica.

**a gelding** (693). A gelding is a castrated male horse. The Pardoner's high voice and beardlessness may indicate that he is a eunuch—a man who does not have and perhaps never did have testicles.

**the Belle** (721). Presumably the name of a rival tavern . Southwark.

**best sentence and most solas** (800). Here Chaucer suggests what has become the standard double-test for literary excellence, instruction and amusement. Chaucer never finished *The Canterbury Tales,* so we never find out who gets the free supper. Indeed, the pilgrims never quite reach Canterbury.

**the watering of Seint Thomas** (828). A brook not far outside of London where people and horses could refresh themselves on the way to Canterbury.

# THE PROLOGE

*Here biginneth the Book of the Tales of Caunterbury*

Whan that Aprill with his shoures sote
　　The droghte of Marche hath perced to the rote,
And bathed every veyne in swich licour
Of which vertu engendred is the flour;
Whan Zephirus* eek with his swete breeth　　　　5
Inspired hath in every holt and heeth
The tendre croppes, and the yonge sonne
Hath in the Ram* his halfe cours y-ronne,
And smale fowles maken melodye,
That slepen al the night with open yë　　　　　　10
(So priketh hem Nature in hir corages):
Than longen folk to goon on pilgrimages
And palmers for to seken straunge strondes,
To ferne halwes, couthe in sondry londes;
And specially, from every shires ende　　　　　　15
Of Engelond, to Caunterbury they wende,
The holy blisful martir* for to seke
That hem hath holpen, whan that they were seke.
　Bifel that in that seson on a day,
In Southwerk at the Tabard as I lay　　　　　　　20
Redy to wenden on my pilgrimage
To Caunterbury with ful devout corage,
At night was come into that hostelrye
Wel nyne and twenty in a companye
Of sondry folk, by aventure y-falle　　　　　　　25
In felawshipe, and pilgrims were they alle,
That toward Caunterbury wolden ryde.
The chambres and the stables weren wyde,

# THE GENERAL PROLOGUE

*Here begins the Book of the Canterbury Tales*

When April with his sweet showers has
pierced the dryness of March to the root,
and bathed every vein in such moisture
as has power to bring forth the flower;
when, also, Zephyrus with his sweet breath          5
has breathed spirit into the tender new shoots
in every wood and meadow, and the young sun
has run half his course in the sign of the Ram,
and small birds sing melodies and
sleep with their eyes open all the night          10
(so Nature pricks them in their hearts):
then people long to go on pilgrimages,
and palmers long to seek strange shores
and far-off shrines known in various lands,
and, especially, from the ends of every shire          15
in England they come to Canterbury,
to seek the holy, blissful martyr
who helped them when they were sick.
   It befell that one day in that season,
as I was in Southwark at the Tabard Inn,          20
ready to go on my pilgrimage
to Canterbury with a most devout heart,
at night there came into that hostelry
a company of nine-and-twenty people—
all sorts of people—who had met by chance;          25
and all of them were pilgrims
who were riding toward Canterbury.
The chambers and the stables were spacious,

And wel we weren esed atte beste.
And shortly, whan the sonne was to reste,    30
So hadde I spoken with hem everichon,
That I was of hir felawshipe anon,
And made forward erly for to ryse,
To take our wey, ther as I yow devyse.

But natheles, whyl I have tyme and space,    35
Er that I ferther in this tale pace,
Me thinketh it acordaunt to resoun
To telle yow al the condicioun
Of ech of hem, so as it semed me,
And whiche they weren, and of what degree,    40
And eek in what array that they were inne:
And at a knight than wol I first biginne.

A KNIGHT ther was, and that a worthy man,
That fro the tyme that he first bigan
To ryden out, he loved chivalrye,    45
Trouthe and honour, fredom and curteisye.
Ful worthy was he in his lordes werre,
And therto hadde he riden, no man ferre,
As wel in Cristendom as hethenesse,
And ever honoured for his worthinesse.    50
At Alisaundre he was, whan it was wonne;
Ful ofte tyme he hadde the bord bigonne
Aboven alle naciouns in Pruce;
In Lettow hadde he reysed and in Ruce,
No Cristen man so ofte of his degree;    55
In Gernade at the sege eek hadde he be
Of Algezir, and riden in Belmarye;
At Lyeys was he, and at Satalye,
Whan they were wonne; and in the Grete See
At many a noble armee hadde he be.    60
At mortal batailles hadde he been fiftene,
And foughten for our feith at Tramissene
In listes thryes, and ay slayn his fo.
This ilke worthy Knight had been also
Somtyme with the lord of Palatye,    65
Ageyn another hethen in Turkye:

and we were made most comfortable.
And shortly, when the sun had gone down,                          30
I had spoken with every one of them
so that I had soon become one of their group,
and made an arrangement to rise early
to be on our way, as I shall tell you.

But none the less, while I have time and space,                  35
before I pass on further in this tale,
it seems to me in order
to tell you all about
each of them, as they seemed to me—
and who they were, and of what rank in life,                     40
and also what they wore—
and with a knight, then, I will begin.
There was a KNIGHT, a valiant man,
who, from the time when he had first begun
to venture out, had loved chivalry,                              45
truth and honor, liberality and courtesy.
He had proved his worth in his lord's wars,
in which he had ridden as far as any man,
both in Christendom and in heathen lands,
and he had always been honored for his valor.                   50

He was at Alexandria when it was won;
many times he had sat at the head of the table
in Prussia, above knights of all nations;
he had campaigned in Lithuania, and in Russia,
more often than any other Christian man of his rank;            55
he had also been in Granada at the siege
of Algeciras, and had fought in Benmarin.
He had been at Lyas and at Attalia
when they were won; and he had sailed upon
the Mediterranean with many a noble host.                       60
He had been in fifteen mortal battles,
and fought for our faith at Tlemcen
three times in tournaments, and always slain his foe.
This same worthy Knight had also been
at one time with the lord of Balat,                             65
against another heathen in Turkey:

And evermore he hadde a sovereyn prys.
And though that he were worthy, he was wys,
And of his port as meke as is a mayde.
He never yet no vileinye ne sayde                          70
In al his lyf, unto no maner wight.
He was a verray, parfit, gentil* knight.
But for to tellen yow of his array,
His hors were gode, but he was nat gay.
Of fustian he wered a gipoun                               75
Al bismotered with his habergeoun;
For he was late y-come from his viage,
And wente for to doon his pilgrimage.

    With him there was his sone, a yong SQUYER,
A lovyere, and a lusty bacheler,                            80
With lokkes crulle as they were leyd in presse.
Of twenty yeer of age he was, I gesse.
Of his stature he was of evene lengthe,
And wonderly deliver, and of greet strengthe.
And he had been somtyme in chivachye,                      85
In Flaundres, in Artoys, and Picardye,
And born him wel, as of so litel space,
In hope to stonden in his lady grace.
Embrouded was he, as it were a mede
Al ful of fresshe floures, whyte and rede.                 90
Singinge he was, or floytinge, al the day;
He was as fresh as is the month of May.
Short was his goune, with sleves longe and wyde.
Wel coude he sitte on hors, and faire ryde.
He coude songes make and wel endyte,                       95
Juste and eek daunce, and well purtreye and wryte.
So hote he lovede, that by nightertale
He slepte namore than dooth a nightingale.
Curteys he was, lowly, and servisable,
And carf biforn his fader at the table.                    100
    A YEMAN hadde he, and servaunts namo

and always he had won the highest honor.
Although he was valiant, he was prudent,
and bore himself as meekly as a maiden;
never in all his life had he been                               70
rude to anyone at all.
He was a true, perfect, gentle knight.
But to tell you about his array—
His horses were good, but he was not gaily dressed.
He wore a fustian tunic,                                        75
much stained by his hauberk;
for he had just come back from his expedition,
and was on his way to make his pilgrimage.
    With him was his son, a young SQUIRE,
a lover, and a gay youth on his way to knighthood,             80
with locks as curly as if they had been pressed.
He was about twenty years old, I guess;
he was of normal height
and wonderfully agile, and of great strength.
He had been on cavalry expeditions for a while—               85
in Flanders, in Artois, and in Picardy—
and in this short time he had borne himself well,
in the hope of winning his lady's favor.
His clothing was embroidered so as to look like
    a meadow
all full of fresh flowers, white and red.                      90
He sang or fluted all the day long;
he was as youthful as the month of May.
His gown was short, with long, wide sleeves.
He knew how to sit his horse well, and ride
    beautifully;
he could compose songs and poems,                              95
joust and dance, too, and draw and write.
So hotly did he love that at night
he slept no more than a nightingale.
He was courteous, humble, and serviceable,
and carved for his father at the table.                       100
    A YEOMAN was also with the Knight, and no other
        servants

At that tyme, for him liste ryde so;
And he was clad in cote and hood of grene;
A sheef of pecok-arwes brighte and kene
Under his belt he bar ful thriftily;                                    105
Wel coude he dresse his takel yemanly:
His arwes drouped noght with fetheres lowe;
And in his hand he bar a mighty bowe.
A not-heed hadde he, with a broun visage.
Of wode-craft wel coude he al the usage.                    110
Upon his arm he bar a gay bracer,
And by his syde a swerd and a bokeler,
And on that other syde a gay daggere,
Harneised wel, and sharp as point of spere;
A Cristofre on his brest of silver shene;                        115
An horn he bar, the bawdrik was of grene.
A forster was he, soothly, as I gesse.
    Ther was also a Nonne, a PRIORESSE,
That of hir smyling was ful simple and coy.
Hir gretteste ooth was but "by Seinte Loy";           120
And she was cleped Madame Eglentyne.
Ful wel she song the service divyne,
Entuned in hir nose ful semely;
And Frensh she spak ful faire and fetisly,
After the scole of Stratford atte Bowe,*                      125
For Frensh of Paris was to hir unknowe.
At mete wel y-taught was she withalle;
She leet no morsel from hir lippes falle,
Ne wette hir fingres in hir sauce depe.
Wel coude she carie a morsel, and wel kepe,             130
That no drope ne fille upon hir brest.
In curteisye was set ful muchel hir lest.
Hir over-lippe wyped she so clene
That in hir coppe was no ferthing sene
Of grece, whan she dronken hadde hir draughte.    135
Ful semely after hir mete she raughte,
And sikerly she was of greet disport,
And ful plesaunt, and amiable of port,
And peyned hir to countrefete chere

at the time (so it pleased him to ride);
the yeoman was dressed in a coat and hood of green;
beneath his belt he carefully carried a
sheaf of bright, keen peacock-feathered arrows          105
(well did he know how to take care of his equipment:
his arrows never drooped with tired feathers!);
and in his hand he carried a mighty bow.
He was a brown-faced man, with a close-cropped head.
He knew all there is to know about woodcraft.           110
On his arm was a fine wrist guard,
and by one side a sword and shield;
on the other, a bright dagger,
well mounted and sharp as the point of a spear.
A silver Saint Christopher medal shone on his breast;   115
he carried a horn, with a green baldric.
I suppose that he must have been a forester.
    There was also a nun, a PRIORESS,
whose smile was modest and sweet.
Her greatest oath was only "By Saint Loy!"              120
She was called Madame Eglantine.
She sang the divine service well,
entuning it in her nose in a most seemly way;
and she spoke French well and properly,
after the school of Stratford-at-Bow—                   125
for the French of Paris was unknown to her.
Her table manners were admirable:
she never let a morsel fall from her lips,
nor wet her fingers too deeply in the sauce;
daintily she carried a morsel to her lips, taking care  130
that no drop should fall on her breast:
she took much pleasure in proper etiquette.
She wiped her upper lip so carefully that no
trace of grease could be seen in her cup
when she had taken a drink from it;                     135
she helped herself to food in a very proper way.
And certainly she was very cheerful,
most pleasant, and amiable in bearing,
and took great pains to behave in a well-

Of court, and been estatlich of manere, 140
And to ben holden digne of reverence.
But, for to speken of hir conscience,
She was so charitable and so pitous
She wolde wepe if that she sawe a mous
Caught in a trappe, if it were deed or bledde. 145
Of smale houndes had she, that she fedde
With rosted flesh, or milk and wastel-breed.
But sore wepte she if oon of hem were deed,
Or if men smoot it with a yerde smerte:
And al was conscience and tendre herte. 150
Ful semely hir wimpel pinched was;
Hir nose tretys; hir eyen greye as glas;
Hir mouth ful smal, and thereto softe and reed.
But sikerly she hadde a fair forheed;
It was almost a spanne brood, I trowe; 155
For, hardily, she was nat undergrowe.
Ful fetis was hir cloke, as I was war.
Of smal coral aboute hir arm she bar
A peire of bedes, gauded al with grene,
And theron heng a broche of gold ful shene, 160
On which ther was first write a crowned A,
And after, *Amor vincit omnia.**
     Another NONNE with hir hadde she,
That was hir chapeleyne, and PREESTES THREE.
     A MONK ther was, a fair for the maistrye, 165
An out-rydere, that lovede venerye;*
A manly man, to been an abbot able.
Ful many a deyntee hors hadde he in stable:
And whan he rood men mighte his brydel here
Ginglen in a whistling wind as clere 170
And eek as loude as dooth the chapel-belle
Ther as this lord was keper of the celle.
The reule of Seint Maure* or of Seint Beneit,*
By cause that it was old and somdel streit,
This ilke Monk leet olde thinges pace, 175
And held after the newe world the space.

bred fashion, to be stately in manner,                    140
and to appear worthy of reverence.
But to speak of her tender feelings:
she was so charitable and so full of pity
that she would weep if she saw a mouse
caught in a trap and dead or bleeding.                    145
She had a few small dogs that she fed
with roast meat, or milk and fine bread;
but she wept indeed if one of them died,
or if someone hit it smartly with a stick—
she was all feeling and tender heart.                    150
Her wimple was suitably pleated;
her nose well-shaped; her eyes bright as glass;
her mouth very small, and soft and red;
and indeed she had a fine forehead—
it was almost a handspan broad, I believe,                    155
for certainly she was not undersized.
I noticed that her cloak was becoming.
Around her arm she wore a rosary of
tiny coral beads, marked off with green,
and on it hung a lovely golden brooch,                    160
on which was written first a crowned *A,*
and then, *Amor vincit omnia.*
    With her she had another Nun,
who was her assistant, and Three Priests.
    There was a Monk—a splendid sort;                    165
an inspector of his monastery's estates, who loved
    venery;
a manly man, capable of being an abbot.
He had many a dainty horse in the stable,
and when he rode one might hear the
bells on his bridle jingle in the wind as                    170
loud and clear as the chapel bell
in the place where this Monk was in charge.
As for the rule of Saint Maurus or Saint Benedict:
since it was old and somewhat strict,
this same Monk let old-fashioned things pass away                    175
and held to the ways of the modern world.

He yaf nat of that text a pulled hen
That seith that hunters been nat holy men,
Ne that a monk, whan he is recchelees
Is lykned til a fish that is waterlees;                    180
This is to seyn, a monk out of his cloistre.
But thilke text held he nat worth an oistre;
And I seyde his opinioun was good.
What sholde he studie, and make himselven wood,
Upon a book in cloistre alwey to poure,                   185
Or swinken with his handes and laboure,
As Austin* bit? How shal the world be served?
Lat Austin have his swink to him reserved.
Therefore he was a pricasour aright;
Grehoundes he hadde, as swifte as fowel in flight;        190
Of priking and of hunting for the hare
Was al his lust, for no cost wolde he spare.
I seigh his sleves purfiled at the hond
With grys, and that the fyneste of a lond;
And, for to festne his hood under his chin,               195
He hadde of gold y-wroght a curious pin:
A love-knotte in the gretter ende ther was.
His heed was balled, that shoon as any glas,
And eek his face, as he had been anoint.
He was a lord ful fat and in good point;                  200
His eyen stepe, and rollinge in his heed,
That stemed as a forneys of a leed;
His botes souple, his hors in greet estat.
Now certeinly he was a fair prelat:
He was nat pale as a forpyned goost;                      205
A fat swan loved he best of any roost.
His palfrey was as broun as is a berye.
    A FRERE ther was, a wantown and a merye,
A limitour, a ful solempne man.
In alle the ordres foure is noon that can                 210
So muche of daliaunce and fair langage.
He hadde maad ful many a mariage

He didn't give a plucked hen for that text
which says that hunters are not holy men,
and that a monk, when he is heedless of duty,
is like a fish out of water—                                         180
that is to say, a monk out of his cloister;
but he held that text was not worth an oyster.
And I said his opinion was good.
Why should he study and drive himself mad,
always poring over a book in the cloister,                 185
or work with his hands and labor
as Saint Augustine ordered? How shall the world
    be served?
Let Augustine have his labor to himself.
Therefore he was a really hard-riding horseman.
He had greyhounds as swift as a bird in flight;          190
riding and hunting the hare
were all his joy; for this he spared no cost.
I saw that his sleeves were edged at the cuff
with gray fur, and that the finest in the land;
and to fasten his hood under his chin                        195
he had a very intricate pin made of gold;
there was a love knot in the bigger end.
His head was bald and shone like glass,
and his face did, too, as if he had been anointed.
He was a fine fat lord, in splendid shape;                   200
his protruding eyes rolled in his head and
glowed like a furnace under a pot;
his boots were supple, his horse well-groomed:
now certainly he was a handsome prelate—
he was not pale, like a wasted ghost;                        205
his favorite roast was a good fat swan;
his palfrey was as brown as a berry.
    There was a FRIAR, who was wanton and merry.
He was one licensed to beg in a limited area—a
    dignified
man. In all the four orders of friars no one else knew    210
as much about dalliance and sweet talk.
He had married off many a

Of yonge wommen, at his owene cost.
Unto his ordre he was a noble post.
Ful wel biloved and famulier was he                    215
With frankeleyns* overal in his contree,
And eek with worthy wommen of the toun:
For he had power of confessioun,
As seyde himself more than a curat,
For of his ordre he was licentiat.                     220
Ful swetely herde he confessioun,
And plesaunt was his absolucioun.
He was an esy man to yeve penaunce
Ther as he wiste to han a good pitaunce;
For unto a povre ordre for to yive                     225
Is signe that a man is wel y-shrive;
For if he yaf, he dorste make avaunt,
He wiste that a man was repentaunt;
For many a man so hard is of his herte,
He may nat wepe althogh him sore smerte.               230
Therefore, in stede of weping and preyeres,
Men moot yeve silver to the povre freres.
His tipet was ay farsed ful of knyves
And pinnes, for to yeven faire wyves.
And certeinly he hadde a mery note;                     235
Wel coude he singe and pleyen on a rote.
Of yeddinges he bar utterly the prys.
His nekke whyt was as the flour-de-lys;
Therto he strong was as a champioun.
He knew the tavernes wel in every toun,                240
And everich hostiler and tappestere
Bet than a lazar or a beggestere;
For unto swich a worthy man as he
Acorded nat, as by his facultee,
To have with seke lazars aqueyntaunce:                 245
It is nat honest, it may nat avaunce
For to delen with no swich poraille,
But al with riche and sellers of vitaille,
And overal, ther as profit sholde aryse,

young woman at his own expense.
He was a noble pillar of his order!
He was a well-beloved and familiar figure     215
among the franklins all over his part of the country,
and among the respectable townswomen, too:
for, as he himself said, he had powers connected with
confession which were greater than those of a
    curate,
since he was a licentiate of his order.     220
Most sweetly he heard confession,
and his absolution was pleasant.
He was an easy man in giving penance
where he knew he would gain a good pittance;
for to give to a poor order     225
is a sign that a man is well shriven;
if one gave, the friar could swear that
he knew that a man was repentant;
many a man is so hardhearted
he cannot weep, although he is very sorrowful.     230
Therefore, instead of weeping and praying,
men can give silver to the poor friars.
His cape was always stuffed full of knives
and pins, to give to fair young wives;
certainly he could carry a merry tune;     235
well could he sing and play a fiddle.
His ballads absolutely took the prize.
His neck was as white as the fleur-de-lis;
moreover, he was strong as a champion.
He knew the taverns well in every town,     240
and every innkeeper and barmaid
better than a leper or a beggarwoman; for
it is not fitting for such a respectable
man as he, in his position,
to be acquainted with sick lepers:     245
it is not right, there is no profit
in dealing with such paupers,
but with the rich and the sellers of food,
and in general wherever it might be profitable,

Curteys he was, and lowly of servyse.                                    250
Ther nas no man nowher so vertuous.
He was the beste beggere in his hous,
And yaf a certeyn ferme for the graunt;
Noon of his bretheren cam ther in his haunt;
For thogh a widwe hadde noght a sho,                                     255
So plesaunt was his *"In principio,"**
Yet wolde he have a ferthing, er he wente.
His purchas was wel bettre than his rente.
And rage he coude, as it were right a whelpe.
In love-dayes ther coude he muchel helpe,                                260
For there he was nat lyk a cloisterer,
With a thredbar cope, as is a povre scoler,
But he was lyk a maister or a pope:
Of double worsted was his semi-cope,
That rounded as a belle out of the presse.                               265
Somwhat he lipsed, for his wantownesse,
To make his English swete upon his tonge;
And in his harping, whan that he had songe,
His eyen twinkled in his heed aright
As doon the sterres in the frosty night.                                 270
This worthy limitour was cleped Huberd.

A MARCHANT was ther with a forked berd,
In mottelee, and hye on horse he sat,
Upon his heed a Flaundrish bever hat,
His botes clasped faire and fetisly.                                     275
His resons he spak ful solempnely,
Souninge alway th'encrees of his winning.
He wolde the see were kept for any thing
Bitwixe Middelburgh* and Orewelle.*
Wel coude he in eschaunge sheeldes selle.                                280
This worthy man ful wel his wit bisette;
Ther wiste no wight that he was in dette,
So estatly was he of his governaunce,
With his bargaynes, and with his chevisaunce.
For sothe he was a worthy man withalle;                                  285
But, sooth to seyn, I noot how men him calle.

A CLERK ther was of Oxenford also,

he was courteous and humbly serviceable. 250
There was nowhere a better man.
He was the best beggar in his house
and gave a definite rent for his area;
none of his brethren came into his domain;
For though a widow might not have a shoe, 255
his *In principio* was so pleasant
that he would still get a farthing before he went.
His takings were a good deal better than his rent.
He could wanton as if he were a puppy.
He was a great help with legal settlements, 260
at these he did not look like a cloistered monk,
with a threadbare cloak, as a poor scholar does,
but more like a master or a pope:
his robe was made of double worsted
and was rounded like a bell right out of the mold. 265
He affected somewhat of a lisp
to make his English sweet upon his tongue;
and when he harped at the end of a song,
his eyes twinkled in his head just
like the stars on a frosty night. 270
This worthy licensed beggar was called Hubert.

There was a MERCHANT with a forked beard;
dressed in motley, he sat high on his horse.
On his head was a Flemish beaver hat;
his boots were clasped handsomely and well. 275
He delivered his remarks very solemnly,
always emphasizing how his profits grew.
He wanted the sea to be guarded at all costs
between Middelburg and Orwell.
He did well on the exchange, selling Flemish currency. 280
This worthy man made good use of his wits;
no one knew he was in debt,
he conducted himself in such a stately way,
with his bargainings and his borrowings.
In any case, he was indeed a worthy man; 285
but to tell the truth, I don't know what his name is.

There was also a CLERK of Oxford,

That unto logik hadde longe y-go.
As lene was his hors as is a rake,
And he nas nat right fat, I undertake,          290
But loked holwe, and therto soberly.
Ful thredbar was his overest courtepy,
For he hadde geten him yet no benefyce,
Ne was so worldly for to have offyce.
For him was lever have at his beddes heed      295
Twenty bokes, clad in blak or reed,
Of Aristotle and his philosophye,
Than robes riche, or fithele, or gay sautrye.
But al be that he was a philosophre,
Yet hadde he but litel gold in cofre;          300
But al that he mighte of his freendes hente,
On bokes and on lerninge he it spente,
And bisily gan for the soules preye
Of hem that yaf him wherwith to scoleye.
Of studie took he most cure and most hede.     305
Noght o word spak he more than was nede,
And that was seyd in forme and reverence,
And short and quik, and ful of hy sentence.
Souninge in moral vertu was his speche,
And gladly wolde he lerne, and gladly teche.   310
   A SERGEANT OF THE LAWE, war and wys,
That often hadde been at the Parvys,*
Ther was also, ful riche of excellence.
Discreet he was, and of greet reverence:
He semed swich, his wordes weren so wyse.      315
Justyce he was ful often in assyse,
By patente, and by pleyn commissioun;
For his science, and for his heigh renoun
Of fees and robes hadde he many oon.
So greet a purchasour was no-wher noon;        320
Al was fee simple to him in effect,
His purchasing mighte nat been infect.
Nowher so bisy a man as he ther nas,

who had long since devoted himself to the course
    of logic.
His horse was as lean as a rake,
and he himself was not exactly fat, I assure you,                    290
but looked hollow and serious.
His outer cloak was very threadbare,
for as yet he had not got himself a benefice,
nor was he worldly enough to hold a secular office.
He would rather have twenty volumes                    295
of Aristotle and his philosophy, bound in
black or red, at the head of his bed than
rich robes, or a fiddle or lively harp.
But although he was a philosopher,
he still had little gold in his coffers;                    300
he spent all that he could get from his friends
on books and learning,
and diligently prayed for the souls
of those who gave him money to carry on his
    studies with.
He gave most of his attention to studying.                    305
He never spoke a word more than was necessary,
and what he did say was in due form, and reverent,
and short and to the point, and full of lofty thought:
his talk tended toward moral qualities,
and gladly would he learn, and gladly teach.                    310
    A SERGEANT OF THE LAW, wary and wise,
who had often been in the portal of Saint Paul's
for consultation, was also there—an excellent man.
He was discreet, and greatly to be respected:
or so he seemed, his words were so wise.                    315
He had often been a justice in assizes,
by appointment and by full commission;
his knowledge and his high renown had
won him many fees and robes.
Nowhere was there a greater buyer of land;                    320
all was fee-simple to him, in effect:
his title could never be found defective.
Nowhere was there a man as busy as he—

And yet he semed bisier than he was.
In termes hadde he caas and domes alle          325
That from the tyme of King William were falle.
Therto he coude endyte, and make a thing,
Ther coude no wight pinche at his wryting;
And every statut coude he pleyn by rote.
He rood but hoomly in a medlee cote          330
Girt with a ceint of silk, with barres smale;
Of his array telle I no lenger tale.

   A FRANKELEYN was in his companye;
Whyt was his berd, as is the dayesye.
Of his complexioun* he was sangwyn.*          335
Wel loved he by the morwe a sop in wyn.
To liven in delyt was ever his wone,
For he was Epicurus owne sone,
That heeld opinioun that pleyn delyt
Was verray felicitee parfyt.          340
An housholdere, and that a greet, was he;
Seint Julian he was in his contree.
His breed, his ale, was alwey after oon;
A bettre envyned man was nowher noon.
Withoute bake mete was never his hous,          345
Of fish and flesh, and that so plentevous
It snewed in his hous of mete and drinke,
Of alle deyntees that men coude thinke.
After the sondry sesons of the yeer,
So chaunged he his mete and his soper.          350
Ful many a fat partrich hadde he in mewe,
And many a breem and many a luce in stewe.
Wo was his cook but if his sauce were
Poynaunt and sharp, and redy al his gere.
His table dormant in his halle alway          355
Stood redy covered al the longe day.
At sessiouns ther was he lord and sire;
Ful ofte tyme he was knight of the shire.
An anlas and a gipser al of silk

and yet he seemed busier than he was.
he knew the exact terms of all the cases and judgments   325
occurring since the time of King William the
    Conquerer.
Also, he could write and draw up a deed
so that no man could find fault with his drafts;
and he knew every statute absolutely by heart.
He rode simply dressed in a coat of mixed weave,   330
gathered with a silk belt with small metal ornaments.
I shall not say any more about his dress.
  A FRANKLIN accompanied him;
his beard was as white as a daisy.
His temperament was sanguine. He dearly   335
loved a morning sop of bread in wine.
It was always his custom to live pleasurably,
for he was own son to Epicurus,
who believed that complete pleasure
equaled true and perfect happiness.   340
He was a householder, and a great one:
the patron saint of hospitality of his part of
    the country.
The quality of his bread and ale never varied;
a man better furnished in his wine cellar did not exist.
His house was never without baked dishes,   345
both fish and meat, and these so plenteous
that it seemed to snow food and drink in his house,
with all the delicacies thinkable.
He varied his dinner and supper
according to the various seasons of the year.   350
He had many a fat partridge in his coop,
and many a carp and pike in his fishpond.
Woe betide his cook unless his sauce was
pungent and sharp, and all his utensils ready.
In his great hall the table stood   355
always ready, fully set all the day long.
At court sessions he was lord and master.
He was often in Parliament as Knight of the Shire.
A dagger and a purse made of silk

Heng at his girdel, whyt as morne milk.                         360
A shirreve hadde he been, and a countour;
Was nowher such a worthy vavasour.

    An HABERDASSHER and a CARPENTER,
A WEBBE, a DYERE, and a TAPICER,
Were with us eek, clothed in o liveree                          365
Of a solempne and greet fraternitee.
Ful fresh and newe hir gere apyked was;
Hir knyves were y-chaped noght with bras,
But al with silver; wroght ful clene and weel
Hir girdles and hir pouches every-deel.                         370
Wel semed ech of hem a fair burgeys
To sitten in a yeldhalle on a deys.
Everich, for the wisdom that he can,
Was shaply for to been an alderman;
For catel hadde they ynogh and rente,                           375
And eek hir wyves wolde it wel assente;
And elles certein were they to blame:
It is ful fair to been y-clept *"ma dame,"*
And goon to vigilyës al bifore,
And have a mantel royalliche y-bore.                            380

    A COOK they hadde with hem for the nones,
To boille the chiknes with the marybones,
And poudre-marchant tart, and galingale.
Wel coude he knowe a draughte of London ale.
He coude roste, and sethe, and broille, and frye,              385
Maken mortreux, and wel bake a pye.
But greet harm was it, as it thoughte me,
That on his shine a mormal hadde he.
For blankmanger, that made he with the beste.

    A SHIPMAN was ther, woning fer by weste:                   390
For aught I woot, he was of Dertemouthe.
He rood upon a rouncy, as he couthe,
In a gowne of falding to the knee.
A daggere hanging on a laas hadde he

hung at his girdle, white as morning milk. 360
He had been a sheriff and a county auditor.
Nowhere else was there such a worthy landholder.
   A HABERDASHER and a CARPENTER,
a WEAVER, a DYER, and a TAPESTRY MAKER were
     with us, too,
all clothed in the same livery— 365
that of a great and dignified guild.
Their gear was all freshly and newly adorned;
Their knives were mounted not with brass,
but entirely with silver; their belts and their
purses were beautifully made in every respect. 370
Each of them seemed indeed a burgess imposing
     enough
to sit on the dais in a guildhall;
every one of them, because of his wisdom,
was suited to be an alderman,
for they had enough property and income, 375
and also their wives would certainly agree to it
(otherwise they would surely be to blame):
it is very nice to be called "Madame,"
to go into church first on feast eves,
and to have your mantle borne right royally. 380
   They had a COOK with them for the occasion,
to boil the chickens with the marrowbones
and tart spices and seasonings.
He could easily recognize a draft of London ale.
He could roast, and boil, and broil, and fry, 385
make stews, and bake a pie well.
But it was a shame, it seemed to me,
that he had an ulcer on his shin.
For making an elegant chicken stew, he was among
     the best.
   A SHIPMAN was there, who lived far in the west; 390
for all I know, he came from Dartmouth.
In a coarse knee-length woolen gown, he
rode a large nag as best he could.
He had a dagger hanging on a strap

Aboute his nekke under his arm adoun.                          395
The hote somer* had maad his hewe al broun.
And certeinly he was a good felawe;
Ful many a draughte of wyn had he y-drawe
From Burdeux-ward, whyl that the chapman sleep:
Of nyce conscience took he no keep;                           400
If that he faught and hadde the hyer hond,
By water he sente hem hoom to every lond.
But of his craft to rekene wel his tydes,
His stremes and his daungers him bisydes,
His herberwe and his mone, his lode-menage,                   405
Ther nas noon swich from Hulle to Cartage.
Hardy he was, and wys to undertake;
With many a tempest hadde his berd been shake.
He knew wel alle the havenes, as they were,
From Gootlond to the cape of Finistere,                       410
And every cryke in Britayne and in Spayne;
His barge y-cleped was the Maudelayne.
      With us ther was a DOCTOUR OF PHISYK;
In al this world ne was ther noon him lyk
To speke of phisik and of surgerye.                           415
For he was grounded in astronomye;
He kepte his pacient a ful greet del
In houres by his magik naturel.
Wel coude he fortunen the ascendent
Of his images for his pacient.                                420
He knew the cause of everich maladye,
Were it of hoot* or cold,* or moiste,* or drye,*
And where engendred, and of what humour;*
He was a verray, parfit practisour.
The cause y-knowe, and of his harm the rote,                  425
Anon he yaf the seke man his bote.
Ful redy hadde he his apothecaries
To sende him drogges and his letuaries,
For ech of hem made other for to winne;
Hir frendschipe nas nat newe to biginne.                      430
Wel knew he th'olde Esculapius,*

which went about his neck and down under his arm.                395
The hot summer had tanned him.
And certainly he was a good fellow;
he had drawn many a draft of wine
on the way from Bordeaux while the wine merchant
     slept.
He paid no mind to fussy conscience;                             400
if he fought and had the upper hand,
he sent his captives home to every land by water.
But when it came to his craft of reckoning his tides,
his currents and the hazards around him,
his anchorage and his moon and his compass work,               405
there was no other such man from Hull to Cartagena.
He was a hardy man, prudent in his undertakings;
many a tempest had shaken his beard.
He knew all the havens as they appear
from Gotland to the cape of Finisterre,                          410
and every creek in Brittany and Spain;
his ship was called the *Magdalen*.
     With us there was a DOCTOR OF MEDICINE;
in all this world there was none other like him
when it comes to medicine and surgery.                          415
For he was grounded in astronomy, and he
tended his patients at the proper astrological
hours through his knowledge of natural magic.
He could tell when the right planet was in
the ascendant for the use of images to help                     420
his patient. He knew the cause of every malady,
be it hot or cold or moist or dry,
and where it is engendered, and from what humor:
he was a really perfect practitioner.
Having learned the cause and root of the evil,                  425
he gave the sick man a remedy at once.
He had his apothecaries quite ready
to send him drugs and medicines,
for each of them helped the other to profit;
their friendship was not recently begun.                        430
Well did he know ancient Aesculapius,

And Deiscorides,* and eek Rufus,*
Old Ypocras,* Haly,* and Galien,*
Serapion,* Razis,* and Avicen,*
Averrois,* Damascien,* and Constantyn,*          435
Bernard,* and Gatesden,* and Gilbertyn.*
Of his diete mesurable was he,
For it was of no superfluitee,
But of greet norissing and digestible.
His studie was but litel on the Bible.*          440
In sangwin and in pers he clad was al,
Lyned with taffata and with sendal;
And yet he was but esy of dispence;
He kepte that he wan in pestilence.
For gold in phisik is a cordial,          445
Therfore he lovede gold in special.
    A good WYF was ther of bisyde BATHE,
But she was somdel deef, and that was scathe.
Of clooth-making she hadde swiche an haunt
She passed hem of Ypres* and of Gaunt.*          450
In al the parisshe wyf ne was ther noon
That to th' offring bifore hir sholde goon;
And if ther dide, certeyn so wrooth was she,
That she was out of alle charitee.
Hir coverchiefs ful fyne were of ground:          455
I dorste swere they weyeden ten pound
That on a Sonday were upon hir heed.
Hir hosen weren of fyn scarlet reed,
Ful streite y-teyd, and shoos ful moiste and newe.
Bold was hir face, and fair, and reed of hewe.          460
She was a worthy womman al hir lyve;
Housbondes at chirche-dore* she hadde fyve,
Withouten* other companye in youthe;
But therof nedeth nat to speke as nouthe.
And thryes hadde she been at Jerusalem;*          465
She hadde passed many a straunge streem;
At Rome* she hadde been, and at Boloigne,*
In Galice* at Seint Jame, and at Cologne.*
She coude muche of wandring by the weye.

Dioscorides, and Rufus, too;
ancient Hippocrates, Hali and Galen, Serapion,
Rhazes, and Avicenna, Averroes,
Damascenus, and Constantine, 435
Bernard, and Gatesden, and Gilbert.
He was temperate in his diet,
for it did not include anything superfluous,
but was very nourishing and digestible.
His study was but rarely of the Bible. 440
He was dressed entirely in bright red and blue,
lined with taffeta and finest silk;
and yet he was far from free in his spending;
he kept the money he gained in time of pestilence.
Since gold in medicine is a stimulant, 445
therefore he loved gold especially.
    A good WIFE was there, from near Bath.
She was somewhat deaf, which was a shame.
She had such a talent for making cloth
that she surpassed the weavers of Ypres and Ghent. 450
In all the parish there was no wife
entitled to make her offering before her,
and if one did, certainly she was so angry
that she was out of all charity.
Her kerchiefs were of very fine fabric: 455
I dare say that the ones that were on her head of
a Sunday must have weighed ten pounds.
Her hose were of fine scarlet red,
laced tightly, and her shoes very new and supple.
Her face was bold and handsome and ruddy. 460
She had been a worthy woman all her life;
she had had five husbands at the church door,
aside from other company in youth;
but of that there is no need to speak now.
And three times had she been at Jerusalem; 465
she had crossed many a strange river;
she had been at Rome and at Boulogne,
in Galicia at the shrine of Saint James, and at Cologne.
She knew much about wandering by the way.

Gat-tothed was she, soothly for to seye.                    470
Upon an amblere esily she sat,
Y-wimpled wel, and on hir heed an hat
As brood as is a bokeler or a targe;
A foot-mantel* aboute hir hipes large,
And on hir feet a paire of spores sharpe.                   475
In felawschip wel coude she laughe and carpe.
Of remedyes of love she knew perchaunce,
For she coude of that art the olde daunce.

    A good man was ther of religioun,
And was a povre PERSOUN of a toun,                          480
But riche he was of holy thoght and werk.
He was also a lerned man, a clerk,
That Cristes gospel trewely wolde preche;
His parisshens devoutly wolde he teche.
Benigne he was, and wonder diligent,                        485
And in adversitee ful pacient,
And swich he was y-preved ofte sythes.
Ful looth were him to cursen for his tythes,
But rather wolde he yeven, out of doute,
Unto his povre parisshens aboute                            490
Of his offring and eek of his substaunce.
He coude in litel thing han suffisaunce.
Wyd was his parisshe, and houses fer asonder,
But he ne lafte nat, for reyn ne thonder,
In siknes nor in meschief, to visyte                        495
The ferreste in his parisshe, muche and lyte,
Upon his feet, and in his hand a staf.
This noble ensample to his sheep he yaf,
That first he wroghte, and afterward he taughte;
Out of the gospel he tho wordes caughte;                    500
And this figure he added eek therto,
That if gold ruste, what shal iren do?
For if a preest be foul, on whom we truste,
No wonder is a lewed man to ruste;
And shame it is, if a preest take keep,                     505
A shiten shepherde and a clene sheep.
Wel oghte a preest ensample for to yive

She was gap-toothed, to tell the truth.                470
On an ambling horse she sat easily,
well wimpled; and on her head was a hat
as broad as a buckler or a shield;
a foot-mantle was loose about her hips,
and on her feet a pair of sharp spurs.                475
In company she could laugh and gossip well.
She knew of the remedies of love, as it happened,
for she knew that art's old dance.

    There was a good man of religion
who was a poor PARSON of a town;                480
but he was rich in holy thoughts and works.
He was also a learned man, a clerk,
who would truly preach Christ's gospel;
he would teach his parishioners devoutly.
He was benign, and wonderfully diligent,                485
and most patient in adversity,
and had been proved to be such many times.
He was loath to condemn a man for not paying his tithes,
but would, without a doubt, rather give
his poor parishioners thereabouts                490
part of his own offerings and property.
He was satisfied with very little.
His parish was wide and its houses far apart,
but he never neglected—for rain or thunder,
sickness or trouble—to visit on foot,                495
with a staff in his hand,
the furthest in his parish, great or humble.
He gave this noble example to his sheep:
that he practiced first and preached afterwards.
He took this motto from the gospel                500
and further added this saying:
that if gold rusts, what shall iron do?
For if a priest in whom we trust be corrupt,
it is no wonder if an ignorant man go to rust.
And it is indeed shameful (if a priest will but note)                505
to find a filthy shepherd and a clean sheep.
Surely a priest ought to give an example,

By his clennesse how that his sheep shold live.
He sette nat his benefice to hyre
And leet his sheep encombred in the myre          510
And ran to London, un-to Seinte Poules,
To seken him a chaunterie for soules,
Or with a bretherhed to been withholde,
But dwelte at hoom and kepte wel his folde,
So that the wolf ne made it nat miscarie;          515
He was a shepherde and no mercenarie.
And though he holy were, and vertuous,
He was to sinful men nat despitous,
Ne of his speche daungerous ne digne,
But in his teching discreet and benigne.          520
To drawen folk to heven by fairnesse
By good ensample, this was his bisinesse:
But it were any persone obstinat,
What-so he were, of heigh or lowe estat,
Him wolde he snibben sharply for the nones.          525
A bettre preest I trowe that nowher noon is.
He wayted after no pompe and reverence,
Ne maked him a spyced conscience,
But Cristes lore, and his apostles twelve,
He taughte, and first he folwed it himselve.          530

    With him ther was a PLOWMAN, was his brother,
That hadde y-lad of dong ful many a fother.
A trewe swinker and a good was he,
Livinge in pees and parfit charite;
God loved he best with al his hole herte          535
At alle tymes, thogh him gamed or smerte,
And thanne his neighebour right as himselve.
He wolde thresshe, and therto dyke and delve,
For Cristes sake, for every povre wight,
Withouten hyre, if it lay in his might.          540
His tythes payed he ful faire and wel,
Bothe of his propre swink and his catel.
In a tabard he rood upon a mere.

    Ther was also a Reve and a Millere,
A Somnour and a Pardoner also,          545

by his own spotlessness, of how his sheep should live.
He did not hire out his benefice
and leave his sheep encumbered in the mire                    510
while he ran off to London, to Saint Paul's,
to find himself a chantry for souls
or be shut up with a religious order,
but stayed at home and kept his fold well,
so that the wolf could not harm it:                           515
he was a shepherd and not a mercenary.
And although he was holy and virtuous,
he was not scornful to sinful men,
or haughty and proud in his speech,
but discreet and benign in his teaching.                      520
To draw folk to heaven by fair behavior
and good example—that was his business.
But if any person were obstinate,
whoever he was, of high or low degree,
he would scold him sharply on that occasion.                  525
I believe there is no better priest anywhere.
He did not look for pomp and reverence,
nor affect an overly scrupulous conscience;
he taught the lore of Christ and his twelve
Apostles—but first he followed it himself.                    530
    With him there was a PLOWMAN, his brother,
who had pulled many a cartload of dung.
He was a good and faithful laborer,
living in peace and perfect charity.
He loved God best with all his heart,                         535
at all times, whether he was pleased or grieved,
and next he loved his neighbor as himself.
He would thresh, and also dig and delve
for Christ's sake, for every poor man,
without pay, if it were in his power.                         540
He paid his tithes fairly and well,
both on his own earnings and on his property.
Wearing a tunic, he rode upon a mare.
    There were also a Reeve and a Miller,
a Summoner and a Pardoner, too,                               545

A Maunciple, and myself; ther were namo.
　　The MILLER was a stout carl, for the nones;
Ful big he was of braun, and eek of bones;
That proved wel, for overal ther he cam
At wrastling he wolde have alwey the ram.　　　　550
He was short-sholdred, brood, a thikke knarre.
Ther nas no dore that he nolde heve of harre,
Or breke it, at a renning, with his heed.
His berd as any sowe or fox was reed,
And therto brood, as though it were a spade.　　　555
Upon the cop right of his nose he hade
A werte, and theron stood a tuft of heres,
Reed as the bristles of a sowes eres;
His nose-thirles blake were and wyde.
A swerd and bokeler bar he by his syde.　　　　560
His mouth as greet was as a greet forneys.
He was a janglere and a goliardeys;
And that was most of sinne and harlotryes.
Wel coude he stelen corn, and tollen thryes;
And yet he hadde a thombe of gold, pardee.　　　565
A whyt cote and a blew hood wered he.
A baggepype wel coude he blowe and sowne,
And therwithal he broghte us out of towne.
　　A gentil MAUNCIPLE was ther of a temple,
Of which achatours mighte take exemple　　　　570
For to be wyse in bying of vitaille,
For whether that he payde, or took by taille,
Algate he wayted so in his achat
That he was ay biforn and in good stat.
Now is not that of God a ful fair grace,　　　　575
That swich a lewed mannes wit shal pace
The wisdom of an heep of lerned men?
Of maistres hadde he mo than thryes ten,
That were of lawe expert and curious,
Of which ther were a doseyn in that hous　　　　580
Worthy to been stiwardes of rente and lond
Of any lord that is in Engelond,

a Manciple and myself—there were no more.
   The MILLER was a stout fellow indeed;
he was huge—brawny, and large-boned, too;
this was well proved, for wherever he came
he always won the ram at wrestling matches. 550
He was short-shouldered and broad—a thick-set knave.
There was no door that he could not heave from
    its hinges
or break at a run with his head.
His beard was as red as a sow or a fox,
and as broad as a spade as well; 555
right on top of his nose he had
a wart, and on it stood a tuft of hairs,
red as the bristles of a sow's ears;
his nostrils were black and wide.
He bore a sword and buckler by his side. 560
His mouth was as wide as a great furnace.
He was a chatterer and a teller of tavern tales,
mostly about sin and ribaldry.
He knew well how to steal corn and charge threefold;
and yet he had a thumb of gold, all right. 565
He wore a white coat and a blue hood.
He could blow and play a bagpipe well,
and to its tune he brought us out of town.
   There was a gentle MANCIPLE of the Inner Temple,
from whom buyers might take an example 570
of how to be wise in purchasing food supplies;
for whether he paid or bought on account,
he was always so careful in his buying
that he was always ahead and prosperous.
Now, isn't it a fair example of God's favor 575
that such an ignorant man's wit can surpass
the wisdom of a heap of learned men?
He had more than thirty masters
who were cunning experts in the law
and of whom there were a dozen in that house 580
worthy to be stewards of the income and land
of any lord in England,

To make him live by his propre good,
In honour dettelees, but he were wood,
Or live as scarsly as him list desire,                                585
And able for to helpen al a shire
In any cas that mighte falle or happe;
And yit this Maunciple sette hir aller cappe.

    The REVE was a sclendre colerik man.
His berd was shave as ny as ever he can;                         590
His heer was by his eres round y-shorn;
His top was dokked lyk a preest biforn;
Ful longe were his legges and ful lene,
Ylyk a staf: ther was no calf y-sene.
Wel coude he kepe a gerner and a binne;                         595
Ther was noon auditour coude on him winne.
Wel wiste he, by the droghte and by the reyn,
The yelding of his seed and of his greyn.
His lordes sheep, his neet, his dayerye,
His swyn, his hors, his stoor, and his pultrye,                   600
Was hoolly in this reves governing,
And by his covenaunt yaf the rekening,
Sin that his lord was twenty yeer of age;
Ther coude no man bringe him in arrerage.
Ther nas baillif, ne herde, ne other hyne,                         605
That he ne knew his sleighte and his covyne;
They were adrad of him as of the deeth.
His woning was ful fair upon an heeth;
With grene trees yshadwed was his place.
He coude bettre than his lord purchace;                            610
Ful riche he was astored prively.
His lord wel coude he plesen subtilly,
To yeve and lene him of his owne good,
And have a thank, and yet a cote and hood.
In youthe he lerned hadde a good mister;                         615
He was a wel good wrighte, a carpenter.
This reve sat upon a ful good stot
That was al pomely grey and highte Scot.

to help him live on his own wealth
honorably and without debt (unless he were out of
   his wits)
or to live as economically as he might wish— 585
men who could help a whole county
in any case that might come up:
and yet this Manciple got the best of them all!
   The REEVE was a slender, choleric man.
His beard was shaved as close as could be; 590
his hair was shorn around his ears;
the top of his head was clipped like a priest's in front.
His legs were very long and lean,
like a staff—no calf was visible.
He knew very well how to watch over a granary and
   a bin; 595
no auditor could catch him short.
He could calculate, according to droughts and
rains, what the yield of his seed and grain should be.
His lord's sheep, his cattle, his dairy,
his pigs, his horses, his stores, and his poultry 600
were wholly in this Reeve's power,
and under his contract he had given his reckoning
since his lord was twenty years old.
No man could find him to be in arrears.
There was no bailiff, or shepherd or other laborer 605
whose tricks and plots were unknown to him;
they were scared to death of him.
His home was a pleasant one, in a meadow;
his place was shaded with green trees.
He was a better buyer than his lord; 610
he had privately laid by considerable riches.
He knew how to please his lord well, underhandedly
giving and lending him the lord's own goods,
and got thanks and a coat and hood besides.
In youth he had learned a good trade; 615
he was a good craftsman, a carpenter.
He sat on a very good farm horse,
a dappled gray called Scot.

A long surcote of pers upon he hade,
And by his syde he bar a rusty blade.                    620
Of Northfolk was this Reve, of which I telle,
Bisyde a toun men clepen Baldeswelle.
Tukked he was, as is a frere, aboute,
And ever he rood the hindreste of our route.

A SOMNOUR was ther with us in that place,       625
That hadde a fyr-reed cherubinnes face,
For sawcefleem he was, with eyen narwe.
As hoot he was, and lecherous, as a sparwe,
With scalled browes blake and piled berd;
Of his visage children were aferd.                      630
Ther nas quiksilver, litarge, ne brimstoon,
Boras, ceruce, ne oille of tartre noon,
Ne oynement that wolde clense and byte
That him mighte helpen of his whelkes whyte,
Nor of the knobbes sitting on his chekes.            635
Wel loved he garleek, oynons, and eek lekes,
And for to drinken strong wyn, reed as blood.
Than wolde he speke, and crye as he were wood.
And whan that he wel dronken hadde the wyn,
Than wolde he speke no word but Latyn.             640
A fewe termes hadde he, two or three,
That he had lerned out of som decree;
No wonder is, he herde it al the day;
And eek ye knowen wel how that a jay
Can clepen "Watte" as well as can the pope.       645
But who-so coude in other thing him grope,
Thanne hadde he spent al his philosophye;
Ay *"Questio quid iuris"** wolde he crye.
He was a gentil harlot and a kinde;
A bettre felawe sholde men noght finde.             650
He wolde suffre, for, a quart of wyn,
A good felawe to have his concubyn
A twelf-month, and excuse him atte fulle:
Ful prively a finch eek coude he pulle.
And if he fond owher a good felawe,                  655
He wolde techen him to have non awe

He wore a long blue outer coat,
and he carried a rusty blade by his side.
This Reeve I am telling you about came fr
near a town which is called Bawdeswell.
His coat was tucked up around him like a fr
and he always rode last in our company.

A SUMMONER was with us there,                    625
who had a fire-red face like a cherub in a painting,
for he was pimply, with narrow eyes.
He was as hot and lecherous as a sparrow,
with scabby black brows and a scanty beard;
his face frightened little children.              630
There was no quicksilver, lead, or brimstone,
borax, white lead, or oil of tartar,
or any kind of cleansing or astringent ointment,
that could cure him of his white blotches
or of the knobs on his cheeks.                    635
He loved garlic, onions, and leeks,
and he liked to drink strong wine as red as blood.
Then he would talk and shout as if he were mad.
And when he had drunk deep of his wine,
then he would not speak a word except Latin.      640
He knew a few terms—two or three—
that he had learned out of some decree;
which was no wonder, for he heard it all day long,
and, too, you know that a parrot
can say "Walt!" as well as the pope.              645
But if anyone wanted to try him further,
he had exhausted his learning;
he would just keep crying, *"Questio quid juris."*
He was a gentle, kindly rascal;
no one could find a better fellow.                650
For a quart of wine he would allow
a good fellow to have his concubine
for a year, and would excuse him fully:
he could pluck a finch in secrecy himself.
And if he found a good fellow anywhere,           655
he would teach him not to stand in awe,

ɪɪ cas of the erchedeknes curs,
ɪf a mannes soule were in his purs;
ʃor in his purs he sholde y-punisshed. be.
"Purs is the erchedeknes helle," seyde he.                    660
But wel I woot he lyed right in dede;
Of cursing oghte ech gilty man him drede—
For curs wol slee, right as assoilling saveth—
And also war him of a *significavit*.*
In daunger hadde he at his owne gyse                          665
The yonge girles of the diocyse,
And knew hir counseil, and was al hir reed.
A gerland hadde he set upon his heed,
As greet as it were for an ale-stake;
A bokeler hadde he maad him of a cake.                        670
With him ther rood a gentil PARDONER
Of Rouncival,* his freend and his compeer.
That streight was comen fro the court of Rome.
Ful loude he song, "Com hider, love,* to me."
This Somnour bar to him a stiff burdoun:                      675
Was never trompe of half so greet a soun.
This Pardoner hadde heer as yelow as wex,
But smothe it heng as dooth a strike of flex;
By ounces henge his lokkes that he hadde,
And therwith he his shuldres overspradde;                    680
But thinne it lay, by colpons oon and oon;
But hood, for jolitee, ne wered he noon,
For it was trussed up in his walet.
Him thoughte he rood al of the newe jet;
Dischevele, save his cappe, he rood al bare.                 685
Swiche glaringe eyen hadde he as an hare.
A vernicle* hadde he sowed on his cappe;
His walet lay biforn him in his lappe,
Bretful of pardoun come from Rome al hoot.
A voys he hadde as smal as hath a goot;                       690
No berd hadde he, ne never sholde have,
As smothe it was as it were late y-shave;
I trowe he were a gelding* or a mare.

in such a case, of the archdeacon's curse,
unless the man's soul were in his purse;
for it was in his purse that he was to be punished.
"Purse is the Archdeacon's hell," said he.                           660
But I know well that he lied indeed;
every guilty man should dread excommunication—
for it will slay, just as absolution saves—
and beware of a writ of *significavit* (which ends in jail).
He had the young wenches of the diocese                              665
under control, at his own wish,
and knew their secrets, and was their sole advisor.
He had set a garland on his head, as big as the ones
that hang from the ale-stake before a drinking house;
he had made himself a shield out of a cake.                          670
    With him there rode a gentle PARDONER
of Rouncivalle; he was the Summoner's friend and
comrade, who had come straight from the court of
Rome. Loudly he sang, "Come hither, love, to me,"
and the Summoner accompanied him powerfully—                         675
never did a trumpet make half so great a sound.
The Pardoner had hair as yellow as wax,
but it hung as smoothly as a hank of flax;
wisp by wisp his locks hung down,
and he had spread them over his shoulders—                           680
but they lay thinly, in strands, one by one;
however, for sport, he wore no hood;
it was trussed up in his pack.
He thought he rode all in the latest style:
with his hair down, he rode bareheaded except for
        his cap.                                                     685
He had staring eyes just like a hare's.
He had sewed a veronica on his cap;
his bag was in his lap before him,
brimful of pardons, all come hot from Rome.
He had a voice as thin as a goat's;                                  690
no beard did he have, nor would ever have—
his face was as smooth as if he had just shaved;
I expect he was a gelding or a mare.

But of his craft, fro Berwik into Ware,
Ne was ther swich another pardoner:                    695
For in his male he hadde a pilwe-beer,
Which that, he seyde, was Our Lady veyl;
He seyde he hadde a gobet of the seyl
That Seinte Peter hadde whan that he wente
Upon the see, til Jesu Crist him hente;                700
He hadde a croys of latoun, ful of stones,
And in a glas he hadde pigges bones—
But with thise relikes, whan that he fond
A povre person dwelling upon lond,
Upon a day he gat him more moneye                      705
Than that the person gat in monthes tweye.
And thus, with feyned flaterye and japes,
He made the person and the peple his apes.
But trewely to tellen atte laste,
He was in chirche a noble ecclesiaste.                 710
Wel coude he rede a lessoun or a storie,
But alderbest he song an offertorie;
For wel he wiste whan that song was songe
He moste preche, and wel affyle his tonge
To winne silver, as he ful wel coude;                  715
Therefore he song the murierly and loude.
    Now have I told you shortly, in a clause,
Th'estat, th'array, the nombre, and eek the cause
Why that assembled was this companye
In Southwerk, at this gentil hostelrye                 720
That highte the Tabard, faste by the Belle.*
But now is tyme to yow for to telle
How that we baren us that ilke night
Whan we were in that hostelrye alight,
And after wol I telle of our viage                     725
And al the remenaunt of our pilgrimage.
But first I pray yow, of your curteisye,
That ye n'arette it nat my vileinye,
Thogh that I pleynly speke in this matere,
To telle yow hir wordes and hir chere,                 730
Ne thogh I speke hir wordes properly;

But to speak of his craft, from Berwick to Ware
there was no other such pardoner;                              695
for in his bag he had a pillowcase
which, he said, was Our Lady's veil;
he said he had a piece of the sail
Saint Peter had when he sailed
on the sea, until Jesus Christ took him;                       700
he had a cross of brass, set with stones,
and in a glass he had pigs' bones;
but with these "relics," whenever he found
a poor country parson,
he in one day got himself more money                           705
than the parson got in two months.
And thus, with false flattery and tricks,
he made monkeys of the parson and the people.
But in the end, to do him justice,
in church he was a noble ecclesiastic.                         710
He could read a lesson or a history beautifully,
but best of all he sang an offertory;
for well he knew that when that song was sung
he must preach and smooth his tongue
to win silver, as he indeed could do—                          715
therefore he sang the more merrily and the louder.

  Now I have told you truthfully, in a few words,
the condition, the clothing and display, the number, and
the reason for the gathering of this company
in Southwark, at the fine hostelry                             720
that is called the Tabard, right near the Bell.
But now it is time to tell you
what we did that same night,
when we had alighted at that hostelry,
and afterwards I will tell you about our trip,                 725
and all the rest of our pilgrimage.
But first I pray you, by your courtesy,
not to interpret it as my vulgarity
even though I speak plainly in this matter,
in telling you their words and behavior—                       730
not even though I give you their exact words;

For this ye knowen also wel as I,
Who-so shal telle a tale after a man,
He moot reherce, as ny as ever he can,
Everich a word, if it be in his charge,                    735
Al speke he never so rudeliche and large;
Or elles he moot telle his tale untrewe,
Or feyne thing, or finde wordes newe.
He may nat spare, althogh he were his brother;
He moot as wel seye o word as another.                     740
Crist spak himself ful brode in Holy Writ,
And wel ye woot no vileinye is it.
Eek Plato seith, who-so that can him rede,
The wordes mote be cosin to the dede.
Also I prey yow to foryeve it me                           745
Al have I nat set folk in hir degree
Here in this tale, as that they sholde stonde;
My wit is short, ye may wel understonde.

   Greet chere made our Hoste us everichon,
And to the soper sette us anon,                            750
And served us with vitaille at the beste.
Strong was the wyn, and wel to drinke us leste.
A semely man our Hoste was withalle
For to han been a marshal in an halle;
A large man he was, with eyen stepe,                       755
A fairer burgeys is ther noon in Chepe:
Bold of his speche, and wys, and wel y-taught,
And of manhod him lakkede right naught.
Eek therto he was right a mery man,
And after soper pleyen he bigan,                           760
And spak of mirthe amonges othere thinges—
Whan that we hadde maad our rekeninges—
And seyde thus: "Now, lordinges, trewely,
Ye been to me right welcome hertely:
For by my trouthe, if that I shal nat lye,                 765
I saugh nat this yeer so mery a companye
At ones in this herberwe as is now.

for you know as well as I do
that whoever repeats a man's story
is obligated to report, as nearly as he can,
every word that is within the area he has been
    charged with,                                                   735
however rudely and broadly he may speak;
otherwise, he would have to falsify his tale,
or invent new matter, or find new words.
He may not forbear, even if his brother told the tale;
he must speak one word as well as another.           740
Christ himself spoke very broadly in Holy Writ,
and you well know that that isn't vulgarity;
also Plato says (as whoever can read him knows)
the words must be cousin to the deed.
Also I pray you to forgive me                                  745
if I have not presented people according to their
proper ranks in this account:
my wit is short, as you can easily understand.

    Our Host made each one of us welcome,
and he set us down to supper at once                     750
and served us with the best of food.
The wine was strong, and we were glad to drink.
Our HOST was indeed a seemly enough man
to have been a master of ceremonies in a hall;
he was a large man, with prominent eyes;            755
there isn't a more imposing burgher in all Cheapside:
he was bold in his speech, prudent, and well taught;
and he lacked no manly quality.
Besides that, he was indeed a merry man.
After supper he began to joke,                                760
and spoke of amusements among other things—
when we had all paid our bills—
and said as follows: "Now, my lords, truly
you are right welcome here, with all my heart.
For on my word, to tell the truth,                          765
I haven't seen all year so merry a company
all at one time in this inn as now.

Fayn wolde I doon yow mirthe, wiste I how.
And of a mirthe I am right now bithoght,
To doon yow ese, and it shal coste noght.          770
  Ye goon to Caunterbury; God yow spede,
The blisful martir quyte yow your mede.
And wel I woot as ye goon by the weye
Ye shapen yow to talen and to pleye;
For trewely, confort ne mirthe is noon.            775
To ryde by the weye doumb as a stoon;
And therfore wol I maken yow disport,
As I seyde erst, and doon yow som confort.
And if yow lyketh alle, by oon assent,
Now for to stonden at my jugement,                 780
And for to werken as I shal yow seye,
Tomorwe, whan ye ryden by the weye,
Now, by my fader soule that is deed,
But ye be merye, I wol yeve yow myn heed.
Hold up your hond, withouten more speche."         785
  Our counseil was nat longe for to seche;
Us thoughte it was noght worth to make it wys,
And graunted him withouten more avys,
And bad him seye his verdit, as him leste.
  "Lordinges," quod he, "now herkneth for the beste;  790
But tak it not, I prey yow, in desdyn;
This is the poynt, to speken short and pleyn,
That ech of yow, to shorte with your weye
In this viage, shal telle tales tweye—
To Caunterbury-ward, I mene it so—                 795
And homward he shal tellen othere two
Of aventures that whylom han bifalle;
And which of yow that bereth him best of alle,
That is to seyn, that telleth in this cas
Tales of best sentence and most solas,*           800
Shal have a soper at our aller cost
Here in this place, sitting by this post,
Whan that we come agayn fro Caunterbury.

I would be glad to give you some amusement, if I
    knew how.
And just now a way to please you
has occurred to me, and it shall cost nothing.      770
    "You are going to Canterbury—God speed you;
may the blissful martyr give you your reward.
Well I know that as you go along the way
you plan to tell tales and amuse yourselves,
for surely there is no consolation or mirth      775
in riding along the way dumb as a stone;
and therefore I wish to amuse you,
as I said before, and give you pleasure.
If you all agree, with one accord,
to abide by my judgment      780
and to do as I shall direct you
tomorrow when you ride on your way,
then, by the soul of my dead father,
I swear I shall give you my own head unless you are
    amused!
Hold up your hands, without any more talk."      785
    Our decision was not long in forthcoming;
it did not seem worth a long consultation;
we granted what he asked without further conferring
and told him to give whatever verdict he pleased.
    "Lords," said he, "now listen carefully;      790
but don't, I pray you, take what I say amiss.
This is the point, to speak shortly and plainly:
that each of you, for something to shorten our way with
on this trip, shall tell two tales—
that is, on the way to Canterbury, I mean—      795
and on the homeward way, two more,
about adventures that happened formerly;
and whichever one of you acquits himself the best—
that is to say, whoever tells in this case
the most instructive and amusing tales—      800
shall have a supper at the cost of all the rest of us,
right here by this pillar,
when we come back again from Canterbury.

And for to make yow the more mery,
I wol myselven goodly with yow ryde,          805
Right at myn owne cost, and be your gyde.
And who-so wol my jugement withseye
Shal paye al that we spenden by the weye.
And if ye vouche-sauf that it be so,
Tel me anon, withouten wordes mo,          810
And I wol erly shape me therfore."
    This thing was graunted, and our othes swore
With ful glad herte, and preyden him also
That he wold vouche-sauf for to do so,
And that he wolde been our governour          815
And of our tales juge and reportour,
And sette a soper at a certeyn prys;
And we wold reuled been at his devys,
In heigh and lowe; and thus, by oon assent,
We been acorded to his jugement.          820
And therupon the wyn was fet anon;
We dronken, and to reste wente echon,
Withouten any lenger taryinge.
    A-morwe whan that day bigan to springe,
Up roos our Host, and was our aller cok,          825
And gadrede us togidre alle in a flok,
And forth we riden, a litel more than pas,
Unto the watering of Seint Thomas;*
And there our Host bigan his hors areste,
And seyde: "Lordinges, herkneth, if yow leste.          830
Ye woot your forward, and I it yow recorde.
If even-song and morwe-song acorde,
Lat see now who shal telle the firste tale.
As ever mote I drinke wyn or ale,
Who-so be rebel to my jugement          835
Shal paye for al that by the weye is spent.
Now draweth cut, er that we ferrer twinne;
He which that hath the shortest shal biginne.
Sire Knight," quod he, "my maister and my lord,
Now draweth cut, for that is myn acord.          840
Cometh neer," quod he, "my lady Prioresse;

And to make you all the merrier,
I will patiently ride with you myself 805
(completely at my own cost) and be your guide.
And whoever shall gainsay my judgment
shall pay all that we spend on the way.
If you agree that it be so done,
tell me at once, without more words, 810
and I will prepare myself early for the purpose."

This was granted, and we gladly took our oaths,
and also prayed him
that he would agree to do so,
and that he would be our governor, 815
and be judge of our tales and keep count of them,
and set a supper at a certain price;
we would be ruled at his command
in large and small matters. Thus with one accord
we agreed to his judgment. 820
Thereupon the wine was fetched at once;
we drank and went to rest, every one of us,
without any further tarrying.

The next day, when it began to lighten,
our Host got up and like a cock aroused us, 825
and gathered us together in a flock.
We rode forth at a little more than footpace,
as far as the watering place of Saint Thomas.
There our Host checked his horse
and said, "Lords, listen if you will: 830
you know your agreement, and I remind you of it;
If evening song and morning song agree,
let's see now who shall tell the first tale.
As sure as ever I drink either wine or ale,
whoever is rebellious toward my judgment 835
shall pay for all that is spent by the way.
Now draw a lot before we go any further:
he who gets the shortest shall begin.
Sir Knight," said he, "my master and my lord,
now draw your lot, for that is my decision. 840
Come near," said he, "my lady Prioress;

And ye, sir Clerk, lat be your shamfastnesse,
Ne studieth noght; ley bond to, every man."
   Anon to drawen every wight bigan,
And shortly for to tellen, as it was,           845
Were it by aventure, or sort, or cas,
The sothe is this, the cut fil to the Knight,
Of which ful blythe and glad was every wight;
And telle he moste his tale, as was resoun,
By forward and by composicioun,           850
As ye han herd; what nedeth wordes mo?
And whan this gode man saugh it was so,
As he that wys was and obedient
To kepe his forward by his free assent,
He seyde: "Sin I shal beginne the game,       855
What, welcome be the cut, a Goddes name!
Now lat us ryde, and herkneth what I seye."
   And with that word we riden forth our weye;
And he bigan with right a mery chere
His tale anon, and seyde in this manere.        860

and you, sir Clerk, leave off your bashfulness,
don't deliberate; lay a hand to, everyone!"
    At once each one drew,
and to tell you in short what happened,                    845
whether it was by luck, or fate, or chance,
the truth is that the lot fell to the Knight,
for which everyone was very glad;
he had to tell his tale, as was right,
according to the agreement and the treaty,                 850
as you have heard. What need is there to say more?
When this good man saw that it was so,
then as a man who was prudent and obedient
in keeping his agreement without being urged,
he said, "Since I shall begin the game,                    855
well, welcome be the lot, in God's name!
Now let us ride, and listen to what I say."
    And with these words we rode forth on our way.
He began his tale at once most cheerfully,
and spoke as follows.                                      860

# THE KNIGHT'S TALE

# INTRODUCTION

❦

THE KNIGHT'S TALE, which mostly takes place in ancient Athens, is the conflicted love story of two royal Theban cousins who love the same woman. Because "The Knight's Tale" is by far the longest and most complex of the *Canterbury Tales* presented in this volume, a quick summary of the action of the four parts of the tale may help readers encountering it for the first time:

*Part I.* On his way back to Athens with his bride, Hypolita, and his sister-in-law, Emily, Duke Theseus responds to the pleas of some grieving widows by defeating Creon, the tyrant of Thebes. Among the bodies of the defeated army, he finds near death the royal cousins Palamon and Arcite. Rather than kill them, Theseus takes them back to Athens and places them in prison. From their barred prison window, the two young men see the lovely Emily and both fall in love with her. Arcite after a time is released but banished from Athens on pain of death, while Palamon remains in prison. The two are envious of each other's condition.

*Part II.* Arcite disguises himself as a common laborer and comes back to Athens, where he gets a job working in Emily's household. Meanwhile, Palamon escapes from prison, and the rival cousins chance to meet in a grove near Athens. While Palamon and Arcite are fighting a bloody duel, Theseus, Hypolita, and Emily, out hunting, by chance come upon them in a grove. At first angry, Theseus soon relents, sets both of his enemies free, and invites them to return in a year, each with a hundred knights, to take part in a glorious tournament, with Emily's hand going to the winner.

*Part III.* Theseus builds a splendid amphitheater in preparation for the tournament and places on its west, east, and north borders elaborately decorated temples to Mars, Venus, and Diana. When the two troops of warriors come back for the tournament, the three principals each pray to one of the planetary deities. Palamon prays to Venus, not for victory but for the hand of Emily. Emily prays to Diana to be spared marriage to either Palamon or Arcite, praying instead to remain a maiden always. Arcite prays to Mars for victory in the tournament.

*Part IV.* Just before the tournament begins Theseus declares that he wants no lives to be lost and restricts the kinds of weapons that may be used. He sets out the rules of the game, the primary one being that the winning side will be the one that takes the loser to a stake at the end of the field. After vigorous fighting, Arcite's men drag the wounded Palamon to the stake. No sooner is Arcite declared the winner than Saturn commands Pluto, god of the underworld, to send a diabolical fury to frighten Arcite's horse. Arcite is thrown and crushed by his own saddle bow. After an elaborate funeral and the passage of some years, Theseus tells Palamon and Emily to marry, and they happily do so.

Arching over the story of the warriors and lovers down on the earth below is a heavenly conflict among the gods or, more precisely, among the planetary or astrological influences that were thought to control the affairs of men. Indeed, a key feature of "The Knight's Tale" is the prayers of the three principal characters to these influences. Closely tied up with the question of whether Palamon or Arcite will get the young woman they both love is the question of how the powerful Saturn will settle the conflicting demands on him of Mars, Venus, and Diana.

Chaucer's main source for "The Knight's Tale" is Giovanni Boccaccio's several-hundred-page-long *Teseida.* Readers who are upset at having to read Chaucer's long and leisurely story of Palamon, Arcite, and Emily should thank Chaucer for streamlining a story that is less than a quarter the length of Boccaccio's Italian story of Palemone, Arcita, and Emilia. Chaucer reduced the story in lots of ways, particularly by staying focused on the love story. He cut out, for example, Boccaccio's long opening description of Theseus's journey to the land of the Amazons, his defeat of them, and his acquiring as his bride the Amazonian queen Hypolita. But Chaucer did more than reduce the *Teseida,* which focuses on Arcite as the main character, who in Boccaccio is almost a tragic figure who makes the mistake of praying to the wrong deity. For Chaucer, Palamon is raised to equal importance, if not more importance, than his rival. And Chaucer transforms the vain and coquettish Emilia of his source into a more innocent object of the love of rival cousins.

One of Chaucer's most important changes was to give the story a philosophical overlay by introducing into it the ideas of the ancient philosopher Boethius. One of Boethius's key ideas was that there is a great God who designs a far better plan for human beings than they could possibly design for themselves. That design sometimes involves what looks like adversity, but the adversity is always (for Boethius) part of a design that leads to happiness. We should then, according to Boethius, not resist or fight against the troubles that come our way, but cheerfully accept them, trusting that in the end things will work out for the best. The ending of "The Knight's Tale," then, reflects this reassuring philosophy by showing that although the three principal characters all seem at first not to get what they want most, in the end all of them do get what they want, or perhaps something even better.

For this and the other tales in this volume, readers should reread the portrait of the teller given by Chaucer in the General Prologue. The portrait of the Knight (lines 43–78) shows him to be the idealized Christian soldier who fought with valor and honor at most of the important late-fourteenth-century battles against heathens. We know less of his marital than of his martial life, but he does have a son who is with him on this pilgrimage. The Knight seems, all in all, an ideal teller for the long tale of war, romance, honor, and philosophy that Chaucer assigns to him.

## NOTES

### Part I

**Femenye** (line 8). A race of warlike women, led by Hypolita, who decided that they could live and protect themselves without the help of men. They are sometimes called Amazons, their land Scithia.

**Saturne, Juno** (470–71). Two forces that Palamon blames for the setbacks that Thebes has suffered. Saturn is the powerful planet. Juno is the jealous wife of Jupiter, who had made love to two Theban women.

### Part II

**Hereos** (516). Eros, a sickness associated with the intense emotion of falling in love.

**manye** (516). A kind of melancholy madness or mania brought on by the frustration of his love for an inaccessible woman.

**Argus** (532). In classical mythology, the jealous Juno had set the hundred-eyed Argus as guard to Io, who was a lover of her husband, Jupiter. Argus was killed by Mercury (see line 527), who first sang all of Argus's hundred eyes to sleep.

**Cadme and Amphioun** (688). Cadmus and Amphion are the legendary founders of the city of Thebes, home to Palamon and Arcite.

**regne of Trace** (780). The reference in this and the next lines is to the Thracian kingdom in which a hunter prepares himself at a mountain pass to meet a charging lion or bear.

**Part III**

**Citheroun** (1078). Venus's supposed mountainous island of
Cytherea, though Chaucer may have confused the name
with the name of a different location.

**Ydelnesse, Salamon, Hercules, Medea, Circes, Turnus,
Cresus** (1082–88). Various literary, historical, and classi-
cal allusions, most of them demonstrating the follies and
miseries associated with the snares of love.

**qualm** (1156). Probably a reference to the "pestilence" or
bubonic plague that killed millions in Europe during
Chaucer's lifetime. See also line 1611 below, where Saturn
claims to have the power to send the plague. The reference
to the bubonic plague here is anachronistic, since "The
Knight's Tale" is set in the classical pre-Christian era.

**Julius, Nero, Antonius** (1173–74). Three famous rulers
slaughtered in time of war—exemplary of the mayhem and
death caused by mighty Mars. The last is Marcus Aurelius
Antoninus Caracalla, a Roman emperor murdered in AD
217.

**Puella, Rubeus** (1187). Two astrological references to Mars
as cast by a complicated process called geomancy, a pseudo-
science involving dots and lines.

**Calistopee, Dane, Attheon, Atthalante, Meleagre** (1198–
1213). Various classical and legendary allusions to hunters
or the hunted whose unfortunate tales are depicted on the
walls of the temple of Diana, goddess of the hunt.

**griffon** (1275). A griffin was in Greek mythology a fearsome
beast with the head and wings of an eagle on the body of
a lion.

**in hir houre** (1359). Palamon picks his hour of prayer care-
fully. The various planets were supposed to have special
powers on certain hours of the day, hours in which it was
particularly propitious to make prayers for their astrologi-
cal influence. Venus would have had special strength on the
twenty-third hour of Sunday night (see line 1351), when it

was not yet two hours before dawn on Monday morning (line 1352).

**the thridde houre inequal** (1413). The medieval astrological day was divided into twenty-four "inequal" or planetary hours. In this system the time between dawn and dusk was divided equally into twelve hours, the time between dusk and the following dawn into twelve more. Except at the two equinoxes, when the daylight hours would have been exactly equal in length to the nighttime hours (that is, sixty minutes), the daylight hours would have been longer or shorter than the hours of darkness, depending on the time of the year—thus the inequality. Emily prays to Diana on the third inequal hour after Palamon prayed to Venus. That would have been the first hour of Monday ("moon day"), or the dawn hour, the hour at which Diana's power would have been the greatest. Like Palamon, Emily picks her prayer time very carefully.

**Stace of Thebes** (1436). The *Thebaid* of Statius, though Chaucer's more direct source was actually Boccaccio's *Teseida,* which he does not mention by name here or elsewhere. Chaucer was often eager to claim an ancient source, not a contemporary one.

**Attheon** (1445). While hunting, Acteon accidentally saw Diana while she was bathing. In her anger she changed him into a stag, which Acteon's hunting dogs then killed, not realizing that they were killing their master. See lines 1207–10 above, where Acteon's unhappy story is artistically summarized on the walls of Diana's temple.

**thre formes** (1455). As suggested in lines 1439–42 above, the goddess was imagined to have appeared in various forms. The three referred to here are probably Luna, the moon (in the heavens), the chaste Diana, the huntress (on earth), and Proserpina, the reluctant wife of Pluto (in the underworld).

**the nexte houre of Mars** (1509). Mars's next hour, the hour that Arcite would have selected for his prayer to Mars, would have been the fourth hour of that Monday.

Part IV

**al that Monday** (1628). Monday is given over to partying and celebrations so that the tournament itself takes place the next day, on a Tuesday, or Mars's day ("Mardi" in French). Since Tuesday is the day when the influence of Mars is strongest, it would not have surprised a medieval audience that Arcite, who had prayed to Mars, wins the tournament.

**Galgopheye** (1768). Probably a valley in another part of Greece, perhaps Gargaphia.

**Belmarye** (1772). Probably Benmarin in Morocco but, like the previous name, perhaps just meant to be an exotic place where wild animals were rampant and dangerous.

**furie infernal** (1826). A fury was an avenging spirit usually confined to the underworld but released from time to time to influence the affairs of men, sometimes to see that justice was done.

**vertu expulsif** (1891). This "virtue" involved the ability to expel certain harmful poisons from the body. This complex account of the mechanics of Arcite's dying, the technical details of which are not important here, shows Chaucer's awareness of the medical terminology of his day.

**Firste Moevere** (2129). This First Mover who creates the links in the great "chain of love," though later in the passage identified as Jupiter, may perhaps be read as an anachronistic stand-in for the Judeo-Christian godhead, the all-loving deity who stands above and beyond the planetary gods and goddesses that seem to control the fates of men. This prime mover determines the number of years individual men and women get to live on earth and arranges things better for them than they could arrange them for themselves.

# THE KNIGHTES TALE

Whylom, as olde stories tellen us,
    Ther was a duk that highte Theseus;
Of Athenes he was lord and governour,
And in his tyme swich a conquerour
That gretter was ther noon under the sonne.     5
Ful many a riche contree hadde he wonne;
What with his wisdom and his chivalrye,
He conquered al the regne of Femenye,*
That whilom was y-cleped Scithia,
And weddede the quene Ipolita,     10
And broghte hir hoom with him in his contree
With muchel glorie and greet solempnitee,
And eek hir yonge suster Emelye.
And thus with victorie and with melodye
Lete I this noble duk to Athenes ryde,     15
And al his hoost in armes him bisyde.
   And certes, if it nere to long to here,
I wolde han told yow fully the manere,
How wonnen was the regne of Femenye
By Theseus, and by his chivalrye;     20
And of the grete bataille for the nones
Bitwixen Athenës and Amazones;
And how asseged was Ipolita,
The faire, hardy quene of Scithia;
And of the feste that was at hir weddinge,     25
And of the tempest at hir hoom-cominge;
But al that thing I moot as now forbere.
I have, God woot, a large feeld to ere,
And wayke been the oxen in my plough.

# THE KNIGHT'S TALE

Once upon a time, as ancient stories tell us,
    there was a duke who was named Theseus.
He was lord and ruler of Athens,
and such a conqueror in his day
that there was no greater under the sun.                          5
He had won many a rich country
by virtue of his wisdom and his knightly prowess.
He conquered the whole realm of the Amazon women,
which formerly was called Scythia,
and took in marriage Queen Hippolyta                             10
and brought her home with him to his country
with much glory and great pomp;
and he brought as well her young sister Emily.
And thus, with victory and the sound of music,
I leave this noble duke riding to Athens                         15
and, with him, all his force in arms.

    And, indeed, if it were not too long to listen to,
I would have wanted to tell you fully the way
in which the realm of the Amazons was won
by Theseus and his knightly company;                             20
and of the singularly great battle
between the Athenians and the Amazons;
and how siege was laid to Hippolyta,
the fair bold queen of Scythia;
and of the feast that there was at their wedding,               25
and of the tempest at their homecoming.
But for now I must shun all that matter.
I have, God knows, a broad field to till,
and the oxen pulling my plow are weak;

The remenant of the tale is long y-nough.                    30
I wol nat letten eek noon of this route;
Lat every felawe telle his tale aboute.
And lat see now who shal the soper winne;
And ther I lefte, I wol ageyn biginne.

  This duk, of whom I make mencioun,                         35
When he was come almost unto the toun,
In al his wele and in his moste pryde,
He was war, as he caste his eye asyde,
Wher that ther kneled in the hye weye
A companye of ladies, tweye and tweye,                       40
Ech after other, clad in clothes blake;
But swich a cry and swich a wo they make,
That in this world nis creature livinge,
That herde swich another weymentinge;
And of this cry they nolde nevere stenten,                   45
Til they the reynes of his brydel henten.

  "What folk ben ye, that at myn hoom-cominge
Perturben so my feste with cryinge?"
Quod Theseus, "have ye so greet envye
Of myn honour, that thus compleyne and crye?                 50
Or who hath yow misboden or offended?
And telleth me if it may been amended,
And why that ye ben clothed thus in blak."

  The eldeste lady of hem alle spak,
When she hadde swowned with a deedly chere,                  55
That it was routhe for to seen and here.
She seyde: "Lord, to whom Fortune hath yiven
Victorie, and as a conquerour to liven,
Nat greveth us your glorie and your honour;
But we biseken mercy and socour.                             60
Have mercy on our wo and our distresse.
Some drope of pitee, thurgh thy gentilesse,
Upon us wrecched wommen lat thou falle.
For certes, lord, ther nis noon of us alle,
That she nath been a duchesse or a quene;                    65
Now be we caitifs, as it is wel sene:
Thanked be Fortune, and hir false wheel,

the rest of the tale is long enough.     30
Besides, I don't want to hinder any in this company;
let each of our companions tell his tale in turn,
and let us see, now, who is to win the supper.
Where I left off, I'll begin again.

    The duke of whom I speak,     35
when he had come almost to the town *Athens*
in all his felicity and in his fullest glory,
became conscious, as he cast his eye to one side,
that in the highway there was kneeling
a company of ladies, two by two,     40
each pair behind another, dressed in black.
They made such an outcry and grieved so *ladies*
that no creature living in this world
has heard such another lamentation. *in*
They would not leave off this shrieking
until they had grasped his bridle reins. *black*     45

    "What people are you, who at my homecoming
thus disturb my celebration with your cries?"
said Theseus. "Have you such great envy
of my honor that you thus complain and cry out?     50
Or who has mistreated or offended you?
Tell me if your wrong can be righted,
and why you are thus clothed in black."

    The eldest lady of them all spoke *metaphor*
(after she had reeled faintly, looking like death,     55
so that it was pitiable to see and hear her),
"My lord, to whom Fortune has given
victory and the life due a conqueror,
your glory and honor do not grieve us at all.
Rather, we beg for mercy and aid. *mercy*     60
Have mercy on our woe and our distress!
By reason of your gentleness let some drop of pity fall
upon us wretched women.
For indeed, my lord, there is not one of us all
who has not been a duchess or a queen.     65
Now we are "wretches," as is evident:
thanks to Fortune and her false wheel—

That noon estat assureth to be weel.
And certes, lord, t'abyden your presence,
Here in this temple of the goddesse Clemence        70
We han ben waytinge al this fourtenight;
Now help us, lord, sith it is in thy might.

"I wrecche, which that wepe and waille thus,
Was whylom wyf to king Capaneus,
That starf at Thebes, cursed be that day!        75
And alle we, that been in this array
And maken al this lamentacioun,
We losten alle our housbondes at that toun,
Whyl that the sege ther-aboute lay.
And yet now th'olde Creon, weylaway!        80
That lord is now of Thebes the citee,
Fulfild of ire and of iniquitee,
He, for despyt, and for his tirannye,
To do the dede bodyes vileinye,
Of alle our lordes, whiche that ben y-slawe,        85
Hath alle the bodyes on an heep y-drawe,
And wol nat suffren hem, by noon assent,
Neither to been y-buried nor y-brent,
But maketh houndes ete hem in despyt."
And with that word, withouten more respyt,        90
They fillen gruf, and cryden pitously,
"Have on us wrecched wommen som mercy,
And lat oure sorwe sinken in thyn herte."

This genil duk doun from his courser sterte
With herte pitous, whan he herde hem speke.        95
Him thoughte that his herte wolde breke,
Whan he saugh hem so pitous and so mat,
That whylom weren of so greet estat.
And in his armes he hem alle up hente,
And hem conforteth in ful good entente;        100
And swoor his ooth, as he was trewe knight,
He wolde doon so ferforthly his might
Upon the tyraunt Creon hem to wreke,
That al the peple of Grece sholde speke
How Creon was of Theseus y-served,        105

her who assures happiness to no condition of man.
Indeed, my lord, to wait for your presence
we have been attending here in 70
the temple of the goddess Clemency for a fortnight.
Now help us, lord, since it is in your power.

   "Wretch that I am, thus weeping and wailing,
I was formerly the wife of King Capaneus, *widow*
who died at Thebes, cursed be the day! 75
All of us, who are dressed as you see
and uttering all this lamentation—
we all lost our husbands at that city *7 black =*
while it was being besieged. *death of*
And just recently, alas, old Creon— *husbands*
who is now lord of the city of Thebes 80
and is full of wrath and evil—
out of his spitefulness and tyranny
has piled all the corpses in a heap
in order to do an ungentle deed to the dead bodies 85
of all our husbands, who have been slain.
He will not allow them, by any agreement,
either to be buried or to be burned,
but for spite has dogs eat them."
With that word and without further pause, 90
the women fell prostrate and cried out piteously,
"Have some mercy on us wretched women
and let our sorrow sink into your heart." *cries*

   The gentle duke jumped down from his horse
with pitying heart as he heard them speak. *duke's* 95
He thought that his heart would break *heart*
when he saw how pitiable and dejected they were,
who formerly were of such high estate.
He took up each of them in his arms
and comforted them with a good will *avenge* 100
and swore, as he was a faithful knight,
that he would perform what was in his power
in order to avenge them upon the tyrant Creon
to such an extent that all the people of Greece would talk
of how Creon was treated by Theseus 105

As he that hadde his deeth ful well deserved.
And right anoon, withouten more abood,
His baner he desplayeth, and foorth rood
To Thebes-ward, and al his host bisyde;
No neer Athenes wolde he go ne ryde,                    110
Ne take his ese fully half a day,
But onward on his wey that night he lay;
And sente anoon Ipolita the quene,
And Emelye hir yonge suster shene,
Unto the toun of Athenës to dwelle;                    115
And forth he rit; ther is namore to telle.
    The rede statue of Mars, with spere and targe,
So shyneth in his whyte baner large,
That alle the feeldes gliteren up and doun;
And by his baner born is his penoun                    120
Of gold ful riche, in which ther was y-bete
The Minotaur, which that he slough in Crete.
Thus rit this duk, thus rit this conquerour,
And in his host of chivalrye the flour,
Til that he cam to Thebes, and alighte                  125
Faire in a feeld, ther as he thoghte to fighte.
But shortly for to speken of this thing,
With Creon, which that was of Thebes king,
He faught, and slough him manly as a knight
In pleyn bataille, and putte the folk to flight;       130
And by assaut he wan the citee after,
And rente adoun bothe wal, and sparre and rafter;
And to the ladyes he restored agayn
The bones of hir housbondes that were slayn,
To doon obsequies as was tho the gyse.                 135
But it were al to long for to devyse
The grete clamour and the waymentinge
That the ladyes made at the brenninge
Of the bodyes, and the grete honour
That Theseus, the noble conquerour,                    140
Doth to the ladyes, whan they from him wente;

as a villain who had fully deserved death.
And immediately, without further delay,
he displayed his banner and rode forth
toward Thebes with all his army.
He would not walk or ride any nearer to Athens,                110
nor would he rest for half a day,
but lodged that night further along on his route.
He sent Queen Hippolyta
and Emily, her fair young sister,
to stay in the city of Athens.                                 115
And he rode off; there is no more to say.

    The red statue of Mars, with spear and shield,
so gleamed in Theseus's broad white banner
that all the fields roundabout glistened.
Beside his banner was borne his pennon                         120
of richest cloth of gold, on which was embroidered
an image of the Minotaur, which he had slain in Crete.
Thus rode this duke and conqueror,
with the flower of knighthood in his host,
until he came to Thebes and lighted down                       125
in splendor in a field where he intended to wage battle.
But to make a long story short:
he fought with Creon, king of Thebes,
and slew him in manly and knightly fashion
in open battle and put Creon's people to flight.               130
Thereafter he won the city by assault
and tore down wall and beam and rafter.
To the ladies he returned
their slain husbands' bones, so that
the funeral rites might be celebrated in the way that
    was                                                        135
then the custom. But it would take all too long to
    describe
the great clamor and lamentation
that the ladies made at the burning
of the bodies and the great honor
that the noble conqueror Theseus                               140
paid to the ladies when they departed from him;

But shortly for to telle is myn entente.
Whan that this worthy duk, this Theseus,
Hath Creon slayn, and wonne Thebes thus,
Stille in that feeld he took al night his reste,　　　　145
And dide with al the contree as him leste.
To ransake in the tas of bodyes dede,
Hem for to strepe of harneys and of wede,
The pilours diden bisinesse and cure,
After the bataille and disconfiture.　　　　150
And so bifel, that in the tas they founde,
Thurgh-girt with many a grevous blody wounde,
Two yonge knightes ligginge by and by,
Bothe in oon armes, wroght ful richely,
Of whiche two, Arcita highte that oon,　　　　155
And that other knight highte Palamon.
Nat fully quike, ne fully dede they were,
But by hir cote-armures, and by hir gere,
The heraudes knewe hem best in special
As they that weren of the blood royal　　　　160
Of Thebes, and of sustren two y-born.
Out of the tas the pilours han hem torn,
And han hem caried softe unto the tente
Of Theseus, and he ful sone hem sente
To Athenes, to dwellen in prisoun　　　　165
Perpetuelly; he nolde no raunsoun.
And whan this worthy duk hath thus y-don,
He took his host, and hoom he rit anon
With laurer crowned as a conquerour;
And there he liveth, in joye and in honour,　　　　170
Terme of his lyf; what nedeth wordes mo?
And in a tour, in angwish and in wo,
Dwellen this Palamoun and his felawe Arcite,
For evermore; ther may no gold hem quyte.
This passeth yeer by yeer, and day by day,　　　　175
Til it fil ones, in a morwe of May,
That Emelye, that fairer was to sene
Than is the lilie upon his stalke grene,

to narrate briefly is my intent.
   When this valiant Duke Theseus
had killed Creon and thus won Thebes,
he took his rest all night upon that same field          145
and dealt with all the country as he wished.
   Searching in the pile of dead bodies
in order to strip them of armor and clothes,
the pillagers worked hard and carefully
after the battle and defeat.          150
It so happened that they found in the pile,
thrust through with many a grievous bloody wound,
two young knights lying side by side,
both in identical arms, which were made most richly.
Of the two, one was named Arcite          155
and the other knight was called Palamon.
They were neither fully alive nor fully dead,
but by their coats of arms and other equipment
the heralds knew them especially well
as the ones who were of the royal line          160
of Thebes, and sons of two sisters.
The pillagers pulled them from the heap of bodies
and carried them gently to the tent
of Theseus. He immediately sent them
to Athens, to remain in prison          165
forever; he would not take ransom for them.
When the valiant duke had thus taken action,
he took his army and soon rode home,
crowned with laurel as a conqueror.
And there he lived in joy and honor          170
to the end of his life; what more need be said?
And in a tower, in anguish and woe,
Palamon and Arcite remain
for evermore; no amount of gold might pay for their
    release.
   This went on day after day and year after year,          175
until it once happened, of a May morning,
that Emily—who was lovelier to look at
than the lily is upon its green stalk,

And fressher than the May with floures newe—
For with the rose colour stroof hir hewe,                    180
I noot which was the fairer of hem two—
Er it were day, as was hir wone to do,
She was arisen, and al redy dight;
For May wol have no slogardye a-night.
The sesoun priketh every gentil herte,                      185
And maketh him out of his sleep to sterte,
And seith, "Arys, and do thyn observaunce."
This maked Emelye have remembraunce
To doon honour to May, and for to ryse.
Y-clothed was she fresh, for to devyse;                     190
Hir yelow heer was broyded in a tresse,
Bihinde hir bak, a yerde long, I gesse.
And in the gardin, at the sonne upriste,
She walketh up and doun, and as hir liste
She gadereth floures, party whyte and rede,                 195
To make a subtil gerland for hir hede,
And as an aungel hevenly she song.
    The grete tour, that was so thikke and strong,
Which of the castel was the chief dongeoun,
(Ther as the knightes weren in prisoun,                     200
Of whiche I tolde yow, and tellen shal)
Was evene joynant to the gardin-wal,
Ther as this Emelye hadde hir pleyinge.
Bright was the sonne, and cleer that morweninge,
And Palamon, this woful prisoner,                           205
As was his wone, by leve of his gayler,
Was risen, and romed in a chambre on heigh,
In which he al the noble citee seigh,
And eek the gardin, ful of braunches grene,
Theras this fresshe Emelye the shene                        210
Was in hire walk, and romed up and doun.
This sorweful prisoner, this Palamoun,
Goth in the chambre, rominge to and fro,
And to himself compleyning of his wo;
That he was born, ful ofte he seyde, "alas!"                215

and fresher than May with its spring flowers
(for her complexion vied with the color of roses;                    180
I do not know which of the two was fairer)—
this Emily was up and already dressed
before daybreak, as it was her wont to be,
for May won't stand for slug-a-beds:
the season arouses every gentle heart,                    185
and makes him start up from his sleep,
and says, "Get up, pay me your due homage."
All this made Emily take thought
to do honor to May and to arise.
Her clothes were bright and new in appearance;                    190
her blond hair was twined in a braid
down her back—a yard long, by my guess.
In the garden at sunrise
she walked up and down; according to her fancy,
she gathered flowers, some white, some red,                    195
to make an artful garland for her head;
and she sang in a voice as heavenly as an angel's.
　　The great tower, very thick and strong,
which was the chief dungeon of the castle
(where those knights of whom I told you,                    200
and shall tell you more, were in prison)
adjoined the wall of the garden
where Emily took her amusement.
The sun was bright and the morning fair;
Palamon, the woeful prisoner,                    205
as was his custom by his jailer's leave,
was up and was walking to and fro in a high chamber
　　in the
tower, from which he saw all of the noble city
and the garden, too, full of green branches,
where lively and shining Emily the fair                    210
was at her walk, roaming up and down.
The sorrowful prisoner, this Palamon,
walked to and fro in the chamber
and complained to himself of his woe.
Often he said, "Alas!" that he was born.                    215

And so bifel, by aventure or cas,
That thurgh a window, thikke of many a barre
Of yren greet and square as any sparre,
He caste his eye upon Emelya,
And therwithal he bleynte, and cryde "A!"          220
As though he stongen were unto the herte.
And with that cry Arcite anon up-sterte,
And seyde, "Cosin myn, what eyleth thee,
That art so pale and deedly on to see?
Why crydestow? who hath thee doon offence?          225
For Goddes love, tak al in pacience
Oure prisoun, for it may non other be;
Fortune hath yeven us this adversitee.
Som wikke aspect or disposicioun
Of Saturne, by sum constellacioun,          230
Hath yeven us this, although we hadde it sworn;
So stood the heven whan that we were born;
We moste endure it: this is the short and pleyn."
    This Palamon answerde, and seyde ageyn,
"Cosyn, for sothe, of this opinioun          235
Thou hast a veyn imaginacioun.
This prison caused me nat for to crye.
But I was hurt right now thurghout myn yë
Into myn herte; that wol my bane be.
The fairnesse of that lady that I see          240
Yond in the gardin romen to and fro,
Is cause of al my crying and my wo.
I noot wher she be womman or goddesse;
But Venus is it, soothly, as I gesse."
And therwithal on kneës doun he fil,          245
And seyde: "Venus, if it be thy wil
Yow in this gardin thus to transfigure
Bifore me, sorweful, wrecche creature,
Out of this prisoun help that we may scapen.
And if so be my destinee be shapen          250
By eterne word to dyen in prisoun,

It so happened, by chance or luck,
that through a window (thick with many an iron bar
as large and squared as any beam)
he cast his eye on Emily.
Therewith he paled and cried out, "Ah!"                          220
as though he had been stung to the heart.   *hyperbole*
At that cry Arcite at once jumped up
and said, "My cousin, what ails you?
You are so pale and deathlike to look at.
Why did you cry out? Who has done you wrong?          225
For the love of God, resign yourself in all patience to
our prison, for it may not be otherwise;    *fortune*
Fortune has given us this adversity.
Some unfavorable aspect or disposition
of Saturn, through some arrangement of the heavenly
   bodies,   *planets → astronomy*                           230
has bestowed this on us; it would have been so even
   if we
had taken oath to do the opposite.
The heavens stood thus when we were born;
we must endure it: this is the brief, plain truth."

   Palamon answered, "In fact, cousin, in this opinion of   235
what is wrong you are harboring vain imaginings.
It was not this prison that made me cry out,
but I was hurt just now through my eyes and   *pain*
to my heart—the hurt will be my destruction.   *of*
The beauty of the lady whom I see   *beauty*                    240
wandering yonder in the garden
is the cause of all my cries and my woe.
I do not know whether she is a woman or a goddess,
but my guess is that she is in truth Venus."   *goddess*
With that he fell down on his knees                              245
and said, "Venus, if it be your will
thus to take this shape upon yourself in this garden
before me, sorrowful, wretched creature,
then help us to escape from this prison.
And if it be that my destiny is fashioned,                       250
by eternal decree, to die in prison,

Of oure linage have som compassioun,
That is so lowe y-broght by tirannye."
And with that word Arcite gan espye
Wheras this lady romed to and fro.                    255
And with that sighte hir beautee hurte him so,
That, if that Palamon was wounded sore,
Arcite is hurt as muche as he, or more.
And with a sigh he seyde pitously:
"The fresshe beautee sleeth me sodeynly             260
Of hir that rometh in the yonder place;
And, but I have hir mercy and hir grace,
That I may seen hir atte leeste weye,
I nam but deed; ther nis namore to seye."

This Palamon, whan he tho wordes herde,            265
Dispitously he loked, and answerde:
"Whether seistow this in ernest or in pley?"

"Nay," quod Arcite, "in ernest, by my fey!
God help me so, me list ful yvele pleye."

This Palamon gan knitte his browes tweye:          270
"It nere," quod he, "to thee no greet honour
For to be fals, ne for to be traytour
To me, that am thy cosin and thy brother
Y-sworn ful depe, and ech of us til other,
That nevere, for to dyen in the peyne,             275
Til that the deeth departe shal us tweyne,
Neither of us in love to hindre other,
Ne in non other cas, my leve brother;
But that thou sholdest trewely forthren me
In every cas, as I shal forthren thee:             280
This was thyn ooth, and myn also, certeyn;
I wot right wel, thou darst it nat withseyn.
Thus artow of my counseil, out of doute.
And now thou woldest falsly been aboute
To love my lady, whom I love and serve,            285
And evere shal, til that myn herte sterve.
Nay, certes, fals Arcite, thou shalt nat so.

have some compassion on our family,
which is brought so low by tyranny."
At that word Arcite espied
where the lady wandered to and fro,                          255
and at the sight her beauty touched him so
that, if Palamon was sorely wounded,
Arcite was hurt as much or more.
With a sigh he said pitiably,
"The fresh beauty of her who wanders in that                 260
place yonder works sudden death upon me;
unless I have mercy and favor from her,
so that I may at least see her,
I am but dead; there is no more to say."
    Palamon, hearing these words,                            265
gave an angry look and answered,
"Do you say this in earnest or as a joke?"
    "No," said Arcite, "in earnest, on my honor!
God help me, I have little desire to joke."
    Palamon knitted his brows;                               270
"It would not," he said, "be any great honor for you
to be false, or to be a traitor
to me, who am your cousin and your sworn brother,
bound most solemnly by oath (as each of us is to the
        other)
to the pact that never—even under pain of torture to
        death,                                               275
and never until death shall part us two—
shall either of us hinder the other in love,
or in any other case, my dear brother.
Rather that you should faithfully help me
in every situation, and that I should help you:             280
this was your oath, and mine, too, in certainty.
I know quite well that you dare not deny this.
Thus, without a doubt, you belong to my side.
And now you would treacherously plan
to love my lady, whom I love and serve,                     285
and ever shall do, until my heart perishes.
Now, false Arcite, indeed you shall not do so.

I loved hir first, and tolde thee my wo
As to my counseil, and my brother sworn
To forthre me, as I have told biforn.          290
For which thou art y-bounden as a knight
To helpen me, if it lay in thy might,
Or elles artow fals, I dar wel seyn."

    This Arcite ful proudly spak ageyn,
"Thou shalt," quod he, "be rather fals than I;          295
And thou art fals, I telle thee utterly;
For *par amour* I loved hir first er thow.
What wiltow seyn? thou wistest nat yet now
Whether she be a womman or goddesse!
Thyn is affeccioun of holinesse,          300
And myn is love, as to a creature;
For which I tolde thee myn aventure
As to my cosin, and my brother sworn.
I pose, that thou lovedest hir biforn;
Wostow nat wel the olde clerkes sawe,          305
That 'who shal yeve a lover any lawe?'
Love is a gretter lawe, by my pan,
Than may be yeve to any erthely man.
And therefore positif lawe and swich decree
Is broken al-day for love, in ech degree.          310
A man moot nedes love, maugree his heed.
He may nat fleen it, thogh he sholde be deed,
Al be she mayde, or widwe, or elles wyf.
And eek it is nat lykly, al thy lyf,
To stonden in hir grace; namore shal I;          315
For wel thou woost thyselven, verraily,
That thou and I be dampned to prisoun
Perpetuelly; us gayneth no rausoun.
We stryve as dide the houndes for the boon:
They foughte al day, and yet hir part was noon;          320
Ther cam a kyte, whyl that they were so wrothe,
And bar awey the boon bitwixe hem bothe.
And therfore, at the kinges court, my brother,
Ech man for himself, ther is non other.
Love if thee list; for I love and ay shal;          325

I loved her first and told my sorrow to you
as to my counselor and my brother, sworn
to aid me, as I said before.                                    290
For which cause you are bound as a knight
to help me, if it lies in your power.
Otherwise you are false: I dare to say it."
    Arcite replied, in all his pride,
"You will be false sooner than I;                              295
and you *are* false; I tell you straight out;
for, before you, I loved her first as a woman.
What can you say? Even now you don't know
whether she is a woman or a goddess!
You love a holy deity;                                         300
I love a created human being.
For which reason I told you what had happened to me—
I told it to you as my cousin and my sworn brother.
Even if I suppose that you loved her first,
don't you know the old proverb of learned men,               305
'All's fair in love'?
On my head I swear, love is a greater law
than any other that may be given to any earthly man.
Therefore man-made law, and decrees like that,
are broken every day for love, among all classes of men.     310
A man must needs love, in spite of himself.
He may not flee love, even if he dies for not doing it,
whether his object is maid, or widow, or wife.
Besides, it is not likely that at any time in your life
you will be in her grace, and no more shall I.               315
For well you yourself know, in fact,
that you and I are condemned to prison
forever; no ransom will recover us.
We vie like dogs fighting for the bone:
they fought all day, and yet had no part of it;             320
while they were raging, a kite-bird came
and bore off the bone from between the two of them.
Therefore, at the king's court, my brother, it is
every man for himself; there's no other way.
Love if you like; for I love her and ever shall,            325

And soothly, leve brother, this is al.
Here in this prisoun mote we endure,
And everich of us take his aventure."
    Greet was the stryf and long bitwixe hem tweye,
If that I hadde leyser for to seye;                           330
But to th'effect. It happed on a day,
(To telle it yow as shortly as I may)
A worthy duk that highte Perotheus,
That felawe was unto duk Theseus
Sin thilke day that they were children lyte,                  335
Was come to Athenes, his felawe to visyte,
And for to pleye, as he was wont to do.
For in this world he loved no man so:
And he loved him als tendrely ageyn.
So wel they loved, as olde bokes seyn,                        340
That whan that oon was deed, sothly to telle,
His felawe wente and soghte him doun in helle;
But of that story list me nat to wryte.
    Duk Perotheus loved well Arcite,
And hadde him knowe at Thebes yeer by yere;                   345
And fynally, at requeste and preyere
Of Perotheus, withouten any raunsoun,
Duk Theseus him leet out of prisoun,
Freely to goon, wher that him liste overal,
In swich a gyse as I you tellen shal.                         350
    This was the forward, pleynly for t'endyte,
Bitwixen Theseus and him Arcite:
That if so were that Arcite were y-founde
Ever in his lyf, by day or night, o stounde
In any contree of this Theseus,                              355
And he were caught, it was acorded thus,
That with a swerd he sholde lese his heed;
Ther nas non other remedye ne reed,
But taketh his leve, and homward he him spedde;
Let him be war, his nekke lyth to wedde!                      360
    How greet a sorwe suffreth now Arcite!
The deeth he feleth thurgh his herte smyte;

and truthfully, dear brother, that's all.
We must endure this prison here,
and each of us must take his chance."
 The strife between the two of them was great
  and lasting,
as I could describe if I had leisure;     330
but on to the outcome: it happened one day
(to tell it to you as briefly as I can)
that a valiant duke who was named Pirithous,
and who had been a friend of Duke Theseus
since the day they had been little children,   335
had come to Athens to visit his friend
and enjoy himself, as he was accustomed to do;
for he loved no other man in the world as much,
and Theseus, in turn, loved him just as strongly.
They loved each other so well, as ancient books say, 340
that when one of them was dead, to tell the truth
his friend went to look for him in hell—
but I don't want to write about that story.
 Duke Pirithous held Arcite in high esteem
and had known him at Thebes for many years.  345
Finally, at the request and supplication
of Pirithous, Duke Theseus let Arcite
out of prison, without any ransom,
to go freely anywhere that he pleased,
subject to a special arrangement I shall describe. 350
 This was the agreement, to relate plainly,
between Theseus and Arcite:
if it happened that Arcite were found
ever in his life—for a single hour by day or by night—
within any country belonging to Theseus,  355
and if Arcite were then caught, it was agreed
that he should lose his head by the sword.
There was no other remedy or plan,
except to take his leave and hurry homeward.
Let him beware; his head is in pawn!   360
 What great sorrow Arcite now suffered!
He felt death smiting his heart.

He wepeth wayleth, cryeth pitously;
To sleen himself he wayteth prively.
He seyde, "Allas that day that I was born!        365
Now is my prison worse than biforn;
Now is me shape eternally to dwelle
Noght in purgatorie, but in helle.
Allas! that evere knew I Perotheus!
For elles hadde I dwelled with Theseus        370
Y-fetered in his prisoun evermo.
Than hadde I been in blisse, and nat in wo.
Only the sighte of hir, whom that I serve,
Though that I never hir grace may deserve,
Wolde han suffised right ynough for me.        375
O dere cosin Palamon," quod he,
"Thyn is the victorie of this aventure,
Ful blisfully in prison maistow dure;
In prison? certes nay, but in paradys!
Wel hath fortune y-turned thee the dys,        380
That hast the sighte of hir, and I th'absence.
For possible is, sin thou hast hire presence,
And art a knight, a worthy and an able,
That by som cas, sin fortune is chaungeable,
Thou mayst to thy desyr sometime atteyne.        385
But I, that am exyled, and bareyne
Of alle grace, and in so greet despeir,
That ther nis erthe, water, fyr, ne eir,
Ne creature, that of hem maked is,
That may me helpe or doon confort in this:        390
Wel oughte I sterve in wanhope and distresse;
Farwel my lyf, my lust, and my gladnesse!
    "Allas, why pleynen folk so in commune
Of purveyaunce of God, or of Fortune,
That yeveth hem ful ofte in many a gyse        395
Wel bettre than they can hemself devyse?
Som man desyreth for to han richesse,
That cause is of his mordre or greet siknesse.
And som man wolde out of his prison fayn,
That in his hous is of his meynee slayn.        400

He wept, he wailed, he cried out pitiably;
he sought occasion to kill himself secretly.
He said, "Alas the day that I was born!                       365
Now my prison is worse than before;
now I am destined to dwell eternally,
not in purgatory, but in hell.
Alas, that I ever knew Pirithous!
Otherwise I would have stayed with Theseus,              370
fettered in his prison evermore.
Then I would have been in bliss, and not in woe.          *greater woe*
Just the sight of her whom I serve,
even though I might never deserve her favor,
would have been quite enough for me.                        375
Oh, dear cousin Palamon," he said,
"the victory is yours in this adventure;
most happily you may stay in prison.                         *worse off*
In prison? Indeed, no, but in paradise!
Fortune has well set the dice for you,                       380
who have sight of Emily, while I am absent from her.
For it is possible—since you are near her,
and are a valiant and able knight—
that by some chance, since Fortune is changeable,       *Emily*
you may some time attain your desire.                        385
But I, exiled and out
of all favor, and in such great despair
that there is neither earth, water, fire, nor air,
nor creature made from them,
that can help or comfort me in this affair—               *dramatic*   390
I ought indeed to perish in hopelessness and distress.
Farewell my life, my desire, and my joy!
    "Alas, why do people so commonly complain
over God's providence, or over Fortune,
which often gives them, in many a fashion,                  395
something much better than they themselves can devise?
One man desires to have wealth, which becomes
the cause of his being murdered or greatly diseased.
Another man would willingly get out of his prison,
who in his home will be slain by one of his household.   400

Infinite harmes been in this matere;
We witen nat what thing we preyen here.
We faren as he that dronke is as a mous;
A dronke man wot wel he hath an hous,
But he noot which the righte wey is thider;          405
And to a dronke man the wey is slider.
And certes, in this world so faren we;
We seken faste after felicitee,
But we goon wrong ful often, trewely.
Thus may we seyen alle, and namely I,                410
That wende and hadde a greet opinioun,
That, if I mighte escapen from prisoun,
Than hadde I been in joye and perfit hele,
Ther now I am exyled fro my wele.
Sin that I may nat seen yow, Emelye,                 415
I nam but deed; ther nis no remedye."
    Upon that other syde Palamon,
Whan that he wiste Arcite was agon,
Swich sorwe he maketh that the grete tour
Resouneth of his youling and clamour.                420
The pure fettres on his shines grete
Weren of his bittre salte teres wete.
"Allas!" quod he, "Arcita, cosin myn,
Of al oure stryf, God woot, the fruyt is thyn.
Thow walkest now in Thebes at thy large,             425
And of my wo thou yevest litel charge.
Thou mayst, sin thou hast wisdom and manhede,
Assemblen alle the folk of oure kinrede,
And make a werre so sharp on this citee
That by som aventure, or som tretee,                 430
Thou mayst have hir to lady and to wyf,
For whom that I moste nedes lese my lyf.
For, as by wey of possibilitee,
Sith thou art at thy large, of prison free,
And art a lord, greet is thyn avauntage,             435
More than is myn, that sterve here in a cage.
For I mot wepe and wayle, whyl I live,

There are infinite evils under this heading;
we do not know what we pray for in this connection;
we are like the man who is drunk as a mouse:
a drunken man knows that he has a house,
but he docs not know which is the right way to it;          405
and for a drunken man any path is slippery.
Certainly we all prosper in this same way in the world.
we continually seek felicity,
but, truly, we often go far astray.
We may all say so, and chiefly may I,                        410
who imagined and was perfectly convinced
that, if I might have escaped from prison,
then I would have been in joy and perfect satisfaction
in the situation where I am now exiled from my
    happiness.
Since I may not see you, Emily,                              415
I am as good as dead; there is no help for it."

    On the other hand, Palamon,
having learned that Arcite was gone,
made such lamentation that the great tower
echoed with his howls and clamor.                            420
The very fetters on his powerful shins
were wet with his bitter, salt tears.
"Alas!" he said, "Arcite, my cousin,
God knows you have the best of our quarrel.
You now walk at liberty in Thebes,                           425
and you take small account of my sorrow.
Since you have shrewdness and valor, you can
assemble all our kindred
and make so sharp an attack on this city
that, by some chance or some treaty,                         430
you may have for lady and for wife her
for whom I must needs lose my life.
In terms of what is possible
(since you are at large, freed from prison,
and arc a ruler), your chance of success is great—           435
greater than I have, who perish here in a cage.
I must weep and wail as long as I live,

With al the wo that prison may me yive,
And eek with peyne that love me yiveth also,
That doubleth al my torment and my wo."          440
Therwith the fyr of jelousye up-sterte
Withinne his brest, and hente him by the herte
So woodly, that he lyk was to biholde
The box-tree, or the asshen dede and colde.
Thanne seyde he, "O cruel goddes, that governe          445
This world with binding of your word eterne,
And wryten in the table of athamaunt
Youre parlement, and youre eterne graunt,
What is mankinde more unto yow holde
Than is the sheep that rouketh in the folde?          450
For slayn is man right as another best,
And dwelleth eek in prison and arest,
And hath siknesse, and greet adversitee,
And ofte tymes giltelees, pardee!

    "What governaunce is in this prescience,          455
That giltelees tormenteth innocence?
And yet encreseth this al my penaunce,
That man is bounden to his observaunce,
For Goddes sake, to letten of his wille,
Ther as a beest may al his lust fulfille.          460
And whan a beest is deed, he hath no peyne;
But man after his deeth moot wepe and pleyne,
Though in this world he have care and wo:
Withouten doute it may stonden so.
Th' answere of this I lete to divynis,          465
But wel I woot, that in this world gret pyne is.
Allas! I see a serpent or a theef,
That many a trewe man hath doon mescheef,
Goon at his large, and wher him list may turne.
But I mot been in prison thurgh Saturne,*          470
And eek thurgh Juno,* jalous and eek wood,
That hath destroyed wel ny al the blood
Of Thebes, with his waste walles wyde.
And Venus sleeth me on that other syde
For jelousye, and fere of him Arcite."          475

with all the woe that prison can give me
and, also, the pain which love, too, gives me,
and which doubles all my torment and sorrow." 440
With that the fire of jealousy leaped up
within his breast and caught his heart
so madly that, to look at, he was like
the white boxtree or the ashes that are dead and cold.
Then he said, "Oh, cruel gods, who govern 445
this world by the constraint of your eternal decree
and inscribe upon a tablet of adamant
your decision and eternally unchanging allotment,
in what way is mankind more esteemed by you
than is the sheep that cowers in the fold? 450
For man is slain like any other beast,
and also remains in prison and detention,
and suffers sickness and other great adversity;
often, in fact, these things happen to a guiltless man!

"How much reason is in this divine foreknowledge 455
that torments innocence, all guiltless?
And yet another point increases my suffering:
that man is bound to his moral duty,
so as to restrain his own desire for the sake of God,
where a beast may fulfill all its desire. 460
And when an animal is dead, it feels no more pain;
but man must weep and sorrow after his death,
even though he has had care and woe on earth:
beyond doubt, this is the way it all may be.
I leave the final question to the theologians, 465
but well I know there is great suffering in this world.
Alas, I see a serpent or a thief,
who has done mischief to many a true man,
allowed to go at large; he may go where he pleases.
But I must stay in prison, by the will of Saturn 470
and also of Juno, the jealous and wrathful;
she has destroyed nearly all the royal blood
of Thebes, with its wide walls laid waste.
And Venus slays me on the other hand
for jealousy and fear of Arcite." 475

Now wol I stinte of Palamon a lyte,
And lete him in his prison stille dwelle,
And of Arcita forth I wol yow telle.

The somer passeth, and the nightes longe
Encresen double wyse the peynes stronge                           480
Bothe of the lovere and the prisoner.
I noot which hath the wofuller mester.
For, shortly for to seyn, this Palamoun
Perpetuelly is dampned to prisoun,
In cheynes and in fettres to ben deed;                            485
And Arcite is exyled upon his heed
For evermo, as out of that contree,
Ne nevere mo he shal his lady see.

Yow loveres axe I now this questioun.
Who hath the worse, Arcite or Palamoun?                           490
That oon may seen his lady day by day,
But in prison he moot dwelle alway.
That other wher him list may ryde or go,
But seen his lady shal he nevere mo.
Now demeth as yow liste, ye that can,                             495
For I wol telle forth as I bigan.

## II

Whan that Arcite to Thebes comen was,
Ful ofte a day he swelte and seyde "allas,"
For seen his lady shal he never-mo.
And shortly to concluden al his wo,                               500
So muche sorwe had never creature
That is, or shal, whyl that the world may dure.
His sleep, his mete, his drink is him biraft,
That lene he wex, and drye as is a shaft.
His eyen holwe, and grisly to biholde;                            505
His hewe falwe, and pale as asshen colde,
And solitarie he was, and ever allone,
And wailling al the night, making his mone.
And if he herde song or instrument,

Now I wish to stop talking about Palamon
    for a while
and leave him dwelling quietly in his prison;
I want to tell you further of Arcite.
    The summer passed, and the long nights
increased with doubled strength the extreme tortures    480
of both the lover and the prisoner.
I don't know which one had the more sorrowful lot.
To put it briefly, Palamon
is condemned forever to prison,
to die in chains and fetters;    485
and Arcite is exiled, on pain of death,
from that country forever;
and he may nevermore see his lady.
    I ask this question of you lovers:
which has the worse part, Arcite or Palamon?    490
The one may see his lady daily,
but always has to stay in prison.
The other may ride or walk wherever he pleases,
but is never supposed to see his lady again.
Now decide as you like—you who can—    495
and I shall go on narrating as I began.

II

    When Arcite had come to Thebes
he swooned and said, "Alas" many times a day,
for he was nevermore to see his lady.
To sum up his woe briefly,
so much sorrow never came to any other created being    500
which is or shall be as long as the world endures.
His sleep, his food, his drink were banished from him
so that he grew lean and dry as the shaft of a spear.
His eyes were hollow and frightening to look at;    505
his complexion was sallow and pale as dead ashes.
He was given to solitude and ever alone,
and wailing all night as he uttered his complaint.
If he heard song, or an instrument being played,

Then wolde he wepe, he mighte nat be stent;                  510
So feble eek were his spirits, and so lowe,
And chaunged so, that no man coude knowe
His speche nor his vois, though men it herde.
And in his gere, for al the world he ferde
Nat oonly lyk the loveres maladye                  .          515
Of Hereos,* but rather lyk manye*
Engendred of humour malencolyk,
Biforen, in his celle fantastyk.
And shortly, turned was al up-so-doun
Bothe habit and eek disposicioun                            520
Of him, this woful lovere daun Arcite.
    What sholde I al-day of his wo endyte?
Whan he endured hadde a yeer or two
This cruel torment, and this peyne and wo,
At Thebes, in his contree, as I seyde,                      525
Upon a night in sleep as he him leyde,
Him thoughte how that the winged god Mercurie
Biforn him stood and bad him to be murye.
His slepy yerde in hond he bar uprighte;
An hat he werede upon his heres brighte.                    530
Arrayed was this god (as he took keep)
As he was whan that Argus* took his sleep;
And seyde him thus: "To Atthenes shaltou wende;
Ther is thee shapen of thy wo an ende."
And with that word Arcite wook and sterte.                  535
"Now trewely, how sore that me smerte,"
Quod he, "To Atthenes right now wol I fare;
Ne for the drede of deeth shal I nat spare
To see my lady, that I love and serve;
In hir presence I recche nat to sterve."                    540
    And with that word he caughte a greet mirour,
And saugh that chaunged was al his colour,
And saugh his visage al in another kinde.
And right anoon it ran him in his minde,
That, sith his face was so disfigured                       545
Of maladye, the which he hadde endured,

he would weep so that he could not be stopped. 510
Also his spirits were so feeble, low,
and changed that no one could recognize
his speech or his voice, even if one were listening to it.
In his moodiness he behaved for all the world
not only like one afflicted with the lovers' malady 515
called "Hereos," but also rather more as having the
    mania
caused by the humor of melancholy
in the front cell of his brain, where fantasy resides.
Briefly, both the habits and the state of mind
of this woeful lover, sir Arcite, 520
were turned completely upside down.
    Why should I continually relate his woe?
When for a year or two he had endured
this cruel torment and this pain and woe,
then (in Thebes, in his country, as I said) 525
one night as he was lying asleep
it seemed to him that the winged god Mercury
stood before him and told him to be of good cheer.
Mercury held his sleep-inducing staff upright in his hand
and wore a hat upon his shining hair. 530
This god was dressed (as Arcite noticed)
as he had been when Argus had his slumber.
He said to Arcite, "You are to go to Athens;
the end of your woe is destined for you there."
At those words Arcite awoke and jumped up. 535
"Now truly, no matter how much I suffer for it,"
he said, "I shall go to Athens at once,
and I shall not hesitate for dread of death
to see my lady, whom I love and serve.
In her presence I care not if I die." 540
    With these words he caught up a large mirror
and saw that his complexion was completely changed
and that his face looked entirely different.
Instantly it came into his mind
that, since his face was so disfigured 545
with the sickness which he had undergone,

He mighte wel, if that he bar him lowe,
Live in Athenes evermore unknowe,
And seen his lady wel ny day by day.
And right anon he chaunged his array,                       550
And cladde him as a povre laborer,
And al allone, save oonly a squyer,
That knew his privetee and al his cas,
Which was disgysed povrely, as he was,
To Atthenes is he goon the nexte way.                       555
And to the court he wente upon a day,
And at the gate he profreth his servyse,
To drugge and drawe, what so men wol devyse.
And shortly of this matere for to seyn,
He fil in office with a chamberleyn,                        560
The which that dwelling was with Emelye;
For he was wys, and coude soon aspye
Of every servaunt, which that serveth here.
Wel coude he hewen wode, and water bere,
For he was yong and mighty for the nones,                   565
And therto he was strong and big of bones
To doon that any wight can him devyse.
A yeer or two he was in this servyse,
Page of the chambre of Emelye the brighte;
And "Philostrate" he seide that he highte.                  570
But half so wel biloved a man as he
Ne was ther never in court, of his degree;
He was so gentil of condicioun,
That thurghout al the court was his renoun.
They seyden that it were a charitee                         575
That Theseus wolde enhauncen his degree,
And putten him in worshipful servyse,
Ther as he mighte his vertu excercyse.
And thus, with-inne a whyle, his name is spronge,
Bothe of his dedes and his goode tonge,                     580
That Theseus hath taken him so neer
That of his chambre he made him a squyer,
And yaf him gold to mayntene his degree;

he might well, if he bore himself humbly,
live unknown in Athens ever after
and see his lady nearly every day.
Immediately he changed his clothes                        550
and dressed himself as a poor laborer.
All alone, except for a squire
who knew his secret and his whole situation
and who was disguised, like Arcite, as a poor man,
he traveled the shortest way to Athens.                   555
He went one day to the court
and at the gate offered his services
to fetch and carry at whatever kind of labor
        anyone devised.
To speak shortly of this matter,
he got employment with a chamberlain                      560
who attended upon Emily,
for Arcite was shrewd and could soon find out
which of all the servants served her.
He could hew wood and carry water handily,
for he was young and really strong,                       565
and also big and powerfully boned
enough to do whatever anyone could devise for him.
He was in this service for a year or two
as page of the chamber of lovely Emily;
he said that he was called Philostrato.                   570
There was never a man of his rank who was
half so well liked in the court:
he was so gentle in his manners
that his fame ran throughout the court.
They said it would be a good deed                         575
for Theseus to raise his rank
and put him into honorable service
where he might exercise his ability.
Thus in a little while his reputation,
both for his deeds and his speech, had spread             580
to the point that Theseus took him so near him
as to make him a squire of his chamber
and gave him money to maintain his station.

And eek men broghte him out of his contree
From yeer to yeer, ful prively, his rente;                 585
But honestly and slyly he it spente,
That no man wondred how that he it hadde.
And three yeer in this wyse his lyf he ladde,
And bar him, so in pees and eek in werre,
Ther was no man that Theseus hath derre.                   590
And in this blisse lete I now Arcite,
And speke I wol of Palamon a lyte.

     In derknesse and horrible and strong prisoun
This seven yeer hath seten Palamoun,
Forpyned, what for wo and for distresse;                   595
Who feleth double soor and hevinesse
But Palamon that love destreyneth so,
That wood out of his wit he gooth for wo?
And eek therto he is a prisoner
Perpetuelly, noght oonly for a yeer.                       600
Who coude ryme in English properly
His martirdom? for sothe, it am nat I;
Therefore I passe as lightly as I may.

     It fel that in the seventhe yeer, in May,
The thridde night (as olde bokes seyn,                     605
That al this storie tellen more pleyn).
Were it by aventure or destinee
(As, whan a thing is shapen, it shal be)
That, sone after the midnight, Palamoun,
By helping of a freend, brak his prisoun,                  610
And fleeth the citee, faste as he may go;
For he had yive his gayler drinke so
Of a clarree, maad of a certeyn wyn,
With nercotikes and opie of Thebes fyn,
That al that night, thogh that men wolde him shake,        615
The gayler sleep, he mighte nat awake;
And thus he fleeth as faste as ever he may.
The night was short, and faste by the day,
That nedes-cost he moste himselven hyde,
And til a grove, faste ther besyde,                        620
With dredeful foot than stalketh Palamoun.

Also there was brought to him from his country
(yearly, and very privately) his income;                    585
but he spent it suitably and discreetly
so that no one wondered how he got it.
He led his life in this fashion for three years
and conducted himself in peace—and in war, too—
so well that Theseus held no one else dearer.               590
And I now leave Arcite in this bliss
and will speak a little of Palamon.

    In darkness, in the horror of a strong prison,
Palamon had sat these seven years,
wasted away, what with sorrow and distress.                 595
Who but Palamon felt twofold sorrow and grief?
Love afflicted him so
that for grief he was completely out of his mind.
And, besides, he was a prisoner
forever, not simply for a year.                             600
Who could properly tell his martyrdom
in English verse? Indeed, I am not the one;
therefore I pass over as lightly as I may.

    It happened in the seventh year that on
the third night of May (as ancient books say,              605
which tell all this story more fully),
whether it was by chance or destiny
(as, when a thing is fated, it shall be),
Palamon, soon after midnight and
with the help of a friend, broke out of prison              610
and fled the city as fast as he could go.
He had given his jailer so much to drink
of a spiced, honeyed potion made of a certain wine
with narcotics and refined opium of Thebes
that all that night, even if the jailer were shaken,        615
he slept and could not wake up.
And thus Palamon fled as fast as he could.
The night was short and the dawn close by,
when (as need was) he would have to hide.
With fearful footstep, then, Palamon crept                  620
to a grove close by.

For shortly, this was his opinioun,
That in that grove he wolde him hyde al day,
And in the night than wolde he take his way
To Thebes-ward, his freendes for to preye                      625
On Theseus to helpe him to werreye;
And shortly, outher he wolde lese his lyf,
Or winnen Emelye unto his wyf;
This is th'effect and his entente pleyn.

   Now wol I torne to Arcite ageyn,                         630
That litel wiste how ny that was his care,
Til that Fortune had broght him in the snare.

   The bisy larke, messager of day,
Saluëth in hir song the morwe gray;
And fyry Phebus ryseth up so bright,                           635
That al the orient laugheth of the light,
And with his stremes dryeth in the greves
The silver dropes hanging on the leves.
And Arcita, that in the court royal
With Theseus is squyer principal,                              640
Is risen, and loketh on the myrie day.
And, for to doon his observaunce to May,
Remembring on the poynt of his desyr,
He on a courser, startlynge as the fyr,
Is riden into the feeldes him to pleye,                        645
Out of the court, were it a myle or tweye;
And to the grove, of which that I yow tolde,
By aventure, his wey he gan to holde,
To maken him a gerland of the greves,
Were it of wodebinde or hawethorn-leves,                       650
And loude he song ageyn the sonne shene:
"May, with alle thy floures and thy grene,
Welcome be thou, faire fresshe May,
In hope that I som grene gete may."
And from his courser, with a lusty herte,                      655
Into the grove ful hastily he sterte,
And in a path he rometh up and doun,
Theras, by aventure, this Palamoun

Briefly, it was his expectation
that he would hide himself in that grove all day
and then take his way during the night
in the direction of Thebes, in order to ask his friends          625
to help him make war on Theseus.
To put it in a few words, either he would lose his life
or he would win Emily to wife:
this was his aim and full intention.

    Now I shall return to Arcite,                                   630
who little knew how near trouble was
until Fortune had brought him into the snare.

    The busy lark, the messenger of day,
saluted the bright morning with her song,
and fiery Phoebus rose up so bright                              635
that all the east laughed with his light;
among the branches he dried with his rays
the silver drops hanging on the leaves.
Arcite, who was in the royal court
as chief squire to Theseus,                                     640
rose and looked out upon the merry day.
In order to pay his respects to May,
and bringing to mind the object of his longing,
he rode out into the fields on a courser as spirited
as fire in order to amuse himself                              645
outside the court, perhaps a mile or two away.
To the grove that I told you of
he by chance took his way
to make himself a garland of the branches,
whether they were woodbine or hawthorn,                         650
and he loudly sang this song in the face of the
    shining sun:
"May, with all your flowers and green—
be welcome, fair, fresh May;
in hope that I may get some green."
And with a happy heart he sprang                                655
from his courser and into the grove,
and walked up and down in a path
where Palamon by chance

Was in a bush, that no man mighte him see,
For sore afered of his deeth was he.                          660
Nothing ne knew he that it was Arcite:
God wot he wolde have trowed it ful lyte.
But sooth is seyd, go sithen many yeres,
That "feeld hath eyen, and the wode hath eres."
It is ful fair a man to bere him evene,                       665
For al-day meteth men at unset stevene.
Ful litel woot Arcite of his felawe,
That was so ny to herknen al his sawe,
For in the bush he sitteth now ful stille.

    Whan that Arcite hadde romed al his fille,                670
And songen al the roundel lustily,
Into a studie he fil sodeynly,
As doon thise loveres in hir queynte geres,
Now in the croppe, now doun in the breres,
Now up, now doun, as boket in a welle.                        675
Right as the Friday, soothly for to telle,
Now it shyneth, now it reyneth faste,
Right so can gery Venus overcaste
The hertes of hir folk; right as hir day
Is gereful, right so chaungeth she array.                     680
Selde is the Friday al the wowke ylike.

    Whan that Arcite had songe, he gan to syke,
And sette him doun withouten any more:
"Alas!" quod he, "that day that I was bore!
How longe, Juno, thurgh thy crueltee,                         685
Woltow werreyen Thebes the citee?
Allas! y-broght is to confusioun
The blood royal of Cadme and Amphioun;*
Of Cadmus, which that was the firste man
That Thebes bulte, or first the toun bigan,          ·        690
And of the citee first was crouned king,
Of his linage am I, and his ofspring
By verray ligne, as of the stok royal:
And now I am so caitif and so thral,
That he, that is my mortal enemy,                             695
I serve him as his squyer povrely.

was in a bush where no one could see him;
he was terribly afraid that he would be killed.            660
He had no idea that the intruder was Arcite; God knows
there is small chance that he would have imagined it.
But it has been said truthfully, for many years past,
"The field has eyes and the wood has ears."
It is very fitting for a man to behave coolly,            665
for one is faced every day with unexpected meetings.
Little did Arcite know of his friend,
who was so near as to hear all that he said,
for Palamon now sat in the bush in complete silence.

     When Arcite had had his fill of roaming            670
and had gaily sung all the roundel,
he suddenly began to brood,
as lovers do, in their curious moods:
sometimes in the treetop, other times in the briars,
now up, now down, like a bucket in a well.            675
To tell truly, just as on Friday (Venus's day)
it sometimes shines and at other times rains continually,
just so, changeable Venus overcasts
the hearts of her followers; just as her day
is changeable, so she changes her arrangements.            680
Seldom is Friday like the rest of the week.

     When Arcite had sung, he began to sigh
and sat down without further ado.
He said, "Alas, the day that I was born!
How long, Juno, in your cruelty            685
will you make war on the city of Thebes?
Alas! brought to confusion is
the royal blood of Cadmus and Amphion—
of Cadmus, who was the first man
to build Thebes, the first to begin it,            690
and was first crowned king of the city:
I am of his lineage, and am his offspring
by the true line, being of the royal stock.
And now, I am so wretched and enslaved
that the man who is my mortal enemy            695
I serve meanly as his squire.

And yet doth Juno me wel more shame,
For I dar noght biknowe myn owne name;
But ther as I was wont to highte Arcite,
Now highte I Philostrate, noght worth a myte.            700
Allas! thou felle Mars, allas! Juno,
Thus hath your ire our lynage al fordo,
Save only me, and wrecched Palamoun,
That Theseus martyreth in prisoun.
And over al this, to sleen me outrely,                   705
Love hath his fyry dart so brenningly
Y-stiked thurgh my trewe careful herte,
That shapen was my deeth erst than my sherte.
Ye sleen me with your eyen, Emelye;
Ye been the cause wherefore that I dye.                  710
Of al the remenant of myn other care
Ne sette I nat the mountaunce of a tare,
So that I coude don aught to youre plesaunce!"
And with that word he fil doun in a traunce
A longe tyme; and after he up-sterte.                    715
    This Palamoun, that thoughte that thurgh his herte
He felte a cold swerd sodeynliche glyde,
For ire he quook, no lenger wolde he byde.
And whan that he had herd Arcites tale,
As he were wood, with face deed and pale,                720
He sterte him up out of the buskes thikke,
And seyde: "Arcite, false traitour wikke,
Now artow hent, that lovest my lady so,
For whom that I have al this peyne and wo,
And art my blood, and to my counseil sworn,              725
As I ful ofte have told thee heer-biforn,
And hast by-japed here duk Theseus,
And falsly chaunged hast thy name thus;
I wol be deed, or elles thou shalt dye.
Thou shalt nat love my lady Emelye,                      730
But I wol love hir only, and namo;
For I am Palamoun, thy mortal fo.

And Juno does me yet more shame,
in that I dare not declare my own name;
whereas I was accustomed to be called Arcite,
I am now called Philostrato, worth nothing.          700
Alas, cruel Mars, alas, Juno:
thus your wrath has destroyed all our line
except for me, and wretched Palamon,
whom Theseus torments in prison.
And on top of all this, so as to slay me utterly,          705
Love has so ardently thrust his fiery dart
through my faithful, troubled heart that it seems that my
death was prepared for me before my first clothes
     were made.
You slay me with your eyes, Emily;
you are the cause of my dying.          710
On all the rest of my cares
I would not set the worth of one weed,
if I could do anything that would please you!"
At that he fell down in a trance
for a long time; then he got up.          715
    Palamon, who thought that he felt
a cold sword suddenly gliding through his heart,
quaked with wrath; he would wait no longer.
When he had heard what Arcite said,
he jumped from the thick bushes          720
as if he were mad, with a face of deadly pallor;
he said, "Arcite, false and wicked traitor,
now you are caught, you who so love my lady
(for whom I have all this pain and sorrow),
you who are of my blood, and are sworn to be
     on my side          725
(as I have often told you before this),
you who have deceived Duke Theseus here
and thus falsely changed your name,
either you shall die, or I will.
You shall not love my lady Emily,          730
for only I, and no others, shall love her.
I am Palamon, your mortal foe.

And though that I no wepene have in this place,
But out of prison am astert by grace,
I drede noght that outher thou shalt dye,                    735
Or thou ne shalt nat loven Emelye.
Chees which thou wolt for thou shalt nat asterte."
     This Arcite, with ful despitous herte,
Whan he him knew, and hadde his tale herd,
As fiers as leoun pulled out a swerd,                        740
And seyde thus: "by God that sit above,
Nere it that thou are sik, and wood for love,
And eek that thou no wepne hast in this place,
Thou sholdest never out of this grove pace,
That thou ne sholdest dyen of myn hond.                      745
For I defye the seurtee and the bond
Which that thou seyst that I have maad to thee.
What, verray fool, think wel that love is free,
And I wol love hir, maugre al thy might!
But, for as muche thou art a worthy knight,                  750
And wilnest to darreyne hir by batayle,
Have heer my trouthe, to-morwe I wol nat fayl
Withoute witing of any other wight,
That here I wol be founden as a knight,
And bringen harneys right ynough for thee;                   755
And chees the beste, and leef the worste for me
And mete and drinke this night wol I bringe
Ynough for thee, and clothes for thy beddinge.
And, if so be that thou my lady winne,
And slee me in this wode ther I am inne,                     760
Thou mayst wel have thy lady, as for me."
This Palamon answerd, "I graunte it thee."
And thus they been departed til a-morwe,
Whan ech of hem had leyd his feith to borwe.
     O Cupide, out of alle charitee!                         765
O regne, that wolt no felawe have with thee!
Ful sooth is seyd that love ne lordshipe
Wol noght, his thankes, have no felaweshipe;
Wel finden that Arcite and Palamoun.

Though I have no weapon here,
but have just escaped by luck from prison,
let there be no fear: either you shall die 735
or you shall not love Emily.
Choose which you want, for you shall not escape."
   With scornful heart, Arcite,
when he recognized Palamon and had heard
    what he said,
pulled out a sword; he was fierce as a lion. 740
He said, "By God who sits above,
if it were not that you are sick and crazed through love,
and also that you have no weapon here,
you should never go from this grove
without dying at my hand. 745
I spurn the covenant and the bond
which you say I have entered into with you.
Why, you absolute fool, recall that love is free,
and that I will love her, in spite of all you can do!
Yet, as you are a valiant knight, 750
and desire to decide the claim to her by battle,
take here my promise: tomorrow, without anyone's
knowing of it, I shall not fail
to be found here, on my faith as a knight,
and to bring quite enough armor for you; 755
you choose the better and leave the worse for me.
Tonight I shall bring food and drink
enough for you, and bedding;
if it be that you win my lady
and kill me in this wood where I am now, 760
you are welcome to your lady, as for me."
Palamon answered, "I agree to this plan."
Thus they parted until the next day,
for which time each had faithfully pledged himself.
   O Cupid, beyond all charity! 765
O sovereignty that wants none equal with yourself!
It is said most truly that neither love nor rule
will willingly endure a shared role.
Arcite and Palamon indeed discovered this.

Arcite is riden anon unto the toun,                                    770
And on the morwe, er it were dayes light,
Ful prively two harneys hath he dight,
Bothe suffisaunt and mete to darreyne.
The bataille in the feeld bitwix hem tweyne.
And on his hors, allone as he was born,                               775
He carieth al the harneys him biforn;
And in the grove, at tyme and place y-set,
This Arcite and this Palamon ben met.
Tho chaungen gan the colour in hir face;
Right as the hunter in the regne of Trace,*                           780
That stondeth at the gappe with a spere,
Whan hunted is the leoun or the bere,
And hereth him come russhing in the greves,
And breketh bothe bowes and the leves,
And thinketh, "heer cometh my mortel enemy,                           785
Withoute faile, he moot be deed, or I;
For outher I mot sleen him at the gappe,
Or he mot sleen me, if that me mishappe":
So ferden they, in chaunging of hir hewe,
As fer as everich of hem other knewe.                                 790
Ther nas no "good day," ne no saluing;
But streight, withouten word or rehersing,
Everich of hem halp for to armen other,
As freendly as he were his owne brother;
And after that, with sharpe speres stronge                            795
They foynen ech at other wonder longe.
Thou mightest wene that this Palamoun
In his fighting were a wood leoun,
And as a cruel tygre was Arcite:
As wilde bores gonne they to smyte,                                   800
That frothen whyte as foom for ire wood.
Up to the ancle foghte they in hir blood.
And in this wyse I lete hem fighting dwelle;
And forth I wol of Theseus yow telle.

    The destinee, ministre general,                                   805
That executeth in the world over-al
The purveyaunce, that God hath seyn biforn,

Arcite then rode to town, 770
and before daylight the next day
he secretly provided two suits of armor,
both of them sufficient and suitable for deciding
the lonely battle between them.
On his horse, utterly alone, 775
he carried all the armor before him;
in the thicket, at the set time and place,
Arcite and Palamon met.
Then their complexions began to change color;
just as the Thracian hunter, 780
who stands at the gap with a spear,
when the lion or the bear is being hunted,
and hears the beast come rushing among the branches,
breaking both twigs and leaves,
thinks, "Here comes my mortal enemy; 785
without fail either he or I must die,
for either I must slay him at this gap
or he must kill me, if I do badly";
just so they fared, as their complexions changed
as soon as each recognized the other. 790
There was no "Good day" or other greeting,
but straightaway, without speech or rehearsal of their
agreement, each helped to arm the other,
as friendly as if one were the other's brother.
After that, with sharp, strong spears, 795
they thrust at each other a very long time.
You might have thought that Palamon
in his fighting was a wrathful lion,
and that Arcite was a cruel tiger;
they smote each other like wild boars 800
which froth themselves white as foam in their wild wrath.
They fought up to the ankles in their blood.
And I leave them continuing the fight in this manner;
I shall go on to tell about Theseus.

Destiny, the governor general 805
who executes everywhere in this world
the providence that God has foreseen,

So strong it is, that, though the world had sworn
The contrarie of a thing, by ye or nay,
Yet somtyme it shal fallen on a day          810
That falleth nat eft with-inne a thousand yere.
For certeinly, our appetytes here,
Be it of werre, or pees, or hate, or love,
Al is this reuled by the sighte above.
This mene I now by mighty Theseus,          815
That for to hunten is so desirous,
And namely at the grete hert in May,
That in his bed ther daweth him no day;
That he nis clad, and redy for to ryde
With hunte and horn, and houndes him bisyde.          820
For in his hunting hath he swich delyt,
That it is al his joye and appetyt
To been him-self the grete hertes bane:
For after Mars he serveth now Diane.

   Cleer was the day, as I have told er this,          825
And Theseus, with alle joye and blis,
With his Ipolita, the fayre quene,
And Emelye, clothed al in grene,
On hunting be they riden royally.
And to the grove, that stood ful faste by,          830
In which ther was an hert, as men him tolde,
Duk Theseus the streighte wey hath holde.
And to the launde he rydeth him ful right,
For thider was the hert wont have his flight,
And over a brook, and so forth on his weye.          835
This duk wol han a cours at him, or tweye,
With houndes, swiche as that him list comaunde.

   And whan this duk was come unto the launde,
Under the sonne he loketh, and anon
He was war of Arcite and Palamon,          840
That foughten breme, as it were bores two;
The brighte swerdes wenten to and fro
So hidously, that with the leeste strook
It seemed as it wolde felle an ook;
But what they were, nothing he ne woot.          845

is so strong that, even if the world had sworn,
by yea or nay, the contrary of an event,
still yet one day that event should befall, 810
though it should not happen again in a thousand years.
For certainly, our desires here below,
be it for war or peace, or hate or love,
are all ruled by the providence above.
I intend all this now in reference to mighty Theseus, 815
who was so fond of hunting—
especially for the great hart in May—
that no day dawned upon him
when he was not dressed and ready to ride
with hunt and horn, and hounds beside him. 820
He had such delight in hunting
that all his joy and longing was
to be, himself, the scourge of the great hart;
for, after Mars, he now served Diana the huntress.

    The day was clear, as I have said before, 825
and with joy Theseus,
with his fair queen Hippolyta
and with Emily—all dressed in green—
had ridden royally to the hunt.
He went straight to the grove, 830
which stood nearby and
in which there was a hart, as he was told.
He rode right to the glade among the trees,
for the hart in his flight was likely to go there,
and then across a brook, and forth on his way. 835
The duke wanted to have him in chase once or twice
with such dogs as it pleased him to direct.

    When the duke had come to the glade,
he squinted below the low-lying sun and
immediately became aware of Arcite and Palamon, 840
who were fighting as furiously as if they were two boars.
The bright swords thrust to and fro
so hideously that with the least of their strokes
it seemed as if they would fell an oak.
He had no idea, however, who they were. 845

This duk his courser with his spores smoot,
And at a stert he was bitwix hem two,
And pulled out a swerd and cride, "Ho!
Namore, up peyne of lesing of your heed.
By mighty Mars, he shal anon be deed,                   850
That smyteth any strook, that I may seen!
But telleth me what mister men ye been,
That been so hardy for to fighten here
Withouten juge or other officere,
As it were in a listes royally?"                        855
    This Palamon answerde hastily
And seyde: "Sire, what nedeth wordes mo?
We have the deeth deserved bothe two.
Two woful wrecches been we, two caytyves,
That been encombred of our owne lyves;                  860
And as thou art a rightful lord and juge,
Ne yeve us neither mercy ne refuge,
But slee me first, for seynte charitee;
But slee my felawe eek as wel as me.
Or slee him first; for, though thou knowest it lyte,    865
This is thy mortal fo, this is Arcite,
That fro thy lond is banished on his heed,
For which he hath deserved to be deed.
For this is he that cam unto thy gate,
And seyde that he highte Philostrate.                   870
Thus hath he japed thee ful many a yeer,
And thou hast maked him thy chief squyer:
And this is he that loveth Emelye.
For sith the day is come that I shal dye,
I make pleynly my confessioun,                          875
That I am thilke woful Palamoun,
That hath thy prison broken wikkedly.
I am thy mortal fo, and it am I
That loveth so hote Emelye the brighte,
That I wol dye present in hir sighte.                   880
Wherfore I axe deeth and my juwyse;
But slee my felawe in the same wyse,
For both han we deserved to be slayn."

The duke struck spurs to his courser
and at a lunge he was between the two of them;
he pulled out a sword and cried "Halt!
No more, on pain of losing your heads!
By mighty Mars, the man shall die instantly          850
who gives another stroke that I can see!
Tell me what kind of men you are
who are so rash as to fight here
without judge or other officer
just as though you were in the lists under royal control?"   855
    Palamon hastily answered,
"Sire, what need is there for further words?
We have both deserved death.
We are two woeful wretches, two captives,
whose lives are an encumbrance to us;                860
and as you are a just lord and judge,
do not give us mercy or refuge,
but kill me first, for holy charity,
but kill my companion too, as well as me.
Or kill him first; for though you little know it,      865
this is your mortal enemy; this is Arcite,
who was banished from your land on pain of death,
for which reason he has deserved to die.
For he is the one that came to your gate
and said his name was Philostrato.                 870
Thus he has deceived you many a year
and you have made him your chief squire;
and I am one who loves Emily.
And since the day has come when I shall die,
I fully make my confession                        875
that I am that same woeful Palamon
who has wickedly broken from your prison.
I am your mortal enemy, and I am one
who loves lovely Emily so ardently
that I wish to die in her sight.                    880
Therefore I ask for my punishment and for death,
but on the same principle kill my companion,
for we have both deserved to be slain."

This worthy duk answerde anon agayn,
And seyde, "This is a short conclusioun:                    885
Youre owene mouth, by youre confessioun,
Hath dampned you, and I wol it recorde;
It nedeth noght to pyne yow with the corde.
Ye shal be deed, by mighty Mars the rede!"

The quene anon, for verray wommanhede,                      890
Gan for to wepe, and so dide Emelye,
And alle the ladies in the companye.
Gret pitee was it, as it thoughte hem alle,
That evere swich a chaunce sholde falle;
For gentil men they were, of greet estat,                   895
And nothing but for love was this debat;
And sawe hir blody woundes wyde and sore;
And alle crieden bothe lasse and more,
"Have mercy, lord, upon us wommen alle!"
And on hir bare knees adoun they falle,                     900
And wolde have kist his feet theras he stood,
Til at the laste aslaked was his mood;
For pitee renneth sone in gentil herte.
And though he first for ire quook and sterte,
He hath considered shortly, in a clause,                    905
The trespas of hem bothe, and eek the cause:
And although that his ire hir gilt accused
Yet in his reson he hem bothe excused;
As thus: he thoghte wel, that every man
Wol helpe himself in love, if that he can,                  910
And eek delivere himself out of prisoun;
And eek his herte hadde compassioun
Of wommen, for they wepen ever in oon;
And in his gentil herte he thoghte anoon,
And softe unto himself he seyde: "Fy                        915
Upon a lord that wol have no mercy,
But been a leoun, bothe in word and dede,
To hem that been in repentaunce and drede
As wel as to a proud despitous man
That wol maynteyne that he first bigan!                      920

The valiant duke answered immediately,
"This is a quick settlement:                                            885
by your confession your own mouth
has condemned you, and I will remember it;
there is no need of torture to make you confess.
You shall be slain, by mighty Mars the red!"
Then in true womanhood Queen Hypolita                                   890
began to weep, and so did Emily
and all the other ladies of the company.
It seemed to all of them a great pity
that such a chance should ever befall;
for the young men were gentle and of high station,                     895
and their quarrel was for nothing but love;
the ladies saw their bloody wounds, great and painful,
and all of the ladies, both least and greatest, cried out,
"Have mercy, lord, upon all us women!"
They fell down on their knees                                          900
and would have kissed his feet where he stood,
until at last his anger was slaked,
for pity soon arises in a gentle heart.
Though at first he quaked and shook with anger,
he gave brief, concise consideration                                   905
to the misdeeds of the two, and to the cause of these as
well: and although his anger affirmed their guilt,
he still excused both of them in his reason,
thus: he well considered that every man
will help himself in love, if he can,                                  910
and also will escape from prison;
and, besides, his heart took pity
on the women, for they continued to weep.
And in that gentle heart he now considered,
and whispered to himself, "Shame                                       915
upon a ruler that will have no mercy
but be a ravening lion, both in word and deed,
to those who are repentant and fearful
as much as to a proud, scornful man
who will persist in the same course of action that
    he began                                        920

That lord hath litel of discrecioun,
That in swich cas can no divisioun,
But weyeth pryde and humblesse after oon."
And shortly, whan his ire is thus agoon,
He gan to loken up with eyen lighte,                    925
And spak thise same wordes al on highte:
"The god of love, a! *benedicite,*
How mighty and how greet a lord is he!
Ayeins his might ther gayneth none obstacles,
He may be cleped a god for his miracles;               930
For he can maken at his owene gyse
Of everich herte, as that him list devyse.
Lo heer, this Arcite and this Palamoun,
That quitly weren out of my prisoun,
And mighte han lived in Thebes royally,                935
And witen I am hir mortal enemy,
And that hir deeth lyth in my might also;
And yet hath love, maugree hir eyen two,
Broght hem hider bothe for to dye!
Now loketh, is nat that an heigh folye?                940
Who may been a fool, but if he love?
Bihold, for Goddes sake that sit above,
Se how they blede! be they noght well arrayed?
Thus hath hir lord, the god of love, y-payed
Hir wages and hir fees for hir servyse!                945
And yet they wenen for to been ful wyse
That serven love, for aught that may bifalle!
But this is yet the beste game of alle,
That she, for whom they han this jolitee,
Can hem therefore as muche thank as me;                950
She woot namore of al this hote fare,
By God, than woot a cokkow or an hare!
But al mot been assayed, hoot and cold;
A man mot been a fool, or yong or old;
I woot it by myself ful yore agoon:                    955
For in my tyme a servant was I oon.
And therfore, sin I knowe of loves peyne,

with. That ruler has little discernment
who knows no dividing line in such a case,
but weighs pride and humility by one measure."
Shortly, when his anger had thus passed off,
he looked up with cheerful eyes                                    925
and pronounced the following in a loud voice:
"The god of love—ah, bless us all—
how great and mighty a ruler he is!
No obstacles withstand his might;
he may be called a god for his miracles,                           930
for according to his own desire he can make
whatever he pleases of every heart.
Look at this Arcite and Palamon here,
who were clean out of my prison
and might have lived as kings in Thebes,                           935
and who know that I am their mortal enemy
and that their death, too, lies within my power;
yet Love, in spite of what they can do, has
brought both of them here to die!
Consider now; isn't that the height of folly?                      940
Who may be a real fool unless he is in love?
For the sake of God who sits above,
see how they bleed! Aren't they finely equipped?
Thus their lord, the god of love, has paid
their wages and fees for their service!                            945
And yet those think themselves very wise
who serve love, no matter what may happen!
But the best joke of all is
that the lady for whom they are having this diversion
knows as little to thank them for in it as I do;                   950
she knows no more of these hot-blooded goings-on,
by God, than a cuckoo or a hare does!
But everything has to be tried, hot or cold;
a man must be a fool, either young or old;
I know that from very long ago through my
        own experience,                                            955
for in my time I was one of those servants of Love.
Therefore, since I know of the pain of Love,

And woot how sore it can a man distreyne,
As he that hath ben caught ofte in his las,
I yow foryeve al hoolly this trespas,                    960
At requeste of the quene that kneleth here,
And eek of Emelye, my suster dere.
And ye shul bothe anon unto me swere,
That nevere mo ye shul my contree dere,
Ne make werre upon me night ne day;                      965
But been my freendes in al that ye may;
I yow foryeve this trespas every del."
And they him swore his axing fayre and wel,
And him of lordshipe and of mercy preyde,
And he hem graunteth grace, and thus he seyde:          970
     "To speke of royal linage and richesse,
Though that she were a quene or a princesse,
Ech of yow bothe is worthy, doutelees,
To wedden whan tyme is, but nathelees
I speke as for my suster Emelye,                         975
For whom ye have this stryf and jalousye.
Ye woot yourself she may not wedden two
At ones, though ye fighten evermo:
That oon of yow, al be him looth or leef,
He moot go pypen in an ivy-leef;                         980
This is to seyn, she may nat now han bothe,
Al be ye never so jalouse ne so wrothe.
And for-thy I yow putte in this degree,
That ech of yow shal have his destinee
As him is shape; and herkneth in what wyse;             985
Lo heere your ende of that I shal devyse.
     My wil is this, for plat conclusioun,
Withouten any replicacioun—
If that yow lyketh, tak it for the beste,
That everich of yow shal gon wher him leste             990
Frely, withouten raunson or daunger;
And this day fifty wykes, fer ne ner,
Everich of you shal bringe an hundred knightes,
Armed for listes up at alle rightes,

and realize, as one who has often been caught in his net,
how sorely this pain can cripple a man,
I wholly forgive you this misdeed,                    960
at the request of the queen, who kneels here,
and also of my dear sister, Emily.
You must both swear to me at once
that you will never harm my country,
or make war upon me by night or day,                    965
but be my friends in every matter that you can;
I forgive you every bit of this misdeed."
They swore to him fairly and well what he had asked for
and sued for his patronage and mercy.
He granted them favor and spoke thus:                    970
    "In the matter of royal lineage and wealth,
even if the lady were a queen or princess,
each of you is no doubt worthy
to marry when the time comes, but all the same
I am speaking for my sister Emily,                    975
for whose sake you sustain this conflict and jealousy.
You yourselves know that she may not marry two
at the same time, even if you fight forever:
one of you, whether he likes it or not,
must go blow on an ivy leaf;                    980
that is to say, she may not now have you both,
no matter how jealous or angry you are.
Therefore I am placing you in the following position
so that each of you shall have his destiny
as it is shaped for him. Listen to how;                    985
see, here is your solution in terms of what I devise:
    "My will is as follows, as a flat conclusion to
        the matter
without any arguing;
if it pleases you, take it willingly:
each of you shall go where he wishes,                    990
freely and without reason or control,
and fifty weeks from this day, neither more nor less,
each of you shall bring here a hundred knights,
armed properly for the tournament

Al redy to darreyne hir by bataille.                              995
And this bihote I yow, withouten faille,
Upon my trouthe, and as I am a knight,
That whether of yow bothe that hath might—
This is to seyn, that whether he or thou
May with his hundred, as I spak of now,                          1000
Sleen his contrarie, or out of listes dryve—
Him shal I yeve Emelya to wyve,
To whom that Fortune yeveth so fair a grace.
The listes shal I maken in this place,
And God so wisly on my soule rewe,                               1005
As I shal evene juge been and trewe.
Ye shul non other ende with me maken,
That oon of yow ne shal be deed or taken.
And if yow thinketh this is wel y-sayd,
Seyeth your avys, and holdeth yow apayd.                         1010
This is youre ende and youre conclusion."
    Who loketh lightly now but Palamoun?
Who springeth up for joye but Arcite?
Who couthe telle, or who couthe it endyte,
The joye that is maked in the place                              1015
Whan Theseus hath doon so fair a grace?
But doun on knees wente every maner wight,
And thanked him with al hir herte and might,
And namely the Thebans often sythe.
And thus with good hope and with herte blythe                    1020
They taken hir leve, and hom-ward gonne they ryde
To Thebes, with his olde walles wyde.

### III

    I trowe men wolde deme it necligence.
If I foryete to tellen the dispence
Of Theseus, that goth so bisily                                  1025
To maken up the listes royally,
That swich a noble theatre as it was,
I dar wel seyn that in this world ther nas.
The circuit a myle was aboute,

and ready to decide the claim to her by battle.                995
I promise you without fail,
on my faith and as I am a knight,
that whichever of you two has the might—
that is to say, whichever, he or you,
can, with the hundred knights I spoke of,                1000
kill his opponent or drive him from the arena—
then to him, to whom Fortune gives such fair favor,
I shall give Emily in marriage.
I shall set up the arena in this spot;
and, as God shall have pity on my soul,                1005
I shall be a fair and faithful judge;
you shall not come to terms with me
unless one of you is dead or captured.
If you think this is a good plan,
say so, and consider yourselves well treated.                1010
This is your settlement and decision."
    Who but Palamon now looks happy?
Who but Arcite jumps for joy?
Who could say or sing
the joy that was made in that spot                1015
when Theseus had performed so fair a favor?
Every kind of person present went down on his knees
and thanked him with all his heart and might,
and especially the two Thebans thanked him often.
Thus with good hope and happy heart                1020
they took their leave and began to ride homeward
to Thebes, with its ancient wide walls.

### III

    I imagine that it would be considered negligence
if I forgot to tell of the outlay
of Theseus, who worked so hard                1025
to construct the arena in royal fashion
that there was not, I may well say, anywhere else
in the world such a noble amphitheater as it was.
The distance around it was a mile;

Walled of stoon, and diched al withoute.                    1030
Round was the shap, in maner of compas,
Ful of degrees, the heighte of sixty pas,
That, whan a man was set on o degree,
He letted nat his felawe for to see.

Estward ther stood a gate of marbel whyt,          1035
Westward, right swich another in the opposit.
And shortly to concluden, swich a place
Was noon in erthe, as in so litel space;
For in the lond ther nas no crafty man,
That geometrie or ars-metrike can,                        1040
Ne purtreyour, ne kerver of images,
That Theseus ne yaf him mete and wages
The theatre for to maken and devyse.
And for to doon his ryte and sacrifyse,
He estward hath, upon the gate above,                  1045
In worship of Venus, goddesse of love,
Don make an auter and an oratorie;
And on the gate westward, in memorie
Of Mars, he maked hath right swich another,
That coste largely of gold a fother.                         1050
And northward, in a touret on the wal,
Of alabastre whyt and reed coral
An oratorie riche for to see,
In worship of Dyane of chastitee,
Hath Theseus doon wroght in noble wyse.          1055

But yet hadde I foryeten to devyse
The noble kerving and the portreitures,
The shap, the countenaunce, and the figures,
That weren in thise oratories three.

First in the temple of Venus maystow see          1060
Wroght on the wal, ful pitous to biholde,
The broken slepes, and the sykes colde;
The sacred teres, and the waymentynge,
The fyry strokes of the desirynge
That Loves servaunts in this lyf enduren;          1065

it was walled with stone and provided with a moat
   on the                                                                    1030
outside. The shape was round, an exact circle,
and it was filled, with tiered seats, to the height of
   sixty feet,
so that when a man sat on one tier
he did not keep his neighbor from seeing.

   To the east there stood a gate of white marble;         1035
and to the west just such another opposite it.
To conclude briefly, there was not such another place
in all the earth arranged in so small a space.
For in all the land there was no skilled workman
who knew geometry or arithmetic,                                           1040
nor any painter or sculptor,
to whom Theseus did not give food and wages
to plan and construct the amphitheater.
For conducting his rites and making his sacrifices
he had an altar and an oratory made                                        1045
at the east end, above the gate,
in honor of Venus, the goddess of love;
and over the gate to the west, in memory
of Mars, he made just such another,
which cost a generous pile of gold.                                        1050
To the north, in a turret on the wall,
Theseus caused to be constructed in noble fashion
an oratory, richly adorned,
of white alabaster and red coral,
in worship of chaste Diana.                                                1055

   But I have forgotten to describe
the noble sculptures and paintings,
the shape, the appearance, and the markings
of these three oratories.

   First, in the temple of Venus you may see                1060
depicted on the wall (and very pitiable to look at)
interrupted slumbers, sad sighs,
devoted tears, and lamentation,
the fiery strokes of desire
which the servants of Love endure in this life;                            1065

The othes that hir covenants assuren;
Plesaunce and Hope, Desyr, Foolhardinesse,
Beautee and Youthe, Bauderie, Richesse,
Charmes and Force, Lesinges, Flaterye,
Dispense, Bisynesse, and Jelousye,                     1070
That wered of yelwe goldes a gerland,
And a cokkow sitting on hir hand;
Festes, instruments, caroles, daunces,
Lust and Array, and alle the circumstaunces
Of love, whiche that I rekne and rekne shal,           1075
By ordre weren peynted on the wal,
And mo than I can make of mencioun.
For soothly al the mount of Citheroun,*
Ther Venus hath hir principal dwellynge,
Was shewed on the wal in portreyynge,                  1080
With al the gardin and the lustinesse.
Nat was foryeten the porter Ydelnesse,*
Ne Narcisus the faire of yore agon,
Ne yet the folye of king Salamon,*
Ne yet the grete strengthe of Hercules*—               1085
Th'enchauntements of Medea* and Circes*—
Ne of Turnus,* with the hardy fiers corage,
The riche Cresus,* caytif in servage.
Thus may ye seen that wisdom ne richesse,
Beautee ne sleighte, strengthe, ne hardinesse,         1090
Ne may with Venus holde champartye;
For as hir list the world than may she gye,
Lo, alle thise folk so caught were in hir las,
Til they for wo ful ofte seyde "allas!"
Suffyceth heer ensamples oon or two,                   1095
And though I coude rekne a thousand mo.
  The statue of Venus, glorious for to see,
Was naked fleting in the large see,
And fro the navele doun all covered was
With wawes grene, and brighte as any glas.             1100
A citole in hir right hand hadde she,
And on hir heed, ful semely for to see,
A rose gerland, fresh and wel smellinge;

the pledges that seal their covenants;
Pleasure and Hope, Desire, Foolhardiness,
Beauty and Youth, Bawdry, Riches,
Enchantments and Force, Lies, Flattery,
Extravagance, Anxious Labor, and Jealousy,          1070
who wore a garland of marigolds
and had a cuckoo sitting on her hand;
banquets, musical instruments, carols, dances,
Joy and Adornment, and all the circumstances
of love which I have reckoned and shall reckon up   1075
were painted in order on the wall
and others more than I can mention.
For in fact all the mountain of Cithaeron,
where Venus has her principal dwelling,
was portrayed on the wall,                          1080
with all its garden and its pleasures.
The porter Idleness was not forgotten,
nor Narcissus the fair of long ago,
nor yet the folly of King Solomon,
the great strength of Hercules,                     1085
the enchantments of Medea and Circe,
Turnus with his brave, fierce disposition,
rich Croesus, captive in servitude.
Thus you may see that neither wisdom nor riches,
beauty nor trickery, strength nor boldness          1090
may share power equally with Venus,
for as she wishes she may guide the world.
Behold, all these people were caught in her snare
until for sorrow they often said, "Alas!"
One or two examples suffice here,                    1095
although I could reckon up a thousand more.
    The statue of Venus, glorious to behold,
was naked, floating in the sea,
and from the navel down was covered
with green waves, glittering like glass.            1100
She had a stringed instrument in her right hand
and on her head a garland of roses,
handsome, fresh, and fragrant;

Above hir heed hir dowves flikeringe.
Biforn hir stood hir sone Cupido,                              1105
Upon his shuldres winges hadde he two;
And blind he was, as it is often sene;
A bowe he bar and arwes brighte and kene.

Why sholde I noght as wel eek telle yow al
The portreiture that was upon the wal                         1110
Withinne the temple of mighty Mars the rede?
Al peynted was the wal, in lengthe and brede,
Lyk to the estres of the grisly place,
That highte the grete temple of Mars in Trace,
In thilke colde, frosty regioun,                              1115
Theras Mars hath his sovereyn mansioun.

First on the wal was peynted a forest,
In which ther dwelleth neither man ne best,
With knotty, knarry, bareyn treës olde
Of stubbes sharpe and hidous to biholde;                      1120
In which ther ran a rumbel in a swough,
As though a storm sholde bresten every bough.
And downward from an hille, under a bente,
Ther stood the temple of Mars armipotente,
Wroght al of burned steel, of which the entree                1125
Was long and streit, and gastly for to see.
And therout cam a rage and such a vese,
That it made al the gates for to rese.
The northren light in at the dores shoon,
For windowe on the wal ne was ther noon,                      1130
Thurgh which men mighten any light discerne.
The dore was alle of adamant eterne,
Y-clenched overthwart and endelong
With iren tough; and, for to make it strong,
Every piler, the temple to sustene,                           1135
Was tonne-greet, of iren bright and shene.

Ther saugh I first the derke imagining
Of Felonye, and al the compassing;
The cruel Ire, reed as any glede;
The pykepurs, and eek the pale Drede;                         1140
The smyler with the knyf under the cloke;

above her head her doves were fluttering.
Before her, stood her son Cupid;                              1105
he had two wings upon his shoulders,
and he was blind, as is often seen;
he carried a bow and shining, keen arrows.

Why should I not tell you as well of all
the pictures upon the wall                                   1110
within the temple of mighty Mars the red?
The wall was covered with pictures just as was
the interior of the grisly place
which is called the great temple of Mars in Thrace,
in that cold and frosty region                              1115
where Mars has his principal seat.

First on the wall was depicted a forest
in which dwelled neither man nor beast,
with knotty, gnarled, barren old trees
having splintered stubs of branches, hideous to see.        1120
In it there ran a rumbling sound and a soughing
as though a storm would break every branch.
Down a hill, at the bottom of the slope,
stood the temple of Mars the powerful in arms;
it was made entirely of burnished steel; the entry          1125
was long, narrow and ghastly to look at.
From it came such a blast and rush of wind
that it made all the gates tremble.
The northern lights shone in at the doors;
there was no window in the wall                             1130
through which one could discern any light.
All the doors were of eternal adamant,
clamped together crosswise and lengthwise
with hard iron; and, to make the temple strong,
every pillar supporting the temple                         1135
was as big as a cask, and made of bright, glittering iron.

There I first saw the dark plannings
of Treachery, and all the execution of the plan;
cruel Ire, red as a glowing coal;
the pickpurse, and pale Dread;                              1140
the smiler with the knife beneath his cloak;

The shepne brenning with the blake smoke;
The treson of the mordring in the bedde;
The open werre, with woundes al bibledde;
Contek, with blody knyf and sharp manace;                1145
Al ful of chirking was that sory place.
The sleere of himself yet saugh I ther;
His herte-blood hath bathed al his heer;
The nayl y-driven in the shode a-night;
The colde Deeth, with mouth gaping upright.              1150
Amiddes of the temple sat Meschaunce,
With disconfort and sory contenaunce.
Yet saugh I Woodnesse laughing in his rage;
Armed Compleint, outhees, and fiers Outrage.
The careyne in the bush, with throte y-corve:            1155
A thousand slayn, and nat of qualm* y-storve;
The tiraunt, with the prey by force y-raft;
The toun destroyed, then was nothing laft.
Yet saugh I brent the shippes hoppesteres;
The hunte strangled with the wilde beres;                1160
The sowe freten the child right in the cradel;
The cook y-scalded, for al his longe ladel.
Noght was foryeten by th'infortune of Marte;
The carter overriden with his carte,
Under the wheel ful lowe he lay adoun.                   1165
Then were also, of Martes divisioun,
The barbour, and the bocher, and the smith,
That forgeth sharpe swerdes on his stith.
And al above, depeynted in a tour,
Saw I Conquest sittinge in greet honour,                 1170
With the sharpe swerde over his heed
Hanginge by a sotil twynes threed.
Depeynted was the slaughtre of Julius,*
Of grete Nero,* and of Antonius;*
Al be that thilke tyme they were unborn,                 1175
Yet was hir deeth depeynted ther-biforn,
By manasinge of Mars, right by figure;

the stable burning with its black smoke;
the treason of the murder in the bed;
open warfare, with wounds covered with gore;
Strife, with bloody knife and sharp menace;                    1145
the whole sorry place was full of strident noise.
More, I saw there the suicide
(his heart's blood had soaked his hair);
the nail driven by night into a man's temple; and
cold Death, on his back with his mouth gaping.                  1150
In the midst of the temple sat Misfortune
with discouraged and sorry countenance.
I further saw Madness, laughing in his rage;
armed Grievance, Outcry, and fierce Outrage;
the corpse in the bush, with his throat cut;                    1155
a thousand slain, not dead of the plague;
the tyrant, with his prey snatched by force; and
the town so destroyed that nothing was left.
I saw further the ships being burned as they danced
    on the
waves, the hunter strangled by the wild bears,                 1160
the sow devouring the child right in the cradle,
the cook scalded in spite of the length of his ladle.
Nothing was forgotten of the ill fortune caused by
    Mars;
the carter run over by his cart,
beneath the wheel he lay right low.                             1165
Also there, of Mars's people, were
the barber-surgeon and the butcher and the smith,
who forges sharp swords on his anvil.
I saw at the top, depicted in a tower,
Conquest sitting in great honor,                               1170
with the sharp sword hanging over his head
by a thin thread of twine.
Depicted there were the murders of Julius Caesar,
of great Nero, and of Caracalla;
although they were not born at that time,                       1175
their deaths were depicted beforehand, by the menacing
of Mars, according to astrological calculation.

So was it shewed in that portreiture,
As is depeynted in the sterres above
Who shal be slayn or elles deed for love.          1180
Suffyceth oon ensample in stories olde,
I may not rekne hem alle though I wolde.

The statue of Mars upon a carte stood,
Armed, and loked grim as he were wood;
And over his heed ther shynen two figures          1185
Of sterres, that been cleped in scriptures,
That oon Puella,* that other Rubeus.*
This god of armes was arrayed thus:
A wolf ther stood biforn him at his feet
With eyen rede, and of a man he eet;          1190
With sotil pencel depeynted was this storie,
In redoutinge of Mars and of his glorie.

Now to the temple of Diane the chaste
As shortly as I can I wol me haste,
To telle yow al the descripcioun.          1195
Depeynted been the walles up and doun
Of hunting and shamefast chastitee.
Ther saugh I how woful Calistopee,*
Whan that Diane agreved was with here,
Was turned from a womman til a bere,          1200
And after was she maad the lode-sterre;
Thus was it peynt, I can say yow no ferre;
Hir sone is eek a sterre, as men may see.
Ther saugh I Dane,* y-turned til a tree—
I mene nat the goddesse Diane,          1205
But Penneus doughter, which that highte Dane.
Then saugh I Attheon* an hert y-maked,
For vengeaunce that he saugh Diane al naked;
I saugh how that his houndes have him caught,
And freten him, for that they knewe him naught.          1210
Yet peynted was a litel forther moor,
How Atthalante* hunted the wilde boor,
And Meleagre,* and many another mo,
For which Diane wroghte him care and wo.
Ther saugh I many another wonder storie,          1215

Thus were they revealed in those paintings
as in the stars above is delineated
who is to be killed or to die for love.                                    1180
One example is enough in ancient stories;
I may not reckon up all of them even if I wanted to.

The statue of Mars stood armed upon a chariot
and looked as fierce as if he were mad with anger;
over his head there shone two constellations,                              1185
of which, in writings on the subject,
one is called Puella, the other Rubeus.
This god of arms was thus equipped:
before him at his feet there stood a wolf,
red-eyed, who was eating at a man;                                         1190
with skillful brush this history was depicted
in fearful reverence of Mars and of his glory.

Now, as short a way as I can, I shall hasten to
the temple of Diana the chaste
to describe it to you fully.                                               1195
The walls were covered from top to bottom with pictures
of hunting and modest chastity.
There I saw how woeful Callisto,
when Diana was offended by her,
was changed from a woman into a bear,                                      1200
and how, afterward, she was made into the North Star;
thus it was painted; I can say no more;
her son is also a star, as may be seen.
I saw there Daphne, turned into a tree
(I do not mean the goddess Diana,                                          1205
but the daughter of Peneus, who was called Daphne).
I saw there Actaeon, turned into a hart
in vengeance for his having seen Diana naked;
I saw how his dogs caught
and ate him, because they did not recognize him.                          1210
In addition there was painted a little further along
how Atalanta and Meleager and many another
hunted the wild boar,
for which reason Diana gave Meleager care and sorrow.
I saw there many another marvelous story                                   1215

The which me list nat drawen to memorie.
This goddesse on an hert ful hye seet,
With smale houndes al aboute hir feet;
And undernethe hir feet she hadde a mone,
Wexing it was, and sholde wanie sone.　　　　　1220
In gaude grene hir statue clothed was,
With bowe in honde, and arwes in a cas.
Hir eyen caste she ful lowe adoun,
Ther Pluto hath his derke regioun.
A womman travailinge was hir biforn,　　　　　1225
But, for hir child so longe was unborn,
Ful pitously Lucyna gan she calle,
And seyde, "Help, for thou mayst best of alle."
Wel couthe he peynten lyfly that it wroghte;
With many a florin he the hewes boghte.　　　　1230

　　Now been thise listes maad, and Theseus,
That at his grete cost arrayed thus
The temples and the theatre every del,
Whan it was doon, him lyked wonder wel.
But stinte I wol of Theseus a lyte,　　　　　　1235
And speke of Palamon and of Arcite.

　　The day approcheth of hir retourninge,
That everich sholde an hundred knightes bringe,
The bataille to darreyne, as I yow tolde;
And til Athenes, hir covenant for to holde,　　　1240
Hath everich of hem broght an hundred knightes
Wel armed for the werre at alle rightes.
And sikerly ther trowed many a man
That nevere, sithen that the world bigan,
As for to speke of knighthod of hir hond,　　　　1245
As fer as God hath maked see or lond,
Nas, of so fewe, so noble a companye.
For every wight that lovede chivalrye,
And wolde, his thankes, han a passant name,
Hath preyed that he mighte ben of that game;　　1250
And wel was him, that therto chosen was.

which I do not want to bring to memory.
On high the goddess sat upon a hart
and had small hounds about her feet;
beneath her feet she had a moon;
it was waxing, but should soon wane.                    1220
Her statue was clothed in bright green;
she had a bow in hand and arrows in a quiver.
She was casting her eyes far down
to where Pluto holds his dark region.
A woman in labor was before her,                        1225
but, because childbirth was so long delayed,
the woman called upon Lucina piteously,
saying, "Help me, for you may do it best of all."
He who made the picture could indeed paint to the life;
he bought the paints with many a florin.               1230
    Now the arena was constructed, and Theseus,
who at great cost had thus arranged
every part of the temples and the amphitheater,
liked the work marvelously well when it was done.
But I shall cease for a while on the subject of Theseus  1235
and speak of Palamon and Arcite.
    The day approached for their return,
when each of them should bring a hundred knights
to decide the battle, as I told you;
to keep their agreement, each of them brought           1240
a hundred knights to Athens,
well armed in all respects for the battle.
And, indeed, many a man believed
that never since the world began,
as far as God extended sea or land,                     1245
had there been concentrated in such a small
        number of men
such a noble company in respect of knightly valor.
For every man that loved chivalry
and wanted, for his part, to have a surpassing
        reputation
had asked that he might take part in that affair;       1250
and happy was he who was chosen for it.

For if ther fille to-morwe swich a cas,
Ye knowen wel that every lusty knight
That loveth paramours, and hath his might,
Were it in Engelond, or elleswhere,                           1255
They wolde, hir thankes, wilnen to be there.
To fighte for a lady, *ben'cite*!
It were a lusty sighte for to see.
    And right so ferden they with Palamon.
With him ther wenten knightes many oon;                       1260
Som wol ben armed in an habergeoun,
And in a brestplate and a light gipoun;
And somme wol have a peyre plates large;
And somme wol have a Pruce sheld or a targe;
Somme wol ben armed on hir legges weel,                        1265
And have an ax, and somme a mace of steel;
Ther is no newe gyse that it nas old;
Armed were they, as I have you told,
Everich after his opinioun.
    Ther maistow seen coming with Palamoun                     1270
Ligurge himself, the grete king of Trace;
Blak was his berd, and manly was his face.
The cercles of his eyen in his heed,
They gloweden bitwixen yelow and reed,
And lyk a griffon* loked he aboute,                            1275
With kempe heres on his browes stoute;
His limes grete, his braunes harde and stronge,
His shuldres brode, his armes rounde and longe.
And as the gyse was in his contree,
Ful hye upon a char of gold stood he,                          1280
With foure whyte boles in the trays.
Instede of cote-armure over his harnays,
With nayles yelwe and brighte as any gold
He hadde a beres skin, col-blak for old.
His longe heer was kembd bihinde his bak;                      1285
As any ravenes fether it shoon for blak;
A wrethe of gold, arm-greet, of huge wighte,
Upon his heed, set ful of stones brighte,
Of fyne rubies and of dyamaunts.

For, if such a matter came up tomorrow,
you well know that every lusty knight
who loves in the manner of man and woman and has his
strength would, whether in England or elsewhere,          1255
desire for his part to be there.
To fight for a lady, Lord bless us,
would be a joyous sight to see.

   And so it was for those who were with Palamon.
Many a knight went with him;                              1260
some preferred to be armed in a coat of mail,
a breastplate, and a light tunic;
some would wear two steel plates, front and back.
and some would have a Prussian shield or a round one;
some wanted to be well armed on their legs,               1265
and have an ax, and some wanted a steel mace:
there is no new fashion which is not also old.
They were armed, as I have told you,
each one according to his own idea.

   There you might see coming with Palamon              1270
Lycurgus himself, the great king of Thrace;
his beard was black and his face manly.
The pupils of his eyes
glowed between yellow and red,
and he looked about him like a griffin,                   1275
with thick hair on his strong brows;
his limbs were large, his muscles hard and strong,
his shoulders broad, his arms long and rounded.
As the custom was in his country,
he sat high upon a golden chariot                         1280
with four white bulls in the traces.
Instead of a coat of arms over his battle dress
he had a bearskin, coal-black with age,
its yellow claws glittering like gold.
His long hair was combed down his back;                   1285
it shone like a raven's feather in its blackness;
a gold wreath, as thick as an arm and of huge weight,
was upon his head and shone with bright stones—
fine rubies and diamonds.

Aboute his char ther wenten whyte alaunts,          1290
Twenty and mo, as grete as any steer,
To hunten at the leoun or the deer,
And folwed him, with mosel faste y-bounde,
Colered of gold, and torets fyled rounde.
An hundred lordes hadde he in his route          1295
Armed ful wel, with hertes sterne and stoute.

     With Arcita, in stories as men finde,
The grete Emetreus, the king of Inde,
Upon a stede bay, trapped in steel,
Covered in cloth of gold diapred weel,          1300
Cam ryding lyk the god of armes, Mars.
His cote-armure was of cloth of Tars,
Couched with perles whyte and rounde and grete.
His sadel was of brend gold newe y-bete;
A mantelet upon his shuldre hanginge,          1305
Bret-ful of rubies rede, as fyr sparklinge.
His crispe heer lyk ringes was y-ronne,
And that was yelow, and glitered as the sonne.
His nose was heigh, his eyen bright citryn,
His lippes rounde, his colour was sangwyn,          1310
A fewe fraknes in his face y-spreynd,
Betwixen yelow and somdel blak y-meynd,
And as a leoun he his loking caste.
Of fyve and twenty yeer his age I caste.
His berd was wel bigonne for to springe;          1315
His voys was as a trompe thunderinge.
Upon his heed he wered of laurer grene
A gerland fresh and lusty for to sene.
Upon his hand he bar, for his deduyt,
An egle tame, as eny lilie whyt.          1320
An hundred lordes hadde he with him there,
Al armed, save hir heddes, in al hir gere,
Ful richely in alle maner thinges.
For trusteth wel that dukes, erles, kinges,
Were gadered in this noble companye,          1325
For love, and for encrees of chivalrye.

About his chariot moved white wolfhounds,                1290
twenty and more, and large as steers,
for hunting lion or deer;
they followed him, with their muzzles tightly bound
and gold collars with leash holes filed round.
He had a hundred lords in his company,                1295
well armed, with stern, proud spirits.
. With Arcite, as we find in histories,
came riding, like Mars, god of arms,
the great Emetreus, king of India,
upon a bay steed; its trappings were of steel                1300
and it was covered with cloth of gold patterned skillfully.
His coat of arms was of cloth of Tartary,
set with pearls that were white and smooth and large.
His saddle was of burnished gold newly hammered;
a short mantle hanging upon his shoulders                1305
was brimful of rubies, sparkling like fire.
His curly hair was clustered in ringlets;
it was yellow and glittered like the sun.
His nose was highly arched, his eyes bright citron-
        colored,
his lips rounded, his color sanguine.                1310
A few freckles were sprinkled in his face,
mixed between yellow and something near black,
and he cast his glance forth like a lion.
I estimate his age to have been twenty-five.
His beard had made a good beginning;                1315
his voice was like a trumpet thundering.
Upon his head he wore a garland
of green laurel, fresh and pleasant to the eye.
Upon his hand he bore for his pleasure
a tame falcon, white as a lily.                1320
He had a hundred lords there with him,
all armed, except for their heads, in all their gear,
very richly in all respects.
For you can be sure that dukes, earls, and kings
were gathered together in this noble company                1325
for love and for the glory of chivalry.

Aboute this king ther ran on every part
Ful many a tame leoun and lepart.
And in this wyse thise lordes, alle and some,
Ben on the Sonday to the citee come                     1330
Aboute pryme, and in the toun alight.

This Theseus, this duk, this worthy knight,
Whan he had broght hem into his citee,
And inned hem, everich in his degree,
He festeth hem, and dooth so greet labour               1335
To esen hem, and doon hem al honour,
That yet men wenen that no mannes wit
Of noon estat ne coude amenden it.
The minstralcye, the service at the feste,
The grete yiftes to the meeste and leste,               1340
The riche array of Theseus paleys,
Ne who sat first ne last upon the deys,
What ladies fairest been or best daunsinge,
Or which of hem can dauncen best and singe,
Ne who most felingly speketh of love;                   1345
What haukes sitten on the perche above,
What houndes liggen on the floor adoun:
Of al this make I now no mencioun;
But al th'effect, that thinketh me the beste;
Now comth the poynt, and herkneth if yow leste.         1350

The Sonday night, er day bigan to springe,
When Palamon the larke herde singe,
(Although it nere nat day by houres two,
Yet song the larke), and Palamon right tho,
With holy herte, and with an heigh corage               1355
He roos, to wenden on his pilgrimage
Unto the blisful Citherea benigne—
I mene Venus, honurable and digne.
And in hir houre* he walketh forth a pas
Unto the listes, ther hire temple was,                  1360
And doun he kneleth, and with humble chere
And herte soor, he seyde as ye shul here:

"Faireste of faire, o lady myn, Venus,
Doughter to Jove and spouse of Vulcanus,

There ran about this king on every side
many a tame lion and leopard.
And in this fashion these lords, one and all,
came to the city on the Sunday                                    1330
about nine in the morning, and lighted down in the town.

    Theseus, the duke and valiant knight,
after having escorted them into his city,
and lodged them, each according to his rank,
feasted them, and expended so much energy                         1335
to make them comfortable and do them all honor
that people still think the wit of no man of any rank
could improve on what he did.
The music, the service at the feast,
the noble gifts for the great and small,                          1340
the rich adornment of Theseus's palace,
who sat highest or lowest on the dais,
which ladies were the most beautiful or danced best,
or which of them could both sing and dance best,
or who talked most feelingly of love;                             1345
what hawks sat above on the perch,
or what dogs lay below on the floor:
all these things I do not mention now,
but only what resulted; that seems to be best;
now comes the point, and listen if you will.                      1350

    That Sunday night, before daybreak,
When Palamon heard the lark singing
(although it was not yet light by two hours,
the lark nevertheless sang), he immediately rose
with reverent heart and exalted mind                              1355
to go on his pilgrimage
to blissful and benign Cytherea—
that is to say, Venus, worthy of honor and reverence.
In her hour he went forth at a footpace
to where her temple was in the arena,                             1360
and kneeled down, and with humility
and a troubled heart spoke as you shall hear:

    "Fairest of fair ones, my lady Venus,
daughter to Jove and spouse of Vulcan,

Thou glader of the mount of Citheroun,                    1365
For thilke love thou haddest to Adoun,
Have pitee of my bittre teres smerte,
And tak myn humble preyer at thyn herte.
Allas, I ne have no langage to telle
Th'effectes ne the torments of myn helle;                    1370
Myn herte may myne harmes nat biwreye;
I am so confus, that I can noght seye
But, 'mercy, lady bright, that knowest weele
My thought, and seest what harmes that I feele.'
Considere al this, and rewe upon my sore,                    1375
As wisly as I shal for evermore,
Emforth my might, thy trewe servant be,
And holden werre alwey with chastitee;
That make I myn avow, so ye me helpe.
I kepe noght of armes for to yelpe,                    1380
Ne I ne axe nat tomorwe to have victorie,
Ne renoun in this cas, ne veyne glorie
Of pris of armes blowen up and doun;
But I wolde have fully possessioun
Of Emelye, and dye in thy servyse.                    1385
Find thou the maner how and in what wyse:
I recche nat but it may bettre be
To have victorie of hem, or they of me,
So that I have my lady in myne armes.
For though so be that Mars is god of armes,                    1390
Youre vertu is so greet in hevene above
That, if yow list, I shal wel have my love.
Thy temple wol I worshipe evermo,
And on thyn auter, wher I ryde or go,
I wol don sacrifice and fyres bete.                    1395
And if ye wol nat so, my lady swete,
Than preye I thee, tomorwe with a spere
That Arcita me thurgh the herte bere.
Thanne rekke I noght, whan I have lost my lyf,
Though that Arcita winne hir to his wyf.                    1400
This is th'effect and ende of my preyere:
Yif me my love, thou blisful lady dere."

giver of joy on Mount Cithaeron: 1365
for the sake of the love you felt for Adonis,
have pity on my bitter, painful tears
and take my humble prayer to your heart.
Alas, I have no speech to describe
the causes or the torments of my hell; 1370
my heart may not disclose my sufferings;
I am so abashed that I can ask nothing
but, 'Mercy, fair lady, who know well
my thought and see what wounds I feel.'
Consider all this and take pity on my pain, 1375
as surely as I shall for evermore
be your true servant to the extent of my strength
and always be a foe to foolish chastity;
I make that my vow, if you help me.
I do not care to boast of arms, 1380
and I do not ask to have the victory tomorrow,
or renown in this matter, or vain glory
of reputation in arms rumored to and fro;
but I would have full possession
of Emily, and die in your service; 1385
I implore you, find how and by what means to do this.
I do not care whether it may be better
to have victory over them or for them to have it over me,
if I may have my lady in my arms.
Though it is true that Mars is god of arms, 1390
your power is so great in heaven above
that, if you desire it, I shall indeed have my love.
I will worship your temple forever,
and wherever I ride or walk, I will do sacrifice
and make fires upon your altar. 1395
And if, my sweet lady, you do not wish it so,
then I pray to you that tomorrow Arcite
pierce me through the heart with a spear.
Then, when I have lost my life, I shall not care
even if Arcite wins her to his wife. 1400
This is the point and purpose of my prayer:
give me my love, dear and blissful lady."

Whan th'orisoun was doon of Palamon,
His sacrifice he dide, and that anon,
Ful pitously, with alle circumstaunces,                     1405
Al telle I noght as now his observaunces.
But atte laste the statue of Venus shook,
And made a signe, wherby that he took
That his preyere accepted was that day.
For thogh the signe shewed a delay,                         1410
Yet wiste he wel that graunted was his bone;
And with glad herte he wente him hoom ful sone.

The thridde houre inequal* that Palamon
Bigan to Venus temple for to goon,
Up roos the sonne, and up roos Emelye,                      1415
And to the temple of Diane gan hye.
Hir maydens, that she thider with hire ladde,
Ful redily with hem the fyr they hadde,
Th'encens, the clothes, and the remenant al
That to the sacrifyce longen shal;                          1420
The hornes fulle of meth, as was the gyse;
Ther lakked noght to doon hir sacrifyse.
Smoking the temple, ful of clothes faire,
This Emelye, with herte debonaire.
Hir body wessh with water of a welle;                       1425
But how she dide hir ryte I dar nat telle,
But it be any thing in general.
And yet it were a game to heren al;
To him that meneth wel, it were no charge;
But it is good a man ben at his large.                      1430
Hir brighte heer was kempt, untressed al;
A coroune of a grene ook cerial
Upon hir heed was set ful fair and mete.
Two fyres on the auter gan she bete,
And dide hir thinges, as men may biholde                    1435
In Stace of Thebes,* and thise bokes olde.
Whan kindled was the fyr, with pitous chere
Unto Diane she spak, as ye may here:
    "O chaste goddesse of the wodes grene,

When Palamon's prayer was done,
he made his sacrifice; he did it immediately,
very pitiably, and with all attendant ceremonies,        1405
although for now I do not relate his observances.
At last the statue of Venus shook
and made a sign, by which he gathered
that his prayer that day was accepted.
For though the sign showed a delay,                      1410
he well knew that his request was granted;
with happy heart he went quickly home.

In the third unequal hour after Palamon
had started for Venus's temple,
the sun rose, and so did Emily,                          1415
and started out for the temple of Diana.
Her maidens, whom she took there with her,
had ready with them the fire,
the incense, the vestments, and all the rest
that must go with the sacrifice—                         1420
the horns full of mead, as was the custom;
nothing lacked to make sacrifice to Diana.
When the temple was smoking with incense and full
         of fair
vestments, Emily, with a pious heart,
washed her body with water of the well;                  1425
but how she performed her rite I dare not tell,
except in general.
Yet it would be a satisfaction to hear all of it;
for him that means well, it would be no burden;
but it is good for a man to be free to omit what he wants. 1430
Her shining hair was combed, completely loose;
a crown of evergreen oak
was set fairly and becomingly on her head.
She began to make two fires upon the altar
and performed her duties as we may read                  1435
in Statius's *Thebaid* and other ancient books.
When the fire was kindled, with a piteous countenance
she spoke to Diana as you may hear:
    "O chaste goddess of the green wood,

To whom bothe heven and erthe and see is sene,        1440
Quene of the regne of Pluto derk and lowe,
Goddesse of maydens, that myn herte hast knowe
Ful many a yeer, and woost what I desire,
As keep me fro thy vengeaunce and thyn ire,
That Attheon* aboughte cruelly.        1445
Chaste goddesse, wel wostow that I
Desire to been a mayden al my lyf,
Ne nevere wol I be no love ne wyf.
I am, thou woost, yet of thy companye
A mayde, and love hunting and venerye,        1450
And for to walken in the wodes wilde,
And noght to been a wyf and be with childe.
Noght wol I knowe companye of man.
Now help me, lady, sith ye may and can,
For tho thre formes* that thou hast in thee.        1455
And Palamon, that hath swich love to me,
And eek Arcite, that loveth me so sore,
This grace I preye thee withoute more,
As sende love and pees bitwixe hem two;
And from me turne awey hir hertes so,        1460
That al hir hote love and hir desyr,
And al hir bisy torment and hir fyr
Be queynt, or turned in another place.
And if so be thou wolt not do me grace,
Or if my destinee be shapen so,        1465
That I shal nedes have oon of hem two,
As sende me him that most desireth me.
Bihold, goddesse of clene chastitee,
The bittre teres that on my chekes falle.
Sin thou are mayde, and keper of us alle,        1470
My maydenhede thou kepe and wel conserve,
And whyl I live a mayde, I wol thee serve."
    The fyres brenne upon the auter clere,
Whyl Emelye was thus in hir preyere;
But sodeinly she saugh a sighte queynte,        1475
For right anon oon of the fyres queynte,
And quiked agayn, and after that anon

to whom both heaven and earth and sea are visible,     1440
queen of the dark, deep kingdom of Pluto,
goddess of virgins, who have known my heart
for many a year, and who know what I desire,
keep me from your vengeance and your anger,
which Actacon paid for painfully.     1445
Chaste goddess, well you know
that I desire to be a maiden all my life;
I never want to be either a beloved or a wife.
You know that I am still one of your company,
a virgin, and love hunting     1450
and roaming in the wild wood,
and do not desire to be a wife and to be with child.
I do not want to know the company of man.
Now help me lady, since you may and can,
by virtue of the three forms which you possess.     1455
As for Palamon, who bears such love to me,
and Arcite, too, who loves me so strongly
(this boon I beg without another),
send love and peace between the two of them;
and so turn away their hearts from me     1460
that all their fervent love and their desire,
and all their vexatious torment and their ardor
is quenched or turned in another direction.
And if it be that you will not grant me this favor,
or if my destiny is so shaped     1465
that I must have one of the two,
send me the one who most desires me.
Behold, goddess of pure chastity,
the bitter tears that fall upon my cheeks.
Since you are a maid and the preserver of us all,     1470
keep and preserve my maidenhood,
and as long as I live as a maiden I will serve you."

The fires burned upon the splendid altar
while Emily was thus engaged in her prayer;
but suddenly she saw a strange vision,     1475
for just then one of the fires was quenched,
and then caught again, and after that

That other fyr was queynt, and al agon;
And as it queynte it made a whistelinge,
As doon thise wete brondes in hir brenninge,          1480
And at the brondes ende out-ran anoon
As it were blody dropes many oon;
For which so sore agast was Emelye,
That she was wel ny mad, and gan to crye;
For she ne wiste what it signifyed,          1485
But only for the fere thus hath she cryed,
And weep, that it was pitee for to here.
And therwithal Diane gan appere,
With bowe in hond, right as an hunteresse,
And seyde: "Doghter, stint thyn hevinesse.          1490
Among the goddes hye it is affermed,
And by eterne word write and confermed,
Thou shalt ben wedded unto oon of tho
That han for thee so muchel care and wo;
But unto which of hem I may nat telle.          1495
Farwel, for I ne may no lenger dwelle.
The fyres which that on myn auter brenne
Shulle thee declaren, er that thou go henne,
Thyn aventure of love, as in this cas."
And with that word, the arwes in the cas          1500
Of the goddesse clateren faste and ringe,
And forth she wente, and made a vanisshinge;
For which this Emelye astoned was,
And seyde, "What amounteth this, allas?
I putte me in thy proteccioun,          1505
Diane, and in thy disposicioun."
And hoom she gooth anon the nexte weye.
This is th'effect, ther is namore to seye.

The nexte houre of Mars* folwinge this,
Arcite unto the temple walked is          1510
Of fierse Mars, to doon his sacrifyse,
With alle the rytes of his payen wyse.
With pitous herte and heigh devocioun,
Right thus to Mars he seyde his orisoun:
      "O stronge god, that in the regnes colde          1515

the other fire was quenched and completely extinguished;
and as it was quenched, it crackled
as wet wood does as it burns,                                1480
and at the end of the firebrands then ran out
many of what seemed bloody drops;
Emily was so terribly frightened at this
that she was very nearly out of her wits, and cried out.
She did not know what the meaning of all this was;         1485
it was only for shock that she cried out
and wept, so that it was pitiable to hear her.
At that, Diana appeared
with bow in hand, clad as a huntress,
and said, "Daughter, stop your sorrow.                      1490
Among the high gods it is declared
and by eternal word written and confirmed
that you shall be wedded to one of them
who have had so much care and trouble for you;
but which of them I may not tell.                           1495
Farewell, for I may stay no longer.
The fires that burn on my altar
shall declare to you, before you go hence,
your fortune in love, in this present situation."
With that word, the arrows in the quiver                   1500
of the goddess rattled and rang loudly,
and she went forth and disappeared;
Emily was astonished at this
and said, "Alas, what does this mean?
Diana, I put myself under your protection,                 1505
to be disposed of as you wish."
Then she went home the nearest way.
This is what happened; there is no more to say.
     At the hour of Mars next following this:
Arcite proceeded to the temple                             1510
of fierce Mars to make his sacrifice
with all the rites of his pagan custom.
With piteous heart and exalted devotion
he thus said his prayer to Mars:
     "O strong god, who are honored and held              1515

Of Trace honoured art and lord yholde,
And hast in every regne and every lond
Of armes al the brydel in thyn hond,
And hem fortunest as thee list devyse,
Accept of me my pitous sacrifyse.                          1520
If so be that my youthe may deserve,
And that my might be worthy for to serve
Thy godhede, that I may been oon of thyne,
Than preye I thee to rewe upon my pyne
For thilke peyne, and thilke hote fyr                      1525
In which thou whylom brendest for desyr,
Whan that thou usedest the beautee
Of fayre, yonge, fresshe Venus free,
And haddest hir in armes at thy wille—
Although thee ones on a tyme misfille                      1530
Whan Vulcanus had caught thee in his las,
And fond thee ligging by his wyf, allas.
For thilke sorwe that was in thyn herte,
Have routhe as wel upon my peynes smerte.
I am yong and unkonning, as thou wost,                     1535
And, as I trowe, with love offended most
That evere was any lyves creature;
For she that dooth me al this wo endure,
Ne reccheth never wher I sinke or flete.
And wel I woot, er she me mercy hete,                      1540
I moot with strengthe winne hir in the place;
And wel I woot, withouten help or grace
Of thee ne may my strengthe noght availle.
Than help me, lord, tomorwe in my bataille,
For thilke fyr that whylom brende thee,                    1545
As well as thilke fyr now brenneth me,
And do that I tomorwe have victorie.
Myn be the travaille, and thyn be the glorie.
Thy soverein temple wol I most honouren
Of any place, and alwey most labouren                      1550
In thy plesaunce and in thy craftes stronge,
And in thy temple I wol my baner honge,
And all the armes of my companye;

a lord in the cold realm of Thrace,
and who have, in every realm and land,
the whole bridle of war in your hand
and whose desires control destiny,
accept from me my piteous sacrifice.                    1520
If it be that my youth deserves it,
and that my strength is worthy to serve
your godhead, so that I may be one of your own,
then I pray you to take pity upon my pain
for the sake of the same pain and same ardent fire      1525
in which you once burned for desire,
when you enjoyed the beauty
of the fair, young, fresh, and gracious Venus,
and had her at your will in your arms—
even though misfortune befell you                       1530
when Vulcan had caught you in his net
and found you, alas, lying by his wife.
For the sake of the pain which was in your heart,
take pity upon my exceeding pain as well.
I am young and inexperienced, as you know,             1535
and, as I think, more injured by love
than was ever any other living creature;
for she that makes me endure all this woe
never cares whether I sink or swim.
Well I know that before she offers me mercy            1540
I must win her by force on the spot;
and well I know that without help or favor
from you, my strength may not avail.
Then, lord, help me tomorrow in my battle,
for the sake of that fire that once burned you         1545
as much as that fire now burns me,
and arrange it that I shall have victory tomorrow.
Mine be the pains, and yours the glory.
I will honor your sovereign temple above
any other place, and always labor most                 1550
for your pleasure and in your mighty skills,
and in your temple I will hang my banner
and all the arms of my company;

And everemo unto that day I dye
Eterne fyr I wold biforn thee finde.                           1555
And eek to this avow I wol me binde:
My berd, myn heer, that hongeth long adoun,
That nevere yet ne felte offensioun
Of rasour nor of shere, I wol thee yive,
And been thy trewe servant whyl I live.                        1560
Now, lord, have routhe upon my sorwes sore:
Yif me victorie, I aske thee namore."

The preyere stinte of Arcita the stronge,
The ringes on the temple dore that honge,
and eek the dores, clatereden ful faste,                       1565
Of which Arcita somwhat him agaste.
The fyres brende upon the auter brighte,
That it gan al the temple for to lighte;
A swete smel anon the ground up yaf;
And Arcita anon his hand up haf,                               1570
And more encens into the fyr he caste,
With othere rytes mo; and atte laste
The statue of Mars bigan his hauberk ringe.
And with that soun he herde a murmuringe
Ful lowe and dim, that sayde thus, "Victorie";                1575
For which he yaf to Mars honour and glorie.
And thus with joye and hope wel to fare
Arcite anon unto his inne is fare,
As fayn as fowel is of the brighte sonne.

And right anon swich stryf ther is bigonne,                   1580
For thilke graunting, in the hevene above,
Bitwixe Venus, the goddesse of love,
And Mars, the sterne god armipotente,
That Jupiter was bisy it to stente;
Tis that the pale Saturnus the colde,                         1585
That knew so manye of aventures olde,
Fond in his old experience an art,
That he ful sone hath plesed every part.
As sooth is sayd, elde hath greet avantage;
In elde is bothe wisdom and usage;                            1590
Men may the olde at-renne, and noght at-rede.

and from now on until the day I die
I will provide eternal fire before you.                              1555
I will bind myself to this vow also:
I will give to you my beard and my hair that hangs
far down my back and that never yet has felt the injury
of razor or shears,
and I will be your faithful servant while I live.                    1560
Now, lord, take pity upon my bitter sorrows:
give me victory, I ask no more of you."

The prayer of Arcite the strong having ended,
the rings that hung on the temple door,
and the doors, too, set up a loud clattering,                        1565
at which Arcite was somewhat afraid.
The fires so burned upon the splendid altar
that they lighted up all the temple;
then the floor gave off a sweet smell,
and Arcite lifted up his hand                                        1570
and cast more incense into the fire,
performing other rites; at last
the statue of Mars began to make its coat of mail jingle.
With that sound he heard a murmuring,
very low and indistinct, which said, "Victory";                     1575
for this he gave honor and glory to Mars.
And thus with joy and hope of faring well
Arcite then went to his lodging,
as happy as a bird is for the bright sun.

Immediately, on account of this grant, such strife                   1580
began in heaven above
between Venus, the goddess of love,
and Mars, the stern god powerful in arms,
that Jupiter strove to stop it;
until pale Saturn the cold,                                          1585
who had known so many ancient turns of fortune,
thought of a solution from his aged experience
so that he had very soon pleased all sides.
It is truly said, age has a great advantage;
in age there is both wisdom and practice;                            1590
one may outrun the old but not surpass them in

Saturne anon, to stinten stryf and drede,
Al be it that it is agayn his kynde,
Of al this stryf he gan remedie fynde.
  "My dere doghter Venus," quod Saturne,                1595
"My cours, that hath so wyde for to turne,
Hath more power than wot any man.
Myn is the drenching in the see so wan;
Myn is the prison in the derke cote;
Myn is the strangling and hanging by the throte,       1600
The murmure and the cherles rebelling,
The groyning, and the pryvee empoysoning:
I do vengeance and pleyn correccioun
Whyl I dwelle in the signe of the Leoun.
Myn is the ruine of the hye halles,                    1605
The falling of the toures and of the walles
Upon the mynour or the carpenter.
I slow Sampsoun, shaking the piler;
And myne be the maladyes colde,
The derke tresons, and the castes olde;                1610
My loking is the fader of pestilence.
Now weep namore, I shal doon diligence
That Palamon, that is thyn owene knight,
Shal have his lady, as thou hast him hight.
Though Mars shal helpe his knight, yet nathelees       1615
Bitwixe yow ther moot be som tyme pees,
Al be ye noght of o complexioun,
That causeth al day swich divisioun.
I am thyn aiel redy at thy wille;
Weep thou namore, I wol thy lust fulfille."            1620
  Now wol I stinten of the goddes above,
Of Mars, and of Venus, goddesse of love,
And telle yow as pleynly as I can
The grete effect, for which that I bigan.

counsel. Saturn, then, to stop strife and fear
(although such action is against his nature),
began to find a remedy for all this strife.
    "My dear daughter Venus," said Saturn,     1595
"my planetary course, which has to make so wide
    an orbit,
has more astrological power than any man knows.
    Mine is
the drowning in the pale sea;
mine is the prison in the dark hut;
mine is the strangling and hanging by the throat,     1600
mine is the uproar and the revolt of the underlings,
the discontent and the poisoning;
I take vengeance and do full chastisement
while I dwell in the zodiacal sign of the Lion.
Mine is the collapse of the lofty halls,     1605
the falling of the towers and of the walls
upon the miner and the carpenter.
I slew Samson, shaking the pillar,
and mine are the chilling sicknesses,
the hidden treasons, and the hoariest plots.     1610
My look is the father of pestilence.
Now weep no more; I shall see to it carefully
that Palamon, who is your own knight,
shall have his lady as you have promised him.
Although Mars shall help his knight, nevertheless     1615
there must some time be peace between you,
even if the two of you are not of one humor,
which fact causes such argument continually.
I am your grandfather, ready at your will;
now weep no more, I will fulfill your desire."     1620
    Now I will stop talking about the gods above—
about Mars and about Venus, goddess of love—
and tell you, as plainly as I can,
the great climax for the sake of which I began.

## IV

Greet was the feeste in Athenes that day,                    1625
And eek the lusty seson of that May
Made every wight to been in swich plesaunce
That al that Monday* justen they and daunce,
And spenden it in Venus heigh servyse.
But by the cause that they sholde ryse                       1630
Erly, for to seen the grete fight,
Unto hir reste wente they at night.
And on the morwe whan that day gan springe,
Of hors and harneys noyse and clateringe
Ther was in hostelryes al aboute;                            1635
And to the paleys rood ther many a route
Of lordes upon stedes and palfreys.
Ther maystow seen devysing of herneys
So uncouth and so riche, and wroght so weel
Of goldsmithrie, of browding, and of steel;                  1640
The sheeldes brighte, testers, and trappures;
Gold-hewen helmes, hauberks, cote-armures;
Lordes in paraments on hir courseres;
Knightes of retenue, and eek squyeres
Nailinge the speres and helmes bokelinge,                    1645
Gigginge of sheeldes, with layneres lacinge—
Ther as need is they weren no thing ydel—
The fomy stedes on the golden brydel
Gnawinge, and faste the armurers also
With fyle and hamer prikinge to and fro;                     1650
Yemen on fote and communes many oon
With shorte staves, thikke as they may goon;
Pypes, trompes, nakers, clariounes,
That in the bataille blowen blody sounes;
The paleys ful of peples up and doun—                        1655
Heer three, ther ten, holding hir questioun,
Divyninge of thise Thebane knightes two.
Somme seyden thus, somme seyde it shall be so;
Somme helden with him with the blake berd,

## IV

There was a great festival in Athens that day,           1625
and, besides, the joyful season of May
made all of them so happy
that they jousted and danced all of Monday
and spent it in the noble service of Venus.
But because they were to get up                          1630
early the next day to see the great battle,
they went to bed at nightfall.
At daybreak the next day
there was noise and rattling of horse and battle gear
in inns on all sides;                                    1635
many a train of lords on chargers and palfreys
rode to the palace.
Thereabouts you might see contrivances of battle gear
that were very strange, rich, and well-made
in goldsmith's work, embroidery, and steel;             1640
you might see glittering shields, head armor, and horse
armor; gold-hued helmets, coats of mail, coats of arms;
lords in clothes of state upon their coursers;
knights in service, and squires, too,
fastening points on spearshafts and buckles on helmets, 1645
putting straps on shields, inserting thongs in the rings—
where need was, they were by no means idle—
the foam-flecked horses gnawing on their golden bridles,
and the armorers also continually
riding hard to and fro with file and hammer;            1650
yeomen on foot and many commoners
with short staves, as crowded together as they could
     be and
still walk; pipes, trumpets, kettledrums, clarions
that blow the bloody sounds of battle;
the palace full of people up and down,                  1655
here three, there ten, discussing and
conjecturing about these two Theban knights. Some said
it would be thus and such, others said that was the way
it would be; some chose the one with the black beard,

Somme with the balled, somme with the thikke-herd; 1660
Somme sayde he loked grim and he wolde fighte;
"He hath a sparth of twenty pound of wighte."
Thus was the halle ful of divyninge
Longe after that the sonne gan to springe.

The grete Theseus, that of his sleep awaked 1665
With minstralcye and noyse that was maked,
Heeld yet the chambre of his paleys riche,
Til that the Thebane knightes, bothe yliche
Honoured, were into the paleys fet.
Duk Theseus was at a window set, 1670
Arrayed right as he were a god in trone.
The peple preesseth thiderward ful sone
Him for to seen and doon heigh reverence,
And eek to herkne his heest and his sentence.

An heraud on a scaffold made an "Oo!" 1675
Til al the noyse of peple was y-do;
And whan he saugh the peple of noyse al stille,
Thus shewed he the mighty dukes wille:
"The lord hath of his heigh discrecioun,
Considered that it were destruccioun 1680
To gentil blood to fighten in the gyse
Of mortal bataille now in this empryse;
Wherfore, to shapen that they shul nought dye,
He wol his firste purpos modifye.
No man therfor, up peyne of los of lyf, 1685
No maner shot, ne pollax, ne short knyf
Into the listes sende, or thider bringe;
Ne short swerd for to stoke with poynt bytinge,
No man ne drawe, ne bere it by his syde.
Ne no man shal unto his felawe ryde 1690
But o cours with a sharp y-grounde spere;
Foyne, if him list, on fote, himself to were.
And he that is at meschief shal be take,
And noght slayn, but be broght unto the stake
That shal ben ordeyned on either syde; 1695

others the one that was bald, still others, the one
    with thick hair;                                    1660
others said that one looked grim: he would fight;
"He has a battle-ax that weighs twenty pounds."
Thus the hall was full of guesses
long after the sun had come up.

    Great Theseus, who woke from his sleep          1665
because of the music and noise that was being made,
still stayed in the bedchamber of his rich palace
until the Theban knights, both alike
honored, were brought into the palace.
Duke Theseus then sat at a window,                      1670
situated and adorned as if he were a god upon his throne.
The people crowded that way very quickly
to see him and to show him high respect,
and also to listen to his bidding and announced intention.

    A herald on a scaffold cried out, "Hear ye!"   1675
until the noise of the crowd was done;
and when he saw that the people were completely quiet,
he thus disclosed the mighty duke's will:

    "Our lord in his noble discretion
has considered that it would be destruction            1680
of gentle blood to fight in the manner
of mortal combat in this present enterprise;
wherefore, to arrange things so that the contestants
    shall not die,
it is his will to modify his first plan.
Therefore, no man, on pain of losing his life,        1685
shall send into the lists, or bring there,
any kind of missile, or battle-ax, or dagger;
no man shall draw, or bear at his side,
any short sword with a piercing point to thrust with.
No man shall ride more than one course against        1690
his fellow with a spear ground to sharpness; he may
parry with it, if he wishes, on foot, to defend himself.
And anyone who is in trouble shall be taken prisoner,
not killed, and be brought to the stake
which shall be placed on each side;                    1695

But thider he shal by force, and ther abyde.
And if so falle the chieftayn be take
On either syde, or elles slee his make,
No lenger shal the turneyinge laste.
God spede yow: goth forth and ley on faste.          1700
With long swerd and with maces fight your fille.
Goth now your wey. This is the lordes wille."
  The voys of peple touchede the hevene,
So loude cride they with mery stevene,
"God save swich a lord, that is so good:             1705
He wilneth no destruccioun of blood!"
Up goon the trompes and the melodye,
And to the listes rit the companye,
By ordinaunce, thurghout the citee large,
Hanged with cloth of gold, and nat with sarge.      1710
  Ful lyk a lord this noble duk gan ryde,
Thise two Thebanes upon either syde;
And after rood the quene and Emelye,
And after that another companye
Of oon and other, after hir degree.                 1715
And thus they passen thurghout the cittee,
And to the listes come they by tyme—
It nas not of the day yet fully pryme.
Whan set was Theseus ful riche and hye,
Ipolita the quene and Emelye,                       1720
And othere ladies in degrees aboute,
Unto the seetes preesseth al the route.
And westward, thurgh the gates under Marte,
Arcite and eek the hundred of his parte,
With baner reed, is entred right anon;              1725
And in that selve moment Palamon
Is under Venus, estward in the place,
With baner whyt, and hardy chere and face.
In al the world, to seken up and doun,
So evene withouten variacioun,                      1730
Ther nere swiche companyes tweye;
For ther was noon so wys that coude seye

there he shall be conveyed by force, and there he
    shall stay.
And if it happens that the chieftain is captured
on either side, or else if he kills his opposite,
then the tourney shall last no longer.
God speed you: go out and hit hard. 1700
Fight your fill with the long sword and with maces.
Now go your way. This is our lord's will."
    The people's voice reached the heavens,
so loud they cried out with joyful voice,
"God save such a lord, who is so good; 1705
he wills that there be no loss of blood!"
Up start the trumpets and the music,
and the company rides to the lists
in order through the large city,
which was hung with cloth of gold, not with dark serge. 1710
    In very lordly fashion this noble duke rode,
one of these two Thebans on either side;
next rode the queen and Emily,
and after them another company
of various people according to their rank. 1715
In this way they passed through the city
and arrived in good time at the lists—
it was not yet quite nine o'clock.
When Theseus was seated in a noble and lofty position,
Queen Hippolyta, Emily, 1720
and other ladies being in tiers about him,
all the crowd pressed to the seats.
On the west, through the gates under Mars,
Arcite and also the hundred on his side
entered immediately with their red banner; 1725
and in the same moment Palamon
entered under Venus, on the east of the field,
with his white banner and with a bold bearing.
Nowhere, no matter where you searched,
were there two such companies 1730
so evenly matched, without differentiation.
For there was none so wise as to be able to say

That any hadde of other avauntage
Of worthinesse, ne of estaat, ne age,
So evene were they chosen, for to gesse.              1735
And in two renges faire they hem dresse.

    Whan that hir names rad were everichoon,
That in hir nombre gyle were ther noon,
Tho were the gates shet, and cryed was loude,
"Do now youre devoir, yonge knightes proude!"        1740
    The heraudes lefte hir priking up and doun;
Now ringen trompes loude and clarioun;
Ther is namore to seyn, but west and est
In goon the speres ful sadly in arest;
In goth the sharpe spore into the syde.               1745
Ther seen men who can juste and who can ryde;
Ther shiveren shaftes upon sheeldes thikke;
He feleth thurgh the herte-spoon the prikke.
Up springen speres twenty foot on highte;
Out goon the swerdes as the silver brighte;          1750
The helmes they to-hewen and to-shrede;
Out brest the blood with sterne stremes rede;
With mighty maces the bones they to-breste;
He thurgh the thikkeste of the throng gan threste;
Ther stomblen stedes stronge, and doun goth al;      1755
He rolleth under foot as dooth a bal;
He foyneth on his feet with his tronchoun,
And he him hurtleth with his hors adoun;
He thurgh the body is hurt and sithen take,
Maugree his heed, and broght unto the stake:         1760
As forward was, right ther he moste abyde;
Another lad is on that other syde.

    And som tyme dooth hem Theseus to reste,
Hem to refresshe and drinken if hem leste.
Ful ofte a day han thise Thebanes two                1765
Togidre y-met and wroght his felawe wo;
Unhorsed hath ech other of hem tweye.
Ther nas no tygre in the vale of Galgopheye,*
Whan that hir whelp is stole whan it is lyte,
So cruel on the hunte as is Arcite                   1770

that any of them had an advantage over another
in respect to valor, nobility, or age,
so evenly were they chosen, as far as one could guess.   1735
They drew themselves up fairly in two ranks.

When each of their names had been read, so that
there would be no deception in the total on each side,
then the gates were shut, and the cry was loudly given,
"Do now what you ought, proud young knights!"              1740

The heralds left off their spurring up and down;
now the loud trumpets and clarions ring out;
there is no more to say; but east and west
the spears go firmly into the spear rests;
the sharp spurs go into the horses' sides.                 1745
There they see who can joust and ride;
there spear shafts shatter on thick shields;
one feels the thrust through the breastbone.
Up spring the spears twenty feet in the air;
out come the swords glittering like silver;                1750
they hew and cut to pieces the helmets;
out bursts the blood in violent red streams;
the knights break bones with strong maces;
that one thrusts through the thickest of the press;
there strong steeds stumble, and down go horse and man;    1755
this one rolls underfoot like a ball;
that one, on foot, parries with the shaft of his spear;
another crashes down with his horse.
Another is wounded through the body and then captured,
in spite of all he can do, and brought to the stake:      1760
as the rule said, he must stay right there;
another is led to the stake on the other side.

At times Theseus has them rest,
to refresh themselves and to drink if they wish.
The two Thebans have very often                            1765
met together, and each has caused the other pain;
each has unhorsed the other twice.
In the vale of Gargaphia no tiger
whose whelp has been stolen when it was young
is as cruel to the hunter as Arcite is                     1770

For jelous herte upon this Palamoun;
Ne in Belmarye* ther nis so fel leoun,
That hunted is, or for his hunger wood,
Ne of his praye desireth so the blood,
As Palamon to sleen his fo Arcite.                    1775
The jelous strokes on hir helmes byte;
Out renneth blood on both hir sydes rede.

Som tyme an ende ther is of every dede:
For er the sonne unto the reste wente,
The stronge king Emetreus gan hente              1780
This Palamon, as he faught with Arcite,
And made his swerd depe in his flesh to byte;
And by the force of twenty is he take
Unyolden, and y-drawe unto the stake.
And in the rescous of this Palamoun              1785
The stronge king Ligurge is born adoun;
And king Emetreus, for al his strengthe,
Is born out of his sadel a swerdes lengthe,
So hitte him Palamon er he were take;
But al for noght, he was broght to the stake.    1790
His hardy herte mighte him helpe naught;
He moste abyde, whan that he was caught,
By force, and eek by composicioun.

Who sorweth now but woful Palamoun,
That moot namore goon agayn to fighte?          1795
And whan that Theseus hadde seyn this sighte,
Unto the folk that foghten thus echoon
He cryde "Ho! namore, for it is doon!
I wol be trewe juge, and no partye.
Arcite of Thebes shal have Emelye,               1800
That by his fortune hath hir faire y-wonne."
Anon ther is a noyse of peple bigonne
For joye of this, so loude and heigh withalle,
It seemed that the listes sholde falle.

What can now faire Venus doon above?             1805
What seith she now? what dooth this quene of love?
But wepeth so, for wanting of hir wille,
Til that hir teres in the listes fille;

for the jealousy of his heart against Palamon;
and in Benmarin there is no lion
hunted or maddened with hunger which is so cruel
or so desires the blood of his prey
as Palamon desires to kill his foe Arcite.                    1775
The jealous strokes bite into their helmets;
the blood runs red down the sides of both.

There is an end some time for every action:
before the sun went down
strong King Emetreus caught                                   1780
Palamon as he fought with Arcite;
the king's sword bit deeply into Palamon's flesh;
and by the strength of twenty men he was captured,
without having surrendered, and was pulled to the stake.
In the attempt to rescue him                                 1785
strong King Lycurgus was borne down;
and King Emetreus, in spite of all his strength,
was carried a sword's length out of his saddle,
Palamon hit him so hard before being captured;
but all this was for nothing; he was brought to the stake.  1790
His brave heart could not help him;
he had to stay there, when he was captured,
by force and also by the rules.

Who sorrows now more than woeful Palamon,
who may no longer resume the fight?                          1795
And when Theseus had seen this sight,
he cried out to the people still fighting,
"Stop! No more; it's finished!
I will be an impartial judge, not a friend of one party.
Arcite of Thebes shall have Emily;                           1800
by his good fortune he has won her fairly."
Then such a clamor arose—
for joy at this—so loud and high
that it seemed the walls of the arena would collapse.

What could fair Venus do now in heaven?                      1805
What did she say now? What did the queen of love do?
She only wept, for not having her way—but so hard
that her tears fell into the arena;

She seyde, "I am ashamed, doutelees."
Saturnus seyde, "Doghter, hold thy pees.    1810
Mars hath his wille, his knight hath al his bone,
And, by myn heed, thou shalt ben esed sone.
The troumpours, with the loude minstralcye,
The heraudes that ful loude yelle and crye
Been in hir wele for joye of daun Arcite—    1815
But herkneth me, and stinteth now a lyte."
    Which a miracle ther bifel anon.
This fierse Arcite hath of his helm y-don,
And on a courser, for to shewe his face,
He priketh endelong the large place,    1820
Loking upward upon this Emelye;
And she agayn him caste a freendlich yë
(For wommen, as to speken in comune,
They folwen al the favour of fortune),
And she was al his chere, as in his herte.    1825
Out of the ground a furie infernal* sterte,
From Pluto sent at requeste of Saturne,
For which his hors for fere gan to turne,
And leep asyde, and foundred as he leep;
And, er that Arcite may taken keep,    1830
He pighte him on the pomel of his heed,
That in the place he lay as he were deed,
His brest to-brosten with his sadel-bowe.
As blak he lay as any cole or crowe,
So was the blood y-ronnen in his face.    1835
Anon he was y-born out of the place,
With herte soor, to Theseus paleys.
Tho was he corven out of his harneys,
And in a bed y-brought ful faire and blyve,
For he was yet in memorie and alyve,    1840
And alway crying after Emelye.
    Duk Theseus, with al his companye,
Is comen hoom to Athenes his citee,
With alle blisse and greet solempnitee;
Al be it that this aventure was falle,    1845
He nolde noght disconforten hem alle.

she said, "I am put to shame, beyond a doubt."
Saturn said, "Daughter, stop complaining and wait.    1810
Mars has his wish, his knight has all his request,
and, by my head, you shall soon be comforted.
The trumpeters with their loud music,
the heralds, who loudly cry and shout,
are in a bliss of joy for Sir Arcite.    1815
But listen to me, and stop your noises for a little."
    What a miracle then befell there.
Fierce Arcite had taken off his helmet,
and to show his face he spurred on a courser along
the length of the large field,    1820
looking up at Emily;
and she cast a friendly eye toward him
(for, to speak in general, women
all follow the favor of fortune),
and she was the source of all the happiness in his heart.    1825
A fury from the infernal regions started up from the
ground, sent by Pluto at the request of Saturn,
which made his horse turn
and leap to the side, and he foundered as he leaped;
and, before Arcite could take heed,    1830
the horse pitched him on the pommel of the saddle and
over his head so hard that he lay in the field as if dead,
his breast crushed in with his saddle bow.
He lay looking as black as a coal or a crow,
blood had so suffused his face.    1835
He was immediately borne out of the field,
with a painful heart, to Theseus's palace.
Then he was cut out of his armor
and put into a bed easily and quickly,
for he was still alive and in his senses,    1840
and always he cried out for Emily.
    Duke Theseus with all his company
came home to his city of Athens
with all joy and ceremony;
in spite of this mischance    1845
he did not want to disconcert them all.

Men seyde eek that Arcite shal nat dye;
He shal ben heled of his maladye.
And of another thing they were as fayn:
That of hem alle was ther noon y-slayn,                    1850
Al were they sore y-hurt, and namely oon,
That with a spere was thirled his brest-boon.
To othere woundes and to broken armes
Some hadden salves, and some hadden charmes;
Fermacies of herbes and eek save                          1855
They dronken, for they wolde hir limes have.
For which this noble duk, as he wel can,
Conforteth and honoureth every man,
And made revel al the longe night
Unto the straunge lordes, as was right.                   1860
Ne ther was holden no disconfitinge,
But as a justes or a tourneyinge;
For soothly ther was no disconfiture:
For falling nis nat but an aventure;
Ne to be lad with fors unto the stake                     1865
Unyolden, and with twenty knightes take,
O persone allone, withouten mo,
And haried forth by arme, foot, and to,
And eek his stede driven forth with staves,
With footmen, bothe yemen and eek knaves—                 1870
It nas aretted him no vileinye;
Ther may no man clepen it cowardye.
    For which anon duk Theseus leet crye,
To stinten alle rancour and envye,
The gree as wel of o syde as of other,                    1875
And either syde ylik, as otheres brother;
And yaf hem yiftes after hir degree,
And fully heeld a feste dayes three;
And conveyed the kinges worthily
Out of his toun a journee largely.                        1880
And hoom wente every man the righte way.
Ther was namore, but "Fare wel, have good day."
Of this bataille I wol namore endyte,

Also it was said that Arcite would not die;
that he would be healed of his sickness.
For another matter they were just as glad:
that none of them all was killed,                             1850
although they were badly wounded, and especially one of
them whose breastbone was pierced with a spear.
For other wounds and for broken arms
some had salves, others had incantations;
they drank herb medicines and decoctions,                    1855
for they wanted to keep their limbs.
For their sakes the noble duke (as he well could)
gave comfort and honor to every man
and feasted the foreign lords the long
night through, as it was right to do.                         1860
And there was held to have been no vanquishing in this
affair, except as in a joust or tourney;
for in fact there was no defeat:
falling is a result of nothing but luck;
likewise, to be led by force to the stake,                   1865
without surrendering, and having been captured by
     twenty
knights—one person by himself, without more—
and dragged on by arm, foot, and toe,
and also his horse driven on with staves
by footmen—both yeomen and servants—                         1870
all this was not reckoned a disgrace to Palamon;
no one could call it cowardice.

   For these reasons Duke Theseus caused to be publicly
announced, in order to prevent all rancor and envy,
the success of each side as well as the other,               1875
and either side alike as though they had been brothers;
he gave them gifts according to their rank,
and held a feast for fully three days,
and conveyed the kings nobly
out of his town the distance of a generous day's journey. 1880
Every man went home the direct way.
There was nothing further but "Farewell! Good-bye!"
I shall not write any more of this battle,

But speke of Palamon and of Arcite.
　Swelleth the brest of Arcite, and the sore　　　　1885
Encreesseth at his herte more and more.
The clothered blood, for any lechecraft,
Corrupteth and is in his bouk y-laft,
That neither veyne-blood, ne ventusinge,
Ne drinke of herbes may ben his helpinge.　　　　1890
The vertu expulsif* or animal
Fro thilke vertu cleped natural
Ne may the venim voyden, ne expelle.
The pypes of his longes gonne to swelle,
And every lacerte in his brest adoun　　　　1895
Is shent with venim and corrupcioun.
Him gayneth neither, for to gete his lyf,
Vomyt upward, ne dounward laxatif;
Al is to-brosten thilke regioun,
Nature hath now no dominacioun,　　　　1900
And certeinly, ther nature wol nat wirche,
Farewel, phisyk: go ber the man to chirche.
This al and som, that Arcita moot dye,
For which he sendeth after Emelye,
And Palamon, that was his cosin dere;　　　　1905
Than seyde he thus, as ye shal after here:
　"Naught may the woful spirit in myn herte
Declare o poynt of alle my sorwes smerte
To yow, my lady, that I love most;
But I biquethe the service of my gost　　　　1910
To yow aboven every creature,
Sin that my lyf may no lenger dure.
Allas the wo, allas the peynes stronge,
That I for yow have suffred, and so longe;
Allas the deeth, allas myn Emelye;　　　　1915
Allas, departing of our companye;
Allas, myn hertes quene, allas, my wyf,
Myn hertes lady, endere of my lyf!
What is this world? what asketh men to have?
Now with his love, now in his colde grave,　　　　1920
Allone, withouten any companye.

but speak of Palamon and Arcite.
    The breast of Arcite swelled, and the pain    1885
at his heart increased more and more.
No matter what medical skill was tried, the clotted blood
corrupted and remained in his body,
so that neither bleeding nor cupping
nor herb decoctions could help him.    1890
The expulsive, or animal, power
could not void or expel the poison
from that power named the natural one.
The tubes of his lungs began to swell,
and every muscle down in his breast    1895
was damaged with venom and corruption.
Nothing helped to save his life, neither
vomiting upward nor laxative downward;
that region was completely shattered.
Nature now had no dominion,    1900
and, certainly, where nature will not work,
farewell, medicine: go bear the man to church.
In a word, Arcite had to die,
for which reason he sent for Emily,
and for Palamon, who was his dear cousin;    1905
then he spoke thus, as you shall hear:
    "The woeful spirit within me
cannot declare the smallest part of the pain of my sorrow
to you, my lady, whom I most love;
but I bequeath the service of my spirit    1910
to you above any other creature,
since my life may last no longer.
Alas, the woe, alas, the bitter pains
that I have suffered for you, and for so long;
alas, death, and alas, my Emily;    1915
alas, the parting of our company;
alas, heart's queen, alas, my wife,
lady of my heart, ender of my life!
What is this world? What does man ask to have?
One instant with his love, the next in his cold grave,    1920
alone, and without company.

Fare wel, my swete fo, myn Emelye,
And softe tak me in your armes tweye,
For love of God, and herkneth what I seye.

"I have heer with my cosin Palamon          1925
Had stryf and rancour many a day agon,
For love of yow, and for my jalousye;
And Juppiter so wis my soule gye—
To speken of a servant proprely,
With alle circumstaunces trewely,          1930
That is to seyn, trouthe, honour, knighthede,
Wisdom, humblesse, estaat, and heigh kinrede,
Fredom, and al that longeth to that art—
So Juppiter have of my soule part,
As in this world right now ne knowe I non   1935
So worthy to ben loved as Palamon,
That serveth yow, and wol doon al his lyf.
And if that evere ye shul been a wyf,
Foryet nat Palamon, the gentil man."

And with that word his speche faille gan,    1940
For from his feet up to his brest was come
The cold of deeth, that hadde him overcome;
And yet more over, for in his armes two
The vital strengthe is lost and al ago.
Only the intellect withouten more,           1945
That dwelled in his herte syk and sore,
Gan faillen whan the herte felte deeth:
Dusked his eyen two, and failled breeth.
But on his lady yet caste he his yë.
His laste word was, "Mercy, Emelye."         1950
His spirit chaunged hous and wente ther
As I cam never, I can nat tellen wher.
Therfor I stinte, I nam no divinistre;
Of soules finde I nat in this registre,
Ne me ne list thilke opiniouns to telle      1955
Of hem, though that they wryten wher they dwelle.
Arcite is cold, ther Mars his soule gye.
Now wol I speken forth of Emelye.

Shrighte Emelye, and howleth Palamon,

Farewell, my sweet foe, my Emily,
and softly take me in your two arms,
for the love of God, and listen to what I say.
    "With my cousin Palamon here                              1925
I have had strife and rancor for a long time,
for the love of you, and for my jealousy.
Jupiter so wise, guide my soul—
to speak properly of a servant of love,
faithfully with all his qualities—                            1930
that is to say, faithfulness, honor, chivalry,
wisdom, humility, nobility, high descent,
magnanimity, and all else that belongs to that calling—
as I hope Jupiter will take my soul,
I know at this very moment none in this world                 1935
so worthy to be loved as Palamon,
who serves you, and will do so all his life.
And if you are ever to be a wife,
don't forget Palamon, the gentle man."
    At those words his speech began to fail,                  1940
for from his feet up to his breast had come
the cold of death that had overcome him;
and, yet more, in his two arms
the vital strength was lost and gone.
Without the other powers, the intellect, last and alone,     1945
which dwelt in his sick and painful heart,
began to fail when the heart felt death:
his two eyes darkened, and his breath failed.
But yet he cast his eye on his lady.
His last word was, "Mercy, Emily."                           1950
His spirit changed its house and went where
I have never gone; I cannot say where.
Therefore I cease; I am no theologian;
I find nothing about souls in my book,
and I do not wish to relate the opinions                     1955
of theologians, even if they write where souls dwell.
Arcite is dead; may Mars guide his soul thither.
Now I will speak of Emily.
    Emily shrieked and Palamon howled,

And Theseus his suster took anon                        1960
Swowninge, and bar hir fro the corps away.
What helpeth it to tarien forth the day
To tellen how she weep, bothe eve and morwe?
For in swich cas wommen have swich sorwe,
Whan that hir housbondes been from hem ago,    1965
That for the more part they sorwen so,
Or elles fallen in swich maladye,
That at the laste certeinly they dye.

　　Infinite been the sorwes and the teres
Of olde folk and folk of tendre yeres,          1970
In al the toun for deeth of this Theban;
For him ther wepeth bothe child and man;
So greet weping was ther noon, certayn,
Whan Ector was y-broght, al fresh y-slayn,
To Troye; allas, the pitee that was ther,        1975
Cracching of chekes, renting eek of heer;
"Why woldestow be deed," thise wommen crye,
"And haddest gold ynough, and Emelye?"
No man mighte gladen Theseus,
Savinge his olde fader Egeus,                    1980
That knew this worldes transmutacioun,
As he had seyn it chaungen bothe up and doun—
Joye after wo, and wo after gladnesse,
And shewed hem ensamples and lyknesse:
　　"Right as ther deyed nevere man," quod he,   1985
"That he ne livede in erthe in som degree,
Right so ther livede nevere man," he seyde,
"In al this world, that some tyme he ne deyde.
This world nis but a thurghfare ful of wo,
And we been pilgrimes, passinge to and fro;      1990
Deeth is an ende of every worldly sore."
And over al this yet seyde he muchel more
To this effect, ful wisely to enhorte
The peple, that they sholde hem reconforte.

　　Duk Theseus, with al his bisy cure,          1995
Caste now wher that the sepulture
Of good Arcite may best y-maked be,

and Theseus soon took his sister                                    1960
swooning and bore her away from the corpse.
What good is it to spend time
in telling how she wept, both evening and morning?
For in such cases women feel such sorrow—
when their husbands are gone from them—                            1965
that for the most part they mourn thus,
or else fall into such sickness
that in the end they certainly die.

　　The sorrows and tears
of old and young were endless                                       1970
in all the town for the death of this Theban,
both child and adult wept for him;
there was not such great weeping, certainly,
when Hector, only just killed, was brought
into Troy; alas, the pity here:                                     1975
scratching of cheeks, and also tearing of hair.
"Why would you be dead," these women cry,
"when you had money enough, and Emily?"
No one could raise the spirits of Theseus
except his old father Aegeus,                                       1980
who had come to know the mutability of this world
as he had seen it changing, both up and down—
joy after sorrow, and sorrow after happiness;
he expounded precedents and analogies to Theseus:

　　"Just as no man," he said, "ever died                          1985
who did not in some condition live on earth,
so," he said, "there never lived a man
in all this world who did not some time die.
This world is but a highway full of sorrow,
and we are pilgrims, passing to and fro;                            1990
death is an end of every earthly pain."
And besides this he said much more still
to this effect, in order to exhort
the people to take comfort.

　　Duke Theseus with all diligent care                            1995
now planned where the funeral
of good Arcite might be best held

And eek most honurable in his degree.
And at the laste he took conclusioun,
That ther as first Arcite and Palamoun          2000
Hadden for love the bataille hem bitwene,
That in that selve grove swote and grene,
Ther as he hadde his amourouse desires,
His compleynt, and for love his hote fires,
He wolde make a fyr in which the office         2005
Funeral he mighte al accomplice;
And leet comaunde anon to hakke and hewe
The okes olde, and leye hem on a rewe
In colpons wel arrayed for to brenne.
His officers with swifte feet they renne        2010
And ryde anon at his comaundement.
And after this, Theseus hath y-sent
After a bere, and it al over-spradde
With cloth of gold, the richeste that he hadde.
And of the same suyte he cladde Arcite;         2015
Upon his hondes hadde he gloves whyte,
Eek on his heed a coroune of laurer grene,
And in his hond a swerd ful bright and kene.
He leyde him, bare the visage, on the bere.
Therwith he weep that pitee was to here.        2020
And for the peple sholde seen him alle,
Whan it was day he broghte him to the halle,
That roreth of the crying and the soun.
    Tho cam this woful Theban Palamoun,
With flotery berd and ruggy, asshy heres,        2025
In clothes blake, y-dropped al with teres;
And, passing othere of weping, Emelye,
The rewfulleste of al the companye.
In as muche as the service sholde be
The more noble and riche in his degree,          2030
Duk Theseus leet forth three stedes bringe,
That trapped were in steel al gliteringe,
And covered with the armes of daun Arcite.
Upon thise stedes, that weren grete and whyte,

in a manner honorable to his rank.
In the end he decided
that in the place where Arcite and                          2000
Palamon first battled for love—
in the same fresh, green grove
where Arcite showed his amorous desires,
his plaint, and the ardent fires of love—
a fire would be built, in which the funeral                 2005
rites might be wholly accomplished;
Theseus then had the order given to lop and cut down
the old oaks and lay them in rows
of piles well arranged for burning.
His officers then ran swiftly                               2010
and rode at his command.
After this Theseus sent for
a bier and covered it completely
with cloth of gold, the richest that he had.
He clothed Arcite correspondingly;                          2015
he had white gloves on his hands;
also, upon his head he had a crown of green laurel,
and in his hand a bright, keen sword.
Theseus laid him with his face bare upon the bier,
at the same time he wept so that it was a pity to
    hear him.                                               2020
And, in order that all the people should see him,
Theseus brought him into the hall when daylight came;
it resounded with the weeping and the noise.
    Then came the woeful Theban Palamon,
with fluttering beard and wild hair covered with ashes,     2025
in black dress, all sprinkled with tears;
and Emily, surpassing all others in weeping,
the saddest of all the company.
So that the service would be
the more noble and rich of its kind,                        2030
Duke Theseus had three steeds brought forth,
which were furnished with trappings of glittering steel
and covered with the arms of Arcite.
On these steeds (which were large and white)

Ther seten folk, of which oon bar his sheeld,　　　2035
Another his spere up in his hondes heeld,
The thridde bar with him his bowe Turkeys—
Of brend gold was the caas, and eek the harneys;
And riden forth a paas with sorweful chere
Toward the grove, as ye shul after here.　　　2040
The nobleste of the Grekes that ther were
Upon hir shuldres carieden the bere,
With slakke paas, and eyen rede and wete,
Thurghout the citee by the maister-strete,
That sprad was al with blak, and wonder hye　　　2045
Right of the same is the strete y-wrye.
Upon the right hond wente old Egeus,
And on that other syde duk Theseus,
With vessels in hir hand of gold ful fyn,
Al ful of hony, milk, and blood, and wyn;　　　2050
Eek Palamon, with ful greet companye;
And after that cam woful Emelye,
With fyr in honde, as was that tyme the gyse,
To do the office of funeral servyse.

Heigh labour and ful greet apparaillinge　　　2055
Was at the service and the fyr-makinge,
That with his grene top the heven raughte,
And twenty fadme of brede the armes straughte—
This is to seyn, the bowes were so brode.
Of stree first ther was leyd ful many a lode.　　　2060
But how the fyr was maked up on highte,
And eek the names how the treës highte—
As ook, firre, birch, asp, alder, holm, popler,
Wilow, elm, plane, ash, box, chasteyn, lind, laurer,
Mapul, thorn, beech, hasel, ew, whippel-tree—　　　2065
How they weren feld shal nat be told for me;
Ne how the goddes ronnen up and doun,
Disherited of hir habitacioun,
In which they woneden in reste and pees—
Nymphes, faunes, and amadrides;　　　2070
Ne how the bestes and the briddes alle

there sat men of whom one bore his shield,                2035
a second held up Arcite's spear in his hands,
and the third carried his Turkish bow—
the quiver and the trappings were of burnished gold;
they rode forth sorrowfully at footpace
toward the grove, as you shall hereafter hear.           2040
The noblest there of the Greeks
carried the bier on their shoulders,
at a slow pace and with reddened eyes,
through the city by the main street,
which was wholly spread with black cloth; and all        2045
the street fronts to a great height were hung with
    the same.
On the right hand walked old Aegeus,
and on the other side Duke Theseus
with vessels of fine gold in hand,
all filled with honey, milk, blood, and wine;            2050
Palamon also came, with a great company,
and after them came sad Emily,
with fire in hand, as was then the custom,
to perform the funeral rite.

Noble activity and great preparation                     2055
were given to the service and the making of the pyre,
which reached the heavens with its green top;
its sides stretched out twenty fathoms in breadth
(that is to say, the boughs were so broad).
There was first laid many a load of straw.               2060
But how the pyre was constructed above,
and also what were the names of the trees—
such as oak, fir, birch, aspen, alder, holm-oak, poplar,
willow, elm, plane, ash, box, chestnut, linden, laurel,
maple, thorn, beech, hazel, yew, dogwood—                2065
and how they were felled shall not be told by me;
nor how the divinities ran up and down,
disinherited of their habitation,
in which they had lived in calm and peace—
nymphs, fauns, hamadryads;                               2070
nor how the beasts and birds all

Fledden for fere, whan the wode was falle;
Ne how the ground agast was of the light,
That was nat wont to seen the sonne bright;
Ne how the fyr was couched first with stree, 2075
And than with drye stikkes cloven a three,
And than with grene wode and spycerye,
And than with cloth of gold and with perrye,
And gerlandes hanging with ful many a flour,
The mirre, th'encens, with al so greet odour; 2080
Ne how Arcite lay among al this,
Ne what richesse aboute his body is;
Ne how that Emelye, as was the gyse,
Putte in the fyr of funeral servyse;
Ne how she swowned whan men made the fyr, 2085
Ne what she spak, ne what was hir desyr;
Ne what jeweles men in the fire caste,
Whan that the fyr was greet and brente faste;
Ne how some caste hir sheeld and some hir spere,
And of hir vestiments, whiche that they were, 2090
And cuppes ful of wyn, and milk, and blood,
Into the fyr, that brente as it were wood;
Ne how the Grekes with an huge route
Thryës riden al the fyr aboute
Upon the left hand with a loud shoutinge, 2095
And thryës with hir speres clateringe;
And thryës how the ladies gonne crye;
Ne how that lad was homward Emelye;
Ne how Arcite is brent to asshen colde;
Ne how that liche-wake was y-holde 2100
Al thilke night; ne how the Grekes pleye
The wake-pleyes, ne kepe I nat to seye—
Who wrastleth best naked, with oille enoynt,
Ne who that bar him best, in no disjoynt;
I wol nat tellen eek how that they goon 2105
Hoom til Athenes whan the pley is doon;
But shortly to the poynt than wol I wende,
And maken of my longe tale an ende.

fled for fear when the woods were felled;
nor how at the light the ground was shocked,
not being accustomed to see the bright sun;
nor how the fire was first laid with straw,                    2075
and then with dry sticks split into threes,
and then with green wood and spices,
and then with cloth of gold and jewels
and hanging garlands with many a flower,
and myrrh and incense with so strong a fragrance;              2080
nor how Arcite lay among all this,
nor what riches lay about his body;
nor how Emily, as was the custom,
put in the ceremonial funeral fire;
nor how she swooned when the fire was made up,                 2085
nor what she said, nor what was her desire;
nor what jewels were cast into the fire
when it had grown and was burning hard;
nor how some cast their shields, and some their spears
and part of the clothes they wore,                            2090
and cups full of wine, milk, and blood
into the fire, which raged madly;
nor how the Greeks in a huge troop
rode thrice around the fire
leftward, with loud shouting,                                 2095
and thrice rattled their spears;
nor how the ladies thrice cried out;
nor how Emily was led homeward;
nor how Arcite was burned to cold ashes;
nor how the funeral wake was held                             2100
all that night; nor how the Greeks performed
the funeral games, I do not care to say—
who wrestled best naked and anointed with oil,
nor who bore himself best, not getting into any
     predicament.
I don't wish to tell, either, how they went                   2105
home to Athens when the games were finished;
I will move briefly to the point
and make an end of my long tale.

By processe and by lengthe of certeyn yeres
Al stinted is the moorning and the teres          2110
Of Grekes, by oon general assent.
Than semed me ther was a parlement
At Athenes, upon certeyn poynts and cas;
Among the whiche poynts y-spoken was
To have with certeyn contrees alliaunce,          2115
And have fully of Thebans obeisaunce:
For which this noble Theseus anon
Leet senden after gentil Palamon,
Unwist of him what was the cause and why;
But in his blake clothes sorwefully              2120
He cam at his comaundement in hye.
Tho sente Theseus for Emelye.
Whan they were set, and hust was al the place,
And Theseus abiden hadde a space
Er any word cam from his wyse brest,             2125
His eyen sette he ther as was his lest,
And with a sad visage he syked stille,
And after that right thus he seyde his wille:
    "The Firste Moevere* of the cause above,
Whan he first made the faire cheyne of love,      2130
Greet was th'effect, and heigh was his entente—
Wel wiste he why and what therof he mente:
For with that faire cheyne of love he bond
The fyr, the eyr, the water, and the lond
In certeyn boundes, that they may nat flee;       2135
That same Prince and that Moevere," quod he,
"Hath stablissed in this wrecched world adoun
Certeyne dayes and duracioun
To al that is engendred in this place,
Over the whiche day they may nat pace,            2140
Al mowe they yet tho dayes wel abregge:
Ther needeth non auctoritee t'allegge,
For it is preved by experience,
But that me list declaren my sentence.
Thanne may men by this ordre wel discerne         2145

By course of time and passing of a certain number
  of years
the mourning and tears wholly ceased. 2110
Then, it seems to me, there was, by a general agreement,
a meeting of the Greeks
at Athens on certain questions and affairs,
among which questions it was proposed
to have alliance with certain countries 2115
and to have the Thebans fully in submission:
for which purpose noble Theseus then
had gentle Palamon sent for,
without the latter's knowing the matter or the reason.
But Palamon came sorrowfully in his black clothes 2120
at Theseus's high command.
Then Theseus sent for Emily.
When they had sat down, and all the place was quiet,
and Theseus had waited for a time
before any word came from his wise breast, 2125
he set his eyes there where he wished
and sighed quietly with a sad face;
after that he said his will just thus:

"When the First Mover of the supernal cause
first made the fair chain of love, 2130
great was the outcome, and his plan was exalted;
he well knew why and what he intended by it;
for with that fair chain of love he bound
the fire, the air, the water, and the earth
within sure limits, so that they might not flee. 2135
That same Prince and Mover," said Theseus,
"has established down in this wretched world
certain periods and durations
for all that is engendered here,
beyond which limits they may not pass, 2140
although they may well shorten their days;
it is not necessary to cite any authority;
for this is proved by experience;
but I desire to make my meaning clear.
We may well discern, then, by this orderliness 2145

That thilke Moevere stable is and eterne:
Wel may men knowe, but it be a fool,
That every part deryveth from his hool,
For nature hath nat take his beginning
Of no partie ne cantel of a thing,                    2150
But of a thing that parfit is and stable,
Descending so, til it be corrumpable.
And therfore, of his wyse purveyaunce,
He hath so wel biset his ordinaunce
That speces of thinges and progressiouns               2155
Shullen enduren by successiouns,
And nat eterne, withouten any lyë:
This maistow understonde and seen at yë.

   "Lo the ook, that hath so long a norisshinge
From tyme that it first biginneth springe,             2160
And hath so long a lyf, as we may see,
Yet at the laste wasted is the tree;
Considereth eek how that the harde stoon
Under oure feet, on which we trede and goon,
Yit wasteth it as it lyth by the weye;                 2165
The brode river somtyme wexeth dreye;
The grete tounes see we wane and wende—
Than may ye see that al this thing hath ende.

   "Of man and womman seen we wel also,
That nedeth, in oon of thise termes two—               2170
This is to seyn, in youthe or elles age—
He moot ben deed, the king as shal a page:
Som in his bed, som in the depe see,
Some in the large feeld, as men may se;
Ther helpeth noght, al goth that ilke weye.            2175
Thanne may I seyn that al this thing moot deye.
What maketh this but Juppiter the king,
That is prince and cause of alle thing,
Converting al unto his propre welle
From which it is deryved, sooth to telle?              2180
And here-agayns no creature on lyve,

that that Mover is immovable and eternal.
Anyone but a fool may easily see
that every part derives from the whole to
    which it belongs,
for nature did not take its beginning
from a mere part or portion of a thing,                    2150
but from a thing that is complete and unchangeable,
descending until the point where it is subject
    to destruction.
And therefore in his wise providence
he has beyond doubt so well arranged his scheme
that particular things and happenings                    2155
are to last by succeeding themselves
and not by being individually eternal:
this you may comprehend and perceive at a glance.
    "Look at the oak, that has so long a period of growth
from the time it first begins to sprout,                    2160
and has so long a life, as we may see:
yet at last the tree is destroyed.
Consider also beneath our feet the stone
on which we tread and travel,
hard as it is, yet wastes away as it lies by the road.                    2165
The broad river at some time goes dry.
We see great towns diminish and pass away.
You may see, then, that all these things have an end.
    "In the case of man and woman also, we see
that necessarily in one of two periods—                    2170
that is to say, in youth or else in age—
the king as well as the page must die:
one in his bed, another in the deep sea,
another in the broad field, as one may perceive;
nothing helps; all go that same way.                    2175
I may then say that everything around us must die.
What causes this but Jupiter the ruler,
who, truthfully, is prince and cause of all things,
converting everything into its proper source
from which it was derived?                    2180
Against this no living creature

Of no degree, availleth for to stryve.
　"Thanne is it wisdom, as it thinketh me,
To maken vertu of necessitee,
And take it wel, that we may nat eschue,          2185
And namely that to us alle is due.
And whoso gruccheth ought, he dooth folye,
And rebel is to him that al may gye.
And certeinly a man hath most honour
To dyen in his excellence and flour,              2190
Whan he is siker of his gode name;
Thanne hath he doon his freend, ne him, no shame.
And gladder oghte his freend ben of his deeth
Whan with honour up-yolden is his breeth,
Than whan his name apalled is for age,            2195
For al forgeten is his vasselage.
Thanne is it best, as for a worthy fame,
To dyen whan that he is best of name.
　"The contrarie of al this is wilfulnesse.
Why grucchen we? why have we hevinesse,           2200
That good Arcite, of chivalrye flour,
Departed is with duetee and honour
Out of this foule prison of this lyf?
Why grucchen heer his cosin and his wyf
Of his welfare that loved hem so weel?            2205
Can he hem thank?—nay, God wot, never a deel—
That bothe his soule and eek hemself offende,
And yet they mowe hir lustes nat amende.
　"What may I conclude of this longe serie,
But after wo I rede us to be merie                2210
And thanken Juppiter of al his grace?
And, er that we departen from this place,
I rede that we make of sorwes two
O parfyt joye, lasting everemo;
And loketh now, wher most sorwe is herinne,       2215
Ther wol we first amenden and biginne.

of any condition succeeds in striving.
    "Then it is wisdom, as it seems to me,
to make a virtue of necessity,
and to accept willingly what we may not avoid,                    2185
and particularly what happens to all of us.
Whoever complains at all is guilty of folly
and is rebellious against the one who has power to
control all. And, certainly, a man gains most honor
in dying in his excellence and flower,                    2190
when he is sure of his good name;
then he has done no shame to his friend, or to himself.
And his friend ought to be happier for his death
when his breath is given up with honor,
than when his name is faded with age;                    2195
for then his prowess is all forgotten.
Then it is best, for the sake of a worthy reputation,
for a man to die when his name is most esteemed.
    "To deny all this is willfulness.
Why do we grumble? Why are we sad                    2200
that good Arcite, the flower of chivalry,
has departed in the line of duty and with honor
from the foul prison of this life?
Why do his cousin and his bride here complain
about the good fortune of him who loved them so well?  2205
Can he thank them for it? No, God knows, not a bit—
not them, who offer offense to both his soul
        and themselves,
and still cannot cheer themselves up.
    "What may I conclude from this long chain of
        reasoning
except that, after woe, I advise us to be merry                    2210
and thank Jupiter for all his favors?
And, before we leave this place,
I advise that we make out of two sorrows
one complete joy, lasting evermore;
and consider now, where there is most sorrow
        in this matter,                    2215
there will we first start the improvement.

"Suster," quod he, "this is my fulle assent,
With al th'avys heer of my parlement,
That gentil Palamon, your owne knight,
That serveth yow with wil and herte and might,　　2220
And evere hath doon sin ye first him knewe,
That ye shul of your grace upon him rewe,
And taken him for housbonde and for lord:
Lene me youre hond, for this is our acord.
Lat see now of your wommanly pitee.　　2225
He is a kinges brother sone, pardee;
And though he were a povre bacheler,
Sin he hath served yow so many a yeer,
And had for yow so greet adversitee,
It moste been considered, leveth me;　　2230
For gentil mercy oghte to passen right."
　　Than seyde he thus to Palamon the knight:
"I trowe ther nedeth litel sermoning
To make yow assente to this thing.
Com neer, and taak youre lady by the hond."　　2235
Bitwixen hem was maad anon the bond
That highte matrimoine or mariage,
By al the counseil and the baronage.
And thus with alle blisse and melodye
Hath Palamon y-wedded Emelye.　　2240
And God, that al this wyde world hath wroght,
Sende him his love, that hath it dere aboght.
For now is Palamon in alle wele,
Living in blisse, in richesse, and in hele;
And Emelye him loveth so tendrely,　　2245
And he hir serveth al so gentilly,
That nevere was ther no word hem bitwene
Of jalousie, or any other tene.
Thus endeth Palamon and Emelye;
And God save al this faire companye. —Amen.　　2250

"Sister," he said, "this is my final opinion,
with the advice of my councillors here,
concerning Palamon, your own knight,
who serves you with will and heart and strength,          2220
and has always done so since you first knew him:
that you should by your favor take pity on him
and accept him as husband and lord:
give me your hand, for this is our agreement.
Now let's see your womanly pity.          2225
By heaven, he is son to the brother of a king;
and if he were nothing but a poor youth not yet a knight,
his service to you for so many a year,
and the great adversity he has suffered for you
would have to be considered, believe me; for gentle
     mercy          2230
ought to be more esteemed than standing on one's
     rights."
   Then he spoke thus to Palamon, the knight:
"I imagine that little preaching is needed
to make you agree to this.
Come near and take your lady by the hand."          2235
Between them was then made the bond
that is called matrimony or marriage,
in the presence of all the council and nobility.
And thus with full bliss and melody
Palamon married Emily.          2240
And God, who has wrought all this wide world,
send him his love who has paid for it dearly.
Now is Palamon in complete happiness,
living in bliss, in riches, and in health;
and Emily loves him so tenderly,          2245
and he serves her just so gently,
that there has never been between them a word
of jealousy or any other vexation.
Thus ends the story of Palamon and Emily,
and God save all this fair company —Amen.          2250

# THE MILLER'S TALE

# INTRODUCTION

✿

THE MILLER'S TALE is a perennial favorite of read-
ers of Chaucer. It was once seen as an obscene embar-
rassment in the Chaucerian canon. Editors, translators, and
some teachers tended to shy away from it as generally unsa-
vory, inappropriate for most readers, and not really all that
funny anyhow. More recent criticism takes the tale to be one
of Chaucer's most delightful and realistic masterpieces, a
welcome change of pace after the static list of portraits in the
General Prologue and the stagy unreality of "The Knight's
Tale." One of the most delightful aspects of "The Miller's
Tale" is that it is just that—a miller's tale. The General Pro-
logue description of the Miller (see lines 547–68) shows him
to be a big quarrelsome bully who likes to tell raunchy tales.
The interchange between him and the Host shows him to be
a belligerent drunk who intrudes himself into the tale-telling
by bumping aside the Monk and demanding to tell a story
that will be a proper reply to the aristocratic Knight's tale of
Theseus, Arcite, Palamon, and the virginal Emily.

"The Miller's Tale" is in some ways an upside-down mir-
ror of "The Knight's Tale," with old John now in the role of
Theseus, randy Nicholas and fruity Absalom in the roles of
Arcite and Palamon, and sexy Alison showing us the Miller's
version of what real young women are like—or should be
like. To put it differently, we have in "The Miller's Tale" an-
other narrative of a love triangle in which two young men be-
come the jealous rivals for the affections of a beautiful young
woman who is not readily available to either of them because
her life is controlled by the conservative protection of an
older male relative. As in "The Knight's Tale," one of the

young suitors is victorious in the contest but soon receives his just punishment.

For many readers the crowning achievement of "The Miller's Tale" is young Alison, whose thirty-eight-line description (lines 47–84) near the start of the tale portrays her as precisely the kind of sleek, frisky, and flighty young barnyard creature—weasel, sheep, colt, calf, goat kid, barn swallow— who would so readily accept the seductive onslaught of the bold Nicholas and then reject so boldly the less manly seduction of the fastidious Absalom. With his portrayal of Alison the Miller gives us a satirical yet appreciative look at women who are young and pretty, yes, but possessed of a fun-loving spirit of resistance that would be unthinkable for the sedately bored and boring Emily. While Emily's response to men who adore her is to pray to the chaste goddess of the moon for eternal virginity, Alison's is to give one of them access to her haunches and the other to her moon-out-the-window. And then there is that window. The window in "The Knight's Tale" is in a prison wall and has iron bars in it that symbolize Emily's distant inaccessibility to the men trapped on the other side. The window in "The Miller's Tale," on the other hand, is easily opened at the will of the woman herself and of her lover who needs to relieve himself after a night of joyous lust.

Chaucer's most likely source for "The Miller's Tale" is the fourteenth-century Middle Dutch story about an unmarried Antwerp prostitute named Heile. Needing money, Heile of Beersele makes appointments with three men on the same night—a miller, a priest, and a blacksmith. The fun of the story is in its hastily reached climax, where three appointments that were meant to be consecutive turn out to be simultaneous. The three men are all with Heile, or wanting to be, at the same time. Heile hides the miller in a hanging trough while she entertains the priest in the bed below and afterward hears his prediction that a great flood is coming. When her neighbor the blacksmith knocks at her window, Heile tries to send him away, but he asks for at least a kiss. The priest is happy to comply by sticking his buttocks out the dark window to receive the kiss, and the angry smith then rushes to his nearby forge to bring back a hot iron.

Whereas Chaucer had greatly reduced the length of his source when he wrote "The Knight's Tale," he greatly expanded his source when he wrote "The Miller's Tale." Most of the expansion comes at the opening of the tale as he gives full scope to the descriptions, the motivations, and the preclimax actions of the four principal characters. These prepare for what happens at foolish old John's house on that fateful Monday night. So carefully integrated are the parts of the tale that Chaucer's version seems more fast-paced than the much shorter story of Heile. Chaucer has taken a tale that turns on a clever plot and transformed it into one that turns on cleverly constructed characters.

## NOTES

### The Miller's Prologue

**Pilates vois** (line 16). The reference here is to the voice of Pontius Pilate in medieval biblical drama, the man who ordered the execution of Jesus. It is usually thought to be a loud, ranting, and commanding voice, though the Miller's reference to the sound of his drunken voice (line 31) may indicate a wheezy or squeaky voice.

**clerk** (35). A student or "cleric." Chaucer usually uses the term to indicate a young man, probably in training ultimately for a priestly vocation, but still enrolled in college. That designation certainly works well enough for the clerks in this and the next tale.

### The Miller's Tale

**gnof** (line 2). The term generally meant something like "churl" or "boor." The fact that John is also in the same line said to be "riche," coupled with the fact that he has a spacious house with rooms to let out and at least two servants, suggests that he has been successful in his building trade. Perhaps the term "nouveau riche" is appropriate.

**art** (5). The term refers not to pictorial art but more generally to the "liberal arts," which in Chaucer's time would have included a deep study of Aristotelian logic.

**hende** (13). This term, which Chaucer uses repeatedly of Nicholas, has several possible translations: "gracious," "pleasant," "clever," and perhaps, given his easy accessibility to Alison, "near at hand," or, considering the role his roving hands play in the tale, "handy."

*Almageste* (22). A book of astrology, probably based ultimately on the work of Ptolomy.

*Angelus ad virginem* (30). A religious song of the annunciation of the angel Gabriel to the Virgin Mary telling her that she will be the mother of God.

**kinges note** (31). Apparently the name of a well-known song in Chaucer's time, but no song that answers to that name or title has been found.

**Catoun** (41). The supposed author of a collection of maxims and proverbs in Latin. The work surely existed and was used in schools in Chaucer's time, but little is known of the author. John's failure to know it suggests that he is ignorant and probably illiterate.

**noble** (70). Gold coins that were minted in the Tower of London.

**Oseneye** (88). There was an Augustinian abbey in the nearby village of Osney. It is now part of Oxford, but in Chaucer's time, it was a short distance from the town.

**Absolon** (127). We adopt the spelling "Absalom" in the translation to remind readers that this foppish parish clerk is apparently named after the Old Testament Absalom, an unusually pretty son of Abraham. The biblical Absalom is killed for rebelling against his father.

**Powles window** (132). Prettily latticed shoe tops modeled after the carved windows in St. Paul's Cathedral in London.

**shot-windowe** (172). The term is variously taken to mean a hinged casement window or possibly a window out of which to shoot intruders. It more likely refers to a window "shuttered" for privacy and security on the street level. In this case the shutter or shutters must have opened into the room, so that those inside could open and close it safely.

**Herodes upon a scaffold hye** (198). A reference to the biblical drama of Chaucer's time. The scaffold would have been a stationary open-air stage or possibly a raised portion on a pageant wagon. It is curious that Absalom would have thought to impress Alison by portraying Herod, the evil king who as part of his plan to get rid of Jesus ordered the slaying of all male children under age two in Bethlehem.

**"Jesu ... soster"** (297–300). The superstitious John recites a near-nonsensical charm to protect his house from the evil spirits that he fears have attacked Nicholas.

**gete his wyf to shipe** (354). The story of how much trouble Noah had getting his wife into the ark is not in the Bible, but it was a humorous addition to the biblical account of the flood in some cycles of the mystery plays.

*Pater-noster* (452). Latin for the prayer beginning, "Our father..."

**corfew-tyme** (459). The curfew was usually at dusk.

**belle of Laudes** (469). The bell marking the second canonical service was rung before dawn.

**cokkes crowe** (489). Roosters traditionally crowed just at dawn.

**cultour** (590). The colter was the knifelike part of a plow that cut a vertical slice in the ground before the plowshare turned the soil over. It was adjustable for depth, designed to be easily removable for sharpening, and readily portable.

# THE MILLERE

*Wordes bitwene the Host and the Millere*

Whan that the Knight had thus his tale y-told,
   In al the route nas ther yong ne old
That he ne seyde it was a noble storie,
And worthy for to drawen to memorie,
And namely the gentils everichoon. 5
Our Hoste lough and swoor, "So moot I goon,
This gooth aright: unbokeled is the male.
Lat see now who shal tell another tale,
For trewely the game is well bigonne.
Now telleth ye, sir Monk, if that ye conne, 10
Sumwhat to quyte with the Knightes tale."
The Miller, that for dronken was all pale,
So that unnethe upon his hors he sat,
He nolde avalen neither hood ne hat,
Ne abyde no man for his curteisye, 15
But in Pilates vois* he gan to crye,
And swoor, "By armes and by blood and bones,
I can a noble tale for the nones,
With which I wol now quyte the Knightes tale!"

   Our Hoste saugh that he was dronke of ale, 20
And seyde, "Abyd, Robin, my leve brother;
Som bettre man shal telle us first another.
Abyd, and lat us werken thriftily."

   "By Goddes soul," quod he, "that wol nat I;
For I wol speke or elles go my wey." 25
Our Hoste answerde, "Tel on, a devel wey!
Thou art a fool, thy wit is overcome."

# THE MILLER

*Words between the Host and the Miller*

When the Knight had thus told his tale
   in all that company ther was no one, young
  or old,
who did not say it was a noble story,
and worthy to be remembered,
particularly the gentlefolk, each and every one.     5
Our Host laughed, and swore, "As I may walk,
this goes well: the pouch is unbuckled.
Now let's see who shall tell another tale,
for the game is indeed well begun.
Now, sir Monk, if you can, tell     10
something to match the Knight's tale."
The Miller, who was all pale with drunkenness,
so that he could hardly sit on his horse,
was not minded to doff his hood or hat
nor wait on any man for courtesy's sake,     15
but began to cry out in a voice like Pilate's,
and swore, "By God's arms and blood and bones,
I know a splendid tale for the occasion,
with which I'll now match the Knight's tale!"

    Our Host saw that he was drunk with ale,     20
and said, "Wait, Robin, my dear brother;
first some better man shall tell us another.
Wait, and let us do things properly."

    "By God's soul," said he, "that I will not;
for I will speak or else go on my way."     25
Our Host answered, "Tell on, in the devil's name!
You are a fool; your wits are drowned."

"Now herkneth," quod the Miller, "alle and some.
But first I make a protestacioun
That I am dronke, I knowe it by my soun;                    30
And therefore if that I misspeke or seye,
Wyte it the ale of Southwerk, I yow preye;
For I wol tell a legende and a lyf
Bothe of a carpenter and of his wyf,
How that a clerk* hath set the wrightes cappe."            35
      The Reve answerde and seyde, "Stint thy clappe!
Lat be thy lewed dronken harlotrye.
It is a sinne and eek a greet folye
To apeiren any man or him diffame,
And eek to bringen wyves in swich fame.                    40
Thou mayst ynogh of othere thinges seyn."
      This dronken Miller spak ful sone ageyn
And seyde, "Leve brother Osewold,
Who hath no wyf, he is no cokewold.
But I sey nat therfore that thou art oon;                  45
Ther been ful gode wyves many oon,
And ever a thousand gode ayeyns oon badde;
That knowestow wel thyself, but if thou madde.
Why artow angry with my tale now?
I have a wyf, pardee, as well as thou;                     50
Yet nolde I, for the oxen in my plogh,
Take upon me more than ynogh
As demen of myself that I were oon;
I wol beleve wel that I am noon.
An housbond shal nat been inquisitif                       55
Of Goddes privetee, nor of his wyf.
So he may finde Goddes foyson there,
Of the remenant nedeth nat enquere."
      What sholde I more seyn but this Millere
He nolde his wordes for no man forbere,                    60
But tolde his cherles tale in his manere,
M'athinketh that I shal reherce it here,
And therfore every gentil wight I preye,
For Goddes love, demeth nat that I seye

"Now listen," said the Miller, "everyone.
But first I will proclaim that
I am drunk; I know it by the sound of my voice.      30
And therefore, if I speak amiss,
blame it on the ale of Southwark, I pray you;
for I am going to tell a legend, a history,
of both a carpenter and his wife,
and how a clerk made a fool of the carpenter."      35

The Reeve answered and said, "Stop your gabble!
Leave off your stupid, drunken obscenity.
It is sinful and very foolish
to injure any man or defame him,
and also to bring wives into such repute.      40
You can say enough about other things."

This drunken Miller replied at once,
and said, "Dear brother Oswald,
he who has no wife is no cuckold.
But I don't say that therefore you are one;      45
there are a great many good wives,
and always a thousand good ones to one bad one;
you know that perfectly well yourself, unless
    you're crazy.
Why are you angry with my story already?
I have a wife, by God, just as you do;      50
yet I wouldn't, for the oxen in my plow,
take more than enough on myself so
as to think that I am a cuckold;
I will believe firmly that I am none.
A husband should not be inquisitive      55
about God's secrets—or his wife's.
If he can find God's plenty in his wife,
there's no need to inquire about the rest."

What more should I say but that this Miller
would not spare his words for any man,      60
but told his churl's tale in his own way.
I regret that I must repeat it here,
and therefore I ask every well-bred person,
for God's love, don't think that I speak

wife morals

Of evel entent, but for I moot reherce　　　　65
Hir tales alle, be they bettre or werse,
Or elles falsen some of my matere.
And therfore, whoso list it nat y-here,
Turne over the led and chese another tale,
For he shal finde ynowe, grete and smale,　　　　70
Of storial thing that toucheth gentillesse,
And eek moralitee and holinesse.
Blameth nat me if that ye chese amis.
The Miller is a cherl, ye knowe wel this;
So was the Reve, and othere mo,　　　　75
And harlotrye they tolden bothe two.
Avyseth yow and putte me out of blame;
And eek men shal nat make ernest of game.

*Here biginneth the Millere his Tale*

Whylom ther was dwellinge at Oxenforde
A riche gnof,* that gestes heeld to borde,
And of his craft he was a carpenter.
With him ther was dwellinge a poure scoler,
Hadde lerned art,* but al his fantasye　　　　5
Was turned for to lerne astrologye,
And coude a certeyn of conclusiouns
To demen by interrogaciouns,
If that men axed him in certein houres
Whan that men sholde have droghte or elles shoures,　　　　10
Or if men axed him what sholde bifalle
Of every thing—I may nat rekene hem alle.
　　This clerk was cleped hende* Nicholas;
Of derne love he coude, and of solas;
And therto he was sleigh and ful privee,　　　　15
And lyk a mayden meke for to see.
A chambre hadde he in that hostelrye
Allone, withouten any companye,

with evil intentions; but I must repeat                         65
all their tales, be they better or worse,
or else be false to some of my material.
And therefore whoever does not wish to hear it,
turn over the leaf and choose another tale;
for he shall find enough, long and short,                       70
of narratives that deal with nobility,
and also morality and holiness.
Don't blame me if you choose amiss.
The Miller is a churl, you know this well;
so was the Reeve, as well as some of the others.               75
Both of them recited ribaldry.
Take heed, and don't put the blame on me;
and then, too, one should not take a game seriously.


*Here begins the Miller's Tale*


Once upon a time there lived at Oxford
a rich churl who boarded paying guests;
he was a carpenter by trade.
At his house lived a poor scholar
who had completed part of his arts course, but
his whole                                                        5
imagination was directed to learning astrology.
He knew a number of propositions
by which to make a decision in astrological analyses
in certain hours if you asked him
when you would have drought or else showers,                    10
or if you asked him what should come
of all sorts of things; I can't mention all of them.
    This clerk was named pleasant Nicholas;
he knew all about secret love and pleasurable
        consolations,
and, besides, he was sly and very discreet                      15
and looked as meek as a maiden.
In that boardinghouse he had a room,
alone, without further company,

Ful fetisly y-dight with herbes swote;
And he himself as swete as is the rote          20
Of licorys or any cetewale.
His *Almageste** and bokes grete and smale,
His astrelabie, longinge for his art,
His augrim-stones layen faire apart
On shelves couched at his beddes heed;          25
His presse y-covered with a falding reed;
And al above ther lay a gay sautrye,
On which he made a-nightes melodye
So swetely that al the chambre rong;
And *Angelus ad virginem** he song;            30
And after that he song the kinges note;*
Ful often blessed was his myrie throte.
And thus this swete clerk his tyme spente
After his freendes finding and his rente.

This carpenter had wedded newe a wyf            35
Which that he lovede more than his lyf;
Of eightetene yeer she was of age.
Jalous he was, and heeld hire narwe in cage,
For she was wilde and yong, and he was old,
And demed himself ben lyk a cokewold.          40
He knew nat Catoun,* for his wit was rude,
That bad man sholde wedde his similitude:
Men sholde wedden after hir estaat,
For youthe and elde is often at debaat.
But sith that he was fallen in the snare,       45
He moste endure, as other folk, his care.

Fair was this yonge wyf, and therwithal
As any wesele hir body gent and smal.
A ceynt she werede barred al of silk,
A barmclooth eek as whyt as morne milk         50
Upon hir lendes, ful of many a gore.
Whyt was hir smok and broyden al bifore
And eek bihinde, on hir coler aboute,
Of col-blak silk, withinne and eek withoute.
The tapes of hir whyte voluper                  55

and nicely decked with fragrant herbs;
and he himself was as sweet and clean as the root          20
of licorice or any ginger.
His *Almagest* and books large and small,
his astrolabe, proper to his art,
and his counters for arithmetic lay neatly separated
on shelves set at the head of his bed;          25
his storage chest was covered with a red woolen cloth.
At the top there lay a pretty psaltery
on which by night he made melody
so sweetly that all the room rang with it;
he sang *Angelus ad virginem,*          30
and after that he sang the King's Tune;
people often blessed his merry voice.
And thus this sweet clerk spent his time,
depending upon his friends' support and his income.

   This carpenter had recently married a wife          35
whom he loved more than his life;
she was eighteen years of age.
He was jealous and kept her on a short leash,
for she was wild and young, and he was old,
and judged himself near to being a cuckold.          40
He did not know (for his understanding was crude)
   Cato's
saying that a man should marry someone like himself:
people should wed according to their condition,
for youth and age are often at odds.
But since he had fallen into the trap,          45
he had to endure his trouble, like other people.
   This young wife was lovely;
her body was as graceful and slim as a weasel's.
She wore a sash threaded with silk,
and around her loins a flared apron          50
white as morning-fresh milk;
her smock was white, and embroidered with
black silk around the collar,
inside and outside, front and back.
The ribbons of her cap          55

Were of the same suyte of hir coler;
Hir filet brood of silk, and set ful hye;
And sikerly she hadde a likerous yë.
Ful smale y-pulled were hir browes two,
And tho were bent and blake as any sloo.          60
She was ful more blisful on to see
Than is the newe pere-jonette tree;
And softer than the wolle is of a wether.
And by hir girdel heeng a purs of lether,
Tasseld with silk, and perled with latoun.        65
In al this world, to seken up and doun,
There nis no man so wys that coude thenche
So gay a popelote or swich a wenche.
Ful brighter was the shyning of hir hewe
Than in the tour the noble* y-forged newe.        70
But of hir song, it was as loude and yerne
As any swalwe sittinge on a berne.
Therto she coude skippe and make game
As any kide or calf folwinge his dame.
Hir mouth was swete as bragot or the meeth,       75
Or hord of apples leyd in hey or heeth.
Winsinge she was as is a joly colt,
Long as a mast, and upright as a bolt.
A brooch she baar upon hir lowe coler
As brood as is the bos of a bocler.               80
Hir shoes were laced on hir legges hye.
She was a prymerole, a pigges-nye,
For any lord to leggen in his bedde,
Or yet for any good yeman to wedde.

　　Now sire, and eft sire, so bifel the cas,      85
That on a day this hende Nicholas
Fil with this yonge wyf to rage and pleye,
Whyl that hir housbond was at Oseneye,*
As clerkes ben ful subtile and ful queynte;
And prively he caughte hir by the queynte,        90
And seyde, "y-wis, but if ich have my wille,
For derne love of thee, lemman, I spille."
And heeld hir harde by the haunche-bones,

matched her collar,
and her broad silk headband sat well back from her face.
And—certainly—she had a wanton eye.
Her eyebrows were closely plucked,
and they arched gracefully and were black as a sloe. 60
She was more of a treat to look at
than a pear tree, just come into bloom,
and she was softer to touch than the wool of a sheep.
At her waist hung a leather purse,
tasseled with silk and beaded in bright metal. 65
In all this world, if you search up and down,
you can find no man clever enough to imagine
so gay a poppet or such a wench. The brilliance
of her coloring was better than the gleam of a
gold noble newly minted in the Tower of London. 70
As for her singing, it was as clear and lively
as the notes of a barn swallow.
Besides all this, she could gambol and play
like any kid or calf following his mother.
Her mouth was as sweet as drinks made from honey, 75
or as a hoard of apples laid away in hay or heather.
She was skittish as a colt,
tall as a mast, and straight as an arrow.
On her low collar she wore a brooch
as broad as the boss of a buckler. 80
Her shoes were laced far up her legs.
She was a morning glory, she was a daisy,
fit for any lord to lay in his bed,
or yet for any good yeoman to marry.

Now sir, and again sir, it so happened 85
that one day this pleasant Nicholas
happened to flirt and play with this young wife
while her husband was at Osney
(these clerks are very subtle and sly),
and privily he grabbed her by the crotch 90
and said, "Unless I have my will of you,
sweetheart, I'm sure to die for suppressed love."
And he held her hard by the hips

And seyde, "lemman, love me al at-ones,
Or I wol dyen, also God me save!"                              95
And she sprong as a colt doth in the trave,
And with hir heed she wryed faste awey,
And seyde, "I wol nat kisse thee, by my fey.
Why, lat be," quod she, "lat be, Nicholas!
Or I wol crye 'out, harrow' and 'allas.'                      100
Do wey your handes, for your curteisye!"

This Nicholas gan mercy for to crye,
And spak so faire, and profred hir so faste,
That she hir love him graunted atte laste,
And swoor hir ooth, by Seint Thomas of Kent,                 105
That she wol been at his comandement,
Whan that she may hir leyser wel espye.
"Myn housbond is so ful of jalousye
That, but ye wayte wel and been privee,
I woot right wel I nam but deed," quod she.                   110
"Ye moste been ful derne, as in this case."

"Nay, therof care thee noght," quod Nicholas,
"A clerk hadde litherly biset his whyle,
But if he coude a carpenter bigyle."
And thus they been acorded and y-sworn                       115
To wayte a tyme, as I have told biforn.
Whan Nicholas had doon thus everydeel,
And thakked hir aboute the lendes weel,
He kist hir swete, and taketh his sautrye,
And pleyeth faste, and maketh melodye.                       120

Thanne fil it thus, that to the parissh chirche,
Cristes owne werkes for to wirche,
This gode wyf wente on an haliday:
Hir forheed shoon as bright as any day,
So was it wasshen whan she leet hir werk.                     125

Now was ther of that chirche a parissh clerk,
The which that was y-cleped Absolon.*
Crul was his heer, and as the gold it shoon,
And strouted as a fanne large and brode;
Ful streight and even lay his joly shode.                     130

and said, "Sweetheart, love me right away
or I'll die, so help me God!"                                    95
She jumped like a colt imprisoned in a shoeing frame
and twisted her head away hard
and said, "I won't kiss you, on my faith;
why let be," she said, "let be, Nicholas,
or I'll cry 'Help!' and 'Alas!'                              100
Take away your hands; where are your manners!"
    This Nicholas started begging for mercy
and spoke so prettily and pushed himself so hard
that she finally granted him her love
and made her oath, by Saint Thomas à Becket,             105
that she would be his to command
when she could see her opportunity.
"My husband is so filled with jealousy
that, unless you are on guard and keep it a secret,
I know for sure that I'm as good as dead," she said.    110
"You must be very discreet in this matter."
    "No, don't bother about that," said Nicholas,
"A clerk would certainly have spent his time poorly
if he couldn't fool a carpenter."
And thus they agreed and promised                        115
to look out for an occasion, as I told before.
When Nicholas had accomplished all this,
and patted her thoroughly about the loins,
he kissed her sweetly, and took his psaltery
and played it hard and made music.                       120
    Then it happened that this good wife
went to the parish church on a holy day
to perform Christ's own works:
her forehead shone as bright as day,
it had been washed so thoroughly when she left
    her work.                                            125
    Now, there was a parish clerk of that church
who was called Absalom.
His hair was curly and shone like gold
and spread out like a big, wide fan;
the pretty parting of his hair lay straight and even.    130

His rode was reed; his eyen greye as goos;
With Powles window* corven on his shoos,
In hoses rede he wente fetisly.
Y-clad he was ful smal and proprely,
Al in a kirtel of a light wachet—                        135
Ful faire and thikke been the poyntes set.
And therupon he hadde a gay surplys
As whyt as is the blosme upon the rys.
A merye child he was, so God me save.
Wel coude he laten blood and clippe and shave,          140
And maken a chartre of lond, or acquitaunce.
In twenty manere coude he trippe and daunce,
After the scole of Oxenforde tho,
And with his legges casten to and fro,
And pleyen songes on a small rubible;                   145
Therto he song somtyme a loud quinible;
And as wel coude he pleye on a giterne.
In al the toun nas brewhous ne taverne
That he ne visited with his solas,
Ther any gaylard tappestere was.                        150
But sooth to seyn, he was somdel squaymous
Of farting, and of speche daungerous.
    This Absolon, that jolif was and gay,
Gooth with a sencer on the haliday,
Sensinge the wyves of the parish faste;                 155
And many a lovely look on hem he caste,
And namely on this carpenteres wyf:
To loke on hir him thoughte a merye lyf,
She was so propre and swete and likerous.
I dar wel seyn, if she had been a mous,                 160
And he a cat, he wolde hire hente anon.
This parissh clerk, this joly Absolon,
Hath in his herte swich a love-longinge
That of no wyf ne took he noon offringe;
For curteisye, he seyde, he wolde noon.                 165
    The mone, whan it was night, ful brighte shoon,
And Absolon his giterne hath y-take,

His complexion was red, his eyes as gray as a goose;
he went very elegantly in red hose,
with St. Paul's window tooled into his shoes.
He was dressed very properly and with a close fit
in a light blue tunic;                                                135
its laces were set in neatly and close together.
In addition he had a handsome surplice
as white as a blossom on the bough.
He was a merry lad, God help me.
He well knew how to let blood, to clip hair,
    and to shave,                                                    140
and how to draw up a charter of land or a release.
He could trip and dance twenty different ways
according to the then manner of Oxford
and prance to and fro on his legs,
and play song tunes on a small fiddle                               145
(he sometimes sang the high treble loudly);
and he could play as well on his guitar.
There wasn't a beer house or tavern in the whole town
that he didn't visit with his entertainment,
if there was any gay barmaid there.                                 150
But, to tell the truth, he was a little squeamish
about farting and prim in his speech.
    This Absalom, who was lively and playful,
went with a censer on the holy day
censing the wives of the parish zealously,                          155
and many a loving look he cast upon them,
particularly on the carpenter's wife:
looking at her seemed a merry life to him,
she was so neat and sweet and appetizing.
I daresay that if she had been a mouse                              160
and he a cat, he would have grabbed her right away.
Jolly Absalom, this parish clerk,
had such love-longing in his heart
that he accepted no offering from any wife;
he said that he wouldn't for the sake of his manners.               165
    When night came, the moon shone brightly
and Absalom took his guitar,

For paramours he thoghte for to wake.
And forth he gooth, jolif and amorous,
Til he cam to the carpenteres hous            170
A litel after cokkes hadde y-crowe,
And dressed him up by a shot-windowe*
That was upon the carpenteres wal.
He singeth in his vois gentil and smal,
"Now, dere lady, if thy wille be,            175
I preye yow that ye wol rewe on me,"
Ful wel acordaunt to his giterninge.
This carpenter awook and herde him singe,
And spak unto his wyf, and seyde anon,
"What, Alison, herestow nat Absolon            180
That chaunteth thus under our boures wal?"
And she answerde hir housbond therwithal,
"Yis, god wot, John, I here it every-del.
This passeth forth. What wol ye bet than wel?"
    Fro day to day this joly Absolon            185
So woweth hire, that him is wo-bigon:
He waketh al the night and al the day;
He kempte hise lokkes brode and made him gay;
He woweth hir by menes and brocage,
And swoor he wolde been hir owne page;            190
He singeth, brokkinge as a nightingale;
He sente hir piment, meeth, and spyced ale,
And wafres, pyping hote out of the glede;
And, for she was of toune, he profred mede.
For som folk wol ben wonnen for richesse,            195
And som for strokes, and som for gentillesse.
    Somtyme to shewe his lightnesse and maistrye,
He pleyeth Herodes upon a scaffold hye.*
But what availleth him as in this cas?
She loveth so this hende Nicholas            200
That Absolon may blowe the bukkes horn;
He ne hadde for his labour but a scorn;
And thus she maketh Absolon hir ape,
And al his ernest turneth til a jape.

for he planned to stay up as lovers do.
Forth he went, lusty and amorous,
until he came to the carpenter's house 170
a little after cockcrow,
and took his stand by a shuttered window
in the carpenter's wall.
He sang in his refined, dainty voice,
"Now, dear lady, if it be your will, 175
I pray you to take pity on me,"
nicely in tune with his playing.
The carpenter woke up and heard him sing
and spoke to his wife saying,
"Why, Alison, don't you hear Absalom 180
singing that way below our chamber wall?"
And she thereupon answered her husband,
"Yes, God knows, John, I hear every bit of it.
Such things go on. What do you expect?"
    From day to day this pretty Absalom 185
wooed her until he was woebegone:
he stayed awake all night and all day;
he combed his wide-spreading locks and made
    himself look
pretty; he wooed her by go-betweens and proxy
and swore he would be her very own page; 190
he sang quaveringly, like a nightingale;
he sent her sweetened wine, mead, spiced ale,
and pastries piping hot out of the coals;
and (since she was a townswoman) he offered bribes.
For some will be won with riches, 195
some with blows, and some with kindness.
    Once, to show his agility and skill,
he played Herod on a high scaffold.
But what use was anything to him in this case?
She loved pleasant Nicholas so much 200
that Absalom could go whistle to the wind;
he earned nothing but scorn for his labors;
thus she made a monkey of Absalom
and turned all his seriousness into a joke.

Ful sooth is this proverbe, it is no lye;                    205
Men seyn right thus, "Alwey the nye slye
Maketh the fere leve to be looth."
For though that Absolon be wood or wrooth,
By cause that he fer was from hir sighte,
This nye Nicholas stood in his lighte.                       210

    Now bere thee wel, thou hende Nicholas,
For Absolon may waille and singe "Allas."
And so bifel it on a Saterday
This carpenter was goon til Osenay;
And hende Nicholas and Alisoun                               215
Acorded been to this conclusioun,
That Nicholas shal shapen him a wyle
This sely jalous housbonde to bigyle;
And if so be the game wente aright,
She sholde slepen in his arm al night,                       220
For this was his desyr and hir also.
And right anon, withouten wordes mo,
This Nicholas no lenger wolde tarie,
But doth ful softe unto his chambre carie
Bothe mete and drinke for a day or tweye,                    225
And to hir housbonde bad hire for to seye,
If that he axed after Nicholas,
She sholde seye she niste where he was—
Of al that day she saugh him nat with yë;
She trowed that he was in maladye,                           230
For no cry hir mayde coude him calle;
He nolde answere, for nothing that mighte falle.

    This passeth forth al thilke Saterday
That Nicholas stille in his chambre lay,
And eet, and sleep, or dide what him leste,                  235
Til Sonday that the sonne gooth to reste.

    This sely carpenter hath greet merveyle
Of Nicholas, or what thing mighte him eyle,
And seyde, "I am adrad, by Seint Thomas,
It stondeth nat aright with Nicholas.                        240
God shilde that he deyde sodeynly!
This world is now ful tikel, sikerly:

There's no doubt that this proverb is very true;                    205
men say just this: "Always the nearby sly one
makes the distant dear one to be hated."    *men*
Though Absalom may be raging and furious
because he was far from her sight,
this nearby Nicholas stood in his light.                    210

Now play your part well, you pleasant Nicholas,
for Absalom may wail and sing "Alas."
And so it happened on a Saturday
that this carpenter had gone to Osney;
and pleasant Nicholas and Alison    *away*                    215
agreed to this effect,
that Nicholas should invent himself a wily trick
to fool this simple-minded, jealous husband;
and if the game went right,
she would sleep in his arms all night,                    220
for this was his desire, and hers, too.    *Plans*
Right away, without another word,
Nicholas wouldn't stand for further tarrying
but very quietly carried to his room
both food and drink for a day or two,                    225
and told her to say to her husband
if he asked for Nicholas
that she didn't know where he was—
that she hadn't laid eyes on him all that day;
and that she imagined he was sick,                    230
for her maid couldn't rouse him, despite her shouting;
he wouldn't answer, no matter what happened.

It followed that all that Saturday
and until sundown on Sunday
Nicholas stayed quiet in his room                    235
and ate and slept, or did whatever he wanted.

This foolish carpenter was astonished
at Nicholas and wondered what ailed him;
he said, "By St. Thomas, I am afraid
that things aren't right with Nicholas.                    240
God forbid that he should die suddenly!
This world now is very ticklish, in truth:

I saugh today a cors y-born to chirche
That now, on Monday last, I saugh him wirche.
Go up," quod he unto his knave anoon;                    245
"Clepe at his dore, or knokke with a stoon.
Loke how it is, and tel me boldely."
   This knave gooth him up ful sturdily,
And at the chambre-dore, whyl that he stood,
He cryde and knokked as that he were wood,                250
"What! how! what do ye, maister Nicholay?
How may ye slepen al the longe day?"
   But al for noght; he herde nat a word.
An hole he fond, ful lowe upon a bord,
Ther as the cat was wont in for to crepe;                255
And at that hole he looked in ful depe,
And at the laste he hadde of him a sighte.
This Nicholas sat evere caping uprighte,
As he had kyked on the newe mone.
Adoun he gooth, and tolde his maister sone                260
In what array he saugh this ilke man.
   This carpenter to blessen him bigan,
And seyde, "Help us, Seinte Frideswyde!
A man woot litel what him shal bityde.
This man is falle, with his astromye,                    265
In som woodnesse or in som agonye:
I thoghte ay wel how that it sholde be!—
Men sholde nat knowe of Goddes privetee.
Ye, blessed be alwey a lewed man,
That noght but only his bileve can.                      270
So ferde another clerk with astromye:
He walked in the feeldes for to prye
Upon the sterres, what ther sholde bifalle,
Til he was in a marle-pit y-fall—
He saugh nat that. But yet, by Seint Thomas,             275
Me reweth sore of hende Nicholas.
He shal be rated of his studying,
If that I may, by Jesus, hevene king!
Get me a staf, that I may underspore,
Whyl that thou, Robin, hevest up the dore.               280

I saw a corpse being borne to church today
who just last Monday I saw going about his business.
Go up," he said then to his servant,                        245
"call at his door or knock with a stone.
See how matters stand, and tell me straight out."

    This servant went up sturdily,
and as he stood at the chamber door
he shouted and knocked like mad.                            250
"How now, what are you doing, Master Nicholas?
How can you sleep all day long?"
    But all for nothing; he heard not a word.
He found a hole low down on one of the boards
where the cat was accustomed to creep in,                   255
and he looked far in there;
at last he had a sight of him,
Nicholas sat there, continuously gaping up in the air,
as though he were gazing at the new moon.
The servant went down and soon told his master             260
in what state he had seen this man.

    The carpenter set to crossing himself
and said, "Help us, Saint Frideswide!
A man little knows what is going to happen to him.
This man has fallen, with his astronomy,                    265
into some madness or fit;
I always thought it would be this way!—
men shouldn't pry into the secret things of God.
Yea, ever blessed be an unschooled man
who knows nothing but his creed.                            270
Another clerk fared the same way with astronomy:
he walked in the fields to pry
into the stars and find out what was to occur
until he fell into a clay pit—
he didn't see that. And yet, by St. Thomas,                275
I sorely pity pleasant Nicholas.
He shall be scolded for his studying
if I can do it, by Jesus, heaven's king!
Get me a staff, so that I can pry underneath
while you, Robin, heave up the door.                        280

He shal out of his studying, as I gesse."
And to the chambre-dore he gan him dresse.
His knave was a strong carl for the nones,
And by the haspe he haf it up atones:
Into the floor the dore fil anon.                          285
This Nicholas sat ay as stile as stoon,
And ever caped upward into the eir.
This carpenter wende he were in despeir,
And hente him by the sholdres mightily,
And shook him harde, and cryde spitously.                 290
"What, Nicholay! what, how! what! loke adoun!
Awaak, and thenk on Cristes passioun!
I crouche thee from elves and fro wightes."
Therwith the night-spel seyde he anon-rightes
On foure halves of the hous aboute,                       295
And on the threshfold of the dore withoute:
    "Jesu Crist and seinte Benedight,
    Blesse this hous from every wikked wight;
    For nightes nerye the white *pater-noster*.
    Where wentestow, seynt Petres soster?"*             300
And atte laste this hende Nicholas
Gan for to syke sore, and seyde, "Allas,
Shal al the world be lost eftsones now?"
    This carpenter answerde, "What seystow?
What! thenk on God, as we don, men that swinke."          305
    This Nicholas answerde, "Fecche me drinke,
And after wol I speke in privetee
Of certeyn thing that toucheth me and thee;
I wol telle it non other man, certeyn."
    This carpenter goth doun and comth ageyn.            310
And broghte of mighty ale a large quart;
And whan that ech of hem had dronke his part,
This Nicholas his dore faste shette,
And doun the carpenter by him he sette.
    He seyde, "John, myn hoste lief and dere,            315
Thou shalt upon thy trouthe swere me here

He shall come out of his studying, I'll bet."
And he began to apply himself to the chamber door.
His servant was a strong fellow for the purpose,
and he heaved it up at once by the hasp:
the door then fell on the floor.                                    285
Nicholas continued to sit as still as stone
and kept gaping up in the air.
The carpenter thought that Nicholas was in a fit,
and seized him strongly by the shoulders
and shook him hard, crying roughly,                                290
"What! Nicholas, what! Look down!
Awake, and think on Christ's Passion!
I sign you with the cross against elves and evil
    creatures."
Then he immediately said the night charm
toward the four quarters of the house                             295
and on the threshold of the outside door:
    "Jesus Christ and Saint Benedict,
    bless this house against every wicket creature;
    let the white *pater-noster* defend us by night.
    Where did you go, Saint Peter's sister?"                      300
At last pleasant Nicholas
began to sigh sorely and said, "Alas,
shall all this world now be lost again?"
    The carpenter answered, "What are you saying?
How now! Think on God, as we do—we men
    who work."                                                    305
    Nicholas answered, "Bring me something to drink,
and afterwards I want to speak in private
of a certain thing that concerns you and me;
I won't tell it to another man, for sure."
    The carpenter went down and came back up,                     310
bringing a generous quart of strong ale;
and when each of them had drunk his share,
Nicholas shut his door tight
and sat the carpenter down beside him.
    He said, "John, my beloved and esteemed host,                 315
you shall swear to me here on your word of honor

That to no wight thou shalt this conseil wreye;
For it is Cristes conseil that I seye,
And if thou telle it man, thou are forlore,
For this vengeaunce thou shalt han therfore,                    320
That if thou wreye me, thou shal be wood."
"Nay, Crist forbede it, for his holy blood!"
Quod tho this sely man, "I nam no labbe;
Ne, though I seye, I nam nat lief to gabbe.
Sey what thou wolt, I shal it nevere telle                    325
To child ne wyf, by Him that harwed helle."
     "Now John," quod Nicholas, "I wol nat lye;
I have y-founde in myn astrologye,
As I have loked in the mone bright,
That now a Monday next, at quarter night,                    330
Shal falle a reyn, and that so wilde and wood,
That half so greet was never Noës flood.
This world," he seyde, "in lasse than an hour
Shal al be dreynt, so hidous is the shour;
Thus shal mankynde drenche, and lese hir lyf."                    335
     This carpenter answerde, "Allas, my wyf!
And shal she drenche? allas, myn Alisoun!"
For sorwe of this he fil almost adoun,
And seyde, "Is ther no remedie in this cas?"
     "Why, yis, for Gode," quod hende Nicholas,                    340
"If thou wok werken after lore and reed—
Thou mayst nat werken after thyn owene heed;
For thus seith Salomon, that was ful trewe,
'Werk al by conseil, and thou shalt nat rewe.'
And if thou werken wolt by good conseil,                    345
I undertake, withouten mast and seyl,
Yet shal I saven hir and thee and me.
Hastow nat herd how saved was Noë,
Whan that oure Lord hadde warned him biforn
That al the world with water sholde be lorn?"                    350
     "Yis," quod this carpenter, "ful yore ago."
     "Hastow nat herd," quod Nicholas, "also

that you will not betray this secret to any creature;
for it is Christ's secret that I am going to utter,                    *Secrecy*
and if you tell it to anyone, you are lost,
because for doing so you shall suffer this vengeance:                    320
if you betray me, you shall go mad."
"No, Christ forbid it for the sake of his holy blood!"
said this simple man, "I am no blabber;
no, though I say it myself, I don't like to gossip.
Say what you will, I shall never tell it                    325
to child or wife, by Him who harrowed hell."
    "Now, John," said Nicholas, "I won't lie;
I have discovered in my astrology,
as I was looking at the bright moon,
that on Monday next, when a quarter of the night
    is still                    330
to go, there shall fall a rain, so wild and furious
that Noah's flood was never half so great.
In less than an hour," he said, "this world
shall be drowned, so hideous will be the downpour;
thus all mankind shall drown and lose their lives."                    335
    The carpenter answered, "Alas, my wife!
Shall she drown? Alas, my Alison!"
For his sorrow at this he almost collapsed,
and said, "Is there no remedy in this matter?"
    "Why, yes, indeed, by God," said pleasant Nicholas,                    340
"if you will act according to learning and advice—
you may not act according to your own idea;
for thus says Solomon, who was very truthful,
'Do everything according to advice and you will not
    be sorry.'
And if you will act on good advice,                    345
I promise that, without mast or sail,
I shall yet save her and you and myself.
Haven't you heard how Noah was saved
when our Lord had forewarned him
that all the world should be lost by water?"                    350
    "Certainly," said the carpenter, "long ago."
    "Haven't you heard also," said Nicholas,

The sorwe of Noë with his felaweshipe,
Er that he mighte gete his wyf to shipe?*
Him hadde be lever, I dar wel undertake,          355
At thilke tyme, than alle hise wetheres blake
That she hadde had a ship hirself allone.
And therfore, wostou what is best to done?
This asketh haste, and of an hastif thing
Men may nat preche or maken tarying.          360

    "Anon go gete us faste into this in
A kneding-trogh or elles a kimelin
For ech of us, but loke that they be large,
In whiche we mowe swimme as in a barge,
And han ther-inne vitaille suffisant          365
But for a day—fy on the remenant!
The water shal aslake and goon away
Aboute pryme upon the nexte day.

    "But Robin may nat wite of this, thy knave,
Ne eek thy mayde Gille I may nat save;          370
Axe nat why, for though thou aske me,
I wol nat tellen Goddes privetee.
Suffiseth thee, but if thy wittes madde,
To han as greet a grace as Noë hadde.
Thy wyf shal I wel saven, out of doute.          375
Go now thy wey, and speed thee heer-aboute.

    "But whan thou hast, for hir and thee and me,
Y-geten us thise kneding-tubbes three,
Thanne shaltow hange hem in the roof ful hye,
That no man of oure purveyaunce spye.          380
And whan thou thus hast doon as I have seyd,
And hast our vitaille faire in hem y-leyd,
And eek an ax to smyte the corde atwo
When that the water comth, that we may go,
And broke an hole an heigh upon the gable          385
Unto the gardin-ward, over the stable,
That we may frely passen forth our way
Whan that the grete shour is goon away—
Than shaltow swimme as myrie, I undertake,
As doth the whyte doke aftir hir drake.          390

"of the anxiety of Noah and his companions
until he could get his wife on board?
I'll bet that that time he would rather have          355
had her have a ship to herself
than keep all his fine black wethers.
And do you know what's best to do for all this?
This requires haste, and about an urgent matter
you mayn't preach or make delay.          360

"Go promptly and bring right into this house
a kneading trough, or else a shallow tub,
for each of us, but be sure they are large ones,
in which we can float as in a ship,
and have in them victuals enough          365
for a day only—fie on the rest!
The water shall diminish and go away
about nine in the morning the next day.

"But Robin, your servant, may not know of this,
and I mayn't save Jill, your maid, either;          370
don't ask why, for even if you do,
I won't reveal God's private affairs.
It is enough for you, unless you are mad,
to have as great grace as Noah had.
I shall indeed save your wife, beyond a doubt.          375
Now go your way, and hurry about our business.

"But when, for her and yourself and me, you have
got us these three kneading tubs,
then you are to hang them high up in the rafters,
so that no one will spy out our preparations.          380
And when you've done as I have said,
and have stowed our victuals in them safely,
and an ax, too, to cut the rope in two
when the water comes, so that we may float,
and when you've broken a hole high up on the gable          385
toward the garden and over the stable,
so that we can get out freely on our way
when the great rain is over—
then you'll float as merrily, I promise,
as the white duck does after her drake.          390

Than wol I clepe, 'how, Alison! how, John!
Be myrie, for the flood wol passe anon.'
And thou wolt seyn, 'Hayl, master Nicholay!
Good morwe, I se thee wel, for it is day!'
And thanne shul we be lordes al oure lyf          395
Of al the world, as Noë and his wyf.

"But of o thyng I warne thee ful right:
Be wel avysed on that ilke night
That we ben entred into shippes bord
That noon of us ne speke nat a word,            400
Ne clepe, ne crye, but been in his preyere,
For it is Goddes owne heste dere.

"Thy wyf and thou mote hange fer a-twinne,
For that bitwixe yow shal be no sinne—
Namore in looking than ther shal in dede.        405
This ordinance is seyd; go, God thee spede.
Tomorwe at night, whan men ben alle aslepe,
Into oure kneding-tubbes wol we crepe,
And sitten ther, abyding Goddes grace.
Go now thy wey, I have no lenger space          410
To make of this no lenger sermoning.
Men seyn thus, 'send the wyse, and sey nothing';
Thou art so wys it nedeth thee nat teche:
Go, save our lyf, and that I thee biseche."

This sely carpenter goth forth his wey.          415
Ful ofte he seide "Allas" and "Weylawey,"
And to his wyf he tolde his privetee;
And she was war, and knew it bet than he,
What al this queynte cast was for to seye.
But nathelees she ferde as she wolde deye,        420
And seyde, "Allas! go forth thy wey anon,
Help us to scape, or we been dede echon.
I am thy trewe verray wedded wyf:
Go, dere spouse, and help to save oure lyf."

Lo! which a greet thyng is affeccioun:          425
Men may dyen of imaginacioun,
So depe may impressioun be take.
This sely carpenter biginneth quake;

Then I'll call out, 'How now, Alison! How now, John!
Cheer up; the flood will go away soon,'
and you will say, 'Hail, Master Nicholas!
Good morning, I see you well, it's light.'
And then we shall be lords for all our lives                    395
of all the world, like Noah and his wife.

"But I caution you about one thing for sure:
be well forewarned that on that same night
when we have gone on shipboard,
none of us may speak a word,                                   400
or call, or cry out, but be in prayer,
for it is God's own precious command.

"Your wife and you must hang far apart
so that there shall be no sin between you,     *plan*
any more in looking than in deed.                              405
I've described our arrangement; go, Godspeed.
Tomorrow night, when everyone is asleep,
we'll creep into our kneading tubs
and sit there, awaiting God's grace.
Now go on your way, I have no more time                        410
to make a longer sermon of this.
People speak thus, 'Send the wise and say nothing';
you are so wise that there is no need to teach you:
go, save our lives, I beseech you."

    The foolish carpenter went his way.                        415
Often he said, "Alas" and "Alack,"
and he told his secret to his wife;      *master-*
she was aware of it, and knew better than he     *plan*
what all this elaborate contrivance amounted to.
Nevertheless, she behaved as though she would die,            420
and said, "Alas! Go your way immediately,
help us to escape, or we are lost, each one of us.
I am your faithful, true, wedded wife:   *ironic*
go, dear spouse, and help to save our lives."

    Look what a great thing emotion is!                        425
one may die by force of imagining things,
so deeply may a notion be imprinted.
This foolish carpenter began to shake;

Him thinketh verraily that he may see
Noës flood come walwing as the see                    430
To drenchen Alisoun, his hony dere.
He wepeth, weyleth, maketh sory chere;
He syketh with ful many a sory swogh;
He gooth and geteth him a kneding-trogh,
And after that a tubbe and a kimelin,                 435
And prively he sente hem to his in,
And heng hem in the roof in privetee.
His owne hand he made laddres three
To climben by the ronges and the stalkes
Unto the tubbes hanginge in the balkes,               440
And hem vitailled, bothe trogh and tubbe,
With breed and chese, and good ale in a jubbe,
Suffysinge right ynogh as for a day.
But er that he hadde maad al this array.
He sente his knave, and eek his wenche also,          445
Upon his nede to London for to go.
And on the Monday whan it drow to night,
He shette his dore withouten candel-light,
And dressed alle thing as it sholde be.
And shortly, up they clomben alle three;              450
They sitten stille wel a furlong wey.
    "Now, *pater-noster,** clom," seyde Nicholay,
And "Clom," quod John, and "Clom," seyde Alisoun.
This carpenter seyde his devocioun,
And stille he sit and biddeth his preyere,            455
Awaytinge on the reyn, if he it here.
    The dede sleep, for wery bisinesse,
Fil on this carpenter right, as I gesse,
Aboute corfew-tyme,* or litel more;
For travail of his goost he groneth sore,             460
And eft he routeth, for his heed mislay.
Doun of the laddre stalketh Nicholay,
And Alisoun ful softe adoun she spedde;
Withouten wordes mo they goon to bedde
Ther as the carpenter is wont to lye.                 465
Ther was the revel and the melodye,

he thinks in truth that he can see
Noah's flood come surging like the sea                      430
to drown Alison, his honey-dear.
He weeps, wails, looks mournful;
he sighs with many a sorry gust;
he went and got himself a kneading trough,
and after that two tubs,                                    435
and secretly he sent them to his home
and hung them under the roof in privacy.
With his own hands he made three ladders
on which they might climb by the rungs and uprights
to the tubs hanging in the rafters,                         440
and victualed both trough and tub
with bread and cheese and good ale in a jug,
quite sufficient for a day.
But before he installed all this array,
he sent his manservant, and also the maid,                  445
to go to London on an errand for him.
On Monday, when night drew on,
he shut his door without lighting any candles
and arranged everything as it was supposed to be.
And, shortly, they all three climbed up;                    450
they sat still for the time it takes to go a furlong.
  "Now, *pater-noster,* hush!" said Nicholas,
and "Hush," said John, and "Hush," said Alison.
The carpenter recited his devotions,
and sat still, offering his prayers                         455
and waiting to see whether he might hear the rain.
  Wearied by his own diligence, the carpenter
fell into a dead sleep—as I judge, just
about curfew time, or a little later.
He groaned painfully for the affliction of his spirit,      460
and then he snored, for his head lay uncomfortably.
Nicholas crept down from the ladder
and Alison hurried down very softly;
without more words they went to bed
where the carpenter was wont to lie.                        465
There was the revel and the harmony,

And thus lyth Alison and Nicholas
In bisinesse of mirthe and of solas
Til that the belle of Laudes* gan to ringe
And freres in the chauncel gonne singe.          470
   This parissh clerk, this amorous Absolon,
That is for love alwey so wo-bigon,
Upon the Monday was at Oseneye,
With companye him to disporte and pleye,
And axed upon cas a cloisterer          475
Ful prively after John the carpenter;
And he drough him apart out of the chirche,
And seyde, "I noot, I saugh him here nat wirche
Sin Saterday; I trow that he be went
For timber ther oure abbot hath him sent,          480
For he is wont for timber for to go
And dwellen at the grange a day or two—
Or elles he is at his hous, certeyn;
Where that he be I can nat sothly seyn."
   This Absolon ful joly was and light,          485
And thoghte, "Now is tyme to wake al night,
For sikirly I saugh him nat stiringe
Aboute his dore sin day bigan to springe.
So moot I thryve, I shal, at cokkes crowe,*
Ful prively knokken at his windowe          490
That stant ful lowe upon his boures wal.
To Alison now wol I tellen al
My love-longing, for yet I shal nat misse
That at the leste wey I shal hir kisse.
Som maner confort shal I have, parfay.          495
My mouth hath icched al this longe day;
That is a signe of kissing atte leeste.
Al night me mette eek I was at a feeste.
Therfor I wol go slepe an houre or tweye,
And al the night thanne wol I wake and pleye."          500
   Whan that the firste cok hath crowe, anon
Up rist this joly lover Absolon,
And him arrayeth gay, at point-devys.

and thus lay Alison and Nicholas
in diligence of mirth and pleasure *slept together*
until the bell of Lauds began to ring
and friars began to sing in the chancel.                    470

   The parish clerk, this amorous Absalom,
who was always so woebegone for love,
was at Osney on Monday
to have a good time with some clerical friends;
he chanced to ask a member of the order                     475
very secretly about John the carpenter;
the man drew him apart, out of the church,
and said, "I don't know, I haven't seen him doing
      anything
here since Saturday; I imagine that he went
for timber where our abbot sent him,                        480
for he is accustomed to go for timber
and stay at the farm for a day or two;
or else he's certainly at home;
I cannot truthfully say where he is."

   This Absalom grew frolicsome and lighthearted,           485
and thought, "Now is the time to stay up all night,
for surely I haven't seen him stirring
about his door since dawn.
As I may thrive, at cockcrow I shall
knock very secretly at the window                           490
that is quite low in the wall of his bedchamber.
Now I'll tell Alison all
my love-sickness, for still it won't fail    *his*
at the very least that I'll kiss her.        *plan*
I shall have some kind of comfort, for sure.               495
My mouth has itched all this livelong day;
that is a sign of kissing, at least.
Besides, I dreamed all night that I was at a feast.
Therefore, I'll go sleep for an hour or two,
and then I'll stay up and amuse myself all night."         500
   When the first cock had crowed, then
rose up this lusty lover Absalom,            *cock?!*
and dressed himself handsomely to perfection.

But first he cheweth greyn and lycorys,
To smellen swete, er he hadde kembd his heer. 505
Under his tonge a trewe-love he beer,
For therby wende he to ben gracious.
He rometh to the carpenteres hous,
And stille he stant under the shot-windowe—
Unto his brest it raughte, it was so lowe— 510
And softe he cougheth with a semi-soun.
"What do ye, hony-comb, swete Alisoun,
My faire brid, my swete cinamome?
Awaketh, lemman myn, and speketh to me.
Wel litel thenken ye upon my wo, 515
That for your love I swete ther I go.
No wonder is thogh that I swelte and swete:
I moorne as doth a lamb after the tete.
Ywis, lemman, I have swich love-longinge
That lyk a turtel trewe is my moorninge; 520
I may nat ete na more than a mayde."
  "Go fro the window, Jakke fool," she sayde.
"As help me, God, it wol nat be 'com-pa-me.'
I love another—and elles I were to blame—
Wel bet than thee, by Jesu, Absolon. 525
Go forth thy wey or I wol caste a ston,
And lat me slepe, a twenty devel wey!"
  "Allas," quod Absolon, "and weylawey,
That trewe love was ever so yvel biset.
Thanne kisse me, sin it may be no bet, 530
For Jesus love and for the love of me."
  "Wiltow thanne go thy wey therwith?" quod she.
  "Ye, certes, lemman," quod this Absolon.
  "Thanne make thee redy," quod she, "I come anon."
And unto Nicholas she seyde stille, 535
"Now hust, and thou shalt laughen al thy fille."
  This Absolon doun sette him on his knees,
And seyde, "I am a lord at alle degrees,
For after this I hope ther cometh more.
Lemman, thy grace, and swete brid, thyn ore!" 540
  The window she undooth, and that in haste.

But first he chewed cardamon and licorice,
in order to smell sweet, before he combed his hair.       505
He carried a sprig of clover under his tongue,
for by its means he expected to be pleasing.
He strolled to the carpenter's house
and stood quietly under the shuttered window—
it reached only to his chest, it was so low—             510
and he coughed softly with a small sound.
"What do you, honeycomb, sweet Alison?
My fair bird, sweet cinnamon,
awake, my sweetheart, and speak to me.
Little do you think of my woe, which is                   515
so great that I sweat upon the ground as I walk.
It is no wonder though I melt and sweat:
I yearn as does the lamb for the teat.
Indeed, sweetheart, I have such love-sickness
that my mourning is like that of the faithful turtledove;  520
I may not eat any more than a girl."
    "Go away from the window, Jack-fool," she said.
"So help me God, it won't be 'come-kiss-me.'
By Jesus, Absalom, I love another a lot better
than you, and otherwise I'd be to blame.                 525
Go your way or I'll throw a stone,
and let me sleep, in the name of twenty devils!"
    "Alas," said Absalom, "and alack
that ever true love was so ill-used.
Kiss me, then—since it may be no better—                 530
for Jesus's love and love of me."
    "Will you go your way then?" she said.
    "Yes, certainly, sweetheart," said Absalom.
    "Then get ready," she said, "I'm coming right away."
And she said quietly to Nicholas,                        535
"Now keep quiet, and you shall laugh your fill."
    Absalom got down on his knees,
and said, "I am a lord in every way,
for after this I expect more will be coming.
Your favor, beloved; and sweet bird, your mercy!"        540
    She undid the window quickly.

"Have do," quod she, "com of and speed thee faste,
Lest that our neighebores thee espye."
   This Absolon gan wype his mouth ful drye:
Derk was the night as pich or as the cole,     545
And at the window out she putte hir hole,
And Absolon, him fil no bet ne wers,
But with his mouth he kiste hir naked ers,
Ful savourly, er he was war of this.
   Abak he sterte, and thoghte it was amis,     550
For wel he wiste a womman hath no berd:
He felte a thing al rough and long y-herd,
And seyde, "Fy! allas! what have I do?"
   "Tehee," quod she, and clapte the window to;
And Absolon goth forth a sory pas.     555
   "A berd, a berd!" quod hende Nicholas,
"By Goddes corpus, this goth faire and weel."
   This sely Absolon herde every deel,
And on his lippe he gan for anger byte,
And to himself he seyde, "I shal thee quyte!"     560
   Who rubbeth now, who froteth now his lippes
With dust, with sond, with straw, with clooth,
   with chippes,
But Absolon, that seith ful ofte, "Allas"?
"My soule bitake I unto Sathanas,
But me were levere than al this toun," quod he,     565
"Of this despyt awroken for to be.
Allas," quod he "allas, I ne hadde y-bleynt!"
His hote love was cold and al y-queynt,
For fro that tyme that he had kiste hir ers
Of paramours he sette nat a kers,     570
For he was heled of his maladye.
Ful ofte paramours he gan deffye,
And weep as dooth a child that is y-bete.
A softe paas he wente over the strete
Until a smith men cleped daun Gerveys,     575
That in his forge smithed plough-harneys:
He sharpeth shaar and cultour bisily.

"Finish up," she said, "come on and do it quickly,
so that our neighbors won't see you."

Absalom wiped his mouth very dry;
the night was dark as pitch or coal,                             545
and she stuck her hole out the window,
and Absalom fared neither better nor worse
than with his mouth to kiss her naked arse
with much relish, before he knew what he was doing.

He started back and thought that something
    was wrong,                                 550
for he well knew that a woman doesn't have a beard;
he felt something that was all rough and long haired,
and said, "Fie, alas, what have I done?"

"Tee-hee," she said, and slammed the window shut;
and Absalom went forth with sorry step.                         555

"A beard, a beard," said pleasant Nicholas,
"by God's body, this goes nicely."

The foolish Absalom heard it all,
and he bit his lip for anger
and said to himself, "I'll pay you back!"                        560

Who now rubs, who wipes his lips
with dust, with sand, with straw, with cloth,
    with chips,
but Absalom; who says "Alas" again and again?
"I'll give my soul to Satan,
if I wouldn't rather be revenged for this insult                 565
than have all this town," he said.

"Alas," he said, "alas, that I didn't turn aside!"
His hot love had grown cold and was all quenched,
for from the time that he had kissed her arse,
he didn't care a jot for woman's love,
for he was cured of his love-sickness.                           570
He renounced love over and over,
and wept like a child that is beaten.
He crossed the street softly
to a smith called Master Gervase,                               575
who was shaping plowing equipment in his forge:
he was busily sharpening plowshares and colters.

This Absolon knokketh al esily,
And seyde, "Undo, Gerveys, and that anon."
"What, who artow?" "It am I, Absolon."                                580
"What, Absolon! for Cristes swete tree!
Why ryse ye so rathe? Ey, *benedicite,*
What eyleth yow? som gay gerl, God it woot,
Hath broght yow thus upon the viritoot:
By Seynte Note, yet woot wel what I mene."                            585
    This Absolon ne roghte nat a bene
Of al his pley. No word agayn he yaf:
He hadde more tow on his distaf
Than Gerveys knew, and seyde, "Freend so dere,
That hote cultour* in the chimenee here,                              590
As lene it me, I have therwith to done,
And I wol bringe it thee agayn ful sone."
    Gerveys answerde, "Certes, were it gold,
Or in a poke nobles alle untold,
Thou sholdest have, as I am trewe smith.                              595
Ey, Cristes foo, what wol ye do therwith?"
    "Therof," quod Absolon, "be as be may;
I shal wel telle it thee to-morwe day,"
And caughte the cultour by the colde stele.
Ful softe out at the dore he gan to stele,                            600
And wente unto the carpenteres wal:
He cougheth first, and knokketh therewithal
Upon the windowe, right as he dide er.
    This Alison answerde, "Who is there
That knokketh so? I warante it a theef."                              605
    "Why, nay," quod he, "God woot, my swete leef,
I am thyn Absolon, my dereling.
Of gold," quod he, "I have thee broght a ring—
My moder yaf it me, so God me save;
Ful fyn it is and thereto wel y-grave;                                610
This wol I yeve thee if thou me kisse."
    This Nicholas was risen for to pisse,
And thoughte he wolde amenden al the jape:
He sholde kisse his ers er that he scape.

Absalom knocked quietly
and said, "Open up, Gervase, right away."
    "What, who are you?" "It's me, Absalom."          580
"How now, Absalom! Christ's cross!
Why do you rise so early, eh, bless us!
What's wrong with you? Some pretty girl, God knows,
has got you on the prowl this way:
by Saint Neot, you know well what I mean."          585
    Absalom didn't care a bean
for all his joking. He replied not a word:
he had more wool on his distaff
than Gervase knew, and said, "Dear friend,
that hot colter in the chimney there—          590
lend it to me, I have something I want to do with it
and I'll return it to you very soon."
    Gervase answered, "Certainly, if it were gold
or uncounted gold nobles in a bag,
you should have it, as I am an honest smith;          595
eh, the devil, what will you do with it?"
    "Concerning that," said Absalom, "let it be as
        it may;
I'll tell you indeed tomorrow,"
and he grabbed the colter by its cool handle.
He stole out softly at the door          600
and walked to the carpenter's wall:
first he coughed and then knocked
on the window, just as he had done before.
    Alison answered, "Who's there
knocking so hard? It's a thief, I warrant."          605
    "Why, no," he said, "God knows, sweet love,
I am your Absalom, my darling.
I have brought you a gold ring," he said—
"my mother gave it to me, God save me;
it's very fine, and well engraved, too;          610
I'll give it to you if you'll kiss me."
    Nicholas had risen to urinate,
and thought he would improve on the joke:
Absalom should kiss his arse before escaping.

And up the windowe dide he hastily,                    615
And out his ers he putteth prively
Over the buttok to the haunche-bon;
And therwith spak this clerk, this Absolon,
"Spek, swete brid, I noot nat wher thou art."
    This Nicholas anon leet flee a fart,              620
As greet as it had been a thonder-dent,
That with the strook he was almost y-blent;
And he was redy with his iren hoot,
And Nicholas amidde the ers he smoot:
Of gooth the skin an hande-brede aboute;              625
The hote cultour brende so his toute
That for the smert he wende for to dye.
As he were wood for wo he gan to crye,
"Help! water! water! help, for Goddes herte!"
    This carpenter out of his slomber sterte,        630
And herde oon cryen "Water!" as he were wood,
And thoughte, "Allas, now comth Nowélis flood!"
He sit him up withouten wordes mo,
And with his ax he smoot the corde a-two,
And doun goth al; he fond neither to selle           635
Ne breed ne ale, til he cam to the celle
Upon the floor; and ther aswowne he lay.
    Up sterte hire Alison, and Nicholay,
And cryden "Out" and "Harrow" in the strete.
The neighebores, bothe smale and grete,              640
In ronnen, for to gauren on this man,
That yet aswowne lay bothe pale and wan,
For with the fal he brosten hadde his arm;
But stonde he moste unto his owne harm,
For whan he spak he was anon bore doun               645
With hende Nicholas and Alisoun:
They tolden every man that he was wood—
He was agast so of "Nowélis flood,"
Thurgh fantasye, that of his vanitee
He hadde y-boght him kneding-tubbes three,           650
And hadde hem hanged in the roof above;
And that he preyed hem, for Goddes love,

He raised the window quickly                                    615
and quietly stuck his arse out
beyond the buttocks, as far back as the thigh bone;
then this clerk Absalom said,
Speak, sweet bird, I don't know where you are."
    Nicholas then let fly a fart                                620
as strong as a thunderclap,
so that Absalom was almost blinded with its force;
but he was ready with his hot iron
and struck Nicholas in the middle of his arse:
off went the skin a handsbreadth wide;                          625
the hot colter burned his buttocks so badly
that he thought he would die with the pain.
He began to cry out as if he were mad,
"Help! Water! Water! Help, for God's heart!"
    The carpenter started out of his slumber                    630
and heard someone crying "Water!" like mad,
and he thought, "Alas, now Noel's flood is coming!"
He sat up without another word
and hacked the rope in two with his ax,
and down went all; he didn't find time to sell                 635
either bread or ale before he hit the flooring
at ground level; and there he lay in a faint.
    Alison and Nicholas jumped up
and cried "Alas" and "Help" in the street.
The neighbors high and low                                      640
ran in to gape at this man
who still lay in a faint, pale and wan,
for he had broken his arm with the fall;
but he had to take the blame for his own mishap,
for when he spoke he was soon put down                          645
by pleasant Nicholas and Alison:
they told everyone that he was mad—
he was so afraid of "Noel's flood"
through hallucination that in his folly
he had bought himself three kneading tubs                       650
and had hanged them up under the roof;
and that he had asked them, for God's love,

To sitten in the roof, *par compaignye.*
  The folk gan laughen at his fantasye.
Into the roof they kyken and they cape,       655
And turned al his harm unto a jape,
For what so that this carpenter answerde,
It was for noght: no man his reson herde;
With othes grete he was so sworn adoun,
That he was holden wood in al the toun,      660
For every clerk anon-right heeld with other:
They seyde "The man is wood, my leve brother";
And every wight gan laughen of this stryf.
  Thus swyved was the carpenteres wyf,
For al his keping and his jalousye;      665
And Absolon hath kist hir nether yë;
And Nicholas is scalded in the toute:
This tale is doon, and God save al the route!

to sit under the roof for in good company.

    The people set to laughing at his delusion.

They peered and gaped up at the roof     655

and turned all his misfortune into a joke,

for whatever the carpenter said in answer,

it did no good: no one listened to his explanation;

he was cursed with strong oaths and

was considered mad through all the town,     660

for every clerk immediately stuck with the

     other's story.

They said, "The man is mad, dear brother":

and everyone laughed at this fuss.

    Thus was the carpenter's wife screwed,

in spite of all his guarding and jealousy;     665

and Absalom has kissed her lower eye;

and Nicholas is scalded on the bum:

this tale is done, and God save all the company!

*reveals all facts* [handwritten marginal note]

# THE REEVE'S TALE

# INTRODUCTION

✣

THE REEVE'S TALE, newly edited and translated for this second edition, follows naturally after "The Miller's Tale." Not only is it, like the one before it, a fabliau (a short comic tale, often about low-life people involved in sexual and scatological shenanigans), but it picks up on the quarrel that we have seen developing between the Miller and the Reeve. That quarrel is anticipated by the age, physical build, degree of hairiness, weaponry, and position on the pilgrimage of the two tellers as described in the General Prologue. (For the Miller see lines 547–68; for the Reeve see lines 589–624.) That the two don't much like each other would not have surprised a medieval audience, which would have understood that one of a reeve's duties on a medieval manor would have been to supervise the work and financial dealings of the mill. No greedy miller would have welcomed a suspicious reeve poking his own greedy nose into his profits and dishonest winnings.

The Reeve's own acerbic response to the lighthearted "Miller's Tale," however, is the result of his own angry, jealous, choleric, and paranoid character. He takes personal offense at the fact that "The Miller's Tale" makes fun of old John, a carpenter—though of course it also makes fun of others in the tale. Remembering that he himself had once followed the profession of carpenter, Oswald the Reeve feels honor bound to tell a tale in retribution. His tale makes fun of a proud miller named Symkyn, whose very description appears to be based in large measure on the Miller who is on the pilgrimage. Just as the old carpenter, John, is left a physically damaged and cuckolded laughingstock at the end of

"The Miller's Tale," so is Symkyn the miller left at the end of "The Reeve's Tale."

The basic plot of "The Reeve's Tale" itself was told and retold in several languages, among them French, Middle Dutch, and Italian. Chaucer probably knew several of these other versions of the tale, but he adapted them to his own narrative needs. In the French tale, for example, the parts of Chaucer's Alan and John are played by two poor parsons in a time of famine. Having decided to become bakers in these hard times to make ends meet, they borrow a nag to take some borrowed wheat to a miller to be ground. In both the Middle Dutch and the Italian tales the man with a pretty wife and daughter is not a miller at all. In none of these tales is the host's wife said to be unrealistically proud of her highborn status as the daughter of the local priest (and, presumably, a nun, since she had been raised in a nunnery). In none of the other versions do we see or hear about the father of the wife (grandfather of the young daughter).

Indeed, the whole theme of pride in one's social status, one's intellectual superiority, and one's reputation among fellow students back at college is Chaucer's own addition to the tale. The local English setting in Cambridge is also new in Chaucer, as is the specific location of the mill at Trumpington, a real place a couple of hours' walk from downtown Cambridge, both in Chaucer's time and today. Also original in Chaucer's version is that the two students speak in a dialect from the north of England: *swa* in stead of *so, til and fra* instead of *to and fro,* and so on. For this tale, more than most others, the nasty tone of the tale reflects as badly on the character of the teller as it does on any of the characters in the tale.

## NOTES

### The Reeve's Prologue

**Depeford** (line 52). A town about five miles from London on the usual road to Canterbury.

**Grenewych** (53). A town about six miles from London. Chaucer's statement that many a rascal lives in Greenwich may well be a bit of ironical self-mockery, since he himself is known to have lived in Greenwich for a time.

## The Reeve's Tale

**Sheffeld** (13). A town in Yorkshire still known for its fine cutlery.

**sokene** (67). A monopoly. John and Alan have no choice about where to have their grain ground since they must take it to Symkyn. For his part, Symkyn has no particular reason to be nice to them, since their continued business is assured.

**Soler Halle** (70). An earlier name for King's Hall, in Cambridge.

**Strother** (94). A town in the north of England. It is probably a fictional name since no records of a town by that name have been found.

**wolf, mare** (135). The reference is to a story about a mare who tricked a wolf into examining her hoof, and then kicked him with it.

**fen** (160). A low-lying marshy area, possibly referring to Lingley Fen below Trumpington.

**toun** (216). Presumably the nearby village of Trumpington, not Cambridge.

**pale, nat reed** (230). The miller's paleness was a sign of advanced drunkenness, well past the rosy-cheeked flush to be seen in earlier stages of inebriation.

**two furlong** (246). A furlong, originally the length of a furrow in a ten-acre square plot of ground, was about an eighth of a mile long.

**complyn** (251). The complin is the last of the liturgical songtimes of the day for clergymen.

**furlong wey or two** (279). The time it would take to walk, or more likely plow, one or two furrows (see note to line 246 above), probably a half-hour or more.

**thridde cok** (313). The third cock-a-doodle-do would have come an hour or so before dawn.

**Bromeholm** (366). Town in Norfolk with a well-known Christian shrine.

*In manus tuas* (367). Latin for "Into your hands," the opening phase of a dying person's prayer to God: "Into your hands I commend my spirit." In this phrase and the reference to Bromeholm, the miller's wife is presumably spouting phrases she learned from her priestly father or from the nuns who raised her.

# THE REVE'S TALE

Whan folk hadde laughen at this nyce cas
Of Absolon and hende Nicholas,
Diverse folk diversely they seyde,
But for the moore part they loughe and pleyde.
Ne at this tale I saugh no man hym greve,          5
But it were oonly Osewold the Reve.
By cause he was of carpenteris craft
A litel ire is in his herte ylaft.
He gan to grucche, and blamed it a lite.
"So theek," quod he, "ful wel koude I thee quite    10
With bleryng of a proud milleres ye,
If that me liste speke of ribaudye.
But ik am oold, me list not pley for age.
Gras tyme is doon, my fodder is now forage.
This white top writeth myne olde yeris.            15
Myn herte is also mowled as myne heris,
But if I fare as dooth an open-ers.
That ilke fruyt is ever lenger the wers:
Til it be roten in mullok or in stree.
We olde men, I drede, so fare we.                  20
Til we be roten, kan we nat be rype.
We hoppen alwey whil the world wol pype,
For in oure wyl ther stiketh evere a nayl,
To have an hoor heed and a grene tayl,
As hath a leek. For thogh oure myght be goon,      25
Oure wyl desireth folie evere in oon.

# THE REEVE'S TALE

*Prologue to the Reeve's Tale*

When people had had a good laugh at this
    foolish situation
of Absalom and courteous Nicholas,
various listeners said various things,
but most of them just laughed and enjoyed it.
I saw no man show any grief at the tale                          5
except maybe Oswald the Reeve.
Because he had once followed the craft of carpenter,
a little annoyance lingered in his heart.
He began to grumble and find fault with the tale.

  "I swear," said he, "I could easily repay you              10
with a tale about how a proud miller was tricked,
if I wanted to talk in ribald terms.
But I'm too old to play around with such things.
My green-grass grazing is over, and now I just eat
    chopped fodder.
This white hair on my head reveals my many years,      15
and my heart is as moldy as my hair is,
except that I am more like the medlar fruit—
that fruit just grows worse and worse
until it is all rotted up in a pile of rubbish or straw.
I fear that we old men are just like that.                        20
We never ripen until we are rotten.
We limp along while the world prances merrily on.
Our will always keeps a sharp nail of desire.
We have a white head but a green tail,
just like a scallion. Though our sexual potency is gone,   25
we still make fools of ourselves whenever we can.

For whan we may nat doon, than wol we speke.
Yet in oure asshen olde is fyr y-reke.
Foure gleedes han we, which I shal devyse:
Avauntyng, liyng, anger, coveitise.                    30
Thise foure sparkles longen unto eelde.
Oure olde lemes mowe wel been unweelde,
But wyl ne shal nat faillen, that is sooth.
And yet ik have alwey a coltes tooth,
As many a yeer as it is passed henne                   35
Syn that my tappe of lif bigan to renne.
For sikerly, whan I was bore, anon,
deeth drough the tappe of lyf and leet it gon.
And ever sithe hath so the tappe y-ronne
Til that almoost al empty is the tonne.                40
The streem of lyf now droppeth on the chymbe.
The sely tonge may wel rynge and chymbe
Of wrecchednesse that passed is ful yoore.
With olde folk, save dotage, is namoore."

    Whan that oure Hoost hadde herd this sermonyng,    45
He gan to speke as lordly as a kyng.
He seide, "What amounteth al this wit?
What? Shul we speke alday of hooly writ?
The devel made a reve for to preche,
Or of a soutere a shipman or a leche.                  50
Sey forth thy tale, and tarie nat the tyme
Lo Depeford!* and it is half-wey pryme.
Lo Grenewych,* ther many a shrewe is inne!
It were al tyme thy tale to bigynne."

    "Now, sires," quod this Osewold the Reve,          55
"I pray yow alle that ye nat yow greve,

When we can no longer do it, we still talk about it.
Even so, in our dead ashes you can still rake up
    a little fire!
Let me tell you about the four coals we old
    men have—
boasting, fibbing, anger, and greed.                         30
These four sparks last into old age.
These old limbs of ours may be feeble,
but our strong willfulness never fails us, and that's
    the truth.
I still have the frisky desires of a colt,
even though many a year has passed                           35
since the tap of my life was opened up.
To tell the truth, the day I was born a long time ago,
death opened up the spigot of my life and left it on.
And ever since that day, that old tap has just run
    and run
until now the barrel is practically empty.                   40
The stream of my life now drops almost to the bottom
    of the barrel.
My silly old tongue just clatters on
about the wretchedness of what lies ahead for me.
With us old guys, there is nothing left but our dotage."
    After our Host had heard this silly sermon,               45
he started to talk as lordly as a king.
He said, "What's the point of all this wit?
What? Are we going to gab on all day about
    holy writs?
The devil turned a reeve into a preacher,
just as if he turned a shoemaker into a sailor or
    a doctor.                                                 50
Just tell your tale and stop wasting time.
Look, there's Deptford up ahead, and it is already half
    past seven.
And there's Greenwich. Many a scoundrel lives there!
Hey, it's time to start your tale."
    "Now, sirs," said Oswald the Reeve,                       55
"please don't complain when I answer this Miller

Thogh I answere, and somdeel sette his howve,
For leveful is with force force of-showve.
This dronke Millere hath y-toold us heer
How that bigyled was a carpenteer,                    60
Peraventure in scorn, for I am oon.
And, by youre leve, I shal hym quite anoon,
Right in his cherles termes wol I speke.
I pray to God his nekke mote to-breke.
He kan wel in myn eye seen a stalke,                  65
But in his owene he kan nat seen a balke."


*Heere bigynneth the Reves Tale*


At Trumpington, nat fer fro Cantebrigge,
Ther gooth a brook, and over that a brigge,
Upon the whiche brook ther stant a melle—
And this is verray sooth that I yow telle.
  A millere was ther dwellynge many a day.            5
As any pecok he was proud and gay.
Pipen he koude and fisshe, and nettes beete,
And turne coppes, and wel wrastle and sheete.
Ay by his belt he baar a long panade,
And of a swerd ful trenchant was the blade.           10
A joly poppere baar he in his pouche.
Ther was no man, for peril, dorste hym touche.
A Sheffeld* thwitel baar he in his hose.
Round was his face, and camus was his nose.
As piled as an ape was his skulle.                    15
He was a market-betere atte fulle.
Ther dorste no wight hand upon hym legge
That he ne swoor he sholde anon abegge.
A theef he was for sothe of corn and mele,
And that a sly, and usaunt for to stele.              20
  His name was hoote deynous Symkyn.
A wyf he hadde, y-comen of noble kyn—
The person of the toun hir fader was.

and set things right. Turnabout is fair play,
and I have a right to answer nastiness with nastiness.
This drunk Miller has told us
how a carpenter got tricked,                                    60
probably because he knows I'm a carpenter.
But, by your leave, I intend to repay him right now,
and speak in churlish language, just like he did.
I pray to God that Miller breaks his neck.
He can see a speck in my eye                                    65
but he can't see a boulder in his own."

*Here begins the Reeve's Tale*

A t Trumpington, not far from Cambridge,
there runs a brook, and over that is a bridge,
and upon that brook stands a mill—
and this is the absolute truth that I am saying.
A miller had dwelt there many a day.                            5
He was as proud and gay as any peacock.
He could play pipes and fish and mend fishnets
and tip a cup of booze, and wrestle and shoot.
Always on his belt he wore a long cutlass
with a really sharp blade.                                      10
He also carried a jolly little dagger in his pocket.
No man dared touch him, for peril of his life.
He also concealed a Sheffield knife in his socks.
He had a round face with a pug nose.
His head was as bald as an ape's.                               15
He was a regular market-bully.
No man dared lay a hand on him
without his swearing that he'd pay for it.
He cleverly stole grain and flour
from his clients. He made a regular habit of it.               20
He was called arrogant Symkyn.
He had a wife who came of noble kin—
the town parson was her father.

With hire he yaf ful many a panne of bras,
For that Symkyn sholde in his blood allye.                    25
She was y-fostred in a nonnerye,
For Symkyn wolde no wyf, as he sayde,
But she were wel y-norissed and a mayde,
To saven his estaat of yomanrye.
And she was proud, and peert as is a pye.                     30
A ful fair sighte was it upon hem two!
On halydayes biforn hire wolde he go
With his typet bounden aboute his heed.
And she cam after in a gyte of reed.
And Symkyn hadde hosen of the same.                          35
Ther dorste no wight clepen hire but "dame."
Was noon so hardy that wente by the weye
That with hire dorste rage or ones pleye,
But if he wolde be slayn of Symkyn
With panade, or with knyf, or boidekyn.                       40
For jalous folk ben perilous everemo,
Algate they wolde hire wyves wenden so.
And eek, for she was somdel smoterlich,
She was as digne as water in a dich,
And ful of hoker and of bisemare.                            45
Hir thoughte that a lady sholde hire spare,
What for hire kynrede and hir nortelrie
That she hadde lerned in the nonnerie.

   A doghter hadde they bitwixe hem two
Of twenty yeer, withouten any mo,                            50
Savynge a child that was of half yeer age.
In cradel it lay and was a propre page.
This wenche thikke and wel y-growen was,
With kamus nose, and eyen greye as glas,
With buttokes brode, and brestes rounde and hye.            55
But right fair was hire heer, I wol nat lye.

   This person of the toun, for she was feir,
In purpos was to maken hire his heir,
Bothe of his catel and his mesuage.

As her dowry he gave many a brass dish
to get Symkyn to make alliance with his family.                    25
She had been fostered in a nunnery,
because Symkyn said he would not marry any woman
who was not well educated and a maiden,
so he could uphold his yeomanly estate.
She was as proud and perky as a magpie.                    30
It was a pretty sight to see those two together!
On holy days he would walk in front of her
with the tassel of his hood wrapped around his head,
and she came after him wearing her red cape,
with Symkyn wearing socks of the same material.                    35
They insisted that everyone call her "madam."
No one walking by was so hardy
that he would flirt or josh with her,
unless he wanted Symkyn to kill him
with his cutlass, knife, or dagger.                    40
Jealous folk are always dangerous—
or at least they hope their wives will think they are.
And because people knew she was somewhat
     besmirched—
she was about as dignified as ditchwater
and so full of disdain and arrogance—                    45
she thought that ladies like her should remain aloof
because of her high kinship and the education
that she had received in the nunnery.

They had a daughter between them,
aged twenty, and no more children                    50
except a baby that was only six months old.
This proper young lad lay in a cradle.
The wench was strong and well-grown
with her father's pug nose and eyes as grey as glass.
She had nice broad buttocks and breasts that were
     round and high.                    55
I won't lie: she had pretty hair.
The town parson, because she was pretty,
hoped to make her the heir
of both his house and his personal property.

And straunge he made it of hir mariage.                    60
His purpos was for to bistowe hire hye
Into som worthy blood of auncetrye,
For hooly chirches good moot been despended
On hooly chirches blood, that is descended.
Therfore he wolde his hooly blood honoure,                 65
Though that he hooly chirche sholde devoure.
    Greet sokene* hath this millere, out of doute,
With whete and malt of al the land aboute,
And nameliche ther was a greet collegge
Men clepen the Soler Halle* at Cantebregge.                70
Ther was hir whete and eek hir malt y-grounde.
And on a day it happed, in a stounde,
Sik lay the maunciple on a maladye.
Men wenden wisly that he sholde dye,
For which this millere stal bothe mele and corn            75
An hundred tyme moore than biforn.
For therbiforn he stal but curteisly,
But now he was a theef outrageously,
For which the wardeyn chidde and made fare.
But therof sette the millere nat a tare:                   80
He craketh boost, and swoor it was nat so.
    Thanne were ther yonge povre scolers two
That dwelten in this halle, of which I seye.
Testif they were, and lusty for to pleye.
And oonly for hire myrthe and revelrye.                    85
Upon the wardeyn bisily they crye
To yeve hem leve, but a litel stounde,
To goon to mille and seen hir corn y-grounde.
And hardily they dorste leye hir nekke
The millere sholde not stele hem half a pekke              90
Of corn by sleighte, ne by force hem reve.
And at the laste the wardeyn yaf hem leve.
John highte that oon, and Aleyn highte that oother.

He made certain difficulties about her marriage                60
because he proposed to bestow her highly
into some pedigreed family with noble ancestry.
After all, the wealth of the holy church should be spent
on the offspring of holy churchmen!
And so he wanted to do honor to his own holy blood        65
even though in the process he should consume the
     holy church.

    This miller had a large and profitable monopoly
on the wheat and malt in all the surrounding land,
and to be specific, his monopoly included a big college
that men call the Soler Hall at Cambridge.                   70
At his mill their wheat and malt were ground
     into flour.
One day, as it chanced to be,
the manciple lay sick of a certain malady.
Indeed, men thought he would die.
Because of that this miller stole grain and meal             75
a hundred times more than he did before.
He usually stole carefully and on the sly,
but now he was an outrageous thief.
That caused the warden of the college to make a fuss,
but the miller didn't give a straw about that.               80
He just blustered it through and swore he
     was innocent.

   At that time there were two young scholars
who dwelt in that hall—the hall I told you about.
They were headstrong and loved to play around.
Just for fun and revelry                                     85
they begged the warden
to give them permission, for just a little while,
to go to the mill to see their grain ground.
They bravely dared to bet their necks
that the miller wouldn't steal even half a peck             90
of grain by his sleight of hand, nor take any from them
     by force.
At last the warden gave them permission to go.
One was called John, Alan the other.

Of o toun were they born, that highte Strother,*
Fer in the north, I kan nat telle where.                        95
This Aleyn maketh redy al his gere,
And on an hors the sak he caste anon.
Forth goth Aleyn the clerk, and also John,
With good swerd and with bokeler by hir syde.
John knew the wey—hem nedede no gyde—            100
And at the mille the sak adoun he layth.
    Aleyn spak first: "Al hayl, Symond, y-fayth!
Hou fares thy faire doghter and thy wyf?"
    "Aleyn, welcome," quod Symkyn, "by my lyf!
And John also. How now, what do ye heer?"          105
    "Symond," quod John, "by God, nede has na peer.
Hym boes serve hymself that has na swayn,
Or elles he is a fool, as clerkes sayn.
Oure manciple, I hope he wil be deed,
Swa werkes ay the wanges in his heed.                   110
And forthy is I come, and eek Alayn,
To grynde oure corn and carie it ham agayn.
I pray yow spede us heythen that ye may."
    "It shal be doon," quod Symkyn, "by my fay!
What wol ye doon whil that it is in hande?"             115
    "By God, right by the hopur wil I stande,"
Quod John, "and se howgates the corn gas in.
Yet saugh I nevere, by my fader kyn,
How that the hopur wagges til and fra."
    Aleyn answerde, "John, and wiltow swa?             120
Thanne wil I be bynethe, by my croun,
And se how that the mele falles doun
Into the trough. That sal be my disport.
For John, y-faith, I may been of youre sort.
I is as ille a millere as ar ye."                               125
    This millere smyled of hir nycetee,
And thoghte, "Al this nys doon but for a wyle.
They wene that no man may hem bigyle,
But, by my thrift, yet shal I blere hir ye,

They both came from the town of Strother,
way up in the north. I'm not sure where up there.          95
Alan got his gear all ready
and he threw the sack of grain on a horse.
Alan the clerk then went off with John,
wearing a good sword and buckler by his side.
John knew the way—they needed no guide—          100
and at the mill he lay down the sack.

Alan spoke first: "All hail, Symond, by my faith!
How are your fair daughter and your wife?"

"Alan, welcome," said Symkyn, "by my life.
And John also. Say, now, what brings you here?"          105

"Symond," said John, "by God, it is all a matter
of need.
He who has no servant must serve himself,
or else he's a fool, as clerks say.
I'm afraid our manciple is in danger of dying,
to judge by the ache in the infected tooth in his head.          110
And therefore I have come, along with Alan,
To grind our grain and carry the flour home again.
I pray you, help us get home as quickly as possible."

"I shall do it," said Symkyn, "by my faith!
And what will you two do while I have the job
in hand?"          115

"By God, I'll stand right by the hopper,"
said John, "and see how the grain goes in.
You know, by my father's kin, I never yet saw
how the hopper wags to and fro."

Alan answered, "John, will you really do that?          120
Then I'll be here beneath, by my head,
and see how the meal falls down
into the trough. That'll be my job,
because, John, by my faith, I'm like you—
I'm just as bad a miller as you are."          125

The miller smiled at their foolishness
and thought, "They're doing all this just to trick me.
They think no man can trick them,
but, by golly, I'll blur their eyes for them,

For al the sleighte in hir philosophye.                             130
The moore queynte crekes that they make,
The moore wol I stele whan I take.
In stide of flour yet wol I yeve hem bren.
'The gretteste clerkes been noght wisest men,'
As whilom to the wolf thus spak the mare.*                          135
Of al hir art ne counte I noght a tare."

   Out at the dore he gooth ful pryvely,
Whan that he saugh his tyme. Softely
He looketh up and doun til he hath founde
The clerkes hors, ther as it stood y-bounde                         140
Bihynde the mille, under a levesel.
And to the hors he goth hym faire and wel.
He strepeth of the brydel right anon.
And whan the hors was laus, he gynneth gon
Toward the fen, ther wilde mares renne,                             145
And forth with "Wehee," thurgh thikke and thurgh
      thenne.

This millere gooth agayn, no word he seyde,
But dooth his note, and with the clerkes pleyde,
Til that hir corn was faire and well y-grounde.

   And whan the mele is sakked and y-bounde,              150
This John goth out and fynt his hors away,
And gan to crie "Harrow!" and "Weylaway,
Oure hors is lorn, Alayn, for Goddes banes,
Step on thy feet! Com of, man, al atanes!
Allas, our wardeyn has his palfrey lorn."                           155

   This Aleyn al forgat bothe mele and corn.
Al was out of his mynde his housbondrie.
"What? Whilk way is he geen?" he gan to crie.

   The wyf cam lepynge inward with a ren.
She seyde, "Allas! youre hors goth to the fen*                      160
With wilde mares, as faste as he may go.
Unthank come on his hand that boond hym so,
And he that bettre sholde han knyt the reyne!"

   "Allas," quod John, "Aleyn, for Cristes peyne
Lay doun thy swerd, and I wil myn alswa.                            165
I is ful wight, God waat, as is a raa.

in spite of all their college-kid cleverness.                    130
The more cute tricks they try,
the more I'll steal from them.
Instead of flour, I'll see that they get only bran.
'The greatest clerks are not the wisest men,'
as the mare once said to the wolf.                               135
I don't care a weed for all their artfulness."
     He went outside secretly
when he saw the right time. Stealthily
he looked up and down until he found
the clerks' horse where it stood tied up                        140
behind the mill under a tree.
He went right up to the horse.
He stripped off the bridle right away,
and when the horse was loose it went
toward the fen where wild mares ran.                             145
He galloped forth whinnying, "Wehee," through
     thick and thin.
This miller went inside again, saying no word,
but set about his work while the clerks played
until their grain was all ground up into flour.
     When the meal was sacked and tied,                         150
John went out and found his horse missing
and cried out, "Help!" and "Alas,
our horse is loose, Alan, for God's bones
get a move on! Come on, man, right now!
Alas, our warden's horse is loose."                             155
     Alan completely forgot about both meal and grain—
his proper task went way out of his mind.
"What? Which way is he gone?" he cried.
     The miller's wife came leaping in.
She said, "Alas, your horse went to the fen                     160
to be with the wild mares as fast as he could.
A curse upon the hand that bound him so,
on him who should have tied the reins better!"
     "Alas," said John, "Alan, for Christ's pains
lay your sword down, as I will mine.                            165
I'm as strong, God knows, as a buck.

By Goddes herte, he sal nat scape us bathe!
Why ne had thow pit the capul in the lathe?
Il-hayl! By God, Alayn, thou is a fonne!"

Thise sely clerkes han ful faste y-ronne          170
Toward the fen, bothe Aleyn and eek John,
And whan the millere saugh that they were gon,
He half a busshel of hir flour hath take,
And bad his wyf go knede it in a cake.
He seyde, "I trowe the clerkes were aferd.          175
Yet kan a millere make a clerkes berd,
For al his art. Now lat hem goon hir weye.
Lo, wher he gooth! Ye, lat the children pleye.
They gete hym nat so lightly, by my croun."

Thise sely clerkes rennen up and doun          180
With "Keep! Keep! Stand! Stand! Jossa! Warderere!
Ga whistle thou, and I shal kepe hym heere!"

But shortly, til that it was verray nyght,
They koude nat, though they dide al hir myght,
Hir capul cacche—he ran alwey so faste—          185
Til in a dych they caughte hym atte laste.

Wery and weet, as beest is in the reyn,
Comth sely John, and with him comth Aleyn.
"Allas," quod John, "the day that I was born!
Now are we dryve til hethyng and til scorn.          190
Oure corn is stoln, men wil us fooles calle,
Bathe the wardeyn and oure felawes alle,
And namely the millere, weylaway!"
Thus pleyneth John as he gooth by the way
Toward the mille, and Bayard in his hond.          195

The millere sittynge by the fyr he fond,
For it was nyght, and forther myghte they noght.
But, for the love of God, they hym bisoght
Of herberwe and of ese, as for hir peny.

The millere seyde agayn, "If ther be eny,          200
Swich as it is, yet shal ye have youre part.

By God's heart, the horse won't escape both of us!
Why didn't you put the horse in the barn?
Bad luck to you! By God, Alan, you're an idiot!"
   These silly clerks ran right off                          170
toward the fen, both Alan and John,
and when the miller saw that they were gone,
he took half a bushel of their flour
and told his wife to go knead it into a cake.
He said, "I guess those clerks were leery of me,              175
but a miller can still pull a clerk's beard,
for all his artfulness. Now let them go their way.
Look where that one runs! Yes, let the children play.
They won't catch that horse so lightly, by my head."
   These silly clerks ran up and down                          180
with "Stay! Stay! Stand! Stand! Down here!
   Look out!
You go whistle and I'll keep him here!"
   But shortly, until it was night,
they couldn't, though they did all they could,
catch their horse—he ran away too fast—                      185
until they finally trapped him in a ditch.
   Tired and wet, like an animal in the rain,
foolish John and Alan came back.
"Alas," John said, "the day that I was born!
Now are we driven to contempt and scorn.                     190
Our grain is stolen. Men will say we're fools,
particularly the warden and our fellow students,
and most especially the miller. Alas!"
Thus John complained as he went back
toward the mill, with Bayard's reins in his hand.            195
   He found the miller sitting beside the fire
because it was night. They could go no further in the
    darkness
so, for the love of God, they begged him
for lodging and a place to lie down, in exchange for
    their money.
   The miller answered, "If there is space,                    200
such as it is, you shall have your part of it.

Myn hous is streit, but ye han lerned art.
Ye konne by argumentes make a place
A myle brood of twenty foot of space.
Lat se now if this place may suffise,                        205
Or make it rowm with speche, as is youre gise."
   "Now, Symond," seyde John, "by Seint Cutberd,
Ay is thou myrie, and this is faire answerd.
I have herd seyd, 'Man sal taa of twa thynges,
Slyk as he fyndes, or taa slyk as he brynges.'              210
But specially I pray thee, hooste deere,
Get us som mete and drynke, and make us cheere,
And we wil payen trewely atte fulle:
'With empty hand men may na haukes tulle.'
Loo, heere oure silver, redy for to spende."                215
   This millere into toun* his doghter sende
For ale and breed, and rosted hem a goos,
And boond hire hors, it sholde namoore go loos!
And in his owene chambre hem made a bed,
With sheetes and with chalons faire y-spred                 220
Noght from his owene bed ten foot or twelve.
His doghter hadde a bed, al by hirselve,
Right in the same chambre, by and by.
It myghte be no bet, and cause why?
Ther was no roumer herberwe in the place.                   225
   They soupen and they speke, hem to solace,
And drynken evere strong ale atte beste.
   Aboute mydnyght wente they to reste.
Wel hath this millere vernysshed his heed.
Ful pale he was for dronken, and nat reed.*                 230
He yexeth, and he speketh thurgh the nose
As he were on the quakke, or on the pose.
To bedde he goth, and with hym goth his wyf.
As any jay she light was and jolyf,

My house is small, but you college boys, by your
    clever artfulness
and your logical arguments can make a place
of only twenty feet a full mile wide.
Now you can see if this place will be sufficient,    205
or you can make it roomier with your talking, as is
    your custom."
    "Now, Symond," said John, "by Saint Cuthbert,
since you are so merry, you deserve a merry answer.
I have heard it said, 'A man shall have one of
    two things,
such as he finds, or such as he brings.'    210
But I beg you, dear host,
get us some meat and drink, so we can all make merry,
we'll pay you, honestly and in full:
'With empty hand no man can lure a hawk.'
Lo, here's our silver, ready to spend."    215
    This miller sent his daughter into town
to fetch ale and bread, and roasted them a goose,
and tied up their horse—it wouldn't get loose
    anymore!
Then in his own bedroom he made them a bed,
with sheets and blankets spread comfortably    220
not ten or twelve feet away from his own bed.
His daughter had a bed, all by herself,
right there in the same room nearby.
There was no choice. Do you know why?
Because there was no other room in that lodging.    225
    They supped and they talked to give each other
    solace,
and drank lots of the very best strong ale.
    About midnight they went to bed.
The miller was pretty well shellacked!
He was all pale in his drunkenness, not red anymore.    230
He belched and spoke through his nose
as if he were hoarse or had a cold
He went to bed, and with him went his wife.
She was as fluttery and jolly as a bird,

So was hir joly whistle wel y-wet.                                    235
The cradel at hir beddes feet is set,
To rokken, and to yeve the child to sowke.
   And whan that dronken al was in the crowke,
To bedde wente the doghter right anon.
To bedde goth Aleyn and also John.                                    240
Ther nas na moore. Hem nedede no dwale!
   This millere hath so wisely bibbed ale
That as an hors he fnorteth in his sleep,
Ne of his tayl bihynde he took no keep.
His wyf bar hym a burdon, a ful strong.                               245
Men myghte hir rowtyng heere two furlong.*
The wenche rowteth eek, par compaignye.
   Aleyn the clerk, that herde this melodye,
He poked John, and seyde, "Slepestow?
Herdestow evere slyk a sang er now?                                   250
Lo, swilk a complyn* is ymel hem alle!
A wilde fyr upon thair bodyes falle!
Wha herkned evere slyk a ferly thyng?
Ye, they sal have the flour of il endyng.
This lange nyght ther tydes me na reste.                              255
But yet, nafors, al sal be for the beste.
For, John," seyde he, "als evere moot I thryve,
If that I may, yon wenche wil I swyve.
Som esement has lawe y-shapen us.
For, John, ther is a lawe that says thus,                             260
That gif a man in a point be agreved,
That in another he sal be releved.
Oure corn is stoln, sothly, it is na nay,
And we han had an il fit al this day.
And syn I sal have neen amendement                                    265
Agayn my los, I will have esement.
By Goddes sale, it sal neen other bee!"
   This John answerde, "Alayn, avyse thee!
The millere is a perilous man," he seyde,

because she, too, had really wet her whistle with
    the ale.                                                    235
She set the cradle at the foot of her bed,
so she could rock it and let the baby nurse.
    And when the last drop was drunk from the crock of
    ale,
the daughter went to bed right away,
and then Alan and John went to bed too.                           240
That's all there were. They needed no sleeping potion
    that night!
    This miller had imbibed so much ale
That he snored like a horse in his sleep,
nor did he keep control of his bottom.
His wife played a good strong bass accompaniment.                 245
Men could hear their snoring a quarter mile away.
Their daughter snored also, keeping them company.
    Alan the clerk heard this melody,
poked John, and said, "Are you asleep?
Have you ever heard such a song before?                           250
Lo, such a compline is among them!
May a wild hot itching scrofula fall upon their bodies!
Who ever heard such an awful noise?
Yes, may they have the very flower of bad endings.
I am not destined to sleep this whole night long.                255
But no matter, all shall be for the best,
because, John," he said, "as I may ever thrive,
if I can, I am going to screw yonder wench.
The law guarantees some easement,
because, John, there is a law that says                          260
that if a man in is harmed in one point of the law,
then in another point he shall find relief.
Our grain is stolen, truly, no denying that,
and you and I have had one hell of a day.
And since there is no amending                                   265
the loss, I will have compensation for it.
By God's soul, it shall happen!"
    John answered, "Alan, be careful!
The miller is a dangerous man," he said,

"And gif that he out of his sleep abreyde,                    270
He myghte doon us bathe a vileynye."
    Aleyn answerde, "I counte hym nat a flye!"
And up he rist, and by the wenche he crepte.
    This wenche lay uprighte, and faste slepte,
Til he so ny was, er she myghte espie,                         275
That it had been to late for to crie,
And shortly for to seyn, they were aton.
    Now pley, Aleyn, for I wol speke of John.
This John lith stille a furlong wey or two,*
And to hymself he maketh routhe and wo.                        280
"Allas," quod he, "This is a wikked jape.
Now may I seyn that I is but an ape.
Yet has my felawe somwhat for his harm.
He has the milleris doghter in his arm.
He auntred hym, and has his nedes sped,                        285
And I lye as a draf-sak in my bed.
And when this jape is tald another day,
I sal been halde a daf, a cokenay.
I wil arise and auntre it, by my fayth.
'Unhardy is unseely,' thus men sayth."                         290
    And up he roos, and softely he wente
Unto the cradel, and in his hand it hente,
And baar it softe unto his beddes feet.
    Soone after this the wyf hir rowtyng leet,
And gan awake, and wente hire out to pisse,                    295
And cam agayn, and gan hir cradel mysse,
And groped heer and ther, but she foond noon.
    "Allas!" quod she. "I hadde almoost mysgoon.
I hadde almoost goon to the clerkes bed.
Ey, benedicite! thanne hadde I foule y-sped."                  300
    And forth she gooth til she the cradel fond.
She gropeth alwey forther with hir hond,
And foond the bed, and thoghte noght but good,
By cause that the cradel by it stood.

"and if he should wake up,                                              270
he might do harm to both of us."
    Alan answered, "I don't give a fly for him!"
And he got up and crept in beside the girl.
She lay face up, sleeping soundly.
He was so close before she could see him                                275
that it was too late for her to cry out.
To tell you quickly, they were soon at one.
    Now play, Alan, for I will speak of John.
John lay still for a short while
upbraiding himself, full of self-pity and sadness.                      280
"Alas," he said, "this is a sad state of affairs.
Now I see that I am just an ape.
Now my pal has some compensation for the harm
    done us.
He has the miller's daughter in his arms.
He took a chance, and now has his needs taken care of,  285
but I lie in my bed like a bag of trash.
And when this joke is told some later day,
I shall be thought to be a fool, a weak little coward.
By my faith, I'm going to get up and do something
    about it!
'The weak man has no luck,' as men say."                                290
    He got up, quietly went
over to the cradle, picked it up,
and carried it softly to the lower end of his own bed.
    Soon after that the wife stopped her snoring,
woke up, and went outside to take a piss.                               295
Then she came in again, missed the cradle gone
    from its usual place,
and groped here and there, but she couldn't find it.
    "Alas!" she said, "I almost went wrong!
I almost got into the clerks' bed.
Oh, my goodness, then I would have been in trouble."  300
    She felt around until she found the cradle.
Then she groped still further with her hand,
and found the bed—thinking only good thoughts
because the cradle was right there by it.

And nyste wher she was, for it was derk.                          305
But faire and wel she creep in to the clerk,
And lith ful stille, and wolde han caught a sleep.
  Withinne a while this John the clerk up leep,
And on this goode wyf he leith on soore.
So myrie a fit ne hadde she nat ful yoore!                        310
He priketh harde and depe as he were mad.
  This joly lyf han thise two clerkes lad
Til that the thridde cok* bigan to synge.
Aleyn wax wery in the dawenynge,
For he had swonken al the longe nyght,                            315
And seyde, "Fare weel, Malyne, sweete wight!
The day is come, I may no lenger byde.
But everemo, wher so I go or ryde,
I is thyn awen clerk, swa have I seel!"
  "Now, deere lemman," quod she, "go, far weel!                   320
But er thow go, o thyng I wol thee telle.
Whan that thou wendest homward by the melle,
Right at the entree of the dore bihynde
Thou shalt a cake of half a busshel fynde
That was y-maked of thyn owene mele,                             325
Which that I heelp my sire for to stele.
And, goode lemman, God thee save and kepe!"
  And with that word almoost she gan to wepe.
Aleyn up rist, and thoughte, er that it dawe,
"I wol go crepen in by my felawe."                                330
And fond the cradel with his hand anon.
"By God," thoughte he, "al wrang I have mysgon.
Myn heed is toty of my swynk to-nyght,
That makes me that I ga nat aright.
I woot wel by the cradel I have mysgo.                            335
Heere lith the millere and his wyf also."
  And forth he goth, a twenty devel way,
Unto the bed ther as the millere lay.
He wende have cropen by his felawe John,
And by the millere in he creep anon,                              340
And caughte hym by the nekke, and softe he spak.

She didn't know where she was, because it was
    so dark. 305
But all innocent, she crept in by the clerk,
lay all quiet, and tried to get to sleep again.

    After a short while John the clerk leaped up
and landed eagerly on this good woman.
She hadn't had such a merry fit for a long time! 310
He plunged hard and deep, like a madman.

    These two clerks led this happy life
until the third rooster started crowing.
Alan grew tired as the dawn came on,
for he had labored all night long, 315
and said, "Farewell, Malyne, sweet lady!
Day has come, and I can stay no longer,
but always, wherever I walk or ride,
I am your own clerk, that I swear."

    "Now, dear love," said she, "go, farewell! 320
But before you go, I want to tell you something.
When you head home beside the mill,
just at the entrance, right behind the door,
you'll find a half-bushel cake
that was made from your own flour, 325
that I helped my father steal from you.
And, my fine lover, God save you and keep you well!"
And with that word she almost started to weep.

Alan rose up before dawn and thought,
"I'll go get in beside my pal," 330
and soon his hand found the cradle.
"By God," he thought, "I've gone all wrong.
My head is confused from all my drinking tonight.
That made me get all turned around.
I know by this cradle that I almost went wrong. 335
Here lie the miller and his wife."

    And he pushed on, as if chased by twenty devils,
to the other bed where the miller lay.
He thought he crept in by his fellow John,
but he actually crept in beside the miller, 340
and caught him by the neck, and spoke softly to him.

He seyde, "Thou John, thou swynes-heed, awak,
For Cristes saule, and heer a noble game.
For by that lord that called is Seint Jame,
As I have thries in this shorte nyght               345
Swyved the milleres doghter bolt upright,
Whil thow hast, as a coward, been agast."
 "Ye, false harlot!" quod the miller. "Hast?
A false traitour, false clerk!" quod he,
"Thow shalt be deed, by Goddes dignitee!           350
Who dorste be so boold to disparage
My doghter, that is come of swich lynage?"
 And by the throte-bolle he caughte Alayn,
And he hente hym despitously agayn,
And on the nose he smoot hym with his fest.        355
Doun ran the blody streem upon his brest.
And in the floor, with nose and mouth tobroke,
They walwe as doon two pigges in a poke.
And up they goon, and doun agayn anon,
Til that the millere sporned at a stoon,           360
And doun he fil bakward upon his wyf,
That wiste no thyng of this nyce stryf.
For she was falle aslepe a lite wight
With John the clerk, that waked hadde al nyght.
And with the fal out of hir sleep she breyde.      365
 "Help! Hooly croys of Bromeholm,"* she seyde.
"*In manus tuas,** Lord, to thee I calle!
Awak, Symond, the feend is on me falle.
Myn herte is broken. Help! I nam but deed!
Ther lyth oon upon my wombe and on myn heed.       370
Help, Symkyn, for the false clerkes fighte!"
 This John stirte up as faste as ever he myghte,
And graspeth by the walles to and fro,
To fynde a staf. And she stirte up also,
And knew the estres bet than dide this John,       375

He said, "You, John, you stupid pig-head, wake up
for Christ's sake, and let me tell you about a
    noble game.
For by that lord named Saint James,
I have thrice in this short night                                345
screwed the miller's daughter flat on her back,
while you have, like a coward, been afraid to get
    out of bed."
    "Oh yeah, you false harlot!" said the miller. "Have
        you really?
Ah, you false traitor, false clerk," he said.
"Now, by the dignity of God, you die!                            350
Who is this who dares to make bold to degrade
my daughter, who comes of such fine lineage?"
    And by the throat he caught Alan,
who in turn angrily grabbed him back
and punched him on the nose with his fist.                       355
The bloody stream ran down upon his chest
and on the floor, with nose and mouth all broken,
they wallowed like two pigs in a sack.
They no sooner got up than they went down again,
until the miller stumbled on a stone,                            360
and tumbled over backward on his wife,
who knew nothing of this foolish battle,
because she had fallen asleep for a short time
with John the clerk, who had stayed awake all that
    night.
At the fall she woke suddenly from her sleep.                    365
    "Help, by the holy cross of Bromeholm!" she said.
"*In manus tuas,* Lord, I beseech thee!
Wake up, Symond, a devil has fallen on me.
My heart is crushed. Help, I am all but dead!
One lies on my belly, one on my head.                            370
Help, Symkyn, for the false clerks are fighting!"
    John started up just as fast as he could,
and felt around the walls here and there
to find a staff. And the wife got up also.
She knew the nooks and corners better than John did,             375

And by the wal a staf she foond anon,
And saugh a litel shymeryng of a light,
For at an hole in shoon the moone bright.
And by that light she saugh hem bothe two,
But sikerly she nyste who was who.                          380
But as she saugh a whit thyng in hir ye.
And whan she gan this white thyng espye,
She wende the clerk hadde wered a volupeer,
And with the staf she drow ay neer and neer,
And wende han hit this Aleyn at the fulle,                   385
And smoot the millere on the pyled skulle,
That doun he gooth, and cride, "Harrow! I dye!"

    Thise clerkes beete hym weel and lete hym lye,
And greythen hem, and tooke hir hors anon,
And eek hire mele, and on hir wey they gon.                  390
And at the mille yet they tooke hir cake
Of half a busshel flour, ful wel y-bake.

    Thus is the proude millere wel y-bete,
And hath y-lost the gryndynge of the whete,
And payed for the soper everideel                            395
Of Aleyn and of John, that bette hym weel.
His wyf is swyved, and his doghter als.

    Lo, swich it is a millere to be fals!
And therfore this proverbe is seyd ful sooth:
"Hym thar nat wene wel that yvele dooth;                     400
A gylour shal hymself bigyled be."
And God, that sitteth heighe in magestee,
Save al this compaignye, grete and smale.
Thus have I quyt the Millere in my tale.

and by the wall she quickly found a staff.
She saw a little light shimmering
where the bright moon shone in through a hole,
and by that light she saw the two fighters,
but she could not tell which was which.                    380
But then she saw a white thing appear.
When she saw this white thing,
she seemed to remember that the clerk had worn
    a nightcap,
so with the staff she inched nearer and nearer
and tried to hit Alan full on,                    385
but instead smote the miller on his bald head,
so he fell down and cried, "Help, I am dying!"
    The clerks gave him a good beating and let him lie
    there,
then got dressed and took their horse
and their flour, and set out on their way.                    390
At the mill they took the cake
made of the half-bushel of flour, fully baked.
    Thus is the proud miller fully beat up,
and lost the wheat he ground,
and payed for every bit of the supper                    395
of Alan and John, who beat him up.
His wife was screwed, and his daughter, too.
    Lo, such is the reward for a miller who is false!
And therefore we find this very true proverb:
"He who does evil cannot expect good;                    400
A beguiler shall himself be beguiled."
And God, who sits in high majesty,
save all this company, both great and small.
Now I have repaid the Miller with my tale.

# THE WIFE OF BATH

# INTRODUCTION

✠

THE WIFE OF BATH is perhaps the most memorable of the pilgrims on the road to Canterbury. She is memorable in part simply because we know far more about her than we know about any other pilgrim. In addition to the thirty-two-line description of her in the General Prologue to *The Canterbury Tales* (see lines 447–78), we have the amazing 856-line prologue to her tale in which she gives a confessional account of her life, her philosophy of love and marriage, and her various husbands. But Alisoun of Bath is memorable mostly just because of who she is: a wonderfully varied, funny, garrulous, abrasive, pushy, honest, dishonest, hateful, lovable, and contradictory woman who knows how to yield, flowerlike, to get what she wants from men, but also how to stand up to them, bulldozer-like, when she needs to.

The Wife of Bath draws on many learned, religious, and literary sources for the materials we find in her prologue. One is the long allegorical work in French, *The Romance of the Rose*. There is no question that Chaucer knew this work since he translated at least parts of it into English. Of particular interest to readers concerned with the Wife of Bath is the long speech of the Old Woman to a young man named Fair Welcoming. In that speech in *The Romance of the Rose* she tells him in blunt language about the wiles and nastiness of women in their relations with men. The other is Jerome's long Latin tractate *Against Jovinian*. In that document he takes Jovinian to task for what he considers to be Jovinian's wrong-headed ideas about virginity and marriage. The Wife of Bath rejects Jerome's opinions, much preferring Jovinian's more liberal ideas on the nonnecessity of virginity, on the marriage debt that men owe their wives, on the acceptability of successive marriages, and so on.

We have no head-link to "The Wife of Bath's Prologue." That is, her prologue is not connected to a previous tale, and the Host never calls upon her to speak up and tell a tale. Rather, the Wife of Bath just charges into action by proclaiming that she will speak from experience, and then proceeds, uninvited, to do just that. Her long prologue seems like the wandering outpouring of a sloppy-minded narcissist—and of course it is that. But a closer look shows that the prologue is carefully organized into two large sections. In the first part, where the mode is expository, Alisoun explains why she prefers virginity to chastity and why she prefers multiple or successive marriages to a state of widowhood. That section ends after 162 lines with the interruption of the Pardoner, who requests that she teach young men like him about her marital practices.

In the second large section of the prologue, where the mode is autobiographical, Alisoun tells about her own five marriages in chronological order, three to rich old men and then two to more desirable but more impoverished younger men. That section ends after 636 lines with another interruption, this time by the Friar, who is himself immediately interrupted by the Summoner. After a short altercation between the two, the Host commands them to "let the woman tell her tale" (851).

That initiates the third portion of her performance, the tale itself, told in the narrative mode. "The Wife of Bath's Tale" is a 408-line romance about one of King Arthur's young knights who rapes a woman. To pay for his crime the knight is sent by Arthur's queen on a year-long quest to discover what women most desire. At the center of the tale is an enigmatic old woman who teaches several lessons to the impulsive young knight and in the end rewards him for learning those lessons. Chaucer's source for this tale was one of several narratives about ugly old women who marry much younger men and are ultimately transformed into lovely young brides. One of these is John Gower's "Tale of Florent" from the

*Confessio Amantis*. Another is the anonymous "Wedding of Sir Gawain and Dame Ragnell." Chaucer's version is similar to both of these, but different in many ways. In both of those tales, for example, the young man is exemplary in almost all ways, whereas in Chaucer he is a morally repugnant rapist who deserves punishment. In the other two tales the choice offered the bridegroom on his wedding night is having his bride lovely by day but foul by night, or vice versa. In Chaucer the choice involves a moral element about a lovely wife's possible infidelity.

All in all, the Wife of Bath turns in an amazingly varied performance, each piece of which adds to our understanding of one of Chaucer's finest creations.

## NOTES

### The Wife of Bath's Prologue

**at chirche dore** (line 6). The official or public part of the wedding took place outside the church, where there would be more witnesses to it. Then the wedding party moved inside for the religious and more private part of the nuptials.

**Cane of Galilee** (11). See John 2:1.

**Samaritan** (16). See John 4:17–18.

**wexe and multiplye** (28). See Genesis 1:28. Curiously enough, there is no evidence that the Wife of Bath ever had any children.

**th'Apostle** (49). St. Paul. See 1 Corinthians 7:39.

**Lameth, Abraham, Jacob** (54–56). These three men are said in Jerome's *Against Jovinian* to have had multiple wives: Lamech two, Abraham three, and Jacob four. There is biblical support for some of these, as in Genesis 4:19.

**maydenhede** (64). See 1 Corinthians 7:25.

**swich as he** (81). That is, remain a virgin. See 1 Corinthians 7:7.

**al of gold** (100). See 2 Timothy 2:20.

**a propre yifte** (103). See 1 Corinthians 7:7.

**hir dette** (130). That is, sexual debt. See 1 Corinthians 7:3. Compare line 153 below.

**barly breed** (144). See John 6:9–11. A similar reference can be found in Mark 6:38–41, though without the specific reference to barley.

**tribulacioun** (156). See 1 Corinthians 7:28.

**and noght he** (159). See 1 Corinthians 7:7.

*Almageste* (183). A book on astrology by Ptolemy, though the proverbs (see also lines 325–27 below) that Alisoun refers to are not there.

**Dunmowe** (218). A town in Essex where a side of bacon was said to have been awarded annually to a married couple that could assert it had not quarreled all year long.

**cow is wood** (232). The chough, a crowlike bird, was supposed to tell husbands of their wives' infidelities. A wise wife, of course, will proclaim the accusing bird mad.

*bele chose* (447). French for "pretty thing," a reference to her genitalia. She uses the same euphemism in line 510 below.

**Seint Joce** (483). Little is known of St. Jodicus, a seventh-century Breton saint, whose relics were kept in an abbey in London and who was apparently identified as having carried the staff of a pilgrim.

**rode-beem** (496). Important citizens could be buried in the church itself, under the rood-beam that divided the nave from the chancel. On the rood beam was often nailed a cross.

**Darius, Appelles** (498–99). Appelles was a Jewish craftsman who was supposed to have constructed an elaborate tomb for the wealthy Darius.

**Gat-tothed** (603). To have gaps in one's front teeth may have indicated a heightened sexuality. The term "gat" comes from the word for goat, known in medieval times for its horniness. Compare line 470 in the description of the Wife of Bath in the General Prologue to *The Canterbury Tales*.

**Venus seel** (604). A reference to the notion that the astrological alignment at one's birth could leave a physical sign on the body. Possibly Alisoun refers to the gap teeth as this "seal." Compare Mars's mark in line 619 below.

*quoniam* (608). A Latin euphemism for the female genitalia.

**Venerien ... Marcien** (609–10). In these and the following lines Alisoun explains her divided nature and why she is both seductive enough (from Venus, goddess of love) to win men, and tough enough (from Mars, god of war) to control them.

**Martes mark** (619). Evidence of her birth under the sign of Mars is apparent in a mole or some other mark or blemish on a "private place"—presumably her genitalia.

**Simplicius Gallus** (643). The text says enough about the unreasonable bossiness of this Roman and the unnamed man referred to in line 647 that no further explanation is needed.

**Ecclesiaste** (651). The apocryphal book of Ecclesiasticus, not the biblical Ecclesiastes.

**Valerie, Theophraste, Jerome, Tertulan, Crisippus, Trotula, Helowys** (671–77). Various authors of antifeminist and antimatrimonial tracts that are bound together in a "book of wicked wives" that Alisoun's husband gleefully reads to her at night. It was perhaps designed to convince candidates for the priesthood that they ought to stay away from women.

**Who peyntede the leoun** (692). Refers to Aesop's fable about the lion who sees a painting of a lion vanquished by a man. The lion reflects that if the artist were a lion, then the picture would be quite different. Alisoun's point is that if women told the stories, it is the men who would look weak, foolish, and evil.

**children of Mercurie** (697). Mercury was the god or planet associated with learning and clerks, as opposed to Venus, whose "children" are associated with lust, fun, and procreation.

**Sampson, Hercules, Socrates, Amphiorax** (721–41). These are all men whose death or other mistreatment was caused by the actions of women in the stories recounted. Alisoun gives enough details about the various women mentioned in these and the following lines that no explication is needed— but see next item.

**Phasipha** (733). Alisoun is reluctant to give details of the "grisly" act of Pasiphaë, who had a love affair with a bull and later gave birth to the Minotaur.

**Sidingborne** (847). Sittingbourne is a town some fifteen miles from Canterbury—apparently some distance ahead of where they are now on the road to Canterbury.

## The Wife of Bath's Tale

**king Arthour** (1). Arthur was the legendary sixth-century king of England. Alisoun is careful to set her tale back in the early days of British history, well before the fourteenth-century England of the pilgrimage, back in the days when there were still elves and magic in the land.

**limitours** (10). A friar who had permission to preach within a certain "limit" or jurisdiction. Alisoun may be taking a swipe at the Friar on the pilgrimage who had criticized her prologue for its length. He is referred to as a "limitour" in the General Prologue to *The Canterbury Tales,* line 271.

**incubus** (24). A demon who had intercourse with women while they were sleeping—apparently without their permission. Sometimes these unions resulted in demon offspring.

**bacheler** (27). In this context the term refers to a young knight just starting out in his profession, a kind of knight-apprentice. Elsewhere in the story he is referred to as a knight.

**Ovyde** (96). In his *Metamorphoses,* Ovid tells the story of King Midas's ears. In that version, however, it is Midas's barber, not his wife, who cannot keep the secret. The barber digs a hole in the ground and whispers into it about Midas's ears, but the winds blow the secret about.

**Dant** (270). The Italian poet Dante Alighieri. The actual reference in the following lines is to Dante's *Purgatorio* 7, 121–23. The idea is that gentility comes not from the branches of our family tree, but from God.

**Caucasus** (284). A mountain in faraway Russia. The idea of this passage is that fire burns whether anyone is watching it or not, and so does true gentility. The false nobles, on the other hand, demonstrate gentility only when there are witnesses.

**Valerius, Tullius Hostilius** (309–10). The author Valerius describes how Tullius, born a peasant, rose through his true gentility to be king of Rome.

**Senek, Boece** (312). Seneca and Boethius were Roman philosophers. Chaucer particularly admired Boethius's *Consolation of Philosophy*.

**Juvenal** (336). A Roman poet.

# THE WYF OF BATHE

*The Prologe of the Wyves Tale of Bathe*

Experience, though noon auctoritee
Were in this world, were right ynough to me
To speke of wo that is in mariage;
For, lordinges, sith I twelf yeer was of age,
Thonked be God that is eterne on lyve,                    5
Housbondes at chirche dore* I have had fyve—
If I so ofte myghte have wedded be;
And alle were worthy men in hir degree.
But me was told certeyn, nat longe agon is,
That sith that Crist ne wente never but onis             10
To wedding in the Cane of Galilee,*
That by the same ensample taughte he me
That I ne sholde wedded be but ones.
Herke eek, lo! which a sharp word for the nones
Besyde a welle Jesus, God and man,                       15
Spak in repreve of the Samaritan:*
'Thou hast y-had fyve housbondes,' quod he,
'And thilke man, the which that hath now thee,
Is noght thyn housbond'; thus seyde he certeyn;
What that he mente therby, I can nat seyn.               20
But that I axe, why that the fifthe man
Was noon housbond to the Samaritan?
How manye mighte she have in mariage?
Yet herde I never tellen in myn age
Upon this nombre diffinicioun.                           25
Men may devyne and glosen up and doun,
But wel I woot, expres, withoute lye,
God bad us for to wexe and multiplye;*

# THE WIFE OF BATH

*The Prologue of the Wife of Bath's Tale*

Experience, even if there were no other authority
in this world, would be grounds enough for me
to speak of the woe that is in marriage;
for, my lords, since I was twelve years old,
thanks be to eternal God,                                    5
I have had five husbands at the church door—
if I may have been legally married so often;
and all were worthy men in their different ways.
But I was definitely told, not long ago,
that since Christ went but once                              10
to a wedding, in Cana of Galilee,
by that example he taught me
that I should not be married more than once.
Also, consider what sharp words
Jesus, God and man, spoke beside a                           15
well in reproof of the Samaritan:
'Thou hast had five husbands,' he said,
'and he whom thou now hast
is not thy husband'; thus he spoke, certainly;
what he meant by it, I cannot say.                           20
But I ask this, why was the fifth man
no husband to the Samaritan?
How many was she allowed to have in marriage?
Never yet in my life have I heard
this number defined.                                         25
People may guess and interpret the text up and down,
but I know well, without a doubt, God bade
us expressly to increase and multiply;

That gentil text can I wel understonde.
Eek wel I woot he seyde myn housbonde          30
Sholde lete fader and moder, and take me;
But of no nombre mencioun made he
Of bigamye or of octogamye;
Why sholde men speke of it vileinye?
   "Lo, here the wyse king, dan Salomon;          35
I trowe he hadde wyves mo than oon;
As, wolde god, it leveful were to me
To be refresshed half so ofte as he!
Which yifte of God hadde he for alle his wyvis!
No man hath swich that in this world alyve is.          40
God woot, this noble king, as to my wit,
The firste night had many a mery fit
With ech of hem, so wel was him on lyve!
Blessed be God that I have wedded fyve!
Welcome the sixte, whan that ever he shal.          45
For sothe, I wol nat kepe me chast in al;
Whan myn housbond is fro the world y-gon,
Som Cristen man shal wedde me anon;
For thanne th'Apostle* seith that I am free
To wedde, a Goddes half, wher it lyketh me.          50
He seith that to be wedded is no sinne;
Bet is to be wedded than to brinne.
What rekketh me, thogh folk seye vileinye
Of shrewed Lameth* and his bigamye?
I woot wel Abraham* was an holy man,          55
And Jacob* eek, as ferforth as I can;
And ech of hem hadde wyves mo than two,
And many another holy man also.
Wher can ye seye in any maner age,
That hye God defended mariage          60
By expres word? I pray you, telleth me;
Or wher comanded he virginitee?
I woot as wel as ye, it is no drede,
Th'Apostel, whan he speketh of maydenhede,*
He seyde, that precept thereof hadde he noon.          65
Men may conseille a womman to been oon,

that pleasant text I can well understand.
And also I well know that he said my husband      30
should leave father and mother, and take me;
but he made no mention of number—
of bigamy or of octogamy;
why should men speak evil of it?

"Look at the wise king, Lord Solomon;      35
I think he had more than one wife;
I would to God I could
be refreshed half so often as he!
What a gift from God he had with all his wives!
No man living in this world has such.      40
God knows this noble king to my thinking
had many a merry bout with each of them
the first night; he had a good life.
Blessed be God that I have married five!
Welcome the sixth, whenever he comes along.      45
For indeed, I don't want to keep myself entirely chaste;
when my husband has gone from the world,
some Christian man shall wed me soon.
for the Apostle says that then I am free
to marry in God's name where I please.      50
He says it's no sin to be married;
it is better to marry than to burn.
What do I care if folk speak evil
of cursed Lamech and his bigamy?
I know very well that Abraham was a holy man,      55
and Jacob too, as far as I can see;
and each of them had more than two wives,
and so did many another holy man.
Tell me, where, in any time,
did God on high expressly prohibit marriage?      60
I pray you, tell me;
or where did he command virginity?
I know as well as you do—not a doubt!—
that the Apostle, when he spoke of maidenhood,
said that he had no commandment for it.      65
One may counsel a woman to be a virgin,

But conseilling is no comandement;
He putte it in our owene jugement.
For hadde God comanded maydenhede,
Thanne hadde he dampned wedding with the dede;            70
And certes, if ther were no seed y-sowe,
Virginitee, whereof than sholde it growe?
Poul dorste nat comanden atte leste
A thing of which his maister yaf noon heste.
The dart is set up for virginitee;            75
Cacche who so may, who renneth best lat see.
    "But this word is nat take of every wight,
But ther as God list give it of his might.
I woot wel that th'Apostel was a mayde;
But natheless, thogh that he wroot and sayde            80
He wolde that every wight were swich as he,*
Al nis but conseil to virginitee;
And for to been a wyf, he yaf me leve
Of indulgence; so it is no repreve
To wedde me, if that my make dye,            85
Withoute excepcioun of bigamye—
Al were it good no womman for to touche
(He mente as in his bed or in his couche),
For peril is bothe fyr and tow t'assemble—
(Ye knowe what this ensample may resemble).            90
This is al and som: he heeld virginitee
More parfit than wedding in freletee.
Freletee clepe I, but if that he and she
Wolde leden al hir lyf in chastitee.
    "I graunte it wel, I have noon envye,            95
Thogh maydenhede preferre bigamye.
Hem lyketh to be clene, body and goost;
Of myn estaat I nil nat make no boost.
For wel ye knowe a lord in his household,
He hath nat every vessel al of gold*;            100
Somme been of tree, and doon hir lord servyse.
God clepeth folk to him in sondry wyse,
And everich hath of God a propre yifte.*
Som this, som that, as him lyketh shifte.

but counseling is not commandment;
he left it to our own judgment.
For if God had decreed maidenhood, then
he would have condemned marriage in effect;                    70
and certainly if there were no seed sown,
then where should virginity grow from?
Paul did not dare in the least to decree
a thing for which his master gave no order.
The prize is set up for virginity;                             75
grab it who may, let's see who wins the race.

    "But this saying does not apply to every man,
but only where it pleases God to give it, of his might.
I very well know that the Apostle was a virgin;
but nevertheless, although he wrote and said                   80
that he wished that everyone were such as he,
all this is only advice in favor of virginity;
and he gave me, as an indulgence, leave
to be a wife; so it is no reproach
for me to marry if my mate dies;                               85
it is without any taint of bigamy—
although it may be good not to touch a woman
(he meant in a bed or couch;
for it is dangerous to assemble fire and tow—
you know what this example means).                             90
This is the sum of the matter, he held virginity to be
more perfect than marrying in the frailty of the flesh.
It is frailty, that is, unless the man and woman
intend to live all their lives in chastity.

    "I grant it freely; I'm not envious,                       95
although maidenhood be preferred to bigamy.
It pleases some to be pure, body and soul;
I won't make any boast about my own estate.
As you well know, a lord doesn't have every
vessel in his household made of gold;                          100
some are made of wood, and are serviceable to their lord.
God calls people to him in sundry ways,
and each one has an appropriate gift of God,
some this, some that—as it pleases him to provide.

"Virginitee is greet perfeccioun,                      105
And continence eek with devocioun,
But Crist, that of perfeccioun is welle,
Bad nat every wight he sholde go selle
All that he hadde, and give it to the pore,
And in swich wyse folwe him and his fore;              110
He spak to hem that wolde live parfitly:
And lordinges, by your leve, that am nat I.
I wol bistowe the flour of al myn age
In th' actes and in fruit of mariage.

"Telle me also, to what conclusioun               115
Were membres maad of generacioun,
And of so parfit wys a wight y-wroght?
Trusteth right wel, they were nat maad for noght.
Glose whoso wole, and seye bothe up and doun,
That they were maked for purgacioun                    120
Of urine, and our bothe thinges smale
Were eek to knowe a femele from a male,
And for noon other cause: sey ye no?
The experience woot wel it is noght so;
So that the clerkes be nat with me wrothe,             125
I sey this, that they maked been for bothe;
This is to seye, for office, and for ese
Of engendrure, ther we nat God displese.
Why sholde men elles in hir bokes sette,
That man shal yelde to his wyf hir dette?*             130
Now wherwith sholde he make his payement
If he ne used his sely instrument?
Than were they maad upon a creature
To purge uryne, and eek for engendrure.

"But I seye noght that every wight is holde,       135
That hath swich harneys as I to yow tolde,
To goon and usen hem in engendrure;
Than sholde men take of chastitee no cure.
Crist was a mayde, and shapen as a man,
And many a seint, sith that the world bigan,           140
Yet lived they ever in parfit chastitee.

"Virginity is a great perfection,                                    105
and also devoted continence,
but Christ, who is the well of perfection,
did not bid every man to go and sell
all that he had and give it to the poor,
and in that way to follow in his footsteps;                          110
He spoke to them that wished to live perfectly:
and by your leave, my lords, that isn't me.
I will bestow the flower of my whole life
in the acts and fruits of marriage.

"Tell me also, to what end                                           115
were reproductive organs made,
why are people made so perfectly?
Believe me, they were not made for nothing.
whoever wants to, let him enlarge on the matter
     and argue to
and fro that they were made for the purgation                        120
of urine, and that both our private parts
were made to distinguish a female from a male,
and for no other cause—do you say no?
Experience knows well it is not so;
so that the clerics won't be angry with me,                          125
I'll say this: they were made for both;
that is to say, for necessary business and for pleasure
in engendering, when we do not displease God.
Why else should men set it down in their books
that a man shall yield his wife her debt?                            130
Now how shall he make his payment
unless he uses his simple instrument?
Then, they were given to creatures
for purging urine and also for propagation.

"But I don't say that everyone who has                               135
such equipment as I mentioned is bound
to go and use it in engendering;
then we wouldn't care about chastity.
Christ, who was formed as a man, was a virgin,
and many a saint since the world began                               140
lived always in perfect chastity.

I nil envye no virginitee;
Lat hem be breed of pured whete seed
And lat us wyves hoten barly breed;*
And yet with barly breed, Mark telle can,                    145
Our Lord Jesu refresshed many a man.
In swich estaat as God hath cleped us
I wol persevere, I nam nat precious.
In wyfhode I wol use myn instrument
As frely as my maker hath it sent.                           150
If I be daungerous, God yeve me sorwe!
Myn housbond shal it have bothe eve and morwe,
Whan that him list com forth and paye his dette.
An housbonde I wol have, I nil nat lette,
Which shal be bothe my dettour and my thral,                 155
And have his tribulacioun* withal
Upon his flessh, whyl that I am his wyf.
I have the power duringe al my lyf
Upon his propre body, and noght he.*
Right thus th'Apostel tolde it unto me,                      160
And bad our housbondes for to love us weel.
Al this sentence me lyketh every deel—"
    Up sterte the Pardoner, and that anon,
"Now dame," quod he, "by God and by Seint John,
Ye been a noble prechour in this cas!                        165
I was aboute to wedde a wyf; allas!
What sholde I bye it on my flesh so dere?
Yet hadde I lever wedde no wyf to-yere!"
    "Abyde!" quod she, "my tale is nat bigonne;
Nay, thou shalt drinken of another tonne                     170
Er that I go, shal savoure wors than ale.
And whan that I have told thee forth my tale
Of tribulacioun in mariage,
Of which I am expert in al myn age—
This to seyn, myself have been the whippe—                   175
Than maystow chese whether thou wolt sippe
Of thilke tonne that I shal abroche.

I won't envy them virginity:
let them be white bread of finest wheat,
and let us wives be called barley bread;
and yet, with barley bread, as Mark tells us,          145
Our Lord Jesus refreshed many a man.
In such estate as God has called us to
I'll persevere; I'm not particular.
In marriage I'll use my equipment
as freely as my maker sent it.                          150
If I should be grudging, God give me sorrow!
My husband shall have it both evening and
    morning,
whenever he wants to come forth and pay his debt.
I'll have a husband—I won't make it difficult—
who shall be both my debtor and my slave,              155
and have his trouble
in the flesh while I'm his wife.
All through my life I have the power
over his own body, and not he.
Just so the Apostle explained it to me,                160
and he bade our husbands to love us well.
Every bit of this lesson pleases me—"
    Just then the Pardoner started up;
"Now, dame," he said, "by God and by Saint John,
you are a noble preacher in this matter!               165
I was about to wed a wife; alas,
why should I purchase it so dearly with my flesh?
I'd rather not wed a wife this year!"
    "Wait," said she, "my tale is not begun;
no, you'll drink from another barrel                   170
before I am through—one that shall taste worse
    than ale.
And when I have told you my tale
of the tribulation of marriage,
in which I have been an expert all my life—
that is to say, I myself have been the whip—          175
then you may choose whether you wish to sip
of the tun that I shall broach.

Be war of it, er thou to ny approche;
For I shal telle ensamples mo than ten.
Whoso that nil be war by othere men,                    180
By him shul othere men corrected be.
The same wordes wryteth Ptholomee;
Rede in his *Almageste,** and take it there."

　　"Dame, I wolde praye yow, if your wil it were,"
Seyde this Pardoner, "as ye bigan,                      185
Telle forth your tale; spareth for no man,
And teche us yonge men of your praktike."

　　"Gladly," quod she, "sith it may yow lyke.
But yet I praye to al this companye,
If that I speke after my fantasye,                      190
As taketh not agrief of that I seye;
For myn entente nis but for to pleye.

　　"Now sires, now wol I telle forth my tale.—
As ever mote I drinken wyn or ale,
I shal seye sooth, tho housbondes that I hadde,         195
As three of hem were gode and two were badde.
The three men were gode, and riche, and olde;
Unnethe mighte they the statut holde
In which that they were bounden unto me—
Ye woot wel what I mene of this, pardee!                200
As help me God, I laughe whan I thinke
How pitously a-night I made hem swinke;
And by my fey, I tolde of it no stoor.
They had me yeven hir lond and hir tresoor;
Me neded nat do lenger diligence                        205
To winne hir love, or doon hem reverence.
They loved me so wel, by God above,
That I ne tolde no deyntee of hir love!
A wys womman wol sette hir ever in oon
To gete hir love, ye, ther as she hath noon;            210
But sith I hadde hem hoolly in myn hond,
And sith they hadde me yeven all hir lond,
What sholde I taken hede hem for to plese,
But it were for my profit and myn ese?

Be wary of it, before you approach too near;
for I shall tell more than ten examples.
By him who won't be warned by other men                    180
shall other men be warned.
These same words were written by Ptolemy;
read in his *Almagest,* and find it there."

    "Dame, I pray you, if it be your will,"
said this Pardoner, "tell your tale                        185
as you began; leave off for no man,
and teach us young men some of your practice."

    "Gladly," said she, "since it may please you.
But yet I pray all this company
that if I speak according to my fancy,                     190
you do not take what I say amiss;
for I only intend to amuse you.

    "Now, sirs, I'll go on with my tale.—
As ever I hope to drink wine or ale,
I'll tell the truth; of those husbands that I had,         195
three of them were good and two were bad.
The first three men were good, and rich, and old;
they were scarcely able to keep the statute
by which they were bound to me—
you know quite well what I mean by this, by heaven!        200
So help me God, I laugh when I think
how pitifully I made them work at night;
and by my faith I set no store by it.
They had given me their land and their treasure;
I no longer needed to be diligent                          205
to win their love, or show them reverence.
They loved me so well, by God above,
that I didn't prize their love!
A wise woman will concentrate on getting
that love which she doesn't possess;                       210
but since I had them wholly in my hand,
and since they had given me all their land,
why should I take pains to please them,
unless it should be for my own profit and
        pleasure?

I sette hem so a-werke, by my fey,                                    215
That many a night they songen 'weilawey!'
The bacoun was nat fet for hem, I trowe,
That som men han in Essex at Dunmowe.*
I governed hem so well, after my lawe,
That ech of hem ful blisful was and fawe                              220
To bringe me gaye thinges fro the fayre.
They were ful glad whan I spak to hem fayre;
For God it woot, I chidde hem spitously.

  " 'Now herkneth, how I bar me proprely,
Ye wyse wyves, that can understonde.                                  225
Thus shoulde ye speke and bere hem wrong on honde;
For half so boldely can ther no man
Swere and lyen as a womman can.
I sey nat this by wyves that ben wyse,
But if it be whan they hem misavyse.                                  230
A wys wyf, if that she can hir good,
Shal bere him on hond the cow is wood,*
And take witnesse of hir owene mayde
Of hir assent; but herkneth how I sayde:

  " 'Sir olde kaynard, is this thyn array?                            235
Why is my neighebores wyf so gay?
She is honoured overal ther she goth;
I sitte at hoom, I have no thrifty cloth.
What dostow at my neighebores hous?
Is she so fair? Artow so amorous?                                     240
What rowne ye with our mayde, ben'cite!
Sir olde lechour, lat thy japes be!
And if I have a gossib or a freend,
Withouten gilt, thou chydest as a feend,
If that I walke or pleye unto his hous!                               245
Thou comest hoom as dronken as a mous,
And prechest on thy bench, with yvel preef!
Thou seist to me it is a greet meschief
To wedde a povre womman, for costage;
And if that she be riche, of heigh parage,                           250

I so set them to work, by my faith,                                    215
that many a night they sang 'alas!'
The prize of bacon some people have in
Essex at Dunmow was never brought to them, I know.
I governed them so well in my way
that each of them was most happy and eager               220
to bring me gay things from the fair.
They were glad indeed when I spoke pleasantly
        to them;
for God knows I chided them cruelly.
    " 'Now hear how suitably I behaved myself,
you wise wives who can understand.                            225
You should speak thus and put them in the wrong;
for no man can perjure himself and lie
half so boldly as a woman can.
I don't say this for wives that are wise,
except when they have made a mistake.                        230
A wise wife, if she knows what is good for her,
will convince her husband that the chough is mad,
and call as a witness her own maid,
who conspires with her; but listen to how I spoke:
    " 'Old sluggard, is this the way you dress me?        235
Why is my neighbor's wife so smart?
She is honored everywhere she goes;
I sit at home, I have no decent clothes.
What do you do at my neighbor's house?
Is she so fair? Are you so amorous?                              240
What are you whispering to our maid, for
        heaven's sake?
Old sir, lecher, stop your tricks!
Why, if I have a friend or acquaintance
in all innocence, you chide like a fiend
if I walk to his house and visit!                                    245
You come home as drunk as a mouse
and preach from your bench, bad luck to you!
You tell me it is a great misfortune
to marry a poor woman, as far as cost is concerned;
and if she is rich and of high lineage,                          250

Than seistow that it is a tormentrye
To suffre hir pryde and hir malencolye.
And if that she be fair, thou verray knave,
Thou seyst that every holour wol hir have:
She may no whyle in chastitee abyde,        255
That is assailled upon ech a syde.

"'Thou seyst som folk desyre us for richesse,
Som for our shap, and som for our fairnesse;
And som, for she can outher singe or daunce,
And som, for gentillesse and daliaunce;        260
Som, for hir handes and hir armes smale;
Thus goth al to the devel by thy tale.
Thou seyst men may nat kepe a castel wal,
It may so longe assailled been overal.

"'And if that she be foul, thou seist that she        265
Coveiteth every man that she may see;
For as a spaynel she wol on him lepe,
Til that she finde som man hir to chepe;
Ne noon so grey goos goth ther in the lake,
As, seistow, that wol been withoute make;        270
And seyst it is an hard thing for to welde
A thing that no man wol, his thankes, helde.
Thus seistow, lorel, whan thow goost to bedde,
And that no wys man nedeth for to wedde,
Ne no man that entendeth unto hevene.        275
With wilde thonder-dint and firy levene
Mote thy welked nekke be tobroke!

"'Thow seyst that dropping houses, and eek smoke,
And chyding wyves, maken men to flee
Out of hir owene hous; a, ben'cite!        280
What eyleth swich an old man for to chyde?
Thow seyst we wyves wol our vyces hyde
Til we be fast, and than we wol hem shewe;
Wel may that be a proverbe of a shrewe!
Thou seist that oxen, asses, hors, and houndes,        285
They been assayed at diverse stoundes;
Bacins, lavours, er that men hem bye,

then you say that it is a torment
to suffer her pride and her melancholy.
And if she is fair, you knave,
you say that every lecher wants to have her;
she who is assaulted on every side                                     255
can't remain chaste very long.

 " 'You say some men desire us for wealth,
some for our shapeliness, and some for our beauty;
some want a woman because she can sing or dance,
some because she is well-bred and flirtatious;                         260
some like her hands and her graceful arms;
thus we all go to the devil by your account.
You say no one can keep a castle wall
when it is assailed all around for so long a time.

 " 'And if she is ugly, you say that she                               265
covets every man she sees;
for she will leap on him like a spaniel
until she finds some man who will buy her wares;
there is no goose swimming in the lake, you say,
that is so gray it cannot find a mate.                                  270
And you say it is very hard to manage
a thing that no man will willingly keep.
You say this, you wretch, as you go to bed,
and that no wise man needs to marry,
nor any man who aspires to heaven.                                      275
May wild thunderbolts and fiery lightning
break your withered neck!

 " 'You say that leaking houses and smoke
and nagging wives make men flee
out of their own houses; bless us,                                     280
what ails such an old man to scold so?
You say we wives will hide our vices
until we are safely married, and then we will show them;
that's certainly a fit proverb for a scolding curmudgeon!
You say that oxen, asses, horses, and hounds                           285
are tested at various times;
and so are basins and washbowls, before people
    buy them—

Spones and stoles, and al swich housbondrye,
And so been pottes, clothes, and array;
But folk of wyves maken noon assay                    290
Til they be wedded; olde dotard shrewe!
And than, seistow, we wol oure vices shewe.
  " 'Thou seist also that it displeseth me
But if that thou wolt preyse my beautee,
And but thou poure alwey upon my face,                295
And clepe me "faire dame" in every place;
And but thou make a feste on thilke day
That I was born, and make me fresh and gay,
And but thou do to my norice honour,
And to my chamberere withinne my bour,                300
And to my fadres folk and his allyes;—
Thus seistow, olde barel ful of lyes!
  " 'And yet of our apprentice Janekyn,
For his crisp heer, shyninge as gold so fyn,
And for he squiereth me bothe up and doun,            305
Yet hastow caught a fals suspecioun;
I wol hym noght, thogh thou were deed tomorwe.
  " 'But tel me this, why hydestow, with sorwe,
The keyes of thy cheste awey fro me?
It is my good as wel as thyn, pardee.                 310
What, wenestow make an idiot of our dame?
Now by that lord that called is Seint Jame,
Thou shalt nat bothe, thogh that thou were wood,
Be maister of my body and of my good;
That oon thou shalt forgo, maugree thyne yën.          315
What helpeth it of me to enquere or spyën?
I trowe, thou woldest loke me in thy cheste!
Thou sholdest seye, "Wyf, go wher thee leste;
Tak your disport; I wol nat leve no talis.
I knowe yow for a trewe wyf, dame Alis."              320
We love no man that taketh kepe or charge
Wher that we goon; we wol ben at our large.
  " 'Of alle men y-blessed moot he be
The wyse astrologien Dan Ptholome,

spoons and stools and all such household goods,
and so are pots, clothes and adornments;
but men don't try out wives                                    290
until they are married; scolding old dotard!
And then, you say, we'll show our vices.

" 'You also say that I am displeased
unless you praise my beauty,
and pore constantly on my face,                                295
and call me "fair dame" everywhere;
and unless you hold a feast on my
birthday, and give me gay new clothing,
and unless you honor my nurse
and my chambermaid,                                            300
and my father's relatives and connections;—
you say all this, old barrel full of lies!

" 'Moreover, you have caught a false
suspicion of our apprentice Jankin,
because he has curly hair, shining like purest gold,           305
and squires me everywhere;
I wouldn't want him even if you died tomorrow.

" 'But tell me this, why do you hide—sorrow to you!—
the keys of your chest away from me?
It is my property as well as yours, by heaven.                 310
Do you think you can make an idiot of the mistress
     of the
house? Now by the lord who is called Saint James,
you shall not be master of both my body and my goods,
even if you rage with anger;
you'll go without one of them, like it or not.                 315
What use is it to snoop and spy on me?
I think you'd like to lock me in your chest!
You should say, "Wife, go where you like;
amuse yourself, I won't believe any gossip.
I know you for a true wife, Dame Alice."                       320
We don't love a man who carefully watches
where we go; we want to be at large.

" 'Beyond all other men, may the wise
astrologer Lord Ptolemy be blessed,

That seith this proverbe in his *Almageste:*                           325
"Of alle men his wisdom is the hyeste
That rekketh never who hath the world in honde."
By this proverbe thou shalt understonde,
Have thou ynough, what thar thee recche or care
How merily that othere folkes fare?                                     330
For certeyn, olde dotard, by your leve,
Ye shul have queynte right ynough at eve.
He is to greet a nigard that wol werne
A man to lighte his candle at his lanterne;
He shal have never the lasse light, pardee;                            335
Have thou ynough, thee thar nat pleyne thee.

   " 'Thou seyst also that if we make us gay
With clothing and with precious array
That it is peril of our chastitee;
And yet, with sorwe, thou most enforce thee,                          340
And seye thise wordes in the Apostles name:
"In habit maad with chastitee and shame
Ye wommen shul apparaille yow," quod he,
"And noght in tressed heer and gay perree,
As perles, ne with gold, ne clothes riche."                            345
After thy text, ne after thy rubriche,
I wol nat wirche as muchel as a gnat.
Thou seydest this, that I was lyk a cat;
For whoso wolde senge a cattes skin,
Thanne wolde the cat wel dwellen in his in;                            350
And if the cattes skin be slyk and gay,
She wol nat dwelle in house half a day,
But forth she wole, er any day be dawed,
To shewe hir skin and goon a-caterwawed;
This is to seye, if I be gay, sir shrewe,                               355
I wol renne out, my borel for to shewe.

   " 'Sire olde fool, what helpeth thee to spyën?
Thogh thou preye Argus, with his hundred yën,
To be my warde-cors, as he can best,
In feith, he shal nat kepe me but me lest;                             360
Yet coude I make his berd, so moot I thee.

for in his *Almagest* he speaks this proverb:                     325
"The wisest of all men is he
that never cares who has the world in his hand."
You should understand by this proverb
that if you have enough, why should you care
how merrily other folks fare?                                      330
For certainly, old dotard, by your leave,
you'll have quite sex enough at night.
He who forbids another man to light a candle
at his lantern is too great a niggard;
he'll have none the less light, by heaven;                          335
if you have enough, you needn't complain.

    " 'You also say that if we make ourselves attractive
with fine clothing and adornments
it imperils our chastity;
and further—sorrow take you—you must back
    yourself up                                    340
by saying these words in the Apostle's name:
"You women shall adorn yourselves
in shamefastness and sobriety," said he,
"and not in braided hair and gay jewels,
as pearls or gold, or rich array";                                  345
I won't conform to this text and
rubric one gnat's worth!
You said this: that I was like a cat;
for if someone singes a cat's fur,
then the cat will stay in its dwelling;                             350
and if the cat's fur is sleek and attractive,
she won't stay in the house half a day,
but out she'll go, before the break of day,
to show her fur and go a-caterwauling;
this is to say, sir grouch, that if I'm gaily dressed,              355
I'll run out to show off my clothes.

    " 'You old fool, what use is it for you to spy?
Even if you ask Argus, with his hundred eyes,
to be my bodyguard (as he can do it best),
in faith, he can't guard me unless I please;                        360
I still could deceive him, as I hope to thrive.

" 'Thou seydest eek, that ther ben thinges three,
The whiche thinges troublen al this erthe,
And that no wight may endure the ferthe;
O leve sir shrewe, Jesu shorte thy lyf!                365
Yet prechestow, and seyst an hateful wyf
Y-rekened is for oon of thise meschances.
Been ther none othere maner resemblances
That ye may lykne your parables to,
But if a sely wyf be oon of tho?                        370
" 'Thou lykenest wommanes love to helle,
To bareyne lond, ther water may not dwelle.
Thou lyknest it also to wilde fyr:
The more it brenneth, the more it hath desyr
To consume every thing that brent wol be.              375
Thou seyst right as wormes shende a tree,
Right so a wyf destroyeth hir housbonde;
This knowe they that been to wyves bonde.'

"Lordinges, right thus, as ye have understonde,
Bar I stifly myne olde housbondes on honde,            380
That thus they seyden in hir dronkenesse;
And al was fals, but that I took witnesse
On Janekin and on my nece also.
O Lord, the peyne I dide hem and the wo,
Ful gilteless, by Goddes swete pyne!                   385
For as an hors I coude byte and whyne;
I coude pleyne, thogh I were in the gilt,
Or elles often tyme hadde I ben spilt.
Whoso that first to mille comth, first grint;
I pleyned first, so was our werre y-stint.             390
They were ful glad t'excusen hem ful blyve
Of thing of which they never agilte hir lyve.

"Of wenches wolde I beren hem on honde,
Whan that for syk unnethes mighte they stonde.
Yet tikled it his herte, for that he                   395
Wende that I hadde of him so greet chiertee.
I swoor that al my walkinge out by nighte
Was for t'espye wenches that he dighte;
Under that colour hadde I many a mirthe,

" 'You also said that there are three things
which trouble all this earth,
and that no man can endure a fourth;
O dear sir tartar, Jesus shorten your life!                365
Still you preach and say that a hateful wife
is reckoned as one of these misfortunes.
Are there no other kind of comparisons
you can apply your parables to—
must a poor wife be one of them?                          370
    " 'You compare a woman's love to hell,
to barren land where water can't remain.
You compare it also to wild fire:
the more it burns, the more it wants
to consume everything that will burn.                     375
You say that just as worms destroy a tree,
just so a wife destroys her husband; and
that all who are bound to wives know this.'
    "My lords, just so, as you have learned,
I boldly accused my old husbands                          380
of speaking in their drunkenness;
and all was false, but I called on
Jankin and my niece as witnesses.
Oh Lord, the pain and woe I gave them,
though they were guiltless, by God's sweet suffering!     385
For I could bite and whinny like a horse;
I could complain, though I was the guilty one;
else many time I would have been ruined.
Whoever comes first to the mill, grinds first;
I complained first, and so our fight was ended.           390
They were quite glad to excuse themselves quickly
for things they had never been guilty of in their lives.
    "I would accuse them about wenches
when they were so sick they could hardly stand.
Yet it tickled a husband's heart, since he                395
thought I showed such great fondness for him.
I swore that all my walking out by night
was to spy out the wenches he lay with;
under this pretense I had many a merry time,

For al swich wit is yeven us in our birthe;                    400
Deceite, weping, spinning God hath yive
To wommen kindely, whyl they may live.
And thus of o thing I avaunte me,
Atte ende I hadde the bettre in ech degree,
By sleighte, or force, or by som maner thing,    405
As by continuel murmur or grucching;
Namely abedde hadden they meschaunce,
Ther wolde I chyde and do hem no plesaunce;
I wolde no lenger in the bed abyde,
If that I felte his arm over my syde,              410
Til he had maad his raunson unto me;
Than wolde I suffre him do his nycetee.
And therfore every man this tale I telle,
Winne whoso may, for al is for to selle:
With empty hand men may none haukes lure;         415
For winning wolde I al his lust endure,
And make me a feyned appetyt;
And yet in bacon hadde I never delyt—
That made me that ever I wolde hem chyde.
For thogh the pope had seten hem bisyde,           420
I wolde nat spare hem at hir owene bord;
For by my trouthe, I quitte hem word for word.
As help me verray God omnipotent,
Thogh I right now sholde make my testament,
I ne owe hem nat a word that it nis quit.          425
I broghte it so aboute by my wit
That they moste yeve it up, as for the beste;
Or elles hadde we never been in reste.
For thogh he loked as a wood leoun,
Yet sholde he faille of his conclusioun.           430
    "Thanne wolde I seye, 'Gode lief, tak keep
How mekely loketh Wilkin oure sheep;
Com neer, my spouse, let me ba thy cheke!
Ye sholde been al pacient and meke,
And han a swete spyced conscience,                 435
Sith ye so preche of Jobes pacience.
Suffreth alwey, sin ye so wel can preche;

for all such wit is given us at our birth;                              400
God has given women by nature deceit, weeping,
and spinning, as long as they live.
And thus I can boast of one thing:
in the end I got the better of them in every case,
by trick, or force, or by some kind of method,                         405
such as continual complaining or whining,
in particular, they had misfortune in bed,
where I would chide and give them no pleasure;
I would no longer stay in the bed
if I felt my husband's arm over my side                                410
until he had paid his ransom to me;
then I'd allow him to do his bit of business.
Therefore I tell this moral to everyone—
profit whoever may, for all is for sale:
you cannot lure a hawk with an empty hand;                             415
for profit I would endure all his lust,
and pretend an appetite myself;
and yet I never had a taste for aged meat—
that's what made me scold them all the time.
For even if the pope had sat beside them,                              420
I wouldn't spare them at their own board;
I swear I requited them word for word.
So help me almighty God,
even if I were to make my testament right now,
I don't owe them a word which has not been repaid.                     425
I brought it about by my wit
that they had to give up, as the best thing to do,
or else we would never have been at rest.
For though he might look like a raging lion,
yet he would fail to gain his point.                                   430
    "Then I would say, 'Dear friend, notice
the meek look on Wilkin, our sheep;
come near, my spouse, let me kiss your cheek!
You should be quite patient and meek,
and have a scrupulous conscience,                                      435
since you preach so of the patience of Job.
Always be patient, since you preach so well;

And but ye do, certein we shal yow teche
That it is fair to have a wyf in pees.
Oon of us two moste bowen, doutelees;    440
And sith a man is more resonable
Than womman is, ye moste been suffrable.
What eyleth yow to grucche thus and grone?
Is it for ye wolde have my queynte allone?
Why taak it al, lo, have it everydeel;    445
Peter! I shrewe yow but ye love it weel!
For if I wolde selle my *bele chose*,*
I coude walke as fresh as is a rose;
But I wol kepe it for your owene tooth.
Ye be to blame, by God, I sey yow sooth.'    450
    "Swiche maner wordes hadde we on honde.
Now wol I speken of my fourthe housbonde.
    "My fourthe housbonde was a revelour—
This is to seyn, he hadde a paramour;
And I was yong and ful of ragerye,    455
Stiborn and strong, and joly as a pye.
How coude I daunce to an harpe smale,
And singe, ywis, as any nightingale,
Whan I had dronke a draughte of swete wyn!
Metellius, the foule cherl, the swyn,    460
That with a staf birafte his wyf hir lyf
For she drank wyn, thogh I hadde been his wyf,
He sholde nat han daunted me fro drinke;
And after wyn on Venus moste I thinke:
For al so siker as cold engendreth hayl,    465
A likerous mouth moste han a likerous tayl.
In womman vinolent is no defence;
This knowen lechours by experience.
    "But, Lord Crist! whan that it remembreth me
Upon my yowthe and on my jolitee,    470
It tikleth me aboute myn herte rote;
Unto this day it dooth myn herte bote
That I have had my world as in my tyme.
But age, allas! that al wol envenyme,
Hath me biraft my beautee and my pith;    475

for unless you do, we shall certainly teach you
that it is a fine thing to have a wife in peace.
One of us two must bend, without a doubt;          440
and since a man is more reasonable
than a woman is, you must be patient.
What ails you to grumble and groan so?
Is it because you want to have my thing to yourself?
Why take it all, then, have every bit of it!          445
Peter! I swear you love it well!
Now if I would sell my *belle chose,*
I could walk as fresh as a rose;
but I will keep it for your own taste.
You're to blame, by God, I tell you the truth.'          450
    "We would have words like this.
Now I will speak of my fourth husband.

    "My fourth husband was a reveller—
that is to say, he had a paramour;
and I was young and full of wantonness,          455
stubborn and strong and merry as a magpie.
How gracefully I could dance to a harp,
and sing just like a nightingale,
when I had drunk a draught of sweet wine!
Metellius, the foul churl, the swine,          460
who took his wife's life with a staff
because she drank wine—if I had been his wife
he wouldn't have daunted me from drink;
and after wine I must needs think of Venus:
for just as surely as cold brings hail,          465
a lickerish mouth must have a lecherous tail.
A drunken woman has no defense;
this, lechers know by experience.

    "But Lord Christ! When I remember
my youth and my gaiety,          470
it tickles me to the bottom of my heart;
to this day it does my heart good
that I have had my world in my time.
But age, alas, that poisons everything,
has robbed me of my beauty and my pith;          475

Lat go, farewel, the devel go therwith!
The flour is goon, ther is namore to telle:
The bren, as I best can, now moste I selle;
But yet to be right mery wol I fonde.
Now wol I tellen of my fourthe housbonde.        480
    "I seye, I hadde in herte greet despyt
That he of any other had delyt.
But he was quit, by God and by Seint Joce!*
I made him of the same wode a croce;
Nat of my body in no foul manere,        485
But, certeinly, I made folk swich chere,
That in his owene grece I made him frye
For angre and for verray jalousye.
By God, in erthe I was his purgatorie,
For which I hope his soule be in glorie.        490
For God it woot, he sat ful ofte and song
Whan that his shoo ful bitterly him wrong.
Ther was no wight, save God and he, that wiste,
In many wyse, how sore I him twiste.
He deyde whan I cam fro Jerusalem,        495
And lyth y-grave under the rode-beem,*
Al is his tombe noght so curious
As was the sepulcre of him Darius,*
Which that Appelles* wroghte subtilly;
It nis but wast to burie him preciously.        500
Lat him fare wel, God yeve his soule reste;
He is now in the grave and in his cheste.
    "Now of my fifthe housbond wol I telle:
God lete his soule never come in helle!
And yet was he to me the moste shrewe;        505
That fele I on my ribbes al by rewe,
And ever shal, unto myn ending day.
But in our bed he was so fresh and gay,
And therwithal so wel coude he me glose
Whan that he wolde han my *bele chose,*        510
That thogh he hadde me bet on every boon
He coude winne agayn my love anoon.
I trowe I loved him beste for that he

let it go, farewell, the devil with it!
The flour is gone, there is no more to say:
now I must sell the bran, as best I can;
but still I will contrive to be right merry.
Now I'll tell about my fourth husband.                    480
    "I tell you I was angry in my heart
that he had delight in any other.
But he was repaid, by God and by Saint Joce!
I made him a staff of the same wood—
not with my body in a filthy way,                         485
but indeed my manner with other men was such
that I made him fry in his own grease
for anger and pure jealousy.
By God, I was his purgatory on earth,
by which help I hope his soul is in glory.                490
For God knows he often sat and sang out
when his shoe pinched him bitterly.
No one but God and he knew
how sorely I wrung him in many ways.
He died when I came back from Jerusalem,                  495
and lies buried under the rood-beam,
although his tomb is not so elaborate
as the sepulchre of that Darius was
which Appelles wrought so skillfully;
it would have been just a waste to bury him expensively.  500
Farewell to him, may God rest his soul;
he is now in his grave and in his coffin.
    "Now I will tell of my fifth husband:
God never let his soul go down to hell!
And yet he was the most brutal to me;                     505
that I can feel on my ribs, all down the row,
and always shall, to my dying day.
But in our bed he was so tireless and wanton,
and moreover he could cajole me so well
when he wanted to have my *belle chose,*                  510
that even if he had beaten me on every bone,
he could soon win my love again.
I think I loved him best because

Was of his love daungerous to me.
We wommen han, if that I shal nat lye,          515
In this matere a queynte fantasye;
Wayte what thing we may nat lightly have,
Therafter wol we crye al day and crave.
Forbede us thing, and that desyren we;
Prees on us faste, and thanne wol we flee.          520
With daunger oute we al our chaffare;
Greet prees at market maketh dere ware,
And to greet cheep is holde at litel prys;
This knoweth every womman that is wys.

"My fifthe housbonde, God his soule blesse,          525
Which that I took for love and no richesse,
He somtyme was a clerk of Oxenford,
And had left scole, and wente at hoom to bord
With my gossib, dwellinge in oure toun:
God have hir soule! Hir name was Alisoun.          530
She knew myn herte and eek my privetee
Bet than our parisshe preest, so moot I thee!
To hir biwreyed I my conseil al.
For had myn housebonde pissed on a wal
Or doon a thing that sholde han cost his lyf,          535
To hir, and to another worthy wyf,
And to my nece, which that I loved weel,
I wolde han told his conseil every deel.
And so I dide ful often, God it woot,
That made his face ful often reed and hoot          540
For verray shame, and blamed himself for he
Had told to me so greet a privetee.

"And so bifel that ones, in a Lente—
So often tymes I to my gossib wente,
For ever yet I lovede to be gay,          545
And for to walke, in March, Averille, and May,
Fro hous to hous, to here sondry talis—
That Jankin clerk and my gossib dame Alis
And I myself into the feldes wente.
Myn housbond was at London al that Lente;          550
I hadde the bettre leyser for to pleye,

he was so cool in his love to me.
We women have, to tell the truth,                                    515
an odd fancy in this matter;
whatever we cannot easily get
we will cry after and crave all day.
Forbid us a thing, and we desire it;
press it upon us, and then we will flee.                             520
Faced with coyness we bring out all our wares;
a great crowd at the market makes wares expensive,
and what is too cheap is held to be worth little;
every wise woman knows this.

    "My fifth husband, God bless his soul,                         525
whom I took for love and not money,
was at one time a scholar at Oxford,
and had left school, and went home to board
with my close friend, who dwelt in our town:
God bless her soul! Her name was Alison.                             530
She knew my heart and private affairs
better than our parish priest, as I may thrive!
To her I revealed all my secrets.
For whether my husband had pissed on a wall
or done something which should have cost him his life,               535
to her, and to another worthy wife,
and to my niece, whom I loved well,
I would have betrayed every one of his secrets.
And so I did often enough, God knows,
and that often made his face red and hot                             540
for very shame, so that he blamed himself
for having told me so great a confidence.

    "And so it happened that once, in Lent
(thus many times I went to my friend's house,
for I always loved to be merry,                                      545
and to walk, in March, April, and May,
from house to house, to hear various tidings),
that Jankin the clerk and my dear friend Dame Alice
and I myself went into the fields.
My husband was at London all that Lent;                              550
I had the better leisure to enjoy myself

And for to see, and eek for to be seye
Of lusty folk; what wiste I wher my grace
Was shapen for to be, or in what place?
Therefore I made my visitaciouns                    555
To vigilies and to processiouns,
To preching eek and to thise pilgrimages,
To pleyes of miracles and to mariages,
And wered upon my gaye scarlet gytes:
Thise wormes ne thise motthes ne thise mytes,      560
Upon my peril, frete hem never a deel;
And wostow why? For they were used weel.
    "Now wol I tellen forth what happed me.
I seye that in the feeldes walked we,
Til trewely we hadde swich daliance,               565
This clerk and I, that of my purveyance
I spak to him, and seyde him how that he,
If I were widwe, sholde wedde me.
For certeinly, I sey for no bobance,
Yet was I never withouten purveyance              570
Of mariage, n'of othere thinges eek:
I holde a mouses herte nat worth a leek
That hath but oon hole for to sterte to,
And if that faille, thanne is al y-do.
    "I bar him on honde he hadde enchanted me;     575
My dame taughte me that soutiltee.
And eek I seyde I mette of him al night:
He wolde han slayn me as I lay upright
And al my bed was ful of verray blood,
But yet I hope that he shal do me good;           580
For blood bitokeneth gold, as me was taught.
And al was fals, I dremed of it right naught,
But as I folwed ay my dames lore,
As wel of this as of other thinges more.
    "But now sir, lat me see, what I shal seyn?    585
Aha! By God, I have my tale ageyn.
    "Whan that my fourthe housbond was on bere,
I weep algate, and made sory chere,

and to see, and be seen by,
lusty people; how could I know how my favor
was destined to be bestowed, or where?
Therefore I made my visits                              555
to feast-eves and processions,
to sermons and these pilgrimages,
to miracle plays and to marriages,
and wore my gay scarlet clothes:
on my life, worms or moths or mites                     560
never ate a bit of them;
and do you know why? Because they were
    used constantly.
    "Now I'll tell what happened to me.
As I was saying, we walked in the fields,
until truly this clerk and I enjoyed                    565
such dalliance that in my foresight
I spoke to him and told him that
if I were a widow he should marry me.
For certainly (I don't say it as a boast)
I was never yet unprovided for                          570
in marriage, and other matters too;
I hold that a mouse that has but one hole
to run to has a heart not worth a leek;
for if that should fail, then all is finished.
    "I made him believe he had enchanted me;           575
my mother taught me that trick.
And also I said I had dreamed of him all night:
he wanted to slay me as I lay on my back,
and all my bed was full of blood;
but yet I expected that he would bring me luck;        580
for blood signifies gold, as I was taught.
And all this was false, I had dreamed none of it;
I was just following my mother's lore, as I
always did, in this as well as in other matters.
    "But now sir, let me see, what am I talking about?  585
Aha! By God, I have my tale back again
    "When my fourth husband was on his bier,
I wept, all the same, and acted sorrowful,

As wyves moten, for it is usage,
And with my coverchief covered my visage;          590
But for that I was purveyed of a make,
I weep but smal, and that I undertake.
    "To chirche was myn housbond born amorwe
With neighebores, that for him maden sorwe;
And Janekin oure clerk was oon of tho.          595
As help me God, whan that I saugh him go
After the bere, me thoughte he hadde a paire
Of legges and of feet so clene and faire,
That al myn herte I yaf unto his hold.
He was, I trowe, a twenty winter old,          600
And I was fourty, if I shal seye sooth;
But yet I hadde alwey a coltes tooth.
Gat-tothed* was, and that bicam me weel:
I hadde the prente of Seinte Venus seel.*
As help me God, I was a lusty oon,          605
And faire and riche and yong and wel bigoon;
And trewely, as myne housbondes tolde me,
I had the beste *quoniam*\* mighte be.
For certes, I am al Venerien*
In felinge, and myn herte is Marcien:*          610
Venus me yaf my lust, my likerousnesse,
And Mars yaf me my sturdy hardinesse.
Myn ascendent was Taur, and Mars therinne.
Allas, allas, that ever love was sinne!
I folwed ay myn inclinacioun          615
By vertu of my constellacioun;
That made me I coude noght withdrawe
My chambre of Venus from a good felawe.
Yet have I Martes mark* upon my face,
And also in another privee place.          620
For, God so wis be my savacioun,
I ne loved never by no discrecioun,
But ever folwede myn appetyt,
Al were he short or long, or blak or whyt;
I took no kepe, so that he lyked me,          625

as wives must, for it is customary,
and covered my face with my handkerchief;                      590
but since I was provided with a mate,
I wept but little, that I guarantee.

"My husband was brought to church in the morning,
with neighbors who mourned for him;
and Jankin our clerk was one of them.                          595
So help me God, when I saw him walk
behind the bier, it seemed to me he had a pair
of legs and feet so neat and handsome
that I gave all my heart into his keeping.
He was, I think, twenty years old,                             600
and I was forty, if the truth be told;
but yet I always had a colt's tooth.
I was gap-toothed, and that became me well;
I had the print of St. Venus's seal.
So help me God, I was a lusty one,                             605
and fair and rich and young and well off;
and truly, as my husbands told me,
I had the best *quoniam* that might be.
For certainly, my feelings all come
from Venus, and my heart from Mars:                            610
Venus gave me my lust, my lecherousness,
and Mars gave me my sturdy hardiness,
because Taurus was in the ascendant when I was
     born, and
Mars was in that sign. Alas, alas, that ever love was sin!
I always followed my inclination                               615
according to the stellar influences at my birth;
I was so made that I could not withhold
my chamber of Venus from a good fellow.
I still have the mark of Mars on my face,
and also in another private place.                             620
For, as surely as God is my salvation,
I never had any discrimination in love,
but always followed my appetite,
be he short or tall, dark or fair;
I didn't care, so long as he pleased me,                       625

How pore he was, ne eek of what degree.
    "What sholde I seye, but, at the monthes ende,
This joly clerk Jankin, that was so hende
Hath wedded me with greet solempnitee,
And to him yaf I al the lond and fee                    630
That ever was me yeven therbifore;
But afterward repented me ful sore:
He nolde suffre nothing of my list.
By God, he smoot me ones on the list,
For that I rente out of his book a leef,                635
That of the strook myn ere wex al deef.
Stiborn I was as is a leonesse,
And of my tonge a verray jangleresse,
And walke I wolde, as I had doon biforn,
From hous to hous, although he had it sworn;            640
For which he often tymes wolde preche,
And me of olde Romayn gestes teche,
How he Simplicius Gallus* lefte his wyf,
And hir forsook for terme of al his lyf,
Noght but for open-heeded he hir say                    645
Lokinge out at his dore upon a day.
    "Another Romayn tolde he me by name,
That, for his wyf was at a someres game
Withoute his witing, he forsook hir eke.
And than wolde he upon his Bible seke                   650
That ilke proverbe of Ecclesiaste,*
Wher he comandeth and forbedeth faste
Man shal nat suffre his wyf go roule aboute;
Than wolde he seye right thus, withouten doute:
    'Whoso that buildeth his hous al of salwes,         655
    And priketh his blinde hors over the falwes,
    And suffreth his wyf to go seken halwes,
    Is worthy to been hanged on the galwes.'
But al for noght; I sette noght an hawe
Of his proverbes n'of his olde sawe,                    660
Ne I wolde nat of him corrected be.
I hate him that my vices telleth me,

how poor he was, nor of what rank.
   "What should I say, except that at the end of the
      month
this gay clerk Jankin, that was so pleasant,
wedded me with great ceremony,
and to him I gave all the lands and property          630
that had ever been given to me before,
but afterward I repented this sorely:
he would not allow anything I wanted.
By God, he hit me once on the ear
because I had torn a leaf out of his book;            635
as a result of that stroke, my ear became totally deaf.
I was stubborn as a lioness,
and as for my tongue, an absolute ranter;
and I'd walk, as I'd done before,
from house to house, although he'd sworn I wouldn't;  640
because of this he would often preach
and teach me of the deeds of ancient Romans:
how Simplicius Gallus left his wife
and forsook her for the rest of his life
just because he saw her looking out                   645
of his door bareheaded one day.
   "He told me by name of another Roman
who also, because his wife was at a summer
game without his knowledge, forsook her.
And then he would seek in his Bible                   650
for that proverb of Ecclesiasticus
where he makes a command strictly forbidding
a man to allow his wife to go roaming about;
then you could be sure he would say this:
   'Whoever builds his house of willows,             655
   and rides his blind horse over plowed land,
   and allows his wife to visit shrines,
   is worthy to be hanged on the gallows.'
But all for nought; I didn't care a berry
for his proverbs and old saw,                         660
nor would I be corrected by him.
I hate that man who tells me my vices,

And so do mo, God woot, of us than I.
This made him with me wood al outrely;
I nolde noght forbere him in no cas.                           665
    "Now wol I seye yow sooth, by Seint Thomas,
Why that I rente out of his book a leef,
For which he smoot me so that I was deef.
He hadde a book that gladly, night and day,
For his desport he wolde rede alway.                           670
He cleped it Valerie* and Theofraste,*
At whiche book he lough alwey ful faste;
And eek ther was somtyme a clerk at Rome,
A cardinal, that highte Seint Jerome,*
That made a book agayn Jovinian;                               675
In whiche book eek ther was Tertulan*
Crisippus,* Trotula,* and Helowys,*
That was abbesse nat fer fro Parys;
And eek the Parables of Salomon,
Ovydes Art, and bokes many on,                                680
And alle thise wer bounden in o volume.
And every night and day was his custume,
Whan he had leyser and vacacioun
From other worldly occupacioun,
To reden on this book of wikked wyves.                         685
He knew of hem mo legendes and lyves
Than been of gode wyves in the Bible.
For trusteth wel, it is an impossible
That any clerk wol speke good of wyves,
But-if it be of holy seintes lyves,                           690
Ne of noon other womman never the mo.
Who peyntede the leoun,* tel me who?
By God, if wommen hadde writen stories,
As clerkes han withinne hir oratories,
They wolde han writen of men more wikkednesse                  695
Than all the mark of Adam may redresse.
The children of Mercurie* and of Venus
Bee in hir wirking ful contrarious;
Mercurie loveth wisdom and science,
And Venus loveth ryot and dispence.                           700

and so, God knows, do more of us than I.
This made him utterly furious with me;
I wouldn't give in to him in any case.                                665
    "Now I'll tell you truly, by Saint Thomas,
why I tore a leaf out of his book,
for which he hit me so that I became deaf.
He had a book that he always loved to read
night and day to amuse himself.                                      670
He called it Valerius and Theophrastus;
at which book he was always laughing heartily;
and also there was at some time a clerk at Rome,
a cardinal, that was called St. Jerome,
who wrote a book against Jovinian;                                   675
in this book there was also Tertulian,
Chrysippus, Trotula, and Heloise,
who was an abbess not far from Paris;
and also the Parables of Solomon,
Ovid's *Art of Love,* and many other books,                         680
and all these were bound in one volume.
And every day and night it was his custom,
when he had leisure and could rest
from other worldly occupation,
to read in this book of wicked wives.                                685
He knew more legends and lives of them
than there are of good wives in the Bible.
For believe me, it is an impossibility
for any clerk to speak good of wives—
unless it be of the lives of holy saints,                            690
but never of any other woman.
Who painted the lion, tell me who?
By God, if women had written stories,
as clerks have in their oratories,
they would have written more of men's wickedness                     695
than all of the sex of Adam can redress.
The children of Mercury and of Venus
are quite contrary in their ways;
Mercury loves wisdom and learning,
and Venus loves revelry and expenditure.                             700

And, for hir diverse disposicioun,
Ech falleth in otheres exaltacioun;
And thus, God woot, Mercurie is desolat
In Pisces, wher Venus is exaltat;
And Venus falleth ther Mercurie is reysed;     705
Therfor no womman of no clerk is preysed.
The clerk, whan he is old, and may noght do
Of Venus werkes worth his olde sho,
Than sit he doun, and writ in his dotage
That wommen can nat kepe hir mariage!     710

  "But now to purpos, why I tolde thee
That I was beten for a book, pardee.
Upon a night Jankin, that was our syre,
Redde on his book, as he sat by the fyre,
Of Eva first, that, for hir wikkednesse     715
Was al mankinde broght to wrecchednesse,
For which that Jesu Crist himself was slayn,
That boghte us with his herte blood agayn.
Lo, here expres of womman may ye finde,
That womman was the los of al mankinde.     720

  "Tho redde he me how Sampson* loste his heres:
Slepinge, his lemman kitte hem with hir sheres;
Thurgh whiche tresoun loste he bothe his yën.

  "Tho redde he me, if that I shal nat lyen,
Of Hercules* and of his Dianyre,     725
That caused him to sette himself afyre.

  "No thing forgat he the care and the wo
That Socrates* had with hise wyves two;
How Xantippa caste pisse upon his heed;
This sely man sat stille as he were deed;     730
He wyped his heed, namore dorste he seyn
But 'Er that thonder stinte, comth a reyn.'

  "Of Phasipha,* that was the quene of Crete,
For shrewednesse, him thoughte the tale swete;
Fy, spek namore—it is a grisly thing—     735
Of hir horrible lust and hir lyking.

  "Of Clitemistra, for hir lecherye,
That falsly made hir housbond for to dye,

And, because of their diverse dispositions,
each loses power when the other is dominant;
and thus, God knows, Mercury is powerless
in the Sign of the Fish, where Venus is dominant;
and Venus falls when Mercury ascends;                    705
therefore no woman is praised by any clerk.
The clerk, when he is old, and unable to do
any of Venus's work worth his old shoe,
then sits down and writes in his dotage
that women cannot keep their marriage vows!              710

"But now to the purpose, as to why I was beaten,
as I told you, because of a book, for heaven's sake.
One night Jankin, who was the head of the household,
read in his book as he sat by the fire,
first, concerning Eve, that all mankind was brought      715
to wretchedness by her wickedness,
for which Jesus Christ himself was slain,
who redeemed us with his heart's blood.
Here you can expressly find this of woman:
that woman caused the fall of all mankind.               720

"Then he read to me how Samson lost his hair:
while he was sleeping, his mistress cut it with her shears;
through this treason he lost both his eyes.

"Then he read to me, and this is no lie,
about Hercules and his Dejanira,                         725
who caused him to set himself on fire.

"He forgot none of the sorrow and woe
that Socrates had with his two wives;
how Xantippe cast piss upon his head;
this poor man sat as still as if he were dead;           730
he wiped his head; he dared to say no more
than, 'Before the thunder stops, comes the rain.'

"The tale of Pasiphaë, who was the queen of Crete,
he maliciously thought sweet;
fie, speak no more—it is a grisly thing—                 735
about her horrible lust and her preference.

"Of Clytemnestra, who because of her lechery
with falseness caused her husband's death,

He redde it with ful good devocioun.

"He tolde me eek for what occasioun    740
Amphiorax*at Thebes loste his lyf;
Myn housbond hadde a legende of his wyf,
Eriphilem, that for an ouche of gold
Hath prively unto the Grekes told
Wher that hir housbonde hidde him in a place,    745
For which he hadde at Thebes sory grace.

"Of Lyvia tolde he me, and of Lucye;
They bothe made hir housbondes for to dye,
That oon for love, that other was for hate;
Lyvia hir housbond, on an even late,    750
Empoysoned hath, for that she was his fo.
Lucya, likerous, loved hir housbond so,
That, for he sholde alwey upon hir thinke,
She yaf him swich a maner love-drinke,
That he was deed er it were by the morwe;    755
And thus algates housbondes han sorwe.

"Than tolde he me how oon Latumius
Compleyned to his felawe Arrius
That in his gardin growed swich a tree,
On which he seyde how that his wyves three    760
Hanged hemself for herte despitous.

" 'O leve brother,' quod this Arrius,
'Yif me a plante of thilke blissed tree,
And in my gardin planted shal it be.'

"Of latter date, of wyves hath he red    765
That somme han slayn hir housbondes in hir bed,
And lete hir lechour dighte hir al the night
Whyl that the corps lay in the floor upright.
And somme han drive nayles in hir brayn
Whyl that they slepte, and thus they han hem slayn.    770
Somme han hem yeve poysoun in hir drinke.
He spak more harm than herte may bithinke;
And therwithal he knew of mo proverbes
Than in this world ther growen gras or herbes.

" 'Bet is,' quod he, 'thyn habitacioun    775
Be with a leoun or a foul dragoun,

he read with great devotion.

"He told me also why 740
Amphiaraus lost his life at Thebes;
my husband had a story about his wife,
Eriphyle, who for a trinket of gold
secretly told the Greeks
where her husband had hidden himself, 745
which is why he had sad luck at Thebes.

"He told me of Livia and of Lucilla;
they both caused their husbands to die,
one for love and the other for hate;
Livia, late one night, poisoned 750
her husband, because she was his foe.
Lustful Lucilla loved her husband so
that in order to make him think of her always
she gave him a love potion of such a kind
that he was dead before morning; 755
and thus husbands always suffer.

"Then he told me how one Latumius
complained to his friend Arrius
that in his garden there grew a tree
on which, he said, his three wives 760
had spitefully hanged themselves.

" 'O dear brother,' said this Arrius,
'give me a cutting of that blessed tree,
and it shall be planted in my garden.'

"He read of wives of a later date 765
some of whom had slain their husbands in their beds,
and let their lechers make love to them all the night
while the corpse lay flat on the floor.
And some have driven nails into their husband's brain
while they slept, and thus slain them. 770
Some have given them poison in their drink.
He told of more evil than the heart can imagine;
and along with that, he knew more proverbs
than there are blades of grass or herbs in the world.

" 'It is better,' said he, 'to dwell 775
with a lion or a foul dragon

Than with a womman usinge for to chyde.
Bet is,' quod he, 'hye in the roof abyde
Than with an angry wyf doun in the hous;
They been so wikked and contrarious,                    780
They haten that hir housbondes loveth ay.'
He seyde, 'A womman cast hir shame away,
Whan she cast of hir smok,' and forthermo,
'A fair womman, but she be chaast also,
Is lyk a gold ring in a sowes nose.'                    785
Who wolde wenen, or who wolde suppose
The wo that in myn herte was, and pyne?

"And whan I saugh he wolde never fyne
To reden on this cursed book al night,
Al sodeynly three leves have I plight                   790
Out of his book, right as he radde, and eke
I with my fist so took him on the cheke,
That in our fyr he fil bakward adoun.
And he up stirte as dooth a wood leoun,
And with his fist he smoot me on the heed              795
That in the floor I lay as I were deed.
And when he saugh how stille that I lay,
He was agast, and wolde han fled his way,
Til atte laste out of my swogh I breyde:
'O, hastow slayn me, false theef?' I seyde,            800
'And for my land thus hastow mordred me?
Er I be deed, yet wol I kisse thee.'

"And neer he cam, and kneled faire adoun,
And seyde, 'Dere suster Alisoun,
As help me God, I shal thee never smyte;               805
That I have doon, it is thyself to wyte.
Foryeve it me, and that I thee biseke.'
And yet eftsones I hitte him on the cheke,
And seyde, 'Theef, thus muchel am I wreke;
Now wol I dye, I may no lenger speke.'                  810
But atte laste, with muchel care and wo,
We fille acorded, by us selven two.
He yaf me al the brydel in myn hond
To han the governance of hous and lond,

than with a woman accustomed to scold.
It is better,' said he, 'to stay high on the roof
than with an angry wife down in the house;
they are so wicked and contrary            780
they always hate what their husbands love.'
He said, 'A woman casts her shame away
when she casts off her smock,' and furthermore,
'A fair woman, unless she is also chaste,
is like a gold ring in a sow's nose.'         785
Who would suppose or imagine
the woe and pain that was in my heart?

   "And when I saw he would never stop
reading in this cursed book all night,
suddenly I plucked three leaves         790
out of his book, right as he was reading, and also
I hit him on the cheek with my fist, so
that he fell down into our fire backward.
He started up like a raging lion
and hit me on the head with his fist        795
so that I lay on the floor as if I were dead.
And when he saw how still I lay,
he was aghast, and would have fled away,
until at last I awoke from my swoon:
'Oh! Have you slain me, false thief?' I said,    800
'And have you murdered me thus for my land?
Before I die, I yet want to kiss you.'

   "He came near, and kneeled down gently,
and said, 'Dear sister Alisoun,
so help me God, I shall never hit you again;    805
what I have done, you are to blame for yourself.
Forgive me for it, I beseech you.'
But yet again I hit him on the cheek,
and said, 'Thief, this much I am avenged;
now I shall die, I can speak no longer.'     810
But at last, after much care and woe,
we fell into accord between ourselves.
He gave the bridle completely into my hand
to have control of house and land,

And of his tonge and of his hond also, 815
And made him brenne his book anon right tho.
And whan that I hadde geten unto me
By maistrie al the soveraynetee,
And that he seyde, 'Myn owene trewe wyf,
Do as thee lust the terme of al thy lyf, 820
Keep thyn honour, and keep eek myn estaat,'
After that day we hadden never debaat.
God help me so, I was to him as kinde
As any wyf from Denmark unto Inde,
And also trewe, and so was he to me. 825
I prey to God that sit in magestee,
So blesse his soule, for his mercy dere!
Now wol I seye my tale, if ye wol here."

*Biholde the wordes bitween the Somonour
and the Frere*

The Frere lough whan he hadde herd al this:
"Now, dame," quod he, "so have I joye or blis, 830
This is a long preamble of a tale!"
And whan the Somnour herde the Frere gale,
"Lo," quod the Somnour, "Goddes armes two!
A frere wol entremette him evermo.
Lo, gode men, a flye and eek a frere 835
Wol falle in every dish and eek matere.
What spekestow of preambulacioun?
What! amble, or trotte, or pees, or go sit doun;
Thou lettest our disport in this manere."

"Ye, woltow so, sir Somnour?" quod the Frere, 840
"Now, by my feith, I shal, er that I go,
Telle of a somnour swich a tale or two
That alle the folk shal laughen in this place."

"Now elles, Frere, I bishrewe thy face,"
Quod this Somnour, "and I bishrewe me, 845
But if I telle tales two or three
Of freres er I come to Sidingborne,*

and also of his tongue and hand;                                  815
and I made him burn his book right then.
And when I had got for myself,
through superiority, all the sovereignty,
and he had said, 'My own true wife,
do as you wish the rest of your life,                             820
preserve your honor, and my public position, too,'
after that day we never argued.
So God help me, I was as kind to him
as any wife from Denmark to India,
and as true, and so was he to me.                                825
I pray to God who sits in majesty
to bless his soul, for his dear mercy's sake!
Now I'll tell my tale, if you will listen."


*Behold the words between the Summoner
and the Friar*


The Friar laughed when he had heard all this:
"Now, dame," said he, "as I may have joy or bliss,              830
this is a long preamble to a tale!"
And when the Summoner heard the Friar exclaim,
"Lo!" said the Summoner, "By God's two arms!
A friar will always be butting in.
See, good people, a fly and a friar                             835
will fall into every dish and also every matter.
What do you mean, talking about perambulation?
Oh, amble or trot or pace, or go sit down;
you're spoiling our fun by behaving in this manner."

      "Oh, is that so, sir Summoner?" said the Friar,           840
"Now by my faith, before I go, I'll
tell such a tale or two about a summoner
that everyone here shall laugh."

      "Now, Friar, damn your eyes,"
said this Summoner, "and damn me                                845
if I don't tell two or three tales
about friars before I get to Sittingbourne,

That I shal make thyn herte for to morne;
For wel I woot thy patience is goon."
    Our Hoste cryde, "Pees, and that anoon!"     850
And seyde, "Lat the womman telle hir tale.
Ye fare as folk that dronken been of ale.
Do, dame, tel forth your tale, and that is best."
    "Al redy, sir," quod she, "right as yow lest,
If I have licence of this worthy Frere."     855
"Yis, dame," quod he, "tel forth, and I wol here."


*Here biginneth the Tale of the Wyf of Bathe*


In th'olde dayes of the king Arthour*
Of which that Britons speken greet honour,
Al was this land fulfild of fayerye.
The elf-queen with hir joly companye
Daunced ful ofte in many a grene mede;     5
This was the olde opinion, as I rede.
I speke of manye hundred yeres ago.
But now can no man see none elves mo,
For now the grete charitee and prayeres
Of limitours* and othere holy freres,     10
That serchen every lond and every streem,
As thikke as motes in the sonne-beem,
Blessinge halles, chambres, kichenes, boures,
Citees, burghes, castels, hye toures,
Thropes, bernes, shipnes, dayeryes;     15
This maketh that ther been no fayeryes.
For ther as wont to walken was an elf,
Ther walketh now the limitour himself,
In undermeles and in morweninges,
And seyth his Matins and his holy thinges     20
As he goth in his limitacioun.
Wommen may go saufly up and doun;
In every bush or under every tree
Ther is noon other incubus* but he—
And he ne wol doon hem but dishonour.     25

so that I shall make your heart mourn;
I can easily see that your patience is gone."

Our Host cried "Peace! And that at once!" 850
And said, "Let the woman tell her tale.
You behave like people who have got drunk on ale.
Tell your tale, dame; that is best."

"All ready, sir," said she, "just as you wish,
if I have the permission of this worthy Friar." 855

"Yes, dame," said he, "tell on and I will listen."

*Here begins the Wife of Bath's Tale*

In the old days of King Arthur,
of whom Britons speak great honor,
this land was all filled with fairies.
The elf queen with her jolly company
danced often in many a green meadow— 5
this was the old belief, as I have read;
I speak of many hundred years ago.
But now no one can see elves anymore,
for now the great charity and prayers
of limiters and other holy friars, 10
who search every field and stream,
as thick as specks of dust in a sunbeam,
blessing halls, chambers, kitchens, bedrooms,
cities, towns, castles, high towers,
villages, barns, stables, dairies: 15
this is the reason that there are no fairies.
For where an elf was wont to walk,
there now walks the limiter himself,
in afternoons and in mornings,
and says his Matins and his holy things, 20
as he goes about within his limits.
Women may go up and down safely;
in every bush or under every tree
there is no other incubus but he—
and he won't do anything but dishonor to them. 25

And so bifel it that this King Arthour
Hadde in his hous a lusty bacheler*
That on a day cam rydinge fro river;
And happed that, allone as she was born,
He saugh a mayde walkinge him biforn,                    30
Of whiche mayde anon, maugree hir heed,
By verray force he rafte hir maydenheed;
For which oppressioun was swich clamour
And swich pursute unto the King Arthour,
That dampned was this knight for to be deed              35
By cours of lawe, and sholde han lost his heed—
Paraventure, swich was the statut tho—
But that the quene and othere ladies mo
So longe preyeden the king of grace,
Til he his lyf him graunted in the place,                40
And yaf him to the quene, al at hir wille,
To chese whether she wolde him save or spille.

The quene thanketh the king with al hir might,
And after this thus spak she to the knight,
Whan that she saugh hir tyme, upon a day:                45
"Thou standest yet," quod she, "in swich array
That of thy lyf yet hastow no suretee.
I grante thee lyf if thou canst tellen me
What thing is it that wommen most desyren.
Be war, and keep thy nekke-boon from yren.               50
And if thou canst nat tellen it anon,
Yet wol I yeve thee leve for to gon
A twelfmonth and a day, to seche and lere
An answere suffisant in this matere.
And suretee wol I han, er that thou pace,                55
Thy body for to yelden in this place."

Wo was this knight and sorwefully he syketh;
But what, he may nat do al as him lyketh.
And at the laste, he chees him for to wende,
And come agayn, right at the yeres ende,                 60
With swich answere as God wolde him purveye;
And taketh his leve, and wendeth forth his weye.

He seketh every hous and every place

It so happened that this King Arthur
had in his house a lusty bachelor,
who one day came riding from the river;
and it happened that he saw a maiden
walking before him, alone as she was born. 30
And from this maiden then, against her will,
and by pure force, he took her maidenhood.
Because of this violation, there was such a clamor
and such petitioning to King Arthur
that this knight was condemned to die 35
according to law, and should have lost his head—
it happened that such was the statute then—
except that the queen and various other ladies
prayed to the king for grace so long
that he granted him his life on the spot, 40
and gave him to the queen, completely at her will,
to choose whether she would save or destroy him.

The queen thanked the king heartily,
and then spoke thus to the knight,
one day, when she saw a fitting time: 45
"You are still in such a position," said she,
"that you have no guarantee of your life as yet.
I will grant you life if you can tell me
what thing it is that women most desire.
Be wary, and keep your neck from the ax. 50
And if you cannot tell it to me now,
I will still give you leave to go
a year and a day to seek and learn
a sufficient answer in this matter.
And I want a guarantee, before you go, 55
that you will yield up your person in this place."

The knight was woeful, and he sighed sorrowfully;
but then, he could not do as he pleased.
And in the end he decided to go off,
and to come back again just at the end of the year, 60
with such an answer as God would provide for him;
he took his leave and went forth on his way.

He sought in every house and every place

Wher as he hopeth for to finde grace,
To lerne what thing wommen loven most;                    65
But he ne coude arryven in no cost
Wheras he mighte finde in this matere
Two creatures accordinge in fere.

   Somme seyde wommen loven best richesse;
Somme seyde honour; somme seyde jolynesse;                70
Somme, riche array; somme seyden, lust abedde,
And ofte tyme to be widwe and wedde.
Somme seyde that our hertes been most esed
Whan that we been y-flatered and y-plesed:
He gooth ful ny the sothe, I wol nat lye;                 75
A man shal winne us best with flaterye,
And with attendance and with bisinesse
Been we y-lymed, bothe more and lesse.

   And somme seyen that we loven best
For to be free, and do right as us lest,                  80
And that no man repreve us of our vyce,
But seye that we be wyse, and no thing nyce.
For trewely, ther is noon of us alle,
If any wight wol clawe us on the galle,
That we nil kike, for he seith us sooth;                  85
Assay, and he shal finde it that so dooth.
For be we never so vicious withinne,
We wol been holden wyse and clene of sinne.

   And somme seyn that greet delyt han we
For to ben holden stable and eek secree,                  90
And in o purpos stedefastly to dwelle,
And nat biwreye thing that men us telle.
But that tale is nat worth a rake-stele;
Pardee, we wommen conne no thing hele;
Witnesse on Myda; wol ye here the tale?                   95

   Ovyde,* amonges othere thinges smale,
Seyde Myda hadde, under his longe heres,
Growinge upon his heed two asses eres,
The whiche vyce he hidde, as he best mighte,
Ful subtilly from every mannes sighte,                    100
That, save his wyf, ther wiste of it namo.

where he hoped to find favor,
in order to learn what thing women most love;⠀⠀⠀⠀65
but he reached no land where he could find
two people who were in agreement
with each other on this matter.

⠀⠀Some said women love riches best;
some said honor; some said amusement;⠀⠀⠀⠀70
some, rich apparel; some said pleasure in bed,
and often to be widowed and remarried.
Some said that our hearts are most soothed
when we are flattered and pampered:
he came near the truth, I will not lie;⠀⠀⠀⠀75
a man can win us best with flattery,
and with constant attendance and assiduity
we are ensnared, both high and low.

⠀⠀And some said that we love best
to be free, and do just as we please,⠀⠀⠀⠀80
and to have no man reprove us for our vice,
but say that we are wise and not at all foolish.
For truly, if anyone will scratch us
on a sore spot, there is not one of us
who will not kick for being told the truth;⠀⠀⠀⠀85
try it, and he who does shall find this out.
No matter how full of vice we are within,
we wish to be thought wise and clean from sin.

⠀⠀And some said that we take delight
in being thought reliable and able to keep a secret⠀⠀⠀⠀90
and hold steadfast to a purpose
and not betray anything that people tell us.
But that idea isn't worth a rake handle;
by heaven, we women can't conceal a thing;
witness Midas; would you hear the tale?⠀⠀⠀⠀95
Ovid, among other brief matters,
said Midas had two ass's ears growing
on his head under his long hair;
which evil he hid from everyone's sight
as artfully as he could,⠀⠀⠀⠀100
so that no one knew of it except his wife.

He loved hir most, and trusted hir also;
He preyede hir, that to no creature
She sholde tellen of his disfigure.
 She swoor him nay, for al this world to winne,  105
She nolde do that vileinye or sinne
To make hir housbond han so foul a name;
She nolde nat telle it for hir owene shame.
But nathelees, hir thoughte that she dyde
That she so longe sholde a conseil hyde;  110
Hir thoughte it swal so sore aboute hir herte
That nedely som word hir moste asterte;
And sith she dorste telle it to no man,
Doun to a mareys faste by she ran—
Til she came there, hir herte was afyre—  115
And, as a bitore bombleth in the myre,
She leyde hir mouth unto the water doun:
"Biwreye me nat, thou water, with thy soun,"
Quod she. "To thee I telle it, and namo:
Myn housbond hath longe asses eres two!  120
Now is myn herte all hool, now is it oute;
I mighte no lenger kepe it, out of doute."
Heer may ye se, thogh we a tyme abyde,
Yet out it moot, we can no conseil hyde.
The remenant of the tale if ye wol here,  125
Redeth Ovyde, and ther ye may it lere.
 This knight, of which my tale is specially,
Whan that he saugh he mighte nat come therby—
This is to seye, what wommen loven moost—
Withinne his brest ful sorweful was the goost;  130
But hoom he gooth, he mighte nat sojourne:
The day was come that hoomward moste he tourne.
And in his wey it happed him to ryde,
In al this care, under a forest syde,
Wher as he saugh upon a daunce go  135
Of ladies foure and twenty and yet mo;
Toward the whiche daunce he drow ful yerne,
In hope that som wisdom sholde he lerne.
But certeinly, er he came fully there,

He loved her most, and also trusted her;
he prayed her not to tell anyone
of his disfigurement.

   She swore to him that not for all the world   105
would she do such villainy and sin
as to give her husband so bad a name;
out of her own shame she wouldn't tell it *his secret*
But nonetheless she thought that she would die
for having to keep a secret so long;   110
it seemed to her that her heart swelled so painfully
some word must needs burst from her;
and since she dared not tell it to anybody,
she ran down to a marsh close by—
her heart was on fire until she got there—   115
and, as a bittern booms in the mire,
she laid her mouth down to the water:

   "Betray me not, you water, with your sound,"
said she. "To you I tell it, and to no one else:
my husband has two long ass's ears!   *tells water*   120
Now my heart is all cured, for the secret is out!
I simply couldn't keep it any longer."
In this you can see that though we wait a time,
yet out it must come: we cannot hide a secret.
If you wish to hear the rest of the tale,   125
read Ovid, and there you can learn of it.

   When this knight whom my tale specially concerns
saw that he couldn't come by it—
that is to say, what women love most—
his spirit was very sorrowful within his breast;   130
but home he went, he might not linger:
the day was come when he must turn homeward.
And on his way, burdened with care, he happened
to ride by the edge of a forest,
where he saw more than twenty-four   135
ladies moving in a dance;
he drew eagerly toward that dance
in the hope that he might learn something.
But indeed, before he quite got there,

Vanisshed was this daunce, he niste where.                    140
No creature saugh he that bar lyf,
Save on the grene he saugh sittinge a wyf;
A fouler wight ther may no man devyse.
Agayn the knight this olde wyf gan ryse
And seyde, "Sir knight, heer forth ne lyth no wey.     145
Tel me what that ye seken, by your fey.
Parventure it may the bettre be;
Thise olde folk can muchel thing," quod she.

    "My leve mooder," quod this knight, "certeyn,
I nam but deed, but if that I can seyn              150
What thing it is that wommen most desyre;
Coude ye me wisse, I wolde wel quyte your hyre."

    "Plight me thy trouthe, heer in myn hand," quod she,
"The nexte thing that I requere thee,
Thou shalt it do, if it lye in thy might;            155
And I wol tell it yow er it be night."
"Have here my trouthe," quod the knight." I grante."

    "Thanne," quod she, "I dar me wel avante
Thy lyf is sauf, for I wol stonde therby,
Upon my lyf, the queen wol seye as I.                160
Lat see which is the proudeste of hem alle
That wereth on a coverchief or a calle
That dar seye nay of that I shal thee teche;
Lat us go forth withouten lenger speche."
Tho rouned she a pistel in his ere,                 165
And bad him to be glad, and have no fere.

    Whan they be comen to the court, this knight
Seyde he had holde his day, as he hadde hight,
And redy was his answere, as he sayde.
Ful many a noble wyf, and many a mayde,              170
And many a widwe, for that they ben wyse,
The quene hirself sittinge as a justyse,
Assembled been, his answere for to here;
And afterward this knight was bode appere.

    To every wight comanded was silence,              175
And that the knight sholde telle in audience
What thing that worldly wommen loven best.

the dancers vanished, he knew not where.        140
He saw no living creature,
except a woman sitting on the green:
no one could imagine an uglier creature.
This old woman rose before the knight
and said, "Sir knight, no road lies this way.        145
Tell me, by your faith, what you seek for.
Perhaps it may be the better;
these old folks know many things," said she.

  "Dear mother," said this knight, "certainly
I am as good as dead unless I can say        150
what thing it is that women most desire;
if you could tell me, I would repay your trouble well."

  "Give me your promise, here upon my hand," said she,
"that you will do the next thing I require
of you, if it lies in your power,        155
and I will tell it to you before nightfall."
"Here is my promise," said the knight, "I grant it."

  "Then," said she, "I dare to boast
that your life is safe, for I'll swear
upon my life that the queen will say as I do.        160
Let's see whether the proudest of all those
that wear a coverchief or headdress
dares deny what I shall teach you;
let's go on without any more talk."
Then she whispered a message in his ear,        165
and told him to be glad and not afraid.

  When they had come to the court, this knight
said he had kept his day as he had promised,
and his answer, he said, was ready.
Many a noble wife and many a maiden,        170
and many a widow (since widows are so wise),
were assembled to hear his answer
with the queen herself sitting as judge;
and then the knight was ordered to appear.

  Everyone was commanded to keep silence,        175
and the knight was commanded to tell in open assembly
what thing it is that secular women love best.

This knight ne stood nat stille as doth a best,
But to his questioun anon answerde
With manly voys, that al the court it herde:    180
  "My lige lady, generally," quod he,
"Wommen desyren to have sovereyntee
As wel over hir housbond as hir love,
And for to been in maistrie him above;
This is your moste desyr, thogh ye me kille,    185
Doth as yow list, I am heer at your wille."
  In al the court ne was ther wyf ne mayde
Ne widwe that contraried that he sayde,
But seyden he was worthy han his lyf.
  And with that word up stirte the olde wyf,    190
Which that the knight saugh sittinge in the grene:
"Mercy," quod she, "my sovereyn lady quene!
Er that your court departe, do me right.
I taughte this answere unto the knight;
For which he plighte me his trouthe there,    195
The firste thing I wolde of him requere,
He wolde it do, if it lay in his might.
Bifore the court than preye I thee, sir knight,"
Quod she, "that thou me take unto thy wyf;
For wel thou wost that I have kept thy lyf.    200
If I sey fals, sey nay, upon thy fey."
  This knight answered, "Alas and weylawey!
I woot right wel that swich was my biheste.
For Goddes love, as chees a newe requeste;
Tak al my good, and lat my body go."    205
  "Nay than," quod she, "I shrewe us bothe two!
For thogh that I be foul and old and pore,
I nolde for al the metal, ne for ore,
That under erthe is grave, or lyth above,
But if thy wyf I were and eek thy love."    210
  "My love?" quod he; "Nay, my dampnacioun!
Allas, that any of my nacioun
Sholde ever so foule disparaged be!"
But al for noght, the ende is this, that he
Constreyned was, he nedes moste hir wedde;    215

This knight did not stand in beastlike silence,
but answered to his question at once
with manly voice, so that all the court heard it:          180

"My liege lady," he said, "generally
women desire to have dominion
over their husbands as well as their lovers,
and to be above them in mastery;
this is your greatest desire, though you may kill me;          185
do as you please, I am at your will here."

In all the court there was neither wife nor maiden
nor widow who contradicted what he said,
but all said he deserved to have his life.

And at that word up jumped the old woman          190
whom the knight had seen sitting on the green:
"Mercy," said she, "my sovereign lady queen!
Before your court depart, do right by me,
I taught this answer to the knight;
for this he gave me his promise there          195
that he would do the first thing
I required of him, if it lay in his power.
Before the court, then, I pray you, sir knight,"
said she, "to take me as your wife;
for well you know that I have saved your life.          200
If I say false, deny me, on your faith!"

The knight answered, "Alas and woe is me!
I know quite well that such was my promise.
For the love of God ask for something else;
take all my property and let my body go."          205

"No then," said she. "Curse the two of us!
For though I am ugly and old and poor,
I wouldn't want all the metal or ore
that is buried under the earth or lies above
unless I were your wife and your love as well."          210
"My love?" said he; "No, my damnation!
Alas, that any of my birth
should ever be so foully disgraced!"
But it was all for nothing; the end was this, that he
was forced to accept the fact that he must needs wed her;          215

And taketh his olde wyf and gooth to bedde.
   Now wolden som men seye, paraventure,
That for my necligence I do no cure
To tellen yow the joye and al th'array
That at the feste was that ilke day. 220
To whiche thing shortly answere I shal;
I seye ther nas no joye ne feste at al,
Ther nas but hevinesse and muche sorwe;
For prively he wedded hir on the morwe,
And al day after hidde him as an oule— 225
So wo was him, his wyf looked so foule.
   Greet was the wo the knight hadde in his thoght,
Whan he was with his wyf abedde y-broght;
He walweth, and he turneth to and fro.
His olde wyf lay smylinge evermo, 230
And seyde, "O dere housbond, *ben'cite!*
Fareth every knight thus with his wyf as ye?
Is this the lawe of King Arthures hous?
Is every knight of his so dangerous?
I am your owene love and eek your wyf; 235
I am she which that saved hath your lyf;
And certes, yet dide I yow never unright.
Why fare ye thus with me this firste night?
Ye faren lyk a man had lost his wit.
What is my gilt? for Goddes love, tel me it, 240
And it shal been amended, if I may."
   "Amended?" quod this knight, "Allas, nay, nay!
It wol nat been amended never mo!
Thou art so loothly and so old also,
And therto comen of so lowe a kinde, 245
That litel wonder is thogh I walwe and winde.
So wolde God myn herte wolde breste!"
   "Is this," quod she, "the cause of your unreste?"
   "Ye, certainly," quod he, "no wonder is."
   "Now, sire," quod she, "I coude amende al this, 250
If that me liste, er it were dayes three,
So wel ye mighte bere yow unto me.
   "But for ye speken of swich gentillesse

and he took his old wife and went to bed.

Now some people might say, perhaps,
that out of negligence I am not bothering
to tell you about the joy and the pomp
at the feast that day,                                    220
to which objection I shall answer briefly:
I am telling you that there was no joy or feast at all,
there was nothing but gloom and much sorrow;
for he married her privately in the morning
and afterward hid himself like an owl all day—          225
he was so dejected because his wife looked so ugly.

Great was the woe in the knight's mind
when he was brought with his wife to bed;
he tossed and he turned to and fro.
His old wife lay smiling all the time,                   230
and said, "O dear husband, bless my soul!
Does every knight behave with his wife as you do?
Is this the law of King Arthur's house?
Is every one of his knights so cold?
I am your own love and your wife;                        235
I am she who saved your life;
and certainly I never yet did wrong to you.
Why do you act thus with me the first night?
You act like a man who has lost his mind.
What am I guilty of? For God's sake, tell me,           240
and it shall be corrected, if I can manage it."

"Corrected?" said this knight, "Alas, no, no!
It will never be corrected!
You are so loathsome and so old,
and what is more, of such low birth,                     245
that it is little wonder if I toss and turn.
I wish to God my heart would break!"

"Is this," said she, "the cause of your unrest?"

"Yes, certainly," said he, "it's no wonder."

"Now, sir," said she, "I could rectify all this,        250
if I wanted to, before three days were up,
if you behaved yourself to me well.

"But in the matter of your speaking of such nobility

As is descended out of old richesse,
That therfore sholden ye be gentil men,                       255
Swich arrogance is nat worth an hen.
Loke who that is most vertuous alway,
Privee and apert, and most entendeth ay
To do the gentil dedes that he can,
And tak him for the grettest gentil man.                      260
Crist wol we clayme of him our gentillesse,
Nat of our eldres for hir old richesse:
For thogh they yeve us al hir heritage,
For which we clayme to been of heigh parage,
Yet may they nat biquethe for nothing                         265
To noon of us hir vertuous living,
That made hem gentil men y-called be;
And bad us folwen hem in swich degree.
  "Wel can the wyse poete of Florence,
That highte Dant,* speken in this sentence;                   270
Lo in swich maner rym is Dantes tale:
'Ful selde up ryseth by his branches smale
Prowesse of man; for God, of his goodnesse,
Wol that of him we clayme our gentillesse.'
For of our eldres may we nothing clayme                       275
But temporel thing, that man may hurte and mayme.
Eek every wight wot this as wel as I;
If gentillesse were planted naturelly
Unto a certeyn linage, doun the lyne,
Privee and apert, than wolde they never fyne                  280
To doon of gentillesse the faire offyce;
They mighte do no villeinye or vyce.
  "Tak fyr, and ber it in the derkeste hous
Bitwix this and the Mount of Caucasus,*
And lat men shette the dores and go thenne;                   285
Yet wol the fyr as faire lye and brenne
As twenty thousand men mighte it biholde;
His office naturel ay wol it holde,
Up peril of my lyf, til that it dye.
  "Heer may ye see wel how that genterye                      290

as descends from ancient wealth,
claiming that because of it you are supposed to be          255
noblemen—such arrogance is not worth a hen.
Find the man who is always the most virtuous,
privately and publicly, and who always tries hardest
to do what noble deeds he can,
and consider him the greatest nobleman.          260
Christ wants us to claim our nobility from him,
not from our ancestors because of their ancient wealth:
for though they give us all their heritage,
on the strength of which we claim to be of noble descent,
yet they cannot bequeath by any means          265
or to any of us their virtuous manner of life
which made them be called noblemen;
and which summoned us to follow them at the
          same level.
   "Well can the wise poet of Florence
who is called Dante speak on this subject;          270
in this sort of rhyme is Dante's tale:
'Not oft by branches of a family tree
Does human prowess rise; for gracious God
Wants us to claim from him nobility.'
For from our elders we may claim nothing          275
but perishable matter, to which man may do hurt and
injury. And everyone knows as well as I that
if nobility were implanted by nature
in a certain lineage, down the line of descent,
they would never cease, in private or public,          280
to do the fair offices of nobility;
they could do nothing shameful or evil.
   "Take fire, and bear it into the darkest house
from here to the Mount of Caucasus,
and let men shut the doors and go away;          285
yet the fire will blaze and burn as well
as if twenty thousand men were looking at it;
it will maintain its natural function always
until it dies, I'll stake my life.
   "By this you can easily see that nobility          290

Is nat annexed to possessioun,
Sith folk ne doon hir operacioun
Alwey, as dooth the fyr, lo, in his kinde.
For, God it woot, men may wel often finde
A lordes sone do shame and vileinye;                        295
And he that wol han prys of his gentrye
For he was boren of a gentil hous,
And hadde hise eldres noble and vertuous,
And nil himselven do no gentil dedis,
Ne folwe his gentil auncestre that deed is,                 300
He nis nat gentil, be he duk or erl;
For vileyns, sinful dedes make a cherl.
For gentillesse nis but renomee
Of thyne auncestres, for hir heigh bountee,
Which is a strange thing to thy persone.                    305
Thy gentillesse cometh fro God allone;
Than comth our verray gentillesse of grace,
It was no thing biquethe us with our place.
    "Thenketh how noble, as seith Valerius,*
Was thilke Tullius Hostilius,*                              310
That out of povert roos to heigh noblesse.
Redeth Senek,* and redeth eek Boece,*
Ther shul ye seen expres that it no drede is
That he is gentil that doth gentil dedis.
And therfore, leve housbond, I thus conclude,               315
Al were it that myne auncestres were rude,
Yet may the hye God, and so hope I,
Grante me grace to liven vertuously;
Thanne am I gentil, whan that I biginne
To liven vertuously and weyve sinne.                        320
    "And theras ye of povert me repreve,
The hye God, on whom that we bileve,
In wilful povert chees to live his lyf;
And certes every man, mayden, or wyf
May understonde that Jesus, hevene king,                    325
Ne wolde nat chese a vicious living.

is not tied to possessions,
since people do not perform their function
without variation as does the fire, according to
    its nature.
For, God knows, men may very often find
a lord's son committing shameful and vile deeds; 295
and he who wishes to have credit for his nobility
because he was born of a noble house,
and because his elders were noble and virtuous,
but will not himself do any noble deeds
or follow the example of his late noble ancestor, 300
he is not noble, be he duke or earl;
for villainous, sinful deeds make him a churl.
This kind of nobility is only the renown
of your ancestors, earned by their great goodness,
which is a thing apart from yourself. 305
Your nobility comes from God alone;
then our true nobility comes of grace,
it was in no way bequeathed to us with our station
    in life.
    "Think how noble, as Valerius says,
was that Tullius Hostilius 310
who rose out of poverty to high nobility.
Read Seneca, and read Boethius, too;
there you shall see expressly that there is no doubt
that he is noble who does noble deeds.
And therefore, dear husband, I thus conclude 315
that even if my ancestors were low,
yet God on high may—and so I hope—
grant me grace to live virtuously;
then I am noble, from the time when I begin
to live virtuously and avoid sin. 320
    "And as for the poverty you reprove me for,
high God in whom we believe
chose to live his life in willing poverty;
and certainly every man, maiden, or wife
can understand that Jesus, heaven's king, 325
would not choose a vicious way of life.

Glad povert is an honest thing, certeyn;
This wol Senek and othere clerkes seyn.
Whoso that halt him payd of his poverte,
I holde him riche, al hadde he nat a sherte,
He that coveyteth is a povre wight,
For he wolde han that is nat in his might.
But he that noght hath, ne coveyteth have,
Is riche, although ye holde him but a knave.
    "Verray povert, it singeth proprely;
Juvenal* seith of povert, 'Merily
The povre man, whan he goth by the weye,
Bifore the theves he may singe and pleye.'
Povert is hateful good, and, as I geese,
A ful greet bringer out of bisinesse;
A greet amender eek of sapience
To him that taketh it in pacience.
Povert is this, although it seme elenge:
Possessioun, that no wight wol chalenge.
Povert ful ofte, whan a man is lowe,
Maketh his God and eek himself to knowe.
Povert a spectacle is, as thinketh me,
Thurgh which he may his verray frendes see.
And therfore, sire, sin that I noght yow greve,
Of my povert namore ye me repreve.
    "Now, sire, of elde ye repreve me;
And certes, sire, thogh noon auctoritee
Were in no book, ye gentils of honour
Seyn that men sholde an old wight doon favour,
And clepe him fader, for your gentillesse;
And auctours shal I finden, as I gesse.
    "Now ther ye seye that I am foul and old,
Than drede you noght to been a cokewold;
For filthe and elde, also mote I thee,
Been grete wardeyns upon chastitee.
But nathelees, sin I knowe your delyt,
I shal fulfille your worldly appetyt.

330

335

340

345

350

355

360

Contented poverty is an honorable thing, indeed;
this is said by Seneca and other learned men.
Whoever is content with his poverty
I hold to be rich, even if he hasn't a shirt.          330
He who covets anything is a poor man,
for he wants to have something which is not in
    his power.
But he who has nothing and desires nothing is rich,
although you may consider him nothing but a
    lowly man.
   "True poverty sings of its own accord;          335
Juvenal says of poverty, 'Merrily can
the poor man sing and joke before the
thieves when he goes by the road.'
Poverty is a good that is hated, and, I guess,
a great expeller of cares;          340
a great amender of knowledge, too,
to him that takes it in patience.
Poverty is this, although it seem unhealthy:
possession of that which no man will challenge.
Poverty will often, when a man is low,          345
make him know his God and himself as well.
Poverty is a glass, it seems to me,
through which he can see his true friends.
And therefore, sir, since I do not harm you by it,
do not reprove me for my poverty anymore.          350
   "Now, sir, you reprove me for age;
but certainly, sir, aside from bookish
authority, you nobles who are honorable
say that one should honor an old person,
and call him father, for the sake of your nobility;          355
and I can find authors to that effect, I imagine.
   "Now as to the point that I am ugly and old—
then you need not dread being a cuckold;
for ugliness and age, as I may thrive,
are great wardens of chastity.          360
But nevertheless, since I know what pleases you,
I shall fulfill your fleshly appetite.

"Chees now," quod she, "oon of thise thinges tweye:
To han me foul and old til that I deye,
And be to yow a trewe humble wyf,          365
And never yow displese in al my lyf;
Or elles ye wol han me yong and fair,
And take your aventure of the repair
That shal be to your hous, by cause of me,
Or in som other place, may wel be.          370
Now chees yourselven, whether that yow lyketh."

This knight avyseth him and sore syketh,
But atte laste he seyde in this manere,
"My lady and my love, and wyf so dere,
I put me in your wyse governance;          375
Cheseth yourself which may be most plesance,
And most honour to yow and me also.
I do no fors the whether of the two;
For as yow lyketh, it suffiseth me."

"Thanne have I gete of yow maistrye," quod she,          380
"Sin I may chese, and governe as me lest?"

"Ye certes, wyf," quod he, "I holde it best."

"Kis me," quod she, "we be no lenger wrothe;
For, by my trouthe, I wol be to yow bothe;
This is to seyn, ye, bothe fair and good.          385
I prey to God that I mot sterven wood
But I to yow be al so good and trewe
As ever was wyf sin that the world was newe.
And, but I be tomorn as fair to sene
As any lady, emperyce or quene          390
That is bitwixe the est and eke the west,
Doth with my lyf and deeth right as yow lest.
Cast up the curtin, loke how that it is."

And whan the knight saugh verraily al this,
That she so fair was, and so yong therto,          395
For joye he hente hir in his armes two,
His herte bathed in a bath of blisse;
A thousand tyme arewe he gan hir kisse.
And she obeyed him in every thing

"Choose now," said she, "one of these two things:
to have me ugly and old until I die,
and be a faithful, humble wife to you,                    365
and never displease you in all my life;
or else to have me young and fair,
and take your chances on the flocking
of people to your house because of me—
or to some other place, it may well be.                   370
Now choose yourself, whichever you like."

The knight considered and sighed sorely,
but at last he spoke in this manner,
"My lady and my love, and wife so dear,
I put myself under your wise control;                     375
you yourself choose which may be most pleasurable
and most honorable to you and to me also.
I don't care which of the two I get;
for whatever pleases you suffices for me."

"Then have I got mastery over you," said she,             380
"since I may choose and rule as I please?"

"Yes, certainly, wife," said he, "I consider that best."

"Kiss me," said she, "we won't be angry anymore;
for I swear I will be both these things to you;
that is to say, both fair indeed and good.               385
I pray to God that I may die mad
if I am not just as good and true to you
as ever was wife since the world began.
And, if I am not tomorrow as fair to see
as any lady, empress, or queen                            390
between the east and the west,
do with the question of my life and death just as
    you wish.
Raise the curtain, and see how it is."

And when the knight actually saw all this—
that she was so fair and so young, too,                   395
he seized her in his two arms for joy,
his heart was bathed in bliss;
he kissed her a thousand times in a row.
And she obeyed him in everything

That mighte doon him plesance or lyking.          400
    And thus they live, unto hir lyves ende,
In parfit joye; and Jesu Crist us sende
Housbondes meke, yonge, and fresshe abedde,
And grace t'overbyde hem that we wedde.
And eek I preye Jesu shorte hir lyves          405
That wol nat be governed by hir wyves;
And olde and angry nigardes of dispence,
God sende hem sone verray pestilence!

that might give him pleasure or joy.                              400
    And thus they lived to the end of their lives
in perfect joy; and Jesus Christ send us
husbands who are meek, young, and lively in bed,
and grace to outlive those that we marry.
And also I pray Jesus to shorten the lives                        405
of those that won't be governed by their wives;
and as for old and angry niggards with their money,
God send them soon a true pestilence.

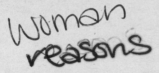

# THE
# MERCHANT'S TALE

# INTRODUCTION

❦

THE MERCHANT'S TALE is a curious combination of medieval romance and raunchy fabliau. What starts off as a story about a wealthy knight who falls for a beautiful young woman quickly degenerates into one in which that same beautiful young woman is unfaithful to him with an ignoble squire in the branches of a pear tree. Although pieces of the story have their own individual sources, Chaucer's unique combination of them makes "The Merchant's Tale" one of Chaucer's most original and unusual creations.

The foundational plot about a rich man who goes blind and whose wife takes advantage of his blindness to take a lover in the branches of a fruit tree probably came to Chaucer by way of a short two-page thirteenth-century Italian tale from a collection now known as the *Novellino*. In that tale the rich man's blindness causes him to be so jealous of his wife that he will not allow her to leave his side. She takes pity on a gentleman from the neighborhood and finds a way to communicate with him by whispering through a long hollow tube. She tells him to wait for her in the branches of a pear tree in the garden. She then persuades her husband to let her climb the tree while he embraces the trunk so that no one can climb up to join her. Her husband does not realize, of course, that her lover is already there. While she is in the tree engaged in sex with the gentleman, Christ and St. Peter come by. St. Peter feels sorry for the husband and asks Jesus to give him back his eyesight. Jesus does so, but predicts that the sly woman will find a ready excuse for her adultery.

Chaucer altered that plot in some fundamental ways, such as making the husband an old man and changing the identity of the supernatural interveners. More important, he preceded the man's blindness and the pear-tree part of his story with a much longer account—some 70 percent of "The Merchant's Tale"—of the deliberations of old January about whether and whom to marry, his seeking the counsel of his friends, his wedding and wedding night, and his sending his new wife to pay attention to his sick squire.

Two interconnected critical issues relating to "The Merchant's Tale" are the tone of the tale and the relationship of the tale to the Merchant who tells it. Is the tale to be read as a lighthearted comedy about the foolishness of men and the devious ways of wives or, alternatively, as the bitterly cynical confessional outpourings of a misogynist husband who has made a botch of his own marriage? To try to answer that question, readers will want to read the description of the Merchant in the General Prologue to *The Canterbury Tales* (see lines 272–86) and the self-revealing thirty-two-line prologue that immediately precedes the tale. That prologue briefly discusses his own two-month marriage to a shrew. To what extent should we allow that prologue, which was not present in the authoritative Hengwrt manuscript of *The Canterbury Tales* but was inserted in the more polished Ellesmere version, to color our reading of the tone of the tale itself? Are we to assume that the Merchant somehow identifies with the foolish January, or can we take him at his word when he tells us in his prologue that he is specifically not telling a tale about "my own misery" (31)? Some readers find that the literary and classical allusiveness of the tale, as well as its poetically elaborate references to time and astrology, sort poorly with the character of a man of the merchant class. They wonder whether the tale may have been written originally for Chaucer's own separate reading at some occasion— perhaps a court entertainment, a bachelor party for a friend, or a gathering of clerics.

Whatever the occasion, "The Merchant's Tale" makes much that could be lovely into something ugly. Falling in love, marriage, marital sex, and even extramarital affairs can be beautiful and uplifting. Here they are sordid and depressing. For a woman to read a love letter can be a warmly romantic experience, but here May reads it in a privy and then disposes of it in the same place. When a supernatural being miraculously cures an old man's blindness, we should feel joy, but here it just proves that the foolish old man is still blind since he refuses to use his new vision to see the truth about himself or his wife.

## NOTES

### The Merchant's Prologue

**Grisildis grete pacience** (line 12). The Merchant refers here to the preceding Clerk's Tale (not included in this collection) about patient Griselda, a peasant woman who is selected to be the wife of the marquis Walter, but who is then repeatedly and cruelly tested by him to satisfy his whim of making sure that she really is as obedient to her husband as he thinks a woman should be.

**Seint Thomas of Inde** (18). One of the original apostles—"doubting Thomas"—who was thought to have converted many people in India to Christianity.

### The Merchant's Tale

**Lumbardye** (1). A region of Italy known for its involvement in international trade, finance, and usury—presumably the sources of January's wealth.

**Pavye** (2). A principal city in the Lombard region.

**foles that ben seculeer** (7). Some have taken this puzzling reference to secular fools as evidence that the tale might have been originally written for a religious teller, perhaps the Monk or the Friar, but few now accept such a supposition. Compare line 78 below, where the speaker makes reference to folks of the secular estate.

**Theofraste** (50). An early antifeminist writer whose works are known now only indirectly through references to him in the works of other writers, such as Jerome.

**Jacob** (118). In Genesis 27:1–29, Rebecca helps her son Jacob to trick the blind Isaac into blessing him rather than the intended Esau.

**Judith** (122). In the apocryphal book of Judith, chapters 11–13, Judith beheads the evil Holofernes as he sleeps.

**Abigayl** (125). In 1 Samuel 25:1–35, Abigail intercepts David, who has come to slay her husband, Nabal. Soon afterward Nabal dies anyhow and Abigail marries David.

**Ester** (127). In Esther 5–7, Queen Esther persuades King Ahasuerus to save her uncle Mordecai by hanging Haman on the gallows intended for Mordecai.

**pyk, pikerel** (175). January compares young pike fish to old pickerel, just as in the next line he compares old beef to tender veal.

**Wades boot** (180). The reference to Wade's boat has never been convincingly explained.

**his bretheren two** (231). The term "brothers" refers not to his biological brothers but to January's friends or close counselors.

**Placebo** (232). Literally "I shall please."

**Justinus** (233). Literally "the just man."

**sinnes sevene** (396). The seven deadly sins are those for which a sinner, at death, will go immediately to hell, unless they are confessed and atoned for. In order of importance, they are pride, envy, anger, sloth, greed, gluttony, and lechery. As the next lines show, they were sometimes portrayed pictorially as a tree with seven large branches, each of which has a number of smaller branches identifying varieties or subcategories of the seven major sins.

**the Wyf of Bathe** (441). It is curious indeed that an Italian character in "The Merchant's Tale" should make reference to a Canterbury pilgrim whose tale he has not heard. There is no good explanation for the reference here, except perhaps that Chaucer meant it as a private joke as he recited the tale before some specific audience to which he had also recited some portion of "The Wife of Bath's Prologue."

**Sarra and Rebekke** (460). These two biblical wives were considered to exemplify wisdom and faithfulness.

**Orpheus, Amphioun** (472). Two musicians who played with legendary skill.

**Joab** (475). One of King David's generals who used a trumpet to give signals to his army.

**Theodomas** (476). A legendary Theban seer whose invocation was followed by trumpeting.

**Bacus** (478). God of wine.

**Venus** (479). Goddess of love, sometimes depicted with a firebrand (see lines 483, 533 below).

**Marcian** (488). Martianus Capella was the fifth-century author of an allegorical Latin poem about the marriage of Philology and Mercury.

**Constantyn** (566). The eleventh-century author of *De Coitu,* or *About Coitus,* mentioned in the next line, that contains recipes for aphrodisiacs and other cures for male impotence.

***Romance of the Rose*** (788). An elaborate thirteenth-century allegory of a lover's assault on the virginity of the rose. Chaucer had translated a version of the allegory from the French of Guillaume de Lorris and Jean de Meun, in which a magnificent garden of love is described.

**Priapus** (790). The god of gardens and, because of his proverbially frustrated lust, the god of the phallus.

**Pluto, Proserpina** (794–95). The god and goddess of the underworld, bearing various literary associations as the king and queen of the fairies who danced around a well at the center of a garden. Pluto was said to have carried off Proserpina against her consent to be his wife in the underworld.

**scorpion** (814). A common symbol of treachery. The scorpion is said to charm her victim with her head before suddenly stinging him with her tail. On many medieval illustrations of the human body, a scorpion is drawn over the genital region.

**Argus** (867). The mythological Argus was appointed by Hera to watch over Io. His hundred eyes were to no avail.

**Ovyde** (881). Ovid's Latin *Metamorphoses* was well known in the Middle Ages. It contained the story of Pyramus and Thisbe (referred to in lines 884–87 below). Pyramus loved his beautiful neighbor but was forbidden to see her by both his own parents and hers. By talking through a chink in the wall they arranged to meet in a nearby wood. The story ends tragically with the death of both.

**"Rys up, my wyf ..."** (894–904). January's lines are an almost blasphemous parallel to the Song of Solomon (see, for example, 2:10–12, 4:1, and 4:7–12). Chaucer may have learned the phrases in Jerome's *Against Jovinian*.

**Phebus** (976). Apollo or the sun god.

**Claudian** (988). Author of the fourth-century epic poem *De Raptu Proserpinae,* which is about Pluto's ravishment of his wife. Some readers have seen a distant parallel with the way January carries off the lovely young May into the unhappy underworld of marriage.

**Jesus *filius* Syrak** (1006). Not, of course, Christ, but rather the supposed author of the apocryphal book of Ecclesiasticus. For the reference quoted above in lines 1003–04, see Ecclesiasticus 7:29.

**a womman in my plyt** (1091). The desire of pregnant women for strange foods was as well known in medieval times as it is now. Of course, May is probably only pretending to be pregnant to play on January's desire for an heir (see lines 28 and 193–96 above).

# THE MARCHANT

## *The Prologe of the Marchantes Tale*

"Weping and wayling, care and other sorwe
I knowe ynogh, on even and a-morwe,"
Quod the Marchant, "and so doon othere mo
That wedded been. I trowe that it be so,
For wel I woot it fareth so with me.                                    5
I have a wyf, the worste that may be;
For thogh the feend to hire y-coupled were,
She wolde him overmacche, I dar wel swere.
What sholde I yow reherce in special
Hir hye malice? She is a shrewe at al.                                10
Ther is a long and large difference
Bitwix Grisildis grete pacience*
And of my wyf the passing crueltee.
Were I unbounden, also moot I thee,
I wolde nevere eft comen in the snare.                                15
We wedded men live in sorwe and care—
Assaye whoso wole and he shal finde
I seye sooth, by Seint Thomas of Inde,*
As for the more part—I sey nat alle:
God shilde that it sholde so bifalle.                                 20
A, goode sire Hoost, I have y-wedded be
Thise monthes two, and more nat, pardee;
And yet I trowe he that all his lyve
Wyflees hath been, though that men wolde him ryve
Unto the herte, ne coude in no manere                                25
Tellen so muchel sorwe, as I now here
Coulde tellen of my wyves cursednesse!"

# THE MERCHANT

## The Prologue of the Merchant's Tale

Weeping and wailing, care and sorrow
I know well enough, evening and morning,"
said the Merchant, "and so do many others
who are married: I believe it's so,
for I well know that so it goes with me.                              5
I have a wife, the worst that can be;
for even if the devil were coupled with her
she would master him, I dare to give my oath.
Why should I repeat to you in detail
her proud malice? She is a shrew in every way.          10
There is a long and large difference
between Griselda's great patience
and the surpassing cruelty of my wife.
If I were unshackled, I swear
I would never get in the trap again.                            15
We married men live in unhappiness and anxiety—
whoever wants to, let him try it, and he shall find
that, by Saint Thomas of India, I'm saying the truth
about the majority—I don't say it for all:
God forbid that it should happen that way.                 20
Ah, good sir Host, I have been married
these two months and no more, by heaven;
and yet I think that a man who for all his life
has been without a wife could not, even if he were
        to be
stabbed to the heart, in any way                               25
recount as much unhappiness as I could tell
here and now concerning my wife's cursedness!"

"Now," quod oure Hoost, "Marchaunt, so God yow
  blesse,
Sin ye so muchel knowen of that art,
Ful hertely I pray yow telle us part."                    30
  "Gladly," quod he, "but of myn owene sore
For sory herte I telle may namore."

*Here biginneth the Marchantes Tale*

Whylom ther was dwellinge in Lumbardye*
     A worthy knight that born was of Pavye,*
In which he lived in greet prosperitee;
And sixty yeer a wyflees man was he,
And folwed ay his bodily delyt                            5
On wommen ther as was his appetyt,
As doon thise foles that ben seculeer.*
And whan that he was passed sixty yeer—
Were it for holinesse or for dotage,
I can nat seye—but swich a greet corage                   10
Hadde this knight to been a wedded man,
That day and night he dooth al that he can
T'espyen where he mighte wedded be,
Preyinge our Lord to graunten him that he
Mighte ones knowe of thilke blisful lyf                   15
That is bitwixe an housbond and his wyf,
And for to live under that holy bond
With which that first God man and womman bond.
"Non other lyf," seyde he, "is worth a bene,
For wedlok is so esy and so clene                         20
That in this world it is a paradys."
Thus seyde this olde knight that was so wys.
  And certeinly, as sooth as God is king,
To take a wyf, it is a glorious thing,
And namely whan a man is old and hoor:                    25
Thanne is a wyf the fruit of his tresor;
Thanne sholde he take a yong wyf and a feir,

"Now, Merchant," said our Host, "as God may
    bless you,
since you have so much of that knowledge,
I pray you heartily to tell us a part of it."          30
    "Willingly," he said, "but of my own misery
I can say no more, for heavyheartedness."

*Here begins the Merchant's Tale*

There once resided in Lombardy
    a worthy knight whose birth was of Pavia,
where he lived in great prosperity.
He was a bachelor for sixty years,
and all that time followed fleshly pleasure          5
in women wherever his appetite led,
as do these fools who are not in clerical orders.
When he had passed his sixtieth year
(I cannot say whether it was for religious motive
or because he was in his dotage), this knight          10
felt such a strong desire to be a wedded man
that day and night he did everything he could
to discover whom he might be married to,
imploring our Lord to grant that he
might sometime come to know that blissful life          15
which is between a husband and his wife,
and that he might live under that holy bond
with which God first bound together man and
    woman.
"No other life," he said, "is worth a bean,
for wedlock is so comforting and so pure          20
that it is an earthly paradise."
Thus said this old knight who was so wise.
    And indeed, as surely as God is our ruler,
it is a glorious thing to take a wife,
especially when a man is old and hoary:          25
then a wife is the best part of his treasure;
then he should take a young and beautiful wife

On which he mighte engendren him an heir,
And lede his lyf in joye and in solas,
Wheras thise bacheleres singe "Allas,"                    30
Whan that they finden any adversitee
In love, which nis but childish vanitee.
And trewely it sit wel to be so,
That bacheleres have often peyne and wo:
On brotel ground they builde, and brotelnesse            35
They finde whan they wene sikernesse.
They live but as a brid or as a beste
In libertee and under non areste,
Ther as a wedded man in his estaat
Liveth a lyf blisful and ordinaat,                       40
Under the yok of mariage ybounde:
Wel may his herte in joye and blisse habounde,
For who can be so buxom as a wyf?
Who is so trewe, and eek so ententyf
To kepe him, syk and hool, as is his make?               45
For wele or wo, she wol him nat forsake.
She nis nat wery him to love and serve,
Thogh that he lye bedrede til he sterve.
And yet somme clerkes seyn it nis nat so,
Of whiche he Theofraste* is oon of tho—                  50
What force though Theofraste liste lye?
"Ne take no wyf," quod he, "for housbondrye,
As for to spare in houshold thy dispence;
A trewe servant dooth more diligence,
Thy good to kepe, than thyn owene wyf,                    55
For she wol clayme half part al hir lyf.
And if that thou be syk, so God me save,
Thy verray frendes or a trewe knave
Wol kepe thee bet than she that waiteth ay
After thy good, and hath don many a day.                 60
And if thou take a wyf unto thyn hold,
Ful lightly maystow been a cokewold."
This sentence and an hundred thinges worse

on whom he can engender an heir,
and lead his life in joy and in delights,
while bachelors sing another song 30
when they find any reverses
in the game of love, which is nothing but childish folly.
And in fact it is very suitable
that bachelors should often have pain and sorrow:
they build on unstable ground, and they shall 35
find instability when they expect security.
They live but as a bird or beast,
at liberty and with no control,
whereas a wedded man in his condition
lives a blissful and orderly life, 40
controlled in the yoke of marriage;
his heart may well be filled with joy and bliss.
For who may be so obedient as a wife?
Who is so faithful and also so attentive
in watching over him, sick or healthy, as is his wife? 45
For better or for worse she will not forsake him.
She does not grow weary of loving and serving him,
even if he lies bedridden until he dies.
And yet some learned men say this is not so,
of whom Theophrastus is one— 50
but what difference does it make if Theophrastus
    wants to
lie? "Do not take a wife for economy's sake," he said,
"so as to save expense in your household;
a faithful servant takes more trouble
to watch over your possessions than does your own wife, 55
for she will make a claim to half of it all her life.
And if you are sick, as God may save me,
your true friends or a faithful servant will
take better care of you than she will, who continually lies
in wait for your possessions, and has done so for
    many a day. 60
And if you take a wife into your keeping,
you may very easily become a cuckold."
This man wrote this maxim and a hundred

Wryteth this man, ther God his bones corse!
But take no kepe of al swich vanitee;                    65
Deffye Theofraste and herke me.
    A wyf is Goddes yifte verraily;
Alle other maner yiftes hardily,
As londes, rentes, pasture, or commune,
Or moebles, alle ben yiftes of fortune,                  70
That passen as a shadwe upon a wal.
But drede nat, if pleynly speke I shal,
A wyf wol laste and in thyn hous endure
Wel lenger than thee list, paraventure.
    Mariage is a ful gret sacrement.                     75
He which that hath no wyf, I holde him shent:
He liveth helplees and al desolat
(I speke of folk in seculer estaat).
And herke why, I sey nat this for noght,
That womman is for mannes help y-wroght:                 80
The hye God, whan he hadde Adam maked
And saugh him al allone, bely-naked,
God of his grete goodnesse seyde than,
"Lat us now make an help unto this man
Lyk to himself." And thanne he made him Eve.             85
Heer may ye se, and heerby may ye preve,
That wyf is mannes help and his confort,
His paradys terrestre and his disport.
So buxom and so vertuous is she,
They moste nedes live in unitee,                         90
O flesh they been, and o flesh, as I gesse
Hath but on herte in wele and in distresse.
    A wyf! a, Seinte Marie, *benedicite,*
How mighte a man han any adversitee
That hath a wyf? Certes, I can nat seye.                  95
The blisse which that is bitwixe hem tweye
Ther may no tonge telle or herte thinke.
If he be povre, she helpeth him to swinke;
She kepeth his good and wasteth never a deel;
Al that hir housbonde lust hire lyketh weel;            100
She seith not ones "nay," when he seith "ye."

things worse, God curse his bones!
But pay no attention to all such foolishness; 65
scorn Theophrastus and listen to me.

 A wife is truly a gift of God.
All other kinds of gifts, like arable lands,
revenues, pasture or pasturage rights, or
moveable goods are surely gifts of fortune, 70
which pass like shadows on a wall.
But, do not fear—if I am to speak plainly—
a wife will last and endure in your house
longer indeed than you perhaps wish.

 Marriage is a very great sacrament. 75
I hold the man who has no wife to be ruined:
he lives unhelped and forsaken
(I am talking about laymen).
Listen to why—I am not saying this for nothing:
woman was created for a help to man: 80
God on high, having created Adam
and seeing him all alone and destitute,
then said in his great goodness,
"Let us now make a help unto this man
like himself." And then he made him Eve. 85
Here you may see, and hereby you may prove,
that a wife is man's help and comfort,
his earthly paradise and his source of pleasure.
She is so obedient and virtuous
that by necessity they must live in unity. 90
They are one flesh, and, as I suppose, one flesh
has but one will, in happiness and in sorrow.

 A wife! Ah, Saint Mary bless us,
How might a man have any adversity
if he has a wife? Certainly I cannot say. 95
No tongue may tell, or heart think,
the bliss that is between the two.
If he is poor, she helps him in his labor;
she watches over his possessions and does not waste a bit;
all that her husband desires seems desirable to her; 100
she does not once say "No" when he says "Yes."

"Do this," seith he; "al redy, sire," seith she.
O blisful ordre of wedlok precious,
Thou art so merye, and eek so vertuous,
And so commended and appreved eek,                    105
That every man that halt him worth a leek
Upon his bare knees oughte al his lyf
Thanken his God that him hath sent a wyf,
Or elles preye to God him for to sende
A wyf to laste unto his lyves ende,                   110
For thanne his lyf is set in sikernesse.
He may nat be deceyved, as I gesse,
So that he werke after his wyves reed;
Thanne may he boldly beren up his heed,
They been so trewe and therwithal so wyse;            115
For which, if thou wolt werken as the wyse,
Do alwey so as wommen woi thee rede.

  Lo how that Jacob,* as thise clerkes rede,
By good conseil of his moder Rebekke
Bond the kides skin aboute his nekke,                 120
For which his fadres benisoun he wan.

  Lo Judith,* as the stone eek telle can,
By wys conseil she Goddes peple kepte,
And slow him Olofernus whyl he slepte.

  Lo Abigayl,* by good conseil how she              125
Saved hir housbond Nabal whan that he
Sholde han be slayn; and loke Ester* also
By good conseil delivered out of wo
The peple of God, and made him Mardochee
Of Assuere enhaunced for to be.                       130

  Ther nis nothing in gree supenlatyf,
As seith Senek, above an humble wyf.

  Suffre thy wyves tonge, as Caton bit:
She shal comande and thou shalt suffren it,
And yet she wol obeye of curteisye.                   135

  A wyf is keper of thyn hounbondrye;
Wel may the syke man biwaille and wepe,
Ther as ther nis no wyf the hous to kepe.

"Do this," says he; "All ready, sir," says she.
O blissful order of precious wedlock,
you are so joyous, and also so virtuous,
and also so commended and approved                    105
that every man who holds himself worth a leek
ought to thank, upon his bare knees
throughout his life, the God who has sent him a wife,
or else pray God to send him
a wife to last to the end of his life,                110
for then his life will be soundly based.
As I think, he may not be deceived,
if he acts according to his wife's advice;
then he may carry his head high,
wives are so faithful and at the same time so wise;   115
for which reason, if you would act as the wise do,
always do as women advise you.

Consider how Jacob, as learned men relate,
by the good advice of his mother Rebecca
tied the kid's skin around his neck,                  120
whereby he won his father's blessing.

Consider Judith: as history tells in this case, too,
she preserved God's people by wise counsel
and killed Holofernes while he slept.

Consider how Abigail by good advice                   125
saved her husband Nabal when he
was to be killed; and consider, too, how Esther
by good advice delivered God's people from their
    suffering
and caused Mordecai
to be exalted by Ahasuerus.                            130

There is nothing of higher degree,
As Seneca says, than an humble wife.

Endure your wife's tongue, as Cato bids you:
she shall command, and you shall suffer it,
and yet she will obey you by courtesy.                135

A wife is the guardian of your domestic affairs;
well may the sick man wail and weep
where there is no wife to watch over the house.

I warne thee, if wisely thou wolt wirche,
Love wel they wyf as Crist loved his chirche;     140
If thou lovest thyself, thou lovest thy wyf:
No man hateth his flesh, but in his lyf
He fostreth it, and therfore bidde I thee
Cherisse thy wyf or thou shalt never thee.
Housbond and wyf, what so men jape or pleye,     145
Of worldly folk holden the siker weye.
They been so knit, ther may noon harm bityde,
And namely, upon the wyves syde.

For which this Januarie, of whom I tolde,
Considered hath, inwith his dayes olde,          150
The lusty lyf, the vertuous quiete,
That is in mariage hony swete;
And for his freendes on a day he sente
To tellen hem th'effect of his entente.

With face sad his tale he hath hem told;         155
He seyde, 'Freendes, I am hoor and old,
And almost, God woot, on my pittes brinke;
Upon my soule somwhat moste I thinke.
I have my body folily despended;
Blessed be God, that it shal been amended!       160
For I wol be, certeyn, a wedded man,
And that anoon in al the haste I can,
Unto som mayde fair and tendre of age.
I prey yow, shapeth for my mariage
Al sodeynly, for I wol nat abyde;                165
And I wol fonde t'espyen, on my syde,
To whom I may be wedded hastily.
But for as muche as ye ben mo than I,
Ye shullen rather swich a thing espyen
Than I, and wher me best were to allyen.         170

But o thing warne I yow, my freendes dere:
I wol non old wyf han in no manere;
She shal nat passe twenty yeer, certayn;
Old fish and yong flesh wolde I have ful fayn.
Bet is," quod he, "a pyk than a pikerel;*        175

I warn you: if you want to act wisely,
love your wife well, as Christ loved his church; 140
if you love yourself, you love your wife:
no man hates his own flesh, but during his life
he cares for it tenderly, and therefore I bid you
to cherish your wife, or you shall never prosper.
However people may joke, husband and wife 145
hold to the sure path for laymen.
They are so firmly knit together that no harm may arise,
particularly on the wife's side.

    For these reasons, this January of whom I was
      telling you
considered in his latter days 150
the merry life and the virtuous peace
that is in honey-sweet marriage;
he sent for his friends one day
to tell them the outcome of his plans.

    He told them his tale with sober face; 155
he said, "Friends, I am white-haired and old,
and almost, God knows, at the brink of my grave;
I must give a little thought to my soul.
I have expended my body in folly;
blessed be God that this shall be corrected! 160
For I will be married,
and that as fast as I can,
to some fair maiden of tender age.
I entreat you, plan for my marriage
hastily, for I don't want to wait; 165
and I on my side will try to search out
whom I may be married to quickly.
But because there are more of you, you are likely
to discern more quickly than I such a possibility,
and where it would be best for me to ally myself. 170

    But I warn you of one thing, dear friends:
I won't have any kind of old wife;
she shall not be over twenty, for certain;
I would very willingly have old fish but fresh meat.
A pike is better than a pickerel," he said, 175

And bet than old boef is the tendre veel:
I wol no womman thritty yeer of age—
It is but bene-straw and greet forage.
And eek thise olde widwes, God it woot,
They conne so muchel craft on Wades boot,*          180
So muchel broken harm whan that hem leste,
That with hem sholde I never live in reste.
For sondry scoles maketh sotile clerkis:
Womman of manye scoles half a clerk is.
But certeynly a yong thing may men gye,          185
Right as men may warm wex with handes plye.
Wherfore I sey yow pleynly, in a clause,
I wol non old wyf han right for this cause.
For if so were I hadde swich mischaunce
That I in hire ne coude han no plesaunce,          190
Thanne sholde I lede my lyf in avoutrye,
And go streight to the devel whan I dye;
Ne children sholde I none upon hire geten,
Yet were me levere houndes hadde me eten
Than that myn heritage sholde falle          195
In straunge hand; and this I tell yow alle:
I dote nat, I woot the cause why
Men sholde wedde, and forthermore woot I
Ther speketh many a man of mariage,
That woot namore of it than woot my page          200
For whiche causes man sholde take a wyf:
If he ne may nat liven chast his lyf,
Take him a wyf with greet devocioun,
By cause of leveful procreacioun
Of children, to th'onour of God above,          205
And nat only for paramour or love;
And for they sholde lecherye eschue,
And yelde hir dette whan that it is due;
Or for that ech of hem sholde helpen other
In meschief, as a suster shal the brother,          210

"but tender veal is better than old beef.
I don't want any woman thirty years of age;
that's nothing but straw and coarse fodder.
And besides, God knows, these old widows
have so much skill in Wade's boat—                              180
can cause so much vexation when they want to—
that I should never live in peace with them.
Studying in different schools makes cunning scholars:
a woman who has been at many schools is half a
    scholar.
But one may certainly guide a young thing,                      185
just as one may ply warm wax with the hands.
Therefore I say to you plainly and briefly
that for just this cause I won't take an old wife.
For if it were to happen that I had such a misfortune
as not to be able to take any pleasure in my wife,             190
then I should lead my life in adultery
and go straight to the devil when I die.
Nor should I engender any children upon her,
yet I would rather have had dogs eat me
than to have my inheritance fall                                195
into the hands of strangers; and to all of you I say this:
I am not doting; I know why
we should marry, and furthermore I know
that many a man speaks of marriage
who knows no more than my page does                            200
of the reasons for which man should take a wife;
if a man cannot live his life chastely,
let him take himself a wife with great devoutness
for the sake of lawful procreation
of children to the honor of God above,                         205
and not simply for sexual pleasure or love;
and let him do this because, also, they should
    eschew lechery
and pay their debt to each other when it is due;
or let him take a wife because one should help
    the other
in tribulation, as a sister should help her brother,          210

And live in chastitee ful holily—
But sires, by your leve, that am nat I,
For God be thanked, I dar make avaunt,
I fele my limes stark and suffisaunt
To do al that a man bilongeth to;                        215
I woot myselven best what I may do.
Though I be hoor, I fare as dooth a tree
That blosmeth er that fruyt y-woxen be;
And blosmy tree nis neither drye ne deed:
I fele me nowher hoor but on myn heed;                   220
Myn herte and alle my limes been as grene
As laurer thurgh the yeer is for to sene.
And sin that ye han herd al myn entente,
I prey yow to my wil ye wol assente."

    Diverse men diversely him tolde                      225
Of mariage manye ensamples olde:
Somme blamed it, somme preysed it, certeyn;
But atte laste, shortly for to seyn,
As al day falleth altercacioun
Bitwixen freendes in disputisoun,                        230
Ther fil a stryf bitwixe his bretheren two,*
Of which that oon was cleped Placebo;*
Justinus* soothly called was that other.

    Placebo seyde, "O Januarie brother,
Ful litel nede hadde ye, my lord so dere,               235
Conseil to axe of any that is here;
But that ye been so ful of sapience
That yow ne lyketh, for your heighe prudence,
To weyven fro the word of Salomon;
This word seyde he unto us everichon:                    240
'Wirk alle thing by conseil,' thus seyde he,
'And thanne shaltow nat repenten thee.'
But though that Salomon spak swich a word,
Myn owene dere brother and my lord,
So wisly God my soule bringe at reste,                   245
I hold your owene conseil is the beste.
For brother myn, of me tak this motyf:

and live in chastity with great holiness—
but by your leave, sirs, I am not in the latter class,
for, God be thanked, I dare to boast that
I feel my limbs to be strong and competent
to do all that belongs to a man;                                    215
I myself know best what I can do.
Although I am white-haired, I fare like a tree
that blossoms before the fruit has grown;
a blossoming tree is neither dry nor dead:
I feel gray nowhere except on my head;                             220
my heart and all my limbs seem as green
as laurel looks throughout the year.
Now, since you have heard my full purpose,
I pray that you will assent to my desire."

    Diverse men advised him diversely with many         225
ancient stories to illustrate their points about marriage:
it is sure that some gave it blame, others gave
    it praise;
but at last (to speak briefly)
as altercation constantly occurs
between friends in dispute,                                        230
an argument arose between his two brothers,
of whom one was called Placebo
and the other was in truth named Justinus.

    Placebo said, "O brother January,
you had little need, my lord so dear,                              235
to ask advice of anyone who is here;
it was only that you are so full of wisdom
that in your exalted prudence it does not please you
to depart from the proverb of Solomon.
He pronounced this maxim for each of us:                          240
'Do everything by advice,' thus he said,
'and then you shall not repent of your action.'
But although Solomon uttered such a proverb,
my dear brother and my lord,
as surely as I hope God may bring my soul to peace,               245
I hold that your own counsel is the best.
For, brother mine, take this policy from me:

I have now been a court-man al my lyf,
And, God it woot, though I unworthy be,
I have stonden in ful greet degree                          250
Abouten lordes of ful heigh estaat,
Yet hadde I never with noon of hem debaat;
I never hem contraried, trewely;
I woot wel that my lord can more than I;
What that he seith, I holde it ferme and stable;            255
I seye the same or elles thing semblable.
A ful gret fool is any conseillour,
That serveth any lord of heigh honour,
That dar presume, or elles thenken it
That his conseil sholde passe his lordes wit.               260
Nay, lordes been no foles, by my fay.
Ye han yourselven shewed heer today
So heigh sentence, so holily and weel,
That I consente and conferme everydeel
Youre wordes alle and youre opinioun.                       265
By God, ther nis no man in al this toun,
Ne in Itaille, that coude bet han sayd:
Crist halt him of this conseil wel apayd.
And trewely it is an heigh corage
Of any man that stapen is in age                            270
To take a yong wyf! By my fader kin,
Your herte hangeth on a joly pin!
Dooth now in this matere right as yow leste,
For finally I holde it for the beste."

    Justinus, that ay stille sat and herde,                 275
Right in this wyse he to Placebo answerde:
"Now, brother myn, be pacient, I preye,
Sin ye han seyd, and herkneth what I seye.
Senek amonges othere wordes wyse
Seith that a man oghte him right wel avyse                   280
To whom he yeveth his lond or his catel;
And sin I oghte avyse me right wel
To whom I yeve my good awey fro me,
Wel muchel more I oghte avysed be

I have now been a courtier all my life,
and God knows, although I am unworthy,
I have stood in a very superior rank          250
in attendance on lords of very high estate,
yet I never argued with them;
truly, I never contradicted them;
I know well that my lord knows more than I;
whatever he says, I hold it to be firm and established.          255
I say the same or else something like it.
Any counselor is a great fool
who, serving a lord of great honor,
dares to presume, or else to think,
that his advice should be better than his lord's wisdom.          260
No, lords are no fools, by my faith.
You yourself have manifested here today
such noble sentiments in so holy and good a fashion
that I agree with and confirm in every part
all your words and your opinion.          265
By God, there isn't a man in all this town,
or in all Italy, who could have said better:
Christ holds himself well pleased with this plan,
and, truly, it shows a fine spirit
in any man who is advanced in age          270
to take a young wife! By my father's race,
your heart is taking a merry way!
Do now just as you wish in this matter,
for, finally, I consider that best."

    Justinus, who all this time had sat still and listened,          275
answered Placebo in just this way:
"Now, my brother, I pray you to be patient,
since you have had your say, and listen to what
    I shall say.
Among his other wise proverbs, Seneca
says that a man ought to consider right well          280
to whom he is giving his land or his riches;
and since I ought to consider right well
to whom I am giving away my goods,
all the more ought I consider

To whom I yeve my body for alwey.                               285
I warn yow wel, it is no childes pley
To take a wyf withouten avysement.
Men moste enquere—this is myn assent—
Wher she be wys, or sobre, or drokelewe,
Or proud, or elles otherweys a shrewe;                          290
A chidestere, or wastour of thy good,
Or riche, or poore, or elles mannish wood—
Al be it so that no man finden shal
Noon in this world that trotteth hool in al,
Ne man ne beest swich as men coude devyse;                      295
But nathelees, it oghte y-nough suffise
With any wyf, if so were that she hadde
Mo gode thewes than hir vyces badde;
And al this axeth leyser for t'enquere.
For God it woot, I have wept many a tere                        300
Ful prively sin I have had a wyf:
Preyse whoso wole a wedded mannes lyf,
Certein I finde in it but cost and care,
And observances, of alle blisses bare.
And yet, God woot, my neighebores aboute,                       305
And namely of wommen many a route,
Seyn that I have the moste stedefast wyf,
And eek the mekeste oon that bereth lyf—
But I wot best wher wringeth me my sho.
Ye mowe, for me, right as yow lyketh do;                        310
Avyseth yow—ye been a man of age—
How that ye entren into mariage,
And namely with a yong wyf and a fair.
By him that made water, erthe, and air,
The yongeste man that is in al this route                       315
Is bisy ynogh to bringen it aboute
To han his wyf allone. Trusteth me,
Ye shul nat plesen hire fully yeres three—
This is to seyn, to doon hir ful plesaunce:
A wyf axeth ful many an observaunce.                            320
I prey yow that ye be nat yvel apayd."
    "Wel," quod this Januarie, "and hastow sayd?

to whom I am giving my body forever. 285
I give you firm warning, it is no child's play
to take a wife without deliberation.
One must inquire, in my opinion,
whether she is discreet, or sober, or inclined to drink,
or proud, or shrewish in other ways; 290
whether she is a chider or a waster of your goods,
or rich, or poor, or inclined to unwomanly rages—
although it is true that no man shall find
any in the world that runs soundly in every respect,
neither man nor beast such as could be imagined; 295
but nevertheless, it ought to be enough
in the case of any wife, if she has
more good qualities than evil vices;
and all this demands leisure for inquiry.
For, God knows, I have wept many a tear 300
in secret since I have had a wife:
let who so will praise a married man's life,
I certainly find in it only cost and misery,
and duties, devoid of every bliss.
And yet, God knows, my neighbors roundabout, 305
and especially many a host of women,
say that I have the most steadfast wife,
and also the meekest one, alive.
But I know best where my shoe pinches me.
You may do what you want for my part; 310
but you are a man of age—consider
that you are entering into marriage,
and, particularly, with a young, pretty wife.
By him who made the water, earth, and air,
the youngest man in this group 315
has enough trouble
to keep his wife to himself. Believe me,
you shall not please her for as much as three years—
that is to say, please her fully:
a wife requires much to be performed. 320
Please don't be annoyed."
    "Well," said this January, "and have you finished?

Straw for thy Senek and for thy proverbes!
I counte nat a panier ful of herbes
Of scole-termes; wyser men than thow,                    325
As thou hast herd, assenteden right now
To my purpose; Placebo, what sey ye?"
    "I seye it is a cursed man," quod he,
"That letteth matrimoigne, sikerly."
And with that word they rysen sodeynly,                  330
And been assented fully that he sholde
Be wedded whanne him list and wher he wolde.
    Heigh fantasye and curious bisinesse
Fro day to day gan in the soule impresse
Of Januarie aboute his mariage.                          335
Many fair shap and many a fair visage
Ther passeth thurgh his herte night by night.
As whoso toke a mirour polished bright,
And sette it in a commune market-place,
Thanne sholde he see ful many a figure pace              340
By this mirour; and in the same wyse
Gan Januarie inwith his thoght devyse
Of maydens whiche that dwelten him bisyde.
He wiste nat wher that he mighte abyde:
For if that oon have beautee in hir face,                345
Another stant so in the peples grace
For hir sadnesse and hir benignitee,
That of the peple grettest voys hath she;
And some were riche and hadden badde name.
But nathelees, bitwixe ernest and game,                  350
He atte laste apoynted him on oon,
And leet alle othere from his herte goon,
And chees hir of his owene auctoritee—
For Love is blind al day and may nat see.
And whan that he was in his bed y-broght,                355
He purtreyed in his herte and in his thoght
Hir fresshe beautee and hir age tendre,
Hir myddel smal, hir armes longe and sclendre,
Hir wyse governaunce, hir gentillesse,

A straw for your Seneca and for your proverbs!
I don't give a basket of greens
for pedantries; wiser men than you,                              325
as you heard, just now assented
to my intention; Placebo, what do you say?"
     "I say," he said, "that it's an abominable man
who hinders matrimony, surely."
And at that word they abruptly all got up                        330
and were in full agreement that January should
be married when he liked and to whomever he wanted.
     Lofty fancies and minute solicitude
from day to day made their imprint upon the soul
of January concerning his marriage.                              335
Many fair shapes and many a pretty face
passed through his heart night by night.
As, if anyone took a brightly polished mirror
and set it in a public market place,
he would then see many figures passing                          340
by his mirror, so in the same fashion
January in his thoughts commenced to muse
about girls who lived near him.
He didn't know where he might rest:
for if one of them had a beautiful face,                         345
another was so established in popular favor
for her sobriety and benevolence
that she had the majority's voice;
and some were rich and had an evil name.
But nevertheless, partly for sober reasons, partly
          for lighter                                            350
ones, he at last settled on one
and let all the others pass from his heart,
and chose her on his own authority—
for Love is ever blind and cannot see.
When he was conveyed to bed,                                     355
he pictured in his heart and mind
her fresh beauty and tender age,
her slim waist, her long, slender arms,
her discreet behavior, her genteel courtesy,

Hir wommanly beringe and hir sadnesse.                    360
And whan that he on hire was condescended,
Him thoughte his chois mighte nat ben amended.
For whan that he himself concluded hadde,
Him thoughte ech other mannes wit so badde,
That inpossible it were to replye                          365
Agayn his chois: this was his fantasye.
His freendes sente he to at his instaunce,
And preyed hem to doon him that plesaunce
That hastily they wolden to him come:
He wolde abregge hir labour alle and some;                 370
Nedeth namore for him to go ne ryde;
He was apoynted ther he wolde abyde.

    Placebo cam, and eek his freendes sone,
And alderfirst he bad hem alle a bone,
That noon of hem none argumentes make                      375
Agayn the purpos which that he hath take;
Which purpos was plesant to God, seyde he,
And verray ground of his prosperitee.

    He seyde ther was a mayden in the toun,
Which that of beautee hadde greet renoun;                  380
Al were it so she were of smal degree,
Suffyseth him hir youthe and hir beautee;
Which mayde he seyde he wolde han to his wyf,
To lede in ese and holinesse his lyf.
And thanked God that he mighte han hire al,                385
That no wight his blisse parten shal;
And preyde hem to labouren in this nede,
And shapen that he faille nat to spede;
For thanne, he seyde, his spirit was at ese.

    "Thanne is," quod he, "no thing may me displese,       390
Save o thing priketh in my conscience,
The which I wol reherce in youre presence.
I have," quod he, "herd seyd ful yore ago
Ther may no man han parfite blisses two—
This is to seye, in erthe and eek in hevene.               395
For though he kepe him fro the sinnes sevene,*

her womanly bearing, and her steadfastness. 360
And when he had determined on her,
he thought that his choice might not be improved on.
For when he himself had come to a decision,
he thought that every other man's wit was so lacking
that it would be impossible to object 365
to his choice: this was his delusion.
He sent urgently to his friends
and asked them to do him the pleasure
of coming to him hastily:
he would shorten all their labors; 370
he no longer needed to walk or to ride;
he had determined where he would rest.

Soon Placabo came, and his other friends as well,
and first of all January made a request of all of them
that no one would make any arguments 375
against the design which he had adopted;
which design he said was pleasing to God
and the very basis of his own welfare.

He said that there was a girl in the town
who had a great reputation for beauty; 380
although she was of low estate,
her youth and beauty were enough for him;
which girl, he said, he wanted to have for wife
so as to lead his life in comfort and holiness.
And he thanked God that he might have her
    completely 385
so that no man might share in his bliss;
and he asked them to do their offices in this matter
and arrange things so that he should not fail to gain his
    end; for then, he said, his spirit would be at rest.

"Then," he said, "nothing can displease me, 390
except for one thing that pricks my conscience,
which I shall relate in your presence.
I have heard it said long ago," he remarked,
"that no man may have two kinds of perfect bliss—
that is to say, on earth and in heaven as well. 395
For even if he keep himself from the seven deadly sins,

And eek from every branche of thilke tree,
Yet is ther so parfit felicitee
And so greet ese and lust in mariage,
That ever I am agast now in myn age          400
That I shal lede now so mery a lyf,
So delicat, withouten wo and stryf,
That I shal have myn hevene in erthe here.
For sith that verray hevene is boght so dere
With tribulacioun and greet penaunce,          405
How sholde I thanne, that live in swich plesaunce
As alle wedded men doon with hir wyvis,
Come to the blisse ther Crist eterne on lyve is?
This is my drede, and ye, my bretheren tweye,
Assoileth me this questioun, I preye."          410
   Justinus, which that hated his folye,
Answerde anonright in his japerye;
And for he wolde his longe tale abregge,
He wolde noon auctoritee allegge,
But seyde, "Sire, so ther be noon obstacle          415
Other than this, God of his heigh miracle
And of his mercy may so for yow wirche,
That, er ye have youre right of holy chirche,
Ye may repente of wedded mannes lyf,
In which ye seyn ther is no wo ne stryf.          420
And elles, God forbede but he sente.
A wedded man him grace to repente
Wel ofte rather than a sengle man.
And therfore, sire, the beste reed I can:
Dispeire yow noght, but have in your memorie,          425
Paraunter she may be your purgatorie:
She may be Goddes mene and Goddes whippe!
Thanne shat youre soule up to hevene skippe
Swifter than dooth an arwe out of the bowe.
I hope to God, herafter shul ye knowe          430
That their nis no so greet felicitee
In mariage, ne nevere mo shal be,
That you shal lette of your savacioun,

and every subbranch of that tree,
yet there is such perfect felicity
and such great comfort and joy in marriage
that here in my old age I am continually afraid          400
that I shall now have so merry a life,
one of such delight, without sorrow and conflict,
that I shall have my heaven here upon earth.
For since true heaven is purchased so dearly,
with tribulation and heavy penance,                     405
how then should I, who live in such pleasure
as all married men have with their wives,
come to that bliss where Christ lives eternally?
This is my fear, and you, my two brothers,
please resolve this question for me."                    410
    Justinus, who despised his folly,
answered immediately in his derisive way;
and because he wanted to cut short his long tale,
he would not cite authorities
but said, "Sir, if there is no obstacle                  415
other than this, God with his miraculous power
and mercy may so arrange for you
that, before having your final due of holy church,
you may repent of the life of a married man,
in which you say there is no sorrow or conflict.         420
Put it another way: God forbid but that he should send
the grace of frequent repentance sooner to a
       married man
than he should to a single man.
And therefore, sir, the best advice I can give is
not to despair, but to keep in mind                      425
that perhaps a wife may be your purgatory:
she may be God's means and God's scourge!
Then your soul shall skip up to heaven
more swiftly than an arrow from the bow.
I expect, by God, that hereafter you will learn          430
there is no such great felicity
in marriage, nor evermore shall be,
as would keep you from your salvation,

So that ye use, as skile is and resoun,
The lustes of youre wyf attemprely,                    435
And that ye plese hir nat too amorously,
And that ye kepe yow eek from other sinne.
My tale is doon, for my wit is thinne.
Beth nat agast herof, my brother dere,
But lat us waden out of this matere.                    440
The Wyf of Bathe,* if ye han understonde,
Of mariage which ye have on honde
Declared hath ful wel in litel space.
Fareth now wel; God have yow in his grace."

    And with this word this Justin and his brother    445
Han take hir leve, and ech of hem of other.
For whan they saw that it moste nedes be,
They wroghten so, by sly and wys tretee,
That she this mayden, which that Maius highte,
As hastily as evere that she mighte,                    450
Shal wedded be unto this Januarie.
I trowe it were too longe you to tarie
If I you tolde of every scrit and bond
By which that she was feffed in his lond,
Or for to herknen of hir riche array;                    455
But finally y-comen is the day
That to the chirche bothe be they went
For to receyve the holy sacrement.

    Forthcomth the preest with stole aboute his nekke,
And bad hire be lyk Sarra and Rebekke*                 460
In wisdom and in trouthe of mariage,
And seyde his orisons as is usage,
And croucheth hem, and bad God sholde hem blesse,
And made al siker ynogh with holinesse.

    Thus been they wedded with solempnitee.            465
And at the feste sitteth he and she
With other worthy folk upon the deys.
Al ful of joye and blisse is the paleys,
And ful of instruments and of vitaille,
The moste deyntevous of al Itaille.                     470

if, as is reasonable, you enjoy
the pleasures of your wife moderately,                    435
and if you do not delight her too amorously,
and if you keep yourself from other sin.
My tale is told, for my wit is slight.
Don't be afraid of this, dear brother,
but let us leave this subject.                            440
The Wife of Bath, if you have understood,
has pronounced very well and briefly on this matter
of marriage which we have in hand.
Now farewell, God have you in his grace."

     And at this word Justinus and his brother           445
took their leave of him and of each other.
When they saw it had to be,
they so arranged, by clever and prudent negotiations,
that this girl, who was named May,
should, as hastily as possible,                          450
be married to January.
I believe it would delay you too long
if I told you of every writ and bond
by which she was endowed with his land,
or if you were to hear of her rich array,                455
but finally the day came
when they both went to church
to receive the holy sacrament.

     The priest came forth with his stole about his neck
and enjoined her to be like Sarah and Rebecca           460
in prudence and faithfulness in marriage,
and said his prayers according to custom, and signed
them with the cross, and bade that God should
     bless them,
and made everything secure enough with holiness.

     Thus they were married with ceremony,              465
and at the feast he and she sat
with other worthy folk on the dais.
The palace was brimming with joy and bliss
and filled with provisions and food,
the most delicious in all Italy.                        470

Biforn hem stoode instruments of swich soun,
That Orpheus,* ne of Thebes Amphioun*
Ne maden nevere swich a melodye.
   At every cours thanne cam loud minstralcye,
That nevere tromped Joab,* for to here,                    475
Nor he Theodomas,* yet half so clere
At Thebes whan the citee was in doute.
Bacus* the wyn hem shinketh al aboute,
And Venus* laugheth upon every wight,
For Januarie was bicome hir knight,                        480
And wolde bothe assayen his corage
In libertee and eek in mariage;
And with hir fyrbrond in hir hand aboute
Daunceth biforn the bryde and al the route.
And certeinly, I dar right wel seyn this,                  485
Ymeneüs, that god of wedding is,
Saugh never his lyf so mery a wedded man.
Hold thou thy pees, thou poete Marcian,*
That wrytest us that ilke wedding murie
Of hire Philologye and him Mercurie,                       490
And of the songes that the Muses songe—
Too smal is bothe thy penne and eek thy tonge
For to descryven of this mariage.
Whan tendre youthe hath wedded stouping age,
Ther is swich mirthe that it may nat be writen;            495
Assayeth it yourself, than may ye witen
If that I lye or noon in this matere.
   Maius, that sit with so benigne a chere,
Hire to biholde it semed fayërÿe—
Quene Ester loked never with swich an ÿe                   500
On Assuer, so meke a look hath she—
I may yow nat devyse al hir beautee,
But thus muche of hir beautee telle I may,
That she was lyk the brighte morwe of May,
Fulfild of alle beautee and plesaunce.                     505
   This Januarie is ravisshed in a traunce
At every time he loked on hir face;
But in his herte he gan hir to manace

Before them were instruments of such sweetness
that neither Orpheus nor Amphion of Thebes
ever made such melody.
   At every course there came such loud music
that, to listen to it, neither Joab                  475
nor Thiodamas at Thebes, when the fate of the city
was in doubt, trumpeted even half so splendidly.
Bacchus poured the wine out all around,
and Venus smiled on every man,
for January had become her knight                  480
and willed to try his mettle
not only in liberty but also in marriage;
and with her firebrand in her hand
she danced about before the bride and all the company.
And certainly I may hazard to say this,           485
that Hymen, who is god of weddings,
never in his life saw so merry a wedded man.
Hold your peace, you poet Martianus,
who created for us that merry wedding
of Philology and Mercury,                     490
and wrote about the songs the Muses sang—
too limited are both your pen and tongue
to describe this marriage.
When tender youth has wedded stooping age,
there is such merriment that it may not be written;    495
try it yourself, then you may know
whether or not I am lying about this matter.
   It seemed like magic to look on
May, she sat with so gracious a countenance—
so meek a look she had that Queen Esther never    500
gazed with such an eye on Ahasuerus.
I cannot describe all her beauty to you,
but I may tell this much—
that she was like a bright May morning,
filled with all beauty and delight.                505
   January was ravished away into a trance
every time he looked upon her face;
but in his heart he commenced to threaten

That he that night in armes wolde hir streyne
Harder than ever Paris dide Eleyne.                        510
But nathelees yet hadde he greet pitee
That thilke night offenden hire moste he,
And thoughte, "Allas, O tendre creature,
Now wolde God ye mighte wel endure
Al my corage, it is so sharp and kene;                      515
I am agast ye shul it nat sustene—
But God forbede that I dide al my might!
Now wolde God that it were woxen night,
And that the night wolde lasten everemo.
I wolde that al this peple were ago."                       520
And finally he doth al his labour,
As he best mighte, savinge his honour,
To haste hem fro the mete in subtil wyse.

The tyme cam that reson was to ryse,
And after that men daunce and drinken faste,               525
And spyces al aboute the hous they caste,
And ful of joye and blisse is every man—
All but a squyer, highte Damian,
Which carf biforn the knight ful many a day:
He was so ravisshed on his lady May                        530
That for the verray peyne he was ny wood;
Almost he swelte and swowned ther he stood,
So sore hath Venus hurt him with hir brond,
As that she bar it daunsinge in hir hond.
And to his bed he wente him hastily.                       535
Namore of him as at this tyme speke I,
But ther I lete him wepe ynough and pleyne,
Til fresshe May wol rewen on his peyne.

O perilous fyr that in the bedstraw bredeth!
O famulier foo, that his servyce bedeth!                   540
O servant traitour, false hoomly hewe,
Lyk to the naddre in bosom, sly, untrewe!
God shilde us alle from your aqueyntaunce!
O Januarie, dronken in plesaunce
In mariage, see how thy Damian,                            545
Thyn owene squyer and thy borne man,

that he would constrain her that night in his arms
more violently than Paris ever did Helen.                    510
Nevertheless, he felt great pity that
he would have to assail her that night,
and thought, "Alas, tender creature,
now would to God that you might easily endure
all my vigor, it is so sharp and keen;                       515
I am fearful that you will not sustain it—
but God forbid that I should do all I can!
Now would God that it had grown to night,
and that the night would last forever.
I wish that all these people were gone."                     520
Finally, as best he could, he did what he
might, saving his honor as a host,
to hasten them unostentatiously from the food.

The time came when it was proper to rise,
and after that they danced and drank deep,                   525
and cast spices all about the house,
and every man was full of joy and contentment—
all but a squire named Damian,
who had carved before the knight for many a day:
he was so ravished with his lady May                         530
that for the very pain he was nearly mad;
he almost languished and fainted where he stood,
so painfully had Venus wounded him with her brand
as she bore it in her hand while she danced.
Hastily he took to his bed.                                  535
I speak no more of him at this time,
but leave him there weeping and grieving his fill
until fresh May will take pity on his suffering.

O perilous fire that grows within the bedding!
O family foe, who proffers his service!                      540
O traitorous servant, false household menial,
sly and treacherous like an adder in the bosom!
God defend us all from knowing you!
O January, drunk with the pleasures
of marriage, see how Damian,                                 545
your own squire, born your man,

Entendeth for to do thee vileinye!
God graunte thee thyn hoomly fo t'espye,
For in this world nis worse pestilence
Than hoomly foo al day in thy presence.          550
    Parfourned hath the sonne his ark diurne;
No lenger may the body of him sojurne
On th'orisonte as in that latitude.
Night with his mantel that is derk and rude
Gan oversprede the hemisperie aboute,          555
For which departed is this lusty route
Fro Januarie, with thank on every syde.
Hom to hir houses lustily they ryde,
Whereas they doon hir thinges as hem leste,
And whan they sye hir tyme, goon to reste.      560
Sone after that, this hastif Januarie
Wolde go to bedde—he wolde no lenger tarie.
He drinketh ipocras, clarree, and vernage
Of spyces hote, t'encresen his corage;
And many a letuarie hadde he ful fyn,          565
Swiche as the cursed monk dan Constantyn*
Hath writen in his book De Coitu;
To eten hem alle he nas no-thing eschu.
And to his privee freendes thus seyde he,
"For Goddes love, as sone as it may be,         570
Lat voyden al this hous in curteys wyse."
And they han doon right as he wol devyse.
Men drinken and the travers drawe anon;
The bryde was broght abedde as stille as stoon.
And whan the bed was with the preest y-blessed,  575
Out of the chambre hath every wight him dressed.
And Januarie hath faste in armes take
His fresshe May, his paradys, his make;
He lulleth hire, he kisseth hir ful ofte.
With thikke bristles of his berd unsofte,        580
Lyk to the skin of houndfish, sharp as brere
For he was shave al newe in his manere,
He rubbeth hir aboute hir tendre face,

aims to do you a foul deed!
God grant you the boon of discerning your
    domestic foe,
for there is no worse plague in this world
than a household foe continually in your presence.    550
    The sun had run his daily arc;
no longer might his sphere linger
on the horizon in that latitude.
Night with his harsh, dark mantle
began to overspread the whole hemisphere of the sky,    555
so that this merry crowd left
January, with thanks on every side.
They rode home merrily to their houses
where they minded their business as they wished,
and when they saw their time, went to bed.    560
Soon afterward this urgent January
wanted to go to bed—he would wait no longer.
He drank cordials and wine
containing hot spices to increase his ardor;
and he had many a concentrated medicine,    565
such as the accursed monk master Constantinus
has written of in his book *De Coitu*;
he did not scruple in the least to eat them all.
He spoke thus to his intimate friends,
"For the love of God, as soon as possible    570
clear this house in a courteous way."
And they did just as he wanted to contrive.
They drank a toast and then drew the curtains;
the bride was brought to bed as still as stone.
And when the bed had been blessed by the priest,    575
everyone went out of the room.
January took close in his arms
his fresh May, his paradise, his mate;
he soothed her, he kissed her again and again.
He rubbed about her tender face    580
with the thick bristles of his harsh beard,
like a dogfish's skin, sharp as briar
(for he was newly shaven according to his custom),

And seyde thus, "Allas, I moot trespace
To you, my spouse, and you gretly offende          585
Er tyme come that I wil doun descende.
But nathelees, considereth this," quod he,
"Ther nis no werkman, whatsoevere he be,
That may bothe werke wel and hastily;
This wol be doon at leyser parfitly.               590
It is no fors how longe that we pleye:
In trewe wedlok coupled be we tweye,
And blessed be the yok that we been inne,
For in our actes we mowe do no sinne;
A man may do no sinne with his wyf,                595
Ne hurte himselven with his owene knyf;
For we han leve to pleye us by the lawe."
Thus laboureth he till that the day gan dawe,
And than he taketh a sop in fyn clarree,
And upright in his bed thanne sitteth he;          600
And after that he sang ful loude and clere,
And kiste his wyf and made wantoun chere:
He was al coltish, ful of ragerye,
And ful of jargon as a flekked pye.
The slakke skin aboute his nekke shaketh,          605
Whyl that he sang, so chaunteth he and craketh,
But God woot what that May thoughte in hir herte
Whan she him saugh up sittinge in his sherte,
In his night-cappe, and with his nekke lene.
She preyseth nat his pleying worth a bene.         610
Thanne seide he thus, "my reste wol I take;
Now day is come I may no lenger wake."
And doun he leyde his heed, and sleep til pryme.

    And afterward whan that he saugh his tyme
Up ryseth Januarie. But fresshe May               615
Heeld hir chambre unto the fourthe day,
As usage is of wyves for the beste,
For every labour somtyme moot han reste,
Or elles longe may he nat endure—
This is to seyn, no lyves creature,               620

and said, "Alas, I must do you injury,
my spouse, and great offense                               585
before the time comes when I shall come down.
Nevertheless, consider this," he said,
"there is no workman, whatever kind he is,
who may work both well and in haste;
this shall be done at leisure perfectly.                    590
It makes no difference how long we are at play:
we two are coupled in faithful wedlock,
and blessed be our yoke,
for in our acts we may do no sin;
a man can do no sin with his wife,                          595
any more than he will hurt himself with his own knife;
for we have leave by law to take our pleasure."
Thus he labored until day dawned,
and then he ate a sop of bread in fine wine,
and then he sat up in bed;                                  600
and after that he sang loud and clear,
and kissed his wife, and behaved wantonly:
he was very frisky, brimful of dalliance,
and full of chatter as a magpie.
The slack skin around his neck shook                        605
as he sang, he trilled and croaked so much,
but God knows what May thought in her heart
when she saw him sitting up in his nightshirt
and nightcap, with his lean neck.
She didn't think his diversions worth a bean.              610
Then he said, "I'll take my rest;
now day is come, I can't stay awake any longer."
And he laid his head down and slept until nine in the
     morning.
   Afterward, when the time seemed right to him,
he got up. But fresh May                                    615
kept her chamber until the fourth day,
as the custom is of wives, all for the best,
for every laborer must have rest some time,
or otherwise he cannot last long—
that is to say, any creature alive,                          620

Be it of fish, or brid, or beest, or man.
　　Now wol I speke of woful Damian
That languissheth for love, as ye shul here;
Therefore I speke to him in this manere:
I seye, "O sely Damian, allas, 625
Answere to my demaunde as in this cas:
How shaltow to thy lady fresshe May
Telle thy wo? She wole alwey seye nay;
Eek if thou speke, she wol thy wo biwreye.
God be thyn help, I can no bettre seye." 630
　　This syke Damian in Venus fyr
So brenneth that he dyeth for desyr,
For which he putte his lyf in aventure.
No lenger mighte he in this wyse endure,
But prively a penner gan he borwe, 635
And in a lettre wroot he al his sorwe,
In manere of a compleynt or a lay,
Unto his faire fresshe lady May;
And in a purs of silk, heng on his sherte,
He hath it put and leyde it at his herte. 640
　　The mone that, at noon, was, thilke day
That Januarie hath wedded fresshe May,
In two of Taur, was into Cancre gliden:
So longe hath Maius in hir chambre biden,
As custume is unto thise nobles alle: 645
A bryde shal nat eten in the halle
Til dayes foure or three dayes atte leste
Y-passed been; than lat hir go to feste.
The fourthe day compleet fro noon to noon,
Whan that the heighe masse was y-doon, 650
In halle sit this Januarie and May,
As fresh as is the brighte someres day.
And so bifel how that this gode man
Remembred him upon this Damian,
And seyde, "Seinte Marie! how may this be 655
That Damian entendeth nat to me?

whether it is fish or bird or beast or man.
   Now I will speak of woeful Damian,
who languishes for love as you shall hear;
therefore I speak to him thus:
I say, "O poor Damian, alas,                                    625
answer my question about this matter:
how shall you tell your sorrow to your lady,
fresh May? She will always deny you;
also, if you speak, she will disclose your sorrow.
God be your help; I have no better answer."                    630
   Sick Damian so burned in Venus's
fire that he died for desire,
for which cause he risked his life.
He could not last any longer in this fashion,
but secretly he borrowed a pencase                             635
and wrote all his sorrow in a letter,
in the manner of a complaint or poem,
to his fair, fresh lady May;
and he put it in a purse of silk
that hung on his shirt, and laid it over his heart.            640
   The moon, which at noon on the day
that January married fresh May was
two degrees inside the sign of the Bull, had glided
      into the
Crab: May had stayed thus long in her chamber,
as the custom is among noble people:                           645
a bride must not eat in the hall
until four, or at least three, days
have passed; then let her go to the feast.
The fourth full day, running from noon to noon,
when High Mass was finished,                                    650
January and May sat in the hall;
she was as fresh as a bright summer day.
And it so happened that this good man
bethought him of Damian,
and said, "By Saint Mary! How may it be                         655
that Damian does not attend on me?

Is he ay syk, or how may this bityde?"
His squyeres whiche that stoden ther bisyde
Excused him by cause of his siknesse,
Which letted him to doon his bisinesse:          660
Noon other cause mighte make him tarie.
    "That me forthinketh," quod this Januarie.
"He is a gentil squyer, by my trouthe.
If that he deyde, it were harm and routhe.
He is as wys, discreet, and as secree          665
As any man I woot of his degree,
And thereto manly and eek servisable,
And for to been a thrifty man right able.
But after mete as sone as ever I may,
I wol myself visyte him, and eek May,          670
To doon him al the confort that I can."
And for that word him blessed every man,
That of his bountee and his gentillesse
He wolde so conforten in siknesse
His squyer—for it was a gentil dede.          675
"Dame," quod this Januarie, "tak good hede,
At after mete ye with your wommen alle,
Whan ye han been in chambre out of this halle,
That alle ye go see this Damian;
Doth him disport—he is a gentil man—          680
And telleth him that I wol him visyte,
Have I no thing but rested me a lyte;
And spede yow faste, for I wol abyde  ·
Til that ye slepe faste by my syde."
And with that word he gan to him to calle          685
A squyer that was marchal of his halle,
And tolde him certeyn thinges what he wolde.
    This fresshe May hath streight hir wey y-holde
With alle hir wommen unto Damian.
Doun by his beddes syde sit she than,          690
Confortinge him as goodly as she may.
This Damian, whan that his tyme he say,
In secree wise his purs, and eek his bille,

Is he sick all this time, or how may it happen?"
His squires, who stood nearby,
excused him on the grounds of illness,
which kept him from performing his duties:          660
no other reason might keep him back.
    "I regret that," said January.
"He is a gentle squire, by my faith!
If he died, it would be a loss and a pity.
He is as prudent, discreet, and trusty          665
as any man I know of his rank,
and in addition manly and ready to give service,
and quite capable of being a successful man.
But after dinner, just as soon as I may,
I will visit him myself, and May will, too,          670
to give him all the comfort that I can."
And at this speech every man blessed him
for being thus willing in his goodness and courtesy
to give to his squire comfort
in sickness; it was a courteous deed.          675
"Madame," said January, "be sure that
after dinner when you have left this hall
and been in your chamber, you and all
your women go see Damian;
cheer him up—he is a well-bred man—          680
and tell him that I will visit him
when I have rested just a little;
and go quickly, for I will be waiting
until you come to bed close by my side."
And thereupon he called to him          685
a squire who was the major-domo in his hall
and told him what he wanted done about certain
        matters.
    Fresh May took her way with all
her women straight to Damian.
She then sat down by his bedside,          690
comforting him as kindly as she could.
When Damian saw his opportunity,
he secretly put into her hand his purse,

In which that he y-writen hadde his wille,
Hath put into hir hand withouten more,                           695
Save that he syketh wonder depe and sore,
And softely to hir right thus seyde he,
"Mercy, and that ye nat discovere me,
For I am deed if that this thing be kid."
This purs hath she inwith hir bosom hid,                          700
And wente hir wey—ye gete namore of me.
    But unto Januarie y-comen is she,
That on his beddes syde sit ful softe.
He taketh hir and kisseth hire ful ofte,
And leyde him doun to slepe, and that anon.                       705
She feyned hire as that she moste gon
Ther as ye woot that every wight moot nede;
And whan she of this bille hath taken hede,
She rente it al to cloutes atte laste
And in the privee softely it caste.                              710
    Who studieth now but faire fresshe May?
Adoun by olde Januarie she lay,
That sleep til that the coughe hath him awaked.
Anon he preyde hire strepen hire al naked;
He wolde of hir, he seyde, han som plesaunce,                    715
And seyde hir clothes dide him encombraunce,
And she obeyeth, be hire lief or looth.
But lest that precious folk be with me wrooth,
How that he wroghte I dar not to yow telle,
Or whether hir thoughte it paradys or helle;                     720
But here I lete hem werken in hir wyse
Til evensong rong, and that they moste aryse.
    Were it by destinee or aventure,
Were it by influence or by nature,
Or constellacion, that in swich estat                            725
The hevene stood that tyme fortunat
As for to putte a bille of Venus werkes
(For alle thing hath tyme, as seyn thise clerkes)
To any womman, for to gete hir love,

and also his note, in which he had written
his desire. He did this without explanation,    695
except that he sighed most deeply and bitterly,
and whispered to her just thus,
"Your mercy! Do not reveal me,
for I am dead if this thing is made known."
She hid the purse in her bosom    700
and went her way—you get no more from me.
     She came to January,
who was sitting very comfortably on the side of
     his bed.
He embraced her and kissed her again and again,
and at once lay down to sleep.    705
She pretended that she had to go
where you know everyone must;
and when she had perused the note,
she finally tore it to shreds
and threw it quietly in the privy.    710
     Who ponders now but fresh and pretty May?
She lay down by old January,
who slept until his cough awakened him.
Then he asked her to strip naked;
he would, he said, have some pleasure from her,    715
and, he said, her clothes hampered him.
She obeyed, whether it was agreeable to her
     or loathsome.
But lest fastidious people would be angry with me,
I dare not tell you how he acted
or whether she thought it paradise or hell; but here    720
I leave them conducting themselves in their fashion
until the bell for evensong rang and they had to get up.
     Whether it was by destiny or chance,
by occult influence or by nature,
or by astrological influence—so that, being in such a    725
position, the heavens were at that time at a point
favorable for presenting a petition of Venus's works
to any woman in order to get her love
(everything has its time, say these learned men),

I can nat seye; but grete God above,                             730
That knoweth that non act is causelees,
He deme of al, for I wol holde my pees.
But sooth is this, how that this fresshe May
Hath take swich impression that day,
For pitee of this syke Damian,                                   735
That from hir herte she ne dryve can
The remembrance for to doon him ese.
"Certeyn," thoghte she, "whom that this thing displese
I rekke noght. For here I him assure
To love him best of any creature,                                740
Though he namore hadde than his shcrte."
Lo, pitee renneth sone in gentil herte!
     Heer may ye se how excellent franchyse
In wommen is whan they hem narwe avyse.
Som tyrant is, as ther be many oon,                              745
That hath an herte as hard as any stoon,
Which wolde han lete him sterven in the place
Wel rather than han graunted him hir grace,
And hem rejoysen in hir cruel pryde
And rekke nat to been an homicyde.                               750
     This gentil May, fulfilled of pitee,
Right of hir hande a lettre made she,
In which she graunteth him hir verray grace:
Ther lakketh noght but only day and place
Wher that she mighte unto his lust suffyse,                      755
For it shall be right as he wol devyse.
And whan she saugh hir time upon a day
To visite this Damian goth May,
And sotilly this lettre doun she threste
Under his pilwe: rede it if him leste.                           760
She taketh him by the hand and harde him twiste
So secrely that no wight of it wiste,
And bad him been al hool; and forth she wente
To Januarie whan that he for hir sente.
     Up ryseth Damian the nexte morwe:                           765
Al passed was his siknesse and his sorwe.

I do not know; but let great God above,          730
who knows no act is without a cause,
judge all, for I will hold my peace.
But the truth is that fresh May
was that day so impressed
with pity for sick Damian          735
that she could not drive from her heart
the thought of comforting him.
"Indeed," she thought, "I do not care whom
     this matter
displeases, for here I promise
to love him best of all,          740
even if he had no more than his shirt."
Behold, pity soon arises in the gentle heart!
     Here you may see what excellent generosity
there is in women when they take careful thought.
There is some tyrant (there are many such)          745
who has a heart as hard as any stone
and who would have left him dying where he lay
sooner than have granted him her favor;
such ones would rejoice in their cruel pride
and do not scruple to be murderers.          750
     This gentle May, filled with pity,
wrote a letter in her own hand
in which she promised him her favor:
nothing lacked but time and place
in which she might satisfy his desire,          755
for it was to be just as he should arrange.
And one day, when she saw her opportunity,
May went to visit Damian,
and cunningly she thrust the letter down
under his pillow: let him read it if he wants.          760
She took him by the hand and wrung it hard,
so secretly that no one knew of it,
and told him to get well; and forth she went
to January when he sent for her.
     Damian got up the next morning:          765
his sickness and his depression were all over.

He kembeth him, he preyneth him and pyketh,
He dooth al that his lady lust and lyketh.
And eek to Januarie he gooth as lowe
As evere dide a dogge for the bowe.                          770
He is so plesant unto every man—
For craft is al, whoso that do it can—
That every wight is fayn to speke him good;
And fully in his lady grace he stood.
Thus lete I Damian aboute his nede,                         775
And in my tale forth I wol procede.

   Somme clerkes holden that felicitee
Stant in delyt, and therefore certeyn he
This noble Januarie, with al his might
In honest wyse as longeth to a knight,                      780
Shoop him to live ful deliciously:
His housinge, his array as honestly
To his degree was maked as a kinges.
Amonges othere of his honest thinges,
He made a gardin walled al with stoon;                      785
So fair a gardin woot I nowher noon,
For out of doute I verraily suppose
That he that wroot the *Romance of the Rose**
Ne coude of it the beautee wel devyse;
Ne Priapus* ne mighte nat suffyse—                          790
Though he be god of gardins—for to telle
The beautee of the gardin, and the welle
That stood under a laurer alwey grene.
Ful ofte tyme he Pluto* and his quene
Proserpina* and al hir fayërye                              795
Disporten hem and maken melodye
Aboute that welle, and daunced, as men tolde.
This noble knight, this Januarie the olde,
Swich deintee hath in it to walke and pleye
That he wol no wight suffren bere the keye                  800
Save he himself; for of the smale wiket
He bar alwey of silver a cliket,
With which whan that him leste he it unshette.

He combed his hair, he preened himself, he tidied up,
he did everything that pleased his lady.
And also to January he was as obedient and humble
as a well-trained hunting dog.                                    770
He was so pleasant to every man
—for craft is everything, if you can manage it—
that everyone was glad to speak well of him;
and he stood fully in his lady's favor.
Thus I leave Damian busy about his needs,                         775
and I shall proceed with my tale.
     Some learned men hold that felicity
consists in sensuous pleasure, and for that end
noble January certainly contrived with all his might
to live most delightfully in honorable fashion                    780
as befits a knight:
his buildings, his finery were
made as honorably for their rank as a king's.
Among other honorable possessions of his,
he had built a garden, walled on all sides with stone;            785
I do not know of so fair a garden anywhere else,
for beyond doubt I truly believe
that he who wrote the *Romance of the Rose*
could not suitably describe the beauty of it;
nor might Priapus suffice—                                        790
although he is god of gardens—to tell
the beauty of the garden and of its well,
which lay beneath an ever-green laurel tree.
Frequently Pluto and his queen
Proserpina and all their fairy crew                               795
played and sang
and danced around that well, as we are told.
This noble knight, old January,
took such delight in strolling and disporting
      himself there
that he would allow no one to carry the key                       800
except himself; for the narrow wicket gate
he always carried a small key of silver
with which he opened the gate when he wanted.

And whan he wolde paye his wyf hir dette
In somer seson, thider wolde he go, 805
And May his wyf, and no wight but they two;
And thinges whiche that were nat doon abedde,
He in the gardin parfourned hem and spedde.
And in this wyse many a merye day
Lived this Januarie and fresshe May. 810
But worldly joye may nat alwey dure
To Januarie, ne to no creature.

O sodeyn hap, o thou Fortune instable,
Lyk to the scorpion* so deceivable,
That flaterest with thyn heed when thou wolt stinge, 815
Thy tayl is deeth, thurgh thyn enveniminge!
O brotil joye, o swete venim queynte!
O monstre, that so subtilly canst peynte
Thy yiftes under hewe of stedfastnesse,
That thou deceyvest bothe more and lesse! 820
Why hastow Januarie thus deceyved,
That haddest him for thy fulle frend receyved?
And now thou hast biraft him bothe his yën,
For sorwe of which desyreth he to dyen.

Allas, this noble Januarie free, 825
Amidde his lust and his prosperitee,
Is woxen blind, and that al sodeynly.
He wepeth and he wayleth pitously;
And therwithal the fyr of jalousye,
Lest that his wyf sholde falle in som folye, 830
So brente his herte that he wolde fayn
That som man bothe hire and him had slayn;
For neither after his deeth nor in his lyf
Ne wolde he that she were love ne wyf,
But evere live as widwe in clothes blake, 835
Soul as the turtle that hath lost hir make.
But atte laste, after a monthe or tweye,
His sorwe gan aswage, sooth to seye;
For whan he wiste it may noon other be,
He paciently took his adversitee— 840

And when, in the summer, he wanted to pay
his wife her debt, he and May would                          805
go there, no one except those two;
and things that were not done in bed,
he successfully performed in the garden.
For many a merry day January
and fresh May lived in this fashion.                         810
But worldly joy may not always last
for January, or for any other created being.
    O sudden chance, O unstable Fortune,
deceitful as the scorpion,
you flatter with your head when you intend to sting;         815
your tail is death by your poisoning!
O brittle joy! O sweet, subtle venom!
O monster, who can so cleverly color
your gifts with the hue of constancy
that you deceive both great and small!                       820
Why have you, who had accepted January fully
as your friend, thus deceived him?
Now you have robbed him of the sight of both
    his eyes,
for sorrow at which he desires to die.
    Alas, this noble, generous January,                      825
in the midst of his pleasure and well-being,
became blind, and without any warning.
He wept and wailed piteously,
and, besides, the fire of jealousy,
for fear that his wife would fall into some folly,           830
so burned his heart that he would have been glad
if someone had slain both her and himself;
for no more after his death than in his life
did he want her to be either paramour or wife;
he wanted her to live ever after as a widow in black,        835
alone as the dove that has lost her mate.
But at last, after a month or two,
his sorrow began to be assuaged, if the truth be known;
for when he knew it could not be otherwise,
he took his adversity in patience—                           840

Save out of doute he may nat forgoon
That he nas jalous everemore in oon;
Which jalousye it was so outrageous
That neither in halle, n'in noon other hous,
Ne in noon other place, neverthemo,                      845
He nolde suffre hire for to ryde or go,
But if that he hadde hand on hire alway;
For which ful ofte wepeth fresshe May,
That loveth Damian so benignly
That she moot outher dyen sodeynly,                      850
Or elles she moot han him as hire leste;
She wayteth whan hir herte wolde breste.

   Upon that other syde Damian
Bicomen is the sorwefulleste man
That evere was, for neither night ne day                 855
Ne mighte he speke a word to fresshe May,
As to his purpos, of no swich matere,
But if that Januarie moste it here,
That hadde an hand upon hire evermo;
But nathelees, by wryting to and fro                     860
And privee signes, wiste he what she mente,
And she knew eek the fyn of his entente.

   O Januarie, what mighte it thee availle
Though thou mightest see as fer as shippes saille?
For also good is blind deceyved be                       865
As to be deceyved whan a man may see.
Lo Argus,* which that hadde an hondred yën,
For al that evere he coude poure or pryen,
Yet was he blent, and God wot so ben mo
That wenen wisly that it be nat so.                       870
Passe over is an ese, I sey namore.

   This fresshe May that I spak of so yore,
In warme wex hath emprented the cliket
That Januarie bar of the smale wiket,
By which into his gardin ofte he wente.                  875
And Damian, that knew al hir entente,
The cliket countrefeted prively—

except, beyond doubt, that he could not forgo
being constantly jealous;
this jealousy was so excessive
that even in his hall, or any other house,
or any other place 845
he would not allow her to go in any manner
unless he always had a hand on her;
on this account fresh May often wept;
she loved Damian so cordially
that either she must have him as she wished 850
or suddenly die: she stood
in expectation of the time when her heart would break.
   On the other side Damian
became the most sorrowful man
that ever was, for neither night nor day 855
might he speak a word of any matter
to fresh May concerning his purpose
without January's having to hear it,
who had his hand on her always.
Nevertheless, by writing back and forth 860
and by secret signs, he knew what she thought,
and she, too, knew the goal of his intention.
   O January, what might it avail you
if you could see as far as ship can sail?
It is just as well to be deceived when one is blind 865
as to be deceived when one may see.
Consider Argus, who had a hundred eyes:
no matter how intently he could peer and pry,
he was still hoodwinked; and, God knows, so are
   others
who think that it is surely not so. 870
Letting the matter drop is a relief; I say no more.
   This fresh May, whom I first mentioned so long ago,
took in warm wax an imprint of the key
carried by January for the narrow wicket gate
by which he so often entered his garden. 875
Damian, who knew all her plan,
secretly made a copy of the key—

Ther nis namore to seye, but hastily
Som wonder by this cliket shal bityde.
Which ye shul heren if ye wole abyde.                    880
    O noble Ovyde,* ful sooth seystou, God woot,
What sleighte is it, thogh it be long and hoot,
That he nil finde it out in som manere!
By Piramus and Tesbee may men lere;
Thogh they were kept ful longe streite overal,          885
They been accorded, rouninge thurgh a wal,
Ther no wight coude han founde out swich a sleighte.
    But now to purpos: er that dayes eighte
Were passed, er the monthe of Juil, bifil
That Januarie hath caught so greet a wil—               890
Thurgh egging of his wyf—him for to pleye
In his gardin, and no wight but they tweye,
That in a morwe unto his May seith he,
"Rys up, my wyf,* my love, my lady free;
The turtles vois is herd, my douve swete;               895
The winter is goon with alle his reynes wete.
Com forth now with thyn eyën columbyn.
How fairer been thy brestes than is wyn!
The gardin is enclosed al aboute:
Com forth, my whyte spouse; out of doute,               900
Thou hast me wounded in myn herte. O wyf,
No spot of thee ne knew I al my lyf.
Com forth and lat us taken our disport;
I chees thee for my wyf and my comfort."
    Swiche olde lewed wordes used he.                    905
On Damian a signe made she
That he sholde go biforn with his cliket:
This Damian thanne hath opened the wiket,
And in he stirte, and that in swich manere
That no wight mighte it see neither y-here;             910
And stille he sit under a bush anoon.
    This Januarie, as blind as is a stoon,

there is no more to say except that soon
an amazing thing will happen because of this key,
which you shall hear if you will wait.                           880
     O noble Ovid, God knows you speak truth in saying
that, whatever trick it is, though it take time and sweat,
love will find it out somehow!
One may learn this by the example of Pyramus
     and Thisbe;
although they were long guarded closely on all sides,
     they                                                         885
came to an understanding by whispering through
     a wall,
where no one else could have discovered such a trick.
     But now back to the story: before eight days
had passed in the month before July, it happened
that January fell into so strong a desire                        890
(through his wife's urging) to dally
in his garden with no one there but the two of them,
that one morning he said to May,
"Rise up, my wife, my love, my gracious lady;
the voice of the turtle is heard, my sweet dove;                 895
the winter is past, with its wet rain;
now come away, with your eyes like those of the dove.
Thy breasts are fairer than wine!
The garden is enclosed all about:
come away, my lily-white spouse; beyond doubt                    900
you have ravished my heart. O wife,
I knew no fault in thee all my life.
Come forth, and let us take our pleasure;
I choose you for my wife and my comfort."
     He made use of such old, wanton speeches as this.           905
She made a sign to Damian
to go in advance with his key:
Damian then opened the wicket
and went in quickly, in such fashion
that no one might see or hear him;                               910
and then he sat still beneath a bush.
     January, blind as a stone,

With Maius in his hand and no wight mo,
Into his fresshe gardin is ago,
And clapte to the wiket sodeynly.          915
    "Now, wyf," quod he, "here nis but thou and I,
That art the creature that I best love.
For, by that Lord that sit in heven above,
Levere ich hadde to dyen on a knyf
Than thee offende, trewe dere wyf.          920
For Goddes sake, thenk how I thee chees,
Noght for no coveityse, doutelees,
But only for the love I had to thee.
And though that I be old, and may nat see,
Beth to me trewe, and I wol telle yow why.          925
Three thinges, certes, shul ye winne ther-by:
First, love of Crist, and to yourself honour,
And al myn heritage, toun and tour—
I yeve it yow: maketh chartres as yow leste;
This shal be doon tomorwe er sonne reste,          930
So wisly god my soule bringe in blisse.
I prey yow first in covenant ye me kisse;
And thogh that I be jalous, wyte me noght.
Ye been so depe enprented in my thoght,
That whan that I considere youre beautee,          935
And therwithal the unlykly elde of me,
I may nat, certes, thogh I sholde dye,
Forbere to been out of youre companye
For verray love; this is withouten doute.
Now kis me, wyf, and lat us rome aboute."          940
    This fresshe May, whan she thise wordes herde,
Benignely to Januarie answerde,
But first and forward she bigan to wepe.
"I have," quod she, "a soule for to kepe
As wel as ye, and also myn honour,          945
And of my wyfhod thilke tendre flour,
Which that I have assured in youre hond
Whan that the preest to yow my body bond;
Wherfore I wole answere in this manere,
By the leve of yow, my lord so dere:          950

with May held by his hand and no one else,
went into his fresh garden
and slammed the wicket shut quickly. 915
    "Now, wife," he said, "here is no one but you and me,
and you are the creature whom I love best.
By the Lord who sits in heaven above,
I would rather die by the knife
than do you any injury, faithful dear wife. 920
Think, for God's sake, how I chose you—
not for avarice, surely,
but only for the love I felt for you.
And though I am old and cannot see,
be true to me; I shall tell you why you should. 925
By doing so you shall certainly win three things:
Christ's love, honor to yourself,
and all my inheritance, town and castle—
I give it to you: make charters for it as you wish;
this shall be done tomorrow before sundown, 930
as surely as I hope God may bring my soul to joy.
I ask you first to seal this covenant with a kiss;
and although I am jealous, don't blame me for it.
You have made so deep an impression on my mind
that, when I consider your beauty 935
and, with it, my unsuitable age,
certainly I cannot, though I should die,
bear for very love to be out of your company;
this is beyond doubt.
Now kiss me, wife, and let us stroll here and there." 940
    When fresh May had heard these words,
she answered January graciously,
but first of all she began to weep.
"I have," she said, "a soul to save
as well as you do, and also my honor 945
and the tender flower of my womanhood
which I entrusted to your hands
when the priest bound my body to you;
therefore I will answer in this manner,
by your leave, my dear lord: 950

I prey to God that nevere dawe the day
That I ne sterve as foule as womman may,
If ever I do unto my kin that shame,
Or elles I empeyre so my name,
That I be fals. And if I do that lak,                               955
Do strepe me, and putte me in a sak,
And in the nexte river do me drenche:
I am a gentil womman and no wenche.
Why speke ye thus? But men ben ever untrewe,
And wommen have repreve of yow ay newe.                            960
Ye han non other contenance, I leve,
But speke to us of untrust and repreve."
    And with that word she saugh wher Damian
Sat in the bush, and coughen she bigan,
And with hir finger signes made she                                965
That Damian sholde climbe upon a tree
That charged was with fruit; and up he wente,
For verraily he knew al hir entente,
And every signe that she coude make,
Wel bet than Januarie, hir owene make,                             970
For in a lettre she hadde told him al
Of this matere how he werchen shal.
And thus I lete him sitte upon the pyrie,
And Januarie and May rominge myrie.
    Bright was the day, and blew the firmament;                    975
Phebus* hath of gold his stremes doun sent
To gladen every flour with his warmnesse.
He was that tyme in Geminis, as I gesse,
But litel fro his declinacioun
Of Cancer, Jovis exaltacioun.                                      980
And so bifel, that brighte morwe-tyde,
That in that gardin in the ferther syde
Pluto, that is king of fayërye,
And many a lady in his compaignye,
Folwinge his wyf, the quene Proserpina,                            985
Which that he ravisshed out of Etna

I pray God that the day may never dawn
when I do not die as disgracefully as a woman can
if I ever do such shame to my family
or so mar my name
as to be false. And if I commit that sin,                    955
have me stripped, and put in a sack,
and drowned in the nearest river:
I am a gentlewoman and no wanton commoner.
Why do you talk this way? But men are always
  unfaithful,
and women have reproof from you ever anew.              960
I believe you have no face to put upon your faults
except to talk to us of unfaithfulness and reproof."

  At that word she saw where Damian
was sitting beneath the bush, and she began to cough
and made signs with her finger                    965
to him to climb up into a tree
that was full of fruit; and up he went,
for indeed he knew all her mind
and every sign that she could make
much better than January, her own husband,            970
for she had told him in a letter everything
concerning how he should go about this matter.
I leave him thus sitting in the pear tree,
and January and May strolling about happily.

  The day was bright and the sky was blue;            975
Phoebus had sent down his golden rays
to gladden every flower with his warmth.
He was at that time in the sign of the Twins, as I judge,
only a little way from his northernmost declination
in the sign of Cancer, which sign is Jupiter's
  exaltation.                                          980
It so happened that sunny morning
that on the further side of that garden were
Pluto, who is the king of fairyland,
and many a lady in his company
following his wife, Queen Proserpina,               985
whom he had ravished away from Mount Aetna

Whyl that she gadered floures in the mede—
In Claudian* ye may the stories rede,
How in his grisly carte he hire fette—
This king of fairye thanne adoun him sette          990
Upon a bench of turves fresh and grene,
And right anon thus seyde he to his quene:
    "My wyf," quod he, "ther may no wight seye nay;
Th'experience so preveth every day
The treson whiche that wommen doon to man.         995
Ten hondred thousand tales tellen I can
Notable of your untrouthe and brotilnesse.
O Salomon, wys and richest of richesse,
Fulfild of sapience and of worldly glorie,
Ful worthy been thy wordes to memorie            1000
To every wight that wit and reson can—
Thus preiseth he yet the bountee of man:
'Amonges a thousand men yet fond I oon,
But of wommen alle fond I noon.'
Thus seith the king that knoweth youre wikkednesse.   1005
And Jesus *filius Syrak,** as I gesse,
Ne speketh of yow but selde reverence.
A wilde fyr and corrupt pestilence
So falle upon your bodies yet tonight!
Ne see ye nat this honurable knight?              1010
By-cause, allas, that he is blind and old,
His owene man shal make him cokewold.
Lo wher he sit, the lechour; in the tree!
Now wol I graunten of my magestee
Unto this olde, blinde worthy knight              1015
That he shal have ayeyn his eyen sight,
Whan that his wyf wolde doon him vileinye;
Than shal he knowen al hir harlotrye,
Both in repreve of hir and othere mo."
    "Ye shal," quod Proserpyne. "Wol ye so?         1020
Now, by my modres sires soule I swere
That I shal yeven hire suffisant answere,

while she was gathering flowers in the meadow—
you can read the story in Claudian
of how he fetched her in his horrible chariot;
this king of fairies sat down                                        990
on a bench of fresh green turf
and then said to his queen:
     "My wife, no one may contradict this;
experience proves every day
the treachery which women commit against men.       995
I can tell ten hundred thousand stories
which are remarkable for your infidelity and
          fickleness.
O Solomon, wise, most abounding in riches,
full of knowledge and worldly glory,
your words are very worthwhile to commit to mind       1000
for everyone who recognizes wisdom and reason—
thus he still praises the goodness of man:
'Among a thousand men I yet found one,
but among all women I found none.'
Thus speaks the king who knows your wickedness.       1005
And Jesus, son of Sirach, as I believe,
seldom speaks well of you.
May wildfire and a destroying pestilence
yet fall upon your bodies this night!
Don't you see this honorable knight?                       1010
Because he is blind and old, alas,
his own servant is to cuckold him.
Look where he sits, the lecher, in the tree!
Now I will in my majesty make the grant
to this old, blind, worthy knight                              1015
that he shall recover his eyesight
when his wife does him shame;
then he shall know all her harlotry,
in reproof both of her and of others."
     "Shall you?" said Proserpina. "Do you want to
          do that?                                                      1020
Now, by the soul of my mother's father I swear
that I shall give a good enough answer to her,

And alle wommen after for hir sake,
That, though they be in any gilt y-take,
With face bold they shulle hemself excuse,          1025
And bere hem doun that wolden hem accuse:
For lakke of answer noon of hem shal dyen.
Al hadde man seyn a thing with bothe his yën,
Yit shul we wommen visage it hardily,
And wepe, and swere, and chyde subtilly,          1030
So that ye men shul been as lewed as gees—
What rekketh me of youre auctoritees?

    "I woot wel that this Jew, this Salomon,
Fond of us wommen foles many oon;
But though that he ne fond no good womman,          1035
Yet hath ther founde many another man
Wommen ful trewe, ful gode, and vertuous.
Witnesse on hem that dwelle in Cristes hous:
With martirdom they preved hir constance.
The Romayn gestes maken remembrance          1040
Of many a verray, trewe wyf also.
But sire, ne be nat wrooth, al be it so,
Though that he seyde he fond no good womman,
I prey yow, take the sentence of the man:
He mente thus, that in sovereyn bontee          1045
Nis noon but God, but neither he ne she.

    "Ey, for verray God, that nis but oon,
What make ye so muche of Salomon?
What though he made a temple, Goddes hous?
What though he were riche and glorious?          1050
So made he eek a temple of false goddis:
How mighte he do a thing that more forbode is?
Pardee, as faire as ye his name emplastre,
He was a lechour and an ydolastre;
And in his elde he verray God forsook.          1055
And if that God ne hadde, as seith the book,
Y-spared him for his fadres sake, he sholde
Have lost his regne rather than he wolde.

and to all women thereafter, for her sake,
so that, even if they are taken in any guilty act,
they shall boldfacedly give an excuse for themselves 1025
and bear down those that would accuse them:
none of them shall die for lack of an answer.
Even if a man has seen a thing with both his eyes,
yet shall we women face it out confidently
and weep, and take our oath and scold deviously, 1030
so that you men will be as ignorant as geese—
what do I care about your authorities?

"I certainly know that this Jew, this Solomon,
found many a fool among us women;
but even if he didn't find any good woman, 1035
many another man has found
very faithful, good, and virtuous ones.
Take witness on those of them who dwell in Christ's
abode:
they proved their constancy by martyrdom.
The stories of Rome also make mention 1040
of many a true, faithful wife.
But, sir, don't be angry, even though this is the way it is:
although Solomon said that he found no good woman,
I pray you, take the man's meaning:
he meant this, that in the matter of sovereign goodness 1045
there is no one but God in Trinity.

"Ah, by the one true God,
why do you make so much of Solomon?
What if he made a temple, a house of God?
What if he was rich and glorious? 1050
So he made a temple of false gods, too:
how could he do a thing that is more forbidden?
By heaven, no matter how you whitewash his
reputation,
he was a lecher and an idolater;
and in his old age he forsook the true God. 1055
And, as the book says, if God hadn't
spared him for his father's sake, he would
have lost his rule sooner than he wanted.

I sette right noght of al the vileinye,
That ye of wommen wryte, a boterflye.                    1060
I am a womman, nedes moot I speke,
Or elles swelle til myn herte breke.
For sithen he seyde that we been jangleresses,
As evere hool I moote brouke my tresses,
I shal nat spare for no curteisye                        1065
To speke him harm that wolde us vileinye."

    "Dame," quod this Pluto, "be no lenger wrooth;
I yeve it up. But sith I swoor myn ooth
That I wolde graunten him his sighte ageyn,
My word shal stonde, I warne yow certeyn.               1070
I am a king: it sit me noght to lye."

    "And I," quod she, "a queene of fayërye:
Hir answere shal she have, I undertake.
Lat us namore wordes heerof make.
Forsoothe, I wol no lenger yow contrarie."              1075

    Now lat us turne agayn to Januarie,
That in the gardin with his faire May
Singeth ful merier than the papejay,
"Yow love I best, and shal, and other noon."
So longe aboute the aleyes is he goon                   1080
Til he was come agaynes thilke pyrie,
Wher as this Damian sitteth ful myrie
An heigh among the fresshe leves grene.

    This fresshe May, that is so bright and shene,
Gan for to syke and seyde, "Allas, my syde!             1085
Now sire," quod she, "for ought that may bityde,
I moste han of the peres that I see,
Or I moot dye, so sore longeth me
To eten of the smale peres grene.
Help, for hir love that is of hevenc quene!             1090
I telle yow wel, a womman in my plyt*
May han to fruit so greet an appetyt
That she may dyen but she of it have."

    "Allas," quod he, "that I ne hadde heer a knave

I don't give a butterfly for all
the shame that you write about women. 1060
I am a woman, I have to speak,
or else swell until my heart bursts.
Since he said that we are idle talkers,
as ever I hope to possess my tresses unshorn I shall not,
for the sake of any courteous forbearance, refrain 1065
from speaking harm of this man who wished shame
   upon us."

   "My lady," said Pluto, "don't be angry any longer;
I give up. But since I swore an oath
that I would give him back his sight,
my word shall stand, I warn you for a certainty. 1070
I am a king: it does not suit me to lie."

   "And I," she said, "a queen of faery:
she shall have her answer, I guarantee it.
Let us have no more words about this.
Truly, I won't contradict you any longer." 1075

   Now let us turn to January again,
who sang more merrily than a parrot
in the garden with his pretty May,
"I love you best, and always shall, and no other."
He walked around the paths far enough 1080
to come up to that pear tree
where Damian was sitting happily
on high, among the fresh green leaves.

   Fresh May, who was so bright and shining,
began to sigh, and said, "Alas, my side! 1085
Now, sir," she said, "no matter what happens,
I must have some of the pears that I see,
or I must die, I have so strong a longing
to eat some of the small green pears.
Help, for the love of her who is heaven's queen! 1090
I tell you indeed, a woman in my condition
may have so great an appetite for fruit
that she may die unless she gets some."

   "Alas," he said, "that I don't have a young
   manservant here

That coude climbe! Allas, allas," quod he,                    1095
"For I am blind!" "Ye, sire, no fors," quod she:
"But wolde ye vouche sauf, for Goddes sake,
The pyrie inwith youre armes for to take
(For wel I woot that ye mistruste me),
Thanne sholde I climbe wel ynogh," quod she,                 1100
"So I my foot mighte sette upon your bak."

     "Certes," quod he, "thereon shal be no lak,
Mighte I yow helpen with myn herte blood."
He stoupeth doun, and on his bak she stood,
And caughte hir by a twiste, and up she gooth.              1105
Ladies, I preye yow that ye be nat wrooth;
I can nat glose, I am a rude man.
And sodeynly anon this Damian
Gan pullen up the smok, and in he throng.

     And whan that Pluto saugh this grete wrong,              1110
To Januarie he gaf agayn his sighte,
And made him see as wel as evere he mighte.
And whan that he hadde caught his sighte agayn,
Ne was ther nevere man of thing so fayn.
But on his wyf his thoght was everemo:                       1115
Up to the tree he caste his eyen two,
And saugh that Damian his wyf had dressed
In swich manere it may nat been expressed,
But if I wolde speke uncurteisly;
And up he yaf a roring and a cry,                            1120
As doth the moder whan the child shal dye.
"Out! help! allas! harrow!" he gan to crye,
"O stronge lady store, what dostow?"

     And she answerde, "Sire, what eyleth yow?
Have pacience and reson in youre minde.                      1125
I have yow holpe on bothe your eyen blinde.
Up peril of my soule, I shal nat lyen,
As me was taught, to hele with your yën,
Was no thing bet to make yow to see
Than strugle with a man upon a tree:                         1130
God woot I dide it in ful good entente."

     "Strugle!" quod he, "Ye, algate in it wente!

that could climb! Alas, alas," he said,                    1095
"that I am blind." "Yea, sir, it doesn't matter," she said:
"but if you would deign, for God's sake,
to put your arms around the pear tree
(for I well know that you don't trust me),
then I would climb well enough," she said,                 1100
"provided that I might put my foot on your back."
     "Certainly," he said, "you should not lack
if I could help you with my heart's blood."
He stooped down, and she stood on his back
and caught hold of a branch, and up she went.              1105
Ladies, I ask you not to be angry with me;
I cannot gloss, I am a blunt man.
Without warning, then, this Damian
pulled up the smock, and in he thrust.
     When Pluto saw this great wrong,                       1110
he restored January's sight,
and made him see as well as he ever could.
And when he had got his sight back,
there was never another man so glad of anything.
But his thoughts continued to dwell on his wife:          1115
he cast his two eyes up to the tree,
and saw that Damian had managed his wife
in such a way as may not be expressed
unless I would speak discourteously;
and he gave a roar and cry                                  1120
like a mother's when her child is on the point of death.
"Alas! Help, thief!" he cried,
"Outrageous, gross woman, what are you doing?"
     And she answered, "Sir, what ails you?
Be patient and reasonable.                                  1125
I have given help to your two blind eyes.
On my soul, I shall not lie:
as I was taught, there was nothing better
to heal your eyes with and give you vision
than to struggle with a man in a tree:                     1130
God knows, I meant well."
     "Struggle!" said he, "yes, but it went in!

God yeve yow bothe on shames deeth to dyen!
He swyved thee—I saugh it with myne yën,
And elles be I hanged by the hals."                    1135
    "Thanne is," quod she, "my medicyne al fals;
For certeinly if that ye mighte see,
Ye wolde nat seyn thise wordes unto me;
Ye han som glimsing and no parfit sighte."
    "I see," quod he, "as wel as evere I mighte,        1140
Thonked be God, with bothe myne eyen two,
And by my trouthe, me thoughte he dide thee so."
    "Ye maze, maze, gode sir," quod she.
"This thank have I for I have maad yow see;
Allas," quod she, "that evere I was so kinde!"          1145
    "Now, dame," quod he, "lat al passe out of minde.
Com doun, my lief, and if I have missayd,
God help me so as I am yvel apayd.
But, by my fader soule, I wende han seyn
How that this Damian had by thee leyn,                  1150
And that thy smok had leyn upon his brest."
    "Ye, sire," quod she, "ye may wene as yow lest;
But, sire, a man that waketh out of his sleep,
He may nat sodeynly wel taken keep
Upon a thing, ne seen it parfitly,                      1155
Till that he be adawed verraily;
Right so a man that longe hath blind y-be
Ne may nat sodeynly so wel y-see,
First whan his sighte is newe come ageyn,
As he that hath a day or two y-seyn.                    1160
Til that your sighte y-satled be a whyle,
Ther may ful many a sighte yow bigyle.
Beth war, I preye yow; for, by hevene king,
Ful many a man weneth to seen a thing,
And it is al another than it semeth:                    1165
He that misconceyveth, he misdemeth."
And with that word she leep doun fro the tree.
    This Januarie, who is glad but he?
He kisseth hire and clippeth hir ful ofte,

God give you both to die a shameful death!
He plumbed you—I saw it with my eyes;
else let me be hanged by the neck."    1135
    "Then," said she, "my medicine is all false;
for if you could see, certainly
you would not utter these words to me;
you have some glimmering but no perfect sight."
    "I see," he said, "as well as I ever could,    1140
with both my eyes, thanked be God,
and by my faith, I thought he handled you that way."
    "You are dazed, dazed, good sir," she said.
"This is the thanks I get for having made you see;
alas," she said, "that I was ever so kind!"    1145
    "Now, my lady," he said, "let everything be forgotten.
Come down, my dear, and if I have misspoken
God help me in respect to my being ill-pleased.
But, on my father's soul, I thought I saw
that Damian was lying by you    1150
and that your smock lay on his breast."
    "Yea, sir," she said, "you may think as you wish;
but, sir, a man that wakes from his sleep
cannot suddenly grasp
a thing, or see it perfectly,    1155
until he is really awake;
just so, a man who has been blind for a long time
may not immediately see as well
at first when his sight has just recently returned
as a man that has seen for a day or two.    1160
Until your sight has settled for a while,
many a view may fool you.
Be cautious, I implore you; for, by the king of heaven,
many a man thinks he is seeing something,
and it is completely different from what it seems to be.    1165
Whoever misapprehends, misjudges."
And so saying she jumped down from the tree.
    Who was happy but January?
He kissed her and hugged her again and again,

And on hir wombe he stroketh hire ful softe,          1170
And to his palays hoom he hath hire lad.
Now, gode men, I praye yow to be glad.
Thus endeth here my tale of Januarie.
God blesse us and his moder Seinte Marie.

he stroked her belly very gently,                                    1170
and he led her home to his palace.
Now, good people, I ask you to be satisfied.
Thus ends here my tale of January.
God and his mother Saint Mary bless us.

# THE FRANKLIN'S TALE

# INTRODUCTION

❦

THE FRANKLIN'S TALE has long been a favorite of students of Chaucer. Like "The Knight's Tale," it is a romance, but it is shorter and less military, and it has a more genial ending. Unlike the story of Palamon and Arcite, which ends when one of them weds the reluctant Emily, in this one the two major characters are already married. Their challenge is to find a way to manage, together, a mutually satisfying and honorable continuation of a good marriage. Like "The Merchant's Tale," it is about a married woman who is approached by a lovesick would-be adulterer, but this assignation ends not ignobly in the branches of a pear tree, but nobly with everyone doing the right thing. It leaves a sweet taste in the mouth by emphasizing the essential goodness of human nature. That goodness permits a generosity of spirit that can overcome baser drives like lust and greed. People make mistakes, yes, but by following the basic principle of the importance of keeping one's promises and by following the moral leadership of good men and women, they can grow to be better people.

Chaucer's most likely source for "The Franklin's Tale" is the *Filocolo,* in which Giovanni Boccaccio tells a somewhat similar story. In the *Filocolo* story, the loyal wife of a gentleman tells Tarolfo, her would-be lover who is also a gentleman, that he must stop pestering her unless he can perform an impossible task—to create for her in January a garden that blooms as if it were May. Instead of taking her meaning that he should get lost, Tarolfo determines to find a way to provide the garden. When he chances upon a sorcerer-botanist named

Tebano, Tarolfo offers him half of his castles and treasure if he will produce such a garden. Tebano does produce such a garden, and when Tarolfo shows the lovely garden to the woman he loves, she agrees to give in to him. She asks, however, for a delay before she has to deliver herself to him. In that grace period, she confesses to her husband what she has done and says she would kill herself rather than keep her promise to Tarolfo. Her husband tells her to keep her promise but not to make a similar mistake again. Tarolfo is impressed with the husband's generosity and releases her from her promise, and the sorcerer subsequently releases Tarolfo from his payment. The *Filocolo* tale ends with a long discussion—almost as long as the narrative portion of the tale—about which of the three men is the most generous. The queen who is running the discussion concludes that the husband is the most honorable since he offered to sacrifice honor, which is more important than either the sexual gratification Tarolfo gave up or the mere riches that the sorcerer gave up. (Interestingly, Boccaccio told the same basic story once again as the fifth tale of the tenth day of the *Decameron*. In that version the teller of the tale suggests— much more briefly—that the lover gave up more than the husband.)

Chaucer's tale gives readers much to think and talk and write about: the morality of Arveragus's going off to England and his decision to send his wife to Aurelius; the degree to which we can blame Dorigen for making her rash promise; why Chaucer adds her long catalogue of other women who chose death rather than dishonor; the reason Chaucer changes the impossible task from a spring garden in January to removing the black rocks from the bay; the religious implications of Dorigen's, Aurelius's, and the magician's attempts to alter the shape of creation to further their own personal needs; the seriousness with which we should take young Aurelius's lovesickness; and, of course, the answer in this story to the closing question: who was the most "free" or generous?

"The Franklin's Tale" is sometimes seen as Chaucer's "solution" to what is sometimes called the "marriage debate" in *The Canterbury Tales*. The idea here is that the Wife of Bath introduces the debate by arguing that in the ideal marriage wives should be in charge. The Clerk (in a tale not included in this collection) then argues, rather, that husbands should be in charge. Then the Merchant expresses his cynical view that any marriage can go sour, no matter who is in control. And then the Franklin comes along and offers up a tale about the ideal marriage in which there is mutual respect and enduring love. Some readers question the whole notion of a four-tale debate about marriage, preferring to see a more fundamental concern in these and other *Canterbury Tales* about what it means to be gentle in a world in which there is so little true gentility. Such a concern about the nature of gentility would in any case have been natural to the Franklin, a wealthy landholder who seems to think that a man's gentleness is measured by the sumptuousness and quantity of the food he serves (see General Prologue lines 333–62). His own tale challenges that idea.

## NOTES

**Armorik, Britayne** (line 1). The northwest corner of what is now France, particularly that part of France that extends out into the Atlantic between the English Channel and the Bay of Biscay.

**bothe his lady and his love** (68). According to the tenets of courtly love, a man could not love his wife, since the term "love" was by definition adulterous—the desire of a man for another man's wife, and hers for him. Arveragus seems to challenge that notion because his wife or "lady" and his "love" are the same person. Similarly, he is both her lord through marriage and her servant in love (see line 65 above).

**Penmark** (73). A location on the Breton cape or peninsula.

**Kayrrud** (80). A village of Kerru. Like the previous place name, it is difficult to place it precisely on a modern map. Chaucer may have imagined some of the geographical details.

**Briteyne** (82). Britain. The words for Brittany (line 1 above) and Britain were almost identical, but this one clearly refers to England.

**Ekko, Narcisus** (223–24). In Ovid's *Metamorphoses*, the nymph Echo falls in love with the self-admiring Narcissus, who has affection only for himself. Echo gradually wastes away in her grief until nothing but her voice remains.

**Appollo** (303). The god of the sun, later referred to as Phoebus (line 308).

**Lucina** (317). The goddess of the moon, often referred to as Luna. Chaucer surely knew that there was a causal connection between the phases of the moon and the tides. In the following lines Aurelius asks Apollo to arrange that the sun and moon stay in conjunction so that the tides would remain at the highest for the longest period, and thus cover the rocks.

**fyve fadme** (332). Five fathoms was around thirty feet, which would give plenty of clearance for virtually any ship then afloat.

**Delphos** (349). Delphi, or perhaps Delos, where Apollo was born.

**Pamphilus, Galathee** (382). Pamphilus loved and ultimately seduced Galatea in a thirteenth-century poem in Latin.

**magik naturel** (397). The manipulation of astrological influences as opposed to black magic.

**Orliens** (425). Orléans is a town south and a little west of Paris.

**Gerounde, Sayne** (494). Two large rivers. The Gironde emp-
ties into the Bay of Biscay, the Seine into the English
Channel. The huge expanse between them took in more
than half the northern and western coastline of what we
now call France. The magician's feat, then, was by no means
localized to the coastline that Dorigen could see from her
cliff.

**round** (500). This line shows that it is a myth that all men be-
fore Columbus thought the earth was flat. Sailors, at least,
must have known that it was round.

**Janus** (524). The double-faced god. His looking both ways
may indicate that the actual date is December 21, the win-
ter solstice, with Janus looking back to warm weather and
forward to the real chills of winter.

**"Nowel!"** (527). The reference is apparently to the season of
Christ's birth, though Christ is not mentioned explicitly in
"The Franklin's Tale."

**tables Toletanes** (545). Astronomical tables adopted in
the late thirteenth century for the city of Toledo in Spain.
It is not necessary to try to be precise about the meanings
of the technical and astrological terms in these and the
following lines (through 569). The magician understood
what he was doing to make the rocks seem to disappear.
As with any magician, it is all right for us to remain puz-
zled about how he does his tricks.

**collect, expans yeres** (547). The magician had tables show-
ing the movements of the planets over a year (expanse) and
over a twenty-year span of years (collect).

**rotes** (548). The day for which the data on a given table
starts.

**centres, arguments** (549). Astronomical figures used in
making calculations.

**proporcionels convenients** (550). Tables, ratios, and formu-
las for making calculations.

**Phidoun** (641). Chaucer probably learned in Jerome's *Against Jovinian* this story and the others in this section about virgins and wives who died rather than be dishonored.

**free** (894). The word "free" is used here in the sense of "generous," or "liberal with one's possessions," or merely "gentle."

# THE FRANKLIN

In Armorik,* that called is Britayne,*
Ther was a knight that loved and dide his payne
To serve a lady in his beste wyse;
And many a labour, many a greet empryse
He for his lady wroghte er she were wonne,                    5
For she was oon the faireste under sonne,
And eek thereto come of so heigh kinrede
That wel unnethes dorste this knight, for drede,
Telle hir his wo, his peyne, and his distresse.
But atte laste, she, for his worthinesse,                     10
And namely for his meke obeysaunce,
Hath swich a pitee caught of his penaunce
That prively she fil of his accord
To take him for hir housbonde and hir lord,
Of swich lordshipe as men han over hir wyves;                 15
And for to lede the more in blisse hir lyves,
Of his free wil he swoor hir as a knight
That never in all his lyfe he, day ne night,
Ne sholde upon him take no maistrye
Agayn hir wil, ne kythe hir jalousye,                         20
But hir obeye and folwe hir wil in al
As any lovere to his lady shal;
Save that the name of soveraynetee,
That wolde he have for shame of his degree.

# THE FRANKLIN'S TALE

In Armorica, which is called Brittany,
there was a knight who loved a lady and took pains
to serve her as best he could;
and he performed many a labor, many a great
    enterprise,
for her, before she was won,                                    5
for she was one of the fairest under the sun,
and also she came of such a noble family
that, for fear, this knight scarcely dared
tell her his woe, his pain, and his distress.
But at last, because of his great worth,                        10
and particularly because of his meek obedience,
she took such pity on his suffering
that privately she agreed
to take him for her husband and her lord—
in such lordship as men have over their wives;                  15
and in order that they might lead their lives
    together the
more blissfully, of his free will he swore to her
    as a knight
that never in all his life, by day or night,
would he take an authoritarian role over her
against her will, nor show jealousy to her,                     20
but would obey her and always follow her will in
    all things,
as any lover ought to his lady;
except that he wanted to have the title of sovereignty:
that he wanted for the sake of the dignity of his
    position.

She thanked him, and with ful greet humblesse 25
She seyde, "Sire, sith of your gentillesse
Ye profre me to have so large a reyne,
Ne wolde never God bitwixe us tweyne,
As in my gilt, were outher werre or stryf.
Sir, I wol be your humble trewe wyf, 30
Have heer my trouthe, til that myn herte breste."
Thus been they bothe in quiete and in reste.

For o thing, sires, saufly dar I seye:
That frendes everich other moot obeye,
If they wol longe holden compayne. 35
Love wol nat ben constreyned by maistrye;
Whan maistrie comth, the god of love anon
Beteth hise winges, and farwel—he is gon.
Love is a thing as any spirit free;
Wommen of kinde desiren libertee, 40
And nat to ben constreyned as a thral;
And so doon men, if I sooth seyen shal.
Loke who that is most pacient in love,
He is at his avantage al above.
Pacience is an heigh vertu certeyn, 45
For it venquisseth, as thise clerkes seyn,
Thinges that rigour sholde never atteyne.
For every word men may nat chyde or pleyne.
Lerneth to suffre, or elles, so moot I goon,
Ye shul it lerne wherso ye wole or noon. 50
For in this world, certein, ther no wight is
That he ne dooth or seith somtyme amis.
Ire, siknesse, or constellacioun,
Wyn, wo, or chaunginge of complexioun
Causeth ful ofte to doon amis or speken. 55
On every wrong a man may nat be wreken;
After the tyme, moste be temperaunce
To every wight that can on governaunce.
And therfore hath this wyse worthy knight,
To live in ese, suffrance hir bihight, 60
And she to him ful wisly gan to swere
That never sholde ther be defaute in here.

She thanked him, and with great humility          25
she said, "Sir, since in your courtesy
you offer me so free a rein,
God forbid that there should ever be between us two,
through my fault, any quarrel or strife.
Sir, I will be your humble, true wife,          30
I give you my pledge, until my heart stops beating."
Thus they were both in peace and accord.

For there is one thing, sirs, I can safely say:
that those bound by love must obey each other
if they are to keep company long.          35
Love will not be constrained by mastery;
when mastery comes, the god of love at once
beats his wings, and farewell—he is gone.
Love is a thing as free as any spirit;
women naturally desire liberty,          40
and not to be constrained like slaves;
and so do men, if I shall tell the truth.
See who is the most patient in love:
he has the greatest advantage.
Patience is surely a great virtue,          45
for it vanquishes, as these scholars say,
things that rigor would never manage.
One cannot scold or complain at every word.
Learn to endure patiently, or else, as I live and breathe,
you shall learn it whether you want to or not.          50
For certainly there is no one in this world
who doesn't sometimes do or say something amiss.
Anger, sickness, or planetary influences,
wine, sorrow, or changing of the balance of humors
often causes one to do or speak amiss.          55
A man cannot be avenged for every wrong;
according to the occasion, everyone who knows
how to manage himself must use temperance.
And therefore this wise, valiant knight, in order to
live in comfort, promised her forbearance,          60
and she wisely gave her promise to him
that there would never be any lack of it on her part.

Heer may men seen an humble wys accord:
Thus hath she take hit servant and hir lord,
Servant in love and lord in mariage;                    65
Thanne was he bothe in lordship and servage.
Servage? Nay, but in lordshipe above,
Sith he hath bothe his lady and his love;*
His lady, certes, and his wyf also,
The which that lawe of love acordeth to.                70
And whan he was in this prosperitee,
Hoom with his wyf he gooth to his contree,
Nat fer fro Penmark,* ther his dwelling was,
Wheras he liveth in blisse and in solas.

Who coude telle but he hadde wedded be               75
The joye, the ese, and the prosperitee
That is bitwixe an housbonde and his wyf?
A yeer and more lasted this blisful lyf,
Til that the knight of which I speke of thus,
That of Kayrrud* was cleped Arveragus,               80
Shoop him to goon and dwelle a yeer or tweyne
In Engelond, that cleped was eek Briteyne,*
To seke in armes worship and honour—
For al his lust he sette in swich labour—
And dwelled ther two yeer, the book seith thus.      85
Now wol I stinte of this Arveragus,
And speken I wole of Dorigene his wyf,
That loveth hir housbonde as hir hertes lyf.
For his absence wepeth she and syketh,
As doon thise noble wyves whan hem lyketh.           90
She moorneth, waketh, wayleth, fasteth, pleyneth;
Desyr of his presence hir so distreyneth
That al this wyde world she sette at noght.
Hir frendes, whiche that knewe hir hevy thoght,
Conforten hir in al that ever they may;              95
They prechen hir, they tell hir night and day,
That causelees she sleeth hirself, allas;
And every confort possible in this cas
They doon to hir with al hir bisinesse,
Al for to make hir leve hir hevinesse.               100

Here one may see a humble, wise agreement:
she has thus accepted her servant and her lord,
servant in love and lord in marriage;                    65
he was, then, both in lordship and in servitude.
Servitude? No, but in the higher state of lordship,
since he had both his lady and his love;
his lady, certainly, and his wife too,
which is in accordance with the law of love.             70
And when he was in this happy state,
he went home with his wife to his own country,
not far from Penmarch, where his home was,
and there he lived in bliss and happiness.

Who could tell, unless he had been married,              75
the joy, the comfort, and the happiness
there is between a husband and his wife?
This blissful life lasted for a year and more,
until the knight of whom I am speaking,
who was called Arveragus of Kerru,                       80
prepared to go and stay a year or two
in England, which was also called Britain,
to seek glory and honor at arms—
for all his joy was in such feats—
and he stayed there two years, as the book says.         85

Now I will stop talking of this Arveragus,
and speak of Dorigen his wife,
who loved her husband as her own heart's life.
On account of his absence she wept and sighed,
as these noble wives do when they please.                90
She mourned, lost sleep, wailed, fasted, lamented;
desire for his presence so afflicted her
that she cared nothing for all this wide world.
Her friends, who knew her distress of mind,
comforted her in every way they could;                   95
they preached to her, night and day they told her
that she was killing herself without cause, alas;
and they diligently gave her
every possible comfort in this situation,
all in order to make her stop grieving.                  100

By proces, as ye knowen everichoon,
Men may so longe graven in a stoon
Til som figure therinne emprented be.
So longe han they conforted hir til she
Receyved hath, by hope and by resoun,                    105
Th'emprenting of hir consolacioun,
Thurgh which hir grete sorwe gan aswage;
She may nat aiwey duren in swich rage.

And eek Arveragus, in al this care,
Hath sent hir lettres hoom of his welfare,                110
And that he wol come hastily agayn;
Or elles hadde this sorwe hir herte slayn.

Hir freendes sawe hir sorwe gan to slake,
And preyed hir on knees, for Goddes sake,
To come and romen hir in companye,                        115
Awey to dryve hir derke fantasye.
And finally she graunted that requeste;
For wel she saugh that it was for the beste.

Now stood hir castel faste by the see,
And often with hir freendes walketh she                   120
Hir to disporte upon the bank an heigh,
Wheras she many a ship and barge seigh
Seilinge hir cours wheras hem liste go;
But thanne was that a parcel of hir wo,
For to hirself ofte "Allas!" seith she,                   125
"Is ther no ship of so manye as I see
Wol bringen hom my lord? Thanne were myn herte
Al warisshed of his bittre peynes smerte."

Another tyme ther wolde she sitte and thinke
And caste hir eyen dounward fro the brinke;               130
But whan she saugh the grisly rokkes blake,
For verray fere so wolde hir herte quake
That on hir feet she mighte hir noght sustene.
Thanne wolde she sitte adoun upon the grene
And pitously into the see biholde,                        135
And seyn right thus, with sorweful sykes colde:
  "Eterne God, that thurgh thy purveyaunce

In due process of time, as you all know,
one may scrape on a stone so long
that some figure is imprinted there.
They comforted her so long that she
received, through hope and reason,                     105
the imprint of their consolation,
through which her great sorrow began to diminish;
she could not go on forever in such grief.

And also, while she was in this sorrow, Arveragus
had sent her letters home assuring her of his welfare   110
and saying that he would return quickly;
otherwise this sorrow would have slain her heart.

Her friends saw that her sorrow began to abate,
and prayed her on their knees for the love of God
to come and stroll about with them,                    115
to drive away her dark fantasies.
And finally she granted that request,
for she saw well that it was for the best.

Now her castle stood close by the sea,
and often she walked with her friends                  120
to amuse herself high up on the precipitous coast.
From there she saw many a ship and barge
sailing their courses, wherever they chose to go;
but then that added to her sorrow,
for she often said to herself, "Alas,                  125
is there no ship of the many I see
which will bring home my lord? Then my heart
     would be
all healed of its keen and bitter pain."

Another time she would sit there thinking,
and direct her eyes down from the cliff edge;          130
but when she saw the grisly black rocks,
her heart would quake so for pure fear
that she couldn't keep on her feet.
Then she would sit down on the grass
and piteously look at the sea,                         135
and say, with sorrowful, bitter sighs,

"Eternal God, who through your providence

Ledest the world by certein governaunce,
In ydel, as men seyn, ye nothing make;
But, Lord, thise grisly feendly rokkes blake,          140
That semen rather a foul confusioun
Of werk than any fair creacioun
Of swich a parfit wys God and a stable,
Why han ye wroght this werk unresonable?
For by this werk, south, north, ne west, ne eest,          145
Ther nis y-fostered man, ne brid, ne beest;
It dooth no good, to my wit, but anoyeth.
See ye nat, Lord, how mankinde it destroyeth?
An hundred thousand bodies of mankinde
Han rokkes slayn, al be they nat in minde,          150
Which mankinde is so fair part of thy werk
That thou it madest lyk to thyn owene merk.
Thanne semed it ye hadde a greet chiertee
Toward mankinde; but how thanne may it be
That ye swiche menes make it to destroyen,          155
Which menes do no good, but ever anoyen?
I woot wel clerkes wol seyn, as hem leste,
By arguments, that al is for the beste,
Though I ne can the causes nat y-knowe.
But thilke God that made wind to blowe,          160
As kepe my lord! This my conclusioun;
To clerkes lete I al disputisoun.
But wolde God that alle thise rokkes blake
Were sonken into helle for his sake!
Thine rokkes sleen myn herte for the fere."          165
Thus wolde she seyn, with many a pitous tere.

   Hir freendes sawe that it was no disport
To romen by the see, but disconfort;
And shopen for to pleyen somwher elles.
They leden hir by riveres and by welles,          170
And eek in othere places delitables;
They dauncen and they pleyen at ches and tables.

   So on a day, right in the morwe-tyde,
Unto a gardin that was ther bisyde,

guides the world with sure control,
men say you make nothing in vain;
but, Lord, these grisly, diabolical black rocks, 140
which seem to be a vile, confused work
rather than any fair creation
of a God so perfect, wise, and stable—
why have you made this unreasonable thing?
For neither south, north, west, nor east 145
does this work help man, bird, or beast;
to my mind it does harm, not good.
Don't you see, Lord, how it destroys mankind?
Rocks have slain a hundred thousand men,
although out of memory, 150
and mankind is so fair a part of your work
that you made it in your own image.
At that time, it seemed that you had a great charity
toward mankind; but how then may it be
that you create such means to destroy it, 155
which means do no good, but always do harm?
I know quite well learned men will say, as they like,
with arguments, that all is for the best,
even though I cannot know the causes.
But may the God that made the winds to blow 160
keep my lord safe! This is my conclusion;
to learned men I leave all argument.
But would to God that all these black rocks
were sunk into hell for his sake!
These rocks destroy my heart with fear." 165
Thus, with many a piteous tear, she would speak.

 Her friends saw that it was no diversion
for her to roam by the sea, but a discomfort;
and they arranged to amuse themselves elsewhere.
They led her by rivers and wells, 170
and in other delightful places too;
they danced and they played at chess and
    backgammon.
 So one day, early in the morning,
they went to a garden that was close by,

In which that they hadde maad hir ordinaunce                    175
Of vitaille and of other purveyaunce,
They goon and pleye hem al the longe day.
And this was on the sixte morwe of May,
Which May had peynted with his softe shoures
This gardin ful of leves and of floures;                       180
And craft of mannes hand so curiously
Arrayed hadde this gardin, trewely,
That never was ther gardin of swich prys,
But if it were the verray paradys.
Th' odour of floures and the fresshe sighte                    185
Wolde han maked any herte lighte
That ever was born, but if to gret siknesse
Or to gret sorwe helde it in distresse,
So ful it was of beautee with pleasaunce.
At after-dinner gonne they to daunce,                          190
And singe also, save Dorigen allone,
Which made alwey hir compleint and hir mone,
For she ne saugh him on the daunce go,
That was hir housbonde and hir love also.
But nathelees she moste a tyme abyde,                          195
And with good hope lete hir sorwe slyde.
    Upon this daunce, amonges othere men,
Daunced a squyer biforen Dorigen
That fressher was and jolyer of array,
As to my doom, than is the monthe of May.                     200
He singeth, daunceth, passinge any man
That is, or was, sith that the world bigan.
Therwith he was, if men sholde him discryve,
Oon of the beste faringe man on lyve:
Yong, strong, right vertuous, and riche and wys,              205
And wel biloved, and holden in gret prys.
And shortly, if the sothe I tellen shal,
Unwiting of this Dorigen at al,
This lusty squyer, servant to Venus,
Which that y-cleped was Aurelius,                              210
Hadde loved hir best of any creature
Two yeer and more, as was his aventure,

in which they had made their arrangements    175
for food and other supplies,
and enjoyed themselves all day long.
This was on the sixth morning of May,
and May, with his soft showers, had painted
this garden full of leaves and flowers;    180
and the craft of man's hand had so skillfully
set out this garden that there
really never was one so precious,
unless it were paradise itself.
The scent and the fresh sight of flowers    185
would have lightened any heart
that ever was born, unless too great sickness
or too great sorrow held it in distress,
it was so full of beauty and pleasure.
After dinner they went on to dance,    190
and sing too, save only Dorigen,
who mourned and lamented constantly
because she couldn't see among the dancers him
who was her husband and also her love.
But nonetheless she had to remain awhile,    195
and, hopefully, let her sorrow slip away.
   Among other men in this dance,
a squire danced before Dorigen
who was fresher and gayer in his attire,
in my opinion, than the month of May.    200
He sang and danced surpassing anyone
that is or was since the world began.
Besides, he was, if one should describe him,
one of the handsomest men alive:
young, strong, right virtuous, and rich and prudent,    205
and well-loved, and held in great esteem.
And, if I am to tell the truth, in brief it was this:
completely without Dorigen's knowledge
the lusty squire, who was called Aurelius,
as a servant of Venus had loved Dorigen    210
best of any creature for more than two years,
as it chanced to fall to his lot;

But never dorste he tellen hir his grevaunce;
Withouten coppe he drank al his penaunce.
He was despeyred, no thing dorste he seye,                215
Save in his songes somwhat wolde he wreye
His wo, as in a general compleyning:
He seyde he lovede, and was biloved no thing;
Of swich matere made he manye layes,
Songes, compleintes, roundels, virelayes,                 220
How that he dorste nat his sorwe telle,
But languissheth, as a furie dooth in helle;
And dye he moste, he seyde, as dide Ekko*
For Narcisus,* that dorste nat telle hir wo.
In other manere than ye here me seye                      225
Ne dorste he nat to hir his wo biwreye,
Save that, paraventure, som tyme at daunces,
Ther yonge folk kepen hir observaunces,
It may wel be he loked on hir face
In swich a wyse as man that asketh grace;                 230
But no thing wiste she of his entente.
    Nathelees, it happed, er they thennes wente,
By cause that he was hir neighebour
And was a man of worship and honour,
And hadde y-knowen him of tyme yore,                      235
They fille in speche; and forthe, more and more,
Unto his purpos drough Aurelius,
And whan he saugh his tyme, he seyde thus:
    "Madame," quod he, "by God that this world made,
So that I wiste it mighte your herte glade,               240
I wolde that day that your Arveragus
Wente over the see, that I, Aurelius,
Hadde went ther never I sholde have come agayn;
For wel I woot my service is in vayn.
My gerdon is but bresting of myn herte.                   245
Madame, reweth upon my peynes smerte,
For with a word ye may me sleen or save;
Heer at your feet God wolde that I were grave!
I ne have as now no leyser more to seye;

but he never dared tell her his sorrow;
he drank up all his penance without a cup.
He was in despair; he dared say nothing,                   215
except that in his songs he would disclose
his woe somewhat, as in a general lament:
he said he loved, and was not at all beloved;
of such matter he made many lays,
songs, complaints, roundelays, virelays—                   220
about how he dared not tell his sorrow,
but languished, as a fury does in hell;
and he must die, he said, as Echo,
who dared not tell her woe, did for Narcissus.
In other ways than you have heard me say                   225
he did not dare reveal his woe to her;
except that, perhaps, sometimes at dances,
where young folks perform their devotions,
it may well be he looked into her face
in the manner of a man who asks for favor;                  230
but she knew nothing of his intention.
    Nonetheless, before they went from the garden
        it happened
that, since he was her neighbor
and was a man of reputation and honor
and she had known him from long ago,                        235
they fell into conversation; and Aurelius
drew nearer and nearer to his purpose;
and when he saw an opportunity he spoke as follows:
    "Madame," said he, "by God that made this world,
if I knew that it might gladden your heart,                 240
I wish that on that day when your Arveragus
went over the sea, I, Aurelius,
had gone where I should never have returned again;
for well I know my service is in vain.
My reward is only heartbreak.                               245
Madame, have pity on my bitter pains,
for with a word you can slay or save me;
would to God I were buried here at your feet!
I have no leisure now to say more;

Have mercy, swete, or ye wol do me deye!"                    250
   She gan to loke upon Aurelius:
"Is this your wil," quod she, "and sey ye thus?
Never erst," quod she, "ne wiste I what ye mente.
But now, Aurelie, I knowe your entente,
By thilke God that yaf me soule and lyf,                     255
Ne shal I never been untrewe wyf
In word ne werk, as fer as I have wit:
I wol ben his to whom that I am knit;
Tak this for fynal answer as of me."
But after that in pley thus seyde she:                       260
"Aurelie," quod she, "by heighe God above,
Yet wolde I graunte yow to been your love,
Sin I yow see so pitously complayne:
Loke what day that endelong Britayne
Ye remoeve alle the rokkes, stoon by stoon,                  265
That they ne lette ship ne boot to goon—
I seye, whan ye han maad the coost so clene
Of rokkes that ther nis no stoon y-sene,
Thanne wol I love yow best of any man;
Have heer my trouthe in al that ever I can."                 270
   "Is ther non other grace in yow?" quod he.
   "No, by that Lord," quod she, "that maked me!
For wel I woot that it shal never bityde.
Lat swiche folies out of your herte slyde.
What deyntee sholde a man han in his lyf                     275
For to go love another mannes wyf,
That hath hir body whan so that him lyketh?"
   Aurelius ful ofte sore syketh;
Wo was Aurelie, whan that he this herde,
And with a sorweful herte he thus answerde:                 280
   "Madame," quod he, "this were an inpossible!
Thanne moot I dye of sodein deth horrible."
And with that word he turned him anoon.
Tho come hir othere freendes many oon

have mercy, sweet, or you will cause my death."        250
   She looked at Aurelius:
"Is this what you want," said she, "and do you
   say thus?
Never before," she said, "did I know what you had
   in mind.
But now that I know your intention, Aurelius,
by that God that gave me soul and life,        255
I will never be an unfaithful wife
in word or deed, as far as I can manage:
I will be his to whom I am knit;
take this for my final answer."
But after that she spoke playfully:        260
   "Aurelius," said she, "by high God above,
yet I would like to consent to be your love,
since I see you so piteously complain:
look to the day that along the length of Brittany
you remove all the rocks, stone by stone,        265
so that they do not hinder any ship or boat
   from sailing—
I say, when you have so cleared the coast
of rocks that there is no stone to be seen,
then I will love you best of any man;
here is my word of honor as firm as can be."        270
   "Will you not grant me favor otherwise?" he asked.
   "No," she said, "by that God that made me!
For well I know that it shall never happen.
Let such follies slide from your heart.
What kind of joy can a man have in life        275
if he goes and loves the wife of another man,
who has her body whenever he pleases?"
   Aurelius sighed sorely again and again;
woeful was he when he had heard this,
and with a sorrowful heart he answered,        280
   "Madame, this is an impossibility!
I must, then, die a sudden and horrible death."
And with those words he turned away at once.
Then came many of her other friends

And in the aleyes romeden up and doun,                    285
And no thing wiste of this conclusioun,
But sodeinly bigonne revel newe
Til that the brighte sonne loste his hewe;
For th'orisonte hath reft the sonne his light—
This is as muche to seye as it was night.                 290
And hoom they goon in joye and in solas,
Save only wrecche Aurelius, allas!
He to his hous is goon with sorweful herte;
He seeth he may nat fro his deeth asterte.
Him semed that he felt his herte colde;                   295
Up to the hevene his handes he gan holde,
And on his knowes bare he sette him doun,
And in his raving seyde his orisoun—
For verray wo out of his wit he breyde.
He niste what he spak, but thus he seyde;                 300
With pitous herte his pleynt hath he bigonne
Unto the goddes, and first unto the sonne:

   He seyde, "Appollo,* god and governour
Of every plaunte, herbe, tree and flour,
That yevest, after thy declinacioun,                      305
To ech of hem his tyme and his sesoun,
As thyn herberwe chaungeth lowe or hye,
Lord Phebus, cast thy merciable yë
On wrecche Aurelie, which that am but lorn.
Lo, lord! My lady hath my deeth y-sworn                   310
Withoute gilt, but thy benignitee
Upon my dedly herte have some pitee!
For wel I woot, lord Phebus, if yow lest,
Ye may me helpen, save my lady, best.
Now voucheth sauf that I may yow devyse                   315
How that I may been holpe and in what wyse.

   "Your blisful suster, Lucina* the shene,
That of the see is chief godesse and quene—
Though Neptunus have deitee in the see,
Yet emperesse aboven him is she:                          320
Ye knowen wel, lord, that right as hir desyr

and they strolled up and down the paths,                    285
but they knew nothing of this conversation;
quickly they began new revelry,
lasting until the bright sun faded;
for the horizon had bereft the sun of his light—
this is as much as to say it was night.                     290
And home they went in joy and delight,
save only wretched Aurelius, alas!
He went to his house with a sorrowful heart;
he saw that he could not escape his death,
it seemed to him he felt his heart grow cold;              295
he held his hands up to heaven
and set himself down on his bare knees,
and in his raving said his prayers—
he was going out of his mind with pure grief.
He did not know what he spoke, but this is what
     he said;                                               300
with piteous heart he began his complaint
to the gods, and first to the sun:
     He said, "Apollo, god and ruler
of every plant, herb, tree and flower,
who give to each of them its time and its season           305
according to your position—
as your dwelling changes, low or high—
lord Phoebus, cast your merciful eyes
on wretched Aurelius, who is but lost.
See, lord, my lady has sworn my death,                     310
although I am guiltless, unless your beneficence
have some pity on my dying heart!
For well I know, lord Phoebus, that if you wish
you, next to my lady, can help me best.
Allow me to tell you now                                    315
how I can be helped, and in what way.
     "Concerning your blissful sister, Lucina the bright,
who is chief goddess and queen of the sea
(although Neptune has dominion of the sea,
yet she is empress above him),                              320
you know well, lord, that just as her desire

Is to be quiked and lighted of your fyr,
For which she folweth yow ful bisily,
Right so the see desyreth naturelly
To folwen hir, as she that is goddesse       325
Bothe in the see and riveres more and lesse.
Wherfore, lord Phebus, this is my requeste—
Do this miracle, or do myn herte breste—
That now, next at this opposicioun,
Which in the signe shal be of the Leoun,      330
As preyeth hir so greet a flood to bringe
That fyve fadme* at the leeste it overspringe
The hyeste rokke in Armorik Briteyne,
And lat this flood endure yeres tweyne;
Thanne certes to my lady may I seye:          335
'Holdeth your heste, the rokkes been aweye.'
  "Lord Phebus, dooth this miracle for me:
Preye hir she go no faster cours than ye;
I seye, preyeth your suster that she go
No faster cours than ye thise yeres two       340
Thanne shal she been evene atte fulle alway,
And spring-flood laste bothe night and day.
And, but she vouche-sauf in swiche manere
To graunte me my sovereyn lady dere,
Prey hir to sinken every rok adoun            345
Into hir owene derke regioun
Under the ground, ther Pluto dwelleth inne,
Or nevere mo shal I my lady winne.
Thy temple in Delphos* wol I barefoot seke;
Lord Phebus, see the teres on my cheke,       350
And of my peyne have som compassioun,"
And with that word in swowne he fil adoun.
And longe tyme he lay forth in a traunce.
  His brother, which that knew of his penaunce,
Up caughte him and to bedde he hath him broght.   355
Dispeyred in this torment and this thoght
Lete I this woful creature lye;
Chese he, for me, whether he wol live or dye.

is to be quickened and lighted by your fire
(for which reason she follows you constantly),
just so the sea naturally desires
to follow her, as the goddess who rules    325
both the sea and the rivers, greater and less.
Therefore, lord Phoebus, this is my request—
perform this miracle, or let my heart break—
when you are next in opposition,
in the sign of the Lion,    330
pray her to bring so great a flood
that at the very least it shall rise five fathoms
over the highest rock in Armorican Brittany,
and let this flood last two years;
then certainly I can say to my lady,    335
'Keep your promise, the rocks are gone.'
    "Lord Phoebus, perform this miracle for me:
pray her to go no faster a course than you;
I say pray your sister to make
no faster a course than you for these two years:    340
then she will always be just at the full,
and spring tide shall last both day and night.
And, unless she will deign to grant
me my dear sovereign lady in this way,
pray her to sink every rock down    345
into her own dark region
under the ground, where Pluto dwells,
or I shall nevermore win my lady.
Barefoot I will seek out your temple in Delphos;
lord Phoebus, see the tears on my cheek,    350
and have some compassion on my pain."
And with those words he fell down in a swoon,
and for a long time he lay in a trance.
    His brother, who knew of his suffering,
picked him up and brought him to bed.    355
I shall let this woeful creature lie
despairing in this torment and these imaginings;
let him choose, for my part, whether he will live
    or die.

Arveragus, with hele and greet honour,
As he that was of chivalrye the flour,                      360
Is comen hoom, and othere worthy men.
O blisful artow now, thou Dorigen,
That hast thy lusty housbonde in thyne armes,
The fresshe knight, the worthy man of armes,
That loveth thee as his owene hertes lyf.                   365
No thing list him to been imaginatyf
If any wight had spoke, whyl he was oute,
To hire of love; he hadde of it no doute.
He noght entendeth to no swich matere,
But daunceth, justeth, maketh hir good chere;              370
And thus in joye and blisse I lete hem dwelle,
And of the syke Aurelius wol I telle.

In langour and in torment furious
Two yeer and more lay wrecche Aurelius,
Er any foot he mighte on erthe goon;                        375
Ne confort in this tyme hadde he noon,
Save of his brother, which that was a clerk:
He knew of al this wo and al this werk.
For to non other creature certeyn
Of this matere he dorste no word seyn;                      380
Under his brest he bar it more secree
Than ever dide Pamphilus* for Galathee.*
His brest was hool withoute for to sene,
But in his herte ay was the arwe kene;
And wel ye knowe that of a sursanure                        385
In surgerye is perilous the cure,
But men mighte touche the arwe or come therby.
His brother weep and wayled prively,
Til atte laste him fil in remembraunce
That whiles he was at Orliens in Fraunce,                   390
As yonge clerkes that been likerous
To reden artes that been curious
Seken in every halke and every herne
Particuler sciences for to lerne,
He him remembred that, upon a day,                          395
At Orliens in studie a book he say

Arveragus, with prosperity and great honor,
came home as the flower of chivalry, 360
and other worthy men with him.
Ah, Dorigen, you are blissful now,
with your lusty husband in your arms—
the vigorous knight, the valiant man of arms,
who loves you as his own heart's life. 365
He wasn't inclined to worry about
whether anyone had spoken to her of love
while he was gone; he had no doubts about it.
He paid no attention to such matters,
but danced, jousted, and entertained her; 370
and thus I leave them in joy and bliss,
and will tell you about the sick Aurelius.

In languor and furious torment
wretched Aurelius lay for more than two years
before he could walk a foot; 375
nor did he have any comfort in this time,
except from his brother, a scholar,
who knew of his woe and the whole business.
Of course Aurelius didn't dare say a word
about this matter to any other creature; 380
he bore his love more secretly within his breast
than Pamphilus ever did for Galathea.
To outward appearance his heart was whole,
but within his breast the sharp arrow remained;
and as you well know, in surgery the cure of 385
a superficially healed wound is perilous
unless you can touch the arrow and get at it.
His brother wept and wailed in secret,
until at last he happened to remember
that while he was at Orléans in France, 390
where young scholars who lust
to learn occult arts
seek in every nook and cranny
to learn esoteric sciences—
he remembered that one day 395
while studying at Orléans he saw a book

Of magik naturel,* which his felawe,
That was that tyme a bacheler of lawe,
Al were he ther to lerne another craft,
Had prively upon his desk y-laft;                          400
Which book spak muchel of the operaciouns
Touchinge the eighte and twenty mansiouns
That longen to the mone, and swich folye,
As in our dayes is nat worth a flye;
For holy chirches feith in our bileve                      405
Ne suffreth noon illusion us to greve.
And whan this book was in his remembraunce,
Anon for joye his herte gan to daunce,
And to himself he seyde prively,

   "My brother shal be warisshed hastily;                  410
For I am siker that ther be sciences
By whiche men make diverse apparences
Swiche as thise subtile tregetoures pleye.
For ofte at festes have I wel herd seye
That tregetours withinne an halle large                    415
Have maad come in a water and a barge,
And in the halle rowen up and doun.
Somtyme hath semed come a grim leoun;
And somtyme floures springe as in a mede;
Somtyme a vyne, and grapes whyte and rede;                 420
Somtyme a castel, al of lym and stoon;
And whan hem lyked, voyded it anoon.
Thus semed it to every mannes sighte.

   "Now thanne conclude I thus, that if I mighte
At Orliens* som old felawe y-finde                         425
That hadde this mones mansions in minde,
Or other magik naturel above,
He sholde wel make my brother han his love;
For with an apparence a clerk may make
To mannes sighte that alle the rokkes blake                430
Of Britaigne weren y-voyded everichon,
And shippes by the brinke comen and gon,

about natural magic, which his comrade,
who was at that time a bachelor of law,
had privately left on his desk,
although he was there to learn another skill; 400
this book said much about the operations
concerning the twenty-eight mansions
of the moon, and such folly
as is not worth a fly nowadays;
for Holy Church's faith, which is in our Creed, 405
does not allow such illusions to grieve us.
And when he remembered this book,
at once his heart began to dance for joy,
and he said to himself secretly,

"My brother shall be quickly cured; 410
for I am sure that there are sciences
by means of which illusions can be made
such as these clever conjurers produce.
For I have indeed heard that at feasts
conjurers have often caused water 415
to come into a great hall, with a barge
that rowed up and down in the room.
Sometimes a grim lion has seemed to come;
and sometimes flowers spring up as in a meadow;
sometimes a vine, and grapes, white and red; 420
sometimes a castle, all of limestone and rock;
and when they pleased, the conjurers made everything
    vanish
immediately. Thus it seemed to every man's sight.

"Now then, I conclude that if I could
find some old comrade at Orléans 425
who knew the mansions of the moon,
or other higher natural magic,
he would indeed arrange for my brother to have
    his love;
for with an illusion a learned man can make
it seem to men's sight that all the black rocks 430
of Brittany have disappeared—every one—
and that ships are coming and going by the brink;

And in swich forme enduren a day or two;
Thanne were my brother warisshed of his wo.
Thanne moste she nedes holden hir biheste,　　435
Or elles he shal shame hir atte leste."
　　What sholde I make a lenger tale of this?
Unto his brotheres bed he comen is,
And swich confort he yaf him for to gon
To Orliens that he up stirte anon,　　440
And on his wey forthward thanne is he fare,
In hope for to ben lissed of his care.
　　Whan they were come almost to that citee,
But if it were a two furlong or three,
A yong clerk rominge by himself they mette,　　445
Which that in Latin thriftily hem grette,
And after that he seyde a wonder thing:
"I know," quod he, "the cause of your coming";
And er they ferther any fote wente
He tolde hem al that was in hir entente.　　450
　　This Briton clerk him asked of felawes
The whiche that he had knowe in olde dawes;
And he answerde him that they dede were,
For which he weep ful ofte many a tere.
　　Doun of his hors Aurelius lighte anon,　　455
And with this magicien forth is he gon
Hoom to his hous, and maden hem wel at ese.
Hem lakked no vitaille that mighte hem plese;
So wel arrayed hous as ther was oon
Aurelius in his lyf saugh never noon.　　460
　　He shewed him, er he wente to sopeer,
Forestes, parkes ful of wilde deer;
Ther saugh he hertes with hir hornes hye,
The gretteste that ever were seyn with yë.
He saugh of hem an hondred slayn with houndes,　　465
And somme with arwes blede of bittre woundes.
He saugh, whan voided were thise wilde deer,
Thise fauconers upon a fair river
That with hir haukes han the heron slayn.
Tho saugh he knightes justing in a playn;　　470

this can last a day or two;
then my brother would be cured of his woe.
Dorigen would have to keep her promise,          435
or else he will at least shame her."
    Why should I make a longer tale of this?
He came to his brother's bed
and gave him such encouragement to go
to Orléans that Aurelius got up at once,          440
and then started forth on his way
hoping to be released from his sorrow.
    When they had come almost to that city,
only about two or three furlongs from it,
they met a young scholar walking by himself          445
who greeted them properly in Latin,
and after that he said a remarkable thing:
"I know," said he, "the cause of your coming";
and before they went a foot further
he told them everything they had in mind.          450
    The clerk from Brittany asked him about friends
whom he had known in olden days;
and he answered that they were dead,
which made the brother weep many a tear.
    Aurelius alighted from his horse quickly,          455
and went with this magician, who took them
home to his house and made them most comfortable.
They lacked no food that might please them;
Aurelius had never in his life seen
a house as well provided as this one was.          460
    Before he went to supper, the magician showed him
forests and parks full of wild deer;
there he saw harts with their tall horns,
the largest that were ever seen.
He saw a hundred of them slain by hounds,          465
and some bled with cruel wounds from arrows.
He saw, when these wild deer had disappeared,
falconers on the bank of a beautiful river
who had killed a heron with their hawks.
Then he saw knights jousting on a plain;          470

And after this, he dide him swich plesaunce
That he him shewed his lady on a daunce
On which himself he daunced, as him thoughte.
And whan this maister, that this magik wroughte,
Saugh it was tyme, he clapte his handes two, 475
And farewel—al our revel was ago.
And yet remoeved they never out of the hous
Whyl they saugh al this sighte merveillous,
But in his studie, theras his bookes be,
They seten stille, and no wight but they three. 480
    To him this maister called his squyer,
And seyde him thus: "Is redy our soper?
Almost an houre it is, I undertake,
Sith I yow bad our soper for to make,
Whan that thise worthy men wenten with me 485
Into my studie, theras my bookes be."
    "Sire," quod this squyer, "whan it lyketh yow,
It is al redy, though ye wol right now."
"Go we thanne soupe," quod he, "as for the beste;
This amorous folk som-tyme mote han hir reste." 490
    At after-soper fille they in tretee
What somme sholde this maistres gerdon be
To remoeven alle the rokkes of Britayne,
And eek from Gerounde* to the mouth of Sayne.*
    He made it straunge, and swoor, so God him save, 495
Lasse than a thousand pound he wolde nat have,
Ne gladly for that somme he wolde nat goon.
    Aurelius, with blisful herte anoon,
Answered thus, "Fy on a thousand pound!
This wyde world, which that men seye is round,* 500
I wolde it yeve, if I were lord of it.
This bargayn is ful drive, for we ben knit.
Ye shal be payed trewely, by my trouthe!
But loketh now, for no necligence or slouthe,
Ye tarie us heer no lenger than tomorwe." 505
    "Nay," quod this clerk, "have heer my feith
        to borwe."

and after this, the magician gave him the pleasure
of seeing his lady in a dance
in which he himself danced, as it seemed to him.
And when the master who had made this magic
saw it was time, he clapped his two hands 475
and farewell—all our revel was gone.
And yet they had never moved out of the house
while they saw all this marvelous sight,
but had sat still in his study, where his books were,
and no one else but the three of them. 480
    This master called his squire to him
and spoke to him thus: "Is our supper ready?
It is almost an hour, I'm sure,
since I told you to make our supper;
it was then that these worthy men went with me 485
into my study, where my books are."
    "Sir," said the squire, "when it pleases you—
it is all ready, even if you want it right now."
"Then let us go and eat," said he, "as it is best;
these amorous folk must sometime have their rest." 490
    After supper they fell to bargaining
about what sum this master's reward should be
for removing all the rocks of Brittany
and also from the Gironde to the mouth of the Seine.
He made difficulties, and swore, as God might save
    him, 495
he would not have less than a thousand pounds—
nor would he go gladly for that sum.
    Aurelius, then, with a blissful heart,
answered, "Fie on a thousand pounds!
If I were lord of this wide world, 500
which is said to be round, I would give it.
This bargain is fully driven, for we are agreed.
You shall be faithfully paid, on my honor!
But now see that you don't, through negligence
    or sloth,
cause us to tarry here any longer than tomorrow." 505
    "No," said this clerk, "I give you my word."

To bedde is goon Aurelius whan him leste,
And wel ny al that night he hadde his reste;
What for his labour and his hope of blisse,
His woful herte of penaunce hadde a lisse.          510

Upon the morwe, whan that it was day,
To Britaigne toke they the righte way,
Aurelius and this magicien bisyde,
And been descended ther they wolde abyde;
And this was, as thise bokes me remembre,          515
The colde frosty seson of Decembre.

Phebus wax old and hewed lyk latoun,
That in his hote declinacioun
Shoon as the burned gold with stremes brighte;
But now in Capricorn adoun he lighte,          520
Wheras he shoon ful pale, I dar wel seyn.
The bittre frostes, with the sleet and reyn,
Destroyed hath the grene in every yerd.
Janus* sit by the fyr with double berd,
And drinketh of his bugle-horn the wyn;          525
Biforn him stant braun of the tusked swyn,
And "Nowel!"* cryeth every lusty man.

Aurelius, in al that ever he can,
Doth to his maister chere and reverence,
And preyeth him to doon his diligence          530
To bringen him out of his peynes smerte,
Or with a swerd that he wolde slitte his herte.

This subtil clerk swich routhe had of this man
That night and day he spedde him that he can,
To wayten a tyme of his conclusioun;          535
This is to seye, to make illusioun,
By swich an apparence or jogelrye
(I ne can no termes of astrologye)
That she and every wight sholde wene and seye
That of Britaigne the rokkes were aweye,          540
Or elles they were sonken under grounde.

Aurelius went to bed in due time,
and he had his rest almost all that night;
what with his labor and his hope of bliss,
his troubled heart had some release from suffering.          510
    In the morning, when it was day,
they took the direct road to Brittany,
Aurelius and this magician beside him,
and dismounted when they had arrived at their
        journey's end;
and this was, as the books remind me,                        515
the cold, frosty season of December.
    Phoebus grew old and brassy-colored;
in his hot position he had
shone with bright rays like burnished gold,
but now he lighted down in Capricorn,                        520
where I dare indeed to say he shone quite pale.
The bitter frosts, with the sleet and rain,
had destroyed the green in every yard.
Janus with his double beard sits by the fire
and drinks the wine from his wild ox horn;                   525
before him stands flesh of the tusked swine,
and every lusty man cries out, "Nowell!"
    Aurelius honored and entertained his master
in every way he could,
and begged him to do his utmost                              530
to bring him out of his bitter pains;
otherwise he would stab himself in the heart with
        a sword.
    The clever clerk had such pity for this man
that night and day he hurried as best he could
to find a time for his purpose;                              535
that is to say, to make an illusion,
by such an apparition or jugglery—
I don't know any astrological terms—
that Dorigen and everyone else would both think
        and say
that all the rocks of Brittany were gone,                    540
or else that they had sunk under the ground.

So atte laste he hath his tyme y-founde
To maken his japes and his wrecchednesse
Of swich a supersticious cursednesse.
His tables Toletanes* forth he broght                          545
Ful wel corrected, ne ther lakked noght,
Neither his collect* ne his expans yeres,*
Ne his rotes* ne his othere geres,
As been his centres* and his arguments,*
And his proporcionels convenients*                             550
For his equacions in every thing;
And, by his eighte spere in his wirking,
He knew ful wel how fer Alnath was shove
Fro the heed of thilke fixe Aries above
That in the ninthe speere considered is;                       555
Ful subtilly he calculed al this.
    Whan he hadde founde his firste mansioun,
He knew the remenant by proporcioun,
And knew the arysing of his mone weel,
And in whos face and terme and every deel,                     560
And knew ful weel the mones mansioun
Acordaunt to his operacioun,
And knew also his othere observaunces
For swiche illusiouns and swiche meschaunces
As hethen folk useden in thilke dayes;                         565
For which no lenger maked he delayes,
But thurgh his magik, for a wyke or tweye,
It semed that alle the rokkes were aweye.
    Aurelius, which that yet despeired is
Wher he shal han his love or fare amis,                        570
Awaiteth night and day on this miracle;
And whan he knew that ther was noon obstacle,
That voided were thise rokkes everichon,
Doun to his maistres feet he fil anon,
And seyde, "I woful wrecche, Aurelius,                          575
Thanke yow, lord, and lady myn Venus,
That me han holpen fro my cares colde";

So at last he found his time
to do his tricks and this superstitiously
wicked, wretched business.
He brought out his astronomical tables of Toledo,          545
properly corrected; nothing was lacking,
neither his collect nor his expanse years,
nor his roots nor his other gear,
such as his centers and his arguments
and his tables of proportions                              550
for all his equations of all kinds;
and by the precession of the eighth sphere he well
knew how far Alnath (in the head of the Ram)
     had moved
from the head of the theoretical, fixed Ram higher up,
which is considered to be in the ninth sphere;            555
he calculated all this most skillfully.
     When he had found the first position of the moon,
he knew the rest by the use of proportion,
and understood well the arising of the moon
and in which planet's face and term, and
     everything else,                                      560
and he knew quite well the position of the moon
which was in accordance with his purpose,
and also knew the other rules
for illusions and such mischief
as was practiced by heathen folk in those days;           565
so that now he made no further delay,
but through his magic, for a week or two
it seemed that all the rocks were gone.
     Aurelius, who was still in despair over
whether he would have his love or not,                     570
waited night and day for this miracle;
and when he knew that there was no obstacle,
that every one of these rocks had disappeared,
he fell down at his master's feet at once
and said, "I, Aurelius, woeful wretch,                     575
thank you, lord, and my lady Venus,
who have helped me from my bitter cares":

And to the temple his wey forth hath he holde,
Wheras he knew he sholde his lady see.
And whan he saugh his tyme, anon right he,                    580
With dredful herte and with ful humble chere,
Salewed hath his sovereyn lady dere:
   "My righte lady," quod this woful man,
"Whom I most drede and love as I best can,
And lothest were of al this world displese,                  585
Nere it that I for yow have swich disese
That I moste dyen heer at your foot anon,
Noght wolde I telle how me is wo bigon;
But certes outher moste I dye or pleyne:
Ye slee me giltelees for verray peyne.                       590
But of my deeth thogh that ye have no routhe,
Avyseth yow, er that ye breke your trouthe.
Repenteth yow, for thilke God above,
Er ye me sleen by cause that I yow love.
For madame, wel ye woot what ye han hight—                   595
Nat that I chalange any thing of right
Of yow my sovereyn lady, but your grace;
But in a gardin yond, at swich a place,
Ye woot right wel what ye bihighten me;
And in myn hand your trouthe plighten ye                     600
To love me best, God woot, ye seyde so,
Al be that I unworthy be therto.
Madame, I speke it for the honour of yow,
More than to save myn hertes lyf right now;
I have do so as ye comanded me,                              605
And if ye vouche-sauf, ye may go see.
Doth as yow list, have your biheste in minde,
For quik or deed, right ther ye shal me finde;
In yow lyth al, to do me live or deye:
But wel I woot the rokkes been aweye."                       610
   He taketh his leve, and she astonied stood;
In al hir face nas a drope of blood.
She wende never han come in swich a trappe:
   "Allas!" quod she, "that evere this sholde happe!
For wende I never, by possibilitee,                          615

and he took his way to the temple,
where he knew he would see his lady.
As soon as he saw an opportunity,                                    580
with fearful heart and a humble manner he
greeted his dear and sovereign lady:
    "My own true lady," this woeful man said,
"Whom I most fear and love as best I can,
and would be of all this world most loath to displease:    585
if I were not so sick with love for you
that I am dying here at your feet,
I would tell you nothing of how woebegone I am;
but indeed, I shall die if I do not speak;
you kill me with pain, innocent as I am.                         590
But although you have no pity on my death,
consider before you break your promise.
Repent, for the sake of God above,
before you slay me because I love you.
For, madame, well you know what you promised—    595
not that I claim anything as a right
from you, my sovereign lady, except your grace;
but in a garden yonder, at such a place,
you know right well what you promised me;
putting your hand in mine, you plighted your word    600
to love me best; God knows you said so,
although I am unworthy of it.
Madame, I speak it for the sake of your honor
more than to save my heart's life at this moment;
I have done as you commanded me,                            605
and if you will, you can go and see.
Do as you please, have your pledge in mind,
for you shall find me, alive or dead, right there;
it is up to you, to make me live or die:
but well I know that the rocks are gone."                      610
    He took his leave, and she stood astonished;
in all her face there was not a drop of blood.
She had never expected to fall into such a trap:
    "Alas," she said, "that ever this should happen!
For I never imagined it possible                                       615

That swich a monstre or merveille mighte be;
It is agayns the proces of nature."
And hoom she gooth a sorweful creature.
For verray fere unnethe may she go:
She wepeth, wailleth, al a day or two,                    620
And swowneth, that it routhe was to see;
But why it was to no wight tolde she,
For out of toune was goon Arveragus.
But to hirself she spak, and seyde thus,
With face pale and with ful sorweful chere,               625
In hir compleynt, as ye shal after here:
    "Allas," quod she, "on thee, Fortune, I pleyne,
That unwar wrapped hast me in thy cheyne;
For which t'escape woot I no socour
Save only deeth or elles dishonour;                       630
Oon of thise two bihoveth me to chese.
But natheless, yet have I lever lese
My lyf than of my body have a shame,
Or knowe myselven fals; or lese my name,
And with my deth I may be quit, ywis.                     635
Hath ther nat many a noble wyf, er this,
And many a mayde y-slayn hirself, allas,
Rather than with hir body doon trespas?
    "Yis, certes, lo, thise stories beren witnesse;
Whan thretty tyraunts ful of cursednesse,                 640
Hadde slayn Phidoun* in Athenes, atte feste,
They comanded his doghtres for t'areste,
And bringen hem biforn hem in despyt
Al naked, to fulfille hir foul delyt,
And in hir fadres blood they made hem daunce              645
Upon the pavement, God yeve hem mischaunce!
For which thise woful maydens, ful of drede,
Rather than they wolde lese hir maydenhede,
They prively ben stirt into a welle,
And dreynte hemselven, as the bokes telle.                650
    "They of Messene lete enquere and seke
Of Lacedomie fifty maydens eke,
On whiche they wolden doon hir lecherye;

that such a freak or marvel could be;
it is against the process of nature."
And she went home, a sorrowful creature.
She could scarcely walk for dread:
she wept, she wailed, all through a day or two,                620
and swooned so that it was pitiful to see;
but she told no one why this was,
for Arveragus had gone out of town.
But she spoke to herself, with a pale face
and most sorrowful expression, saying                625
in her lament, as you shall hear:
    "Alas, I complain against you, Fortune,
who have tied me, all unwary, in your chain,
from which I know of no way to escape
except only death or else dishonor;                630
I must choose one of these two.
But nevertheless, I would still rather lose
my life than be shamed in my body,
or know myself false, or lose my good name;
and with my death I can be freed, indeed.                635
Has not many a noble wife before this—
and many a maiden—slain herself, alas,
rather than sin with her body?
    "Yes, surely; see, these stories bear witness;
when thirty tyrants, full of wickedness,                640
had slain Phidon at a feast in Athens,
they commanded his daughters to be arrested
and brought before them for scorn,
all naked, to fulfill their foul delight;
and they made them dance on the pavement                645
in their father's blood—God give them misfortune!
And so these woeful maidens, full of fear,
jumped secretly into a well
and drowned themselves rather than lose
their virginity, as the books tell us.                650
    "The men of Messene also sought out
fifty maidens of Lacedaemonia,
on whom they wished to work their lechery;

But was ther noon of al that companye
That she nas slayn, and with a good entente　　　655
Chees rather for to dye than assente
To been oppressed of hir maydenhede.
Why sholde I thanne to dye been in drede?

　　"Lo, eek, the tiraunt Aristoclides,
That loved a mayden heet Stimphalides,　　　660
Whan that hir fader slayn was on a night,
Unto Dianes temple goth she right
And hente the image in hir handes two,
Fro which image wolde she never go.
No wight ne mighte hir handes of it arace,　　　665
Til she was slayn right in the selve place.
Now sith that maydens hadden swich despyt
To been defouled with mannes foul delyt,
Wel oghte a wyf rather hirselven slee
Than be defouled, as it thinketh me.　　　670

　　"What shal I seyn of Hasdrubales wyf,
That at Cartage birafte hirself hir lyf?
For whan she saugh that Romayns wan the toun,
She took hir children alle and skipte adoun
Into the fyr, and chees rather to dye　　　675
Than any Romayn dide hir vileinye.

　　"Hath nat Lucresse y-slayn hirself, allas,
At Rome whan that she oppressed was
Of Tarquin, for hir thoughte it was a shame
To liven whan that she hadde lost hir name?　　　680

　　"The sevene maydens of Milesie also
Han slayn hemself for verray drede and wo
Rather than folk of Gaule hem sholde oppresse.
Mo than a thousand stories, as I geese,
Coude I now telle as touchinge this matere.　　　685

　　"Whan Habradate was slayn, his wyf so dere
Hirselven slow, and leet hir blood to glyde
In Habradates woundes depe and wyde,
And seyde, 'My body, at the leeste way,
Ther shal no wight defoulen, if I may.'　　　690

　　"What sholde I mo ensamples heerof sayn,

but there was none of all that group
that was not slain, choosing with a good intent          655
to die rather than consent
to be ravished of her maidenhood.
Why then should I be afraid to die?
  "Consider, too, the tyrant Aristoclides,
who loved a maiden called Stymphalis;                    660
when her father was slain one night,
she went right to Diana's temple
and seized the image in her two hands;
she would never go from this image.
No one could tear her hands from it                      665
until she was slain right in that same place.
Now since maidens were so reluctant
to be defiled with man's foul delight,
a wife surely ought to slay herself rather
than be defiled, it seems to me.                         670

  "What shall I say of Hasdrubal's wife,
who took her own life at Carthage?
For when she saw the Romans win the town,
she took all her children and jumped down
into the fire, and chose to die rather                   675
than have any Roman dishonor her.

  "Did not Lucrece slay herself, alas,
at Rome when she was ravished
by Tarquin, since she thought it was shameful
to live when she had lost her good name?                 680

  "Also the seven maidens of Miletus
slew themselves for very fear and woe,
rather than have the men of Gaul ravish them.
I could tell more than a thousand stories,
I believe, touching this matter.                         685

  "When Abradates was slain, his dear wife
slew herself, and let her blood flow
into Abradates's deep, wide wounds,
and said, 'My body, at least,
shall be defiled by no one, if I can help it.'           690

  "Why should I recite more examples of this,

Sith that so manye han hemselven slayn
Wel rather than they wolde defouled be?
I wol conclude that it is bet for me
To sleen myself than been defouled thus.                    695
I wol be trewe unto Arveragus,
Or rather sleen myself in som manere,
As dide Demociones doghter dere,
By cause that she wolde nat defouled be.

　"O Cedasus, it is ful greet pitee                           700
To reden how thy doghtren deyde, allas,
That slowe hemself for swich maner cas.

　"As greet a pitee was it, or wel more,
The Theban mayden that for Nichanore
Hirselven slow, right for swich maner wo.                    705

　"Another Theban mayden dide right so;
For oon of Macedonie hadde hir oppressed,
She with hir deeth hir maydenhede redressed.
What shal I seye of Nicerates wyf,
That for swich cas birafte hirself hir lyf?                  710
How trewe eek was to Alcebiades
His love, that rather for to dyen chees
Than for to suffre his body unburied be!

　"Lo which a wyf was Alceste," quod she.
"What seith Omer of gode Penalopee?                          715
Al Grece knoweth of hir chastitee.

　"Pardee, of Laodomya is writen thus,
That whan at Troye was slayn Protheselaus
No lenger wolde she live after his day.
The same of noble Porcia telle I may;                        720
Withoute Brutus coude she nat live,
To whom she hadde al hool hir herte yive.
The parfit wyfhod of Arthemesye
Honoured is thurgh al the Barbarye.

　"O Teuta queene, thy wyfly chastitee                        725
To alle wyves may a mirour be.
The same thing I seye of Biliea,
Of Rodogone and eek Valeria."

　　Thus pleyned Dorigene a day or tweye,

since so many have slain themselves
rather than be defiled?
I shall conclude that it is better for me
to slay myself than to be so defiled. 695
I will be true to Arveragus,
or else slay myself in some way,
as Demotion's dear daughter did
because she didn't want to be defiled.

"O Scedasus, it is very pitiful 700
to read how your daughters died, alas,
who slew themselves in such a case.

"Just as pitiful, or even more so,
was the Theban maiden who slew herself
because of Nicanor, in just this sort of trouble. 705

"Another Theban maiden did just the same;
because a Macedonian had ravished her,
she avenged her maidenhood with her death.
What shall I say of Nicerates's wife,
who took her own life in such a case? 710
How true, also, was the beloved of
Alcibiades, who chose to die rather
than allow his body to lie unburied!

"See what a wife Alcestis was," said she.
"What does Homer say of good Penelope? 715
All Greece knows of her chastity.

"By heaven, it is written of Laodamia
that when Protesilaus was killed at Troy
she would no longer live after his death.
I can say the same of noble Portia; 720
she could not live without Brutus,
to whom she had given her whole heart.
The perfect wifehood of Artemisia
is honored in all barbarian countries.

"O Teuta, queen, your wifely chastity 725
should be a mirror to all wives.
I say the same thing of Bilia,
of Rhodogone and Valeria too."

Thus Dorigen lamented a day or two,

Purposinge ever that she wolde deye.                              730
But nathelees, upon the thridde night
Hom cam Arveragus, this worthy knight,
And asked hir why that she weep so sore,
And she gan wepen ever lenger the more.

"Allas!" quod she, "that evere was I born!                        735
Thus have I seyd," quod she, "thus have I sworn—"
And told him al as ye han herd bifore;
It nedeth nat reherce it yow namore.

This housbond with glad there in freendly wyse
Answerde and seyde as I shal yow devyse:                          740
"Is ther oght elles, Dorigen, but this?"

"Nay, nay," quod she, "God help me so as wis;
This is to muche, and it were Goddes wille."

"Ye, wyf," quod he, "lat slepen that is stille;
It may be wel, paraventure, yet today.                            745
Ye shul your trouthe holden, by my fay!
For God so wisly have mercy upon me,
I hadde wel lever y-stiked for to be,
For verray love which that I to yow have,
But if ye sholde your trouthe kepe and save.                      750
Trouthe is the hyeste thing that man may kepe."
But with that word he brast anon to wepe,
And seyde, "I yow forbede, up peyne of deeth,
That nevere whyl thee lasteth lyf ne breeth,
To no wight tell thou of this aventure.                           755
As I may best, I wol my wo endure,
Ne make no contenance of hevinesse,
That folk of yow may demen harm or gesse."

And forth he cleped a squyer and a mayde:
"Goth forth anon with Dorigen," he sayde,                         760
"And bringeth hir to swich a place anon."
They take hir leve and on hir wey they gon,
But they ne wiste why she thider wente.
He nolde no wight tellen his entente.

Paraventure an heep of yow, ywis,                                 765
Wol holden him a lewed man in this,
That he wol putte his wyf in jupartye;

resolving always that she would die.                                730
But nevertheless, on the third night
Arveragus, the worthy knight, came home,
and asked her why she wept so sorely,
and she began to weep all the more.

"Alas," said she, "that ever I was born!                             735
I have said this," she said, "I have sworn thus—"
and told him everything as you have heard before;
there is no need to repeat it to you.

Cheerfully and amicably this husband
answered as I shall tell you:                                       740
"Is there nothing else, Dorigen, but this?"

"No, no," she said, "God help me indeed;
this is too much, even if it were divinely intended."

"Now, wife," he said, "let sleeping dogs lie;
perhaps all may yet be well this day.                               745
You shall keep your promise, by my faith!
For as surely as I pray God to have mercy on me,
I would rather be stabbed,
because of the true love I have for you,
than have you fail to keep your word of honor.                      750
Honor is the highest thing that man can hold."
But at that word he burst into tears,
and said, "I forbid you, on pain of death,
ever, while life or breath lasts,
to tell anyone of this misadventure.                                755
As best I can, I will endure my woe,
nor will I show a sorrowful countenance
so that people could guess or think harm of you."

And he called a squire and a maid:
"Go out with Dorigen now," he said,                                 760
"and bring her to such a place at once."
They took their leave and went their way,
but they didn't know why she was going there.
He wouldn't tell anyone his intention.

Perhaps many of you, indeed,                                        765
will hold him to be a foolish man in this,
to put his wife in jeopardy;

Herkneth the tale, er ye upon hir crye.
She may have bettre fortune than yow semeth;
And whan that ye han herd the tale, demeth.          770
    This squyer which that highte Aurelius,
On Dorigen that was so amorous,
Of aventure happed hir to mete
Amidde the toun, right in the quikkest strete,
As she was boun to goon the wey forth right          775
Toward the gardin theras she had hight;
And he was to the gardinward also,
For wel he spyed whan she wolde go
Out of hir hous to any maner place.
But thus they mette, of aventure or grace;          780
And he saleweth hir with glad entente,
And asked of hir whiderward she wente.
    And she answerde half as she were mad,
"Unto the gardin, as myn housbond bad,
My trouthe for to holde, allas, allas!"          785
    Aurelius gan wondren on this cas,
And in his herte hadde greet compassioun
Of hir and of hir lamentacioun,
And of Arveragus, the worthy knight,
That bad hir holden al that she had hight,          790
So looth him was his wyf sholde breke hir trouthe;
And in his herte he caughte of this greet routhe,
Consideringe the beste on every syde,
That fro his lust yet were him lever abyde
Than doon so heigh a cherlish wrecchednesse          795
Agayns franschyse and alle gentillesse;
For which in fewe wordes seyde he thus:
    "Madame, seyth to your lord Arveragus,
That sith I see his grete gentillesse
To yow, and eek I see wel your distresse,          800
That him were lever han shame (and that were routhe)
Than ye to me sholde breke thus your trouthe,
I have wel lever ever to suffre wo

listen to the tale, before you condemn her.
She may have better luck than you think;
and when you have heard the tale, you can judge.        770
    This squire who was called Aurelius,
who was so enamored of Dorigen,
happened to meet her by chance
in the middle of the town, right in the busiest street,
as she was off to go straight        775
toward the garden as she had promised;
and he was also going toward the garden,
for he watched closely to see when she would go
out of her house to any sort of place.
But they met thus, whether by chance or luck;        780
and he greeted her hopefully,
and asked her where she was going.
    And she answered, as if she were half mad,
"To the garden, as my husband ordered,
to keep my promise, alas, alas!"        785
    Aurelius was astonished at this,
and in his heart had great compassion
for her and her lamentation,
and for Arveragus, the worthy knight,
who had ordered her to hold to all she had pledged,        790
because he was so loath to have his wife break
    her promise;
in his heart he felt great pity for this,
and considering what was best on all sides, thought
that now he would rather abstain from his pleasure
than do such a very churlish, wretched deed        795
against generosity and all nobility;
for which reason he spoke in a few words as follows:
    "Madame, say to your lord Arveragus
that since I see his great nobility
to you, and since I well see your distress also,        800
and that he would rather suffer shame (which
    would be a
pity) than have you break your word to me,
I would rather suffer sorrow always

Than I departe the love bitwix yow two.
I yow relesse, madame, into your hond        805
Quit every serement and every bond
That ye han maad to me as heerbiforn,
Sith thilke tyme which that ye were born.
My trouthe I plighte, I shal yow never repreve
Of no biheste; and here I take my leve,        810
As to the treweste and the beste wyf
That ever yet I knew in al my lyf."
But every wyf be war of hir biheste:
On Dorigene remembreth atte leste.
Thus can a squyer doon a gentil dede        815
As well as can a knight, withouten drede.

     She thonketh him upon hir knees al bare,
And hoom unto hir housbond is she fare,
And tolde him al as ye han herd me sayd;
And be ye siker, he was so weel apayd        820
That it were inpossible me to wryte;
What sholde I lenger of this cas endyte?

     Arveragus and Dorigene his wyf
In sovereyn blisse leden forth hir lyf.
Never eft ne was ther angre hem bitwene;        825
He cherisseth hir as though she were a quene,
And she was to him trewe for evermore.
Of thise two folk ye gete of me namore.

     Aurelius, that his cost hath al forlorn,
Curseth the tyme that ever he was born:        830
"Allas," quod he, "allas that I bihighte
Of pured gold a thousand pound of wighte
Unto this philosophre! How shal I do?
I see namore but that I am fordo.
Myn heritage moot I nedes selle,        835
And been a begger; heer may I nat dwelle,
And shamen al my kinrede in this place,
But I of him may gete bettre grace.
But nathelees, I wol of him assaye
At certeyn dayes, yeer by yeer, to paye,        840
And thanke him of his grete curteisye;

than divide the love between you two.
Into your hand, madame, I release, 805
as being discharged, every oath and every bond
that you have before now made to me,
since the time when you were born.
I give you my word of honor, I shall never reprove you
about any promise; and here I take my leave 810
as of the truest and the best woman
that I ever yet knew in all my life."
But every wife should be careful of what she promises,
and remember Dorigen, at least.
Thus a squire can do a courteous deed 815
as well as a knight can, certainly.

She thanked him on her knees,
and went home to her husband,
and told him all, as you have heard me tell it;
and you can be sure he was so well pleased 820
that it would be impossible for me to describe;
why should I write of this matter any longer?
Arveragus and Dorigen his wife
led their life in sovereign bliss.
Never hereafter was there anger between them; 825
he cherished her as though she were a queen,
and she was true to him for evermore.
Of these two folks you'll get no more of me.

Aurelius, whose expenditure had been all in vain,
cursed the time that ever he was born: 830
"Alas," said he, "alas that I promised
a thousand pounds of pure gold
to this philosopher! What shall I do?
I see nothing more than that I am undone.
I must needs sell my heritage 835
and be a beggar; I can't remain here
and shame all my kindred in this place,
unless I can get more forbearance from him.
But nevertheless, I'll propose to pay him
at fixed dates, year by year, 840
and thank him for his great courtesy;

My trouthe wol I kepe, I wol nat lye."
　　With herte soor he gooth unto his cofre
And broghte gold unto this philosophre,
The value of fyve hundred pound, I gesse,　　　845
And him bisecheth, of his gentillesse,
To graunte him dayes of the remenaunt,
And seyde, "Maister, I dar wel make avaunt,
I failed never of my trouthe as yit;
For sikerly my dette shal be quit　　　　　　850
Towardes yow, however that I fare
To goon a-begged in my kirtle bare.
But wolde ye vouche-sauf, upon suretee,
Two yeer or three for to respyten me,
Thanne were I wel; for elles moot I selle　　　855
Myn heritage: ther is namore to telle."
　　This philosophre sobrely answerde,
And seyde thus, whan he thise wordes herde:
"Have I nat holden covenant unto thee?"
"Yes, certes, wel and trewely," quod he.　　　860
"Hastow nat had thy lady as thee lyketh?"
"No, no," quod he, and sorwefully he syketh.
"What was the cause? Tel me if thou can."
Aurelius his tale anon bigan,
And tolde him al, as ye han herd bifore;　　　865
It nedeth nat to yow reherce it more.
　　He seide, "Arveragus, of gentillesse,
Hadde lever dye in sorwe and in distresse
Than that his wyf were of hir trouthe fals."
The sorwe of Dorigen he tolde him als,　　　870
How looth hir was to been a wikked wyf,
And that she lever had lost that day hir lyf,
And that hir trouthe she swoor thurgh innocence:
She never erst hadde herd speke of apparence.
"That made me han of hir so greet pitee;　　　875
And right as frely as he sente hir me,
As frely sente I hir to him ageyn.
This al and som, ther is namore to seyn."
　　This philosophre answerde, "Leve brother,

I will keep my promise, I will not be false."
  With a sore heart he went to his money box
and brought gold to this philosopher,
the value of five hundred pounds, I judge,          845
and begged him, of his courtesy,
to grant him time to pay the rest,
and said, "Master, I can boast
that I never failed to keep my word as yet;
for surely my debt to you shall be          850
discharged, even if it means I must
go begging in my shirt.
But if you would grant, on security,
two or three years of respite to me,
then it would be well for me; for otherwise I must sell          855
my inheritance: there is no more to say."
  The philosopher answered seriously,
and spoke as follows, when he heard those words,
"Have I not kept my covenant with you?"
"Yes, certainly, well and truly," said Aurelius.          860
"Have you not had your lady as you wished?"
"No, no," said he, and he sighed sorrowfully.
"What was the reason? Tell me, if you can."
Aurelius then began his story,
and told him all, as you have heard before;          865
there is no need to repeat it to you.
  He said, "Arveragus, in his nobility,
would rather die in sorrow and distress
than have his wife be false to her word."
He also told him of the sorrow of Dorigen,          870
how loath she was to be a wicked wife,
and that she would rather have lost her life that day,
and that she had sworn her oath in innocence:
she had never before heard of illusions;
"That made me have such great pity on her          875
that just as freely as he sent her to me,
as freely I sent her back to him.
This is the sum of it, there is no more to say."
  "Dear brother," answered the philosopher,

Everich of yow dide gentilly til other.
Thou art a squyer, and he is a knight;
But God forbede, for his blisful might,
But if a clerk coude doon a gentil dede
As wel as any of yow, it is no drede!
   "Sire, I release thee thy thousand pound,          885
As thou right now were cropen out of the ground,
Ne never er now ne haddest knowen me.
For sire, I wol nat take a peny of thee
For al my craft, ne noght for my travaille,
Thou hast y-payed wel for my vitaille;          890
It is ynogh, and farewel, have good day."
And took his hors, and forth he gooth his way.
   Lordinges, this question thanne wol I aske now:
Which was the moste free,* as thinketh yow?
Now telleth me, er that ye ferther wende.          895
I can namore, my tale is at an ende.

"each of you acted nobly toward the other.  880
You are a squire and he is a knight;
but God in his blissful might forbid
that a clerk could not do as noble a deed
as any of you, never fear!

"Sir, I release you of your thousand pounds,  885
as if you had just crept out of the ground
and had never known me before now.
For, sir, I will not take a penny from you
for all my art, or anything for my labor.
You have paid well for my food;  890
it is enough, and farewell, I bid you good day."
and he took his horse and went off on his way.

My lords, I would now like to ask you this question:
which was the most generous, as it seems to you?
Now tell me, before you go any further.  895
I know no more, my tale is at an end.

# THE PARDONER'S TALE

# INTRODUCTION

❦

THE PARDONER'S TALE, one of Chaucer's most frequently taught tales, is about three young rioters who seek to murder Death. They are diverted from their quest by a pile of gold, but then find in that gold the death they sought. Its fast pace, dark setting, swift justice, and clear message all make it memorable. Adding to the interest in the narrative is the fascinating character of the teller, the morally confused Pardoner himself. As with all of Chaucer's tales, readers of "The Pardoner's Tale" will want to reread carefully the description of the teller in the General Prologue to *The Canterbury Tales* (lines 671–716) and try to assess the importance of various pieces of information given there: that he is a close friend and singing companion of the Summoner, that he has no beard and will never be able to grow one, and that he shows unauthentic holy relics to the men and women to whom he preaches. What does it mean that the tale of three rioters who find Death in a hoard of gold is put into the mouth of such a man?

Although it is set in Flanders, just across the English Channel to the southeast of Canterbury, "The Pardoner's Tale" could be set in any region of the world where greed rules the hearts of men. Greed, sometimes known as avarice, is after all one of the seven deadly sins, any one of which, if unconfessed and not atoned for, would take sinners straight to hell when they died. In order of seriousness, the seven deadly sins are pride, envy, anger, sloth, avarice, gluttony, and lechery.

The tale of the three rioters is of ancient origin and has many analogues. The closest to Chaucer's tale involves a hermit who finds gold but flees, knowing the dangers it involves.

In his flight he encounters others and warns them to stay
away from the gold because death awaits them there. Of
course, they ignore his warning, eagerly rush off to find it, and
then murder each other for a larger share of the gold. Chaucer's
version is distinctive in several ways. For example, in his ver-
sion we have the dark background of the bubonic plague,
mentioned in no other of the many versions. That plague, or
pestilence as Chaucer calls it in line 217, was a grim reality
in Chaucer's time. In the tale it serves as a way to motivate
the three rioters who seek to avenge the death of a friend by
charging off to find and destroy Death. A second distinctive
feature in Chaucer's tale is the old man—dark, enigmatic,
hoping Death will find him and return him to his mother
earth. This old man sends the three rioters up the crooked way
to the oak tree that shades the gold. Another change is that
Chaucer embeds the tale of the three rioters in a sermon against
avarice, drunkenness, gambling, and swearing—in other words
a sermon about the very vices that the Pardoner who gives
the sermon is admittedly or demonstrably guilty of.

The little epilogue to that sermon, in which he cheekily in-
vites the Host to buy a pardon and kiss his relics, brings
down upon the Pardoner one of the nastiest retorts in all of
literature. The closing reference to holy relics takes the Par-
doner back full circle to the false relics he brags about in the
General Prologue. He who lives by such relics shall be pun-
ished by them.

### NOTES

#### The Pardoner's Prologue

*Radix malorum est Cupiditas* (line 6). From 1 Timothy 6:10.

#### The Pardoner's Tale

**the Apostel** (67). St. Paul, mentioned six lines earlier.

**turnen substaunce into accident** (77). This reference is ap-
parently to the theological controversy as to whether the

bread and wine of the Eucharist are really turned into the body and blood of Jesus. Gluttonous drunkards, of course, would just as soon have the wine stay wine.

**"Sampsoun, Sampsoun"** (92). The reference is to Samson, known not to drink wine, but apparently Chaucer chose the name also because the *s*, *m*, and *n* sounds would have been easy to slur or speak nasally in imitation of drunken speech. Compare line 110 below.

**Lepe** (101). A town in a wine-producing region of Spain. There is apparently a reference here to the fact that the good wines of France (see line 109) were sometimes watered down with the cheaper wines of Spain. A drunk man would not know the difference.

**Fish-strete or in Chepe** (102). The names of two shopping streets in London. Chepe, probably Cheapside, is mentioned also in line 107.

**Rochel, Burdeux** (109). Towns in France known for their wines.

**Attila** (117). Attila the Hun, the brutal Asiatic leader who invaded Europe in the fifth century, was said to have died of a nosebleed the night he married a new wife.

**Lamuel** (122). A biblical king warned not to drink (see Proverbs 31:4–5) because it would pervert his sense of justice.

**Stilbon** (141). A man not definitely identified except in Chaucer's lines (following) as a philosopher who was appalled at the excess of gambling among the Corinthians. It may be a reference to the Greek philosopher Stilbo.

**Lacidomie** (143). A Spartan town not far south of Corinth, on the Peloponnesian peninsula in Greece.

**Parthes** (160). A region of northern Persia.

**Mathew** (172). See Matthew 5:34.

**Jeremye** (173). See Jeremiah 4:2.

**the seconde** (179). In the Protestant numbering of the Ten Commandments, the commandment against swearing is sometimes listed as the third.

**Hayles** (190). The abbey at Hales in Gloucestershire, England, was said to have a vial of the blood of Jesus, the blood being visible only to people with a clear conscience.

**Holy Writ** (280). See, for example, Leviticus 19:32.

**Avicen** (427). Avicenna was the eleventh-century Arabic writer of a medical treatise that had chapters on poisons.

**Seint Eleyne** (489). Helen was the woman who discovered the true cross, which is presumably meant by the Host to contrast with the false relics of the Pardoner.

# THE PARDONER

## Wordes of the Host to the Pardoner

T hou bel amy, thou Pardoner," he seyde,
  "Tel us some mirthe or japes right anon."
"It shall be doon," quod he, "by Seint Ronyon!
But first," quod he, "heer at this ale-stake
I wol both drinke and eten of a cake."                      5
  But right anon thise gentils gonne to crye,
"Nay, let him telle us of no ribaudye;
Tel us som moral thing, that we may lere
Som wit, and thanne wol we gladly here."
"I graunte, y-wis," quod he, "but I mot thinke          10
Upon som honest thing whyl that I drinke."


## The Prologe of the Pardoners Tale

L ORDINGS," quod he, "in chirches whan I preche,
  I peyne me to han an hauteyn speche
And ringe it out as round as gooth a belle,
For I can al by rote that I telle.
My theme is alwey oon, and ever was—                    5
*Radix malorum est Cupiditas.**
First I pronounce whennes that I come,
And than my bulles shewe I, alle and somme.
Our lige lordes seel on my patente,
That shewe I first, my body to warente,                   10
That no man be so bold, ne preest ne clerk,
Me to destourbe of Cristes holy werk;
And after that than telle I forth my tales,
Bulles of popes and of cardinales,

# THE PARDONER

*Words of the Host to the Pardoner*

"You pretty boy, you Pardoner," he said,
 "tell us some merry stories or jokes right now."
"It shall be done," said he, "by Saint Ronyon!
But first," he said, "I'll have a drink
and eat a cake at this alehouse sign."                        5
 But right away the gentlefolk cried out,
"No, don't let him tell us any ribaldry;
tell us some moral thing, so that we can learn
something worthwhile, and then we shall gladly listen."
"I grant it, certainly," said he, "but I must think          10
up some decent thing while I drink."


*The Prologue of the Pardoner's Tale*

"My lords," said he, "when I preach in church
 I take pains to have a haughty speech,
and ring it out as roundly as a bell,
for I know by heart all that I tell.
My theme is always the same, and ever was—                   5
*The love of money is the root of all evil.*
First I announce where I come from,
and then I show my papal bulls, each and every one.
The papal seal is on my patent—
I show that first, to safeguard my person,                   10
so that no man, priest or clerk, shall be so bold
as to hinder me from Christ's holy work;
and after that I tell my tales;
I show bulls of popes, cardinals,

Of patriarkes, and bishoppes I shewe;                    15
And in Latyn I speke a wordes fewe,
To saffron with my predicacioun,
And for to stire hem to devocioun.
Than shewe I forth my longe cristal stones,
Y-crammed ful of cloutes and of bones;                   20
Reliks been they, as wenen they echoon.
Than have I in latoun a sholder-boon
Which that was of an holy Jewes shepe.
'Good men,' seye I, 'tak of my wordes kepe;
If that this boon be wasshe in any welle,                25
If cow, or calf, or sheep, or oxe swelle
That any worm hath ete or worm y-stonge,
Tak water of that welle, and wash his tonge,
And it is hool anon; and forthermore,
Of pokkes and of scabbe and every sore                   30
Shal every sheep be hool, that of this welle
Drinketh a draughte. Tak kepe eek what I telle:
If that the good-man that the bestes oweth
Wol every wike, er that the cok him croweth,
Fastinge, drinken of this welle a draughte,              35
As thilke holy Jewe our eldres taughte,
His bestes and his stoor shal multiplye.
And, sirs, also it heleth jalousye;
For, though a man be falle in jalous rage,
Let maken with this water his potage,                    40
And never shal he more his wyf mistriste,
Though he the sooth of hir defaute wiste,
Al had she taken preestes two or three.
   "Heer is a miteyn eek that ye may see.
He that his hond wol putte in this miteyn,               45
He shal have multiplying of his greyn,
Whan he hath sowen, be it whete or otes,
So that he offre pens, or elles grotes.
   "Good men and wommen, o thing warne I yow:
If any wight be in this chirche now                      50
That hath doon sinne horrible, that he

patriarchs, and bishops;                                    15
and I speak a few words in Latin,
to give color and flavor to my preaching,
and to stir them to devotion.
Then I bring out my tall glass jars,
crammed full of rags and bones;                             20
these are relics—as they all suppose.
Then I have a shoulder bone, set in
metal, from a holy Jew's sheep.
'Good men,' say I, 'take heed of my words;
if this bone is washed in any well,                         25
and then if a cow, or calf, or sheep, or ox should swell
because of eating a snake, or being stung by one,
take water from that well, and wash its tongue,
and it shall be cured at once; and furthermore,
every sheep that drinks a draft from this well             30
shall be cured of pox and of scabs and every other
    kind of
sore. Pay attention to this also:
if the farmer who owns the beasts
will, fasting, and before the cock crows,
take a drink from this well,                                35
as this holy Jew taught our ancestors,
his beasts and his stock shall multiply.
And, sirs, it also cures jealousy;
for, though a man may have fallen into a jealous rage,
let his soup be made with this water, and then             40
he shall never more mistrust his wife,
although he may know the fact of her sin,
and even if she had taken two or three priests as lovers.
    "Here is a mitten, too, that you can see.
He who puts his hand in this mitten                         45
shall have his grain multiply
when he has sown, be it wheat or oats,
providing he offers pence or groats.
    "Good men and women, I warn you of one thing:
if there is anyone now in this church                       50
who has committed a sin so horrible that he

Dar nat, for shame, of it y-shriven be,
Or any womman, be she yong or old,
That hath y-maad hir housbond cokewold,
Swich folk shul have no power ne no grace 55
To offren to my reliks in this place.
And who-so findeth him out of swich blame,
He wol com up and offre in goddes name,
And I assoille him by the auctoritee
Which that by bulle y-graunted was to me. 60
    "By this gaude have I wonne, yeer by yeer,
An hundred mark sith I was Pardoner.
I stonde lyk a clerk in my pulpet,
And whan the lewed peple is doun y-set,
I preche, so as ye han herd bifore, 65
And telle an hundred false japes more.
Than peyne I me to strecche forth the nekke,
And est and west upon the peple I bekke,
As doth a dowve sitting on a berne.
Myn hondes and my tonge goon so yerne 70
That it is joye to see my bisinesse.
Of avaryce and of swich cursednesse
Is al my preching, for to make hem free
To yeve her pens, and namely unto me;
For my entente is nat but for to winne, 75
And no thing for correccioun of sinne.
I rekke never, whan that they ben beried,
Though that her soules goon a-blakeberied!
For certes, many a predicacioun
Comth ofte tyme of yvel entencioun; 80
Som for plesaunce of folk and flaterye,
To been avaunced by ipocrisye,
And som for veyne glorie, and som for hate.
For, whan I dar non other weyes debate,
Than wol I stinge him with my tonge smerte 85
In preching, so that he shal nat asterte
To been defamed falsly, if that he
Hath trespased to my brethren or to me.
For, though I telle noght his propre name,

dare not, for shame, be shriven of it,
or any woman, be she young or old,
who has made her husband a cuckold,
such folk shall have no power or grace 55
to make an offering to my relics here.
But whoever finds himself free from such faults
will come up and make an offering in God's name,
and I absolve him by the authority
which was granted to me by this bull.' 60
    "By this trick I have won, year after year,
a hundred marks since I became a pardoner.
I stand like a learned man in my pulpit,
and when the ignorant people have sat down,
I preach, as you have just heard, 65
and tell a hundred other falsehoods.
Then I take pains to stretch out my neck
and nod east and west at the people,
like a dove sitting on a barn.
My hands and my tongue go so fast 70
that it is a joy to see my busy activity.
All my preaching is about avarice
and such cursed sins, in order to make them
give freely of their pennies—namely, to me;
for my intention is to win money, 75
not at all to cast out sins.
I don't care, when they are buried,
if their souls go a-blackberrying!
Certainly, many a sermon
proceeds from an evil intention; 80
some are intended to please and flatter folk,
to gain advancement through hypocrisy,
and some are for vanity, and some for hate.
For when I do not dare to argue any other way,
then I will sting my opponent smartly with my tongue 85
in preaching, so that he can't escape
being falsely defamed, if he
has offended my brethren or me.
For, though I don't tell his proper name,

Men shal wel knowe that it is the same                              90
By signes and by othere circumstances.
Thus quyte I folk that doon us displesances;
Thus spitte I out my venim under hewe
Of holynesse, to seme holy and trewe.

"But shortly myn entente I wol devyse:                              95
I preche of no thing but for coveityse.
Therfor my theme is yet, and ever was
*Radix malorum est cupiditas.*
Thus can I preche agayn that same vyce
Which that I use, and that is avaryce.                             100
But, though myself be gilty in that sinne,
Yet can I maken other folk to twinne
From avaryce, and sore to repente.
But that is nat my principal entente.
I preche no thing but for coveityse;                              105
Of this matere it oughte ynogh suffyse.

"Than telle I hem ensamples many oon
Of olde stories, longe tyme agoon:
For lewed peple loven tales olde;
Swich thinges can they wel reporte and holde.                     110
What, trowe ye, that whyles I may preche,
And winne gold and silver for I teche,
That I wol live in povert wilfully?
Nay, nay, I thoghte it never trewely!
For I wol preche and begge in sondry londes;                      115
I wol not do no labour with myn hondes,
Ne make baskettes and live thereby,
Because I wol nat beggen ydelly.
I wol non of the apostles counterfete;
I wol have money, wolle, chese, and whete,                        120
Al were it yeven of the povrest page,
Or of the povrest widwe in a village,
Al sholde hir children sterve for famyne.
Nay! I wol drinke licour of the vyne
And have a joly wenche in every toun.                             125
But herkneth, lordings, in conclusioun;
Your lyking is that I shall telle a tale.

people will easily know it is he 90
by signs and other circumstances.
Thus I repay folk that displease us;
thus I spit out my venom under the color
of holiness, to seem holy and true.

"But I shall explain my intention briefly: 95
I preach for no cause but covetousness.
Therefore my theme is still, and ever was,
*The love of money is the root of all evil.*
Thus I can preach against the same vice
which I practice, and that is avarice. 100
But, though I myself am guilty of that sin,
yet I can make other folk turn
from avarice, and repent sorely.
But that is not my principal intention.
I preach for no reason except covetousness; 105
but that ought to be enough of this matter.

"Then I give them many instances
from old stories of long ago:
for ignorant people love old tales;
such things they can easily repeat and remember. 110
What! Do you think that while I can preach
and win gold and silver for my teaching,
that I will intentionally live in poverty?
No, no, I certainly never considered that!
For I will preach and beg in various lands; 115
I will not labor with my hands,
or live by making baskets
in order to keep from being an idle beggar.
I don't want to imitate any of the apostles;
I want to have money, wool, cheese, and wheat, 120
even if it is given by the poorest page,
or the poorest widow in a village,
although her children die of starvation.
No! I will drink liquor of the vine
and have a jolly wench in every town. 125
But listen, my lords, in conclusion;
your wish is for me to tell a tale.

Now have I dronke a draughte of corny ale,
By God, I hope I shal yow telle a thing
That shal, by resoun, been at your lyking.        130
For, though myself be a ful vicious man,
A moral tale yet I yow telle can,
Which I am wont to preche, for to winne.
Now holde your pees, my tale I wol beginne."

*Here biginneth the Pardoners Tale*

I n Flaundres whylom was a companye
  Of yonge folk that haunteden folye,
As ryot, hasard, stewes, and tavernes,
Whereas, with harpes, lutes, and giternes,
They daunce and pleye at dees bothe day and night,        5
And ete also and drinken over hir might,
Thurgh which they doon the devel sacrifyse
Within that develes temple, in cursed wyse,
By superfluitee abhominable;
Hir othes been so grete and so dampnable        10
That it is grisly for to here hem swere:
Our blissed Lordes body they to-tere—
Hem thoughte Jewes rente him noght y-nough.
And ech of hem at otheres sinne lough.
And right anon than comen tombesteres        15
Fetys and smale, and yonge fruytesteres,
Singers with harpes, baudes, wafereres,
Whiche been the verray develes officeres
To kindle and blowe the fyr of lecherye
That is annexed unto glotonye;        20
The Holy Writ take I to my witnesse
That luxurie is in wyn and dronkenesse.
    Lo, how that dronken Lot unkindely
Lay by his doghtres two, unwitingly;
So dronke he was, he niste what he wroghte.        25
    Herodes, who-so wel the stories soghte,
Whan he of wyn was replet at his feste,

Now that I have had a drink of strong ale,
by God, I hope that I shall tell you something
that shall, with good reason, be to your liking.          130
For although I am myself a very vicious man,
yet I can tell you a moral tale,
which I am accustomed to preach for profit.
Now hold your peace, I will begin my tale."

*Here begins the Pardoner's Tale*

In Flanders once there was a company
of young folk, who devoted themselves to such
          follies
as riotous living, gambling, brothels, and taverns,
where, with harps, lutes, and guitars
they danced and played at dice day and night,          5
and also ate and drank more than they could handle;
and thus they offered sacrifices to the devil
within the devil's temple, in a cursed manner,
through abominable overindulgence;
their oaths were so great and so damnable          10
that it was grisly to hear them swear:
they tore our blessed Lord's body to pieces—
it seemed to them that the Jews had not torn him enough.
And each of them laughed at the others' sins.
And then would come dancing girls,          15
graceful and dainty, and young girls selling fruit,
singers with harps, bawds, girls with cakes—
all truly the devil's agents
to kindle and blow the fire of lechery
that is closely attached to gluttony;          20
I take Holy Writ to my witness
that lechery comes from wine and drunkenness.
    Look how drunken Lot unnaturally
lay by his two daughters unwittingly;
he was so drunk he didn't know what he was doing.          25
    Herod (as anyone who has read the story knows),
when he was full of wine at his feast,

Right at his owene table he yaf his heste
To sleen the Baptist John ful giltelees.
    Senek seith eek a good word doutelees:    30
He seith he can no difference finde
Bitwix a man that is out of his minde
And a man which that is dronkelewe,
But that woodnesse, y-fallen in a shrewe,
Persevereth lenger than doth dronkenesse.    35
O glotonye, ful of cursednesse!
O cause first of our confusioun!
O original of our dampnacioun,
Til Crist had boght us with his blood agayn!
Lo, how dere, shortly for to sayn,    40
Aboght was thilke cursed vileinye:
Corrupt was al this world for glotonye!
    Adam our fader, and his wyf also,
Fro Paradys to labour and to wo
Were driven for that vyce, it is no drede;    45
For whyl that Adam fasted, as I rede,
He was in Paradys; and whan that he
Eet of the fruyt defended on the tree,
Anon he was out cast to wo and peyne.
O glotonye, on thee wel oghte us pleyne!    50
O, wiste a man how many maladyes
Folwen of excesse and of glotonyes,
He wolde been the more mesurable
Of his diete, sittinge at his table.
Allas! The shorte throte, the tendre mouth,    55
Maketh that Est and West, and North and South,
In erthe, in eir, in water men to swinke
To gete a glotoun deyntee mete and drinke!
Of this matere, O Paul, wel canstow trete:
"Mete unto wombe, and wombe eek unto mete,    60
Shal God destroyen bothe," as Paulus seith.
Allas, a foul thing is it, by my feith,
To seye this word, and fouler is the dede,

right at his own table, gave his order
to slay John the Baptist, who was entirely guiltless.
　　Seneca, too, undoubtedly has a good saying:　　　　30
he states that he can find no difference
between a man who is out of his mind
and one who is drunk,
except that madness, occuring in an ill-natured man,
lasts longer than drunkenness does.　　　　35
O gluttony, full of cursedness!
O first cause of our ruin!
O origin of our damnation,
until Christ had redeemed us with his blood!
Lo, how dearly, to sum up,　　　　40
was this cursed villainy paid for;
this whole world was corrupted through gluttony.
　　Adam our father, and his wife, too,
were driven from Paradise to labor and woe
because of that vice—there is no doubt about it;　　　　45
for while Adam fasted, as I read,
he was in Paradise; and when he
ate of the forbidden fruit on the tree,
he was at once cast out to woe and pain.
O gluttony, we certainly ought to complain
　　against you!　　　　50
Oh, if a man knew how many maladies
follow from excess and gluttony,
he would be more temperate
in his diet when he sits at his table.
Alas! The short throat, the sensitive mouth,　　　　55
make men labor east and west and north
and south, in earth, in air, and in water,
to get a glutton dainty food and drink.
Of this matter, Paul, well can you treat:
"Meats for the belly, and the belly for meats:　　　　60
but God shall destroy both it and them," as
　　Saint Paul says.
Alas, it is a foul thing, by my faith,
to say this word, and the deed is fouler,

Whan man so drinketh of the whyte and rede
That of his throte he maketh his privee          65
Thurgh thilke cursed superfluitee.
　　The Apostel* weping seith ful pitously,
"Ther walken many of which yow told have I,
I seye it now weping with pitous voys,
That they been enemys of Cristes croys,          70
Of whiche the ende is deeth, wombe is her god."
O wombe! O bely! O stinking cod,
Fulfild of donge and of corupcioun!
At either ende of thee foul is the soun.
How greet labour and cost is thee to finde!      75
Thise cokes, how they stampe, and streyne, and grinde,
And turnen substaunce into accident,*
To fulfille al thy likerous talent!
Out of the harde bones knokke they
The mary, for they caste noght awey              80
That may go thurgh the golet softe and swote;
Of spicerye, of leef, and bark, and rote
Shal been his sauce y-maked by delyt,
To make him yet a newer appetyt.
But certes, he that haunteth swich delyces       85
Is deed whyl that he liveth in tho vyces.
　　A lecherous thing is wyn, and dronkenesse
Is ful of stryving and of wrecchednesse.
O dronke man, disfigured is thy face,
Sour is thy breeth, foul artow to embrace,       90
And thurgh thy dronke nose semeth the soun
As though thou seydest ay "Sampsoun, Sampsoun";*
And yet, God wot, Sampsoun drank never no wyn.
Thou fallest as it were a stiked swyn;
Thy tonge is lost, and al thyn honest cure;      95
For dronkenesse is verray sepulture
Of mannes wit and his discrecioun.
In whom that drinke hath dominacioun,
He can no conseil kepe, it is no drede.
Now kepe yow fro the whyte and fro the rede,     100

when a man so drinks of white and red wine
that he makes his throat into his privy                          65
through this cursed overindulgence.
    The Apostle says, weeping piteously,
"For many walk, of whom I have told you often,
and now tell you even weeping,
that they are the enemies of the cross of Christ:               70
whose end is destruction, whose God is their belly."
O stomach! O belly! O stinking bag,
filled with dung and corruption!
At either end of you the sound is foul.
How much labor and cost it takes to provide for you!           75
These cooks, how they pound, and strain, and grind,
and turn substance into accident,
to please your gluttonous appetite!
They knock the marrow out of the hard bones,
for they throw away nothing                                     80
that may go softly and sweetly through the gullet;
with spices, of leaf and bark and root,
his sauces shall be made for deliciousness,
to whet a yet keener appetite.
But certainly, he who is accustomed to such delicacies         85
is dead while he lives in those vices.
    Wine is a lecherous thing, and drunkenness
is full of quarreling and wretchedness.
O drunken man, your face is disfigured,
your breath is sour, you are foul to embrace,                  90
and through your drunken nose a sound seems
    to come
as if you were always saying "Samson, Samson";
and yet, God knows, Samson never drank any wine.
You fall as if you were a stuck pig;
your tongue is lost, and all your self-respect;               95
for drunkenness is truly the tomb
of man's wit and discretion.
When drink dominates a man,
he cannot keep secrets—no fear that he can!
Now guard yourself against the white and the red,            100

And namely fro the whyte wyn of Lepe*
That is to selle in Fish-strete or in Chepe;*
This wyn of Spayne crepeth subtilly
In othere wynes, growing faste by,
Of which ther ryseth swich fumositee                    105
That whan a man hath dronken draughtes three,
And weneth that he be at hoom in Chepe,
He is in Spayne, right at the toune of Lepe,
Nat at the Rochel,* ne at Burdeux* toun;
And thanne wol he seye, "Sampsoun, Sampsoun."          110

But herkneth, lordings, a word, I yow preye,
That alle the sovereyn actes, dar I seye,
Of victories in the Olde Testament
Thurgh verray God, that is omnipotent,
Were doon in abstinence and in preyere;                 115
Loketh the Bible and ther ye may it lere.

Loke, Attila,* the grete conquerour,
Deyde in his sleep, with shame and dishonour,
Bledinge ay at his nose in dronkenesse;
A capitayn shoulde live in sobrenesse.                  120
And over al this, avyseth yow right wel
What was comaunded unto Lamuel*—
Nat Samuel, but Lamuel, seye I—
Redeth the Bible, and finde it expresly
Of wyn-yeving to hem that han justyse.                  125
Namore of this, for it may wel suffyse.

And now that I have spoke of glotonye,
Now wol I yow defenden hasardrye.
Hasard is verray moder of lesinges,
And of deceite, and cursed forsweringes,                130
Blaspheme of Crist, manslaughtre, and wast also
Of catel and of tyme; and forthermo,
It is repreve and contrarie of honour
For to ben holde a commune hasardour.
And ever the hyer he is of estaat,                      135

and particularly against the white wine of Lepe
that is sold in Fishstreet and Cheapside;
this wine of Spain creeps subtly
into other wines, growing nearby,
from which there then rise such heady fumes        105
that when a man has taken three drinks,
and thinks he is at home in Cheapside,
he is in Spain, right at the town of Lepe,
not at La Rochelle nor at Bordeaux;
and then he will say, "Samson, Samson."             110
    But listen, my lords, to one fact, I pray:
that all the great actions, I may say,
in the victories of the Old Testament,
by the true God, who is omnipotent,
were performed in abstinence and prayer;           115
look in the Bible, and you can learn it there.
    Look how Attila, the great conquerer,
died in his sleep, shamefully and dishonorably,
bleeding from his nose in drunkenness;
a captain should live soberly.                      120
And besides this, consider well
what Lemuel was told—
not Samuel, but Lemuel, I mean—
read the Bible, and find what is expressly
stated about serving wine to those who administer
    justice.                                        125
No more of this, for what has been said should
    be enough.
    And now that I have spoken of gluttony,
next I shall warn you against gambling.
Gambling is the very mother of lies,
and of deceit, and of cursed perjuries,            130
of blasphemy of Christ, of manslaughter, and also
    of waste
of property and time; and furthermore,
it is a reproof and a dishonor
to be considered a common gambler.
The higher such a man may be in rank,              135

The more is he holden desolaat.
If that a prince useth hasardrye,
In alle governaunce and policye
He is, as by commune opinioun,
Y-holde the lasse in reputacioun.                            140
  Stilbon,* that was a wys embassadour,
Was sent to Corinthe, in ful greet honour,
Fro Lacidomie,* to make hir alliaunce.
And whan he cam, him happede, par chaunce,
That alle the grettest that were of that lond,         145
Pleyinge atte hasard he hem fond.
For which, as sone as it mighte be,
He stal him hoom agayn to his contree,
And seyde, "Ther wol I nat lese my name;
Ne I wol nat take on me so greet defame              150
Yow for to allye unto none hasardours.
Sendeth othere wyse embassadours;
For, by my trouthe, me were lever dye
Than I yow sholde to hasardours allye.
For ye that been so glorious in honours            155
Shul nat allyen yow with hasardours
As by my wil, ne as by my tretee."
This wyse philosophre thus seyde he.
  Loke eek that to the king Demetrius
The king of Parthes,* as the book seith us,         160
Sente him a paire of dees of gold in scorn,
For he hadde used hasard therbiforn;
For which he heeld his glorie or his renoun
At no value or reputacioun.
Lordes may finden other maner pley                      165
Honeste ynogh to dryve the day awey.
  Now wol I speke of othes false and grete
A word or two, as olde bokes trete.
Gret swering is a thing abhominable,
And false swering is yet more reprevable.             170
The heighe God forbad swering at al,
Witnesse on Mathew;* but in special

the more abandoned he is held to be.
If a prince gambles,
in all matters of rule and policy
he is, by general opinion,
the less esteemed.                                                       140
   Stillbon, who was a wise ambassador,
was sent in great pomp to Corinth
from Sparta, to make an alliance between them.
When he arrived, it happened by chance
that he found all the greatest men                                       145
of the land gambling.
For this reason, as soon as possible
he stole home again to his country,
and said, "I don't want to lose my good name there;
nor will I take upon myself such a great dishonor                        150
as to ally you with gamblers.
Send other wise ambassadors;
for I swear I would rather die
than ally you with gamblers.
For you who are so famous for your honors                                155
shall not be allied with gamblers
by my will, or by my treaty."
Thus said this wise philosopher.
   Look, too, how the King of the Parthians,
as the book tells us, sent in scorn                                      160
to King Demetrius a pair of golden dice,
because he had practiced gambling before;
therefore the Parthian held Demetrius's glory and renown
as of no value or repute.
Lords may find other kinds of amusement                                  165
decent enough to while away the day.
   Now I will speak a word or two of
false and strong oaths, as ancient books treat of
      the subject.
Hard swearing is an abominable thing,
and false swearing is more reprehensible yet.                            170
High God forbade swearing entirely—
witness Saint Matthew; and, in particular,

Of swering seith the holy Jeremye,*
"Thou shalt swere sooth thyn othes, and nat lye,
And swere in dome and eek in rightwisnesse"; 175
But ydel swering is a cursednesse.
Bihold and see that in the firste table
Of heighe Goddes hestes honurable
How that the seconde* heste of him is this—
"Tak nat my name in ydel or amis." 180
Lo, rather he forbedeth swich swering
Than homicyde or many a cursed thing;
I seye that, as by ordre, thus it stondeth;
This knowen that his hestes understondeth,
How that the second heste of God is that. 185
And forther over, I wol thee telle al plat
That vengeance shal nat parten from his hous
That of his othes is to outrageous.
By Goddes precious herte, and by his nayles,
And by the blode of Crist, that is in Hayles,* 190
Seven is my chaunce, and thyn is cink and treye;
By Goddes armes, if thou falsly pleye,
This dagger shal thurghout thyn herte go—
This fruyt cometh of the bicched bones two:
Forswering, ire, falsenesse, homicyde. 195
Now, for the love of Crist that for us dyde,
Lete your othes, bothe grete and smale;
But, sirs, now wol I telle forth my tale.


Thise ryotoures three, of whiche I telle,
Longe erst er pryme rong of any belle, 200
Were set hem in a taverne for to drinke;
And as they satte, they herde a belle clinke
Biforn a cors, was caried to his grave;
That oon of hem gan callen to his knave:
"Go bet," quod he, "and axe redily, 205
What cors is this that passeth heer forby;
And look that thou reporte his name wel."

the holy Jeremiah says of swearing,
"And thou shalt swear
in truth, in judgment, and in righteousness";          175
but idle swearing is a sin.
Behold, and see that in the first table
of high God's honorable commandments,
the second of the commandments is this—
"Thou shalt not take the name of the Lord thy God
    in vain."          180
Lo, he forbids such swearing before
homicide or many another cursed sin;
I tell you that it stands in this order;
anyone who understands his commandments knows
that this is the second commandment of God.          185
And furthermore, I will tell you flat
that vengeance shall not forsake the house
of the man who is outrageous in his oaths.
"By God's precious heart, and by his nails,
and by the blood of Christ that is at Hayles,          190
seven is my chance, and yours is five and three;
by God's arms, if you cheat
this dagger shall go through your heart"—
this fruit comes of the two cursed dice:
perjury, ire, falsehood, homicide.          195
Now, for the love of Christ who died for us,
leave off your oaths, both great and small;
but, sirs, now I will tell forth my tale.


THESE three rakes I am telling about,
long before any bell had rung for morning service,          200
had sat themselves in a tavern to drink;
and as they sat, they heard a bell clink
before a corpse that was being carried to its grave;
one of them called to his serving boy:
"Go quickly," said he, "and ask at once          205
whose corpse this is that passes by here;
and look to it that you report his name correctly."

"Sir," quod this boy, "it nedeth never-a-del.
It was me told, er ye cam heer, two houres;
He was, pardee, an old felawe of youres,                   210
And sodeynly he was y-slayn tonight,
Fordronke, as he sat on his bench upright;
Ther cam a privee theef men clepeth Deeth,
That in this contree al the peple sleeth,
And with his spere he smoot his herte a-two,              215
And wente his wey withouten wordes mo.
He hath a thousand slayn this pestilence:
And, maister, er ye come in his presence,
Me thinketh that it were necessarie
For to be war of swich an adversarie;                     220
Beth redy for to mete him evermore.
Thus taughte me my dame, I sey namore."
      "By Seinte Marie," seyde this taverner,
"The child seith sooth, for he hath slayn this yeer,
Henne over a myle, within a greet village,               225
Both man and womman, child and hyne, and page.
I trowe his habitacioun be there;
To been avysed greet wisdom it were,
Er that he dide a man a dishonour."
      "Ye, Goddes armes," quod this ryotour,              230
"Is it swich peril with him for to mete?
I shal him seke by wey and eek by strete,
I make avow to Goddes digne bones!
Herkneth, felawes, we three been al ones;
Lat ech of us holde up his hond til other,               235
And ech of us bicomen otheres brother,
And we wol sleen this false traytour Deeth;
He shal be slayn, which that so many sleeth,
By Goddes dignitee, er it be night."
      Togidres han thise three hir trouthes plight        240
To live and dyen ech of hem for other,
As though he were his owene y-boren brother.
And up they sterte al dronken, in this rage,
And forth they goon towardes that village
Of which the taverner had spoke biforn,                  245

"Sir," said the boy, "there is no need at all for that.
It was told to me two hours before you came here.
He was, indeed, an old companion of yours,                          210
and last night he was suddenly slain,
as he sat upright on his bench, very drunk;
there came a stealthy thief men call Death,
who slays all the people in this country,
and with his spear he smote the man's heart in two,                 215
and went on his way without a word.
He has slain a thousand during this pestilence:
and, master, before you come in his presence,
it seems to me it is necessary
to be wary of such an adversary;                                    220
always be ready to meet him.
Thus my mother taught me, I say no more."

"By Saint Mary," said the tavern keeper,
"The child tells the truth, for this year Death has slain
both man and woman, child and laborer, and page,                    225
in a large village over a mile hence.
I believe he must live there;
it would be wise to be wary,
before he does harm to you."

"Yea, by God's arms," said the rake,                                230
"Is it so dangerous to meet him?
I shall seek him in the highways and byways,
I vow by God's worthy bones!
Listen, comrades, we three are all of one mind;
let each of us hold up his hand to the other two,                   235
and each of us become the others' brother,
and we will slay this false traitor Death;
he shall be slain, who slays so many,
on God's honor, before night falls."

Together these three pledged their word of honor                    240
to live and die each for the other,
as though each were the other's own brother born.
And up they jumped in their drunken rage,
and went forth toward that village
that the taverner had spoken of before;                             245

And many a grisly ooth than han they sworn,
And Cristes blessed body they to-rente—
Deeth shal be deed, if that they may him hente.
  Whan they han goon nat fully half a myle,
Right as they wolde han troden over a style,                    250
An old man and a povre with hem mette.
This olde man ful mekely hem grette,
And seyde thus: "Now, lordes, God yow see!"
  The proudest of thise ryotoures three
Answerde agayn, "What, carl, with sory grace,          255
Why artow al forwrapped save thy face?
Why livestow so longe in so greet age?"
  This olde man gan loke in his visage,
And seyde thus: "For I ne can nat finde
A man, though that I walked into Inde,                           260
Neither in citee nor in no village,
That wolde chaunge his youthe for myn age;
And therfore moot I han myn age stille,
As longe time as it is Goddes wille.
Ne Deeth, allas, ne wol nat han my lyf;                          265
Thus walke I, lyk a restelees caityf,
And on the ground, which is my modres gate,
I knokke with my staf, bothe erly and late,
And seye, 'Leve moder, leet me in!
Lo, how I vanish, flesh, and blood, and skin!                   270
Allas, whan shul my bones been at reste?
Moder, with yow wolde I chaunge my cheste,
That in my chambre longe tyme hath be,
Ye, for an heyre clout to wrappe me!'
But yet to me she wol nat do that grace,                        275
For which ful pale and welked is my face.
But, sirs, to yow it is no curteisye
To speken to an old man vileinye,
But he trespasse in worde, or elles in dede.
In Holy Writ* ye may your-self wel rede,                        280
'Agayns an old man, hoor upon his heed,
Ye sholde aryse'; wherfor I yeve yow reed,
Ne dooth unto an old man noon harm now,

many a grisly oath they then swore,
and they tore Christ's blessed body to pieces—
Death shall be dead, if they can catch him.
    When they had gone not quite half a mile,
just as they were about to step over a stile,                    250
a poor old man met them.
This old man greeted them meekly,
and said, "Now, lords, God protect you."
    The proudest of these three rakes
answered, "What, fellow, may evil come to you!                    255
Why are you all wrapped up except for your face?
Why do you live so long, in such old age?"
    The old man looked into his face
and said, "Because even if I walked to India
I could not find a man,                                            260
either in city or in village,
who would exchange his youth for my age;
and therefore I must still keep my age
for as long as it is God's will.
Nor, alas, will Death take my life;                               265
so I walk like a restless prisoner,
and on the ground, which is my mother's gate,
I knock with my staff, both early and late,
and say, 'Dear mother, let me in!
Lo, how I fade away, flesh and blood and skin!                    270
Alas, when shall my bones be at rest?
Mother, I would gladly exchange my chest,
which has been in my chamber such a long time,
for a haircloth winding sheet to wrap myself in!'
But still she will not do me that favor,                          275
and that is why my face is pale and withered.
But, sirs, it is not courteous of you
to speak rudely to an old man,
unless he injures you by word or deed.
You can read for yourself in Holy Writ,                           280
'Thou shalt rise up before
the hoary head'; therefore I advise you,
do not do harm to an old man now

Namore than ye wolde men dide to yow
In age, if that ye so longe abyde;                               285
And God be with yow, wher ye go or ryde.
I moot go thider as I have to go."
     "Nay, olde cherl, by God, thou shalt nat so,"
Seyde this other hasardour anon;
"Thou partest nat so lightly, by Seint John!               290
Thou spak right now of thilke traitour Deeth,
That in this contree alle our frendes sleeth.
Have heer my trouthe, as thou art his aspye,
Tel wher he is, or thou shalt it abye,
By God, and by the holy sacrament!                         295
For soothly thou art oon of his assent
To sleen us yonge folk, thou false theef!"
     "Now, sirs," quod he, "if that yow be so leef
To finde Deeth, turne up this croked wey,
For in that grove I lafte him, by my fey,                   300
Under a tree, and ther he wol abyde;
Nat for your boost he wol him no thing hyde.
See ye that ook? Right ther ye shul him finde.
God save yow, that boghte agayn mankinde,
And yow amende!"—thus seyde this olde man.            305
     And everich of thise ryotoures ran
Til he cam to that tree, and ther they founde
Of florins fyne of golde y-coyned rounde
Wel ny an eighte busshels, as hem thoughte.
No lenger thanne after Deeth they soughte,              310
But ech of hem so glad was of that sighte,
For that the florins been so faire and brighte,
That doun they sette hem by this precious hord.
The worste of hem he spake the firste word.
     "Brethren," quod he, "tak kepe what I seye;          315
My wit is greet, though that I bourde and pleye.
This tresor hath fortune unto us yiven
In mirthe and jolitee our lyf to liven,
And lightly as it comth, so wol we spende.
Ey, Goddes precious dignitee, who wende                 320
Today that we sholde han so fair a grace?

any more than you would wish others to do to you
in old age, if you live until then;                                      285
and God be with you, wherever you walk or ride.
I must go where I have to go."

"No, old rogue, by God you shall not,"
said another of the gamblers then;
"You aren't going to get away so easily, by Saint John!   290
You spoke just now of this traitor Death,
who slays all our friends in this country.
Take my promise: since you are his spy,
you had better tell where he is, or you shall pay for it,
by God and by the holy sacrament!                          295
For truly you are one of his party, agreed
to slay us young folk, you false thief!"

"Well, sirs," he answered, "if you are so eager
to find Death, turn up this crooked path,
for by my faith I left him in that grove,                          300
under a tree, and there he will stay;
your boasting won't make him hide himself at all.
Do you see that oak? You shall find him right there.
May God, who redeemed mankind, save
and amend you!" Thus said the old man.                          305

And every one of the rakes ran
until he came to that tree; and there they found
almost eight bushels, it seemed,
of fine round florins coined of gold.
Then they did not seek for Death any longer;                          310
each of them was so glad at the sight,
since the florins were so fair and bright,
that they sat themselves down by this precious hoard.
The worst of them spoke first.

"Brothers," he said, "pay attention to what I say;      315
my wits are keen, although I joke and fool.
Fortune has given us this treasure
so that we can live our life in mirth and jollity,
and lightly as it came, so will we spend it
Eh, God's honor! Who would have guessed                          320
that we should have such good luck today?

But mighte this gold be caried fro this place
Hoom to myn hous, or elles unto youres—
For wel ye woot that al this gold is oures—
Than were we in heigh felicitee.
But trewely, by daye it may nat be; 325
Men wolde seyn that we were theves stronge,
And for our owene tresor doon us honge.
This tresor moste y-caried be by nighte,
As wysly and as slyly as it mighte.
Wherfore I rede that cut among us alle 330
Be drawe, and lat see wher the cut wol falle;
And he that hath the cut, with herte blythe
Shal renne to the toune, and that ful swythe,
And bringe us breed and wyn ful prively.
And two of us shul kepen subtilly 335
This tresor wel; and, if he wol nat tarie,
Whan it is night, we wol this tresor carie
By oon assent whereas us thinketh best."

   That oon of hem the cut broughte in his fest, 340
And bad hem drawe, and loke wher it wol falle;
And it fil on the yongeste of hem alle;
And forth toward the toun he wente anon.
And also sone as that he was gon,
That oon of hem spak thus unto that other: 345
"Thou knowest wel thou art my sworne brother;
Thy profit wol I telle thee anon.
Thou woost wel that our felawe is agon;
And heer is gold, and that ful greet plentee,
That shal departed been among us three. 350
But natheles, if I can shape it so
That it departed were among us two,
Hadde I nat doon a freendes torn to thee?"

   That other answerde, "I noot how that may be;
He woot how that the gold is with us tweye. 355
What shal we doon? What shal we to him seye?"

   "Shal it be conseil?" seyde the firste shrewe;
"And I shal tellen thee, in wordes fewe,

But if this gold could be carried from this place
home to my house, or else to yours—
for you know, of course, that all this gold is ours—
then we should be happy as can be.                          325
But, certainly, it cannot be done by day;
people would say that we were bold thieves,
and hang us for our own treasure.
This treasure must be carried by night,
as cunningly and slyly as possible.                         330
Therefore I suggest that we all draw
lots, and see where the lot will fall;
and he whose lot it is shall cheerfully
and quickly run to the town,
and secretly bring us bread and wine.                       335
Two of us shall craftily guard
this treasure well; and, if he does not tarry,
we will carry this treasure when it is night
wherever we all agree is best."

The speaker brought the straws in his fist,         340
and told them to draw, and see where the lot
      would fall;
it fell to the youngest of them all,
and he went off toward the town at once.
As soon as he was gone,
the one spoke thus to the other:                            345
"You know well you are my sworn brother;
I am about to tell you something to your advantage.
You know that our companion is gone;
and here is gold—a great deal of it—
that is to be divided among us three.                       350
Nevertheless, if I could manage it so
that it was divided among us two,
wouldn't I have done you a friendly turn?"

The other answered, "I don't know how that can be;
he knows that the gold is with us two.                      355
What shall we do? What shall we say to him?"

"Will you keep a secret?" said the first villain;
"If so, I shall tell you, in a few words,

What we shal doon, and bringe it wel aboute."

    "I graunte," quod that other, "out of doute,    360
That, by my trouthe, I wol thee nat biwreye."

    "Now," quod the firste, "thou woost wel we be tweye,
And two of us shul strenger be than oon.
Look whan that he is set, that right anoon
Arys as though thou woldest with him pleye;    365
And I shal ryve him thurgh the sydes tweye
Whyl that thou strogelest with him as in game,
And with thy dagger look thou do the same;
And than shal al this gold departed be,
My dere freend, bitwixen me and thee;    370
Than may we bothe our lustes al fulfille,
And pleye at dees right at our owene wille."
And thus acorded been thise shrewes tweye
To sleen the thridde, as ye han herd me seye.

    This yongest, which that wente unto the toun,    375
Ful ofte in herte he rolleth up and doun
The beautee of thise florins newe and brighte.
"O Lord!" quod he, "If so were that I mighte
Have al this tresor to myself allone,
Ther is no man that liveth under the trone    380
Of God that sholde live so mery as I!"
And atte laste the feend, our enemy,
Putte in his thought that he shold poyson beye,
With which he mighte sleen his felawes tweye—
For why the feend fond him in swich lyvinge,    385
That he had leve him to sorwe bringe;
For this was outrely his fulle entente,
To sleen hem bothe, and never to repente.
And forth he gooth, no lenger wolde he tarie,
Into the toun, unto a pothecarie,    390
And preyed him, that he him wolde selle
Som poyson, that he mighte his rattes quelle;
And eek ther was a polcat in his hawe,
That, as he seyde, his capouns hadde y-slawe,
And fayn he wolde wreke him, if he mighte,    395

what we shall do, and bring it off safely."

"I promise," said the other, "you needn't doubt,                360
that, on my word, I will not betray you."

"Now," said the first, "you know well we are two,
and two of us will be stronger than one.
Watch for when he sits down; right away
get up, as if you wanted to play a prank on him;                365
and I shall stab him through from one side to the other
while you struggle with him as if in fun,
and with your dagger see to it that you do the same;
then, my dear friend, all this gold shall be
divided between you and me;                                      370
then we may both satisfy all our desires
and play at dice just as we wish."
And thus these two villains agreed
to slay the third, as you have heard me say.

The youngest, who was going to the town,                         375
kept revolving in his heart
the beauty of the bright, new florins.
"Oh Lord!" he said, "If only I might
have all this treasure to myself alone,
there is no man living beneath the throne                        380
of God who would live as merrily as I!"
And at last, the fiend, our enemy,
put it in his thoughts that he should buy poison
with which he might slay his two comrades—
since the fiend found his manner of living such                  385
that he had leave to bring him to sorrow;
for this was plainly the youth's full intention,
to slay them both, and never to repent.
And on he went, he would tarry no longer,
into the town, to an apothecary,                                 390
and entreated the man to sell him
some poison, so that he might kill his rats;
and also, he said, there was a polecat
in his yard that had slain his capons,
and he wanted to revenge himself, if he could,                   395

On vermin, that destroyed him by nighte.
  The pothecarie answerde, "and thou shalt have
A thing that, also God my soule save,
In al this world ther nis no creature,
That ete or dronke hath of this confiture                    400
Noght but the mountance of a corn of whete,
That he ne shal his lyf anon forlete;
Ye, sterve he shal, and that in lasse whyle
Than thou wolt goon a paas nat but a myle;
This poyson is so strong and violent."                       405
  This cursed man hath in his hond y-hent
This poyson in a box, and sith he ran
Into the nexte strete, unto a man,
And borwed of him large botels three;
And in the two his poyson poured he;                         410
The thridde he kepte clene for his drinke,
For al the night he shoop him for to swinke
In caryinge of the gold out of that place.
And whan this ryotour with sory grace
Had filled with wyn his grete botels three,                  415
To his felawes agayn repaireth he.
  What nedeth it to sermone of it more?
For right as they had cast his deeth bifore,
Right so they han him slayn, and that anon.
And whan that this was doon, thus spak that oon:             420
"Now lat us sitte and drinke, and make us merie,
And afterward we wol his body berie."
And with that word it happed him, par cas,
To take the botel ther the poyson was,
And drank, and yaf his felawe drinke also,                   425
For which anon they storven bothe two.
  But, certes, I suppose that Avicen*
Wroot never in no canon ne in no fen
Mo wonder signes of empoisoning
Than hadde this wrecches two, er hir ending.                 430
Thus ended been this homicydes two,

on the vermin that brought destruction on him
   by night.
   The apothecary answered, "You shall have
such a poison that, as God may save my soul,
there is no creature in all this world
which, if it eats or drinks of this mixture    400
no more than the amount of a grain of wheat,
will not lose his life at once;
yes, he shall die, and that in less time
than it would take you to walk a mile,
this poison is so strong and violent."    405
   The cursed man took the box of poison
in his hand, and then he ran
to a man in the next street,
and borrowed three large bottles from him;
in two of them he poured his poison;    410
the third he kept clean for his own drink,
for he planned to work all night
carrying the gold away from that place.
And when this rascal—may bad come to him—
had filled his three big bottles with wine,    415
he returned again to his comrades.
   What need is there to preach more about it?
For exactly as they had planned his death before,
just so they slew him, and that at once.
And when this was done, the first one said,    420
"Now let us sit and drink, and make merry,
and afterward we will bury his body."
And at that word, he happened, by chance,
to take a bottle which had poison in it,
and drank, and gave his comrade a drink too,    425
so that they both soon died.
   But certainly, I suppose that Avicenna
never wrote in any canon of medicine, or any part
   of one,
more astonishing symptoms of poisoning
than these two wretches suffered before their end.    430
Thus were these two homicides finished,

And eek the false empoysoner also.
   O cursed sinne, of alle cursednesse!
O traytours homicyde, o wikkednesse!
O glotonye, luxurie, and hasardrye!                           435
Thou blasphemour of Crist with vileinye
And othes grete, of usage and of pryde!
Allas, mankinde, how may it bityde,
That to thy creatour which that thee wroghte,
And with his precious herte-blood thee boghte,     440
Thou art so fals and so unkinde, allas!
   Now, goode men, God forgeve yow your trespas,
And ware yow fro the sinne of avaryce.
Myn holy pardoun may yow alle waryce,
So that ye offre nobles or sterlinges,                        445
Or elles silver broches, spones, ringes.
Boweth your heed under this holy bulle!
Cometh up, ye wyves, offreth of your wolle!
Your name I entre heer in my rolle anon;
Into the blisse of hevene shul ye gon;                        450
I yow assoile, by myn heigh power,
Yow that wol offre, as clene and eek as cleer
As ye were born; and, lo, sirs, thus I preche.
And Jesu Crist, that is our soules leche,
So graunte yow his pardon to receyve;                        455
For that is best; I wol yow nat deceyve.


## The Epilogue

But sirs, o word forgat I in my tale:
I have relikes and pardon in my male
As faire as any man in Engelond,
Whiche were me yeven by the popes hond.         460
If any of yow wol, of devocioun,
Offren, and han myn absolucioun,
Cometh forth anon, and kneleth heer adoun,
And mekely receyveth my pardoun:
Or elles, taketh pardon as ye wende,                        465
Al newe and fresh at every miles ende,

and the false poisoner too.
  O cursed sin, full of evil!
O homicidal traitors, O wickedness!
O gluttony, lechery, and gambling!          435
You villainous blasphemer of Christ
with great oaths, coming from habit and from pride!
Alas, mankind, how may it happen
that to your creator that made you
and redeemed you with his precious heart's blood          440
you are so false and so unnatural, alas!
  Now, good men, God forgive you your sin,
and keep you from the sin of avarice.
My holy pardon can save you all,
providing you offer nobles or sterling coins,          445
or else silver brooches, spoons, or rings.
Bow your head under this holy bull!
Come up, you wives, offer some of your wool!
I will enter your name here in my roll at once;
you shall enter into the bliss of heaven;          450
I absolve you by my high power—
you that will make offerings—as clean and pure
as you were born. And lo, sirs, thus I preach.
And Jesus Christ, who is physician of our souls,
grant that you receive his pardon;          455
for that is best; I will not deceive you.


## The Epilogue

But sirs, I forgot one thing in my tale.
I have in my pouch relics and pardons,
as fine as those of any other man in England,
which were given to me by the pope's own hand.          460
If any of you wish, out of devotion,
to make an offering and have my absolution,
come forth now, and kneel down here,
and meekly receive my pardon:
or else take a pardon as you go on your way,          465
all new and fresh at the end of every mile,

So that ye offren alwey newe and newe
Nobles and pens which that be gode and trewe.
It is an honour to everich that is heer
That ye mowe have a suffisant pardoneer          470
T'assoille yow, in contree as ye ryde,
For aventures which that may bityde.
Peraventure ther may falle oon or two
Doun of his hors, and breke his nekke atwo.
Look which a seuretee is it to yow alle          475
That I am in your felaweship y-falle,
That may assoille yow, bothe more and lasse,
Whan that the soule shal fro the body passe.
I rede that our Hoste heer shal biginne,
For he is most envoluped in sinne.               480
Com forth, sir Hoste, and offre first anon,
And thou shalt kisse the reliks everichon,
Ye, for a grote! Unbokel anon thy purs."
    "Nay, nay," quod he, "than have I Cristes curs!
Lat be," quod he, "it shal nat be, so thee'ch!   485
Thou woldest make me kisse thyn olde breech,
And swere it were a relik of a seint,
Thogh it were with thy fundement depeint!
But by the croys which that Seint Eleyne* fond,
I wolde I hadde thy coillons in myn hond         490
In stede of relikes or of seintuarie;
Lat cutte hem of, I wol thee helpe hem carie;
They shul be shryned in an hogges tord."
    This Pardoner answerde nat a word;
So wrooth he was, no word ne wolde he seye.      495
    "Now," quod our Host, "I wol no lenger pleye
With thee, ne with noon other angry man."
But right anon the worthy Knight bigan,
Whan that he saugh that al the peple lough,
"Namore of this, for it is right ynough;         500
Sir Pardoner, be glad and mery of chere;

just so that you offer ever anew
nobles and pennies which are good and genuine.
It is an honor to everyone here
that you may have a competent pardoner                    470
to absolve you, as you ride through the country,
for occasions that may arise.
Perhaps one or two of you
may fall from your horses and break your necks.
Look what a safeguard it is to all of you                 475
that I have fallen in with your company,
since I can absolve you, high and low,
when your soul shall pass from your body.
I recommend that our Host here should begin,
for he is the most enveloped in sin.                      480
Come forth, sir Host, and make the first
        offering now,
and you shall kiss every one of the relics.
Yes, for a groat! Unbuckle your purse at once."
    "No, no," said he, "I would rather be damned
        of Christ!
Let be," he said, "it shall not be, as I hope to thrive!  485
You would make me kiss your old breeches,
and swear they were the relic of a saint,
though they were stained by your buttocks!
But by the cross that Saint Helena found,
I wish I had your testicles in my hand                    490
instead of relics or reliquaries;
Let them be cut off, I'll help you carry them;
they shall be enshrined in a hog's turd."
    The Pardoner answered not a word;
he was so angry he wouldn't say anything.                 495
    "Now," said our Host, "I won't joke with you
any more, or with any other angry man."
But right away the worthy Knight began,
when he saw all the people laughing,
"No more of this, for it is quite enough                  500
Sir Pardoner, be of a glad and merry temper;

And ye, sir Host, that been to me so dere,
I prey yow that ye kisse the Pardoner.
And Pardoner, I prey thee, drawe thee neer,
And, as we diden, lat us laughe and pleye."          505
Anon they kiste, and riden forth hir weye.

and you, sir Host, who are so dear to me,
I beg you to kiss the Pardoner.
And Pardoner, I pray you, draw near;
let us laugh and have fun as we did before."    505
Then they kissed each other, and rode forth.

# THE SHIPMAN'S TALE

# INTRODUCTION

❦

THE CANTERBURY TALES, projected by Chaucer to comprise some 120 tales, four by each of the thirty pilgrims, was never completed. Before he died, Chaucer finished fewer than a fifth of them. The tales we do have are gathered together in ten fragments of one or more tales that are connected to each other within the fragment, but that have no explicit connections to other fragments. We all know that the first fragment, which includes the General Prologue and the tales of the Knight, the Miller, and the Reeve (as well as the unfinished tale of the Cook, not included in this collection), came first, but the other nine fragments are placed by editorial choice, based mostly on references to the location of towns along the way to Canterbury. Such placement assumes a one-way journey. In fact, the tales were to continue on the return journey back to London, and we can never know whether Chaucer planned to use some of the finished tales on that journey.

"The Shipman's Tale," newly edited and translated for this edition, is the first tale in fragment 7, which also includes the tales of the Prioress and the Nun's Priest, included here, and other tales, which are not. There is no head link to "The Shipman's Tale"—that is, no prologue, discussion by other pilgrims, or invitation by the Host to the Shipman to tell the next story. In a curious end link to "The Man of Law's Tale" at the very end of fragment 2, an uncertainly named pilgrim promises to tell a "merry" tale that will wake up all the pilgrims. Different manuscripts give different names as the proposed teller, which suggests that in Chaucer's own handwritten manuscript (now lost), the place for the name was left blank or that the original name was scraped off. The only solid indication of Chaucer's intentions comes after the tale is finished, where the Host thanks the "gentle mariner" for a fine tale and wishes him a long life sailing along the coast.

Because the description of the Shipman in the General Prologue to *The Canterbury Tales* (lines 394–412) focuses more on his piratical and nautical doings than on his literary or domestic ones, we have no strong reason to think that this tale of a monk and his best friend's wife is particularly suitable to him. There is, however, good reason to doubt that the tale was originally written for him. Several *we, us,* and *our* pronouns in lines 10–19 indicate that the original teller of the tale was a married woman. Since there is only one married woman on the pilgrimage, it is useful to think of this tale as having been written originally for the Wife of Bath. Surely the focus of the tale of infidelity in marriage and the qualities a wife expects from a good husband (see lines 173–77) would be a natural for the Alison we know from her long prologue and from her other tale. If the tale was originally written for the Wife of Bath, then when he assigned it to the Shipman, Chaucer never quite got around to altering or removing lines 10–19.

Chaucer's most likely source for "The Shipman's Tale" is the first tale of the eighth day of Giovanni Boccaccio's mid-fourteenth-century *Decameron*. The main character in that story is Gulfardo, a German soldier of fortune who visits Milan on business and falls in love at first sight with Ambruogia, the beautiful wife of Guasparruolo, a local merchant and friend of his. The lovesick Gulfardo one day sends a message to Ambruogia asking her to reward him for his loving devotion to her. After hesitating, she finally agrees to satisfy him, but only if he will give her two hundred gold florins. When Gulfardo learns of her rapaciousness, his love turns to near hatred, and he vows to take revenge against her. He does so by borrowing the two hundred florins from her husband and then, in the presence of a witness, giving it to Ambruogia one day when Guasparruolo is off on business in Genoa. She

counts the money, and then they go to bed—that night and
several other times. When Guasparruolo returns from Genoa,
Gulfardo goes to him and tells him, in the presence of his
wife, that he had, with a witness, given the money back to his
wife. Ambruogia tells her husband that she had forgotten to
tell him about it. Then she brings him the money, which she
has not yet spent.

Of the various changes that Chaucer made in his version
of the tale, two stand out. First, Chaucer made the deceptive
lover a monk rather than a soldier, which introduces a repre-
sentative of the medieval church into the mix. Monks, it should
be remembered, were supposed to live lives of celibacy and
religious devotion, but not all of them did so. Readers might
want to review the gently satirical portrait of the Monk in the
General Prologue to *The Canterbury Tales* (lines 165–207),
where the fancy clothes, love of the hunt, appetite for good
food, and generally questionable morals of some monks are
highlighted. Chaucer's other large change is to replace the
indirect communication between the wife and her lover with
direct communication in the hundred-line garden scene in
which the two principal characters directly negotiate the terms
of their sexual liaison. Other alterations include the curious
presence of the little girl in the garden scene, the enhanced
character of the businessman husband, the motivation of the
wife, and her proposed method of repaying the money.

## NOTES

**Seint-Denys** (line 1). A town north of Paris, now essentially
   part of greater Paris.

**goode man** (29). Not necessarily indicating "good" in the
   moral sense, but just "husband" or "keeper of the goods."
   Similarly, the term "goode wyf" (92) just meant "wife of
   the goodman." There is room, of course, for ironical dou-
   ble meanings in both terms.

**bretherhede** (42). The monk and the husband have become
   sworn brothers, thus entering a near-sacred alliance in
   which they vow to help each other in all things.

**daun John** (43). The term "daun" indicated a certain level of nobility as a leader or a lord. Chaucer never in this tale uses the name "John" without the preceding adjective "daun," which I translate here as "sir."

**Brugges** (55). The capital of Flanders in what is now north-western Belgium. It was the chief commercial and trading center of northern Europe in Chaucer's time. Bruges is famous for its network of lovely canals—"the Venice of the north."

**malvesye, vernage** (70–71). Two kinds of imported white wine, the first Greek, the second Italian.

**hundred frankes** (181). A large amount of money, at least five thousand dollars in early twenty-first century U.S. dollars, but probably lots more than that, depending on how we translate medieval exchange rates across borders and across the centuries.

**Genylon** (194). A man ripped to death by horses for betraying Roland.

**chilyndre** (206). A portable cylindrical sundial that shows the monk that it is around 9:00 A.M., and so time to eat dinner, often served at midmorning in medieval households.

*Quy la?* (214). French for "Who's there?"

**Peter!** (214). Not the name of her husband, who is never named in this tale, but an abbreviated form of "By Saint Peter." Compare the wife's "Marie!" in line 402.

**pilgrymage** (234). To go on a religious pilgrimage was a legal, but often marginally dishonest, way to delay or escape altogether the payment of one's debts.

**creauncc** (289). A complicated form of borrowing against future profits, something like buying on margins today. It was easier to borrow if one had a reputation for paying back all debts in a timely manner. Then, as now, it was very possible to miscalculate future earnings on borrowed money.

**sheeld** (331). A medieval unit of exchange. Twenty thousand of them would have been a lot of money, which the merchant wanted to pay back right away by borrowing from friends in Paris.

**Lumbardes** (367). Bankers from the northern Italian region of Lombardy. Some Lombard families had banks in several cities in Europe.

**my taille** (416). One of the medieval ways to record a debt was to carve markings across the grain of an elongated stick to indicate the amount of the debt, then to split the stick with the grain, with each participant to the agreement keeping half. When the two pieces were fit together, the old markings would still match up, but new ones would not. Of course, there was almost certainly some raunchy punning in the word here and in the final line of the tale.

# THE SHIPMANS TALE

A merchant whilom dwelled at Seint-Denys*
   That riche was, for which men helde hym wys.
A wyf he hadde of excellent beautee,
And compaignable and revelous was she,
Which is a thyng that causeth more dispence      5
Than worth is al the chiere and reverence
That men hem doon at festes and at daunces.
Swiche salutaciouns and contenances
Passen as dooth a shadwe upon the wal.
   But wo is hym that payen moot for al!      10
The sely housbonde, algate he moot paye,
He moot us clothe, and he moot us arraye,
Al for his owene worshipe richely,
In which array we daunce jolily.
And if that he noght may, par aventure,      15
Or ellis list no swich dispence endure,
But thynketh it is wasted and y-lost,
Thanne moot another payen for oure cost,
Or lene us gold, and that is perilous.
   This noble marchaunt heeld a worthy hous,      20
For which ne hadde alday so greet repair
For his largesse, and for his wyf was fair,
That wonder is. But herkneth to my tale.
Amonges alle his gestes, grete and smale,
Ther was a monk, a fair man and a boold      25
(I trowe a thritty wynter he was oold)
That evere in oon was drawynge to that place.

# THE SHIPMAN'S TALE

There was once a merchant who lived in St. Denis
who, because he was rich, was thought to be wise.
He had a wife of great beauty
who was friendly and liked to party,
and that causes more expense                                    5
than all the cheerful reverence and attention
that men pay to women at dinners and dances.
Those gracious greetings and happy faces
pass as quickly as a shadow on the wall.
  But woe to him who has to pay for it all!                     10
The simple husband always has to pay,
he has to clothe us and buy our fine array,
just because he wants us to look prosperous for
      his benefit,
and in that array we do a jolly dance.
And if perhaps he can't buy us fine clothes,                    15
or else prefers not to make such expenses,
thinking it wasteful or just money down the drain,
then we'll find another to pay our expenses
or lend us gold—and that's perilous!
  This noble merchant kept a sumptuous house                    20
and as a result, every day he had so many visitors—
because of his generosity and because of his
      pretty wife—
that it was a wonder. But listen to my story.
Among his important and minor guests,
there was a monk, a bold and handsome man                       25
(I suppose he was around thirty years old),
who time and again visited that place.

This yonge monk, that was so fair of face,
Aqueynted was so with the goode man*
Sith that hir firste knoweliche bigan,                     30
That in his hous as famulier was he
As it is possible any freend to be.
And for as muchel as this goode man,
And eek this monk, of which that I began,
Were bothe two y-born in o village,                       35
The monk hym claymeth as for cosynage,
And he agayn, he seith nat ones nay,
But was as glad therof as fowel of day,
For to his herte it was a greet plesaunce.
Thus been they knyt with eterne alliaunce,                40
And ech of hem gan oother for t'assure
Of bretherhede,* whil that hir lyf may dure.
Free was daun John,* and namely of dispence
As in that hous, and ful of diligence
To doon plesaunce, and also greet costage.                45
He noght forgat to yeve the leeste page
In al that hous. But after hir degree,
He yaf the lord, and sitthe al his meynee,
Whan that he cam, som manere honest thyng.
For which they were as glad of his comyng                 50
As fowel is fayn whan that the sonne up riseth.
Na moore of this as now, for it suffiseth.
    But so bifel, this marchant on a day
Shoop hym to make redy his array
Toward the toun of Brugges* for to fare                   55
To byen there a porcioun of ware,
For which he hath to Parys sent anon
A messager, and preyed hath daun John
That he sholde come to Seint-Denys to pleye
With hym and with his wyf a day or tweye,                 60
Er he to Brugges wente, in alle wise.
This noble monk, of which I yow devyse,
Hath of his abbot, as hym list, licence,

This young monk, who was so handsome to look at,
had been so well acquainted with this husband
for as long as he could remember 30
that he was as familiar in that house
as any friend could possibly be.
And because this husband
and this monk, the one I've been telling you about,
were both born in the same village, 35
the monk claimed him as a cousin,
and for his part, the husband never denied it.
Rather, he was as happy about it as a bird is at sunrise
because to his heart it was a great joy and honor.
They thus formed an eternal alliance, 40
and they each swore to the other
to be brothers as long as they lived.
Sir John was generous in his spending
in that house and very careful
to give pleasure, and went to great expense. 45
He did not forget to give something to the lowliest
    page
in the house. But according to their rank
he gave to the lord, and then to all in his retinue,
whenever he came, some suitable gift.
Because of the gifts they were as happy to have
    him come 50
as a bird is when the sun comes up.
But that's enough. No more of that now.
    But it so happened that one day this merchant
got his things ready
for a trip to the town of Bruges 55
to buy some goods.
He sent a messenger to Paris
to invite sir John
to come to St. Denis for some amusement
with him and his wife for a couple of days 60
before he went to Bruges.
This noble monk, of whom I've told you,
got permission from his abbot, who was happy,

By cause he was a man of heigh prudence,
And eek an officer, out for to ryde,                              65
To seen hir graunges and hire bernes wyde.
And unto Seint-Denys he comth anon.

Who was so welcome as "my lord daun John,
Oure deere cosyn, ful of curteisye"?
With hym broghte he a jubbe of malvesye,*                         70
And eek another, ful of fyn vernage,*
And volatyl, as ay was his usage.
And thus I lete hem ete and drynke and pleye,
This marchant and this monk, a day or tweye.

The thridde day, this marchant up ariseth,                       75
And on his nedes sadly hym avyseth,
And up into his countour-hous gooth he
To rekene with hymself, as wel may be,
Of thilke yeer how that it with hym stood,
And how that he despended hadde his good,                        80
And if that he encressed were or noon.
His bookes and his bagges many oon
He leith biforn hym on his countyng-bord.
Ful riche was his tresor and his hord,
For which ful faste his countour-dore he shette,                 85
And eek he nolde that no man sholde hym lette
Of his acountes, for the meene tyme.
And thus he sit til it was passed pryme.

Daun John was rysen in the morwe also
And in the gardyn walketh to and fro,                            90
And hath his thynges seyd ful curteisly.
This goode wyf cam walkynge pryvely
Into the gardyn, there he walketh softe,
And hym saleweth, as she hath doon ofte.
A mayde child cam in hire compaignye,                            95
Which as hir list she may governe and gye,
For yet under the yerde was the mayde.

"O deere cosyn myn, daun John," she sayde.
"What eyleth yow so rathe for to ryse,
Nece?" quod he. "It oghte ynough suffise                         100
Fyve houres for to slepe upon a nyght,

because the monk was both prudent
and a monastic officer, to let him go                                     65
to check into the monastic granaries and barns.
So he soon came to St. Denis.

Who was so welcome as "my lord, sir John,
our dear courtly cousin"?
With him he brought a jug of white Greek wine,          70
and another jug of fine Italian wine,
and tasty fowl, just as he always did.
And thus I leave them to eat and drink and have fun,
The merchant and the monk, for a day or two.

On the third day, the merchant got up               75
and thought seriously about his business affairs,
and went up into his counting room
to take inventory of his business, as well he might,
to see how matters stood for him that year,
how he had spent his money and goods,                   80
and whether he had prospered or not.
His many account books and money bags
he lay in front of him on his counting bench.
His treasury and his safe were full,
so he closed his counting room door tight              85
and gave instructions that no one should interrupt him
while he took inventory, at least for now.
And thus he sat at work until it was after nine A.M.

Sir John rose up that morning also,
and paced to and fro in the garden                     90
as he said his morning devotions reverently.
The merchant's wife came walking stealthily
into the garden where he paced softly,
and greeted him, as she often did.
With her came a young girl-child                       95
whom she guided and directed as she wanted to,
because the girl was still under her control.

"O my dear cousin, sir John," she said.
"What ails you that you got up so early,
my niece?" he said. "Five hours of sleep          100
a night ought to be enough for everyone

But it were for an old appalled wight,
As been thise wedded men, that lye and dare
As in a fourme sit a wery hare,
Were al forstraught with houndes grete and smale.        105
But deere nece, why be ye so pale?
I trowe, certes, that oure goode man
Hath yow laboured sith the nyght bigan,
That yow were nede to resten hastily."
And with that word he lough ful murily,                  110
And of his owene thought he wax al reed.

    This faire wyf gan for to shake hir heed
And seyde thus, "Ye, God woot al," quod she.
"Nay, cosyn myn, it stant nat so with me,
For, by that God that yaf me soule and lyf,              115
In al the reawme of France is ther no wyf
That lasse lust hath to that sory pley.
For I may synge, 'Allas and weylawey
That I was born,' but to no wight," quod she,
"Dar I nat telle how that it stant with me.              120
Wherfore I thynke out of this land to wende,
Or elles of myself to make an ende,
So ful am I of drede and eek of care."

    This monk bigan upon this wyf to stare,
And seyde, "Allas, my nece, God forbede                  125
That ye, for any sorwe or any drede,
Fordo youreself. But telleth me youre grief.
Paraventure I may, in youre meschief,
Conseille or helpe. And therfore telleth me
Al youre anoy, for it shal been secree.                  130
For on my porthors here I make an ooth
That nevere in my lyf, for lief ne looth,
Ne shal I of no conseil yow biwreye."

    "The same agayn to yow," quod she, "I seye.
By God and by this porthors I yow swere,                 135
Though men me wolde al into pieces tere,
Ne shal I nevere, for to goon to helle,
Biwreye a word of thyng that ye me telle,
Nat for no cosynage ne alliance,

except maybe a near-dead old man,
as these married men are who lie and doze off
like the tired rabbit who cowers in a grassy hollow
as if he were being attacked by dogs of all sizes.          105
But dear niece, why are you so pale?
I suppose, truly, that the master of the house
has kept you so busy in bed all night long
that now you need a nap!"
And when he said that he laughed merrily,          110
then blushed, embarrassed at what he was thinking.

    This pretty wife shook her head
and said, "Truly, God knows everything.
No, my cousin, it is not that way for me,
for, by the Lord who gave me life and a soul,          115
let me tell you that in all of France no wife
has less pleasure in that sorry game than I.
For I can sing, 'Alas, alas
that I was born,' " she said, "but to no one
can I tell how things really stand with me.          120
Therefore I think I shall leave this place
or else put an end to myself,
since I am so upset with fear and anxiety."

    This monk started to stare at the wife
and said, "Alas, my niece, God forbid          125
that you, for any sorrow or fear,
kill yourself. But tell me what grieves you.
Perhaps I can, in your time of trouble,
offer counsel or help. So tell me
all that troubles you, because I'll tell no one.          130
Indeed, I swear on my breviary here
that never in my life, for any reason whatever,
shall I reveal anything you tell me."

    "I swear the same to you, also," she said.
"By God and by your breviary I swear to you,          135
even if men threatened to tear me to pieces,
that I shall never, on pain of hell,
betray a single word of what you tell me.
I promise, not because we are cousins or allies,

But verraily, for love and affiance." 140
    Thus been they sworn, and heerupon they kiste,
And ech of hem tolde oother what hem liste.
    "Cosyn," quod she, "if that I hadde a space,
As I have noon, and namely in this place,
Thanne wolde I telle a legende of my lyf, 145
What I have suffred sith I was a wyf
With myn housbonde, al be he youre cosyn."
    "Nay," quod this monk, "by God and Seint Martyn,
He is na moore cosyn unto me
Than is this leef that hangeth on the tree! 150
I clepe hym so, by Seint Denys of Fraunce,
To have the moore cause of aqueyntaunce
Of yow, which I have loved specially
Aboven alle wommen, sikerly.
This swere I yow on my professioun. 155
Telleth youre grief, lest that he come adoun.
And hasteth yow, and gooth youre wey anon."
    "My deere love," quod she, "O my daun John,
Ful lief were me this conseil for to hyde,
But out it moot, I may namoore abyde. 160
Myn housbonde is to me the worste man
That evere was sith that the world bigan.
But sith I am a wyf, it sit nat me
To tellen no wight of oure privetee,
Neither abedde, ne in noon oother place. 165
God shilde I sholde it tellen, for his grace!
A wyf ne shal nat seyn of hir housbonde
But al honour, as I kan understond,
Save unto yow thus muche I tellen shal:
As helpe me God, he is noght worth at al 170
In no degree the value of a flye.
But yet me greveth moost his nygardye.
And wel ye woot that wommen naturelly
Desiren thynges sixe as wel as I:
They wolde that hir housbondes sholde be 175
Hardy, and wise, and riche, and therto free,

but truly for love and affection."                                    140

Thus they swore, then sealed it with a kiss,
and they told each other whatever they wanted.

"Cousin," she said, "if I had the privacy
that I don't have here in this garden,
then I would tell you a saint's legend about my life,          145
about all that I have suffered since I became the wife
of my husband, even if he is your cousin."

"No way," said the monk, "by God and St. Martin,
is he any more cousin to me
than this leaf that hangs on the tree!                          150
I call him cousin, by St. Denis of France,
so I have more reason to see you
whom I have especially loved
more than all other women, truly.
I swear this to you on my profession as monk.                   155
Tell me what troubles you, lest he comes down.
Hurry, then go your way."

"My dear love," she said, "O my sir John,
I would rather not reveal such things to you,
but it must come out. I just can't take it anymore.            160
My husband treats me worse than any man
ever treated a woman since the world began.
But because I am his wife, it is not fitting for me
to tell anyone about our private life,
not in bed nor in any other place.                              165
God forbid that I should tell such things!
I understand that a wife must say
only honorable things about her husband,
but this much I must tell you:
so help me God, he is not worth in any way,                     170
by any measure imaginable, even the value of a fly.
But you know, what grieves me most is his stinginess.
You fully understand that all women by nature
desire the same six things that I desire:
they want their husband to be                                   175
strong and smart and wealthy, and generous with
    his money,

And buxom unto his wyf, and fressh abedde.
But by that ilke lord that for us bledde,
For his honour, myself for to arraye,
A Sonday next I moste nedes paye                          180
An hundred frankes,* or ellis I am lorn.
Yet were me levere that I were unborn
Than me were doon a sclaundre or vileynye.
And if myn housbonde eek it myghte espye,
I nere but lost. And therfore I yow preye,                185
Lene me this somme, or ellis moot I deye.
Daun John, I seye, lene me thise hundred frankes.
Pardee, I wol nat faille yow my thankes,
If that yow list to doon that I yow praye.
For at a certeyn day I wol yow paye,                      190
And doon to yow what plesance and service
That I may doon, right as yow list devise.
And but I do, God take on me vengeance
As foul as evere hadde Genylon* of France."
    This gentil monk answerde in this manere:            195
"Now trewely, myn owene lady deere,
I have," quod he, "on yow so greet a routhe
That I yow swere, and plighte yow my trouthe,
That whan youre housbonde is to Flaundres fare,
I wol delyvere yow out of this care.                      200
For I wol brynge yow an hundred frankes."
    And with that word he caughte hire by the flankes,
And hire embraceth harde, and kiste hire ofte.
    "Gooth now youre wey," quod he, "al stille and softe,
And lat us dyne as soone as that ye may,                  205
For by my chilyndre* it is pryme of day.
Gooth now, and beeth as trewe as I shal be."
    "Now elles God forbede, sire," quod she.
And forth she gooth as jolif as a pye,
And bad the cookes that they sholde hem hye,              210
So that men myghte dyne, and that anon.
    Up to hir housbonde is this wyf y-gon,
And knokketh at his countour boldely.

and obedient to his wife, and vigorous in bed.
But, by the lord that died for us,
so that I can clothe myself in such a way as to
    do honor to him,
next Sunday I must pay back                               180
a hundred francs, or else I am lost.
I would rather never have been born
than have a slanderous or villainous act done to me.
And if my husband saw me doing such an act,
I'd be a goner. And therefore I ask you,                 185
lend me this sum or else I will surely die.
Sir John, I say, lend me these hundred francs.
Be assured, I will not fail in my thanks to you
if you find a way to do what I ask.
For on a certain day I will pay you back                 190
and also give you any pleasure or service
I can give, whatever you desire.
And if I don't, may God take on me a vengeance
as awful as any taken against Ganelon of France."

    The gentle monk answered,                             195
"Now truly, my own dear lady,
I have such great pity on you
that I swear, and plight my troth to you,
that when your husband goes to Flanders
I will deliver you from your troubles,                   200
for I will bring you a hundred francs."

    And with that word he grabbed her by the haunches,
gave her a good hard hug, and kissed her often.

    "Go your way now," he said, "all soft and quietly,
and let's dine as soon as possible,                      205
for by my cylinder it is midmorning already.
Go now, and be as true as I shall be."

    "God forbid anything else, sir," she said.
She went out as jolly as a magpie,
and asked the cooks to hurry things up                   210
so that they could dine soon.
Then this wife went up to her husband
and knocked boldly at his counting house door.

    *"Quy la?"** quod he. "Peter!* It am I,"
Quod she."What, sire, how longe wol ye faste?                    215
How longe tyme wol ye rekene and caste
Youre sommes, and youre bookes, and youre thynges?
The devel have part on alle swiche rekenynges!
Ye have ynough, pardee, of Goddes sonde.
Com doun to-day, and lat youre bagges stonde.                    220
Ne be ye nat ashamed that daun John
Shal fasting al this day alenge goon?
What? Lat us heere a messe, and go we dyne."
    "Wyf," quod this man, "litel kanstow devyne
The curious bisynesse that we have.                               225
For of us chapmen, also God me save,
And by that lord that clepid is Seint Yve,
Scarsly amonges twelve tweye shul thryve
Continuelly, lastynge unto oure age.
We may wel make chiere and good visage,                          230
And dryve forth the world as it may be,
And kepen oure estaat in pryvetee,
Til we be deed. Or elles that we pleye
A pilgrymage,* or goon out of the weye.
And therfore have I greet necessitee                             235
Upon this queynte world t'avyse me.
For everemoore we moote stonde in drede
Of hap and fortune in oure chapmanhede.
To Flaundres wol I go to-morwe at day,
And come agayn, as soone as evere I may.                         240
For which, my deere wyf, I thee biseke,
As be to every wight buxom and meke,
And for to kepe oure good be curious,
And honestly governe wel oure hous.
Thou hast ynough, in every maner wise,                           245
That to a thrifty houshold may suffise.
Thee lakketh noon array ne no vitaille.
Of silver in thy purs shaltow nat faille."

   *"Quy la?"* he said. "By saint Peter, it is I,"
she said. "Come on, sire, how long are you planning
    to fast? 215
How long does it take to reckon up and figure out
your sums, your books, and your accounting things?
The devil take all such calculations!
You have plenty with what God has sent you.
Come down and let your bags of gold stay where
    they are. 220
Aren't you ashamed that sir John
has been fasting all this long morning?
Come on, let's hear a mass, and then go eat."
   "My wife," said this man, "you don't understand
the curious business I am in. 225
For among us many merchants, I swear to God,
and by that lord named St. Ivo,
scarcely two in twelve will succeed
continually, all the way to old age.
We may pretend good cheer and a happy face, 230
fend off the troubles of the world,
and keep our business affairs private
until we are dead. Or else we can pretend to go
on a pilgrimage, or escape in some other way.
And therefore we have to consider carefully 235
the uncertainties of this treacherous world.
We must always fear the role
of chance and fortune in our business affairs.
Tomorrow at dawn I will leave for Flanders,
but I'll return just as soon as I can. 240
And so, my dear wife, I beseech you
to be meek and obedient to everyone,
to protect our belongings carefully,
and to govern our house honestly.
You have enough money 245
for a thrifty household.
You have plenty of clothing and food,
and you'll have enough silver in your purse."

And with that word his countour-dore he shette,
And doun he gooth, no lenger wolde he lette. 250
But hastily a messe was ther seyd,
And spedily the tables were y-leyd,
And to the dyner faste they hem spedde,
And richely this monk the chapman fedde.

At after-dyner daun John sobrely 255
This chapman took apart, and prively
He seyde hym thus: "Cosyn, it standeth so,
That wel I se to Brugges wol ye go.
God and Seint Austyn spede yow and gyde!
I prey yow, cosyn, wisely that ye ryde. 260
Governeth yow also of youre diete
Atemprely, and namely in this hete.
Bitwix us two nedeth no strange fare.
Farewel, cosyn, God shilde yow fro care!
And if that any thyng by day or nyght, 265
If it lye in my power and my myght,
That ye me wol comande in any wyse,
It shal be doon, right as ye wol devyse.
O thyng, er that ye goon, if it may be,
I wolde prey yow for to lene me 270
An hundred frankes, for a wyke or tweye,
For certein beestes that I moste beye,
To stoore with a place that is oures.
God helpe me so, I wolde it were youres!
I shal nat faille surely of my day, 275
Nat for a thousand frankes, a mile way.
But lat this thyng be secree, I yow preye,
For yet to-nyght thise beestes moot I beye.
And fare now wel, myn owene cosyn deere.
Graunt mercy of youre cost and of youre cheere." 280
    This noble marchant gentilly anon
Answerde and seyde, "O cosyn myn, daun John,

And with that word he closed his counting house
   door
and went down with no further delay. 250
A quick mass was said
and the tables were speedily set,
and then they all made haste to dinner.
The merchant fed the monk sumptuously.

   After dinner sir John with a serious face 255
took the merchant aside privately
and said to him, "Cousin, here's the situation.
I know you are heading to Bruges.
May God and St. Augustine speed and guide you.
I pray you, cousin, ride with caution. 260
Be careful of your diet
and eat moderately, especially in this heat.
Between us there need be no elaborate good-byes.
So, farewell, cousin, God protect you from all cares.
If you need anything, by day or night, 265
and it lies in my power to provide it,
just ask for it, and
it will be done, just as you like.
But there's one thing you can do for me. If possible,
   before you go,
I wonder if you could lend me 270
a hundred francs, just for a week or two,
for certain animals that I need to purchase
to stock one of our monastic farms.
By God, I would that it were your farm!
I absolutely won't fail to repay you on the due date, 275
not even to gain a thousand francs, just a mile away.
But, if you don't mind, let's keep this little transaction
   a secret,
because even tonight I need to purchase these animals.
And now farewell, my own dear cousin.
I thank you for your trouble, and for our cheerful
   friendship." 280

   This noble merchant right off answered gently
and said, "O my cousin, sir John,

Now sikerly this is a smal requeste.
My gold is youres, whan that it yow leste,
And nat oonly my gold, but my chaffare.                    285
Take what yow list, God shilde that ye spare.
But o thyng is, ye knowe it wel ynogh,
Of chapmen, that hir moneie is hir plogh.
We may creaunce* whil we have a name,
But goldlees for to be, it is no game.                      290
Paye it agayn whan it lith in youre ese.
After my myght ful fayn wolde I yow plese."
    Thise hundred frankes he fette forth anon,
And prively he took hem to daun John.
No wight in al this world wiste of this loone,             295
Savynge this marchant and daun John allone.
They drynke, and speke, and rome a while and pleye,
Til that daun John rideth to his abbeye.
    The morwe cam, and forth this marchant rideth
To Flaundres-ward. His prentys wel hym gydeth,            300
Til he came into Brugges murily.
Now gooth this marchant faste and bisily
Aboute his nede, and byeth and creaunceth.
He neither pleyeth at the dees ne daunceth,
But as a marchaunt, shortly for to telle,                  305
He let his lyf, and there I lete hym dwelle.
    The Sonday next the marchant was agon,
To Seint-Denys y-comen is daun John,
With crowne and berd al fressh and newe y-shave.
In al the hous ther nas so litel a knave,                  310
Ne no wight elles, that he nas ful fayn
For that "my lord daun John" was come agayn.
And shortly to the point right for to gon,
This faire wyf acorded with daun John
That for thise hundred frankes he sholde al nyght  ·       315
Have hire in his armes bolt upright.

surely this is but a small request.
My gold is yours whenever you want it,
and not just my gold, but my goods. 285
Take what you like, God forbid that you hold back.
But one thing, you know it well enough,
a merchant's money is his plow.
We can borrow money while our name is good,
but if we have no gold, the game is up. 290
Please repay it when you can.
To the best of my power, I will do all I can to
    please you."
    He right away fetched the hundred francs
and privately took them to sir John.
Nobody in the whole world knew of this loan, 295
just the merchant and sir John.
They drank, and spoke, and amused themselves, and
    strolled around
until sir John rode back to his abbey.
    The next morning the merchant rode off
to Flanders. His apprentice guided him carefully 300
until he came merrily into Bruges.
Now this merchant quickly went
about his needs by buying and borrowing.
He neither gambled nor danced,
but, to be brief about it, as a merchant and nothing else 305
he led his life in Bruges, and there I leave him.
    The next Sunday after the merchant left
sir John went to St. Denis
with his tonsure and his beard all freshly shaved.
In the whole house even the most menial servant boy, 310
and everyone else, was delighted
that "sir John, my lord" had come again.
And to get straight to the point,
the pretty wife of the merchant had agreed with sir
    John
that for the hundred francs he would for the
    whole night 315
have her on her back in his arms.

And this acord parfourned was in dede.
   In myrthe al nyght a bisy lyf they lede
Til it was day, that daun John wente his way,
And bad the meynee, "Farewel, have good day!"    320
For noon of hem, ne no wight in the toun,
Hath of daun John right no suspecioun.
And forth he rydeth hoom to his abbeye,
Or where hym list. Namoore of hym I seye.
   This marchant, whan that ended was the faire,    325
To Seint-Denys he gan for to repaire,
And with his wyf he maketh feeste and cheere,
And telleth hire that chaffare is so deere
That nedes moste he make a chevyssaunce.
For he was bounden in a reconyssaunce    330
To paye twenty thousand sheeld* anon.
For which this marchant is to Parys gon
To borwe of certeine freendes that he hadde
A certeyn frankes, and somme with him he ladde.
And whan that he was come into the toun,    335
For greet chiertee and greet affeccioun,
Unto daun John he gooth first, hym to pleye,
Nat for to axe or borwe of hym moneye,
But for to wite and seen of his welfare,
And for to tellen hym of his chaffare,    340
As freendes doon whan they been met yfeere.
   Daun John hym maketh feeste and murye cheere,
And he hym tolde agayn, ful specially,
How he hadde wel y-boght and graciously,
Thanked be God, al hool his marchandise,    345
Save that he moste, in alle maner wise,
Maken a chevyssaunce, as for his beste,
And thanne he sholde been in joye and reste.
   Daun John answerde, "Certes, I am fayn
That ye in heele ar comen hom agayn.    350
And if that I were riche, as have I blisse,
Of twenty thousand sheeld sholde ye nat mysse,

And this agreement was performed not just in words
    but in deeds.
  In joy all that night they led a busy life
until it was day. Then sir John went his way,
and told the servants, "Farewell, and have a good day."    320
Not a one of them, nor anyone in St. Denis,
had the slightest suspicion of sir John.
He rode home to his abbey,
or wherever he wanted. I say no more of him now.
  When he left the market in Bruges, the merchant    325
headed back to St. Denis.
He had a fine and cheerful meal with his wife
and told her that interest rates had gone up so much
that he had to take out a loan,
because he was bound by a formal contract    330
to repay twenty thousand shields right away.
Because of that contract the merchant went off to Paris
to borrow from some of his friends there
a certain number of francs, and some francs he took
    with him.
When he got to town,    335
for friendship and affection,
he went first to sir John to have some amusement,
not to ask for or borrow money from him,
but just to ask after his welfare,
and to tell him of his business dealings,    340
as good friends do when they get together.
  Sir John offered him a fine feast and happy cheer,
and the merchant told him, in detail,
how he had purchased well and with good grace,
thanks be to God, all of his merchandise,    345
except that he must, at all costs,
borrow some money, in his own best interests,
and then he would be in joy and able to relax.
  Sir John answered, "Certainly, I am delighted
that you have come home again in good health.    350
And if I were rich, by heaven,
I'd give you the twenty thousand shields,

For ye so kyndely this oother day
Lente me gold. And, as I kan and may,
I thanke yow, by God and by Seint Jame! 355
But nathelees, I took unto oure dame,
Youre wyf, at hom, the same gold ageyn
Upon youre bench. She woot it wel, certeyn,
By certeyn tokenes that I kan hire telle.
Now, by youre leve, I may no lenger dwelle. 360
Oure abbot wole out of this toun anon,
And in his compaignye moot I goon.
Grete wel oure dame, myn owene nece sweete,
And fare wel, deere cosyn, til we meete!"

This marchant, which that was ful war and wys, 365
Creanced hath, and payd eek in Parys
To certeyn Lumbardes,* redy in hir hond,
The somme of gold, and gat of hem his bond.
And hoom he gooth, murie as a papejay,
For wel he knew he stood in swich array 370
That nedes moste he wynne in that viage
A thousand frankes aboven al his costage.
His wyf ful redy mette hym atte gate,
As she was wont of oold usage algate.
And al that nyght in myrthe they bisette, 375
For he was riche and cleerly out of dette.
Whan it was day, this marchant gan embrace
His wyf al newe, and kiste hire on hir face,
And up he gooth and maketh it ful tough.

"Namoore," quod she, "by God, ye have ynough!" 380
And wantownly agayn with hym she pleyde,
Til atte laste thus this marchant seyde:
"By God," quod he, "I am a litel wrooth
With yow, my wyf, although it be me looth.
And woot ye why? By God, as that I gesse 385
That ye han maad a manere straungenesse
Bitwixen me and my cosyn daun John.

since you so generously the other day
lent me gold. In the best way I know how,
I thank you, by God and by St. James.                    355
Nevertheless, I took to our lady,
your wife at home, that same gold and put it
on your counting bench. She knows this very well, I
     assure you,
by certain tokens that I could mention.
Now, by your leave, I can't stay any longer.             360
Our abbot is leaving town very soon,
and I must accompany him.
Give my regards to our lady, my own sweet niece,
and farewell, dear cousin, until we meet again."

     The merchant, who had lots of business smarts,       365
borrowed what he needed and paid in Paris
to certain Lombards, cash in hand,
the correct sum of gold, and retrieved his bond
     from them.
Then he went home, happy as a parrot
because he now knew that he                              370
would clear from his business trip
a thousand francs above his expenses.
His wife was ready to greet him at the gate,
as she always was when he came home.
All that night in good spirits they went at it,          375
for he was rich and clear of his debt.
When it was morning, this merchant embraced
his wife afresh, and kissed her on the face,
and right on up he went, and made it pretty wild
     for her.

     "No more," she said, "by God, you've had enough!"    380
But she again played wantonly with him,
until at last this merchant spoke.
"By God," he said, "I am just a bit annoyed
with you, my wife, although I am loath to be.
You know why? Because, by God, I guess                   385
you've created a bit of awkwardness
between me and my cousin sir John.

Ye sholde han warned me, er I had gon,
That he yow hadde an hundred frankes payed
By redy token, and heeld hym yvele apayed,                    390
For that I to hym spak of chevyssaunce,
Me semed so, as by his contenaunce.
But nathelees, by God, oure hevene kyng,
I thoughte nat to axen hym no thyng.
I prey thee, wyf, ne do namoore so.                    395
Telle me alwey, er that I fro thee go,
If any dettour hath in myn absence
Y-payed thee, lest thurgh thy necligence
I myghte hym axe a thing that he hath payed."

    This wyf was nat afered nor affrayed,                    400
But boldely she seyde, and that anon,
"Marie! I deffie the false monk, daun John!
I kepe nat of his tokenes never a deel.
He took me certeyn gold, that woot I weel.
What? Yvel thedam on his monkes snowte!                    405
For, God it woot, I wende, withouten doute,
That he hadde yeve it me bycause of yow,
To doon therwith myn honour and my prow,
For cosynage, and eek for beele cheere
That he hath had ful ofte tymes heere.                    410
But sith I se I stonde in this disjoynt,
I wol answere yow shortly to the poynt.
Ye han mo slakkere dettours than am I!
For I wol paye yow wel and redily
Fro day to day, and if so be I faille,                    415
I am youre wyf. Score it upon my taille,*
And I shal paye as soone as ever I may.
For by my trouthe, I have on myn array,
And nat on wast, bistowed every deel.
And for I have bistowed it so weel                    420
For youre honour, for Goddes sake, I seye,
As be nat wrooth, but lat us laughe and pleye.

You should have warned me, before I left for Paris,
that he had paid you a hundred francs
in certain cash tokens. He felt badly treated 390
because I spoke to him of borrowing—
anyhow, it seemed that way, to judge from his face.
Nevertheless, by God, our heavenly king,
I did not mean to ask him anything about the money.
I pray you, my wife, don't do that again. 395
Always tell me, before I leave here,
whether any debtor has in my absence
payed you, lest through your negligence
I might ask someone for money he's already paid."
      This wife was neither nervous nor afraid 400
but boldly spoke right up:
"By St. Mary, I defy that false monk, sir John!
I kept none of his 'tokens,' not even a penny.
He did bring me a certain amount of gold, I
      know that.
Sure. But bad luck fall on that monk's snout 405
because, God knows, I thought, without a doubt,
that he had given it to me because of you,
to spend for my own honor and benefit,
because of our cousinly relationship and the good
      hospitality
that he so often had here. . 410
But since I see that he has put me in a pickle here,
I will answer you quickly and to the point.
You'll have far more slacker debtors than I
because I will pay you fully and readily
a bit each day, and if it so happens that I miss
      a payment, 415
well, I'm your wife, so just score it on my 'tally.'
I shall pay you just as soon as I can.
But I promise you that I have spent it on clothes,
not on waste, every bit of it.
And, I assure you, I have spent it on these clothes 420
to do you honor, for God's sake.
So don't be annoyed, but let's laugh and play!

Ye shal my joly body have to wedde.
By God, I wol nat paye yow but abedde!
Forgyve it me, myn owene spouse deere.                425
Turne hiderward, and maketh bettre cheere."

   This marchant saugh ther was no remedie,
And for to chide it nere but folie,
Sith that the thyng may nat amended be.
   "Now wyf," he seyde, "and I foryeve it thee.          430
But, by thy lyf, ne be namoore so large.
Keep bet my good, this yeve I thee in charge."
Thus endeth now my tale, and God us sende
Taillynge ynough unto oure lyves ende.

You shall have my jolly body to wed whenever
   you like.
By God, I won't pay you except in bed.
Forgive me, my own dear spouse. 425
Turn over here and give me a happier face."

   The merchant saw that there was no remedy,
that it was folly to chide her anymore,
since the thing could no longer be amended.

   "Now, my wife," he said, "I forgive the debt, 430
but, on your life, don't be so generous.
I charge you to keep my goods better next time."

   Thus ends my tale, and may God send us
enough "tallying" to last us all our lives.

# THE PRIORESS'S TALE

# INTRODUCTION

꩜

A T THE END of "The Shipman's Tale," the Host thanks the gentle mariner for his tale about the corrupt monk, then courteously invites the "lady Prioress" to tell the next tale. The Prioress gladly complies and launches immediately into her prologue in praise of Jesus and, especially, of his chaste mother, Mary. "The Prioress's Tale" itself is as different as it can possibly be in style, genre, subject matter, tone, and even verse form from the preceding "Shipman's Tale." Here there is no love triangle, no adultery, no borrowed money, no humor. Some readers have found thematic connections between the two tales—the reference to money lending, for example, and the presence of small children and monks in both tales—but the connections are unemphatic and may be accidental.

"The Prioress's Tale" is an example of a genre popular in the Middle Ages known as the miracle of the Virgin—a narrative in which Mary performs a miraculous event that shows her goodness, mercy, and power. There are many such stories from medieval times. Chaucer could have chosen from among many variations of this particular tale about a miracle involving the murder of a Christian boy at the hands of Jews. A version close to his own concerns a Christian cleric who carries food each day across the Jewish quarter of the town to feed his ailing father. The Jews grow increasingly annoyed when they hear him repeatedly sing an anthem to the Virgin Mary, and one day they seize him, take him off to one of their chambers, cut the shape of a cross in his belly, rip his guts out, and throw his body into a latrine. He miraculously keeps singing, however, though only Christians, not the Jews, can

hear his song. The next day the cleric's aging mother goes out
to seek him, hears his song in the Jewish quarter, and sum-
mons the town authorities. They too hear the song, search for
and find the body, and take it to the church for burial. Only
after his body is buried does the singing praise of the Virgin
Mary stop.

In form "The Prioress's Tale" is written in seven-line stan-
zas each with only three rhyme sounds. That stanza form,
now known as rhyme royal, marks this tale as probably one
of Chaucer's earlier creations. If it is true that he wrote it be-
fore he had conceived the scheme of the Canterbury proj-
ect, then it is interesting to speculate about why he assigned
this tale to the ambiguously devout Prioress (see the Gen-
eral Prologue to *The Canterbury Tales,* lines 118–62). Did
Chaucer want to emphasize the sensitive feelings of a woman
who cares about the safety of little mice and dogs by having
her tell about a little boy who is undeservedly killed by his
satanic enemies? Did he want, rather, to emphasize the con-
trast between her concern for the welfare of little animals
and the brutal treatment of the Jews in her tale? Other read-
ers have wondered about the source of the anti-Semitism of
the tale. Is the anti-Semitism Chaucer's own, or does the ge-
nial Chaucer criticize the hypocritical Prioress for her anti-
Semitism? Whatever the answer, in fact most English men
and women had no personal contact with Jews since the Jews
had been by decree banished from England in 1290. Jews
were, then, officially the "other" to the people of England. It
was easy to vilify them as the killers of Jesus and to blame
them when any innocent Christian was slain through the evil
of personal revenge, of war, or of pestilence.

## NOTES

### The Prioress's Prologue

**O bussh unbrent** (line 16). Like the lily in line 9, the un-
burnt bush (see Exodus 3:2) was seen as a symbol for the
unblemished purity of Mary.

**Gydeth my song** (35). Mary is invoked almost as if she were a poetic muse to help the speaker sing a song of praise.

The Prioress's Tale

**Asie, in a greet citee** (1). The tale is set in what we now think of as Asia Minor—in the Near East (perhaps Turkey), not the Far East. Chaucer is vague about the place and what native language the little Christian boy would have spoken in his home city.

**Jewerye** (2). The section of town set aside for Jews, where they were permitted to lend money. Christians were not permitted to lend money at interest, though some borrowed from Jewish moneylenders.

*Ave Marie* (21). A Latin song in praise of Mary.

**Seint Nicholas** (27). The fourth-century St. Nicholas, bishop of Myra, had been known for his piety even as a very young child.

**prymer** (30). A schoolbook with lessons on the alphabet, containing certain prayers, hymns, and devotions.

*Alma redemptoris* (31). The expanded title of this anthem to Mary is given below in line 154, *O Alma redemptoris mater,* which can be translated from the Latin as "O nourishing mother of the redeemer." It is abbreviated to *O Alma* in line 168.

**blood out cryeth** (91). See Genesis 4:2 for a biblical precedent for the blood of the slain Abel bespeaking Cain's terrible crime against an innocent victim.

**Seint John** (95). The apostle John who was believed to have written the book of Revelation in a cave on the Aegean island of Patmos. See Revelation 14:1–4 for John's vision that those who die in the purity of presexual innocence would follow the Lamb to heaven.

**Rachel** (140). The reference here is to Matthew 2:18, where Rachel weeps for her children who were murdered by Herod when he slaughtered the innocents.

**greyn** (175). This kernel or seed of grain was Chaucer's addition to his version of the story, though Chaucer is vague about what it means. Perhaps we are not meant to pin down its exact symbolic significance. A miracle is, after all, a miracle. The innocent child himself does not speculate any more than to say that it seemed to him that Mary placed the grain on his tongue to permit him to sing after his throat was cut. When it is removed (line 184), he stops singing.

**Hugh of Lincoln** (197). The young Hugh was a historical or legendary youth who was said to have been murdered by Jews in the English town of Lincoln in 1255. His supposed martyrdom has been called into serious question by modern historians.

# THE PRIORESSE

*The Prologe of the Prioresses Tale*

O Lord, oure Lord, thy name how merveillous
  Is in this large worlde y-sprad—quod she—
For noght only thy laude precious
Parfourned is by men of dignitee,
But by the mouth of children thy bountee           5
Parfouned is, for on the brest soukinge
Som tyme shewen they thyn heryinge.

Wherfore in laude, as I best can or may,
Of thee and of the whyte lilye flour
Which that thee bar, and is a mayde alway,        10
To telle a storie I wol do my labour—
Nat that I may encresen hir honour,
For she hirself is honour, and the rote
Of bountee, next hir sone, and soules bote.

O moder Mayde, O mayde Moder free!        15
O bussh unbrent,* brenninge in Moyses sighte,
That ravishedest doun fro the deitee,
Thurgh thyn humblesse, the goost that in th'alighte,
Of whos vertu, whan he thyn herte lighte,
Conceived was the Fadres sapience:        20
Help me to telle it in thy reverence.

Lady, thy bountee, thy magnificence,
Thy vertu, and thy grete humilitee
Ther may no tonge expresse in no science;
For somtyme, Lady, er men praye to thee,        25

# THE PRIORESS

*The Prologue of the Prioress's Tale*

O Lord our governor, how marvelous is your name,
 spread through this wide world—she said—
for not only is your precious praise
celebrated by worthy men,
but by the mouths of children your bounty                    5
is expressed: suckling at the breast
sometimes they show forth your praise.

Therefore in praise (as best I know or can)
of you and of the white lily flower
who bore you, and is forever a virgin,                        10
I shall take pains to tell a story—
not so that I may increase her honor,
for she herself is honor, and next to her son
the root of bounty and the help of souls.

O mother-maid, O gracious maiden-mother,                     15
O bush unconsumed, burning in Moses's sight,
who ravished down from the deity,
by your humility, the spirit who alighted within you,
of whose power, when he made light your heart,
the wisdom of the Father was conceived:                      20
help me to tell my tale in reverence of you.

Lady, your bounty, your glory,
your power, and your great humility
no tongue has knowledge to express;
for sometimes, Lady, before men pray to you,                 25

Thou goost biforn of thy benignitee,
And getest us the light, of thy preyere,
To gyden us unto thy sone so dere.

My conning is so wayk, O blisful Quene,
For to declare thy grete worthinesse,
That I ne may the weighte nat sustene,
But as a child of twelf month old, or lesse,
That can unnethes any word expresse,
Right so fare I, and therfore I yow preye,
Gydeth my song* that I shall of yow seye.          30

                                                   35

*Rime Royale*

*Here biginneth the Prioresses Tale*

Ther was in Asie, in a greet citee,*
Amonges Cristen folk, a Jewerye,*
Sustened by a lord of that contree
For foule usure and lucre of vilanye,
Hateful to Crist and to his companye;
And thurgh the strete men mighte ryde or wende,
For it was free, and open at either ende.

*dainty hanky weeps prissy clean revisions Mary*

A litel scole of Cristen folk ther stood
Doun at the ferther ende, in which ther were
Children an heep, y-comen of Cristen blood,          10
That lerned in that scole yeer by yere
Swich maner doctrine as men used there;
This is to seyn, to singen and to rede,
As smale children doon in hir childhede.

Among thise children was a widwes sone,          15
A litel clergeon, seven yeer of age,
That day by day to scole was his wone,
And eek also, whereas he saugh th'image
Of Cristes moder, hadde he in usage,
As him was taught, to knele adoun and seye          20
His *Ave Marie,** as he goth by the weye.

you go before in your benignity
and get us by your prayer the light
to guide us to your dear son.

My skill is so weak, O blessed Queen,
to declare your great worth,                                    30
that I cannot sustain the weight of my burden;
it is with me as with a child of twelve months or less,
who can express scarcely a word;
therefore I pray you,
guide the song that I shall sing of you.                        35

*Here begins the Prioress's Tale*

In a great city in Asia there was,
among the Christian folk, a community of Jews,
maintained by the lord of that country
for purposes of foul usury and filthy lucre,
hateful to Christ and his followers;
and through their street people might ride or walk,
for it was free and open at either end.

A little Christian school stood there,
down at the farther end, in which were
many children of Christian blood,                               10
who learned in the school year by year
such subjects as were customary there;
that is to say, to sing and read,
as small children do in their childhood.

Among these children was a widow's son,                         15
a little scholar seven years of age,
who day by day was wont to go to school;
and also, whenever he saw the image
of Christ's mother, he would customarily,
as he had been taught, kneel down and say              20
his *Ave Maria,* on his way.

Thus hath this widwe hir litel sone y-taught
Our blisful Lady, Cristes moder dere,
To worshipe ay, and he forgat it naught,
For sely child wol alday sone lere;                        25
But ay whan I remembre on this matere,
Seint Nicholas* stant ever in my presence,
For he so yong to Crist did reverence.

This litel child, his litel book lerninge,
As he sat in the scole at his prymer,*                    30
He *Alma redemptoris** herde singe,
As children lerned hir antiphoner;
And, as he dorste, he drough him ner and ner,
And herkned ay the wordes and the note,
Til he the firste vers coude al by rote.                  35

Noght wiste he what this Latin was to seye,
For he so yong and tendre was of age;
But on a day his felaw gan he preye
T'expounden him this song in his langage,
Or telle him why this song was in usage;                  40
This preyde he him to construe and declare
Ful ofte tyme upon his knowes bare.

His felaw, which that elder was than he,
Answerde him thus: "This song, I have herd seye,
Was maked of our blisful Lady free,                       45
Hir to salue, and eek hir for to preye
To been our help and socour whan we deye.
I can no more expounde in this matere;
I lerne song, I can but smal grammere."

"And is this song maked in reverence                      50
Of Cristes moder?" seyde this innocent;
"Now certes, I wol do my diligence
To conne it al, er Cristemasse is went;
Though that I for my prymer shal be shent,

Thus the widow had taught her little son
always to worship our blissful Lady,
Christ's dear mother, and he did not forget it,
for an innocent child will always learn quickly; 25
but whenever I think about this subject,
Saint Nicholas always comes to my mind,
since he did reverence to Christ so young.

This little child studied his little book:
as he sat in the school reading his primer, 30
he heard *Alma redemptoris* being sung,
as older children learned their anthem books;
and, as much as he dared, he drew nearer and nearer
and listened to the words and notes
until he knew the first verse all by heart. 35

He knew not at all what this Latin meant,
since he was of so young and tender an age;
but one day he asked his comrade
to explain the song to him in his own language,
or tell him why this song was sung; 40
on his bare knees he begged him many times
to translate and explain this.

His comrade, who was older than he,
answered him thus: "This song, I have heard said,
was composed about our blissful gracious Lady, 45
to greet her, and also to pray her
to be our help and succor when we die.
I can explain no more about it;
I am learning to sing, I know very little Latin grammar."

"And is this song written in reverence 50
of Christ's mother?" said this innocent;
"Now certainly, I will try diligently
to learn it all before Christmas has gone by;
even if I shall be punished for neglecting my primer

And shal be beten thryës in an houre,                         55
I wol it conne, Our Lady for to honoure."


His felaw taughte him homward prively,
Fro day to day, til he coude it by rote,
And than he song it wel and boldely
Fro word to word, acording with the note;                    60
Twyës a day it passed thurgh his throte,
To scoleward and homward whan he wente;
On Cristes moder set was his entente.


As I have seyd, throughout the Jewerye
This litel child, as he cam to and fro,                       65
Ful merily than wolde he singe, and crye
*O Alma redemptoris* everemo.
The swetnes hath his herte perced so
Of Cristes moder, that, to hir to preye,
He can nat stinte of singing by the weye.                     70


Our firste fo, the serpent Sathanas,
That hath in Jewes herte his waspes nest,
Up swal, and seide, "O Hebraik peple, allas!
Is this to yow a thing that is honest,
That swich a boy shal walken as him lest                      75
In your despyt, and singe of swich sentence,
Which is agayn your lawes reverence?"


Fro thennes forth the Jewes han conspyred
This innocent out of this world to chace;
An homicyde thereto han they hyred,                           80
That in an aley hadde a privee place;
And as the child gan forby for to pace,
This cursed Jew him hente and heeld him faste,
And kitte his throte, and in a pit him caste.


I seye that in a wardrobe they him threwe                     85
Whereas these Jewes purgen hir entraille.
O cursed folk of Herodes al newe,

and shall be beaten three times in an hour,          55
I will learn it, to honor Our Lady."

Day by day his comrade taught it to him secretly
on the way home, until he knew it by heart,
and then he sang it well and boldly
word for word according with the tune;          60
twice a day it issued from his throat,
on the way to school and on the way home;
his heart was set on Christ's mother.

As I have said, this little child, as he
went to and fro through the ghetto,          65
would sing most merrily, and cry
O Alma redemptoris constantly.
The sweetness of Christ's mother had so
pierced his heart that, in order to pray to her,
he could not stop singing on his way.          70

Our first foe, the serpent Satan,
who has his wasp's nest in the hearts of Jews,
swelled up, and said, "O Hebrew people, alas!
Is this a thing that is seemly to you,
that such a boy should walk as it pleases him          75
in contempt of you, and sing of such a doctrine,
which is contrary to the reverence due to your laws?"

Thenceforth the Jews conspired
to hunt this innocent out of this world;
for this purpose they hired a murderer,          80
who had a hiding place in an alley;
and when the child was passing by,
this cursed Jew seized him and held him fast,
and cut his throat, and cast him into a pit.

I tell you they threw him into a privy          85
where these Jews purged their entrails.
O folk of Herod cursed yet again,

What may your yvel entente yow availle?
Mordre wol out, certein, it wol nat faille,
And namely ther th'onour of God shal sprede,       90
The blood out cryeth* on your cursed dede.

O martir, souded to virginitee,
Now maystou singen, folwing ever in oon
The whyte lamb celestial—quod she—
Of which the grete evangelist, Seint John,*       95
In Pathmos wroot, which seith that they that goon
Biforn this lamb, and singe a song al newe,
That never fleshly wommen they ne knewe.

This povre widwe awaiteth al that night
After hir litel child, but he cam noght;       100
For which, as sone as it was dayes light,
With face pale of drede and bisy thoght,
She hath at scole and elleswher him soght,
Til finally she gan so fer espye
That he last seyn was in the Jewerye.       105

With modres pitee in hir brest enclosed,
She gooth, as she were half out of hir minde,
To every place wher she hath supposed
By lyklihede hir litel child to finde;
And ever on Cristes moder meke and kinde       110
She cryde, and atte laste thus she wroghte:
Among the cursed Jewes she him soghte.

She frayneth and she preyeth pitously
To every Jew that dwelte in thilke place,
To tell hir, if hir child wente oght forby.       115
They seyde nay; but Jesu, of his grace,
Yaf in hir thought, inwith a litel space,
That in that place after hir sone she cryde,
Wher he was casten in a pit bisyde.

what can your evil intent avail you?
Murder will out, certainly, it will not fail,
especially when the honor of God shall thereby
    be increased;                                                                90
the blood cries out on your cursed deed.

O martyr consecrated to virginity,
now you may sing, ever following
the white lamb of heaven—she said—
of which the great evangelist Saint John                          95
wrote in Patmos, saying that they who walk
before this lamb, and sing a new song,
never knew women carnally.

This poor widow waited all that night
for her little child, but he did not come;                       100
therefore, as soon as it was daylight,
with the pale face of dread and a disturbed mind,
she looked for him at school and elsewhere,
until finally she got so far as to discern
that he was last seen in the ghetto.                             105

With a mother's fear in her breast,
she went, as if she were half out of her mind,
to every place where she supposed
it likely to find her little child;
and ever she called upon Christ's mother,                        110
so meek and kind, who at last led her
to look for him among the cursed Jews.

She asked and she begged piteously
of every Jew that dwelled in that place
to tell her if her child had gone by at all.                     115
They said no, but Jesus of his grace
put it in her mind, after a little while,
to call out for her son in the place
next to which he was cast in a pit.

O grete God, that parfournest thy laude                    120
By mouth of innocents, lo heer thy might!
This gemme of chastitee, this emeraude,
And eek of martirdom the ruby bright,
Ther he with throte y-corven lay upright,
He *Alma redemptoris* gan to singe                         125
So loude that al the place gan to ringe.

The Cristen folk, that thurgh the strete wente,
In coomen, for to wondre upon this thing,
And hastily they for the provost sente;
He cam anon withouten tarying,                             130
And herieth Crist that is of heven king,
And eek his moder, honour of mankinde;
And after that, the Jewes leet he binde.

This child with pitous lamentacioun
Up taken was, singing his song alway;                      135
And with honour of greet processioun
They carien him unto the nexte abbay.
His moder swowning by the bere lay;
Unnethe might the peple that was there
This newe Rachel* bringe fro his bere.                     140

With torment and with shamful deth echon
This provost dooth thise Jewes for to sterve
That of this mordre wiste, and that anon;
He nolde no swich cursednesse observe.
Yvel shal have, that yvel wol deserve.                     145
Therfor with wilde hors he dide hem drawe,
And after that he heng hem by the lawe.

Upon his bere ay lyth this innocent
Biforn the chief auter, whyl masse laste,
And after that, the abbot with his covent                  150
Han sped hem for to burien him ful faste;
And whan they holy water on him caste,

O great God, who manifest your praise 120
by the mouths of innocents, behold here thy might!
This gem of chastity, this emerald,
the ruby bright of martyrdom also,
there as he lay with his throat cut, his face upturned,
he began to sing *Alma redemptoris* 125
so loudly that all the place rang with it.

The Christian folk who were going through this street
came in to marvel at this thing,
and they hastily sent for the provost;
he came at once without tarrying, 130
and praised Christ who is king of heaven,
and his mother too, honor of mankind;
and after that he had the Jews bound.

This child was taken up with piteous lamentation,
continually singing his song, 135
and with full processional honor
they carried him to the nearest abbey.
His mother lay swooning by the bier;
the people there could scarcely
bring this latter-day Rachel from it. 140

With torment and with shameful death
this provost put every one of the Jews that
knew of this murder to death, and that at once;
he would not countenance any such cursedness.
Evil shall get what it deserves. 145
Therefore he had them drawn with wild horses,
and after that he hanged them according to law.

This innocent still lay upon his bier
before the high altar, while mass lasted,
and after that, the abbot with his convent 150
diligently made haste to bury him.
And when they cast holy water on him,

Yet spak this child, whan spreynd was holy water,
And song *O Alma redemptoris mater*!

This abbot, which that was an holy man                       155
As monkes been, or elles oghten be,
This yonge child to conjure he bigan,
And seyde, "Oh dere child, I halse thee,
In vertu of the Holy Trinitee,
Tel me what is thy cause for to singe,
Sith that thy throte is cut, to my seminge?"                 160

"My throte is cut unto my nekke-boon,"
Seyde this child, "and, as by wey of kinde,
I sholde have deyed, ye, longe tyme agoon,
But Jesu Crist, as ye in bokes finde,                        165
Wil that his glorie laste and be in minde;
And, for the worship of his moder dere,
Yet may I singe *O Alma* loude and clere.

"This welle of mercy, Cristes moder swete,
I lovede alwey, as after my connnige;                        170
And whan that I my lyf sholde forlete,
To me she cam, and bad me for to singe
This antem verraily in my deyinge,
As ye han herd, and, whan that I had songe,
Me thoughte, she leyde a greyn* upon my tonge.               175

"Wherfor I singe, and singe I moot certeyn
In honour of that blisful mayden free,
Til fro my tonge of-taken is the greyn;
And afterward thus seyde she to me,
'My litel child, now wol I fecche thee                       180
Whan that the greyn is fro thy tonge y-take;
Be nat agast, I wol thee nat forsake.' "

This holy monk, this abbot, him mene I,
His tonge out caughte and took awey the greyn,
And he yaf up the goost ful softely.                         185

still this child spoke, when the holy water had been
sprinkled, and sang *O Alma redemptoris mater!*

The abbot, who was a holy man,                                    155
as monks are (or else ought to be),
began to entreat this young child,
and said, "O dear child, I beseech thee,
by the power of the holy Trinity,
tell me what causes you to sing,                                 160
for your throat has been cut, as far as I can see."

"My throat is cut through to the neck bone,"
said this child, "and by the law of nature
I should have died—indeed, long ago;
but Jesus Christ, as you will find in books,                     165
desires that his glory last and be kept in mind;
and, for the honor of his dear mother,
yet shall I sing *O Alma* loud and clear.

"I always loved this well of mercy,
Christ's mother sweet, as best I could;                          170
and when I was about to lose my life,
she came to me, and truly told me to sing
this anthem as I died,
as you have heard, and when I had sung,
it seemed to me she laid a grain upon my tongue.                 175

"Therefore I sing, and certainly must go on singing
in honor of that blissful, gracious maiden,
until the grain is taken from my tongue;
and afterward she said to me,
'My little child, now I will fetch you                           180
when the grain is taken from your tongue;
do not be afraid, I will not forsake you.' "

This holy monk, this abbot (him I mean),
pulled out the tongue and took away the grain,
and quietly the child gave up the ghost.                         185

And whan this abbot had this wonder seyn,
His salte teres trikled doun as reyn,
And gruf he fil al plat upon the grounde,
And stille he lay as he had been y-bounde.

The covent eek lay on the pavement 190
Weping, and herien Cristes moder dere,
And after that they ryse, and forth ben went,
And toke awey this martir fro his bere,
And in a tombe of marbul stones clere
Enclosen they his litel body swete; 195
Ther he is now, God leve us for to mete.

O yonge Hugh of Lincoln,* slayn also
With cursed Jewes, as it is notable
(For it nis but a litel whyle ago),
Preye eek for us, we sinful folk unstable, 200
That, of his mercy, God so merciable
On us his grete mercy multiplye,
For reverence of his moder Marye. Amen.

When the abbot had seen this miracle,
his salt tears trickled down like rain, *simile*
and he fell flat upon the ground
and lay as still as if he had been bound.

The rest of the monks also lay on the floor,　　190
weeping and praising Christ's dear mother,
and after that they rose and went forth,
taking this martyr from his bier,
and they enclosed his sweet little body *buried*
in a tomb of shining marble;　　195
where he is now, God grant that we may meet.

O young Hugh of Lincoln, also slain
by cursed Jews, everyone knows
(for it was but a little while ago),
pray for us unstable, sinful folk,　　*moral*　200
that of his mercy God so merciful will　　*theme*
multiply his great mercy toward us,
for reverence of his mother Mary. Amen.

# THE NUN'S PRIEST'S TALE

# INTRODUCTION

✣

THE NUN'S PRIEST is a shadowy figure just barely
mentioned in the General Prologue to *The Canterbury
Tales* (line 164) as one of three priests who accompany the
Prioress. He is given no description there. We can surmise
that he worked under the authority of the Prioress and joined
her on the pilgrimage to Canterbury to protect her and to
hear her confessions. Of course, he might well have wanted
to pay homage to St. Thomas for spiritual reasons of his own,
but in fact we are not told that. All we really have to go on is
the strangely brilliant tale he tells about a poor widow's chick-
ens who talk about the significance of dreams and whose safe
little yard is invaded by a flattering fox. What that tale lets us
infer about the character of the Nun's Priest—if anything—
is open to debate. Most readers read the tale for its own sake
and don't worry much about the teller, except perhaps inso-
far as his personality and antifeminist leanings are revealed
in that tale.

"The Nun's Priest's Tale" is a beast fable in which animals
talk and behave very much as humans do. The closing event,
where Chauntecleer is carried off by a hungry fox who by
making the mistake of speaking lets Chauntecleer escape,
came to Chaucer through a brief (35-line) fable of Marie de
France. That fable accounts for some 150 lines of Chaucer's
much expanded version, but even that part of the story (roughly
lines 462–615) is only the last quarter of "The Nun's Priest's
Tale." The opening three-fourths is taken up with a short ac-
count of the old widow and her chicken yard, a much longer
debate about the significance of Chauntecleer's dream that a
doglike animal wanted to kill him, and various associated

bits of medical information, philosophical explanation, and scholastic debate. Chaucer drew some of this material from one or more of the stories about Reynard the fox. In these earlier analogues the cock's wife, named Pinte in one of them, correctly interprets her hero's dream as a warning of dangers that lie ahead, while the arrogant Chauntecleer tells her she is wrong and cockily ignores her warning.

Chaucer's tale is a delightful combination of plot, innuendo, allegory, learned citations, and mock-heroic humor aimed at making human pretensions look silly when imposed on mere chickens. The tale purports to have a serious moral: "But you that think this tale is a trifle about a fox, or a cock, and a hen, accept the moral. . . . Take the fruit and let the chaff alone" (lines 618–20, 623). No one clear moral is given, however, and it is easy enough to suppose that pointing to the absent fruit is part of the joke.

## NOTES

**rede colera** (line 108). Like the **malencolye** of line 113, this red *choler* is the result of an imbalance of the bodily fluids or "humors" sometimes thought to control human complexion, temperament, personality, and happiness. The four humors are blood, phlegm, *choler* or red bile, and melancholy or black bile. An imbalance of these was thought to cause sanguinary, phlegmatic, choleric (bad tempered), and melancholy dispositions.

**Catoun** (120). Dionysius Cato, who wrote a series of Latin maxims. Chauntecleer picks up on the reference in line 151, below. The allusion to Cato is vague, the main point of it being the humor of chickens citing ancient authors as authorities.

**tak som laxatyf** (123). Pertelote thinks that Chauntecleer's troubled dream has a physical or natural cause, probably indigestion, and urges him to take a laxative to purge his system.

**wormes, lauriol, centaure, fumetere** (142–43). These are all substances prescribed in medieval medical tractates for various conditions. It is not clear that they would have helped Chauntecleer, even if his dreams had been caused by what he ate or by the imbalance of his four humors. There is no great need for modern readers to understand the complex details of these conditions or the proposed treatments. The main point seems to be that Pertelote does not understand them well herself.

**dremes ben significaciouns** (159). Unlike his wife Pertelote, Chauntecleer believes that his strange dream has predictive value and is a serious warning of a disastrous event to come.

**Oon of the gretteste auctours** (164). Probably Cicero is referred to, though Chaucer apparently read the following stories about dreams elsewhere.

**Kenelm** (290). According to legend, Kenelm was murdered at age seven, not long after he dreamed that he had climbed a lovely tree that was then cut from beneath him, freeing him to fly to heaven as a bird.

**Macrobeus** (303). Fifth-century author of a well-known commentary on the dreams of Scipio.

**Daniel** (308). See Daniel, chapters 7 ff., for several of Daniel's visions.

**Joseph** (310), **Cresus** (318), **Andromacha** (321). These are all references to people known in medieval times for their dreams or their ability to interpret them accurately. The brief descriptions in the text tell us all that we need to know about them, except perhaps the humor of a rooster citing biblical and classical sources.

*In principio, / Mulier est hominis confusio* (343–44). A well-known proverb in Latin: "In the beginning, woman was the downfall of man." The allusion is ultimately to the story of Eve's succumbing to the influence of Satan and thus causing all mankind to be exiled from paradise. (Compare lines 436–38, below.) Immediately afterward Chauntecleer takes advantage of Pertelote's ignorance of Latin by giving a translation that she will like better. Of course, it may be that he himself misunderstands the Latin he quotes.

**Launcelot de Lake** (392). A romance story about the love of Lancelot and Guinevere, King Arthur's wife.

**Scariot** (407), **Genilon** (407), **Sinon** (408). Judas Iscariot, Ganelon of France, and Sinon of Greece were all well-known traitors. They provide unflattering company for the sly fox who tricks Chauntecleer.

**Augustyn** (421), **Boëce** (422), **Bradwardyn** (422). St. Augustine, Boethius, and Thomas Bradwardine were three authorities on scholastic questions of fate and free will. At stake in the various debates was whether God's foreknowledge of certain events makes them "necessary" or certain to happen, and whether that foreknowledge robs men of the ability to make their own free choices.

**Phisiologus** (451). Refers to the supposed author, "the Naturalist," of a book about the qualities associated with certain real and legendary animals.

**Burnel the Asse** (492). The reference is to a brief story about a boy who broke a rooster's leg by throwing a rock at it. Much later the rooster got his revenge by crowing late on the morning the man was to get ordained and be awarded a benefice. He missed out on both because he overslept.

**Allas, ye lordes** (505). This reference to the flattery of lords by the men around them is puzzling in connection with the Canterbury pilgrimage, on which no lords are present. It may well indicate that Chaucer wrote the tale earlier than *The Canterbury Tales* project, perhaps initially for his own separate reading in a royal court.

**Ecclesiaste** (509). The exact source of this statement on flattery has not been identified, but there are several biblical warnings about the evils of flattery.

**Friday** (521). Friday, associated with the special powers of Venus (see next line), has traditionally been considered a day of bad luck, and still is, as in "Friday the thirteenth."

**Gaufred** (527). Geoffrey of Vinsauf, a thirteenth-century author of a book on medieval rhetoric, wrote in his *Poetria nova* a rhetorically overblown poem lamenting the death of King Richard I on a Friday.

**Pirrus** (537), **Priam** (538), *Eneydos* (539), **Hasdrubales wyf** (543), **Nero** (550). Chaucer continues the list of classical parallels to the lives and trials of chickens. Pyrrhus was the son of Achilles who attacked Priam, the king of Troy. The *Eneydos* (the *Aeneid*) is a long poem by Virgil about the destruction of Troy. Hasdrubal was a king of Carthage whose wife took her own life. Nero burned Rome and murdered the wives of the senators.

**Jakke Straw** (574). A leader of the English Rising (sometimes called the Peasants' Revolt) of 1381. Straw was supposed to have been among those who attacked a group of Flemish wool-traders, rivals for the English wool trade.

# THE NONNES PREESTES TALE

A povre widwe, somdel stape in age,
  Was whylom dwelling in a narwe cotage,
Bisyde a grove, stonding in a dale.
This widwe, of which I telle yow my tale,
Sin thilke day that she was last a wyf,                    5
In pacience ladde a ful simple lyf,
For litel was hir catel and hir rente;
By housbondrye of swich as God hir sente
She fond hirself and eek hir doghtren two.
Three large sowes hadde she, and namo,                    10
Three kyn, and eek a sheep that highte Malle.
Ful sooty was hir bour and eek hir halle,
In which she eet ful many a sclendre meel.
Of poynaunt sauce hir neded never a deel:
No deyntee morsel passed thurgh hir throte;               15
Hir dyete was accordant to hir cote.
Repleccioun ne made hir never syk;
Attempree dyete was al hir phisyk,
And exercyse, and hertes suffisaunce.
The goute lette hir nothing for to daunce,                20
N'apoplexye shente nat hir heed;
No wyn ne drank she, neither whyt ne reed:
Hir bord was served most with whyt and blak,
Milk and broun breed, in which she fond no lak;
Seynd bacoun, and somtyme an ey or tweye,                 25
For she was as it were a maner deye.
  A yerd she hadde, enclosed al aboute
With stikkes, and a drye dich withoute,

# THE NUN'S PRIEST'S TALE

A poor widow, somewhat advanced in age,
once dwelt in a humble cottage
beside a grove in a valley.
This widow whom I am telling you about
had patiently lived a simple life                                      5
since the day that she lost her husband.
Her property and her income were meager;
by frugal management of such as God gave her
she supported herself, and her two daughters as well.
She had three large sows (no more),                                    10
three cows, and, besides, a sheep named Molly.
Grimed with soot was her bedchamber and hall,
in which she ate many a scanty meal.
She had no need at all of sharp sauce;
no dainty morsel went down her throat—                                15
her diet accorded with her condition in life.
Overeating never made her sick;
a temperate diet, exercise,
and a contented heart were her only medicine.
Gout didn't in the least hinder her from dancing,                     20
nor did apoplexy ever hurt her head.
She drank no wine—neither white nor red;
her board was more likely to be set with white and
        black—
milk and dark bread, of which she found no lack—
broiled bacon and sometimes an egg or two,                            25
for she was something of a dairywoman.
    She had a farmyard, enclosed
with a fence and a dry ditch.

In which she hadde a cok, hight Chauntecleer:
In al the land of crowing nas his peer.                    30
His vois was merier than the mery orgon
On messe-dayes that in the chirche gon;
Wel sikerer was his crowing in his logge
Than is a clokke, or an abbey orlogge.
By nature knew he ech ascencioun                          35
Of equinoxial in thilke toun;
For whan degrees fiftene were ascended,
Thanne crew he, that it mighte nat ben amended.
His comb was redder than the fyn coral,
And batailed, as it were a castel wal.                    40
His bile was blak, and as the jeet it shoon;
Lyk asur were his legges and his toon;
His nayles whytter than the lilie flour,
And lyk the burned gold was his colour.

This gentil cok hadde in his governaunce                  45
Sevene hennes, for to doon al his plesaunce,
Whiche were his sustres and his paramours,
And wonder lyk to him as of colours;
Of which the faireste hewed on hir throte
Was cleped faire damoysele Pertelote.                     50
Curteys she was, discreet, and debonaire,
And compaignable, and bar hirself so faire,
Sin thilke day that she was seven night old,
That trewely she hath the herte in hold
Of Chauntecleer, loken in every lith;                     55
He loved hir so that wel was him therwith.
But such a joye was it to here hem singe,
Whan that the brighte sonne gan to springe,
In swete accord, "My lief is faren in londe."
For thilke tyme, as I have understonde,                   60
Bestes and briddes coude speke and singe.

And so bifel that in a daweninge,
As Chauntecleer among his wyves alle
Sat on his perche, that was in the halle,
And next him sat this faire Pertelote,                    65
This Chauntecleer gan gronen in his throte,

In the yard she had a cock named Chauntecleer:
in all the land he had no equal in crowing. 30
His voice was merrier than the merry organ
that was played in the church on holy days,
and in his dwelling his crowing was more dependable
than any clock, even the great one of an abbey.
He knew by instinct the daily 35
movement of the heavens,
for when they had moved fifteen degrees
he crowed in a way that could not be bettered.
His comb was redder than fine coral,
and crenellated like a castle wall; 40
his bill was black and shone like jet;
his legs and toes were like azure;
his nails whiter than the lily;
and his color like the burnished gold.

This courtly cock had at his command 45
seven hens to do his pleasure.
They were his sisters and his paramours,
and marvelously like him in coloring;
of them the one with the most beautifuly colored throat
was called the fair damsel Pertelote: 50
she was courteous, discreet, debonaire,
and companionable, and she conducted herself so
handsomely that since the day she was seven
nights old she had truly held the heart
of Chauntecleer bound and captive. 55
He loved her so much that all was well with him.
But what a joy it was to hear them,
when the bright sun began to rise, singing
"My love has gone away" in sweet harmony—
for at that time, as I understand, 60
beasts and birds could speak and sing.

It befell one morning at dawn,
as Chauntecleer was sitting on his perch
in the hall among all his wives,
and as Pertelote sat next to him, 65
that he began to groan in his throat,

As man that in his dreem is drecched sore.
And whan that Pertelote thus herde him rore,
She was agast, and seyde, "O herte dere,
What eyleth yow, to grone in this manere?      70
Ye been a verray sleper, fy, for shame!"
    And he answerde and seyde thus, "Madame,
I pray yow that ye take it nat agrief.
By God, me mette I was in swich meschief
Right now, that yet myn herte is sore afright.      75
Now God," quod he, "my swevene recche aright,
And keep my body out of foul prisoun!
Me mette how that I romed up and doun
Withinne our yerde, whereas I saugh a best,
Was lyk an hound, and wolde han maad arest      80
Upon my body, and wolde han had me deed.
His colour was bitwixe yelwe and reed;
And tipped was his tail, and bothe his eres,
With blak, unlyk the remenant of his heres;
His snowte smal, with glowinge eyen tweye.      85
Yet of his look for fere almost I deye;
This caused me my groning, doutelees."
    "Avoy!" quod she, "Fy on yow, hertelees!
Allas!" quod she, "For by that God above,
Now han ye lost myn herte and al my love;      90
I can nat love a coward, by my feith.
For certes, what so any womman seith,
We alle desyren, if it mighte be,
To han housbondes hardy, wyse, and free,
And secree, and no nigard, ne no fool,      95
Ne him that is agast of every tool,
Ne noon avauntour, by that God above!
How dorste ye seyn for shame unto your love
That any thing mighte make yow aferd?
Have ye no mannes herte, and han a berd?      100
Allas, and conne ye been agast of swevenis?
Nothing God wot, but vanitee in sweven is.
Swevenes engendren of repleccliouns,
And ofte of fume, and of compleccliouns,

like a man who is sorely troubled in his dream.
And when Pertelote heard him roaring this way,
she was aghast, and said, "Dear heart,
what ails you to groan in this manner? 70
You're a great sleeper, aren't you?—Fie, for shame!"
    And he answered thus: "Madame,
I pray you not to take it amiss.
By God, I dreamed I was in such mischief
just now that my heart is still sore afraid. 75
Now may God," he said, "help to interpret my dream
correctly, and keep my body from foul captivity!
I dreamed that I was roaming up and down
in our yard, when I saw a beast
that was like a dog and that wanted to seize 80
my body and kill me.
His color was between yellow and red,
and his tail and both his ears were tipped
with black, unlike the rest of his coat.
His snout was small and he had two glowing eyes. 85
I am still almost dying for fear of the look of him.
This caused my groaning, doubtless."
    "Avaunt!" she said, "Fie on you, faint heart!
Alas," she said, "for, by God above,
now you have lost my heart and all my love. 90
I cannot love a coward, by my faith.
For certainly, whatever any woman says,
we all desire, if it might be,
to have husbands who are bold, prudent, generous,
and able to keep a secret—neither niggards nor fools 95
nor someone who is frightened of every weapon,
nor a boaster, by God above!
How dare you for shame say to your love
that anything might make you afraid?
Have you no man's heart, and yet you have a man's beard? 100
Alas, and can you be afraid of dreams?
Nothing but nonsense is in dreams, God knows!
Dreams come from overeating,
and often from gas and from temperamental

Whan humours been to habundant in a wight.            105
Certes this dreem, which ye han met to-night,
Cometh of the grete superfluitee
Of youre rede *colera*,* pardee,
Which causeth folk to dreden in hir dremes
Of arwes, and of fyr with rede lemes,                 110
Of grete bestes, that they wol hem byte,
Of contek, and of whelpes grete and lyte;
Right as the humour of malencolye
Causeth ful many a man in sleep to crye
For fere of blake beres or boles blake,               115
Or elles, blake develes wole hem take.
Of othere humours coude I telle also
That werken many a man in sleep ful wo;
But I wol passe as lightly as I can.

   "Lo Catoun,* which that was so wys a man,     120
Seyde he nat thus, 'Ne do no fors of dremes'?
Now, sire," quod she, "whan we flee fro the bemes,
For Goddes love, as tak som laxatyf;*
Up peril of my soule and of my lyf,
I counseille yow the beste, I wol nat lye,            125
That bothe of colere and of malencolye
Ye purge yow; and for ye shul nat tarie,
Though in this toun is noon apothecarie,
I shal myself to herbes techen yow,
That shul ben for your hele, and for your prow;       130
And in our yerd tho herbes shal I finde,
The whiche han of hir propretee, by kinde,
To purgen yow binethe and eek above.
Forget not this, for Goddes owene love!
Ye been ful colerik of complexioun.                   135
Ware the sonne in his ascencioun
Ne fynde yow nat repleet of humours hote:
And if it do, I dar wel leye a grote
That ye shul have a fevere terciane,
Or an agu, that may be youre bane.                    140

dispositions when humors are too abundant in a man.     105
Certainly this dream that you had this night
comes from the great superfluity
of your red bile,
which causes folk in their dreams to dread
arrows and fire with red flames,     110
or huge beasts that want to bite them,
and strife, and dogs great and small—
just as the humor of melancholy
causes full many a man to cry out in sleep
either for fear of black bears and black bulls     115
or else because he thinks that black devils want to seize
him. I could tell of other humors, too,
that work woe to many a man in sleep,
but I want to pass over as lightly as I can.

   "Look at Cato, who was so wise a man—didn't he     120
pronounce on the subject thus: 'Pay no attention
   to dreams'?
Now sir," said she, "when we fly down from the beams,
take some laxative, for the love of God.
On peril of my life and soul,
I am counseling you for the best; I don't want to deceive     125
you: you should purge yourself of both choler
and melancholy; and in order to keep you
   from dallying—
there is, after all, no apothecary in this town—
I myself shall teach you about herbs
that will work for your health and profit,     130
and in our yard I shall find those herbs
that by nature have properties
to purge you below, and above, too.
Don't forget this, for God's own love!
You are of a very choleric temperament;     135
beware lest the sun in his ascension
find you overfull of hot humors;
if it does, I'll venture to bet a groat
that you will have a tertian fever
or an ague that may be your bane.     140

A day or two ye shul have digestyves
Of wormes,* er ye take your laxatyves
Of lauriol,* centaure,* and fumetere,*
Or elles of ellebor, that groweth there,
Of catapuce, or of gaytres beryis,                             145
Of erbe yve growing in our yerd, ther mery is;
Pekke hem up right as they growe, and ete hem in.
Be mery, housbond, for your fader kin!
Dredeth no dreem; I can say yow namore."
    "Madame," quod he, "graunt mercy of your lore.           150
But nathelees, as touching daun Catoun,
That hath of wisdom swich a greet renoun,
Though that he bad no dremes for to drede,
By God, men may in olde bokes rede
Of many a man more of auctoritee                              155
Than ever Catoun was, so mote I thee,
That al the revers seyn of his sentence,
And han wel founden by experience
That dremes ben significaciouns,*
As wel of joye as tribulaciouns                               160
That folk enduren in this lyf present.
Ther nedeth make of this noon argument;
The verray preve sheweth it in dede.
    "Oon of the gretteste auctours* that men rede
Seith thus, that whylom two felawes wente                     165
On pilgrimage, in a ful good entente;
And happed so, thay come into a toun,
Wheras ther was swich congregacioun
Of peple, and eek so streit of herbergage
That they ne founde as muche as o cotage                      170
In which they bothe mighte y-logged be.
Wherfor thay mosten, of necessitee,
As for that night, departen compaignye;
And ech of hem goth to his hostelrye,
And took his logging as it wolde falle.                        175
That oon of hem was logged in a stalle,
Fer in a yerd, with oxen of the plough;

You shall have digestives of worms
for a day or two before you take your laxatives
of spurge-laurel, centaury, fumitory,
or else of hellebore growing down there,
of caper-spurge or of berries of the gaytree,          145
and of ground ivy growing in our pleasant yard.
Peck them up right as they grow and swallow them down.
Be merry, husband, for the honor of your father's
     family!
Dread no dream; I can say no more to you."
     "Madame," said he, "I thank you for your lore.          150
But nevertheless, in regard to Master Cato,
who had such a great reputation for wisdom:
although he said not to dread dreams,
you can, by God, read in ancient books
of many a man of more authority          155
than ever Cato was, as I hope to thrive,
who says just the opposite of his opinion,
and has found by experience
that dreams are signs
of joy as well as of tribulations          160
that people endure in this present life.
There is no need to make an argument of this;
real experience shows it clearly.
     "One of the greatest authors men read
says thus: once two friends went          165
on a pilgrimage, with very pious intentions;
it happened that they came into a town
where there was such a press
of people and such a shortage of lodgings
that they didn't find so much as a cottage          170
in which they could both be lodged.
Therefore they found that they must, of necessity,
part company for that night;
and each of them went to a hostelry,
and took his lodging as his luck might fall.          175
One of them was lodged in a stall,
far away in a barnyard, with the plow oxen;

That other man was logged wel ynough,
As was his aventure or his fortune,
That us governeth alle as in commune.                    180
    "And so bifel that, longe er it were day,
This man mette in his bed, theras he lay,
How that his felawe gan upon him calle,
And seyde, 'Allas, for in an oxes stalle
This night I shal be mordred ther I lye.                 185
Now help me, dere brother, er I dye;
In alle haste com to me,' he sayde.
This man out of his sleep for fere abrayde;
But whan that he was wakned of his sleep,
He turned him, and took of this no keep;                 190
Him thoughte his dreem nas but a vanitee.
Thus twyës in his sleping dremed he.
And atte thridde tyme yet his felawe
Cam, as him thoughte, and seide; 'I am now slawe;
Bihold my blody woundes, depe and wyde!                   195
Arys up erly in the morwe-tyde,
And at the west gate of the toun,' quod he,
'A carte ful of dong ther shaltow see,
In which my body is hid ful prively;
Do thilke carte aresten boldely.                         200
My gold caused my mordre, sooth to sayn';
And tolde him every poynt how he was slayn,
With a ful pitous face, pale of hewe.
And truste wel, his dreem he fond ful trewe;
For on the morwe, as sone as it was day,                 205
To his felawes in he took the way;
And whan that he cam to this oxes stalle,
After his felawe he bigan to calle.
    "The hostiler answered him anon,
And seyde, 'Sire, your felawe is agon;                    210
As sone as day he wente out of the toun.'
This man gan fallen in suspecioun,
Remembring on his dremes that he mette,
And forth he goth, no lenger wolde he lette,

the other man was lodged well enough,
as was his luck or fortune,
which governs all of us equally.                               180
    "It so happened that long before it was day
the second man dreamed as he lay in his bed
that his comrade called to him,
and said, 'Alas, for tonight
I shall be murdered where I lie in an ox's stall.             185
Now help me, dear brother, before I die;
come to me in all haste,' he said.
The man started up out of his sleep for fear;
but when he was awake
he turned over and took no notice of this;                   190
he thought the dream was only nonsense.
He dreamed thus twice in his sleep.
Yet a third time his friend
came, as it seemed to him, and said, 'I have now been
slain; behold my bloody wounds, deep and wide!              195
Get up early tomorrow morning,
and at the west gate of the town,' he said,
'you shall see a cart full of dung,
in which my body is secretly hidden;
stop that cart boldly.                                        200
My gold was the cause of my murder, it is true';
and with a piteous, pale face
he told his friend every detail of how he was slain.
And believe me, the friend found that his dream
        was true;
for on the next day, as soon as it was light,               205
he made his way to his companion's inn,
and when he came to the ox's stall
he began to call for his comrade.
    "The innkeeper answered him quickly,
and said, 'Sir, your companion is gone:                      210
as soon as it was day he went out of the town.'
The man became suspicious,
remembering the dreams he had had,
and he went immediately

Unto the west gate of the toun, and fond                          215
A dong-carte, wente as it were to donge lond,
That was arrayed in the same wyse
As ye han herd the dede man devyse;
And with an hardy herte he gan to crye
Vengeaunce and justice of this felonye:                           220
'My felawe mordred is this same night,
And in this carte he lyth gapinge upright.
I crye out on the ministres,' quod he,
'That sholden kepe and reulen this citee;
Harrow! Allas! Her lyth my felawe slayn!'                         225
What sholde I more unto this tale sayn?
The peple out sterte and caste the cart to grounde,
And in the middel of the dong they founde
The dede man, that mordred was al newe.
O blisful God, that art so just and trewe!                        230
Lo, how that thou biwreyest mordre alway!
Mordre wol out, that see we day by day.
Mordre is so wlatsom and abhominable
To God, that is so just and resonable,
That he ne wol nat suffre it heled be;                            235
Though it abyde a yeer, or two, or three,
Mordre wol out, this my conclusioun.
And right anoon, ministres of that toun
Han hent the carter, and so sore him pyned,
And eek the hostiler so sore engyned,                             240
That thay biknewe hir wikkednesse anoon,
And were anhanged by the nekke-boon.
    "Here may men seen that dremes been to drede.
And certes, in the same book I rede,
Right in the nexte chapitre after this—                           245
I gabbe nat, so have I joye or blis—
Two men that wolde han passed over see,
For certeyn cause, into a fer contree,
If that the wind ne hadde been contrarie;
That made hem in a citee for to tarie,                            250
That stood ful mery upon an haven-syde.

to the west gate of the town, where he found                215
a dung cart, which looked as if it were on the way
    to spread
dung on the land, that was in the same state
as the dead man had described;
so with a bold heart he cried out
for vengeance and justice for this felony:                  220
'My friend was murdered tonight,
and in this cart he lies dead on his back.
I call upon the authorities,' he said,
'who are supposed to guard and rule this city;
Help! Alas, my comrade lies here slain!'                    225
What more should I add to this story?
The people rushed out and turned the cart over,
and in the middle of the dung they found
the dead man, who had just been murdered.
O blissful God, who art so just and true!                   230
Lo, how you always reveal murder!
Murder will out; that we see day by day.
Murder is so loathsome and abominable
to God, who is so just and reasonable,
that he will not suffer it to be concealed;                 235
though it may wait a year, or two or three,
murder will out, this is my conclusion.
And right away officials of that town
seized the carter, and tortured him so sorely,
and also the innkeeper, whom they racked,                   240
that these soon acknowledged their wickedness,
and were hanged by the neck.
    "Thus one can see that dreams are to be dreaded.
And, certainly, I read in the same book,
right in the next chapter after this—                       245
I'm not making it up, as I hope for joy or bliss—
of two men who would have crossed the sea
for a certain reason, to a distant country,
if the wind had not been unfavorable;
that made them wait in a city                               250
which was pleasantly located by a harborside.

But on a day, agayn the even-tyde,
The wind gan chaunge, and blew right as hem leste.
Jolif and glad they wente unto hir reste,
And casten hem ful erly for to saille.                          255
But to that oo man fil a greet mervaille:
That oon of hem, in sleping as he lay,
Him mette a wonder dreem, agayn the day;
Him thoughte a man stood by his beddes syde,
And him comaunded that he sholde abyde,                         260
And seyde him thus, 'If thou tomorwe wende,
Thou shalt be dreynt; my tale is at an ende.'
He wook, and tolde his felawe what he mette,
And preyde him his viage for to lette;
As for that day, he preyde him to abyde.                        265
    His felawe, that lay by his beddes syde,
Gan for to laughe, and scorned him ful faste.
'No dreem,' quod he, 'may so myn herte agaste
That I wil lette for to do my thinges.
I sette not a straw by thy dreminges,                           270
For swevenes been but vanitees and japes.
Men dreme alday of owles or of apes,
And eke of many a maze therwithal;
Men dreme of thing that never was ne shal.
But sith I see that thou wolt heer abyde,                        275
And thus forsleuthen wilfully thy tyde,
God wot it reweth me; and have good day.'
And thus he took his leve and wente his way.
But er that he hadde halfe his cours y-seyled,
Noot I nat why, ne what mischaunce it eyled,                     280
But casuelly the shippes botme rente,
And ship and man under the water wente
In sighte of othere shippes it byside
That with hem seyled at the same tyde.
And therfor, faire Pertelote so dere,                           285
By swiche ensamples olde maistow lere
That no man sholde been to recchelees
Of dremes, for I sey thee doutelees
That many a dreem ful sore is for to drede.

But one day, toward evening,
the wind changed and blew just as they wanted.
They went to their rest joyfully,
planning to sail early the next day.                              255
But a great wonder befell one of the men:
as he lay sleeping,
he had a marvelous dream, toward daybreak;
it seemed to him a man stood by his bedside
and ordered him to wait,                                          260
and said to him, 'If you sail tomorrow,
you will be drowned; that's all I have to say.'
He woke up, and told his comrade what he had dreamed,
and begged him to delay his voyage;
he asked him to wait another day.                                265

    His friend, who lay in the next bed,
laughed, and scorned him thoroughly.
'No dream,' he said, 'can so dismay my heart
that I will put off going about my business.
I don't care a straw for your dreams,                             270
for dreams are nothing but illusions and frauds.
Men are always dreaming of owls or apes,
and other bewildering nonsense;
men dream of things that never were and never shall be.
But since I see you intend to stay here,                          275
and thus willfully waste your tide,
God knows I'm sorry; and good day to you.'
And thus he took his leave and went his way.
But before he had sailed half his course—
I don't know why, or what was the trouble with it—               280
but accidentally the ship's bottom was split,
and ship and man sank
in the sight of other ships alongside,
which had sailed with them on the same tide.
And therefore, fair Pertelote so dear,                            285
by such ancient examples you may learn
that no man should be too heedless
of dreams, for I tell you that without
a doubt many a dream is sorely to be dreaded.

"Lo, in the lyf of Seint Kenelm* I rede—                    290
That was Kenulphus sone, the noble king
Of Mercenrike—how Kenelm mette a thing
A lyte er he was mordred, on a day;
His mordre in his avisioun he say.
His norice him expouned every del                          295
His sweven, and bad him for to kepe him wel
For traisoun; but he nas but seven yeer old,
And therfore litel tale hath he told
Of any dreem, so holy was his herte.
By God, I hadde lever than my sherte                       300
That ye had rad his legende as have I.
Dame Pertelote, I sey yow trewely,
Macrobeus,* that write th'avisioun
In Affrike of the worthy Cipioun,
Affermeth dremes, and seith that they been                 305
Warning of thinges that men after seen.

     "And forthermore, I pray yow loketh wel
In th' Olde Testament, of Daniel,*
If he held dremes any vanitee.
Reed eek of Joseph,* and ther shul ye see                  310
Wher dremes ben somtyme (I sey nat alle)
Warning of thinges that shul after falle.
Loke of Egipt the king, daun Pharao,
His bakere and his boteler also,
Wher they ne felte noon effect in dremes.                  315
Whoso wol seken actes of sondry remes
May rede of dremes many a wonder thing.

     "Lo Cresus,* which that was of Lyde king,
Mette he nat that he sat upon a tree,
Which signified he sholde anhanged be?                      320
Lo heer Andromacha,* Ectores wyf,
That day that Ector sholde lese his lyf
She dremed on the same night biforn
How that the lyf of Ector sholde be lorn,
If thilke day he wente into bataille;                       325
She warned him, but it mighte nat availle;
He wente for to fighte nathelees,

"Lo, I read in the life of Saint Kenelm                              290
(who was the son of Kenulphus, the noble king
of Mercia) how Kenelm dreamed something
one day, a little before he was murdered;
he saw his murder in a vision.
His nurse explained his dream to him                                 295
completely, and warned him to guard himself well
against treason; but he was only seven years old,
and therefore he set little store
by any dream, his heart was so holy.
By God, I'd give my shirt                                            300
to have had you read his legend as I have.
Dame Pertelote, I tell you truly
that Macrobius, who wrote the vision
of the worthy Scipio in Africa,
affirms the truth of dreams, and says that they are                 305
warnings of things that men perceive afterward.

"And furthermore, I beg you to look carefully
in the Old Testament, at the story of Daniel,
and see if he held dreams to be any nonsense.
Read of Joseph, too, and there you shall see                         310
whether dreams are sometimes (I don't say *all* of them)
warnings of things that shall happen later.
Look at the king of Egypt, Lord Pharaoh,
and his butler and baker, too,
and see if they found no effect in dreams.                           315
Whoever studies the history of various realms
may read many marvelous things about dreams.

"Look at Croesus, who was king of Lydia;
didn't he dream that he sat in a tree,
which meant that he would be hanged?                                 320
There is Andromache, Hector's wife;
on the very night before the day that Hector
was to lose his life, she dreamed
of how his life would be lost
if he went into battle that day;                                     325
she warned him, but it was of no avail;
he went to fight anyway,

But he was slayn anoon of Achilles.
But thilke tale is al to long to telle,
And eek it is ny day, I may nat dwelle.                      330
Shortly I seye, as for conclusioun,
That I shal han of this avisioun
Adversitee; and I seye forthermore
That I ne telle of laxatyves no store,
For they ben venimous, I woot it wel;                        335
I hem defye, I love hem never a del.
    "Now let us speke of mirthe, and stinte al this;
Madame Pertelote, so have I blis,
Of o thing God hath sent me large grace;
For whan I see the beautee of your face—                     340
Ye ben so scarlet reed about your yën—
It maketh al my drede for to dyen;
For, also siker as *In principio,*
*Mulier est hominis confusio;* *
Madame, the sentence of this Latin is,                       345
'Womman is mannes joye and al his blis.'
For whan I fele a-night your softe syde,
Albeit that I may nat on you ryde,
For that our perche is maad so narwe, alas!
I am so ful of joye and of solas                             350
That I defye bothe sweven and dreem."
    And with that word he fley doun fro the beem,
For it was day, and eek his hennes alle;
And with a chuk he gan hem for to calle,
For he had founde a corn, lay in the yerd.                   355
Royal he was, he was namore aferd;
He fethered Pertelote twenty tyme,
And trad as ofte, er that it was pryme.
He loketh as it were a grim leoun,
And on his toos he rometh up and doun;                       360
Him deyned not to sette his foot to grounde.
He chukketh, whan he hath a corn y-founde,
And to him rennen thanne his wyves alle.
Thus royal, as a prince is in his halle,
Leve I this Chauntecleer in his pasture;                     365

but was soon slain by Achilles.
But that story is all too long to tell,
and also it is nearly day, I may not tarry.                           330
Briefly, I say in conclusion,
that this vision means I shall have
some adversity; and I say furthermore
that I set no store by laxatives,
for they are venomous, I know it well;                                335
I defy them, I don't like them a bit.

"Now let us speak of pleasant things, and stop all this;
Madame Pertelote, as I hope for bliss,
In one respect God has shown me great favor;
for when I see the beauty of your face—                               340
you are so scarlet red about your eyes—
it destroys all my dread;
for it is just as certain as *In principio*,
*Mulier est hominis confusio;*
Madame, the meaning of this Latin is,                                 345
'Woman is man's joy and all his bliss.'
For at night when I feel your soft side,
although I cannot ride on you
since our perch was made so narrow, alas!
I am so full of joy and delight                                       350
that I defy nightmares and dreams."

And with those words he flew down from the beam,
and so did all his hens, for it was day;
and with a chuck he called for them
since he had found a bit of grain lying in the yard.                  355
He was regal, no longer afraid;
he feathered Pertelote twenty times
and rode her as often, before midmorning.
He looked like a grim lion,
as he roamed to and fro on tiptoes;                                   360
he did not deign to set his foot on the ground.
He chucked when he had found a grain,
and then his wives all ran to him.
Thus I leave this Chauntecleer to his dinner,
royal as a prince in his hall,                                        365

And after wol I telle his aventure.

Whan that the month in which the world bigan,
That highte March, whan God first maked man,
Was complet, and passed were also,
Sin March bigan, thritty dayes and two,                          370
Bifel that Chauntecleer, in al his pryde,
His seven wyves walking by his syde,
Caste up his eyen to the brighte sonne,
That in the signe of Taurus hadde y-ronne
Twenty degrees and oon, and somwhat more;                        375
And knew by kynde, and by noon other lore,
That it was pryme, and crew with blisful stevene.

"The sonne," he sayde, "is clomben up on hevene
Fourty degrees and oon, and more, ywis.
Madame Pertelote, my worldes blis,                               380
Herkneth thise blisful briddes how they singe,
And see the fresshe floures how they springe;
Ful is myn herte of revel and solas."
But sodeinly him fil a sorweful cas;
For ever the latter ende of joye is wo.                          385
God woot that worldly joye is sone ago;
And if a rethor coude faire endyte,
He in a cronique saufly mighte it wryte,
As for a sovereyn notabilitee.
Now every wys man, lat him herkne me;                            390
This storie is also trewe, I undertake,
As is the book of Launcelot de Lake,*
That wommen holde in ful gret reverence.
Now wol I torne agayn to my sentence.

A col-fox, ful of sly iniquitee,                                 395
That in the grove hadde woned yeres three,
By heigh imaginacioun forncast,
The same night thurghout the hegges brast
Into the yerd, ther Chauntecleer the faire
Was wont, and eek his wyves, to repaire;                         400
And in a bed of wortes still he lay
Til it was passed undern of the day,

and next I will tell of his adventure.

When the month that is called March,
in which the world began and God first made man,
was over, and when, in addition, since the
beginning of March thirty-two days had passed,          370
it befell that Chauntecleer, in all his pride,
with his seven wives walking by his side,
cast up his eyes to the bright sun,
which had passed through somewhat more
than twenty-one degrees in the sign of Taurus;          375
he knew by instinct, and by no other lore,
that it was nine o'clock, and crowed with a blissful
    voice.
"The sun," he said, "has climbed up the heavens
forty-one degrees and a fraction.
Madame Pertelote, my earthly bliss,          380
listen to how the blissful birds sing,
and see how the fresh flowers spring up;
my heart is full of joy and content."
But suddenly a sad mischance befell him;
for the latter end of joy is ever woe.          385
God knows that worldly joy is soon gone;
and a rhetorician who could write well
might safely put this in a chronicle
as a notable maxim.
Now let every wise man listen to me;          390
this story is just as true, I guarantee,
as the book of Lancelot du Lac,
which women hold in such high regard.
Now I will turn again to my theme.

A fox with black markings, full of sly iniquity,          395
who had lived in the wood three years,
that same night (as was destined by divine planning)
burst through the hedges
into the yard where noble Chauntecleer
and his wives were wont to repair;          400
and he lay quietly in a bed of cabbages
until midmorning had passed,

Wayting his tyme on Chauntecleer to falle,
As gladly doon thise homicydes alle,
That in awayt liggen to mordre men.                    405
O false mordrer, lurking in thy den!
O newe Scariot,* newe Genilon!*
False dissimilour, O Greek Sinon,*
That broghtest Troye al outrely to sorwe!
O Chauntecleer, acursed be that morwe              410
That thou into that yerd flough fro the bemes:
Thou were ful wel y-warned by thy dremes
That thilke day was perilous to thee.
But what that God forwoot mot nedes be,
After the opinioun of certeyn clerkis.               415
Witnesse on him that any perfit clerk is,
That in scole is gret altercacioun
In this matere, and greet disputisoun,
And hath ben of an hundred thousand men.
But I ne can not bulte it to the bren                 420
As can the holy doctour Augustyn,*
Or Boëce,* or the bishop Bradwardyn,*
Whether that Goddes worthy forwiting
Streyneth me nedely for to doon a thing
(Nedely clepe I simple necessitee);                   425
Or elles, if free choys be graunted me
To do that same thing, or do it noght,
Though God forwoot it, er that it was wroght;
Or if his witing streyneth nevere a del
But by necessitee condicionel.                         430
    I wol not han to do of swich matere;
My tale is of a cok, as ye may here,
That took his counseil of his wyf, with sorwe,
To walken in the yerd upon that morwe
That he had met the dreem that I yow tolde.          435
Wommennes counseils been ful ofte colde;
Wommannes counseil broughte us first to wo,
And made Adam fro paradys to go,
Theras he was ful mery, and wel at ese.
But for I noot to whom it mighte displese            440

biding his time to fall on Chauntecleer,
as all these homicides usually do,
who lie in wait to murder men.                                405
O false murderer, lurking in your den!
O new Iscariot, new Ganelon!
False dissembler, Greek Sinon,
who brought Troy utterly to sorrow!
O Chauntecleer, accursed be that day                         410
when you flew into that yard from the beams:
you were well warned by your dreams
that this day was perilous to you.
But what God foresees must needs be,
according to the opinion of certain clerks.                  415
Any learned clerk will bear witness
that in the schools there is much altercation
and dispute about this matter,
it has been debated among a hundred thousand men.
But I cannot sift the grain from the chaff in this matter,   420
as the holy doctor Augustine can,
or Boethius or Bishop Bradwardine:
whether God's worthy foreknowledge
constrains me to do a thing
(by "constraint" I refer to simple necessity);              425
or else, whether I am granted free choice
to do that same thing or not to do it,
though God foresaw it before it was done;
or whether his foreknowledge doesn't constrain at all
except by conditional necessity.                             430
    I won't have anything to do with such matters;
my tale is about a cock, as you can hear,
who, unfortunately, took advice from his wife
to walk in the yard the day after
he had had the dream I told you about.                       435
Women's counsel is often baneful;
woman's counsel brought us first to woe,
and caused Adam to leave paradise,
where he had been merry and well at ease.
But since I don't know whom it might displease             440

If I counseil of wommen wolde blame,
Passe over, for I seyde it in my game.
Rede auctours, wher they trete of swich matere,
And what thay seyn of wommen ye may here.
Thise been the cokkes wordes, and nat myne;          445
I can noon harm of no womman divyne.

Faire in the sond, to bathe hir merily,
Lyth Pertelote, and alle hir sustres by,
Agayn the sonne; and Chauntecleer so free
Song merier than the mermayde in the see;          450
For Phisiologus* seith sikerly
How that they singen wel and merily.
And so bifel that as he caste his yë
Among the wortes on a boterflye,
He was war of this fox that lay ful lowe.          455
Nothing ne liste him thanne for to crowe,
But cryde anon, "Cok, cok," and up he sterte,
As man that was affrayed in his herte.
For naturelly a beest desyreth flee
Fro his contrarie, if he may it see,          460
Though he never erst had seyn it with his yë.

This Chauntecleer, whan he gan him espye,
He wolde han fled, but that the fox anon
Seyde, "Gentil sire, allàs, wher wol ye gon?
Be ye affrayed of me that am your freend?          465
Now certes, I were worse than a feend
If I to yow wolde harm or vileinye.
I am nat come your counseil for t'espye;
But trewely, the cause of my cominge
Was only for to herkne how that ye singe.          470
For trewely ye have as mery a stevene
As eny aungel hath that is in hevene;
Therwith ye han in musik more felinge
Than hadde Boëce, or any that can singe.
My lord your fader (God his soule blesse!)          475
And eek your moder, of hir gentilesse,
Han in myn hous y-been, to my gret ese;
And certes, sire, ful fayn wolde I yow plese.

If I disparage the counsel of women,
overlook that, for I said it in sport.
Read the authorities where they treat of such matters,
and you'll hear what they say about women;
these are the cock's words, and not mine;                         445
I can't find any harm in any woman.
    Pertelote lay in the sand, merrily
bathing in the sun, and all
her sisters with her; noble Chauntecleer
sang more merrily than a mermaid in the sea            450
(for Physiologus says reliably
that mermaids sing well and merrily).
And it happened that as he cast his eye
on a butterfly among the cabbages,
he became aware of the fox who was lying low there.   455
He had no desire to crow then,
but cried at once, "Cok, cok," and started up
like a man terrified in his heart,
for a beast instinctively wants to flee
from his natural enemy, if he should see it,                    460
although he may never before have seen it with his eyes.
    This Chauntecleer, when he saw the fox,
would have fled, but the fox at once
said, "Gentle sir, alas, where are you going?
Are you afraid of me, your friend?                              465
Now certainly, I would be worse than a fiend
if I wished to harm or dishonor you.
I didn't come to spy on your secrets;
but truly, the reason I came
was only to hear how you sing.                                   470
For indeed you have as merry a voice
as any angel in heaven;
and moreover you have more feeling for music
than had Boethius, or any other singer.
My lord your father (God bless his soul!)                       475
and your gentle mother
have been at my house, to my great pleasure;
and certainly, sir, I would gladly entertain you.

But for men speke of singing, I wol saye,
So mote I brouke wel myn eyen tweye,   480
Save yow, I herde never man so singe
As dide your fader in the morweninge;
Certes, it was of herte, al that he song.
And for to make his voys the more strong,
He wolde so peyne him that with bothe his yën  485
He moste winke, so loude he wolde cryen,
And stonden on his tiptoon therwithal,
And strecche forth his nekke long and smal.
And eek he was of swich discrecioun
That ther nas no man in no regioun   490
That him in song or wisdom mighte passe.
I have wel rad in daun Burnel the Asse,*
Among his vers, how that ther was a cok,
For that a preestes sone yaf him a knok
Upon his leg whyl he was yong and nyce,  495
He made him for to lese his benefyce.
But certeyn, ther nis no comparisoun
Bitwix the wisdom and discrecioun
Of youre fader, and of his subtiltee.
Now singeth, sire, for seinte charitee:   500
Let see, conne ye your fader countrefete?"
This Chauntecleer his winges gan to bete,
As man that coude his tresoun nat espye,
So was he ravisshed with his flaterye.

 Allas, ye lordes,* many a fals flatour  505
Is in your courtes, and many a losengeour,
That plesen yow wel more, by my feith,
Than he that soothfastnesse unto yow seith.
Redeth Ecclesiaste* of flaterye;
Beth war, ye lordes, of hir trecherye.   510

 This Chauntecleer stood hye upon his toos,
Strecching his nekke, and heeld his eyen cloos,
And gan to crowe loude for the nones;
And daun Russel the fox sterte up at ones

But speaking of singing, I will say,
as I hope to enjoy the use of my two eyes,                         480
that, except for you, I never heard anyone sing
the way your father did in the morning;
certainly all that he sang came from the heart.
And to make his voice the stronger,
he would exert himself so much that he had              485
to close both his eyes, he would crow so loudly,
and stand on his tiptoes at the same time,
and stretch forth his long, slender neck.
And also he was so judicious
that there was no one anywhere                          490
who could surpass him in song or wisdom.
I have, indeed, read in the book of Sir Brunellus
      the Ass,
among its verses, that there was once a cock:
because a priest's son who was young and foolish
gave him a knock on his leg, the cock                   495
caused him to lose a benefice.
But certainly there is no comparison
between his cleverness and the wisdom
and discretion of your father.
Now sing, sir, for holy charity:                        500
let's see, can you imitate your father?"
Chauntecleer began to beat his wings
like a man who could not see the treason which
      threatened
him, he was so ravished by the fox's flattery.
      Alas, you lords, in your courts are many           505
false flatterers and deceivers
who please you much more, by my faith,
than he who tells you the truth.
Read what Ecclesiastes says of flattery;
beware, you lords, of their treachery.                   510
      Chauntecleer stood high on his toes,
stretching his neck out; he held his eyes closed,
and then began to crow very loudly;
and Sir Russell the fox started up at once

And by the gargat hente Chauntecleer,                    515
And on his bak toward the wode him beer,
For yet ne was ther no man that him sewed.
O Destinee, that mayst nat been eschewed!
Allas, that Chauntecleer fleigh from the bemes!
Allas, his wyf ne roghte nat of dremes!                  520
And on a Friday* fil al this mechaunce.·
O Venus, that art goddesse of plesaunce,
Sin that thy servant was this Chauntecleer,
And in thy service dide al his poweer,
More for delyt, than world to multiplye,                 525
Why woldestow suffre him on thy day to dye?
O Gaufred,* dere mayster soverayn,
That, whan thy worthy king Richard was slayn
With shot, compleynedest his deth so sore,
Why ne hadde I now thy sentence and thy lore,            530
The Friday for to chyde, as diden ye?
For on a Friday soothly slayn was he.
Than wolde I shewe yow how that I coude pleyne
For Chauntecleres drede and for his peyne.
    Certes, swich cry ne lamentacioun                    535
Was never of ladies maad whan Ilioun
Was wonne, and Pirrus* with his streite swerd,
Whan he hadde hent King Priam* by the berd,
And slayn him, as saith us *Eneydos,**
As maden alle the hennes in the clos                     540
Whan they had seyn of Chauntecleer the sighte.
But sovereynly dame Pertelote shrighte
Ful louder than dide Hasdrubales wyf*
Whan that hir housbond hadde lost his lyf,
And that the Romayns hadde brend Cartage;                545
She was so ful of torment and of rage
That wilfully into the fyr she sterte,
And brende hirselven with a stedfast herte.
O woful hennes, right so cryden ye
As, whan that Nero* brende the cittee                    550
Of Rome, cryden senatoures wyves,

and seized Chauntecleer by the throat,                                    515
and carried him on his back toward the woods,
for as yet no one was pursuing him.
O Destiny, which may not be eschewed!
Alas, that Chauntecleer flew from the beams!
Alas, that his wife didn't believe in dreams!                             520
And on a Friday fell all this misfortune.
O Venus who is goddess of pleasure,
since Chauntecleer was your servant
and did all that he could in your service,
more for delight than to multiply the world's beings,                     525
why would you allow him to die on your day?
O Geoffrey, dear sovereign master,
who lamented the death of your worthy
King Richard so sorely when he was shot,
why don't I now have your expressive wisdom
        and learning,                                                      530
to chide the Friday, as you did?
(For, truly, he was slain on a Friday.)
Then I would show you how I could mourn
for Chauntecleer's dread and pain.

    Certainly, never was made such a cry and lamentation                  535
by the Trojan ladies when Ilion
was won, and Pyrrhus with his unsparing sword
had taken king Priam by the beard
and slain him (the *Aeneid* tells us),
as made all the hens in the yard                                          540
when they had seen the sight of Chauntecleer.
But chiefly Dame Pertelote shrieked—
much louder than did Hasdrubal's wife
when her husband had lost his life
and the Romans had burned Carthage                                        545
(that lady was so full of torment and rage
that she threw herself into the fire of her own will
and burned herself with a steadfast heart).
O woeful hens, just so cried you
as, when Nero burned the city of                                          550
Rome, the senators' wives cried,

For that hir housebondes losten alle hir lyves;
Withouten gilt this Nero hath hem slayn.
Now wol I torne to my tale agayn:

This sely widwe and eek hir doghtres two          555
Herden thise hennes crye and waken wo,
And out at dores sterten they anoon,
And syen the fox toward the grove goon,
And bar upon his back the cok away;
And cryden, "Out!" "Harrow!" and "Weylaway!"          560
"Ha, ha, the fox!" and after him they ran,
And eek with staves many another man;
Ran Colle our dogge, and Talbot and Gerland,
And Malkin with a distaf in hir hand;
Ran cow and calf, and eek the verray hogges,          565
For-fered for berking of the dogges
And shouting of the men and wimmen eke;
They ronne so hem thoughte hir herte breke.
They yelleden as feendes doon in helle;
The dokes cryden as men wolde hem quelle;          570
The gees for fere flowen over the trees;
Out of the hyve cam the swarm of bees—
So hidous was the noyse, a, *benedicite*!
Certes, he Jakke Straw* and his meynee
Ne made never shoutes half so shrille          575
Whan that they wolden any Fleming kille,
As thilke day was maad upon the fox.
Of bras thay broghten bemes, and of box,
Of horn, of boon, in whiche they blewe and pouped,
And therwithal thay shryked and they houped;          580
It semed as that heven sholde falle.
Now, gode men, I pray yow herkneth alle!

Lo, how Fortune turneth sodeinly
The hope and pryde eek of hir enemy!
This cok, that lay upon the foxes bak,          585
In al his drede unto the fox he spak,
And seyde, "Sire, if that I were as ye,
Yet sholde I seyn, as wis God helpe me,
'Turneth agayn, ye proude cherles alle!

because their husbands had all lost their lives;
Nero had them slain, innocent as they were.
Now I will turn to my tale again.

    This poor widow, and her two daughters, too,     555
heard the hens cry and lament,
and they quickly rushed outdoors
and saw the fox go toward the grove,
bearing away the cock on his back;
and they cried, "Out! Help, woe, alas!     560
Hah, hah, the fox!" and they ran after him,
and many others followed with staves in hand;
out ran Colle our dog, and Talbot and Garland,
and Malkin with a distaff in her hand;
cow and calf ran, and even the hogs,     565
they were so frightened by the barking of the dogs
and the shouting of the men and women;
they ran so that they thought their hearts would break.
They yelled like fiends in hell;
the ducks cried out as if they were going to be killed;     570
the geese, terrified, flew over the trees;
the swarm of bees came out of the hive—
so hideous was the noise, God bless us!
Surely even Jack Straw and his throng
never gave shouts half so shrill     575
when they wanted to kill a Fleming
as were uttered that day at the fox.
They brought trumpets of brass and of boxwood,
of horn and of bone, on which they blew and tooted,
and at the same time they shrieked and whooped;     580
it seemed as if heaven should fall.
Now good men, I pray you all listen!

    See how Fortune suddenly reverses
the hope and pride of their enemy!
This cock, who lay on the fox's back,     585
spoke in all his dread to the fox,
and said, "Sir, if I were as you,
I would say, so help me God,
'Turn again, all you silly fools!

A verray pestilence upon yow falle! 590
Now am I come unto this wodes syde,
Maugree your heed, the cok shal heer abyde;
I wol him ete, in feith, and that anon.' "
The fox answerde, "In feith, it shal be don,"
And as he spak that word, al sodeinly 595
This cok brak from his mouth deliverly,
And heighe upon a tree he fleigh anon.

And whan the fox saugh that he was y-gon,
"Allas!" quod he, "O Chauntecleer, allas!
I have to yow," quod he, "y-doon trespas, 600
In as muche as I maked yow aferd
Whan I yow hente and broghte out of the yerd;
But, sire, I dide it in no wikke entente;
Com doun, and I shal telle yow what I mente.
I shal seye sooth to yow, God help me so." 605
"Nay than," quod he, "I shrewe us bothe two,
And first I shrewe myself, bothe blood and bones,
If thou bigyle me ofter than ones.
Thou shalt namore thurgh thy flaterye
Do me to singe and winke with myn yë. 610
For he that winketh whan he sholde see,
Al wilfully, God lat him never thee!"
"Nay," quod the fox, "but God yeve him meschaunce
That is so undiscreet of governaunce
That jangleth whan he sholde holde his pees." 615

Lo, swich it is for to be recchelees,
And necligent, and truste on flaterye.
But ye that holden this tale a folye,
As of a fox, or of a cok and hen,
Taketh the moralitee, good men. 620
For Seint Paul seith that al that writen is
To our doctryne it is y-write, ywis.
Taketh the fruyt, and lat the chaf be stille.

Now, gode God, if that it be thy wille,
As seith my Lord, so make us alle good men; 625
And bringe us to his heighe blisse. Amen.

A pox upon you! 590
Now that I have come to the edge of the wood,
in spite of you the cock shall stay here;
in faith, I will eat him, and right now at that.' "
The fox answered, "In faith, it shall be done,"
and the moment he spoke those words, the cock 595
nimbly broke away from his mouth,
and immediately flew high up into a tree.
      And when the fox saw that he was gone,
he said, "Alas, O Chauntecleer, alas!
I have wronged you," he said, 600
"inasmuch as I frightened you
when I took you and brought you out of the yard;
but, sir, I did it with no wicked intent;
come down, and I shall tell you what I meant.
I shall tell you the truth, so help me God." 605
"No indeed," said the cock, "may we both be damned,
but may I be damned first, both blood and bones
if you beguile me more than once.
No more shall you, through your flattery,
get me to close my eyes and sing. 610
For he who knowingly blinks when he should see,
God let him never thrive!"
"No," said the fox, "but God give him misfortune
who is so indiscreet in his conduct
as to jabber when he should hold his peace." 615
      Lo, this is what it is like to be careless
and negligent, and to trust in flattery.
But you that think this tale is a trifle
about a fox, or a cock and a hen,
accept the moral, good people. 620
For Saint Paul says that all that is written
is certainly written for our learning.
Take the fruit, and let the chaff alone.
Now, gracious God, if it be your will,
as my Lord says, make us all good men; 625
and bring us to his exalted bliss. Amen.

MANUAL OF

# PSYCHIATRIC NURSING CARE PLANNING

## Assessment Guides • Diagnoses • Psychopharmacology

# MANUAL OF
# PSYCHIATRIC NURSING CARE PLANNING

## Assessment Guides • Diagnoses • Psychopharmacology

### Elizabeth M. Varcarolis, RN, MA

Professor Emeritus
Formerly Deputy Chairperson, Department of Nursing
Borough of Manhattan Community College
Associate Fellow
Albert Ellis Institute for Rational Emotive Behavioral
Therapy (REBT)
New York, New York

SAUNDERS

ELSEVIER

# SAUNDERS
ELSEVIER

3251 Riverport Lane
St. Louis, Missouri 63043

*Manual of Psychiatric Nursing Care Planning:*
*Assessment Guides, Diagnoses, and Psychopharmacology*  ISBN: 978-1-4377-1782-2
© **2011 by Saunders, an affiliate of Elsevier, Inc. All rights reserved.**

---

### Notices

Knowledge and best practice in this field are constantly changing. As new research and experience broaden our understanding, changes in research methods, professional practices or medical treatment may become necessary.

Practitioners and researchers must always rely on their own experience and knowledge in evaluating and using any information, methods, compounds, or experiments described herein. In using such information or methods they should be mindful of their own safety and the safety of others, including parties for whom they have a professional responsibility.

With respect to any drug or pharmaceutical products identified, readers are advised to check the most current information provided (i) on procedures featured or (ii) by the manufacturer of each product to be administered, to verify the recommended dose or formula, the method and duration of administration, and contraindications. It is the responsibility of practitioners, relying on their own experience and knowledge of their patients, to make diagnoses, to determine dosages and the best treatment for each individual patient, and to take all appropriate safety precautions.

To the fullest extent of the law, neither the Publisher nor the authors, contributors, or editors, assume any liability for any injury and/or damage to persons or property as a matter of products liability, negligence or otherwise, or from any use or operation of any methods, products, instructions, or ideas contained in the material herein.

---

Previous editions copyrighted 2006, 2004, 2000.

**Library of Congress Cataloging-in-Publication Data**
Varcarolis, Elizabeth M.
    Manual of psychiatric nursing care planning : assessment guides, diagnoses, and psychopharmacology / Elizabeth M. Varcarolis. – 4th ed.
        p. ; cm.
    Rev. ed. of: Manual of psychiatric nursing care plans / Elizabeth M. Varcarolis. 3rd. ed. c2005.
    Includes bibliographical references.
    ISBN 978-1-4377-1782-2 (pbk. : alk. paper) 1. Psychiatric nursing–Handbooks, manuals, etc. 2. Nursing care plans–Handbooks, manuals, etc. I. Varcarolis, Elizabeth M. Manual of psychiatric nursing care plans. II. Title.
    [DNLM: 1. Mental Disorders–nursing–Handbooks. 2. Nursing Assessment–Handbooks. 3. Psychiatric Nursing–methods–Handbooks. WY 49 V289m 2010]
    RC440.V374 2010
    616.89'023 1–dc22                                                    2009050799

*Senior Editor:* Yvonne Alexopoulos
*Senior Developmental Editor:* Lisa P. Newton
*Publishing Services Manager:* Anne Altepeter
*Project Manager:* Cindy Thoms
*Senior Book Designer:* Amy Buxton

Printed in the United States of America
Last digit is the print number:  9  8  7  6  5  4  3  2  1

---

## Working together to grow
## libraries in developing countries

www.elsevier.com | www.bookaid.org | www.sabre.org

ELSEVIER   BOOK AID International   Sabre Foundation

*To my Paul*
*Whose love, friendship, and needed distractions*
*into the land of cherished books*
*keep my mind full of life*
*and my heart full of love.*

# Preface

This updated edition of our clinical guide will enable students and practitioners to plan realistic, evidence-based, and individualized nursing care for their patients. It is important that we address our patients' crucial needs at their present level of functioning. To assist with this process, **assessment guides** are included to help identify the signs and symptoms of the most frequently encountered mental disorders and psychiatric emergencies. Accurate and thorough assessments are crucial for the planning of appropriate, effective, and safe nursing care. The assessment tools for children and adolescents can be found in Appendix C, and Appendix D provides the tools needed to assess adults.

In addition to updates to the content and slight revision of format for easier access, this edition includes **outcomes, long-term goals,** and **short-term goals** that are "stated in attainable and measurable terms and include a time estimate for attainment" as required by the *2007 American Psychiatric-Mental Health Nursing: Scope and Standards of Practice* (ANA, APNA, and ISPMHN).

The evidence-based interventions are stated clearly in applicable actions that allow the nurse to make decisions regarding which interventions will best meet the patient's most pressing needs.

Unit Five, **Psychopharmacology,** will help the reader better understand the uses and workings of psychotropic agents. When a specific neurotransmitter (e.g., $5 HT^1$, $D^1$, $D^2$, $H^1$) is either increased or decreased, to improve symptoms, it is necessary to understand that the effectiveness of a drug may be accompanied by certain adverse reactions and toxic effects. Through an understanding of transmitter-receptor actions, health care professionals can identify agents that would best serve individual patient needs. When a patient is able to mitigate the effects of adverse reactions, compliance may be increased. Therefore, **patient and family medication teaching tools** are included at the end of the discussion of each psychotropic agent in Chapter 21. An overview of specific medications and dosages, as well as drug tables, remain in the relevant clinical chapters.

Wishing you success,

**Elizabeth Varcarolis**

# Acknowledgments

I wish to thank Yvonne Alexopoulos, senior editor, for keeping this project moving along in a timely fashion. And to Heather Rippetoe, editorial assistant, for providing everything I needed to easily move the process along.

Genuine appreciation to Lisa Newton, senior developmental editor, for her timely queries, clarifications, and detail work on the manuscript. And of course, big thanks to Cindy Thoms, project manager, for pulling all the details together, producing a handsome and reader-friendly edition for students and clinical nurses.

# PART I

# GUIDELINES FOR PLANNING PSYCHIATRIC NURSING CARE

# CHAPTER 1

# The Nursing Process and Assessment Tools for Psychiatric Nursing

The nursing process is the basic framework for nursing practice with patients. The Psychiatric-Mental Health Nursing Scope and Standards of Practice (APNA, ANA, ISPN, 2007) contain the authoritative statements that describe the responsibilities for which nurses are accountable and provide direction for professional nursing practice and a framework for the evaluation of practice. The Psychiatric-Mental Health Clinical Nursing Practice Standards define the nursing process within the context of six standards of care (Figure 1-1):

| | |
|---|---|
| **Standard I— Assessment** | Collects, organizes, and synthesizes pertinent data using evidence-based assessment techniques |
| **Standard II— Nursing Diagnosis** | Identifies problems in order of priority and formulates nursing diagnosis defined by the collected data |
| **Standard III— Outcomes Identification** | Constructs outcomes as realistic, measurable, and time-limited goals (short-term and long-term) |
| **Standard IV— Planning** | Develops a personalized plan of care using strategies and alternatives to attain expected outcomes |

| | |
|---|---|
| **Standard V—Implementation** | Implements plan safely using evidence-based interventions and treatments |
| **Standard VI—Evaluation** | Performs an ongoing evaluation of the desired outcomes and documents results of evaluation |

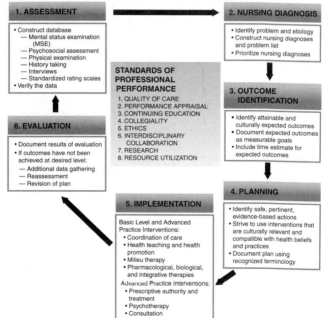

**Figure 1-1** The nursing process in psychiatric mental health nursing. (From Varcarolis, E. [2009]. *Essentials of psychiatric mental health nursing: A communication approach to evidence-based care.* Philadelphia, Saunders.)

# ASSESSMENT

The assessment of a patient's mental health status is part of the nursing assessment, along with the assessment of the patient's physical health. Depression, suicidal thoughts, anger, disorientation, delusions, and hallucinations might be encountered in medical-surgical wards, obstetric and intensive care units, outpatient settings, extended-care facilities, emergency departments, community centers, and home settings. Many emotional and/or psychiatric symptoms can be the result of medical/chemical imbalances and disease. The purpose of the assessment is to identify and clearly articulate specific problems in the individual's life that are causing physical or mental disequilibrium or harm.

The purpose of the psychosocial assessment is to:
- Establish a rapport
- Obtain an understanding of current problems/illness
- Review physical status and obtain baseline vital signs
- Understand how this illness/process has affected the patient's life (self-esteem, loss of intimacy, role change, change in family dynamics, lifestyle change, employment issues)
- Assess for risk factors affecting the safety of the patient (suicidal, confused, homicidal thoughts); obtain information on previous psychiatric problems or disorder(s)
- Assess psychosocial status (social patterns, interests and abilities, stress factors, substance use and abuse, relationship issues, social supports)
- Perform a mental status examination (MSE) (Refer to Chapter 12 for a tool to evaluate mental status.)
- Formulate a plan of care

The basic components of the *psychosocial/psychiatric nursing assessment* include a patient history and a mental and emotional status evaluation. Because it is always preferable to verify the patient's data, family members and/or friends and relatives should be a part of the assessment whenever possible. If a police officer is the one who brought the patient into the psychiatric emergency department, it is important for the nurse to know as much as possible about what the patient was doing that warranted police intervention.

Past medical and psychiatric history can supply valuable information. This is particularly important if the patient is too psychotic, withdrawn, or agitated to provide a history. In many places, this information might be easily available through the use of computer-based patient records (CBRs). Laboratory reports also provide important information. As mentioned, abnormal body chemistry can cause personality changes and violent behavior. For example, abnormal liver enzymes can explain irritability, depression, and lethargy.

The use of a standardized nursing assessment tool facilitates the assessment process. For an example of a general assessment tool refer to Appendix B-1. Today most all hospitals and clinics have their own assessment tools. With practice the nurse becomes proficient in gathering information in an informal fashion, with the nurse clarifying, focusing, and exploring pertinent data with the patient. This method allows patients to state their perceptions in their own words and enables the nurse to observe a wide range of nonverbal behaviors. When the order and the questions on the assessment tool are too rigidly applied, spontaneity is reduced. Assessment is a skill that is learned over time. Practice, supervision, and patience enhance the development of this skill. A personal style of interviewing congruent with the nurse's personality develops as comfort and experience increase.

Box 1-1 is an example of a psychosocial assessment tool for use in the clinical area.

---

### Box 1-1 Psychosocial Assessment Tool

A. Previous hospitalizations
B. Educational background
C. Occupational background
   1. Employed? Where? What length of time?
   2. Special skills
D. Social patterns
   1. Describe family.
   2. Describe friends.
   3. With whom does the patient live?
   4. To whom does the patient go in time of crisis?
   5. Describe a typical day.

| Box 1-1 | **Psychosocial Assessment Tool—cont'd** |
|---|---|

E. Sexual patterns
   1. Sexually active? Practices safe sex? Practices birth control?
   2. Sexual orientation
   3. Sexual difficulties
F. Interest and abilities
   1. What does the patient do in his or her spare time?
   2. What sport, hobby, or leisure activity is the patient good at?
   3. What gives the patient pleasure?
G. Substance use and abuse
   1. What medications does the patient take? How often? How much?
   2. What herbal or over-the-counter drugs does the patient take? How often? How much?
   3. What psychotropic drugs does the patient take? How often? How much?
   4. How many drinks of alcohol does the patient take per day? Per week?
   5. What recreational drugs does the patient take? How often? How much?
   6. Does the patient identify the use of drugs as a problem?
H. Coping abilities
   1. What does the patient do when he or she gets upset?
   2. To whom can the patient talk?
   3. What usually helps to relieve stress?
   4. What did the patient try this time?
I. Spiritual assessment
   1. What importance does religion or spirituality have in the patient's life?
   2. Do the patient's religious or spiritual beliefs relate to the way the patient takes care of himself or herself or of the patient's illness? How?
   3. Does the patient's faith help the patient in stressful situations?
   4. Whom does the patient see when he or she is medically ill? Mentally upset?
   5. Are there special health care practices within the patient's culture that address his or her particular mental problems?

| Box 1-2 *DSM-IV-TR* **Multiaxial Assessment System** |
| --- |

| Axis I | Clinical Disorders |
| | Other Conditions That Might Be a Focus of Clinical Attention |
| Axis II | Personality Disorders |
| | Mental Retardation |
| Axis III | General Medical Conditions |
| Axis IV | Psychosocial and Environmental Problems |
| Axis V | Global Assessment of Functioning |

From American Psychiatric Association. (2000). *Diagnostic and statistical manual of mental disorders* (4th ed., text rev.). Washington, DC: Author.

Another helpful tool that can give nurses and other health care workers important information about the patient is the Multiaxial Assessment System of the American Psychiatric Association (American Psychiatric Association [APA], 2000) (Box 1-2).

Axes IV and V can give the nurse and others information that is important for setting realistic goals and planning effective care. **Axis IV—Psychosocial and Environmental Problems** identifies things going on in the patient's life that might greatly affect the patient's life and might become the primary focus of clinical attention. Examples of Axis IV problems include (APA, 2000):

- **Problems with primary support groups** (death, illness, divorce, sexual/physical abuse, neglect of child, discord with siblings, birth of a sibling)
- **Problems related to the social environment** (death or loss of friends, inadequate social support, living alone, difficulty with acculturation, discrimination, adjustment to life-cycle transition [e.g., retirement])
- **Educational problems** (illiteracy, academic problems, discord with teachers or classmates, inadequate school environment)
- **Occupational problems** (unemployment, threat of job loss, stressful work schedule, difficult work conditions, job dissatisfaction, job change, discord with boss or co-workers)
- **Economic problems** (extreme poverty, inadequate finances, insufficient welfare support)

- **Problems with access to health care services** (inadequate health care services, transportation to health care facilities unavailable, inadequate health insurance)
- **Problems related to interaction with the legal system/ crime** (arrest, incarceration, litigation, victim of crime)

**Axis V—Global Assessment of Functioning** is the clinician's judgment of the patient's overall level of functioning. This information helps the health care team plan treatment and predict outcomes. Box 1-3 summarizes the Global Assessment of Functioning Scale.

---

### Box 1-3  *DSM-IV-TR* Global Assessment of Functioning (GAF) Scale

Consider psychological, social, and occupational functioning on a hypothetical continuum of mental health–illness. Do not include impairment in functioning caused by physical (or environmental) limitations.

Code (**Note**: Use intermediate codes when appropriate; e.g., 45, 68, 72.)

100 **Superior functioning in a wide range of activities, life's problems never seem to get out of hand, is sought out by others because of his or her many positive qualities. No symptoms**.

91

90 **Absent or minimal symptoms** (e.g., mild anxiety before an examination), **good functioning in all areas, interested and involved in a wide range of activities, socially effective, generally satisfied with life, no more than everyday problems or concerns** (e.g., an occasional argument with family members).

81

80 **If symptoms are present, they are transient and expectable reactions to psychosocial stressors** (e.g., difficulty concentrating after family argument); **no more than slight impairment in social, occupational, or school functioning** (e.g., temporarily falling behind in schoolwork).

71

70 **Some mild symptoms** (e.g., depressed mood and mild insomnia) **OR some difficulty in social, occupational, or school functioning** (e.g., occasional truancy, theft within the household), **but generally functioning pretty well, has some meaningful interpersonal relationships**.

---

*Continued*

---

Box 1-3  *DSM-IV-TR* **Global Assessment of Functioning (GAF) Scale—cont'd**

61
60 **Moderate symptoms** (e.g., flat affect and circumstantial speech, occasional panic attacks) **OR moderate difficulty in social, occupational, or school functioning** (e.g., few friends, conflicts with peers or co-workers).
51
50 **Serious symptoms** (e.g., suicidal ideation, severe obsessional rituals, frequent shoplifting) **OR any serious impairment in social, occupational, or school functioning** (e.g., no friends, unable to keep a job).
41
40 **Some impairment in reality testing or communication** (e.g., speech is at times illogical, obscure, or irrelevant) **OR major impairment in several areas, such as work or school, family relations, judgment, thinking, or mood** (e.g., depressed man avoids friends, neglects family, and is unable to work; child frequently beats up younger children, is defiant at home, and is failing at school).
31
30 **Behavior is considerably influenced by delusions or hallucinations OR serious impairment in communication or judgment** (e.g., is sometimes incoherent, acts grossly inappropriately, is preoccupied with suicide) OR inability to function in almost all areas (e.g., stays in bed all day; has no job, home, or friends).
21
20 **Some danger of hurting self or others** (e.g., suicide attempts without clear expectation of death; frequent violence; manic excitement) **OR occasionally fails to maintain minimal personal hygiene** (e.g., smears feces) **OR gross impairment in communication** (e.g., largely incoherent or mute).
11
10 **Persistent danger of severely hurting self or others** (e.g., recurrent violence) **OR persistent inability to maintain minimal personal hygiene OR serious suicidal act with clear expectation of death.**
1
0 Inadequate information

---

From American Psychiatric Association. (2000). *Diagnostic and statistical manual of mental disorders* (4th ed., text rev.). Washington, DC: Author.

After the initial assessment, it is useful to summarize pertinent data with the patient. This summary provides patients with reassurance that they have been heard, and it allows them the opportunity to clarify any misinformation. They should then be told what will happen next. For example, if the initial assessment takes place in the hospital, the nurse should tell the patient about the clinicians he or she will be seeing. If a psychiatric nurse in a mental health clinic conducts the initial assessment, the nurse will let the patient know when and how often they will meet to work on the patient's problems. If the nurse thinks a referral is necessary (e.g., to a psychiatrist, social worker, or medical physician), this should be discussed with the patient.

## Assessment of a Non–English-Speaking Patient

If a nurse does not speak the patient's language, data gathering may be inaccurate, incomplete, and extremely difficult to obtain. The Americans with Disabilities Act (ADA) has established federal standards that ensure that communication does not interfere with equal access to health care for all people. For patients who have difficulty with the English language or have other language difficulties, federal law maintains the use of a trained interpreter (Arnold & Boggs, 2007). All health care establishments are to establish systems for identifying available language interpreters, interpreters trained in sign language, telecommunication devices for the deaf (TDDs), closed-caption decoders for televisions, and amplifiers on phones.

Nurses must often rely on interpreters. Using family members, friends, or neighbors to act as interpreters could have significant drawbacks. For example, a family interpreter might want to protect the patient and filter out information given to the patient. Conversely, the family member might want to filter out information about a problem or crisis in the family and not clearly relay the information back to the nurse. It is best to avoid a family member acting as an interpreter. Friends and neighbors might find it embarrassing to discuss private and personal matters. Family members acting as interpreters should be avoided altogether when the patient is a child.

Guidelines for nurses working through an interpreter have been suggested:

- **Address the patient directly** rather than speaking to the interpreter. Maintain eye contact with the patient to ensure patient involvement and strengthen personal contact.
- **Avoid interrupting the patient and interpreter.** At times, their interaction might take longer because of the need to clarify issues. Descriptions might require more time because of dialect differences or the interpreter's awareness that the patient needs more preparation before being asked a particular question.
- **Instruct the interpreter to give you verbatim translations.**
- **Avoid using medical jargon** the interpreter or the patient might not understand.
- **Avoid talking or commenting to the interpreter at length;** the patient might feel left out and distrustful.
- **Always ask for permission to discuss intimate or emotionally laden topics first,** and prepare the interpreter for the content of the interview.
- **Be aware that asking intimate or emotionally laden questions might be difficult for the patient as well as for the interpreter.** Lead up to these questions slowly.
- **Whenever possible, arrange for the interpreter and the patient to meet each other ahead of time** to establish some rapport.
- **Try to use the same interpreter** for subsequent interviews with the patient.

When an interpreter is not immediately available, aids such as picture charts or flash cards can help the nurse and patient communicate important basic information about the patient's immediate needs (e.g., degree of pain or need for elimination). Because of cultural backgrounds or wanting to be helpful, some patients with limited English might seem agreeable and nod "yes" even though they do not understand. Asking questions that require more than a yes or no answer can provide a better idea of the patient's level of understanding.

## Cultural and Social Assessment

More frequently nurses are called on to plan care for culturally diverse populations. Many advocate that nurses have a broader understanding of how health and illness are influenced by cultural and social factors. Refer to Box 1-4 for a brief cultural and social assessment.

# NURSING DIAGNOSIS

A nursing diagnosis is a clinical judgment about individual, family, or community responses to actual or potential health problems/life processes. A well-stated nursing diagnosis provides the basis for selection of nursing interventions to achieve outcomes for which the nurse is accountable (approved at the 9th NANDA Conference, 1990).

A nursing diagnosis must be expressed concisely and include the Influencing Causes (Related Factors, "Related To's") of the condition and is supported by Defining Characteristics, which include both objective and subjective data ("As Evidenced By's"). (See Appendix B-2 for currently used 2009–2011 nursing diagnoses.) Nursing diagnoses are updated and added to every 2 years by NANDA International, based on research and clinical evaluation.

Physicians and researchers also have formulated clear and accurate guidelines for identifying and categorizing clinical psychiatric disorders and syndromes. The APA provides specific criteria that must be met before a medical psychiatric diagnosis can be reached. The most current of these criteria are found in the *Diagnostic and Statistical Manual of Mental Disorders*, fourth edition, text revision (*DSM-IV-TR*) see Appendix B-3 (APA, 2000). In each clinical chapter in this manual, both the *DSM-IV-TR* criteria and the appropriate nursing diagnosis are provided. The classification system used for medical diseases and medical treatments is found in the *International Statistical Classification of Diseases and Related Health Problems*, tenth edition (ICD-10) (World Health Organization, 1992).

The psychiatric mental health nurse uses nursing diagnoses, standard classifications of mental disorders (*DSM-IV-TR*), and standard international classification of diseases (ICD-10) to develop a treatment plan based on assessment data and theoretical premises.

A nursing diagnosis has three structural components: (1) problem/process, (2) related factors (Related To's), and the (3) defining characteristic (As Evidenced By's).

Box 1-4 **Brief Cultural and Social Assessment**

**Brief Guide to Cultural Assessment**
A. **Language**
   1. What is your primary spoken language?
   2. How would you rate your fluency in English?
   3. Would you like an interpreter?
B. **Communication style**
   1. *Observe nonverbal communication (gesture, posture, eye movement).*
   2. What are your feelings about touch?
   3. *Observe how much eye contact the patient is comfortable with.*
   4. How much or little do people make eye contact in your culture?
C. **Family group**
   1. Describe the members of your family.
   2. Who makes the decisions in your family?
   3. Which family member can you confide in?
D. **Social supports**
   1. Are there people outside the family (friends, neighbors) that you are close to and feel free to confide in?
   2. Is there a place where you can go for support (church, school, work, club)?
E. **Religious beliefs and practices**
   1. How important are religious or spiritual practices in your life?
   2. Does your faith help in times of stress?
   3. Who do you seek when you are medically ill? Mentally upset?
   4. Are there any restrictions on diet or medical interventions within your religious, spiritual, or cultural beliefs?
   5. To whom can the patient talk to in times of stress or sickness?
F. **Health and illness beliefs**
   1. When you become ill what it the first thing you do to take care of the illness?
   2. How is this condition (medical or mental) viewed by your culture?
   3. Are there special health care practices within your culture that address your medical/mental problem?
   4. What are the attitudes of mental illness in your culture?

## Problem/Process

The nursing diagnostic title states what should change; for example:

**RISK FOR INJURY**

## Related Factors (Related To's)

The related factors include factors that contribute to or are related to the development or maintenance of a nursing diagnosis title. Stating the probable cause or contributing factors tell us what needs to be done to effect change and identifies causes the nurse can target through interventions. Related factors are linked to the diagnostic title with the words *related to*, so the "related to" component of the nursing diagnosis should be defined as clearly as possible because it discerns what must be targeted. For example:

Risk for injury: *related to extreme agitation and constant, uncontrollable motor activity*

This activity is a probable nursing diagnosis for a patient in the manic phase of bipolar disorder. In this case, the potential for injury is related to uncontrollable hyperactivity in a person who is unable to use his or her usual problem-solving skills to avoid harm. Contrast this with the same nursing diagnostic title for a woman who is being constantly battered by her mate:

Risk for injury: *related to mate's poor impulse control and rage reaction*

In this case, probable cause for injury is related to a woman living with a physically violent partner in a situation she believes she cannot leave (fear for her life, no way to support herself financially, fear for her children).

## Defining Characteristics—The Supporting Data (As Evidenced By's)

Supporting signs and symptoms (As Evidenced By's) are the "defining characteristics" that cluster in patterns and support the validity of the diagnosis (NANDA International, 2009–2011). After interventions have been made and are successful, the goal is that these signs and symptoms would be greatly minimized or no longer be present.

For example, using the earlier situation of a patient with mania, he or she might have observable signs and symptoms that alert the medical staff that injury or potential for injury is present and requires nursing/medical intervention. The defining characteristics/supporting signs and symptoms might be bruises or wounds resulting from falls, suffering from lack of sleep as a result of constant physical activity, dehydration from not drinking or eating (related to hyperactivity or an inability to concentrate on the task of eating/drinking), and/or being near exhaustion or even cardiac collapse. A complete nursing diagnosis statement would then read:

Risk for injury: *related to extreme agitation and constant, uncontrollable motor activity as evidenced by fewer than 2 hours rest a night, poor skin turgor, and abrasions on hands and arms*

As the final outcome of effective medical and nursing interventions, members of the health team could expect to see the patient obtain adequate rest or sleep (e.g., 6 hours per night), good skin turgor, and an ability to rest and refrain from agitated physical activity for frequent periods during the day.

## SUMMARY

From data, nurses make clinical judgments about an individual's, family's, or community's response to actual or potential health problems/life processes and formulate nursing diagnoses accordingly. The nurse then plans and provides nursing actions that target the patient's health problem or life process.

## OUTCOMES IDENTIFICATION

Outcome criteria described in behavioral or measurable terms are the desired results of nursing interventions planned for a patient. Outcome criteria also provide the basis for evaluating the effectiveness of care since, outcome criteria are the desired results of care. The nurse identifies outcomes as short- and long-term goals that (once met) will help ensure that the outcome criteria are met, partially met, or not met. The short- and long-term goals are stated in behavioral and measurable terms and might have time factors (in 1 week, by discharge, within 2 days), or end results, or hoped-for results. They might also indicate a future steady state. For example:

- Patient will function independently in the community with aid of social support.
- Patient will refrain from self-harm.

These goals can be evaluated and revised as the patient progresses or doesn't progress, and the plan might need to be revised. Goals are always patient centered (not staff centered). Goals are only useful if they are reasonable and attainable within a specified period of time. The short-term goals for each nursing diagnosis can include several steps that lead to the final outcome criteria. The amount of time needed to attain some of these goals will vary among patients. For some patients, the final outcome criteria might not be realistic goals, whereas for other patients the goals might be not only realistic but easily attainable. For these reasons, the nurse must use good judgment based on the patient's database to identify realistic outcome criteria and select appropriate goals for reaching the outcome criteria.

For the previously stated nursing diagnosis:

**Risk for injury:** *related to extreme agitation and constant, uncontrollable motor activity as evidenced by fewer than 2 hours rest a night, poor skin turgor, and abrasions on hands and arms*

---

Possible long-term goals (outcomes) might include:

- By discharge, patient will be sleeping 6 to 8 hours per night.
- Patient will willingly maintain an adequate diet (1500 to 2000 cal/day) and sufficient daily fluid intake by the time of discharge.
- Patient will be free from infections, and abrasions/wounds will be in final healing stages by time of discharge.
- Patient will continue attendance at support group within the community.
- Patient will adhere to medication regimen.

Possible short-term goals (outcomes) might include:

- Patient will sleep 3 to 4 hours per night within 2 days, with the aid of medication.
- Patient will drink 8 oz of fluid (juice, milk, milkshake) every hour with the aid of nursing intervention.
- Patient's skin turgor will be within normal limits within 24 hours.
- Patient will spend 10 minutes in a quiet, nonstimulating area with nurse each hour during the day.

## PLANNING

Each stated goal should include nursing interventions, which are instructions for all people working with the patient. These written plans aid in the continuity of care for the patient and are points of information for all members of the health team. Increasingly, units in both inpatient and community-based facilities use standardized care plans or clinical/critical pathways for patients with specific diagnoses. However, even standardized care plans and critical pathways must be tailored to specific patients, and there are often spaces on the standardized forms for patient-centered revisions. Nursing interventions planned for meeting a specific goal should be:

*Safe:* They must be safe for the patient as well as for other patients, staff, and family.

*Appropriate:* They must be compatible with other therapies and with the patient's personal goals and cultural values as well as with institutional rules.

*Evidenced-based:* They should be based on scientific principles.

*Individualized:* They should be realistic: (1) written within the capabilities of the patient's age, physical strength, condition, and willingness to change; (2) based on the number of staff available; (3) reflective of actual available community resources; and (4) within the student's or nurse's capabilities.

The *Nursing Outcomes Classification (NOC)* (2008) is a useful guide for identifying appropriate guidelines for intervention. The outcomes here are consistent with NOC.

## IMPLEMENTATION

Implementation is the action the nursing staff takes to carry out the nursing measures identified in the care plan to achieve the expected outcome criteria. Nursing interventions might be called *actions, approaches, nursing orders,* or *nursing prescriptions.* Whenever possible, interventions should be evidenced based. When carrying out the nursing interventions, additional data might be gathered, and further refinements of the care plan can be made.

The *Psychiatric Mental Health Nursing Scope and Standards of Practice* (APNA, ANA, ISPN, 2007) identifies four areas for intervention for the psychiatric mental health registered nurse (RN-PMH). Recent graduates and practitioners new to the psychiatric setting will participate in many of these activities. Interventions at the basic level include:

- Coordination of care
- Health teaching and health promotion
- Milieu therapy
- Pharmacological, biological, and integrative techniques

The advanced practice psychiatric mental health registered nurse (APRN-PMH) is prepared at the master's level or beyond. Advanced practice interventions include:

- Psychotherapy
- Prescription authority and treatment
- Consultations

## EVALUATION

Evaluation is an ongoing process that includes evaluating the effectiveness of plans and strategies and documenting the results. Evaluation is often the most neglected part of the nursing process. Evaluation of short- and long-term goals can have three possible outcomes: The goal is met, not met, or partially met. Using our original example for the nursing diagnosis:

**Risk for injury:** *related to extreme agitation and constant, uncontrollable motor activity as evidenced by fewer than 2 hours rest a night, poor skin turgor, and abrasions on hands and arms*

For the short-term goal (outcome):

- Patient will drink 8 oz of fluid (juice, milk, milkshake) every hour during the day with the aid of nursing intervention.

In evaluation, the nurse might chart:

*Goal met:* **Patient takes frequent sips of fluid equaling 8 oz an hour provided in portable containers with lid, during the hours of 9 AM to 4 PM, with reminders from nursing staff.**

For the short-term goal (outcome):

- Patient will spend 10 minutes in a quiet, nonstimulating area with nurse each hour during the day.

In evaluation, the nurse might chart:

*Goal partially met:* **After 2 days, patient continues restless and purposeless pacing up and down the halls; only able to stay quiet with nurse for 4 to 6 minutes an hour.**

For the short-term goal (outcome):

- Patient's skin turgor will be within normal limits within 24 hours as evidenced by skin pinched over sternum and released; raised area disappears in 3 seconds or fewer.

In evaluation, the nurse might chart:

*Goal not met:* **At 8:00 AM this morning, patient's skin turgor still poor. Pinched skin over sternum disappeared 4 seconds post release. Evaluate need for increasing daytime fluids from 9 AM to 9 PM.**

The chapters in Parts II and III of this book present specific psychiatric clinical disorders and phenomena that might require nursing interventions. Under each disorder or phenomenon, the most common nursing diagnoses are presented. Suggested outcomes and short-term goals are offered for each nursing diagnosis. Outcome criteria are the final long-term goals that signal that the nursing diagnosis should no longer be a target for intervention.

Keep in mind that all goals are tailored to each patient's current level of functioning and realistic potential. Therefore, one person's short-term outcome might be another's long-term outcome.

For each nursing diagnosis, specific nursing actions are suggested with supporting rationales. This clinical reference guide is intended to help nurses formulate well-stated nursing diagnoses and set realistic outcome criteria with suggested steps (short-term goals) to reach the final outcome. Realistic and appropriate nursing interventions are provided, and nurses identify those that are appropriate for their patients. Some of the interventions are well within the student's realm; others might be better suited to a more advanced practitioner. They are all included to help give a more thorough overview of what constitutes nursing interventions. **This clinical nursing guide is intended for students in planning care, as a guide to staff members who are new to a psychiatric unit, and for clinicians as a quick clinical reference.**

 # INTERNET SITES

**Nursing Net**
www.nursingnet.org
Information and web links for both students and seasoned
   nurses.

**American Nurses Association**
www.nursingworld.org

# CHAPTER 2

# Maximizing Communication Skills

Communication and interviewing techniques are acquired skills. Nurses learn to increase their ability to use communication and interviewing skills through practice and supervision. Communication is a complex process that can involve a variety of personal and environmental factors that might distort the sending and receiving of messages. Examples include:

*Personal factors:* Emotions (mood), knowledge level, language use, attitudes, and bias

*Social factors:* Previous experience, culture, language, and health beliefs and practice

*Environmental factors:* Physical factors (background noise, lack of privacy, uncomfortable accommodations) and societal factors (presence of others, expectations of others)

Communication is said to be 10% to 20% verbal and 80% to 90% nonverbal.

Cultural and social factors influence concepts of what is health and what is illness, and practices vary greatly among cultures; thus it is important that mental health nurses learn a much broader understanding of the complexities of various cultures than are the norm today. Look back to Box 1-4 in Chapter 1 for a Brief Cultural and Social Questionnaire that may provide some questions to ask of the patient who comes from a different cultural/social background.

# VERBAL COMMUNICATION

Verbal communication comprises all words a person speaks. Talking is our most common activity. Talking links us with others, it is our primary instrument of instruction, and it is one of the most personal aspects of our private life. When we speak, we:

- Communicate our beliefs, values, attitudes, and culture
- Communicate perceptions and meanings
- Convey interests and understanding *or* insult and convey judgment
- Convey messages clearly *or* convey conflicting or implied messages
- Convey clear, honest feelings *or* disguised, distorted feelings

Verbal communication can become misunderstood and garbled even among people with the same primary language and/or the same cultural background. In our multiethnic society, keeping communication clear and congruent takes thought and insight. Communication styles, eye contact, and touch all have different meanings and are used and interpreted very differently among cultures. Ensuring that your verbal message is what you mean to convey, and that the message you send is the same message the other person receives, is a complicated skill.

At times people convey conflicting messages. A person says one thing verbally, but conveys the opposite in non verbal behavior. This is called a **double message** or **mixed message.** As in the saying, "actions speak louder than words," actions are often interpreted as the true meaning of a person's intent, whether that intent is conscious or unconscious. For example:

A young man goes to counseling because he is not making good grades in school and fears that he will not be able to get into medical school. He appears bright and resourceful and states he has good study habits. In the course of the session, he tells the nurse that he is a star on the tennis team, is president of his fraternity, and has an active and successful social life, "If you know what I mean." Implied in this exchange appears to be a *double message*. The verbal message is "I want good grades to get into medical school." The nonverbal message is that what is important to him is spending a great deal of time excelling at a sport, heading a social club, and engaging in dating activities.

One way nurses can respond to verbal and nonverbal incongruity (double messages) is to reflect and validate the individual's thoughts and feelings. For example:

"You say you are unhappy with your grades and as a consequence might not be able to get into medical school. Yet, from what I hear you say, you seem to be filling up your time excelling in so many other activities that there is very little time left for adequate preparation for excelling in your main goal, getting into medical school. I wonder what you think about this apparent contradiction in priorities?"

# NONVERBAL COMMUNICATION

Nonverbal communication consists of the behaviors displayed by an individual and as mentioned may account for 80% to 90% of the information being conveyed. Tone of voice and manner in which a person paces speech are examples of nonverbal communication. Other common examples of nonverbal communication (called *cues*) are facial expressions, body posture, amount of eye contact, eye cast (emotion expressed in the eyes), hand gestures, sighs, fidgeting, and yawning. Nonverbal communication consists of an amalgam of feelings, feedback, local wisdom, cultural rhythms, ways to avoid confrontation, and unconscious views of how the world works. Table 2-1 identifies some key components of nonverbal communication.

Sometimes gestures and other nonverbal cues can have opposite meanings, depending on culture and context. For example, eye contact can be perceived as comforting and supportive or invasive and intimidating. Touching a patient gently on the arm can be experienced as supportive and caring or threatening or sexual. Facial expressions such as a smile can appear to convey warmth and interest or hide feelings of fear or anger.

Many nonverbal cues have cultural meaning. In some Asian cultures, avoiding eye contact shows respect. Conversely, in many people with French, British, and African backgrounds, avoidance of eye contact by another person might be interpreted as disinterest, not telling the

Table 2-1 **Nonverbal Behaviors**

| Type | Possible Behaviors | Example |
|------|-------------------|---------|
| **Body behavior** | Posture, body movements, gestures, gait | The patient is slumped in a chair, puts her face in her hands, and occasionally taps her right foot. |
| **Facial expressions** | Frowns, smiles, grimaces; raised eyebrows, pursed lips, licking lips, tongue movements | The patient grimaces when speaking to the nurse; when alone, he smiles and giggles to himself. |
| **Eye cast** | Angry, suspicious, and accusatory looks | The patient's eyes hardened with suspicion. |
| **Voice-related behaviors** | Tone, pitch, level, intensity, inflection, stuttering, pauses, silences, fluency | The patient talks in a loud, sing-song voice. |
| **Observable autonomic physiological responses** | Increase in respirations, diaphoresis, pupil dilation, blushing, paleness | When the patient mentions discharge, she becomes pale, her respirations increase, and her face becomes diaphoretic. |
| **General appearance** | Grooming, dress, hygiene | The patient is dressed in a wrinkled shirt, his pants are stained, his socks are dirty, and he wears no shoes. |
| **Physical characteristics** | Height, weight, physique, complexion | The patient appears grossly overweight for his height, and his muscle tone appears flabby. |

Varcarolis, E. (2010). *Foundations of psychiatric mental health nursing* (6th ed.). Philadelphia, Saunders, p. 177.

truth, avoiding the sharing of important information, or dictated by social order.

There are numerous ways to interpret verbal and nonverbal communication for each cultural and subcultural group. Even if a nurse is aware of how a specific cultural group responds to, for example, touch, the nurse could still be in error when dealing with an individual within that cultural group. Sustaining effective and respectful communication is very complex. It is the task of nurses to identify and explore the meaning of patients' nonverbal and verbal behaviors. Listed at the end of the chapter are Internet sites that provide further cultural information for health care professionals.

# EFFECTIVE COMMUNICATION TECHNIQUES

## Degree of Openness

Any question or statement can be classified as (1) an open-ended verbalization, (2) a focused question, or (3) a closed-ended verbalization. Furthermore, any question or statement can be classified along the *continuum of openness*. There are three variables that influence where any given verbalization sits on this openness continuum (Shea, 1998):

1. The degree to which the verbalization tends to produce spontaneous and lengthy response
2. The degree to which the verbalization does not limit the patient's answer set
3. The degree to which the verbalization opens up a moderately resistant patient

Refer to Table 2-2 during the following discussion.

### Open-Ended Questions

Open-ended questions require more than one-word answers (e.g., a "yes" or "no"). Even with a patient who is sullen, resistant, or guarded, open-ended questions can encourage lengthy information on experiences, perceptions of events, or responses to a situation. Examples of an open-ended question are: "What are some of the stresses you are grappling with?" "What do you perceive to be

Table 2-2 **Degree of Openness Continuum**

| Verbalization | Example |
|---|---|
| Open-ended | These questions are to be stated with a gentle tone of voice while expressing a genuine interest. They invite the patient to share personal experiences. They cannot be answered with a "yes" or a "no." |
| 1. Open-ended questions (giving broad openings) | 1. What would you like to discuss?<br>2. What are your plans for the future?<br>3. How will you approach your father?<br>4. What are some of your thoughts about the marriage? |
| 2. Gentle commands (encouraging descriptions of perceptions) | 1. Tell me something about your home life.<br>2. Share with me some of your hopes about your future.<br>3. Describe for me the problem with your boss. |
| Focused | These questions represent a middle ground with regard to openness. When the relationship is strong, these questions can result in spontaneous lengthy speech. Used with a resistant patient, these questions might be answered tersely. |
| 1. Exploring/focusing | 1. Can you describe your feelings?<br>2. Can you tell me a little about your boss?<br>3. Can you say anything positive about your marriage?<br>4. Can you tell me what the voices are saying? |
| 2. Qualitative questions | 1. How's your appetite?<br>2. How's your job going?<br>3. How's your mood been? |

*Continued*

Table 2-2 **Degree of Openness Continuum—cont'd**

| Verbalization | Example |
|---|---|
| 3. Statements of inquiry (restating, reflecting, paraphrasing, clarifying) | 1. You say you were fifth in your class?<br>2. So you left the marriage after 3 years?<br>3. So when she cries you feel guilty?<br>4. You seem to be saying that you're viewed as the bad guy in the family.<br>5. Give me an example of your being "no good." |
| 4. Empathetic statements (making observations, sharing perceptions, seeking clarification) | 1. It sounds like a troubling time for you.<br>2. It's difficult to end a marriage after 10 years.<br>3. It looks like you're feeling sad.<br>4. You seem very disappointed about... |
| 5. Facilitatory statements (accepting, offering general leads) | 1. Uh-huh.<br>2. Go on.<br>3. I see. |
| **Closed-ended** | These techniques tend to decrease a patient's response length, but they can be effective in focusing a wandering patient. Closed-ended questions help obtain important facts or ask for specific details. Closed-ended statements give information or explanations or have an educational slant. |
| 1. Closed-ended questions (seeking information) | 1. How long have you been hearing voices?<br>2. Are you feeling happy, sad, or angry?<br>3. What medications are you taking? |

Table 2-2  **Degree of Openness Continuum—cont'd**

| Verbalization | Example |
|---|---|
| 2. Closed-ended statements (giving information) | 1. Anxiety can be helped with behavioral therapies. |
| | 2. This test will determine... |
| | 3. I read in your chart that you tried suicide once before. |
| | 4. We will begin by taking a blood sample to check your medication level. |

Modified from Shea, S.C. (1998). *Psychiatric interviewing: The art of understanding* (2nd ed.). Philadelphia, Saunders, p. 82; reprinted with permission.

your biggest problem at the moment?" "Will you tell me something about your family?"

Generally, nurses/clinicians applying the principles of therapeutic communication are encouraged to use open-ended questions or gentle inquiries (e.g., "Tell me about...." "Share with me....") with our patients. This is especially helpful when beginning a relationship and in the early interviews. Although the initial responses might be short, with time the responses often become more informative as the patient grows more at ease. This is an especially valuable technique to use with patients who are resistant or guarded, but it is also a good rule for opening phases of any interview, especially in the early phase of establishing a rapport with an individual.

## Closed-Ended Questions

Closed-ended questions, in contrast, are questions that ask for specific information (dates, names, numbers, yes-or-no information). These are closed-ended questions because they limit the patient's freedom of choice. Students are often discouraged from using closed-ended questions. When closed-ended questions are used frequently during a counseling session, or especially during an initial interview, they can close an interview down rapidly. This is especially true with a guarded or resistant patient. However, in some cases the answers to closed-ended questions are necessary and can provide important information. For example:

"Do you feel like killing yourself now?"

"How long have you been hearing the voices that tell you 'bad things'?"

"Did you seek therapy after your first suicide attempt?"

"Do you think the medication is helping you?"

Closed-ended questions give specific information when needed, such as during an initial assessment or intake interview or to ascertain results, as in "Are the medications helping you?" They are usually answered by a "yes," a "no," or a short answer.

Useful tools for nurses in communicating with their patients are (1) clarifying/validating techniques, (2) the use of silence, and (3) active listening.

## Clarifying/Validating Techniques

Understanding depends on clear communication, which is aided by verifying with a patient the nurse's interpretation of the patient's messages. The nurse must request feedback on the accuracy of the message received from verbal and nonverbal cues. The use of clarifying techniques helps both participants to identify major differences in their frames of reference, giving them the opportunity to correct misperceptions before they cause any serious misunderstandings. The patient who is asked to elaborate on or clarify vague or ambiguous messages needs to know that the purpose is to promote mutual understanding. For example, "I hear you saying that you are having difficulty trusting your son after what happened. Is that correct?"

### Paraphrasing

For clarity, the nurse might use paraphrasing, which means to restate in different (often fewer) words the basic content of a patient's message. Using simple, precise, and culturally relevant terms, the nurse can readily confirm interpretation of the patient's previous message before the interview proceeds. By prefacing statements with a phrase such as "I am not sure I understand" or "In other words, you seem to be saying...," the nurse helps the patient form a clearer perception of what might be a bewildering mass of details. After paraphrasing, the nurse must validate the accuracy of the restatement and its helpfulness to the discussion. The patient might confirm or deny the perceptions through nonverbal cues or by directly responding to a question such as "Was I correct in saying...?" As a result, the patient is made aware that the interviewer is actively involved in the search for understanding.

## Restating

With restating, the nurse mirrors the patient's overt and covert messages; this technique can be used to echo feeling as well as content. Restating differs from paraphrasing in that it involves repetition of the same key words the patient has just spoken. If a patient remarks, "My life has been full of pain," additional information might be gained by restating, "Your life has been full of pain." The purpose of this technique is to more thoroughly explore subjects that might be significant. However, too frequent and indiscriminate use of restating might be interpreted by patients as inattention or disinterest. It is very easy to over-use this tool and become mechanical. Inappropriately parroting or mimicking what another has said might be perceived as ridiculing, making this nondirective approach a definite drawback to communication. To avoid overuse of restating, the nurse can combine restating with use of other clarifying techniques that encourage descriptions. For example:

"Tell me about how your life has been full of pain."
"Give me an example of how your life has been full of pain."

## Exploring

A technique that enables the nurse to examine important ideas, experiences, or relationships more fully is exploring. For example, if a patient tells the nurse that he does not get along well with his wife, the nurse should explore this area further. Possible openers might include:

"Tell me more about your relationship with your wife."
"Describe your relationship with your wife."
"Give me an example of you and your wife not getting along."

Asking for an example can greatly clarify a vague or generic statement made by a patient:

*Mary:* No one likes me.

*Nurse:* Give me an example of one person who doesn't like you.

*Jim:* Everything I do is wrong.

*Nurse:* Give me an example of one thing you do that you think is wrong.

## Use of Silence

In many cultures in our society, including nursing, there is an emphasis on action. In communication, we tend to expect a high level of verbal activity. Many students and practicing nurses find that when the flow of words stops, they become uncomfortable. The effective use of silence, however, is a helpful communication technique.

Silence is not the absence of communication. Silence is a specific channel for transmitting and receiving messages. The practitioner needs to understand that silence is a significant means of influencing and being influenced by others.

In the initial interview, the patient might be reluctant to speak because of the newness of the situation, the unfamiliarity with the nurse, self-consciousness, embarrassment, shyness, or anger. Talking is highly individualized. Some find the telephone a nuisance; others believe they cannot live without it. The nurse must recognize and respect individual differences in styles and tempos of responding.

Although there is no universal rule about how much silence is too much, silence has been said to be worthwhile only so long as it is serving some function and not frightening the patient. Knowing when to speak during the interview is largely dependent on the nurse's perception about what is being conveyed through the silence. Icy silence might be an expression of anger and hostility. Being ignored or "given the silent treatment" is recognized as an insult and is a particularly hurtful form of communication. For example, it has been observed that silence among some African-American patients might relate to anger, insulted feelings, or acknowledgment of a nurse's lack of cultural sensitivity.

Silence can also convey a person's acceptance of another person; comfort in being with someone and sharing time together; that a person is pondering an idea or forming a response to what has just been said; or that a person is comfortable when there is nothing more to say at that moment. Successful interviewing might be dependent on the nurse's "will to abstain"—that is, to refrain from talking more than necessary. Silence might provide meaningful moments of reflection for both participants. It gives each an opportunity to contemplate thoughtfully what has been said and felt, weigh alternatives, formulate new ideas, and gain a new perspective of the matter under discussion. If the nurse waits to speak and allows the patient to break the silence, the patient might share thoughts and feelings that could otherwise have been withheld. Nurses who feel compelled to fill every void with words often do so because of their own anxiety, self-consciousness, and embarrassment. When this occurs, the nurse's need for comfort tends to take priority over the needs of the patient.

Conversely, prolonged and frequent silences by the nurse can hinder an interview that requires verbal articulation. Although the untalkative nurse might be comfortable with silence, this mode of communication might make the patient feel like a fountain of information to be drained dry. Moreover, without feedback, patients have no way of knowing whether what they said was understood.

In naturally evolving interviews, open-ended techniques are interwoven with empathetic and facilitatory statements and closed-ended statements, all of which serve to clarify issues and demonstrate the interviewer's interest (Shea, 1998).

## Active Listening

People want more than just physical presence in human communication. Most people are looking for the other person to be there for them psychologically, socially, and emotionally (Egan, 1994). Active listening includes:

- Observing and paraphrasing the patient's nonverbal behaviors
- Listening to and seeking to understand patients in the context of the social setting of their lives

- Listening for the "false notes" (e.g., inconsistencies or things the patient says that need more clarification)

We have already noted that effective interviewers need to become accustomed to silence. It is just as important, however, for effective interviewers to learn to become active listeners when the patient is talking, as well as when the patient becomes silent. During active listening, we carefully note what the patient is saying verbally and nonverbally, and we monitor our own nonverbal responses (Parsons and Wicks, 1994). Using silence effectively and learning to listen on a deeper, more significant level to both the patient and our own thoughts and reactions are key ingredients in effective communications. Both these skills take time, profit from guidance, and can be learned.

Here is a word of caution about listening. It is important for all of us to recognize that it is impossible to listen to people in an unbiased way. In the process of socialization, we develop *cultural filters* through which we listen to ourselves, others, and the world around us (Egan, 1994). Cultural filters are a form of cultural bias or cultural prejudice.

One of the functions of culture is to provide a highly selective screen between us and the outside world. In its many forms, culture designates what we pay attention to and what we ignore. This screening provides structure for the world (Hall, 1997, p. 85).

We humans seem to need these cultural filters to provide structure for ourselves and help us interpret and interact with the world. But unavoidably, these cultural filters also introduce various forms of bias in our listening, because they are bound to influence our personal, professional, familial, and sociological values and interpretations.

When nurses employ active listening techniques, they help strengthen a patient's ability to solve personal problems. By giving the patient undivided attention, the nurse communicates that the patient is not alone; rather, the nurse is working along with the patient, seeking to understand and help. This kind of intervention enhances self-esteem and encourages the patient to direct energy toward finding ways to deal with problems. Serving as a sounding board, the nurse listens as the patient tests thoughts by voicing them aloud. This form of interpersonal interaction often enables the patient to clarify thinking, link ideas, and tentatively decide what should be done and how best to do it.

# TECHNIQUES TO MONITOR AND AVOID

Some techniques health care workers might employ are not useful and can negatively affect the interview and threaten rapport between the nurse and patient. Using ineffective techniques that set up barriers to communication is something we all have done and will do again. However, with thoughtful reflection and appropriate alternative therapeutic behaviors and methods, communication skills will become more effective, and confidence in interviewing abilities will be gained. Most importantly, the ability to work with patients will be improved—even those patients who present the greatest challenges. Supervision and peer support are immensely valuable in identifying techniques to target and change.

Some of the most common approaches that can cause problems and are especially noticeable in the nurse who is new to psychosocial nursing are (1) asking excessive questions, (2) giving advice, (3) giving false reassurance, (4) requesting an explanation, and (5) giving approval.

## Asking Excessive Questions

Excessive questioning, especially *closed-ended* questions, puts the nurse in the role of interrogator, demanding information without respect for the patient's willingness or readiness to respond. This approach conveys lack of respect and sensitivity to the patient's needs. Excessive questioning controls the range and nature of response and can easily result in a therapeutic stall or a shut-down interview. It is a controlling tactic and might reflect the interviewer's lack of security in letting the patient tell his or her own story. It is better to ask more open-ended questions and follow the patient's lead. For example:

*Excessive questions:*
"Why did you leave your wife?" "Did you feel angry at her?" "What did she do to you?" "Are you going back to her?"

*Better to say*:
"Tell me about the situation between you and your wife."

## Giving Advice

When a nurse offers patients solutions, the inference could be that the nurse does not view the patient as capable of making effective decisions. Giving people advice can undermine their feelings of adequacy and competence. It can also foster dependence on the advice giver and shift problem-solving responsibility from the patient to the nurse. Giving constant advice to patients (or others for that matter) devalues the other individual and prevents the other person from working through and thinking through other options, either on their own or with the nurse. It keeps the "advice giver" in control and feeling like the strong one, although this might be unconscious on the nurse's part. This is very different from giving information to people. People need information to make informed decisions.

*Giving advice*:
*Patient*: "I don't know what to do about my brother. He is so lost."
*Nurse*: "You should call him up today and explain to him you can't support him any longer, and he will have to go on welfare." (If I were you...Why don't you...It would be best...)
*Better to say*:
*Patient*: "I don't know what to do about my brother. He is so lost."
*Nurse*: "What do you see as some possible actions you can take?" (encourages problem solving)
**OR**
*Nurse*: "Have you thought about discussing this with the rest of your family?" (offers alternatives the patient can consider)
Patients often ask nurses for solutions. It is best to avoid this trap.

## Giving False Reassurance

Giving false reassurance underrates a person's feelings and belittles a person's concerns. This usually causes people to stop sharing feelings because they feel they are not taken seriously or are being ridiculed. As a result, the person's real feelings remain undisclosed and unexplored. False reassurance in effect invalidates the patient's experience and can lead to increased negative effect.

*False reassurance:*
"Everybody feels that way."
"Don't worry, things will get better."
"It's not that bad."
"You're doing just fine."

*Better to say:*
"What specifically are you worried about?"
"What do you think could go wrong?"
"What do you see as the worst thing that could happen?"

## Requesting an Explanation: "Why" Questions

A "why" question from a person in authority (nurse, doctor, teacher) can be experienced as intrusive and judgmental. "Why" questions might put people on the defensive and serve to close down communication. It is much more useful to ask, "What is happening?" rather than why it is happening. People often have no idea why they did something, although almost everyone can make up a ready answer on the spot. Unfortunately, the answer is mostly defensive and not useful for further exploration.

*Why questions:*
"Why don't you leave him if he is so abusive?"
"Why didn't you take your medications?"
"Why didn't you keep your appointment?"

*Better to say:*
"What are the main reasons you stay in this relationship?"
"Tell me about the difficulties you have regarding taking your medications."
"I notice you didn't keep your appointment, even though you said that was a good time for you. What's going on?"

## Giving Approval

We often give our friends and family approval when we believe they have done something well. Even when what they have done is not that great, we make a big point of it.

It is natural to bolster up friends' and loved ones' egos when they are feeling down.

You might wonder what is wrong with giving a person a pat on the back once in a while. The answer is nothing, as long as it is done without involving a judgment (positive or negative) by the nurse. Giving approval in the nurse-patient relationship is a much more complex matter than giving approval or "a pat on the back" to a friend or colleague. People coming into the psychiatric setting are often feeling overwhelmed and alienated and might be down on themselves. During this time, patients are vulnerable and might be needy for recognition, approval, and attention. Yet, when people are feeling vulnerable, a value comment can be misinterpreted. For example:

*Value judgment:*
"You did a great job of holding your temper when Sally started screaming at you. You are really getting good at maintaining your 'cool.'"

Implied in this message is that the nurse was *pleased* by the way the patient kept his temper in a volatile situation. In many instances, the patient might see this as a way to please the nurse or get recognition from others. Therefore, the behavior becomes a way to gain approval. This can be a much healthier and more useful behavior for the patient, but when the motivation for any behavior starts to focus on getting recognition and approval from others, it stops coming from the individual's own volition or conviction. When the people the patient wants approval from are not around, the motivation for the new behavior might not be there either, so it is not really a change in behavior as much as a ploy to win approval and acceptance from others.

*Better to say:*
"I notice you kept your temper when Sally screamed at you. You seem to be acting more even-tempered lately. How does it feel to be more in control of your emotions?"

This response opens the door to finding out how the patient is feeling. Is this new behavior becoming easier? Was this situation of holding back anger difficult? Does the patient want to learn more assertiveness skills? Was it useful for the patient? Is there more about this situation the patient wants to discuss? The response by the nurse also makes it clear that this was a self-choice the patient made. The patient is given recognition for the change in behavior, and the topic is also open for further discussion.

# ASSESSING YOUR COMMUNICATIONS SKILLS

Gaining communication and counseling skills is a process that takes time. Self-assessment over time and noting areas of improvement and areas to target for the future might be helpful. Table 2-3 is a communication self-assessment checklist. It is helpful to check yourself frequently over time and note your progress.

## Table 2-3 **Nurse's Communication Self-Assessment Checklist**

*Instructions*: Periodically during your clinical experience, use this checklist to identify areas needed for growth and progress made. Think of your clinical patient experiences. Indicate the extent of your agreement with each of the following statements by marking the scale:

**SA, strongly agree; A, agree; NS, not sure; D, disagree; SD, strongly disagree**

| | | | | | |
|---|---|---|---|---|---|
| 1. I maintain appropriate eye contact. | SA | A | NS | D | SD |
| 2. Most of my verbal comments follow the lead of the other person. | SA | A | NS | D | SD |
| 3. I encourage others to talk about feelings. | SA | A | NS | D | SD |
| 4. I ask open-ended questions. | SA | A | NS | D | SD |
| 5. I restate and clarify a person's ideas. | SA | A | NS | D | SD |
| 6. I paraphrase a person's nonverbal behaviors. | SA | A | NS | D | SD |
| 7. I summarize in a few words the basic ideas of a long statement made by a person. | SA | A | NS | D | SD |
| 8. I make statements that reflect the person's feelings. | SA | A | NS | D | SD |

*Continued*

Table 2-3 **Nurse's Communication Self-Assessment Checklist—cont'd**

| | | | | | |
|---|---|---|---|---|---|
| 9. I share my feelings relevant to the discussion when appropriate to do so. | SA | A | NS | D | SD |
| 10. I give feedback. | SA | A | NS | D | SD |
| 11. At least 75% or more of my responses help enhance and facilitate communication. | SA | A | NS | D | SD |
| 12. I assist the person in listing some available alternatives. | SA | A | NS | D | SD |
| 13. I assist the person in identifying some goals that are specific and observable. | SA | A | NS | D | SD |
| 14. I assist the person in specifying at least one next step that might be taken toward the goal. | SA | A | NS | D | SD |

Myrick, D., & Erney, T. (1984). *Caring and sharing.* Educational Media Corporation, p. 154.

# INTERNET SITES

**Transcultural Nursing Society**
www.tcns.org

**JAMARDA Resources, Inc.**
Cultural diversity in the health care field
www.jamardaresources.com

**Natural Health Village**
Alternative systems of health practice
www.naturalhealthvillage.com

# CHAPTER 3

# Guidelines for the Nurse Conducting a Clinical Interview

The foundation of nursing practice is the ability of the nurse to engage in interpersonal interactions in a goal-directed manner for the purpose of assisting patients with their emotional or physical health needs. This definition by Hagety (1984) remains the most concise and relevant in today's practice. The relationship between nurse and patient is a professional relationship and as such implies certain responsibilities. Responsibilities inherent in the nurse-patient relationship for all levels of nursing include:

- **Accountability**—The nurse assumes responsibility for the conduct and consequences of the assignment and for the nurse's actions.
- **Focus on the patient's needs**—The interest of the patient, *not* that of other health care workers or the institution, is given first consideration. *The nurse's role is that of patient advocate.*
- **Clinical competence**—The nurse bases his or her conduct on the principles of knowledge of and appropriateness to the specific situation. This involves awareness and incorporation of the latest knowledge made available from research.
- **Delaying judgment**—Ideally, nurses refrain from judging patients and avoid imposing their own values and beliefs on others.

- **Supervision**—Validation of performance quality is through regularly scheduled supervisory sessions. Supervision is conducted either by a more experienced clinician or through discussion with the nurse's peers in professionally conducted supervisory sessions.

# RESPONSIBILITIES OF THE NURSE DURING THE PHASES OF A THERAPEUTIC RELATIONSHIP

Any disciplines describe the phases of a therapeutic relationship during counseling. These phases are the same for all disciplines, although different disciplines might have their own names for them. We will use the names that are generally recognized in the practice of nursing: (1) the orientation phase, (2) the working phase, and (3) the termination phase.

In some situations, the nurse might only meet with the patient once or for only a few sessions. The time spent together might be brief, but the relationship or encounters can be substantial, useful, and important to the patient. This limited relationship is often referred to as a *therapeutic encounter*. Many of the following principles and practices apply to even a limited encounter (e.g., issues of confidentiality, goals, tasks), although the working phase is brief and adapted to the brief encounter. Termination per se might not apply; however, the nurse might want to find out what the patient thought was helpful or whether there is an issue the patient wishes to pursue that was discussed during the encounter. This might warrant referring the patient to appropriate staff or members of the treatment team.

There are certain tasks and phenomena that are specific to each phase, although they might overlap. For example, the issue of confidentiality, first addressed in the orientation phase, can be discussed and reiterated throughout all phases of the nurse-patient relationship. The following discussion highlights important aspects and responsibilities of the nurse during each phase.

## Orientation Phase

The orientation phase can last for a few meetings or can extend for a longer period of time. The first time the nurse and patient meet, they are strangers to each other.

When strangers meet for the first time, they interact according to their own backgrounds, standards, values, and experiences. This fact underlies the need for self-assessment and self-awareness on the part of the nurse.

## Goals of the Orientation Phase

1. **To establish trust.** Establishing trust is essentially establishing a sound engagement with the patient in a therapeutic alliance. Trust is something that will or will not develop between the two parties. Establishing an atmosphere in which trust can grow is the responsibility of the nurse. Trust is nurtured by demonstrating genuineness (congruence) and empathy, developing a positive regard for the patient, demonstrating consistency, and offering assistance in alleviating the patient's emotional pain or problems.
2. **To effect some degree of anxiety reduction in the patient.**
3. **To instill hope and ensure that the patient will remain adherent to treatment.**
4. **To develop an assessment from which nursing diagnoses can be formulated,** if a nursing assessment has not already been done.
5. **To develop appropriate treatment goals (outcome criteria) and a plan of care.**

## Tasks of the Orientation Phase

During the orientation phase, the nurse addresses four specific issues: (1) the parameters of the relationship, (2) the formal or informal contract, (3) confidentiality, and (4) termination.

### Parameters of the Relationship

Patients have the right to know about the nurse or counselor with whom they will be working. For example, who is this nurse and what is the nurse's background? They also need to know the stated purpose of the meetings. For a student, this providing of information might be conveyed thus:

"Hello, Mrs. Gonzales, I am Sylvia Collins from Sullivan College. I am in my senior year, and I am doing my psychiatric rotation. I will come to City College for the next 8 Thursdays, and I would like to meet with you each Thursday if you are still here. I am here to be a support person for you as you work on your treatment goals."

**OR**

"Hello, Mrs. Gonzales. I am Jim Santos from Ohio State College. I am here only once this week, so we will have today to discuss your most important issues."

For a psychiatric–mental health advanced practice registered nurse (APRN-PMH) working in the clinical setting, the parameters might be altered.

"Hello, Mrs. Gonzales, I am John Horton. I am an advanced-practice psychiatric nurse, and I have been counseling patients for about 4 years now. Dr. Sharp referred you to me and stated that you wished to work out some issues in counseling/therapy."

### Formal or Informal Contract

A contract emphasizes the patient's participation and responsibilities. It implies that the nurse does something *with* the patient, not just *for* the patient. The contract, either stated or written, includes the time, place, date, and duration of the meetings as well as mutual agreement as to goals. If a fee is to be paid, the patient is told how much it will be and when the fee is due.

For a student, the statement of the contract might sound something like this:

"Mr. Snyder, we will meet at 10:00 AM each Monday in the consultation room at the clinic for 45 minutes from September 15th to October 27th. We can use that time to further discuss your feelings of loneliness and explore some things you could do to make things better for yourself."

For an APRN-PMH, the contract might be:

"Mrs. Lang, we will meet on Thursdays at 10:00 AM in my office at the clinic. Our sliding-scale fee is $45 per session. Our policy states that if you can't make a session, it is important to let us know 24 hours in advance; otherwise we will charge you for the session. We can use our time together to further explore your feelings of loneliness and anger with your husband and any other issues you wish to work on."

**Confidentiality**

The patient has the right to know who else knows about the information being shared with the nurse. He or she needs to know that the information might be shared with specific people, such as a clinical supervisor, the physician, the treatment team, or other students in conference. The patient also needs to know that the information will *not* be shared with the patient's family, friends, or others outside the treatment team, except in extreme situations. Extreme situations include:

- When the patient reveals information that might be harmful to the patient or others (child abuse, elder abuse)
- When the patient threatens self-harm
- When the patient does not intend to follow through with the treatment plan

When information must be given to others, it is usually done by the physician, according to legal guidelines. The nurse must be aware of the patient's right to confidentiality and must not violate that right. Refer to Box 3-1 for guidelines for confidentiality.

A student might phrase the issue of confidentiality something like:

"Mrs. Martin, I will be sharing some of what we discuss with my nursing instructor, and at times I might discuss certain concerns with my peers in conference or with the staff. I will *not* share this information with your husband or any other members of your family or your friends without your permission."

For a psychiatric nurse specialist, the issue can be broached in the following manner:

"Mr. Shapiro, I might share some of what we discuss with Dr. Lean during bimonthly supervision or in peer-group supervision here at the clinic. I will *not* discuss this information outside the clinic setting or with any members of your family or friends unless I have your permission, or if I am concerned that your life or someone else's life is in danger."

**Termination**

The issue of termination is always discussed in the first interview. It can also be brought up during the working phase. In some cases, the termination date is known,

---

| Box 3-1 **Ethical Guidelines for Confidentiality** |
|---|

1. Keep all patient records secure.
2. Consider carefully the content to be entered into the record.
3. Release information only with written consent and full discussion of the information to be shared, except when release is required by law.
4. Use professional judgment deliberately regarding confidentiality when the patient is a danger to self or others.
5. Use professional judgment deliberately when deciding how to maintain the confidentiality of a minor. The rights of the parent/guardian must also be considered deliberately.
6. Disguise clinical material when used professionally for teaching and writing.
7. Maintain confidentiality in consultation and peer review situations.
8. Maintain anonymity of research subjects.
9. Safeguard the confidentiality of the student in teaching/learning situations.

From Colorado Society of Clinical Specialists in Psychiatric Nursing. (1990). Ethical guidelines for confidentiality. *Journal of Psychosocial Nursing and Mental Health Services* 28, 42–44.

---

such as in a student rotation, in short-term therapy in which sessions are specifically limited, or when insurance issues dictate only a specific number of sessions. At other times, when the nurse-patient relationship is open-ended, the termination date might not be known. A student can address termination by saying:

"Mrs. Tacinelli, as I mentioned earlier, our last clinical day is October 27th. We will have three more meetings after today."

A clinical specialist can broach termination by saying something like:

"Mr. Middelstaedt, you are here to work on your phobia of using public transportation. Many people become more comfortable with their phobias in 12 to 14 sessions. At the end of 14 sessions, we can evaluate your goals and/or see if there is anything else you want to work on."

In summary, the initial interview includes the following elements:

1. The nurse's role is clarified, and the responsibilities of both the patient and the nurse are defined.
2. The contract containing the time, place, date, and duration of the meetings is discussed.
3. Confidentiality is discussed and assumed.
4. The terms of termination are introduced.

## Working Phase

During the working phase, the nurse and patient together identify and explore areas in the patient's life that are causing problems. Some of the specific tasks of the working phase of the nurse-patient relationship include (Moore & Hartman, 1988):

1. Maintaining the relationship
2. Gathering additional data
3. Promoting the patient's problem-solving ability
4. Facilitating behavior change
5. Overcoming resistance
6. Evaluating problems and goals and redefining them as necessary
7. Practicing and experiencing alternative adaptive behaviors

It is important, however, to keep in mind that chronically ill patients, particularly those with severe and persistent mental illness (SMI), frequently are unable to define problem areas or goals. The illness impairs their cognitive functioning and ability to establish relationships. It is important to recognize that establishing a trusting relationship with a chronically ill patient, and even temporarily relieving the patient's feelings of isolation and social withdrawal that accompany the illness, are significant goals to pursue.

During the orientation and working phase, patients often unconsciously employ "testing behaviors." The patient might want to know if the nurse will:

- Be able to set limits
- Still show concern if the patient gets angry, babyish, unlikable, or dependent
- Still be there if the patient is late, leaves early, refuses to speak, or is angry

Table 3-1 gives examples of common testing behaviors patients employ and some suggested nursing responses.

Table 3-1 **Testing Behaviors Used by Patients**

| Patient Behavior | Patient Example | Nurse Response | Rationale |
|---|---|---|---|
| Shifts focus of interview *to* the nurse, *off* the patient | "Do you have any children?" or "Are you married?" | "This time is for you." If appropriate, the nurse should add: <br> 1. "Do you have any children?" or "What about your children?" <br> 2. "Are you married?" or "What about your relationships?" | The nurse refocuses attention to the patient and patient's concerns. The nurse sticks to the contract. |
| Tries to get the nurse to take care of him or her | "Could you tell my doctor..." | "I'll leave a message with the ward clerk that you want to see him" or "You know best what you want him to know. I'll be interested in what he has to say." | 1. The nurse validates that the patient can do many things for himself or herself. This aids in increasing self-esteem. |
| | "Should I take this job?" | "What do you see as the pros and cons of this job?" | 2. The nurse always encourages the person to function at the highest level, even if he or she does not want to. |

| Makes sexual advances toward the nurse, such as touching the nurse's arm, wanting to hold hands, or kiss the nurse | "Would you go out with me?... Why not?" or "Can I kiss you?... Why not?" | "I am not comfortable having you touch (kiss) me." | 1. The nurse needs to set clear limits on expected behavior. |
| | | The nurse briefly reiterates the nurse's role: "This time is for you to focus on your problems and concerns." | 2. Frequently restating the nurse's role throughout the relationship can help maintain boundaries. |
| | | If the patient stops: "I wonder what this is all about?" 1. Is the patient afraid the nurse will not like him or her? 2. Is the patient trying to take the focus off of problems? | 3. Whenever possible, the meaning of the patient's behavior should be explored. |
| | | If the patient continues: "If you can't cease this behavior, I'll have to leave. I'll be back at (time) to spend time with you then." | 4. Leaving gives the patient time to gain control. The nurse returns at the stated time. |

*Continued*

Table 3-1  **Testing Behaviors Used by Patients—cont'd**

| Patient Behavior | Patient Example | Nurse Response | Rationale |
|---|---|---|---|
| **Continues to arrive late for meetings** | "I'm a little late because (excuse)." | The nurse arrives on time and leaves at the scheduled time. (The nurse does not let the patient manipulate him or her or bargain for more time.)<br><br>After a couple of times, the nurse can explore behavior (e.g., "I wonder if there is something going on you don't want to deal with?" or "I wonder what these late arrivals mean to you?") | 1. The nurse keeps the contract. Patients feel more secure when "promises" are kept, even though patients might try to manipulate the nurse through anger or helplessness, for example.<br><br>2. The nurse does not tell the patient what to do, but the nurse and patient need to explore what the behavior is all about. |

From Varcarolis, E. (2002). *Foundations of psychiatric mental health nursing* (4th ed.). Philadelphia, Saunders; p. 234; reprinted with permission.

## Termination Phase

Termination has been discussed in the first interview; it might also have been broached during the working phase of the relationship. Reasons for terminating include:

- Symptom relief
- Improved social functioning
- Greater sense of identity
- More adaptive behaviors in place
- Accomplishment of the patient's goals
- An impasse in therapy
- End of student rotation
- End of health maintenance organization (HMO) contract
- Discharge or death

Termination is an integral part of the nurse-patient relationship, and without it, the relationship remains incomplete. Summarizing the goals and objectives achieved in the relationship is part of the termination process. Reviewing situations that occurred during the time spent together and exchanging memories can help validate the experience for both the nurse and the patient, and can facilitate closure of the relationship.

During the termination process, old feelings of loss, abandonment, or loneliness might be reawakened in the patient. Therefore, the termination phase should offer the patient an opportunity to express these feelings, perhaps for the first time. Similar feelings might also be reawakened in the nurse, perhaps to a different degree or intensity if he or she has strong issues of loss. Nurses can benefit from discussing these feelings with more experienced nurses, supervisors, trusted instructors, and their mature peers. Because loss is an integral part of life, it is also an integral part of the human condition. Many feelings can be reawakened at termination, and patients might feel vulnerable and at a loss. Although many patients can talk about their feelings, patient behaviors vary widely. For example, a patient might respond with anger toward the nurse or demonstrate symptoms thought to be resolved. A patient might withdraw from the nurse during the last session or refuse to spend time with the nurse at all. It is always a good idea to acknowledge what seems to be going on and explore this with the patient:

> "You seem very quiet today and haven't made eye contact with me. Goodbyes often stir up memories of past separations. Do you remember any past separations that were painful?"

Throughout the process (introduction, working, termination), pertinent clinical information is recorded in the patient's record and verbally passed along to members of the treatment team.

# THE CLINICAL INTERVIEW

Anxiety during the first clinical interview is to be expected, as in any meeting between strangers. Patients might be anxious about their problems, about the nurse's reaction to them, or about their treatment. Shea (1998) identifies some common patient fears and concerns during the first interview:

- Who is this nurse/clinician?
- Is he or she competent?
- Is this person understanding?
- What does he or she already know about me?
- Am I going to be hurt?
- Do I have any control in this matter?

Students and clinicians new to psychosocial nursing might have other concerns:

- What should I say?
- What should I do?
- Will the patient like me?
- How will the patient respond to me?
- Can I help this person?
- Can I hurt the patient if I say the wrong thing?
- What will the instructor/supervisor think of what I am doing?
- How will I do compared with my peers?

## How to Begin the Interview

Helping a person with an emotional or medical problem is rarely a straightforward task. The goal of assisting a patient to regain psychological or physiological functional normality can be difficult to reach. It is extremely important in any kind of counseling to permit the patient to set the pace of the interview, no matter how slow the progress might be (Parsons & Wicks, 1994).

### Setting

Effective communication can take place almost anywhere. The quality of the interaction—whether in a clinic, a ward, an office, or the patient's home—depends on the degree to which the nurse and patient feel safe, so establishing a setting that enhances feelings of security can be important to the relationship. A health care setting, a conference room, or a quiet part of the unit that has relative privacy but is within view of others is ideal. Home visits offer the nurse a valuable opportunity to assess the person in the context of everyday life.

## Seating

In all settings, chairs need to be arranged so that conversation can take place in normal tones of voice, and eye contact can be comfortably maintained or avoided. A nonthreatening physical environment for the nurse and patient would involve:

- Assuming the same height—either both sitting or both standing
- Avoiding a face-to-face stance when possible—a 90-degree angle or side-by-side might be less intense
- Leaving plenty of space between patient and nurse
- Making sure that the door is easily accessible to both patient and nurse. This is particularly important if the patient suffers from paranoia or has a history of violence
- Avoiding a desk barrier between the nurse and patient

## Introductions

In the orientation phase, nurses tell the patient who they are, the purpose of the meetings, and how long and at what time they will be meeting with the patient. The issue of confidentiality is also covered at some point during the initial interview. The nurse can then ask the patient how he or she would like to be addressed. This question accomplishes a number of tasks (Shea, 1998); for example:

- It conveys respect.
- It gives the patient direct control.

## How to Start

Once introductions have been made, the nurse can turn the interview over to the patient by using one of a number of open-ended statements:

- "Where should we start?"
- "Tell me a little about what has been going on with you."

- "What are some of the stresses you have been coping with recently?"
- "Tell me a little about what has been happening in the past couple of weeks."
- "Perhaps you can begin by letting me know what some of your concerns have been recently."
- "Tell me about your difficulties."

The appropriate use of offering leads (e.g., "Go on"), statements of acceptance (e.g., "Uh-huh"), or other conveyances of the nurse's interest can facilitate communication.

## Tactics to Avoid

The nurse needs to avoid some behaviors (Moscato, 1988):

- Do not argue with, minimize, or challenge the patient.
- Do not praise the patient or give false reassurance.
- Do not verbally interpret the patient or speculate on the dynamics of the patient's problem.
- Do not question the patient about sensitive areas until trust is established.
- Do not try to "sell" the patient on accepting treatment.
- Do not join in attacks the patient launches on his or her mate, parents, friends, or associates.
- Do not participate in criticism of another nurse or any other staff member with the patient.
- Do not barrage the patient with many questions, especially closed-ended questions.

## Helpful Guidelines

Some guidelines for conducting the initial interviews are offered by Meier and Davis (1989):

- Speak briefly.
- When you do not know what to say, say nothing.
- When in doubt, focus on feelings.
- Avoid advice; rather, look at how the patient feels about the situation and what he or she wants to change.
- Avoid relying on questions.
- Pay attention to nonverbal cues.
- Keep the focus on the patient.

## Guidelines for Specific Patient Behaviors

There are a number of common patient behaviors that arise during the process of the nurse-patient relationship in mental health settings. New nurses might not know how best to handle these situations. These behaviors include patients who (1) cry, (2) ask the nurse to keep a secret, (3) leave before the session is over, (4) say they want to kill themselves, (5) do not want to talk, (6) seek to prolong the interview, (7) give the nurse a present, and (8) ask personal questions. Table 3-2 identifies common nursing reactions to these situations and offers the nurse useful responses.

Table 3-2 **Common Patient Behaviors and Nurse Responses**

| Patient Behavior | Possible Reactions by Nurse | Useful Responses by Nurse |
|---|---|---|
| **The patient cries.** | The nurse might feel uncomfortable and experience increased anxiety or feel somehow responsible for making the person cry. | The nurse should stay with the patient and reinforce that it is all right to cry. Often, it is at that time that feelings are closest to the surface and can be best identified. "You seem ready to cry." "What are you thinking right now?" The nurse offers tissues when appropriate. |
| **The patient asks the nurse to keep a secret.** | The nurse might feel conflict because he/she wants the patient to share important information but is unsure about making such a promise. | The nurse *cannot* make such a promise. This information might be important to the health and safety of the patient or others. "I cannot make that promise. It might be important for me to share it with other staff." The patient then decides whether to share the information or not. |
| **Another patient interrupts during time with your selected patient.** | The nurse might feel a conflict. The nurse does not want to appear rude. Sometimes the nurse tries to engage both patients in conversation. | The time the nurse had contracted with a selected patient is that patient's time. By keeping their part of the contract, nurses demonstrate that they mean what they say and that they view the sessions as important. I am with Mr. Rob for the next 20 minutes. At 10 AM, after our time is up, I can talk to you for 5 minutes." |

| | | |
|---|---|---|
| **The patient says he wants to kill himself.** | The nurse might feel overwhelmed or responsible to "talk the patient out of it." The nurse might pick up some of the client's feelings of hopelessness. | The nurse tells the patient that this is serious, that he or she does not want harm to come to the patient, and that this information needs to be shared with other staff. "This is very serious, Mr. Lamb. I do not want any harm to come to you. I will have to share this with the other staff." The nurse can then discuss with the patient the feelings and circumstances that led up to this decision. (Refer to Chapter 16 for strategies in suicide intervention.) |
| **The patients says she does not want to talk.** | A nurse who is new to this situation might feel rejected or ineffective. | At first, the nurse might say: "It's all right. I would like to spend time with you. We don't have to talk." The nurse might spend short, frequent periods (e.g., 5 minutes) with the patient throughout the day. "Our 5 minutes are up. I'll be back at 10 AM and stay with you 5 more minutes." This gives the patient the opportunity to understand that the nurse means what he or she says and is back on time consistently. It also gives the patient time between visits to assess the nurse and perhaps feel less threatened. |

*Continued*

Table 3-2   **Common Patient Behaviors and Nurse Responses—cont'd**

| Patient Behavior | Possible Reactions by Nurse | Useful Responses by Nurse |
|---|---|---|
| **The patient gives the nurse a present.** | The nurse might feel uncomfortable when offered a gift. The meaning needs to be examined. Is the gift:<br>1. A way of getting better care?<br>2. A way to maintain self-esteem?<br>3. A way to make the nurse feel guilty?<br>4. A sincere expression of thanks?<br>5. A cultural expectation? | *Possible guidelines:*<br>If the gift is expensive, the best policy is to perhaps graciously refuse.<br>If it is inexpensive and<br>1. given *at the end* of hospitalization when a relationship has developed, graciously accept.<br>2. given *at the beginning* of hospitalization, graciously refuse and explore the meaning behind the present.<br>"Thank you, but it is our job to care for our clients. Are you concerned that some aspect of your care will be overlooked?"<br>If the gift is money, it might be best to graciously refuse. |
| **The client asks you a personal question.** | The nurse might think it is rude not to answer the client's question.<br>*or*<br>A new nurse might feel relieved to put off the start of the interview. | The nurse may or may not answer the client's query. If the nurse decides to answer a natural question, he or she answers in a word or two, then refocuses back on the client. |

*or*

The nurse might feel embarrassed and want to leave the situation.

New nurses are often manipulated by a client to change roles. This keeps the focus off the client and prevents the building of a relationship.

P: Are you married?
N: Yes, do you have a spouse?
P: Do you have any children?
N: This time is for you—tell me about yourself.
P: You can tell me if you have any children.
N: This is your time to focus on your concerns. Tell me something about your family.

Varcarolis, E.M. and Halter, M.J. (2009). *Essentials of Psychiatric Mental Health Nursing.* St. Louis, Saunders; pp. 110–111.
Varcarolis, E.M. (2002). *Foundations of psychiatric mental health nursing* (4th ed.) Philadelphia, Saunders; pp 246–247.

# PART II

# DIAGNOSIS AND CARE PLANNING

# CHAPTER 4

# Selected Disorders
# of Childhood
# and Adolescence

## OVERVIEW

About 15% to 20% of children and adolescents in the
United States suffer from some form of mental disorder
(WHO, 2005) that causes significant impairment in their
functioning in school, at home, and with their peers. If left
untreated, all areas of the youth's life will be tragi-
cally impeded, leaving young people socially isolated,
stigmatized, and unable to live up to their potential and/or
contribute to society.

The risk factors for mental disorders in childhood or
adolescence are many. Genetic, biochemical, prenatal, and
postnatal influences; individual temperament; personal
psychosocial development, and personal resiliency are
all potential risk factors. The vulnerability to risk factors is
the result of a complex interaction among many factors
(e.g., constitutional endowment, trauma, disease, and inter-
personal experiences). Vulnerability changes over time as
children/adolescents grow and the emotional and physical
environment changes. As children and adolescents mature,
they develop competencies that enable them to communi-
cate, remember, test reality, solve problems, make decisions,
control drives and impulses, modulate affect, tolerate
frustration, delay gratification, adjust to change, establish

satisfying interpersonal relationships, and develop healthy self-concepts. These competencies reduce the risk for developing emotional, mental, or health problems.

Although it is true that the majority of mental suffering experienced by children and adolescents is related to situational stresses that respond to psychological treatment, it is also true that many mental illnesses begin in childhood.

The following disorders, most commonly seen in children and adolescents, are discussed in this chapter: (1) **Attention Deficit Disorders (ADD)** or **Attention Deficit Hyperactivity Disorders (ADHD)**, (2) **Disruptive Behavioral Disorders (Conduct Disorder)**, and (3) **Pervasive Developmental Disorders.** Anxiety disorders are covered in Chapter 5 and depression and bipolar disorders are addressed in Chapters 6 and 7, respectively. Currently accepted psychopharmacological agents used in the treatment of anxiety disorders in children and adolescents are included in Table 4-2.

## Initial Assessment

The observation/interaction part of a mental health assessment begins with a semistructured interview in which the child or adolescent is asked about life at home with parents and siblings and life at school with teachers and peers. Because the interview is not structured, children are free to describe their current problems and give information about their own developmental history. Play activities, such as games, drawing, puppets, and free play, are used for younger children who cannot respond to a direct approach. An important part of the first interview is observing interactions among the child, caregiver, and siblings (if possible).

### Assessment Tools

Nurses working with children and adolescents need to have a good grasp of growth and development. A chart comparing and contrasting the psychosexual stages of development according to Erickson, Freud, and Sullivan is found in Appendix C-1.

The **developmental assessment** (Appendix C-2) provides information about the child's current maturational level. This can help the nurse identify current lags or deficits. The

**Mental Status Assessment** (Appendix C-3) provides information about the child's/adolescent's current mental state. The developmental and mental status assessments have many areas in common, and for this reason any observation and interaction will provide data for both assessments.

# Attention Deficit and Disruptive Behavior Disorders

Most children and adolescents receiving treatment for mental disorders have behaviors that disrupt their lives at home and at school. The distinguishing characteristics for these disorders—**attention deficit hyperactivity disorder, oppositional defiant disorder**, and **conduct disorder**—are presented in the following sections.

## ASSESSMENT

### Attention Deficit Hyperactivity Disorder

Attention deficit hyperactivity disorder (ADHD) is a persistent pattern of inattention and/or hyperactivity/impulsivity that is *more frequently displayed* and *more severe* than that typically observed in individuals at a comparable level of development (American Psychiatric Association [APA], 2000). ADHD occurs in 3% to 7% of school-aged children. Children with ADHD might have a higher incidence of problems with temper outbursts, bossiness, stubbornness, labile moods, poor school performance, rejection by peers, low self-esteem, and enuresis and/or encopresis. It is important to note that about 5% to 7% of children are affected by ADHD, and two-thirds of those will have symptoms into adulthood (Preston et al., 2008). ADHD is often dually diagnosed with oppositional defiant disorder or conduct disorder (APA, 2000).

### Presenting Signs and Symptoms

#### Inattention

- Has difficulty paying attention in tasks or play
- Does not seem to listen, follow through, or finish tasks

- Does not pay attention to details and makes careless mistakes
- Dislikes activities that require sustained attention
- Is easily distracted, loses things, and is forgetful in daily activities (with symptoms worsening in situations requiring sustained attention)

### Hyperactivity

- Fidgets or is unable to sit still or stay seated in school
- Runs and climbs excessively in inappropriate situations
- Has difficulty playing quietly in leisure activities
- Acts as though "driven by a motor" and is constantly "on the go"
- Talks excessively

### Impulsivity

- Blurts out an answer before question is completed
- Has difficulty waiting for turns
- Interrupts or intrudes in others' conversations and games

### Other

- Some hyperactivity, impulsiveness, or inattention present before age 7
- Clear evidence of impairment in social, academic, or occupational functioning
- Impairment from symptoms in at least two settings (home, school, work)

## Oppositional Defiant Disorder

Oppositional defiant disorder is a recurrent pattern of negativistic, disobedient, hostile, defiant behavior toward authority figures, without serious violations of the basic rights of others (APA, 2000). The behavior is usually evident before age 8 years and no later than early adolescence. It is more common in males until puberty, when the male-to-female ratio might become equal. The behavior is evident at home and might not be evident elsewhere. The behavior persists for at least 6 months and might be a precursor of a **conduct disorder**.

## Presenting Signs and Symptoms

- Often loses temper
- Often argues with adults
- Often actively defies or refuses to comply with requests
- Deliberately annoys others and is easily annoyed by others
- Blames others for his or her mistakes
- Is often angry, resentful, spiteful, and vindictive

Other behaviors that often accompany this disorder are low self-esteem, labile moods, low frustration tolerance, swearing, early use of alcohol and illicit drugs, and conflicts with parents, teachers, and peers.

## Conduct Disorder

Conduct disorder is a persistent pattern of behavior in which the rights of others and age-appropriate societal norms or rules are violated (APA, 2000). The prevalence of conduct disorders appears to have increased during the past decade. The onset of this disorder might be as early as preschool years, but it is usually noted from middle adolescence through middle adulthood.

**Childhood-onset type** occurs prior to age 10 and mainly in males who are physically aggressive, have poor peer relationships with little concern for others, and lack guilt or remorse. Although they try to project a "tough" image, they have low self-esteem, low frustration tolerance, irritability, and temper outbursts. They are more likely to have their conduct disorder persist through adolescence and develop into **antisocial personality disorder.**

In the **adolescent-onset type,** no conduct problems occurred prior to age 10. These children are less likely to be aggressive, have more normal peer relationships, and act out their misconduct with their peer group. Males are more apt to fight, steal, vandalize, and have school discipline problems, whereas girls lie, are truant, run away, abuse substances, and engage in prostitution.

Complications associated with conduct disorders are school failures, suspension and dropout, juvenile delinquency, and the need for the juvenile court system to assume responsibility for youths who cannot be managed by their parents. Psychiatric disorders that frequently coexist with conduct disorder are anxiety, depression, ADHD, and learning disabilities.

## Presenting Signs and Symptoms

### *Aggression Toward People and Animals*

- Often bullies, threatens, and intimidates others
- Often initiates physical fights
- Has used a weapon that could cause serious injury
- Has been physically cruel to others and/or animals
- Has stolen while confronting a victim
- Has forced someone into sexual activity

### *Destruction of Property*

- Has deliberately set fires intending to cause damage
- Has deliberately destroyed another's property

### *Deceitfulness or Theft*

- Has broken into a house, building, or car
- Often lies to obtain goods or favors
- Has stolen items of trivial value (shoplifting)

### *Serious Violations of Rules*

- Often stays out at night, despite parental prohibition, before age 13
- Has run away from home at least twice, or once for a lengthy period of time
- Often truant from school before age 13

## Assessment Questions

### *Attention Deficit and Disruptive Behavior Disorders (for the Parent or Caregiver)*

*The nurse uses a variety of therapeutic techniques to obtain the answers to the following questions. Use your discretion and decide which questions are appropriate to complete your assessment.*

1. Describe the child's temperament. (easy, highly reactive, difficult)
2. Describe the child's overall activity level. (high energy, hyperactive)
3. Who is/was the primary caregiver? Any disruptions in that relationship?

4. Problems going to sleep or staying asleep? (nightmares, sleepwalking)
5. Describe the child's adjustment to feeding schedules or new foods. (food refusal, food fetishes)
6. Any difficulty separating from you if left in the care of others?
7. How does the child show affection toward you, siblings, peers?
8. What comforts the child when stressed?
9. Does the child express concern when others are injured or distressed? Express remorse or guilt when hurtful to others?
10. How does the child respond to limits? Being told 'no'? Having to wait, share, or end a favorite activity? (protests, tantrums)
11. How motivated is the child to learn new skills? (persistence, patience, response to frustration)
12. How long will the child attend to an activity? Easily distracted?
13. Can the child follow 1-, 2-, and 3-part directions?
14. Does the child have difficulty organizing or completing tasks? Lose personal belongings?
15. Does the child have friends? How well do they play together?
16. Does the child frequently seek attention? Talk a lot? Interrupt or intrude on other's activities or body space?
17. At what grade level is the child? How is the child's academic progress?
18. Describe any problematic behaviors. (acts impulsively or recklessly, is physically aggressive, is hostile, is cruel to people and animals, is manipulative, lies and cheats, steals, destroys property, sets fires, swears, skips school, runs away from home, uses drugs or alcohol, sexually acts out)

## Assessment Guidelines

### Attention Deficit and Disruptive Behavior Disorders

1. Assess the quality of the relationship between the child and parent/caregiver for evidence of bonding, anxiety, tension, and difficulty of fit between the parents' and

the child's temperament, which can contribute to the development of disruptive behaviors.

2. Assess the parent/caregiver's understanding of growth and development, parenting skills, and handling of problematic behaviors, because lack of knowledge contributes to the development of these problems.

3. Assess cognitive, psychosocial, and moral development for lags or deficits, because immature developmental competencies result in disruptive behaviors.

## Attention Deficit Hyperactivity Disorder

1. Observe the child for level of physical activity, attention span, talkativeness, and the ability to follow directions and control impulses. Medication is often needed to ameliorate these problems.

2. Assess for difficulty in making friends and performing in school. Academic failures and poor peer relationships lead to low self-esteem, depression, and further acting out.

3. Assess for problems with enuresis and encopresis.

## Oppositional Defiant Disorder

1. Identify issues that result in power struggles, when they began, and how they are handled.

2. Assess the severity of the defiant behavior and its impact on the child's life at home, at school, and with peers.

## Conduct Disorder

1. Assess the seriousness of the disruptive behavior, when it started, and what has been done to manage it. Hospitalization or residential placement, as well as medication, might be necessary.

2. Assess the child's levels of anxiety, aggression, anger, and hostility toward others and the ability to control destructive impulses.

3. Assess the child's moral development for the ability to understand the impact of the hurtful behavior on others, empathize with others, and feel remorse.

## Nursing Diagnoses with Interventions

### Discussion of Potential Nursing Diagnoses

Children and adolescents with attention deficit hyperactivity disorder, oppositional defiant disorder, and conduct disorder have disruptive behaviors that are impulsive, angry/aggressive, and often dangerous **(Risk for Violence).** These children and adolescents are often in conflict with parents and authority figures, refuse to comply with requests, do not follow age-appropriate social norms, or have inappropriate ways of getting needs met **(Defensive Coping).** When their behavior is disruptive or aggressive and hostile, they have difficulty making or keeping friends **(Impaired Social Interaction).** Their problematic behaviors can impair learning and result in academic failure. Interpersonal and academic problems lead to high levels of anxiety, low self-esteem, and blaming others for one's troubles **(Chronic Low Self-Esteem).** Parents/caregivers have difficulty handling disruptive behaviors and being effective parents, so their participation in the therapeutic program is essential **(Impaired Parenting).**

## Overall Guidelines for Nursing Interventions

### Attention Deficit and Disruptive Behavior Disorders

Help the child reach his or her full potential by fostering developmental competencies and coping skills:

1. Protect the child from harm and provide for biological and psychosocial needs while acting as a parental surrogate.
2. Increase the child's ability to trust, control impulses, modulate the expression of affect, tolerate frustration, concentrate, remember, reality test, recognize cause and effect, make decisions, problem solve, use interpersonal skills to maintain satisfying relationships, form a realistic self-identity, and play with enjoyment and creativity.
3. Foster the child's identification with positive role models so positive attitudes and moral values that enable the child to experience feelings of empathy, remorse, shame, and pride can develop.
4. Provide support, education, and guidance for the parents/caregivers.

## Selected Nursing Diagnoses and Nursing Care Plans

### RISK FOR VIOLENCE: SELF-DIRECTED OR OTHER-DIRECTED

At risk for behaviors in which an individual demonstrates that he/she can be physically, emotionally, and/or sexually harmful to self or to others

### *Some Risk Factors (Related To)*

▲ Impaired neurological development or dysfunction
▲ Cognitive impairment (e.g., learning disabilities, attention deficit disorder, decreased intellectual functioning)
▲ Impulsivity
▲ History of childhood abuse or witnessing family violence
▲ History of violent antisocial behavior toward others
▲ Psychotic symptomatology (hallucinations, paranoid delusions, illogical thought process)
▲ Emotional problems (e.g., hopelessness, despair, increased anxiety, panic, anger, hostility)
▲ History of substance abuse; pathological intoxication

### *Some Defining Characteristics: Presenting Behaviors (As Evidenced By)*

● Bullying, threatening, and having physical fights with others
● Physical cruelty to people and animals
● Setting fires and/or destroying property
● Forcing someone into sexual activity (attempted rape, rape, sexual molestation)
● History of aggressive behavior (e.g., mugs or robs others)
● Inability to control temper

---

▲ NANDA International accepted;  ● In addition to NANDA International

## Outcome Criteria

- Control aggressive, impulsive behaviors
- Demonstrate respect for the rights of others

## Long-Term Goals

Child/adolescent will:
- Demonstrate the ability to control aggressive impulses and delay gratification within 3 to 4 months with counseling and support

## Short-Term Goals

Child/adolescent will:
- Respond to limits on aggressive and cruel behaviors within 2 to 4 weeks
- Identify at least three situations that trigger violent behaviors within 1 to 2 months
- Channel aggression into constructive activities and appropriate competitive games within 2 to 4 weeks
- State the effects of his or her behavior on others within 2 to 4 weeks
- Demonstrate the ability to control aggressive impulses and delay gratification within 2 to 8 weeks

## Interventions and Rationales

| Intervention | Rationale |
|---|---|
| 1. Use one-on-one or appropriate level of observation to monitor rising levels of anxiety; determine emotional and situational triggers. | 1. External controls are needed for ego support and to prevent acts of aggression and violence. |
| 2. Intervene early to calm the patient and defuse a potential incident. | 2. Learning can take place before the patient loses control; new ways to cope can be discussed and role modeled. |
| 3. Use graduated techniques for managing disruptive behaviors (Table 4-1). | 3. Techniques such as signals/warnings, proximity and touch control, humor, and attention might be all that is needed. |
| 4. Set clear, consistent limits in a calm, nonjudgmental | 4. A child gains a sense of security with clear |

| Intervention | Rationale |
|---|---|
| manner; remind patient of consequences of acting out. | limits and calm adults who follow through on a consistent basis. |
| 5. Avoid power struggles and repeated negotiations about rules and limits. | 5. When limits are realistic and enforceable, manipulation can be minimized. |
| 6. Use strategic removal if the patient cannot respond to limits (time out, quiet room, therapeutic holding). | 6. Removal allows the patient to express feelings and discuss problems without losing face in front of peers. |
| **7. Process incidents with the patient to make it a learning experience.** | **7. Reality testing, problem solving, and testing new behaviors are necessary to foster cognitive growth.** |
| 8. Use a behavior modification program that rewards the patient for seeking help with handling feelings and controlling impulses to act out. | 8. Rewarding the patient's efforts can increase positive behaviors and foster development of self-esteem. |
| 9. Redirect expressions of disruptive feelings into nondestructive, age-appropriate behaviors; channel excess energy into physical activities. | 9. Learning how to modulate the expression of feelings and use anger constructively is essential for self-control. |
| 10. Help the patient see how acting out hurts others; appeal to the child's sense of "fairness" for all. | 10. These children are insensitive to the feelings of others. However, they can understand the concept of "fairness" and generalize it to other persons. |
| 11. Encourage feelings of concern for others and remorse for misdeeds. | 11. Development of empathy is a therapeutic goal with these children. |
| 12. Use medication if indicated to reduce anxiety and aggression or to modulate moods. | 12. A variety of medications are effective in children who experience behavioral dyscontrol. |

## Table 4-1 **Techniques for Managing Disruptive Behaviors in Children**

| | |
|---|---|
| 1. Planned ignoring | 1. Evaluate surface behavior, and intervene when the intensity is becoming too great. |
| 2. Use of signals or gestures | 2. Use a word, gesture, or eye contact to remind child/adolescent to use self-control. |
| 3. Physical distance and touch control | 3. Move closer to the child/adolescent for a calming effect—maybe put arm around child/adolescent. |
| 4. Increase involvement in the activity | 4. Redirect child/adolescent's attention to the activity and away from a distracting behavior by asking a question. |
| 5. Additional affection | 5. Ignore the provocative content of the behavior, and give the child emotional support for the current problem. |
| 6. Use of humor | 6. Use well-timed kidding as a diversion to help the child/adolescent save face and relieve feelings of guilt or fear. |
| 7. Direct appeals | 7. Appeal to the child's/adolescent's developing self-control (e.g., "Please, not now.") |
| 8. Extra assistance | 8. Give early help to the child/adolescent who "blows up" and is easily frustrated when trying to achieve a goal; do not overuse this technique. |
| 9. Clarification as intervention | 9. Help child/adolescent understand the situation and his or her own motivation for the behavior. |
| 10. Restructuring | 10. Change the activity in ways that will lower the stimulation or the frustration (e.g., shorten a story or change to a physical activity). |
| 11. Regrouping | 11. Use total or partial changes in the group's composition to reduce conflict and contagious behaviors. |
| 12. Strategic removal | 12. Remove child/adolescent who is disrupting or acting dangerously, but consider whether it gives too much status or makes the child a scapegoat. |
| 13. Physical restraint | 13. Use "therapeutic holding" to control, give comfort, and assure a child that |

*Continued*

Table 4-1 **Techniques for Managing Disruptive Behaviors in Children\*—cont'd**

| | he or she is protected from his or her own impulses to act out. |
|---|---|
| 14. Setting limits and giving permission | 14. Use sharp, clear statements about what behavior is not allowed, and give permission for the behavior that is expected. |
| 15. Promises and rewards | 15. Use very carefully and very infrequently to avoid situations in which the child/adolescent bargains for a reward. |
| 16. Threats and punishment | 16. Use very carefully; the child/adolescent needs to internalize the frustration generated by the punishment and use it to control impulses rather than externalizing the frustration in further acting out. |

Redl, F., & Wineman, D. (1957). *The aggressive child*. Glencoe, IL: The Free Press.

## DEFENSIVE COPING

Repeated projection of falsely positive self-evaluation based on a self-protective pattern that defends against underlying perceived threats to positive self-regard

### Some Related Factors (Related To)

▲ Deficient support system
▲ Low level of self-confidence
▲ Fear of failure/humiliation
● Disturbance in pattern of tension release (problems in impulse control and frustration tolerance)
● Impaired neurological development or dysfunction
● Birth temperament (highly reactive, difficult to comfort, high motor activity)
● Disturbed relationship with parent/caregiver (lack of trust, abuse, neglect, conflicts, inadequate role models, disorganized family system)

▲ NANDA International accepted; ● In addition to NANDA International

## *Defining Characteristics: Presenting Behaviors (As Evidenced By)*

▲ Denial of obvious problems/weaknesses
▲ Uses projection of blame
▲ Difficulty in perception of reality testing
▲ Hypersensitive to criticism or slights
▲ Superior attitude toward others and/or ridicule of others
● Uses forms of coping that impede adaptive behavior (defiant, negative, and/or hostile toward authority figures)
● Refuses to follow directions or comply with limits set on behaviors
● Tests limits persistently
● Is argumentative, stubborn, and unwilling to give in or negotiate

## *Outcome Criteria*

● Complies with requests and limits on behaviors in the absence of arguments, tantrums, or other acting-out behaviors

## *Long-Term Goals*

Child/adolescent will:
● Question the requests or limits that seem unreasonable and negotiate a settlement within 2 to 3 months

## *Short-Term Goals*

Child/adolescent will:
● Demonstrate increased impulse control within 2 weeks using a scale of 1 to 10 (1 being the most controlled)
● Demonstrate the ability to tolerate frustration and delay gratification within 6 weeks
● Demonstrate an absence of tantrums, rage reactions, or other acting-out behaviors within 4 to 8 weeks

---

▲ NANDA International accepted; ● In addition to NANDA International

- Discuss requests and behavioral limits and understand their rationale with the authority figure within 4 to 6 weeks
- Accept responsibility for misbehaviors within 2 to 6 weeks

## Interventions and Rationales

| Intervention | Rationale |
|---|---|
| 1. Use one-on-one or appropriate level of observation to monitor rising levels of frustration; determine emotional and situational triggers. | 1. External controls are needed for emotional support and to prevent tantrums and rage reactions. |
| 2. Intervene early to calm the patient, problem solve, and defuse a potential outburst. | 2. Learning can take place before the patient loses control; new solutions and compromises can be proposed. |
| 3. Avoid power struggles and "no-win" situations. | 3. Therapeutic goals are lost in power struggles. |
| 4. Use a behavior modification program to reward tolerating frustration, delaying gratification, and responding to requests and behavioral limits. | 4. Rewarding the patient's efforts will increase the positive behaviors and help with development of self-control. |
| 5. Allow the patient to question the requests or limits *within reason*; give simple, understandable rationale for requests or limits. | 5. Discussion allows the patient to maintain some sense of autonomy and power. (Rationale is tailored to the developmental age and promotes socialization.) |
| 6. When feasible, negotiate an agreement on the expected behaviors. Avoid giving bribes or allowing the patient to manipulate the situation. | 6. An agreement on expected behavior will result in better compliance. However, constant negotiations can result in increased manipulation and testing of limits. |

| **Intervention** | **Rationale** |
|---|---|
| 7. Use medication if indicated to reduce anxiety, rage, and aggression, and to modulate moods. | 7. A variety of medications are effective in children who experience behavioral and emotional dyscontrol. |

## IMPAIRED SOCIAL INTERACTION

Insufficient or excessive quantity or ineffective quality of social exchange

### *Some Related Factors (Related To)*

▲ Sociocultural dissonance
▲ Disturbed thought processes
▲ Limited physical mobility
▲ Absence of significant others
▲ Communication barriers
● Impaired neurological development or dysfunction
● Disturbance in the development of impulse control, frustration tolerance, or empathy for others
● Disturbed relationship with parents/caregiver (lack of trust, abuse, neglect, conflicts, disorganized family system)
● Lack of appropriate role models and/or identification with aggressive/abusive models
● Loss of friendships due to disruptions in family life and living situations

### *Defining Characteristics: Presenting Behaviors (As Evidenced By)*

▲ Discomfort in social situations
▲ Dysfunctional interaction with peers and others (teases, taunts, bullies, and fights with others)
▲ Use of unsuccessful social interaction behavior
▲ Inability to communicate a satisfying sense of social engagement (e.g., belonging, caring, interest, shared history)

---

▲ NANDA International accepted; ● In addition to NANDA International

- Difficulty making friends because of immature, disruptive, destructive, cruel, or manipulative behaviors
- Isolated, having few or no friends and/or poor sibling relationships
- Blames others for poor peer relationships
- Sad/depressed about not being liked by peers
- Low self-esteem or unrealistic, inflated esteem as the aggressor

## Outcome Criteria

- Use age-appropriate interpersonal skills to establish genuine and equal-status friendship with at least one person

## Long-Term Goals

Child/adolescent will:
- Interact with others using age-appropriate and acceptable behavior within 4 months

## Short-Term Goals

Child/adolescent will:
- Participate in one-on-one and group activities without attempts to interrupt, intimidate, or manipulate others within 4 to 6 weeks
- Use age-appropriate skills in play activities and interpersonal exchanges within 4 to 8 weeks
- Describe a realistic sense of self using feedback from adults and peers within 4 to 8 weeks

## Interventions and Rationales

| **Intervention** | **Rationale** |
|---|---|
| 1. Use one-on-one relationship to engage the patient in a working relationship. | 1. The patient needs positive role models for healthy identification. |

▲ NANDA International accepted; ● In addition to NANDA International

| Intervention | Rationale |
|---|---|
| 2. Monitor for negative behaviors, and identify maladaptive interaction patterns. | 2. Negative behaviors are identified and targeted to be replaced with age-appropriate social skills. |
| 3. Intervene early, give feedback and alternative ways to handle the situation. | 3. Children learn from feedback; early intervention prevents rejection by peers and provides immediate ways to cope. |
| 4. Use therapeutic play to teach social skills such as sharing, cooperation, realistic competition, and manners. | 4. Learning new ways to interact with others through play allows the development of satisfying friendships and self-esteem. |
| 5. Use role-playing, stories, therapeutic games, and the like to practice skills. | 5. Solidifies new skills in a safe environment. |
| 6. Help patient find and develop a special friend; set up one-on-one play situations; be available for problem solving peer relationship conflicts; role model social skills. | 6. The abilities to reality test, problem solve, and resolve conflicts in peer relationships are important competencies needed for interpersonal skills. |
| 7. Help the patient develop equal-status peer relationships with reciprocity for honest, appropriate expression of feelings and needs. | 7. When people can identify personal feelings and needs, they are better prepared to use more direct communication rather than manipulation and/or intimidation. |

## CHRONIC LOW SELF-ESTEEM

Longstanding negative self-evaluation/feelings about self or self-capabilities

## Some Related Factors (Related To)

▲ Perceived lack of belonging
▲ Perceived lack of respect from others
▲ Repeated failures
▲ Repeated negative reinforcement
▲ Psychiatric disorder
● Disturbed relationship with parent/caregiver (lack of trust, abuse, neglect, conflicts, inadequate role models, disorganized family system)
● Being targeted by peers for rejection or abuse

## Defining Characteristics: Presenting Behaviors (As Evidenced By)

▲ Rejects positive feedback about self
▲ Excessively seeks reassurance
▲ Dependent on others' opinions
▲ Exaggerates negative feedback
▲ Nonassertive behavior
▲ Lack of eye contact
▲ Frequent lack of success in life events
● Self-negating verbalization.
● Uses defense mechanisms (denial, rationalization, projection, reaction formation) to protect against threats to self-esteem

## Outcome Criteria

● Develop cognitive and emotional competencies needed for self-concept development

## Long-Term Goals

Child/adolescent will:
● Participate in three new activities and new situations with relative comfort
● Identify four positive personal attributes

---

▲ NANDA International accepted; ● In addition to NANDA International

- Develop genuine positive self-regard based on a more realistic appraisal of personal abilities/talents within 2 months

## Short-Term Goals

Child/adolescent will:
- Recognize when feeling threatened in unfamiliar situations and seek adult help in reducing anxiety and enhancing self-esteem within 2 to 4 weeks
- Demonstrate one new way to cope with new situations using reality testing, problem solving, and positive affirmations within 4 to 8 weeks
- Identify at least two realistic goals and start to develop desired skills/abilities that will increase self-esteem within 2 to 8 weeks
- Name two things he/she likes about self within 1 week
- Use social skills to develop rewarding peer relationships within 4 to 8 weeks

## Interventions and Rationales

| Intervention | Rationale |
|---|---|
| 1. Give "unconditional positive regard" without reinforcing negative behaviors. | 1. The patient often sets up situations in which the behavior brings rejection and further confirms the lack of self-worth. |
| 2. Reinforce the patient's self-worth with time and attention. | 2. Giving one-on-one time or attention in a group activity confirms the patient's self-worth. |
| 3. Help the patient identify positive qualities and accomplishments. | 3. An accurate appraisal of accomplishments can help dispel unrealistic expectations. |
| 4. Help the patient identify behaviors needing change and set realistic goals. | 4. To change, the patient needs goals and knowledge of new behaviors. |
| 5. Use a behavior modification program that rewards the patient for trying new behaviors and evaluates results. | 5. Rewarding the patient's efforts will increase the positive behaviors and foster the development of self-esteem. |

## IMPAIRED PARENTING

Inability of the primary caregiver to create, maintain, or regain an environment that promotes the optimum growth and development of the child

### *Some Risk Factors (Related To)*

▲ Physical illness (impaired neurological development or dysfunction; handicapped condition)
▲ Attention deficit hyperactivity disorder
▲ Lack of parent/caregiver fit with child
▲ Lack of knowledge about parenting/child development or the special needs of the child
▲ Role strain or overload (multiple stressors)
▲ Mental or physical illness, either parent(s) or child
● Constraints of child's birth temperament
● History of being abused or history of being abusive

### *Some Defining Characteristics (As Evidenced By)*

▲ Behavioral disorders
▲ Failure to thrive
▲ Rejection of child or hostility toward child
▲ Unsafe home environment
▲ Frequent accidents, illness, incidence of abuse or trauma
▲ Inappropriate caretaking skills and or child care arrangements
● Disturbed relationship between parent/caregiver and child (lack of trust, abuse, neglect, conflicts, inadequate role models, disorganized family system)
● Unrealistic expectations of self or the child

### *Outcome Criteria*

● Parent/caregiver has the resources to help patient reach his or her age-related potential
● Home situation will be safe (free of abuse, neglect, undue stress, environmental risks)

---

▲ NANDA International accepted; ● In addition to NANDA International

## Long-Term Goals

Parent/caregiver will:
- Learn the appropriate parenting skills to deal with the patient's individual problematic behavior within 3 months
- Will have at least four alternative ways to deal with stress and parenting.
- Will be in treatment for any mental or physical problems related to inability to parent in an effective manner within 1 to 4 months

## Short-Term Goals

Parent/caregiver will:
- Participate in the patient's therapeutic program within 1 to 2 weeks
- Increase knowledge of normal growth and development, the patient's diagnosis, medications, and parenting skills needed within 2 to 6 weeks
- Set realistic, age-appropriate behavioral goals for patient when at home within 4 weeks
- Learn at least four new skills that will help provide patient's biological and psychosocial needs when at home within 2 to 4 weeks
- Learn the skills necessary to facilitate the development of patient's competencies and coping skills when at home within 4 to 6 weeks
- Develop a support system to assist themselves with parenting within 4 to 6 weeks
- Use available resources to advocate for the patient's needs within 2 to 4 weeks

## Interventions and Rationales

| Intervention | Rationale |
|---|---|
| 1. Explore the impact of the problematic behavior on the life of the family. | 1. Helps nurse understand the parent/caregiver situation. Feeling understood and supported can help foster an alliance. |
| 2. Assess the parent's/caregiver's knowledge of childhood growth and development and parenting skills. | 2. Problem identification and analysis of learning needs are necessary before intervention begins. |

| **Intervention** | **Rationale** |
|---|---|
| 3. Assess the parent's/caregiver's understanding of the child's diagnosis, treatment, and medications. | 3. Knowledge will increase parent/caregiver participation, motivation, and satisfaction. |
| 4. Help the parent/caregiver identify the child's biological and psychosocial needs. | 4. Adequate parenting involves being able to identify the child's actual age-appropriate needs. |
| 5. Involve the parent in identifying a realistic plan for how these needs will be met when the client is at home. | 5. Parents/caregivers have the opportunity to learn the skills necessary to meet the child's needs. |
| 6. Work with the parent/caregiver to set behavioral goals; help set realistic goals for when the child is at home. | 6. Mutually setting goals provides continuity and prevents the child from using splitting or manipulation to sabotage treatment. |
| 7. Teach behavior modification techniques; give parent/caregiver support in using them and evaluating effectiveness. | 7. Education and follow-up support is the key to a successful treatment program. |
| 8. Assess the parent/caregiver support system; use referrals to establish additional supports. | 8. Self-help groups and special programs such as respite care can increase the caregiver's ability to cope. |
| 9. Give information on legal rights and available resources that can assist in advocating for child services. | 9. Parent/caregiver frequently lacks information on how to secure services for the child. |

# Pervasive Developmental Disorders

Pervasive developmental disorders are characterized by their severe and pervasive impairment in reciprocal social interaction and communication skills. The four subtypes of pervasive developmental disorders are autistic, Asperger's, Rett's, and childhood disintegrative disorders. These disorders are usually evident in the first years of life and might be associated with some degree of mental retardation (APA, 2000).

# ASSESSMENT

## Autistic Disorder

Predominant features include markedly abnormal or impaired development in social interaction and communication. The impairment in reciprocal social interaction and communication skills is gross and sustained (APA, 2000).

Autistic disorder is usually recognized before the age of 3. What is most notable is the restrictive, repetitive, and stereotypic patterns of behavior, interests, and activities.

The prognosis is generally poor. Few can live and work independently; approximately 33% can achieve partial independence.

## Presenting Signs and Symptoms

### Impairment in Social Interactions

- Lack of responsiveness to and interest in others
- Lack of eye-to-eye contact and facial responses
- Indifference or aversion to affection and physical contact
- Failure to cuddle or be comforted
- Lack of seeking or sharing enjoyment, interest, or achievement with others
- Failure to develop cooperative play or imaginative play with peers
- Lack of friendships

### Impairment in Communication and Imaginative Activity

- Language delay or total absence of language
- Immature grammatical structure; pronoun reversal; inability to name objects
- Stereotyped or repetitive use of language (echolalia, idiosyncratic words, inappropriate high-pitched squealing/giggling, repetitive phrases, sing-song speech quality)

- Lack of spontaneous make-believe play or imaginative play
- Failure to imitate

## *Markedly Restricted, Stereotyped Patterns of Behavior, Interests, and Activities*

- Rigid adherence to routines and rituals with catastrophic reactions to minor changes in them or changes made in the environment (moving furniture)
- Stereotyped and repetitive motor mannerisms (hand/finger flapping, clapping, rocking, dipping, swaying, spinning, dancing around and walking on toes, head banging, or hand biting)
- Preoccupation with certain objects (buttons, parts of the body, wheels on toys) that is abnormal in intensity or focus
- Preoccupation with certain repetitive activities (pouring water/sand, spinning wheels on toys, twirling string) that is abnormal in intensity or focus

## Asperger's Disorder

This disorder differs from autistic disorder in that it appears to have a later onset and there is no significant delay in cognitive and language development (APA, 2000). Mental retardation is not usually observed. This is a continuum and a lifelong disorder.

## Presenting Signs and Symptoms

- Recognized later than autistic disorder
- No significant delays in cognitive and language development
- Severe and sustained impairment in social interactions
- Development of restricted, repetitive patterns of behavior, interests, and activities resembling autistic disorder
- Might have delayed motor development milestones, with clumsiness noted in preschool
- Social interaction problems more noticeable when child enters school
- Problems with empathy and modulating social relationships might continue into adulthood

## Rett's Disorder

This disorder differs from autistic and Asperger's disorders in that it has been observed only in females, with the onset before the age of 4 (APA, 2000). Rett's disorder is usually associated with profound mental retardation.

## Presenting Signs and Symptoms

- Development of multiple deficits after a normal prenatal and postnatal period of development
- Normal head circumference at birth, but growth rate slows between the 5th and 48th months of life
- Persistent and progressive loss of previously acquired hand skills between the 5th and 30th months of life
- Development of stereotyped hand movements (hand wringing, handwashing)
- Problems with coordination of gait and trunk movements
- Severe psychomotor retardation
- Severe problems with expressive and receptive language
- Loss of interest in social interactions but might develop this interest later in childhood or adolescence

## Childhood Disintegrative Disorder

This disorder is marked by regression in multiple areas of functioning following a period of at least 2 years of normal development (APA, 2000). The onset can be abrupt or insidious. This disorder is usually associated with severe mental retardation.

## Presenting Signs and Symptoms

- Marked regression in multiple areas of function after at least 2 years of normal development
- Loss of previously acquired skills in at least two areas (communication, social relationships, play, adaptive behavior, motor skills, and bowel/bladder control)
- Deficits in communication and social interactions (same as autistic disorder)
- Stereotyped behaviors (same as autistic disorder)
- Loss of skills reaches a plateau, followed by limited improvement

## Assessment Questions

### *Pervasive Developmental Disorders (for the Parent or Caregiver)*

*The nurse uses a variety of therapeutic techniques to obtain the answers to the following questions. Use your discretion and decide which questions are appropriate to complete your assessment.*

1. Describe the child's temperament and adjustment as a newborn.
2. Describe any unusual responses to stimuli. (sounds, lights, or being touched)
3. When did the child develop a social smile? Become responsive to words and physical contact?
4. Can the child be comforted? How does the child comfort self?
5. Does the child show interest in others? Concern when others are hurt?
6. When did speech develop? Unusual characteristics? (in rate, rhythm, tone, inflection pattern, echolalia, made-up words)
7. Describe any unusual behaviors. (hand/finger flapping, clapping, rocking, dipping, swaying, spinning, dancing around, and walking on toes)
8. What, if any, behaviors cause self-injury? (head banging, slapping, or hand biting)
9. What are the child's favorite toys? Any preoccupation with round or shiny objects, objects that can spin or move, or parts of the body?
10. What is the child's favorite activity? Any preoccupation with repetitive activities? (pouring water/sand, spinning/twirling objects, chewing or eating inedible items)
11. How does the child respond to limit setting? Tantrum behaviors?
12. How does the child respond to changes? (routines, schedules, activities or rituals, changes in furniture arrangements)
13. How well does the child do at self-care activities? (dressing, toileting, eating)
14. Have previously learned skills or abilities changed or been lost?

**Assessment Guidelines**

*Pervasive Developmental Disorders*

1. Assess for developmental spurts, lags, uneven development, or loss of previously acquired abilities. (Use baby books/diaries, photographs, films/videotapes. First-time mothers might not be aware of developmental lags, and family members might need to be consulted.)
2. Assess the quality of the relationship between the child and parent/caregiver for evidence of bonding, anxiety, tension, and difficulty-of-fit between the parents' and child's temperaments.
3. Be aware that children with behavioral and developmental problems are at risk for abuse.

# NURSING DIAGNOSES WITH INTERVENTIONS

## Discussion of Potential Nursing Diagnoses

The child with pervasive developmental disorders has severe impairments in social interactions and communications skills. Often these are accompanied by stereotyped behavior, interests, and activities. The severity of the impairment is demonstrated by the child's lack of responsiveness to or interest in others, lack of empathy or sharing with peers, and lack of cooperative or imaginative play with peers. Therefore, **Impaired Social Interaction** is almost always present. Language delay or absence of language and the unusual stereotyped or repetitive use of language is another area for nursing interventions. Therefore, **Impaired Verbal Communication** and **Delayed Growth and Development** (language delay) are useful nursing diagnoses. Stereotyped and repetitive motor behaviors can include behaviors such as head banging, face slapping, and hand biting. The child's apparent indifference to pain can result in serious self-injury, so **Risk for Self-Mutilation** and/or **Risk for Injury** can become a priority. If the child's rigid adherence to specific routines and rituals is disrupted, the child might have a catastrophic reaction such as severe temper tantrums or rage reactions, leading to **Risk for Self-Directed Violence** or **Risk for Other-Directed Violence**. The child's lack of interest in activities outside of self and the frequent disregard for bodily needs interfere with the development of a personal identity, so **Disturbed Personal Identity** might be an appropriate nursing diagnosis.

## Overall Guidelines for Nursing Interventions
### *Pervasive Developmental Disorders*

Help the child reach his or her full potential by fostering developmental competencies and coping skills:

1. Increase the child's interest in reciprocal social interactions.
2. Foster the development of social skills.
3. Facilitate the expression of appropriate emotional responses, including the development of trust, empathy, shame, remorse, anger, pride, independence, joy, and enthusiasm.
4. Foster the development of reciprocal communication, especially language skills.
5. Provide for the development of psychomotor skills in play and activities of daily living (ADLs).
6. Facilitate the development of cognitive skills (attention, memory, cause and effect, reality testing, decision making, and problem solving).
7. Foster the development of self-concepts (identity, self-awareness, body image, and self-esteem).
8. Foster the development of self-control, including controlling impulses and tolerating frustration and the delay of gratification.

## Selected Nursing Diagnoses and Nursing Care Plans

### IMPAIRED SOCIAL INTERACTION

Insufficient or excessive quantity or ineffective quality of social exchange

## *Some Related Factors (Related To)*

▲ Self-concept disturbance (immaturity or developmental deviation)
▲ Absence of available significant others/peers
▲ Disturbed thought process
● Impaired neurological development or dysfunction
● Disturbance in response to external stimuli
● Disturbance in attachment/bonding with the parent/caregiver

## *Defining Characteristics (As Evidenced By)*

Assessment findings/diagnostic cues:
▲ Dysfunctional interaction with peers and others
● Lack of responsiveness to or interest in others (eye contact, facial expressions, verbalizations)
● Lack of bonding or affectional ties to parental figures (indifference or aversion to physical contact)
● Lack of interest or ability to play and share with peers
● Lack of empathy or concern for others

## *Outcome Criteria*

• Child initiates actions with peers and trusted friends

## *Long-Term Goals*

Child will:
• Participate in at least four activities that reflect reciprocal social interactions within 1 year

## *Short-Term Goals*

Child will:
• Seek out nurse/caregiver for activities/ADLs and for comfort when distressed within 1 to 3 months
• Show interest and begin to participate in play activities with others, especially peers, within 2 to 6 months
• Use at least two social skills to initiate contact with peers at the same developmental level within 6 to 12 months

---

▲ NANDA International accepted; ● In addition to NANDA International

*Interventions and Rationales*

| Intervention | Rationale |
|---|---|
| 1. Use one-on-one interaction to engage the patient in a working alliance. | 1. Assigning the same primary nurse who will be a parental surrogate can promote attachment. |
| 2. Monitor for signs of anxiety/distress. Intervene early to provide comfort. | 2. Anticipating need for help in managing stress enhances the patient's feelings of security. |
| 3. Provide emotional support and guidance for ADLs and other activities; use a system of rewards for attempts and successes. | 3. Learning occurs through meaningful social interactions involving imitation, modeling, feedback, and reinforcement. |
| 4. Set up play situations starting with play with parallel peers and moving toward cooperative play. | 4. Learning to play with peers is sequential. |
| 5. Help the patient find a special friend. | 5. Having a special friend enhances learning experience. |
| 6. Role model social interaction skills (interest, empathy, sharing, waiting, and required language). | 6. Facilitates the development of needed social/emotional skills. |
| 7. Reward attempts to interact and play with peers and the use of appropriate emotional expressions. | 7. Behaviors that are rewarded are repeated. |
| 8. Role-play situations that involve conflicts in social interactions to teach reality testing, cause and effect, and problem solving. | 8. These cognitive skills are needed for successful social/emotional reciprocity. |

## IMPAIRED VERBAL COMMUNICATION

Decreased, delayed, or absent ability to receive, process, transmit, and use a system of symbols

## Related To (Etiology)

▲ Physiological conditions and/or emotional conditions
▲ Alteration of central nervous system
▲ Impaired neurological development or dysfunction
● Disturbance in attachment/bonding with the parent/caregiver

## As Evidenced By (Assessment Findings/Diagnostic Cues)

● Language delay or total absence of language
● Immature grammatical structure; pronoun reversal; inability to name objects
● Stereotyped or repetitive use of language (echolalia, idiosyncratic words, inappropriate high-pitched squealing/giggling, repetitive phrases, sing-song speech quality)
● Lack of response to communication attempts by others

## Outcome Criteria

● Communicate in words/gestures that are understood by others

## Long-Term Goals

Child will:
● Communicate to parent/caregiver and peers at least four basic needs (hunger, thirst, fatigue, pain), verbally and/or through gestures and body language

## Short-Term Goals

Child will:
● Communicate through eye contact, facial expressions, and other nonverbal gestures within 1 month
● Attempt to use language and begin to communicate with words within 5 to 6 months
● Increase language skills needed for social and emotional reciprocal interactions within 6 to 8 months
● Use language or gestures to identify self, others, objects, feelings, needs, plans, and desires within 12 months

---

▲ NANDA International accepted; ● In addition to NANDA International

## Interventions and Rationales

| Intervention | Rationale |
|---|---|
| 1. Use one-on-one interactions to engage the patient in nonverbal play. | 1. The nurse enters the patient's world in a nonthreatening interaction to form a trusting relationship. |
| 2. Recognize subtle cues indicating the patient is paying attention or attempting to communicate. | 2. Cues are often difficult to recognize (glancing out of the corner of the eye). |
| 3. Describe for the patient what is happening, and put into words what the patient might be experiencing. | 3. Naming objects and describing actions, thoughts, and feelings helps the patient to use symbolic language. |
| 4. Encourage vocalizations with sound games and songs. | 4. Children learn through play and enjoyable activities. |
| 5. Identify desired behaviors and reward them (e.g., hugs, treats, tokens, points, or food). | 5. Behaviors that are rewarded will increase in frequency. Desire for food is a powerful incentive in modifying behavior. |
| 6. Use names frequently, and encourage the use of correct pronouns (e.g., I, me, he). | 6. Problems with self-identification and pronoun reversal are common. |
| 7. Encourage verbal communication with peers during play activities using role modeling, feedback, and reinforcement. | 7. Play is the normal medium for learning in a child's development. |
| 8. Increase verbal interaction with parents and siblings by teaching them how to facilitate language development. | 8. Education and emotional support help parents and siblings to become more therapeutic in their interactions with the patient. |

## RISK FOR SELF-MUTILATION

Deliberate self-injurious behavior causing tissue damage with the intent of causing nonfatal injury to attain relief of tension

### Some Risk Factors (Related To)

▲ Autistic individuals
● Impaired neurological development or dysfunction
● Need for painful stimuli to increase opiate levels and reduce tension
● Rage reactions and aggression turned toward self
● Lack of impulse control and the ability to tolerate frustration

### Some Defining Characteristics (As Evidenced By)

● History of self-injury (head banging, biting, scratching, hair pulling) when frustrated or angry
● Old scars or new areas of tissue damage
● Self-injurious tantrums when changes are made in routines, rituals, or the environment, or when asked to end a pleasurable activity

### Outcome Criteria

● Demonstrate new behaviors and skills to cope with anxiety and feelings

### Long-Term Goals

Child will:
● Be free of self-inflicted injury

### Short-Term Goals

Child will:
● Respond to a parent or surrogate's limits on self-injurious behaviors within 1 to 6 months

---

▲ NANDA International accepted; ● In addition to NANDA International

- Seek help when anxiety and tension rise within 1 to 6 months
- Express feelings and describe tensions verbally and/or with noninjurious body language within 6 months to 1 year
- Use appropriate play activities for the release of anxiety and tension within 1 to 6 months

## Interventions and Rationales

| Intervention | Rationale |
|---|---|
| 1. Monitor the patient's behavior for cues of rising anxiety. | 1. Behavioral cues signal increasing anxiety. |
| 2. Determine emotional and situational triggers. | 2. Knowledge of triggers is used in planning ways to prevent or manage outbursts. |
| 3. Intervene early with verbal comments or limits and/or removal from the situation. | 3. Potential outbursts can be defused through early recognition, verbal interventions, or removal. |
| 4. Give plenty of notice when having to change routines or rituals or end pleasurable activities. | 4. Children often react to change with catastrophic reactions and need time to adjust. |
| 5. Provide support for the recognition of feelings, reality testing, impulse control. | 5. These competencies are often underdeveloped in these children. |
| 6. If the patient does not respond to verbal interventions, use therapeutic holding. Some might need special restraints (helmets, mittens, special padding). | 6. Therapeutic holding reassures the patient that the adult is in control; feelings of security can become feelings of comfort and affection. |
| 7. Help the patient connect feelings and anxiety to self-injurious behaviors. | 7. Self-control is enhanced through understanding the relationship between feelings and behaviors. |

| **Intervention** | **Rationale** |
|---|---|
| 8. Help the patient develop ways to express feelings and reduce anxiety verbally and through play activities. Use various types of motor and imaginative play (e.g., swinging, tumbling, role-playing, drawing, singing). | 8. Methods for modulating and directing the expression of emotions and anxiety must be learned to control destructive impulses |

## DISTURBED PERSONAL IDENTITY

Inability to maintain an integrated and complete perception of self.

### *Related Factors (Related To)*

▲ Biochemical imbalance
● Impaired neurological development or dysfunction
● Failure to develop attachment behaviors, resulting in fixation at autistic phase of development
● Interrupted or uncompleted separation/individuation process resulting in extreme separation anxiety

### *Some Defining Characteristics (As Evidenced By)*

● Seemingly unaware of or uninterested in others or their activities
● Unable to identify parts of the body or bodily sensations (enuresis, encopresis)
● Fails to imitate others or unable to stop imitating others' actions or words (echolalia, echopraxis)
● Fails to distinguish parent/caregiver as a whole person, instead relates to body parts (e.g., takes person's hand and places it on doorknob)
● Becomes distressed by bodily contact with others
● Spends long periods of time in self-stimulating behaviors (self-touching, sucking, rocking)

---

▲ NANDA International accepted; ● In addition to NANDA International

- Needs ritualistic behaviors and sameness to control anxiety
- Has extreme distress reactions to changes in routines or the environment
- Cannot tolerate being separated from parent/caregiver

## *Outcome Criteria*

- Demonstrate recognition of self-boundaries and being separate from others

## *Long-Term Goals*

Child will:
- Adjust to changes in activities and the environment within 9 months

## *Short-Term Goals*

Child will:
- Seek comfort and physical contact from others within 1 to 2 months
- Relate to caregiver by name with eye contact and verbal requests within 6 months
- Recognize body parts, body boundaries, and sexual identity within 6 months
- Show an interest in the activities of others and tolerate their presence within 3 to 6 months
- Spend more time in purposeful activities rather than rituals and self-stimulating activities in 2 to 6 months
- Recognize body sensations (pain, hunger, fatigue, elimination needs) within 2 to 6 months
- Express a full range of feelings within 4 to 6 months
- Recognize the feelings and activities of others as separate within 6 months
- Adjust to changes in activities and the environment within 5 to 9 months

---

▲ NANDA International accepted; ● In addition to NANDA International

## Interventions and Rationales

| Intervention | Rationale |
|---|---|
| 1. Use one-on-one interaction to engage the patient in a safe relationship with the nurse/caregiver. | 1. A consistent caregiver provides for the development of trust needed for a sense of safety and security. |
| 2. Use names and descriptions of others to reinforce their separateness. | 2. Consistent reinforcement will help break into the patient's autistic world. |
| 3. Draw the patient's attention to the activities of others and events that are happening in the environment. | 3. Interrupts the patient's self-absorption and stimulates outside interests. |
| 4. Limit self-stimulating and ritualistic behaviors by providing alternative play activities or by providing comfort when stressed. | 4. Redirecting the patient's attention to favorite or new activities, or giving comfort, reduces anxiety. |
| 5. Foster self-concept development; reinforce identity, sexual identity, and body boundaries through drawing, stories, and play activities. | 5. Learning body parts and sexual identity is necessary and fun in play activities. |
| 6. Help patient distinguish body sensations and how to meet bodily needs by picking up on cues and using ADLs to teach self-care. | 6. The lack of self-awareness contributes to problems with self-care, especially toileting. |
| 7. Provide play opportunities for the patient that identify the feelings of others (stories, puppet play, peer interactions). | 7. Consistent feedback about the feelings of others helps with self-differentiation and the development of empathy. |

# MEDICAL TREATMENTS

## Psychopharmacology

Most likely, the majority of emotional suffering experienced by children and adolescents is related to situational stress and best treated through a variety of therapeutic modalities. However, it is also becoming increasingly apparent that many major mental diseases have their origin in childhood (Preston et al., 2005).

Medications that target specific symptoms can make a decided difference in the family's ability to cope and their quality of life, and they can enhance the child's or adolescent's optimal potential for growth (Table 4-2). However, psychoactive medications should be used with caution with children and adolescents and monitored closely, especially the SSRIs.

## Psychosocial Treatment for Childhood and Adolescent Disorders

Treatment of childhood and adolescent disorders requires a multimodal approach in most instances. Close work with schools, the availability of remediation services, and the incorporation of behavior modification techniques should all be part of the intervention.

Therapies include cognitive-behavioral therapies. Effective behavioral techniques for supporting desirable behaviors include:

- Positive reinforcement
- Time out
- Token economy—earning points for privileges/rewards
- Response costs—withdrawing privileges based on undesirable behavior

Other therapies, including social skills groups, family therapy, parent training in behavioral techniques, and individual therapy focused on esteem issues, have all been found to be useful. Skills training might focus on a variety of areas, depending on the child's or adolescent's presenting symptoms. For example, some children need to learn basic ADLs, others have difficulty with their impulse control and frustration tolerance, and those with anxiety disorders might benefit from anxiety-reduction

**Table 4-2  Psychopharmacology and Therapeutic Modalities for Child and Adolescent Disorders\***

| Disorder | Pharmacological Treatment | Therapeutic Modalities |
|---|---|---|
| **Pervasive Developmental Disorders** (Autistic disorder, Asperger's syndrome, Rett's disorder, childhood disintegrative disorder) | **Treatment of symptoms only:**<br>• Aggression and self-injurious behavior: Atypical antipsychotics (e.g. Risperidone)<br>• Hyperactivity: alpha-2 agonists; stimulants<br>• Repetitive behaviors, rituals, compulsions: selective serotonin uptake inhibitors (SSRIs) (e.g., clomipramine) | • Educational and behavioral interventions<br>• Training parents in skills of behavior modification<br>• Resolution of parents' concerns may result in gains in child's language, cognitive, and social areas of behavior |
| Attention deficit hyperactivity disorder (ADHD) | **Medication treatment alone is rarely effective.**<br>• Psychostimulants (methylphenidate or amphetamine compounds) remain the first line of treatment. | • Parent education and training in behavioral techniques<br>• Structure home and school environment using behavior modification with rewards and consequences |
| Conduct disorders | **Psychopharmacological intervention for comorbid conditions:**<br>• Lithium: bipolar diagnosis<br>• Antidepressants: depression<br>• Beta-blockers and clonidine have been used for aggression and impulsivity (with mixed results) | • Course and prognosis limited due to lack of motivation<br>• Behavioral techniques toward altering destructive patterns<br>• Intensive family-focused and community-based programs |

*Continued*

Table 4-2 **Psychopharmacology and Therapeutic Modalities for Child and Adolescent Disorders*—cont'd**

| Disorder | Pharmacological Treatment | Therapeutic Modalities |
|---|---|---|
| **Anxiety Disorders** | | |
| Panic disorder and agoraphobia* | **Pharmacology alone is not considered adequate treatment.**<br>Short-term: short-acting benzodiazepines for immediate anxiety relief<br>Long-term: antidepressants (e.g., SSRIs) | • Cognitive behavioral therapy (CBT) effective with minimizing panic and panic attacks<br>• Individual, family, and group therapy helpful if complicated issues |
| Obsessive-compulsive disorder (OCD) | • Antidepressants (SSRIs) Clomipramine (Anafranil)<br>• Atypical anxiolytic, buspirone (BuSpar), used as adjunct treatment in refractory OCD | • CBT using exposure response prevention<br>• In tandem with treatment of other psychopathology, individual, family, and educational interventions apply. |
| General anxiety disorder (GAD) | • Buspirone (BuSpar) may decrease anxiety<br>• Antidepressant SSRIs when severe | • Multimodal approach including school, primary care provider, psychotherapy (family), and pharmacology |

| Disorder | Medication | Therapy/Notes |
|---|---|---|
| Separation anxiety disorder* | Antidepressants (tricyclic antidepressants [TCAs], SSRIs) | • Therapy: multimodal approach (individual, family, and behavioral strategies such as CBT<br>• CBT promotes successful experiences in social situations<br>• Individual/group psychotherapy promotes social skills, assertiveness, etc.<br>• Behavioral therapy and CBT may be helpful<br>• Complicated cases may require family and individual therapy<br>• Outpatient psychotherapy is preferred initial treatment |
| Social phobia | TCAs such as protriptyline (Vivactil) Antianxiety agents such as buspirone (BuSpar) | |
| Specific phobia | Transient, developmentally appropriate fears do not require treatment | |
| Posttraumatic stress disorder (PTSD) | Antidepressants, SSRIs first line for depression or panic symptoms Atypical antipsychotic, risperidone (Risperdal), being used to control the flashbacks and aggression in PTSD | |

*Continued*

Table 4-2 **Psychopharmacology and Therapeutic Modalities for Child and Adolescent Disorders\*—cont'd**

| Disorder | Pharmacological Treatment | Therapeutic Modalities |
|---|---|---|
| **Mood Disorders** | | |
| Depression | Pharmacology alone is not considered adequate treatment. The SSRI, fluoxetine (Prozac), is the only FDA-approved medication for treatment in children and adolescents* | • CBT effective for reducing symptoms<br>• Long-term social skills interventions may be needed. |
| Bipolar disorder | • Combination of mood-stabilizing medications (e.g., lithium and divalproex) | • Multimodal approach combining medications with psychotherapeutic interventions |

\*Psychopharmacology is always used with caution in children and adolescents, and treatment choices change as more studies support or reject current practice. Research on the psychopharmacology for anxiety disorders in children is sparse.
Data from Preston, J.D., O'Neal, J.H., & Talaga, M.C. (2008). *Handbook of clinical psychopharmacology for therapists* (5th ed.). Oakland, CA: New Harbinger Publications, Inc; Goldberg, R.J. (2007). *The care of the psychiatric patient* (3rd ed.). Philadelphia: Mosby.

skills. Many children and adolescents benefit from a variety of social skills (problem solving, decision making, initiating and maintaining contacts with peers) that will help them negotiate satisfying and productive relationships and friendships in the outside world. Many young people suffer from severe symptoms of depression, and although medication might be immediately useful, family and individual therapies should be made a pivotal part of the patient's treatment. *Rarely, if ever, is medication alone the treatment of choice.*

## Nurse, Client, and Family Resources

## INTERNET SITES

**Autism Society of America Home Page**
www.autism-society.org

**Autism Resources**
www.autism-resources.com

**Children and Adults with Attention
Deficit Hyperactivity Disorder**
www.chadd.org

**ADD Medical Treatment Center of Santa Clara Valley**
www.addmtc.com

**Conduct Disorders Support Site**
www.conductdisorders.com

**Anxiety Disorders in Children and Adults**
www.algy.com/anxiety/children.html

**American Academy of Child & Adolescent Psychiatry**
www.aacap.org

**Association of Child and Adolescent Psychiatric Nurses**
www.ispn-psych.org/html/acapn.html

# CHAPTER 5

# Anxiety and Anxiety Disorders

## OVERVIEW

### Anxiety

Anxiety is a normal response to threatening situations. **Anxiety** is conceptualized on four levels, mild (+), moderate (++), severe (+++), and panic (++++).

Anxiety levels from *mild* to *moderate* can be positive motivating factors (e.g., student experiences before taking a test can heighten awareness and sharpen focus). However, anxiety at moderate to severe levels can:

- Interfere with adaptive behavior
- Cause physical symptoms
- Become intolerable

Therefore, it is helpful to distinguish between mild/moderate and severe/panic levels of anxiety, since the interventions for these continuum of levels differ. Defenses against anxiety are called *defense mechanisms*. They can be used in adaptive or healthy ways or maladaptive ways. Please refer to Appendix D-1.

### Anxiety Disorders

Anxiety disorders are often the most common of all psychiatric disorders and result in considerable distress and functional impairment. Anxiety disorders are a group of disorders that have as their primary symptom anxiety levels that are so high they interfere with personal, occupational, or social functioning. These disorders produce symptoms that range from mild to severe and even panic, and they tend to be persistent and are often disabling. People often suffer from more than one anxiety disorder, and anxiety and depression often occur together.

**Physicians and nurses need to be alerted to the fact that anxiety can be a symptom of a physical disease, medical problem, or substance use problem. Medical causes and drug-induced anxiety must be ruled out before a diagnosis of anxiety disorder can be made.**

People who have anxiety disorders are usually treated in the community setting. Rarely is hospitalization needed unless the patient is suicidal or the symptoms are severely out of control (e.g., patient is employing self-mutilating behaviors). The best treatment for anxiety disorders is often a combination of medication and therapy (often cognitive or behavioral therapies). In the last section of this chapter, we discuss medications and therapies that seem to prove most effective for each of the anxiety disorders. Anxiety disorders include **Panic Disorder** (with or without agoraphobia), **Phobias, Obsessive-Compulsive Disorder, Generalized Anxiety Disorder,** and **Stress Disorders.**

## Panic Disorder (with or without Agoraphobia)

Evolving evidence seems to support that panic disorder (PD) is a biochemical dysfunction, not a psychological disorder, and responds well to medications (Preston & Johnson, 2009) during the initial phase of treatment. A diagnosis of PD is made in the presence or history of recurrent, unexpected panic attacks that do not have an underlying medical or chemical etiology. A **panic attack** involves extreme apprehension or fear, usually associated with feelings of impending doom or terror. During an attack, normal functioning is suspended, the peripheral field of vision is severely limited, and misinterpretations of reality might occur. Individuals experiencing panic attacks often have the terrifying belief that they are having a heart attack. These signs and symptoms can be mistaken for a heart attack by hospital personnel because the symptoms of a panic attack can be similar to those of a myocardial infarction (shortness of breath, chest pain, feelings of impending doom). Box 5-1 identifies the *DSM IV-TR* signs and symptoms of a panic attack. Panic attacks can also be present in other

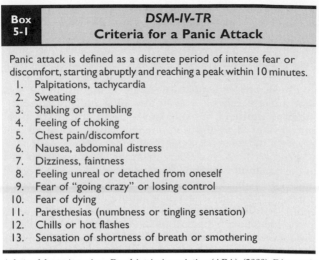

Adapted from American Psychiatric Association (APA). (2000). *Diagnostic and statistical manual of mental disorders* (4th ed., text rev.) (*DSM-IV-TR*). Washington, DC: Author, p. 432; reprinted with permission.

anxiety disorders, including social phobia, simple phobia, and posttraumatic stress disorder (PTSD). Box 5-2 presents the *Diagnostic and Statistical Manual of Mental Disorders* (4th edition, text revision) (*DSM-IV-TR*) diagnostic criteria for panic disorder.

**Agoraphobia** is frequently seen with panic disorder. Individuals who are agoraphobic avoid places or situations from which escape might be difficult or embarrassing, or where help might not be available if a panic attack occurred. Agoraphobia is a phobia and is discussed further under phobias. One in three people with PD will go on to have agoraphobia and lose or quit their jobs because they can no longer tolerate traveling to their place of business. PD can be a devastating disease, and people with panic disorder have a disproportionate rate of suicide attempts.

## Phobias

**Phobias** are irrational fears of an object or situation that persist even though the person recognizes them as unreasonable. There are three categories of phobias: agoraphobia, social phobia, and specific phobia. See Box 5-3 for *DSM-IV-TR* diagnostic criteria for phobias.

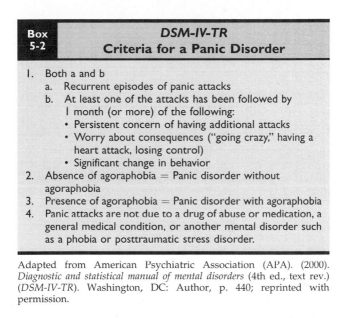

| Box 5-2 | *DSM-IV-TR* **Criteria for a Panic Disorder** |

1. Both a and b
   a. Recurrent episodes of panic attacks
   b. At least one of the attacks has been followed by 1 month (or more) of the following:
      - Persistent concern of having additional attacks
      - Worry about consequences ("going crazy," having a heart attack, losing control)
      - Significant change in behavior
2. Absence of agoraphobia = Panic disorder without agoraphobia
3. Presence of agoraphobia = Panic disorder with agoraphobia
4. Panic attacks are not due to a drug of abuse or medication, a general medical condition, or another mental disorder such as a phobia or posttraumatic stress disorder.

Adapted from American Psychiatric Association (APA). (2000). *Diagnostic and statistical manual of mental disorders* (4th ed., text rev.) (*DSM-IV-TR*). Washington, DC: Author, p. 440; reprinted with permission.

| Box 5-3 | *DSM-IV-TR* **Criteria for Phobias** |

1. Irrational fear of an object or situation that persists, although the person might recognize it as excessive or unreasonable.
2. Types include:
   - **Agoraphobia:** Fear of being alone in open or public places where escape might be difficult. Person might not leave home.
   - **Social Phobia:** Fear of situations in which one might be seen and embarrassed or criticized; speaking to authority figures, public speaking, or performing
   - **Specific Phobia:** Fear of a single object, activity, or situation (e.g., snakes, closed spaces, flying)
3. Anxiety is severe if the object, situation, or activity cannot be avoided.

Adapted from American Psychiatric Association (APA). (2000). *Diagnostic and statistical manual of mental disorders* (4th ed., text rev.) (*DSM-IV-TR*). Washington, DC: Author, pp. 449–450; reprinted with permission.

## Obsessive-Compulsive Disorder

**Obsessive-compulsive disorder** (OCD) results in severe emotional suffering. People with OCD have either *obsessions* (intrusive thoughts, impulses, or images) that break into their conscious awareness and are perceived as senseless and intrusive, *compulsions* (repetitive behaviors or mental acts that the person feels driven to perform in order to reduce distress or prevent a dreaded event or situation), or both. Common compulsions involve touching, counting, cleaning, and arranging things. People with OCD often present in a physician's office with a complaint of compulsive handwashing, compulsive cleanliness, or alopecia resulting from pulling out their hair (trichotillomania). Box 5-4 presents the *DSM-IV-TR* diagnostic criteria for OCD.

## Generalized Anxiety Disorder

People are diagnosed with **generalized anxiety disorder** (GAD) when they have chronic and excessive anxiety or

---

| Box 5-4 | DSM-IV-TR Criteria for Obsessive-Compulsive Disorder |
|---|---|

1. Either obsessions or compulsions:
   - Preoccupation with persistent, intrusive thoughts, impulses, or images (obsession) that cannot be ignored or suppressed

     *or*
   - Repetitive behaviors or mental acts the person feels driven to perform to reduce distress or prevent a dreaded event or situation (**compulsion**); behaviors are not connected in a realistic way with what they are designed to neutralize or prevent
2. Person knows the obsessions/compulsions are excessive and unreasonable
3. Obsession/compulsion can cause increased distress and is time-consuming

---

Adapted from American Psychiatric Association (APA). (2000). *Diagnostic and statistical manual of mental disorders* (4th ed., text rev.) (*DSM-IV-TR*). Washington, DC: Author, p. 462; reprinted with permission.

worry most of the time during a 6-month period of time. Other symptoms include restlessness, fatigue, difficulty concentrating, irritability, muscle tension, and sleep problems. The symptoms cause the individual to have significant distress, and these individuals tend to have impairment in their social and occupational functioning. Box 5-5 presents the *DSM-IV-TR* diagnostic criteria for GAD.

## Stress Disorders

Two other disorders that are included in the anxiety disorders are **posttraumatic stress disorder** (PTSD) and **acute stress disorder** (ASD). Both of these disorders follow exposure to an extremely traumatic event, usually outside the range of normal experience (e.g., natural disasters, crime-related events, prisoner of war, diagnosis of

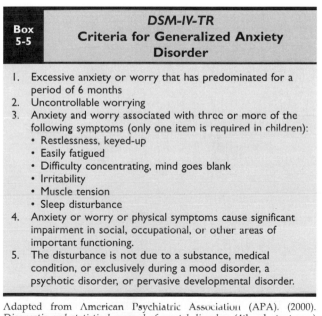

| Box 5-5 | *DSM-IV-TR* Criteria for Generalized Anxiety Disorder |
|---|---|

1. Excessive anxiety or worry that has predominated for a period of 6 months
2. Uncontrollable worrying
3. Anxiety and worry associated with three or more of the following symptoms (only one item is required in children):
   • Restlessness, keyed-up
   • Easily fatigued
   • Difficulty concentrating, mind goes blank
   • Irritability
   • Muscle tension
   • Sleep disturbance
4. Anxiety or worry or physical symptoms cause significant impairment in social, occupational, or other areas of important functioning.
5. The disturbance is not due to a substance, medical condition, or exclusively during a mood disorder, a psychotic disorder, or pervasive developmental disorder.

Adapted from American Psychiatric Association (APA). (2000). *Diagnostic and statistical manual of mental disorders* (4th ed., text rev.) (*DSM-IV-TR*). Washington, DC: Author, p. 476; reprinted with permission.

a life-threatening disease, rape). They also share similar symptoms:

- Reexperiencing the symptoms through dreams or images
- Reliving the event through flashbacks, illusions, hallucinations
- Marked symptoms of anxiety
  - Difficulty falling/staying asleep
  - Irritability/outbursts of anger
  - Difficulty concentrating
- Avoidance of stimuli associated with the trauma that could arouse memory of the trauma

The main difference is one of time. ASD lasts from 2 days to 4 weeks and occurs within 4 weeks of the traumatic event. PTSD lasts for more than 1 month and might last for years. Boxes 5-6 and 5-7 present *DSM-IV-TR* diagnostic criteria for these two stress responses.

## ASSESSMENT

### Presenting Signs and Symptoms

- Might state they have a sense of impending doom or feel as though they are going to die
- Narrowing of perceptions, difficulty concentrating, problem solving inefficient
- Increased vital signs (blood pressure, pulse, respirations), increased muscle tension, sweat glands activated, pupils dilated
- Palpitations, urinary urgency/frequency, nausea, tightening of throat, unsteady voice
- Complaints of fatigue, difficulty sleeping, irritability, disorganization

### Assessment Tools

There are a number of tools that help the health care worker assess for anxiety symptoms. The Hamilton Rating Scale for Anxiety helps the clinician to identify a patient's level of anxiety. Refer to Appendix D-2 for this tool. Box 5-8 presents a simple screening guide that can be done quickly and can elicit specific anxiety symptoms the patient might not offer without being asked. Any positive answers alert the nurse clinician that more detailed assessment is needed.

| Box 5-6 | *DSM-IV-TR* **Criteria for Posttraumatic Stress Disorder** |
|---|---|

1. The person experienced, witnessed, or was confronted with an event that involved actual or threatened death to self or others and responded in fear, helplessness, or horror.
2. The event is persistently reexperienced:
   - Recurring, distressing recollections of the event including thoughts or perceptions
   - Distressing dreams or images
   - Reliving the event through flashbacks, illusions, hallucinations
   - Intense psychological distress to exposure to internal or external cues that symbolize or resemble an aspect of the traumatic event
3. Persistent avoidance of stimuli associated with trauma and numbing of general responsiveness as indicated by three or more of the following:
   - Efforts to avoid thoughts, feelings, conversations that trigger trauma
   - Efforts to avoid people, places, activities that trigger trauma
   - Inability to recall aspects of trauma
   - Decreased interest in usual activities
   - Feelings of detachment, estrangement from others
   - Restriction in feelings (love, enthusiasm, joy)
   - Sense of shortened feelings
4. Persistent symptoms of increased arousal (two or more):
   - Difficulty falling/staying asleep
   - Irritability/outbursts of anger
   - Difficulty concentrating
   - Hypervigilance
   - Exaggerated startle response
5. Duration more than 1 month:
   - Acute: Duration less than 3 months
   - Chronic: Duration 3 months or more
   - Delayed: Onset of symptoms is at least 6 months after stress

Adapted from American Psychiatric Association (APA) (2000), *Diagnostic and statistical manual of mental disorders* (4th ed., text rev.) (*DSM-IV-TR*). Washington, DC: Author, p. 468; reprinted with permission.

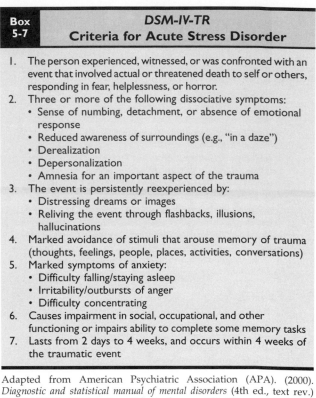

| Box 5-7 | *DSM-IV-TR*<br>**Criteria for Acute Stress Disorder** |
|---|---|

1. The person experienced, witnessed, or was confronted with an event that involved actual or threatened death to self or others, responding in fear, helplessness, or horror.
2. Three or more of the following dissociative symptoms:
   - Sense of numbing, detachment, or absence of emotional response
   - Reduced awareness of surroundings (e.g., "in a daze")
   - Derealization
   - Depersonalization
   - Amnesia for an important aspect of the trauma
3. The event is persistently reexperienced by:
   - Distressing dreams or images
   - Reliving the event through flashbacks, illusions, hallucinations
4. Marked avoidance of stimuli that arouse memory of trauma (thoughts, feelings, people, places, activities, conversations)
5. Marked symptoms of anxiety:
   - Difficulty falling/staying asleep
   - Irritability/outbursts of anger
   - Difficulty concentrating
6. Causes impairment in social, occupational, and other functioning or impairs ability to complete some memory tasks
7. Lasts from 2 days to 4 weeks, and occurs within 4 weeks of the traumatic event

Adapted from American Psychiatric Association (APA). (2000). *Diagnostic and statistical manual of mental disorders* (4th ed., text rev.) (*DSM-IV-TR*). Washington, DC: Author; p. 471–472; reprinted with permission.

## Assessment Guidelines

### Anxiety Disorders

1. A sound **physical and neurological examination** helps determine if the anxiety is primary or secondary to another psychiatric disorder, medical condition, or substance abuse.
2. Assess for history of childhood abuse.
3. Assess for **potential for self-harm. Severe anxiety disorder is associated with suicide attempt or completed**, as well as certain **medications.**

---

Box 5-8 **Sample Questions for Assessing Anxiety Symptoms**

1. Do you ever experience a sudden, unexplained attack of intense fear, anxiety, or panic for no apparent reason?
2. Have you been afraid of not being able to get help or not being able to escape in certain situations, such as being on a bridge, in a crowded store, or in similar situations?
3. Do you find it difficult to control your worrying?
4. Do you spend more time than necessary doing things over and over again, such as washing your hands, checking things, or counting things?
5. Do you either avoid or feel very uncomfortable in situations involving people, such as parties, weddings, dating, dances, or other social events?
6. Have you ever had an extremely frightening, traumatic, or horrible experience such as being a victim of a crime, being seriously injured in a car accident, being sexually assaulted, or seeing someone injured or killed?

---

Provided by Screening for Mental health, Inc., 1 Washington Street, Suite 304, Welksky Hills, MA, 20481–1706; (701) 239–0071; www.mental-healthscreening.org.

4. **Assess patient's community for appropriate clinics, groups, and counselors who offer anxiety-reduction techniques.** Table 5-1 identifies which approaches and medications seem to be the most effective for each of the anxiety disorders.
5. Be aware that differences in culture can affect how anxiety is manifested.

## NURSING DIAGNOSES WITH INTERVENTIONS

### Discussion of Potential Nursing Diagnoses

Several nursing diagnoses target symptoms for people with high levels of anxiety and anxiety disorders. The nursing diagnosis **Anxiety** is most often used. When using the nursing diagnosis of Anxiety, the nurse needs to clarify the level of anxiety, because different levels of anxiety call for different intervention strategies. For example, the diagnosis should be stated **Anxiety—Moderate Level,** or **Anxiety—Severe/Panic Level.**

**Ineffective Coping** is another frequently used diagnosis, because high levels of anxiety lead to interference in ability to work, disruptions in relationships, and changes in ability to interact satisfactorily with others. For example, people with phobias often develop avoidance behaviors, and people with obsessions and compulsions make it difficult for others to relate to them other than under rigid circumstances.

**Disturbances in Thought Processes** are almost always present in people with anxiety disorders, although this diagnosis may be retired from NANDA 2012-2014. Individuals with OCD are preoccupied with their obsessive thoughts, and people with panic disorder are filled with fear and terror during anxiety attacks when their ability to problem solve, use sound judgment, or understand directions is totally impaired. Individuals with PTSD and ASD suffer from intrusive thoughts and memories that increase levels of anxiety so that their ability to function and think clearly is greatly hampered for brief periods of time. They would then qualify for **Posttrauma Syndrome.** Most people with anxiety disorders also suffer from **Disturbed Sleep Pattern.** Sleep deprivation can lead to the inability to function at work, school, and in social situations.

The nursing diagnoses Anxiety, Ineffective Coping, Disturbed Thought Processes, Posttrauma Syndrome, and Disturbed Sleep Pattern are presented here with suggested nursing interventions for each diagnosis.

## Overall Guidelines for Nursing Interventions

### Anxiety Disorders

1. Identify community resources that can help the patient develop skills that have been proven to be highly effective for people with a variety of anxiety disorders:
   - Cognitive restructuring
   - Relaxation training
   - Modeling techniques
   - Systematic desensitization/graduated exposure
   - Flooding (implosion therapy)
   - Behavior therapy

2. Identify community support groups for people with specific anxiety disorders.
3. Assess need for interventions with families and significant others (support groups, family therapy) and help with issues that might lead to relationship stress and turmoil.
4. When medications are used in conjunction with therapy, patients and their significant others will need thorough teaching. Written information and instructions should be given to patient/family/partner.
5. Refer to Table 5-1 for the accepted treatment for psychopharmacological and therapeutic modalities for selected anxiety disorders.

## Selected Nursing Diagnoses and Nursing Care Plans

### ANXIETY

Vague uneasy feeling of discomfort or dread accompanied by an autonomic response (the source often nonspecific or unknown to the individual); a feeling of apprehension caused by anticipation of danger; it is an alerting signal that warns of impending danger and enables the individual to take measures to deal with the threat

### Some Related Factors (Related To)

▲ Changes in or a threat to economic status, environment, health status, interaction patterns, role function, role status, or self-concept. Perceived threat to self-concept, health status, socioeconomic status, role function, interaction patterns, or environment
▲ Threat of death
▲ Unconscious conflicts about life goals or essential values
▲ Unmet needs
▲ Substance abuse
● Crisis (situational, maturational)
● Exposure to phobic object or situation

---

▲ NANDA International accepted; ● In addition to NANDA International

- Cessation of ritualistic behavior
- Traumatic experience
- Fear of panic attack
- Intrusive, unwanted thoughts
- Flashbacks

## Some Defining Characteristics (As Evidenced By)

▲ *Sympathetic* signs and symptoms (e.g., tachycardia, rapid breathing, palpitations, muscle tension, diaphoresis, increased blood pressure)
▲ *Parasympathetic* (e.g., fatigue, nausea, urinary frequency, urgency, etc.)
▲ *Cognitive* (e.g., narrowing focus of attention, diminished ability to problem solve and learn, confusion, etc.)
▲ *Behavioral* (e.g., restlessness, purposeless activity, immobilization, insomnia, scanning, vigilance, diminished productivity)
▲ *Affective* (e.g., feelings of dread, anguish, painful increased helplessness, apprehension, irritability, etc.)
- Increase in symptoms (compulsions, phobias, obsessions, nightmares/flashbacks)
- Inability to complete tasks

## Outcome Criteria

- Controls anxiety response
- Reports absence of physical manifestations of anxiety
- Behavioral manifestations of anxiety absent
- Uses effective coping strategies

## Long-Term Goals

Patient will:
- Demonstrate three anxiety-reducing skills that work for him or her by (date)
- State that he or she feels comfortable, and physical symptoms of anxiety are reduced
- Electively solve problems without assistance much of the time by (date)

---

▲ NANDA International accepted; ● In addition to NANDA International

- Identify negative "self-talk," and reframe thoughts successfully by (date)
- Demonstrate ability to reframe problems in solvable terms by (date)
- Demonstrate ability to get needs met using assertive communication skills by (date)
- Decrease time spent in ritualistic behaviors by (date)

## Short-Term Goals

Patient will:
- Demonstrate skills at reframing anxiety-provoking situations with aid of nurse/clinician (date)
- Demonstrate one relaxation technique that works well for him or her (date)
- Role-play with the nurse two behavioral techniques that help reduce feelings of anxiety to tolerable levels by (date)
- Decrease anxiety level from severe (+++) to moderate (++) within 2 hours on (date)
- Role-play assertive communication skills with nurse
- Attend a support group if warranted (e.g., PTSD)

## Interventions and Rationales

| Intervention | Rationale |
|---|---|
| 1. Provide a safe, calm environment:<br>  a. Decrease environmental stimuli.<br>  b. Listen to and reassure patient that he or she can feel more in control. | 1. When people feel fearful and vulnerable, being heard in an atmosphere of calm helps to foster a sense of connectedness with someone and control over what will happen. |
| 2. Encourage patient to talk about feelings and concerns. | 2. When concerns are stated out loud, problems can be discussed and feelings of isolation decreased. |
| 3. Reframe the problem in a way that is solvable. Provide a new perspective and correct distorted perceptions. | 3. Correcting distortions increases the possibility of finding workable solutions to a realistically defined problem. |

| Intervention | Rationale |
|---|---|
| 4. Identify thoughts or feelings prior to the onset of anxiety: "What were you doing/thinking right before you started to feel anxious?" | 4. Identifies triggers for escalating anxiety and a chance to understand why these triggers are so frightening to the patient. |
| 5. Identify any "self-talk" patients might use at this time (e.g., "I'll never be able to do this right." "This means I'll never succeed in anything."). | 5. Identify what thoughts trigger anxious feelings. Then cognitive skills can be used to help patient to reframe his or her thinking so that problems can be solved. |
| 6. Teach relaxation techniques (deep breathing exercises, meditation, progressive muscle relaxation). | 6. When patients learn to lower levels of anxiety, their ability to assess a situation and utilize their own problem-solving skills are improved. |
| 7. Refer patient and significant others to support groups, self-help programs, or advocacy groups when appropriate. | 7. Patients with specific problems are known to greatly benefit from being around others who are grappling with similar issues. Provides the patient with information and support and lowers feelings of isolation in stressful and difficult situations. |
| 8. Administer medications or obtain an order for medications when appropriate. | 8. Use least restrictive interventions to decrease anxiety. |

## INEFFECTIVE COPING

Inability to form a valid appraisal of the stressors; inadequate choices of practical responses; and/or inability to use available resources

## Some Related Factors (Related To)

- Severe to panic levels of anxiety—panic attack, GAD
- Excessive negative beliefs about self—GAD, OCD, other
- Hypervigilance after a traumatic event—PTSD, ASD
- Presence of obsessions and compulsions associated with fear of contamination—OCD, phobia
- Avoidance behavior associated with phobia (list phobia)—phobia

## Some Defining Characteristics (As Evidenced By)

Assessment Findings/Diagnostic Cues:

- ▲ Verbalization of inability to cope or inability to ask for help
- ▲ Inability to problem solve
- ▲ Change in usual communication patterns
- ▲ Difficulty organizing information
- Disturbance in vocational and social functioning related to (phobias, obsessions, compulsions, panic attacks, posttrauma symptoms)
- Panic attacks, severe obsessive acts, disturbing thoughts, disabling phobias, posttrauma symptoms

## Outcome Criteria

- Uses multiple new coping strategies
- Verbalizes a sense of control
- Functions at previous level of independence without interference from phobias, compulsions, obsessions, posttrauma event, panic attacks, disabling anxiety

## Long-Term Goals

Patient will:

- Verbalize ability to cope effectively with anxiety, using two new stress-reducing skills by (date)
- Demonstrate new coping skills (cognitive, behavioral, relaxation techniques, insight) that allay anxiety symptoms, such as visualization, deep breathing, and thought-stopping techniques by (date)
- Report increase in psychological comfort by (date)

---

▲ NANDA International accepted; ● In addition to NANDA International

## Short-Term Goals

Patient will:
- Demonstrate knowledge of breathing techniques and relaxation skills by end of first/second session with nurse
- Describe the different therapies that are effective in treating their particular anxiety disorder (cognitive, behavioral, group) (see Table 5-1)
- Demonstrate one new anxiety-reduction technique that works best for him or her within 2 weeks
- Accurately describe the desired effects, side effects, and toxic effects of any medication he or she might be given as an adjunct to therapy within 2 days

## Interventions and Rationales

| Intervention | Rationale |
|---|---|
| 1. Monitor and reinforce patient's use of positive coping skills and healthy defense mechanisms. | 1. Identifies what does and does not work for patient. Nurse uses patient's strengths to build upon. |
| 2. Teach new coping skills to substitute for ineffective ones. | 2. Gives patient options. |
| 3. At patient level of understanding, explain the *fight-or-flight response* and the *relaxation response* of the autonomic nervous system. Address how breathing can be used to elicit the *relaxation response*. | 3. Understanding the physiological aspects of anxiety and that people have some degree of control over their physiological responses gives patients hope and a sense of control in their lives. Such knowledge aids them in mastering relaxation techniques. |
| 4. When the patient's level of anxiety is mild to moderate, teach patient proper **breathing techniques,** and breathe with the patient. (See Box 5-9 for patient instructions for abdominal breathing.) | 4. Breathing techniques can prevent anxiety from escalating. Doing exercises with patient helps foster adherence. |

| Intervention | Rationale |
|---|---|
| 5. When the patient's level of anxiety is mild to moderate, teach patient **relaxation techniques** (such as imaging, visualization [Box 5-10]). | 5. Help the patient gain some control over switching the autonomic nervous system from the fight-or-flight response to the relaxation response. |
| 6. Identify for patient which therapies have been highly effective with individuals who have the same disorder (cognitive, behavioral) (see Table 5-1). | 6. Not only do cognitive and behavioral approaches work to decrease patients' anxiety and improve quality of life, they also foster chemical changes in the brain that lessen the brain's response to anxiety. |
| 7. Use a cognitive approach. | 7. Helps the patient recognize that thoughts and beliefs can cause anxiety. |
| 8. Teach patient proven behavioral techniques. | 8. Cognitive and behavioral techniques |

---

### Box 5-9 Teaching Abdominal Breathing

Instruct the patient to:
1. Place one hand on the abdomen beneath the rib cage.
2. Inhale slowly and deeply through the nose, sending air as far down into the lungs as possible. The hand should rise.
3. After taking the full breath, pause for a moment, then exhale slowly and fully.
4. While exhaling, allow the entire body to go limp.
5. Count each breath up to 10 by saying the appropriate number after each exhalation.
6. Do two or three "sets" of 10 abdominal breaths to produce a state of considerable relaxation.

From Varcarolis E. (2002). *Foundations of psychiatric mental health nursing* (4th ed.). Philadelphia: Saunders, reprinted with permission.

| Intervention | Rationale |
|---|---|
| Patient can become desensitized to a feared object or situation over time. | are extremely effective interventions for treating anxiety disorders. Once they are learned, patients can draw upon these skills for the rest of their lives. |
| 9. Keep focus on manageable problems; define them simply and concretely. | 9. Concrete, well-defined problems lend themselves to intervention. |
| 10. Provide behavioral rehearsals (role-play) for anticipated stressful situations. | 10. Predetermination of previous effective or new coping strategies, along with practice, increases potential for success. |

---

### Box 5-10  Script for Visualizing a Peaceful Scene

Imagine releasing all the tension in your body . . . letting it go.

Now, with every breath you take, feel your body drifting down deeper and deeper into relaxation . . . floating down . . . deeper and deeper.

Imagine your peaceful scene. You're sitting beside a clear, blue mountain stream. You are barefoot, and you feel the sun-warmed rock under your feet. You hear the sound of the stream tumbling over the rocks. The sound is hypnotic, and you relax more and more. You see the tall pine trees on the opposite shore bending in the gentle breeze. Breathe the clean, pine-scented air, each breath moving you deeper and deeper into relaxation. The sun warms your face.

You are very comfortable. There is nothing to disturb you. You experience a feeling of well-being.

You can return to this peaceful scene by taking time to relax. The positive feelings can grow stronger and stronger each time you choose to relax.

You can return to your activities now, feeling relaxed and refreshed.

| **Intervention** | **Rationale** |
|---|---|
| 11. Some patients respond well to biofeedback and feel more comfortable with physiological manipulations than one-on-one therapy. | 11. Biofeedback is extremely useful for decreasing anxiety levels. Some patients might feel less "shame" in getting help. |
| 12. Many anxiety disorders respond to medications along with therapy (e.g., selective serotonin reuptake inhibitors [SSRIs] for OCD and PD, buspirone [BuSpar] for GAD). Therefore, medication teaching is extremely important, especially with the anxiolytics. | 12. Patients need to know what the medications can and cannot do. They need to know that "more is not better," the side effects and toxic effects, and what to do if an untoward reaction occurs. This information should always be given to patients in writing after it is verbally explained by the nurse clinician. |

## DISTURBED THOUGHT PROCESSES

Disruption in cognitive operations and activities

### *Related Factors (Related To)*

- Severe levels of anxiety
- Distorted perceptions
- Intrusive, obsessive thoughts
- Anticipatory anxiety
- Automatic thoughts set off escalating anxiety
- Faulty thinking

### *Some Defining Characteristics (As Evidenced By)*

▲ Hypervigilance
▲ Distractibility
▲ Inaccurate interpretation of the environment

▲ NANDA International accepted; ● In addition to NANDA International

▲ Inappropriate thinking
● Flashbacks
● Intrusive, obsessive thinking
● Disturbing, recurring thoughts

## Outcome Criteria

● Is able to control intrusive thoughts to a comfortable level
● Demonstrates increase in concentration and attentiveness
● Is able to reframe faulty thinking
● Demonstrates control over selected events and situations
● Maintains focus without being distracted
● Is able to problem solve

## Long-Term Goals

Patient will:
● Recognize when anxiety begins to escalate and link anxiety to precipitating thoughts or feelings by (date)
● Demonstrate techniques that can distract and distance self from thoughts and feelings that are anxiety producing by (date)
● Reframe automatic thoughts and self-judgments that lead to increase in anxiety and lowering of self-worth by (date)

## Short-Term Goals

Patient will:
● Identify two thoughts or feelings that precede increases in anxiety and will discuss with the nurse within 1 week or (date)
● Share daily journal with counselor/nurse regarding thoughts/feelings preceding anxiety (date)
● Rate the anxiety on a scale from 1 to 10, then re-rate anxiety after using breathing, relaxation, cognitive, behavioral, or other anxiety-reducing skills
● Demonstrate one cognitive or behavioral technique after 1 week (date)

---

▲ NANDA International accepted; ● In addition to NANDA International

## *Interventions and Rationales*

| **Intervention** | **Rationale** |
| --- | --- |
| 1. Explore with patient the thoughts that lead up to patient's anxious feelings and relief behaviors. | 1. Recognition of precipitating thoughts or feelings leading to anxiety behaviors might give clues about how to arrest escalating anxiety. |
| 2. Link patient's relief behaviors to thoughts and feelings. | 2. Patient becomes aware of how anxiety can be the result of thoughts and feelings and realizes that with practice, people can have some control over their thoughts and therefore their anxiety levels. |
| 3. Teach cognitive principles.<br>  a. Anxiety is the result of dysfunctional appraisal of a situation.<br>  b. Anxiety is the result of automatic thinking. | 3. Again, introduces the concept to patients that they can have some control over their thoughts and feelings; instills hope and stimulates trying new ways of thinking. |
| 4. Teach some brief **cognitive techniques** that the patient can try out right away (Box 5-11). | 4. Increases self-awareness while distancing self from own anxiety. In a sense, helps distract patient from feelings of anxiety and allows him or her to be more of an observer. |
| 5. Teach patient **behavioral techniques** that can interrupt intrusive, unwanted thoughts (Box 5-12). | 5. Can help distract patient and interrupt escalating anxiety. During this time, alternative coping skills can be employed. |
| 6. Role-play and rehearse with patient alternative coping strategies that can be used in threatening or anxiety-provoking situations. | 6. Gives patient a chance to be proactive, giving patient a choice of alternatives instead of patient employing usual unsatisfactory automatic reactions. |

| **Intervention** | **Rationale** |
|---|---|
| 7. Encourage patient to keep a daily journal of thoughts and situations that seem to precede anxiety and coping strategies used. | 7. Allows patient to monitor "triggers" and evaluate useful coping strategies over time. |
| 8. Teach patient to rate his or her anxiety levels on a scale from 1 to 10, where 1 is the least and 10 the highest. Have situations and anxiety levels in the journal. | 8. Allows patient to evaluate effectiveness of coping strategies and monitor decrease in anxiety levels over time. |

---

### Box 5-11 **Brief Cognitive Techniques**

1. Instruct patient to refer to self by first name and comment on own anxiety or thoughts (e.g., "Mary's heart is beating fast." "Ted thinks everyone is looking at him now.")

2. Work with the patient to recognize his or her automatic thinking and how certain words can trigger anxiety (e.g., *should, never, always*). Help patient use words that are more objective and neutral; for example:
   - *Change* "I should have gone to college." *to* "I would have benefited from going to college, and if I still wish to go, I can."
   - *Change* "I always use poor judgment when it comes to money; I'll never get it right!" *to* "Although I have made mistakes regarding money in the past, it would be useful for me to get some advice and check out my ideas more thoroughly in the future."

---

### Box 5-12 **Thought Stopping: Brief Behavioral Techniques**

- Have patient wear a rubber band around his or her wrist. When intrusive repetitive thoughts start to occur (as in obsessive compulsive disorder), have patient snap the rubber band hard on the wrist.
- When patient is experiencing intrusive painful memories, clap your hands loudly in front of patient, then teach patient and family to do the same thing.

| Intervention | Rationale |
|---|---|
| 9. Review journal with patient and identify which strategies worked and which did not work. Review with patient progress made, and give credit for the patient's hard work. | 9. Helps patient see what seems to be working and what does not and encourages adherence when going through phases of feeling discouraged. |
| 10. Teach patient to recognize triggers of anxiety. | 10. Gives patient opportunity to use alternative responses and skills. |
| 11. Refer patient to support groups in the community in which people are dealing with similar issues. | 11. Groups can foster a sense of belonging and diminish feelings of isolation and alienation. Positive feedback from others helps foster adherence and enhances self-esteem. |
| 12. Review **stress-reduction techniques** with patient, family, and significant others during family and patient teaching (Box 5-13). Encourage patient and family members to practice relaxation techniques; give handouts and references. | 12. Everyone around the patient might be tense. Sometimes simple steps make big differences in people's lives. |
| 13. Refer family members and significant others to appropriate resources in the community. Resources might include family therapy, couples counseling, financial counseling, support groups, or classes in meditation and other relaxation techniques. | 13. Family and others close to the patient might need a great deal of support. They might benefit from learning new coping strategies that can lessen conflicts and stress on the whole family unit. |

## Box 5-13 **Selected Stress Reduction Techniques**

**Relaxation Techniques**
1. Induce a relaxation state more physiologically refreshing than sleep
2. Neutralize stress energy, producing a calming effect

**Reframing**
1. Changes the way we look and feel about things
2. There are many ways to interpret the same reality (seeing the glass as half full rather than half empty).
3. Reassess situation. We can learn from most situations. Ask:
   "What positive thing came out of the situation/experience?"
   "What did you learn in this situation?"
   "What would you do differently next time?"
4. Walking in another person's shoes can help dissipate tension and help us step outside of ourselves.
   We might even feel some compassion toward the person.
   • "What might be going on with your (spouse, boss, teacher, friend) that would cause him/her to (say, do) that?"
   • "Is he/she having problems? Feeling insecure? Under pressure?"

**Sleep**
1. Chronically stressed people are often fatigued.
2. Go to sleep 30 to 60 minutes earlier each night for a few weeks.
3. If still fatigued, try going to bed another 30 minutes earlier.
4. Sleeping later in the morning is not helpful and can throw off body rhythms.

**Exercise (Aerobic)**
1. Exercise can dissipate chronic and acute stress.
2. Recommended amount: at least 30 minutes three times a week

**Lower/Eliminate Caffeine Intake**
1. Such a simple thing can lead to more energy and fewer muscle aches and help people feel more relaxed.
2. Wean off coffee, tea, colas, and chocolate drinks.

Box 5-13  **Selected Stress Reduction Techniques—cont'd**

**Stress-Lowering Tips For Living**
1.  Engage in meaningful, satisfying work.
2.  Don't let work dominate your entire life.
3.  Associate yourself with gentle people who affirm your personhood.
4.  Guard your personal freedom, your freedom to:
    - Choose your friends
    - Live with and/or love whom you choose
    - Think and believe as you choose
    - Structure your time as you see fit
    - Set your own life's goals

## POSTTRAUMA SYNDROME

Sustained maladaptive response to a traumatic, overwhelming event

### Some Related Factors (Related To)

▲ Wars
▲ Sexual assault/abuse
▲ Terrorism
▲ Torture
▲ Disasters
▲ Events outside the range of usual human experience (e.g., adventitious crisis)
▲ Military combat
▲ Physical and psychological abuse
▲ Serious accidents
▲ Witnessing violent death or mutilations
▲ Motor vehicle and industrial accidents
▲ Being held prisoner of war
▲ Natural disasters and man-made disasters

### Some Defining Characteristics (As Evidenced By)

Assessment Findings/Diagnostic Cues:
▲ Difficulty concentrating
▲ Intrusive thoughts/dreams

---

▲ NANDA International accepted; ● In addition to NANDA International

▲ Flashbacks
▲ Exaggerated startle response
▲ Anger and/or rage
▲ Hopelessness
▲ Panic attacks
▲ Depression
▲ Anxiety
▲ Psychogenic amnesia
▲ Detachment
▲ Numbing
▲ Compulsive behavior
▲ Flashbacks
▲ Avoidance
▲ Regression

## Outcome Criteria

• Diminished symptoms of PTSD (e.g., nightmares, flashbacks, depression, isolation, headaches, confusion, difficulty concentrating)
• Maintains self-control without supervision
• Satisfaction with coping ability
• Satisfaction with close relationships
• Use of available social supports
• Increased psychological comfort

## Long-Term Goals

Patient will:
• Report feelings of support and comfort within support group of people sharing similar experiences by (date)
• Use three new effective relaxation strategies to help reduce tension and anxiety by (date)
• Talk about a traumatic event, fears, terrors, and experiences and demonstrate congruent feelings within ___ weeks
• Participate in social skills training targeting specific previously identified behaviors
• Demonstrate a new sense of control over certain situations or events by (date)
• Agree to continue with treatment goals and management strategies by (date)

---

▲ NANDA International accepted; ● In addition to NANDA International

## Short-Term Goals

Patient will:
- Identify one person or group that patient is willing to talk to or spend time with working on issues of PTSD
- Identify three coping skills patient believes would improve his/her sense of well-being and functioning and agree to work on them with (nurse/staff/clinician) within 1 week
- Identify two problems that, if addressed, would improve patient's quality of life and those of family/friends/coworkers/boss (e.g., impulse control, assertiveness, social skills)

## Interventions and Rationales

| Intervention | Rationale |
|---|---|
| 1. Assess for any suicidal or homicidal thoughts and feelings. (See Chapters 16 and 17 for nursing care plans related to suicide behaviors and anger and aggression.) | 1. Priority of concern and nursing measures would be for patient and other safety. |
| 2. Assess the patient's anxiety level. | 2. Identify what level of intervention might be needed to minimize further escalation of anxiety. |
| 3. Assess for alcohol or drug abuse. If yes, assess readiness for substance use/abuse therapies (e.g., support groups, counseling). Offer referrals if patient is ready. | 3. Most patients cannot participate in learning coping skills, reliving traumatic memories, and making positive changes while impaired. |
| 4. Identify the patient's symptoms, and clarify that they are anxiety related and not the product of a physiological condition (e.g., chest tightness, headaches, dizziness, numbness). | 4. Physical causes of symptoms need to be ruled out before assumptions of psychological causes are made. (A patient might well have PTSD along with a cardiac problem, etc.) |

| **Intervention** | **Rationale** |
|---|---|
| 5. Identify and document the psychological response the patient is experiencing (e.g., shock, anger, withdrawal, panic, confusion, psychotic episodes, emotional instability, nightmares, flashbacks). | 5. The psychological symptoms are often many, and different ones might require different intervention strategies. When the symptoms begin to diminish, you know that goals are being reached. |
| 6. Identify if patient has been or is exposed to groups in which others deal with similar traumatic issues. If not, offer referrals to groups in the patient's community. | 6. Support groups of people with similar experiences are perhaps pivotal to healing. Allows for expressing similar feelings in a safe environment. |
| 7. Spend time with patient, allowing patient to go at own speed regarding describing present or past traumatic events. | 7. Often feelings and memories of trauma are buried. It often takes time and trust for a person to open up to a "stranger" or discuss a topic he/she might not have shared with anyone. |
| 8. Monitor your own feelings in response to your patient's experience. | 8. Many of the stories patients tell are horrifying and difficult to listen to. |
| 9. Refrain from interrupting or minimizing the horror or overidentifying with the events. | 9. Venting with other staff or supervisor helps nurse process feelings and discharge tensions. |
| 10. Remain nonjudgmental in your interactions. | 10. Avoid reinforcing blame, shame, guilt, and so on. |
| 11. Listen attentively to patient's description of the event. | 11. Although it might be difficult to listen to the trauma, sharing the pain with others can be the beginning of healing. |
| 12. Encourage the expression of feelings through talking, | 12. The description of the events and the expression of feelings |

| **Intervention** | **Rationale** |
|---|---|
| writing, crying, role playing, or other ways the patient is comfortable with. | associated with the event are paramount to the healing process. |
| 13. Teach the patient adaptive cognitive and behavioral strategies to manage symptoms of emotional and physical reactivity:<br>a. Deep breathing (see Box 5-9)<br>b. Relaxation exercises (see Box 5-10)<br>c. Cognitive techniques (see Box 5-11)<br>d. Desensitization<br>e. Assertive behavior<br>f. Thought-stopping techniques (see Box 5-12)<br>g. Stress reduction techniques (see Box 5-13) | 13. Once repressed areas are opened up, accompanying, often unbearable, feelings will emerge. |
| 14. Assess family and social support system. Is there a need for family interventions or counseling? | 14. Often family and friends become confused, afraid, hurt, angry, or feel hopeless and depressed over time. |
| 15. Instruct patient and family on the signs and symptoms of PTS. | 15. Often when actions and behaviors that seemed totally chaotic and unrelated are viewed in terms of an identifiable syndrome, relief is experienced, especially when treatment is available. |
| 16. Assess if the patient found comfort in religious or spiritual activities in the past. Are they still practicing? Do they wish to resume | 16. Deep spiritual convictions, when activated, can provide a sense of hope and meaning for patients struggling with feelings |

| Intervention | Rationale |
|---|---|
| practice or contact with supportive spiritual persons? | of helplessness and hopelessness. |
| 17. Offer the patient access to coping skills training when patient is ready and when appropriate (e.g., anger management, assertive skills, anxiety reduction techniques, coping skills training, social skills training). | 17. Patients might need to learn or relearn a variety of coping skills once they begin to function again. |
| 18. Identify the need for social services (e.g., employment, legal issues, living arrangements) and give patient referrals. | 18. Some patients might have multiple social needs related to long-term, entrenched behaviors. |

## DISTURBED SLEEP PATTERN

Time-limited disruption of sleep (natural, periodic suspension of consciousness), amount, and quality

### Related Factors (Related To)

- Fear
- Anxiety
- Fatigue
- Inadequate sleep hygiene
- Biochemical agents
- Nightmares
- Obsessional thoughts
- Fears (e.g., dark, intrusion, death)
- Panic attacks

### Defining Characteristics (As Evidenced By)

Assessment Findings/Diagnostic Cues:
▲ Decreased ability to function
▲ Verbal complaints of not feeling well rested

▲ NANDA International accepted; ● In addition to NANDA International

- Arising earlier or later than desired
- Three or more nighttime awakenings

## Outcome Criteria

- Develops an uninterrupted sleep pattern of 5 to 8 hours per night
- Reports feeling rejuvenated after sleep
- Establishes an effective sleep routine

## Long-Term Goals

Patient will:
- State he/she begins to see improvement in quality of sleep and pattern of sleep after 2 weeks
- State that the relaxation exercises (tapes) are useful sleep aids by (date)
- Work with nurse to review and revise plan if sleep pattern has not improved after 2 weeks

## Short-Term Goals

Patient will:
- Identify personal habits that disrupt sleep pattern and those things that could augment quality of sleep after first interview
- Form a "sleep plan" with nurse that the patient is willing to try within 2 days
- Identify any other issues that might need attention that are contributing to sleep pattern disturbance and be open for referrals

## Interventions and Rationales

| Intervention | Rationale |
|---|---|
| 1. Assess patient and family usual sleep pattern, any changes that have occurred, and what was happening at the time. Identify if there | 1. Information from both patient and family clarifies specific sleep disturbance. |

---

▲ NANDA International accepted; ● In addition to NANDA International

| **Intervention** | **Rationale** |
|---|---|
| was a precipitating event around onset of sleep problem or if it is chronic. | |
| 2. Identify the patient's usual sleep patterns, including the following:<br>• Bedtime rituals<br>• Time of rising, time of retiring<br>• Use of alcohol and/or caffeine before sleep<br>• Use of sleep aids (prescribed or over-the-counter medications) | 2. Establish a baseline and help identify problems:<br>• Sleeping medications and alcohol interfere with rapid eye movement (REM) sleep.<br>• Caffeine and exercise before retiring can interfere with sleep. |
| 3. Review sleep hygiene measures with the patient. Determine if the patient does any of the following: refrains from naps, alcohol, and caffeine at night; follows a regular retiring and arising schedule; exercise pattern. | 3. Identifying baseline helps target needed interventions. |
| 4. Develop a sleep relaxation program with patient (e.g., self-hypnosis, progressive muscle relaxation, imagery). | 4. Employing both physical and mental relaxation can help minimize anxiety and promote sleep. |
| 5. Demonstrate and rehearse these techniques with patient until patient feels relaxed and is able to practice them at bedtime. | 5. Have patient practice chosen relaxation method with nurse. Allow time for patient to begin to feel results of relaxation. |
| 6. Suggest use of relaxation tapes. | 6. If patient has racing thoughts or is troubled by a problem, tapes can help the patient focus on relaxation. |

| **Intervention** | **Rationale** |
|---|---|
| 7. Encourage patient to:<br>• Use decaffeinated beverages until sleep pattern improves.<br>• Limit fluid intake 3 to 5 hours before retiring.<br>• Increase physical activity during the day, even if fatigued.<br>• Avoid daytime naps.<br>• Establish regular times of retiring and waking. | 7. These are known sleep aids. |
| 8. Establish with patient a sleep program that incorporates the elements of good sleep hygiene and relaxation tools. | 8. Patient is more likely to follow plan if he/she is involved with the incorporation of known effective techniques. |
| 9. Suggest to patient that if he/she does not feel drowsy after 20 minutes, get up and engage in a quiet activity that is "boring"—*not* stimulating. | 9. Waiting for sleep that will not come can increase anxiety and frustration. Doing something monotonous at bedtime might help the patient become drowsy. |
| 10. Encourage patient to practice the agreed-upon bedtime routine for 2 weeks even if there does not seem to be a benefit. | 10. It might take 2 weeks or longer for habits to settle in. |
| 11. Encourage patient to simultaneously work on any issues that might be adversely affecting sleep (e.g., anxiety disorders, social or personal problems, job-related issues, interpersonal difficulties). Offer referrals when appropriate. | 11. Disturbances in sleep are often secondary to other issues, either emotional or physical. If such issues are present, they need to be addressed. |

# MEDICAL TREATMENTS

## Psychopharmacology

Although psychopharmacology is often an important adjunct to treating anxiety disorders, it is important to be aware of cognitive-behavioral modalities (CBT) that are proven effective for these disorders and might be superior in some instances in the long run. CBT teaches patients coping skills and behaviors that might enhance their quality of life.

At one time, the predominant treatment for anxiety disorders was antianxiety medications, or *anxiolytics*, as they are currently referred to. The benzodiazepines were often the treatment of choice and still are used for severe anxiety. However, there are currently many groups of medications that can be used effectively for patients with anxiety disorders. Each group seems to be helpful for specific disorders. For example, the tricyclic antidepressants (TCAs) (e.g., *imipramine*) seem to be effective in targeting **panic attacks.** The monoamine oxidase inhibitor (MAOI) antidepressants seem to have **anti-agoraphobic effects.** Although the benzodiazepines are useful in **GAD,** they are best used for a short time, because they can become addicting. Benzodiazepines might also cause "rebound anxiety" when they are stopped. Clinicians might prefer to start with *buspirone*, which is not addicting, nor does the patient develop a tolerance for the drug. The downside of buspirone (BuSpar) is that it can take a long time to work (3 weeks or much longer for some). The patient can be maintained with buspirone for a long time. Although anxiolytics might be the most widely used treatment for GAD, the World Federation of Societies of Biological Psychiatry (2002) recently recommended SSRIs as first-line therapy. The SSRI antidepressants (e.g., fluvoxamine [Luvox], fluoxetine [Prozac]) have also been found to be very effective for people with **OCD.**

Table 5-1 gives a good example of effective drugs for each of the anxiety disorders. Note that it is best when these drugs are given as an adjunct to therapy. Drugs are not a cure. Therapy gives patients options on how to assess situations and how to deal with situations in ways that are appropriate and effective, and in doing so enhances the patient's quality of life. Drugs cannot do that. Refer to Chapter 21 for the neurotransmitters targeted, the negative side effects related to receptor-blocking activity, and patient and family teaching to optimize adherence and drug safety and effectiveness. Table 5-2 offers a more comprehensive list of specific antianxiety medications, their trade names, and usual daily dosage.

## Psychosocial Treatment for Anxiety Disorders

Among the therapeutic modalities used to treat anxiety disorders, the **cognitive-behavioral therapies are those with the strongest empirical support** and are the treatments of choice.

Cognitive strategies focus on altering or reframing one's perception of anxiety-producing stimuli. These interventions often make use of "coping skills," which involve teaching people various ways to help manage anxiety or fear. Coping skills are any behaviors that help people feel more secure; these often involve the use of self-statement.

Cognitive-behavioral interventions include:
- Challenging dysfunctional thoughts and irrational beliefs
- Cognitive restructuring
- Desensitization
- Anxiety-management training

In addition to these general cognitive-behavioral strategies, several specific behavioral and cognitive-behavioral interventions have been developed for certain anxiety disorders. These involve:
- Panic control therapy for panic disorders
- Social effectiveness therapy for social phobia
- Applied relaxation for blood or injury phobia
- Flooding and response prevention for OCD

Table 5-1 identifies useful medications and therapies for each of the anxiety disorders. Brief stress-reduction techniques that can be used during health teaching are outlined in Box 5-13.

Table 5-1 **Accepted Treatment for Selected Anxiety Disorders**

| Disorder | Pharmacotherapy | Therapeutic Modality | Comments |
|---|---|---|---|
| Panic disorder | 1. High-potency benzodiazepines<br>2. Antidepressants (TCAs and SSRIs)<br>3. MAOIs | **CBT (Cognitive-behavioral therapy)**<br>• Relaxation techniques<br>• Breathing techniques<br>• Cognitive restructuring<br>• Systematic desensitization<br>• In vivo exposure aimed at eliminating avoidance behaviors | Benzodiazepines (short term) to reduce or eliminate panic attacks in initial phase of treatment)<br>Antidepressants may decrease panic episodes and treat underlying depression<br>**CBT**<br>Teaches new coping skills and ways to reframe thinking |
| Generalized anxiety disorder | **When medications are indicated:**<br>a. Benzodiazepines—short term only, danger of abuse<br>c. Buspirone (BuSpar) reduces rumination and worry, not addictive<br>a. SSRIs and TCA anti-depressants—effective with chronic anxiety<br>d. Gabapentin (antiseizure drug) used to reduce anxiety | • Cognitive therapy<br>• Behavioral therapy<br>• Stress management<br>• Relaxation training<br>• Aerobic level exercises | Many patients are helped with psychological approaches and may not need medications |

| | | |
|---|---|---|
| **Posttraumatic stress disorder** | a. MAOIs (panic)<br>b. TCAs (imipramine and amitriptyline) and SSRIs (depressive symptoms, hyperarousal, diminish nightmares and flashbacks)<br>c. Low-dose antipsychotics (if transient psychosis, derealization and treatment-resistant PTSD)<br>d. Anticonvulsant for treatment-resistant PTSD | • Psychotherapy<br>• Family therapy<br>• Vocational rehabilitation<br>• Group therapy<br>• Relaxation techniques | More than one treatment modality should be used.*<br>a. Establish support<br>b. Focus on abreaction, survivor guilt or shame, anger, and helplessness |
| **Obsessive-compulsive disorder** | a. SSRIs (fluvoxamine [Luvox] and fluoxetine [Prozac])<br>b. Clomipramine (Anafranil) (TCA) | Cognitive-behavioral therapy | Effective and necessary in addition to serotonergic medications<br>Exposure in vivo plus response prevention are the crucial essential factors |

*The sooner treatment begins, the more successful recovery is likely to be.

*MAOI,* Monoamine oxidase inhibitor; *SSRI,* selective serotonin reuptake inhibitor; *TCA,* tricyclic antidepressant.

Updated from original in Varcarolis, E. (2002). *Foundations of psychiatric mental health nursing* (4th ed.). Philadelphia: Saunders, p. 331; reprinted with permission; Preston, J.D., O'Neal, J.H., & Talaga, M.C. (2008). *Handbook of clinical psychopharmacology for therapists* (5th ed.). Oakland, CA: New Harbinger Publications; and Preston, J.D. & Johnson, J. (2009). *Clinical psychopharmacology made ridiculously simple* (6th ed.). Miami, FL: MedMaster Inc.

Table 5-2 **Medications Commonly Used in the Treatment of Anxiety Disorders**

| Generic Name | Trade Name | Usual Daily Dose (mg/day) | Comments |
|---|---|---|---|
| **Benzodiazepines** | | | |
| Alprazolam* | Xanax | 0.5–6 | Anxiolytic effects result from depressing neurotransmission in the limbic system and cortical areas. Useful for short-term treatment of anxiety; dependence and tolerance develop. These drugs are NOT indicated as a primary treatment for OCD or PTSD. |
| | Xanax XR | 3–6 | |
| Diazepam | Valium | 4–40 | |
| Lorazepam* | Ativan | 2–6 | |
| Oxazepam | Serax | 30–120 | |
| Chlordiazepoxide | Librium | 15–100 | |
| Clorazepate | Tranxene | 15–60 | |
| **Buspirone** | | | |
| Buspirone hydrochloride† | BuSpar | 30–60 | Alleviates anxiety but works best before benzodiazepines have been tried. Less sedating than benzodiazepines. Does not appear to produce physical or psychological dependence. Requires 3 or more weeks to be effective. |

**Selective Serotonin Reuptake Inhibitors (SSRIs)**

**First Line**

| | | | |
|---|---|---|---|
| Citalopram | Celexa | 20–60 | |
| Escitalopram | Lexapro | 10–20 | Escitalopram not useful with SAD or PD. |
| Fluoxetine | Prozac | 20–80 | |
| Fluvoxamine | Luvox | 100–300 | |
| Paroxetine | Paxil | 20–50 | |
| Sertraline | Zoloft | 50–200 | |

**Dual-Action Reuptake Inhibitors (Serotonin & Norepinephrine) (SNRIs)**

**First Line**

| | | | |
|---|---|---|---|
| Duloxetine | Cymbalta | 40–60 | Acts within 1 to 2 weeks. |
| Venlafaxine | Effexor | 75–225 | |

**Tricyclic Antidepressants (TCAs)**

**Second or Third Line**

| | | | |
|---|---|---|---|
| Amitriptyline | Elavil | 100–200 | Clomipramine effective with OCD, PD, GAD, SAD; may also respond to Surmontil. |
| Clomipramine | Anafranil | 100–200 | |
| Desipramine | Norpramin | 100–200 | |
| Doxepin | Sinequan | 75–150 | |
| Imipramine | Tofranil | 75–150 | |

*Continued*

Table 5-2 **Medications Commonly Used in the Treatment of Anxiety Disorders—cont'd**

| Generic Name | Trade Name | Usual Daily Dose (mg/day) | Comments |
|---|---|---|---|
| Maprotiline | Ludiomil | 100–150 | |
| Nortriptyline | Pamelor | 75–150 | |
| Trimipramine | Surmontil | 50–150 | |
| Amoxapine | Asendin | 200–300 | |
| **β-Blockers** | | | |
| Propranolol | Inderal | 20–160 | Used to relieve physical symptoms of anxiety, as in performance anxiety (stage fright). Act by attaching to sensors that direct arousal messages. |
| Atenolol | Tenormin | 25–100 | |

*Most commonly used benzodiazepines for treating chronic or unpredictable anxiety syndromes.
†Useful as a first-line treatment in GAD.
*GAD*, Generalized anxiety disorder; *OCD*, obsessive-compulsive disorder; *PTSD*, posttraumatic stress disorder; *PD*, panic disorder; *SAD*, seasonal affective disorder.

Adapted from Varcarolis, E.M. (2006). *Manual of psychiatric mental health nursing care plans* (3rd ed.). St. Louis: Saunders, p. 151.
Lehne, R.A. (2007). *Pharmacology for nursing care* (6th ed.). St. Louis: Saunders.

# COMPLEMENTARY APPROACHES

A general caveat for all herbal and dietary supplements is that they are not subjected to rigorous testing, not required to be uniform, and problems can occur due to their interaction with other substances. Problems that may arise with the use of *psychotropic* herbs include side effects and herb-drug interactions.

That said, there are some "natural" substances that are purported to relieve anxiety and are now undergoing randomized control studies; however, the scientific evidence for any of these is sparse.

**Kava-kava** (*Piper methysticum*) is one drug that has proved promising in the treatment of anxiety. Kava has also been used to reduce pain and relax muscles, and it has anticonvulsant effects as well. Kava products might be beneficial in the management of anxiety and tension of nonpsychotic origin, and they do not adversely affect cognitive function, mental acuity, or coordination, in contrast with the benzodiazepines. Kava should not be taken with other substances that act on the central nervous system, such as alcohol, barbiturates, antidepressants, and antipsychotics, or by those with liver disease. In 2002 the FDA warned that hepatic toxicity is possibly associated with kava-containing products. There have also been reports of hearing impairment, leukopenia, and thrombocytopenia associated with kava. Check *consumerLab.com* for reputable brands.

# NURSE, PATIENT, and FAMILY RESOURCES

## ASSOCIATIONS

**Anxiety Disorders Association of America**
8730 Georgia Avenue, Suite 600
Silver Spring, MD 20910
(240) 485-1001
www.adaa.org

**Obsessive-Compulsive Foundation, Inc.**
337 Notch Hill Road
North Branford, CT 06471

(203) 315-2190
www.ocdfoundation.org

# INTERNET SITES

**Panic/Anxiety Disorders Guide**
www.panicdisorder.about.com

**Panic Disorder**
www.nlm.nih.gov/medlineplus/panicdisorder.html

**David Baldwin's Trauma Information Pages**
www.trauma-pages.com
Site focuses on emotional trauma and traumatic stress, including PTSD

**National Center for PTSD**
www.ncptsd.org

**Mental Help Net**
mentalhelp.net

# CHAPTER 6

# Depressive Disorders

## OVERVIEW

Happiness and unhappiness are appropriate responses to life events. When sadness, grief, or elation is extremely intense and the mood unduly prolonged, a mood disorder results. **Depressive symptoms often coexist in people with alcohol or substance abuse problems. Depressive symptoms are common in people who have other psychiatric disorders or behaviors** (anorexia nervosa, borderline disorders, phobias, and schizophrenia), or **people who have been physically or mentally abused** (posttrauma behaviors). **Depression might be a critical symptom of many medical disorders or conditions** (hepatitis, mononucleosis, multiple sclerosis, dementia, cancer, diabetes, chronic pain). **Depression might also be directly related to the intake of many commonly prescribed medications** (e.g., antihypertensive medications, steroids, hormones, digitalis, stimulants). Therefore, mood disorders can be caused by a medical condition, psychoactive drugs, medications, and a host of psychiatric conditions. However, interventions for depression can be helpful, regardless of the etiology. **Risk for Suicide** is an essential component of a thorough assessment, regardless of the cause of depression. Refer to Chapter 16 for more on the diagnoses and interventions specific for suicide.

### Major Depressive Disorder

In major depressive disorder, a severely depressed mood, usually recurrent, causes clinically significant distress or impairment in social, occupational, or other important areas of the person's life. The depressed mood can be distinguished from the person's usual functioning and might occur suddenly or gradually. Major depression is considered to be a "severe biologically based mental illness" as determined by medical science in conjunction with the *Diagnostic and Statistical Manual of Mental Disorders* (4th edition, text revision) (*DSM-IV-TR*) (National Alliance for the Mentally III [NAMI], 1999).

Major depression might be characterized by certain features. For example:

- **Psychotic features**—delusions or hallucinations
- **Seasonal affective disorder (SAD)**—most prominent during certain seasons (e.g., winter or summer); SAD is more prevalent in climates with longer periods of darkness in a 24-hour cycle
- **Catatonic features**—for example, peculiarities of voluntary movement, motor immobility, purposeless motor activity, echolalia, or echopraxia
- **Melancholic features**—severe symptoms, loss of feelings of pleasure, worse in morning, early morning awakening, significant weight loss, excessive feelings of guilt
- **Postpartum onset**—within 4 weeks of delivery

Box 6-1 presents the *DSM-IV-TR* diagnostic criteria for a major depressive disorder.

### Dysthymic Disorder

Dysthymic disorder (dysthymia) is characterized by less severe, usually chronic depressive symptoms that have been present for at least 2 years (1 year for children or adolescents). Although dysthymia is not as severe as a major depression, the symptoms can cause significant distress or impairment in major areas of the person's life.

Box 6-2 provides a summary of the *DSM-IV-TR* diagnostic criteria for dysthymia.

## ASSESSMENT

### Presenting Signs and Symptoms

- Depressed mood (or irritability in children or adolescents)

| Box 6-1 | ***DSM-IV-TR*** <br> **Criteria for Major Depressive Episode** |
|---|---|

1.  Represents a change in previous functions.
2.  Symptoms cause clinically significant distress or impair social, occupational, or other important areas of functioning.
3.  **Five or more** of the following occur nearly every day for most waking hours during the same 2-week period. At least one of the symptoms is either a (1) depressed mood or (2) loss of interest or pleasure (anhedonia).
    *   Depressed mood
    *   Anhedonia
    *   Significant weight loss or gain (more than 5% of body weight in 1 month)
    *   Insomnia or hypersomnia nearly every day
    *   Increased or decreased motor activity
    *   Anergia (fatigue or loss of energy)
    *   Feelings of worthlessness or inappropriate guilt (might be delusional)
    *   Decreased concentration, indecisiveness, or inability to think clearly
    *   Recurrent thoughts of death or suicidal ideation (with or without pain)
4.  Symptoms are not due to (1) psychological effects of substance, (2) a general medical condition, or (3) recent bereavement.

Adapted from American Psychiatric Association (APA). (2000). *Diagnostic and statistical manual of mental disorders* (4th ed., text rev.) (*DSM-IV-TR*). Washington DC: Author, p. 356; reprinted with permission.

*   Diminished interest in or pleasure in almost all activities (anhedonia)
*   Alterations in eating, sleeping, activity level (fatigue), and libido
*   Feelings of worthlessness or guilt
*   Difficulty with concentration, memory, and making decisions
*   Recurrent thoughts of death and/or self-harm

## Assessment Tools

There are many useful assessment tools available to evaluate for depression such as the Zung Self-Rating Scale. See Appendix D-4.

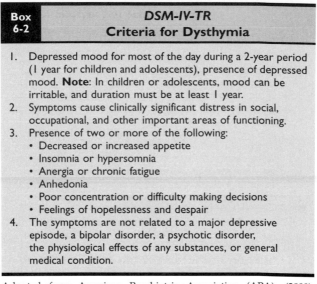

| Box 6-2 | *DSM-IV-TR*<br>**Criteria for Dysthymia** |
|---|---|

1. Depressed mood for most of the day during a 2-year period (1 year for children and adolescents), presence of depressed mood. **Note:** In children or adolescents, mood can be irritable, and duration must be at least 1 year.
2. Symptoms cause clinically significant distress in social, occupational, and other important areas of functioning.
3. Presence of two or more of the following:
   - Decreased or increased appetite
   - Insomnia or hypersomnia
   - Anergia or chronic fatigue
   - Anhedonia
   - Poor concentration or difficulty making decisions
   - Feelings of hopelessness and despair
4. The symptoms are not related to a major depressive episode, a bipolar disorder, a psychotic disorder, the physiological effects of any substances, or general medical condition.

Adapted from American Psychiatric Association (APA). (2000). *Diagnostic and statistical manual of mental disorders* (4th ed., text rev.) (*DSM-IV-TR*). Washington DC: Author, p. 380; reprinted with permission.

## Assessment Guidelines

### Depression

1. A thorough physical and neurological examination helps determine if the depression is primary or secondary to another disorder. Depression is a mood that can be secondary to a host of medical or other psychiatric disorders, as well as drugs/medications. Essentially, the nurse evaluates whether:
   - The patient is psychotic
   - The patient has taken drugs or alcohol
   - Medical conditions are present
2. Always evaluate the patient's risk of harm to self or others. Overt hostility is highly correlated with suicide.

# NURSING DIAGNOSES WITH INTERVENTIONS

## Discussion of Potential Nursing Diagnoses

There are many areas in a person's life that can be severely affected by depression. **Risk for Self-Directed Violence** is the number one priority for assessment and intervention. **Risk for Suicide** is a concern for people who have a variety of psychiatric disorders (schizophrenia, bipolar disorder, substance abuse, borderline personality disorder), as well as medical disorders and syndromes. Refer to Chapter 16.

Depression drastically affects a person's life and often affects cognitive ability. Poor concentration, lack of judgment, and difficulties with memory can all affect cognitive abilities **(Disturbed Thought Processes).** Feelings of self-worth plummet **(Chronic Low Self-Esteem),** and ability to gain strength from usual religious activities dwindles **(Spiritual Distress).** Feelings of hopelessness are common. Most noticeably, the ability to interact and gain solace from others is markedly reduced **(Impaired Social Interaction).**

The vegetative signs of depression can lead to physical complications such as lack of sleep **(Disturbed Sleep Pattern),** change in eating patterns **(Imbalanced Nutrition),** and change in elimination (most often **Constipation,** although diarrhea can also occur in agitated patients). Therefore, **Self-Care Deficit** is often an obvious occurrence.

Table 6-1 identifies some potential nursing diagnoses for depressed patients.

Table 6-1 **Potential Nursing Diagnoses for Depressive Disorders**

| Signs and Symptoms | Potential Nursing Diagnoses |
|---|---|
| Previous suicide attempts, putting affairs in order, giving away prized possessions, suicidal ideation (has a plan and the ability to carry it out), makes overt or covert statements regarding killing self, feelings of worthlessness, hopelessness, helplessness | **Risk for Self-Directed Violence** **Risk for Self-Mutilation** **Risk for Suicide** |

*Continued*

Table 6-1 **Potential Nursing Diagnoses for Depressive Disorders—cont'd**

| Signs and Symptoms | Potential Nursing Diagnoses |
| --- | --- |
| Lack of judgment, memory difficulty, poor concentration, inaccurate interpretation of environment, negative ruminations, cognitive distortions | **Disturbed Thought Processes** |
| Difficulty with simple tasks, inability to function at previous level, poor problem solving, poor cognitive functioning, verbalizations of inability to cope | **Ineffective Coping Interrupted Family Processes Risk for Impaired Parenting Ineffective Role Performance** |
| Difficulty making decisions, poor concentration, inability to take action | **Decisional Conflict** |
| Feelings of helplessness, hopelessness, powerlessness | **Hopelessness Powerlessness** |
| Questions meaning of life, own existence; unable to participate in usual religious practices, conflict over spiritual beliefs, anger toward spiritual deity or religious representatives | **Spiritual Distress Impaired Religiosity** |
| Feelings of worthlessness, poor self-image, negative sense of self, self-negating verbalizations, feels like a failure, expressions of shame or guilt, hypersensitive to slights or criticism | **Chronic Low Self-Esteem Situational Low Self-Esteem** |
| Withdrawn, uncommunicative, speaks only in monosyllables, shies away from contact with others | **Impaired Social Interaction Social Isolation Risk for Loneliness** |
| Vegetative signs of depression: changes in sleep, eating, grooming and hygiene, elimination, sexual patterns | **Self-Care Deficit (bathing/ hygiene, dressing/ grooming, feeding, toileting) Imbalanced Nutrition Disturbed Sleep Pattern Constipation Sexual Dysfunction** |

The section that identifies specific nursing diagnoses, goals, and interventions is useful when working with depressed patients and targeting discrete problems. However, the following overall guidelines are important throughout your work with depressed patients.

## Overall Guidelines for Nursing Interventions

### Depression

1. Convey caring, empathy, and potential for change by spending time with the patient, even in silence, anticipating patient's needs.
2. **The instillation of hope is a key tool for recovery.**
3. Enhance the person's sense of self by highlighting past accomplishments and strengths.
4. Whether in the hospital or in the community:
   - Assess needs for self-care and offer support when appropriate.
   - Monitor and intervene to help maintain adequate nutrition, hydration, and elimination.
   - Monitor and intervene to help provide adequate balance of rest, sleep, and activity.
   - Monitor and record increases/decreases in symptoms and which nursing interventions are effective.
   - Involve the patient's support system and find supports for the patient and family members in the community that are appropriate to their needs.
5. The dysfunctional attitude or learned helplessness and hopelessness seen with depressed people can be alleviated through cognitive therapy or other psychotherapeutic interventions.
6. **Continuously assess for the possibility of suicidal thoughts and ideation throughout the patient's course of recovery.** (See Chapter 16, Suicide.)
7. Primary depression is a medical disease. People respond well to psychopharmacology and electroconvulsive therapy (ECT). Be sure patients and those closely involved with them understand the nature of the disease and have written information about the specific medications the patient is taking. **Psychoeducation and a support system are essential.**

8. Assess family's and significant others' needs for teaching, counseling, self-help groups, knowledge of community resources.

## Selected Nursing Diagnoses and Nursing Care Plans

The following section offers key nursing diagnoses, goals, and nursing interventions that can help practitioners plan care for depressed patients.

### RISK FOR SELF-DIRECTED VIOLENCE*

At risk for behaviors in which an individual demonstrates that he/she can be physically, emotionally, and/or sexually harmful to self

### *Some Related/Risk Factors (Related To)*

▲ Emotional problems (hopelessness, despair, increased anxiety, panic, anger, hostility)
▲ Impulsivity
▲ History of violence to self or others
▲ Mental health problems (severe depression, psychosis, severe personality disorder, eating disorder, addictions)
▲ Lack of social resources (e.g., poor rapport, socially isolated, unresponsive family)
● Psychotic symptoms (command hallucinations, paranoid delusion, illogical thought)

### *Some Defining Characteristics (As Evidenced By)*

Assessment Findings/Diagnostic Cues:
▲ Behavioral clues (e.g., writing, giving away personal items, making a will, taking out a large insurance policy, etc.)

---

*Refer to Chapter 16 for more detailed intervention for Risk for Suicide.

▲ NANDA International accepted; ● In addition to NANDA International

▲ Suicidal behavior (attempts, talk, ideation, plan, available means)
  ○ Suicide plan (clear, specific, lethal method and available means)
  ○ Previous attempts
  ○ When depression begins to lift, patients may have energy to carry out a suicide plan
▲ Threatening gestures (verbal, actual) toward others

## Outcome Criteria

● Behavioral manifestations of depression are absent
● Satisfaction with social circumstances and achievement of life goals
● Seeks help when experiencing self-destructive/other-destructive impulses

## Long-Term Goals

Patient will:
● Demonstrate alternative ways of dealing with negative feelings and emotional stress by (date)
● Identify supports and support groups with whom he/she is in contact within 1 month
● State that he/she wants to live
● Start working on constructive plans for the future
● Demonstrate adherence with any medication or treatment plan within 2 weeks

## Short-Term Goals

Patients will:
● Not harm self or others
● Identify at least two people he/she can call for support and emotional guidance when he/she is feeling self-destructive before discharge

---

▲ NANDA International accepted; ● In addition to NANDA International

## *Interventions and Rationales*

| Intervention | Rationale |
|---|---|
| 1. Determine level of suicide precautions needed. If high, does patient need hospitalization? If low, will patient be safe to go home with supervision from a friend or family member? For example, does patient:<br>• Have a suicide plan<br>• Admit previous suicide attempts<br>• Abuse substances<br>• Have no friends | 1. A high-risk patient will need constant supervision and a safe environment. |
| 2. Does patient have more than a week's supply of medication? | 2. Usually, when a patient is suicidal, medication supply should be limited to 3 to 5 days. |
| 3. Encourage patients to talk freely about feelings (anger, disappointments), and help patient plan alternative ways to handle anger and frustration. | 3. Patient can learn alternative ways of dealing with overwhelming emotions and gain a sense of control over his/her life. |
| 4. Implement a written no-suicide contract if appropriate. | 4. Reinforces action the patient can take when feeling suicidal. |
| 5. Contact family, arrange for crisis counseling. Activate links to self-help groups. | 5. Patients need a network of resources to help diminish personal feelings of worthlessness, isolation, and helplessness. |
| 6. If hospitalized, follow unit protocols. | 6. Refer to Chapter 16 for detailed interventions for the suicidal patient in either the hospital or community. |

## DISTURBED THOUGHT PROCESSES

A state in which an individual experiences a disruption in cognitive operations and activities

## Some Related Factors (Related To)

▲ Severe anxiety or depressed mood
▲ Biochemical/neurophysical imbalances
▲ Overwhelming life circumstances
▲ Persistent feelings of extreme anxiety, guilt, or fear
▲ Biological/medical factors
▲ Prolonged grief reaction

## Some Defining Characteristics (As Evidenced By)

Assessment findings/diagnostic cues:

▲ Memory deficit/problems
▲ Inaccurate interpretation of the environment
▲ Hypovigilance
▲ Inappropriate thinking
● Impaired perception, judgment, decision making
● Impaired attention span/easily distracted
● Impaired ability to grasp ideas or order thoughts
● Negative ruminations
● Impaired insight
● Decreased problem-solving abilities

## Outcome Criteria

● Recalls recent and remote information accurately
● Processes information and makes appropriate decisions
● Exhibits organized thought process

## Long-Term Goals

Patient will:

● Give examples showing that short-term memory and concentration have improved to usual levels by (date)
● Demonstrate an increased ability to make appropriate decisions when planning with nurse by (date)
● Identify negative thoughts and rationally counter them and/or reframe them in a positive manner within 2 weeks
● Show improved mood as demonstrated by a standard depression rating scale (e.g. Zungs).

---

▲ NANDA International accepted; ● In addition to NANDA International

## Short-Term Goals

Patient will:
- Remember to keep appointments, attend activities, and attend to grooming with minimal reminders from others within 1 to 3 weeks
- Identify two goals he or she wants to achieve from treatment, with aid of nursing intervention, within 1 to 2 days
- Discuss with nurse two irrational thoughts about self and others by the end of the first day
- Reframe three irrational thoughts with nurse by (date)

## Interventions and Rationales

| Intervention | Rationale |
|---|---|
| 1. Identify patient's previous level of cognitive functioning (from patient, family, friends, previous medical records). | 1. Establishing a baseline of ability allows for evaluation of patient's progress. |
| 2. Help patient postpone making important major life decisions. | 2. Making rational major life decisions requires optimal psycho-physiological functioning. |
| 3. Minimize patient's responsibilities while he/she is severely depressed. | 3. Decreases feelings of pressure and anxiety and minimizes feelings of guilt. |
| 4. Use simple, concrete words. | 4. Slowed thinking and difficulty concentrating impair comprehension. |
| 5. Allow patient plenty of time to think and frame responses. | 5. Slowed thinking necessitates time to formulate a response. |
| 6. Help patient and significant others structure an environment that can help reestablish set schedules and predictable routines during severe depression. | 6. A routine that is fairly repetitive and nondemanding is easier to both follow and remember. |

**Intervention**

7. Allow more time than usual for patient to finish usual activities of daily living (ADL) (e.g., dressing, eating).

8. Work with patient to recognize negative thinking and thoughts. Teach patient to reframe and/or refute negative thoughts.

**Rationale**

7. Usual tasks might take long periods of time; demands for patient to hurry only increase anxiety and slow down ability to think clearly.

8. Negative ruminations add to feelings of hopelessness and are part of a depressed person's faulty thought processes. Intervening in this process aids in a healthier and more useful outlook.

## CHRONIC LOW SELF-ESTEEM

Longstanding negative self-evaluation/feelings about self or self-capabilities

### *Some Related Factors (Related To)*

▲ Perceived lack of respect from others
▲ Repeated past failures
▲ Repeated negative reinforcement
● Biochemical/neurophysiological imbalances
● Impaired cognitive self-appraisal
● Unrealistic expectations of self

### *Defining Characteristics (As Evidenced By)*

Assessment findings/diagnostic cues:
▲ Rejects positive feedback about self
▲ Self-negating verbalizations/negative view of abilities
▲ Evaluation of self as unable to deal with events
▲ Expression of shame and/or guilt

---

▲ NANDA International accepted; ● In addition to NANDA International

- Repeated expressions of worthlessness
- Inability to recognize own achievements

## Outcome Criteria

- Expresses belief in self
- Demonstrates a zest for life and ability to enjoy the present
- Maintains self-esteem

## Long-Term Goals

Patient will:

- Give an accurate and nonjudgmental account of four positive qualities and identify two areas he or she wishes to improve by (date)
- Demonstrate the ability to modify unrealistic self-expectations by (date)
- Report decreased feelings of shame, guilt, and self-hate by using a scale of 1 to 10 (1 lowest, 10 highest)

## Short-Term Goals

Patient will:

- Identify one or two strengths by the end of the day
- Identify two unrealistic self-expectations and reformulate more realistic life goals with nurse by the end of the day
- Keep a daily log and identify on a scale of 1 to 10 (1 lowest, 10 highest) feelings of shame, guilt, self-hate
- Identify three judgmental terms patient uses to describe self (e.g., "I am lazy"), and identify objective terms to replace them (e.g., "I do not feel motivated to") by (date)

## Interventions and Rationales

| Intervention | Rationale |
|---|---|
| 1. Work with the patient to identify cognitive distortions that encourage negative self-appraisal. For example: | 1. Cognitive distortions reinforce negative, inaccurate perception of self and the world. |

---

▲ NANDA International accepted; ● In addition to NANDA International

| Intervention | Rationale |
|---|---|
| a. Overgeneralizations | a. Taking one fact or event and making a general rule of it ("He always"; "I never") |
| b. Self-blame | b. Consistent self-blame for everything perceived as negative. |
| c. Mind reading | c. Assuming others "do not like me," for example, without any real evidence that assumptions are correct. |
| d. Discounting positive attributes | d. Focusing on negative qualities |
| 2. Teach visualization techniques that help patient replace negative self-images with more positive thoughts and images. | 2. Promotes a healthier and more realistic self-image by helping the patient choose more positive actions and thoughts. |
| 3. Work with patient on areas that he or she would like to improve using problem-solving skills. Evaluate need for more teaching in this area. | 3. Feelings of low self-esteem can interfere with usual problem-solving abilities. |
| 4. Evaluate patient's need for assertiveness training tools to pursue things he or she wants or needs in life. Arrange for training through community-based programs, personal counseling, literature, etc. | 4. People with low self-esteem often feel unworthy and have difficulty asking appropriately for what they need and want. |
| 5. Role model assertiveness. | 5. Patients can follow examples. |
| 6. Encourage participation in a support/therapy group where others are experiencing similar thoughts, feelings, and situations. | 6. Decrease feelings of isolation and provide an atmosphere where positive feedback and a more realistic appraisal of self are available. |

## SPIRITUAL DISTRESS

Impaired ability to experience and integrate meaning and purpose in life through a person's connectedness with self, others, art, music, literature, nature, or a power greater than oneself

### Some Related Factors (Related To)

▲ Self-alienation
▲ Sociocultural deprivation
▲ Death or dying of self or others
▲ Chronic illness of self or others
▲ Life changes
▲ Pain
● Lack of purpose and meaning in life

### Some Defining Characteristics (As Evidenced By)

▲ Expresses lack of hope, meaning, or purpose in life, forgiveness of self, peace/serenity, acceptance
▲ Questions meaning of own existence
▲ Refuses interactions with friends/families/religious leaders
▲ Expresses concern with meaning of life/death or belief systems
▲ Expresses being abandoned by or having anger toward God
▲ Unable to participate in usual religious practices
▲ Inability to pray
▲ Expresses hopelessness and helplessness
● Inability to express previous state of creativity (e.g., singing, listening to music, writing)

### Outcome Criteria

● Expression of purpose and meaning in life
● Participates in spiritual rites and passages
● Connectedness with others to share thoughts, feelings, and beliefs
● Connectedness with inner self

---

▲ NANDA International accepted; ● In addition to NANDA International

## *Long-Term Goals*

Patient will:
- State that he/she gained comfort from previous spiritual practices by (date)
- State that he/she feels a sense of forgiveness by (date)
- State that he/she wants to participate in former creative activities by (date)

## *Short-Term Goals*

Patient will:
- Talk to nurse or spiritual leader about spiritual conflicts and concerns within 3 days
- Discuss with nurse two things that gave his or her life meaning in the past within 3 days
- Keep a journal tracking thoughts and feelings for 1 week

## *Interventions and Rationales*

| Intervention | Rationale |
|---|---|
| 1. Assess what spiritual practices have offered comfort and meaning to the patient's life when not ill. | 1. Evaluates neglected areas in the person's life that, if reactivated, might add comfort and meaning during a painful depression. |
| 2. Discuss what has given meaning and comfort to the patient in the past. | 2. When depressed, patients often struggle for meaning in life and reasons to go on when feeling hopeless and despondent. |
| 3. Encourage patient to write in a journal every day, expressing daily thoughts and reflections. | 3. Helps some to identify significant personal issues and thoughts and feelings surrounding spiritual issues. Journal writing is an excellent way to explore deeper meanings of life. |
| 4. If patient is unable to write, have patient use a tape recorder. | 4. Often, speaking aloud helps a person clarify thinking and explore issues. |

| **Intervention** | **Rationale** |
|---|---|
| 5. Provide information on referrals, when needed, for religious or spiritual information (e.g., readings, programs, tapes, community resources). | 5. When hospitalized, spiritual tapes and readings can be useful; when the patient is in the community, patient might express other needs. |
| 6. Suggest that the spiritual leader affiliated with the facility contact patient. | 6. Spiritual leaders in an institution or community are familiar with spiritual distress and might offer comfort to patient. |

## IMPAIRED SOCIAL INTERACTION

Insufficient or excessive quantity or ineffective quality of social exchange

### Some Related Factors (Related To)

▲ Self-concept disturbance (negative view of self)
▲ Absence of available significant others/peers (support system deficit)
▲ Disturbed thought processes
▲ Self-concept disturbance
● Fear of rejection
● Feelings of worthlessness
● Anergia (lack of energy and motivation)

### Some Defining Characteristics (As Evidenced By)

▲ Discomfort in social situations verbalized or observed (e.g., inability to receive or communicate a satisfying sense of belonging, caring, interest, or shared history)
▲ Family reports change of style or patterns of interaction
● Dysfunctional interaction with peers, family, and/or others
● Remains secluded, lacks eye contact, and avoids contact with others

---

▲ NANDA International accepted; ● In addition to NANDA International

## Outcome Criteria
- Interacts with family/friends/neighbors
- Participation in community activities (e.g., church member, club officer, volunteer group, leisure activity)
- Performance of premorbid role behaviors

## Long-Term Goals
Patient will:
- State and demonstrate progress in the resumption of sustaining relationships with friends and family members within 1 month
- State that he/she enjoys interacting with others in activities and one-to-one interactions to the extent they did before becoming depressed by (date)

## Short-Term Goals
Patient will:
- Participate in one activity by the end of each day
- Discuss three alternative actions to take when feeling the need to withdraw by (date)
- Identify two personal behaviors that might discourage others from seeking contact by (date)
- Eventually voluntarily attend individual/group therapeutic meetings within a therapeutic milieu (hospital or community) by (date)

## Interventions and Rationales

| Intervention | Rationale |
|---|---|
| 1. While patient is most severely depressed, involve the patient in one-to-one activity. | 1. Maximizes the potential for interactions while minimizing anxiety levels. |
| 2. Engage the patient in activities involving gross motor activity that call for limited concentration (e.g., taking a walk). | 2. Physical activities can help relieve tensions and might help to elevate mood. |
| 3. Initially, provide activities that require | 3. Concentration and memory are poor in |

| Intervention | Rationale |
|---|---|
| very little concentration (e.g., playing simple card games, looking through a magazine, drawing). | depressed people. Activities that have no "right or wrong" or "winners or losers" minimize opportunities for self-diminishment. |
| 4. Eventually increase the patient's contacts with others (first one other, then two others, etc.). | 4. Contact with others distracts the patient from self-preoccupation. |
| 5. Eventually involve the patient in group activities (e.g., dance therapy, art therapy, group discussions). | 5. Socialization decreases feelings of isolation. Genuine regard for others can increase self-worth. |
| 6. Refer both patient and family to self-help groups in the community. | 6. Both patient and family can gain tremendous support and insight from people through sharing their experiences. |

## SELF-CARE DEFICIT (SPECIFY LEVEL)

Impaired ability to perform or complete bathing/hygiene, dressing/grooming, feeding, or toileting activities for oneself

### Some Related Factors (Related To)

▲ Perceptual or cognitive impairment
▲ Decreased or lack of motivation (anergia)
▲ Severe anxiety
▲ Fatigue
▲ Severe preoccupation

### Some Defining Characteristics (As Evidenced By)

● Consuming insufficient food or nutrients to meet minimum daily requirements
● Decreased ability to function secondary to sleep deprivation

---

▲ NANDA International accepted; ● In addition to NANDA International

- Weight loss
- Body odor/hair unwashed and unkempt
- Clothes dirty, disheveled, mismatched etc.
- Inability to organize simple steps in hygiene and grooming
- Constipation related to lack of exercise, roughage in diet, and poor fluid intake

## Outcome Criteria

- Performs all tasks of self-care consistently (all ADL)
- Experiences normal elimination
- Sleeps 6 to 8 hours a night without medication
- Appears groomed and dressed clean and appropriate

## Long-Term Goals

Patient will:
- Gradually return to weight consistent for height and age or baseline before illness by (date)
- Sleep between 6 and 8 hours per night within 1 month
- Demonstrate progress in the maintenance of adequate hygiene and be appropriately groomed and dressed (shave/makeup, clothes clean and neat) by (date)
- Experience normal elimination with the aid of diet, fluids, and exercise within 3 weeks

## Short-Term Goals

Patient will:
- Gain 1 pound a week with encouragement from family, significant others, and/or staff if significant weight loss exists
- Sleep between 4 and 6 hours with aid of medication and/or nursing measures
- Groom and dress appropriately with help from nursing staff and/or family
- Regain more normal elimination pattern with aid of foods high in roughage, increased fluids, and daily exercise (also with aid of medications)

---

▲ NANDA International accepted; ● In addition to NANDA International

## *Interventions and Rationales*

| Intervention | Rationale |
|---|---|

**Imbalanced Nutrition**

1. Encourage small, high-calorie, high-protein snacks and fluids frequently throughout the day and evening if weight loss exists.

   1. Minimize weight loss, dehydration, and constipation.

2. Encourage eating with others.

   2. Increase socialization, decrease focus on food.

3. Serve foods or drinks the patient likes.

   3. Patients are more likely to eat the foods they like.

4. Weigh the patient weekly and observe the patient's eating patterns.

   4. Give the information needed for revising the intervention.

**Disturbed Sleep Pattern**

1. Provide rest periods after activities.

   1. Fatigue can intensify feelings of depression.

2. Encourage the patient to get up and dress and to stay out of bed during the day.

   2. Minimizing sleep during the day increases the likelihood of sleep at night.

3. Encourage relaxation measures in the evening (e.g., backrub, tepid bath, or warm milk).

   3. These measures induce relaxation and sleep.

4. Reduce environmental and physical stimulants in the evening; provide decaffeinated coffee, soft lights, soft music, and quiet activities.

   4. Decreasing caffeine and epinephrine levels increases the possibility of sleep.

5. Teach relaxation exercises (see Chapter 5).

   5. Besides deeply relaxing the body, relaxation exercises often lead to sleep.

**Bathing/Hygiene Self-Care Deficit**

1. Encourage the use of toothbrush, washcloth, soap, makeup, shaving equipment, and so forth.

   1. Being clean and well groomed can temporarily raise self-esteem.

**Intervention**

2. Give step-by-step reminders, such as "Wash the right side of your face, now the left . . ."

**Constipation**
1. Monitor intake and output, especially bowel movements.

2. Offer foods high in fiber, and provide periods of exercise.

3. Encourage the intake of nonalcoholic/ noncaffeinated fluids, 6 to 8 glasses/day.

4. Evaluate the need for laxatives and enemas.

**Rationale**

2. Slowed thinking and difficulty concentrating make organizing simple tasks difficult.

1. Many depressed patients are constipated. If this condition is not checked, fecal impaction can occur.

2. Roughage and exercise stimulate peristalsis and help evacuation of fecal material.

3. Fluids help prevent constipation.

4. These prevent the occurrence of fecal impaction.

# MEDICAL TREATMENTS

## Psychopharmacology

Depression is a recurring disorder. About 50% to 60% of people with primary depression have multiple episodes. However, the discovery of effective antidepressants has resulted in depression being one of the most "treatable" disorders (Preston et al., 2008). It has been noted that:

- The majority of depression patients "respond" to antidepressant treatment.
- Roughly one-fourth (25%) to one-third (33%) of patients with a major depression fail to respond meaningfully to currently available treatment.
- **Waiting too long to start treatment can lead to:**
  - Greater morbidity
  - Greater disability
  - Greater expense
  - Greater resistance to treatment and increased potential for relapse

All depressed individuals need to be evaluated for suicide risk, whether they are in the hospital or the community. When a depressed person is hospitalized, staff members must check to make sure that all medications are swallowed (not placed in the cheek or under the tongue). To minimize the risk of a patient overdosing, if a severely depressed person is being treated in an outpatient setting, only a week's supply of medication should be given.

Antidepressant drugs can improve poor self-concept, degree of withdrawal, vegetative signs of depression, and activity level. The major types of antidepressant drugs are:

- Selective serotonin reuptake inhibitors (SSRIs)
- Tricyclic antidepressants (TCAs)
- Monoamine oxidase inhibitors (MAOIs)
- Novel (atypical) antidepressants

### Selective Serotonin Reuptake Inhibitors

SSRIs are recommended as first-line therapy in all depressions except severe inpatient depression (in which electroconvulsive therapy [ECT] might be the first choice), melancholic depression, or mild outpatient depression.

SSRI antidepressant drugs have a lower incidence of anticholinergic side effects (dry mouth, blurred vision, urinary retention), less cardiotoxicity, and faster onset than the TCAs. For most patients, the SSRIs are better tolerated than the TCAs. The SSRIs are also being used successfully with many individuals who have anxiety disorders and eating disorders. See Table 6-2 for a list of SSRIs and dosages. Refer to Chapter 21 for pharmacology and a guide to patient and family teaching for SSRIs.

### Tricyclic Antidepressants

TCAs benefit approximately 65% to 80% of people with nondelusional depressive disorders. It can take up to 10 to 14 days before these agents start to work. The full effect might not be seen for 4 to 8 weeks. As with all drugs, side effects and toxic effects can occur. As mentioned, the SSRIs are considered the drugs of choice.

People taking TCAs can have adverse reactions to numerous other medications. For example, use of an MAOI along with a TCA is contraindicated.

**Table 6-2 Adult Dosages for Antidepressants**

| Generic Name | Trade Name | Range of Usual Dose (mg/day) | Advantages of Selective Drugs | Disadvantages of Selective Drugs |
|---|---|---|---|---|
| **Tricyclic Antidepressants (TCAs)** | | | | |
| Amitriptyline | Elavil | 75–300 | | |
| Clomipramine | Anafranil | 75–200 | | |
| Desipramine | Norpramin | 75–300 | | |
| Doxepin | Sinequan | 75–300 | | |
| Imipramine | Tofranil | 75–300 | | |
| Maprotiline | Ludiomil | 75–225 | | |
| Nortriptyline | Pamelor | 50–150 | | |
| Protriptyline | Vivactil | 15–60 | | |
| Trimipramine | Surmontil | 75–300 | | |
| Amoxapine | Asendin | 150–400 | | |
| **Monoamine Oxidase Inhibitors (MAOIs)** | | | | |
| Isocarboxazid | Marplan | 20 | MAOIs potent in treating treatment-resistant depression | Interact with some drugs and food, causing severe to fatal results (HBP, stroke, death) **Special diet crucial.** (See Chapter 21.) |
| Phenelzine | Nardil | 30–90 | | |
| Tranylcypromine | Parnate | 20–60 | | |

*Continued*

Table 6-2 **Adult Dosages for Antidepressants—cont'd**

| Generic Name | Trade Name | Range of Usual Dose (mg/day)* | Advantages of Selective Drugs | Disadvantages of Selective Drugs |
|---|---|---|---|---|
| **Selective Serotonin Reuptake Inhibitors (SSRIs)** | | | | |
| Citalopram | Celexa | 10–60 | Minimal interaction with other drugs, weight gain, sedation | Possible initial anxiety |
| Escitalopram | Lexapro | 15–20 | Minimal interaction, sedation, and weight gain | Possible initial anxiety |
| Fluoxetine | Prozac | 20–80 | Energizing | Possible interaction with other drugs, anxiety |
| Fluvoxamine | Luvox | 50–300 | | |
| Paroxetine | Paxil | 20–60 | Good antianxiety benefit | Weight gain, interacts with other meds |
| Sertraline | Zoloft | 50–200 | Not too sedating, not prone to increase anxiety | Prone to GI upset |
| **Atypical Antidepressants** | | | | |
| Bupropion | Wellbutrin | 150–400 | Energizing, few sexual side effects, less weight gain | Can cause seizures at doses over 400 mg; possible increase in anxiety/insomnia |
| Trazodone | Desyrel | | | |

**Dual Action Reuptake Inhibitors (Serotonin and Norepinephrine) (SNRIs)**

| | | | |
|---|---|---|---|
| Mirtazapine | Remeron | 15–45 | Good for severe depression, insomnia, less sexual dysfunction | High weight gain and sedation |
| Duloxetine | Cymbalta | 20–100 | Good for severe depression | Possible nausea, sedation |
| Venlafaxine | Effexor | 75–300 | Good for severe depression, social anxiety, GAD | Possible HBP, GI upset |

**Selective Norepinephrine Reuptake Inhibitors (SNRIs)**

| | | | |
|---|---|---|---|
| Atomoxetine | Strattera | 60–120 | Good for cognitive symptoms, low SE profile | Possible sedation and/or anxiety |
| Reboxetine | Vestra | 2–8 | | |

* Doses for children and adolescents are different.
† Doses listed are average daily doses from low to high. Depending on the drug and the patient, the total dose might be given in a single dose or in divided doses.
‡ Doses higher than these might be needed for some people with severe depression.
From Lehne RA. (2004). Preston et al., 2008, Preston and Johnson, 2009.

Patients and families should be aware of the side effects and toxic effects of the medications, as well as other relevant information. This information should be written down and given to the family and patient once teaching is complete. See Table 6-2 for a list of TCAs and dosages. Refer to Chapter 21 for pharmacology and a guide to patient and family teaching for the TCAs.

## Monoamine Oxidase Inhibitors

These drugs are usually *not* first-line drugs because of their serious side effects, one being that they interact with foods containing tyramine, a natural product of bacterial fermentation found in many cheeses, some wines, and chopped liver, as well as certain medications, including sympathomimetic amines. The interaction results in a hypertensive crisis that can cause a stroke or even death.

Because these drugs have the danger of hypertensive crisis, they are usually contraindicated for people who are debilitated, elderly, or hypertensive; those who have cardiac or cerebrovascular disease; those who have severe renal and hepatic disease; and those unwilling or unable to adhere to dietary restrictions.

Patient teaching is as important with these drugs as with all others, perhaps even more so because of the danger of hypertensive crisis with tyramine-containing foods and with medications. Patients and their families should know contraindicated foods and drugs and be taught to read food labels very carefully; tyramine-containing foods might be present as an ingredient. Patients should also be told that before they take *any* over-the-counter medication, they should first check with their physician. See Table 6-2 for a list of MAOIs and dosages. Refer to Chapter 21 for pharmacology, a list of "forbidden" foods, and patient and family teaching.

## Novel (Atypical) Antidepressants

Novel (atypical) antidepressants are among a group of drugs that differ structurally or in their pharmacological action from the medications in the categories mentioned earlier. Included in this group are trazodone (Desyrel), nefazodone (Serzone), bupropion (Wellbutrin), venlafaxine (Effexor), mirtazapine (Remeron), reboxetine (Vestra), and atomoxetine (Strattera). See Table 6-2 for a list of atypical antidepressants and dosages. Refer to Chapter 21 for further discussion of the atypical antidepressants and for more on antidepressants in general.

### Electroconvulsive Therapy

ECT is the gold standard for severe (psychotic) depressions and for treatment-resistant depressions. ECT is most effective in depression with psychotic features, catatonic stupor, severe suicidality, extreme mania, or when self-starvation is present (Preston et al., 2008).

Essentially, ECT is the use of electrically induced repetitive firings of the neurons in the central nervous system. Electrodes are placed on the patient's temples (either bilaterally or unilaterally), and they are given a well-measured electric shock. These electrical firings cause grand mal seizures in the brain. Patients are under a short-acting anesthesia and given a muscle-paralyzing agent to help prevent fractures. A course of ECT for depressed patients is approximately 6 to 12 treatments given two or three times per week. See Appendix F for a better understanding of the actual procedure and the nursing responsibilities involved in ECT.

ECT can terminate an ongoing episode of depression; therefore, some people greatly benefit from "maintenance" treatments on a weekly or monthly basis to prevent recurrence. ECT improves mood quite rapidly, so antidepressant medications, antipsychotic medications (if psychosis is present), and mood stabilizers in case of mania. The chief side effects of ECT are cognitive. Treatment is most often associated with transient confusional states after single treatments and with a longer period of anterograde and retrograde memory interference (APA, 2000b).

Depressed patients with various medical conditions might be at risk: patients with cardiovascular disease, increased intracranial pressure, or cerebrovascular fragility might be poor candidates and would require careful pretreatment medical work-up.

## INTEGRATED APPROACHES AND OVER-THE-COUNTER PRODUCTS

Accordingly to Preston and Johnson (2009), there are three products that have some research support for treating depression. Perhaps the best known of herbal remedies for depression is **St. John's wort**. St. John's wort has been reported in some studies to be effective for mild to moderate depression. The herb should not be taken in certain situations (e.g., major depression, pregnancy, or by children younger than 2 years [Fuller & Sajatovic, 2000]). St. John's wort is not regulated as a drug by the FDA. It has significant effects on liver metabolism and poses a danger of potentially harmful drug-drug interactions (Preston et al., 2009). For example, the combined use of St. John's wort can have harmful effects with digoxin, birth control pills, anesthesia, amphetamines and other stimulants, and all antidepressants.

**SAM-e (S-adenosylmethionine),** a synthetic form of a chemical produced naturally in the body, is also proposed to be of possible benefit for depression. To date, the benefits and long-term risks remain unclear (UC Berkeley Wellness Letter, 2005). One important problem with SAM-e is that it is converted into homocystine in the body, and high levels of homocystine appear to raise the risk of heart disease (UC Berkeley Wellness Letter, 2004). SAM-e should be used with caution in persons with bipolar disorder, because it may induce mania. It should not be taken with any other serotonin-enhancing drugs, since it may increase the risk of serotonin syndrome. Check out **consumerlab.com** for reputable brands of herbal and dietary supplements.

# NURSE, PATIENT, and FAMILY RESOURCES

## ASSOCIATIONS

**National Alliance for the Mentally Ill (NAMI)**
Colonial Place Three
2107 Wilson Boulevard, Suite 300
Arlington, VA 22201-3042
(800) 950-NAMI
www.nami.com

**Depressed Anonymous: Recovery from Depression**
http://www.nami.org
PO Box 17471
Louisville, KY 40217
(502) 569-1989
www.depressedanon.com

**National Foundation for Depressive Illness, Inc**.
PO Box 2257
New York, NY 10016
(800) 239-1265
www.depression.org

**National Organization for Seasonal Affective Disorders (NOSAD)**
PO Box 40190
Washington, DC 20016

**Depression and Bipolar Support Alliance**
730 N. Franklin, Suite 501
Chicago, IL 60610
(312) 642-0049
www.dbsalliance.org

# INTERNET SITES

**Depression Central**
www.psycom.net/depression.central.html

**Depression.com**
www.depression.com
Great general source

**Internet Mental Health**
www.mentalhealth.com
Great resource for everything

**NIMH: Depression**
www.nimh.nih.gov/publicat/depression.cfm

# CHAPTER 7

# Bipolar Disorders

## OVERVIEW

Bipolar disorders are serious neurobiological disorders that often leave people destitute, shatter friendships, family, and partner relationships, and result in jobs lost. They are a group of disorders with different courses and treatments. Simplistically stated, *bipolar disorders* are mood disorders that include one or more episodes of mania or hypomania (elevated, expansive, or irritable mood) and usually one or more depressive episodes. These disorders are essentially related to biochemical imbalances in the brain, and the disease is thought to be genetically transferred. Medication adherence is key if nursing and counseling interventions are to be effective.

An acute or severe manic phase usually warrants hospitalization. A person experiencing hypomania, however, rarely needs hospitalization unless there is a danger to self or others.

Bipolar disorders consist of three different categories of disorders: **(1) cyclothymia, (2) bipolar disorder (bipolar I and bipolar II)**, and **(3) bipolar disorder not otherwise specified.** The symptoms seen in bipolar disorder I and II are more serious than those seen in cyclothymia.

### Cyclothymia

*Cyclothymia* is a chronic mood disturbance of at least 2 years duration with the recurrent experience of some of the symptoms of *hypomania* alternating with *dysthymic depression*. People with cyclothymia *do not* have severe impairment in their social or occupational functioning, nor do they experience psychotic symptoms such as delusions.

## Bipolar Disorder (Bipolar I and Bipolar II)

The manic episode in bipolar I might begin suddenly and last a few days to months. There can be impairments in reality testing; when severe, these impairments can take the form of grandiose or persecutory *delusions*. Considerable impairment in social, occupational, and interpersonal functioning exists. Hospitalization is often required to protect the person from the consequences of poor judgment and hyperactivity. **Bipolar disorder is classified as a severe, biologically based mental illness by medical science,** in conjunction with the *Diagnostic and Statistical Manual of Mental Disorders* (4th edition, text revision) (*DSM-IV-TR*).

**Bipolar I** consists of one or more episodes of *major depression* plus one or more periods of clear-cut *mania*.

**Bipolar II** consists of one or more periods of *major depression* plus at least one *hypomanic episode*.

The distinction between hypomania and mania is made clear for diagnostic purposes in the *DSM-IV-TR* and is presented in Box 7-1.

| Box 7-1 | ***DSM-IV-TR***<br>**Criteria for Manic Episode and<br>Hypomanic Episode** |
| --- | --- |

1. A distinct period of abnormality and persistently elevated, expansive, or irritable mood for at least:
   - 4 days for hypomania
   - 1 week for mania
2. During the period of mood disturbance, **at least three (or more)** of the following symptoms have persisted (four if the mood is only irritable) and have been present to a significant degree:
   - Inflated self-esteem or grandiosity
   - Decreased need for sleep (e.g., the person feels rested after only 3 hours of sleep)

*Continued*

| Box 7-1 | *DSM-IV-TR*<br>**Criteria for Manic Episode and Hypomanic Episode—cont'd** |
|---|---|

- Increased talkativeness or pressure to keep talking
- Flight of ideas or subjective experience that thoughts are racing
- Distractibility (i.e., the person's attention is too easily drawn to unimportant or irrelevant external stimuli)
- Increase in goal-directed activity (either socially, at work or school, or sexually) or psychomotor agitation
- Excessive involvement in pleasurable activities that have a high potential for painful consequences (e.g., the person engages in unrestrained buying sprees, sexual indiscretions, or foolish business investments)

**Hypomania**
1. The episode is associated with an unequivocal change in functioning that is uncharacteristic of the person when not symptomatic.
2. Absence of marked impairment in social or occupational functioning
3. Delusions are never present.
4. Hospitalization is not indicated.

**Mania**
1. Severe enough to cause marked impairment in occupational activities, usual social activities, or relationships
   *or*
2. Hospitalization is needed to protect patient and others from irresponsible or aggressive behavior
   *or*
3. There are psychotic features (e.g., grandiose and/or paranoid delusions)

Adapted from American Psychiatric Association (APA). (2000). *Diagnostic and statistical manual of mental disorders* (4th ed., text rev.) (*DSM-IV-TR*). Washington DC: Author, pp. 362, 368; reprinted with permission.

Bipolar disorder can be grouped into three phases:

1. **Acute Phase**—Hospitalization is usually indicated for a patient in the acute manic or severe manic phase of bipolar disorder (particularly bipolar I). Hospitalization protects patients from harm (cardiac collapse, financial loss) and allows time for medication stabilization.
2. **Continuation Phase**—Usually lasts for 4 to 9 months, and the goal during this phase is to prevent relapse.
3. **Maintenance Treatment Phase**—Aimed at preventing the recurrence of an episode of bipolar illness.

Many of the interventions in this chapter address the patient in the acute phase, because that is the phase that often requires hospitalization and immediate and complex nursing care. A thorough physical work up will most likely identify medical conditions associated with mania and/or drugs (prescription, over the counter, recreational) that can induce mania.

# ASSESSMENT

## Presenting Signs and Symptoms

- Periods of hyperactivity (pacing, restlessness, accelerated actions)
- Overconfident, exaggerated view of own abilities
- Decreased need for sleep, no acknowledgment of fatigue
- Poor social judgment, engaging in reckless and self-destructive activities (foolish business ventures, sexual indiscretions, buying sprees)
- Rapid-fire speech; pressured speech; loud, garrulous, rhyming or punning
- Brief attention span, easily distractible, flights of ideas, loosened associations, delusions
- Expansive, irritable, or paranoid behaviors
- Impatient, uncooperative, abusive, obscene, manipulative

## Assessment Tools

See Appendix D-4 for a questionnaire for mania. Patients might want to take this test frequently to monitor symptoms.

**Assessment Guidelines**

Assessment will, of course, include identification of manic symptoms (Appendix D-4) and depressive symptoms (Appendix D-3). However, there are very important areas that need to be identified to secure safety, not just for the patient, but perhaps others as well. Important overall assessment guidelines follow.

*Elated-Phase Bipolar*

1. Assess if patient is a danger to self or others:
   - Manic patients can exhaust themselves to the point of death.
   - Patient might not eat or sleep for days at a time.
   - Poor impulse control might result in harm to others or self.
   - Uncontrolled spending.
2. Patients might give away all of their money or possessions, so might need controls to protect them from bankruptcy.
3. Assess for need for hospitalization to safeguard and stabilize patient.
4. Assess medical status. A thorough medical examination helps determine if mania is primary (a mood disorder—bipolar/cyclothymia) or secondary to another condition. Mania can be:
   - Secondary to a general medical condition
   - Substance induced (use or abuse of drug, medication, or toxin exposure)
5. Assess the patient's and family's understanding of bipolar disorder, knowledge of medications, support groups, and organizations that provide information on bipolar disorder.

# NURSING DIAGNOSES WITH INTERVENTIONS

## Discussion of Potential Nursing Diagnoses

During an acutely or extremely manic episode, hospitalization is recommended to prevent physical exhaustion and to initiate and stabilize medication. The primary consideration is the prevention of exhaustion and death from cardiac collapse. Because of the patient's poor judgment, excessive and constant motor activity, probable dehydration, and difficulty evaluating reality, the patient is at risk for injury **(Risk for Injury).**

Aggression is a common feature in mania. At times, intrusive and taunting behaviors can induce others to strike out against these patients. Conversely, when in a manic state, a patient might evidence inability to control behavior, and destructive, hostile, and aggressive behaviors (range reaction) might occur and pose danger to the well-being of others and/or property **(Risk for Violence: Self-Directed or Other Directed).**

Grandiosity and poor judgment can result in the patient giving away money and possessions indiscriminately, bankruptcy, and neglect of family. Patients might get involved in making foolish business deals or make impulsive major life changes (e.g., divorce, marriage, or career changes). Getting involved in impossible schemes, shady legal deals, and questionable business ventures can also be part of the picture. Because of the patient's grandiose thinking and extremely poor judgment, **Disturbed Thought Processes** are present. The behaviors that stem from the patient's faulty thinking usually result in **Ineffective Coping.**

Patients in the manic phase can be extremely manipulative, fault finding, and adept at exploiting other's vulnerabilities. They constantly push limits. Often the motivation for this manipulation is an attempt to gain a sense of control, when in fact the person is totally unable to control any aspect of his or her life—thoughts, feelings, and particularly behaviors. Therefore, **Defensive Coping** might be evidenced by the patient's manipulative, angry, and hostile verbal behaviors.

The families of individuals with bipolar disorder often experience extreme disruptions in their lives and might be in crises when their family member is in acute and severe mania. Infidelity and divorce is common; family savings might be wiped out and debt accumulated; relationships within the family unit might be strained beyond endurance; and friendships can be ruined. **Interrupted Family Processes** must always be assessed and information and referrals for support provided.

The patient in the acute or extreme manic state might have numerous unmet physical needs. The manic patient is too agitated and hyperactive to eat, sleep, or be appropriately groomed or dressed and can be constipated. Therefore, **Deficient Fluid Volume, Imbalanced Nutrition, Disturbed Sleep Pattern, Constipation, Dressing/Grooming Self-Care Deficit, and Bathing/Hygiene Self-Care Deficit** are all areas that need to be carefully assessed. When the patient is severely manic, the nurse could target interventions for all of the above using **Total Self-Care Deficit** (eating, sleeping, dressing/grooming, bathing/hygiene, bowel functioning).

Table 7-1 provides a list of potential nursing diagnoses.

Table 7-1 **Potential Nursing Diagnoses for Bipolar Disorder**

| Signs and Symptoms | Nursing Diagnoses |
|---|---|
| Excessive and constant motor activity | **Risk for Injury** |
| Poor judgment | |
| Lack of rest and sleep | |
| Poor nutritional intake (Excessive/relentless mix of above behaviors can lead to cardiac collapse.) | |
| Loud, profane, hostile, combative, aggressive, demanding | **Risk for Violence: Self-Directed or Other-Directed** |
| Intrusive and taunting behaviors | **Ineffective Coping** |
| Inability to control behavior | |
| Rage reaction | |
| Manipulative, angry, or hostile verbal and physical behaviors | **Defensive Coping** |
| Racing thoughts, grandiosity, poor judgment | **Disturbed Thought Processes** |
| | **Ineffective Coping** |
| Gives away valuables, neglects family, makes impulsive major life changes (divorce, career changes) | **Interrupted Family Processes** |
| | **Caregiver Role Strain** |
| Continuous, pressured speech jumping from topic to topic (flights of ideas) | **Impaired Verbal Communication** |

*Continued*

Table 7-1  **Potential Nursing Diagnoses for Bipolar Disorder—cont'd**

| Signs and Symptoms | Nursing Diagnoses |
| --- | --- |
| Constant motor activity, going from one person or event to another; might annoy or taunt others; speech loud and crass, provocative behaviors | Impaired Social Interaction |
| Too distracted, agitated, and disorganized to eat, groom, bathe, dress self | Imbalanced Nutrition: Less than Body Requirements |
| Too frantic and hyperactive to sleep; sleep deprivation can lead to exhaustion and death | Deficient Fluid Volume Self-Care Deficit (bathing/ hygiene, dressing/ grooming) Disturbed Sleep Pattern |

## Overall Guidelines for Nursing Interventions

Specific behaviors demonstrated by the manic patient should be addressed separately, as follows in this chapter. Overall guidelines that are effective with bipolar patients during periods of mania include:

### Elated-Phase Bipolar

1. Use a firm and calm approach.
2. Use short, concise explanations or statements.
3. Remain neutral, avoid power struggles.
4. Provide a consistent and structured environment.
5. Firmly redirect energy into appropriate and constructive channels.
6. Decrease environmental stimuli whenever possible.
7. Provide structured solitary activities; tasks that take minimal concentration are best. Avoid groups and stimulating activities until patient can tolerate that level of activity.
8. Spend one-on-one time with the patient if he/she is psychotic or anxious.
9. Provide frequent rest periods.
10. Provide high-calorie fluids and finger foods frequently throughout the day.

11. On a daily basis, monitor patient's:
    - Sleep pattern
    - Food intake
    - Elimination (constipation often a problem)
12. Teach patient and family about illness, and be sure patient has written information regarding his or her medications.
13. Ascertain that patient and family have information on supportive services in their community for further information and support.

## Selected Nursing Diagnoses and Nursing Care Plans

The following sections identify primary nursing diagnoses for use with a manic patient, particularly in the acute and severely manic phases of the illness. Included are specific nursing interventions that are appropriate for meeting outcome criteria for each diagnosis.

### RISK FOR INJURY

A risk of injury as a result of environmental conditions interacting with the individual's adaptive and defensive resources

### Some Related/Risk Factors (Related To)

Cognitive, affective, and psychomotor factors:
- ▲ Biochemical/neurological imbalances
- ● Extreme hyperactivity/physical agitation
- ● Rage reaction
- ● Dehydration and exhaustion

### Some Defining Characteristics (As Evidenced By)

Impaired judgment (reality testing, risk behavior):
- ● Excessive and constant motor activity—unable to rest for even short periods
- ● Lack of fluid ingestion/dehydration
- ● Abrasions, bruises, cuts from running/falling into objects

---

▲ NANDA International accepted; ● In addition to NANDA International

## Outcome Criteria

- Response to medication will have expected therapeutic effects
- Maintenance of therapeutic blood levels (0.6 to 1.2 mEq/L)
- Sustain optimum physical health through medication management and therapeutic regimen

## Long-Term Goals

Patient will:
- Be free of injury within 2 to 3 weeks:
  - Cardiac status stable
  - Well hydrated
  - Skin free of abrasions and scrapes
- Be free of excessive physical agitation and purposeless motor activity within 2 weeks
- Take short voluntary rest periods during the day by (date)

## Short-Term Goals

- Patient's cardiac status will remain stable while in the hospital
- While acutely manic, patient will drink 8 oz of fluid every hour throughout the day
- Patient will spend time with the nurse in a quiet environment three to four times a day between 7 AM and 11 PM with the aid of nursing guidance
- Patient will remain free from falls and abrasions every day while in the hospital
- Patient will be free of dangerous levels of hyperactive motor behavior with the aid of medications and nursing interventions within 24 hours

## Interventions and Rationales

| Intervention | Rationale |
|---|---|
| 1. Maintain low level of stimuli in patient's environment (e.g., away from loud noises, bright lights, and people). | 1. Helps decrease escalation of anxiety. |
| 2. Provide structured solitary activities with nurse or aide. | 2. Structure provides security and focus. |

| **Intervention** | **Rationale** |
|---|---|
| 3. Provide frequent high-calorie fluids. | 3. Prevents serious dehydration. |
| 4. Provide frequent rest periods. | 4. Prevents exhaustion. |
| 5. Redirect violent behavior. | 5. Physical exercise can decrease tension and provide focus. |
| 6. Acute mania might warrant the use of phenothiazines and seclusion to minimize physical harm. | 6. Exhaustion and death result from dehydration, lack of sleep, and constant physical activity. |
| 7. Observe for signs of lithium toxicity. | 7. There is a small margin of safety between therapeutic and toxic doses. |
| 8. Protect patient from giving away money and possessions. Hold valuables in hospital safe until rational judgment returns. | 8. Patient's "generosity" is a manic defense that is consistent with irrational, grandiose thinking. |

## RISK FOR VIOLENCE: SELF-DIRECTED OR OTHER-DIRECTED

At risk for behaviors in which an individual demonstrates that he/she can be physically, emotionally, and/or sexually harmful to self or others

### Some Related Factors (Related To)

▲ Psychotic symptomatology
▲ History of violence toward others
▲ Impulsivity
● Manic excitement
● Biochemical/neurological imbalances

---

▲ NANDA International accepted; ● In addition to NANDA International

## *Some Defining Characteristics (As Evidenced By)*

▲ Verbal threats against others
▲ Verbal threats against self (suicidal threats/attempts, hitting or injuring self, banging head against wall)
▲ Provocative behaviors (e.g., argumentative)
● Loud, threatening, profane speech
● Poor impulse control
● Agitated behaviors (e.g., slamming doors, prowling hallways, increased muscle tension, knocking things over)

## *Outcome Criteria*

● Displays nonviolent behaviors toward self and others
● Verbalizes control of feelings
● Interacts with others appropriately

## *Long-Term Goals*

Patient will:
● Refrain from verbal threats and loud, profane language toward others by (date)
● Seek help when experiencing aggressive impulses by (date)
● Demonstrate healthier ways to deal with stress (e.g., walking, sports, etc.)

## *Short-Term Goals*

Patient will:
● Display nonviolent behavior toward others in the hospital, with the aid of medications and nursing interventions by (date)
● Refrain from provoking others to physical harm, with the aid of seclusion or nursing interventions by (date)
● Respond to external controls (medications, seclusion, nursing interventions) when potential or actual loss of control occurs by (date)

---

▲ NANDA International accepted; ● In addition to NANDA International

*Interventions and Rationales*

| Intervention | Rationale |
|---|---|
| 1. Use a calm and firm approach. | 1. Provides structure and control for a patient who is out of control. |
| 2. Use short and concise explanations or statements. | 2. Short attention span limits comprehension to small bits of information. |
| 3. Maintain a consistent approach, employ consistent expectations, and provide a structured environment. | 3. Clear and consistent limits and expectations minimize potential for patient's manipulation of staff. |
| 4. Remain neutral: avoid power struggles and value judgments. | 4. Patient can use inconsistencies and value judgments as justification for arguing and escalating mania. |
| 5. Decrease environmental stimuli (keep away from loud music/noises, people, and bright lights). | 5. Helps decrease escalation of anxiety and manic symptoms. |
| 6. Assess patient's behavior frequently (every 15 minutes) for signs of increased agitation and hyperactivity. | 6. Early detection and intervention of escalating mania might help prevent harm to patient or others and decrease need for seclusion. |
| 7. Redirect agitation and potentially violent behaviors with physical outlets in area of low stimulation (e.g., punching bag). | 7. Can help to relieve pent-up hostility and relieve muscle tension. |
| 8. Alert staff if potential for seclusion appears imminent. Usual priority of interventions would be:<br>  a. Firmly setting limits | 8. If nursing interventions (quiet environment and firm limit setting) and chemical restraints (tranquilizers—e.g., haloperidol [Haldol]) have not helped dampen |

| Intervention | Rationale |
|---|---|
| b. Chemical restraints (tranquilizers) | escalating manic behaviors, then seclusion |
| c. Seclusion | might be warranted. **See Chapter 17 for guidelines on secluding an individual.** |
| 9. Include in nurse's notes: patient behaviors; interventions; what seemed to escalate agitation; what helped to calm agitation, when as-needed (PRN) medications were given and their effect; and what proved most helpful. | 9. Staff will begin to recognize potential signals for escalating manic behaviors and have a guideline for what might work best for the individual patient. |

## INEFFECTIVE COPING

Inability to form a valid appraisal of stressors, inadequate choice of practical responses, and/or inability to use available resources

### *Some Related Factors (Related To)*

▲ Disturbance in tension release
▲ Inadequate level of perception of control
● Ineffective problem-solving strategies/skills
● Biochemical/neurological changes in the brain

### *Defining Characteristics (As Evidenced By)*

▲ Inability to ask for help
▲ Inability to meet basic needs
▲ Inadequate problem-solving
▲ Destructive behavior toward self or others
● Change in usual communication patterns
● Presence of delusions (grandeur, persecution)

---

▲ NANDA International accepted; ● In addition to NANDA International

- Using extremely poor judgment in business and financial negotiations
- Giving away valuables and financial savings indiscriminately, often to strangers

## Outcome Criteria

- Patient reports an absence of delusions, racing thoughts, and irresponsible actions as a result of medication adherence and environmental structures
- Is protected from making any major life decisions (legal, business, marital) during an acute or severe manic phase
- Demonstrates an absence of destructive behavior toward self or others
- Ceases use of manipulation to obtain needs and control others
- Returns to pre-crisis level of functioning after acute/severe manic phase is past

## Long-Term Goals

Patient will:
- Demonstrate a decrease in manipulative behavior by (date)
- Demonstrate a decrease in demanding and provocative behavior by (date)
- Seek competent medical assistance and legal protection when signing any legal documents regarding personal or financial matters during manic phase of illness

## Short-Term Goals

Patient will:
- Retain valuables or other possessions while in the hospital
- Respond to external controls (medication, seclusion, nursing interventions) when potential or actual loss of control occurs
- Respond to limit-setting techniques with aid of medication during acute and severe manic phase by (date)

---

▲ NANDA International accepted; ● In addition to NANDA International

## *Interventions and Rationales*

| **Intervention** | **Rationale** |
|---|---|
| 1. Administer an antimanic medication and PRN tranquilizers, as ordered, and evaluate for efficacy, side effects, and toxic effects. | 1. Bipolar disorder is caused by biochemical/neurological imbalances in the brain. Appropriate antimanic medications allow psychosocial and nursing interventions to be effective. |
| 2. Observe for destructive behavior toward self or others. Intervene in the early phases of escalation of manic behavior. Intervene using **Risk for Violence** in this Chapter and **Chapter 17 (Anger and Aggression)** as a guide for interventions. | 2. Hostile verbal behaviors, poor impulse control, provocative behaviors, and violent acting out against others or property are some of the symptoms of this disease and are seen in extreme and/or acute mania. Early detection and intervention can prevent harm to patient or others in the environment. |
| 3. Have valuables, credit cards, and large sums of money sent home with family or put in hospital safe until patient is discharged. | 3. During manic episodes, individuals may give away valuables and money indiscriminately to strangers, often leaving themselves without money and in debt. |
| 4. Maintain a firm, calm, and neutral approach at all times.<br>**Avoid:**<br>   a. Getting involved in power struggles<br>   b. Arguing with the patient<br>   c. Joking or "clever" repartee in response to patient's "cheerful and humorous" mood | 4. a-c. These behaviors by staff can escalate environmental stimulation and, consequently, manic activity. Once the manic patient is out of control, seclusion might be required, which can be traumatic to the manic individual as well as the staff and other patients. |

| **Intervention** | **Rationale** |
|---|---|
| 5. Provide hospital legal service when and if patient is involved in making or signing important legal documents during an acute manic phase. | 5. Judgment and reality testing are both impaired during acute mania. Patients might need legal advice and protection against making important decisions that are not in their best interest. |
| 6. Assess and recognize early signs of manipulative behavior, and intervene appropriately. | 6. Setting limits is an important step in the intervention of bipolar patients, especially when intervening in manipulative behaviors. Staff agreement on limits set and consistency is imperative if the limits are to be carried out effectively. **Refer to Chapter 19** for more on interviewing with manipulative behaviors. |

For example:
  a. Taunting staff by pointing out faults or oversights
  b. Pitting one staff member against another ("You are much more understanding than Nurse X...do you know what he did?") or pitting one group against another (evening versus day shift)
  c. Aggressively demanding behaviors that can trigger exasperation and frustration in staff

## IMPAIRED SOCIAL INTERACTION

Insufficient or excessive quantity or ineffective quality of social exchange

## Some Related Factors (Related To)

▲ Disturbed thought processes
● Use of profanity, manipulation, flights of ideas
● Excessive hyperactivity and agitation

## Some Defining Characteristics (As Evidenced By)

▲ Use of unsuccessful social interaction behaviors
▲ Dysfunctional interaction with peers, family, and/or others
▲ Family reports change of style of interaction
● Intrusive and manipulative behaviors antagonizing others
● Loud, obscene, or threatening verbal behavior
● Poor attention span and difficulty focusing on one thing at a time
● Increase of manic behaviors when patient is in a highly stimulating environment (e.g., with groups of people, loud music)

## Outcome Criteria

● Patient initiates and maintains goal-directed and mutually satisfying activities/verbal exchanges with others
● Patient and family state that there is an increase in stability and meaningfulness in social interactions

## Long-Term Goals

Patient will:
● Put feelings into words instead of actions when experiencing anxiety or loss of control before discharge
● Participate in unit activities without disruption or demonstrating inappropriate behavior by discharge
● Demonstrate ability to remove self from stimulating environment in order to "cool down" by discharge

---

▲ NANDA International accepted; ● In addition to NANDA International

## Short-Term Goals

Patient will:

- Focus on one activity requiring a short attention span for 5 minutes three times a day with nursing assistance by (date)
- Find one or two solitary activities that can help relieve tensions and minimize escalation of anxiety with aid of nurse or occupational/activity therapist by (date)
- Sit through a short, small group meeting free from disruptive outbursts by (date)

## Interventions and Rationales

| Intervention | Rationale |
|---|---|
| 1. When possible, provide an environment with minimum stimuli (e.g., quiet, soft music, dim lighting). | 1. Reduction in stimuli lessens distractibility. |
| 2. Solitary activities requiring short attention spans with mild physical exertion are best initially (e.g., writing, painting [finger painting, murals], woodworking, or walks with staff). | 2. Solitary activities minimize stimuli; mild physical activities release tension constructively. |
| 3. When less manic, patient might join one or two other patients in quiet, nonstimulating activities (e.g., board games, drawing, cards). *Avoid competitive games.* | 3. As mania subsides, involvement in activities that provide a focus, and social contact becomes more appropriate. Competitive games can stimulate aggression and increase psychomotor activity. |

## TOTAL SELF-CARE DEFICIT

Impaired ability to perform or complete bathing/hygiene, dressing/grooming, feeding, or toileting activities for oneself

## Some Related Factors (Related To)

▲ Perceptual or cognitive impairment
▲ Severe anxiety
● Manic excitement
● Racing thoughts and poor attention span
● Inability to concentrate on one thing at a time

## Defining Characteristics (As Evidenced By)

● Observation or valid report of inability to eat, bathe, toilet, dress, and/or groom self independently

## Outcome Criteria

● Maintenance of pre-crisis level of self-care

## Long-Term Goals

● Patient's weight will be within normal limits for age and height by (date)
● Patient will sleep 6 to 8 hours per night by (date)
● Patient will dress and groom self in appropriate manner consistent with pre-crisis level of dress and grooming by (date)
● Patient's bowel habits will be within normal limits by (date)

## Short-Term Goals

Patient will:
● Eat one half to one third of each meal plus one snack between meals with aid of nursing intervention by (date)
● Sleep 6 hours out of 24 with aid of medication and nursing measures within 3 days
● Wear appropriate attire each day while in hospital
● Bathe at least every other day while in hospital
● Have normal bowel movements within 2 days with the aid of high-fiber foods, fluids, and, if needed, medication

---

▲ NANDA International accepted; ● In addition to NANDA International

## Interventions and Rationales

| Intervention | Rationale |
|---|---|

### Imbalanced Nutrition
1. Monitor intake, output, and vital signs.

1. Ensures adequate fluid and caloric intake; minimizes dehydration and cardiac collapse.

2. Encourage frequent high-calorie protein drinks and finger foods (e.g., sandwiches, fruit, milkshakes).

2. Constant fluid and calorie replacement are needed. Patient might be too active to sit at meals. Finger foods allow "eating on the run."

3. Frequently remind the patient to eat (e.g., "Tom, finish your milkshake." "Sally, eat this banana.").

3. The manic patient is unaware of bodily needs and is easily distracted. Needs supervision to eat.

### Disturbed Sleep Pattern
1. Encourage frequent rest periods during the day.

1. Lack of sleep can lead to exhaustion and death.

2. Keep patient in areas of low stimulation.

2. Promotes relaxation and minimizes manic behavior.

3. At night, encourage warm baths, soothing music, and medication when indicated. Avoid giving the patient caffeine.

3. Promotes relaxation, rest, and sleep.

### Dressing/Grooming Self-Care Deficit
1. If warranted, supervise choice of clothes; minimize flamboyant and bizarre dress and sexually suggestive dress, such as bikini tops and bottoms.

1. Lessens the potential for inappropriate attention, which can increase level of mania, or ridicule, which lowers self-esteem and increases the need for manic defense. Assists patient in maintaining dignity.

| Intervention | Rationale |
|---|---|
| 2. Give simple step-by-step reminders for hygiene and dress (e.g., "Here is your razor. Shave the left side. . .now the right side." "Here is your toothbrush. Put the toothpaste on the brush."). | 2. Distractibility and poor concentration are countered by simple, concrete instructions. |

**Constipation**

| | |
|---|---|
| 1. Monitor bowel habits; offer fluids and food that is high in fiber. Evaluate the need for a laxative. Encourage patient to go to the bathroom. | 1. Prevents fecal impaction resulting from dehydration and decreased peristalsis. |

## INTERRUPTED FAMILY PROCESSES

Change in family relationships and/or functioning

### Some Related Factors (Related To)

▲ Shift in health status of family member
▲ Situational crisis or transition (e.g., illness, manic episode of one member)
▲ Family role shift
● Erratic and out-of-control behavior of one family member with the potential for dangerous behavior affecting all family members (violence, leaving family in debt, risky behaviors in relationships and business, flagrant infidelities, unprotected and promiscuous sex)
● Nonadherence to antimanic and other medications

### Some Defining Characteristics (As Evidenced By)

▲ Changes in effectiveness in completing assigned tasks
▲ Changes in participation in problem solving

---

▲ NANDA International accepted; ● In addition to NANDA International

▲ Changes in participation in decision making
▲ Changes in communication patterns
▲ Changes in stress-related behaviors
● Deficient knowledge regarding bipolar disorder, need for medication adherence, and available support systems for both family members and patient
● Family in crisis

## Outcome Criteria

All members:
● Perform expected roles
● Adapt to unexpected crises
● Use stress reduction techniques

## Long-Term Goals

Family members/significant others:
● State that they find needed support and information in a support group(s) by (date)
● Can identify the signs of increased manic behavior in their family member by (date)
● State what they will do (whom to call, where to go) when patient's mood begins to escalate to dangerous levels by (date)
● Demonstrate an understanding of what a bipolar disorder is, the medications, the need for adherence to medication and treatment by (date)

## Short-Term Goals

Family members/significant others will:
● Discuss with nurse/counselor three areas of family life that are most disruptive and seek alternative options with aid of nursing/counseling interventions by (date)
● State and have in writing the names and telephone numbers of at least two bipolar support groups by (date)
● State that they have gained support from at least one support group on how to work with family member when he or she is manic by (date)
● State their understanding for the need for medication adherence and be able to identify three signs that indicate

---

▲ NANDA International accepted; ● In addition to NANDA International

possible need for intervention when their family member's mood escalates by (date)
- Briefly discuss and have in writing the names and addresses of two bipolar organizations, two Internet site addresses, and medication information regarding bipolar disorder by (date)

## *Interventions and Rationales*

| Intervention | Rationale |
|---|---|
| 1. During the first or second day of hospitalization, spend time with family identifying their needs during this time; for example:<br>a. Need for information about the disease<br>b. Need for information about lithium or other antimanic medications (e.g., need for adherence, side effects, toxic effects)<br>c. Knowledge about bipolar support groups in the family's community and how they can help families going through crises | 1. This is a disease that can devastate and destroy some families. During an acute manic attack, families experience a great deal of disruption and confusion when their family member begins to act bizarre, out of control, and at times aggressive. Families need to understand about the disease, what can and cannot be done to help control the disease, and where to go for help for their individual issues. |

# MEDICAL TREATMENTS

The following discussion is for current treatment of bipolar patients. Please keep in mind that the treatment plan for a particular patient needs to include treatment for any comorbid conditions. Is the patient at risk for suicide, homicide, or violence? Is there evidence of psychotic or catatonic features? Does the patient have a co-occurring substance abuse disorder as well? Are there other psychiatric comorbidities, such as personality disorder or conduct disorder in a child or adolescent? Although there are clear-cut, acceptable primary treatments for bipolar disorder, the treatment plan often includes a multimodal approach targeting a variety of patient needs.

## Psychopharmacology—Mood Stabilizers

It is important for clinicians—nurses and physicians alike—to keep in mind from the outset that patients with bipolar disease often resist mood stabilizers. On the continuum of mania, many patients want to keep the desired state of a higher level of energy, creativity, and confidence. Unfortunately, if left untreated, that state either escalates to more disastrous mania or painful depression.

*Mood stabilizers* are those medications with both antimanic and antidepressive action and therefore the medications used to treat bipolar disorder. For example, lithium is 60% to 80% effective for "typical" acute mania and for the prevention of further manic-depressive episodes (Preston et al., 2008). Lithium and divalproex (Depakote) (an antiepileptic) are considered by many as first-line treatments.

Besides divalproex, other FDA-approved antiepileptic drugs (AEDs) found to be effective in treating bipolar disease are carbamazepine (Tegretol) and lamotrigine (Lamictal). A brief discussion of FDA-approved mood stabilizers follows. Refer to Chapter 21 for specific information on these drugs, including side/toxic effects, nursing considerations, and patient and family teaching.

### Lithium

Lithium or other mood stabilizers (particularly divalproex [Depakote]) are an essential part of treatment. Lithium is particularly effective in mania, reducing:
- Elation
- Flights of ideas
- Irritability and manipulativeness
- Anxiety

To a lesser extent, lithium controls:
- Insomnia
- Psychomotor agitation
- Threatening or assaultive behavior
- Distractibility
- Paranoia
- Hypersexuality

Lithium can calm manic patients, prevent or modify future manic episodes, and protect against future depressive episodes. Lithium must reach therapeutic levels in the patient's blood to be effective. This usually takes from 7 to 14 days to be effective. Therefore, when a patient is first brought to the hospital, he or she might be started on an antipsychotic (atypical antipsychotic medications are more apt to be favored [e.g., Olanzapine] to help decrease psychomotor activity and aggressive behaviors and prevent exhaustion, coronary collapse, and death).

As lithium reaches therapeutic levels, the antipsychotics are usually discontinued. A narrow range exists between the therapeutic dose and the toxic dose of lithium. Initially, blood levels can be checked every 3 to 7 days for the first few weeks and once the patient is stable, every 1 to 3 months. Initially, levels should be from 1.0 to 1.2 mEq/L (sometimes higher) when the patient is in acute mania. Maintenance blood levels of lithium range from 0.6 to 1.2 mEq/L. To avoid serious toxicity, lithium levels should not exceed 1.5 mEq/L (Skidmore & Roth, 2009).

Before the administration of lithium, a medical evaluation is performed to assess the patient's ability to tolerate the drug. Lithium should not be given to people who are pregnant, have brain damage, or have cardiovascular, renal, or thyroid disease. Lithium is often the drug of choice for bipolar patients; however, some bipolar patients might not respond or might respond insufficiently to lithium, particularly those who have four or more cycles per year (rapid cyclers), mixed manic/depressive features, or psychosis or neurological disorders.

## Other Mood Stabilizers—Antiepileptic Drugs

Antiepileptic drugs seem to be effective for certain patients who are resistant to lithium—those with:

- Rapid cycling (four or more episodes a year)
- Dysphoric mania (depressive thoughts/feelings during manic episodes)
- Severe paranoia and anger

As mentioned earlier, three anticonvulsants have demonstrated efficacy in the treatment of individuals with bipolar disease: carbamazepine (Tegretol), divalproex (Depakote), and lamotrigine (Lamictal) (Preston et al.,

2008). Divalproex is particularly useful in mixed-state and rapid-cycling bipolar patients. Some clinicians find that divalproex is better tolerated than lithium and as effective in preventing subsequent bipolar episodes.

Blood-level monitoring is required for both carbamazepine and divalproex. The major worry with divalproex is the risk of severe, even fatal, hepatotoxicity. Carbamazepine (Tegretol) is used either alone or in combination with other mood stabilizers and can be useful in patients with mixed states. Carbamazepine use is associated with potentially serious adverse reactions. Lamotrigine is a first-line agent for bipolar depression and a second-line agent for rapid cycling (Preston et al., 2008).

## Adjunctive and New or Atypical Medicines

Other antimanic drugs include some anticonvulsant drugs, such as gabapentin (Neurontin) and topiramate (Topamax). Gabapentin (Neurontin) appears effective as an adjunct in the treatment of refractory bipolar patients, as does topiramate (Topamax), which seems to be effective in acute mania as well as in adjunctive use in combination with other mood stabilizers. Some also report success with rapid cycling. These drugs do not have well-controlled studies to back their efficacy but may be used when other drugs fail.

Some benzodiazepines (e.g., clonazepam [Klonopin] and lorazepam [Ativan]) have been found to facilitate other antimanic treatments useful in treatment-resistant manic patients. Refer to Chapter 21 for a more thorough discussion of the mood stabilizers and specific information on these drugs, including adverse reactions, nursing considerations, and patient and family teaching. Table 7-2 lists FDA-approved drugs for mood disorders, usual doses, and adverse reactions.

## Other Medical Treatments

### Electroconvulsive Therapy (ECT)

ECT is a primary consideration when a highly manic patient is unable to wait until a medication starts to become effective, cannot tolerate one of the first-line medications listed earlier, or does not respond to the first-line medications. ECT has been found especially effective with rapid-cycling

Table 7-2 **Mood Stabilizers for Bipolar Disorders (FDA Approved)**

| Drug | Dosage | Major Adverse Effects |
|---|---|---|
| Lithium | 1200–2400 mg daily<br>600–1800 mg daily | For acute mania<br>Maintenance dose<br>• Lithium blood levels are drawn every 3–7 days initially, then once every 1–3 months when stable<br>• Serum levels when acute: 0.8–1.5 mEq/L<br>• Maintenance serum levels: 0.6–1.2 mEq/L<br>• Symptoms range from early signs of toxicity, advanced signs of toxicity, to severe toxicity. See Chapter 21 for side effects at various blood levels and related interventions. |
| **Antiepileptic Drugs (AEDs)**<br>Carbamazepine (Tegretol) | 600–1600 mg daily | • Agranulocytosis and aplastic anemia are most serious side effects.<br>• Blood levels should be monitored throughout first 8 weeks because drug induces liver enzymes that speed its own metabolism. Dosage may need to be adjusted to maintain serum level of 6–8 mg/L. |

*Continued*

Table 7-2 **Mood Stabilizers for Bipolar Disorders (FDA Approved)—cont'd**

| Drug | Dosage | Major Adverse Effects |
|------|--------|----------------------|
| Divalproex (Depakote) | 750–1500 mg daily | • Sedation is most common problem; tolerance usually develops.<br>• Diplopia, incoordination, and sedation can signal excessive levels.<br>• Baseline liver function tests should be performed and results monitored at regular intervals. Hepatitis, although rare, has been reported, with fatalities in children.<br>• Signs and symptoms to watch for include fever, chills, right upper quadrant pain, dark urine, malaise, and jaundice.<br>• Common side effects include tremors, gastrointestinal upset, weight gain, and (rarely) alopecia. |
| Lamotrigine (Lamictal) | 50–400 mg daily | • Life-threatening rash reported in 3 out of every 1000 individuals (Stevens-Johnson syndrome).<br>• Use caution when renal, hepatic, or cardiac function is impaired.<br>• Dizziness, diplopia, headache, ataxia, and somnolence are among frequent side effects. |

Data from Preston and O'Neal (2008); Lehne (2007)

patients (those who suffer four or more episodes of illness a year), as well as those with paranoid-destructive features that often respond poorly to lithium therapy (Abou-Saleh, 1992). ECT should be considered for severe and dangerous manic patients and those in highly agitated states. ECT should also be considered for pregnant women. Refer to Appendix F for the nurse's responsibilities in ECT therapy.

## Psychotherapeutic Treatments

The primary goal of all therapies is to reduce the patient's distress, improve the patient's ability to function between episodes, and decrease the frequency of future episodes (APA, 2000b). Because of the behaviors associated with the disorder, there are usually severe psychosocial consequences from past episodes. Bipolar disease appears to be a chronic, recurrent disease. Many patients do not fully recover between episodes. Some research suggests that between 30% and 60% of patients fail to regain full occupational and social functioning (Steinhauer, 2003). Therefore it becomes clear that adjuvant treatments are necessary along with medications.

No matter which therapy is chosen for a specific patient, an approach that enforces clear limits in a firm and unprovocative manner is most recommended (APA, 2000b). There are a number of psychotherapeutic approaches that can be helpful to some patients. Group/family therapy focuses on acceptance of the disease, the need for long-term medication treatment, and medication teaching. Therapy with medication-stabilized patients includes:
- Cognitive
- Behavioral
- Psychoeducation

# NURSE, PATIENT, and FAMILY RESOURCES

## ASSOCIATIONS

**National Alliance for the Mentally III (NAMI)**
Colonial Place Three
2107 Wilson Boulevard, Suite 300
Arlington, VA 22201-3042
(800) 950-NAMI
www.nami.org

**Depressed Anonymous: Recovery from Depression**
PO Box 17471
Louisville, KY 40217
(502) 569-1989
www.depressedanon.com

**National Foundation for Depressive Illness, Inc.**
PO Box 2257
New York, NY 10116
(800) 239-1265
www.depression.org

**Depression and Bipolar Support Alliance**
730 N. Franklin, Suite 501
Chicago, IL 60610
(800) 82N-DMDA
www.dbsalliance.org

**Depression and Related Affective Disorders Association**
2330 West Joppa Road, Suite 100
Lutherville, MD 21093
(410) 583-2919
www.drada.org

## INTERNET SITES

**National Institute of Mental Health**
www.nimh.nih.gov/publicat/index.cfm
List of publications on bipolar disorder

**Bipolar Disorder Page**
www.mentalhelp.net/poc/center_index.php?id=4&cn=4

**Med Help International**
www.medhelp.org
Many good links

**Bipolar Website**
www.bipolar.com
Good information and links

**Bipolar Disorder Guide at about.com**
www.bipolar.about.com

# CHAPTER 8

# Schizophrenia and Other Psychotic Disorders

## OVERVIEW

The word *psychosis* refers to symptoms that include hallucinations (seriously impaired perception, e.g., seeing, hearing, smelling something which is not there), *delusions* (false beliefs, e.g., paranoid beliefs that people are out to harm them when it is not true), and *disorganized thinking* as evidenced in behavior and speech. Psychosis is either a *primary or secondary psychosis*. *Primary psychoses* are those that have a biological or neurobiological origin. Examples of disorders that are considered *primary psychotic disorders* are schizophrenia, depression with psychotic features, schizoaffective disorder, bipolar disorder, manic. *Secondary psychoses* are those that are referred to as "Psychotic Disorders Due to a General Medical Condition" such as metabolic disorders, head injuries, dementia, intracranial tumors or drug and alcohol intoxication or withdrawal.

## Some Primary Psychotic Disorders
### Schizophreniform Disorder

The essential features of this disorder are exactly those of schizophrenia, except that:
- The total duration of the illness is at least 1 month but less than 6 months.

- Impaired social or occupational functioning during some part of the illness is not apparent (although it might occur).

This disorder might or might not have a good prognosis.

## Brief Psychotic Disorder

This is a disorder in which there is a sudden onset of psychotic symptoms (delusions, hallucinations, disorganized speech) or grossly disorganized or catatonic behavior. The episode lasts at least 1 day but less than 1 month, and then the individual returns to his or her premorbid level of functioning. Brief psychotic disorders often follow extremely stressful life events.

## Schizoaffective Disorder

This disorder is characterized by an uninterrupted period of illness during which there is a major depressive, manic, or mixed episode, concurrent with symptoms that meet the criteria for schizophrenia. The symptoms must not be due to any substance use or abuse or general medical condition.

## Delusional Disorder

This disorder involves nonbizarre delusions (situations that occur in real life, such as being followed, infected, loved at a distance, deceived by a spouse, or having a disease) of at least 1 month's duration. The person's ability to function is not markedly impaired, nor is the person's behavior obviously odd or bizarre. Common types of delusions seen in this disorder are delusions of grandeur, persecution, jealousy, or somatic or mixed delusions.

## Shared Psychotic Disorder (Folie à Deux)

A shared psychotic disorder is an occurrence in which one individual, who is in a close relationship with another who has a psychotic disorder with a delusion, eventually comes to share the delusional beliefs either in total or in part. Apart from the shared delusion, the person who takes on the other's delusional behavior is not otherwise odd or unusual. Impairment of the person who shares the delusion is usually much less than the person who has the psychotic disorder with the delusion. The cult phenomenon is an example, as was demonstrated at Waco and Jonestown.

## Induced or Secondary Psychosis

Psychosis can be induced by substances (drugs of abuse, alcohol, medications, or toxin exposure) or caused by the physiological consequences of a general medical condition (delirium, neurological conditions, metabolic conditions, hepatic or renal diseases, and many more). **Medical conditions and substances of abuse must always be ruled out before a primary diagnosis of schizophrenia or other psychotic disorder can be made**.

## Schizophrenia

Schizophrenia is a chronic primary disorder that is prone to recurring psychotic episodes. Is not a single disease, but rather a syndrome that involves cerebral blood flow, neuroelectrophysiology, neuroanatomy, and neurobiochemistry. Schizophrenia affects approximately 1% of the population, and 95% of individuals who become schizophrenic have the condition throughout their lifetime. The symptoms of schizophrenia usually become apparent during adolescence or early adulthood (age 15 to 25 for men, 25 to 35 for women). Paranoid schizophrenia has a later onset. Although schizophrenias are not caused by psychological events, stressful life events can trigger an exacerbation of the illness. Preston and Johnson (2009) break schizophrenia into three groups. The first, schizophreniform disorder, was described earlier. Actual schizophrenic disorders include:

a. **Positive symptom schizophrenia.** This type of schizophrenia is thought to occur because of an overactive dopamine system. Symptoms in positive symptom schizophrenia occur suddenly, and patients have a normal premorbid personality and normal CT findings. Positive symptoms are active and include alterations in:
   - Perceptions (hallucinations and delusions)
   - Thinking (delusions, paranoia, disorganized thinking)

- Agitation and emotional dyscontrol
- Language (associative looseness, poverty of speech)

Hallucinations and delusions can be very frightening, often terrifying for individuals. They also can be very disconcerting initially and even frightening to nurses and other health care individuals, as well as family and friends. Communicating with patients who are delusional and hallucinatory and have disorganized thinking is a skill learned with guidance and practice.

b. **Negative symptom schizophrenia.** This is a neurodevelopmental disorder and occurs earlier starting in childhood. Often children with this were viewed as odd and withdrawn by others. The symptoms are more insidious and the most damaging to the patient's quality of life. Negative symptoms include alterations in:

- Emotions—apathy, anhedonia, depression, feelings of emptiness, amotivational states.
- Social behavior—aggression, bizarre conduct, or extreme social withdrawal.
- Cognitive symptoms—poor problem solving, poor decision-making skills, illogical thinking—also need to be targeted when planning care for all patients with schizophrenia, but most specifically for negative-symptom schizophrenia.

The *Diagnostic and Statistical Manual of Mental Disorders* (4th edition, text revision) (*DSM-IV-TR*) criteria for the diagnosis of schizophrenia are listed in Box 8-1. Box 8-2 identifies five subtypes of schizophrenia.

## Phases of Schizophrenia

Schizophrenia has been divided into three phases:

**Phase I—Onset.** This phase (acute phase) includes the prodromal symptoms (e.g., acute or chronic anxiety, phobias, obsessions, compulsions, dissociative features) and the acute psychotic symptoms of hallucinations, delusions, and/or disorganized thinking.

**Phase II—Years following onset.** Patterns that characterize this phase are the ebb and flow of the intensity and disruption caused by symptoms, which might in some cases be followed by complete or relatively complete recovery.

| Box 8-1 | *DSM-IV-TR* **Criteria for Schizophrenia** |
|---|---|

1. *Characteristic symptoms*: Two (or more) of the following, each present for a significant portion of the time during a 1-month period (or less if successfully treated):
   • Delusions
   • Hallucinations
   • Disorganized speech (e.g., frequent derailment or incoherence)
   • Grossly disorganized or catatonic behavior
   • Negative symptoms, (i.e., affective flattening, alogia, or avolition)
   NOTE: Only one Criterion 1 symptom is required if delusions are bizarre or hallucinations consist of a voice keeping up a running commentary on the person's behavior or thoughts, or two or more voices conversing with each other.

2. *Social/occupational dysfunction*: For a significant portion of the time since the onset of the disturbance, one or more major areas of functioning, such as work, interpersonal relations, or self-care, are markedly below the level achieved prior to the onset (or when the onset is in childhood or adolescence, failure to achieve expected level of interpersonal, academic, or occupational achievement).

3. *Duration*: Continuous signs of the disturbance persist for at least 6 months. This 6-month period must include at least 1 month of symptoms (or less if successfully treated) that meet Criterion 1 (i.e., active-phase symptoms) and might include periods of prodromal or residual symptoms.

4. Symptoms are not caused by (a) another psychotic disorder; (b) a substance or general medical disorder; or (c) a pervasive developmental disorder, unless prominent delusions or hallucinations are also present for at least 1 month.

Adapted from American Psychiatric Association. (2000). *Diagnostic and statistical manual of mental disorders* (4th ed., text rev.). Washington, DC: Author, p. 312; reprinted with permission.

**Phase III—Long-term course and outcome.** This is the course a severely and persistently mentally ill patient follows when the disease becomes chronic. For some patients, the intensity of the psychosis might diminish with age, but the long-term dysfunctional effects of the disorder are not as amenable to change.

## Box 8-2 **Subtypes of Schizophrenia**

**Paranoid**
Onset usually in the late 20s to 30s. People who develop this disorder usually function well before the onset of the disorder (good premorbid functioning). *Paranoia* (any intense and strongly defended irrational suspicion) is the main characteristic; the main defense is projection. *Hallucinations, delusions, and ideas of reference* are dominant.

**Disorganized**
The most *regressed and socially impaired* of all the schizophrenias. The person has highly disorganized speech and behavior and inappropriate affect. Bizarre mannerisms include grimacing, along with other oddities of behavior.

**Catatonia**
The essential feature is abnormal motor behavior. Two extreme motor behaviors are seen in catatonia. One extreme is psychomotor agitation, which can lead to exhaustion. The other extreme is psychomotor retardation and *withdrawal* to the point of stupor. The onset is usually acute, and the prognosis is good with medications and swift interventions. Other behaviors might include autism, waxy flexibility, and negativism.

**Undifferentiated (Mixed Type)**
Patients experience active hallucinations and delusions, but no one clinical picture dominates (e.g., not paranoid, catatonic, or disorganized; rather, the clinical picture is one of a *mixture* of symptoms).

**Residual**
A person who is referred to as having residual schizophrenia no longer has active symptoms of the disease, such as delusions, hallucinations, or disorganized speech and behaviors. However, there is a persistence of some symptoms—for example, marked social withdrawal; impairment in role function (wage earner, student, or homemaker); eccentric behavior or odd beliefs; poor personal hygiene; lack of interest, energy, initiative; and inappropriate affect.

# ASSESSMENT

## Presenting Signs and Symptoms

1. Positive symptoms
   - Delusions
   - Hallucinations
   - Disorganized thinking/speech
   - Disorganized or catatonic behavior
2. Negative symptoms
   - Flat emotional affect
   - Sparse productivity of thought (alogia)
   - Lack of goal-directed activity (avolition)
3. Cognitive symptoms
   - Memory and attention deficits
   - Language difficulties (e.g., poverty of thought)
   - Ability to monitor personal behavior, ability to establish goals and maintain tasks, and so on

## Assessment Tool

The Brief Psychiatric Rating Scale (BPRS) (Appendix D-5) is a useful tool for evaluating overall psychiatric functioning. It is particularly helpful in evaluating the degree to which psychotic symptoms affect a person's ability to function.

## Assessment Guidelines
### Schizophrenias
**Assessing Positive Symptoms**
1. Assess for command hallucinations (e.g., voices telling the person to harm self or another).

If yes:
   - Do you plan to follow the command?
   - Do you believe the voices are real?
2. Assess whether the patient has fragmented, poorly organized, well-organized, systematized, or extensive system of beliefs that are not supported by reality (delusions).

If yes:
   - Assess whether delusions have to do with someone trying to harm the patient and whether the patient is planning to retaliate against a person or organization.
   - Assess whether precautions need to be taken.

3. Assess for pervasive suspiciousness about everyone and their actions, for example:
   • Is on guard, hyperalert, vigilant
   • Blames others for consequences of own behavior
   • Is hostile, argumentative, or often threatening in verbalization or behavior

**Assessing Negative Symptoms**

1. Assess for negative symptoms of schizophrenia (Table 8-1 lists definitions and suggested interventions).
2. Assess whether patient is on medications, what the medications are, and if treatment is adherent with medications.
3. How does the family respond to increased symptoms? Overprotective? Hostile? Suspicious?
4. How do family members and patient relate?
5. Assess support system. Is family well informed about the disorder (e.g., schizophrenia)? Does family understand the need for medication adherence? Is family familiar with family support groups in the community or where to go for respite and family support?

# NURSING DIAGNOSES WITH INTERVENTIONS

People with schizophrenia often have multiple needs. Basic to these is safety. Refer to Chapters 16 and 17 for nursing care plans identifying nursing interventions for **suicide intent and violence toward others.** Suicide and threat of violence to others are basic to nursing interventions for all patients in all settings, not just for people with schizophrenia or the hospitalized person. Table 8-2 lists potential nursing diagnoses for patients with schizophrenia.

Relating to people with schizophrenia can be a challenge, especially in the acute phase; therefore guidelines for **Impaired Verbal Communication** are included. Again, during the acute phase, relating to others is difficult. Guidelines for interacting and gradually adding social skills are included in **Impaired Social**

Table 8-1 **Negative (Deficit) Symptoms of Schizophrenia**

| Symptoms | Clinical Findings | Treatment |
|---|---|---|
| Apathy<br>Poverty of speech or content of speech<br>Poor social functioning<br>Anhedonia<br>Social withdrawal | Slow onset<br>Interferes with a person's life<br>Positive premorbid history<br>Chronic deterioration<br>Family history of schizophrenia<br>Cerebellar atrophy and lateral and third ventricular enlargement on computed tomography scan<br>Abnormalities on neuropsychological testing<br>Poor response to antipsychotics | The newer atypical (novel) antipsychotics might target some of the negative symptoms.<br>The most used interventions include:<br>1. Skills training interventions.<br>  • Identify areas of skill deficit person is willing to work on.<br>  • Prioritize skills important to the person.<br>2. Working with person to identify stressors:<br>  • Identify which stressors contribute to maladaptive behaviors.<br>3. Work with person on increasing appropriate coping skills. |

**Interaction.** Working with patients who are hallucinating **(Disturbed Sensory Perception)**, delusional **(Disturbed Thought Processes)**, and paranoid **(Defensive Coping)** can be a great challenge. Therefore, these are included.

Importantly, families are often left to cope with the exhaustive needs of their mentally ill family member. **Interrupted Family Processes** should always be assessed, and referrals and teaching should be readily available.

Table 8-2 **Potential Nursing Diagnoses for Schizophrenia**

| Symptoms | Nursing Diagnoses |
| --- | --- |
| **Positive Symptoms** *Hallucinations:* | |
| • Hears voices (loud noises) others do not hear | Disturbed Sensory Perception: Auditory/ Visual |
| • Hears voices telling them to hurt self or others (*command hallucinations*) | Risk for Violence: Self-Directed and Other-Directed |
| *Distorted thinking not based in reality, for example:* | Disturbed Thought Processes |
| • **Persecution:** thinking others are trying to harm them | Defensive Coping |
| • **Jealousy:** thinking spouse or lover is being unfaithful, or thinks others are jealous when they are not | |
| • **Grandeur:** thinking they have powers they do not possess, or they are someone powerful or famous | |
| • **Reference:** believing all events within the environment are directed at or hold special meaning for them | |
| • Loose association of ideas **(looseness of association)** | Impaired Verbal Communication |
| • Uses words in a meaningless, disconnected manner **(word salad)** | Disturbed Thought Processes |
| • Uses words that rhyme in a nonsensical fashion **(clang association)** | |
| • Repeats words that are heard (*echolalia*) | |
| • Does not speak **(mutism)** | |
| • Delays getting to the point of communication because of unnecessary and tedious details **(circumstantiality)** | |
| • Concrete thinking: the inability to abstract; uses literal translations concerning aspects of the environment | |

*Continued*

Table 8-2 **Potential Nursing Diagnoses for Schizophrenia—cont'd**

| Symptoms | Nursing Diagnoses |
|---|---|
| **Negative Symptoms** | |
| Uncommunicative, withdrawn, no eye contact | Social Isolation |
| Preoccupation with own thoughts | Impaired Social Interaction |
| Expression of feelings of rejection or of aloneness (lies in bed all day; positions back to door) | Risk for Loneliness |
| Talks about self as "bad" or "no good" | Chronic Low Self-Esteem |
| Feels guilty because of "bad thoughts"; extremely sensitive to real or perceived slights | Risk for Self-Directed Violence |
| Lack of energy (anergia) | Ineffective Coping |
| Lack of motivation (avolition); unable to initiate tasks (social contact, grooming, and other aspects of daily living) | Self-Care Deficit (bathing/ hygiene, dressing/ grooming) Constipation |
| **Other** | Compromised Family Coping |
| Families and significant others become confused, overwhelmed, lack knowledge of disease or treatment, feel powerless in coping with patient at home | Disabled Family Coping Impaired Parenting Caregiver Role Strain |
| **Nonadherence to medications and treatment:** patient stops taking medication (often because of side effects), stops going to therapy groups. | Deficient Knowledge Nonadherence (Noncompliance) |

## Selected Nursing Diagnoses and Nursing Care Plans

### IMPAIRED VERBAL COMMUNICATION

Decreased, delayed, or absent ability to receive, process, transmit, or use a system of symbols

## Some Related Factors (Related To)

▲ Psychological barriers (e.g., psychosis, lack of stimuli)
▲ Side effects of medication
▲ Altered perceptions
● Biochemical alterations in the brain of certain neuro-transmitters

## Defining Characteristics (As Evidenced By)

▲ Inappropriate verbalization
▲ Difficulty expressing thoughts verbally
▲ Difficulty comprehending and maintaining the usual communication pattern
● Poverty of speech
● Disturbances in cognitive associations (e.g., looseness of association, perseveration, neologisms)
● Inability to distinguish internally stimulated thoughts from actual environmental events or commonly shared knowledge

## Outcome Criteria

● Communicates thoughts and feelings in a coherent, goal-directed manner (to patient's best ability)
● Demonstrates reality-based thought processes in verbal communication (to patient's best ability)

## Long-Term Goals

Patient will:
● With the aid of medication and attentive listening, be able to speak in a manner that can be understood by others by discharge
● Learn two diversionary tactics that work for him/her to lower anxiety, thus enhancing ability to think clearly and speak more logically by (date)

---

▲ NANDA International accepted; ● In addition to NANDA International

## Short-Term Goals

Patient will:
- Spend three 5-minute periods with nurse, sharing observations in the environment within 4 days
- Spend time with one or two other people in structured activity involving neutral topics by (date)

## Interventions and Rationales

| Intervention | Rationale |
|---|---|
| 1. Assess whether incoherence in speech is chronic or more sudden, as in an exacerbation of symptoms. | 1. Establishing a baseline facilitates the establishment of realistic goals, the cornerstone for planning effective care. |
| 2. Identify how long patient has been on antipsychotic medication. | 2. Therapeutic levels of an antipsychotic helps clear thinking and diminishes looseness of association (LOA). |
| 3. Plan short, frequent periods with patient throughout the day. | 3. Short periods are less stressful, and periodic meetings give patient a chance to develop familiarity and safety. |
| 4. Use simple words, and keep directions simple. | 4. Patient might have difficulty processing even simple sentences. |
| 5. Keep voice low and speak slowly. | 5. High pitched/loud tone of voice can raise anxiety levels; slow speaking aids understanding. |
| 6. Look for themes in what is said, even though spoken words appear incoherent (e.g., anxiety, fear, sadness). | 6. Often patient's choice of words is symbolic of feelings. |
| 7. When you do not understand a patient, let him/her know you are having difficulty understanding (e.g., "I want to understand what you are saying, but I am having difficulty.") | 7. Pretending to understand (when you do not) limits your credibility in the eyes of your patient and lessens the potential for trust. |

| **Intervention** | **Rationale** |
|---|---|
| 8. Use therapeutic techniques to try to understand patient's concerns (e.g., "Are you saying...?" "You mentioned demons many times. Are you feeling frightened?"). | 8. Even if the words are hard to understand, try getting to the feelings behind them. |
| 9. Focus on and direct patient's attention to concrete things in the environment. | 9. Helps draw focus away from delusions and focus on reality-based things. |
| 10. Keep environment quiet and as free of stimuli as possible. | 10. Keeps anxiety from escalating and increasing confusion and hallucinations/delusions. |
| 11. Use simple, concrete, and literal explanations. | 11. Minimizes misunderstanding and/ or incorporating those misunderstandings into delusional systems. |
| 12. When patient is ready, introduce tactics that can lower anxiety and minimize voices and "worrying" thoughts. Teach patient to do the following:<br>• Take time out.<br>• Read aloud to self.<br>• Seek out staff, family, or other supportive person.<br>• Listen to music.<br>• Learn to replace irrational thoughts with rational statements.<br>• Learn to replace "bad" thoughts with constructive thoughts.<br>• Perform deep-breathing exercises. | 12. Helping patient to use tactics to lower anxiety can help enhance functional speech. |

## IMPAIRED SOCIAL INTERACTION

The state in which an individual participates in an insufficient or excessive quantity or ineffective quality of social exchange

### *Some Related Factors (Related To)*

▲ Self-concept disturbance (might feel "bad" about self or "no good")
● Difficulty with communication (e.g., associative looseness)
● Inappropriate or inadequate emotional responses
● Feeling threatened in social situations
● Exaggerated response to stimuli
● Difficulty with concentration
● Impaired thought processes (hallucinations or delusions)

### *Some Defining Characteristics (As Evidenced By)*

▲ Discomfort in social situations
▲ Use of unsuccessful social interactions behaviors
▲ Dysfunctional interaction with peers
● Spends time alone by self
● Inappropriate or inadequate emotional response
● Does not make eye contact or initiate or respond to social advances of others
● Appears agitated or anxious when others come too close or try to engage him in an activity

### Outcome Criteria

● Improves social interaction with family, friends, and neighbors
● Engages in social interactions in goal-directed manner
● Uses appropriate social skills in interactions
● Seeks out supportive social contacts

---

▲ NANDA International accepted; ● In addition to NANDA International

## Long-Term Goals

Patient will:

- Engage in one or two activities, with minimal encouragement from nurse or family members by (date)
- Use appropriate skills to initiate and maintain an interaction by (date)
- State that he or she is comfortable in at least three structured activities that are goal directed by (date)
- Demonstrate interest in starting coping skills training when ready for learning

## Short-Term Goals

Patient will:

- Engage in one activity with nurse by the end of the day
- Attend one structured group activity within 1 week
- Maintain an interaction with another patient while doing an activity (drawing, playing cards, cooking a meal)

## Interventions and Rationales

| Intervention | Rationale |
|---|---|
| 1. Assess whether medication has reached therapeutic levels. | 1. Many of the positive symptoms (paranoia, delusions, and hallucinations) will subside with medications, which will facilitate interactions. |
| 2. Ensure that the goals set are realistic, whether in the hospital or community. | 2. Avoids pressure on patient and sense of failure on part of nurse/ family. This sense of failure can lead to mutual withdrawal. |
| 3. Keep patient in an environment as free of stimuli (loud noises, high traffic areas) as possible. | 3. Patient might respond to noises and crowding with agitation, anxiety, and increased inability to concentrate on outside events. |

| Intervention | Rationale |
| --- | --- |
| 4. Avoid touching the patient. | 4. Touch by a "stranger" can be misinterpreted as a sexual or threatening gesture. This is particularly true for a patient with paranoia. |
| 5. If patient is unable to respond verbally or in a coherent manner, spend frequent, short periods with her/him. | 5. An interested presence can provide a sense of being worthwhile. |
| 6. Structure times each day to include planned times for brief interactions and activities with the patient on a one-on-one basis. | 6. Helps patient develop a sense of safety in a nonthreatening environment. |
| 7. If patient is delusional/hallucinating or is having trouble concentrating at this time, provide very simple, concrete activities (e.g., looking at a picture book with nurse, drawing, painting). | 7. Even simple activities may shift the patient's attention from delusional thinking to reality in the environment. |
| 8. Structure activities that work at the patient's pace and ability. | 8. Patient can lose interest in activities that are too ambitious, which can increase a sense of failure. |
| 9. Try to incorporate the strengths and interests the patient had when not as impaired into the activities planned. | 9. Increases likelihood of patient's participation and enjoyment. |
| 10. If patient is experiencing **paranoid thoughts**, solitary or one-on-one activities that require concentration are appropriate. | 10. Patient is free to choose level of interaction; however, the concentration can help minimize distressing paranoid thoughts or voices (e.g., chess). |

| **Intervention** | **Rationale** |
|---|---|
| 11. If patient is very **withdrawn**, one-on-one activities with a "safe" person initially should be planned. | 11. Learns to feel safe with one person, then gradually might participate in a structured group activity. |
| 12. As patient progresses, provide graded activities according to level of tolerance: (1) simple games with one "safe" person; (2) slowly add a third person into "safe" activities; (3) introduce simple group activities; and then (4) groups in which patients participate more. | 12. Gradually the patient learns to feel safe and competent with increased social demands. |
| 13. Eventually engage other patients and significant others in social interactions and activities with the patient (card games, ping-pong, sing-a-longs, group outings, etc.) at patient's level. | 13. Patient continues to feel safe and competent in a graduated hierarchy of interactions. |
| 14. Identify with patient symptoms experienced when he/she feels aggressive, begins to feel anxious around others, and so forth. | 14. Increased anxiety can intensify agitation, aggressiveness, and suspiciousness. |
| 15. Teach patient to remove self briefly when feeling agitated and work on anxiety-relief exercises (e.g., deep breathing, thought stopping). | 15. Teaches patient skills in dealing with anxiety and increases sense of control. |

| Intervention | Rationale |
|---|---|
| 16. Provide opportunities for the patient to learn adaptive social skills in a nonthreatening environment. Initial social skills training could include basic social behaviors (e.g., maintain good eye contact, appropriate distance, calm demeanor, moderate voice tone). | 16. Social skills training helps patient adapt and function at a higher level in society; increases patient's quality of life. These simple skills might take time for a patient with schizophrenia, but can increase both self-confidence and positive responses from others. |
| 17. As patient progresses, coping skills training should be available to him/her (nurse, staff, or others). Basically, the process is:<br>a. Define the skill to be learned.<br>b. Model the skill.<br>c. Rehearse skills in a safe environment, then in the community.<br>d. Give corrective feedback on the implementation of skills. | 17. Increases patient's ability to derive social support and decrease loneliness. Patients will not give up substances of abuse unless they have alternative means to facilitate socialization and feel they belong. |
| 18. Useful coping skills that patient will need include conversational and assertiveness skills. | 18. These are fundamental skills for dealing with the world, which everyone uses daily with more or less skill. |
| 19. Remember to give acknowledgment and recognition for positive steps patient takes in increasing social skills and appropriate interactions with others. | 19. Recognition and appreciation go a long way toward sustaining and increasing a specific behavior. |

# HALLUCINATIONS

## Three Presenting Signs and Symptoms

- Patients state they hear voices.
- Patient denies hearing voices, but observer notes patient('s):
  - Eyes following something in motion that observer cannot see
  - Staring at one place in room
  - Head turning to side as if listening
  - Mumbling to self or conversing when no one else is present
  - Inappropriate facial expressions, eye blinking
- If hallucinations are from other causes (e.g., drugs, alcohol, delirium), the underlying cause must be treated as soon as possible using accepted medical and nursing protocols.

## Assessment Guidelines

### Hallucinations

1. Assess for command hallucinations (e.g., voices telling the person to harm self or another).
2. Assess when hallucinations seem to occur the most (e.g., times of stress, at night).

## Selected Nursing Diagnoses and Nursing Care Plans

### DISTURBED SENSORY PERCEPTION: SPECIFY TYPE (e.g., AUDITORY/VISUAL)

Change in the amount or patterning of incoming stimuli accompanied by a diminished, exaggerated, distorted, or impaired response to such stimuli

### Some Related Factors (Related To)

▲ Altered sensory reception: transmission or integration
▲ Biochemical imbalance

▲ Biochemical imbalance (neurological/biochemical changes)
▲ Chemical alterations (e.g., drugs, electrolyte imbalances)
▲ Altered sensory integration/perception
▲ Psychological stress

## Some Defining Characteristics (As Evidenced By)

▲ Change in sensory acuity
▲ Disorientation
▲ Hallucinations
▲ Change in problem-solving pattern
▲ Impaired communication
● Tilting head as if listening to someone
● Frequent eye blinking and grimacing
● Mumbling to self, talking or laughing to self

## Outcome Criteria

● Maintains social relationships
● Maintains role performance
● States that the voices are no longer threatening, nor do they interfere with his or her life
● Learns ways to refrain from responding to hallucinations

## Long-Term Goals

Patient will:
● Demonstrate techniques that help distract him or her from the voices by (date)
● Monitor intensity of anxiety

## Short-Term Goals

Patient will:
● State, using a scale from 1 to 10, that "the voices" are less frequent and threatening when aided by medication and nursing intervention by (date)

---

▲ NANDA International accepted; ● In addition to NANDA International

- State three symptoms they recognize when their stress levels are high by (date)
- Identify two stressful events that trigger hallucinations by (date)
- Demonstrate one stress-reduction technique by (date)
- Identify two personal interventions that decrease or lower the intensity or frequency of hallucinations (e.g., listening to music, wearing headphones, reading aloud, jogging, socializing) by (date)

## Interventions and Rationales

| Intervention | Rationale |
|---|---|
| 1. If voices are telling the patient to harm self or others, take necessary environmental precautions. | 1. People often obey hallucinatory commands to kill self or others. Early assessment and intervention might save lives. |
|   a. Notify others and police, physician, and administration according to unit protocol. | |
|   b. If in the hospital, use unit protocols for **threats of suicide or violence** if patient plans to act on commands. | |
|   c. If in the community, evaluate need for hospitalization. | |
|   d. Clearly document what patient says; if he/she is a threat to others, document who was contacted and notified (use agency protocol as a guide). | |
| 2. Decrease environmental stimuli when possible (low noise, minimal activity). | 2. Decrease potential for anxiety that might trigger hallucinations. Helps calm patient. |

| Intervention | Rationale |
|---|---|
| 3. Accept the fact that the voices are real to the patient, but explain that you do not hear the voices. Refer to the voices as "your voices" or "voices that you hear." | 3. Validating that your reality does not include voices can help patient cast "doubt" on the validity of his or her voices. |
| 4. Stay with patients when they are starting to hallucinate, and direct them to tell the "voices they hear" to go away. Repeat often in a matter-of-fact manner. | 4. Patients can sometimes learn to push voices aside when given repeated instruction, especially within the framework of a trusting relationship. |
| 5. Keep to simple, basic, reality-based topics of conversation. Help patient to focus on one idea at a time. | 5. Patient's thinking might be confused and disorganized; this intervention helps patient focus and comprehend reality-based issues. |
| 6. Explore how the hallucinations are experienced by the patient. | 6. Exploring the hallucination and sharing the experience can help give the person a sense of power that he or she might be able to manage the hallucinatory voices. |
| 7. Help patient identify the needs that might underlie the hallucination. What other ways can these needs be met? | 7. Hallucinations might reflect needs for: a. Power b. Self-esteem c. Anger d. Sexuality |
| 8. Help patient identify times the hallucinations are most prevalent and frightening. | 8. Helps both nurse and patient identify situations and times that might be most anxiety producing and threatening to patient. |

| **Intervention** | **Rationale** |
|---|---|
| 9. Engage patient in simple physical activities or tasks that channel energy (writing, drawing, crafts, noncompetitive sports, treadmill, walking on track, exercise bike). | 9. Redirecting patient's energies to acceptable activities can decrease the possibility of acting on hallucinations and help distract from voices. |
| 10. Work with the patient to find which activities help reduce anxiety and distract the patient from hallucinatory material. Practice new skills with patient. | 10. If stress triggers hallucinatory activity, the patient might be more motivated to find ways to remove self from a stressful environment or try distraction techniques. |
| 11. Be alert for signs of increasing fear, anxiety, or agitation. | 11. Might herald hallucinatory activity, which can be very frightening to patient, and patient might act on command hallucinations (harm self or others). |
| 12. Intervene with one-on-one, seclusion, or PRN medication (as ordered) when appropriate. | 12. Intervene before anxiety begins to escalate. If patient is already out of control, use chemical or physical restraints following unit protocols. |

# DELUSIONS
## Presenting Signs and Symptoms
- The patient has fragmented, poorly organized, well-organized, systematized, or extensive system of beliefs that are not supported by reality.
- The content of the delusions can be grandiose, persecutory, jealous, somatic, or based on guilt.

## Assessment Guidelines

### Delusions

1. Assess whether delusions have to do with someone trying to harm the patient, or whether the patient is planning to retaliate against a person or organization.
   a. If patient is a threat to self or others, notify person and authorities.
   b. Confer with physician and administration if precautions need to be taken.
2. Assess when delusional thinking is most prominent (e.g., when under stress, in the presence of certain situations or people, at night).

## Selected Nursing Diagnoses and Nursing Care Plans

### DISTURBED THOUGHT PROCESSES

Disruption in cognitive operations and activities

### Some Related Factors (Related To)

● Biochemical/neurological imbalances
● Panic levels of anxiety/psychosis
● Overwhelming stressful life events
● Chemical alterations (e.g., drugs, electrolyte imbalances neurotransmitter imbalance)

### As Evidenced By

▲ Inaccurate interpretation of environment
▲ Inappropriate thinking (not reality based)
● Delusions

---

▲ NANDA International accepted; ● In addition to NANDA International

## Outcome Criteria

- Refrains from acting on delusional thinking
- Demonstrates satisfying relationships with real people
- Delusions no longer threaten or interfere with ability to function in family, social, work situations
- Perceives environment correctly

## Long-Term Goals

Patient will:
- Demonstrate two effective coping skills that minimize delusional thoughts by (date)

## Short-Term Goals

Patient will:
- State that the "thoughts" are less intense and less frequent with aid of medications and nursing interventions by (date)
- Talk about concrete happenings in the environment without talking about delusions for 5 minutes by (date)
- Begin to recognize that his or her frightening (suspicious) "thinking" occurs most often at times of stress and when he or she is anxious

## Interventions and Rationales

| Intervention | Rationale |
|---|---|
| 1. Utilize safety measures to protect patients or others, if patients believe they need to protect themselves against a specific person. Precautions are needed. | 1. During acute phase, patient's delusional thinking might dictate to them that they might have to hurt others or self to be safe. External controls might be needed. |
| 2. Attempt to understand the significance of these beliefs to the patient at the time of their presentation. | 2. Important clues to underlying fears and issues can be found in the patient's seemingly illogical fantasies. |
| 3. Be aware that patient's delusions represent the way that he or she experiences reality. | 3. Identifying the patient's experience allows the nurse to understand the patient's feelings. |

| **Intervention** | **Rationale** |
|---|---|
| 4. Identify feelings related to delusions. For example: | 4. When people believe that they are understood, anxiety might lessen. |
|   a. If patient believes someone is going to harm him/her, patient is experiencing fear. | |
|   b. If patient believes someone or something is controlling his/her thoughts, patient is experiencing helplessness. | |
| 5. Do not argue with the patient's beliefs or try to correct false beliefs using facts. | 5. Arguing will only increase patient's defensive position, thereby reinforcing false beliefs. This will result in the patient feeling even more isolated and misunderstood. |
| 6. Do not touch the patient; use gestures carefully. | 6. A psychotic person might misinterpret touch as either aggressive or sexual in nature and might interpret gestures as aggressive moves. People who are psychotic need a lot of personal space. |
| 7. Interact with patients on the basis of things in the environment. Try to distract patient from their delusions by engaging in cards, simple board games, simple arts and crafts projects, cooking with another person, and so forth. | 7. When thinking is focused on reality-based activities, the patient is free of delusional thinking during that time. Helps focus attention externally. |

| Intervention | Rationale |
|---|---|
| 8. Teach patient coping skills that minimize "worrying" thoughts. Coping skills include:<br>• Talking to a trusted person<br>• Phoning a helpline<br>• Singing (when auditory hallucinations start)<br>• Going to a gym<br>• Thought-stopping techniques | 8. When patient is ready, teach strategies patient can do alone. |
| 9. Encourage healthy habits to optimize functioning:<br>• Maintain regular sleep pattern.<br>• Reduce alcohol and drug intake.<br>• Maintain self-care.<br>• Maintain medication regimen. | 9. All are vital to help keep patient in remission. |

# PARANOIA

## Presenting Signs and Symptoms

- Pervasive suspiciousness about one or more persons and their actions
- On guard, hyperalert, vigilant
- Blames others for consequences of own behavior
- Hostile, argumentative, often threatening verbalizations or behavior
- Poor interpersonal relationships
- Has delusions of influence, persecution, and grandiosity
- Often refuses medications because "nothing is wrong with me"
- Might refuse food if believes it is poisoned

## Assessment Guidelines

### *Paranoia*

1. Assess for suicidal or homicidal behaviors.
2. Assess for potential for violence.
3. Assess need for hospitalization.

## Selected Nursing Diagnoses and Nursing Care Plans

### DEFENSIVE COPING

Repeated projection of falsely positive self-evaluation based on a self-protective pattern that defends against underlying perceived threats to positive self-regard

### *Related Factors (Related To)*

● Perceived threat to self
● Suspicions of the motives of others
● Perceived lack of self-efficacy/vulnerability

### *Defining Characteristics (As Evidenced By)*

Assessment Findings/Diagnostic Cues:
▲ Projection of blame/responsibility
▲ Reality distortion
▲ Ridicule of others
▲ Superiority to others (grandiosity)
▲ Denial of obvious problems
▲ Rationalization of failures
▲ Hostile laughter or ridicule of others
▲ Difficulty in perception of reality testing
▲ Difficulty establishing/maintaining relationships
● Hostility, aggression, or homicidal ideation

---

▲ NANDA International accepted; ● In addition to NANDA International

- Fearful
- False beliefs about the intentions of others (e.g., paranoia)

## Outcome Criteria

- Interacts with others appropriately
- Maintains adherence to treatment
- Demonstrates decreased suspicious behaviors interacting with others
- Avoids high-risk environments and situations

## Long-Term Goals

Patient will:
- Acknowledge that medications help lower suspiciousness (date)
- State that he/she feels safe and more in control in interactions with environment/family/work/social gatherings by (date)
- Be able to apply a variety of stress/anxiety-reducing techniques on own by (date)

## Short-Term Goals

Patient will:
- Remain safe with the aid of medication and nursing interventions (either interpersonal, chemical, or seclusion), as will others in the patient's environment
- Focus on reality-based activity with the aid of medication/nursing intervention by (date)
- Demonstrate two newly learned constructive ways to deal with stress and feelings of powerlessness by (date)
- With the aid of medications and nursing interventions, demonstrate the ability to remove himself or herself from situations when anxiety begins to increase by (date)
- Identify one action that promotes feeling more in control of his or her life

## Interventions and Rationales

| Intervention | Rationale |
|---|---|
| 1. Use a nonjudgmental, respectful, and neutral approach with the patient. | 1. There is less chance for a suspicious patient to misconstrue intent or meaning if content is neutral and approach is respectful and nonjudgmental. |
| 2. Be honest and consistent with patient regarding expectations and enforcing rules. | 2. Suspicious people are quick to discern dishonesty. Honesty and consistency provide an atmosphere in which trust can grow. |
| 3. Use clear and simple language when communicating with a suspicious patient. | 3. Minimize the opportunity for miscommunication and misconstruing the meaning of the message. |
| 4. Explain to patient what you are going to do before you do it. | 4. Prepares the patient beforehand and minimizes misinterpreting your intent as hostile or aggressive. |
| 5. Be aware of patient's tendency to have ideas of reference; do not do things in front of patient that can be misinterpreted: <br> a. Laughing <br> b. Whispering <br> c. Talking quietly when patient can see but not hear what is being said | 5. Suspicious patients will automatically think they are the target and negatively interpret interactions and behaviors (e.g., you are laughing at them, whispering about them, etc.). |
| 6. Diffuse angry and hostile verbal attacks with a nondefensive stand. | 6. When staff become defensive, anger escalates for both patient and staff. A nondefensive and nonjudgmental attitude provides an atmosphere in which feelings can be explored more easily. |

| Intervention | Rationale |
|---|---|
| 7. Assess and observe patient regularly for signs of increasing anxiety and hostility. | 7. Intervene before patient loses control. |
| 8. Provide verbal/physical limits when patient's hostile behavior escalates: "We won't allow you to hurt anyone here. If you can't control yourself, we will help you." | 8. Often verbal limits are effective in helping a patient gain self-control. |
| 9. Set limits in a clear, matter-of-fact way, using a calm tone. "Threatening John is not acceptable. Let's talk about appropriate ways to deal with your feelings." | 9. Calm and neutral approach may diffuse escalation of anger. Offer an alternative to verbal abuse by finding appropriate ways to deal with feelings. |
| 10. Maintain low level of stimuli and enhance a nonthreatening environment (avoid groups). | 10. Noisy environments might be perceived as threatening. |
| 11. Initially provide solitary, noncompetitive activities that take some concentration. Later, a game with one or more patients that takes concentration (e.g., chess, checkers, thoughtful card games such as bridge or rummy). | 11. If a patient is suspicious of others, solitary activities are the best. Concentrating on environmental stimuli minimizes paranoid rumination. |

## Providing Support to Family/Others

### INTERRUPTED FAMILY PROCESSES

Change in family relationships and/or functioning

## Some Related Factors (Related To)

▲ Shift in health status of a family member
▲ Situational crisis or transition
▲ Family role shift
▲ Developmental crisis or transition
▲ Mental or physical disorder of family member

## Defining Characteristics (As Evidenced By)

▲ Changes in participation in decision making
▲ Changes in mutual support
▲ Changes in stress reduction behavior
▲ Changes in communication patterns
▲ Changes in participation in problem solving
▲ Changes in expression of conflict in family
● Knowledge deficit regarding the disease and what is happening with ill family member (might believe patient is more capable than they are)
● Knowledge deficit regarding community and healthcare support

## Outcome Criteria

Family members/significant others will:
● State they have received needed support from community and agency resources that offer support, education, coping skills training, and/or social network development (psychoeducational approach)
● Demonstrate problem-solving skills for handling tensions and misunderstanding within the family environment
● Recount in some detail the early signs and symptoms of relapse in their ill family member and know whom to contact

## Long-Term Goals

Family members/significant others will:
● Know of at least two contact people when they suspect potential relapse by (date)

---

▲ NANDA International accepted; ● In addition to NANDA International

- Discuss the disease (schizophrenia) knowledgeably by (date):
  - Understand the need for medical adherence
  - Support the ill family member in maintaining optimum health
  - Know about community resources (e.g., help with self-care activities, private respite)
- Have access to family/multiple family support groups and psychoeducational training by (date)

## Short-Term Goals

Family members/significant others will:

- Meet with nurse/physician/social worker the first day of hospitalization and begin to learn about this neurological/biochemical disease, treatment, and community resources
- Attend at least one family support group (single family, multiple family) within 4 days from onset of acute episode
- Problem-solve, with the nurse, two concrete situations within the family that all would like to change
- State what the medications can do for their ill member, the side effects and toxic effects of the drugs, and the need for adherence to medication at least 2 to 3 days before discharge
- Be included in the discharge planning along with patient
- State and have written information identifying the signs of potential relapse and whom to contact before discharge
- Name and have complete list of community supports for ill family member and supports for all members of the family at least 2 days before discharge

## Interventions and Rationales

| Intervention | Rationale |
|---|---|
| 1. Identify family's ability to cope (e.g., experience of loss, caregiver burden, needed supports). | 1. Family's needs must be addressed to stabilize family unit. |
| 2. Provide opportunity for family to discuss feelings related to ill family member and identify their immediate concerns. | 2. Nurses and staff can best intervene when they understand the family's experience and needs. |

| **Intervention** | **Rationale** |
|---|---|
| 3. Assess the family members' current level of knowledge about the disease and medications used to treat the disease. | 3. Family might have misconceptions and misinformation about schizophrenia and treatment, or no knowledge at all. Teach at patient's and family's level of understanding and readiness to learn. |
| 4. Provide information on disease and treatment strategies at family's level of knowledge. | 4. Meet family members' needs for information. |
| 5. Inform the patient and family in clear, simple terms about psychopharmacological therapy: dosage, the need to take medication as prescribed, side effects, and toxic effects. Written information should be given to patient and family members as well. **Refer to the patient and family teaching guidelines in Chapter 21 under Antipsychotic Medication.** | 5. Understanding the disease and its treatment encourages greater family support and patient adherence. |
| 6. Provide information on family and patient community resources for patient and family after discharge: support groups, organizations, day hospitals, psychoeducational programs, respite centers, etc. **See list of associations and Internet sites at end of chapter.** | 6. Schizophrenia is an overwhelming disease for both the patient and family. Agencies, support groups, and psychoeducational centers can help: <br> a. Develop family skills <br> b. Access resources <br> c. Access support <br> d. Access caring <br> e. Minimize isolation <br> f. Improve quality of life for all family members |

| Intervention | Rationale |
|---|---|
| 7. Teach family and patient the warning symptoms of potential relapse. | 7. Rapid recognition of early warning symptoms can help ward off potential relapse when immediate medical attention is sought. |

# MEDICAL TREATMENT

## Psychopharmacology

Antipsychotic medications are indicated for nearly all psychotic episodes of schizophrenia. To delay medication therapy too long can put the patient at risk for suicide or other dangerous behaviors.

Medications used to treat schizophrenia are called *antipsychotic medications*. Two groups of antipsychotic drugs exist: *standard* (traditional/conventional) and the newer *atypical* (or novel) medications. **Many physicians urge the use of the *atypical* medications initially because of their better side-effect profile and their ability to target the negative symptoms (apathy, lack of motivation) and anhedonia (lack of pleasure in life), thereby increasing the quality of life for patients.**

### *Atypical (Novel) Antipsychotic Medications*

During the early 1990s, new types of antipsychotics began appearing on the market, and they are currently used as first-line medications. (Clozapine [Clozaril] is the exception because of its tendency to cause agranulocytosis and its high incidence for seizures.) These drugs not only target the acute and disturbing symptoms seen in acute, active episodes of schizophrenia (hallucinations, delusions, associative looseness, paranoia), called *positive symptoms*, but also target the negative symptoms, promoting improvement in the quality of life (increased motivation, improved judgment, increased energy, ability to experience pleasure, and increased cognitive function). These drugs also have a very low extrapyramidal symptom (EPS) profile and, in general, have a more favorable side-effect profile.

**Pros**
- Target negative and positive symptoms
- Lower risk of EPS
- Lower the incidence of adverse reactions, promote increased adherence
- May improve symptoms of anxiety and depression
- Decreased suicidal behavior

**Cons**
- Increased weight gain
- Metabolic abnormalities (glucose dysregulation, hypercholesterolemia)
- More expensive

Table 8-3 provides a list of atypical antipsychotics, their dosages, and the side effects.

## Standard Medications

Standard antipsychotic drugs target the more flagrant symptoms of schizophrenia (hallucinations, delusions, suspiciousness, associative looseness). These drugs can:
- Reduce disruptive and violent behavior
- Increase activity, speech, and sociability in withdrawn patients
- Improve self-care
- Improve sleep patterns
- Reduce the disturbing quality of hallucinations and delusions
- Improve thought processes
- Decrease resistance to supportive therapy
- Reduce rate of relapse
- Decrease intensity of paranoid reactions

Antipsychotic agents are usually effective 3 to 6 weeks after the regimen is started.

**Adverse Reactions.** There are some troubling side effects of these drugs that can at times limit treatment adherence. One of the most disturbing side effects to patients is EPS. Some side effects can be managed with other medications. EPS, cardiac side effects, and toxic effects of antipsychotic drugs are discussed further in Chapter 21, which also presents a patient and family medication teaching plan. Refer to Table 8-4 for these drugs, maintenance dose, and special considerations.

Table 8-3 **Atypical Antipsychotic Medications**

| Drug | Route(s) | Maintenance Dosage Range (mg/day) | Comments/Notable Adverse Reactions |
|---|---|---|---|
| Clozapine (Clozaril) | Oral PO<br>ODT*: FazaClo | 300–900 | • Not first line; refractory cases only<br>• Agranulocytosis in 0.8%–1%; scheduled WBC required<br>• High seizure rate<br>• Significant weight gain (67%)<br>• High lipid abnormalities<br>• Excessive salivation<br>• Tachycardia<br>• Hypotension<br>• Insomnia<br>• Sedation |
| Risperidone (Risperdal) | Oral<br>ODT*: Risperdal M-TAB<br>Consta<br>Injectable (long-acting): Risperdal Consta | 2–10 | • Rarely NMS, TD<br>• Sexual dysfunction<br>• Weight gain (18%)<br>• Moderate lipid abnormalities |

| Olanzapine (Zyprexa) | Oral ODT*: Zyprexa Injectable (short acting) | 5–20[†] | • Significant weight gain (34%)<br>• High lipid abnormalities<br>• Drowsiness<br>• Agitation and restlessness<br>• Insomnia<br>• Possibly akathisia or parkinsonism |
| Paliperidone (Invega) | Oral | 3–12 | • A metabolite of Risperidone but better tolerated because of the extended release formula<br>• Same side effects as Risperidone |
| Quetiapine (Seroquel) | Oral | 300–750[†] | • Weight gain (23%)<br>• Moderate lipid abnormalities<br>• Headache<br>• Drowsiness<br>• Orthostasis |
| Ziprasidone (Geodon) | Oral Injectable (short acting) | 60–160 | • ECG changes[‡]<br>• QT prolongation, not to be used with other drugs known to prolong QT interval<br>• Low propensity for weight gain<br>• No lipid abnormalities<br>• Targets depressive symptoms |

*Continued*

**Table 8-3 Atypical Antipsychotic Medications—cont'd**

| Drug | Route(s) | Maintenance Dosage Range (mg/day) | Comments/Notable Adverse Reactions |
|---|---|---|---|
| Aripiprazole (Abilify) | Oral/liquid IM | 15–30 | • Little or no weight gain or increase in glucose, HDL, LDL, or triglyceride levels |

*An orally disintegrating tablet (ODT) is a fast-disintegrating tablet or wafer that dissolves on the tongue.

†The safety of olanzapine at dosages of >20 mg/day and quetiapine at dosages of >800 mg/day has not been evaluated in clinical trials.

‡Ziprasidone use may carry a risk for QT prolongation in patients with preexisting cardiac disease, low electrolyte levels, or family history of QTc syndrome or in patients taking other drugs that cause long QTc profiles.

*ACh,* Anticholinergic side effects (dry mouth, blurred vision, urinary retention, constipation, agitation); *ECG,* electrocardiogram; *EPS,* extrapyramidal symptoms; *HDL,* high-density lipoprotein; *IM,* intramuscular; *LDL,* low-density lipoprotein; *NMS,* neuroleptic malignant syndrome; *ODT,* orally disintegrating tablet; *OH,* orthostatic hypotension; *PO,* by mouth; *Sed,* sedation; *TD,* tardive dyskinesia; *WBC,* white blood cell count.

Drug dosages from Preston, J.D., O'Neal, J.H., and Talaga, M.C. (2008). Handbook of clinical psychopharmacology for therapists (5th ed.). Oakland, CA: New Harbinger Publications; Preston, J., and Johnson, J. (2009). Clinical psychopharmacology made ridiculously simple (6th Ed). Miami, Forida:MedMaster, Inc.

Table 8-4 **Typical (First-Generation) Antipsychotics**

| Drug | Route(s) of Administration | Maintenance Dosage (mg/day)* | Special Considerations |
|---|---|---|---|
| **High Potency** | | | |
| Haloperidol (Haldol) | PO, IM | 1–15 | • Has low sedative properties; is used in large doses for assaultive patients to avoid the severe side effect of hypotension<br>• Appropriate for older adults for the same reason; lessens the chance of falls from dizziness or hypotension<br>• High incidence of extrapyramidal side effects |
| Haloperidol decanoate (Haldol) | IM, LAI | 50–250 | • Given deep muscle Z-track IM<br>• **Given every 3–4 weeks** |
| Trifluoperazine (Stelazine) | | 5–30 | • Low sedative effect; good for symptoms of withdrawal or pararoia<br>• High incidence of extrapyramidal side effects<br>• Neuroleptic malignant syndrome may occur |

*Continued*

Table 8-4 **Typical (First-Generation) Antipsychotics—cont'd**

| Drug | Route(s) of Administration | Maintenance Dosage (mg/day)* | Special Considerations |
|---|---|---|---|
| Fluphenazine (Prolixin) | PO, IM, subQ | 1–15 | • Among the least sedating |
| Fluphenazine decanoate (Prolixin) | IM | 6.25–50 | • Given deep muscle Z-track IM<br>• **Effective when given every 2–4 weeks** |
| Thiothixene (Navane) | PO, IM | 6–30 | • High incidence of akathisia |
| **Medium Potency** | | | |
| Loxapine (Loxitane) | PO, IM | 10–60 | • Possibly associated with weight reduction |
| Molindone (Moban) | PO | 15–100 | • Possibly associated with weight reduction |
| Perphenazine (Trilafon) | PO, IM, IV | 8–24 | • Can help control severe vomiting |
| **Low Potency** | | | |
| Chlorpromazine (Thorazine) | PO, IM, R | 50–400 | • Increases sensitivity to sun (as do other phenothiazines)<br>• Highest sedative and hypotensive effects; least potent<br>• May cause irreversible retinitis pigmentosa at 800 mg/day |

| Chlorprothixene (Taractam) | PO, IM | 75–600 | • Weight gain common |
| Thioridazine (Mellaril) | PO | 50–400 | • **Not recommended as first-line antipsychotic**<br>• Dose-related severe ECG changes (prolonged QTC intervals), may cause sudden death |

*Dosages vary with individual response to the antipsychotic agent used.

*IM,* Intramuscular; *IV,* intravenous; *LAI,* long-acting injectable; *PO,* by mouth; *R,* rectal; *subQ,* subcutaneous.

Drug dosages from Lehne, R.A. (2007). *Pharmacology for nursing care* (6th ed.). St. Louis: Saunders; Preston, J.D., Oneal, J.H., and Talaga, M.C. (2005). *Handbook for clinical psychopharmacology for therapists* (4th ed.). Oakland, CA: New Harbinger Publications.

# PSYCHOSOCIAL APPROACHES

## Treatment of Comorbid Conditions

There are many treatment approaches that can help patients with schizophrenia better adjust to their environment and increase their quality of life when used in conjunction with medications. Some of the psychotherapeutic approaches that seem to be useful for many people with these disorders are discussed here. However, treatment should not only be aimed at the symptoms of schizophrenia but also must target comorbid conditions a patient might exhibit. Some of the more common comorbid conditions in people with schizophrenia include:

- Substance use problems
- Depressive symptoms or disorders
- Risk for suicide
- Violent behaviors

If a comorbid condition is identified, it must be treated if overall adherence to a second treatment approach is to be followed and/or successful.

## Specific Psychosocial Treatments

### Individual Therapy

There is evidence that *supportive therapy* that includes problem-solving techniques and social skills training helps reduce relapse and enhance social and occupational functioning when added to medication treatment for schizophrenic individuals who are treated in an outpatient environment. Cognitive behavioral therapy (CBT), cognitive rehabilitation, and social skills training (SST) are particularly helpful in people with chronic schizophrenia who have cognitive impairments.

### Family Intervention

Families with a schizophrenic member endure considerable hardships while coping with the psychotic and residual symptoms of schizophrenia. Often families are the sole caretakers of their schizophrenic member and need education, guidance, support, and training to help them manage (APA, 2000b). A **psychoeducational family approach** provides support, education, coping skills training, and social network expansion and has been proven very successful with both decreasing family stress and increasing patient adherence to treatment. Psychoeducational, family, group, and behavioral approaches can help patients increase their social skills, maximize their ability in self-care and independent living, maintain medical adherence, and most important, increase the quality of their lives. Patient and family education greatly improves the management of schizophrenia. Families can be helped by:

- Understanding the disease and the role of medications
- Setting realistic goals for their family member with schizophrenia
- Developing problem-solving skills for handling tensions and misunderstanding within the family environment
- Identifying early signs of relapse
- Having knowledge of where they can go for guidance and support within the community and nationally

### Group Therapy

The goals of group therapy for individual members are to increase problem-solving ability, enable realistic goal planning, facilitate social interactions, and manage medication side effects. Groups can help patients develop interpersonal skills, work on family problems, and utilize community supports, as well as increase medication adherence by learning to deal with troubling side effects.

## NURSE, PATIENT, and FAMILY RESOURCES

## ASSOCIATIONS

**National Alliance for the Mentally Ill (NAMI)**
Colonial Place Three
2107 Wilson Boulevard, Suite 300
Arlington, VA 22201–3042
(800) 950-NAMI (check this one out!)
www.nami.org

**Schizophrenics Anonymous**
403 Seymour Avenue, Suite 202

Lansing, MI 48933
(517) 485–7168;(800) 482–9534 (consumer line) (check this
    one out!)

**Recovery, Inc**.
802 North Dearborn Street
Chicago, II, 60610
(312) 337–5661

## INTERNET SITES

**Doctors Guide to the Internet**
www.pslgroup.com/schizophr.htm
Many articles; good site for schizophrenia information

**Internet Mental Health**
www.mentalhealth.com
Vast amount of information/booklets/articles and general
    information

**National Alliance for Research on Schizophrenia and
    Depression**
www.narsad.org

**Schizophrenia.com**
www.schizophrenia.com

# CHAPTER 9

# Personality Disorders

## OVERVIEW

People with personality disorders (PD) present complex and difficult behavioral challenges for themselves and people around them. They are often referred to as "difficult patients." *Personality traits* are the enduring styles we use to deal with the world—for example, shyness, rigidity, obsessiveness, manipulativeness, suspiciousness, and the like.

In people with PDs, these traits are maladaptive, persistent, and inflexible and cause dysfunction and disruption in the individual's relationships, jobs, social patterns, and more. The intensity and manifestation of presenting problems can vary widely among patients with PD, depending on diagnoses and specific characteristics. Some patients with PDs have milder forms of disability, whereas other patients' symptoms present as extreme or even psychotic. However, all of the PDs have four common characteristics:

1. Inflexible and maladaptive responses to stress
2. Disability in working and loving
3. Ability to evoke interpersonal conflict in health care providers as well as family and friends
4. Capacity to have an intense effect on others (this process is often unconscious and generally produces undesirable results)

Personality disorders frequently occur in conjunction with other psychiatric disorders or with general medical conditions. For example, both major depression and anxiety disorders have a high rate of comorbidity (co-occurrence)

259

with PDs, estimated to occur in approximately 40% to 70% of patients. Comorbid PDs are likely to be found in patients with somatization, eating disorder, chronic pain, recurrent suicide attempts, and posttraumatic stress disorder (Boerescu, 2007). People with a substance abuse problem might also have a comorbid PD, which can complicate the therapeutic working relationship and interfere with treatment.

Box 9-1 identifies the *Diagnostic and Statistical Manual of Mental Disorders* (4th edition, text revision) (*DSM-IV-TR*) criteria for a person with a PD. The *DSM-IV-TR* organizes

---

| Box 9-1 | DSM-IV-TR<br>Criteria for a Personality Disorder |
|---------|--------------------------------------------------|

1. An enduring pattern of inner experience and behavior that deviates markedly from the expectations of the individual's culture. This pattern is manifested in two (or more) of the following areas:
   - Cognition (i.e., ways of perceiving and interpreting self, other people, and events)
   - Affect (i.e., the range, intensity, liability, and appropriateness of emotional response)
   - Interpersonal functioning
   - Impulse control
2. The enduring pattern is inflexible and pervasive across a broad range of personal and social situations.
3. The enduring pattern leads to clinically significant distress or impairment in social, occupational, or other important areas of functioning.
4. The pattern is stable and of long duration, and its onset can be traced back at least to adolescence or early adulthood.
5. The enduring pattern is not better accounted for as a manifestation or consequence of another mental disorder.
6. The enduring pattern is not due to the direct physiological effects of a substance (e.g., a drug of abuse, a medication) or a general medical condition (e.g., head trauma).

---

Adapted from American Psychiatric Association (APA). (2000). *Diagnostic and statistical manual of mental disorders* (4th ed., text rev.) (*DSM-IV-TR*). Washington DC: Author, p. 689; reprinted with permission.

the 10 PDs into three clusters (Box 9-2). Because each of the PDs has its own characteristics, personality traits, and effects on self and others, it is best to deal with them individually. The following sections describe the defining characteristics, identify some intervention guidelines, and offer the most recent treatment modalities for each PD.

Some of the most problematic behaviors nurses are confronted with in the health care setting are similar for many of the PDs. These behaviors in part include manipulation (see Chapter 19), self-mutilation, suicide (see Chapter 16), anger and hostility (see Chapter 17), low self-esteem, ineffective coping and/or impaired social interaction, and nonadherence to medication or treatment (see Chapter 20). **Self-mutilation, low self-esteem, impaired social interaction, and ineffective coping** are covered in this chapter. The other common nursing diagnoses of patients with PD are covered in separate chapters. All of these behaviors are commonly seen in a host of disorders, and the guidelines for intervention are similar for all patients.

Although people with PDs might be hospitalized briefly during a crisis, generally long-term treatment takes place in clinics and community settings.

| Box 9-2 | *DSM-IV-TR* Personality Disorder Clusters |
|---------|-------------------------------------------|

**Cluster A Disorders—Odd or Eccentric**
Paranoid Personality Disorder
Schizoid Personality Disorder
Schizotypal Personality Disorder

**Cluster B Disorders—Dramatic, Emotional, or Erratic**
Antisocial Personality Disorder
Borderline Personality Disorder
Histrionic Personality Disorder
Narcissistic Personality Disorder

**Cluster C Disorders—Anxious or Fearful**
Dependent Personality Disorder
Obsessive-Compulsive Personality Disorder
Avoidant Personality Disorder

## *DSM-IV-TR* Cluster A Disorders—Odd or Eccentric

Cluster A disorders, often referred to as "odd" or "eccentric," comprise PDs that have been established to have some relationship to schizophrenia. Of the Cluster A disorders, schizotypal PD is most strongly related to schizophrenia. The following discussion gives defining characteristics, guidelines for care, and treatments for the Cluster A disorders.

### Paranoid Personality Disorder (PPD)

*Presenting Signs and Symptoms*

- Vigilant and suspicious of others' motives—believe people mean to exploit, harm, or deceive them in some manner
- Bear grudges; are unforgiving of insults, injuries, or slights
- Read hidden, demeaning, or threatening meanings into benign remarks or events
- Have difficulty establishing close relationships; usually work alone
- Perceived as cold and unemotional, and do not share their thoughts with others; lack a sense of humor
- Very critical of others but have a great deal of difficulty accepting criticism
- Are prone to file lawsuits

### Nursing Guidelines

1. Avoid being too "nice" or "friendly."
2. Give clear and straightforward explanations of tests and procedures beforehand.
3. Use simple, clear language; avoid ambiguity.
4. Project a neutral but kind affect.
5. Warn about any changes, side effects of medications, and reasons for delay. Such interventions might help allay anxiety and minimize suspiciousness.
6. A written plan of treatment might help encourage cooperation.

## Treatment

Paranoid patients will initially mistrust their therapist's motives and find it difficult to share personal information. For that reason, therapy is often not sought or sustained among these patients. However, when a person with PPD does enter therapy, initially supportive therapy might help the patient experience trust and even begin to feel some amount of safety in an interpersonal relationship. If a therapeutic alliance can be achieved, cognitive and behavioral techniques might be useful to the patient. The focus is on counteracting fear and relieving stress and worry that are often expressed as hypervigilance and social withdrawal (Boerescu, 2007). Severe symptoms of paranoia can be attenuated with careful use of antipsychotic medication.

## Schizoid Personality Disorder

### Presenting Signs and Symptoms

- Neither desire nor enjoy close relationships, even within their own family
- Prefer to live apart from others, choose solitary activities, have little interest in sexual activity with others, and might describe themselves as "loners"
- Show emotional coldness, detachment, or flattened affect
- Occupation often involves little interpersonal contact

### Nursing Guidelines

1. Avoid being too "nice" or "friendly."
2. Do not try to resocialize these patients, accept their need to be uninvolved.
3. A thorough diagnostic assessment might be needed to identify symptoms or disorders the patient is reluctant to discuss (Boerescu, 2007).

## Treatment

A schizoid individual is apt to seek treatment only in a crisis situation, and only then to seek relief from acute symptoms. In some cases, supportive psychotherapy with cognitive-behavioral techniques can help reinforce socially outgoing behaviors. Group therapy might be appropriate if the individual needs of each patient are addressed. In some cases, social skills training groups might be an effective intervention (Zale et al., 1997). Short-term use of psychopharmacology might be appropriate for treating anxiety or depression. Low-dose antipsychotic medication can target symptoms such as anger, hostility, paranoia, and ideas of reference if such symptoms are part of the clinical picture.

## Schizotypal Personality Disorders

### Presenting Signs and Symptoms

- Share many of the withdrawn, aloof, and socially distant characteristics listed for the schizoid PD patient described earlier
- Ideas of reference, odd beliefs, magical thinking, or unusual perceptual experiences, including bodily illusions, might be present
- Excessive and unrelieved social anxiety frequently associated with paranoid fears
- Lack of close friends and confidants
- Inappropriate or constricted affect
- Behavior or appearance that is odd, eccentric, or peculiar
- Some individuals diagnosed with schizotypal PD will go on to present with a full-blown schizophrenic illness

### Nursing Guidelines

1. Respect the patient's need for social isolation.
2. Be aware of patient's suspiciousness and employ appropriate interventions (see Chapter 8).
3. As with the schizoid patient, careful diagnostic assessment might be needed to uncover any other medical or psychological symptoms that might need intervention (e.g., suicidal thoughts).

### Treatment

As with the schizoid patient, allowing distance and providing supportive measures might encourage the gradual development of a therapeutic alliance. Cognitive and behavioral measures might help patients gain basic social skills. Low-dose therapy with the newer atypical antipsychotics can be effective in allowing the schizotypal patient to be more comfortable, less anxious, less prone to suspiciousness, and to treat transient psychotic stats.

## *DSM-IV-TR* Cluster B Disorders—Dramatic, Emotional, or Erratic

These four disorders appear to share dramatic, erratic, or flamboyant behavior as part of their presenting symptoms. As yet, no empirical evidence for this manner of clustering exists, but there does seem to be a high degree of overlap among these disorders. There is also a great deal of comorbidity with Axis I disorders such as substance abuse and mood and anxiety disorders, as well as other PDs (cluster A, B, or C) that are found on Axis II. It is often difficult for the clinician to know which disorder is primary and which should take precedence in treatment (Zale et al., 1997).

### Antisocial Personality Disorder (ASPD)

#### *Presenting Signs and Symptoms*

- An extended history of antisocial behaviors (stealing, persistent lying, cruelty to animals or people, vandalism, substance abuse) usually beginning before the age of 15 and continuing into adulthood
- Deceitfulness (use of aliases, conning others for personal profit or pleasure, repeated lying)
- Consistent irresponsibility (failure to honor financial obligations, work responsibilities, family/parenting obligations)
- Impassivity and repeated aggressiveness toward others
- Total lack of remorse for physically or emotionally hurting or mistreating others or swindling or stealing from others
- At times presents as charming, self-assured, and adept

- Interaction with others through **manipulation, aggressiveness,** and **exploitation;** totally lacking in empathy or concern for others
- Substance abuse is the most frequent comorbid Axis I disorder.
- There is a significant familial pattern to criminality in general and ASPD in particular.

## Nursing Guidelines

1. Try to prevent or reduce untoward effects of manipulation (flattery, seductiveness, instilling guilt).
   - Set clear and realistic limits on specific behavior.
   - All limits should be adhered to by all staff involved.
   - Carefully document objective physical signs of manipulation or aggression when managing clinical problems.
   - Document behaviors objectively (give times, dates, circumstances).
   - Provide clear boundaries and consequences.
2. Be aware that antisocial patients can instill guilt when they are not getting what they want. Guard against being manipulated through feeling guilty.
3. Treatment of substance abuse is best handled through a well-organized treatment *before* counseling and other forms of therapy are started.

## Treatment

Very few treatment modalities have proven successful. Nor is there any treatment of choice for ASPD. The most useful approach is to target specific problem behaviors that have been shown to be amenable to modification, combined with other therapies such as psychopharmacology and family therapy. Caregivers need to focus on avoiding to be manipulated and provide clear boundaries with consequences. Some positive results have been obtained through milieu programs (e.g., token economy systems and therapeutic communities).

## Borderline Personality Disorder (BPD)

### Presenting Signs and Symptoms

- Relationships with others are intense, unstable, and alternate between intense dependence and rejection.
- Behaviors are often impulsive and self-damaging (e.g., spending, unsafe sex, substance abuse, reckless driving, binge eating).
- Recurrent suicidal and/or self-mutilating behaviors are common, often in response to perceived threats of rejection, separation.
- Chronic feelings of emptiness or boredom and an absence of self-satisfaction.
- Frantic efforts to avoid real or imagined abandonment.
- Intense affect is manifested in outbursts of anger, hostility, depression, and/or anxiety.
- Intense and primitive rage often complicates therapy and takes the form of extreme sarcasm, enduring bitterness, and angry outbursts at others.
- Major defense is **splitting,** which often manifests in pitting one person or group against another (good guy versus bad guy).
- Splitting is only one form of **manipulation** that individuals with BPD use.
- Rapid idealization-devaluation is a classic signal behavior suggestive of borderline psychopathology or some other primitive personality.
- Transient quasi-psychotic symptoms might develop in the form of paranoid or dissociative symptoms during times of stress.

### Nursing Guidelines

1. Set realistic goals, use clear action words.
2. Be aware of manipulative behaviors (flattery, seductiveness, guilt instilling).
3. Provide clear and consistent boundaries and limits.
4. Use clear and straightforward communication.
5. When behavioral problems emerge, calmly review the therapeutic goals and boundaries of treatment.
6. Avoid rejecting or rescuing.
7. Assess for suicidal and self-mutilating behaviors, especially during times of stress.

## Treatment

Treating people with BPD is a challenge. One method has emerged that has been successful for many people with BPD. Marsha Linehan (1993) developed a behaviorally based treatment that targets the highly dysfunctional behaviors seen in these patients. Her therapeutic approach is called **dialectical behavioral therapy (DBT).** DBT has proven extremely effective in helping borderline individuals gain hope and quality of life.

Therapy for a person with BPD is often marked by a period of improvement with alternating periods of worsening. Short-term hospitalization is not uncommon during periods of suicidal or self-mutilating behaviors or severe depression. Long-term outpatient therapy, and at times carefully chosen group therapy if appropriate for the patient, has provided improvement for many patients.

A combination of psychotherapy and medication seems to provide the best results for treatment of patients diagnosed with BPD. Medications can reduce anxiety, depression, and disruptive impulses. Approximately 50% of people with BPD experience serious episodes of depression. Low-dose antipsychotics might prove useful for severely cognitively disturbed individuals. The newer antidepressants (SSRIs) have helped some BPD patients in dealing with their anger. The anticonvulsant carbamazepine has demonstrated some efficacy in decreasing the frequency and severity of behavioral dyscontrol episodes, suicidality, and temper outbursts (McGee & Linehan, 1997).

Patients with BPD pose great challenges for nurse clinicians, and supervision is advised to help with the inevitable strong countertransference issues.

## Histrionic Personality Disorder (HPD)

### Presenting Signs and Symptoms

- Consistently draw attention to themselves; very concerned about being attractive and use physical appearance to gain center stage
- Show excessive emotionality and attention-getting behavior (e.g., display sexually seductive, provocative, or self-dramatizing behaviors)
- Intense emotional expressions are shallow, with rapid shifts from person to person or idea to idea

- Prone to describe more intimacy in a relationship than is there (e.g., show intense attention to a casual acquaintance)
- Are suggestible (easily influenced by others or circumstances)
- Others experience them as smothering, destructive; unable to understand/insensitive to anyone else's experience
- Without instant gratification or admiration from others, patients can experience depression and become suicidal

## Nursing Guidelines

1. Understand seductive behavior as a response to distress.
2. Keep communication and interactions professional, despite temptation to collude with the patient in a flirtatious and misleading manner.
3. Encourage and model the use of concrete and descriptive rather than vague and impressionistic language.
4. Teach and role model assertiveness.

### Treatment

People with HPD use indirect means to get others to take care of them (physical attractiveness, charm, temper outbursts), and this can greatly complicate the therapeutic process. Therapeutic approaches used are psychoanalytic and cognitive-behavioral methods; however, research on the treatment of HPD is lacking. Most of the literature consists of case reports using various approaches (McGee & Linchan, 1997).

## Narcissistic Personality Disorder (NPD)

### Presenting Signs and Symptoms

- Exploit others to meet their own needs and desires
- Come across as arrogant and demonstrate a demeanor of "persistent entitlement"
- Portray a demeanor of grandiosity, a need for admiration, and a lack of empathy for others (American Psychiatric Association [APA], 2000)
- May begrudge others their success or possessions, feeling that they deserve the admiration and privileges more (APA, 2000)

- Relationships are characterized by disruption (frequently provoke arguments) or control (consistently in power struggles)

## Nursing Guidelines

1. Remain neutral and avoid power struggles or becoming defensive in response to the patient's disparaging remarks, no matter how provocative the situation might be.
2. Convey unassuming self-confidence.

### Treatment

There have been no controlled trials of efficacy for any one therapeutic approach. The main approaches are supportive or insight-oriented psychotherapy. Milieu therapy might be useful for some NPD patients. Treatment difficulties are based on the patient's need to renounce their narcissism to make progress which is ingrained and chronic (Kaplan & Sadock, 2007). Most of these patients do not seek treatment unless they seek treatment for an Axis I disorder and have comorbid NPD.

### *DSM-IV-TR* Cluster C Disorders—Anxious or Fearful

These disorders have been clustered together because their common property is the experience of high levels of anxiety and the outward signs of fear. These personality types also show social inhibitions, mostly in the sexual sphere (e.g., shyness or awkwardness with potential sexual partners; impotence or frigidity). Many people with a Cluster C disorder have a fearful reluctance to express irritation or anger, even in an interpersonal encounter that justifies these feelings (Stone, 1997).

Inhibited patients tend to *internalize* blame for the frustrations in their lives even when they are not to blame for these frustrations. This willingness to accept responsibility for contributing to their own unhappiness can foster a good working relationship between clinician and patient. Therefore, this can be a useful trait. Those who blame others for their problems (*externalize* blame outward), such as antisocial, paranoid, and sadistic people, pose great challenges in therapy and have a guarded prognosis (Stone, 1997).

## Dependent Personality Disorder (DPD)

### Presenting Signs and Symptoms

- Might manifest an unusual degree of agreeableness or friendliness
- These qualities are meant to enhance the dependent person's ability to attach to another who can act as protector; urgently seeks another relationship as a source of care and support when a close relationship ends
- Clinging is a common manifestation, but unfortunately this trait eventually alienates people and threatens to drive them away
- Often perfecting the technique of clinging to others takes the place of outside interests, reading, cultivation of friends, or other sustaining activities
- Have difficulty making everyday decisions without excessive advice and support from others
- Go to excessive lengths to obtain nurture and support from others, even to the point of being mistreated or abused, or suffering extreme self-sacrifice
- Need others to assume responsibility for most major areas of life; when others do not take initiative or take responsibility for them, their needs go unmet
- Have difficulty expressing disagreements with others for fear of loss of support or approval
- At risk for anxiety and mood disorders. DPD can occur in conjunction with BPD, avoidant personality disorder, and HPD
- Fear not getting enough care and often insist on having everything done for them

### Nursing Guidelines

1. Identify and help address current stresses.
2. Try to satisfy patient's needs, but set limits in such a manner that the patient does not feel punished, which might lead to withdrawal.
3. Strong countertransference often develops in clinicians because of the patient's excessive clinging (demands of extra time, nighttime calls, crisis before vacations); therefore, supervision is well advised.
4. Teach and role model assertiveness.

## Treatment

A variety of therapies are useful and might all be appropriate during different phases while working on specific issues. Therapies include supportive therapy, cognitive-behavioral therapy, and group therapy focused on cognitive change, assertive training, and social skills (Boerescu, 2007). Therapy is usually long-term.

## Obsessive-Compulsive Personality Disorder (OCPD)

### Presenting Signs and Symptoms

- Inflexible, rigid, and need to be in control
- Perfectionists to a degree that it interferes with completion of work; cannot delegate
- Overemphasis on work to the exclusion of friendships and pleasurable leisure activities
- Preoccupied with details to the extent that decision making is impaired
- Intimacy in relationships is superficial and rigidly controlled, even though patients with OCPD might feel deep and genuine affection for friends and family
- Highly critical of self and others in matters of morality, ethics, or values
- The term *compulsive* refers to the behavioral aspects: preoccupation with lists, rules, schedules, and more. Other traits include indecisiveness, hoarding, and stinginess with money or time.
- Often overwhelmed with a concern about loss of control (being too messy, sexy, or naughty); hence, their need to overcontrol and dominate people and situations in their lives (Stone, 1997).

## Nursing Guidelines

1. Guard against engaging in power struggles with an OCPD patient. Need for control is very high for these patients.
2. Intellectualization, rationalization, and reaction formation are the most common defense mechanisms that patients with OCPD use.

## Treatment

Individual psychotherapy, supportive therapy, and particularly cognitive-behavioral therapy might all be useful, depending on goals and the ego strengths of the patient. Therapeutic issues usually include those of control, submission, and intellectualization. Some medications found to be useful for the obsessional component are clomipramine (tricyclic antidepressant [TCA]), fluoxetine (SSRI), and clonazepam (anxiolytic). Group therapy can also be a useful adjunct to therapy.

## Avoidant Personality Disorder (APD)

### Presenting Signs and Symptoms

- Pervasive pattern of social inhibition; virtually all people with APD have social phobias
- Strong feelings of inadequacy; APD patients experience fear of rejection and/or criticism; are very reticent in social situations because of this fear
- Avoid occupational activities that involve significant interpersonal contact because of fears of criticism, disapproval, or rejection
- View themselves as socially inept, personally unappealing, or inferior to others
- Might be inhibited and reluctant to involve themselves in new interpersonal situations or new activities
- Not uncommon for some patients with APD to have comorbid agoraphobia and obsessive-compulsive disorder as well as social phobia

### Nursing Guidelines

1. A friendly, gentle, reassuring approach is the best way to treat patients with APD.
2. Being pushed into social situations can cause extreme and severe anxiety for APD patients.

## Treatment

Each patient needs to be assessed individually. For example, if the patient has been taught fearfulness and withdrawal by avoidant parents, treatment would differ from that for the patient whose behavioral and cognitive traits stem from parental brutalization, incest, or sexual molestation in childhood (Stone, 1997). Because of the inherent social phobia, various forms of treatment can prove useful, such as cognitive therapy, desensitization, social skills training, and other cognitive-behavioral techniques. Group therapy has not proven advantageous over one-on-one supportive or exploratory psychotherapies. However, in the case of incest or other interpersonal trauma, special groups that include people with similar backgrounds are considered quite beneficial (Stone, 1997). Social anxiety might respond to a monoamine oxidase inhibitor (MAOI). Benzodiazepine anxiolytics might help to contain brief panic episodes. The lowering of the frightening anxiety can help patients engage more readily in therapy and can aid treatment adherence when patients are very fearful and anxious.

# ASSESSMENT

## Presenting Signs and Symptoms

In assessing for a PD, the patient's history might reveal persistent traits held for long periods of time, causing distress or impairment in functioning. Refer to the sections on individual PDs for specific signs and symptoms. What follows are assessment guidelines for identifying whether a patient fits into a specific Cluster A, B, or C disorder. Does the patient:

### Cluster A

1. Suspect others of exploiting or deceiving him or her? Bear grudges and not forget insults?
2. Detach self from social relationships? Not desire close relationships or being part of a family? Take pleasure in few if any activities?
3. Have a history of social and interpersonal deficits marked by acute discomfort? Have any cognitive or perceptual distortions?

### Cluster B

1. Have a pervasive pattern of disregard for and violation of the rights of others? Act deceitfully (repeated lying,

use others for own needs)? Act consistently irresponsible toward others?
2. Have a pattern of unstable and chaotic personal relationships? Have a history of suicide attempts or self-mutilation? Have chronic feelings of emptiness or show intense anger, intense anxiety, and dysphoria?
3. Have a pattern of excessive emotionality and attention-seeking behaviors (e.g., sexually seductive or provocative)? Have very self-dramatic, theatrical, and exaggerated expressions of emotion?
4. Act grandiose, need admiration, lack empathy for others? Have unreasonable expectations of favored treatment? Act interpersonally exploitive?

## Cluster C

1. Persistently avoid social situations because of feelings of inadequacy and hypersensitivity to negative evaluation? View self as socially inept or inferior to others?
2. Have an excessive need to be taken care of, show clinging behaviors within relationships, have intense fear of separation? Have difficulty making everyday decisions without excessive amount of advice and reassurance from others?
3. Have a preoccupation with neatness, perfectionism, and mental and interpersonal control? Show rigidity and stubbornness?

**Patients with PDs rarely seek treatment. When they do they rarely continue after the crisis is over.**
1. Patient usually comes to the attention of the health care system through a crisis situation.
2. Antisocial patients most often come into the health care system through the courts by means of a court order.
3. Suicide attempts, self-mutilation, or substance abuse are common crises that bring people with PD into treatment.

## Assessment Tools

Refer to Appendix D-6 for a sample questionnaire helpful in identifying personality traits.

## Assessment Guidelines

### Personality Disorders

1. Assessment about personality functioning needs to be viewed within the person's ethnic, cultural, and social background.
2. PDs are often exacerbated following the loss of significant supporting people or in a disruptive social situation.
3. A change in personality in middle adulthood or later signals the need for a thorough medical workup or assessment for unrecognized substance abuse disorder.
4. Be cognizant that social stereotypes can muddy a clinician's judgment in that a particular diagnosis can be over- or underdiagnosed (e.g., for males or females because of sexual bias; because of social class or immigrant status).

# NURSING DIAGNOSES WITH INTERVENTIONS

## Discussion of Potential Nursing Diagnoses

The data the nurse clinician collects provides information about the patient's presenting problem or behaviors, emotional state, precipitating situations, and maladaptive coping behaviors. Patients with PDs present with any number of problematic behaviors. These behaviors can be pathological or maladaptive. Behaviors that are repetitive or rigid, or those that present an obstacle to meaningful relationships or functioning, are considered behaviors that will be focused on during management of care. Many of the dysfunctional thought processes and behaviors were described earlier in the individual presentations of these disorders.

**Short-term goals** usually center on the patient's safety and comfort and are pertinent to the patient's physical and mental well-being. Often, the first goals for the management of an acute crisis are to evaluate the need for medication and to identify appropriate verbal interventions to decrease the patient's immediate emotional stress (Profiri, 1998). **Keep in mind that patients have varied degrees of cognitive functioning and disabilities.**

**What might be a short-term goal for one is likely a long-term goal for another**. The goals cited here and in other chapters are helpful guidelines, but often the clinician is the one to best estimate patient strengths, capabilities, supports, and current level of functioning when setting specific time limits on goals. (For more on this topic, see Chapter 1.)

**Long-term goals** are targeted for the long term and center on skill attainment. It is important to keep goals realistic. Changing lifelong patterns of behaviors that are inflexible and persistent takes a great deal of time, as well as engagement by the patient. Outcome criteria usually include the following areas (Profiri, 1998):

- Linking consequences to both functional and dysfunctional behaviors
- Learning and mastering skills that facilitate functional behaviors
- Practicing the substitution of functional alternatives during crisis
- Ongoing management of anger, anxiety, shame, and happiness
- Creating a lifestyle that prevents regressing (e.g., **HALT:** never getting too Hungry, too Angry, too Lonely, or too Tired)
- Nursing crisis intervention strategies

PD patients often act very impulsively. The nurse will be called on to intervene in many acting-out behaviors, often marked by impulsivity, such as self-mutilation and/or suicide attempts, anger and hostility toward the nurse clinician, extreme paranoia and blaming others for problems, manipulation and splitting, and intense anxiety for example. Acting-out behaviors are often most intense during the initial phases of therapy. Dealing with patients when they are acting out, especially during crises, takes persistence, patience, and learned skill on the part of the clinician. Some of the more common behavioral defenses PD patients employ require rigorous interventions. Because it is impossible to deal with all the problem areas of the 10 PDs, we will identify common behaviors for which all nurses are encouraged to develop skills. Common phenomena related to PD patients are (1) manipulation, (2) self-mutilation/suicide attempts, (3) intense low self-esteem, (4) intense anxiety, (5) anger and physical fighting, (6) projecting identification and blame to others, and (7) impulsivity. PD patients are often very demanding of health care personnel and others.

Four common phenomena and nursing diagnoses are presented here: **Risk for Self-Mutilation** (scratching, burning, cutting), **Chronic Low Self-Esteem, Impaired Social Interaction,** and **Ineffective Coping.** Nursing interventions for minimizing and preventing **manipulation** are presented in Chapter 19. **Suicide** is covered in Chapter 16. Intense **anger and hostility** are addressed in Chapter 17.

People with PDs have great difficulty getting along with others and often elicit intense negative feelings from others. The following behaviors are found in a variety of combinations: demanding, angry, fault finding, suspicious, insensitive to the needs of others, manipulative, clinging, at times withdrawn, and often intensely lonely. Therefore, the interpersonal relationships of those with PDs are often chaotic and unsatisfying for all concerned. **Impaired Social Interaction (Defensive Coping/Avoidance, Ineffective Coping)** are key nursing diagnoses for people with PD; these problems are always present, most often in response to intense feelings of powerlessness. Table 9-1 identifies other possible nursing diagnoses.

Many people with PDs leave therapy after a crisis is over and things have settled down somewhat. Therefore, nonadherence to therapy or medication is common. **Nonadherence to medications or treatment** is addressed in Chapter 20.

The nurse should remember, however, that each patient is uniquely individual, and although many of the phenomena are shared among several of the PDs, the manifestations of these behaviors can take many forms. The difficulty PD patients have in their interpersonal relationships is carried over to the health care setting and poses challenges for nurses, physicians, and other health care personnel.

Supervision and case discussion are usually extremely useful in guarding against getting caught up in countertransferential power struggles and nontherapeutic encounters that threaten any therapeutic alliance.

Whatever nursing diagnoses you choose, keep in mind that nursing diagnoses must be uniquely crafted to the specific individual, the presenting symptoms, the individual circumstances, and the personal manifestation of these symptoms. This is especially true for people with PDs.

Table 9-1 **Potential Nursing Diagnoses for Personality Disorders**

| Symptoms | Nursing Diagnosis |
|---|---|
| Crisis, high levels of anxiety | Ineffective Coping Anxiety Anxiety |
| Anger and aggression; child, elder, or spouse abuse | Risk for Other-Directed Violence |
| | Ineffective Coping |
| | Impaired Parenting |
| | Disabled Family Coping |
| Withdrawal | Social Isolation |
| Paranoia | Fear |
| | Disturbed Sensory Perception |
| | Disturbed Thought Processes |
| | Defensive Coping |
| Depression | Hopelessness |
| | Helplessness |
| | Risk for Self-Directed Violence |
| | Self-Mutilation |
| | Chronic Low Self-Esteem |
| | Spiritual Distress |
| Difficulty in relationships, manipulation | Ineffective Coping |
| | Impaired Social Interaction |
| | Defensive Coping |
| | Interrupted Family Processes |
| | Risk for Loneliness |
| Not keeping medical appointments, late for appointments, not following prescribed medical procedure/ medication | Ineffective Therapeutic Regimen Management |
| | Nonadherence to Medications or Treatments (specify) |

## Overall Guidelines for Nursing Interventions

### Personality Disorders

1. Understand that creating a therapeutic alliance with patients with PD is going to be difficult. A history of interrupted therapeutic alliances, in addition to the

patient's suspiciousness, aloofness, secretive style, and hostility, can be a setup for failure.

2. Giving PD patients some choices (e.g., time they wish to set up appointments) might enhance adherence, because these patients often require a sense of control.

3. A feeling of being threatened and vulnerable might lead to blaming or verbally attacking others.

4. Patients with PD are hypersensitive to criticism; one of the most effective methods of teaching new behaviors is to build on the patient's existing skills.

5. Setting limits is an important part of the work with PD patients. It is important for nurses to take time setting clear boundaries (nurse's responsibilities and patient's responsibility) and repeat the limits frequently when working with PD patients.

## Selected Nursing Diagnoses and Nursing Care Plans

### RISK FOR SELF-MUTILATION

At risk for deliberate self-injurious behavior causing tissue damage with the intent of causing nonfatal injury to attain relief of tension

### *Some Risk Factors (Related To)*

▲ High-risk populations (BPD, psychotic states, eating disorders, etc.)
▲ History of self-injury
▲ History of physical, emotional, or sexual abuse
▲ Feelings of depression, rejection, self-hatred, separation anxiety, guilt, and depersonalization
▲ Psychotic state (e.g., command hallucinations)
▲ Emotionally disturbed or battered children
▲ Mentally retarded and autistic children
▲ Ineffective coping skills
▲ Desperate need for attention
▲ Inability to verbally express tensions
▲ Impulsive behavior

## *Defining Characteristics (As Evidenced By)*

- Signs of old scars on wrists and other parts of the body (cigarette burns, superficial knife/razor marks)
- Fresh superficial slashes on wrists or other parts of the body
- Statements as to self-mutilation behaviors
- Intense rage focused inward

## *Outcome Criteria*

- Is free of self-inflicted injury
- Participates in impulse control training
- Participates in coping skills training
- Seeks help when experiencing self-destructive impulses

## *Long-Term Goals*

Patient will:
- Demonstrate a decrease in frequency and intensity of self-inflicted injury by (date)
- Participate in therapeutic regimen
- Demonstrate two new coping skills that work for patient for when tension mounts and impulse returns by (date)

## *Short-Term Goals*

Patient will:
- Respond to external limits
- Sign a "no-harm" contract that identifies steps he or she will take when urges return by (date)
- Express feelings related to stress and tension instead of acting-out behaviors by (date)
- Discuss alternative ways patient can meet demands of current situation by (date)

---

▲ NANDA International accepted; ● In addition to NANDA International

*Interventions and Rationales*

| Intervention | Rationale |
|---|---|
| 1. Assess patient's history of self-mutilation: <br>   a. Types of mutilating behaviors <br>   b. Frequency of behaviors <br>   c. Stressors preceding behavior | 1. Identifying patterns and circumstances surrounding self-injury helps nurse plan interventions and teaching strategies to fit the individual. |
| 2. Identify feelings experienced before and around the act of self-mutilation. | 2. Feelings are a guideline for future intervention (e.g., rage at feeling left out or abandoned). |
| 3. Explore with patient what these feelings might mean. | 3. Self-mutilation might also be: <br>   a. A way to gain control over others <br>   b. A way to feel alive through pain <br>   c. An expression of guilt or self-hate |
| 4. Secure a written or verbal no-harm contract with the patient. Identify specific steps (e.g., persons to call upon when prompted to self-mutilate). | 4. Patient is encouraged to take responsibility for healthier behavior. Talking to others and learning alternative coping skills can reduce frequency and severity until such behavior ceases. |
| 5. Use a matter-of-fact approach when self-mutilation occurs. Avoid criticizing or giving sympathy. | 5. A neutral approach prevents blaming, which increases anxiety, giving special attention that encourages acting out. |
| 6. After treatment of the wound, discuss what happened right before and the thoughts and feelings the patient had immediately before self-mutilating. | 6. Identify dynamics for both patient and clinician. Allows the identification of less harmful responses to help relieve intense tensions. |

| **Intervention** | **Rationale** |
|---|---|
| 7. Work out a plan identifying alternatives to self-mutilating behaviors. | 7. Plan is periodically reviewed and evaluated. Offers a chance to deal with feelings and struggles that arise. |

   a. Anticipate certain situations that might lead to increased stress (e.g., tension or rage).

   b. Identify actions that might modify the intensity of such situations.

   c. Identify two or three people whom the patient can contact to discuss and examine intense feelings (rage, self-hate) when they arise.

| **Intervention** | **Rationale** |
|---|---|
| 8. Set and maintain limits on acceptable behavior and make clear patient's responsibilities. If patient is hospitalized at the time, be clear regarding the unit rules. | 8. Clear and nonpunitive limit setting is essential for decreasing negative behaviors. |
| 9. Be consistent in maintaining and enforcing the limits, using a nonpunitive approach. | 9. Consistency can establish a sense of security. |

## CHRONIC LOW SELF-ESTEEM

Longstanding negative self-evaluation/feelings about self or self-capabilities

### *Some Related Factors (Related To)*

▲ Repeated failures and negative reinforcement
▲ Lack of affection and/or approval

- Childhood physical/sexual/psychological abuse and/or neglect
- Avoidant and dependent patterns
- Persistent lack of integrated self-view, with splitting as a defense
- Shame and guilt
- Substance use and abuse
- Dysfunctional family of origin

## Defining Characteristics (As Evidenced By)

▲ Longstanding or chronic self-negating verbalizations; expressions of shame/guilt
▲ Evaluates self as unable to deal with events
▲ Rationalizes away/rejects positive feedback and exaggerates negative feedback about self
▲ Hesitant to try new things/situations
▲ Overly conforming, dependent on others' opinions, indecisive
▲ Excessively seeks reassurance
▲ Expresses longstanding shame/guilt

## Outcome Criteria

- Demonstrates ability to reframe negative self-thoughts into more realistic appraisals
- Behavioral manifestations of depression greatly reduced and controlled with medication
- Uses effective coping strategies

## Long-Term Goals

Patient will:
- Demonstrate ability to reframe and dispute cognitive distortions with assistance of nurse/clinician by (date)
- State a willingness to work on two realistic future goals by (date)
- Identify one new skill he or she has learned to help meet personal goals by (date)

---

▲ NANDA International accepted; ● In addition to NANDA International

### Short-Term Goals

Patient will:
- Identify three strengths in work/school life by (date)
- Identify two cognitive distortions that affect self-image
- Reframe and dispute one cognitive distortion with nurse
- Set one realistic goal with nurse that he or she wishes to pursue
- Identify one skill he or she will work on to meet future goals by (date)

### Interventions and Rationales

| Intervention | Rationale |
| --- | --- |
| 1. Maintain a neutral, calm, and respectful manner, although with some patients this is easier said than done. | 1. Helps patient see himself or herself as respected as a person even when behavior might not be appropriate. |
| 2. Keep in mind PD patients might defend against feelings of low self-esteem through blaming, projection, anger, passivity, and demanding behaviors. | 2. Many behaviors seen in PD patients cover a fragile sense of self. Often these behaviors are the crux of patients' interpersonal difficulties in all their relationships. |
| 3. Assess with patients their self-perception. Target different areas of the patient's life: <br> a. Strengths and weaknesses in performance at work/school/daily-life tasks <br> b. Strengths and weaknesses as to physical appearance, sexuality, personality | 3. Identify with patient **realistic** areas of strength and weakness. Patient and nurse can then work on the realities of the self-appraisal and target those areas of assessment that do not appear accurate. |
| 4. Review with the patient the types of cognitive distortions that affect self-esteem (e.g., self-blame, mind reading, over generalization, | 4. These are the most common cognitive distortions people use. Identifying them is the first step to correcting |

| **Intervention** | **Rationale** |
|---|---|
| selective inattention, all-or-none thinking). | distortions that form one's self-view. |
| 5. Work with patient to recognize cognitive distortions. Encourage patient to keep a log. | 5. Cognitive distortions are automatic. Keeping a log helps make automatic, unconscious thinking clear. |
| 6. Teach patient to reframe and dispute cognitive distortions. Disputes need to be strong, specific, and nonjudgmental. | 6. Practice and belief in the disputes over time help patients gain a more realistic appraisal of events, the world, and themselves. |
| 7. Discourage patient from dwelling on and "reliving" past mistakes. | 7. **The past cannot be changed.** Dwelling on past mistakes prevents the patient from appraising the present and planning for the future. |
| 8. Discourage patient from making repetitive self-blaming and negative remarks. | 8. Unacceptable behavior does not make the patient a bad person; it means that the patient made some poor choices in the past. |
| 9. Focus questions in a positive and active light; helps patient refocus on the present and look to the future. For example: **"What could you do differently now?"** *or* **"What have you learned from that experience?"** | 9. Allows patient to look at past behaviors differently and gives the patient a sense that he or she has choices in the future. |
| 10. Give the patient honest and genuine feedback regarding your observations as to his or her strengths, and areas that could use additional skills. | 10. Feedback helps give patients a more accurate view of self, strengths, areas to work on, as well as a sense that someone is trying to understand them. |

| Intervention | Rationale |
|---|---|
| 11. Do not flatter or be dishonest in your appraisals. | 11. Dishonesty and insincerity undermine trust and negatively affect any therapeutic alliance. |
| 12. Set goals realistically, and renegotiate goals frequently. Remember that patient's negative self-view and distrust of the world took years to develop. | 12. Unrealistic goals can set up hopelessness in patients and frustration in nurse clinicians. Patients might blame the nurse for not "helping them," and nurses might blame the patient for not "getting better." |
| 13. Discuss with patient his or her plans for the future. Work with patient to set realistic short-term goals. Identify skills to be learned to help patient reach his or her goals. | 13. Looking toward the future minimizes dwelling on the past and negative self-rumination. When realistic short-term goals are met, patient can gain a sense of accomplishment, direction, and purpose in life. Accomplishing goals can bolster a sense of control and enhance self-perception. |

## IMPAIRED SOCIAL INTERACTION

Insufficient or excessive quantity or ineffective quality of social exchange

*Related Factors (Related To)*

▲ Deficit about ways to enhance mutuality (e.g., knowledge, skills)
▲ Self-concept disturbance

- Unacceptable social behavior or values
- Immature interests
- Biochemical changes in the brain
- Disruptive or abusive early family background

## Defining Characteristics (As Evidenced By)

▲ Use of unsuccessful social interaction behaviors
▲ Dysfunctional interaction with peers, family, and/or others
- Alienating others through angry, clinging, demeaning, and/or manipulative behavior or ridicule toward others
- Destructive behavior toward self or others

## Outcome Criteria

- Demonstrates an ability to use constructive criticism
- Demonstrates newly acquired social skills in social situations
- Identifies and problem solves with counselor factors that interfere with social interaction
- Demonstrates a willingness to participate in follow-up therapy
- Demonstrates a reduction in clinging, splitting, manipulation, and other distancing behaviors

## Long-Term Goals

Patient will:
- Demonstrate, with the aid of the nurse/clinician, the ability to identify at least two unacceptable social behaviors (manipulation, splitting, demeaning attitudes, angry acting out) that patient is willing to work on to change by (date)
- Work with nurse/clinician on substituting positive behaviors for those unacceptable behaviors identified earlier on an ongoing basis by (date)

---

▲ NANDA International accepted; ● In addition to NANDA International.

## Short-Term Goals

Patient will:
- Begin to demonstrate a reduction in manipulative behaviors as evidenced by nurse/staff
- Begin to demonstrate an increase in nonviolent behaviors as evidenced by a reduction in reported outbursts
- Identify two personal behaviors that are responsible for relationship difficulties within 2 weeks
- Verbalize decreased suspicion and increased security
- Identify one specific area that requires change
- Identify and express feelings as they occur with nurse
- State he or she is willing to continue in follow-up therapy
- Keep follow-up appointments

## Interventions and Rationales

| Intervention | Rationale |
|---|---|
| 1. In a respectful, neutral manner, explain expected patient behaviors, limits, and responsibilities during sessions with nurse clinician. Clearly state the rules and regulations of the institution and the consequences when these rules are not adhered to. | 1. From the beginning, patients need to have explicit guidelines and boundaries for expected behaviors on their part, as well as what patient can expect from the nurse. Patients need to be fully aware that they will be held responsible for their behaviors. |
| 2. Set limits on any manipulative behaviors: <br> a. Arguing or begging <br> b. Flattery or seductiveness <br> c. Instilling guilt, clinging <br> d. Constantly seeking attention <br> e. Pitting one person, staff, group against another <br> f. Frequently disregarding the rules <br> g. Constant engagement in power struggles <br> h. Angry, demanding behaviors | 2. From the beginning, limits need to be clear. It will be necessary to refer to these limits frequently, because it is to be expected that the patient will test these limits repeatedly. |

| **Intervention** | **Rationale** |
|---|---|
| 3. Intervene in manipulative behavior.<br><br>  a. **All limits should be adhered to by all staff involved.**<br>  b. **Objective physical signs in managing clinical problems should be carefully documented.**<br>  c. **Behaviors should be documented objectively (give times, dates, circumstances).**<br>  d. **Provide clear boundaries and consequences.**<br>  e. **Enforce the consequences.** | 3. Patients will test limits. Once they understand that the limits are solid, this understanding can motivate them to work on other ways to get their needs met. Hopefully, this will be done with the nurse clinician through problem-solving alternative behaviors and learning new effective communication skills. |
| 4. Expand limits by clarifying expectations for patients in a number of settings. | 4. When time is taken in initial meetings to clarify expectations, confrontations and power struggles with patients can be minimized and even avoided. |
| 5. Collaborate with the patient, as well as the multidisciplinary team, to establish a reward system for adherence to clearly defined expectations (Krupnick & Wade, 1993). | 5. Tangible reinforcement for meeting expectations can strengthen the patient's positive behaviors (Krupnick & Wade, 1993). |
| 6. Monitor own thoughts and feelings constantly regarding your response to the PD patient. Supervision is strongly recommended for new and seasoned clinicians | 6. Strong and intense countertransference reactions to PD patients are bound to occur. When the nurse is enmeshed in his or her own strong reactions |

| Intervention | Rationale |
|---|---|
| alike when working with PD patients. | toward the patient (either positive or negative), nurse effectiveness suffers, and the therapeutic alliance might be threatened. |
| 7. Problem solve and role play with patient acceptable social skills that will help obtain needs effectively and appropriately. | 7. Over time, alternative ways of experiencing interpersonal relationships might emerge. Take one small skill patient is willing to work on, break it down into small parts, and work on it together. |
| 8. Assess need for and encourage skills training workshop. | 8. Skills training workshops offer the patient ways to increase social skills through role play and interactions with others who are learning similar skills. This often acts as a motivating factor where positive feedback and helpful suggestions are readily available. |
| 9. Understand that PD patients in particular will be resistant to change and that this is symptomatic of PDs. This is particularly true in the beginning phases of therapy. | 9. Responding to patient's resistance and seeming lack of change in a neutral manner is part of the foundation for trust. In other words, the nurse does not have a vested interest in the patient "getting better." The nurse remains focused on the patient's needs and issues in any event. |

## INEFFECTIVE COPING

Inability to form a valid appraisal of stressors, inadequate choice of practiced responses, and/or ability to use available resources

### *Some Related Factors (Related To)*

▲ Disturbance in patterns of tension relief
● Intense emotional state
● Failure to intend to change behavior
● Lack of motivation to change behaviors
● Negative attitudes toward health behavior
● Neurobiological factors

### *Defining Characteristics (As Evidenced By)*

▲ Use of forms of coping that impede adaptive behavior
▲ Inadequate problem solving
▲ Inability to meet role expectations
● Failure to achieve optimal sense of control
● Failure to take actions that would prevent further health problems
● Demonstration of nonacceptance of health status
● Anger or hostility
● Dishonesty
● Superficial relationships with others
● Manipulation of others
● Dependency
● Intense emotional dysregulation
● Extreme distrust of others

### *Outcome Criteria*

• Increase in frequency of expressing needs directly without ulterior motives
• Demonstrates decreased manipulative, attention-seeking behaviors

▲ NANDA International accepted; ● In addition to NANDA International.

- Learns and masters skills that facilitate functional behavior
- Ongoing management of anger, anxiety, shame, and loneliness
- Identifies behaviors leading to hospitalization
- Demonstrates use of a newly learned coping skill to modify anxiety and frustration
- Demonstrates increase in impulse control

## *Long-Term Goals*

Patient will:
- State that he/she will continue treatment on an outpatient basis by (date)
- Focus on one problem and work through the problem-solving process with nurse by (date)
- Talk about feelings and perceptions and not act on them at least twice by (date)
- Practice the substitution of functional skills for times of increased anxiety with nurse by (date)

## *Short-Term Goals*

Patient will:
- Remain safe while hospitalized
- Not act out anger toward others while hospitalized
- Spend time with nurse and focus on one thing he/she would like to change

## General Interventions for All Personality Disorders

| Intervention | Rationale |
|---|---|
| 1. Review intervention guidelines for each PD in this chapter. | 1. All patients are individuals, even within the same diagnostic category. However, guidelines for specific categories are helpful for planning. |
| 2. Ascertain from family/friends how the person interacts with | 2. Identifying baseline behaviors helps with setting goals. |

| **Intervention** | **Rationale** |
|---|---|
| significant people. Is the patient always withdrawn, hostile, distrustful? Does he or she have continuous physical complaints? | |
| 3. Identify what the patient sees as the behaviors and circumstances that led to hospitalization. | 3. Ascertain patient's understanding of behaviors and responsibility for own action. |
| 4. Identify behavioral limits and behaviors that are expected. Do not argue, debate, rationalize, or bargain. | 4. Patient needs clear structure. Expect frequent testing of limits initially. Maintaining limits can enhance feelings of safety in the patient. |
| 5. Be clear with the patient as to the unit/hospital/clinic policies. Give brief, concrete reasons for the rules if asked and then move on. | 5. Institutional policies provide structure and safety. |
| 6. Be very clear about the consequences if policies/limits are not adhered to. | 6. Patient needs to understand the consequences of breaking the rules. |
| 7. When limits or policies are not followed, enforce the consequences in a matter-of-fact, nonjudgmental manner. | 7. Enforces that the patient is responsible for his/her own actions. |
| 8. Approach patient in a consistent manner in all interactions. | 8. Enhances feelings of security and provides structure. Exceptions encourage manipulative behaviors. |
| 9. Make a clear and concrete written plan of care so other staff can follow. | 9. Helps minimize manipulations and might help encourage cooperation. |

| **Intervention** | **Rationale** |
|---|---|
| 10. If feasible, devise a care plan with the patient. | 10. If goals and interventions are agreed upon, cooperation with plan is optimized. |
| 11. Refrain from sharing **personal information** with patient. | 11. Opens up areas for manipulation and undermines professional boundaries. |
| 12. Do not take **gifts** from the patient (any patient). | 12. Again, clouds the boundaries and can give patient the idea that he/she is due special consideration. |
| 13. Be aware of **flattery** as an attempt to feed into your needs to feel special. | 13. Giving into patient's thinking that you are "the best" or "the only one" can pit you against other staff and undermine patient's needs for limits. |
| 14. If patient becomes **seductive,** reiterate the therapeutic goals and boundaries of treatment. | 14. The patient is in the hospital/clinic for a reason. Being taken in by seductive behavior undermines effectiveness of treatment. |
| 15. Some patients might attempt to **instill guilt** when they do not get what they want. Remain neutral but firm. | 15. Nurses often want to be seen as "nice." However, being professional and maintaining limits is the better therapeutic approach. |
| 16. If patient becomes **hostile** or **projects blame** onto you or staff, project a neutral, calm demeanor and avoid power struggles. Focus on the patient's underlying feelings. | 16. Defuses tension and opens up productive interaction. |

| **Intervention** | **Rationale** |
|---|---|
| 17. When appropriate, attempt to understand underlying feelings prompting inappropriate behaviors. (Those with ASPD might not be good candidates for this.) | 17. Often, acting-out behaviors stem from underlying feelings of shame, fear, anger, loneliness, insecurity, etc. Talking about feelings can lead to problem solving and growth for patient. |
| 18. Work with patient on problem-solving skills using a situation that is bothering the patient. Go step by step: <br> • Define the problem <br> • Explore alternatives <br> • Make decisions | 18. Patient might not know how to articulate the problem. Helping identify alternatives gives the patient a sense of control. Evaluating the pros and cons of the alternatives facilitates choosing potential solutions. |
| 19. When patient is ready and interested, teach coping skills to help defuse tension and troubling feelings (e.g., anxiety reduction, assertiveness skills). | 19. Increasing skills helps patient use healthier ways to defuse tensions and get needs met. |
| 20. Keep goals very realistic and go in small steps. There are no overnight successes with people with PDs. | 20. It can take a long time to positively change ingrained, lifelong, maladaptive habits; however, change is always possible. |
| 21. Give patient positive attention when behaviors are appropriate and productive. Avoid giving any attention (when possible and not dangerous to self or others) when patient's behaviors are inappropriate. | 21. Reinforcing positive behaviors might increase likelihood of repetition. Ignoring negative behaviors (when feasible) robs patient of even negative attention. |

| Intervention | Rationale |
|---|---|
| 22. Guard against personal feelings of frustration and lack of progress. | 22. Change is often very slow and may seem to take longer than it actually is. Nurture yourself outside the job. Keep your "bucket" full with laughter and high regard from friends and family. |
| 23. Understand that many people with PDs do not stay in treatment and often come to facilities because of crisis or court order. | 23. Even short encounters with therapeutic persons can make a difference when a patient is ready to learn more adaptive ways of living his or her life. |

Three diagnostic categories are the most likely to come into contact with the mental health system. These include people with the diagnoses of **Borderline Personality Disorder** (BPD), **Antisocial Personality Disorder** (ASPD), and **Paranoid Personality Disorder** (PPD). All of the above would apply to all patients with PD, but some additional interventions are suggested for patients with these traits.

## Borderline Personality Disorder (BPD)

| Intervention | Rationale |
|---|---|
| 1. Assess for self-mutilating or suicide thoughts or behaviors (see Chapter 16 for nursing care plans related to suicide behaviors). | 1. Self-mutilating and suicide threats are common behaviors for patients with BPD. |
| 2. Interventions often call for responses to patient's intense and labile mood swings, anxiety, depression, and irritability. | 2. Many of the dysfunctional behaviors of BPD patients (e.g., parasuicidal, anger, manipulation, substance abuse) are used as |

| Intervention | Rationale |
|---|---|
| | "behavioral solutions" to intense pain. |
| a. Anxiety: Teach stress-reduction techniques such as deep breathing, relaxation, mediation, and exercise. | a. Patients experience intense anxiety and fear of abandonment. Stress-reduction techniques help patient focus more clearly. |
| b. Depression: Patient might need medications to help curb depression. Observe for side effects and mood level. | b. Most patients with BPD suffer profound depression. |
| c. Irritability, anger: Use interventions early before anxiety and anger escalate. See Chapter 17 for nursing care plans related to angry and aggressive behaviors. | c. Patients with BPD are extremely uncomfortable and want immediate relief from painful feelings. Anger is a response to this pain. Intervening early can help avoid escalation. |
| 3. Patients with BPD can be manipulative (see Chapter 19 for nursing care plans). Be consistent. Set and maintain limits regarding behavior, responsibilities, and unit/community rules. | 3. Consistent limit setting helps provide structure and decrease negative behaviors. |
| 4. Use assertiveness when setting limits on patient's unreasonable demands for time and attention. | 4. Firm, clear, nonjudgmental limits give patient structure. |
| 5. Be nonjudgmental and respectful when listening to patient's thoughts, feelings, or complaints. | 5. Patients have an intense fear of rejection. |
| 6. Encourage patient to explore feelings and | 6. Patient is used to acting out feelings. |

| Intervention | Rationale |
|---|---|
| concerns (e.g., identify fears, loneliness, self-hate). | |
| 7. Patients with BPD benefit from coping skills training (e.g., interpersonal skills, anger management skills, emotional regulation skills). Provide referrals and/or involve professional experts. | 7. Patient learns to refine skills in changing behaviors, emotions, and thinking patterns associated with problems in living that are causing misery and distress (Linehan, 1993). |
| 8. Treatment of substance abuse is best handled by well-organized treatment systems, not by an individual nurse/clinician. | 8. Keeping detailed records and having a team involved with each patient can minimize manipulation. |
| 9. Provide and encourage the patient to use professionals in other disciplines such as social services, vocational rehabilitation, social work, or the law. | 9. Patients with BPD often have multiple social problems. Often they do not know how to obtain these services. |
| 10. Patients with BPD often drop out of treatment prematurely. However, when they return, they can still draw upon what they have learned from previous encounters with health care personnel. | 10. Patients might become impatient and leave, then return in a crisis situation. It is a good thing when they are able to tolerate longer periods of learning. |

## Antisocial Behaviors

People with antisocial traits are usually hospitalized against their will, often involving law violations, marital discord (battering), or other such conduct. They rarely want to change their behaviors and have no motivation to do so.

These patients relate through manipulation and do not have the ability to care for others' physical or emotional well-being; however, they may be "friendly" with others if there is something in it for them. Often these patients resort to **manipulation or violence** to get what they want. **Refer to Chapter 19 for nursing care plans dealing with manipulative behaviors and Chapter 17 on anger and aggression.**

### Paranoid Behaviors

Often these patients function on the outside, even though they have a deep abiding distrust of the motives of others. Under stress, they might seek crisis help or act out in such a way to require hospitalization. The biggest challenge to nurses and other health care providers is working with the patient's suspiciousness of others. **See Chapter 8 under Defensive Coping for a nursing care plan for a suspicious person.**

## MEDICAL TREATMENTS

### Psychopharmacology

There are no medications for treating PDs per se. There are, however, medications that can target some of the symptoms patients experience. Prescribed on an individual basis, they can be very helpful for many patients as an adjunct in their therapy. Counseling/psychotherapy is probably the best primary approach to care, but psychopharmacology can be an important part of the therapeutic regimen in decreasing a patient's anxiety, paranoia, aggressiveness, or other symptoms. Specific medications that are often used for a particular PD are mentioned in the earlier discussions of each of the PDs. Medications can facilitate a patient's comfort and make people with PDs more amenable to therapy. Refer to the discussion of the individual PDs for those medications that have been helpful for some individuals.

### Other Treatments

Because people with PDs rarely seek treatment or adhere to treatment unless they are under undue stress, depressed, exhibiting suicidal behaviors, remanded by the courts, and so on, therapeutic approaches are sometimes difficult.

## NURSE, PATIENT, and FAMILY RESOURCES

### ASSOCIATIONS

**National Alliance for the Mentally Ill (NAMI)**
Colonial Place Three
2107 Wilson Boulevard, Suite 300
Arlington, VA 22201-3042
(800) 950-NAMI
www.nami.org

### INTERNET SITES

**Borderline Personality Disorder Sanctuary**
www.navicom.com/~patty
Recovery information for people with BPD

**Self-Injury Page**
www.mhsanctuary.com/borderline
Self-mutilation

**BPD Central**
www.bpdcentral.com
Borderline personality disorder website

**Internet Mental Health**
www.mentalhealth.com
A good overview of all the personality disorders

**Personality Disorders**
www.focusas.com/Personality Disorder

# CHAPTER 10

# Addictions

## OVERVIEW

Addictions can be both chemical (e.g., alcohol, cocaine, meth-amphetamines, etc.) or nonchemical (e.g., gambling, compulsive overeating, sex, internet use, etc.). An easy way to define addiction for our purposes is the use of the three Cs:

1. Behavior that is motivated by emotions ranging along the lines of Craving to Compulsive
2. Continued use despite adverse consequences to health, mental state, relationships, occupation, and finances
3. Loss of Control

This chapter will deal with chemical dependencies/substance use disorders. Treatment for individuals with substance use disorders includes an *assessment phase*, the *treatment of the intoxication and/or withdrawal*, and the *development and implementation of an overall treatment strategy* (APA, 2000b). Parent and child/adolescent teaching and recognition of potential harm various drugs can cause is a vital part of prevention.

*Substance-related disorders* refer to those disorders that are related to the taking of a drug of abuse (i.e., alcohol, cocaine, heroin, amphetamines), to the side effects of a prescribed medication (including over-the-counter medications), and to toxin exposure (e.g., heavy metals [lead or aluminum], rat poisons, pesticides, nerve gas). Knowledge of "club drugs" is increasingly important for health care workers to include in their teaching. MDMA (Ecstasy), gamma-hydroxybutyrate (GHB) (G, liquid ecstasy), flunitrazepam (Rohypnol), and methamphetamines are particularly widespread.

1. **Substance Use Disorders (substance dependence and substance abuse).** Refer to Box 10-1 for the *DSM-IV-TR* definitions of substance dependence and substance abuse.

| Box 10-1 | *DSM-IV-TR*<br>Criteria for Substance Abuse and Dependence |
|---|---|

**Substance Abuse**
Maladaptive pattern of substance use leading to clinically significant impairment or distress, manifested by one or more of the following occurring within a 12-month period:
1. Inability to fulfill major role obligations at work, school, and home
2. Recurrent legal or interpersonal problems
3. Continued use despite recurrent social or interpersonal problems
4. Participation in physically hazardous situations while impaired (driving a car, operating a machine, exacerbation of symptoms—e.g., ulcers)

**Substance Dependence**
Maladaptive pattern of substance use leading to clinically significant impairment or distress, manifested by three or more of the following within a 12-month period:
1. Presence of tolerance to the drug
2. Presence of withdrawal syndrome
3. Substance taken in larger amounts or for longer period than intended
4. Reduction or absence of important social, occupational, or recreational activities
5. Unsuccessful or persistent desire to cut down or control use
6. Increased time spent in getting, taking, and recovering from the substance; possibly withdrawn from family or friends
7. Substance use continual despite knowledge of recurrent physical or psychological problems or that problems were caused or exacerbated by one substance

Adapted from American Psychiatric Association (APA). (2000). *Diagnostic and statistical manual of mental disorders* (4th edition, text rev.) *(DSM-IV-TR)*. Washington DC, Author, pp. 197–199; reprinted with permission.

2. **Substance-Induced Disorders include substance intoxication, substance withdrawal, and substance-induced disorders (delirium, substance-induced psychotic disorders, etc.).** Refer to Box 10-2 for the *DSM-IV-TR* definition and criteria for substance intoxication and substance withdrawal.

Substance use disorders (dependence and abuse), substance intoxication, and substance withdrawal are presented here with the more common substances of use

---

| Box 10-2 | *DSM-IV-TR* Criteria for Substance Intoxication and Withdrawal |
|---|---|

**Substance Intoxication**

1. The development of a reversible substance-specific syndrome due to recent ingestion of (or exposure to) a substance
   **Note:** Different substances might produce similar or identical syndromes.
2. Clinically significant maladaptive behavioral or psychological changes that are caused by the effect of the substance on the central nervous system (e.g., belligerence, mood lability, cognitive impairment, impaired judgment, impaired social or occupational functioning) and develop during or shortly after use of the substance
3. The symptoms are not due to a general medical condition and are not better accounted for by another mental disorder.

**Substance Withdrawal**

1. The development of a substance-specific syndrome due to the cessation of (or reduction in) substance use that has been heavy and prolonged.
2. The substance-specific syndrome causes clinically significant distress or impairment in social, occupational, or other important areas of functioning.
3. The symptoms are not due to a general medical condition and are not better accounted for by another medical disorder.

---

Adapted from American Psychiatric Association (APA). (2000). *Diagnostic and statistical manual of mental disorders* (4th edition, text rev.) *(DSM-IV-TR)*. Washington DC, Author, pp. 201–202; reprinted with permission.

(alcohol, amphetamines, cannabis, cocaine, hallucinogens, opioids, phencyclidine [PCP], sedatives, hypnotics, or anxiolytics). Some of these classes of drugs share similar features:

- Alcohol shares features with the sedatives, hypnotics, and anxiolytics.
- Cocaine shares features with amphetamines and similarly acting sympathomimetics.

Table 10-1 identifies common drugs of abuse, therapeutic uses they might have, the properties of these drugs, and the symptoms of intoxication and overdose.

## Other Disorders Associated with Substance Use Disorders

The *DSM-IV-TR* identifies a number of other disorders for each of the substances besides dependence, abuse, intoxication, and withdrawal—for example, substance-induced:

Intoxication delirium
Withdrawal delirium
Persisting dementia
Persisting amnesic disorder
Psychotic disorder
Psychotic disorder with hallucinations/delusions
Mood disorder
Anxiety disorder
Sexual dysfunction
Sleep disorder
Disorder not otherwise specified (NOS)

In this chapter, common drugs of abuse are introduced, and symptoms of use, intoxication, overdose, and withdrawal are discussed. This chapter is focused on assessment data, identifying nursing diagnoses, goals, and interventions the nurse can implement.

## Nurses Need to Know

Before planning nursing care, the nurse needs to be aware of four phenomena that are inherent in the planning of treatment. These four phenomena are:

1. Tolerance
2. Polydrug use
3. Dual diagnoses
4. Medical comorbidity

Text continued on p. 312

Table 10-1 **Common Drugs of Abuse**

| Class | Therapeutic Use | Symptoms of Use | Intoxication | Dependence Physical | Dependence Psychological |
|-------|----------------|-----------------|--------------|---------------------|--------------------------|
| **CNS Depressants** Alcohol (ETOH) Barbiturates Benzodiazepines Chloral hydrate Other sedative-hypnotics | Antidote for methanol consumption | Relaxation, euphoria, decreased inhibitions, lack of concentration, poor judgment, slurred speech, decreased coordination | Slurred speech, nausea, vomiting, incoordination, sedation, drowsiness, emotional instability | Yes | Yes |
| **CNS Stimulants** Cocaine (short-acting) Amphetamines | Topical anesthetic Management of narcolepsy, questionable at present, weight control | Euphoria, initial CNS stimulation, then depression, wakefulness, hypersexuality, impaired judgment, irritability, anxiety, panic attacks, paranoia, agitation, loss of appetite | Psychomotor activation, sweating, ↑ blood pressure, ↑ heart and respirations, tremors, dilated pupils, insomnia, assaultive, grandiose, impaired judgment and social and occupational functioning | Yes | Yes |

| Drug | Therapeutic Use | Effects | | | |
|---|---|---|---|---|---|
| **Opioids**<br>Opium (paregoric)<br>Heroin<br>Meperidine (Demerol)<br>Morphine<br>Codeine<br>Methadone (Dolophine)<br>Hydromorphone (Dilaudid)<br>Fentanyl | Analgesic<br>Methadone use in treatment of heroin dependency<br>• Heroin has NO therapeutic use | Euphoria, sedation, reduced libido, emotional lability, impaired judgment, lack of motivation | Euphoria followed by dysphoria and impairment in attention, judgment, and memory<br>Pupils constrict, ↑ respiration, ↑ blood pressure, slurred speech, psychomotor retardation | Yes | Yes |
| **Hallucinogens**<br>Lysergic acid (LSD) | LSD has no recognized therapeutic application | Euphoria, altered body image, altered perception, alteration in judgment and memory, detachment from surroundings, distortions in | Fear of going crazy, marked anxiety/ depression, depersonalization, grandiosity, hallucinations synesthesia, ↑ blood pressure, ↑ pulse, ↑ temperature | No | No |

*Continued*

Table 10-1 **Common Drugs of Abuse—cont'd**

| Class | Therapeutic Use | Symptoms of Use | Intoxication | Dependence Physical | Dependence Psychological |
|-------|-----------------|-----------------|--------------|---------------------|--------------------------|
| | | thinking (delusions, paranoia, confusion), hallucinations, disorientation, anxiety, panic, increased pulse Experiences range from sublime to terrifying | ↑ respiration, incoordination | | |
| Phencyclidine (PCP) Mescaline Dimethyltryptamine (DMT) | | | Ataxia, muscle rigidity, seizures, regressive behaviors, belligerence, assaultiveness, vertical or horizontal nystagmus, bizarre, violent, labile behavior, ↑ blood pressure, ↑ pulse, ↑ temperature, blank stare | | |

| | | | | | |
|---|---|---|---|---|---|
| **Cannabis**<br>Marijuana<br>Hashish, THC | Marijuana has been known to:<br>• Reduce eye pressure in glaucoma patients<br>• Relieve nausea and vomiting associated with chemotherapy in treatment of cancer patients<br>• Stimulate appetite in AIDS patients | Relaxation, sexual arousal, talkativeness, increased appetite, altered state of awareness, mild euphoria or dysphoria. increased pulse, red eyes, dry mouth | Anxiety, suspiciousness, in high doses sensation of slowed time, social withdrawal, impaired judgment, possible hallucinations, ↑ pulse, conjunctival redness | Yes<br>in high doses | Yes |
| **Inhalants**<br>Glue, lighter fluid, spray paint, paint thinner | None | Euphoria, giddiness, excitation | Excitation, followed by drowsiness staggering, lightheadedness, agitation, disinhibition | Yes | Yes |

*Continued*

Table 10-1 Common Drugs of Abuse—cont'd

| Class | Therapeutic Use | Symptoms of Use | Intoxication | Dependence Physical | Dependence Psychological |
|---|---|---|---|---|---|
| **Club Drugs** Ecstasy (MDMA) | None | Agitation followed by euphoria, sense of profound insight, intimacy, and well-being<br><br>Increased thirst | Sympathetic overload, some of which includes tachycardia, hypertension, arrhythmias, parkinsonism<br><br>Toxic and potentially fatal outcomes are extreme: hyperthermia and the associated "serotonin syndrome," which can result in acute renal and hepatic failure, adult respiratory distress, and end-organ damage are examples | Yes | Yes |

| | | | | | |
|---|---|---|---|---|---|
| Gamma-hydroxybutyrate (GHB) | Narcolepsy | ↓ Social inhibition ↑ Libido, euphoria | Hypersalivation, hypotonia, amnesia, ↑ BP, mood swings, seizures | **Yes** | **Yes** |
| Flunitrazepam (Rohypnol) "date rape drug" | Anesthesia, sedation | Reduced anxiety, muscular tension; drowsiness, headaches; nightmares, confusion | Anterograde amnesia, lack of muscle control, loss of consciousness | **Yes** | **Yes** |

Without thorough considerations of these four phenomena, safe and effective nursing or medical care cannot be implemented.

## Tolerance

Tolerance and withdrawal are two characteristics of physiological addiction to a drug. When the body requires larger and larger amounts of a drug to achieve the same effect, the body builds up a **tolerance** to the drug. When the dose of the drug is reduced or the drug is no longer available, the lack of a certain level of the drug in the body produces **withdrawal symptoms.** Each drug has its own specific withdrawal syndrome. Some drugs, if stopped abruptly, can cause a medical emergency (Table 10-2).

## Polydrug Abuse

Use of two or more substances of abuse (polydrug abuse) is quite common. Alcohol dependence in conjunction with other drug dependence is prevalent, especially but not exclusively for people younger than 30 years of age. This is especially true with drugs taken at nightclubs, raves, or music festivals (club drugs).

## Dual Diagnosis

The co-occurrence of a substance use disorder with another psychiatric disorder is called *dual diagnosis*. It has been reported that more than 50% of substance-abusing individuals also were diagnosed with another psychiatric disorder. Common comorbid psychiatric disorders include personality disorders (borderline and antisocial), major depression, bipolar disorder, and schizophrenia. Dual diagnoses must always be identified and the comorbid disorder treated simultaneously if any change in drug-related behavior is to occur.

## Medical Comorbidity

Many serious and life-threatening medical problems are associated with the consequences of illicit injection drug use and its associated lifestyle. Systemic and

Text continued on p. 320

Table 10-2 **Drug Overdose and Withdrawal**

| Drug | Overdose | | Withdrawal | |
|---|---|---|---|---|
| | Effects | Possible Treatments | Effects | Possible Treatments |
| **CNS Depressants** Barbiturates Benzodiazepines Chloral hydrate Glutethimide Meprobamate Alcohol (ETOH) | Cardiovascular or respiratory depression or arrest (mostly with barbiturates) Coma Shock Convulsions Death | *If awake:* Keep awake. Induce vomiting. Give activated charcoal to aid absorption of drug. Every 15 min, check vital signs (VS) *Coma:* Clear airway; endotracheal tube Intravenous (IV) fluids Gastric lavage with activated charcoal Frequent VS checks for shock and cardiac arrest after patient is stable | *Cessation of prolonged, heavy use:* Nausea-vomiting Tachycardia Diaphoresis Anxiety or irritability Tremors in hands, fingers, eyelids Marked insomnia Grand mal seizures *After 5-15 years of heavy use:* Delirium | Carefully titrated detoxification with similar drug NOTE: **Abrupt withdrawal can lead to death.** |

*Continued*

**Table 10-2 Drug Overdose and Withdrawal—cont'd**

| Drug | Overdose | | Withdrawal | |
|---|---|---|---|---|
| | Effects | Possible Treatments | Effects | Possible Treatments |
| | | Seizure precautions Possible hemodialysis or peritoneal dialysis Flumazenil (Romazicon) IV | | |
| **Stimulants** Cocaine—crack (short-acting) NOTE: High obtained: snorted, for 3 min; injected, for 30 sec; smoked, for 4-6 sec (crack) Average high lasts: cocaine, 15-30 min; crack, 5-7 min | Respiratory distress Ataxia Hyperpyrexia Convulsions Coma Stroke Myocardial infarction Death | Antipsychotics, medical and nursing management for: Hyperpyrexia (ambient cooling) Convulsions (diazepam) Respiratory distress Cardiovascular shock Acidify urine (ammonium chloride for amphetamine) | Fatigue Depression Agitation Apathy Anxiety Sleepiness Disorientation Lethargy Craving | Antidepressants (desipramine) Dopamine agonist |

| | | | |
|---|---|---|---|
| **Amphetamines** (long-acting) Dextroamphetamine Methamphetamine Ice (synthesized for street use) | Same as above | Same as above | Same as above |
| **Opioids** Opium (paregoric) Heroin Meperidine (Demerol) Codeine Methadone (Dolophine) Hydromorph-one (Dilaudid) Fentanyl (Sublimaze) Fentanyl analogs | Pupils might be dilated due to anoxia Respiratory depression/ arrest Coma Shock Convulsions Death | Narcotic antagonist (e.g., naloxone [Narcan]) quickly reverses central nervous | Yawning Insomnia Irritability Runny nose (rhinorrhea) Panic Cramps Diaphoresis Nausea-vomiting Muscle aches ("bone pain") Chills Fever Lacrimation Diarrhea | Methadone/ LAAM tapering Clonidine- raltrexone detoxification Buprenorphine substitution |

*Continued*

Table 10-2 **Drug Overdose and Withdrawal—cont'd**

| | Overdose | | Withdrawal | |
| Drug | Effects | Possible Treatments | Effects | Possible Treatments |
|---|---|---|---|---|
| **Hallucinogens**<br>Lysergic acid (LSD)<br>Mescaline (peyote) | Psychosis<br>Brain damage<br>Death | Keep patient in room with low stimuli: minimal light, sound, activity.<br>Have one person stay with patient, "talk down" patient.<br>Speak slowly and clearly in a low voice.<br>Give diazepam or chloral hydrate for extreme anxiety/tension. | | |
| Psilocybin | | | | |

*Continued*

| Phencyclidine (PCP) | Psychosis | *If alert:* |
| --- | --- | --- |
| | Possible hypertensive crisis/cardiovascular accident | CAUTION: Gastric lavage can lead to laryngeal spasms or aspiration |
| | Respiratory arrest | Acidify urine (cranberry juice, ascorbic acid); in acute stage, ammonium chloride acidifies urine to help excrete drug from body; might continue for 10-14 days. |
| | Hyperthermia | |
| | Seizures | Room with minimal stimuli |
| | | Do not attempt to talk down! Speak slowly, clearly, and in a low voice. |
| | | Diazepam |
| | | Haloperidol can be used for severe behavioral disturbance (not a phenothiazine). |

**Table 10-2 Drug Overdose and Withdrawal—cont'd**

| Drug | Overdose | | Withdrawal | |
|---|---|---|---|---|
| | Effects | Possible Treatments | Effects | Possible Treatments |
| Phencyclidine (cont'd) | | *Medical intervention for:* Hyperthermia High blood pressure Respiratory distress Hypertension | | |
| **Club Drugs** Ecstasy (MDMA) | Hyperthermia Serotonin syndrome Acute hepatic/renal failure Elevated body temperature ↑ Water intake leads to hyponatremia Neurological effects (confusion, delirium, paranoia) | **No Antidote:** Treat symptoms Cardiac monitoring Comprehensive chemistry panel identifies complications (e.g., hepatic or renal damage) | Profound depression secondary to serotonin depletion Repeated use associated with cognitive impairment (potentially permanent memory loss) | |

| | | | Withdrawal symptoms |
|---|---|---|---|
| Gamma-hydroxybutyrate (GBA)<br>Street names:<br>Fantasy<br>GBH<br>Liquid ecstasy<br>Cherry meth<br>(date rape drug) | Cheyne-Stokes respirations<br>Seizures<br>Coma<br>Death | **No Antidote**<br>Treat symptoms<br>Monitor cardiac status<br>Comprehensive chemistry panel (to check renal, hepatic, or other complications) | Withdrawal symptoms include:<br>Anxiety<br>Insomnia<br>Tremors |
| Flunitrazepam<br>Rohypnol<br>(date rape drug) | Hypotension<br>Confusion<br>Visual disturbances<br>Urinary retention<br>Aggressive behavior | **Antidote**<br>Flumazenil | Like other benzodiazepines:<br>↑ Seizure potential<br>Anxiety<br>Muscle pain<br>Photosensitivity<br>Headache |

Data from American Psychiatric Association (APA). (2000). *Diagnostic and statistical manual of disorders* (4th ed., text rev.) (*DSM-IV-TR*). Washington DC: Author; Bohn, M.J. (2000). Alcoholism. *Psychiatric Clinics of North America, 16*(4), 679; O'Connor, P.G., Samet, J.H., & Stein, M.D. (1994). Management of hospitalized drug users: Role of the internist. *American Journal of Medicine, 96,* 551; Bell K. (1992). Identifying the substance abuser in clinical practice. *Orthopedic Nursing,* 11(2);29; Gahlinger, P.M. (2004). Club Drugs: MDMA, Gamma-hydroxybutyrate (GHB), Rohypnol, and ketamine, *American Family Physician,* (69) 11 (June 2004). www.aafp.org/afp/20040601/2619.html. Retrieved 2/22/05.

organ-specific bacterial infections, viral hepatitis, tuberculosis, sexually transmitted disease, complications of pregnancy, pulmonary edema, and trauma are all found in injection drug users.

Another important consideration when working with substance-dependent individuals is that approximately 40% to 50% of patients with substance abuse problems have mild to moderate cognitive problems while actively using. These problems usually get better with long-term abstinence. However, it is best in the beginning to keep their treatment plan simple because these patients are not thinking or functioning at their optimal level (Zerbe, 1999).

Recovering is a lifetime process, and it comes about in steps. Because each patient has different strengths, backgrounds, and supports, goals of treatment should be tailored to the individual's immediate needs and abilities. Initially, however, a 12-step program based on Alcoholics Anonymous **(AA)** is the most effective treatment modality for all addictions. The 12 steps ("working the steps") are designed to help a person refrain from addictive behaviors and to foster individual change and growth.

Such support groups include **PA** (Pills Anonymous), **NA** (Narcotics Anonymous), **WFS** (Women for Sobriety), and **CA** (Cocaine Anonymous), among others. These groups help break down denial in an atmosphere of support, understanding, and acceptance. It is strongly advised that individuals find a reliable sponsor within the support group, especially for the early period of sobriety. A relationship has been established between a person's feelings of "belonging" and treatment outcome. The more the patient feels socially involved with peers, the greater the likelihood of successful treatment outcome, continuation of treatment, and lower relapse rates.

There are self-help groups for families and friends of an addicted person. They are also based on the 12 steps. These groups help patients, family, and friends work through accepting the disease model of addiction. This acceptance can remove the burdens of guilt, hostility, and shame from family members. They also offer pragmatic methods for identifying and avoiding enabling behaviors. Such support groups include **Al-Anon** (for friends and family members of an alcoholic), **Narc-Anon** (for friends and family members of a narcotic addict), and **ACOA** (for Adult Children of Alcoholics). NOTE: **Be aware that several sessions over weeks or months might be necessary for the patient to reach the point of accepting the reality of the problem and the need for treatment** (Dunner, 1997).

# ASSESSMENT

## Presenting Signs and Symptoms

- The patient might exhibit any of the signs and symptoms of **intoxication or withdrawal** (see Table 10-2).
- The patient might have needle tracts in the antecubital fossa, wrist, or feet, or behind the knees.
- The patient might have suicidal thoughts. If yes, assess for lethality of ideations. (See Chapter 16 for discussion on assessment and interventions for suicidal individuals.)
- The patient might have a history of blackouts, delirium, or seizures.
- The patient might have a coexisting medical condition related to the substance of abuse (e.g., AIDS, central nervous system [CNS] disease or deterioration).

## Assessment Tools

It is often less threatening to people when assessing their drug history to start with "safe" questions first, such as:
1. "What prescription drugs do you currently take?"
2. "What over-the-counter drugs do you currently take?"
3. "What social drugs do you currently take?"
   a. Start with nicotine and caffeine.
   b. Ask about alcohol.
   c. Ask about other social drugs (marijuana, cocaine, and heroin).

There are many helpful assessment tools that nurses can use to assess if the individual has an alcohol or drug problem. Three that can be very useful are:
1. Nurse's assessment tool in emergencies (see Appendix D-7A).
2. **Alcohol problems**—The Brief Version of the Michigan Alcohol Screening Test (MAST) (see Appendix D-7B).

3. **Other drug-related problems**—The Drug Abuse Screening Test (DAST) (see Appendix D-7C).

## Assessment Guidelines

### Substance Abuse

1. Is immediate medical attention warranted for a severe or major withdrawal syndrome? For example, alcohol and sedative use can be life threatening during a major withdrawal.
2. Is the patient experiencing an overdose to a drug/alcohol that warrants immediate medical attention? For example, opioids or depressants can cause respiratory depression, coma, and death. Refer to Table 10-2 for symptoms of drug overdose and treatments.
3. Does the patient have any physical complications related to drug abuse (e.g., AIDS, abscess, tachycardia, hepatitis)?
4. Does the patient have suicidal thoughts or indicate, through verbal or nonverbal cues, a potential for self-destructive behaviors?
5. Does the patient seem interested in doing something about his or her drug/alcohol problem?
6. Do the patient and family have information about community resources for alcohol/drug withdrawal (detoxify safely) and treatment; for example:
   - Support groups
   - Treatment for psychiatric comorbidities
   - Family treatment to address enabling behaviors, support adaptive behaviors, and provide support for families and friends

# NURSING DIAGNOSES WITH INTERVENTIONS

Nurses care for chemically impaired patients in a variety of settings and situations. Some interventions call for medical interventions and skilled nursing care, whereas others call for effective use of communication and counseling skills. The following sections offer the nurse guidelines for treatment.

# Discussion of Potential Nursing Diagnoses

## Overdose

**Drug overdoses** can be medical emergencies needing timely medical interventions. Drug overdoses most often seen in hospital emergency rooms are CNS depressants (e.g., barbiturates, benzodiazepines, alcohol), stimulants (e.g., crack/cocaine), opiates (e.g., heroin), and to a lesser extent hallucinogens (e.g., PCP). Table 10-2 lists the signs and symptoms of overdose for these drugs and identifies possible treatments.

## Withdrawal

**Withdrawal from alcohol and other CNS-depressant drugs** is associated with severe morbidity and mortality, unlike withdrawal from other drugs. For example, a person experiencing severe alcohol withdrawal might have delirium tremens (DTs). Death from DTs can be caused by volume depletion, electrolyte imbalance, cardiac arrhythmias, or suicide. Mortality rates range between 5% and 10%, even with treatment (Dunner, 1997).

Therefore, individuals with severe alcohol withdrawal syndrome or withdrawal from a CNS depressant might need hospitalization and close medical attention. Other drug withdrawals might not hold the same dangers, but the patient might benefit from titrating the dose under medical supervision. The major nursing diagnosis that applies for an individual going through withdrawal of a substance of abuse is **Risk for Injury.**

## Initial Drug Treatment and Active Treatment

People who are addicted to alcohol or drugs come from various environments, cultures, and sociological backgrounds. Therefore, people seeking treatment for drug addictions and related problems present with a variety of personal strengths and social backgrounds and have different economic supports. Many patients have legal problems and, certainly, possible medical complications from the drug, as well as coexisting psychiatric problems. One form of treatment for a specific substance will not be effective for everyone addicted to that specific substance. It is probably best to take a long-term view of addictions and remember that lapses or relapses are often part of the long-term course of recovery (Vaillant, 1988).

However, many nursing diagnoses apply to the majority of patients with substance abuse problems. For example, individuals who have been abusing drugs for a long period of time most likely have poor general health. These patients might have nutritional deficits, be susceptible to infections, or be at risk for AIDS and hepatitis. **Ineffective Health Maintenance** is often a nursing focus and an initial priority for patients when they present with life-threatening situations.

A common phenomenon shared among many addicted individuals is that people minimize their drug problems and have a tendency to deny having a "problem" (denial) or minimize the problem by blaming others (projection), rationalizing why they need the drug, or using other methods to deny responsibility for their drug-related behavior. Therefore, **Ineffective Denial** is present. Denial should be broken down so the patient can begin to perceive how his or her life has changed in a negative way because of drug use; motivation for change must be found. Until individuals can admit they have a problem and are ready to start taking responsibility for their drug use, there is little incentive for change as long as they blame others for their problems and think their behavior is justified.

## Relapse Prevention

Relapse prevention is part of most treatment planning for both medical and psychiatric mental health disorders. For people with addictions, the main thrust of relapse prevention is recognizing triggers for abuse and learning different ways to respond to these cues. Because new coping skills are needed, the nursing diagnosis **Ineffective Coping** is used for relapse prevention.

There are many nursing diagnoses that can be a priority for your patients. One important area for assessment is **Risk for Other-Directed or Self-Directed Violence.** Assessment and intervention for **suicide** is addressed in **Chapter 16.** Suggestions for working with patients who are **angry and violent** are found in **Chapter 17.**

Addicted patients often have a lack of concern for the feelings of others and often act entitled or have a sense of grandiosity about them. Many patients who abuse substances learn to manipulate others (family, friends, and institutions) to get their needs met (e.g., money for drugs, shift blame to others, make false promises). Setting limits is key to working with an addicted patient or patients with dual diagnoses. Interventions for **manipulative behaviors** are addressed in **Chapter 19**.

People with a history of long-term substance abuse often have many other needs as well (e.g., medical, social, legal, job-related, personal), warranting a variety of nursing diagnoses. Table 10-3 lists potential nursing diagnoses.

Table 10-3 **Potential Nursing Diagnoses for Substance Abuse**

| Signs and Symptoms | Nursing Diagnoses |
|---|---|
| Vomiting, diarrhea, poor nutritional and fluid intake | **Imbalanced Nutrition** **Risk for Deficient Fluid Volume** |
| Audiovisual hallucinations, impaired judgment, memory deficits, cognitive impairments related to substance intoxication/withdrawal (problem solving, ability to attend to tasks, grasp ideas) | **Disturbed Thought Processes** **Disturbed Sensory Perception: Auditory/Visual** |
| Changes in sleep-wake cycle, interference with stage IV sleep, not sleeping or long periods of sleeping related to effects or withdrawal from substance | **Disturbed Sleep Pattern** |
| Lack of self-care (hygiene, grooming), not caring for basic health needs | **Ineffective Health Maintenance** **Self-Care Deficit** **Nonadherence to Health Care Regimen** |
| Feelings of hopelessness, inability to change, feelings of worthlessness, life has no meaning or future | **Hopelessness** **Impaired Religiosity** **Spiritual Distress** **Chronic Low Self-Esteem** **Risk for Self-Directed Violence** |
| Family crises and family pain, ineffective parenting, emotional neglect of others, increased incidence of physical and sexual abuse toward others, increased self-hate projected to others | **Interrupted Family Processes** **Impaired Parenting** **Risk for Other-Directed Violence** |

*Continued*

Table 10-3 **Potential Nursing Diagnoses for Substance Abuse—cont'd**

| Signs and Symptoms | Nursing Diagnoses |
|---|---|
| Excessive substance abuse affects all areas of person's life: loses friends, has poor job performance, illness rates increase, prone to accidents and overdoses | Ineffective Coping<br>Impaired Verbal Communication<br>Social Isolation<br>Risk for Loneliness<br>Anxiety<br>Risk for Suicide |
| Increased health problems related to substance used and route of use, as well as overdose | Activity Intolerance<br>Ineffective Airway Clearance<br>Ineffective Breathing Pattern<br>Impaired Oral Mucous Membranes<br>Risk for Infection<br>Decreased Cardiac Output<br>Sexual Dysfunction<br>Delayed Growth and Development |
| Total preoccupation and time consumed with taking and withdrawing from drug | Ineffective Coping<br>Impaired Social Interaction<br>Disabled Family Coping |

## Overall Guidelines for Nursing Interventions

### Substance Abuse

1. Detoxify the patient.
2. Assess for feelings of hopelessness, helplessness, and suicidal thinking.
3. Ascertain that the patient is getting interventions for any comorbid medical and/or psychological condition (e.g., liver toxicity, infections, depression, anxiety attacks).
4. Intervene with the patient's use of denial, rationalization, projection, and other defenses that stall motivation for change.
5. Enlist support of family members; confront any tendency on their part to minimize the problem or enable the patient in maintaining his or her addiction.

6. Insist on abstinence.
7. Refer the patient to self-help groups (e.g., AA, NA, CA) early on in treatment.
8. Teach patient to avoid medications that promote dependence.
9. Encourage participation in psychotherapy (e.g., cognitive-behavioral strategies, motivational interviewing, solution-focused therapy).
10. Emphasize personal responsibility—placing control within the patient's grasp removes the nurse from the all-knowing rescuer (Finfgeld, 1999).
11. Support residential treatment when appropriate, particularly for patients with multiple relapses.
12. Expect relapses.
13. Educate the patient and family on the medical and psychological consequences of drug abuse.
14. Educate the patient and family regarding pharmacotherapy for certain addictions (e.g., naltrexone or methadone to help prevent relapse in alcoholism and narcotic addiction).
15. Educate the patient about the physical and developmental effects taking the drug can have on future children (e.g., fetal alcohol syndrome, problems with school, social role performance) (Zerbe, 1999).

## Selected Nursing Diagnoses and Nursing Care Plans
### Withdrawal

Abrupt withdrawal from some drugs can elicit a medical emergency. Overdose of some drugs is also a medical emergency. Review Table 10-2 for common drugs of abuse in which withdrawal or overdose might require immediate nursing and medical attention. NOTE: **Refer to the nursing care plan for violence (Chapter 17) or suicide (Chapter 16) if these apply. If interventions for manipulation are needed, see Chapter 19.**

### RISK FOR INJURY

At risk of injury as a result of environmental conditions interacting with the individual's adaptive and defensive resources

## Some Related Factors (Related To)

▲ Psychological (affective orientation)
▲ Sensory dysfunction—perceptual loss or disorientation
▲ Developmental age (psychological)
▲ Chemical (drugs, alchohol, nicotine)
▲ Malnutrition
● Impaired judgment (disease, drugs, reality testing, risk-taking behaviors)
● Substance withdrawal
● Panic levels of anxiety and agitation
● Potential for electrolyte imbalance or seizures
● Overdose

## Defining Characteristics (As Evidenced By)

● Signs and symptoms of specific drug withdrawal or overdose
● Evidence of hallucinations (bugs, animals, snakes)
● Poor skin turgor
● Elevated temperature, pulse, respirations
● Agitation, trying to "get away" or climb out of bed
● Combative behaviors
● Misrepresentation of reality (illusions)

## Outcome Criteria

● Safe withdrawal
● Free of physical injuries secondary to withdrawal

## Long-Term Goals

Patient will:
● Remain free from injury while withdrawing from substance
● Be free of withdrawal symptoms within given time period for particular drug

---

▲ NANDA International accepted; ▲ In addition to NANDA International

## Short-Term Goals

- Patient's condition will stabilize within 72 hours
- Patient will be oriented during times of lucidity
- Patient will demonstrate decreased aggressive and threatening behavior within 24 hours (using a scale of 1 to 5)

## Interventions and Rationales

| Intervention | Rationale |
|---|---|
| 1. Vital signs should be taken frequently, at least every 15 minutes until stable, then every hour for 4 to 8 hours according to hospital protocol or physician's order. | 1. Pulse is the best indicator of impending DTs, signaling the need for more rigorous sedation. |
| 2. Provide patient with a quiet room free of environmental stimulation, a single room near the nurse's station if possible. | 2. Lowers irritability and confusion. |
| 3. Approach the patient with a calm and reassuring manner. | 3. Patients need to feel that others are in control and that they are safe. |
| 4. Use simple, concrete language and directions. | 4. Patient is able to follow simple commands but unable to process complex or abstract ideas. |
| 5. Orient patient to time/place and person during periods of confusion; inform patient of his or her progress during periods of lucidity. | 5. Fluctuating level of consciousness is the hallmark of delirium. Orientation can help reduce anxiety. |
| 6. Institute seizure precautions according to hospital protocol. | 6. Seizures might occur, and precautions for patient safety are a priority. |
| 7. Carefully monitor intake and output. Check for dehydration or overhydration. | 7. Dehydration can aggravate electrolyte imbalance. Overhydration can lead to congestive heart failure. |

| **Intervention** | **Rationale** |
|---|---|
| 8. If the patient is having **hallucinations**, reassure patient that you do not see them, that you are there and you will see that he remains safe (e.g., "I don't see rats on the wall jumping on your bed. You sound frightened right now. I will stay with you for a few minutes."). | 8. Do not argue with the patient, but share your experience that you do not see anything frightening. Address the fear and let the patient know that you and the staff are here to help him or her remain safe. |
| 9. If the patient is experiencing illusions, correct the patient's misrepresentation in a calm and matter-of-fact manner (e.g., "This is not a snake around my neck ready to strike you, it is my stethoscope...let me show you.") | 9. Illusions can be explained to a patient who is misinterpreting environmental cues. When the patient recognizes normal objects for what they are, anxiety is lessened. |
| 10. Maintain safety precautions at all times; for example:<br>a. Provide electric shaver<br>b. Take away all matches and cigarettes<br>c. Keep siderails up at all times<br>d. Have patient in private room where possible, near nurse's station | 10. During withdrawal, physical safety is the main priority. |
| 11. Administer medications ordered for safe withdrawal. | 11. Abrupt withdrawal from a CNS depressant can be fatal. |

| **Intervention** | **Rationale** |
|---|---|
| 12. Use restraints with caution if patient is combative and dangerous to others. Try to avoid mechanical restraints whenever possible. Always follow unit protocols. | 12. Myocardial infarctions, cardiac collapse, and death have occurred when patients have fought against restraints during experiences of terror. |
| 13. Keep frequent, accurate records of patient's vital signs, behaviors, medication, interventions, and effects of interventions. | 13. Monitor progress; identify what works best; identify potential complications. |

## Initial and Active Drug Treatment

### INEFFECTIVE HEALTH MAINTENANCE

Inability to identify, manage, and/or seek out help to maintain health

## Some Related Factors (Related To)

▲ Inability to make appropriate judgments
▲ Ineffective individual coping
▲ Perceptual/cognitive impairment
● All activities of life focused on obtaining and taking drug
● Money spent on substance of abuse and none left for health care, nourishing food, or safe shelter
● Poor nutrition related to prolonged drug binges, taking drug instead of eating nourishing food, or diminished appetite related to choice of drug (e.g., cocaine)
● Inability to make or keep health care appointments (e.g., mammograms, dentist, yearly physicals) because of

---

▲ NANDA International accepted; ● In addition to NANDA International

either being intoxicated, being hung over, or withdrawing from an illicit substance
- Sleep deprivation related to decreased rapid eye movement (REM) sleep as a result of long-term stimulant, alcohol, or CNS depressant abuse
- Malabsorption of nutrients related to chronic alcohol abuse

## Some Defining Characteristics (As Evidenced By)

▲ History of lack of health-seeking behaviors
▲ Inability to take responsibility for meeting basic health practices
- Physical exhaustion
- Sleep disturbances
- Unattended physical symptoms, for example:
  - Gastrointestinal problems
  - Extreme weight loss
  - Edema of extremities
  - Muscle weakness
  - Ascites
  - Abscesses on extremities
  - Bronchitis

## Outcome Criteria

- Obtains stable health status, meeting minimal requirements for:
  - Sleep
  - Nutrition
  - Weight
- Adheres to medication and treatment regimen

## Long-Term Goals

- Patient will demonstrate responsibility in taking care of health care needs as evidenced by keeping appointments by (date)
- Patient's medical tests will demonstrate a reduced incidence of medical complications related to substance abuse after 6 months
- Patient's weight is within normal range by (date)

---

▲ NANDA International accepted; ● In addition to NANDA International

- Patient's daily nutritional intake will include 5 servings from fruit and vegetables, 2 to 3 from dairy, 2 to 3 from meat/poultry/fish, and 6 from grains (pasta, bread, rice) with help of nurse/nutritionist/family/support group
- Patient will sleep at least 6 hours a night by (date)
- Patient keeps appointments for medical treatment and follow-up within 2 months of treatment

### Short-Term Goals

Patient will:
- Go for medical checkup and treatment of any medical problems within 2 to 3 weeks of starting treatment
- Agree to go for nutrition counseling
- Identify three bodily effects of his or her substance abuse within 1 to 2 weeks and how these can affect self, loved ones, and unborn children

### Interventions and Rationales (If Hospitalized)

| Intervention | Rationale |
|---|---|
| 1. Encourage small feedings if appropriate. Check nutritional status (e.g., conjunctiva, body weight, eating history). | 1. If patient is anorexic, small feedings will be better tolerated. Bland foods are often more appealing. Pale conjunctiva can signal anemia. |
| 2. Monitor fluid intake and output. Check skin turgor. Check for ankle edema. Do urine-specific gravity if skin turgor is poor. | 2. Patients can have potentially serious electrolyte imbalances. Too few fluids can cause or signal renal problems. If patient is retaining too much fluid, there can be a danger of congestive heart failure. |
| 3. When skin turgor is poor, frequently offer fluids containing protein and vitamins (e.g., milk, malts, juices). | 3. Proteins and vitamins help build nutritional status. |

| Intervention | Rationale |
|---|---|
| 4. Promote rest and sleep by placing patient in a quiet environment. | 4. Provide the patient with long rest periods between medical interventions. |
| 5. Identify patient's understanding of how the alcohol/drugs they are taking can cause possible future problems (e.g., fetal alcohol syndrome, hepatitis/ AIDS, fertility issues). | 5. Before teaching, nurse needs to identify what the patient knows about the drugs and evaluate his or her readiness to learn. |
| 6. With physician's approval, review patient's blood work and physical examination with him or her. | 6. Lab results help the nurse identify possible causes of symptoms (e.g., infection) and initiate early counseling. |
| 7. Set up an appointment for medical follow-up in the clinic or community. | 7. Follow-up calls are important reminders. |

## INEFFECTIVE DENIAL

Conscious or unconscious attempt to disavow the knowledge or meaning of an event to reduce anxiety/fear, but leading to the detriment of health

### Some Related Factors (Related To)

- Physical and/or emotional dependence on substance of abuse and a need to maintain the status quo
- Fear of having to change and give up substance of dependence and take responsibility for maladaptive past behaviors and chaotic life situations (legal, family, job problems)
- Underlying feelings of hopelessness and helplessness at having to cope with life without substance
- Long-term self-destructive patterns of behavior and lifestyle

## *Some Defining Characteristics (As Evidenced By)*

▲ Displays inappropriate affect
▲ Minimizes symptoms and substance use
▲ Does not perceive personal relevance of symptoms or danger
● Continues to use substance/drug, knowing it contributes to impaired functioning and exacerbation of physical symptoms
● Uses substance/drug in potentially dangerous situations (e.g., driving while intoxicated)
● Uses rationalization and projection to explain irresponsible, aggressive, manipulative, and other maladaptive behaviors
● Fails to accept responsibility for behaviors that result in disrupted family life, legal problems, serious problems at work/lack of work, disrupted relationships with others
● Reluctant to discuss self or problems

## *Outcome Criteria*

● Maintains abstinence from chemical substances
● Continues attendance for treatment and maintenance of sobriety (e.g., AA, CA, NA, or group therapy, cognitive-behavioral psychotherapy, or other)

## *Long-Term Goals*

Patient will:
● Demonstrate acceptance or responsibility for own behavior at the end of 3 months
● Demonstrate three alternative adaptive responses to stress in family, job, legal, and social situations within 1 month
● Demonstrate three strategies to use in vulnerable situations by (date)
● Identify maladaptive behaviors used in the past and demonstrate three new adaptive behaviors used in the present by (date)
● Attend a relapse program during active course of treatment

---

▲ NANDA International accepted; ● In addition to NANDA International

## Short-Term Goals

Patient will:

- Acknowledge that addiction does not cure itself, and it will worsen until it is treated, by third/fourth week of treatment
- Make a written contract to stay drug-free 1 day at a time within the first week of treatment
- Participate in a support group at least three times a week by second week of treatment
- Agree to contact a support person when he or she feels the need to use substance by the end of the first session
- Recognize and state when using denial, rationalization, and projection when speaking of drug use within the first month of treatment
- Identify at least three areas of his or her life that drugs have negatively affected within the first week
- Work with nurse, sponsor, chemical dependency counselor, therapist, or support group members on ways to change negative situations in his or her life
- Identify at least three positive role models, especially those that have overcome the same addiction themselves, within the first week
- Identify three vulnerable situations and give three strategies to employ
- Take advantage of cognitive-behavioral therapy to increase coping skills during active phase of treatment
- Work with nurse, therapist, chemical-dependency counselor, sponsor (in support group) to develop a relapse program
- Become a member of a relapse-prevention group

## Interventions and Rationales

| Intervention | Rationale |
| --- | --- |
| **Initial Interventions**  | |
| 1. Initially, work with patient on crisis situations and establishing a rapport with patient. | 1. People cannot work on issues when in crisis situations (e.g., practical living problems, family crisis). |

| **Intervention** | **Rationale** |
|---|---|
| 2. Refer the patient to appropriate social services, occupational rehabilitation, or other resources as indicated. | 2. Patient might need help the nurse cannot provide. If patient is to focus on and make changes in drug-related problems and behaviors, all available assistance should be utilized. |
| 3. Maintain an interested, nonjudgmental, supportive approach. | 3. A nonjudgmental, supportive approach based on medical concern is most effective. |
| 4. Refrain from being pulled into power struggles, defending your position, preaching, or criticizing patient's behaviors. | 4. Will only make the patient more defensive. |
| 5. Continue to empathetically confront denial. | 5. Denial is the primary obstacle to receiving treatment. |
| 6. Forge an alliance with the patient on some initial goals and what patient wants to change in his or her life. | 6. Initially, the patient's goal might not be total abstinence. Identifying areas the patient wants to change gives both patient and nurse a basis for working together. |
| 7. Use of *miracle questions* can help identify what patients want to change (e.g., "What if your worst problem were miraculously solved overnight. What would be different about your life the next day?"). | 7. Helps patients perceive their future without some of their problems. Gives direction to moving forward and identifying long- and short-term goals. |
| 8. Help patient analyze specific pro's and con's of substance use/abuse. | 8. Helps patient look at what substances do and do not do for them in a clear light. Can help strengthen motives for change. |

| Intervention | Rationale |
|---|---|
| 9. Discourage the patient's attempts to focus on only external problems (relationships, job-related, legal) without relating them to substance use/abuse. | 9. Helps patient see the relationship between their problems and their drug use. Helps breakdown denial. |
| 10. Work with patient to identify behaviors that have contributed to life problems (e.g., family problems, social difficulties, job-related problems, legal difficulties). | 10. When patient takes responsibility for maladaptive behaviors, he/she is more prepared to take responsibility for learning effective and satisfying behaviors. |
| 11. Encourage patient to stay in the "here and now" (e.g., "You can't change the fact that your mother put you down all your life." "Let's focus on how you want to respond when you perceive that your boss puts you down."). | 11. Dwelling on past disappointments and hurt is not useful to working on new and more adaptive coping behaviors. |
| 12. Refer and encourage patient to attend a 12-step support group. | 12. Research shows that such involvement is the most effective tool in countering addiction (Zerbe, 1999). |
| 13. Encourage patient to find a sponsor within the 12-step program or another therapeutic mode. | 13. Having a sponsor and being a sponsor, according to some research, is important for success (Harvard Mental Health Letter, 1996). |
| 14. Work with patient to identify times he/she might be vulnerable to drinking/drugs and strategies to use at those times. | 14. Having thought out alternative strategies to drinking/drugs in vulnerable situations gives patient ready choice. |

| Intervention | Rationale |
|---|---|
| 15. Encourage family and friends to seek support, education, and ways to recognize and refrain from enabling patient. | 15. Enabling behavior supports the patient's use of drugs by taking away incentive for change. |
| 16. Educate family and patient regarding the physical and psychological effects of the drug, the process of treatment, and aftercare. | 16. An addicted family member greatly changes the dynamics and roles within families. Family and patient need to make decisions based on facts. |
| 17. Attend several open meetings in your local community. | 17. Helps nurse understand how 12-step fellowship process works. |
| 18. Realize that several sessions over weeks or months might pass before patient accepts there is a problem and need for treatment. | 18. When helpers push too hard and become impatient, the patient might leave treatment before making a commitment. |

**Active Treatment**

| | |
|---|---|
| 1. Expect sobriety. Work with patients to view their commitment to *one day at a time*. Thinking that he or she can never take the drug again might seem like an overwhelming responsibility. | 1. Patient is unable to think rationally, make informed decisions, or learn while drug/alcohol impaired. |
| 2. Give feedback constantly when patient tries to rationalize, blame, or minimize effects of drug use. | 2. As long as patient believes that others are responsible, that his or her behavior is normal, or that there is really nothing wrong with his or her drug use, there will be no motivation for change. |

| Intervention | Rationale |
|---|---|
| 3. Teach patient alternative ways to deal with stress:<br>  a. Relaxation techniques<br>  b. Exercise<br>  c. Taking "time out"<br>  d. Getting proper rest and nutrition<br>  e. Strategies for vulnerable situations | 3. Helps both patient and nurse articulate what alternative skills can be identified, rehearsed, and practiced in social situations. |
| 4. Have patient identify his/her stress level on a scale of 1 to 10. Then have patient reevaluate stress after using stress-reduction techniques, and discuss next session. | 4. Helps patient identify what works and what does not work. Nurse then works with patient to learn and try alternative techniques. |
| 5. Assess other coping skills that will help patient maintain sobriety/abstinence—for example:<br>  a. Anger management<br>  b. Impulse control<br>  c. Maintaining relationships<br>  d. Problem-solving skills | 5. Addicted patient's usual method of getting all emotional needs met was through drugs. Problems with impulse control, anger, and problem solving are usually present. Relating to people in a drug-free environment can be very frightening. |
| 6. Refer the patient to social services, vocational rehabilitation, workshops, skills groups, or other resources, when appropriate. | 6. Patient recovering from addictions might have a myriad of needs that must be addressed, which can be key for maintaining sobriety. |
| 7. Continue to encourage group participation. | 7. Group participation provides people with:<br>  a. Sense of belonging<br>  b. Source of friendships<br>  c. Reduction in feelings of isolation<br>  d. Reduction in feelings of despair and shame |

| Intervention | Rationale |
|---|---|
| | e. Alternatives to dealing with common situations and problems |
| | f. Increased motivation toward sobriety |
| 8. Problem-solve with patient realistic future goals, and identify life changes needed to meet these goals. | 8. Drug-free activities and companions need to be established to take the place of usual drug-related activities and drug-abusing companions. |
| 9. Discuss with patient potential difficulty patient might have relating to family and friends who continue to use substances of abuse. | 9. Patient needs to be prepared to communicate with impaired friends and family differently. Patient also needs to identify ways to meet new friends to continue a drug-free lifestyle. |

## Relapse Prevention

### INEFFECTIVE COPING

Inability to form a valid appraisal of the stressors, inadequate choices of practiced response, and/or inability to use available resources

## Some Related Factors (Related To)

- ● Inadequate resources available
- ● Disturbance in pattern of tension release
- ● Inadequate level of or perception of control
- ▲ Knowledge deficit
- ▲ Old coping styles no longer adaptive in present situations

## Some Defining Characteristics (As Evidenced By)

- Abuse of chemical agents
- Inadequate problem solving
- Destructive behavior toward self or others
- Inability to meet role expectations
- Risk taking
- Use of forms of coping that impede adaptive behavior

## Outcome Criteria

- Continues counseling, cognitive-behavioral, interpersonal, or other therapy to deal with arising issues faced in sobriety
- Continues to learn and practice effective coping skills
- Continues to modify lifestyle as needed to maintain sobriety
- Maintains total abstinence from all substances of abuse

## Long-Term Goals

Patient will:
- Participate at least weekly in a relapse prevention program and/or 12-step program
- Continue to verbalize cues or situations that pose increased risk of drug use
- Demonstrate strategies for avoiding and managing these cues
- State that he or she has a stable group of drug-free friends and socialize with them at least three times a week by (date)
- Participate routinely in at least four drug-free activities that give satisfaction and pleasure by (date)
- State that relationships with family members are more enjoyable and stable; family members will agree by (date)

## Short-Term Goals

Patient will:
- Identify at least three situations or events that serve as a source of vulnerability to relapse by (date)

---

▲ NANDA International accepted; ● In addition to NANDA International

- Demonstrate at least three cognitive-behavioral strategies to deal with sources of vulnerability to relapse by (date)
- Form relationships with at least four drug-free individuals that he or she enjoys spending time with in social activities by (date)
- Increase his or her drug-free social circle by two new people by the end of each month within the first month of treatment
- Identify at least two drug-free activities that he or she enjoys that do not trigger drug cravings
- Remain drug-free one day at a time

Family members will:

- State they feel supported in family counseling

## *Interventions and Rationales*

| Intervention | Rationale |
|---|---|
| 1. Work with patient to keep treatment plan simple in the beginning. | 1. Approximately 40% to 50% of patients with substance abuse problems have mild to moderate cognitive problems while using substances. |
| 2. Have patient write notes and self-memos in order to keep appointments and follow treatment plan. | 2. Cognition usually gets better with long-term abstinence, but initially memory aids prove helpful. |
| 3. Encourage patient to join relapse prevention groups (Box 10-3). | 3. Helps patient anticipate and rehearse healthy responses to stressful situations. |
| 4. Encourage patient to find role models (counselors or other recovering people). | 4. Role models serve as examples of how patient can learn effective ways to make necessary life changes. |
| 5. Work with patient on identifying triggers (people, feelings, situations) that help drive the patient's addiction. | 5. Mastering the issues that perpetuate substance use allows for effective change and targets areas for acquiring new skills. |

## Box 10-3 **Relapse Prevention Strategies**

**Basics**
1.  Keep the program simple at first; 40% to 50% of patients who abuse substances have mild to moderate cognitive problems while actively using.
2.  Review instructions with health team members.
3.  Use a notebook and write down important information and telephone numbers.

**Skills**
Take advantage of cognitive-behavioral therapy to increase your coping skills. Identify which important life skills are needed:
1.  What situations do you have difficulty handling?
2.  What situations are you managing more effectively?
3.  For which situations would you like to develop more effective coping skills?

**Relapse Prevention Groups**
Become a member of a relapse prevention group. These groups work on:
1.  Rehearsing stressful situations using a variety of techniques
2.  Finding ways to deal with current problems or ones that are likely to arise as you become drug free
3.  Providing role models to help you make necessary life changes

**Increase Personal Insight**
Therapy—group therapy, individual therapy, family therapy—can help you gain insight and control over many psychological concerns. For example:
1.  What drives your addictions?
2.  What constitutes a healthy supportive relationship?
3.  Increasing your sense of self and self-worth.
4.  What does your addictive substance give you that you think you need and cannot find otherwise?

Adapted from Zerbe, K.J. (1999). *Women's mental health in primary care*. Philadelphia: Saunders, pp. 94–95; reprinted with permission.

| Intervention | Rationale |
|---|---|
| 6. Practice and role-play with patient alternative responses to triggers. | 6. Increases patient confidence of handling drug triggers effectively. |
| 7. Give positive feedback when patient applies new and effective responses to difficult "trigger" situations. | 7. Validates patient's positive steps toward growth and change. |
| 8. Continue to empathetically confront denial throughout recovery. | 8. Denial can surface throughout recovery and can interfere with sobriety during all stages of recovery. |
| 9. Continue to work with patient on the following three areas:<br>a. **Personal issues** (relationship issue)<br>b. **Social issues** (issues of family abuse)<br>c. **Feelings of self-worth** | 9. These areas of human life need to find healing so that growth and change can take place. |
| 10. Recommend family therapy. | 10. Enhanced strategies for dealing with conflict in patient's family are essential to recovery. |
| 11. Stress the fact that substance abuse is a disease the entire family must conquer. | 11. Family members also need encouragement to face their own struggles (Zerbe, 1999). |
| 12. Expect slips to occur. Reaffirm that sobriety can be achieved as emotional pain becomes endurable. | 12. Helps minimize shame and guilt and rebuild self-esteem. |

# MEDICAL TREATMENTS

## Psychopharmacology

In the formulation of a treatment plan for individual drug-dependent patients, treatment for comorbid psychiatric or medical disorders must be included. Some patients, for example, might benefit from an antidepressant for a secondary depressive disorder. The effectiveness of some pharmacological treatments of drug dependencies is not necessarily well established. However, some drugs can be useful in patients with the following dependencies (APA, 2006b). Please keep in mind, these agents should be part of a comprehensive treatment program that includes psychosocial support such as counseling (cognitive-behavioral therapy, psychoeducational family therapy, etc.), relapse prevention groups, and support groups (e.g., 12-step programs, etc.).

## Alcohol

Disulfiram (Antabuse) is an effective adjunct to a comprehensive treatment program for reliable, motivated patients whose drinking is triggered by events that can suddenly increase alcohol cravings.

Naltrexone (Revia), an opiate antagonist, can attenuate some of the reinforcing affects of alcohol and decrease cravings. Alcohol sensitivity drug.

Nalmefene (Revex) is an opiate antagonist similar to naltrexone. Effective in heavy drinkers, with fewer side effects than naltrexone.

Acamprosate (Campral) is an amino acid derivative that has a benign side-effect profile and shows value in alcohol dependence. Acamprosate affects both gamma-aminobutyric acid (GABA) and excitatory amino acid (e.g., glutamate) neurotransmission.

## Cocaine

Pharmacological treatment is not usually indicated as an initial treatment, although patients with more severe dependence might be considered for treatment with dopaminergic medications.

## Opioids

Detoxification may include use of opioid agonists (e.g., methadone), partial agonists (e.g., buprenorphine), antagonists (e.g., naloxone, naltrexone), or nonopioid alternatives such as clonidine or a benzodiazepine.

Maintenance on methadone (suppresses withdrawal for 24 to 36 hours) or levo-alpha-acetyl-methadol (LAAM) (suppresses withdrawal for 48 to 72 hours) can reduce morbidity in patients with prolonged opioid dependence.

Buprenorphine is an opiate approved for the treatment of opioid addiction. Buprenorphine monotherapy (Subutex) and a buprenorphine combination product, Suboxone, a buprenorphine/naloxone derivative, are the two FDA-approved forms at this writing. buprenorphine's potential for abuse is lessened when combined with naloxone. Advantages include less risk of respiratory arrest in overdose, less severe withdrawal symptoms, and the use of a buprenorphine/naloxone combination can be administered in an office-based setting.

Maintenance on naltrexone used in abstinence therapy is beneficial except for lack of patient adherence and low treatment retention.

## Management of Drug Intoxication and Withdrawal

The medical treatment for intoxication and overdose for common drugs of abuse are outlined in Table 10-2.

## Psychosocial

Psychosocial therapies are helpful to many motivated patients with substance use dependencies. Therapies that can be effective in some patients include cognitive behavioral therapies, interpersonal therapy, brief interventions, marital and family therapy, and group therapy. Extremely useful for many are self-help groups such as AA, NA, and PA.

# PATIENT AND FAMILY TEACHING

Patients, families, and significant others all need support and information to guide them during early and middle phases of treatment. Box 10-4 offers the nurse some guidelines.

---

Box 10-4 **Patient and Family Teaching: Chemical Dependence**

---

- Teach patients and families that alcoholism and substance abuse are diseases, not moral weaknesses.
- Like diseases, addictions can be treated through a variety of therapeutic and pharmacological approaches.
- Recognize that substance-related disorders affect all family members.
- Identify "enabling" behaviors, and teach families how to substitute healthier patterns.
- Tell families they are not responsible for their member's substance abuse.
- Tell the patient and family to report any worsening signs of depression or suicidal thoughts.
- Educate about the detrimental effects of alcohol and substance abuse, including depression and sleep disruption.
- Help the patient and family identify community resources such as Adult Children of Alcoholics (ACOA), Al-Anon, and other self-help groups.
- Encourage patients to reveal their urges to use substances before they can act on them.
- Educate patients about the risk of HIV, hepatitis, and other diseases associated with substance abuse.

---

Adapted from Gorman, L.M., Sultan, D.F., & Raines, M.L. (1996). *Davis's manual of psychosocial nursing for general patient care.* Philadelphia: FA Davis, pp. 283–289; reprinted with permission.

# Nurse, Patient, and Family Resources

## ASSOCIATIONS

**Alcoholics Anonymous World Services**
475 Riverside
New York, NY 10115
(212) 870-3400

**Narcotics Anonymous World Services Office**
PO Box 9999
Van Nuys, CA 91409
(818) 773-9999

**Al-Anon Family Group Headquarters, Inc. (for Al-Anon, Alateen, Alatots, ACOA)**
1600 Corporate Landing Parkway
Virginia Beach, VA 23454-5617
(757) 563-1600; (800) 4AL-ANON

**National Clearinghouse for Alcohol and Drug Information**
PO Box 2345
Rockville, MD 20856
www.health.org

**Center for Substance Abuse Treatment (CSAT)**
National Drug Hotline (bilingual)
(800) 662-4357
www.samsha.gov/

**National Institute on Drug Abuse (NIDA)**
American Self-Help Clearinghouse
(201) 625-7101
www.mentalhelp.net/selfhelp

# INTERNET SITES

**Addiction Technology Transfer Center**
www.nattc.org

**Centre for Addiction and Mental Health**
www.camh.net

# CHAPTER 11

# Eating Disorders

## OVERVIEW

**People with eating disorders experience severe disruption in normal eating patterns and severe disruptions in perceptions of body shape and weight.** These disorders are severe and disabling, and successful treatment entails long-term care and follow-up. Unlike most psychiatric conditions, these disorders can cause severe physiological damage. (Refer to Table 11-1 for some medical complications of eating disorders.) Anorexia nervosa and bulimia nervosa are both potentially fatal eating disorders. Because anorexia nervosa and bulimia nervosa are chronic, complex disorders, nursing interventions need to include actions to help minimize harm during the acute phase and help prevent relapse.

Predominantly, these disorders affect adolescents and cause great suffering and frustration to families, friends, and loved ones. Treating these disorders can pose a formidable challenge to the health care system. The two primary categories of eating disorders discussed in this section are anorexia nervosa and bulimia nervosa. When there is evidence that psychological factors are important to the etiology or cause of a particular case of obesity, it is noted as **psychological factors affecting medical condition** (American Psychiatric Association [APA], 2000b). Comorbid personality disorders are frequent among patients with eating disorders, accounting for more than 50% for anorexia and 95% of people with bulimia. Some of the more prominent co-occurring disorders are the mood and anxiety disorders, substance use disorders,

Table 11-1 **Some Medical Complications of Eating Disorders**

| Complication | Laboratory Findings |
|---|---|
| **Cardiovascular** | |
| Bradycardia | Electrocardiographic |
| Postural hypotension | abnormalities |
| Dysrhythmias | |
| **Metabolic** | |
| Acidosis (laxatives) | $\downarrow K^+$ |
| Alkalosis (vomiting) | $\uparrow$Cholesterol |
| Hypokalemia | $\uparrow$Liver function tests |
| Hypocalcemia | $\downarrow Mg^{2+}$ |
| Hypomagnesemia | $\downarrow Na^+$ |
| Osteoporosis | $\downarrow Ca^{2+}$ |
| Dehydration | $\downarrow$Bone density |
| **Renal** | |
| Hematuria | $\uparrow$Blood urea nitrogen |
| Proteinuria | |
| **Gastrointestinal** | |
| Hyperamylasemia | $\uparrow$Serum amylase |
| Parotid swelling— | |
| hypertrophy | |
| Dental erosion (vomiting HCl) | |
| Esophagitis, esophageal tears | |
| (vomiting) | |
| Pancreatitis | |
| Diarrhea (laxative abuse) | |
| Gastric dilation—bingeing | |
| **Hematological** | |
| Leukopenia | $\downarrow$Erythrocyte sedimentation |
| Lymphocytosis | rate |
| Anemias (iron and vitamin $B_{12}$ | Abnormal complete blood |
| deficiency) | count |
| **Endocrine** | |
| Amenorrhea | $\downarrow$Follicle-stimulating hor- |
| Urinary and plasma | mone, luteinizing hormone, |
| gonadotropins | estradiol levels |
| Hypercortisolism | $\uparrow$Corticotropin-releasing |
| Abnormal thyroid | hormone |
| | $\downarrow$Triiodothyronine function |
| | test |

body dysmorphic disorders, personality disorders, and impulse control disorders to name but a few (Sadock & Sadock, 2007). **Eating disorders not otherwise specified (NOS)** is the diagnosis often given when patients have signs and symptoms of both categories. Most people associate eating disorders with females, but up to 10% (or more) of people with eating disorders are males.

# Anorexia Nervosa

The diagnosis of anorexia nervosa is based on psychological and physical criteria. Psychological criteria include an intense fear of gaining weight or becoming fat and a gross disturbance in body image. Physiological requisites for the diagnosis of anorexia nervosa are maintenance of body weight less than 85% of that expected. Box 11-1 presents the *Diagnostic and Statistical Manual of Mental Disorders* (4th edition, text revision) (*DSM-IV-TR*) diagnostic criteria for anorexia nervosa.

Most cases of anorexia nervosa are seen in adolescent females, with over 80% to 85% of cases developing between the ages of 13 and 20. Although most individuals with anorexia nervosa are adolescents, the disorder is being diagnosed in preadolescents, adults, and even the elderly. Males account for approximately 19% to 30% of the younger patients diagnosed with anorexia nervosa (APA, 2000b). The issues and treatment modalities remain the same for both men and women.

Characteristically, patients with anorexia are emaciated, but they still feel "fat" and want to hide their "ugly, fat body." The disorder might cause them to have ritualistic eating patterns and compulsive behaviors; often feel hopeless, helpless, and depressed; and might feel the only control they can exert in their life is through what food they will eat. Suicide is a real concern.

People with this disorder use two methods to control weight:

1. The **bulimic** approach alternates bingeing and starvation (including purging and laxative and/or diuretic abuse). Purging might occur in up to 70% of young patients (*binge eating/purging type*).
2. The **restrictive** approach uses low calorie intake and exercise (*restricting type*).

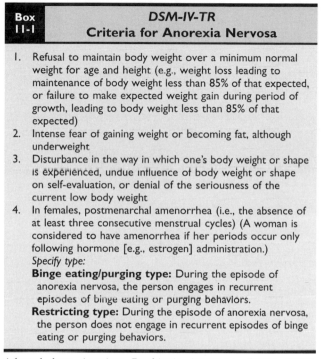

| Box 11-1 | *DSM-IV-TR*<br>Criteria for Anorexia Nervosa |
|---|---|

1. Refusal to maintain body weight over a minimum normal weight for age and height (e.g., weight loss leading to maintenance of body weight less than 85% of that expected, or failure to make expected weight gain during period of growth, leading to body weight less than 85% of that expected)
2. Intense fear of gaining weight or becoming fat, although underweight
3. Disturbance in the way in which one's body weight or shape is experienced, undue influence of body weight or shape on self-evaluation, or denial of the seriousness of the current low body weight
4. In females, postmenarchal amenorrhea (i.e., the absence of at least three consecutive menstrual cycles) (A woman is considered to have amenorrhea if her periods occur only following hormone [e.g., estrogen] administration.)

*Specify type:*

**Binge eating/purging type:** During the episode of anorexia nervosa, the person engages in recurrent episodes of binge eating or purging behaviors.

**Restricting type:** During the episode of anorexia nervosa, the person does not engage in recurrent episodes of binge eating or purging behaviors.

Adapted from American Psychiatric Association (APA). (2000). *Diagnostic and statistical manual of mental disorders* (4th ed., text rev.) (*DSM-IV-TR*). Washington DC: Author, p. 589; reprinted with permission.

The course of anorexia can be (Hoffman & Halmi, 1997):

- A single episode with weight and psychological recovery
- Nutritional rehabilitation with relapses
- An unremitting course resulting in death

The disease has a mortality rate of 5% (most studies) to 20% (long-term studies looking at ultimate mortality rate over 20 years or longer). Death occurs from starvation, fluid and electrolyte imbalance, or suicide in chronically ill patients. Elliot (2007) has identified favorable and negative prognostic indicators for anorexia nervosa:

1. **Favorable prognostic indicators:**
   a. Earlier age at onset
   b. Return of menses
   c. Good premorbid school/work history
2. **Negative prognostic indicators:**
   a. Failure to respond to prior treatments
   b. Multiple hospitalizations
   c. Male
   d. Being married
   e. Disturbed family premorbidly adjustment in childhood
   f. Co-occuring psychiatric condition(s)

# ASSESSMENT

## Presenting Signs and Symptoms

### *Psychosocial*

- Extreme fear of gaining weight
- Poor social adjustment with some areas of high functioning (e.g., intellectual)
- Odd food habits (hoarding, hiding food [e.g., in pockets, under plate])
- Hyperactivity (compulsive and obsessive exercise and/or secretive physical activity in an attempt to burn calories)
- Mood and/or sleep disturbances
- Obsessive-compulsive behaviors (e.g., eating only one pea at a time, arranging and rearranging food on plate before each bite, cutting food into tiny pieces and chewing each piece excessively)
- Perfectionist
- Introverted; avoids intimacy and sexual activity
- Denies feelings of sadness or anger and will often appear pleasant and compliant
- Although cachectic, patients see themselves as fat, a sign of an unrealistic body image
- Families often have rigid rules and high expectations for their members

### *Physiological and Endocrine Symptoms*

- Emaciated physical appearance
- Changes in cardiac status (e.g., bradycardia, hypotension, dysrhythmia)

- Dry, yellowish skin
- Amenorrhea, infertility
- Hair loss, possible presence of lanugo (fine body hair covering)
- Decreased metabolic rate
- Chronic constipation
- Fatigue and lack of energy
- Insomnia
- Loss of bone mass, osteoporosis
- In patients who vomit or use laxatives to purge, loss of tooth enamel and scarring of the back of the hand from inducing vomiting, and enlarged salivary glands might be seen. Serum amylase level is often elevated.
- Dehydration, edema
- Laboratory abnormalities and medical complications (see Table 11-1)

## ASSESSMENT TOOLS

The nurse must be able to make a comprehensive nursing assessment, know when a medical or psychological emergency warrants hospitalization, and alert the medical staff. Refer to Appendix D-8 for a guide that will help the nurse assess whether the patient with an eating disorder is a candidate for hospital admission.

### Assessment Guidelines

#### Anorexia Nervosa

Determine if:
1. The patient has a medical or psychiatric situation that warrants hospitalization.
2. The family has information about the disease and knows where to get support.
3. The patient is amenable to attending appropriate therapeutic modalities and will be adherent.
4. Family counseling has been offered to the family or individual family members for support, or to target a family or individual family member's problem.
5. A thorough physical examination with appropriate blood work has been done.
6. Other medical conditions have been ruled out.

7. The family and patient need further teaching or information regarding patient's treatment plan (e.g., psychopharmacological interventions, behavioral therapy, cognitive therapy, family therapy, individual psychotherapy). If the patient is a candidate for partial hospitalization, can the family/patient discuss their function?
8. The patient and family desire a support group; if yes, provide referrals.

# NURSING DIAGNOSES WITH INTERVENTIONS

## Discussion of Potential Nursing Diagnoses

Eating disorders have both physiological and psychological components. The aims of treatment are survival based (Hill, 1998):

- Regain a healthy weight.
- Restore healthy eating habits.
- Treat physical complications.
- Address dysfunctional beliefs.
- Intervene in those dysfunctional thoughts, feelings, and beliefs.
- Deal with affective and behavioral issues.
- Include family therapy when appropriate and possible.
- Teach relapse prevention.

The first steps in treating the anorexic patient include nutritional rehabilitation and weight restoration. Psychotherapy is not appropriate at this phase because there are profound psychological effects on mood and behavior from self-starvation. Hospitalization is warranted when emaciation is severe, vomiting is present, outpatient treatment has failed, or there is severe depression or suicidal feelings or physical complications (see Appendix D-8).

During hospitalization, treatment goals include:

- Weight restoration
- Normalization of eating behavior
- Change in the pursuit of thinness
- Prevention of relapse

Therefore, **Imbalanced Nutrition: Less Than Body Requirements** is a primary nursing diagnosis.

Because patients with anorexia have extreme distortions of body image (seeing themselves as fat when emaciated) and an intense fear of being fat, **Disturbed Body Image** is an important nursing diagnosis. A realistic perception of body size is important to help the patient refrain from the compulsive need to lose weight. There is real threat for self-harm; therefore, **Risk for Self-Mutilation** or **Risk for Self-Directed Violence** might be appropriate diagnoses for some young patients. Refer to Chapter 16 for guidelines to assessment and care. Patients with anorexia are terrified about gaining weight and will do anything to prevent it; they frequently try to manipulate staff. Although briefly addressed here, Chapter 19 has an in-depth discussion of strategies for dealing with manipulative behaviors.

**Understand that individuals with anorexia nervosa are notoriously disinterested in treatment. Gaining trust and cooperation can be difficult.** Table 11-2 offers potential nursing diagnoses for individuals with eating disorders.

Table 11-2 **Potential Nursing Diagnoses for Eating Disorders**

| Symptoms | Nursing Diagnoses |
|---|---|
| Emaciated, dehydrated, fatigued and lacking energy, edema | **Imbalanced Nutrition: Less Than Body Requirements** <br> **Deficient Fluid Volume** <br> **Impaired Skin Integrity** <br> **Risk for Imbalanced Body Temperature** <br> **Activity Intolerance** <br> **Fatigue** <br> **Risk for Infection** <br> **Decreased Cardiac Output** |
| Chronic constipation or diarrhea, abuse of laxatives | **Constipation** <br> **Diarrhea** |
| Sees self as fat (even when emaciated), has extreme fear of gaining weight, denies feelings of sadness or anger, has obsessive thoughts around food | **Disturbed Thought Processes** <br> **Ineffective Denial** <br> **Disturbed Body Image** |

*Continued*

Table 11-2 **Potential Nursing Diagnoses for Eating Disorders—cont'd**

| Symptoms | Nursing Diagnoses |
|---|---|
| Poor social adjustment, introverted, compulsive behaviors (sexual acting out, shoplifting, bingeing, substance use), perfectionistic, manipulates to avoid calorie intake | Ineffective Coping<br>Social Isolation<br>Impaired Social Interaction |
| Feelings of helplessness, worthlessness, being out of control; mood and sleep disturbances | Hopelessness<br>Powerlessness<br>Chronic Low Self-Esteem<br>Risk for Self-Directed Violence<br>Risk for Self-Mutilation<br>Spiritual Distress<br>Risk for Loneliness<br>Anxiety |
| Disrupted family, family in crisis, family confusion | Interrupted Family Processes<br>Compromised Family Coping<br>Disabled Family Coping |
| Resistance to treatment, denial of problems, shame over bingeing, extreme fear of gaining weight, nonadherence to medications or treatment | Deficient Knowledge<br>Noncompliance<br>Anxiety |

## Overall Guidelines for Nursing Intervention

### Anorexic Individual

1. Gaining an anorexic individual's cooperation is best accomplished by acknowledging his or her desire for thinness and control and stimulating motivation for change.
2. Do a self-assessment and be aware of your own reactions that might hinder your ability to help the patient. Some nurses might (Gorman et al., 1996):
   - Feel shocked or disgusted by the patient's behavior or appearance.

- Resent the patient, believing that the disorder is self-inflicted.
- Feel helpless to change the patient's behavior, leading to anger, frustration, and criticism.
- Become overwhelmed by the patient's problems, leading to feelings of hopelessness or setting rigid limits to feel more in control of the patient's behavior.
- Be swept up into power struggles with the patient, resulting in angry feelings in the nurse toward the patient.

When any of these or other negative feelings toward the patient arise, supervision and/or peer review is needed to help shape the nurse's perspective and lessen feelings of helplessness, guilt, need for control, frustration, or hopelessness.

3. When problems in the family contribute to the feeling of loss of control, family therapy has provided a significant improvement rate.
4. Individual therapy and group therapy are essential in treating patients with eating disorders. Treatment for anorexic patients often includes a behavior modification program, especially initially. Family therapy and family education are often key to a patient's success.
5. Behavior therapy is often used to change the eating patterns of an anorexic who is seriously close to death. This is usually implemented after the anorexic has been tube fed to prevent death.
6. Refrain from focusing on the person's need to eat; recognize that other nonfood factors are the heart of the problem.
7. Monitor lab values, and report abnormal values to primary clinician.

## Selected Nursing Diagnoses and Nursing Care Plans

### IMBALANCED NUTRITION: LESS THAN BODY REQUIREMENTS

Intake of nutrients insufficient to meet metabolic needs

## Some Related Factors (Related To)

▲ Inability to ingest or digest food or to absorb nutrients because of biological, psychological, or economic factors
● Excessive fear of weight gain
● Restricting caloric intake or refusing to eat
● Excessive physical exertion resulting in caloric loss in excess of caloric intake
● Self-induced vomiting related to self-starvation

## Defining Characteristics (As Evidenced By)

▲ Weight loss (with or without adequate intake): 20% or more under ideal body weight
▲ Reported food intake less than RDA (recommended minimum daily allowance)
▲ Diarrhea and/or steatorrhea, abdominal cramping, pain
● Sore buccal cavity
● Emaciated appearance
● Excessive hair loss or increased growth of hair on body (lanugo)
● Serious medical complications resulting from starvation (e.g., electrolyte imbalances, hypothermia, bradycardia, hypotension, cardiac arrhythmias, edema)

## Outcome Criteria

● Food and fluid intake are within normal limits
● Weight is maintained within a medically safe range

## Long-Term Goals

● Patient's electrolytes will be within normal limits by (date)
● Patient's cardiac status will be within normal limits by (date)
● Patient will achieve 85% to 90% of ideal body weight
● Patient will commit to long-term treatment to prevent relapse by (date)
● Patient will demonstrate regular, independent, nutritional eating habits by (date)

---

▲ NANDA International accepted; ● In addition to NANDA International

## Short-Term Goals

Patient will:

- Increase caloric and nutritional intake, showing gradual increases on a weekly basis
- Gain no more than _____ in the first week of refeeding, as decided by patient and health team
- Exercise in limited amounts only when assessed to be both nutritionally and medically stable
- Formulate with the nurse a *nurse-patient contract* facilitating a therapeutic alliance and a commitment to treatment on the part of the patient

## Interventions and Rationales

| Intervention | Rationale |
|---|---|
| **The Severely Malnourished Patient—Nutritional Rehabilitation** | |
| 1. When severely malnourished and refusing nourishment, patient might require tube feedings, either alone or in conjunction with oral or parenteral nutrition. | 1. Tube feedings might be the only means available to maintain patient's life. Patient might not be able to tolerate solid foods at first. The use of nasogastric tube feedings decreases the chance of vomiting. |
| 2. Tube feedings or parenteral nutrition are often given at night. | 2. Using nighttime administration can diminish drawing attention or sympathy from other patients and allows the patient to participate more fully in daytime activities. |
| 3. After completion of nasogastric tube feeding, it is best to supervise patient for 90 minutes initially, then gradually reduce to 30 minutes. | 3. Helps minimize the patient's chance of vomiting or siphoning off feedings. |
| 4. Vital signs at least three times daily until stable, then daily. Repeat | 4. As patient's weight begins to increase, cardiovascular status |

| **Intervention** | **Rationale** |
|---|---|
| electrocardiogram (ECG) and laboratory tests (electrolytes, acid-base balance, liver enzymes, albumin, and others) until stable. | improves to within normal range, and monitoring is needed less frequently. |
| 5. Administer tube feedings in a matter-of-fact, nonpunitive manner. Tube feedings are not to be used as threats, nor are they to be bargained about. | 5. Tube feedings are medical treatments, not a punishment or bargaining chip. Being consistent and enforcing limits lowers the chance of manipulation and the use of power struggles. |
| 6. Give the patient the chance to take foods or liquid supplements orally, and supplement insufficient intake through tube feedings. | 6. Allows the patient some control over whether he or she needs tube feedings or not. The patient's life is the priority, however. |
| 7. Weigh the patient weekly or biweekly at the same time of day each week. Use the following guidelines:<br>• Before the morning meal<br>• After the patient has voided<br>• In hospital gown or bra and pants only | 7. Patients are terrified about gaining weight. Staff members should guard against patients trying to manipulate their weight by drinking excess water before being weighed, having a full bladder, and putting heavy objects in their pockets or on their person. |
| 8. Remain neutral, neither approving nor disapproving. | 8. Keep issues of approval and disapproval separate from issues of health. Weight gain/loss is a health matter, not an area that has to do with the staff's pleasure or disapproval. |

| Intervention | Rationale |
|---|---|

**The Less Severely Malnourished Patient—Nutritional Maintenance**

1. When possible, set up a contract with the patient regarding treatment goals and outcome criteria.

2. Provide a pleasant, calm atmosphere at mealtime. Mealtime should be structured. Patient should be told the specific time and duration of a meal (e.g., 30 minutes).

3. Observe patient *during* meals to prevent hiding or throwing away food. Accompany to the bathroom if purging is suspected. Observe patient for at least 1 hour *after* meals/snacks to prevent purging.

4. Observe patient closely for using physical activity to control weight.

5. Closely monitor and record:
   • Fluid and food intake
   • Vital signs
   • Elimination pattern: discourage the use of laxatives, enemas, or suppositories.

6. Continue to weigh patient as described earlier.

1. When patient agrees to take part in establishing goals, patient is in a position to have some control over his/her care.

2. Mealtimes become episodes of high anxiety, and knowledge of regulations decreases tension in the milieu, particularly when the patient has given up so much control by entering treatment.

3. These behaviors are difficult for the patient to stop. A power struggle might emerge around issues of control.

4. Patients are often discouraged from engaging in planned exercise programs until their weight reaches 85% of ideal body weight.

5. Fluid and electrolyte balance is crucial to patient's well-being and safety. Abnormal data should alert staff to potential physical crises.

6. Monitor progress.

| **Intervention** | **Rationale** |
|---|---|
| 7. As patient approaches target weight, gradually encourage patient to make own choices for menu selection. | 7. Fosters a sense of control and independence. |
| 8. Privileges are based on weight gain (or loss) when setting limits. When weight *loss* occurs, decrease privileges. Use this time to focus on circumstances surrounding the weight loss and feelings of the patient. | 8. By not focusing on eating, physical activity, calorie counts, and the like, there is more emphasis on the patient's feelings and perceptions. |
| 9. When weight gain occurs, increase privileges. | 9. Patient receives positive reinforcements for healthy outcomes and behaviors. |

**Maintenance**

| | |
|---|---|
| 1. Continue to provide a supportive and empathetic approach as patient continues to meet target weight. | 1. For the anorexic patient, eating regularly, even within the framework of restoring health, is extremely difficult. |
| 2. The weight maintenance phase of treatment challenges the patient. This is the ideal time to address more of the issues underlying the patient's attitude toward weight and shape. | 2. At a healthier weight, patient is cognitively better prepared to examine emotional conflicts and themes. |
| 3. Use a cognitive behavioral approach to patient's expressed fears regarding weight gain. Identify dysfunctional thoughts. | 3. Confronting dysfunctional thoughts and beliefs is crucial to changing eating behaviors. |

| **Intervention** | **Rationale** |
|---|---|
| 4. Emphasize social nature of eating. Encourage conversation that does not have the theme of food during mealtimes. | 4. Eating is a social activity shared with others, and participating in conversation serves both as a distraction from obsessional preoccupation and as a pleasurable event. |
| 5. Focus on the patient's strengths, including his or her good work in normalizing weight and eating habits. | 5. The patient has achieved a major accomplishment and should be proud. Explore activities unrelated to eating as sources of gratification. |
| 6. Encourage patient to apply all the knowledge, skills, and gains made from the various individual, family, and group therapy sessions. | 6. The patient should have been receiving intensive therapy (cognitive-behavioral) and education that have provided tools and techniques useful in maintaining healthy eating and living behaviors. |
| 7. Teach and role model assertiveness. | 7. Patient learns to get his or her needs met appropriately. Helps lower anxiety and acting-out behaviors. |

**Follow-Up Care**

| | |
|---|---|
| 1. Involve the patient's family and significant others with teaching, treatment, and discharge and follow-up plans. Teaching includes nutrition, medication, if any, and the dynamics of the illness (Schultz & Videbeck, 2005). | 1. Family involvement is a key factor to patient success. Family dynamics are usually a significant factor in the patient's illness and distress. |

| Intervention | Rationale |
|---|---|
| 2. Make arrangements for follow-up therapy for both the patient and family. | 2. Follow-up therapy for both family and patient is key to prevention of relapse. |
| 3. Offer referrals to the patient and family to local support groups or national groups. (See list at end of chapter for suggestions.) | 3. Support groups offer emotional guidance and support, resources, and important information; help minimize feelings of isolation; encourage healthier coping strategies. |

## DISTURBED BODY IMAGE

Confusion in mental picture of one's physical self

### Some Related Factors (Related To)

▲ Cognitive/perceptual factors
▲ Psychosocial factors
● Morbid fear of obesity
● Low self-esteem
● Feelings of helplessness
● Chemical/biological imbalances

### Defining Characteristics (As Evidenced By)

▲ Verbilization of perceptions that reflect an altered view of one's body in appearance
● Self-destructive behavior (purging, refusal to eat, abuse of laxatives)
● Sees self as fat, although body weight is normal, or patient is severely emaciated
● High to panic levels of anxiety over potential for slight weight gain, although grossly underweight to the point of starvation

---

▲ NANDA International accepted; ● In addition to NANDA International

## Outcome Criteria

- Comfortable with a weight that meets medically safe limits
- Demonstrates pride in self through dress and grooming

## Long-Term Goals

Patient will:
- Describe a more realistic perception of body size and shape in line with height and body type by (date)
- Refer to body in a more positive way by (date)
- Improve grooming, dress, and posture and present self in more socially acceptable and appropriate manner by (date)

## Short-Term Goals

Patient will:
- Challenge dysfunctional thoughts and beliefs about weight with help of nurse/counselor after acute phase of treatment has passed
- State three positive aspects about self

## Interventions and Rationales

| Intervention | Rationale |
|---|---|
| 1. Establish a therapeutic alliance with patient. | 1. Anorexic patients are highly resistant to giving up their distorted eating behaviors. |
| 2. Give the patient factual feedback about the patient's low weight and resultant impaired health. However, do not argue or challenge the patient's distorted perceptions (Ibrahim, 2005). | 2. Focuses on health and benefits of increased energy. Arguments or power struggles will only increase the patient's need to control. |
| 3. Recognize that the patient's distorted image is real to him/her. Avoid minimizing patient's perceptions (e.g., "I understand you see | 3. Acknowledges patient's perceptions, and the patient feels understood, although your perception is different. This kind of feedback is easier to hear |

| **Intervention** | **Rationale** |
|---|---|
| yourself as fat. I do not see you that way.") | than a negation of patient's beliefs. |
| 4. Encourage expression of feelings regarding how the patient thinks and feels about self and body. | 4. Promotes a clear understanding of patient's perceptions and lays the groundwork for working with patient. |
| 5. Assist the patient to distinguish between thoughts and feelings. Statements such as "I feel fat" should be challenged and reframed. | 5. It is important for the patient to distinguish between feelings and facts. The patient often speaks of feelings as though they are reality. |
| 6. Nurses who have training in cognitive-behavioral therapeutic interventions can encourage patient to keep a journal of thoughts and feelings and teach patient how to identify and challenge irrational beliefs. | 6. Cognitive and behavioral approaches can be very effective in helping patient challenge irrational beliefs about self and body image. |
| 7. Encourage patient to identify positive personal traits. Have patient identify positive aspects of personal appearance. | 7. Helps patient refocus on strengths and actual physical and other attributes. Encourages breaking negative rumination. |
| 8. Educate family regarding the patient's illness, and encourage attendance at family and group therapy sessions. | 8. Reactions of others often become triggers for dysphoric reactions and distorted perceptions. Relationships with others, although not causal, are the context in which the eating disorder exists and thrives. |
| 9. Encourage family therapy for family members and significant others. | 9. Families and significant others need assistance in how to communicate and share a relationship with the anorexic patient (Ibrahim, 2005). |

# MEDICAL TREATMENTS

## Psychopharmacology

Medications seem to be useful only after a safe weight has been restored. Although many drugs have proved helpful, no medication has been shown to be effective in maintaining weight gain, changing attitudes, or preventing relapse, either by itself or as an adjunct for treating anorexia nervosa (APA, 2000b).

Selective serotonin reuptake inhibitor (SSRI) antidepressants have helped reduce relapse in patients. Atypical antipsychotics seem to help improve mood and reduce obsessional behavior and resistance to weight gain for many.

A particular challenge with teenagers is that they are often nonadherent to medication regimens and treatment. This knowledge is best factored into the nurse's approach.

## Psychosocial

As mentioned in the opening paragraph, a number of factors should be known when formulating the treatment plan. Box 11-2 summarizes some of the more successful therapeutic modalities for treating anorexia nervosa.

# Bulimia Nervosa

People with bulimia might be slightly overweight, normal weight, or slightly below. The hallmark feature of bulimia nervosa is an excessive intake of food (binge eating), with purging behaviors to maintain body weight. Purging behaviors can include self-induced vomiting or the excessive use of laxatives, diuretics, or enemas. Other behaviors directed at maintaining body weight might include prolonged fasting, excessive exercise, or misuse of diet pills. Purging is used by 80% to 90% of individuals who present for treatment at eating disorder clinics (APA, 2000b).

Individuals with bulimia who use purging behaviors are referred to as having **bulimia nervosa—purging type.** Similarly, **bulimia nervosa—nonpurging type** represents people who use inappropriate compensatory behaviors (fasting, excessive exercise, misuse of diet pills) but do not engage in purging behaviors. *DSM-IV-TR* diagnostic criteria for bulimia nervosa are presented in Box 11-3.

Box 11-2 **Effective Therapeutic Modalities for People Suffering from Anorexia Nervosa**

**Behavioral Therapy**
Behavioral therapy is effective in inducing short-term weight gain in anorexic patients; this approach is incorporated into most structured treatment programs for anorexia, using an operant conditioning paradigm.

**Cognitive Therapy**
Cognitive therapy helps patients challenge the validity of distorted beliefs and perceptions that are perpetuating their illness. The modification of cognitive techniques for the treatment of anorexia nervosa includes examining underlying assumptions, modifying basic assumptions, reinterpreting body image misperceptions, and using the "what if" technique.

**Family Therapy**
Family therapy is advocated not as a single mode of treatment but as an adjunct therapy, especially for anorexic patients with an early age of onset (younger than 18 years). The most commonly found dysfunctional difficulties are enmeshment, rigidity, and failure to resolve conflict. These issues are usually compounded by the pathological family dynamics that usually develop around the eating problems.

**Individual Psychotherapy**
Although most therapists who work with anorexic patients advocate some form of individual psychotherapy, the traditional psychoanalytic approach is thought to be *ineffective* with these patients. Successful psychotherapy needs to be highly interactive, explore relevant issues, educate, negotiate, challenge assumptions underlying behavior, and encourage the patient directly and openly (Dunner, 1997). Themes that are common when treating patients with anorexia nervosa are:
- Low self-esteem
- Self-hatred
- Perfectionist strivings
- Inner emptiness
- Profound sense of ineffectiveness

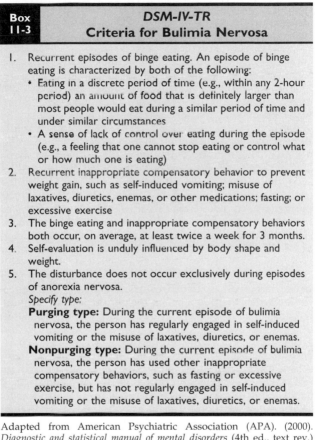

| Box 11-3 | **DSM-IV-TR**<br>**Criteria for Bulimia Nervosa** |
|---|---|

1. Recurrent episodes of binge eating. An episode of binge eating is characterized by both of the following:
   - Eating in a discrete period of time (e.g., within any 2-hour period) an amount of food that is definitely larger than most people would eat during a similar period of time and under similar circumstances
   - A sense of lack of control over eating during the episode (e.g., a feeling that one cannot stop eating or control what or how much one is eating)
2. Recurrent inappropriate compensatory behavior to prevent weight gain, such as self-induced vomiting; misuse of laxatives, diuretics, enemas, or other medications; fasting; or excessive exercise
3. The binge eating and inappropriate compensatory behaviors both occur, on average, at least twice a week for 3 months.
4. Self-evaluation is unduly influenced by body shape and weight.
5. The disturbance does not occur exclusively during episodes of anorexia nervosa.
   *Specify type:*
   **Purging type:** During the current episode of bulimia nervosa, the person has regularly engaged in self-induced vomiting or the misuse of laxatives, diuretics, or enemas.
   **Nonpurging type:** During the current episode of bulimia nervosa, the person has used other inappropriate compensatory behaviors, such as fasting or excessive exercise, but has not regularly engaged in self-induced vomiting or the misuse of laxatives, diuretics, or enemas.

Adapted from American Psychiatric Association (APA). (2000). *Diagnostic and statistical manual of mental disorders* (4th ed., text rev.) (*DSM-IV-TR*). Washington DC: Author, p. 594; reprinted with permission.

Women considered most at risk for bulimia in the United States are Caucasian females between the ages of 14 and 40 years, although most are in late adolescence or their early 20s.

Depressive symptoms often complicate the picture. Suicidal or self-mutilation behaviors can be associated with depression, which usually follows the development of bulimia nervosa (up to 70% of the time). However, in some cases, depression precedes bulimia. Substance abuse is often present (particularly alcohol and stimulants such as cocaine). A substantial number of bulimic patients have personality features of one or more personality disorders, frequently borderline personality disorder (APA, 2000a). This might account for the prevalence of bulimic individuals who present with dysfunctional personal relationships.

Individuals with bulimia are often more socially skilled and sexually active than patients with anorexia nervosa. The bulimic's bingeing is usually done alone and in secret. In one episode of bingeing, a bulimic can consume more than 5000 calories. Excessive vomiting can lead to severe dehydration and electrolyte imbalance, particularly hypokalemia. Teeth might be discolored or rotten as a result of gastric acid erosion related to excessive vomiting. Calluses on fingers result from inducing vomiting.

A sense of being out of control accompanies the excessive and/or compulsive consumption of large amounts of food. Binges are usually recurrent and are only interrupted when there is a social interruption, physical pain, or nausea. Poor impulse control can manifest itself in other impulsive behaviors as well (e.g., shoplifting and promiscuity). Following a binge, individuals often experience tremendous guilt, depression, or disgust with themselves. Young women with bulimia nervosa have an obsessive and persistent overconcern with body shape and weight and experience a distortion of body image. That is, they see themselves as too fat or large even when they are near or below normal body weight.

Treatment is provided in an outpatient setting unless there is a physical or psychological emergency. (Refer to Appendix D-8 for criteria for hospital admittance.)

The clinical course of bulimia nervosa can be either chronic or intermittent, with waxing and waning of symptoms. Many individuals experience the development of other psychiatric or medical problems. Up to 50% or more of bulimics recover; although relapse does sometimes occur. In addition to suicide, death can occur after severe bingeing.

# ASSESSMENT

## Presenting Signs and Symptoms

- Enlarged parotid glands
- Dental erosion, caries
- Calluses on dorsum of hands (from manually stimulating vomiting) and/or finger calluses
- Electrolyte imbalance, especially hypokalemia
- Irregular menses
- Fluid retention and/or dehydration
- Hypotension
- Ulcerations around mouth and cheeks (from emesis splashback)
- Chronic hoarseness, chronic sore throat
- Possible cardiac arrhythmias secondary to electrolyte imbalance
- Fatigue and lack of energy
- Gastrointestinal problems (e.g., constipation, diarrhea, reflux, and esophagitis)
- Alkalosis

## Assessment Tools

Refer to Table 11-3 for a comparison of assessment features between anorexia and bulimia.

Table 11-3 **Comparison of Characteristics of Anorexia and Bulimia**

| Characteristic | Anorexia—Restricting Type | Bulimia |
|---|---|---|
| Prevalence | Approximately 0.5%-1% for presentations that meet full criteria. Those who are subthreshold for the disorder (eating disorder NOS) are more common. | Approximately 1%-3% among adolescent and young adult females. The disorder in males is about 10% of that in females. |

*Continued*

Table 11-3 **Comparison of Characteristics of Anorexia and Bulimia—cont'd**

| Characteristic | Anorexia— Restricting Type | Bulimia |
|---|---|---|
| Appearance | Below 85% of ideal body weight | Normal weight range; might be slightly above or below |
| Onset of illness | Early adolescence, with peaks at 14 and 17 years of age | Late adolescence, early adult |
| Physical signs | Thin, emaciated Amenorrhea Slight yellowing of skin | Altered thyroid and cortisol function Enlarged parotid glands |
| | Bradycardia Hypotension Hypothermia Peripheral edema Bradycardia, electro-cardiogram (ECG) abnormalities | Dental erosion, caries Calluses on dorsum of hands from inducing vomiting Electrolyte imbalance, especially hypokalemia Fluid retention Cardiac problems (heart failure, ECG change, cardiomyopathy) Increased blood urea nitrogen |
| Familial patterns | Increased incidence of mood disorders in first-degree relatives | Increased incidence of mood disorders, substance abuse, dependence in first-degree relatives |
| Personality traits | Perfectionism Social isolation | Poor impulse control Low self-esteem |
| Insight into illness | Denies seriousness of illness Eating disordered behaviors are not viewed as abnormal (egosyntonic) | Aware of illness; disturbed behaviors are egodystonic |

Data from American Psychiatric Association (APA). (2000). *Practice guidelines for the treatment of psychiatric disorders: Compendium 2000.* Washington DC: Author.

## Assessment Guidelines

### Bulimia Nervosa

1. Medical stabilization is the first priority. Problems resulting from purging are disruptions in electrolyte and fluid balance and cardiac function; a thorough medical examination is vital.
2. Medical evaluation usually includes a thorough physical, as well as interpretation of pertinent laboratory values:
   - Electrolytes
   - Glucose
   - Thyroid function tests
   - Neuroimaging of pituitary gland
   - Complete blood count
   - Electrocardiogram
3. Psychiatric evaluation is advised because treatment of psychiatric comorbidity is important to outcome.

# NURSING DIAGNOSES WITH INTERVENTIONS

Individuals with uncomplicated bulimia nervosa are usually treated as outpatients in a clinic setting, a partial hospitalization program, or in private practice. However, hospitalization might be necessary when purging is so severe that it is out of the patient's control or causing severe electrolyte and metabolic disturbances. Psychiatric emergencies such as suicidal ideation or uncontrolled substance abuse might also indicate a need for hospitalization.

## Discussion of Potential Nursing Diagnoses

Because electrolyte and fluid balance and cardiac function can be affected, there is a serious potential for **Risk for Injury.** Because the patient often feels bingeing and purging are beyond their ability to control the behavior, **Powerlessness** is an area that needs to be targeted. **Comorbidity with personality disorders** might play a part in treatment, and the reader is encouraged to refer to Chapter 9. If there are issues of **substance abuse,** Chapter 10 might offer some guidelines for care. Because depression is usually present, there is always the concern with the **potential for suicide.** Refer to Chapter 16 for intervention strategies. Refer to Table 11-2 for potential nursing diagnoses for people with eating disorders.

## Overall Guidelines for Nursing Interventions

### Bulimic Individual

1. Often coexisting disorders complicate the clinical picture (depression, substance use, personality disorders), and these might warrant additional psychotherapy (psychodynamic, interpersonal, family therapy).
2. Cognitive-behavioral psychotherapy has been shown to be useful.
3. Group therapy with other individuals suffering from bulimia is often part of successful therapy.
4. Because anxiety and feelings of stress often precede bingeing, alternative ways of dealing with anxiety and alternative coping strategies to lessen anxiety are useful tools.
5. Family therapy is helpful and encouraged.

### Selected Nursing Diagnoses and Nursing Care Plans

#### RISK FOR INJURY

At risk of injury as a result of environmental conditions interacting with the individual's adaptive and defensive resources

### Some Related Factors (Related To)

- Uncontrollable binge/purge cycles
- Inadequate coping mechanisms to deal with anxiety and stress
- Coexisting conditions, when not addressed, could cause injury or self-injury (suicidal thoughts, self-mutilation, substance abuse)
- Poor impulse control

## *Defining Characteristics (As Evidenced By)*

- Medical complications
  - Electrolyte imbalances (hypokalemia, hypomagnese-mia, hyponatremia, hypocalcemia)
  - Esophageal tears
  - Cardiac problems
  - Altered thyroid and cortisol function
- Overuse of laxatives, diet pills, or diuretics
- Bingeing and purging activities
- Self-destructive behaviors
- Denial of feelings, illness, or problems

## *Outcome Criteria*

- Binge/purge cycle has ceased
- Normal electrolyte balance is maintained
- Uses supports (individual/group therapy, support groups, etc.) when stressed, to help prevent relapse

## *Long-Term Goals*

Patient will:
- Demonstrate at least four newly learned skills for managing stress and anxiety, shame and guilt, and other triggers that induce compulsive eating
- Abstain from binge/purge behaviors
- Be free of self-directed harm
- Demonstrate ability to recognize and refute dysfunctional thoughts and record in journal
- Obtain and maintain normal electrocardiogram readings
- Verbalize a desire to participate in an ongoing treatment program (support groups or therapy as indicated)
- Express feelings in non–food-related ways

## *Short-Term Goals*

Patient will:
- Remain free of self-directed harm
- Identify and role-play with nurse three alternative ways to deal with anxiety and stress by (date)

---

▲ NANDA International accepted; ● In addition to NANDA International

- Identify dysfunctional thoughts that might precede a binge/purge episode, and learn to challenge and refute these thoughts with aid of nurse within 2 weeks
- Identify signs and symptoms of low potassium level and other medical complications that would warrant immediate medical attention within 2 days

## Interventions and Rationales

| Intervention | Rationale |
|---|---|
| 1. Assess for suicidal thoughts and other self-destructive behaviors. | 1. Always be on guard for psychiatric and medical thoughts and emergencies, which take precedence over other forms of treatment. |
| 2. Educate the patient regarding the ill effects of self-induced vomiting (low potassium level, dental erosion, cardiac problems). | 2. Health teaching is crucial to treatment. The patient needs to be reminded of the benefits of normal eating behavior. |
| 3. Educate the patient about the binge/purge cycle and its self-perpetuating nature. | 3. The compulsive nature of the binge/purge cycle is maintained by the cycle of restricting, hunger, bingeing, and then purging accompanied by feelings of guilt. Then the cycle begins again. |
| 4. Identify patient triggers that induce compulsive eating and purging behaviors. | 4. Work with patient to find alternative ways to think and behave when triggers are present. |
| 5. Explore with the patient dysfunctional thoughts that precede the binge/purge cycle. Teach patients to refute these thoughts and reframe them in healthier ways. | 5. Strong rebuttals and nonjudgmental reframing can balance and combat distorted thinking. More rational thinking can lead to healthier behaviors to combat issues of self-esteem, body image, self-worth, and feelings of alienation. |

| **Intervention** | **Rationale** |
|---|---|
| 6. Have patient record thoughts and rebuttals in journal and share with nurse. | 6. Recognizing and reviewing with nurse helps reinforce learning. |
| 7. Work with the patient to identify problems, and mutually establish short- and long-term goals. | 7. Patient needs to develop tools for dealing with personal problems rather than turning to automatic binge/purge behaviors. |
| 8. Assess and teach problem-solving skills when dealing with patient's problem. | 8. Patient is often isolated from close relationships and lacks appropriate skills for getting needs met. |
| 9. Arrange for the patient to learn ways to increase interpersonal communication, socialization, and assertiveness skills. | 9. Patient is often isolated from close relationships and lacks appropriate skills for getting needs met. |
| 10. Encourage attendance at support groups or therapy groups with other bulimic individuals. Provide information for family members as well. | 10. Eating disorders are chronic diseases, and long-term follow-up therapy is critical for success. |

## POWERLESSNESS

Perception that one's own actions will not significantly affect an outcome; a perceived lack of control over a current situation or immediate happening

### Some Related Factors (Related To)

▲ Lifestyle of helplessness
▲ Interpersonal interaction
● Inability to control binge eating and purging behavior
● Severe distortion of body image that perpetuates dysfunctional behavior

- Feelings of low self-worth
- Insufficient coping skills in dealing with stress and anxiety

## Defining Characteristics (As Evidenced By)

▲ Verbal expressions of having no control or influence over situations
▲ Nonparticipation in care or decision making when opportunities are provided
▲ Expression of doubt regarding role performance
▲ Reluctance to express true feelings
- Guilt over uncontrollable behavior
- Distorted perceptions and beliefs regarding eating and self-image (e.g., "If I gain an ounce, I'll feel fat. Being thin is crucial to my success.")

## Outcome Criteria

- Has a sense of control over life
- Has a sense of control over personal choices
- Seeks solution to comorbid issues (e.g., depression, substance abuse) through therapeutic channels

## Long-Term Goals

Patient will:
- Verbalize increased feelings of security and autonomy over his/her life
- Identify people and resources in the community for support and follow-up
- State that he/she feels better able to cope with stress and anxiety
- Demonstrate ability to refrain from binge/purge behaviors

## Short-Term Goals

Patient will:
- Keep a journal of thoughts and feelings and learn to identify automatic thoughts and beliefs that trigger binge/purge behaviors by (date)

---

▲ NANDA International accepted; ● In addition to NANDA International

- Review journal with nurse/counselor on a weekly basis (clinic)
- Demonstrate the ability to dispute dysfunctional negative thoughts about self and abilities by (date)
- Demonstrate ability to do a realistic self-appraisal of strengths by (date)

## *Interventions and Rationales*

| Intervention | Rationale |
|---|---|
| 1. Explore the patient's experience of out-of-control eating behavior. | 1. Listening in an empathetic, nonjudgmental manner helps patient feel that someone understands his/her experience. |
| 2. Encourage the patient to keep a journal of thoughts and feelings surrounding binge/purge behaviors. | 2. Automatic thoughts and beliefs maintain the binge/purge cycle. A journal is an excellent way to identify these dysfunctional thoughts and underlying assumptions. |
| 3. Teach or refer to a counselor who can teach patient how to challenge dysfunctional thoughts and beliefs in a systematic manner. | 3. These automatic dysfunctional thoughts must be examined and challenged if change in patient thinking and behavior is to occur. |
| 4. Review with the patient the kinds of cognitive distortions that affect feelings, beliefs, and behavior. | 4. Cognitive distortions reinforce unrealistic views of self in terms of strengths and future potential. Realistic self-views are necessary for change to occur. |
| 5. Encourage patient's participation in decisions and patient's responsibility in his or her care and future. | 5. Helps patient gain a sense of control over his/her life and realize he/she has options for making important changes. |

| Intervention | Rationale |
|---|---|
| 6. Teach patient alternative stress-reduction techniques and visualization skills to improve self-confidence and feelings of self-worth. | 6. Visualizing a positive self-image and positive outcomes for life goals stimulates problem-solving toward desired goals. |
| 7. Role-play new skills. Encourage patient to apply new skills in individual and group therapy in communications with others, particularly family. | 7. Role-play allows the opportunity for patient to become comfortable with new and different ways of relating and responding to others in a safe environment. |
| 8. Teach the patient that one lapse is not a relapse. One slip of control does not eliminate all positive accomplishments. | 8. At time of lapse, it is helpful to examine what led to the lapse, knowing that one lapse does not eliminate all positive accomplishments. |

# MEDICAL TREATMENTS

## Psychopharmacology

No drug has been proven effective by itself or as an adjunct for treating bulimia nervosa. *Antidepressants*, particularly the SSRIs, have been helpful. Fluoxetine can reduce the number of episodes of bingeing and purging. Cognitive-behavioral therapy in conjunction with SSRIs has been shown to result in higher rates of remission.

## Psychosocial

Currently, cognitive-behavioral psychotherapy is the psychosocial treatment that is the most useful. Controlled trials have shown that interpersonal psychotherapy has also been effective. Family therapy for adolescents who still live with parents is an effective treatment modality.

# PATIENT AND FAMILY TEACHING

The National Association of Anorexia Nervosa and Associated Disorders (ANAD) has provided information that families and friends might find helpful in their dealings with a person with an eating disorder (Box 11-4).

---

**Box 11-4 Do's and Don'ts of Helping Someone Recover from an Eating Disorder**

*This information is provided by the National Association of Anorexia Nervosa and Associated Disorders (ANAD).*

**Do:**
- Gently encourage her to eat properly.
- Express your love and support.
- Try to understand, although this seems impossible.
- Take time to listen, although the talk might seem trivial or insignificant to you.
- Try to see how she (and each family member) perceives the situation.
- Realize that she is terrified of gaining weight and being fat, although she might actually be underweight. These irrational fears are real to her.
- Emphasize her positive, good characteristics, and compliment her on all the things she does right.
- Encourage her to accept support and honestly express her feelings.
- Talk honestly and sincerely, with love and understanding.
- Recognize that other, nonfood factors are at the heart of the problem.
- Help her find someone to support her, who knows what she is going through.
- Realize that although she must have help from others, she must want to get better, and she needs to love herself.

**Don't:**
- Try to force her to eat or stop exercising.
- Get angry or punish her.
- Be impatient (this is really tough).
- Lecture.
- Be too busy, even if you have to give up "important" things.

---

*Continued*

---

Box 11-4 **Do's and Don'ts of Helping Someone Recover from an Eating Disorder—cont'd**

---

- Jump to conclusions or see things only through your eyes and mind.
- Make her feel bad or guilty for having an eating disorder.
- Spy on her.
- Place the blame on anyone.
- Be afraid to talk about problems.
- Pretend it will all just go away.
- Expect an instant recovery.
- Let her feel she is the only one with this problem.

**Do all that you can to help her realize what a beautiful person she really is.**

---

MSI-ANAD014. Copyright 1994-1998 by National Association of Anorexia Nervosa and Associated Disorders, licensed to Medical Strategies, Inc. (MSI); ANAD, PO Box 7, Highland Park, IL 60035, (847) 831-3438; reprinted with permission.

# Nurse, Patient, and Family Resources

## ASSOCIATIONS

**American Anorexia/Bulimia Association**
165 West 46th Street, Suite 1108
New York, NY 10036
(212) 575-6200
For people with eating disorders

**National Association of Anorexia Nervosa and Associated Disorders (ANAD)**
PO Box 7
Highland Park, IL 60035
(847) 831-3438
For people with eating disorders

**National Eating Disorders Association**
603 Stewart Street, Suite 803
Seattle, WA 98101
(206) 382-3438
www.nationaleatingdisorders.org
For people with eating disorders, their families, and their
  friends

# INTERNET SITES

**Mirror Mirror Eating Disorders Home Page**
www.mirror-mirror.org/eatdis.htm

**Anorexia Nervosa and Related Eating Disorders, Inc.**
www.anred.com

**Healthtouch Online**
www.healthtouch.com

# CHAPTER 12

# Cognitive Disorders: Delirium and Dementia

## OVERVIEW

**Delirium** is usually characterized by a *sudden* disturbance of consciousness and a change in cognition, such as impaired attention span and disturbances of consciousness (American Psychiatric Association [APA], 2000). Delirium can have multiple causes but is *always secondary to another condition*, such as a general medical condition (i.e., infections, diabetes), or may be substance induced (drugs, medications, or toxins). Delirium is *usually a transitory condition and reversed when interventions are timely.* Prolonged delirium can lead to dementia.

**Dementia** *develops more slowly* and is characterized by multiple cognitive deficits that include impairment in short-term and long-term memory. Dementia is *usually irreversible.* Dementia can be *primary or secondary* to another condition. (Refer to Table 12-3, p. 398 for a side-by-side comparison of the characteristics of delirium and dementia.)

## Delirium

Box 12-1 presents the *Diagnostic and Statistical Manual of Mental Disorders* (4th edition, text revision) (*DSM-IV-TR*) diagnostic criteria for delirium.

Because delirium is always secondary to a medical disorder or toxicity, it is often seen on medical and surgical units. Delirium is often experienced by elderly patients,

| Box 12-1 | *DSM-IV-TR* Criteria for Delirium |
|---|---|

1. Disturbance of consciousness (i.e., reduced clarity of awareness of the environment with reduced ability to focus, sustain, or shift attention)
2. A change in cognition (memory deficit, disorientation, language disturbance) or the development of a perceptual disturbance that is not better accounted for by a preexisting, established, or evolving dementia
3. The disturbance develops over a short period of time (usually hours to days) and tends to fluctuate during the course of the day
4. The disturbance is due to:
   - A general medical condition, or
   - Substance-induced (intoxication or withdrawal), or
   - Multiple etiologies (both of the above causes), or
   - Not known (not otherwise specified)

Adapted from American Psychiatric Association (APA). (2000). *Diagnostic and statistical manual of mental disorders* (4th ed., text rev.) (*DSM-IV-TR*). Washington DC: Author, pp. 143-147; reprinted with permission.

children with high fevers, postoperative patients, and patients with cerebrovascular disease and congestive heart failure. Delirium can occur in people with infections, metabolic disorders, drug intoxications and withdrawals, medication toxicity, neurological diseases, tumors, and certain psychosocial stressors. Delirium is important to recognize because if it continues without intervention, irreversible brain damage can occur.

# ASSESSMENT

## Presenting Signs and Symptoms

- Fluctuating levels of consciousness. The individual might be disoriented and severely confused at night and during early morning hours (**sundowning**), and remain lucid during the day.
- Impaired ability to reason and carry out goal-directed behavior
- Alternating patterns of *hyperactivity* to *hypoactivity* (slow down activity to stupor or coma)

- Behaviors seen when **hyperactive** include:
  - Hypervigilance
  - Restlessness
  - Incoherent, loud, or rapid speech
  - Irritability
  - Anger and/or combativeness
  - Profanity
  - Euphoria
  - Distractibility
  - Tangentiality
  - Nightmares
  - Persistent abnormal thoughts (delusions)
- Behaviors seen when **hypoactive** include:
  - Lethargy
  - Speaks and moves little or slowly
  - Has spells of staring
  - Reduced alertness
  - Generalized loss of awareness of the environment
- Impaired attention span
- Cognitive changes not accounted for by dementia:
  - Memory impairment
  - Disorientation to time and place
  - Language disturbance; might be incoherent
  - Perceptual disturbance (hallucinations and illusions)
- Alterations in sleep/wake patterns
- Fear and high levels of anxiety

## Assessment Tools

When assessing individuals with confusional states, it is helpful to use structured cognitive screening tests such as the Folstein Mini Mental State Exam or the Functional Dementia Scale. (The latter may be found in Appendix D-9.)

## Assessment Guidelines

### Delirium

1. Assess for fluctuating levels of consciousness, which is key in delirium.
2. Interview family or other caregivers.
3. Assess for past confusional states (e.g., prior dementia diagnosis).

4. Identify other disturbances in medical status (e.g., dyspnea, edema, presence of jaundice).
5. Identify any electroencephalogram (EEG), neuroimaging, or lab abnormalities in patient's record.
6. Assess vital signs, level of consciousness, and neurological signs.
7. Ask the patient (when lucid) or family what they think could be responsible for the delirium (e.g., medications, withdrawal of substance, other medical condition).
8. Assess potential for injury (is the patient safe from falls, wandering).
9. Assess need for comfort measures (pain, cold, positioning).
10. Are immediate medical interventions available to help prevent irreversible brain damage?

# NURSING DIAGNOSES WITH INTERVENTIONS

## Discussion of Potential Nursing Diagnoses

Individuals experiencing delirium often misinterpret environmental cues **(illusions)** or imagine they see things **(hallucinations)** that they most likely believe are threatening or harmful. When patients act on these interpretations of their environment, they are likely to demonstrate a **Risk for Injury.** The symptoms of confusion usually fluctuate, and nighttime is the most severe (this is often called *sundowning*). Therefore, these patients often have **Disturbed Sleep Pattern.** During times of severe confusion, individuals are usually terrified and cannot care for their needs or interact appropriately with others, so **Fear, Self-Care Deficit,** and **Impaired Social Interaction** are also potential diagnoses. This section on delirium concerns **Acute Confusion,** which covers many of the problems mentioned.

Please note that many of the interventions, especially those for communication with the patient with delirium when confused, are also applicable to the patient with dementia when confused. Table 12-1 identifies potential nursing diagnoses useful for all confused patients (delirium or dementia).

Table 12-1 **Potential Nursing Diagnoses for the Confused Patient**

| Symptoms | Nursing Diagnoses |
| --- | --- |
| Wandering, unsteady gait; acts out fear from hallucinations or illusions; forgets things (leaves stove on, doors open) | Risk for Injury |
| Awakes disoriented during the night (sundowning), frightened at night | Disturbed Sleep Pattern<br>Fear |
| Too confused to take care of basic needs | Acute Confusion<br>Self-Care Deficit<br>Ineffective Coping<br>Urinary Incontinence<br>Imbalanced Nutrition<br>Deficient Fluid Volume |
| Sees frightening things that are not there (**hallucinations**), mistakes everyday objects for something sinister and frightening (**illusions**), might become paranoid, thinking that others are doing things to confuse them (**delusions**) | Disturbed Sensory Perception<br>Impaired Environmental Interpretation Syndrome<br>Disturbed Thought Processes |
| Does not recognize familiar people or places, has difficulty with short- and/or long-term memory, forgetful and confused | Impaired Memory<br>Impaired Environmental Interpretation Syndrome<br>Acute Confusion<br>Chronic Confusion |
| Difficulty with communication, cannot find words, difficulty in recognizing objects and/or people, incoherence | Impaired Verbal Communication |
| Devastated over losing their place in life as they know it (during lucid moments); fearful and overwhelmed by what is happening to them | Spiritual Distress<br>Hopelessness<br>Situational Low Self-Esteem<br>Grieving |
| Family and loved ones overburdened and overwhelmed; unable to care for patient's needs | Disabled Family Coping<br>Compromised Family Coping<br>Interrupted Family Processes<br>Impaired Home Maintenance<br>Caregiver Role Strain |

**Overall Guidelines for Nursing Interventions**

*Delirium*

1. Delirium, unlike dementia, is transitory when interventions are instituted and if delirium does not last a prolonged period of time. Therefore, immediate intervention for the underlying cause of the delirium is needed to prevent irreversible damage to the brain. Medical interventions are the first priority.
2. When patients are confused and frightened and are having a difficult time interpreting reality, they might be prone to accidents. Therefore, safety is a high priority.
3. Delirium is a terrifying experience for many patients. When some individuals recover to their premorbid cognitive function, they are left with frightening memories and images. Some clinicians advocate preventive counseling and education after recovery from acute brain failure (Borson, 1997).
4. Refrain from using restraints. Encourage one or two significant others to stay with patient to provide orientation and comfort.

**Selected Nursing Diagnoses and Nursing Care Plans**

## ACUTE CONFUSION

Abrupt onset of a cluster of global, transient changes and disturbances in attention, cognition, psychomotor activity, level of consciousness, and/or sleep/wake cycle

*Some Related Factors (Related To)*

▲ Age older than 60 years
▲ Dementia
▲ Alcohol abuse
▲ Drug abuse
▲ Delirium
● Metabolic disorder, neurological disorder, chemicals, medications, infections, fluid and electrolyte imbalances

## Defining Characteristics (As Evidenced By)

▲ Fluctuation in cognition
▲ Fluctuation in sleep/wake cycle
▲ Fluctuation in level of consciousness
▲ Agitation or restlessness
▲ Misperceptions of the environment (e.g., illusions, hallucinations)
▲ Lack of motivation to initiate and/or follow through with goal-directed or purposeful behavior

## Outcome Criteria

• Oriented to time, place, and person
• Resume usual cognitive and physical activities
• Absence of untoward effects from episode of delirium

## Long-Term Goals

• Patient will correctly state time, place, and person within a few days
• Patient will remain free of injury (e.g., falls) throughout periods of confusion

## Short-Term Goals

• Patient and others will remain safe during patient's periods of agitation or aggressive behaviors
• Patient will respond positively to staff efforts to orient them to time, place, and person throughout periods of confusion
• Patient will take medication as offered to help alleviate their condition

## Interventions and Rationales

| Intervention | Rationale |
|---|---|
| 1. Introduce self and call patient by name at the beginning of each contact. | 1. With short-term memory impairment, person is often confused and needs frequent orienting to time, place, and person. |

▲ NANDA International accepted; ● In addition to NANDA International

| **Intervention** | **Rationale** |
|---|---|
| 2. Maintain face-to-face contact. | 2. If patient is easily distracted, he or she needs help to focus on one stimulus at a time. |
| 3. Use short, simple, concrete phrases. | 3. Patient might not be able to process complex information. |
| 4. Briefly explain everything you are going to do before doing it. | 4. Explanation prevents misinterpretation of action. |
| 5. Encourage the family and friends (one at a time) to take a quiet, supportive role. | 5. Familiar presence lowers anxiety and increases orientation. |
| 6. Keep room well lit. | 6. Lighting provides accurate environmental stimuli to maintain and increase orientation. |
| 7. Keep environment noise to a minimum (e.g., television, visitors). | 7. Noise can be misconstrued as something frightening or threatening. |
| 8. Keep head of bed elevated. | 8. Helps provide important environmental cues. |
| 9. Provide clocks and calendars. | 9. These cues help orient patient to time. |
| 10. Encourage patient to wear prescribed eyeglasses or hearing aid. | 10. Helps increase accurate perceptions of visual, auditory stimuli. |
| 11. Make an effort to assign the same personnel on each shift to care for patient. | 11. Familiar faces minimize confusion and enhance nurse-patient relationships. |
| 12. When hallucinations are present, assure patients they are safe (e.g., "I know you are frightened. I'll sit with you a while and make sure you are safe."). | 12. Patient feels reassured that he or she is safe, and fear and anxiety often decrease. |

| Intervention | Rationale |
|---|---|
| 13. When illusions are present, clarify reality (e.g., "This is a coat rack, not a man with a knife...see? You seem frightened. I'll stay with you for a while."). | 13. With illusion, misinterpreted objects or sounds can be clarified, once pointed out. |
| 14. Inform patient of progress during lucid intervals. | 14. Consciousness fluctuates: patient feels less anxious, knowing where he or she is and who you are during lucid periods. |
| 15. Ignore insults and name calling, and acknowledge how upset the person might be feeling. For example: *Patient:* You incompetent jerk! Get me a real nurse, someone who knows what they are doing. *Nurse:* What you are going through is very difficult. I'll stay with you. | 15. Terror and fear are often projected onto the environment. Arguing or becoming defensive only increases patient's aggressive behaviors and defenses. |
| 16. If patient behavior becomes physically abusive: <br> a. First, set limits on behavior (e.g., "Mr. Jones, you are not to hit me or anyone else. Tell me how you feel." "Mr. Jones, if you have difficulty controlling your actions, we will help you gain control."). <br> b. Second, check orders for use of chemical restraint. | 16. Clear limits need to be set to protect patient, staff, and others. Often patient can respond to verbal commands. Chemical and physical restraints are used as a last resort, if at all. |

| Intervention | Rationale |
|---|---|
| 17. After patient returns to premorbid cognitive state, educate patient and offer counseling for his/her recollection of terrifying, frightening memories and images. | 17. Patient can believe his or her illusions or hallucinations were real, and it may take time for patient to come to terms with the experience. |

# Dementia

Dementia is marked by progressive deterioration in intellectual function, memory, and ability to solve problems and learn new skills. Judgment and moral and ethical behaviors decline as personality is altered. Box 12-2 presents the *DSM-IV-TR* diagnostic criteria for dementia.

Unlike delirium, dementia can be of a primary nature and is usually *NOT* reversible. Dementia is usually a slow and insidious process progressing over months or years. Dementia affects memory and ability to learn new information or to recall previously learned information. Dementia also compromises intellectual functioning and the ability to solve problems. Common causes of dementia are:

- Vascular dementia (multi-infarct)
- HIV disease
- Head trauma
- Parkinson's disease
- Huntington's disease
- Pick's disease
- Creutzfeldt-Jakob disease
- General medical condition (brain tumors, subdural hematoma, etc.)
- Substance use

However, the most prevalent primary dementia is **dementia of the Alzheimer's type (DAT)**. The second most common form of dementia is vascular dementia, which is caused by multiple strokes. As mentioned above, substances can also cause dementia (alcohol, inhalants, phencyclidine, piperidine), as can other medical conditions.

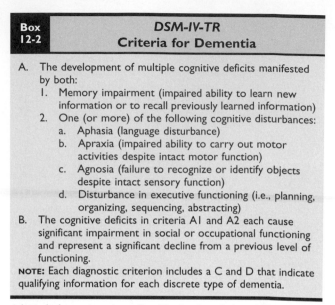

| Box 12-2 | DSM-IV-TR Criteria for Dementia |
|---|---|

A. The development of multiple cognitive deficits manifested by both:
  1. Memory impairment (impaired ability to learn new information or to recall previously learned information)
  2. One (or more) of the following cognitive disturbances:
     a. Aphasia (language disturbance)
     b. Apraxia (impaired ability to carry out motor activities despite intact motor function)
     c. Agnosia (failure to recognize or identify objects despite intact sensory function)
     d. Disturbance in executive functioning (i.e., planning, organizing, sequencing, abstracting)
B. The cognitive deficits in criteria A1 and A2 each cause significant impairment in social or occupational functioning and represent a significant decline from a previous level of functioning.

NOTE: Each diagnostic criterion includes a C and D that indicate qualifying information for each discrete type of dementia.

Adapted from American Psychiatric Association (APA). (2000). *Diagnostic and statistical manual of mental disorders* (4th ed., text rev.) (*DSM-IV-TR*). Washington DC: Author, p. 157; reprinted with permission.

# ASSESSMENT

## Presenting Signs and Symptoms

- Memory impairment, usually short-term memory first
- Cognitive impairment:
  - **Aphasia:** language disturbance, difficulty finding words, using words incorrectly
  - **Apraxia:** inability to carry out motor activities despite motor functions being intact (e.g., putting on one's pants, blouse, etc.)
  - **Agnosia:** loss of sensory ability; inability to recognize or identify familiar objects, such as a toothbrush, or sounds, such as the ringing of the phone; loses ability to problem solve, plan, organize, or abstract
- A significant decline in previous level of functioning; poor judgment

- Mood disturbances, anxiety, hallucinations, delusions, and impaired sleep often accompany dementia

## Assessment Tools

A variety of other medical problems can masquerade as dementia. For example, depression in the elderly is often misdiagnosed as dementia. Table 12-2 highlights the difference between dementia and depression and can be a useful guide for assessment.

At times it is important to distinguish dementia from delirium. Table 12-3 helps the nurse identify differences in the symptoms between one and the other. One always has to keep in mind that delirium can coexist with dementia, and that often clouds the picture.

### Table 12-2 **Dementia Versus Depression**

| Dementia | Depression |
|---|---|
| 1. Recent memory is impaired. In early stages, patient attempts to hide cognitive losses; is skillful at covering up. | 1. Patient readily admits to memory loss; other cognitive disturbances might be present. |
| 2. Symptoms progress slowly and insidiously; difficult to pinpoint onset. | 2. Symptoms are of relatively rapid onset. |
| 3. Approximate or "near-miss" answers are typical; tries to answer. | 3. "Don't know" answers are common; patient does not try to recall or answer. |
| 4. Patient struggles to perform well but is frustrated. | 4. Little effort to perform; is apathetic; seems helpless and pessimistic. |
| 5. Affect is shallow or labile. | 5. Depressive mood is pervasive. |
| 6. Attention and concentration might be impaired. | 6. Attention and concentration are usually intact. |
| 7. Changes in personality (e.g., from cheerful and easygoing to angry and suspicious). | 7. Personality remains stable. |

Varcarolis, E. (1998). *Foundations of psychiatric mental health nursing* (3rd ed.). Philadelphia: Saunders, p. 694.

Table 12-3 **Nursing Assessment: Delirium Versus Dementia**

| | Delirium | Dementia |
|---|---|---|
| Onset | Acute impairment of orientation, memory, intellectual function, judgment, and affect | Slow, insidious deterioration in cognitive functioning |
| Essential feature | Disturbance in consciousness, fluctuating levels of consciousness, and cognitive impairment | Progressive deterioration in memory, orientation, calculation, and judgment; symptoms do not fluctuate |
| Cause | The syndrome is *secondary* to many underlying disorders that cause temporary, diffuse disturbances of brain function. | The syndrome is either *primary* in etiology or *secondary* to other disease states or conditions |
| Course | The clinical course is usually brief (hours to days); prolonged delirium may lead to dementia. | Progresses over months or years; often irreversible |
| Speech | May be slurred; reflects disorganized thinking | Generally normal in early stages; progressive aphasia; confabulation |
| Memory | Short-term memory impaired | Short-term, then long-term, memory destroyed |
| Perception | Visual or tactile hallucinations; illusions | Hallucinations not prominent |
| Mood | Fear, anxiety, and irritability most prominent | Mood labile; previous personality traits become accentuated (e.g., paranoid, depressed, withdrawn, and obsessive-compulsive) |
| Electroen-cephalogram | Pronounced, diffuse slowing or fast cycles. | |

Varcarolis, E. (2002). *Foundations of psychiatric mental health nursing* (4th ed.). Philadelphia: Saunders, p. 694.

## Assessment Guidelines

### Dementia

1. Identify the underlying cause; for example, does the patient have a history of:
   - Depression
   - Substance abuse
   - Pernicious anemia

   See Box 12-3 for laboratory tests that might help root out possible causes.
2. How well is the family prepared and informed about the progress of the patient's dementia (e.g., the phases and course of Alzheimer's disease [AD], vascular dementia, AIDS-related dementia, multiple sclerosis, lupus, brain injury)?
3. How is the family coping with the patient? What are the main issues at this time?
4. What resources are available to the family? Does the family get help from other family members, friends, and community resources? Are the caregivers aware of community support groups and resources?
5. Obtain the data necessary to provide appropriate safety measures for the patient.

---

### Box 12-3  **Basic Workup for Dementia**

- Chest and skull radiograph studies
- Electroencephalography
- Electrocardiography
- Urinalysis
- Sequential multiple analyzer: 12-test serum profile
- Thyroid function tests
- Folate levels
- Venereal Disease Research Laboratories (VDRL), HIV tests
- Serum creatine assay
- Electrolyte assessment
- Vitamin $B_{12}$ levels
- Vision and hearing evaluation
- Neuroimaging (when diagnostic issues are not clear)

6. How safe is the patient's home environment (e.g., wandering, eating inedible objects, falls, provocative behaviors toward others)?
7. For what patient behaviors could the family use teaching and guidance (e.g., catastrophic reaction, lability of mood, aggressive behaviors, nocturnal delirium [increased confusion and agitation at night; sundowning])?
8. Identify family supports in the community.

# NURSING DIAGNOSES WITH INTERVENTIONS

## Discussion of Potential Nursing Diagnoses

The care of a patient with dementia requires a great deal of patience and creativity. These patients have enormous needs and put enormous demands on staff caring for them and on families who carry the burden at home. As some of these diseases progress, most notably AD, so do the demands on the staff, caregivers, and family. Safety is always a major concern. **Risk for Injury** might be related to impaired mobility, sensory deficits, history of accidents, or lack of knowledge of safety precautions.

As time passes, the person loses the ability to perform tasks that were once familiar and routine. The inability of the person to care for basic needs covers all areas (e.g., bathing, hygiene, grooming, feeding, and toileting). Therefore, **Self-Care Deficit** usually involves many functions. The goals are set up so that individuals can do as much for themselves as possible during each phase of the dementia.

**Impaired Verbal Communication** is often related to diminished comprehension, difficulty recognizing objects, aphasia, cerebral impairment, and severe memory impairment. Therefore, family and health care workers need to know ways to interact with a person with this nursing diagnosis.

The burden of caring for a family member with dementia can be enormous, especially over prolonged periods of time. Family members need a great deal of support, education, and guidance from community agencies and well-informed health care workers. Families might experience

**Disabled Family Coping**, which should always be addressed when it is recognized. Therefore, **Risk for Caregiver Role Strain** should be part of the initial assessment and must be continuously assessed as the dementia progresses. Most families will need information, support, and periods of respite.

There are numerous nursing diagnoses that might be appropriate. Refer back to Table 12-1 for nursing diagnoses appropriate for confused patients.

## Overall Guidelines for Nursing Interventions

1. Educate family on safety features for impaired family member living at home:
   a. Precautions for wandering (e.g., MedicAlert bracelet, "Home Safe Program," effective locks)
   b. Home safety features (e.g., eliminating slippery rugs, labeling of rooms and drawers, installing complex locks on top of doors)
   c. Self-care guidelines on maintaining optimal nutrition, bowel and bladder training, optimal sleep patterns, and working to optimal ability in activities of daily living
2. Educate family (and staff) on effective communication strategies with a confused patient:
   a. Teaching alternative modes of communication when patient is aphasic
   b. Teaching basic communication techniques with confused patients (e.g., introduce self each time; use simple, short sentences; maintain eye contact; focus on one topic at a time; talk about familiar and simple topics)
3. **Family/caregiver support is a priority.** Provide names and telephone numbers of support groups, respite care, day care, protective services, recreational services, Meals on Wheels, hospice services, and so on that are within the family/caregivers' community. Encourage the use of support groups for caregivers.
4. Provide family with information on all medications patient is taking (use for each, potential side and toxic effects, any interactions that could occur) and name and number of whom to call with future questions.

## Selected Nursing Diagnoses and Nursing Care Plans

### RISK FOR INJURY

At risk of injury as a result of environmental conditions interacting with the individual's adaptive and defensive resources

### *Related Factors (Related To)*

▲ Sensory dysfunction
▲ Cognitive or emotional difficulties
● Confusion, disorientation
● Faulty judgment
● Loss of short-term memory
● Previous falls
● Unsteady gait
● Wandering
● Provocative behavior

### *Some Defining Characteristics (As Evidenced By)*

● Getting into fights with others
● Choking on inedible objects
● Wandering
● Burns
● Falls
● Getting lost
● Poisoning—wrong medication, wrong dose

### *Outcome Criteria*

● Highest level of functioning will be supported
● Optimal health is maintained (nutrition, sleep, elimination)
● Free of fractures, bruises, contusions, burns, and falls

---

▲ NANDA International accepted; ● In addition to NANDA International

## Long-Term Goals

- With guidance and environmental manipulation, patient will not hurt himself/herself if falls occur
- With the aid of an identification bracelet, neighborhood or hospital alert, and enrollment in the Safe Return Program, patient will be returned within 3 hours of wandering
- Patient will ingest only correct doses of prescribed medication and appropriate food and fluids

## Short-Term Goals

- Patient will remain injury free, whether at home or in the hospital, with the aid of environmental manipulation and family or nursing staff precautions and interventions

## Interventions and Rationales

| Intervention | Rationale |
|---|---|
| **Safe Environment** | |
| 1. Restrict driving. | 1. Impaired judgment can lead to accidents. |
| 2. Remove throw rugs and other objects. | 2. Minimizes tripping and falling. |
| 3. Minimize sensory stimulation. | 3. Decreases sensory overload, which can increase anxiety and confusion. |
| 4. If patients become verbally upset, listen, give support, then change the topic. | 4. When attention span is short, patients can be briefly distracted to more productive topics and activities. |
| 5. Label all rooms and drawers with pictures. Label often-used objects (e.g., hairbrushes and toothbrushes). | 5. Might keep patient from wandering into other patient's rooms. Increases environmental clues to familiar objects. |
| 6. Install safety bars in bathroom. | 6. Prevents falls. |
| 7. Supervise patients when they smoke. | 7. Danger of burns is always present. |

| Intervention | Rationale |
|---|---|
| 8. If patient wanders during the night, put mattress on the floor. | 8. Prevents falls when patient is confused. |
| 9. Have patient wear MedicAlert bracelet that cannot be removed (with name, address, and telephone number). Provide police department with recent pictures. | 9. Patient can easily be identified by police, neighbors, or hospital personnel. |
| 10. Alert local police and neighbors about wanderer. | 10. Can reduce time necessary to return patient to home or hospital. |
| 11. Put complex locks on door. | 11. Reduces opportunity to wander. |
| 12. Place locks at top of door. | 12. In moderate and late DAT, ability to look up and reach upward is lost. |
| 13. Encourage physical activity during the day. | 13. Physical activity during the day might decrease wandering at night. |
| 14. Explore the feasibility of installing sensor devices. | 14. Provides warning if patient wanders. |
| 15. Enroll the patient in the Alzheimer's Association's Safe Return program (www.alz.org). | 15. Helps track individuals with dementia who wander and are at risk of getting lost or injured. |

## SELF-CARE DEFICIT

Impaired ability to perform or complete feeding, bathing, toileting, dressing, and grooming activities for oneself

### Some Related Factors (Related To)

▲ Perceptual or cognitive impairment
▲ Neuromuscular impairment
▲ Decreased strength and endurance

▲ Confusion
● Apraxia (inability to perform tasks that were once routine)
● Severe memory impairment

## Defining Characteristics (As Evidenced By)

▲ Inability to wash properly
▲ Impaired ability to put on or take off necessary items of clothing
▲ Inability to maintain appearance at a satisfactory level
▲ Inability to get to toilet or commode
▲ Inability to carry out proper toilet hygiene

## Outcome Criteria

● Patient's self-care needs will be met with optimal participation by patient

## Long-Term Goals

● Patient will participate in self-care at optimal level with supervision and guidance
● Patient's skin will remain intact despite incontinence or prolonged pressure
● Patient will maintain nutrition, hygiene, dress, and toileting activities with appropriate support from others (e.g., caregivers, family, staff)

## Short-Term Goals

Patient will:
● Be able to follow step-by-step instructions for dressing, bathing, and grooming
● Put on own clothes appropriately with aid of fastening tape (Velcro) and supervision
● Participate in toilet training procedures daily
● Ingest adequate calories (1500 to 2200 calories/day)
● Maintain an adequate fluid intake (2400 to 3200 mL/day)

---

▲ NANDA International accepted; ● In addition to NANDA International

*Interventions and Rationales*

| Intervention | Rationale |
|---|---|

**Dressing and Bathing**

1. Always have patients perform all tasks they are capable of.

2. Always have patient wear own clothes, even if in the hospital.

3. Use clothing with elastic, and substitute fastening tape (Velcro) for buttons and zippers.

4. Label clothing items with name and name of item.

5. Give step-by-step instructions whenever necessary (e.g., "Take this blouse...put in one arm...now the other arm...pull it together in the front...now...").

**Rationale**

1. Maintains self-esteem, uses muscle groups, and minimizes further regression.

2. Helps maintain patient's identity and dignity.

3. Minimizes patient's confusion and increases independence of functioning.

4. Helps identify patients if they wander, and gives caregivers additional clues when aphasia or agnosia occurs.

5. Patient can focus on small pieces of information more easily; allows patient to perform at optimal level.

**Nutrition**

1. Monitor food and fluid intake.

2. Offer finger food that patient can walk around with.

3. During period of hyperorality, watch that patient does not eat nonfood items (e.g., ceramic fruit or food-shaped soaps).

**Rationale**

1. Patient might have anorexia or be too confused to eat.

2. Increases input throughout the day; patient might eat only small amounts at meals.

3. Patient puts everything into mouth; might be unable to differentiate inedible objects.

| Intervention | Rationale |
|---|---|
| **Bowel and Bladder Function** | |
| 1. Begin bowel and bladder program early; start with bladder control. | 1. Same time of day for bowel movements and toileting—in early morning, after meals and snacks, and before bedtime—can help prevent incontinence. |
| 2. Evaluate use of adult disposable undergarments. | 2. Prevents embarrassment if incontinent. |
| 3. Label bathroom door, as well as doors to other rooms, with a picture. | 3. Additional environmental clues can maximize independent toileting. Pictures are more readily interpreted. |
| **Sleep** | |
| 1. Because patient might awaken frightened and disoriented at night, keep area well lit. | 1. Reinforces orientation, minimizes possible illusions. |
| 2. Nonbarbiturates might be ordered (e.g., chloral hydrate). | 2. Barbiturates can have a paradoxical reaction, causing agitation. |
| 3. Avoid the use of restraints. | 3. Can cause patient to become more terrified and fight against restraints until exhausted to a dangerous degree. |

## IMPAIRED VERBAL COMMUNICATION

Decreased, delayed, or absent ability to receive, process, transmit and use a system of symbols

### Related Factors (Related To)

▲ Decrease in circulation to the brain
▲ Physical barrier (e.g., brain tumor, subdural hematoma)
▲ Deterioration or damage to the neurological centers in the brain that regulate speech and language

▲ Biochemical changes in the brain, physiological conditions
● Severe memory impairment
● Escalating anxiety
● Delusions or illusions

## Defining Characteristics (As Evidenced By)

▲ Difficulty forming words or sentences (e.g., aphasia)
▲ Difficulty expressing thoughts verbally
▲ Speaks or verbalizes with difficulty
▲ Does not or cannot speak
● Has difficulty identifying objects (agnosia)
● Inability to focus or concentrate on a train of thought
● Impaired comprehension
● Reverts back to first language

## Outcome Criteria

● Communicates with aid of variety of verbal and nonverbal techniques for optimal period of time

## Long-Term Goals

● Patient will communicate basic needs with the use of visual and verbal clues when needed
● Patient will communicate important thoughts with the use of visual and verbal clues when needed
● Patient's family and caregivers demonstrate ability to minimize patient's agitation and fear when patient is delusional or having illusions

## Short-Term Goals

● Patient's basic needs will be met when in the hospital (hydration and nutrition, hygiene, dress, bowel and bladder function)
● Patient will learn to adopt alternative modes of communication with the use of nonverbal techniques (e.g., writing, pointing, demonstrating an action [pantomime])

---

▲ NANDA International accepted; ● In addition to NANDA International

- Patient's anxiety and fear will be decreased when delusions or illusions occur through the use of appropriate nursing techniques

## *Interventions and Rationales*

Follow the guidelines for intervention with a confused patient in the first half of this chapter. Communication techniques specific for dementia follow.

| Intervention | Rationale |
|---|---|
| 1. Use a variety of nonverbal techniques to enhance communication: <br> a. Point, touch, or demonstrate an action while talking about it. <br> b. Ask patients to point to parts of their body or things they want to communicate about. <br> c. When patient is searching for a particular word, guess at what is being said and ask if you are correct (e.g., "You are pointing to your mouth, saying pain. Is it your dentures? No. Is your mouth sore? Yes. OK, let me take a look to see if I can tell what is hurting you."). Always ask patient to confirm whether your guess is correct. <br> d. Use of cue cards, flash cards, alphabet letters, signs, and pictures on doors to various rooms is often helpful for many patients and their families (e.g., bathroom, | 1. Both delirium and dementia can pose huge communication problems, and often alternative nonverbal or verbal methods have to be used. |

| Intervention | Rationale |
|---|---|
| "Charles's bedroom"). Use of pictures is helpful when ability to read decreases. | |
| 2. Encourage reminiscing about happy times in life. | 2. Remembering accomplishments and shared joys helps distract patient from deficit and gives meaning to existence. |
| 3. If a patient gets into an argument with another patient, stop the argument and get them out of each other's way. After a short while (5 minutes), explain to each patient matter-of-factly why you had to intervene. | 3. Prevents escalation to physical acting out. Shows respect for patient's right to know. Explaining in an adult manner helps maintain self-esteem. |
| 4. Reinforce patient's speech through pictures, nonverbal gestures, X's on calendars, and other methods used to anchor patient in reality. | 4. When aphasia starts to hinder communication, alternate methods of communication need to be instituted. |

Burnside (1988) suggests useful guidelines for implementing nursing interventions or teaching a severely cognitively impaired person (Box 12-4).

---

**Box 12-4 Guidelines for Caring for the Cognitively Impaired**

1. Provide only one visual clue (object) at a time.
2. Know that the patient might not understand the task assigned.
3. Remember that relevant information is remembered longer than irrelevant information.
4. Break tasks into very small steps.
5. Give only one instruction at a time.
6. Report, record, and document all data.

## CAREGIVER ROLE STRAIN

A caregiver's felt or exhibited difficulty in performing the family caregiver role

*Some Related Factors (Related To)*

**Complexity of activites and severity of the care receiver's illness:**
▲ 24-hour care responsibility
▲ Years of caregiving
▲ Lack of support
▲ Unadequate community support (e.g., respite and recreation for the caregiver)
▲ Inadequate physical environment, (transportation, housing) for providing care
▲ Family's and/or caregiver's isolation

*Defining Characteristics (As Evidenced By)*

**Expressions by caregiver of:**
▲ Difficulty in performing required activities
▲ Altered caregiver health status (hypertension, cardiovascular disease, etc.)
▲ Feelings of stress/frustration in relationship with patient
▲ Feelings of anger and/or depression
▲ Family conflict regarding issues of providing care
▲ Lack of time to meet personal needs

*Outcome Criteria*

• Satisfaction with physical health
• Satisfaction with social support
• Satisfaction with professional support

---

▲ NANDA International accepted; ● In addition to NANDA International

## Long-Term Goals

Caregivers will:
- State that they have help from family and/or friends, and/or the community, that has helped stabilize their situation
- Demonstrate adaptive coping strategies for dealing with the stress of the caregiver role
- Demonstrate effective problem-solving techniques they can use to deal with issues of caring for their family member
- Identify resources they can use when new situations arise that appear to need new coping strategies
- State that they now maintain social relationships with other individuals and families, as evidenced by involvement in community groups, with extended family members, and with friends

## Short-Term Goals

Caregivers will:
- State they understand and have written information on their family member's/friend's type of dementia (e.g., AD, multi-infarct dementia) and appropriate caregiving techniques by (date)
- Know and discuss the available resources in their community, national resources, and sites on the Internet that will provide information, support, and how to arrange respite by (date)
- Identify at least three steps they can take to relieve some of the family stress and enhance well-being to all members of the family unit by (date)
- Learn at least three new coping strategies and coping mechanisms to diffuse the tension and strain on caregiver and family by (date)
- Care for their own needs through diet, exercise, and plenty of rest and give five examples of healthy changes by (date)
- Be aware of where to go to get legal and financial planning advice early in the disease process by (date)
- Acknowledge realistic goals of treatment for their family member by (date)

## *Interventions and Rationales*

| Intervention | Rationale |
|---|---|
| 1. Assess what caregivers and family know about patient's dementia, and educate regarding the patient's specific illness. | 1. Points out areas that will benefit from planning and preparation (e.g., legal issues, financial issues, additional caregiving techniques, and knowing what they can and what they cannot change or accomplish). |
| 2. Provide a list of community agencies and support groups where family and primary caregiver can receive support, further education, and information regarding how to arrange respite. | 2. Helps diminish a sense of hopelessness and increase a sense of empowerment. |
| 3. Help the caregiver and family identify areas that need intervention and those areas that are presently stable. | 3. Identifies specific areas needing assistance and those that will need assistance in the future. |
| 4. Teach the caregiver and family specific interventions to use in response to behavioral or social problems brought on by the dementia. | 4. Caregivers need to learn many new ways to intervene in situations that are common with demented patients (agitation, catastrophic reactions, sleep/wake disturbances, wandering). |
| 5. Safety is a major concern. Box 12-5 identifies some steps caregivers and family can take to make the home a safer place. | 5. These steps, prepared by the Alzheimer's Association, can help make the home safe for the person with dementia. |

## Box 12-5 **Home Safety**

### Make Potentially Dangerous Places Less Accessible
- Install door locks out of sight.
- Use special safety devices, such as child-proof locks and door knobs, to limit access to places where knives, appliances, equipment, and cleaning fluids are stored.

### Accommodate Visual Changes
- Add extra lighting in entries, outside landings, areas between rooms, stairways, and bathrooms, because changes in level of light can be disorienting.
- Place contrasting colored rugs in front of doors or steps to help the individual anticipate staircases and room entrances.

### Avoid Injury During Daily Activities
- Monitor the temperature of water faucets and food, because the person might have a decreased sensitivity to temperature.
- Install walk-in showers, grab bars, and decals on slippery surfaces in the bathroom to prevent falls.
- Supervise the person in taking prescription and over-the-counter medications.

### Beware of Hazardous Objects and Substances
- Limit the use of certain appliances and equipment such as mixers, grills, knives, and lawnmowers.
- Supervise smoking and alcohol consumption.
- Remove objects such as coffee tables, floor lamps, and the like to create safe wandering areas and reduce the possibility of injury.

### Be Prepared for Emergencies
- Keep a list of emergency phone numbers and addresses for the local police departments, hospitals, and poison control help lines.
- Check fire extinguishers and smoke alarms, and conduct fire drills regularly.
- If the person with Alzheimer's Disease tends to wander, enroll him or her in the Safe Return program.

| Intervention | Rationale |
|---|---|
| 6. Encourage spending nonstressful time with the patient at patient's present level of functioning (e.g., watching a favorite movie together, reading with patient a simple book with pictures, performing simple tasks like setting the table, washing dishes, washing the car). | 6. Encourages the patient to participate as much as possible in family life. Helps diminish feelings of isolation and alienation temporarily. |
| 7. Encourage caregiver/family members to follow family traditions (church activities, holidays, and vacations). | 7. Helps family maintain their family rituals and helps patient's sense of belonging. |
| 8. Encourage caregivers/family members to use respite care during regular intervals (e.g., vacations). | 8. Regular periods of respite can help caregivers/family prevent burnout, can allow caregivers to continue participating in their life, and can help minimize feelings of resentment. |
| 9. Identify financial burdens placed on caregiver/family. Refer to community, national associations, or other resources that might help. | 9. Any kind of long-term illness within a family can place devastating financial burdens on all members. |

# MEDICAL TREATMENTS

## Psychopharmacology for Dementia

**Alzheimer's disease (AD)** is the most common dementia, accounting for 70% of all dementias, and is the fourth most prevalent cause of death in the adult population.

Three cholinesterase inhibitors approved by the FDA can help in Alzheimer's dementia during the early phases of AD (mild to moderate). They are **galantamine (Razadyne)**, **rivastigmine (Exelon)**, and **donepezil (Aricept)** and demonstrate positive effects on cognition and activites of daily living (Rabins, 2006).

**Memantine (Namenda)** is the first drug to demonstrate significant effectiveness in patients with moderate to severe AD. Memantine works differently than the cholinesterase inhibitors, being an NMDA (N-methyl-D-aspartate) receptor antagonist. Besides being useful in cases of moderate to severe AD, it may also slow down functional decline and may even help improve function in some people.

## Other Agents Used for Targeting Specific Symptoms in Dementia

### Agitation, Aggression, and Delusions

Current research strongly advises *not* using antipsychotics in cases of agitation, anxiety, aggression, and delusional behaviors but non-drug treatments instead. The modest benefits that might be gained through the use of medications are cancelled out by the side effects (worsening of cognitive impairment, oversedation, falls, etc.). Even the atypical antipsychotics, risperidone (Risperdal) and olanzapine (Zyprexa), which may have modest benefits, may increase the rate of mortality from cardiovascular or infectious causes (Lehne, 2007). Instead, the APA (2008) advocates structural education programs for staff to help them manage disruptive behaviors and cognitive techniques to reduce the need for medications or restraints. In any event, the use of antipsychotics should be used sparingly and with great caution.

### Anxiety

Buspirone is not a sedative and does not produce many unwanted side effects, such as psychomotor impairment, drowsiness, or cognitive impairment. For this reason, many prefer this drug to the benzodiazepines. Beta-blockers (e.g., propranolol) may be useful in patients with dementia.

## Depression

The selective serotonin reuptake inhibitor (SSRI) anti-depressants are effective and are best tolerated by patients with dementia. The tricyclic antidepressants (TCAs) are not recommended because of the high anticholinergic side effects, orthostasis (leading to falls or fractures), and cardiac conduction delays.

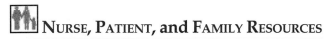 # NURSE, PATIENT, and FAMILY RESOURCES

## ASSOCIATIONS

**Alzheimer's Disease and Related Disorders Association**
225 North Michigan Avenue, Suite 1700
Chicago, IL 60601-7633
(312) 335-8700; (800) 272-3900
For caregivers of Alzheimer's patients

**Alzheimer's Disease Education and Referral Center Hotline**
(800) 438-4380
Information, referrals, and publications regarding clinical trials

## INTERNET SITES

**Alzheimer's Association**
www.alz.org

**Alzheimer Society of Canada**
www.alzheimer.ca

# PART III

# PSYCHIATRIC EMERGENCIES AND FORENSIC ISSUES

# CHAPTER 13

# Crisis Intervention and Rehabilitation

## OVERVIEW

A **crisis** is an acute, time-limited phenomenon experienced as an overwhelming emotional reaction to a:
- Stressful situational event
- Developmental event
- Societal event
- Cultural event or perception of that event

A crisis is not a pathological state, and being in crisis is not pathological. It is a struggle for equilibrium and adjustment when problems are perceived as insolvable.

Nurses intervene through a variety of crisis-intervention modalities, such as disaster nursing, mobile crisis units, group work, health education and crisis prevention, victim outreach programs, and telephone hotlines.

It is important to keep in mind that in crisis work, particularly, the patient might be an individual, a group, or a community:
- **Individual patient** (e.g., physical abuse)
- **Group** (e.g., students after a classmate's suicide or a school shooting)
- **Community** (e.g., disaster nursing—tornado, flood, airplane crash, terror attack)

It is difficult to predict what one person will perceive as a disastrous event constituting a crisis. A pregnancy, a breakup of a relationship, failing a test, or being given an adverse medical diagnosis can be catastrophic for one person but not to another. Some crises are more universal, such as the death of a child or spouse; these events are experienced as crises to almost everyone.

Crisis by definition is self-limiting and is resolved within 4 to 6 weeks. The goal of crisis intervention is to maintain the precrisis level of functioning. However, a person can emerge from the crisis at a higher level of functioning, at the same level, or at a lower level of functioning. Crisis intervention deals with the present (here-and-now) only, and nurses take a much more active and directive role with their patients in crisis.

## Types of Crises

There are basically three types of crises: maturational, situational, and adventitious.

### Maturational

Erikson identified eight stages of growth and development that must be completed to reach maturity. Each stage identifies a specific task that must be successfully mastered to progress through the growth process. When a person arrives at a new stage, former coping styles might no longer be age appropriate, and new coping mechanisms have yet to be developed. During this period of transition, psychological disequilibrium might occur. This temporary disequilibrium might affect interpersonal relationships, body image, and social and work roles (Hoff, 1995).

### Situational

A situational crisis arises from an external rather than an internal source. Examples of internal situations that could precipitate a crisis include loss of job, the death of a loved one, witnessing a crime, abortion, a change of job, a change in financial status, "coming out" as to homosexual orientation, divorce, and school problems. These external situations are often referred to as *life events* or *crucial life problems*, because most people encounter some of these problems during the course of their lives.

## *Adventitious*

An adventitious crisis is a crisis of disaster and not part of everyday life; it is unplanned and accidental. Adventitious crises can be divided into three subcategories:
1. Natural disaster (floods, earthquakes, fires, tornadoes)
2. National disasters (wars, riots, airplane crashes, terror attacks)
3. Crimes of violence (assault or murder in the workplace, bombing in crowded places, spousal or child abuse, sexual assault)

## Phases of Crisis

1. A problem arises that contributes to increased anxiety levels. The anxiety stimulates the use of usual problem-solving techniques.
2. If the usual problem-solving techniques do not work, anxiety continues to rise, and trial-and-error attempts at restoring balance are tried.
3. If trial-and-error attempts fail, anxiety escalates to severe or panic levels, and the person adopts automatic relief behaviors.
4. If these measures do not reduce anxiety, anxiety can overwhelm the person and lead to serious personality disorganization, which signals the person is in crisis.

## Levels of Crisis Intervention

There are three levels of crisis intervention: (1) preventive, (2) crisis intervention, and (3) rehabilitation. Psychotherapeutic nursing interventions are directed toward these three levels of care.

## *Preventive (Primary Care)*

Primary preventions are interventions that promote mental health and reduce the incidence of mental illness in an individual, group, or community. Interventions are aimed at altering causative factors before they can do harm—for example, anticipating and preparing people for stressful events by offering parenting classes, premarital counseling, preoperative teaching, respite care, or childbirth classes.

Environmental manipulation can also help allay a crisis by providing support or removing the patient from the stressor. Examples include finding shelter for an abused woman and her children, offering sick leave to an individual, or obtaining shelter for a homeless individual.

### Crisis Intervention (Secondary Care)

Intervention during an acute crisis aims to prevent prolonged anxiety from diminishing personal effectiveness and personality organization.

### Rehabilitation (Tertiary Care)

Rehabilitation provides support for those who have experienced and are now recovered from a disabling mental state and are, as a result, psychologically disabled. There are notably different aspects of response between a mentally healthy person and a severely and persistently mentally ill person in crisis. The mentally healthy person can make good use of crisis intervention (secondary care). The severely mentally ill or psychologically disabled person, in contrast, will fare much better with rehabilitation (tertiary care). Table 13-1 gives the reader an idea of some of the basic differences between a person with adequate coping skills and a person with persistent and severe mental illness (SMI).

## ASSESSMENT

### Assessing History

A positive history for potential crises might include:
- Overwhelming life event (situational, maturational, or adventitious)
- History of violent behavior
- History of suicidal behavior
- History of a psychiatric disorder (e.g., depression, personality disorder, bipolar disorder, schizophrenia, anxiety disorder)
- History of or concurrent serious medical condition (cancer, ongoing cardiac problems, uncontrolled diabetes, lupus, multiple sclerosis)
- Religious or cultural beliefs that can affect the way the person experiences the crisis event

Table 13-1 **The Mentally Healthy Versus the Severely Mentally Ill Person in Crisis**

| Mentally Healthy Person | Long-Term Mentally Ill Person |
|---|---|
| 1. Has realistic perception of potential crisis event. | 1. Because of severe biologically based mental illness or psychologically disabling illness, potential crisis event is usually distorted by minimizing or maximizing the event. |
| 2. Has healthy sense of self, place, and purpose in life. Good problem-solving abilities. | 2. Inadequate sense of self and purpose or abilities. Inadequate problem-solving abilities. Nurse becomes more active in assisting a person with severe mental illness in crisis. |
| 3. Usually has adequate situational supports. | 3. Person often has no family or friends and might be living an isolated existence or may even be homeless. |
| 4. Usually has adequate coping skills. Has a number of techniques that can be used to lower anxiety and adapt to the situation. | 4. Because coping ability for the severely and persistently mentally ill is poor, coping mechanisms are usually inadequate or poorly utilized. |

## Presenting Signs and Symptoms

People in crisis present with a variety of behaviors. Examples are:

- Confusion; disorganized thinking
- Immobilization; social withdrawal
- Violence against others; suicidal thoughts or attempts
- Running about aimlessly; agitated, increased psychomotor activity
- Crying; sadness
- Flashbacks; intrusive thoughts; nightmares
- Forgetfulness; poor concentration

## Sample Questions

*Nurses use a variety of therapeutic techniques to obtain the answers to the following questions. Use your discretion and decide which questions are appropriate to complete your assessment.*

The nurse assesses three main areas during a crisis: (1) the meaning of the precipitating event, (2) support system, and (3) coping skills.

## Determine the Meaning of the Precipitating Event

1. "What happened in your life before you started to feel this way?"
2. If this is an ongoing problem, ask the person, "What is different about (the problem) today than it was yesterday? Be specific."
3. "What does this event/problem mean to you?"
4. "How does this event/problem affect your life?"
5. "How do you see this event/problem affecting your future?"

## Evaluate the Patient's Support System

1. "Who do you talk to when you feel overwhelmed?"
2. "Who can you trust?"
3. "Who is available to help you?"
4. "Are these people available now?"
5. "Where do you worship (talk to God)? Go to school? Are there community-based activities you are involved in?"

## Identify Personal Coping Skills

1. "What do you usually do when you feel stressed or overwhelmed?"
2. "What has helped you get through difficult times in the past?"
3. "When these things have not helped, why do you think your previous coping skills are not working now?"
4. "What have you done so far to cope with this situation?"
5. "Have you thought of killing yourself or someone else?"

### Assessment Tools

Many factors can influence how a person responds to a potential crisis situation. Some factors that can limit a person's ability to cope with stressful life events are:
  • The number of other stressful life events the person is currently coping with

- The presence of other unresolved losses the person is dealing with
- The presence of concurrent medical problems
- Experiencing excessive fatigue or pain

Assessing for stressful life events can be a very useful tool (see Appendix D-10 for the Life-Changing Events Questionnaire)

## Assessment Guidelines

### Crisis

1. Identify whether the patient's response to the crisis warrants psychiatric treatment or hospitalization to minimize decompensation (suicidal behavior, psychotic thinking, violent behavior).
2. Do the nurse and patient have a clear understanding of the *precipitating event*?
3. Assess patient's understanding of his or her present *situational supports*.
4. What *coping styles* does the patient usually use? What coping mechanisms might help the situation in the present?
5. Are there certain religious or cultural beliefs that need to be considered in assessing and intervening in this person's crisis?
6. Is this situation one in which the patient needs primary (education, environmental manipulation, or new coping skills), secondary (crisis intervention), or tertiary (rehabilitation) intervention?

# NURSING DIAGNOSES WITH INTERVENTIONS

## Discussion of Potential Nursing Diagnoses

During a crisis, a person might exhibit a variety of behaviors that indicate a number of human problems. When anxiety levels escalate to high-moderate, severe, or panic levels, the ability to problem solve is impaired, if present at all. Essentially, what happens in an acute crisis is that a person's usual coping skills are not effective in meeting the crisis situation. In a person with already compromised coping skills, this situation is compounded. **Ineffective Coping** is evidenced by inability to meet basic needs, use of inappropriate defense mechanisms, and/or alteration in social participation.

**Anxiety** (moderate, severe, panic) is always present, and lowering of anxiety so that patients can start problem solving on their own is key in crisis management.

**Compromised Family Coping** or **Disabled Family Coping** can be related to a situational or maturational event within the family, or two or more events going on simultaneously. Family members might have difficulty responding to each other in a helping manner. Communications become confused, and an inability to express feelings is evident.

## Overall Guidelines for Nursing Interventions

### Acute Crisis

1. Safety first: Assess for any suicidal or homicidal thoughts or plans.
2. Initial steps focus on increasing feelings of safety and decreasing anxiety.
3. Initially, the nurse can take an active approach (make phone calls, set up and mobilize social supports, etc.).
4. Plan with patient interventions acceptable to both nurse and patient.
5. Crisis intervention calls for creative directive approaches.
6. Plan follow-up on patient's progress.

### Crisis Stabilization and Rehabilitation

1. People with severe and long-term mental health problems are readily susceptible to crisis.
2. Adapting the crisis model to this group includes focusing on patient's strengths, modifying and setting realistic goals, and taking a more active role.

## After Crisis Stabilization

1. Assess and provide for patient's and family's psycho-educational needs.
2. Assess and provide for needed social skills training.
3. Assess and refer to a vocational rehabilitation program when appropriate.
4. Evaluate and refer to supportive group therapy.
5. Teach or refer patients to cognitive-behavioral therapy programs, where they can learn to manage their psychotic symptoms.

## Selected Nursing Diagnoses and Nursing Care Plans

The following sections thread **Ineffective Coping** through **Acute Crisis Intervention** and then to **Rehabilitation.**

## Acute Crisis Intervention

### INEFFECTIVE COPING

Inability to form a valid appraisal of the stressors, inadequate choices of practiced responses, and/or inability to use available resources

## Some Related Factors (Related To)

▲ Inadequate social support created by characteristics of relationships
▲ Inadequate level of perception of control
▲ Inadequate resources available
▲ High degree of threat (situational or maturational crises)
▲ Inadequate opportunity to prepare for stressors
▲ Disturbance in pattern of appraisal of threat
▲ Disturbance in pattern of tension release
● Mass disaster (bombing, tornado, flood, hostage situation)
● Act of terrorism/threat or actual attack
● Crime of violence (rape, witnessing robbery or murder, spouse/child abuse)

## Defining Characteristics (As Evidenced By)

▲ Inability to meet basic needs
▲ Destructive behavior toward self or others
▲ Inability to meet role expectations
▲ Use of forms of coping that impede adaptive behavior
▲ Substance use/abuse
▲ Change in usual communication patterns
▲ Difficulty organizing information
▲ Decreased use of social support
▲ Inadequate problem solving
▲ Verbalization of inability to cope or inability to ask for help

## Outcome Criteria

• Uses effective coping strategies
• Reports increase in psychological comfort
• Verbalizes sense of control
• Functions well at precrisis level or higher

## Long-Term Goals

Patient will:

• Return to precrisis level of functioning within 4 to 6 weeks
• Identify skills and information that can help prevent future crises
• State that he/she has learned more adaptive ways to cope with stress
• State that he/she has a stronger existing support system

## Short-Term Goals

• Patient's anxiety level will go from severe to moderate or moderate to mild by end of first encounter (a person in mild to moderate levels of anxiety can still problem solve)

---

▲ NANDA International accepted;  ● In addition to NANDA International

- Patient and nurse will clarify the problem in solvable terms by end of first session
- Patient and nurse will identify existing supports and identify other needed supports by end of first session
- Patient and nurse will set realistic goals to deal with problem situations by end of first session
- Patient and nurse will identify a clear step-by-step plan of action by end of first session, revised throughout
- Patient will remain safe throughout crisis situation

## *Interventions and Rationales*

| Intervention | Rationale |
|---|---|
| 1. Provide liaison to social agencies to take care of emergency needs. | 1. Physical needs such as shelter, food, protection from abuser need to be handled immediately. |
| 2. Make appointments for needed medical or other health care providers. Write out time of appointment and directions for patient. | 2. For example, child or elder might have acute physical problems that need emergency attention. |
| 3. Assess for patient's safety. Examples: Are there suicidal thoughts? Is there child or spouse abuse? Are there unsafe living conditions? | 3. Patient safety is first consideration. |
| 4. Identify patient's perception of the event. Reframe perception of the event if event is seen as overwhelming or hopeless and/or patient views self as helpless. | 4. Distorted perception raises anxiety. Help patient experience event as a problem that can be solved. |
| 5. Assess stressors and precipitating cause of the crisis. | 5. Identify areas for change and intervention. |
| 6. Identify patient's current skills, resources, and knowledge to deal with problems. | 6. Encourage patient to use strengths and usual coping skills. |

| Intervention | Rationale |
|---|---|
| 7. Identify other skills patient might need to develop (e.g., decision-making skills, problem-solving skills, communication skills, relaxation techniques). | 7. Additional skills can help minimize crisis situations in the future and help patients regain more control over their present situation. |
| 8. Assess patient's support systems. Rally existing supports *(with patient's permission)* if patient is overwhelmed at present. | 8. Patient might be immobilized initially. Nurses often need to take an active role during crisis intervention. |
| 9. Identify and arrange for extra supports if current support system is either not available or insufficient. | 9. Patient might have lost important supports (death, divorce, distance) or simply not have sufficient supports in place. |
| 10. Nurse often needs to take an active role in crisis intervention (e.g., make telephone calls; arrange temporary child care; arrange for shelters, emergency food, first aid, etc.). | 10. Patients in crisis are often temporarily immobilized by anxiety and unable to problem solve. Nurse organizes situation so that it is seen as solvable and controllable. |
| 11. Give only small amounts of information at a time. | 11. Only small pieces of information can be understood when a person's anxiety level is high. |
| 12. Encourage patient to stay in the "here and now" to deal with the immediate situation only. | 12. Crisis intervention deals with the immediate problem disrupting patient's present situation. |
| 13. Listen to patient's story. Refrain from interrupting. | 13. Telling the story can in itself be healing. |
| 14. Help patient set achievable goals. | 14. Working in small, achievable steps helps patient gain sense of control and mastery. |

| **Intervention** | **Rationale** |
|---|---|
| 15. Work with patient on devising a plan to meet goals. | 15. A realistic and specific plan helps decrease anxiety and promote hopefulness. |
| 16. Identify and contact other members of the health team who can work with patient to solve crisis event. | 16. Provides a broad base of support to intervene with problem, and enlarges patient's network for future problems. |
| 17. In some situations, **debriefing** is a valuable technique for use with a group of people. Examples of debriefing: with staff on a unit when a patient attempts suicide; in a disaster situation (e.g., plane crashes, bombings, natural disasters). | 17. Survivors, family members, and staff all need to discuss the impact of a disaster, and debriefing provides a structure in which to do so (Weeks, 1999). |

## *Rehabilitation*

People with severe mental disorders are also subject to crisis situations that can negatively affect their functioning and exacerbate their condition. The nursing diagnosis **Ineffective Coping** also applies for people with severe mental illness (SMI), but here the interventions are more geared toward regaining some kind of stabilization.

### INEFFECTIVE COPING

Inability to form a valid appraisal of the stressors, inadequate choices of practiced responses, and/or inability to use available resources

## *Some Related Factors (Related To)*

▲ Inadequate social supports
▲ Disturbance in pattern of tension release
▲ Disturbance in pattern of appraisal of threat

- Poor coping skills
- Inability to problem solve
- Inadequate level of personal resources

## Defining Characteristics (As Evidenced By)

▲ Inability to meet role expectations
▲ High illness rate
▲ Inability to meet basic needs
▲ Substance use/abuse
▲ Destructive behavior toward self and others
▲ Verbalization of inability to cope or inability to ask for help
- Lack of ability to function at precrisis level
- Altered thought processes or inappropriate mood states
- Prolonged confusion

## Outcome Criteria

Maintenance of optimal level of functioning in:
- Work
- Home
- Community

## Long-Term Goals

Patient will:
- Function in the community with minimal use of inpatient services
- Increase life skills and available supports to use during times of stress
- Maintain stable functioning between episodes of exacerbation

## Short-Term Goals

Patient will:
- Retain positive coping strategies during times of stress with aid of nurse/family/friends
- Work with nurse to find needed supports (e.g., residential, financial, employment/education, medical, social, recreational)

---

▲ NANDA International accepted; ● In addition to NANDA International

## *Interventions and Rationales*

| Intervention | Rationale |
|---|---|
| 1. Nurse works with patient and family to assess the variety of needs the patient has. | 1. Patient with psychiatric disabilities has a wide range of needs. |
| 2. Identify patient's highest level of functioning in terms of: <br> a. Living skills <br> b. Learning skills <br> c. Working skills <br> Table 13-2 lists skills that promote psychiatric rehabilitation. | 2. Identifies patient's potential so that arrangements can incorporate the patient's potential. |
| 3. Identify the social supports available to the family: <br> a. Education about the disease, treatment, prognosis, and medications <br> b. Community supports to help patient function optimally <br> c. Community supports that offer family support/groups/ongoing psychoeducation | 3. Family members need a variety of supports to prevent family deterioration. |
| 4. Identify specific community supports that can provide individuals to help patient and family with continuity of care, such as (Public Policy Committee, 1999): <br> a. Residential support services <br> b. Transportation support services <br> c. Intensive case management | 4. The National Alliance for the Mentally Ill (NAMI) (Public Policy Committee, 1999) contends that a comprehensive array of community support services must be available for individuals to help people function at optimal levels and slow down relapse rate. |

Table 13-2 **Living, Learning, and Working Skills for Psychiatrically Disabled Patients** *(Potential skilled activities needed to achieve goal of psychiatric rehabilitation)*

| Physical | Emotional | Intellectual |
|---|---|---|
| **Living Skills** | | |
| Personal hygiene | Human relations | Money management |
| Physical fitness resources | Self-control | Use of community resources |
| Use of public transportation | Selective reward | Goal setting |
| Cooking | Stigma reduction | Problem development |
| Shopping | Problem solving | |
| Cleaning | Conversational skills | |
| Participating in sports | | |
| Using recreational facilities | | |
| **Learning Skills** | | |
| Being quiet | Making speeches | Reading |
| Paying attention | Asking questions | Writing |
| Staying seated | Volunteering answers | Arithmetic |
| Observing | Following directions | Study skills |
| Being punctual | Asking for directions | Hobby activities |
| | Listing | Typing |
| **Working Skills** | | |
| Punctuality | Job interviewing | Job qualifying |
| Use of job tools | Job decision making | Job seeking |
| Job strength | Human relations | Specific job tasks |
| Job transportation | Self-control | |
| Specific job tasks | Job keeping | |
| | Specific job tasks | |

Anthony, W.A. (1980). *Principles of psychiatric rehabilitation.* Baltimore, MD: University Park Press.

| **Intervention** | **Rationale** |
|---|---|
| d. Psychosocial rehabilitation | |
| e. Peer support | |
| f. Consumer-run services | |
| g. Around-the-clock crisis services | |
| h. Outpatient services with mobile capabilities | |
| 5. Provide *social skills training*, especially if patient is living with family. | 5. Some studies have shown that social skills training lowers relapse over time, especially for those living with families (Public Policy Committee, 1999). |
| 6. Work with family and patient to identify patient's prodromal (early) signs of impending relapse. | 6. Patient and family can secure medical help before exacerbation of illness occurs. |
| 7. Work with patient and family to identify an appropriate vocational rehabilitation service for patient. Box 13-1 describes types of vocational rehabilitation services available. | 7. Employment makes a significant contribution to relapse prevention, improved clinical outcomes, and improved self-image. |
| 8. Teach patient and family about psychoactive medications: | 8. Medication teaching can do a lot to reduce relapse rate and prolong time between relapses. |
| a. Side effects | |
| b. Toxic effects | |
| c. What medication can do | |
| d. What medication cannot do | |
| e. Who/where to call with questions, or in emergencies | |

438 PART III Psychiatric Emergencies and Forensic Issues

---

### Box 13-1 **Some Vocational Rehabilitation Models**

**Supported Employment (SE) Programs**
This model has proven to be most successful in assisting persons with the most serious disabilities to attain and maintain an attachment to the work force. It is individualized, provides on-site, one-on-one supports and job-coaching services, and occurs in competitive "real work" settings; job coach services are gradually reduced and removed.

**Transitional Employment (TE) Programs**
This model offers a temporary work experience to individuals, with the same supports and services as SE. TE positions are contracted to a service program that fills openings and staffs positions to meet contractual obligations. No individual participants receive permanent TE positions; they must move on to competitive employment within an agreed-upon length of time. Staff often cover contract positions, working on the job for a day in cases of illness or with changes in participants' schedules.

**Clubhouses**
Programs are "member directed," with *members* defined as individuals with serious mental illness. Clubhouse services and supports are provided to members according to the structure of the "work-ordered day." Members have individual daily responsibilities and schedules to fulfill as preparation for entry or reentry into the world of work. Membership in a clubhouse is lifelong, and members provide each other ongoing support.

**Job Clubs**
There are two main types: in-house clubs and postprogram graduate clubs. Members discuss issues, uncertainties, and problems they face while seeking employment or maintaining employment gains. In-house clubs can provide practical guidelines in résumé writing, guidelines for work exploration, opportunities to practice interviewing skills, and in some cases vocational assessment and interest identification. Postprogram graduate clubs provide essential off-site support services, such as working with new coworkers, adjusting to job requirements, handling issues of stigma and disclosure, and feelings of isolation.

---

Box 13-1   **Some Vocational Rehabilitation Models—cont'd**

**Peer and Natural Supports**
These circles of support are central to the continued success of individuals with serious psychiatric conditions who are attaining and maintaining employment. Circles expand connections beyond the usual family and friends to include wider community links to religious organizations, recreational/activity groups, public libraries, volunteer activities, and peer support activities (such as job clubs, support groups that meet regularly, one-on-one relationships, "warm lines" for crisis intervention and supports, and Internet chat rooms).

---

Donegan, K.R., & Palmer-Erbs, V.K. (1998). Promoting the importance of work for persons with psychiatric disabilities. *Journal of Psychosocial Nursing, 36,* 13–23.

## NURSE, PATIENT, and FAMILY RESOURCES

## ASSOCIATIONS

**Emotions Anonymous**
PO Box 4245
St. Paul, MN 55104-0245
(612) 647-9712
12-Step program of recovery from emotional difficulties

**Workaholics Anonymous**
PO Box 289
Menlo Park, CA 94026-0289
(510) 273-9253
12-Step program of recovery from compulsive overworking

**Red Cross Disaster Mental Health Services (DMHS)**
Contact local Red Cross for information

# INTERNET SITES

**Alliance for Psychosocial Nursing**
www.psychnurse.org

**NAMI (National Alliance for the Mentally Ill)**
www.nami.org

**Mental Help Net**
www.mentalhelp.net

# CHAPTER 14

# Family Violence

## OVERVIEW

One of the most disturbing aspects of family violence or victimization is the horrifying legacy of violence. Physical and psychological trauma causes long-lasting and devastating damage to people's lives, their children's lives, and lives of generations to come. Violence has moved from the home into schools, the workplace, neighborhoods, onto the road, and into air travel; it touches every corner of community life. This chapter deals with child, partner, and elder abuse.

### Child, Partner, and Elder Abuse

Victims of abuse are often debilitated when their ability to cope is overwhelmed. Zerbe (1999) states that during a course of a lifetime, few escape traumatic events, but the victims are often left to deal with the devastating consequences by themselves.

The nurse is often the first point of contact for people experiencing family violence and is in the ideal position to contribute to prevention, detection, and effective intervention. All forms of interpersonal abuse can be devastating. Abuse can take the form of emotional, physical, and/or sexual abuse, as well as neglect. Emotional abuse kills the spirit and the ability to succeed later in life, to feel deeply, or to make emotional contact with others. Physical abuse includes emotional abuse in addition to the potential for long-term physical deformity, internal damage, and acute painful tissue damage, bone damage, and in some cases death. The consequences of being sexually abused as a child are devastating and often never ending. Survivors of sexual abuse experience low self-esteem, self-hatred, affective instability, poor control of aggressive impulses, and disturbed interpersonal relationships compounded by an inability to trust and difficulty in protecting themselves. Sexual abuse occurs all too often in conjunction with partner abuse and elder abuse.

## ASSESSMENT

Sensitivity is required on the part of the nurse who suspects family violence. Interview guidelines are suggested in Box 14-1. A person who feels judged or accused of wrongdoing is most likely to become defensive, and any attempts at changing coping strategies in the family will be thwarted. It is better for the nurse to ask about ways of solving disagreements or methods of disciplining children,

---

### Box 14-1 **Interview Guidelines**

**Do's**
- Conduct the interview in private.
- Be direct, honest, and professional.
- Use language the patient understands.
- Ask patient to clarify words not understood.
- Be understanding.
- Be attentive.
- Inform the patient if you must make a referral to child/adult protective services, and explain the process.
- Assess safety and help reduce danger (at discharge).

**Don'ts**
- Do *not* try to "prove" abuse by accusations or demands.
- Do *not* display horror, anger, shock, or disapproval of the perpetrator or situation.
- Do *not* place blame or make judgments.
- Do *not* allow the patient to feel "at fault" or "in trouble."
- Do *not* probe or press for responses or answers the patient is not willing to give.
- Do *not* conduct the interview with a group of interviewers.
- Do *not* force a child to remove clothing.

rather than use the word *abuse* or *violence*, which appear judgmental and therefore are threatening to the family.

1. **Child:** Is there a history of unexplained "accidents" and physical injuries?
2. **Child:** Does the child appear well nourished, appropriately dressed, clean, and appropriately groomed?
3. **Adult woman:** Does she have a history of abuse as a child?
4. **Adult man:** Does he have a history of abuse as a child?
5. **Elder:** Is there a history of unexplained "accidents" or physical injuries?
6. **Elder:** Does the elder have a history of being abused as a child or abusing his or her children?

**ALL:**

7. Does there seem to be a history of drug or alcohol abuse within the family system?
8. Does the patient reexperience the abuse through flashbacks, dreams or nightmares, or intrusive thoughts?
9. Does the patient or other family member state that he or she has had suicidal or homicidal thoughts in the past?

## Presenting Signs and Symptoms

- Feelings of helplessness or powerlessness
- Repeated emergency room or hospital visits
- Vague complaints, including insomnia, abdominal pain, hyperventilation, headache, or menstrual problems
- Poorly explained bruises in various stages of healing
- Injuries (bruises, fractures, scrapes, lacerations) that do not seem to fit the description of the "accident"
- Frightened, withdrawn, depressed, and/or despondent appearance

## Assessment Questions

*The nurse uses a variety of therapeutic techniques to obtain the answers to the following questions. Use your discretion and decide which questions are appropriate to complete your assessment.*

## For All Patients

1. "Tell me about what happened to you."
2. "Who takes care of you?" (for children or dependent elderly)
3. "What happens when you do something wrong?" (for children)
4. "How do you and your partner/caregiver resolve disagreements?" (for women and elderly)
5. "What do you do for fun?"
6. "Who helps you with your children? Parent?"
7. "What time do you have for yourself?"

## For Partner

1. "Have you been hit, kicked, or otherwise hurt by someone in the past year? By whom?"
2. "Do you feel safe in your current relationship?"
3. "Is there a partner from a previous relationship who is making you feel unsafe now?"

## For Parents

1. "What arrangement do you make when you have to leave your child alone?"
2. "How do you discipline your child?"
3. "When your infant cries for a long time, how do you get him or her to stop?"
4. "What about your child's behavior bothers you the most?"

## Assessment Tools

The Abuse Assessment Screen developed by the Nursing Research Consortium on Violence and Abuse is a helpful tool for nurses in the clinical area and is found in Appendix D-11.

## Assessment Guidelines

### Family Abuse

During your assessment and counseling, maintain an interested and empathetic manner. Refrain from displaying horror, anger, shock, or disapproval of the perpetrator or the situation. Assess for:

1. Presenting signs and symptoms of victims of family violence
2. Potential problems in vulnerable families. For example, some indicators of vulnerable parents who might benefit from education and effective coping techniques are listed in Box 14-2.
3. Physical, sexual, and/or emotional abuse and neglect and economic maltreatment in the case of elders
4. Family coping patterns
5. Patient's support system
6. Drug or alcohol use
7. Suicidal or homicidal ideas
8. Posttrauma syndrome
9. If the patient is a child or an elder, identify the protection agency in your state that will have to be notified.

## NURSING DIAGNOSES WITH INTERVENTIONS

### Discussion of Potential Nursing Diagnoses

Violence brings with it pain, psychological and physical injury and anguish, the potential for disfigurement, and the potential for death. Therefore, **Risk for Injury** is a major concern for nurses and other members of the health care team.

Within all families where violence occurs, severe communication problems are evident. Coping skills are not

---

**Box 14-2 Assessing for Parents Who Are Vulnerable for Child Abuse**

1. New parents whose behavior toward the infant is rejecting, hostile, or indifferent
2. Teenage parents, most of whom are children themselves, require special help and guidance in handling the baby and discussing their expectations of the baby and their support systems
3. Retarded parents, for whom careful, explicit, and repeated instructions on caring for the child and recognizing the infant's needs are indicated
4. People who grew up in abusive homes. This is the biggest risk factor for perpetuation of family violence.

adequate to handle the emotional and environmental events that trigger the crisis situation. Inadequate coping skills among family members result in family members not getting their needs met, including the need for safety, security, and sense of self. Therefore, there exists **Ineffective Role Performance** within the family.

There are many other nursing diagnoses the nurse can use in caring for children and adults who are suffering from abuse at the hands of others. Some include **Anxiety, Fear, Disabled Family Coping, Posttrauma Syndrome, Powerlessness, Caregiver Role Strain, Disturbed Body Image, Chronic Low Self-Esteem, Impaired Parenting,** and **Acute/Chronic Pain.**

This chapter discusses **Risk for Injury** for the child, adult, and elder and **Ineffective Role Performance** geared toward the abuser.

## Overall Guidelines for Nursing Interventions

### Child, Adult, and Elder

1. Establish rapport before focusing on the details of the violent experience.
2. Reassure patient that he or she did nothing wrong.
3. Allow patient to tell his or her story without interruptions.
4. If patient is an **adult,** assure patient of confidentiality, and that any changes are his or hers to make.
5. If patient is a **child,** report abuse to appropriate authorities designated in your state.
6. If patient is an **elder,** check with state laws for reporting information.
7. Establish a safety plan in situations of **partner abuse.** (See Box 14-4 for a full, personalized plan.)
8. **Forensic issues: Follow hospital protocol. Keep your charting detailed, accurate, and up to date.**
   - Verbatim statements of who caused the injury and when it occurred
   - A body map to indicate size, color, shape, areas, and types of injuries with explanation
   - Physical evidence, when possible, of sexual abuse (vaginal/anal swabs, fingernail scrapings, etc.)
   - Ask for permission to take photos

9. Be aware of your own feelings of anger, frustration, and need to rescue.
10. Use peer supervision for validation, support, and guidance.

## Selected Nursing Diagnoses and Nursing Care Plans

### RISK FOR INJURY

At risk of injury as a result of environmental conditions interacting with the individual's adaptive and defensive resources

### *Some Related Factors (Related To)*

- Rage reaction (parents, partner, caregiver)
- Poor coping skills
- History of violence, neglect, or emotional deprivation as a child
- History of drug or alcohol abuse
- Poor impulse control
- Decline in mental status or has a mental illness
- Pathological family dynamics

### *Defining Characteristics (As Evidenced By)*

- Recurrent emergency department (ED) visits for injuries attributed to being "accident prone"
- Presenting problems reflecting signs of high anxiety and chronic stress:
    - Hyperventilation
    - Panic attacks
    - Gastrointestinal disturbances
    - Hypertension
    - Physical injuries
    - Depression
    - Insomnia
    - Violent nightmares

---

- In addition to NANDA International

- ○ Anxiety
- ○ Extreme fatigue
- ○ Eczema, loss of hair
- ○ Inability to concentrate as seen in poor school or work performance
- ○ Poor hygiene and disheveled appearance at school or work or in the home
- ○ Bruises of various ages and specific shapes (fingers, belts)

## Child-Abuse Patient

### Outcome Criteria

- Physical abuse, sexual abuse, and/or neglect has ceased
- Have plans to maintain safety of child

### Long-Term Goals

Child will:

- Know what plans are made for the child's protection and state them to nurse after decision is made by health care team
- Demonstrate renewed confidence and feelings of safety during follow-up visits

### Short-Term Goals

Child will:

- Be safe until adequate home and family assessment is made by (date)
- Be treated by nurse practitioner or physician and receive medical care for injuries within 1 hour
- Participate with therapists (nurse, social worker, counselor) for purpose of ongoing therapy and emotional support (art, play, group, or other) within 24 to 48 hours

### Interventions and Rationales

| Intervention | Rationale |
|---|---|
| 1. Adopt a nonthreatening, nonjudgmental relationship with parents. | 1. If parents feel judged or blamed or become defensive, they may take the child and either seek help elsewhere or seek no help at all. |

| Intervention | Rationale |
|---|---|
| 2. Understand that children do not want to betray their parents. | 2. Even in an intolerable situation, the parents are the only security that child knows. |
| 3. Provide (or have physician provide) a complete physical assessment of child. | 3. To provide competent care and to substantiate reporting to child welfare agency, if required. |
| 4. Use of dolls might help child tell his or her story of how "accident" happened. | 4. Child might not know how to articulate what happened or might be afraid of punishment. Dolls can be an easier way for child to act out what happened. |

**Forensic Issues**

| Intervention | Rationale |
|---|---|
| 1. Be aware of your agency's and state's policy on reporting child abuse. **Contact supervisor and/or social worker to implement appropriate reporting.** | 1. **Health care workers are mandated to report any cases of suspected or actual child abuse.** |
| 2. Ensure that proper procedures are followed and evidence is collected. | 2. If child is temporarily taken to a safe environment, appropriate evidence helps protect the child's future welfare. |
| 3. Keep accurate and detailed records of incident:<br>• Verbatim statements of who caused the injury and when it occurred<br>• A body map to indicate size, color, shape, areas, and types of injuries with explanation<br>• Physical evidence, when possible, of sexual abuse | 3. Accurate records could help ensure child's future safety and court presentation. |

| Intervention | Rationale |
|---|---|
| • Use of photos can be helpful. Check hospital policy (e.g. permissions, etc). | |
| 4. Forensic examination of the sexually assaulted child should be conducted according to specific protocols:<br>• Provided by law enforcement agencies<br>• Particular medical facilities | 4. Proper collection, handling, and storage of forensic specimens are crucial to court presentation. |

## Abused Partner

### Outcome Criteria

• Physical, emotional, sexual, financial abuse has ceased
• Have plans to maintain safety of partner and children

### Long-Term Goals

Partner will:
• Within 3 weeks, state that they believe they do not deserve to be beaten
• Within 3 weeks, state they have joined a support group or are receiving counseling (families, couples, individual)
• State that their living conditions are now safe from partner abuse or potential abuse; or
• Within 2 months, state that they have found safe housing for self and children

### Short-Term Goals

Partner will:
• Have timely access to medical care for fractures, wounds, burns, and other injuries
• After initial interview, name four community resources they can contact (hotlines, shelters, support groups, neighbor, crisis center, or spiritual advisors who do not support violence)
• After initial interview, describe a safety plan to be used in future violent situations
• State their right to live in a safe environment by (date)

*Interventions and Rationales*

| Intervention | Rationale |
|---|---|
| 1. Ensure that medical attention is provided to patient. Ask permission to take photos. | 1. If patient wants to file charges, photos boost victim's confidence to press charges now or in the future. |
| 2. Set up interview in private and ensure confidentiality. | 2. Patient might be terrified of retribution and further attacks from partner for telling someone about the abuse. |
| 3. Assess in a nonthreatening manner information concerning:<br>a. Sexual abuse<br>b. Chemical abuse<br>c. Thoughts of suicide or homicide | 3. These are all vital issues in determining appropriate interventions:<br>a. Increases risk for posttrauma syndrome<br>b. Many victims self-medicate<br>c. Might seem the only way out of an intolerable, catastrophic situation |
| 4. Encourage patient to talk about the battering incident without interruptions. | 4. When you ask patients to share their story, you understand that you are there to listen. |
| 5. Assess for level of violence in the home (Box 14-3). | 5. Each cycle of violence can become more intense. Danger for life of victim and children increases during escalation. |
| 6. Ask how patient is faring with the children in the home. | 6. In homes in which the mother is abused, children also tend to be abused. |
| 7. Assess whether patients have a safe place to go when violence is | 7. When abused patients are ready to go, they will need to go quickly. |

---

Box 14-3 **Partner Abuse—Assessing the Level of Violence in the Home**

1. Does the patient feel safe?
2. Has there been a recent increase in violence?
3. Has the patient been choked?
4. Is there a weapon in the house?
5. Has the abuser used/threatened to use a weapon?
6. Has the abuser threatened to harm the children?
7. Has the abuser threatened to kill the patient?

---

Jezierski, M. (1994). Abuse of women by male partners: Basic knowledge for emergency nurses. *Journal of Emergency Nursing, 20,* 361.

| Intervention | Rationale |
|---|---|
| escalating. If no, include a list of shelters or safehouses with other written information. | |

**Forensic Issues**

| | |
|---|---|
| 1. Identify whether patient is interested in pressing charges. If yes, give information on:<br>  a. Local attorneys who handle partner abuse cases<br>  b. Legal clinics<br>  c. Battered women's advocates | 1. Often patients are afraid of partner or partner retaliation, but when they are ready to seek legal advice, an appropriate list of lawyers well trained in this area is needed. |
| 2. **Know the requirement in your state about reporting suspected partner abuse.** | 2. Many states have or are developing laws and/or guidelines for protecting battered women. |
| 3. Discuss with patient an escape plan during escalation of anxiety, before actual violence | 3. Write out plan, and include shelter and referral numbers. This can prevent further |

| **Intervention** | **Rationale** |
|---|---|
| erupts. (Box 14-4 is an example of a personalized safety plan.) | abuse to children and patient. |
| 4. Throughout work with battered partners, emphasize:<br>  a. *"No one* deserves to be beaten."<br>  b. *"You cannot make anyone hurt you."*<br>  c. "It is *not* your fault." | 4. When self-esteem is eroded, people often buy into the myth that they deserved the beatings because they did something "wrong," and if they had not done X, then it would not have happened. |
| 5. Encourage patients to reach out to family and friends whom they might have been avoiding. | 5. Old friends and relatives can make helpful allies and validate that patient does not deserve to be beaten. |
| 6. Know the psychotherapists in your community who have experience working with battered partners. | 6. Psychotherapy with victims of trauma requires special skills on the part of even an experienced therapist. |
| 7. If patient is not ready to take action at this time, give him/her a list of community resources available:<br>  a. Hotlines<br>  b. Shelters<br>  c. Battered women's groups<br>  d. Battered women's advocates<br>  e. Social services<br>  f. Medical assistance/ Aid to Families with Dependent Children (AFDC) | 7. It can take time for patients to make decisions to change their life situation. People need appropriate information. |

See Box 14-4 for a personalized safety plan for when the abused partner is in the relationship and when the relationship is over.

---

### Box 14-4 **Personalized Safety Plan**

**Suggestions for Increasing Safety—In the Relationship**
- I will have important phone numbers available to my children and myself.
- I can tell _____ and _____ about the violence and ask them to call the police if they hear suspicious noises coming from my home.
- If I leave my home, I can go (list four places) _____, _____, _____, or _____.
- I can leave extra money, car keys, clothes, and copies of documents with _____.
- If I leave, I will bring _____ (see checklist next page).
- To ensure safety and independence, I can: keep change for phone calls with me at all times; open my own savings account; rehearse my escape route with a support person; and review my safety plan on _____ (date).

**Suggestions for Increasing Safety—When the Relationship is Over**
- I can change the locks; install steel/metal doors, a security system, smoke detectors, and an outside lighting system.
- I will inform _____ and _____ that my partner no longer lives with me and ask them to call the police if he or she is observed near my home or my children.
- I will tell people who take care of my children the names of those who have permission to pick them up. The people who have permission are: _____, _____, and _____.
- I can tell _____ at work about my situation and ask _____ to screen my calls.
- I can avoid stores, banks, and _____ that I used when living with my battering partner.
- I can obtain a protective order from _____. I can keep it on or near me at all times, as well as have a copy with _____.
- If I feel down and ready to return to a potentially abusive situation, I can call _____ for support or attend

| Box 14-4 **Personalized Safety Plan—cont'd** |
| --- |

workshops and support groups to gain support and
strengthen my relationships with other people.

**Important Phone Numbers**
Police _____
Hotline _____
Friends _____
Shelter _____

**Items To Take Checklist**
Identification
Birth certificates for me and my children
Social Security cards
School and medical records
Money, bankbooks, credit cards
Keys (house/car/office)
Driver's license and registration
Medications
Change of clothes
Welfare identification
Passports, Green Cards, work permits
Divorce papers
Lease/rental agreement, house deed
Mortgage payment book, current unpaid bills
Insurance papers
Address book
Pictures, jewelry, items of sentimental value
Children's favorite toys and/or blankets

## Abused Elder

### Outcome Criteria

- Physical, emotional, sexual abuse has ceased
- Neglect and/or financial exploitation has ceased
- Have plans to maintain safety of elderly patient

### Long-Term Goals

Elder will:
- State that caregiver has provided adequate food, clothing, housing, and medical care by (date)
- Be free of physical signs of abuse by (date)

## Short-Term Goals

Elder will:
- State that they feel safer and more comfortable by (date) using a scale of 1 to 5 (1 being the safest); *or*
- Ask to be removed from violent situation by (date)
- Name two people who can be called for help by (date)

## Interventions and Rationales

| Intervention | Rationale |
|---|---|
| 1. Assess severity of signs and symptoms of abuse and potential for further abuse on a weekly level. | 1. Determines need for further intervention. |
| 2. Assess environmental conditions as factors in abuse or neglect (Box 14-5). | 2. Identifies areas in need of intervention and degree of abuse or neglect. |
| 3. If abuse is suspected, talk with elder and caregiver separately. | 3. Helps attain a better understanding of what is happening and minimizes friction among parties involved. |
| 4. Discuss with elder factors leading to abuse. | 4. Identifies triggers to abusive behaviors and areas for teaching for abuser. |
| 5. Stress concern for physical safety. | 5. Validates situation is serious. |

### Forensic Issues

| | |
|---|---|
| 1. Know your state laws regarding elder abuse. Notify supervisor, physicians, and social services when a suspected abuse is reported. | 1. Keeps channels of communication open. Emphasizes the need for accurate and detailed records. |
| 2. If **undue influence** is suspected, an expert in geriatric or forensic psychiatry who has | 2. Determine whether the elder is making medical, legal, or financial decisions based on |

| Intervention | Rationale |
|---|---|
| experience should be called. | coercion and manipulations of others to gain control of the elder's finances, home, and/or decision making. |
| 3. Stress that no one has the right to abuse another person. | 3. Often people who have been abused begin to believe they "deserve" the abuse. |
| 4. Discuss with patient:<br>a. Hotlines<br>b. Crisis units<br>c. Emergency numbers | 4. Maximizes elder safety through use of support systems. |
| 5. Explore with elder ways to make changes. | 5. Directs assessment to positive areas. |
| 6. Assist elder in making decisions for future action. | 6. Helps lower feelings of helplessness and identifies realistic options to an abusive situation. |
| 7. Involve community supports to help monitor and support elder. | 7. Involve as many agencies as can take a legitimate role in maintaining elder safety. |

---

### Box 14-5 **Elder Abuse/Neglect—Home Assessment**

**Environmental Conditions**
- House in poor repair
- Inadequate heat, lighting, furniture, cooking utensils
- Presence of garbage or vermin
- Old food in kitchen
- Lack of assistive devices
- Locks on refrigerator
- Blocked stairways
- Elder lying in urine, feces, or food
- Unpleasant odors

**Medication**
- Medication not being taken as prescribed

## For The Perpetrator of Abuse

### INEFFECTIVE ROLE PERFORMANCE

Patterns of behavior and self-expression that do not match the environmental context, norms, and expectations

### Some Related Factors (Related To)

▲ Domestic violence
▲ Inadequate support system
▲ Family conflict
▲ Young age, developmental level
▲ Low socioeconomic status
▲ Substance abuse
▲ Mental illness
▲ Neurological defect
▲ Lack of resources
▲ Lack of knowledge about role skills

### Defining Characteristics (As Evidenced By)

▲ Inadequate external support for role enactment
▲ System conflict
▲ Change in usual patterns of responsibility
▲ Domestic violence
▲ Inadequate role competency and skills
▲ Role overload
▲ Inadequate coping
▲ Anxiety or depression

### Parents of Abused Children

### Outcome Criteria

• Uses alternative coping mechanisms for stress rather than abusive strategies
• Use of emotional, physical, sexual, and neglectful abusive behaviors has ceased

---

▲ NANDA International accepted; ● In addition to NANDA International

## *Long-Term Goals*

Parent will:
- State that group meetings with other parents who have battered are useful
- Demonstrate at least four new parenting skills they find effective
- Share in two planned pleasurable activities twice a day with child when child returns home
- Attend workshops/group classes for effective parenting on an ongoing basis
- Attend an anger management training (AMT) course within 2 weeks

## *Short-Term Goals*

Parent will:
- Be able to name and call three agencies that can help financially during the crisis within 24 hours
- Name two places they can contact to discuss feeling of rage and helplessness by end of first interview
- Be able to name three alternative actions to take when feelings of helplessness and rage start to surface within 1 week

## *Interventions and Rationales*

| Intervention | Rationale |
|---|---|
| **Abusive Parents** | |
| 1. Identify whether the child needs:<br>  a. Hospitalization for treatment and observation, *and/or*<br>  b. Referral to child protective services | 1. Immediate safety of the child is foremost. Temporary removal of the child in volatile situations gives the nurse/counselor time to assess the family situation and coping skills and to rally community resources to lower family stress. |
| 2. Discuss with parents any stresses the family unit is currently facing. Contact appropriate | 2. With the help of outside resources, family stress can be lowered, leading to |

| on | Rationale |
|---|---|
| agencies to help reduce stress: | improved ability to problem solve. |
| *Economic* | |
| a. Job opportunities | |
| b. Social services | |
| c. Family-service agencies | |
| *Social supports* | |
| a. Public health nurse | |
| b. Day care teacher | |
| c. Schoolteacher | |
| d. Social worker | |
| e. Respite worker | |
| f. AMT Encourage and provide family therapy. | |
| 3. Reinforce parents' strengths, and acknowledge the importance of continued medical care for the child. | 3. Gives parents credit and support for positive parenting skills. |
| 4. Work with parents to try out safe methods to effectively discipline the child. | 4. Gives parents alternatives and can help minimize feelings of frustration and helplessness. |
| 5. Strongly encourage parents to join a self-help group (e.g., Parents Anonymous, family counseling, group counseling). | 5. Learning new ways of dealing with stress takes time, and support from others acts as an important incentive to change. |
| 6. Provide written information on hotlines, community supports, and agencies. | 6. Have resources available for immediate use. |

## Perpetrator in Partner Abuse

### Outcome Criteria

- Physical, emotional, sexual, and/or financial abuse of partner has ceased
- Uses alternative coping mechanisms for stress, rather than abuse

### Long-Term Goals

Abuser will:
- State he/she must change in order to stay with family
- Join and attend a group for partners who batter
- Recognize inner states of anger
- Attend a structured *anger management treatment* (AMT) program
- Demonstrate at least four alternative ways to deal with anger and frustration
- Within 6 months, couple will state that violence has ceased altogether; abused partner will be in safe environment

### Short-Term Goals

Patient will:
- State they are interested in knowing about family treatment modalities
- State they no longer choose to live in a situation with violence
- Name three places they can call to receive counseling for self and family
- Obtain a restraining order
- Have information on safe houses, or name people they can stay with

### Interventions and Rationales

| Intervention | Rationale |
|---|---|
| **Perpetrator of Partner Abuse** | |
| 1. If abuser is motivated, make arrangements for | 1. Empirical results show a 6- to 8-week structural |

| Intervention | Rationale |
|---|---|
| abuser to participate in an AMT program. | program trains patients to deactivate angry emotional state (Suinn, 2005). |
| 2. Work with abuser to recognize signs of escalating anger. | 2. Often abuser is unaware of process leading up to rage reaction. |
| 3. Work with abuser to learn ways of channeling anger nonviolently. | 3. Violence is often a learned coping skill. Adaptive skills for dealing with anger must be learned. |
| 4. Encourages abuser to discuss thoughts and feelings with others who have similar problems. | 4. Minimizes isolation and encourages problem solving. |
| 5. Refer to self-help groups in the community (e.g., for abusive men, Batterers Anonymous). | 5. Self-help groups help patients look at own behaviors among those who have similar problems. |

### Perpetrator of Elder Abuse

*Outcome Criteria*

- Physical, emotional, and sexual abuse and neglect of elder have ceased
- Use of **undue influence** for monetary/financial control or all other control of elder has ceased
- Uses alternative coping strategies for stress rather than abuse
- Elder is living in a safe environment

*Long-Term Goals*

- The abused will state the abuse has stopped or state that he or she is now in a safe place (date)
- Family members will state that they will meet the nurse/counselor on a weekly basis for counseling starting by (date)

- Abuser will meet with other family members and discuss feelings on care of elderly by (date)
- Family members will meet together and discuss alternatives for care of elder by (date)
- Patient and family will meet together and discuss resources and supports they feel are important to them by (date)
- Abuser will demonstrate, instead of violence, two appropriate methods of dealing with frustration by (date)

## Short-Term Goals

- Family members will meet together with nurse/counselor and discuss alternative approaches toward their elderly family member within 1 week
- Family members will role-play two strategies for avoiding physical or emotional violence toward elder (relaxation, assertive behaviors, anger management techniques) by (date)
- Family members will demonstrate two safe alternative methods of dealing with their emotions in "hot" situations by (date)
- Family members will name two support services to whom they can turn for help within 2 days
- One other family member or support person will spend time with elder and relieve abuser of caregiving duties for stated periods of time within 1 week

## Interventions and Rationales

| Intervention | Rationale |
| --- | --- |
| **Elder Abuser** | |
| 1. Check your state for laws regarding elder abuse. | 1. Many states have adopted laws to help protect elders and support their needs for safety. |
| 2. Encourage abuser to verbalize feelings about elder and the abusive situation. | 2. The abused might feel overwhelmed, isolated, and unsupported. |

| **Intervention** | **Rationale** |
|---|---|
| 3. Encourage problem solving when identifying stressful areas. | 3. Assesses abuser's approach to problem-solving skills, and explores alternatives. |
| 4. Meet with entire family, and identify stressors and problem areas. | 4. Other family members might not be aware of the strain the abuser is under or the lack of safety to the abused family member. |
| 5. If there are no other family members, notify other community agencies that might help abuser and elder stabilize situation, for example: <br> a. Support group for elder <br> b. Support group for abuser <br> c. Meals on Wheels <br> d. Day care for seniors <br> e. Respite services <br> f. Visiting nurse service | 5. Minimizes family stress and isolation and increases safety. |
| 6. Initiate referrals for available support services. | 6. Rallies needed support for abusive situation. |
| 7. Encourage abuser's use of counseling. | 7. Increases coping skills and social supports. |
| 8. Suggest that family members meet together on a regular basis for problem solving and support. | 8. Encourages family to learn to solve problems together. |
| 9. Act as a facilitator in the beginning to assess and teach problem-solving skills and offer referral information. | 9. Families increase their communication skills, effectiveness in interactions, and self-esteem. |

# ![icon] NURSE, PATIENT, and FAMILY RESOURCES

## ASSOCIATIONS

**Family Violence and Sexual Assault Institute (FVSAI)**
6160 Cornerstone Court East
San Diego, CA 92121
(858) 623-2777
www.fvsai.org

**National Domestic Violence Hotline (NDV Hotline)**
3616 Far West Boulevard, Suite 101-297
Austin, TX 78731-3074
(800) 799-SAFE (hotline)

**Rape, Abuse, and Incest National Network (RAINN)**
(800) 656-HOPE
www.feminist.com/rainn.htm

**Batterers Anonymous**
8485 Tamarinal #D
Fontana, CA 92335
(909) 355-1100
For men who wish to control their anger and eliminate
their abusive behavior

**Sexual Abuse Survivors Anonymous (SASA)**
PO Box 241046
Detroit, MI 48224
(313) 882-6446
12-Step program for survivors of rape, incest, or sexual
abuse

**Survivors of Incest Anonymous (SIA)**
PO Box 190
Benson, MD 21018-9998
(410) 893-3322
12-Step program for survivors of incest

**Child Abuse Prevention—KidsPeace**
(800) 334-4KID
www.kidspeace.org

**Childhelp USA Hotline**
(800) 422-4453 (24 hours)

**Youth Crisis Hotline**
(800) HIT-HOME

**Runaway Hotline**
(800) 231-6946

# INTERNET SITES

**National Coalition Against Domestic Violence**
www.ncadv.org

**Prevent Child Abuse America Home Page**
www.childabuse.org

**Child Abuse Prevention Network**
www.child-abuse.com

**Victim Services Domestic Violence Shelter Tour**
www.dvsheltertour.org

**David Baldwin's Trauma Information Pages**
www.trauma-pages.com/
Site focuses on emotional trauma and traumatic stress

**MaleSurvivor**
www.malesurvivor.org/

**Men Can Stop Rape**
www.mencanstoprape.org
Helping men who rape

# CHAPTER 15

# Sexual Assault

## OVERVIEW

Rape is a violent crime, an act of violence, and sex is the weapon used by the perpetrator. **Rape is a nonconsensual vaginal, anal, or oral penetration, obtained by force or threat of bodily harm, or when a person is incapable of giving consent.** It is usually men who rape, and most of those raped are women. A male who is sexually assaulted is more likely to have physical trauma and to have been victimized by several assailants than is a female. Males experience the same devastating severe and long-lasting trauma as females. Long-term psychological effects of sexual assault might include the development of depression, dysfunction, and somatic complaints in many survivors. Incest victims might experience a negative self-image, self-destructive behavior, and substance abuse. All catastrophic events can result in a posttrauma syndrome. **Rape-trauma syndrome** is a variant of posttraumatic stress disorder (PTSD) and consists of two phases: (1) the acute phase, and (2) the long-term reorganization phase. Nurses might encounter patients right after the sexual assault or weeks, months, or even years after the sexual assault. In either case, the individual will benefit from compassionate and effective nursing interventions.

# ASSESSMENT

## Assessing History

A positive history includes:
1. History of a previous sexual assault
2. History of incest within the family
3. The individual suffers from any of the signs and symptoms of PTSD

## Presenting Signs and Symptoms

### Acute Phase of Rape-Trauma Syndrome (0 to 2 Weeks After the Rape)

Typical reactions to crisis reflecting cognitive, affective, and behavioral disruptions:
- Shock, numbness, and disbelief
- Might appear calm and self-contained
- Might appear hysterical, restless
- Might cry a lot; *or*
- Might smile or laugh a lot
- Complains of disorganization in his or her life
- Complains of somatic symptoms

### Long-Term Reorganization Phase (PSTD) (2 Weeks or More)

- Intrusive thoughts of the rape throughout day and night
- Flashbacks of the incident (reexperiencing the traumatic event)
- Dreams with violent content
- Insomnia
- Increased motor activity (moving, taking trips, changing phone numbers, staying with friends)
- Mood swings, crying spells, depression
- Fears and phobias can develop:
  - Fear of indoors (if rape occurred indoors)
  - Fear of outdoors (if rape occurred outdoors)
  - Fear of being alone
  - Fear of crowds
  - Fear of sexual encounters

Questioning should be done in a very nonthreatening manner, using open-ended types of questions (e.g.,

"It must have been very frightening to know you had no control over what was happening.").

## Assessment Guidelines

### *Sexual Assault*

1. Assess physical trauma—use a body map, and ask permission to take photos.
2. Assess psychological trauma—write down verbatim statements of patient.
3. Assess available support system. Often partners or family members do not understand about rape and might not be the best supports to rally at this time.
4. Assess level of anxiety. If patients are in severe to panic levels of anxiety, they will not be able to problem solve or process information.
5. Identify community supports (e.g., attorneys, support groups, therapists) who work in the area of sexual assault.
6. Encourage patients to tell their story. **Do not** press them to.

# NURSING DIAGNOSES WITH INTERVENTIONS

## Discussion of Potential Nursing Diagnoses

**Rape-Trauma Syndrome** is the nursing diagnosis that applies to the physical and psychological effects resulting from a sexual assault. The diagnosis includes the acute phase of disorganization of the survivor's lifestyle and the long-term phase reorganization.

**FORENSIC NOTE: Each emergency department (ED) or crisis center needs to have its own protocol for the forensic examination of the sexual assault survivor. Most EDs and crisis centers also have rape kits that facilitate collection of specimens such as blood, semen, hair, and fingernail scrapings.**

## Overall Guidelines for Nursing Interventions

### Survivor of Sexual Assault

1. Follow your institution's protocol for sexual assault.
2. Do not leave the person alone.
3. Maintain a nonjudgmental attitude.
4. Ensure confidentiality.
5. Encourage the person to talk; listen empathetically.
6. Emphasize that the person did the right thing to save his or her life.
7. **Forensic issues**
   - Physical trauma—size, color, distribution of trauma with a body map.
   - Ask permission to take photos.
   - Take verbatim statements as to patient's reaction to rape.
   - Document emotional status.
8. Explain everything you are going to do before you do it.
9. Ascertain forensic examination is done and specimens are obtained with patient's written permission.
10. Alert patient as to what he or she might experience during the long-term reorganization phase.
11. Arrange for support follow-up, for example:
    - Support groups
    - Group therapy
    - Individual therapy
    - Crisis counseling

## Selected Nursing Diagnoses and Nursing Care Plans

### RAPE-TRAUMA SYNDROME

Sustained maladaptive response to a forced, violent, sexual penetration against the victim's will and consent

### Related Factors (Related To)

▲ Sexual assault

## Defining Characteristics (As Evidenced By)

▲ Disorganization
▲ Change in relationships
▲ Physical trauma (e.g., bruising, tissue irritation)
▲ Suicide attempts
▲ Denial
▲ Guilt, humiliation, embarrassment
▲ Aggression, muscle tension
▲ Mood swings
▲ Nightmares and sleep disturbances
▲ Sexual dysfunction
▲ Feelings about revenge
▲ Phobias
▲ Loss of self-esteem
▲ Inability to make decisions
▲ Vulnerability, helplessness
▲ Substance abuse
▲ Depression, anxiety
▲ Shame, shock, fear
▲ Self-blame
▲ Dissociative disorders
▲ Hyperalertness

## Outcome Criteria

• Acknowledgment of right to disclose and discuss abusive situations
• Resolution of anger, guilt, hurt, fear, depression, low self-esteem
• Experiences hopefulness and confidence in going ahead with life plans

## Long-Term Goals

Survivor will:
• Discuss the need for follow-up crisis counseling and other supports by (date)
• State that the acuteness of the memory of the rape subsides with time and is less vivid and less frightening within 3 to 5 months

---

▲ NANDA International accepted

- Verbalization of details of abuse
- State that the physical symptoms (e.g., sleep disturbances, poor appetite, and physical trauma) have subsided within 3 to 5 months

## Short-Term Goals

Survivor will:
- Begin to express reactions and feelings about the assault before leaving the ED or crisis center
- Have a short-term plan for handling immediate situational needs before leaving the ED or crisis center
- List common physical, social, and emotional reactions that often follow a sexual assault before leaving the ED or crisis center
- Speak to a community-based rape victim advocate in the ED or crisis center
- State the results of the physical examination completed in the ED or crisis center
- Have access to information on obtaining competent legal council

## Interventions and Rationales

| Intervention | Rationale |
|---|---|
| 1. Have someone stay with the victim (friend, neighbor, or staff member) while he or she is waiting to be treated in the ED. | 1. People experiencing high levels of anxiety need someone with them until anxiety level is down to moderate. |
| 2. **Very important:** Approach victim in a nonjudgmental manner. | 2. Nurses' attitudes can have an important therapeutic impact. Displays of shock, horror, disgust, or disbelief are not appropriate. |
| 3. Confidentiality is crucial. | 3. The client's situation is not to be discussed with anyone other than medical personnel involved unless victim gives consent. |

| Intervention | Rationale |
|---|---|
| 4. Explain to victim the signs and symptoms many people experience during the long-term phase. Examples:<br>a. Nightmares<br>b. Phobias<br>c. Anxiety, depression<br>d. Insomnia<br>e. Somatic symptoms | 4. Many individuals think they are going crazy as time goes on and are not aware that this is a process that many people in their situation have experienced. |
| 5. Listen and let the victim talk. **Do not** press victim to talk. | 5. When people feel understood, they feel more in control of their situation. |
| 6. Stress that they did the right thing to save their life. | 6. Rape victims might feel guilt or shame. Reinforcing that they did what they had to do to stay alive can reduce guilt and maintain self-esteem. |
| 7. Do not use judgmental language. | 7. Use the words (Stern et al., 2004):<br>• *Reported* not *alleged*<br>• *Declined* not *refused*<br>• *Penetration* not *intercourse* |

### Forensic Examination and Issues

| | |
|---|---|
| 1. Assess the signs and symptoms of physical trauma. | 1. Most common injuries are to face, head, neck, extremities. |
| 2. Make a body map to identify size, color, and location of injuries. Ask permission to take photos. | 2. Accurate records and photos can be used as medicolegal evidence for the future. |
| 3. Carefully explain all procedures before doing them (e.g., "We would like to do a vaginal examination and do a swab. Have you had a vaginal examination before?" [rectal | 3. The victim is experiencing high levels of anxiety. Matter-of-factly explaining what you plan to do and why you are doing it can help reduce fear and anxiety. |

| **Intervention** | **Rationale** |
|---|---|
| examination in case of male who has been raped]). | |
| 4. Explain the forensic specimens you plan to collect; inform victim that they can be used for identification and prosecution of the rapist. Examples:<br>a. Combing pubic hairs<br>b. Skin from underneath nails<br>c. Semen samples<br>d. Blood | 4. Collecting body fluids and swabs is essential (DNA) for identifying the rapist. |
| 5. Encourage victim to consider treatment and evaluation for sexually transmitted diseases before leaving the ED. | 5. Many survivors are lost to follow-up after being seen in the ED or crisis center and will not otherwise get protection. |
| 6. Many clinics offer prophylaxis to pregnancy with norgestrel (Ovral). | 6. Approximately 3% to 5% of women who are raped become pregnant. |
| 7. All data must be carefully documented:<br>a. Verbatim statements<br>b. Detailed observations of physical trauma<br>c. Detailed observations of emotional status<br>d. Results from the physical examination<br>e. All lab tests should be noted | 7. Accurate and detailed documentation is crucial legal evidence. |
| 8. Arrange for follow-up support:<br>a. Rape counselor<br>b. Support group<br>c. Group therapy<br>d. Individual therapy<br>e. Crisis counseling | 8. Many individuals carry with them constant emotional trauma. Depression and suicidal ideation are frequent sequelae of rape. The sooner the intervention, the less complicated the recovery may be. |

# Nurse, Patient, and Family Resources

## ASSOCIATIONS

**Family Violence and Sexual Assault Institute (FVSAI)**
6160 Cornerstone Court East
San Diego, CA 92121
(858) 623-2777
www.fvsai.org

**Rape, Abuse, and Incest National Network (RAINN)**
(800) 656-HOPE
www.feminist.com/rainn.htm

**Sexual Abuse Survivors Anonymous (SASA)**
PO Box 241046
Detroit, MI 48224
(313) 882-6446
12-Step program for survivors of rape, incest, or sexual
    abuse

**Survivors of Incest Anonymous (SIA)**
PO Box 190
Benson, MD 21018-9998
(410) 893-3322
12-Step program for survivors of incest

**Child Abuse Prevention—Kids Peace**
(800) 334-4KID
www.kidspeace.org

**Childhelp USA Hotline**
(800) 422-4453 (24 hours)

**Youth Crisis Hotline**
(800) HIT-HOME

**Runaway Hotline**
(800) 231-6946

## INTERNET SITES

**Victim Services Domestic Violence Shelter Tour**
www.dvsheltertour.org

**David Baldwin's Trauma Information Pages**
www.trauma-pages.com
Site focuses on emotional trauma and traumatic stress

**MaleSurvivor**
www.malesurvivor.org

**Men Can Stop Rape**
www.mencanstoprape.org
Helping men who rape

# CHAPTER 16

# Suicide Behaviors

## OVERVIEW

**Suicide** or **completed suicide** is the act of intentionally ending one's own life and opting for nonexistence. Suicide is the 11th leading cause of death in the United States. Although suicide is a behavior that needs careful assessment in depression, alcoholism/substance abuse, schizophrenia, and personality disorders (borderline, paranoid, and anti-social), it is not necessarily synonymous with mental disorders.

Physical illness can play a role in suicide behavior (pain, recent surgery, chronic physical illness). Suicide seems to be most prevalent among patients with diseases that result in suffering and dependency, such as AIDS and cancer. Nurses might encounter suicidal individuals in outpatient settings, intensive care units, nursing homes, medical/surgical units, during home visits, or even among their own circle of family and friends. People who are taking medications that contribute to depression and psychotic symptoms could also be at risk.

Suicide seems to cluster in some families, so family history is pertinent. This could be the result of inherited markers for depression, learned problem-solving behavior within the family, inherited low cerebrospinal fluid (CSF) levels of 5-hydroxyindole-acetic acid (low CSF levels are associated with higher risk of attempted suicide), or some other genetic factor associated with suicide.

Suicidal people share other commonalties. They are often poor problem solvers, have troubled emotional lives (depression, anger, anxiety, guilt, and/or boredom), have a low threshold for emotional pain, are often impulsive, and might engage in extreme solutions sooner than individuals who are not suicide prone (Chiles & Strosahl, 1997). People who are isolated (have poor social supports) and people who are experiencing severe life stress at any age might also be at risk. Risk factors for age were compiled by the National Institute of Mental Health (1995) and remain a valid guide when assessing suicide risk.

- The strongest risk factors for *youth* are alcohol or other drug use disorders and aggressive or disruptive behaviors. Depression and social isolation are also risk factors. Suicide in youths is the second leading cause of death following accidents.
- The strongest risk factors for *adults* are depression, alcohol abuse, cocaine use, and separation or divorce.
- Most *elderly* people who commit suicide have visited their primary care physician in the month before suicide. Recognition and treatment of depression in the medical setting is a promising way to prevent suicide in the elderly. Other risk factors include social isolation, solitary living arrangements, widowhood, lack of financial resources, and poor health. The elderly commit suicide more than any other group in the United States.

## ASSESSMENT

### Assessing History

- Past history of suicide attempts or self-mutilation
- Family history of suicide attempts or completion
- History of a mood disorder, drug or alcohol abuse, or schizophrenia
- History of chronic pain, recent surgery, or chronic physical illness
- Patient has a history of personality disorder (borderline, paranoid, antisocial)
- Patient is bereaved or experiencing another significant loss (divorce, job, home)

### Presenting Signs and Symptoms

Presents with:
- Suicidal ideation—thoughts of harming self
- Suicidal threat—communicates desire to harm/kill self

- Suicide attempt, failed—attempted to kill self
- Deliberate self-harm syndrome—patients who mutilate their bodies
- A high degree of hopelessness, helplessness, and anhedonia, which are crucial factors in suicide
- Patient states they have a plan for how they will kill themselves

## Assessment Tools

There are a number of tools one can use to ascertain risk factors when assessing for potential suicidal behaviors. An acronym can facilitate the health care worker's recall when in the midst of crisis situations. One such acronym, older though still popular and valid, is the SAD PERSONS Scale (Patterson et al., 1983). (See Appendix D-12.)

## Assessment Guidelines

### Suicide

1. Assess risk factors, including history of suicide (family, patient, friends); degree of hopelessness, helplessness, and anhedonia; and lethality of plan.
2. Determine the appropriate level of suicide precautions for the patient (physician or nurse clinician), even in the emergency room. If patient is at a high risk, hospitalization might be necessary. For example, if individuals state they have a *plan* for how to kill themselves, it is important to ascertain concrete behavioral information to assess the measure of lethality. Some guidelines include:
   - Find out what plans have been contemplated.
   - Determine how far the person took suicidal actions or made plans to take action.
   - Determine how much of the person's time is spent on these plans and accompanying ruminations about suicide.
   - Determine how accessible and lethal the mode of action is.
3. A red flag is raised if the patient suddenly goes from sad/depressed to happy and seemingly peaceful. Often a decision to commit suicide "gives a way out of severe emotional pain."

4. If the patient is to be managed on an outpatient basis, then:
   - Assess social supports.
   - Assess friends' and family's knowledge of signs and symptoms of potential suicidal behavior (e.g., increasing withdrawal, preoccupation, silence, and remorse).
   - Identify community supports and groups the patient and family could use for support.

# NURSING DIAGNOSES WITH INTERVENTIONS

## Discussion of Potential Nursing Diagnoses

A sound assessment provides the framework for determining the level of protection the patient warrants at that time. Therefore, **Risk for Suicide** is the first area of concern.

Believing that one's situation or problem is intolerable, inescapable, and interminable leads to feelings of hopelessness. Therefore, **Hopelessness** is most often a crucial phenomenon requiring intervention.

A third area of intervention is to tackle the phenomenon of "tunnel vision" suicidal patients have during times of acute stress and pain. That is, problem-solving skills are poor, and suicidal people have difficulty performing flexible cognitive operations. Teaching the patient or reinforcing the patient's own effective problem-solving skills and helping him or her reframe life difficulties as events that can be controlled is a strategic part of the counseling process with suicidal patients. Therefore, **Ineffective Coping** can be viewed as the third point of intervention. Other potential nursing diagnoses include **Risk for Loneliness, Situational/Chronic Low Self-Esteem, Deficient Knowledge, Social Isolation, Disabled Family Coping,** and **Spiritual Distress.**

## Overall Guidelines for Nursing Interventions

### Suicide

#### Hospitalized: Put on Suicide Precautions

- Suicide precautions range from arm's-length constraint (one-on-one with staff member at arm's length at all times), to one-on-one contact with staff at all times but may attend activities off the unit maintaining one-on-one contact, to knowing the patient's whereabouts at all times on the unit and accompanied by staff while off the unit.

- If there is fear of imminent harm to self, restraints might be required.
- **Follow unit protocols and keep detailed records in patient chart.**

## Outside the Hospital:

- If a patient is to be managed outside the hospital, the family, significant other, or friends should be alerted to the risk and treatment plan and informed of signs of deepening depression, such as a return or worsening of hopelessness.
- When the patient is to be managed on an outpatient basis (Slaby, 1994), then:
  - ○ Social support should be rallied.
  - ○ Appropriate psychopharmacotherapy, psychotherapy, or sociotherapy should be initiated.
  - ○ Patients and their family and friends should be given the psychiatric clinician's telephone number as well as that of a backup clinician or emergency room where they can go if the clinician is unavailable.
  - ○ A return visit (as early as the next day, if decisions concerning hospitalization need to be reconsidered) should be scheduled.
  - ○ Friends and family should be alerted to signs such as increasing withdrawal, preoccupation, silence, remorse, and sudden change from sad to happy and "worry-free."
  - ○ Careful records should be kept in all instances, documenting specific reasons why a patient was or was not hospitalized.
- If the patient is to be managed on an outpatient basis, medication should be given in limited quantity (e.g., 1- to 3-day supply with no refill).

## If an Accepted Procedure at Your Facility/Clinic:

- Form a written no-suicide contract with the patient, such as "I will not kill myself for any reason, and if I should feel suicidal, I will (a) talk to a staff member, or (b) talk to my therapist."
- List support people and agencies to use as outpatient and crisis hotline numbers for patients/family/friends.

## RISK FOR SUICIDE

At risk for self-inflicted, life-threatening injury

### Some Related Factors (Related To)

▲ History of prior suicide attempt
▲ Family history of suicide
▲ Alcohol and substance use/abuse
▲ Abuse in childhood
▲ Fits demographics (elderly, young adult male, adolescent, widowed, Caucasian, Native American)
▲ Physical illness, chronic pain, terminal illness
▲ Grief, bereavement/loss of important relationship, job, home
▲ Legal or disciplinary problems
▲ Poor support system, loneliness
▲ Hopelessness/helplessness
▲ Psychiatric illness (e.g., depression, schizophrenia, bipolar)

### Defining Characteristics (As Evidenced By)

● Suicidal behavior (attempt, talk, ideation, plan, available means)
● Suicide plan (clear and specific, lethal method and available means)
● Suicidal cues
  ○ **Overt**—"No one will miss me"; "Nothing left to live for"; "I'd be better off dead"
  ○ **Covert**—Making out a will, giving valuables away, writing forlorn love notes, taking out large life insurance policy
● Statements of despair, hopelessness, helplessness, and nothing left to live for

### Outcome Criteria

• Refrains from attempting suicide
• Behavior manifestation of depression absent

---

▲ NANDA International accepted; ● In addition to NANDA International

- Satisfaction with quality of life
- Satisfaction with coping ability
- Verbalizes control of impulses

## Long-Term Goals

Patient will:
- State he/she wants to live by (date)
- Name two people he/she can call if thoughts of suicide recur before discharge
- Name at least one acceptable alternative to his/her situation by (date)
- Uphold a suicide contract
- Identify at least one realistic goal for the future by (date)

## Short-Term Goals

Patient will:
- Remain safe while in the hospital, with the aid of nursing intervention and support
- Make a no-suicide contract with the nurse covering the next 24 hours, then renegotiate the terms at that time (if in hospital and accepted at your institution)
- Stay with a friend or family if person still has potential for suicide (if in the community)
- Keep an appointment for the next day with a crisis counselor (if in the community)
- Join family in crisis family counseling
- Have links to self-help groups in the community

## Interventions and Rationales

| Intervention | Rationale |
|---|---|
| **IN THE HOSPITAL** | |
| 1. During the crisis period, health care workers will continue to emphasize the following four points:<br>a. The crisis is temporary.<br>b. Unbearable pain can be survived.<br>c. Help is available.<br>d. You are not alone. | 1. Because of "tunnel vision," patients do not have perspective on their lives. These statements give perspective to the patient and help offer hope for the future. |

| Intervention | Rationale |
|---|---|

**FORENSIC ISSUES**

2. **Follow unit protocol** for suicide regarding creating a safe environment (taking away potential weapons—belts, sharp objects, ties, etc.; see Box 16-1 about ensuring hospital safety.).

2. Provide safe environment during time patient is actively suicidal and impulsive; self-destructive acts are perceived as the only way out of an intolerable situation.

3. Keep accurate and thorough records of patient's behaviors (verbal and physical) and all nursing/physician actions.

3. These might become court documents. If patient checks and attention to patient's needs or requests are not documented, they do not exist in a court of law.

4. Put on either *suicide precaution* (one-on-one monitoring at one arm's length away) or *suicide observation* (15-minute visual check of mood, behavior, and verbatim statements), depending on level of suicide potential.

4. Protection and preservation of the patient's life at all costs during crisis is part of medical and nursing staff responsibility. **Follow hospital protocol.**

5. Keep accurate and timely records, document patient's activity, usually every 15 minutes (what patient is doing, with whom, and so on). **Follow unit protocols.**

5. Accurate documentation is vital. The chart is a legal document as to patient's "ongoing status," interventions taken, and by whom.

6. Construct a *no-suicide contract* between the suicidal patient and nurse. Use clear, simple language. When contract is up, it is renegotiated (if this is accepted

6. The no-suicide contract helps patients know what to do when they begin to feel overwhelmed by pain (e.g., "I will speak to my nurse/counselor/ support group/family

---

### Box 16-1 **Guidelines for a Safe Hospital Environment**

1. Use plastic utensils.
2. Do not allow patients to spend too much time alone in their rooms. Do not assign them to a private room.
3. Jump-proof and hang-proof the bathrooms by installing break-away shower rods and recessed shower nozzles.
4. Keep electrical cords to minimal length.
5. Install unbreakable glass in windows. Install tamper-proof screens or partitions too small to pass through. Keep all windows locked.
6. Lock all utility rooms, kitchens, adjacent stairwells, and offices. All nonclinical staff (e.g., housekeepers and maintenance workers) should receive instructions to keep doors locked.
7. Take all potentially harmful gifts (e.g., flowers in glass vases) from visitors before allowing them to see patients.
8. Go through patient's belongings with patient and remove all potentially harmful objects (e.g., belts, shoelaces, metal nail files, tweezers, matches, and razors).
9. Take care that patient does not hoard medical supplies (e.g., intravenous [IV] tubing) or medications.
10. Ensure that visitors do not leave potentially harmful objects in patient's room (e.g., matches and nail files).
11. Search patients for harmful objects (e.g., drugs, sharp objects, and cords) on return from pass.

---

Schultz, B.M. (1982). *Legal liability in psychotherapy.* San Francisco: Jossey-Bass Publishing.

| Intervention | Rationale |
|---|---|
| procedure at your institution). | member when I first begin to feel the wish to harm myself"). |
| 7. Encourage patient to talk about his/her feelings and problem solve alternatives. | 7. Talking about feelings and looking at alternatives can minimize suicidal acting out. |

| Intervention | Rationale |
|---|---|
| **IN THE COMMUNITY** | |
| 1. Arrange for patient to stay with family or friends. If no one is available and the person is highly suicidal, hospitalization must be considered. | 1. Relieve isolation and provide safety and comfort. |
| 2. Weapons and pills are removed by friends, relatives, or the nurse. | 2. To help ensure safety. |
| 3. Encourage patient to talk freely about feelings (anger, disappointments) and help plan alternative ways of handling anger and frustration. | 3. Gives patient alternative ways of dealing with overwhelming emotions and gaining a sense of control over their lives. |
| 4. Encourage patient to avoid decisions during the time of crisis until alternatives can be considered. | 4. During crisis situations, people are unable to think clearly or evaluate their options. |
| 5. Contact family members, arrange for individual and/or family crisis counseling. Activate links to self-help groups. | 5. Reestablishes social ties. Diminishes sense of isolation and provides contact from individuals who care about the suicidal person. |
| 6. If anxiety is extremely high, or patient has not slept in days, a tranquilizer might be prescribed. | 6. Relief of anxiety and restoration of sleep loss can help the patient think more clearly and might help restore some sense of well-being. |

**Only a 1- to 3-day supply of medication should be given. Family member or significant other should monitor pills for safety.**

## HOPELESSNESS

Subjective state in which an individual sees limited or no alternatives or personal choices available and is unable to mobilize energy on his/her own behalf

### *Some Related Factors (Related To)*

▲ Deteriorating physical condition
▲ Chronic pain
▲ Social isolation
● Lost belief in spiritual power
● Severe lossess (financial reversals, relationship, loss of job)
● Perceiving the future as bleak and wasted

### *Defining Characteristics (As Evidenced By)*

▲ Passivity, decreased verbalization
▲ Decreased affect
▲ Verbal cues (despondent content: "I can't," "Life is hopeless," "What's the use?", "There is no way out")
▲ Lack of involvement in care
● Decreased problem solving
● Loss of interest in life
● Impaired decision making

### *Outcome Criteria*

● Connectedness with others to share thoughts, feelings, and beliefs
● Expression of positive future orientation
● Expression of meaning in life
● Expresses will to live

▲ NANDA International accepted; ● In addition to NANDA International

## Long-Term Goals

Patient will:
- State three optimistic expectations for the future by (date)
- Demonstrate reframing skills when viewing aspects of life that appear all negative by (date)
- Demonstrate two new problem-solving skills that he/she finds effective in making life decisions by (date)
- Describe and plan for at least two future-orientated goals by (date)

## Short-Term Goals

Patient will:
- Identify two alternatives for one life problem area by (date)
- Identify three things that he/she is doing right by (date)
- Reframe two problem areas in life that encourage problem-solving alternative solutions
- Make two decisions related to own care by (date)
- Name one community resource (support group, counseling, social service, family counseling) he/she has attended at least twice

## Interventions and Rationales

| Intervention | Rationale |
|---|---|
| 1. Teach patient steps in the problem-solving process. | 1. Stress that it is not so much *people* who are ineffective, but rather strategies they are using that are not effective. |
| 2. Encourage patient to look into their negative thinking, and reframe negative thinking into neutral objective thinking. | 2. Cognitive reframing helps a person look at situations in ways that allow for alternative approaches. |
| 3. Point out unrealistic and perfectionistic thinking. | 3. Constructive interpretations of events and behavior open up more realistic and satisfying options for the future. |

| **Intervention** | **Rationale** |
|---|---|
| 4. Work with patient to identify strengths. | 4. When people are feeling overwhelmed, they no longer view their lives or behavior objectively. |
| 5. Spend time discussing patient's dreams and wishes for the future. Identify short-term goals they can set for the future. | 5. Renewing realistic dreams and hopes can give promise to the future and meaning to life. |
| 6. Identify things that have given meaning and joy to life in the past. Discuss how these things can be reincorporated into their present lifestyle (e.g., religious or spiritual beliefs, group activities, creative endeavors). | 6. Reawakens in patient abilities and experiences that tapped areas of strength and creativity. Creative activities give people intrinsic pleasure and joy and a great deal of life satisfaction. |
| 7. Encourage contact with religious or spiritual persons or groups that have supplied comfort and support in patient's past. | 7. During times of hopelessness, people might feel abandoned and too paralyzed to reach out to caring people or groups. |

## INEFFECTIVE COPING

Inability to form a valid appraisal of the stressors, inadequate choices of practiced responses, and/or inability to use available resources

### Some Related Factors (Related To)

▲ Situational or maturational crises
▲ Disturbance in pattern of tension release
▲ Inadequate opportunity to prepare for stressor
▲ Inadequate resources available
▲ Inadequate social support created by characteristics of relationship

---

▲ NANDA International accepted; ● In addition to NANDA International

- Inadequate/poorly developed coping skills
- Impulsive use of extreme solutions

## Defining Characteristics (As Evidenced By)

▲ Lack of goal-directed behavior
▲ Verbalization of inability to cope or inability to ask for help
▲ Abuse of chemical agents
▲ Inability to meet basic needs
▲ Decreased use of social supports
▲ Inability to problem solve or poor problem-solving skills
▲ Destructive behavior toward self or others
▲ Inability to meet role expectations
▲ Use of forms of coping that might impede adaptive behavior
▲ Change in usual communication pattern
- Expression of anxiety, depression, fear, impatience, frustration, and/or discouragement

## Outcome Criteria

- Refrains from using or abusing chemical agents
- Reports adequate supportive social contacts
- Identifies multiple coping strategies
- Uses effective coping strategies

## Long-Term Goals

Patient will:
- Demonstrate a reduction of self-destructive behaviors by (date)
- Demonstrate two new behaviors in dealing with emotional pain by (date)
- Name two persons to whom he/she can talk if suicidal thoughts recur in the future by (date)
- State that he/she believes life has value and they have an important role to play (mother, son, husband, father, provider, friend, job-related position, etc.)
- State willingness to learn new coping strategies (through group, individual therapy, coping skills training, cognitive-behavior skills, and so on) by (date)

---

▲ NANDA International accepted; ● In addition to NANDA International

## Short-Term Goals

Patient will:
- Discuss with the nurse/counselor at least three situations that trigger suicidal thoughts, as well as feelings about these situations by (date)
- Name two effective ways to handle difficult situations in the future by (date)
- State that he/she feels comfortable with one new coping technique after three sessions of role playing by (date)

## Interventions and Rationales

| Intervention | Rationale |
|---|---|
| 1. Identify situations that trigger suicidal thoughts. | 1. Identify targets for learning more adaptive coping skills. |
| 2. Assess patient's strengths and positive coping skills (talking to others, creative outlets, social activities, problem-solving abilities). | 2. Use these to build on and draw from in planning alternatives to self-defeating behaviors. |
| 3. Assess patient's coping behaviors that are not effective and result in negative emotional sequelae: drinking, angry outbursts, withdrawal, denial, procrastination. | 3. Identify areas to target for teaching and planning strategies for supplanting more effective and self-enhancing behaviors. |
| 4. Role-play with patient adaptive coping strategies patient can use when situations that lead to suicidal thinking begin to emerge. | 4. Not all new coping strategies are effective. *The idea is that the nurse and patient work together to find what does work, and that there is no one right way to behave.* |
| 5. Assess need for assertiveness training. Assertiveness skills can help patient develop a sense of control and balance. | 5. When people have difficulty getting their needs met or asking for what they need, frustration and anger can build up, leading in some cases to ineffective outlets for stress. |

| **Intervention** | **Rationale** |
|---|---|
| 6. Clarify those things that are not under the person's control. One *cannot* control another's actions, likes, choices, or health status. | 6. Recognizing one's limitations in controlling others is, paradoxically, a beginning to finding one's strength. |
| 7. Assess patient's social supports. | 7. Have patient experiment with attending at least two chosen possibilities. |

## NURSE, PATIENT, and FAMILY RESOURCES

## ASSOCIATIONS

**American Foundation for Suicide Prevention**
120 Wall Street, 22nd Floor
New York, NY 10005
(888) 333-2377; (212) 363-3500
www.afsp.org

**American Suicide Foundation**
1045 Park Avenue, Suite 3C
New York, NY 10028
(800) ASF-4042; (212) 410-1111
Provides referrals to national support groups for suicide survivors

**American Association of Suicidology**
4201 Connecticut Avenue NW, Suite 408
Washington, DC 20008
(202) 237-2280
www.suicidology.org

**Friends for Survival, Inc.**
PO Box 214463
Sacramento, CA 95821
(916) 392-0664
For family, friends, and professionals after a suicide death

**Ray of Hope**
PO Box 2323
Iowa City, IA 52244
(319) 337-9890

**Save Our Sons and Daughters (SOSAD)**
2241 West General Boulevard
Detroit, MI 48208
(313) 361-5200
http://sosad.com
For family and friends of survivors of homicide and suicide

## INTERNET SITES

**Suicide Awareness Voices of Education**
www.save.org

**Samaritans**
www.samaritans.org.uk

**(If You Are Thinking About) Suicide... Read This First**
www.metanoia.org/suicide

# CHAPTER 17

# Anger and Aggression

## OVERVIEW

**Anger** is a primal—and not always logical—human emotion. It can range from mild annoyance to intense fury and rage (APA, 2007). **Aggression** is an intense physical or verbal reaction that reflects rage and may result in physical or verbal destruction that can harm oneself or others. **Violence** is a term that is associated with physical assault.

Control of anger in the health care setting is a top priority. Fortunately, patients most often exhibit some signs of increasing anxiety before it escalates to aggression and violence. Some patients are more prone toward angry and aggressive behaviors than others. Patients who abuse substances or have poor coping skills; patients who are psychotic or have antisocial, borderline, or narcissistic traits; and those with cognitive disorders, paranoia, or mania might at times be at risk for violent behaviors.

Anger, aggression, and violence are the last stages of a response that begins with feelings of vulnerability and then uneasiness, resulting in an increase in anxiety (Alvarez, 2002). Ideally, the most useful nursing interventions would be instituted during these initial phases, before a patient's anger starts to escalate out of control. An understanding of the kinds of situations and patient attributes that might make a patient predisposed to angry and aggressive behaviors is important for nurses. Assessment skills guiding the nurse to signals of escalating anger and aggression are vital.

Accurate assessment and intervention during the early stages of escalating anger are the best prevention of violent or aggressive behavior, which in most instances is the physical attempt to take control (Alvarez, 2002). However, there are times when anger has already escalated, and the threat of violence is imminent. At this time, different intervention strategies are needed; an entirely different set of guidelines is warranted when a patient threatens to become physically violent.

*No nurse need ever accept or tolerate anger or aggression. Preventive measures are required for the safety of the nurse as well as the patient's safety.*

The following sections offer nursing guidelines for assessing (1) anger and potential aggression when a patient is angry and verbally abusive and (2) interventions when a patient's anger has escalated to physical abuse.

**In the hospital, specific protocols that follow legal and ethical guidelines should be followed when restraining or secluding patients.**

There are psychopharmacological agents that have been found useful for angry and aggressive patients as well. Guidelines for working with angry and aggressive patients follow the least restrictive means of helping a patient gain control. Least restrictive usually starts with verbal restraints, then chemical restraints, and finally physical restraints/seclusion.

# ASSESSMENT

## Assessing History

- Any past history of violence (The best predictor of future behavior is past behavior.)
- Paranoia
- Alcohol/drug ingestion
- Certain patients with mania or agitated depression
- Personality disorder patients prone to rage, violence, or impulse dyscontrol (antisocial, borderline, and narcissistic)
- Oppositional defiant disorder or conduct disorder
- Patients experiencing command hallucinations
- Any patient with psychotic features (hallucinations, delusions, illusions)
- Patients with a cognitive disorder (e.g., dementia or delirium)

- Patients known to have intermittent explosive disorder (e.g., domestic violence)
- Certain medical conditions (e.g., chronic illness or loss of body function) can strain a person's coping abilities and lead to uncharacteristic anger

## Presenting Signs and Symptoms

- Violence is usually (but not always) preceded by:
  - Hyperactivity: most important predictor of imminent violence (e.g., pacing, restlessness)
  - Increasing anxiety and tension: clenched jaw or fist, rigid posture, fixed or tense facial expression, mumbling to self—also, shortness of breath, sweating, and rapid pulse
  - Verbal abuse (e.g., uses profanity, is argumentative)
  - Loud voice, change of pitch, or very soft voice, forcing others to strain to hear
  - Intense eye contact or avoidance of eye contact
- Recent acts of violence, including property violence
- Stony silence
- Alcohol or drug intoxication
- Carrying a weapon or object that might be used as a weapon (e.g., fork, knife, rock)
- Milieu conducive to violence:
  - Overcrowding
  - Staff inexperience
  - Staff provocative/controlling
  - Poor limit setting
  - Arbitrarily taking away privileges

## Assessment Tools

Refer to Appendix D-13 for an Overt Aggression Scale.

### Assessment Guidelines

#### Violence and Aggression

1. History of violence is the single best predictor of violence.
2. *Assess patient for risk of violence:*
   - Does patient have a violent wish or intention to harm another?

- Does patient have a plan?
- Does patient have availability or means to carry out plan?
- Consider demographics: sex (male), age (14 to 24), socioeconomic status (low), and support systems (few).
3. Assess situational characteristics (Box 17-1).
4. Assess self for defensive response or taking patient's anger personally, which may accelerate the anger cycle. For example, are you:
   - Responding aggressively toward patient?
   - Avoiding patient?
   - Suppressing or denying either your own or patient's anger?
5. Assess your level of comfort in the situation and the prudence of enlisting other staff to work with you to deal with a potentially explosive situation.

# NURSING DIAGNOSES WITH INTERVENTIONS

## Discussion of Potential Nursing Diagnoses

People who commit acts of violence often lack conflict-resolution skills and resort to more primitive and physical

---

### Box 17-1  Assessing Situational Characteristics for Violence

- Previous history of violence
- **Access to Weapons:** People with martial arts training or combat experience and those who possess great physical strength are capable of inflicting great harm.
- **Substance Use**
- **Stressors:** Daily stressor, such as relationship and financial problems, can reduce a person's frustration tolerance.
- Psychiatric disorders associated with violence.

ways of acting and responding. Many believe that a lack of assertiveness or problem-solving skills is an area of dysfunction in violent people. Teaching patients new coping skills and effective behavioral alternatives to manage their anger is helpful for many patients and is a primary prevention intervention. Many practitioners use psychoeducational and cognitive-behavioral approaches for people with anger, violence, and abuse-control problems. Some of the focus in therapy is directed toward (Mairo, 1997):

- Increasing patient's awareness, appreciation, and accountability for his or her acts
- Enhancing the patient's ability to identify and manage the attitudes and emotions associated with violent behaviors
- Decreasing social isolation and providing a supportive milieu for change
- Decreasing hostile-dependent relationships when they exist
- Developing nonviolent and constructive conflict resolution skills

**Ineffective Coping** is an appropriate nursing diagnosis for patients who have angry and aggressive responses to stressful, frustrating, or threatening situations. When a patient's anxiety and anger escalate to levels at which there is a threat of harm to self or others, **Risk for Other-Directed Violence** is more appropriate and necessitates an entirely different set of interventions. During this time, talking-down skills are employed. If psychopharmacology or chemical restraints are ineffective, restraint or seclusion of an aggressive patient might be warranted.

Nurses are better prepared when they are familiar with the medications that can be effective during an episode of acute aggression or violence. Again, the least restrictive intervention is usually used first: (1) interpersonal (verbal), then (2) chemical (psychopharmacology), and finally (3) physical restraint or seclusion.

The following text discusses two nursing diagnoses: one for intervention with **patients who are angry and hostile,** and a second for intervention with those whose anger has escalated to **threat of violence toward self or others.** Guidelines are given for restraint procedures, and appropriate pharmacological agents for acute anger and aggression are noted.

## Overall Guidelines for Nursing Interventions

### Anger and Violence

1. Always minimize personal risks; stay at least one arm's length away from patient. Give patient lots of space.
2. Set limits at the outset:
   - Use *direct approach* (e.g., "Violence is unacceptable."). Describe the consequences (restraints, seclusion). Best for confused or psychotic patients.
   - Use *indirect approach* if patient is **not** confused or psychotic (e.g., "You have a choice. You can take this medication and go into the interview room [or hallway] and talk, or you can sit in the seclusion room until you feel less anxious.").
3. Follow guidelines for setting limits as identified in Box 17-2.

---

### Box 17-2 **Setting Limits**

1. Set limits only in those areas in which a clear need to protect the patient or others exists.
2. Establish realistic and enforceable consequences of exceeding limits.
3. Make the patient aware of the limits and the consequences of not adhering to the limits before incidents occur. The patient should be told in a clear, polite, and firm manner what the limits and consequences are and should be given the opportunity to discuss any feelings or reactions to them.
4. All limits should be supported by the entire staff. The limits should be written in the care plan if the patient is hospitalized and should also be communicated verbally to all those involved.
5. When the limits are consistently adhered to, a decision to discontinue the limits should be made by the staff and should be noted on the nursing care plan. The decision should be based on consistent behavior, not on promises or sporadic efforts.
6. The staff should formulate a plan to address their own difficulty in maintaining consistent limits.

From Chitty, K.K., & Maynard, C.K. (1986). Managing manipulation. *Journal of Psychosocial Nursing and Mental Health Services, 24,* 9; reprinted with permission.

## Selected Nursing Diagnoses and Nursing Care Plans

*Patients Who Are Angry and Hostile*

---

### INEFFECTIVE COPING

Inability to form a valid appraisal of the stressors, inadequate choices of practiced responses, and/or inability to use available resources

---

### Some Related Factors (Related To)

▲ Inadequate level of perception of control
▲ High degree of threat
▲ Disturbance in pattern of tension release
▲ Inadequate opportunity to prepare for stressors
▲ Disturbance in pattern of appraisal of threat
● Ineffective problem-solving strategies/skills
● Inappropriate/ineffective use of defense mechanisms
● Personal vulnerability
● Knowledge deficit
● Overwhelming crisis situations
● Impaired reality testing
● Excessive anxiety
● Intoxication or withdrawal of substances of chemical abuse
● Chemical or biological brain changes

### Defining Characteristics (As Evidenced By)

▲ Inadequate use of defense mechanisms
▲ Inability to meet role expectations
▲ Use of forms of coping that impede adaptive behavior
▲ Abuse of chemical agents
▲ Destructive behavior toward self and others
▲ Change in usual communication patterns
● Verbal manipulations
● Expresses inability to cope
● Perceptual distortions
● Aggressive rather than assertive behaviors

---

▲ NANDA International accepted; ● In addition to NANDA International

- Immature maladaptive behaviors
- Reports feeling anxious, apprehensive, fearful, and/or depressed, angry

## Outcome Criteria

- Patient and others will remain free from injury
- Destructive behavior toward others, property, animals, and so on will cease
- Use of assertive and healthy behaviors to get needs met is in constant evidence

## Long-Term Goals

Patient will:
- Identify two new safe and appropriate behaviors that will reduce anxiety, frustration, and anger by (date)
- Discuss alternative ways of meeting demands of current situation by (date)
- Recognize when anger and aggressive tendencies begin to escalate and employ tension-reducing behaviors at that time (time outs, deep breathing, talking to a previously designated person, employing an exercise such as jogging) by (date)
- Verbalize an understanding of aggressive behavior, associated disorders, and medications, if any, by (date)
- Identify own strengths and skills to cope with problems, and work with nurse to build on these skills (e.g., problem solving) (ongoing)
- Practice stress-management techniques (exercising, talking, relaxation, journal writing) as evidenced by staff observations and family reports (ongoing)

## Short-Term Goals

Patient will:
- Refrain from harming others or destroying property
- Be free of self-inflicted harm
- Be rule adherent during hospitalization
- Begin to implement at least two new coping techniques when angry and aggressive feelings begin to escalate
- Experience a decrease of anxiety and anger using a self-reported scale of 1 to 10 (1 feeling least anger and 10 feeling the most anger) after trying new coping techniques

## *Interventions and Rationales*

| Intervention | Rationale |
|---|---|
| 1. Assess your own feelings in the situation; guard against taking patient's abusive statements personally or becoming defensive. | 1. Although patients are often skillful at making personal and pointed statements, they do not know nurses personally and have no basis on which they can make accurate judgments. |
| 2. Refrain from responding with sarcasm or ridicule, no matter how threatened or angry you feel. | 2. An angry or sarcastic remark by an authority figure will serve as an attack on the patient's self-esteem and encourage more defensive behaviors (e.g., increased hostility). |
| 3. Pay attention to angry and aggressive behavior; do not minimize such behavior in the hope that it will go away. | 3. *Minimization of angry behaviors* **and** *ineffective limit setting* **are the most frequent factors contributing to the escalation of violence.** |
| 4. Set clear, consistent, and enforceable limits on behavior (see Box 17-2 for guidelines). | 4. Set clear, consistent, understanding of expectations for acceptable behaviors, and stress the consequences of not adhering to those behaviors. |
| 5. Emphasize to patients that they are responsible for all consequences of their aggressive behavior, including legal charges. | 5. Focusing on the here-and-now rules and that patient is responsible for the consequences of any and all aggressive behaviors can help decrease the chronically angry patient's need to "test limits." |
| 6. Emphasize to the patient that you are setting limits on specific | 6. Underlines that behavioral limits are not punitive, while |

**Intervention**

behaviors, not feelings (e.g., "It is okay to be angry with Tom, but it is not okay to threaten him or verbally abuse him").

7. Use a matter-of-fact, neutral approach. Remain calm and use a moderate, firm voice and calming hand gestures.

8. When a patient starts to become abusive and anger threatens to escalate, inform the patient that the nurse will leave the room for a period of time (20 minutes) and will be back when the situation is calmer. Return when time is up.

9. Attend positively to nonabusive communication, such as non-illness-related topics, by responding to requests and by providing emotional support.

10. Avoid power struggles and control battles.

11. Respond to patient anxiety or anger with active listening and validation of patient distress. Apologize when appropriate.

**Rationale**

communicating expectation for positive behaviors.

7. Fear, indignation, and arguing are gratifying to many verbally abusive patients. A matter-of-fact approach can help interrupt the cycle of escalating anger.

8. When this response is given in a neutral, matter-of-fact manner, the patient's abusive behavior does not get rewarded. Always return in the time specified, and focus communication on neutral topics.

9. Reinforces appropriate communication and behaviors. This gives the patient and nurse time to share healthier communication and build up a sounder working relationship.

10. Power struggles and control battles are perceived as a challenge and generally lead to escalation of the conflict.

11. Allows the patient to feel heard and understood; builds trust.

| Intervention | Rationale |
|---|---|
| 12. Work with patient to identify the internal and interpersonal factors that provoke violence or that strengthen a relationship against anger and aggression. | 12. Helps both nurse and patient identify triggers for aggression and factors that can mitigate or reduce the escalation of anger and aggression. **This is the first step in a structured violence-prevention strategy** (Goodwin, 1985). |
| 13. Identify serious risk factors for further violence (family chaos, other mental or environmental risk factors). | 13. Whenever possible, reduce the possibility of continued violence by treating the risk factors (e.g., getting family counseling, finding a job). **This is the second step in a structured violence-prevention strategy** (Goodwin, 1985). |
| 14. Work with patient to identify what supports are lacking, and problem solve ways to achieve needed support. | 14. Advocacy with support is **the third step in intervention for violence** (Goodwin, 1985). |
| 15. Teach the patient (and family) the steps in the problem-solving process. | 15. Many people have never learned a systematic and effective approach to dealing with and mastering tough life situations/problems. |
| 16. Role-play alternative behaviors with patients that they can use in stressful and overwhelming situations when anger threatens. | 16. Role-playing allows patient to rehearse alternative ways of handling stressful and angry feelings in a safe environment. |
| 17. Work with patients to set goals for their behavior. Give positive | 17. Gives patient a sense of control while learning goal-setting skills. |

| Intervention | Rationale |
|---|---|
| feedback when patients reach their goals. | Achieving self-set goals might enhance a person's sense of self, and can foster new and more effective approaches to frustrating feelings. |
| 18. Provide the patient with other outlets for stress and anxiety (exercising, listening to music, reading, talking to a friend, attending support groups, participating in a sport). | 18. Alternative means of channeling aggression and angry feelings can help patients decrease their anxiety and stress and allow for more cognitive approaches to their situation (e.g., using a problem-solving approach). |
| 19. Provide the patient and family with community resources that teach assertiveness training, anger management, and stress reduction techniques. These might take a while to master but will give the patient more satisfying experiences in life. | 19. When patients are motivated, there are a number of techniques they can learn that can aid in helping them get what they want through acceptable and rewarding means. |

## Patients Who Threaten Harm to Self or Others

### RISK FOR OTHER-DIRECTED VIOLENCE

At risk for behaviors in which an individual demonstrates that he/she can be physically, emotionally, and/or sexually harmful to others

## Related Factors (Related To)

▲ History of violent, antisocial behavior
▲ History of childhood abuse or witnessing family violence
▲ History of violence against others (hitting, biting, kicking, spitting, rape, etc.)
▲ Psychotic symptomatology (e.g., command hallucinations, paranoid delusions, illogical thought processes)
▲ Impulsivity
▲ Rage reactions
▲ Neurological impairment (positive electroencephalogram, computed tomography scan, or magnetic resonance image; head trauma, positive neurological findings, seizure disorders)
▲ Manic excitement
▲ Cognitive impairment
▲ Substance abuse or withdrawal

## Defining Characteristics (As Evidenced By)

● Increased motor activity, pacing, excitement, irritability, agitation
● Provocative behavior (argumentative, overactive, complaining, demanding behaviors)
● Hostile, threatening verbalizations (loud, threatening, profane speech)
● Overt aggressive acts; goal-directed destruction of objects in the environment
● Possession of destructive means (gun, knife, other weapon)
● Verbal threats against property/person, threatening notes/letters
● Body language: angry facial expressions, rigid posture, clenched fists, threatening posture

## Outcome Criteria

● Refrains from abusive behaviors (in all forms) toward others
● Controls impulse

---

▲ NANDA International accepted; ● In addition to NANDA International

## Long-Term Goals

Patient will:
- Display nonviolent behaviors toward self and others
- Demonstrate three new ways to deal with tension and aggression in a nondestructive manner
- Make plans to continue with long-term therapy (individual, family, group) to work on violence-prevention strategies and increasing coping skills
- Identify factors contributing to abusive behaviors

## Short-Term Goals

- Patient's behavior will not escalate to aggressive acts toward self, others, or property while in hospital
- Patient will demonstrate increased self-control while in hospital
- Patient will participate in time outs, moving to a less stimulating environment, and verbal limits set by staff during hospital stay
- Patient will refrain from hurting self or others with the aid of verbal, chemical, or physical restraints
- Patient will identify available community resources for help

## Interventions and Rationales

| Intervention | Rationale |
|---|---|
| 1. Keep environmental stimulation at a minimum (e.g., lower lights, keep stereos down, ask patients and visitors to leave the area, or have staff take patient to another area). | 1. Increased stimulation can increase patient's anxiety level, leading to increased agitation or aggressive behaviors. |
| 2. Keep voice calm, speak in a low tone. | 2. High-pitched rapid voice can increase anxiety levels in others; the opposite is true when the tone of voice is low and calm and the words are spoken slowly. |

| Intervention | Rationale |
|---|---|
| 3. Call patient by name, introduce yourself, orient the patient when necessary, tell the patient beforehand what you are going to do. | 3. Calling patient by name helps to establish contact. Orienting and giving information can minimize misrepresentation of nurses' intentions. |
| 4. Always use personal safety precautions:<br>  a. Either leave the door open in the interview room or use a hallway.<br>  b. If you feel uncertain of patient's potential for violence, other staff should be nearby.<br>  c. Never turn your back on an angry patient.<br>  d. Have a quick exit available.<br>  e. If on home visit, go with a colleague if there is concern regarding aggression. **Leave the home immediately if there are any signs that the patient's behavior is escalating out of control.** | 4. **Your safety is always first.** Always call in colleagues or other staff if you feel threatened or in physical danger.<br>Nursing and security staff should have received frequent training in dealing with angry and hostile patients, including frequent training in steps of anger de-escalation and seclusion and restraint procedures.<br>Ask for training, and learn from more experienced staff members.<br>Know well the unit safety precautions for staff as well as patient safety. |

**Forensic Issues**

| | |
|---|---|
| 1. Always document patient's behaviors and staff interventions during each level of restrictive intervention. | 1. Staff can demonstrate the appropriate use for each level of restraint in a court of law, if necessary. |
| 2. When interventions are needed to reduce escalating anger, always | 2. Seclusion or restraints should never be used as punishment or |

| Intervention | Rationale |
|---|---|
| use the least restrictive first when possible:<br>a. Interpersonal—verbal interventions<br>b. Chemical—appropriate medications<br>c. Physical—restraints or seclusion | substitute for staff. Restraints should be used only when there is no less-restrictive alternative. |
| 3. *Verbal interventions:* Encourage the patient to talk about angry feelings, and find ways to tolerate or reduce angry and aggressive feelings. | 3. When patient feels heard and understood and has help with problem-solving alternative options, de-escalation of anger and aggression is often possible. |
| 4. Use *empathetic verbal interventions* (e.g., "It must be frightening to be here and to be feeling out of control."). | 4. Empathetic verbal intervention is the most effective method of calming an agitated, fearful, panicky patient. |
| 5. When interpersonal interventions fail to decrease the patient's anger, consider the need for *chemical* or *physical restraints*. Assessment includes determining whether aggression is acute or chronic. (See Table 17-1 for medications that have antiaggressive effects. | 5. Often psychopharma-cological interventions can help patients gain control of their behavior and prevent continued escalation of anger and hostile impulses. |
| 6. Alert hospital security and other staff in a quiet, unobtrusive manner *before* violent behavior escalates so that security will be prepared to intervene in a | 6. **Hospital staff and security should have frequent training in restraining or secluding patients**. Alerting staff and security beforehand |

| Intervention | Rationale |
|---|---|
| safe and knowledgeable manner if needed. | best ensures that the restraint or seclusion process will be handled safely for patient, staff, and other patients on the unit. |
| 7. When interpersonal and pharmacological interventions fail to control the angry patient, *physical intervention (restraints or seclusion)* is the final resort. **Always follow hospital protocols, which should reflect The Joint Commission (TJC) standards.** Refer to Box 17-3 for some guidelines for use of restraints. | 7. Hospital protocols that are clear and well written tell staff when to restrain, how to restrain, how long before a physician's order is needed, nursing interventions for patient during period of restraints or seclusion, how often to check restraints or patient in seclusion, whom to call, and how often the need for use of restraints/ seclusion needs to be reevaluated by physician. |
| 8. If restraints or seclusion have been used, check on patient every 15 minutes.<br>• check restraints and circulation (color, temperature)<br>• pulses on extremities.<br>• need for toileting, nutrition, and hydration.<br>**Use unit protocol as a guide.** | 8. Patient safety is an important part of our care. Checking patient frequently helps ensure patient safety **(use unit protocol as a guide),** and written records are kept in patient's permanent record. |

# MEDICAL TREATMENTS

## Psychopharmacology

Often anger, aggression, or violence is related to a psychiatric or neurological disorder such as ADHD, paranoid disorder, depression, dementia, conduct disorder, substance-use

| Box 17-3 **Guidelines for Restraining a Patient** |
|---|

1. The specific indications should be clearly documented.
2. There must be a signed physician's order (even if initiated by other staff member).
3. Order should specify a time limit.
4. Anyone impaired enough to require restraints should have continuous staff observation.
5. Restraints are used when there is no less-restrictive alternative.
6. Restraints should be properly used and designed.
7. Five staff members are necessary to restrain a resistant patient.
8. Security should be called to assist.
9. During the procedure, the patient should be told in calm, simple terms what is happening.
   *"You are in a hospital. . .these people are nurses and security staff. . .no one is going to hurt you. . .we are trying to make things safe for you."*
10. Nursing and security staff should receive training in this procedure on a regular basis.

Adapted from Goldberg, R.J. (2007). *Practical guide to the care of the psychiatric patient* (3rd ed). St. Louis, Mosby, p. 284; reprinted with permission.

Table 17-1 **Medications with Antiaggression Effects for Specific Situations**

| Medication | Specific Situation |
|---|---|
| Antipsychotic | Disorganized behavior (psychosis-induced violence) |
| Anticonvulsants | Labile mood, poor impulse control, organicity |
| Beta-blockers (e.g., propranolol) | Organically based violence (e.g., Alzheimer's disease, stroke, Huntington's disease) |
| Buspirone (BuSpar) | Cognitively impaired (e.g., developmentally disabled, head injuries, dementia) |
| SSRIs | Anger attacks |
| Lithium | Labile mood, impulsivity |
| Clonidine | Anxiety, agitation |

Data from Preston, J.D., D'Neal, J.H., and Talaga, M.C. (2008). Handbook of clinical psychopharmacology for therapists (5th ed.). Parkland: New Harbinger publications, Inc.

disorders, schizophrenia, and so forth. In such cases, the patient's treatment is targeted toward the primary disorder. Antidepressants are often helpful in targeting aggression. Table 17-1 lists medications that have been found useful in specific situations.

# NURSE, PATIENT, and FAMILY RESOURCES

## JOURNAL ARTICLES

Barton, S.A., Johnson, R.M., Price, L.V. (2009). Achieving restraint-free on an inpatient behavioral health unit. *Journal of Psychosocial Nursing and Mental Health Services*, 47(1) pp. 34–40

Moylan, L.B. (2009). Physical restraints in acute care psychiatry: A humanistic and realistic approach. *Journal of Psychosocial Nursing and Mental Health Services*, 47(3) pp. 41–47

## INTERNET SITES

**Focus Adolescent Service**
www.focusas.com
Search for "anger" to find relevant articles

**SIUC Mental Health Web**
www.siu.edu/office/counsel/
Managing anger and understanding the dynamics of violence, abuse, and control

**Anger Management Institute**
www.manageanger.com/guidelines.htm
Guidelines for understanding and managing anger

**Centers for Disease Control and Prevention**
www.cdc.gov
Search for "anger" to find multiple articles

**About Anger and Raging**
www.recovery-man.com/abusive/rage_vs_anger.htm

**Anger Management**
www.mentalhelp.net

# CHAPTER 18

# Grieving and Complicated Grieving

## OVERVIEW

Loss is part of the human experience, and grief is the normal response to loss. There can be loss of a relationship (divorce, separation, death, abortion); of health (a body function or part, mental or physical capacity); of status or prestige; of security (occupational, financial, social); of self-confidence; of self-concept; of a dream; or loss can be of a symbolic nature. Loss through death is a major life crisis for most people.

**Grief** is the characteristic painful feelings precipitated by the death of a loved one or by some other significant loss. Grief is not a mood disorder, although a depressive syndrome is often part of the of mourning process. **Bereavement** is the social experience of losing an important person to death. People react within their own cultural patterns and their own values and personality to a devastating loss. **Mourning** refers to the culturally patterned (ethnic, cultural, spiritual, religious) expressions of going through the grief process (1 to 2 years). A person experiences various phenomena during the mourning process which are discussed later.

Most bereaved persons experience a "normal" grief reaction and resolve their loss with help and support from family and friends. However, from 25% to 30% experience *complicated grief* and may require professional support. Acute grief can trigger an exacerbation of any preexisting medical or psychological problems. A history of depression, substance abuse, or posttraumatic stress disorder can complicate grief and require treatment. Unresolved grief reactions account for many of the physical symptoms seen in medical clinics and hospital units. Suicide is higher among people who have had a significant loss, especially if losses are multiple and grieving mechanisms are limited. The death of a child and multiple deaths are regarded as the most severe types of loss. Nurses are not immune to grief reactions. As health care workers, as nurses, as friends, as people who will experience grief and loss throughout our own lifetimes, it is helpful to know what happens during the process of mourning, what might help others through this process, and how to identify a person who is having difficulty resolving his or her pain and sorrow (complicated grieving).

Dr. Elisabeth Kübler-Ross began listening to the terminally ill, and out of her groundbreaking work came a construct of the human response to death that has entered the mainstream (Kramer-Howe, 2010). Most nurses and clinicians are familiar with Kübler-Ross's (1969) classic review of the stages of death and dying (denial, isolation, anger, bargaining, depression, and acceptance). The resolution of the loss usually occurs through these stages, and a person might demonstrate a different clinical picture at each stage of mourning. Each stage has its own characteristics, and the duration and form of each stage varies considerably from person to person.

People react within their own cultural patterns and their own value and personality structure, as well as within their own social environment. Most of us are programmed in our response to death. Distinct characteristics, however, can be identified throughout the grieving process. It is important to keep in mind that these stages do not necessarily progress in an orderly fashion and might overlap during the grief process.

**What we are not often taught is what to say or do to facilitate the healing of those who must learn to live with their anguish.**

Normal grief reaction includes depressed mood, insomnia, anxiety, poor appetite, loss of interest, guilt feelings, dreams about the deceased, and poor concentration. Psychological states include shock, denial, and yearning and searching for the deceased. The acute grief reaction lasts from 4 to 8 weeks; the active symptoms of grief usually last from 3 to 6 months; and the complete work of mourning can take from 1 to 2 years or more to complete. However, acute grief can be a time of exacerbation of any medical or psychiatric problems, as mentioned earlier.

Nurses can care for the bereaved through listening, assisting in communication, teaching families about the process of dying, or facilitating bereavement with opportunities to prevent ill health and to help families find new directions for growth.

# ASSESSMENT

## Assessing History

- Does the bereaved exhibit some of the factors that can complicate the successful completion of mourning?
  - ○ Was the bereaved heavily dependent on the deceased?
  - ○ Were there persistent, unresolved conflicts with the deceased?
  - ○ Was the deceased a child (often the most profound loss)?
  - ○ Does the bereaved have a meaningful relationship/support system?
  - ○ Has the bereaved experienced a number of previous losses?
  - ○ Does the bereaved have sound coping skills?
- Was the deceased's death associated with a cultural stigma (e.g., AIDS, suicide)?
- Was the death unexpected or associated with violence (murder, suicide)?
- Has the bereaved had difficulty resolving past significant losses?
- Does the bereaved have a history of depression, drug or alcohol abuse, or other psychiatric illness?
- If the bereaved is young, are there indications for special interventions?

## Presenting Signs and Symptoms of Complicated Grief

- Prolonged, severe symptoms lasting for 2 or more months
- Limited response to support

- Profound and persistent feelings of hopelessness
- Completely withdrawn or fears being alone
- Inability to work, to create, or to feel emotion and positive states of mind
- Maladaptive behaviors in response to the death, for example:
  - Drug or alcohol abuse
  - Promiscuity
  - Fugue states
  - Feeling dead or unreal
  - Suicidal ideation
  - Aggressive behaviors
  - Compulsive spending
- Recurrent nightmares, night terrors, compulsive re-enactments
- Exhaustion from lack of sleep and hyperarousal
- Prolonged depression, panic attacks
- Self neglect

## Assessment Tools

Table 18-1 presents a comparison of the symptoms seen in a "normal" mourning process, contrasting those seen in a complicated grief reaction. This can be used as a helpful guide in your assessment.

Table 18-1 **Common Experiences During Grief and Their Pathological Intensification**

| Phase | Typical Response | Pathological Intensification |
|---|---|---|
| Dying | Emotional expression and immediate coping with the dying process | Avoidant; overwhelmed, dazed, confused; self-punitive; inappropriately hostile |
| Death and outcry | Outcry of emotions with news of the death and turning to others for help or isolating self with self-succoring | Panic; dissociative reactions, reactive psychoses |

Table 18-1   **Common Experiences During Grief and Their Pathological Intensification—cont'd**

| Phase | Typical Response | Pathological Intensification |
|---|---|---|
| Warding off (denial) | Avoidance of reminders, social withdrawal, focusing elsewhere, emotional numbing, not thinking of implications to self or certain themes | Maladaptive avoidances confronting the implications of death: drug or alcohol abuse, counterphobic frenzy, promiscuity, fugue states, phobic avoidance, feeling dead or unreal |
| Reexperience (intrusion) | Intrusive experiences, including recollections of negative relationship experiences with the deceased, bad dreams, reduced concentration, compulsive reenactments | Flooding with negative images and emotions, uncontrolled ideation, self-impairing compulsive reenactments, night terrors, recurrent nightmares, distraught from intrusion of anger, anxiety, despair, shame, or guilt themes; physiological exhaustion from hyperarousal |
| Working through | Recollection of the deceased and contemplation of self with reduced intrusiveness of memories and fantasies, increased rational acceptance, reduced numbness and avoidance, more "dosing" of recollections, and a sense of working through it | Sense that one cannot integrate the death with a sense of self and continued life. Persistent, warded-off themes can manifest as anxious, depressed, enraged, shame-filled, or guilty moods and psychophysiological syndromes. |

*Continued*

Table 18-1 **Common Experiences During Grief and Their Pathological Intensification—cont'd**

| Phase | Typical Response | Pathological Intensification |
|---|---|---|
| Completion | Reduction in emotional swings, with a sense of self-coherence and readiness for new life experiences and/or relationships | Failure to complete mourning might be associated with inability to work, to create, to feel emotion, or to experience positive states of mind |

Horowitz, M.J. (1990). A model of mourning: Change in schemas of self and others. *Journal of the American Psychoanalytic Association, 38*, 297-324.

## Assessment Guidelines

### Grieving and Complicated Grieving

1. Identify if the individual is at risk for complicated grieving (see Assessing History).
2. Evaluate for psychotic symptoms, agitation, increased activity, alcohol/drug abuse, and extreme vegetative symptoms (anorexia, weight loss, not sleeping).
3. Do not overlook people who do not express significant grief in the context of a major loss. Those individuals might have an increased risk of subsequent complicated or unresolved grief reaction (Kaplan & Sadock, 2007).
4. Complicated grief reactions require significant interventions. Suicidal or severely depressed people might require hospitalization. **Always assess for suicide** with signs of depression or other dysfunctional signs or symptoms.
5. Assess support systems. If support systems are limited, find bereavement groups in the bereaved's community.
6. When grieving is stalled or complicated, a variety of therapeutic approaches have proved extremely beneficial (e.g., cognitive-behavioral interventions). Provide referrals.
7. Grieving can bring with it severe spiritual anguish. Would spiritual counseling or a specific counselor be useful for the bereaved at this time?

# NURSING DIAGNOSES WITH INTERVENTIONS

## Discussion of Potential Nursing Diagnoses

The North American Nursing Diagnosis Association (NANDA International, 2009-2011) identifies three nursing diagnoses for nursing actions: **Grieving, Complicated Grieving,** and **Risk for Complicated Grieving.** However, because nurses are in constant contact with people and their families experiencing painful losses, **Acute Grief Reaction** (*not* a NANDA International nursing diagnosis) can also be the focus of treatment. During this time, the nurse might need to intervene for **Ineffective Coping** or **Compromised Family Coping, Disturbed Sleep Pattern, Risk for Spiritual Distress** or **Spiritual Distress, Disturbed Thought Processes,** or other problems.

## Overall Guidelines for Nursing Interventions

### Grieving and Complicated Grieving

1. Support the family by helping family and friends employ methods that can facilitate the grieving process and give support to a grieving person (Robinson, 1997):
   - Be there for the bereaved; give your full presence.
   - Offer physical touch suited to the moment and your relationship. Do not use touch if it will presume an intimacy that does not exist or as a tool to coerce a person to mourn.
   - Identify family or friends to assist with practical concerns.
   - Try to provide beauty or nourishment in some suitable form.
   - Encourage the individual and family to mourn on their own schedule.
2. Identify and treat/refer an individual with a pathological process.
3. Assess for suicide if there is persistent, severe depression and deep, enduring feelings of hopelessness.

4. Know, share, and support with the bereaved the normal phenomena that occur during the normal mourning process, which might concern some people (intense anger at the deceased, guilt, symptoms the deceased had before death, unbidden flood of memories). Give bereaved a written handout for reference.

5. When the family member dies in the hospital, apply appropriate measures that can help facilitate grieving for families (Table 18-2).

   Remember, we each grieve differently depending on age, culture, and spiritual levels. Make an effort to identify the special/specific needs of the bereaved.

### Table 18-2 **Nursing Interventions for Grieving Families in a Hospital Setting**

| Intervention | Rationale |
|---|---|
| 1. At the death or imminent death of a family member: | |
| • Communicate the news to the family in an area of privacy. | • Family members can support each other in an atmosphere in which they can behave naturally. |
| • If only one family member is available, stay with that member until clergy, a family member, or a friend arrives. | • The presence and comfort of the nurse during the initial stage of shock can help minimize feelings of acute isolation and anxiety. |
| • If the nurse feels unable to handle the situation, the aid of another who can support the family should be enlisted. | • The individual or family will need support, answers to questions, and guidance as to immediate tasks and information. |
| 2. If the family requests to see and take leave of the dying or dead person: | |
| • Grant this request. | • The need to take leave can be of overwhelming importance for some—to kiss good-bye, ask for forgiveness, or take a lock of hair. This helps people face the reality of death. |

Table 18-2  **Nursing Interventions for Grieving Families in a Hospital Setting—cont'd**

| Intervention | Rationale |
|---|---|
| 3. If angry family members accuse the nurse or doctor of abusing or mismanaging the care of the deceased:<br>• Continue to provide the best care for the dying or final care to the dead. Avoid becoming involved in angry and painful arguments and power struggles. | • Complaints are not directed toward the nurse personally. The anger may serve the purpose of keeping grieving relatives from falling apart. Projected anger may be an attempt to deal with aggression and guilt toward the dying person. |
| 4. If relatives behave in a grossly disturbed manner (e.g., refuse to acknowledge the truth, collapse, or lose control):<br>• Show patience and tact, and offer sympathy and warmth. | • Shock and disbelief are the first responses to the news of death, and people need ways to protect themselves from the overwhelming reality of loss. |
| • Encourage the person to cry. | • Crying helps provide relief from feelings of acute pain and tension. |
| • Provide a place of privacy for grieving. | • Privacy facilitates the natural expression of grief. |
| 5. If the family requests specific religious, cultural, or social customs strange or unknown to the nurse:<br>• Help facilitate steps necessary for the family to carry out the desired arrangements. | • Institutional mourning rituals of various cultures provide important external supports for the grief-stricken person. |

Engel, G.L. (1964). Grief and grieving. *American Journal of Nursing*, 64(9), 93.

## Selected Nursing Diagnoses and Nursing Care Plans

### ACUTE GRIEF REACTION

Focuses on the devastating and often overwhelming pain people experience on the death of someone they care about and who was an integral part of their lives; the acute phase lasts from 4 to 8 weeks after the death or a significant loss (The long-term phase follows the acute phase and constitutes the main work of mourning; it might last for 1 to 2 years or more.)

*Related Factors (Related To)*
- Recent death of a loved one (e.g., person, pet) or forced change (e.g., loss of job, home, or body part; disaster; divorce, status)

*Defining Characteristics (As Evidenced By)*
Signs of grief:
- Anguish and pain
- Anger at deceased or health care professionals
- Despair, psychological distress
- Guilt
- Crying
- Vegetative signs (anorexia, insomnia, bowel dysfunction, immobility)
- Disorganization
- Withdrawal from usual activities and preoccupation with the deceased

*Outcome Criteria*
- Expresses positive expectations about the future
- The family will engage in life and pursue other activities

*Long-Term Goals*
- The bereaved will seek support during the grieving process.

---

- In addition to NANDA International

---

Box 18-1 **Behaviors Signaling Successful Mourning**

The person:
1. Can tolerate intense emotions
2. Demonstrates increased periods of stability
3. Takes on new roles and responsibilities
4. Has energy to invest in new endeavors
5. Remembers both positive and negative aspects of the deceased loved one
6. May have brief periods of intense emotions which might occur at significant times, such as anniversaries and holidays.

---

Data from Gorman, L.M., Sultan D.F., & Raines, M.L. (1996). *Davis's manual of psychosocial nursing for general patient care*. Philadelphia: FA Davis.

- The bereaved will demonstrate behaviors that signify the individual is going through the normal process of mourning (Box 18-1).
- The bereaved will participate in planning the funeral.
- The bereaved will state they find comfort and support through their religious/spiritual practices.

### Short-Term Goals

- The bereaved will state the names of two support people he or she can share painful feelings and memories with.
- If the bereaved demonstrates signs of complicated grief reaction, he or she will agree to seek support and treatment.
- The bereaved will express feelings about the loss within 2 days.
- The bereaved will verbalize reality of the loss within 1 week.
- The bereaved will express spiritual beliefs about death.

### Interventions and Rationales

| Intervention | Rationale |
|---|---|
|  **Outside the Hospital** | |
| 1. Employ methods that can facilitate the grieving process (Robinson, 1997): | |
| a. Giving your full presence: use appropriate eye | a. Talking is one of the most important ways of dealing with acute |

| **Intervention** | **Rationale** |
|---|---|
| contact, attentive listening, and appropriate touch. | grief. *Listening patiently* helps the bereaved express all feelings, even ones he or she thinks are negative. *Appropriate eye contact* helps to let him or her know you are there and sharing his or her sadness. *Suitable human touch* can express warmth and nurture healing. Inappropriate touch can leave a person confused and uncomfortable. |
| b. Be patient with the bereaved in times of silence. Do not fill silence with empty chatter. | b. Sharing painful feelings during periods of silence is healing and conveys your concern. |
| 2. **Avoid** euphemisms such as "Sorry James has passed away," "You lost your husband." Instead say something like, "I am really sorry to hear that James died." | 2. Euphemisms can do harm: <br> a. Can cause the bereaved to think we have not caught the gravity of the situation. <br> b. Wanting at one level to deny what is happening, the bereaved might use euphemisms to help postpone facing the painful feelings they desperately need to work through. |
| 3. Avoid banal advice and philosophical statements such as "He's no longer suffering"; "You can always have another child"; or "It's better this | 3. Gives the bereaved the impression that their experience is not understood, and that you are minimizing the experience and pain. |

| Intervention | Rationale |
|---|---|
| way." It is *more helpful* to put into words acknowledgment of the bereaved's painful feelings: <br> a. "His death will be a terrible loss." <br> b. "No one can replace her." <br> c. "He will be missed for a long time." | The fact that the deceased is no longer suffering does not mean that the bereaved is not experiencing a devastating, painful loss. |
| 4. Encourage the support of family and friends. If no supports are available, refer the bereaved to a community bereavement group. (Bereavement groups are helpful even when a person has many friends and/or family support.) | 4. There are routine matters that friends can help with: <br> a. Getting food to the house <br> b. Making phone calls <br> c. Driving to the mortuary <br> d. Taking care of kids or other family members |
| 5. Offer spiritual support and/or referrals when needed. | 5. Dealing with an illness or catastrophic loss can cause the most profound spiritual anguish (Zerbe, 1999). |
| 6. When intense emotions are in evidence, show understanding and support (Box 18-2 offers guidelines). | 6. Empathetic words that reflect acceptance of a bereaved individual's feelings are always healing (Robinson, 1997). |

## COMPLICATED GRIEVING

A disorder that occurs after the death of a significant other, in which the experience of distress accompanying bereavement fails to follow normative expectations and manifests in functional impairment

| Box 18-2 **Guidelines for What to Say** | |
|---|---|
| When you sense an overwhelming *sorrow:* | "This must hurt terribly." |
| When you hear *anger* in the bereaved's voice: | "I hear anger in your voice. Most people go through periods of anger when their loved one dies. Are you feeling anger now?" |
| If you discern *guilt:* | "Are you feeling guilty? This is a common reaction many people have. What are some of your thoughts about this?" |
| If you sense a *fear* of the future: | "It must be scary to go through this." |
| When the bereaved seems *confused:* | "This can be a bewildering time." |
| In almost any *painful* situation: | "This must be very difficult for you." |

Adapted from Robinson, D. (1997). *Good intentions: The nine unconscious mistakes of nice people.* New York: Warner Books, p. 249; reprinted with permission. Copyright 1997 by Duke Robinson.

## Some Related Factors (Related To)

▲ Lack of support systems
▲ Emotional instability
▲ Presence of factors identified in history (e.g., substance abuse, multiple losses, poor physical health, other mental health risks)

## Defining Characteristics (As Evidenced By)

● Verbal expression of distress or loss or denial of loss *and* one of the following:
  • Persistent emotional distress
  • Arrested grieving process before resolution
  • Prolonged grieving beyond expected time for cultural group
  • Emotional response more exaggerated than expected for cultural group (severity of reaction)
● Expression of unresolved issues

- Interference with life functioning
- Suicidal ideation
- Prolonged panic attacks
- Prolonged depression
- Engagement in self-destructive activities
- Self-neglect
- Protracted social withdrawal

## Outcome Criteria

- Can talk about good and bad times during the relationship
- Express optimism about the future
- Expressions of feeling socially engaged
- Takes on new roles and responsibilities

## Long-Term Goals

Bereaved will:
- Resolve blocks to the grieving process (maladaptive avoidance, extreme prolonged denial), and the stages of mourning will be reactivated during grief counseling
- Demonstrate initial integration into their life within 6 months
- Demonstrate physical recuperation from the stress of loss and grieving within 6 months
- Demonstrate reestablished relationships and social supports within 4 weeks

## Short-Term Goals

Bereaved will:
- Be free of self-directed harm
- Demonstrate decreased suicidal, aggressive, depressive, or withdrawn behaviors within 2 weeks
- Express feelings, verbally and nonverbally
- Establish or maintain an adequate balance of rest, sleep, and activity with help from nurse and family
- Establish or maintain adequate nutrition, hydration, and elimination within 2 weeks

---

▲ NANDA International accepted; ● In addition to NANDA International

## Interventions and Rationales

| Intervention | Rationale |
| --- | --- |
| 1. Always assess for presence of suicidal thoughts or ideation. | 1. Severely depressed or suicidal individuals might require hospitalization and protection from self-harm and severe self-neglect. |
| 2. Talk with the bereaved in realistic terms. Discuss concrete changes that have occurred in the person's life after the death and how it might affect the person's future. | 2. Discussing the death and how it has and will continue to affect the person's life can help the death become more concrete and real. |
| 3. If the bereaved cannot talk about the death initially, encourage other means of expression (e.g., keeping a journal, drawing, reading about the experience of grief). | 3. Talking is usually the most important tool for resolving initial pain; however, any avenue for the expression of feelings can help the bereaved identify, accept, and work through their feelings. |
| 4. Stress that people often have strong feelings of anger (even hate) at the deceased, feel guilty, harbor strong feelings of resentment, and the like. | 4. Understanding that strong "negative" feelings are in fact normal and experienced by most people can make the bereaved aware of such feelings and then work through them. |
| 5. Encourage the person to recall memories (happy ones, sad ones, difficult ones); listen actively; and stay silent when appropriate. | 5. Reviewing past memories is an important stage in mourning. Being with the bereaved and sharing painful feelings can be healing. |

| **Intervention** | **Rationale** |
|---|---|
| 6. Encourage the person to talk to others individually, in small groups, or in community bereavement groups. | 6. Talking and listening are the most important activities that can help resolve grief and reactivate the mourning process. |
| 7. Carefully avoid false reassurances that everything will be okay as time passes. | 7. For some, separation through death is never okay; even when the grieving process is complete, the person might be sorely missed. |
| 8. Assess the need for psychotherapy "regrief" work. | 8. Many people find brief counseling (6 to 10 sessions) useful during the work of mourning. |
| 9. Identify religious/ spiritual background, and determine if the bereaved would be receptive to a spiritual advisor. | 9. For many people, spiritual needs and support are extremely comforting at this time, and sharing feelings with a trusted and empathetic religious figure might be comforting. |
| 10. Offer written guidelines for coping with overwhelming grief (see Box 18-3). | 10. When grieving, even simple tasks can become monumental, life becomes confusing, and normal routines are often interrupted. These guidelines offer simple reminders and help validate the bereaved's experience. |

## GUIDELINES FOR COPING WITH GRIEF

Box 18-3 suggests guidelines that can help the bereaved through this period.

## Box 18-3 **Patient Guidelines for Coping with Catastrophic Loss**

1. **Take the time you need to grieve.** The hard work of grief uses psychological energy. Resolution of the "numb state" that occurs after loss requires a few weeks at least. A minimum of 1 year—to cover all the birthdays, anniversaries, and other important dates without your loved one—is required before you can "learn to live" with your loss.

2. **Express your feelings.** Remember that anger, anxiety, loneliness, and even guilt are normal reactions, and that everyone needs a safe place to express them. Tell your personal story of loss as many times as you need to—this repetition is a helpful and necessary part of the grieving process.

3. **Make a daily structure and stick to it.** Although it is hard to do, keeping to some semblance of structure makes the first few weeks after a loss easier. Getting through each day helps restore the confidence you need to accept the reality of loss.

4. **Don't feel that you have to answer all the questions asked of you.** Although most people try to be kind, they might be unaware of their insensitivity. At some point, you might want to read books about how others have dealt with similar circumstances. They often have helpful suggestions for a person in your situation.

5. **As hard as it is, try to take good care of yourself.** Eat well, talk with friends, get plenty of rest. Be sure to let your primary care clinician know if you are having trouble eating or sleeping. Make use of exercise. It can help you let out pent-up frustrations. If you are losing weight, sleeping excessively or intermittently, or still experiencing deep depression after 3 months, be sure to seek professional assistance.

6. **Expect the unexpected.** You may begin to feel a bit better, only to have a brief "emotional collapse." These are expected reactions. You also might dream, visualize, think about, or search for your loved one. This too is a part of the grief process.

7. **Give yourself time.** Do not feel that you have to resume all of life's duties right away.

8. **Make use of rituals.** Those who take the time to "say good-bye" at a funeral or a viewing tend to find it helps the bereavement process.

Box 18-3   **Patient Guidelines for Coping with Catastrophic Loss—cont'd**

9. **If you do not begin to feel better within a few weeks, at least for a few hours every day, be sure to tell your doctor.** If you have had an emotional problem in the past (e.g., depression, substance abuse), be sure to get the additional support you need. Losing a loved one puts you at higher risk for relapse of these disorders.

From Zerbe, K.J. (1999). *Women's mental health in primary care.* Philadelphia: Saunders, pp. 207-208; reprinted with permission.

# NURSE, PATIENT, and FAMILY RESOURCES

## Books

*For People with a Terminally Ill Family Member*
Callahan, M. & Kelley, P. (1997). *Final gifts: Understanding the special awareness, needs and communication of the dying.* New York: Poseidon.

*For Survivors of Suicide*
Chance, S. (1992). *Stronger Than Death.* New York: WW Norton.

*For Widows*
Brothers, J. (1990). *Widowhood.* New York: Ballantine.
Caine, L. (1988). *Being a widow.* New York: Penguin.

*For Bereaved Parents*
Rosof, B.D. (1994). *The worst loss: How families heal from the death of a child.* New York: Henry Holt.

*For Children*
Lionni, L. (1995). *Little blue and little yellow.* New York: Mulberry.

*About Death*
O'Gorman, S. (1998). Death and dying in contemporary society: An evaluation of current attitudes and rituals

associated with death and dying and their relevance to recent understandings of health and healing. *Journal of Advanced Nursing*, 27, 1127–1135.

# EDUCATIONAL RESOURCES

*About Dying*
**National Hospice Foundation**
1700 Diagonal Road, Suite 625
Alexandria, VA 22314
(800) 646-6460
www.hospiceinfo.org

# INTERNET SITES

**American Academy of Hospice and Palliative Medicine**
www.aahpm.org

**Approaching Death: Improving Care at the End of Life**
http://nap.edu/book/html/approaching (Online publication)

**Hospice Foundation of America**
www.hospicefoundation.org

**National Institute on Aging**
www.nia.nih.gov

# PART IV

# CHALLENGING BEHAVIORS

# CHAPTER 19

# Manipulative Behaviors

## OVERVIEW

Healthy manipulation is essentially purposeful behavior directed at getting needs met. It (1) is goal oriented and used only when appropriate, (2) considers others' needs, and (3) is only one of several coping mechanisms used.

Individuals manipulate events every day to manage their lives (e.g., carry out financial obligations, optimize social activities, ensure the welfare of their families) and to keep their lives and the lives of those they care about as secure and stable as possible. Most nurses are good at organizing their daily schedules to provide the optimum care to their patients. This includes consults with other health care professionals, changing time schedules, organizing care into priorities, and countless other ways to ensure quality care. These are all healthy uses of manipulation. Nurses manipulate situations and events not just to complete their assignment but to best serve their patients.

**Manipulation is maladaptive** when (Chitty & Maynard, 1986):

- It is the primary method used for getting needs met.
- The needs, goals, and feelings of others are disregarded.
- Others are treated as objects to fulfill the needs of the manipulator.

Manipulation is, in effect, a matter of gaining a sense of control. When manipulation is used in a maladaptive manner, individuals say or do almost anything to get what they want, even if it is at the expense of others.

Maladaptive manipulation in the health care system presents a real challenge to staff. The staff is most effective when all are working together on intervention for manipulation. One situation in which staff members should be alert to possible manipulation is when each staff member views and experiences the patient in extremely different ways. This inevitably results in staff confusion and disagreements. Infighting can result when discussing caring for the patient. Variations in experiences can occur between nurses and physicians, between shifts, between individuals on the nursing staff, and/or between administrators and staff.

Potential for staff manipulation is particularly high among individuals who:

- Have personality disorders (PDs) (especially borderline and antisocial PDs)
- Have a chemical dependence
- Are in the manic phase of bipolar disorder
- Have long histories of physical complaints without physical cause
- Are children or adolescents who have the diagnosis of conduct disorder

People who manipulate might be trying to gain a variety of different things, although a need for control is usually the underlying force. For example, people might manipulate to get nurturance, power over a situation or person, possessions, or some other material gratification.

Patients manipulate by the use of pitting one person or group against another person or group:

*"Nurse X really understands my situation, so she lets me take my own medications. Why can't you? Please don't tell anyone I told on Nurse X. I don't want her to get into trouble."*

Or, when talking to a member of the day staff, a manipulative patient might say something like:

*"The night staff is awful. They just sit around and drink coffee, yell at the patients when they ring their bells, and really say some nasty stuff about you day people."*

Once staff is all stirred up and angry with each other, the patient is better able to get what he or she wants without interference. *Staff splitting* is a real challenge in the health care setting. Patients also manipulate when they flatter and behave in such a way as to give the impression of sincerity, caring, and appreciation when their only goal is to get their needs met in any manner possible:

*"You are the kindest nurse on the unit and the only one here who cares enough to understand me. You know how much I need to go out on pass, even if I did come in late yesterday. I know I'm not supposed to, but please trust me just this once. I promise I will be on time."*

Patients with *chemical dependence* problems are used to soothing anxiety and denying or postponing unattractive realities through use of their substance. Patients learn to manipulate others through anger, threatening, swindling, cajoling, instilling guilt, flattering, or any other method to get their drugs. For most people dependent on a drug, the drug is the only thing in the world they care about.

Another form of manipulation is seen in patients who are profane, fault finding, and adept at exploring others' vulnerabilities. They constantly push limits. Their manipulative behaviors often alienate family, friends, employers, health care providers, and others.

# ASSESSMENT

## Assessing History

A positive history might include some of the following:
- History of a personality disorder (PD) (borderline, antisocial, passive-aggressive)
- History of mania
- History of substance use or dependence
- History of unreliable or immature behaviors marked by instability, frequent changes in jobs, relationships, and physicians
- Long history of unsubstantiated physical complaints

## Presenting Signs and Symptoms

- Manipulation of staff, family, and others
- Playing one person against another (nurse against nurse, family member against staff, therapist against family member)
- Attempts to get special treatment or privileges
- Attention-seeking behaviors
- Use of somatic complaints to get out of doing things
- Lacks insight
- Denies problems

- Focuses on other people's problems (patients, staff, unit dynamics)
- Uses intimidation to control or feel superior
- Demanding (the more staff try to cater to patient's demands, the more they escalate)
- Frustration causes more intense manipulative behavior
- Lies, cheats, steals
- Exploitive with little concern for others
- Quick to recognize vulnerability in others
- Devalues others to feel good about self
- Resists limits set on negative behaviors

## Assessment Guidelines

### Manipulation

1. Assess for history of physical or psychosocial problems.
2. Identify patient's usual coping responses.
3. Assess medications patient is taking.
4. Assess for a history of substance use or dependence, spouse abuse, legal difficulties, violent behavior.
5. Assess patient's strengths as well as weaknesses.
6. Who does the patient trust?
7. What does he do when he does not get his own way?
8. Is the patient at risk for suicide? Homicide?
9. Is the patient abusing others? Child? Spouse? Elder? Other?

# NURSING DIAGNOSES WITH INTERVENTIONS

## Discussion of Potential Nursing Diagnoses

Patients who employ manipulation as a primary means of getting their needs met often have no motivation to change as long as they can get what they want when they want it, even if it is at the expense of others. **Impaired Social Interaction** is usually present because the individual's actions often impact negatively on others. People who employ maladaptive manipulation in their relationships with others usually present with a history of interpersonal difficulties and unstable relationships. The manipulative individual feels no compunction about lying, stealing, cheating, threatening, tormenting, devaluing, demeaning, or swindling to get what he or she wants.

Staff working with manipulative patients are best prepared when they establish firm rules that are rigidly interpreted and consistently enforced among all members of the health care team. Frequent discussions regarding the patient's progress can help reduce staff frustration and isolation and minimize the patient's attempts at staff splitting. Smith (1994) identifies important guidelines when intervening with manipulative behaviors:

- Ignoring manipulative behaviors will not make them go away; they get worse when ignored.
- Interventions such as employing limit-setting techniques help reduce stress and hostility for both patient and staff.
- To successfully limit problem behavior, limits must be consistent and reinforced by everyone, including all health care personnel as well as family.

Therefore, **confronting** unacceptable, inappropriate, or harmful behavior needs to be done immediately, and **setting limits** on patient behaviors is the pivotal intervention when working with manipulative patients. Clear, enforceable consequences of continuing unacceptable behaviors need to be spelled out and consistently and matter-of-factly enforced by all staff involved in the patient's care.

Schultz and Videbeck (2005) point out that it is not the nurse's purpose to be a friend to the patient, nor the patient a friend to the nurse. The most effective approach with the patient is to maintain a professional therapeutic relationship with clear boundaries. A professional relationship is based on the patient's therapeutic needs, not on being liked or the nurse's personal feelings. People who manipulate others need clear and firm boundaries with clear and firm consequences identified for overstepping those boundaries.

Manipulative patients often have great difficulty with impulse control, become inappropriately angry, might become a risk to others, and are aggressive with little or no provocation when they cannot get their own way. Therefore, anger management is often useful and important for nurses to learn and employ. Refer to Chapter 17.

## Overall Guidelines for Nursing Interventions

### Manipulation

1. Anger is a natural response to being manipulated. Deal with your own feelings of anger toward the patient. Peer supervision can be useful.
2. Assess your feelings toward patients who use manipulation, and work on being assertive in stating limits. Workshops in assertiveness can be very helpful for nurses.
3. State limits and the behavior you expect from the patient in a matter-of-fact, nonthreatening tone.
4. Be sure the limits are:
   - Appropriate, not punitive
   - Enforceable
   - Stated in a nonpersonal way (e.g., "Alcohol is not allowed," *not* "I don't want you to drink alcohol on the unit.")
5. State the consequences if behaviors are not forthcoming. Written limits and consequences can be useful (one copy for patient and one for staff).
6. Be sure all staff members understand the expectations, limits, and consequences discussed with the patient to provide consistency. A written copy should be in Kardex or patient folder.
7. Follow through with the consequences.
8. Enforce all unit, hospital, group, or community center policies. State reasons for not bending the rules.
9. Be direct and assertive, if necessary, in a neutral, factual manner, not in anger.
10. Do *not:*
    - Discuss yourself or other staff members with the patient
    - Promise to keep a secret for the patient
    - Accept gifts from the patient
    - Attempt to be liked, "the favorite," or popular with the patient
11. Withdraw your attention when patient's behavior is inappropriate.
12. Give attention and support when the patient's behavior is appropriate and positive.
13. Emphasize the patient's feelings, not his or her rationalizations or intellectualizations.
14. Encourage the expression of feelings.

15. Set limits on frequency and time of interactions with the patient, especially those that involve therapists who are significant to the patient.
16. Encourage identification of feelings or situations that trigger manipulative behaviors.
17. Role-play situations so that the patient can practice more direct and appropriate ways of relating.
18. Provide positive feedback when the patient interacts without use of manipulation.
19. Where appropriate, see that patients and families have names and numbers of appropriate community resources (e.g., Alanon, Alcoholics Anonymous, Parents Anonymous, Tough Love).
20. Keep detailed records in patient's chart as to patient's responses to limit setting and any increase or decrease in undesirable, unacceptable, maladaptive manipulative behavior. Identify what seems to work and what does not seem to work. Share information with all staff members.

## Selected Nursing Diagnoses and Nursing Care Plans

### IMPAIRED SOCIAL INTERACTION

Insufficient or excessive quantity or ineffective quality of social exchange

### Some Related Factors (Related To)

- Longstanding patterns of maladaptive behaviors
- Biochemical/neurological imbalances
- Impulsive and chronic need for immediate gratification without regard to consequences of others
- Inability or unwillingness to respect the rights and wishes of others

▲ NANDA International accepted; ● In addition to NANDA International

## Defining Characteristics (As Evidenced By)
- ▲ Use of unsuccessful social interactions
- ▲ Dysfunctional interaction with others (peers, family, and others)
- ● Use of forms of coping that impede adaptive behavior
- ● Destructive behavior toward self or others
- ● Inability to meet role expectations
- ● Inability to take responsibility for own actions
- ● Lack of remorse when actions hurt or hinder others

## Outcome Criteria
- ● Increase in assertive ways to get needs met
- ● Decrease in manipulative behaviors to get needs met
- ● Demonstrates responsible behaviors when dealing with others

## Long-Term Goals
Patient will:
- ● Respond in a positive manner to confrontation and limit setting by (date)
- ● Learn and master at least three skills that facilitate adaptive behaviors (particularly anger management) by (date)
- ● Demonstrate an increase in responsible behavior in dealing with others, as witnessed by staff and stated by others (patients, family, acquaintances)
- ● Use acceptable methods of getting needs met
- ● Participate in ongoing management of anger, impulsivity, control issues, and the like
- ● Demonstrate a decrease in manipulative, attention-seeking, or passive-aggressive behaviors as reported by staff, family, and peers within 6 months

## Short-Term Goals
Patients will:
- ● Participate in treatment program, activities, responsibilities, and the like within 1 to 3 days
- ● State understanding of the unit (community center/ rehabilitation program, etc.) rules and the consequences of breaking them by first day

---

▲ NANDA International accepted; ● In addition to NANDA International

- Sign and discuss the content of a contract defining staff and patient expectations by first day
- Participate in articulating a contract to modify specific inappropriate and unacceptable behaviors that spells out the consequences of continuing behaviors by first or second day (a copy goes to the patient and the Kardex/community center/rehabilitation counselor, etc.)
- Target two inappropriate behaviors to work on learning alternative ways of behaving within 2 to 3 days
- Role-play with nurse new skills in dealing with targeted behaviors (ongoing)

## *Interventions and Rationales*

| Intervention | Rationale |
|---|---|
| 1. Assess your own reactions toward patient. If you feel angry, discuss with peers ways to reframe your thinking to defray feelings of anger. | 1. Anger is a natural response to being manipulated. It is also a block to effective nurse-patient interaction. |
| 2. Assess patient's interactions for a short period before labeling them manipulative. | 2. A patient might respond to one particular high-stress situation with maladaptive behaviors but use appropriate behaviors in other situations. |
| 3. Approach patient in a calm, neutral manner when confronting patient with unacceptable behavior. Focus on the behavior, not the patient (e.g., "Drinking alcohol is not allowed here," *not* "I don't want you to drink alcohol on this unit."). | 3. Focusing on behavior (drinking) is less accusing than personalizing the behavior (your drinking). |
| 4. State clearly the limits and behavior the staff expects of patient. | 4. Patient needs to be aware of specific expectations and boundaries. |
| 5. Limits are: <br> a. Appropriate, not punitive. <br> b. Enforceable. | 5. Clear, enforceable limits give patient specific boundaries of expected behaviors. |

| Intervention | Rationale |
|---|---|
| c. Stated in a nonpunitive manner. | |
| d. Written with consequences of nonadherence clearly stated. Make one copy for patient and one copy for patient's record (e.g., Kardex). | |
| 6. Meet with patient to formulate a written contract detailing specific undesirable behaviors that are to be changed, alternatives to those behaviors, and specific consequences of nonadherence. | 6. Encouraging patient to participate in contract drafting might encourage adherence. |
| 7. Both nurse and patient sign the contract; one copy goes to patient and another copy goes to nurse (Kardex). | 7. Validates that the contract is a serious document and will be a guideline for all staff and a reminder for the patient. |
| 8. Communicate frequently to all staff about specific limits and consequences set for patient. Post copy on Kardex. | 8. Limits and consequences have to be adhered to by all of the staff to be effective means for modifying behavior. |
| 9. Follow through with consequences in a nonpunitive manner (e.g., "The unit rules we went over together when you arrived, Mr. Miller, clearly stated that patients were not to have alcohol on the unit, or their weekend passes were to be cancelled. Because you brought alcohol to the unit, your weekend pass is cancelled."). | 9. Patients begin to understand that they will be taking responsibility for their behavior. In this example, the patient chose to drink on the unit, but by doing so, he has also chosen to forgo his weekend pass. |

| Intervention | Rationale |
|---|---|
| 10. Discuss with patient his or her thoughts and feelings immediately before the undesirable behavior. | 10. Identifies specific thoughts and feelings that can be discussed and dealt with in alternative ways. |
| 11. Discuss with patient alternative behaviors he or she could use to effectively deal with these kinds of thoughts, feelings, or situations in the future. | 11. Patient might not be aware of what he/she is feeling (anger, anxiety, and sadness) or the thinking that triggers specific maladaptive behaviors. |
| 12. Teach or refer patient to an appropriate place to learn needed coping skill (e.g., anger management, assertiveness training). | 12. If patient is *not to do* a specific maladaptive behavior, he/she needs to learn *what to do* to deal with intense thoughts/feelings and impulsive behaviors. |
| 13. Role-play situations so that patient can practice the use of new behaviors. | 13. Gives patient chances to practice more direct and appropriate ways of relating and getting needs met. |
| 14. Be vigilant. Avoid:<br>a. Discussing yourself or other staff members with patient<br>b. Promising to keep a secret for the patient<br>c. Accepting gifts from the patient<br>d. Doing special favors for the patient | 14. Patient can use this kind of information to manipulate you and/or split staff. Decline all invitations in a firm but matter-of-fact manner; for example:<br>a. "I cannot keep secrets from other staff. If you tell me something, I may have to share it."<br>b. "If you want to know about Ms. Williams, you will have to ask her."<br>c. "I am here to focus on you." |

| Intervention | Rationale |
|---|---|
| | d. "You are to return to the unit by 4 PM on Sunday, period." |
| 15. Meet frequently with staff to discuss patient's care plan and progress. Revise care plan as a team. | 15. Helps ensure consistency of enforcing limits and minimizes staff splitting. |
| 16. Give patient attention and support when behavior is appropriate and positive. | 16. Reinforces appropriate behaviors. |
| 17. Withdraw attention when patient's behavior is inappropriate (unless there is a need to enforce consequences). | 17. Patient learns that inappropriate behavior will not be rewarded with the attention he or she might be seeking. |
| 18. Maintain a neutral manner at all times. Avoid power struggles or trying to outmanipulate patient. | 18. You cannot win a power struggle or outmanipulate a manipulative patient. In any case, this is not a game. |
| 19. Provide positive feedback when patient interacts without use of manipulation. | 19. Encourages and reinforces appropriate behaviors. |
| 20. Keep detailed and accurate notes on: a. Patient's behaviors b. Frequency of behaviors c. Limits set d. Consequences enforced | 20. Helps staff identify what is working and not working. Can minimize manipulation of staff. |
| 21. Include family in patient education. | 21. The same skills used when working with the patient might be useful for the family. |

# NURSE, PATIENT, and FAMILY RESOURCES

## JOURNAL ARTICLES

Bowers, L. (2003). Manipulation: Description, identification, and ambiguity. *Journal of Psychiatric Mental Health Nursing, 10*(3), 23–28.

## INTERNET ARTICLES

Trimble, T. Recognizing manipulative behaviors by patients.
*Emergency Nursing World*
http://ENW.org/BSQ.htm

### Managing Challenging Behaviors
www.rnceus.com/hiv/challenging.htm
This 4-page article, although targeted to a patient with HIV, is relevant for working with a patient with manipulative behaviors in the hospital and offers clear-cut useful strategies. It can be especially helpful for caregivers.

### Tools for Handling Control Issues: Eliminating Manipulation
www.coping.org/control/manipul.htm
This 8-page article defines manipulation and its negative effects and offers ways to help eliminate manipulation in relationships and life. Included is a "Manipulative Behavior Inventory."

# CHAPTER 20

# Nonadherence (Noncompliance) to Medication or Treatment

## OVERVIEW

When patients do not follow medication and treatment plans, they are often labeled as "noncompliant." Applied to patients, the term *noncompliant* often brings with it negative connotations, because *compliance* traditionally referred to the extent a patient obediently and faithfully followed health care providers' instructions. "That patient is noncompliant" often translates into he or she is "bad" or "lazy," subjecting the patient to blame and criticism. The situation often results in a power struggle between the health care worker and patient that can leave both frustrated and angry. The term *noncompliant* is invariably judgmental of people.

*Adherence* implies a more active, voluntary, and collaborative involvement of the patient in a mutually acceptable course of behavior. Rather than seeing the health care worker's role as trying to "get a noncompliant patient to comply," we should emphasize the importance of negotiation and accommodation within the patient's current understanding of the importance of the medical/mental health regimen and social situation (ability to pay, support from family, supportive others, etc.)—in other words, what is making adherence difficult (Lerner, 1997). Therefore, the term *nonadherence* will be used here.

Nonadherence to medications and treatment alone is not the problem. Nonadherence is usually a *symptom* of more complex, underlying problems. Although inadequate patient education is a common reason for nonadherence to a medical regimen, it is certainly not the only reason.

Many complex issues can complicate a person's willingness to follow a path leading to increased health or health maintenance. These issues, once addressed, can increase a person's adherence to their health care regimen. Table 20-1 presents some factors that will need to be uncovered and dealt with before medical adherence can be a reality.

Table 20-1 **Selected Factors That Contribute to Nonadherence**

| Factor | Suggested Interventions |
|---|---|
| Use of power struggles to gain a sense of control | Devise ways to give patient more control over regimen by giving alternate, effective treatment options. |
| Reluctance to give up a behavior that is a usual coping mechanism (e.g., smoking, diet, drugs/alcohol) | Teach patient alternative coping strategies (relaxation, exercise, creative pursuits), and role-play ceasing the one and employing another. |
| Secondary gains from the "sick" role | Teach family and staff to give positive reinforcement for healthy behavior and use of healthy coping skills, and to draw away from giving attention to problem behavior. |
| Self-destructive behavior (e.g., suicide, anorexia, bulimia, drugs) | Perform good nursing assessment and work or refer patient to competent specially trained clinician. |
| Negative family influence related to denial, lack of understanding, or need for patient to maintain sick role | Family teaching and possibly family therapy to clarify issues, identify long-range consequences of nonadherence, and involve them in treatment plan. |
| Lack of economic resources (e.g., cannot afford medications or time off to keep appointments) | Refer to social services; identify community resources that might be helpful. |

*Continued*

Table 20-1 **Selected Factors That Contribute to Nonadherence—cont'd**

| Factor | Suggested Interventions |
| --- | --- |
| Lack of transportation | Refer to social services. |
| Unsatisfactory relationships with health care personnel | Work to establish a partnership with patient, showing concern and interest; avoid power struggles. |
| Cultural and/or religious beliefs | Identify specific concerns. Emphasize what can happen when regimen is not followed. Attempt to engage patient, family/friends in finding alternative solutions. |
| Language problems, inability to read or understand instructions | Obtain an interpreter, and involve other members of the family who have more facility with English. Have written instructions in patient's primary language. |
| Uncomfortable side effects | Encourage patient and family to share untoward reactions to drug so that adjustments can be made before patient stops taking medication or treatment. |
| Lack of skills to adhere to treatment regimen | Assess and identify needed skills. Some of these skills include decision-making skills, relaxation skills, assertiveness training skills, relapse prevention techniques. |
| Conflict with self-image, especially children and adolescents (e.g., taking medication or imposing limits on activity) | Refer and encourage patient to join a group with others grappling with similar issues. |
| Confusion about: Taking the medication When to take it Whether medication has already been taken | Set up a concrete system for taking medications (e.g., cross-off chart, pillbox with separate compartments). Try to enlist help from family or others if available. |

Data from Gorman, L.M., Sultan D.F., & Raines, M.L. (1996). *Davis's manual of psychosocial nursing for general patient care.* Philadelphia: FA Davis, pp. 243–245; and Schultz, J.M., & Videbeck, S.D. (2005). *Lippincott's manual of psychiatric nursing care plans.* 7th ed. Philadelphia: JB Lippincott.

# ASSESSMENT

## Assessing History

A positive history of nonadherence to medical regime includes:

- History of not keeping appointments
- History of not taking medications
- Escalation of signs and symptoms despite the availability of appropriate medication
- History of emergency visits that are effectively treated with prescribed medication or treatment
- Religious or cultural beliefs that contradict medical/mental health care regimen
- Poor outcome from past medical/mental health treatments
- History of poor relationships with past health care providers
- History of leaving the hospital against medical advice (AMA)

## Presenting Signs and Symptoms

- Objective tests (e.g., blood and urine) inconsistent with reported medication intake (e.g., low lithium levels, low neuroleptic blood levels, high sugar levels)
- Family members or friends state that patient is not adhering to prescribed regimen
- Progression of disease/behaviors despite appropriate medication/treatment ordered
- Fails to follow through with referrals
- Fails to keep appointments
- Denies the need for medication or treatment

## Assessment Guidelines

### Nonadherence

1. Identify any ethnic and/or cultural beliefs that might conflict with the patient adhering to medical management.
2. Does taking medication pose a financial problem?

3. Evaluate age-related issues interfering with adherence to medication/treatment protocols (see Table 20-1).
4. Assess presence of side effects of medications/treatments and how they affect patient's lifestyle. What would he/she like to change?
5. Does patient believe that the medications/treatments are really necessary?
6. Are the directions for taking medications in patient's own language?
7. What does patient identify as being the most difficult aspect of following through with medication/treatment regimen?

# NURSING DIAGNOSES WITH INTERVENTIONS

## Discussion of Potential Nursing Diagnoses

Nonadherence to medications or treatment can be voluntary or a result of a variety of factors that make adherence difficult. The nursing diagnosis of **Noncompliance** coincides with the *active decision of an individual or family to fully or partially fail to adhere to an agreed-on medication/treatment regimen*. In contrast, we should emphasize the importance of negotiation and accommodation within the patient's life situation. As mentioned, the term *nonadherence* frames the behavior more as a problem to be solved and not so much as willful, negative behavior. **Ineffective Therapeutic Regimen Management** refers to the *difficulty or inability to regulate or integrate a medication/treatment plan into daily life*.

The position taken in this chapter is that **Nonadherence** is used to identify *noncompliance* to a medical/psychiatric treatment regimen, the "why's" yet to be determined, and **Ineffective Family Therapeutic Regimen Management** refers to those situations in which the patient *might be willing to comply but is having difficulty* integrating the therapeutic regimen into his or her life or lifestyle.

## Overall Guidelines for Nursing Interventions

### Enhancing Adherence

1. Establish an open and honest relationship with the patient. A *partnering* relationship rather than an *authoritative* one can significantly enhance accurate reporting of adherence difficulties.
2. Educate the patient. Provide information on the disorder, the treatment options, medication side effects, and toxic effects, using booklets, handouts, phone numbers, and websites for further information.
3. After teaching, evaluate patient understanding to clarify misunderstandings and reinforce requests.
4. Keep active follow-up appointments; call if appointment is missed. Definite follow-up appointments enhance adherences.
5. Identify issues that might impede adherence to medications, and work out a needed intervention. For example, weight gain is often associated with many psychotropic agents. Dietary teaching is essential because many medications alter metabolism and predispose the patient to obesity, diabetes, and/or heart disease.
6. Provide feedback on progress and acknowledge and reinforce efforts to adhere.
7. Refer patient and family to a variety of outside resources for education, support, and assistance (e.g., pharmacists, health educators, medication groups, and self-help groups) (Kobayashi, Smith, & Norcross, 1998).

## Selected Nursing Diagnoses and Nursing Care Plans

## NONADHERENCE (NONCOMPLIANCE)*

Behavior of person and/or caregiver that fails to coincide with a health-promoting or therapeutic plan discussed with (agreed on) by the person and/or family and/or community

---

* Terms in parentheses are NANDA International accepted.

and health care professional. In the presence of mutually discussed and agreed-on health-promoting, or therapeutic plan, person's or caregiver's behavior is fully or partially non-adherent and may lead to clinically ineffective or partially ineffective outcomes

## Some Related Factors (Related To)

▲ Access to care
▲ Communication skills of providers/teaching skills of provider
▲ Cost
▲ Intensity
▲ Health beliefs, cultural and/or spiritual values
  ○ Personal and developmental abilities
  ○ Knowledge and skill relevant to the regimen behavior
  ○ Motivational forces
▲ Health system
  ○ Satisfaction with care
  ○ Credibility of provider
  ○ Access and convenience of care
  ○ Financial flexibility of plan
  ○ Provider reimbursement of teaching and follow-up
  ○ Provider continuity and regular follow-up
  ○ Individual health coverage
  ○ Motivation of patient
▲ Involvement of members in health plan
▲ Social value regarding plan
▲ Perceived beliefs of significant others

## Related Factors (As Evidenced By)

● Behavior indicative of failure to adhere
● Evidence of development of complications
● Evidence of exacerbation of symptoms
● Failure to keep appointments
● Failure to progress
● Objective tests (blood, urine, physiological markers)

---

▲ NANDA International accepted; ● In addition to NANDA International

## Outcome Criteria

- Uses health services congruent with needs
- Reports following prescribed regimen
- Seeks external reinforcement for performance of health behaviors

## Long-Term Goals

Patient will:
- State correct information about his/her condition, benefits of treatment, risks of treatment, and treatment options each time changes are made to their treatment plan by (date)
- Participate in decision making concerning treatment plan on an ongoing basis
- Demonstrate adherence to the treatment plan by (date)
- Follow behavioral contract in assuming his/her responsibility for self-care on an ongoing basis

## Short-Term Goals

Patient will:
- Discuss the impact of illness on lifestyle (ongoing)
- Discuss fears, concerns, and beliefs that influence nonadherence (ongoing)
- Identify one barrier to adherence (by end of session)
- With family, problem solve ways to minimize or erase barrier (within 1 week)
- With family, discuss with nurse the potential undesirable consequences of nonadherence to therapeutic regimen (within 1 week)
- Negotiate acceptable changes in the treatment plan that he/she is willing to follow (ongoing)
- Participate in one decision regarding his/her treatment plan (by end of first session)
- Sign a behavioral contract defining his/her mutual participation and responsibility for care (at end of session and review/update frequently)

## Interventions and Rationales

| Intervention | Rationale |
|---|---|
| 1. Explore with patient his or her feelings about the illness/disorder and the need for ongoing treatments (medications). | 1. Setting up a rapport with a patient who believes you are interested in them encourages understanding of patient's perspective. |
| 2. Use therapeutic nursing techniques to encourage patient to share feelings in an atmosphere of acceptance. | 2. When a patient feels understood, he/she is less likely to feel defensive and more likely to be open to suggestions and information regarding optimizing his/her health. |
| 3. Identify communication barriers that might impede patient's (family's) comprehension. Identify need for:<br>a. Interpreters<br>b. Use of nontechnical language<br>c. Need for written material<br>d. Understanding religious barriers<br>e. Ascertaining attitudes toward the health care system | 3. When we make assumptions according to what we teach patients, and not what they might or might not understand, the potential for miscommunication is enhanced. |
| 4. Assess patient's (family's) understanding about the illness/disorder, treatment options, how medications work, and side and toxic effects. | 4. Patient (family) misperceptions about disease/disorder or treatments result in faulty decision making. |

| Intervention | Rationale |
|---|---|
| 5. Assess how the patient's disease/disorder and subsequent treatments/medications impact the patient's (and the family's) lifestyle. | 5. Age, religion, cultural beliefs, and expectations of others all impact on our value system and factor into how we make decisions. |
| 6. Ask patient to share his/her rationale for nonadherence to medical/psychosocial regimen. | 6. Identifies areas of misunderstanding. |
| 7. Do not argue with patient about the value of his or her beliefs; rather, point out the negative outcomes these beliefs might cause. | 7. Arguing or getting into power struggles with patients makes them defensive and not open to alternative actions. |
| 8. Engage family, friends, caregivers to explain negative actions of nonadherence to treatment regimen. | 8. Those whom patient trusts, and who are from similar background, culture, and the like, might inspire trust and open the way for negotiation. |
| 9. Encourage patient to participate in the decision-making process regarding his or her plan of care. | 9. Can give patient a sense of control and the opportunity to choose those interventions he/she might decide to try. |
| 10. Give the patient a range of assignments from which to choose. | 10. Giving patient choices in making a decision increases patient involvement in treatment planning. |
| 11. Negotiate with patient one or two areas he or she will comply with, if patient refuses the whole treatment plan outright. | 11. Patient may "try" one or two items from the treatment regimen to comply with at first. Hopefully this can form a base for further adherence. |

| **Intervention** | **Rationale** |
|---|---|
| 12. Negotiate a behavioral contract with patient, and review it periodically. Give a written copy to patient, and file one in patient's chart. | 12. Contracts have been found to enhance adherence in both adults and children (Kobayashi, Smith, & Norcross, 1998). |
| 13. Reduce the complexity of the treatment plan (prioritize, facilitate schedules, fit to patient lifestyle). | 13. The more complicated a treatment plan, the more likely patients are to be nonadherent. |
| 14. When appropriate, encourage support groups. | 14. While giving support, groups also share information and encourage healthy choices. |
| 15. Determine whether a different medication or type of therapy might be acceptable to the patient. | 15. Patient might engage in treatment if alternative but equally effective treatment options are available. |
| 16. Recognize that it might not be possible to alter strong cultural or religious beliefs. | 16. Ultimately, the final choice rests with the patient. Our job is to provide information and effective treatment options that best suit the patient's lifestyle. |

**Medication Nonadherence**

| | |
|---|---|
| 1. Assess whether the patient believes he/she needs the medication. Identify need for teaching. | 1. If patient denies need for medication, motivation for adherence is lacking. |
| 2. Use a variety of teaching strategies for patient and family members (e.g., pamphlets, videos, role-playing, group teaching with others in similar circumstances, support groups). | 2. Knowledge and understanding can increase adherence to treatment regimen. |
| 3. If patient stops taking medication when he/she "feels better," more | 3. People need to know that in most instances, medications cannot cure |

| **Intervention** | **Rationale** |
|---|---|
| patient teaching is needed. | them but can help stabilize their symptoms with time. |
| 4. Encourage reporting side effects (e.g., "Do these medications affect your ability to function sexually? They affect many people that way."). | 4. Physician can lower dose or give patient an alternative medication when side effects are affecting adherence. |
| 5. Encourage patient to report any disturbing side effects right away, rather than stopping medication. | 5. Some side effects can be minimized through simple actions. |

## INEFFECTIVE FAMILY THERAPEUTIC REGIMEN MANAGEMENT

Pattern of regulating and integrating into daily living a program for treatment of illness and the sequelae of illness that is unsatisfactory for meeting specific health goals

### Some Related Factors (Related To)

▲ Complexity of healthcare system
▲ Complexity of therapeutic regimen
▲ Economic difficulties
▲ Family conflict
● Excessive demands

### Defining Characteristics (As Evidenced By)

▲ Failure to take action to reduce risk factors
▲ Lack of attention to illness
▲ Verbalized difficulty with prescribed regimen(s)
▲ Acceleration of illness symptoms
▲ Verbalized no action was taken to include treatment regimens in daily routines

---

▲ NANDA International accepted; ● In addition to NANDA International

## Outcome Criteria

- Describes diminished barriers to following through with health care regimen (e.g., financial, transportation, family/friends, knowledge and understanding)
- Perceived support of health care workers
- Demonstrates adherence to treatment regimen

## Long-Term Goals

Patient will:

- Verbalize acceptance and adherence to the treatment plan by (date)
- Keep follow-up appointments by (date)
- Demonstrate skills or knowledge needed for adherence by (date)
- Establish a network of referrals to call on if and when difficulties with carrying out treatment regimen arise
- Participate in adjunctive services when appropriate

## Short-Term Goals

Patient will:

- Establish a supportive, therapeutic partnership with health care workers
- Identify obstacles that interfere with carrying out treatment plan
- Identify resources needed to ensure adherence
- Negotiate acceptable changes in the treatment plan that he or she is willing to follow

## Interventions and Rationales

| Intervention | Rationale |
|---|---|
| 1. Establish an open and supportive partnership with patient. | 1. Adherence is positively correlated with patient's perception of health care personnel's caring and interest (DiMatteo & DiNicola, 1982). |
| 2. Identify areas in the treatment regimen that interfere with adherence: a. Economic b. Transportation | 2. Targets areas for interventions. |

| Intervention | Rationale |
|---|---|
| c. Knowledge barrier<br>d. Language barrier<br>e. Lack of or negative family involvement<br>f. Lack of appropriate skills | |
| 3. Involve adjunctive services when appropriate—for example:<br>a. Social services for financial or transportation problems<br>b. Interpreters if language difficulties<br>c. Family teaching and/or alternative teaching strategies if knowledge deficit<br>d. Skills training | 3. Nonadherence is often a symptom of an underlying problem. That problem must be identified. |
| 4. Teach needed skills (e.g., problem-solving skills, assertiveness skills, relaxation skills, decision-making skills). | 4. Skills training can help foster adherence to health care regimen. |
| 5. Keep the treatment plan as clear and simple as possible. | 5. The easier the regimen is to follow, the greater the likelihood of adherence. |
| 6. Evaluate patient comprehension by having patient repeat or demonstrate what is to be done. | 6. Clarifies misunderstandings and reinforces learning. |
| 7. Use behavioral reminders for follow-up:<br>a. Calendars<br>b. Linking appointments | 7. Behavioral reminders have proved successful for long-term adherence (Kobayashi, Smith, & Norcross, 1998). |

| Intervention | Rationale |
|---|---|
| c. Written reminders on refrigerators | |
| d. Sending reminder on postcards | |
| 8. Facilitate short-term goal-setting with patient (explicitly defined, achievable goals). | 8. Patients who use short-term goals rather than long-term goals are most successful at maintenance (Meichenbaum & Turk, 1987). |
| 9. Provide feedback on patient's progress, and develop positive reinforcers for self-regulation. | 9. Encouragement and recognition by clinician as to progress of goals can act as a motivator for positive change. |
| 10. Tailor treatment plan to be congruent with patient's social, cultural, and environmental milieus. | 10. Optimizes patient feeling comfortable with adhering to medications/treatments. |
| 11. Teach relapse prevention skills. | 11. Helps patients learn behavioral cues to potential relapse and how to cope with relapse. |
| 12. Repeat everything. | 12. Information that is repeated is more likely to be retained than information that is not repeated. |

## Nurse, Patient, and Family Resources

### JOURNAL ARTICLES

Centorrino, F., Hernan, M., Drago-Ferrante, G., et al. (2001). Factors associated with noncompliance with psychiatric outpatient visits. *Psychiatric Services*, 52:378–380.

Kemppainen, J.K., Buffum, M., Wike, G. et al. (2003). Psychiatric nursing and medication adherence. *Journal of Psychosocial Nursing and Mental Health Services*, 41(2), 38–49.

# PART V

# PSYCHOPHARMACOLOGY

# CHAPTER 21

# Major Psychotropic Interventions and Patient and Family Teaching

## OVERVIEW

Although the origins of a psychiatric illness are influenced by a number of factors (genetic, neurodevelopment, psychosocial experience, infections, drugs), there will eventually be an alteration in cerebral function that accounts for disturbances in the patient's behavior and mental experience (Varchol and Raynor, 2009). These physiological alterations are the targets of the psychotropic drugs, and reversal of these alterations are the goal of treatment (Varchol and Raynor, 2009).

Ideally, clinicians want a drug that will relieve the mental disturbance of patients, without resulting in either mental or physical adverse effects. Unfortunately, as with all medications, the effectiveness of a specific psychotropic drug might be accompanied by certain adverse or toxic effects. Therefore, it is important for nurses to understand which drugs help target specific mental symptoms, the potential adverse and toxic effects, and of course how to counsel patients and their families about:

- What potential adverse reactions might occur
- Recognizing potential toxic effects and when to notify the health care provider

- Situations in which these drugs are contraindicated or should be used with great caution
- Any dietary or medication restrictions associated with a specific drug
- How and when to take the medication to optimize the action of the drug and minimize the side/toxic effects

Some important guidelines listed in Box 21-1 might enhance patients' medication adherence.

---

### Box 21-1 **Nursing Guidelines for Medication Management**

1. **Patients should be active partners** in managing their symptoms with psychopharmacological agents. Nurses who listen carefully in taking a medication history and educating individuals in how to be proactive in this process might be more successful with patient adherence.
2. **Side effects can cause nonadherence.** Identify with your patients what problems they are having with the medication, and make adjustments. Without examining these issues, the assumption might be made that the drug is not working, not that the patient is not taking the drug because of troublesome side effects.
3. **Psychosocial rehabilitation** can optimize the outcomes of psychopharmacology.
4. **Sleep hygiene** can enhance psychopharmacological treatment (e.g., avoid napping; avoid stimulants such as exercise, television, computer, and alcohol at bedtime).
5. **Evidence-based guidelines** should be used when available.
6. **Individual responses** to medications should be monitored closely in those not responding well to treatment.
7. **Liability** might be an issue for the advanced practice nurse if the diagnosis is incorrect and if the patient is treated from the incorrect medication group.
8. **Full remission** might be expected with medications for anxiety or mood, but outcomes are not as good for psychotic disorders or dementia.

In this chapter, the major classes of psychotropic drugs are reviewed. Within each class of drugs, the neurotransmitters targeted are identified. The neurotransmitter's increase or decrease is responsible for the alleviation of symptoms; however, that same alteration of a specific neurotransmitter can also affect other systems and result in adverse effects. These adverse effects will be identified as well. To encourage patient adherence to medication treatment and protect the patient's safety, patient and family teaching is vital. To aid in patient and family teaching, specific guidelines are provided for each of the major classes of psychotropic medications.

# ANTIANXIETY/ANXIOLYTIC MEDICATIONS

This section introduces:
- Benzodiazepines
- Non-benzodiazepines—azapirones (buspirone)

## Benzodiazepines

### Therapeutic Uses

The benzodiazepines (BZs) have three main indications for use: (1) anxiety, (2) insomnia, and (3) seizure disorders. BZs are also used for alcohol withdrawal.

All BZs share the same pharmacological properties and produce a similar spectrum of responses. However, they differ significantly from one another with respect to time, course, or appropriate use. The downside of the BZs is that they are associated with impaired psychomotor function, cause depression in some individuals, and lead to tolerance and dependence in some individuals. For these reasons, they should only be used on a **short-term** basis. In the treatment of anxiety disorders, high-potency benzodiazepines should be considered only if the adverse effects of all other alternatives are unacceptable to the patient, or if the patient is unwilling or unable to wait out the 4- to 6-week delay in response associated with most antidepressants (selective serotonin reuptake inhibitors [SSRIs] or buspirone. Benzodiazepines are used for:

- Anxiety disorders:
  - o Panic disorder (PD): alprazolam (Xanax), clonazepam (Klonopin), and lorazepam (Ativan) have the most specific antipanic effect.
  - o General anxiety disorder (GAD). The benzodiazepines may be used in severe cases of GAD, but the development of tolerance and dependence is more recently an issue, especially if used with alcohol or by those with a family history of alcohol abuse. See Chapter 5 for psychopharmacology for GAD.
  - o Acute anxiety: for short-term use. Best when used in conjunction with crisis intervention or other psychological interventions.
- Treatment of acute mania: clonazepam (Klonopin) and lorazepam (Ativan)
- As a short-term hypnotic: useful when used short-term to help induce sleep (e.g., temazepam [Restoril], estazolam [ProSom], quazepam [Dural], zolpidem [Ambien], and zaleplon [Sonata])
- Muscle spasms: relaxes muscles (Valium)
- Seizure disorders: anticonvulsant properties help suppress seizure activity (intravenous Valium, Ativan, and Klonopin)
- Treatment of sedative withdrawal syndromes (particularly alcohol withdrawal): long-acting BZs such as diazepam (Valium) or chlordiazepoxide (Librium)
- Preoperative anesthesia (midazolam)

## Mechanism of Action

Benzodiazepines potentiate and intensify the actions of gamma-aminobutyric acid (GABA). GABA is an inhibitory neurotransmitter found throughout the central nervous system (CNS). GABA plays a role in inhibition by reducing aggression, excitation, and anxiety. GABA has anticonvulsant and muscle-relaxing properties and might play a role in pain perception. The BZs work by binding to specific receptors in a supramolecular structure known as the *GABA receptor–chloride channel complex*, thereby intensifying the effects of GABA in the CNS (Lehne, 2007).

## Clinical Dosage

For the usual daily doses for selected BZs and other anxiolytic agents, see Table 5-2 (Anxiety and Anxiety Disorders).

## Metabolism

Benzodiazepines are metabolized by the liver. Oxidation can be impaired through hepatic cirrhosis, old age, or other drugs (cimetidine, estrogens, or isoniazid).

Benzodiazepines can be classified as long-acting or short-acting. The faster acting BZs are more likely to be abused. The **long-acting BZs** (e.g., Librium, clorazepate [Tranxene], Valium, prazepam [Centrex]) have active metabolites with elimination half-lives of approximately 4 days. The longer half-lives can build up the amount of benzodiazepine in the system, which is not desirable, but the long-acting BZs can be discontinued suddenly without serious withdrawal symptoms. The **short-acting BZs** (Xanax, Ativan, oxazepam [Serax]), which are quickly eliminated, have the potential for serious withdrawal reactions.

## Adverse Effects

### Central Nervous System

Benzodiazepines *depress neuronal function* at multiple sites in the CNS and reduce anxiety through the effects on the limbic system. They promote sleep through *effects on cortical areas*, and on the sleep/wakefulness clock. Muscle relaxation is induced through effects on *supraspinal motor areas*, including the cerebellum. Two important side effects, confusion and anterograde amnesia, result from *effects on the hippocampus and cerebral cortex*.

Central nervous system side effects produce:
- Psychomotor impairment and drowsiness
  - ○ Muscle weakness, ataxia, vertigo, confusion, sleepiness
  - ○ Older patients are especially susceptible to psychomotor impairment and falls.
- Cognitive impairment. BZs impair memory
  - ○ Acute anterograde amnesia
  - ○ Impaired long-term memory from interference with memory consolidation, especially with the elderly
- Sedative effects. When taken alone within the proper dose range, the BZs are relatively safe. However, the BZs augment the sedative side effects of other sedatives, such as narcotics, barbiturates, and alcohol. When BZs are taken in combination with other CNS depressants, the combination can lead to respiratory depression, coma, and death.

### Respiratory System

The BZs are weak respiratory muscle depressants and are usually safe when taken orally and without other CNS depression. Respiratory depression is most marked in people with $CO_2$ retention, so people with pulmonary disease should have blood gases taken to test their $P_{CO_2}$ before a BZ is ordered. Respiratory depression is more apt to occur with IV administration of a BZ and, as mentioned earlier, in conjunction with other CNS depressants.

### Cardiovascular Effects

When taken orally, there is no effect on the heart or blood vessels. However, when taken intravenously, the BZs might produce profound hypotension and cardiac arrest.

### Potential for Abuse

Although it is rare that the average person with brief exposure to the drug becomes an abuser, the BZs are potentially drugs of abuse. Addiction-prone individuals are more likely to become physically dependent. BZs should be prescribed for short-term use and be prescribed with caution.

### Overdose

Death from BZs alone is rare, but as previously emphasized, in combination with other CNS depressants, death from overdose can occur. **Flumazenil (Mazicon), a benzodiazepine receptor antagonist**, can reverse excessive sedation and psychomotor impairment.

### Discontinuing Benzodiazepines

The long-acting BZs will often self-taper; the short-acting BZs (e.g., Xanax) should be tapered over several weeks or months. Slowly tapering the BZ helps prevent withdrawal symptoms (e.g., anxiety, insomnia, headache, muscle irritability, blurred vision, dizziness, delirium, paranoia, psychosis). This is especially true if the patient has been taking high doses over a long period of time.

### Pregnancy

The use of BZs is thought to cause a risk of congenital malformations in the fetus. Such risks include cleft lip, inguinal hernia, cardiac anomalies, and CNS depression. Benzodiazepines enter breast milk, so these drugs should be avoided by nursing mothers.

## Drug Interactions

### Drugs That Increase Benzodiazepine Levels

- Fluoxetine (Prozac)
- Cimetidine (Tagamet)
- Low-dose estrogens
- Disulfiram (Antabuse)
- Isoniazid (INH)

### Drugs Whose Levels Might Be Increased by Benzodiazepines

- Phenytoin (Dilantin)
- Warfarin (Coumadin)
- Digoxin (Lanoxin)

### Drugs That Might Impair Benzodiazepine Absorption

- Antacids
- Anticholinergics

### Drugs That Potentiate Central Nervous System Depressant Properties

- Alcohol and other CNS depressants
- Kava Kava

## Use with Caution

- Elderly should be started with lower doses: **"start low, go slow"**; assess potential for falls and confusion/ memory loss
- Patients with pulmonary disease should be medically evaluated (e.g., $P_{CO_2}$ level)
- Used with caution in patients with hepatic or renal disease
- Assess patient safety in depressed or suicidal patients
- Evaluate for drug interactions

## Contraindications

- Driving or around machinery
- Pregnant and nursing women
- History of substance abuse
- Women of childbearing age if they become pregnant
- Narrow-angle glaucoma
- Concurrent alcohol or other CNS depressants

## Patient and Family Teaching

See Box 21-2 for medication teaching guidelines for patients with anxiety disorders.

---

### Box 21-2 **Patient and Family Teaching: Anxiety Disorders**

1. Caution the patient:
   - Not to increase the dose or frequency of administration without previous approval of therapist.
   - That these medications reduce ability to handle mechanical equipment (e.g., cars, saws, and machinery).
   - Not to drink alcoholic beverages or taking other antianxiety drugs, because depressant effects of both would be potentiated.
   - To avoid drinking beverages containing caffeine, because they decrease the desired effects of the drug.
2. Recommend that the patient avoid becoming pregnant, because taking benzodiazepines increases the risk of congenital anomalies.
3. Advise the patient not to breastfeed, because the drug is excreted in the milk and will have adverse effects on the infant.
4. Teach the patient that:
   - Stoppage of the benzodiazepines after 3 to 4 months of daily use can cause withdrawal symptoms (e.g., insomnia, irritability, nervousness, tremors, convulsions, confusion).
   - Medications should be taken with, or shortly after, meals or snacks to reduce gastrointestinal discomfort.
   - Drug interaction can occur: Antacids delay absorption; cimetidine interferes with metabolism of benzodiazepines, causing increased sedation; central nervous system depressants (e.g., alcohol, barbiturates) cause increased sedation; serum phenytoin concentration can build up because of decreased metabolism.
5. Lower doses should be considered for elderly patients.

---

Adapted from Varcarolis, E. and Halter, M. (2009). *Essentials of Psychiatric nursing.* St. Louis: Saunders, p. 148.

# Non-Benzodiazepine Antianxiety Agents: Azapirones (Buspirone [BuSpar])

## Therapeutic Uses

The azapirone group is represented by buspirone (BuSpar). Buspirone differs from other anxiolytics in that it does not cause sedation, has no abuse potential, does not enhance CNS depression, and does not significantly interact with other drugs (except monoamine oxidase inhibitors [MAOIs] and haloperidol). For these reasons, buspirone is particularly useful in treating anxiety or mixed anxiety/depression. Its major disadvantage is that its anxiolytic effects can take several weeks to become effective. Therefore, it cannot be used as an as needed (PRN) medication.

- Anxiety
  - General anxiety disorder (GAD)
  - General anxiety with accompanying depressive symptoms
- Other uses (Goldberg, 2007)
  - Augments response to antidepressants
  - Augments response to drugs that treat obsessive compulsive disorder (OCD)
  - Might reduce the frequency and severity of episodic aggression in some populations with brain damage (developmentally disabled and demented)

## Mechanism of Action

The mechanism for action has not yet been determined. Buspirone does *not* seem to bind to receptors for GABA, as do the benzodiazepines, but seems to show a high affinity for serotonin receptors (5-HT) in the CNS and a low affinity for dopamine ($D_2$ receptors).

## Clinical Dosage

The dosage range for anxiety is between 20 and 40 mg/day, starting at 5 to 10 mg three times daily. Antidepressant effects are usually seen at 40 to 80 mg/day, starting at 10 mg three times daily.

## Metabolism

Buspirone undergoes extensive hepatic metabolism. Its metabolites are excreted primarily in the urine and to a lesser extent in the feces. The elimination half-life of buspirone might be prolonged in persons with renal impairment and cirrhosis. These patients might require lower doses.

## Adverse Effects

Buspirone is well tolerated. The most common reactions (5% to 10% incidence) are as follows:

**Central Nervous System**
Reactions include dizziness, drowsiness, headache, lightheadedness, and excitability.

**Gastrointestinal**
Reactions include nausea and, to a lesser extent, dry mouth, diarrhea, constipation, and vomiting.

**Other Systems**
Buspirone has little if any effect on respiratory system, platelet, smooth muscle, or autonomic nervous system functions.

NOTE: As previously stated, buspirone does *not* seem to instigate a physical or psychological dependency. No withdrawal symptoms seem to occur when the drug is discontinued, nor is there a cross-tolerance or cross-dependency with other sedative-hypnotics.

## Drug Interactions

- Do not take with MAOIs
- Might increase haloperidol levels

## Use with Caution

- Patients who are pregnant or breastfeeding
- Patients who are elderly or debilitated
- Patients who have hepatic or renal dysfunction

## Contraindications

- Main contraindication: patients with a history of hypersensitivity to buspirone
- Patients taking MAOIs or haloperidol

## Patient and Family Teaching

Because of the lag time of several weeks, patients need to be supported through the first few weeks. They need to be told to continue taking the drug, although they are not experiencing any changes as yet.

# ANTIDEPRESSANT MEDICATIONS

Currently there is no conclusive evidence to demonstrate the clinical superiority of one group of antidepressants. One exception is the use of an MAOI for atypical depression. The choice of medication is usually based on the side-effect profile and ease of administration. For example, if a patient is suffering from insomnia, a more sedative antidepressant might be ordered. Conversely, if the patient is sleeping and lethargic, a more energizing antidepressant would be suitable. It might, however, take trial and error to find a drug that will suit a particular patient. There are other considerations as well:

- The SSRIs and other newer-generation antidepressants are usually better tolerated than the tricyclic antidepressants (TCAs) and are safer in overdose.
- **Safety for the use in depressed individuals under 18 years of age is presently heatedly debated, especially children.** The FDA has issued a supplementary warning to follow all individuals closely who are on antidepressants.
- When cost is a consideration, the generic products are less expensive.
- Past experience with a drug or the response of a first-degree relative can be a predictor of an effective medication regimen.
- Most antidepressants are effective in the depressive phase of bipolar disorder; however, use caution because they all carry a risk for inducing mania.
- If a single antidepressant action on serotonin (5-HT) or norepinephrine (NE) receptors is ineffective, a synergistic effect can occur when two independent antidepressant drugs are combined. Therefore, two antidepressants may be prescribed to target specific symptoms.
- Antidepressant medications can take from 1 to 3 weeks or longer before symptoms are relieved.

Table 21-1 **Special Problems and Medications of Choice**

| Problem | Drugs of Choice |
|---|---|
| 1. High suicide risk | 1. Avoid tricyclics and MAOIs |
| 2. Concurrent depression and panic attacks or OCD | 2. Venlafaxine, SSRIs |
| 3. Chronic pain with or without depression | 3. Amitriptyline, doxepin, venlafaxine, duloxetine |
| 4. Weight gain on other antidepressants | 4. Bupropion, SSRIs, avoid mirtazapine |
| 5. Sensitivity to anticholinergic side effects | 5. Avoid tricyclics and paroxetine |
| 6. Orthostatic hypotension | 6. Nortriptyline, bupropion, sertraline |
| 7. Sexual dysfunction | 7. Bupropion, nefazodone |

*MAOI,* Monoamine oxidase inhibitor; *SSRI,* selective serotonin reuptake inhibitor; *TCA,* tricyclic antidepressant.
NOTE: Most antidepressants are quite toxic when taken in an overdose. Extreme caution should be taken in prescribing to high-risk suicidal patients.
From Preston, J., & Johnson, J. (2009). *Clinical psychopharmacology made ridiculously simple* (6th ed.). Miami: MedMaster, Inc.

- Suicide is always a consideration when treating depression. Some patients might be given a limited supply initially to minimize taking an overdose. A precaution in hospitals is to make sure that the medication is taken and not "cheeked."

An overall guide to an effective choice of antidepressants in patients with special needs is presented in Table 21-1.

- First-line agents
  - SSRIs
  - Novel (atypical) new antidepressants
  - TCAs
- Second-line agents
  - MAOIs

# FIRST-LINE AGENTS

## Selective Serotonin Reuptake Inhibitors

SSRIs are as effective as the TCAs but do not have the troubling side effects of TCAs (e.g., hypotension, sedation, anticholinergic effects). Overdose does not cause cardiotoxicity.

The SSRIs are specific for **serotonin (5-HT) reuptake blockage.** The SSRIs currently carry an FDA supplemental warning for individuals under 18 years of age.

## Therapeutic Uses

- **Major depression:** All, except for fluvoxamine (Luvox)
- **Obsessive compulsive disorder (OCD):** fluoxetine (Prozac), sertraline (Zoloft), fluvoxamine (Luvox), paroxetine (Paxil)
- **Bulimia nervosa:** fluoxetine (Prozac)
- **Panic disorder:** sertraline (Zoloft), paroxetine (Paxil), fluoxetine (Prozac), citalopram (Celexa)
- **Social anxiety disorder:** paroxetine (Paxil)
- **Premenstrual syndrome:** fluoxetine (Prozac)

## Unlabeled Uses

- Fluoxetine (Prozac): alcoholism, attention deficit/hyperactivity disorder, bipolar disorder, migraine, Tourette's syndrome, and obesity

## Mechanism of Action

As mentioned, the SSRIs specifically block the reuptake of 5-HT into the presynaptic cell from which it was originally released. Because these drugs are specific to serotonin and have little or no ability to block muscarinic and other receptors, they tend to have fewer untoward autonomic effects than the TCAs. They also do not cause as much sedation or have cardiac toxicity.

## Metabolism

The primary pathway is hepatic metabolism. Impaired hepatic function is associated with impaired metabolism of the SSRIs. There is also metabolic impairment with renal dysfunction. For this reason, a dosage adjustment is made for the elderly and those with hepatic impairment.

## Adverse Effects

### Central Nervous System
Common potential side effects include agitation, anxiety, sleep disturbance, tremor, sexual dysfunction (anorgasmia), and headache.

## Autonomic Nervous System Reactions

Common potential side effects are dry mouth, sweating, weight change, mild nausea, and loose bowel movements.

## Withdrawal Syndrome

Abrupt discontinuation of the SSRIs can cause a withdrawal syndrome. Symptoms begin within days to weeks of discontinuing the medication. Therefore, tapering off is necessary. Withdrawal symptoms include dizziness, headache, nausea, sensory disturbances, tremors, anxiety, and dysphoria.

## Central Serotonin Syndrome

Central serotonin syndrome is a rare and life-threatening event related to overactivation of the central serotonin receptors. This can occur when MAOIs or other drugs that increase the levels of serotonin in the brain are taken concurrently or within 2 weeks of each other. Symptoms include abdominal pain, diarrhea, fever, tachycardia, elevated blood pressure, delirium, myoclonus, increased motor activity, irritability, hostility, and mood change. Severe manifestations can induce hyperpyrexia, cardiovascular shock, and death. For an overview of the adverse and toxic effects of the SSRIs, see Table 21-2.

Table 21-2 **Adverse and Toxic Effects of Selective Serotonin Reuptake Inhibitors**

| Adverse Effects | Comments |
| --- | --- |
| 1. Rash or allergic reaction | 1. Discontinue drug; ask your health care provider about treatment with antihistamines or steroids. |
| 2. Anxiety, nervousness, insomnia | 2. Discontinue the drug. Taking the drug in AM might help decrease insomnia. |
| 3. Anorexia, weight loss, nausea | 3. Particularly common in underweight, depressed patients. If significant weight loss occurs, ask your health care provider about changing to a different drug. |
| 4. Tremors, sweating, dizziness, lightheadedness | 4. Most of the effects listed in 4, 5, and 6 are transient and disappear when drug is discontinued. |

Table 21-2   **Adverse and Toxic Effects of Selective Serotonin Reuptake Inhibitors—cont'd**

| Adverse Effects | Comments |
|---|---|
| 5. Drowsiness and fatigue | 5. SSRIs can affect cognitive and motor ability. |
| 6. Decreased or altered libido/erectile dysfunction | 6. If change in libido or ability to perform becomes a problem, ask your health care provider about changing the drug. |
| 7. Weight gain | 7. Weight gain is a reason for nonadherence to medication in most women and some men. **Dietary teaching is essential when medications alter metabolism and predispose to obesity, diabetes, and/or heart disease.** |
| 8. Nonadherence to drug | 8. Approximately 33% of patients experience sexual dysfunction. |

**Serotonergic Syndrome: Toxic Effects**
1. Hyperactivity/restlessness
2. Tachycardia→cardiovascular shock
3. Fever→hyperpyrexia
4. Elevated blood pressure
5. Confusion→delirium
6. Irrationality, mood swings, hostility
7. Generalized seizures
8. Myoclonus, incoordination, tonic rigidity
9. Abdominal pain, diarrhea, bloating
10. Apnea→death

NOTE: Do not administer SSRIs to patients who are taking MAOIs. The drug interaction can result in serious or fatal reactions.

## Drug Interactions

- MAOIs: SSRIs should **not** be combined with the MAOIs; can produce serotonin syndrome
- Alcohol: CNS depressants antagonize CNS depressant effect
- Oral anticoagulants: can displace highly protein-bound medications from protein-binding sites (e.g., warfarin [Coumadin])

- St. John's wort, which may have harmful additive effects
- TCAs
- Lithium

## Use with Caution

- Patients with impaired renal or hepatic function
- Pregnant women: safety in pregnancy has not been established; unknown whether SSRIs cross the placenta or are distributed in breast milk
- Elderly: often best to start at a lower dose in patients who are elderly
- Patients who are underweight or anorectic
- Patients who have abused drugs or are dependent on drugs
- Patients who are suicidal

## Contraindications

- Do not use within 14 days of MAOI ingestion.
- Do not use in patients who are hypersensitive to the SSRIs.
- Do not use with **St. John's wort** (may be dangerous).

## Patient and Family Teaching

For useful guidelines for family and patient teaching, refer to Box 21-3.

# Novel (Atypical) New-Generation Antidepressants

There are many drugs that have proved to have antidepressant qualities. The drugs and brief side-effect profiles are found in Table 21-3.

# Tricyclic Antidepressants

Tricyclic antidepressants have a long history of effectiveness in major depression. Their main drawback is their side-effect profile, which can affect patient adherence. These drugs can be sedating, cause orthostatic hypertension, and have anticholinergic effects (e.g., dry mouth, blurred vision, photophobia, constipation, urinary hesitancy, and tachycardia). The most hazardous effect is cardiac toxicity.

---

Box 21-3 **Patient and Family Teaching: Selective Serotonin Reuptake Inhibitors**

SSRIs can cause sexual dysfunction or lack of sex drive. Inform your health care provider.

SSRIs can cause insomnia, anxiety, and nervousness. Inform your health care provider.

SSRIs can interact with other medications. Be sure physician knows other medications patient is taking (digoxin, warfarin). SSRIs should not be taken within 14 days of the last dose of an MAOI.

Do not take any over-the-counter drugs without first notifying the physician.

Common side effects include fatigue, nausea, diarrhea, dry mouth, dizziness, tremor, fatigue, and sexual dysfunction or lack of sex drive.

Because of the potential for drowsiness and dizziness, patient should not drive or operate machinery until these side effects are ruled out.

Avoid alcohol.

Patient should have liver and renal function tests performed and blood counts checked periodically.

Do not discontinue medication abruptly. If side effects become bothersome, ask your health care provider about changing to a different drug, but be aware that the medication will have to be phased out over a period of time.

Report any of the following symptoms to your health care provider *immediately*:
- Rash or hives
- Rapid heart beat
- Sore throat
- Difficulty urinating
- Fever, malaise
- Anorexia/weight loss
- Unusual bleeding
- Initiation of hyperactive behavior
- Severe headache

---

Therefore, the TCAs might be poorly tolerated by some because of their side effects.

Because the TCAs have a narrow therapeutic index, there is significant risk for toxicity. A 1-week supply can be fatal in an overdose. A blood concentration higher than 1000 mg/dL

Table 21-3 **Newer Atypical Agents: Dosages and Effects**

| Agent (Trade Name) | Usual Dosage (mg/Day) | Advantages | Adverse Effects |
|---|---|---|---|
| **Bupropion** (Wellbutrin) | 50–300 | • Sexual dysfunction rare<br>• No weight gain<br>• Stimulant properties<br>• Antianxiety properties | *Medication-induced seizures if more than 300 mg<br>*High seizure risk in at-risk individuals<br>*Some nausea |
| (Zyban) | | | |
| **Trazodone** (Desyrel) | 150–300<br>150–400 | • No anticholinergic side effects, *low potential for cardiac effects<br>• In conjunction with other anti-depressants, can aid sleep | *Possible priapism†<br>*Postural hypotension<br>*Weight gain<br>*Memory dysfunction |
| **Dual-Action Reuptake Inhibitors—SNRIs (Serotonin and Norepinephrine)** | | | |
| **Venlafaxine** (Effexor) | 75–225 | • Useful for treatment-resistant chronic depression<br>• Low potential for drug interaction | *Risk of sustained hypertension for some people<br>*Possible somnolence, dry mouth, and dizziness<br>• Rapid discontinuation can cause withdrawal symptoms |

| | | |
|---|---|---|
| **Mirtazapine** (Remeron) | 15–45 | • Antidote to SSRI sexual dysfunction<br>• Noninterference with sleep<br>• Low interference with metabolism of other drugs | *Anxiolytic properties<br>*Strong sedating effect<br>*Possible increased appetite, weight gain, and cholesterol elevation |
| **Duloxetine** (Cymbalta) | 20–30 mg bid | • Response to medication within 1 to 4 weeks<br>• Mild side effects | • Nausea<br>• Somnolence<br>• Dry mouth<br>• Constipation<br>• Decreased appetite<br>• Increased sweating<br>• Fatigue<br>• Twice-a-day dosing |

*Anticholinergic side effects include dry mouth, blurred vision, constipation, urinary retention, tachycardia, and possible confusion.
†Priapism is prolonged painful penile erection that may warrant surgery.
§Catalepsy is characterized by a trancelike state of consciousness and a posture in which the limbs hold any position (waxy flexibility). An anticataleptic agent helps minimize or prevent this phenomenon in patients with schizophrenia.

is correlated with severe cardiac symptoms (prolonged QRS complex and arrhythmias).

## Therapeutic Uses

- **Depression:** acute depression, prevention of relapse, and other depressive syndromes (The TCAs were the first group of drugs effective in the treatment of depression.)
- **Panic attacks:** imipramine (Tofranil), clomipramine (Anafranil), desipramine (Norpramin)
- **Childhood enuresis:** imipramine (Tofranil)
- **Bulimia nervosa:** imipramine (Tofranil), desipramine (Norpramin)
- **Obsessive-compulsive disorder:** clomipramine (Anafranil)—only TCA effective for OCD

*Moderate evidence for:*

- **Chronic pain:** Several TCAs are useful in treating chronic pain (e.g., amitriptyline [Elavil], doxepin [Sinequan]).
- **Chronic insomnia:** amitriptyline (Elavil)
- **Attention-deficit/hyperactivity disorder:** desipramine (Norpramin), imipramine (Tofranil) **(used with caution)**
- **Migraine:** amitriptyline (Elavil)

## Mechanism of Action

The TCAs block NE and serotonin reuptake. Although the blockage is immediate, it takes several weeks for relief of symptoms to occur, as it does with all antidepressants. There is speculation that intermediary neurochemical effects are taking place during the lag time (Lehne, 2001). Along with the desired blockage of serotonin, the TCAs also cause blockage of the receptor sites for histamine (H1), acetylcholine (ACh), and NE, which results in some of the negative side effects of these drugs.

## Metabolism

Clearance of tricyclic compounds is principally the result of hepatic metabolism. Renal clearance accounts for only a small portion of drug elimination. Elimination half-life for most of the TCAs is approximately 24 hours. This allows for once-daily dosing.

## Adverse Effects

### Cardiovascular Effects

Orthostatic hypotension is one of the most common reasons for discontinuation of TCA treatment. Orthostatic hypotension can lead to dizziness and increase risk of falls.

The most serious cardiovascular effects, especially in high doses, are **arrhythmias, tachycardia, myocardial infarction**, and **heart block**. Patients without conduction delay tolerate the tricyclics well. These drugs are used with caution and need to be evaluated in the elderly and in people with cardiac problems.

### Autonomic Nervous System

**Anticholinergic Effects** include dry mouth, blurred vision, tachycardia, constipation, urinary retention, and esophageal reflux. Urinary retention and severe constipation warrant immediate medical attention. The TCAs can cause ocular crisis in people with narrow-angle glaucoma.

### Central Nervous System

Tricyclics can produce confusion or delirium. These effects are dose related. Seizures also are possible side effects with all tricyclics and tetracyclic agents. A fine, rapid hand tremor can be a clinical indication of an elevated blood concentration.

### Hepatic Effects

Tricyclics can cause mild increases of liver enzymes and can be monitored safely. However, drug-induced acute hepatitis develops quickly and is associated with very high enzyme levels. This is a dangerous and potentially fatal condition.

### Sexual Dysfunction

A potential problem with many classes of antidepressants

### Allergic Reactions

Tricyclics are sometimes associated with photosensitivity reactions. Rare reports of various blood dyscrasias have also been reported.

### Psychiatric

Confusion states (especially in the elderly) with hallucinations, disorientation, delusions, anxiety, restlessness, agitation, insomnia, and nightmares; hypomania; and exacerbation of psychosis may occur.

**Toxicity**

Overdose with TCAs can be life threatening. To avoid death by suicide, a patient thought to be at risk for suicide should be given no more than a 1-week supply of TCAs.

## Drug Interactions

- MAOIs, in combination with TCAs, lead to severe hypertension, hypertensive crisis, and potential death.
- Sympathomimetic drugs (e.g., epinephrine and norepinephrine) can lead to increased blood pressure and cardiac effects.
- Anticholinergic agents intensify anticholinergic effects of TCAs; for example:
  - Trihexyphenidyl (Artane)
  - Benztropine (Cogentin)
  - Diphenylamine (Benadryl)
  - Oxybutynin (Ditropan)
  - Propantheline (Pro-Banthine)
  - Meperidine (Demerol)
- CNS depressants (e.g., alcohol, antihistamines, opioids, and barbiturates). These can intensify the CNS depressant effects of the TCAs, increase respiratory depression, and decrease TCA effect.
- Phenothiazines might increase sedative and anticholinergic effects.
- St. John's wort might have additive effects.

## Use with Caution

- Patients with:
  - History of urinary retention or obstruction
  - Glaucoma
  - Diabetes mellitus
  - History of seizures
  - Hyperthyroidism
  - Cardiac/hepatic/renal disease
  - Schizophrenia
  - Increased intraocular pressure
  - Hiatal hernia
- Patients who are elderly or debilitated
- Pregnant or lactating women (safety has not been established)

## Contraindications

- TCAs should not be taken during the acute recovery period following a myocardial infarction.
- TCAs should not be taken within 14 days of MAOI ingestion.

## Patient and Family Teaching

See Box 21-4 for a useful tool in medication teaching.

## Second-Line Agents

### Monoamine Oxidase Inhibitors

MAOIs are seldom first choice, but they are appropriate for those who do not respond to the SSRIs, atypical antidepressants, or TCAs. The MAOIs can cause dangerous side effects. However, many believe they are the drug of choice for atypical depression and depression associated with anxiety, panic, and phobias.

### Therapeutic Uses

- Treatment-resistant major depression
- "Atypical" depression (characterized by anxiety, somatization, feeling better in the morning and worse as the day progresses, hyperphagia, weight gain, sensitivity to rejection, trouble falling or staying asleep)
- Treatment-resistant panic disorder
- Treatment-resistant mixed anxiety-depression
- Treatment-resistant depression in people with bipolar disorder
- Dysthymia not responsive to other antidepressants

### Mechanism of Action

The MAOIs inhibit the action of the monoamine oxidase (MAO) enzyme system at the CNS storage sites. There are two types of MAO in the body: MAO-A and MAO-B. In the brain, MAO-A inactivates NE and serotonin, whereas MAO-B inactivates dopamine.

The reduced MAO activity causes an increased concentration in epinephrine, NE, serotonin, and dopamine at neuron receptor sites producing antidepressant effects. These are all welcome effects.

## Box 21-4 Patient and Family Teaching: Tricyclic Antidepressants

1.  Tell the patient and the patient's family that mood elevation can take from 7 to 28 days. It might take up to 6 to 8 weeks for the full effect to take place and for major depression symptoms to subside.
2.  Have the family reinforce this frequently to the depressed family member because depressed people have trouble remembering, and they respond to ongoing reassurance.
3.  Reassure the patient that drowsiness, dizziness, and hypotension usually subside after the first few weeks.
4.  When the patient starts taking tricyclic antidepressants (TCAs), caution the patient to be careful working around machines, driving cars, and crossing streets because of possible altered reflexes, drowsiness, and/or dizziness.
5.  Alcohol can block the effects of antidepressants. Tell the patient to refrain from drinking.
6.  If possible, the patient should take the full dose at bedtime to reduce the experience of side effects during the day.
7.  If the patient forgets the bedtime dose (or the once-a-day dose), the patient should take the dose within 3 hours; otherwise, the patient should wait for the next day. The patient should *not* double the dose.
8.  Suddenly stopping TCAs can cause nausea, altered heartbeat, nightmares, and cold sweats in 2 to 4 days. Patients should call their health care clinician or take one dose of TCA until the clinician can be contacted.
9.  Patient should have written information as to:
    a.  Side effects
    b.  Possible toxic effects
    c.  The telephone numbers of healthcare clinician and staff
10. Make a thorough assessment of how the patient has been doing since the last visit.

Adapted from Varcarolis, E. and Halter, M. (2009). *Essentials of psychiatric mental health nursing*. St. Louis: Saunders, p. 233.

The inhibition of MAO, therefore, can help relieve depression. But the MAOIs also inhibit the breakdown of the amine, tyramine. Increased levels of tyramine can cause high blood pressure, hypertensive crisis, and eventually cerebrovascular accident. Tyramine is found in many foods, so when a person is on an MAOI, vigilance is required to avoid the long list of prohibited foods rich in tyramine. This avoidance extends to drugs as well.

## Metabolism

The MAOIs are absorbed from the gastrointestinal tract and metabolized in the liver. The metabolites are then excreted in the urine.

## Adverse Effects

### Hypertensive Crisis from Dietary Tyramine

Hypertensive crisis is by far the most dreaded side effect of the MAOIs that can occur if a patient eats food that is rich in tyramine (see Table 21-4). MAOIs can also interact with many drugs (see Box 21-6). The increase in blood pressure can develop into intracranial hemorrhage, hyperpyrexia, convulsions, coma, and death.

Early symptoms include headache, stiff neck, palpitations, increase or decrease in heart rate (often associated with chest pain), nausea, vomiting, and increase in temperature. Immediate medical attention is crucial.

### Other Side Effects

- Hypotension (This is the most critical of the side effects because it can lead to falls, especially in the elderly.)
- Sedation, weakness, fatigue
- Insomnia
- Changes in cardiac rhythm
- Muscle cramps
- Anorgasmia or sexual impotence
- Urinary hesitancy or constipation
- Weight gain

## Use with Caution

- Patients with:
  - Impaired renal function
  - History of seizures

## Table 21-4 **Foods That Can Interact with Monoamine Oxidase Inhibitors**

| | Foods That Contain Tyramine | |
|---|---|---|
| Category | Unsafe Foods (High Tyramine Content) | Safe Foods (Little or No Tyramine) |
| Vegetables | Overripe avocados; fermented bean curd; fermented soybean; sauerkraut; Fava beans | Most vegetables |
| Fruits | Figs, especially if overripe; bananas, in large amounts | Most fruits |
| Meats, Fish | Meats that are fermented, smoked, or otherwise aged; e.g. salmon mousse, lumpfish roe, sliced schmaltz herring in oil. Smoked salmon and pickled herring negligible. Sausages, bologna, pepperoni, salami, spam, chicken liver, and beef liver | Meats that are known to be fresh (exercise caution in restaurants; meats might not be fresh) Nonfermented varieties Fish that is known to be fresh; vacuum-packed fish, if eaten promptly or refrigerated only briefly after opening |
| Milk, milk products | Practically all cheeses | Milk, cottage cheese, cream cheese |
| Foods with yeast | Yeast extract (e.g., Brewer's yeast, Marmite, Bovril) | Baked goods that contain yeast |
| Beer, wine | Red wine, sherry, beer, ale, liquers | Small amounts of white wines and liquor |
| Other foods | Protein dietary supplements; soups (might contain protein extract); shrimp paste; soy sauce | |

**Limit amounts of: chocolate, caffeine, yogurt, sour cream, ripe avacados (guacamole)**

Preston 2008 and 2009

○ Parkinson syndrome
○ Diabetes
○ Hyperthyroidism

## Contraindications

- Patients older than 60 years
- Debilitated/hypertensive patients
- Patients with cerebrovascular/cardiovascular disease
- Foods containing tryptophan, tyramine, and dopamine (see Table 21-4)
- Certain medications (see Box 21-6)
- Pheochromocytoma
- Congestive heart failure (CHF)
- History of liver disease
- Abnormal liver function tests
- Severe renal impairment
- History of severe/recurrent headaches
- Children younger than 16 years of age

Refer to Table 6-2 in Chapter 6, Depressive Disorders, for the most frequently used FDA-approved MAOIs.

## Patient and Family Teaching

Box 21-5 can be used as a guideline for patient and family teaching for a patient on an MAOI. Table 21-4 is a list of forbidden foods, and Box 21-6 is a list of drugs a person on MAOIs must be aware of and avoid.

# ANTIPSYCHOTIC MEDICATIONS

This section presents:

1. **The Conventional/Standard Antipsychotic Agents.** Phenothiazines are used as the prototype for these drugs. They are usually less expensive but have more troubling side effects than the newer generations of antipsychotics. They target predominantly the *positive symptoms* of schizophrenia (e.g., hallucinations, delusions, paranoia, abnormal thought formations).
2. **The Atypical (Novel) Antipsychotic Agents.** These newer agents have a better side-effect profile than the conventional agents. Less troubling side effects can help to increase medication adherence. However, these new generation agents are much more expensive than

---

Box 21-5 **Patient and Family Teaching: Monoamine Oxidase Inhibitors**

- Tell the patient and the patient's family to avoid certain foods and all medications (especially cold remedies) unless prescribed by and discussed with the patient's health care provider/prescriber. Give patient and family a written list of "forbidden" foods and drugs. (See Table 21-4 and Box 21-6.)
- Give the patient a wallet card describing the monoamine oxidase inhibitor (MAOI) regimen.
- Instruct the patient to avoid Chinese restaurants (sherry, brewer's yeast, and other products might be used).
- Tell the patient to go to the emergency room right away if he or she develops a severe headache.
- Ideally, blood pressure should be monitored during the first 6 weeks of treatment (for both hypotensive and hypertensive effects).
- Instruct the patient that after stopping the MAOI, the patient should maintain dietary and drug restrictions for 14 days.

---

Adapted from Varcarolis, E. and Halter, M. (2009). *Essentials of psychiatric mental health nursing*. St. Louis: Saunders, p. 238.

---

Box 21-6 **Drugs That Can Interact with Monoamine Oxidase Inhibitors**

Drug restrictions that apply to patients taking a monoamine oxidase inhibitor include:
- Over-the-counter medications for colds, allergies, or congestion (any product containing ephedrine, phenylephrine, hydrochloride, or phenylpropanolamine)
- Tricyclic antidepressants (imipramine, amitriptyline)
- Narcotics
- Antihypertensives (methyldopa, guanethidine, reserpine)
- Amine precursors (levodopa, L-tryptophan)
- Sedatives (alcohol, barbiturates, benzodiazepines)
- General anesthetics
- Stimulants (amphetamines, cocaine)

---

From Varcarolis, E. and Halter, M. (2009). *Essentials of psychiatric mental health nursing*. St. Louis: Saunders, p. 239.

the traditional agents. These newer agents target both the positive and *negative symptoms* (e.g., apathy, lack of motivation, social withdrawal, communication difficulties, and asocial behavior). By reducing the negative symptoms, many people are able to hold jobs, attend school, and interact with others in a positive and rewarding manner.

## Conventional/Standard Antipsychotic Agents

Refer to Table 8-3 in the chapter on schizophrenia for a list of the traditional antipsychotic medications and their dosages. The conventional/standard antipsychotic agents were the first effective drugs to treat schizophrenia. These neuroleptic agents are characterized by a relatively high tendency to produce extrapyramidal side effects (EPS) and anticholinergic side effects. Unfortunately, as mentioned, they have a poor effect on the negative symptoms of schizophrenia (refer to Chapter 8).

### *Therapeutic Uses*
- Schizophrenia
  - Suppression of symptoms during the acute phase of illness (might take up to 4 weeks for full effects)
  - Taken long-term can decrease the risk of relapse
  - Effective in targeting the positive symptoms of schizophrenia (e.g., hallucinations, delusions, disordered thinking, paranoia)
  - Essentially does not target the troubling negative symptoms (e.g., social and emotional withdrawal, avolition [lack of motivation], anergia [lack of energy], blunted affect, poverty of speech)
- Bipolar disorder: during the acutely manic phase
- Depression with psychotic symptoms
- Tourette's syndrome: helps suppress severe symptoms such as severe motor tics, barking cries, grunts, and outbursts of obscene language that are beyond the control of the individual (haloperidol [Haldol], pimozide)
- Prevention of emesis: chlorpromazine (Thorazine)
- Delusional disorder

- Treatment of choreiform movements of Huntington's disease: haloperidol (Haldol)

## Investigational Uses

- Refractory hiccups: chlorpromazine (Thorazine)
- Relief of acute intermittent porphyria: chlorpromazine (Thorazine)
- Nausea/vomiting associated with chemotherapy: haloperidol (Haldol)
- Psychosis associated with Parkinson's disease and other psychiatric symptoms resulting from organic causes.

## Mechanism of Action

The conventional antipsychotic agents block a variety of receptors within and outside the CNS. The beneficial effects seem to be derived from the blockage of dopamine 2 ($D_2$) receptors in the mesolimbic and mesocortical areas of the brain. However, these drugs also block receptors for acetylcholine (ACh), histamine (H1), and norepinephrine (NE). The wide variety of side effects associated with these drugs can be understood as a logical extension of their receptor-blocking activity (Figure 21-1).

## Clinical Dosage

Table 8-3 identifies the various standard/typical medications and the drug dosage. The drugs are listed from high potency to low potency. This is pertinent information because of what it tells us about the degrees of specific side effects; for example:

- Low Potency = High sedation, high ACh, and low EPS
- High Potency = Low sedation, low ACh, and high EPS (e.g., akathisia)

## Metabolism

These agents undergo hepatic metabolism. All elderly patients should be given lower doses because of increased sensitivity to the side effects. Cigarette smoking significantly increases the metabolism of the conventional

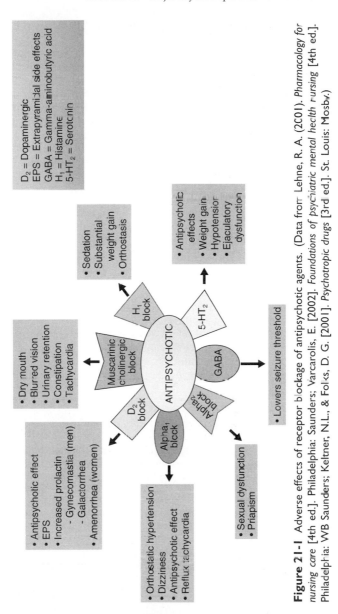

$D_2$ = Dopaminergic
EPS = Extrapyramidal side effects
GABA = Gamma-aminobutyric acid
$H_1$ = Histamine
$5\text{-}HT_2$ = Serotonin

ANTIPSYCHOTIC

**$H_1$ block**
• Sedation
• Substantial weight gain
• Orthostasis

**$5\text{-}HT_2$**
• Antipsychotic effects
• Weight gain
• Hypotension
• Ejaculatory dysfunction

**Muscarinic cholinergic block**
• Dry mouth
• Blurred vision
• Urinary retention
• Constipation
• Tachycardia

**GABA**
• Lowers seizure threshold

**$D_2$ block**
• Antipsychotic effect
• EPS
• Increased prolactin
  - Gynecomastia (men)
  - Galactorrhea
  - Amenorrhea (women)

**Alpha$_2$ block**
• Sexual dysfunction
• Priapism

**Alpha$_1$ block**
• Orthostatic hypertension
• Dizziness
• Antipsychotic effect
• Reflux tachycardia

**Figure 21-1** Adverse effects of receptor blockage of antipsychotic agents. (Data from Lehne, R. A. (2001). *Pharmacology for nursing care* [4th ed.]. Philadelphia: Saunders; Varcarolis, E. [2002]. *Foundations of psychiatric mental health nursing* [4th ed.]. Philadelphia: WB Saunders; Keltner, N.L., & Folks, D. G. [2001]. *Psychotropic drugs* [3rd ed.]. St. Louis: Mosby.)

antipsychotic medications (e.g., thiothixene [Navane], flu-
phenazine [Prolixin].

## Adverse Effects

As previously mentioned, two side effects that contribute
to nonadherence to medication regimens are weight gain
(especially women) and sexual dysfunction (especially
men). Agranulocytosis and neuroleptic malignant syn-
drome (NMS), both relatively rare, are serious and can be
fatal if the patient is not monitored while taking the medi-
cation regimen. Refer to Table 21-5 for more information
on the adverse and toxic reactions and the medical/
nursing interventions.

### Central Nervous System
- Extrapyramidal side effects (EPS): The major neurologi-
  cal side effects involve the extrapyramidal system. They
  occur in 50% to 75% of people taking the standard
  neuroleptics. EPS symptoms include acute dystonia,
  dyskinesia (pseudoparkinsonism), and akathisia.
- Tardive dyskinesia (TD), also an EPS, is a movement dis-
  order that can occur following long-term therapy and is
  often irreversible. See Table 21-5 for the EPS symptoms
  and medical/nursing interventions, as well as other
  untoward effects and nursing interventions for these.
- Lowers the seizure threshold
- Sedation

### Cardiovascular Symptoms
- Hypotension and postural hypotension and tachycardia
  might occur. Refer to Table 21-5.
- Prolongation of $QT_c$ interval is also possible, and pre-
  treatment electrocardiograms should be checked in people
  older than 40 and those with a history of cardiac disease.

### Endocrine Effects
By blocking the inhibitory action of dopamine on prolactin
release, there is an increase in circulating prolactin levels.
This increase can cause breast enlargement (gyneco-
mastia), which can occur in males as well as females,
and irregular menses, including anovulatory cycles and
infertility.

Text continued on p. 603

Table 21-5 **Nursing Measures for Side Effects of Standard/Conventional Antipsychotics**

| Side Effects | Onset | Nursing Measures |
|---|---|---|
| **Anticholinergic Symptoms** | | |
| 1. Dry mouth | | 1. Frequent sips of water and sugarless candy or gum. If severe, provide Xero-Lube, a saliva substitute. |
| 2. Urinary retention and hesitancy | | 2. Check voiding; try warm towel on abdomen; consider catheterization if this does not work. |
| 3. Constipation | | 3. Usually short-term. Stool softeners might be helpful. Assess for adequate water intake. |
| 4. Blurred vision | | 4. Usually abates in 1 to 2 weeks. If patient has been prescribed thioridazine, do not give it, and check with health care provider. |
| 5. Photosensitivity | | 5. Encourage patient to wear sunglasses. |
| 6. Dry eyes | | 6. Use artificial tears. |

*Continued*

**Table 21-5   Nursing Measures for Side Effects of Standard/Conventional Antipsychotics—cont'd**

| Side Effects | Onset | Nursing Measures |
|---|---|---|
| 7. Inhibition of ejaculation or impotence in men | | 7. Alert health care provider that patient might need alternative medication. |
| **Extrapyramidal Side Effects** | | |
| 1. **Pseudoparkinsonism:** Masklike faces, stiff and stooped posture, shuffling gait, drooling, tremor, "pill-rolling" phenomenon | >5–30 days | 1. Alert medical staff. An anticholinergic agent (e.g., trihexyphenidyl [Artane] or benztropine [Cogentin]) might be prescribed. |
| 2. **Acute dystonic reactions:** Acute contractions of tongue, face, neck, and back (tongue and jaw first)<br>• **Opisthotonos:** Titanic heightening of entire body, head and belly up<br>• **Oculogyric crisis:** Eyes locked upward | 1–5 days | 2. **First choice:** Diphenhydramine hydrochloride (Benadryl) 25–50 mg IM/IV. Relief occurs in minutes. **Second choice:** Benztropine, 1–2 mg IM/IV **Prevent further dystonias** with ACh agent. Experience is very frightening. Take person to quiet area and stay with him or her until medicated. |

3. **Akathisia:** Motor inner-driven restlessness (e.g., tapping foot incessantly, rocking forward and backward in chair, shifting weight from side to side)

5–60 days

3. Health care provider may change antipsychotic agent or give antiparkinsonian agent. Tolerance does not develop to akathisia, but akathisia disappears when neuroleptic is discontinued. Propranolol (Inderal), lorazepam (Ativan), or diazepam (Valium) may be used.

4. **Tardive dyskinesia:**
- **Facial:** Protruding and rolling tongue, blowing, smacking, licking, spastic facial distortion, smacking movement
- **Limbs**
- **Choreic:** Rapid, purposeless, and irregular movements
- **Athetoid:** Slow, complex, and serpentine movements.
- **Trunk:** Neck, shoulder, dramatic hip jerks and rocking, twisting pelvic trusts

6–24 mo to years

4. **No known treatment.** Discontinuing the drug does not always relieve symptoms. Possibly 20% of patients taking the drug for >2 years develop tardive dyskinesia. **The health care provider should screen for tardive dyskinesia at least every 3 months.** (Refer to the AIMS Scale in Appendix D-14.)

*Continued*

Table 21-5 **Nursing Measures for Side Effects of Standard/Conventional Antipsychotics—cont'd**

| Side Effects | Onset | Nursing Measures |
|---|---|---|
| **Cardiovascular Effects**<br>1. Hypotension and postural hypotension | | 1. Check blood pressure before giving; advise patient to dangle feet before getting out of bed to prevent dizziness and subsequent falls. A systolic pressure of 80 mm Hg when standing is an indication that the current dose should not be given. This effect usually subsides in 1 to 2 weeks. Elastic bandages might prevent pooling. If condition is serious, the health care provider can order volume expanders or pressure agents |
| 2. Tachycardia | | 2. Patients with existing cardiac problems should *always* be evaluated before the antipsychotic drugs are administered. Haloperidol (Haldol) is usually the preferred drug because of its low ACh effects. |

**Rare and Toxic Effects**

1. **Agranulocytosis:** Symptoms include sore throat, fever, malaise, and mouth sore. It is a rare occurrence, but one the nurse should be aware of; any flulike symptoms should be carefully evaluated.

Usually occurs suddenly and becomes evident in the first 12 weeks

1. Blood work is usually done every week, then every 2 months. Blood work is ordered to determine presence of leukopenia or agranulocytosis If test results are positive, the drug is discontinued, and reverse isolation might be initiated. Mortality is high if the drug is not discontinued and if treatment is not initiated.

2. **Cholestatic jaundice:** Rare, reversible, and usually benign if caught in time; prodromal symptoms are fever, malaise, nausea, and abdominal pain; jaundice appears 1 week later.

2. Drug is discontinued; bed rest and high-protein, high-carbohydrate diet is given. Liver function tests should be performed every 6 months.

*Continued*

**Table 21-5   Nursing Measures for Side Effects of Standard/Conventional Antipsychotics—cont'd**

| Side Effects | Onset | Nursing Measures |
|---|---|---|
| 3. **Neuroleptic malignant syndrome:** Somewhat rare, potentially fatal <ul><li>**Severe extrapyramidal:** Severe muscle rigidity, oculogyric crisis, dysphasia, flexor-extensor posturing, cog wheeling</li><li>**Hyperpyrexia:** Elevated temperature (>103° F)</li><li>**Autonomic dysfunction:** Hypertension, tachycardia, diaphoresis, incontinence</li></ul> | Can occur in the first week of drug therapy but often occurs later; rapidly progresses over 2 to 3 days after initial manifestation <br> RISK FACTORS: <ul><li>Using concomitant psychotropics</li><li>Being older</li><li>Being female (3:2)</li><li>Having a mood disorder (40%)</li><li>Undergoing rapid dose titration</li></ul> | <ul><li>Stop neuroleptic.</li><li>Transfer to medical unit **immediately.**</li><li>**Bromocriptine** can relieve muscle rigidity and reduce fever.</li><li>**Dantrolene** might reduce muscle spasms.</li><li>Cool body to reduce fever.</li><li>Maintain hydration with oral and IV fluids.</li><li>Correct electrolyte imbalance.</li><li>Arrhythmias should be treated.</li><li>Small doses of heparin might decrease possibility of pulmonary emboli.</li><li>**Early detection increases patient's chance of survival.**</li></ul> |

*IM,* Intramuscular; *IV,* intravenous.

## Sexual Dysfunction

Sexual dysfunction manifests as ejaculatory and erectile disturbances in men and anorgasmia and decreased lubrication in women. Both experience decreased libido. These drug-related sexual dysfunctions are often responsible for nonadherence to medications.

## Anticholinergic Effects

Anticholinergic effects are more common with low-potency dopamine receptor antagonists such as chlorpromazine. As previously mentioned, these effects include blurred vision, dry mouth, constipation, and urinary hesitancy, dry eyes, and inhibition of ejaculation or impotence in men (see Table 21-5).

## Skin and Eye Effects

Patients might experience photosensitivity reactions consisting of severe sunburn or rash. It is for this reason that patients should be encouraged to wear sunglasses and use sun block when outside in the sun.

## Adverse Reactions/Toxic Effects

These untoward reactions are serious and can be fatal.
- Agranulocytosis (rare) (see Table 21-5)
- Neuroleptic malignant syndrome (see Table 21-5)

## Drug Interactions

- CNS depressants (alcohol, antihistamines, benzodiazepines, barbiturates): can increase the CNS respiration depression and hypotensive effects
- Antidepressants (TCAs and MAOIs): may increase sedative anticholinergic effects
- Levodopa (a drug used to treat Parkinson's disease) can counteract the antipsychotic effects of the phenothiazines
- Antithyroid agents: may increase risk of agranulocytosis
- Lithium: may decrease absorption and produce adverse neurological effects
- Hypotensives: can increase hypotensive effects of these agents

## Use with Caution

- **Extreme caution in the elderly:** They are extremely susceptible to TD. Always "start low and go slow."
- History of seizures
- Urinary retention
- Glaucoma
- Prostatic hypertrophy
- Hypoglycemia

## Contraindications

- Pregnancy: Gestational weeks 4 to 10 are particularly dangerous. During the remainder of the pregnancy, the lowest possible dosage is desirable. However, it is advised that all antipsychotic medication be discontinued to avoid neonatal toxicity.
- Poorly controlled seizure disorders
- Severe CNS depression, comatose states
- Severe cardiovascular disease
- Bone marrow depression
- Liver, renal, or cardiac insufficiency

## Patient and Family Teaching

Refer to Box 21-7 for guidelines for patient and family teaching with the standard antipsychotic medications. Refer to Table 21-5 for the nursing interventions and teaching points for the various side effects of the standard antipsychotic medications.

## Atypical (Novel) Antipsychotic Agents

These newer atypical agents first emerged in the early 1990s with the advent of clozapine (Clozaril). This was a breakthrough drug in many ways and a miracle drug for some, but unfortunately, this drug causes agranulocytosis in approximately 1% of patients. The atypical agents that eventually followed do not share this same disadvantage. These newer agents not only target the positive symptoms of schizophrenia (hallucinations, delusions) but also allow improvement in the quality of life by mitigating the negative symptoms as well (lack of motivation, poverty of speech, blunted affect, poor self-care, and social

## Box 21-7 **Patient and Family Teaching: Standard Antipsychotics**

1. Full therapeutic response can take at least 6 weeks.
2. Do not abruptly withdraw from long-term therapy. If patient is having sexual difficulty, gaining weight, please contact the physician.
3. Use sun block and wear protective clothing when in the sun. These drugs can potentiate the effects of sunburn.
4. Rise slowly from a sitting or lying position to prevent a sudden drop in blood pressure.
5. Wear sunglasses to minimize the photosensitivity inherent in these medications.
6. Take sips of water and chew sugarless chewing gum. Good oral hygiene can minimize the effects of dry mouth.
7. Do not take alcohol while on these drugs. They potentiate the CNS side effects of each.
8. Smoking might increase the metabolism of some antipsychotics, which might require a dosage adjustment to maintain a therapeutic effect.
9. Do not take any over-the-counter medication without your health care provider's approval.
10. Notify your health care provider if you become pregnant or are planning to become pregnant. These drugs might not be safe during the first trimester.
11. Refer frequently to the written material provided for you by your health care system on the side effects and what might help the side effects of these antipsychotic medications; keep the list in a place where it can be easily referred to.
12. **Report immediately** occurrence of any of the following to your health care provider:
    - Sore throat
    - Fever
    - Malaise
    - Unusual bleeding
    - Difficulty urinating
    - Muscle twitching
    - Severe headache
    - Rapid heart rate
    - Dark-colored urine
    - Pale stools
    - Yellow tinge to skin or eyes

withdrawal). Cognitive enhancement, however, might not be evident for several months.

## Therapeutic Uses

- Schizophrenia
- Management of manifestations of psychotic disorders
- Treatment of acute mania associated with bipolar disorder: olanzapine (Zyprexa)

## Unlabeled Uses

- Anorexia: olanzapine (Zyprexa)
- Maintenance of treatment response in schizophrenic disorders: olanzapine (Zyprexa)
- Treatment of resistant mania and for prophylaxis in bipolar mood disorder: clozapine (Clozaril)

## Overall Benefits

The atypical agents are often chosen as first-line treatment because:
1. They have few or no EPS or tardive dyskinesia side effects.
2. They treat the distressing positive symptoms as well as the disabling negative symptoms of schizophrenia.
3. People on these drugs become more animated and behave in more socially acceptable ways; the rate of rehospitalization is lower for such people than for those on the standard antipsychotic agents.
4. They might improve the neurocognitive defects associated with schizophrenia.
5. Patients who have been refractory with conventional agents frequently respond to these drugs.

## Overall Cautions

Specific cautions for each individual atypical agent are listed in Table 21-6. However, there are universal precautions that need to be applied to all of the atypicals. These newer antipsychotic medications are used with caution in:
1. People who drink alcohol or take other medications
2. Children, the elderly, and pregnant women: The safety of these drugs has not been studied in these groups of people.

Text continued on p. 617

**Table 21-6 Highlights of Atypical/Novel Antipsychotics**

| Drug | Therapeutic Use | Adverse Effects | Toxic Reactions | Contraindication/ Precautions | Nursing Alerts |
|------|-----------------|-----------------|-----------------|-------------------------------|----------------|
| Clozapine (Clozaril) (NOT A FIRST-LINE DRUG) | 1. Refractory schizophrenia<br>2. Has mood stabilizing effects that might be effective in delusional major depression and psychosis associated with Parkinson's | 1. Sedation<br>2. Orthostasis<br>3. Anticholinergic symptoms<br>4. Weight gain<br>5. Dizziness<br>6. Tachycardia<br>7. Hypotension<br>8. Hypersalivation in up to 30% | 1. Agranulocytosis in 0.8% to 1%<br>2. Seizures in 5% | **Do not use:**<br>1. Myeloproliferative disorders<br>2. History of clozapine-induced agranulocytosis<br>3. With drugs having potential to suppress bone marrow function<br>4. Severe CNS depression<br>5. Comatose state<br>6. Breastfeeding<br>**Cautions:**<br>*History of:*<br>1. Seizures<br>2. Cardiovascular disease<br>3. Impaired respiratory function | 1. Requires weekly WBC count<br>2. Expensive because of weekly monitoring at beginning of treatment<br>3. Obtain baseline WBC count before treatment<br>4. Monitor BP for hypertension/ hypotension<br>5. Supervise for suicidal intent<br>6. Weight-gain management |

*Continued*

**Table 21-6 Highlights of Atypical/Novel Antipsychotics—cont'd**

| Drug | Therapeutic Use | Adverse Effects | Toxic Reactions | Contraindication/Precautions | Nursing Alerts |
|---|---|---|---|---|---|
| | | | | 4. Hepatic or renal function<br>5. Alcohol withdrawal<br>6. Urinary retention<br>7. Glaucoma<br>8. Prostatic hypertrophy<br>9. Pregnancy | |
| Risperidone (Risperdal) | 1. Management of symptoms of psychotic disorders | 1. High rate EPS<br>2. Weight gain<br>3. Insomnia<br>4. Sexual dysfunction<br>5. Headache<br>6. Constipation<br>7. Dyspepsia, rhinitis, drowsiness, and dizziness<br>8. Abdominal pain and dry skin<br>9. Tachycardia | **Rare:**<br>1. NMS (see Table 21-4)<br>2. Tardive dyskinesia | **Do not use:**<br>1. Cardiac disease<br>2. Cerebrovascular disease<br>3. Dehydration<br>4. With antihypertensives<br>5. Lactation<br>**Cautions:**<br>1. History of seizures<br>2. Elderly<br>3. Pregnancy | 1. Baseline renal and liver function test first<br>2. Orthostasis often at beginning of treatment; monitor BP<br>3. Caution patient not to drive or use machinery until body adjusts to medication |

| | Uses | Side Effects | Contraindications / Cautions | Nursing Considerations |
|---|---|---|---|---|
| | | 10. Visual disturbances, fever, back pain, and angina<br>11. Agitation<br>12. Anxiety | | 4. Weight-gain management |
| Papiperdone (Invega) | A metabolite of Risperidone and has the same side effects. Is an extended release formula but is better tolerated than Risperidone | | | |
| Olanzapine (Zyprexa) | 1. Psychotic disorders<br>2. Short-term treatment for acute manic states<br>3. Unlabeled uses: Treatment of ulcerative colitis and inflammatory bowel disease | **Frequent:**<br>1. Weight gain<br>2. Somnolence<br>3. Agitation<br>4. Insomnia<br>5. Headache<br>6. Nervousness<br>7. Hostility<br>8. Dizziness<br>9. Rhinitis<br>**Occasional:**<br>1. Anxiety<br>2. Constipation<br>**Rare:**<br>1. Seizures<br>2. NMS<br>3. EPS<br>4. Dysphagia | **No contraindications known at present:**<br>1. Not a first-line treatment for people with increased glucose or people with diabetes; safety in children not established<br>**Cautions:**<br>1. Hepatic or cardiovascular disease | 1. Obtain baseline hepatic function<br>2. Supervise suicidal-risk patients closely<br>3. Tell patient and family to avoid dehydration<br>4. Notify physician if pregnancy occurs or is being planned |

*Continued*

Table 21-6 **Highlights of Atypical/Novel Antipsychotics—cont'd**

| Drug | Therapeutic Use | Adverse Effects | Toxic Reactions | Contraindication/Precautions | Nursing Alerts |
|---|---|---|---|---|---|
| | | 3. Nonaggressive objectionable behavior<br>4. Dry mouth<br>5. Weight gain<br>6. Postural hypotension<br>7. Fever<br>8. Joint pain<br>9. Restlessness<br>10. Cough<br>11. Dimness of vision<br>**Rare:**<br>1. Tachycardia<br>2. Back/chest/abdominal pain<br>3. Tremor<br>4. Extremity pain | | 2. Those who should avoid anticholinergic drugs<br>3. Elderly/debilitated<br>4. Pregnancy<br>5. History of seizures<br>6. Cerebrovascular disease<br>7. Conditions predisposing to hypotension<br>8. Patients at risk for aspiration pneumonia | 5. Avoid driving or tasks that require alertness until response to drug is established<br>6. Dietary teaching is essential with medications that alter metabolism, and predispose to obesity, diabetes, and/or heart disease (personal communication from Dorothy A. Varchol, June 2003) |

| Quetiapine (Seroquel) | 1. Management of manifestations in psychotic disorders | **Frequent:** 1. Headache 2. Sedation/ drowsiness 3. Dizziness 4. Orthostasis **Occasional:** 1. Constipation 2. Postural hypotension 3. Tachycardia 4. Dry mouth 5. Dyspepsia 6. Rash 7. Weakness 8. Abdominal pain 9. Rhinitis **Rare:** 1. Back pain 2. Fever 3. Weight gain | 1. Overdose produces heart block, decreased BP, hypokalemia (weakness), and tachycardia | **No known contraindications:** 1. Not advised for breastfeeding mothers; safety in pregnancy or children not established **Cautions:** 1. Elderly 2. Alzheimer's dementia 3. History of breast cancer 4. Cardiovascular disease 5. Cerebrovascular disease 6. Dehydration 7. History of drug abuse or drug dependencies 8. Hypothyroidism | 1. Obtain baseline (CBC and hepatic function tests before initiation of treatment and periodically 2. Tell patient and family to avoid exposure to extreme heat 3. Take medication as ordered; do not stop or increase dosage 4. Drowsiness generally subsides during continued therapy |

*Continued*

Table 21-6 **Highlights of Atypical/Novel Antipsychotics—cont'd**

| Drug | Therapeutic Use | Adverse Effects | Toxic Reactions | Contraindication/Precautions | Nursing Alerts |
|---|---|---|---|---|---|
| | | | | | 5. Avoid driving or performing tasks that require alertness until response to drug is established<br>6. Avoid alcohol<br>7. Change positions slowly to reduce hypotensive effects |
| Ziprasidone (Geodon) | 1. Treatment of schizophrenia | **Most common:**<br>1. Somnolence<br>2. EPS<br>3. Respiratory disorder | **Cardiac:**<br>1. Prolongation of the $QT_c$ interval; prolonging the $QT_c$ interval can cause cardiac arrhythmias and heart attack, leading to death | **Do not use:**<br>*History of:*<br>1. Irregular heartbeats<br>2. Prolonged $QT_c$ interval (ECG)<br>3. Other heartbeat disturbances | 1. Baseline ECG should be obtained<br>2. Caution your patients to avoid becoming overheated in hot weather and during exercise; |

*Also:*

1. With electrolyte disturbance
2. When other drugs that prolong the $QT_c$ interval are being taken; this is a long list, and these drugs are not to be mixed (e.g., Serentil, Mellaril, Thorazine, Orap, many more); go to *www.health.msn. com* (Drugs and Herbs)

**Cautions:**

1. Elderly
2. Pregnancy
3. Renal problems

ziprasidone might increase risk of heat stroke

**Teach patients:**

1. Do not take over-the-counter drugs/herbs without checking with a health care provider or pharmacist
2. Give patient a list of drugs that can cause heart irregularity so they know what to avoid

*Continued*

Table 21-6 **Highlights of Atypical/Novel Antipsychotics—cont'd**

| Drug | Therapeutic Use | Adverse Effects | Toxic Reactions | Contraindication/ Precautions | Nursing Alerts |
|------|-----------------|-----------------|-----------------|-------------------------------|----------------|
| | | | | | 3. Alert patients to call health care provider immediately if they experience symptoms that might indicate heart rhythm problems such as dizziness, palpitations, or fainting |
| | | | | | 4. Use caution when driving, operating machinery, or performing other hazardous activities; ziprasidone might cause dizziness or drowsiness |

| | | | | |
|---|---|---|---|---|
| | | | | 5. Avoid alcohol or use with caution |
| | | | | 6. Rise slowly to prevent dizziness or falls from dizziness |
| Aripiprazole (Abilify) | 1. Treatment of schizophrenia | **Frequent:**<br>1. Anxiety<br>2. Constipation<br>3. Headache<br>4. Insomnia<br>5. Nausea<br>6. Vomiting | 1. Akathisia<br>2. Fever<br>3. Skin rash<br>4. TD<br>**Rare:**<br>1. Dysphasia<br>2. Heat stroke<br>3. NMS<br>4. Seizures | **Do not use:**<br>1. Breastfeeding<br>**Cautions:**<br>*History of:*<br>1. Heart disease<br>2. Stroke<br>3. Dehydration<br>4. Seizures | 1. Rise slowly to prevent dizziness or falls from dizziness<br>2. Drink plenty of fluids to prevent dehydration |

*Continued*

**Table 21-6 Highlights of Atypical/Novel Antipsychotics—cont'd**

| Drug | Therapeutic Use | Adverse Effects | Toxic Reactions | Contraindication/ Precautions | Nursing Alerts |
|------|-----------------|-----------------|-----------------|-------------------------------|----------------|
| | | **Less frequent:**<br>1. Lightheadedness/ dizziness<br>2. Orthostatic hypotension<br>3. Rhinitis<br>4. Drowsiness<br>5. Tremors<br>**Rare:**<br>1. Blurred vision | | 5. Alzheimer's disease<br>6. Swallowing<br>7. Allergies<br>*Also:*<br>1. Elderly<br>2. Pregnant women | 3. Refrain from driving or using machinery if dizziness or drowsiness occurs |

*BP,* Blood pressure; *CBC,* complete blood count; *CNS,* central nervous system; *ECG,* electrocardiograph; *EPS,* extrapyramidal side effects; *NMS,* neuroleptic malignant syndrome; *TD,* tardive dyskinesia; *WBC,* white blood cell.

3. Lactating women: The newer antipsychotic medications can pass into breast milk and cause problems in a baby, including behavior changes.

### Adverse Effects and Interactions

The following are common adverse effects for the atypical antipsychotic agents. Each drug causes these effects to different degrees. Assess for these in your patients who are taking any of these drugs.

- **Sedation** from blockage of histamine receptors
- **Orthostatic hypotension** from blockage of alpha-adrenergic receptors
- **Weight gain** from blockade of 5HT2 receptors (except ziprasidone and aripiprazole). Weight gain is a major factor in nonadherence and predisposes to obesity, diabetes, and/or heart disease
- Dry mouth, blurred vision, urinary retention, constipation, and tachycardia from blockage of cholinergic receptors
- Medication interactions: Check with the health care provider as to safety with concurrent medications (e.g., with aripiprazole [Abilify]); can have serious interactions with alpha blockers, antihypertensives, diuretics, quinidine, fluoxetine, paroxetine, carbamazepine, antifungals, and more

Because all of the newer novel antipsychotics share different individual properties, they are briefly addressed in Table 21-6. For the usual dosage and highlighted properties of each, please refer to Table 8-3 in the chapter on schizophrenia.

# ANTIMANIC AND MOOD-STABILIZING MEDICATIONS

This section discusses (1) lithium and (2) alternative antimanic and mood-stabilizing agents.

**Lithium** has traditionally been the drug of choice for controlling manic episodes in people with bipolar disorder, and for prophylaxis against recurrent mania and depression. Lithium helps prolong the time before a manic, hypomanic, or mixed episode. Because lithium has such a narrow therapeutic index, lithium serum levels should be monitored regularly, and the patient and family should be aware of the early signs and symptoms of lithium toxicity (Table 21-7).

Lithium is not effective in 30% to 50% of people with bipolar disease, bipolar II, or dysphoric mania, it is less effective in bipolar subtypes (e.g., rapid cycling).

Table 21-7 **Side Effects of Lithium and Signs of Toxicity**

| Level | Sign* | Interventions |
|---|---|---|
| Expected side effects | Fine hand tremors, polyuria, and mild thirst | Symptoms might persist throughout therapy. |
| 0.4–1 mEq/L (therapeutic levels) | Mild nausea and general discomfort | Symptoms often subside during treatment. |
| | Weight gain | Weight gain might be helped with diet, exercise, and nutritional management. |
| Early signs of toxicity <1.5 mEq/L | Nausea, vomiting, diarrhea, thirst, polyuria slurred speech, muscle weakness | Medication should be withheld, blood lithium levels drawn, and the dose reevaluated. |
| Advanced signs of toxicity 1.5–2.0 mEq/L | Coarse hand tremor, persistent gastrointestinal upset, mental confusion, muscle hyperirritability, electroencephalographic changes, incoordination | Use interventions outlined earlier or later, depending on severity of circumstances. |
| Severe toxicity 2.0–2.5 mEq/L | Ataxia, serious electroencephalographic changes, blurred vision, clonic movements, large output of dilute urine, seizures, stupor, severe hypotension, coma. Death is usually | There is no known antidote for lithium poisoning. The drug is stopped and excretion is hastened. Gastric lavage |

Table 21-7   **Side Effects of Lithium and Signs of Toxicity—cont'd**

| Level | Sign* | Interventions |
|-------|-------|---------------|
|  | secondary to pulmonary complications | and treatment with urea, mannitol, and aminophylline all hasten lithium excretion. |
| >2.5 mEq/L | Confusion, incontinence of urine or feces, coma, cardiac arrhythmia, peripheral circulatory collapse, abdominal pain, proteinuria, oliguria, and death | Hemodialysis might also be used in severe cases. |

*Careful monitoring is needed because the toxic levels of lithium are close to the therapeutic levels.

Three anticonvulsants have been found effective in patients who do not respond to lithium or could not tolerate the side effects. These are carbamazepine (Tegretol), divalproex (Depakote), and lamotrigine (Lamictal). Clonazepam (Klonopin), a benzodiazepine, has also been used with some success as treatment or adjunct treatment of acute mania. These and the calcium channel blocker, verapamil, are identified in Table 21-8.

## Lithium

### Therapeutic Uses

- Acute manic phase of bipolar disorder
- Prophylaxis treatment for mania
- Depression
- Bulimia
- Schizophrenia
- Premenstrual syndrome
- Prophylaxis of vascular headache
- Neutropenia

Table 21-8 **Alternative Antimanic and Mood-Stabilizing Drugs**

| FDA-Approved Drugs | Dose | Type | Major Concern/Side Effect |
|---|---|---|---|
| Divalproex (Depakote) | 750–1500 mg/day | Anticonvulsant | **Baseline liver function tests should be done and monitored at regular intervals (6-12 months).**<br>• Hepatotoxicity, although rare, has been reported with fatalities in children.<br>• Thrombocytopenia and platelet dysfunction can occur. Check for bruises and monitor platelet count.<br>• Signs and symptoms to watch for: fever, chills, right upper quadrant pain, dark-colored urine, malaise, and jaundice.<br>• Common side effects: sedation, gastrointestinal upset, tremors, weight gain, and (rarely) alopecia. |
| Lamotrigine (Lamictal) | 50–40 mg/day | Anticonvulsant | • Can be used as initial treatment.<br>• Tolerated well. Low-dose titration to reduce risk (Lamictal) of rashes. **Rarely, the rash can progress to a potentially life-threatening condition** (one person per 1000). |

| | | |
|---|---|---|
| Carbamazepine (Tegretol) (Equetro) a sustained-release form of Carbamazepine | 600–1600 mg/day | Anticonvulsant |

- **Agranulocytosis** and **aplastic anemia** are most serious side effects.

- Blood levels should be monitored through first 8 weeks, because drug induces liver enzymes that speed its own metabolism. (Check complete blood count [CBC] when checking blood levels.) Dose should be adjusted to maintain serum level of 6–8 mg/L.
- Sedation, fatigue, nausea, and dizziness are the most common problems.
- Diplopia, incoordination, and sedation can signal excessive levels.

## Mechanism of Action

Lithium affects storage, release, and reuptake of neuro-transmitters. Antimanic effects result from increase in NE reuptake and increase in serotonin receptors, producing antimanic and antidepressant effects (Hodgson & Kizior, 2003). Besides the serotonergic properties and the effects on NE, lithium stabilizes calcium channels and decreases neuronal activity via effects on second messenger systems, all of which might add to its therapeutic profile.

The major disadvantage of lithium is that improve-ment is gradual. Antimanic effects begin 5 to 7 days after the onset of treatment, but it can take up to 3 weeks to adequately control the symptoms of mania. Therefore, other agents are given in conjunction with lithium to help control the mania until the lithium reaches a therapeutic level (0.8 to 1.4 mEq/L). Effective medications include antipsychotic agents, such as olanzapine or haloperidol, or potent benzodiazepines such as lorazepam or clo-nazepam. Lithium levels are best obtained approximately 12 hours after the administration of the last dose.

## Clinical Dosage

As mentioned in Chapter 7, blood levels are initially drawn weekly or biweekly until therapeutic levels are reached. For acute mania, a blood level of 0.8 to 1.4 mEq/L would be within the initial range. For maintenance therapy, lithium levels should range from 0.4 to 1.0 mEq/L; how-ever, levels of 0.6 to 0.8 mEq/L are effective for most. Levels higher than 1.5 mEq can result in significant toxicity. A typical maintenance dose is 300 mg of lithium carbonate three or four times daily. The therapeutic window between therapeutic levels and toxic levels is very small with lithium, so plasma levels should be monitored routinely. In the beginning, levels should be monitored every 2 to 3 days to keep the levels within the therapeutic range. During maintenance therapy, drug levels should be monitored every 1 to 3 months.

## Metabolism

Lithium has a short half-life, necessitating the drug to be administered in divided daily doses. Lithium is secreted in the kidneys. It must be used with extreme caution in people with renal impairment.

Low sodium levels or sodium depletion will decrease renal excretion of lithium. When this happens, the drug can accumulate in the body, and toxicity results. Therefore, maintaining normal sodium levels is vital, and diuretics, diarrhea, and dehydration can all cause lithium retention by the kidneys, which potentiates the occurrence of lithium toxicity.

## Adverse Effects

There are essentially two categories of adverse effects: (1) adverse effects when lithium levels are excessive and (2) adverse effects when lithium levels are at therapeutic levels.

### Adverse Effects When Lithium Levels Are Excessive

Refer to Table 21-7 for the expected side effects and the early, advanced, and severe signs of toxicity. Interventions for the different levels of toxicity are included.

### Adverse Effects When Lithium Levels Are Within Therapeutic Levels

Several responses occur early in treatment and then usually subside. Refer to Table 21-7 under Expected Side Effects for a list of these. Approximately 30% of people experience transient fatigue, muscle weakness, headache, confusion, and memory impairment. Polyuria and thirst occur in up to 50% of patients and can persist throughout treatment.

Rare reports of weight gain, acne, muscle twitching, eye pain, and headache and vision problems have been made. Other concerns are:

### Renal Toxicity

For some people who have been on lithium for long periods, degenerative changes in the kidney are noted. Kidney function should be assessed before treatment is started and every 6 to 12 months thereafter.

### Goiter

Reports of goiter with chronic administration of lithium have also been identified. This is usually benign, but measurement of thyroid hormones should be obtained prior to treatment and annually thereafter.

## Drug Interactions

- Drugs that might increase effects of lithium
  - Alcohol
  - Diuretics (promote sodium loss)
  - Hypotensive agents
- Drugs that can cause hyperkalemia, such as potassium-sparing diuretics and potassium supplements
- Anticholinergic drugs, which can cause urinary hesitancy, although the administration of these drugs with anticholinergic effects cannot always be avoided (e.g., antipsychotics, antidepressants)
- Drugs that can increase or decrease lithium levels and neurotoxicity, such as calcium channel blockers or Flagyl (metronidazole), and SSRIs

## Use with Caution

- Renal impairment
- Elderly patients
- Those with sodium depletion or on diuretic therapy
- Thyroid disorders
- Dialysis
- Hypovolemia
- Coronary or cerebrovascular insufficiency

## Contraindications

- Pregnancy and lactation
- Myocardial infarction
- Coronary insufficiency
- Angina
- Evidence of coronary artery disease

## Patient and Family Teaching

A useful guideline for patient and family teaching is found in Box 21-8.

## Box 21-8 **Patient and Family Teaching: Lithium**

The patient and the patient's family should be instructed about the following, encouraged to ask questions, and given the material in written form as well.

1. Lithium can treat your current emotional problem and will also help prevent relapse, so it is important to continue with the drug after the current episode is resolved.
2. Because therapeutic and toxic dosage ranges are so close, your lithium blood levels must be monitored very closely, more frequently at first, then once every several months after that.
3. Lithium is not addictive.
4. Maintain a normal diet and normal salt and fluid intake (2500 to 3000 mL/day, or six 12-oz glasses). Lithium decreases sodium reabsorption by the renal tubules, which could cause sodium depletion. A low sodium intake causes a relative increase in lithium retention, which could lead to toxicity.
5. Withhold drug if excessive diarrhea, vomiting, or diaphoresis occurs. Dehydration can raise lithium levels in the blood to toxic levels. Inform your health care provider if you have any of these problems.
6. Diuretics (water pills) are contraindicated with lithium.
7. Lithium is irritating to the gastric mucosa. Therefore, take your lithium with meals.
8. Periodic monitoring of renal and thyroid function is indicated with long-term use. Discuss your follow-up with your health care provider.
9. Avoid taking any over-the-counter medications without checking first with your health care provider.
10. If weight gain is significant, you might need to see a health care provider or nutritionist.
11. Many self-help groups have been developed to provide support for bipolar patients and their families. The local self-help group is (give name and phone number).
12. You can find out more information by calling (give name, phone number, and/or website).

## Alternative Antimanic and Mood-Stabilizing Drugs

Three anticonvulsants have demonstrated efficacy in the treatment of bipolar disease and are FDA approved. These agents are divalproex (Depakote), carbamazepine (Tegretol; including Equetro, sustained- release form of carbamazepine), and lamotrigine (Lamictal) (Preston et al., 2008).

1. **Lamotrigine** (Lamictal) is generally well tolerated. There is one rare and potentially fatal toxic effect, so patients are urged to seek immediate medical advice upon the appearance of a rash. Most rashes that appear with the administration of lamotrigine are benign.

2. **Divalproex sodium (Depakote)** has long been approved for the primary treatment of mania. Divalproex is effective in treating cases of mixed mania and rapid cycling. Divalproex and carbamazepine are both effective in treating mania secondary to general medical conditions. The use of these drugs requires initial evaluation and ongoing monitoring (see Table 21-8). Because of rare reports of elevated liver enzymes, baseline liver function tests should be done and monitored at frequent intervals.

3. **Carbamazepine (Tegretol)** is a good choice for manic episodes when lithium or divalproex are ineffective, contraindicated, or not tolerated. It is especially effective in patients with rapid cycling or secondary mania. The most serious side effect of carbamazepine is agranulocytosis; mild to moderate leukopenia and thrombocytopenia might also occur. A baseline evaluation needs to be done before treatment is started. Complete blood cell count and examination of a blood smear should be performed weekly during the first month of therapy and can be done at progressively longer intervals as treatment continues.

4. **Clonazepam (Klonopin)**, although not an anticonvulsant but rather a BZ, has been effectively used in treatment or as an adjunct for the treatment of acute mania.

# NURSE, PATIENT, and FAMILY RESOURCES

## JOURNAL ARTICLES

Howland, R.H. (2009). What should patients be told about their medications? *Journal of Psychosocial Nursing and Mental Health Services, 47*(2).

Howland, R.H. (2009). Psychopharmacology: Effects of aging on pharmacokinetic and pharmacodynamic drug process, *47*(10).

# APPENDIX A

# References

Abou-Salesh (1992). *Principles and Practice of Geriatric Psychiatry* by Copeland, John R. M., Abou-Salesh, Mohamed T. & Balazer, Dan G. 0471981974/9780471981978. (2nd Ed). 2002, Wiley John & Sons Inc.

American Nurses Association (ANA), & International Society of Psychiatric Mental Health Nurses. (2007). *Psychiatric mental health nursing; Scope and standards of practice.* Washington, DC: Nursebooks.org.

American Psychiatric Association. (2000a). *Diagnostic and statistical manual of mental disorders* (4th ed., text revision). Washington, DC: American Psychiatric Press.

American Psychiatric Association. (2000b). *Practice guidelines for the treatment of psychiatric disorders (compendium 2000).* Washington, DC: American Psychiatric Press.

American Psychiatric Association (APA) (2007). *Controlling anger before it controls you.* Retrieved March 15, 2007 from http://apa.org/topics/controlanger.html.

American Psychiatric Association (APA) (2008). *Practice guidelines for the treatment of patients with Alzheimer's disease and other dementias* (2nd ed.). Retrieved from psychiatryonline.com/pop.aspx?alD-152238.

Anthony, W. A. (1980). *Principles of psychiatric rehabilitation.* Baltimore, MD: University Park Press.

Bell, K. (1992). Identifying the substance abuser in clinical practice. *Orthopedic Nursing, 11*(2), 29.

Boerescu, D. A. (2007). Personality disorders. In Goldberg, R. J. (Ed.). *Practical guide to the care of the psychiatric patient* (3rd ed.). Philadelphia: Mosby/Elsevier.

Bohn, M. J. (2000). Alcoholism. *Psychiatric Clinics of North America, 16*(4), 679.

Borson, S. (1997). Delirium and confusional states. In D. L. Dunner (Ed.), *Current psychiatric therapy* (vol. 2). Philadelphia: Saunders.

Burns, C. M., & Stuart, G. W. (1991). Nursing care in electroconvulsive therapy. *Psychiatric Clinics of North America, 14*(4), 971.

Burnside, I. (1988). *Nursing and the aged* (3rd ed.). New York: McGraw-Hill.

Carson, V. B., & Alvarez, C. (2006). Communication with angry and aggressive clients. In E. M. Varcarolis, V. B. Carson & N. C. Shoemaker (Eds.), *Foundations of psychiatric nursing* (5th ed.). Philadelphia: Saunders.

Chiles, J. A., & Strosahl, K. (1997). Assessment, crisis management, and treatment of the suicidal patient. In D. L. Dunner (Ed.), *Current psychiatric therapy* (2nd ed., pp. 547–551). Philadelphia: Saunders.

Chitty, K. K., & Maynard, C. K. (1986). Managing manipulation. *Journal of Psychosocial and Mental Health Nursing Services, 34*(2), 9.

Colorado Society of Clinical Specialists in Psychiatric Nursing. (1990). Ethical guidelines for confidentiality. *Journal of Psychosocial Nursing and Mental Health Services, 28*, 42–44.

DiMatteo, M. R., & DiNicola, D. D. (1982). *Achieving patient compliance: The psychology of the medical practitioner's role.* Elmsford, NY: Pergamon Press.

Donegan, K. R., & Palmer-Erbs, V. K. (1998). Promoting the importance of work for persons with psychiatric disabilities. *Journal of Psychosocial Nursing, 36*, 13–23.

Dunner, D. L. (1997). *Current psychiatric theory* (2nd ed.). Philadelphia: Saunders.

Egan, G. (2004). *The skilled helper: A problem-management and opportunity-development approach to helping* (7th ed.). Pacific Grove, CA: Brooks/Cole.

Elliot, M. B. (2007). Eating disorders. In Goldberg, R. J. (Ed.), *Practical guide to the care of the psychiatric patient,* (3rd ed.). Philadelphia: Mosby/Elsevier.

Engel, G. L. (1964). Grief and grieving. *American Journal of Nursing, 64*(9), 93.

Fuller, M. A., & Sajatovic, M. (2000). *Drug information handbook* (2nd ed.). Cleveland, OH: Levi-Comp.

Gahlinger, P. M. (2004). Club drugs: MDMA, gamma-hydroxybutyrate (GHB), rohypnol, and ketamine. *American Family Physician, 69*(11), 2004. www.aafp.org/afp/20040601/2619.html. Retrieved 2/25/05.

Goldberg, R. J. (1998). *Practical guide to the care of the psychiatric patient* (2nd ed.). St. Louis: Mosby.

Goodman, J. D., & Sours, J. (1987). *The child mental status examination* (2nd ed.). New York: Basic Books.

Goodwin, J. (1985). *The talk book: The intimate science of communicating in close relationships*. New York: Ballantine.

Hall, E. T. (1997). *Beyond culture*. Garden City, NJ: Anchor Press.

Hill, S. S. (1998). Practice guidelines for major disorders. In G. P. Koocher, J. C. Norcross, & S. S. Hill (Eds.), *Psychologists' desk reference*. New York: Oxford University Press.

Hodgson, B. B., & Kizior, R. J. (2003). *Saunders nursing handbook 2003*. Philadelphia: Saunders.

Hoff, L. A. (1995). *People in crisis: Understanding and helping* (4th ed.). San Francisco: Jossey-Bass.

Hoffman, L., & Halmi, K. A. (1997). Treatment of anorexia nervosa. In D. L. Dunner (Ed.), *Current psychiatric therapy* (Vol. 2). Philadelphia: Saunders.

Horowitz, M. J. (1990). A model of mourning: Change in schemas of self and others. *Journal of the American Psychoanalytic Association, 38*, 297–324.

Ibrahim, K. (2005). People with eating disorders. In E. M. Varcarolis, V. B. Carson, & N. C. Shoemaker (Eds.), *Foundations of psychiatric nursing* (5th ed.). Philadelphia: Saunders.

Jezierski, M. (1994). Abuse of women by male partners: Basic knowledge for emergency nurses. *Journal of Emergency Nursing, 20*, 361.

Kaplan, H. I., & Sadock, B. J. (2002). *Pocket handbook of clinical psychiatry* (9th ed.). Baltimore: Lippincott-Williams & Wilkins.

Keltner, N. L., & Folks, D. G. (2001). *Psychotropic drugs* (3rd ed.). St. Louis: Mosby.

Kobayashi, M., Smith, T. P., & Norcross, J. C. (1998). Enhancing adherence. In G. P. Koocher, J. C. Norcross, S. S. Hill (Eds.), *Psychologists' desk reference*. New York. Oxford University Press.

Kramer-Howe, K., & Varcarolis, E. M. (2010). Care for the dying and for those who grieve. In E. M. Varcarolis &

M. J. Halter (Eds.), *Foundations of Psychiatric Nursing: A Clinical Approach*. St. Louis: Saunders/Elsevier.

Krupnick, S. L. W., & Wade, A. J. (1993). *Psychiatric care planning*. Springhouse, PA: Springhouse.

Kübler-Ross, E. (1969). *On death and dying*. New York: Macmillan.

Lehne, R. A. (2007). *Pharmacology for nursing care* (6th ed.). St. Louis: Saunders.

Lehne, R. A. (2004). *Pharmacology for nursing care* (5th ed.). Philadelphia: Saunders.

Lehne, R. A. (2001). *Pharmacology for nursing* (4th ed.). Philadelphia: Saunders.

Lerner, B. H. (1997). From careless consumptives to recalcitrant patients: The historical construction of noncompliance. *Social Science and Medicine, 45*(9), 1423–1431.

Linehan, M. M. (1993). *Cognitive behavioral treatment of borderline personality disorder*. New York: Guilford Press.

Mairo, R. D. (1997). Anger and aggression. In D. L. Dunner (Ed.), *Current psychiatric therapy* (2nd ed.). Philadelphia: Saunders.

Maxmen, J. S., & Ward, N. G. (2003). *Psychotropic drugs fast facts* (3rd ed.). New York: W.W. Norton.

McGee, D. E., & Linehan, M. M. (1997). Cluster B personality disorders. In D. L. Dunner (Ed.), *Current psychiatric therapy* (2nd ed., pp. 433–438). Philadelphia: Saunders.

Meichenbaum, D., & Turk, D. C. (1987). *Facilitating treatment adherence: A practitioner's guidebook*. New York: Plenum Press.

Meier, S. T., & Davis, S. R. (1989). *The elements of counseling* (2nd ed.). Pacific Grove, CA: Brooks/Cole.

Moore, J. M., & Hartman, C. R. (1988). Developing a therapeutic relationship. In C. K. Beck, R. P. Rawlins, & S. R. Williams (Eds.), *Mental health psychiatric nursing*. St. Louis: Mosby.

Moscato, B. (1988). The one-to-one relationship. In H. S. Wilson & C. S. Kneisel (Eds.), *Psychiatric nursing*. (3rd ed.). Menlo Park, CA: Addison-Wesley.

Myrick, D., & Erney, T. (1984). *Caring and sharing*. Educational Media Corporation, p. 154.

NANDA. (2009). *Nursing Diagnoses-Definitions and Classification 2009-2011* ©2009, 2007, 2005, 2003, 2001, 1998, 1996, 1994 NANDA International. Used by arrangement with Wiley-Blackwell Publishing, a company of John Wiley & Sons, Inc.

National Alliance for the Mentally Ill. (1999). Senators Domenici and Wellstone Introduced Mental Health Equitable Treatment Act of 1999. *NAMI E-News, 99*(116). Available online at http://www.nami.org.

National Institute of Mental Health. (1995). *Suicide.* NIMH.

O'Connor, P. G., Samet, J. H., & Stein, M. D. (1994). Management of hospitalized drug users: Role of the internist. *American Journal of Medicine, 96,* 551.

Parsons, R. D., & Wicks, R. J. (1994). *Counseling strategies and intervention techniques for human services* (4th ed.). Needham Heights, MA: Allyn & Bacon.

Patterson, W., et al. (1983). Evaluation of suicidal patients. The SAD PERSONS Scale. *Psychosomatics, 24*(4), 343.

Preston, J., & Johnson, J. (2009). *Clinical psychopharmacology made ridiculously simple.* Miami, FL: MedMaster, Inc.

Preston, J. D., O'Neal, J. H., & Talaga, M. C. (2005). *Handbook of clinical psychopharmacology for therapists* (4th ed.). Oakland, CA: New Harbinger Publications, Inc.

Preston, J. D., O'Neal, J. H., & Talaga, M. C. (2008). *Handbook of clinical psychopharmacology for therapists* (5th ed.). Oakland, CA: New Harbinger Publications, Inc.

Preston, J. D., & Johnson, J. (2009). *Clinical psychopharmacology made ridiculously simple* (6th ed.). Miami, Fla: MedMaster, Inc.

Prigerson, H. G., Franke, E., Kasl, S. V., et al. (1995). Complicated grief and bereavement-related depression as distinct disorders: Preliminary empirical validation in elderly bereaved spouses. *American Journal of Psychiatry, 152,* 22–30.

Public Policy Committee of the Board of Directors and the NAMI Department of Public Policy and Research. (1999). *Public Policy Platform of the National Alliance for the Mentally Ill (NAMI)* (3rd ed.). Section 4: Services and Supports for Adults. Available at www.nami.org/update/platform/services.htm.

Rabins, P. V. (2006). *Guidelines Watch for the treatment of patients with Alzheimer's disease. Washington,* DC: American Psychiatric Association.

Redl, F., & Wineman, D. (1957). *The aggressive child.* Glencoe, IL: The Free Press.

Robinson, D. (1997). *Good intentions: The nine unconscious mistakes of nice people.* New York: Warner Books.

Sadock, B. J., & Sadock, V. A. (Eds.). (2007). *Kaplan and Sadock's synopsis of Psychiatry* (10th ed.). Philadelphia: Lippincott, Williams and Wilkins.

Schultz, B. M. (1982). *Legal liability in psychotherapy*. San Francisco: Jossey-Bass Publishing.

Schultz, J. M., & Videbeck, S. D. (2005). *Lippincott's manual of psychiatric nursing care plans* (7th ed.). Philadelphia: Lippincott Williams and Wilkins.

Shea, S. C. (1998). *Psychiatric interviewing: The art of understanding* (2nd ed.). Philadelphia: Saunders.

Shoemaker, N. C., & Varcarolis, E. M. (2006). Personality disorders. In E. M. Varcarolis, V. B. Carson & N. C. Shoemaker (Eds.). *Foundations of psychiatric mental health nursing*. (5th ed.). St. Louis, MO: Saunders/Elsevier.

Slaby, A. E. (1994). *Handbook of psychiatric emergencies* (4th ed.). Norwalk, CT: Appleton & Lange.

Smith, L. S. (1994). Coping with the "problem" resident. *Nursing Care, 43*(1), 40–41.

Smith-DiJulio, K. (2002). Families in crisis: Family violence. In E. M. Varcarolis (Ed.), *Psychiatric mental health nursing* (4th ed.). Philadelphia: Saunders.

Stern, T. A., Herman, J. B., & Slavin, P. L. (2004). *Massachusetts General Hospital guide to primary care psychiatry* (2nd ed.). New York: McGraw-Hill Medical Publishing Division.

Stone, M. H. (1997). Cluster C personality disorders. In D. L. Dunner (Ed.), *Current psychiatric therapy* (2nd ed., pp. 439–445). Philadelphia: Saunders.

Suinn, R. M. (2005). Anxiety/Anger management training. In G. Koocher, J. Norcross & S. S. Hill (Eds.). *Psychologists' Desk Reference*, p. 271. Oxford, NY: Oxford University Press.

U.C. Berkley Wellness Letter. (Jan 2004). SAM-e.www.berkleywellness.com/html/ds/dsSAM-e.php. Retrieved February 15, 2005.

Vaillant, G. E. (1988). What can long-term follow-up teach us about relapse and prevention of relapse in addictions? *British Journal of Addictions, 83*, 1147–1157.

Varcarolis, E. (1998). *Foundations of psychiatric mental health nursing* (3rd ed., p. 694). Philadelphia: Saunders.

Varcarolis, E. (2002). *Foundations of psychiatric mental health nursing* (4th ed., p. 694). Philadelphia: Saunders.

Varcarolis, E. (2006). *Foundations of psychiatric mental health nursing* (5th ed.). Philadelphia: Saunders.

Varcarolis, E. (2010). *Foundations of psychiatric mental health nursing* (6th ed.). St. Louis, MO: Saunders/Elsevier, p. 177.

Varcarolis, E.M. (2002). *Foundations of psychiatric mental health nursing* (4th ed.). Philadelphia: Saunders; pp 246–247.

Varcarolis, E. M. (Ed.), (2002). *Psychiatric mental health nursing.* (4th ed.). Philadelphia: Saunders.

Varcarolis, E. M. (2006). *Manual of psychiatric mental health nursing care plans* (3rd ed., p. 151). St. Louis: Saunders.

Varcarolis, E.M. & Halter, M.J. (2009). *Essentials of Psychiatric Mental Health Nursing.* St. Louis: Saunders, pp. 110–111.

Varchol, D. A., & Raynor, J. (2009). Biological basis for understanding psychopharmacology. In E. M. Varcarolis & M. J. Halter (Eds.). *Essentials of Psychiatric Mental Health Nursing.* St. Louis, MO: Saunders/Elsevier.

Weeks, S. M. (1999). Disaster mental health services: A personal perspective. *Journal of Psychosocial Nursing, 37*(2), 14–18.

World Health Organization (WHO). (2005). *Child and adolescent mental health policies (Mental Health Policy and Service Guidance Package).* Geneva: Switzerland. World Health Organization.

Zale, C. F., O'Brian, M. M., Trestman, R. L., & Siever, L. J. (1997). Cluster A personality disorders. In D. L. Dunner (Ed.), *Current psychiatric therapy* (2nd ed., pp. 427–432). Philadelphia: Saunders.

Zerbe, K. J. (1999). *Women's mental health in primary care.* Philadelphia: Saunders.

# APPENDIX B

# Classification and Full Assessment

## APPENDIX B-1: OVERALL ASSESSMENT TOOL

### 1. CLIENT HISTORY

I. GENERAL HISTORY OF CLIENT
   Name _____ Age _____ Sex _____
   Racial and ethnic data _____
   Marital status _____
   Number and ages of children/siblings
   Living arrangements _____
   Occupation _____
   Education _____
   Religious affiliations _____
II. PRESENTING PROBLEM
   A. Statement in the client's own words of why he or she is hospitalized or seeking help
   B. Recent difficulties/alterations in:
      1. Relationships
      2. Usual level of functioning
      3. Behavior
      4. Perceptions or cognitive abilities
   C. Increased feelings of:
      1. Depression
      2. Anxiety
      3. Hopelessness
      4. Being overwhelmed
      5. Suspiciousness
      6. Confusion

   D. Somatic changes, such as:
      1. Constipation
      2. Insomnia
      3. Lethargy
      4. Weight loss or gain
      5. Palpitations
III. RELEVANT HISTORY—PERSONAL
   A. Previous hospitalizations and illnesses
   _____
   B. Educational background _____
   C. Occupational background _____
      1. If employed, where?_____
      2. How long at that job?_____
      3. Previous positions and reasons for
         leaving _____
      4. Special skills _____
   D. Social patterns
      1. Describe friends _____
      2. Describe a usual day_____
   E. Sexual patterns
      1. Sexually active?_____
      2. Sexual orientation _____
      3. Sexual difficulties _____
      4. Practice safe sex or birth control?
      _____
   F. Interests and abilities
      1. What does the client do in his or her spare time?
      _____
      2. What is the client good at?_____
      3. What gives the client pleasure?
      _____
   G. Substance use and abuse
      1. What medication does the client take?
      _____
      How often?_____How much?
      _____
      2. Any herbal or over-the-counter medications?
      _____
      How often?_____ How much?
      _____
      3. What psychotropic drugs does the client take?
      _____
      How often?_____ How much?
      _____

4. How many drinks of alcohol does the client take per day?_____ Per week?
_____

5. Does the client identify use of drugs as a problem?_____

H. How does the client cope with stress?
_____

1. What does the client do when he or she gets upset?_____
2. Who can the client talk to?_____
3. What usually helps to relieve stress?
_____

4. What did the client try this time?
_____

IV. RELEVANT HISTORY—FAMILY
A. Childhood
1. Who was important to the client growing up?
_____

2. Was there physical or sexual abuse?
_____

3. Did the parents drink or use drugs?
_____

4. Who was in the home when the client was growing up?_____

B. Adolescence
1. How would the client describe his or her feelings in adolescence?_____
2. Describe the client's peer group at that time.
_____

C. Use of drugs
1. Was there use or abuse of drugs by any family member?_____ Prescription
_____ Street_____
By whom?_____
2. What was the effect on the family?
_____

D. Family physical or mental problems
1. Is there any family history of violence or physical/sexual abuse?_____
2. Who in the family had physical or mental problems?_____
3. Describe the problems. _____
4. How did it affect the family?_____

E. Was there an unusual or outstanding event the client would like to mention?_____

# 2. MENTAL AND EMOTIONAL STATUS

A. Appearance
Physical handicaps _____
Dress appropriate _____
Sloppy _____
Grooming neat _____
Poor _____
Eye contact held _____
Describe posture _____

B. Behavior
Restless _____ Agitated
_____ Lethargic _____
Mannerisms _____
Facial expressions _____
Other _____

C. Speech
Clear _____ Mumbled
_____ Rapid _____
Slurred _____
Constant _____
Mute or silent _____
Barriers to communications _____
*Specify* (e.g., client has delusions or is confused, withdrawn, or verbose)_____

D. Mood
What mood does the client convey?

_____

E. Affect
Is the client's affect bland, apathetic, dramatic, bizarre, or appropriate? Describe_____

F. Thought process
1. Characteristics
Describe the characteristics of the person's responses:
Flights of ideas _____
Looseness of association _____
Blocking _____
Concrete _____

       Confabulation _____
       Describe _____

  2. Cognitive ability
     Proverbs: Concrete _____
     Abstract _____
     Serial sevens: How far does the client go?
     _____
     Can the client do simple math?
     _____
     What seems to be the reason for poor concentration?_____
     Orientation to time (?), place (?), person (?)
     _____

G. Thought content
  1. Central theme: What is important to the client?
     _____ Describe_____
  2. Self-concept: How does the client view himself
     or herself?_____
     What does the client want to change about
     himself or herself?_____
  3. Insight: Does the client realistically assess his or
     her symptoms?_____
     Realistically appraise his or her situation?
     _____ Describe _____
  4. Suicidal or homicidal ideation? _____
     What is suicide potential? _____
     Family history of suicide or homicide
     attempt or successful completion?
     _____ Explain _____
     Preoccupations. Does the client have
     hallucinations? _____ Delusions?
     _____ Obsessions? _____
     Rituals? _____
     Phobias?_____
     Grandiosity?_____
     Religiosity _____
     Worthlessness _____
     Describe _____

ASK CLIENT:

H. Spiritual assessment
    What importance does religion or spirituality have
    in your life?
    Do your religious or spiritual beliefs influence the
    way you take care of yourself or your illness?
    How? _____

Who or what supplies you with hope?
_____

I. Cultural influences
With what cultural group do you identify?

_____

Have you tried any cultural remedies or practices
for your condition? If so, what?_____
Do you use any alternative or complementary
medicines/herbs/practices?_____

_____

Adapted from Varcarolis, E.M. (2002). *Foundations of psychiatric mental health nursing* (4th ed.). Philadelphia: Saunders, pp. 203–205; reprinted by permission.

# APPENDIX B-2: NANDA 2009–2011 NURSING DIAGNOSIS

## NANDA INTERNATIONAL-APPROVED NURSING DIAGNOSES

Activity intolerance
Activity intolerance, Risk for
Activity planning, Ineffective
Airway clearance, Ineffective
Allergy response, Latex
Allergy response, Risk for latex
Anxiety
Anxiety, Death
Aspiration, Risk for
Attachment, Risk for impaired parent/infant/child
Autonomic dysreflexia
Autonomic dysreflexia, Risk for

Behavior, Risk-prone health
Bleeding, Risk for
Body image, Disturbed
Body temperature, Risk for imbalanced
Bowel incontinence
Breastfeeding, Effective
Breastfeeding, Ineffective

Breastfeeding, Interrupted
Breathing pattern, Ineffective

Cardiac output, Decreased
Cardiac perfusion, Risk for decreased
Cardiac tissue perfusion, Risk for ineffective
Caregiver role strain
Caregiver role strain, Risk for
Cerebral tissue perfusion, Risk for ineffective
Childbearing process, Readiness for enhanced
Comfort, Readiness for enhanced
Comfort, Impaired
Communication, Impaired verbal
Communication, Readiness for enhanced
Conflict, Decisional
Conflict, Parental role
Confusion, Acute
Confusion, Chronic
Confusion, Risk for acute
Constipation
Constipation, Perceived
Constipation, Risk for
Contamination
Contamination, Risk for
Coping, Compromised family
Coping, Defensive
Coping, Disabled family
Coping, Ineffective
Coping, Ineffective community
Coping, Readiness for enhanced
Coping, Readiness for enhanced community
Coping, Readiness for enhanced family

Death syndrome, Risk for sudden infant
Decision making, Readiness for enhanced
Denial, Ineffective
Dentition, Impaired
Development, Risk for delayed
Diarrhea
Dignity, Risk for compromised human
Distress, Moral
Disuse syndrome, Risk for
Diversional activity, Deficient

Electrolyte imbalance, Risk for
Energy field, Disturbed
Environmental interpretation syndrome, Impaired

Failure to thrive, Adult
Falls, Risk for
Family processes: alcoholism, Dysfunctional
Family processes, Interrupted
Family processes, Readiness for enhanced
Fatigue
Fear
Fluid balance, Readiness for enhanced
Fluid volume, Deficient
Fluid volume, Excess
Fluid volume, Risk for deficient
Fluid volume, Risk for imbalanced

Gas exchange, Impaired
Gastrointestinal motility, Dysfunctional
Gastrointestinal motility, Risk for dysfunctional
Gastrointestinal tissue perfusion, Risk for ineffective
Glucose level, Risk for unstable
Grieving
Grieving, Complicated
Grieving, Risk for complicated
Growth and development, Delayed

Health maintenance, Ineffective
Health management, Ineffective self
Health management, Readiness for enhanced self
Health-seeking behaviors
Home maintenance, Impaired
Hope, Readiness for enhanced
Hopelessness
Hyperthermia
Hypothermia

Identity, Disturbed personal
Immunization status, Readiness for enhanced
Incontinence, Functional urinary
Incontinence, Overflow urinary
Incontinence, Reflex urinary
Incontinence, Stress urinary
Incontinence, Total urinary*

Incontinence, Urge urinary
Incontinence, Risk for urge urinary
Infant behavior, Disorganized
Infant behavior, Risk for disorganized
Infant behavior, Readiness for enhanced organized
Infant feeding pattern, Ineffective
Infection, Risk for
Injury, Risk for
Injury, Risk for perioperative-positioning
Insomnia
Intracranial adaptive capacity, Decreased

Jaundice, Neonatal

Knowledge, Deficient
Knowledge, Readiness for enhanced

Lifestyle, Sedentary
Liver function, Risk for impaired
Loneliness, Risk for

Maternal/Fetal dyad, Risk for disturbed
Memory, Impaired
Mobility, Impaired bed
Mobility, Impaired physical
Mobility, Impaired wheelchair

Nausea
Neglect, Self
Neglect, Unilateral
Noncompliance
Nutrition: less than body requirements, Imbalanced
Nutrition: more than body requirements, Imbalanced
Nutrition, Readiness for enhanced
Nutrition: more than body requirements, Risk for
imbalanced

Oral mucous membrane, Impaired

Pain, Acute
Pain, Chronic
Parenting, Readiness for enhanced
Parenting, Impaired
Parenting, Risk for impaired

Peripheral neurovascular dysfunction, Risk for
Peripheral tissue perfusion, Ineffective
Poisoning, Risk for
Post-trauma syndrome
Post-trauma syndrome, Risk for
Power, Readiness for enhanced
Powerlessness
Powerlessness, Risk for
Protection, Ineffective

Rape-trauma syndrome
Rape-trauma syndrome: compound reaction*
Rape-trauma syndrome: silent reaction*
Relationship, Readiness for enhanced
Religiosity, Impaired
Religiosity, Readiness for enhanced
Religiosity, Risk for impaired
Relocation stress syndrome
Relocation stress syndrome, Risk for
Renal perfusion, Risk for ineffective
Resilience, Impaired individual
Resilience, Readiness for enhanced
Resilience, Risk for compromised
Role performance, Ineffective

Self-care, Readiness for enhanced
Self-care deficit, Bathing/hygiene
Self-care deficit, Dressing/grooming
Self-care deficit, Feeding
Self-care deficit, Toileting
Self-concept, Readiness for enhanced
Self-esteem, Chronic low
Self-esteem, Situational low
Self-esteem, Risk for situational low
Self-mutilation
Self-mutilation, Risk for
Sensory perception, Disturbed
Sexual dysfunction
Sexuality pattern, Ineffective
Shock, Risk for
Skin integrity, Impaired
Skin integrity, Risk for impaired
Sleep deprivation
Sleep, Readiness for enhanced
Sleep pattern, Disturbed

Social interaction, Impaired
Social isolation
Sorrow, Chronic
Spiritual distress
Spiritual distress, Risk for
Spiritual well-being, Readiness for enhanced
Stress overload
Suffocation, Risk for
Suicide, Risk for
Surgical recovery, Delayed
Swallowing, Impaired

Therapeutic regimen management, Effective*
Therapeutic regimen management, Ineffective community*
Therapeutic regimen management, Ineffective family
Thermoregulation, Ineffective
Thermoregulation, Ineffective
Thought processes, Disturbed*
Tissue integrity, Impaired
Tissue perfusion, Ineffective
Transfer ability, Impaired
Trauma, Risk for

Urinary elimination, Impaired
Urinary elimination, Readiness for enhanced
Urinary retention

Vascular trauma, Risk for
Ventilation, Impaired spontaneous
Ventilatory weaning response, Dysfunctional
Violence, Risk for other-directed
Violence, Risk for self-directed

Walking, Impaired
Wandering

---

*Retired diagnoses from North American Nursing Diagnosis Association International (NANDA-I). (2007). *NANDA-I nursing diagnoses: Definitions and classification 2007–2008*. Philadelphia: Author.

From North American Nursing Diagnosis Association International (NANDA-I). (2009). *NANDA-I nursing diagnoses: Definitions and classification 2009–2011*. Oxford, United Kingdom: Author.

# APPENDIX B-3: *DSM-IV-TR* CLASSIFICATION

*NOS*, Not Otherwise Specified.

An *x* appearing in a diagnostic code indicates that a specific code number is required.

An ellipsis (...) is used in the names of certain disorders to indicate that the name of a specific mental disorder or general medical condition should be inserted when recording the name (e.g., 293.0 Delirium Due to Hypothyroidism).

If criteria are currently met, one of the following severity specifiers may be noted after the diagnosis:

- Mild
- Moderate
- Severe

If criteria are no longer met, one of the following specifiers may be noted:

- In Partial Remission
- In Full Remission
- Prior History

## DISORDERS USUALLY FIRST DIAGNOSED IN INFANCY, CHILDHOOD, OR ADOLESCENCE

### Mental Retardation

*NOTE: These are coded on Axis II.*

| | |
|---|---|
| 317 | Mild Mental Retardation |
| 318.0 | Moderate Mental Retardation |
| 318.1 | Severe Mental Retardation |
| 318.2 | Profound Mental Retardation |
| 319 | Mental Retardation, Severity Unspecified |

### Learning Disorders

| | |
|---|---|
| 315.00 | Reading Disorder |
| 315.1 | Mathematics Disorder |
| 315.2 | Disorder of Written Expression |
| 315.9 | Learning Disorder NOS |

## Motor Skills Disorder

315.4      Developmental Coordination Disorder

## Communication Disorders

315.31    Expressive Language Disorder
315.32    Mixed Receptive-Expressive Language Disorder
315.39    Phonologic Disorder
307.0     Stuttering
307.9     Communication Disorder NOS

## Pervasive Developmental Disorders

299.00    Autistic Disorder
299.80    Rett's Disorder
299.10    Childhood Disintegrative Disorder
299.80    Asperger's Disorder
299.80    Pervasive Developmental Disorder NOS

## Attention-Deficit and Disruptive Behavior Disorders

314.xx    Attention-Deficit/Hyperactivity Disorder
   .01      Combined Type
   .00      Predominantly Inattentive Type
   .01      Predominantly Hyperactive-Impulsive Type
314.9     Attention-Deficit/Hyperactivity Disorder NOS
312.xx    Conduct Disorder
   .81      Childhood-Onset Type
   .82      Adolescent-Onset Type
   .89      Unspecified Onset
313.81    Oppositional Defiant Disorder
312.9     Disruptive Behavior Disorder NOS

## Feeding and Eating Disorders of Infancy or Early Childhood

307.52    Pica
307.53    Rumination Disorder
307.59    Feeding Disorder of Infancy or Early Childhood

## Tic Disorders

307.23   Tourette's Disorder
307.22   Chronic Motor or Vocal Tic Disorder
307.21   Transient Tic Disorder
         *Specify if:* Single Episode/Recurrent
307.20   Tic Disorder NOS

## Elimination Disorders

\_\_\_.\_   Encopresis
787.6    With Constipation and Overflow Incontinence
307.7    Without Constipation and Overflow Incontinence
307.6    Enuresis (Not Due to a General Medical
         Condition)
         *Specify type:* Nocturnal Only/Diurnal Only/Nocturnal and Diurnal

## Other Disorders of Infancy, Childhood, or Adolescence

309.21   Separation Anxiety Disorder
         *Specify if:* Early Onset
313.23   Selective Mutism
313.89   Reactive Attachment Disorder of Infancy or
         Early Childhood
         *Specify type:* Inhibited Type/Disinhibited Type
307.3    Stereotypic Movement Disorder
         *Specify if:* With Self-Injurious Behavior
313.9    Disorder of Infancy, Childhood, or Adolescence
         NOS

# DELIRIUM, DEMENTIA, AND AMNESTIC AND OTHER COGNITIVE DISORDERS

## Delirium

293.0    Delirium Due to ... *[Indicate the General Medical Condition]*
\_\_\_.\_   Substance Intoxication Delirium (refer to
         Substance-Related Disorders for substance-specific codes)

___.__ Substance Withdrawal Delirium (refer to
Substance-Related Disorders for substance-
specific codes)

___.__ Delirium Due to Multiple Etiologies (code each of
the specific etiologies)

780.09 Delirium NOS

## Dementia

294.xx Dementia of the Alzheimer's Type, With
Early Onset *(also code 331.0 Alzheimer's disease
on Axis III)*

  .10 Without Behavioral Disturbance

  .11 With Behavioral Disturbance

294.xx Dementia of the Alzheimer's Type, With
Late Onset *(also code 331.0 Alzheimer's disease
on Axis III)*

  .10 Without Behavioral Disturbance

  .11 With Behavioral Disturbance

290.xx Vascular Dementia

  .40 Uncomplicated

  .41 With Delirium

  .42 With Delusions

  .43 With Depressed Mood

  *Specify if:* With Behavioral Disturbance

*Code presence or absence of a behavioral disturbance in the
fifth digit for* Dementia Due to a General Medical
Condition:

  0 = Without Behavioral Disturbance

  1 = With Behavioral Disturbance

294.1x Dementia Due to HIV Disease *(also code 042 HIV
on Axis III)*

294.1x Dementia Due to Head Trauma *(also code 854.00
head injury on Axis III)*

294.1x Dementia Due to Parkinson's Disease *(also code
332.0 Parkinson's disease on Axis III)*

294.1x Dementia Due to Huntington's Disease *(also code
333.4 Huntington's disease on Axis III)*

294.1x Dementia Due to Pick's Disease *(also code 331.1
Pick's disease on Axis III)*

294.1x Dementia Due to Creutzfeldt-Jakob Disease
*(also code 046.1 Creutzfeldt-Jakob disease on
Axis III)*

294.1x   Dementia Due to ... *[Indicate the General Medical Condition not listed above] (also code the general medical condition on Axis III)*
___.__   Substance-Induced Persisting Dementia *(refer to Substance-Related Disorders for substance-specific codes)*
___.__   Dementia Due to Multiple Etiologies *(code each of the specific etiologies)*
294.8   Dementia NOS

## Amnestic Disorders

294.0   Amnestic Disorder Due to ... *[Indicate the General Medical Condition]*
   *Specify if*: Transient/Chronic
___.__   Substance-Induced Persisting Amnestic Disorder (refer to Substance-Related Disorders for substance-specific codes)
294.8   Amnestic Disorder NOS

## Other Cognitive Disorders

294.9   Cognitive Disorder NOS

# MENTAL DISORDERS DUE TO A GENERAL MEDICAL CONDITION NOT ELSEWHERE CLASSIFIED

293.89   Catatonic Disorder Due to ... *[Indicate the General Medical Condition]*
310.1   Personality Change Due to ... *[Indicate the General Medical Condition]*
   *Specify type*: Labile Type/Disinhibited Type/ Aggressive Type/Apathetic Type/Paranoid Type/Other Type/Combined Type/Unspecified Type
293.9   Mental Disorder NOS Due to ... *[Indicate the General Medical Condition]*

# SUBSTANCE-RELATED DISORDERS

*The following specifiers may be applied to Substance Dependence as noted:*
   [a]With Physiologic Dependence/Without Physiologic Dependence

[b]Early Full Remission/Early Partial Remission/Sustained
Full Remission/Sustained Partial Remission
[c]In a Controlled Environment
[d]On Agonist Therapy
*The following specifiers apply to Substance-Induced
Disorders as noted:*
[I]With Onset During Intoxication
[W]With Onset During Withdrawal

## Alcohol-Related Disorders

### Alcohol Use Disorders

303.90   Alcohol Dependence[a,b,c]
305.00   Alcohol Abuse

### Alcohol-Induced Disorders

303.00   Alcohol Intoxication
291.81   Alcohol Withdrawal
         *Specify if:* With Perceptual Disturbances
291.0    Alcohol Intoxication Delirium
291.0    Alcohol Withdrawal Delirium
291.2    Alcohol-Induced Persisting Dementia
291.1    Alcohol-Induced Persisting Amnestic Disorder
291.x    Alcohol-Induced Psychotic Disorder
   .5    With Delusions[I,W]
   .3    With Hallucinations[I,W]
291.89   Alcohol-Induced Mood Disorder[I,W]
291.89   Alcohol-Induced Anxiety Disorder[I,W]
291.89   Alcohol-Induced Sexual Dysfunction[I]
291.89   Alcohol-Induced Sleep Disorder[I,W]
291.9    Alcohol-Related Disorder NOS

## Amphetamine (or Amphetamine-Like)–Related Disorders

### Amphetamine Use Disorders

304.40   Amphetamine Dependence[a,b,c]
305.70   Amphetamine Abuse

### Amphetamine-Induced Disorders

292.89   Amphetamine Intoxication
         *Specify if:* With Perceptual Disturbances
292.0    Amphetamine Withdrawal

292.81    Amphetamine Intoxication Delirium
292.xx    Amphetamine-Induced Psychotic Disorder
   .11     With Delusions[I]
   .12     With Hallucinations[I]
292.84    Amphetamine-Induced Mood Disorder[I,W]
292.89    Amphetamine-Induced Anxiety Disorder[I]
292.89    Amphetamine-Induced Sexual Dysfunction[I]
292.89    Amphetamine-Induced Sleep Disorder[I,W]
292.9     Amphetamine-Related Disorder NOS

## Caffeine-Related Disorders

### Caffeine-Induced Disorders

305.90    Caffeine Intoxication
292.89    Caffeine-Induced Anxiety Disorder[I]
292.89    Caffeine-Induced Sleep Disorder[I]
292.9     Caffeine-Related Disorder NOS

## Cannabis-Related Disorders

### Cannabis Use Disorders

304.30    Cannabis Dependence[a,b,c]
305.20    Cannabis Abuse

### Cannabis-Induced Disorders

292.89    Cannabis Intoxication
          *Specify if:* With Perceptual Disturbances
292.81    Cannabis Intoxication Delirium
292.xx    Cannabis-Induced Psychotic Disorder
   .11     With Delusions[I]
   .12     With Hallucinations[I]
292.89    Cannabis-Induced Anxiety Disorder[I]
292.9     Cannabis-Related Disorder NOS

## Cocaine-Related Disorders

### Cocaine Use Disorders

304.20    Cocaine Dependence[a,b,c]
305.60    Cocaine Abuse

## Cocaine-Induced Disorders

292.89 Cocaine Intoxication
 *Specify if:* With Perceptual Disturbances
292.0 Cocaine Withdrawal
292.81 Cocaine Intoxication Delirium
292.xx Cocaine-Induced Psychotic Disorder
 .11 With Delusions[I]
 .12 With Hallucinations[I]
292.84 Cocaine-Induced Mood Disorder[I,W]
292.89 Cocaine-Induced Anxiety Disorder[I,W]
292.89 Cocaine-Induced Sexual Dysfunction[I]
292.89 Cocaine-Induced Sleep Disorder[I,W]
292.9 Cocaine-Related Disorder NOS

## Hallucinogen-Related Disorders

### Hallucinogen Use Disorders

304.50 Hallucinogen Dependence[b,c]
305.30 Hallucinogen Abuse

### Hallucinogen-Induced Disorders

292.89 Hallucinogen Intoxication
292.89 Hallucinogen Persisting Perception Disorder
 (Flashbacks)
292.81 Hallucinogen Intoxication Delirium
292.xx Hallucinogen-Induced Psychotic Disorder
 .11 With Delusions[I]
 .12 With Hallucinations[I]
292.84 Hallucinogen-Induced Mood Disorder[I]
292.89 Hallucinogen-Induced Anxiety Disorder[I]
292.9 Hallucinogen-Related Disorder NOS

## Inhalant-Related Disorders

### Inhalant Use Disorders

304.60 Inhalant Dependence[b,c]
305.90 Inhalant Abuse

### Inhalant-Induced Disorders

292.89 Inhalant Intoxication
292.81 Inhalant Intoxication Delirium

292.82    Inhalant-Induced Persisting Dementia
292.xx    Inhalant-Induced Psychotic Disorder
  .11      With Delusions[I]
  .12      With Hallucinations[I]
292.84    Inhalant-Induced Mood Disorder[I]
292.89    Inhalant-Induced Anxiety Disorder[I]
292.9     Inhalant-Related Disorder NOS

## Nicotine-Related Disorders
### Nicotine Use Disorder
305.1     Nicotine Dependence[a,b]

### Nicotine-Induced Disorder
292.0     Nicotine Withdrawal
292.9     Nicotine-Related Disorder NOS

## Opioid-Related Disorders
### Opioid Use Disorders
304.00    Opioid Dependence[a,b,c,d]
305.50    Opioid Abuse

### Opioid-Induced Disorders
292.89    Opioid Intoxication
          *Specify if:* With Perceptual Disturbances
292.0     Opioid Withdrawal
292.81    Opioid Intoxication Delirium
292.xx    Opioid-Induced Psychotic Disorder
  .11      With Delusions[I]
  .12      With Hallucinations[I]
292.84    Opioid-Induced Mood Disorder[I]
292.89    Opioid-Induced Sexual Dysfunction[I]
292.89    Opioid-Induced Sleep Disorder[I,W]
292.9     Opioid-Related Disorder NOS

## Phencyclidine (or Phencyclidine-Like)–Related Disorders
### Phencyclidine Use Disorders
304.60    Phencyclidine Dependence[b,c]
305.90    Phencyclidine Abuse

## *Phencyclidine-Induced Disorders*

| | |
|---|---|
| 292.89 | Phencyclidine Intoxication |
| | *Specify if:* With Perceptual Disturbances |
| 292.81 | Phencyclidine Intoxication Delirium |
| 292.xx | Phencyclidine-Induced Psychotic Disorder |
| .11 | With Delusions[I] |
| .12 | With Hallucinations[I] |
| 292.84 | Phencyclidine-Induced Mood Disorder[I] |
| 292.89 | Phencyclidine-Induced Anxiety Disorder[I] |
| 292.9 | Phencyclidine-Related Disorder NOS |

## Sedative-, Hypnotic-, or Anxiolytic-Related Disorders

### *Sedative, Hypnotic, or Anxiolytic Use Disorders*

| | |
|---|---|
| 304.10 | Sedative, Hypnotic, or Anxiolytic Dependence[a,b,c] |
| 305.40 | Sedative, Hypnotic, or Anxiolytic Abuse |

### *Sedative-, Hypnotic-, or Anxiolytic-Induced Disorders*

| | |
|---|---|
| 292.89 | Sedative, Hypnotic, or Anxiolytic Intoxication |
| 292.0 | Sedative, Hypnotic, or Anxiolytic Withdrawal |
| | *Specify if:* With Perceptual Disturbances |
| 292.81 | Sedative, Hypnotic, or Anxiolytic Intoxication Delirium |
| 292.81 | Sedative, Hypnotic, or Anxiolytic Withdrawal Delirium |
| 292.82 | Sedative-, Hypnotic-, or Anxiolytic-Induced Persisting Dementia |
| 292.83 | Sedative-, Hypnotic-, or Anxiolytic-Induced Persisting Amnestic Disorder |
| 292.xx | Sedative-, Hypnotic-, or Anxiolytic-Induced Psychotic Disorder |
| .11 | With Delusions[I,W] |
| .12 | With Hallucinations[I,W] |
| 292.84 | Sedative-, Hypnotic-, or Anxiolytic-Induced Mood Disorder[I,W] |
| 292.89 | Sedative-, Hypnotic-, or Anxiolytic-Induced Anxiety Disorder[W] |
| 292.89 | Sedative-, Hypnotic-, or Anxiolytic-Induced Sexual Dysfunction[I] |

292.89   Sedative-, Hypnotic-, or Anxiolytic-Induced Sleep Disorder[I,W]

292.9   Sedative-, Hypnotic-, or Anxiolytic-Related Disorder NOS

## Polysubstance-Related Disorder

304.80   Polysubstance Dependence[a,b,c,d]

## Other (or Unknown) Substance-Related Disorders

### Other (or Unknown) Substance Use Disorders

304.90   Other (or Unknown) Substance Dependence[a,b,c,d]

305.90   Other (or Unknown) Substance Abuse

### Other (or Unknown) Substance-Induced Disorders

292.89   Other (or Unknown) Substance Intoxication
         *Specify if:* With Perceptual Disturbances

292.0   Other (or Unknown) Substance Withdrawal
        *Specify if:* With Perceptual Disturbances

292.81   Other (or Unknown) Substance-Induced Delirium

292.82   Other (or Unknown) Substance-Induced Persisting Dementia

292.83   Other (or Unknown) Substance-Induced Persisting Amnestic Disorder

292.xx   Other (or Unknown) Substance-Induced Psychotic Disorder
   .11   With Delusions[I,W]
   .12   With Hallucinations[I,W]

292.84   Other (or Unknown) Substance-Induced Mood Disorder[I,W]

292.89   Other (or Unknown) Substance-Induced Anxiety Disorder[I,W]

292.89   Other (or Unknown) Substance-Induced Sexual Dysfunction[I]

292.89   Other (or Unknown) Substance-Induced Sleep Disorder[I,W]

292.9   Other (or Unknown) Substance-Related Disorder NOS

# SCHIZOPHRENIA AND OTHER PSYCHOTIC DISORDERS

295.xx   Schizophrenia

*The following Classification of Longitudinal Course applies to all subtypes of Schizophrenia:*

Episodic With Interepisode Residual Symptoms (*specify if:* With Prominent Negative Symptoms)/ Episodic With No Interepisode Residual Symptoms

Continuous (*specify if:* With Prominent Negative Symptoms)

Single Episode in Partial Remission (*specify if:* With Prominent Negative Symptoms)/Single Episode In Full Remission

Other or Unspecified Pattern

   .30   Paranoid Type
   .10   Disorganized Type
   .20   Catatonic Type
   .90   Undifferentiated Type
   .60   Residual Type
295.40   Schizophreniform Disorder
         *Specify if:* Without Good Prognostic Features/ With Good Prognostic Features
295.70   Schizoaffective Disorder
         *Specify type:* Bipolar Type/Depressive Type
297.1    Delusional Disorder
         *Specify type:* Erotomanic Type/Grandiose Type/ Jealous Type/Persecutory Type/Somatic Type/ Mixed Type/Unspecified Type
298.8    Brief Psychotic Disorder
         *Specify if:* With Marked Stressor(s)/Without Marked Stressor(s)/With Postpartum Onset
297.3    Shared Psychotic Disorder
293.xx   Psychotic Disorder Due to . . . *[Indicate the General Medical Condition]*
   .81   With Delusions
   .82   With Hallucinations
___.__   Substance-Induced Psychotic Disorder *(refer to Substance-Related Disorders for substance-specific codes)*
         *Specify if:* With Onset During Intoxication/With Onset During Withdrawal
298.9    Psychotic Disorder NOS

# MOOD DISORDERS

*Code current state of Major Depressive Disorder or Bipolar I Disorder in fifth digit:*

    1 = Mild
    2 = Moderate
    3 = Severe Without Psychotic Features
    4 = Severe With Psychotic Features
    *Specify:* Mood-Congruent Psychotic Features/Mood-
          Incongruent Psychotic Features
    5 = In Partial Remission
    6 = In Full Remission
    0 = Unspecified

*The following specifiers apply (for current or most recent episode) to Mood Disorders as noted:*

    [a]Severity/Psychotic/Remission Specifiers
    [b]Chronic
    [c]With Catatonic Features
    [d]With Melancholic Features
    [e]With Atypical Features
    [f]With Postpartum Onset

*The following specifiers apply to Mood Disorders as noted:*

    [g]With or Without Full Interepisode Recovery
    [h]With Seasonal Pattern
    [i]With Rapid Cycling

## Depressive Disorders

296.xx   Major Depressive Disorder
    .2x   Single Episode[a,b,c,d,e,f]
    .3x   Recurrent[a,b,c,d,e,f,g,h]
300.4    Dysthymic Disorder
         *Specify if:* Early Onset/Late Onset
         *Specify:* With Atypical Features
311      Depressive Disorder NOS

## Bipolar Disorders

296.xx   Bipolar I Disorder
    .0x   Single Manic Episode[a,c,f]
         *Specify if:* Mixed
    .40   Most Recent Episode Hypomanic[g,h,i]
    .4x   Most Recent Episode Manic[a,c,f,g,h,i]

.6x    Most Recent Episode Mixed[a,c,f,g,h,i]
.5x    Most Recent Episode Depressed[a,b,c,d,e,f,g,h,i]
.7     Most Recent Episode Unspecified[g,h,i]
296.89 Bipolar II Disorder[a,b,c,d,e,f,g,h,i]
       *Specify (current or most recent episode):* Hypomanic/
       Depressed
301.13 Cyclothymic Disorder
296.80 Bipolar Disorder NOS
293.83 Mood Disorder Due to ... *[Indicate the General
       Medical Condition]*
       *Specify type:* With Depressive Features/With
       Major Depressive-Like Episode/With Manic
       Features/With Mixed Features
___.__ Substance-Induced Mood Disorder *(refer to
       Substance-Related Disorders for substance-specific
       codes)*
       *Specify type:* With Depressive Features/With
       Manic Features/With Mixed Features
       *Specify if:* With Onset During Intoxication/With
       Onset During Withdrawal
296.90 Mood Disorder NOS

# ANXIETY DISORDERS

300.01 Panic Disorder Without Agoraphobia
300.21 Panic Disorder With Agoraphobia
300.22 Agoraphobia Without History of Panic Disorder
300.29 Specific Phobia
       *Specify type:* Animal Type/Natural Environment
       Type/Blood-Injection-Injury Type/Situational
       Type/Other Type
300.23 Social Phobia
       *Specify if:* Generalized
300.3  Obsessive-Compulsive Disorder
       *Specify if:* With Poor Insight
309.81 Posttraumatic Stress Disorder
       *Specify if:* Acute/Chronic
       *Specify if:* With Delayed Onset
308.3  Acute Stress Disorder
300.02 Generalized Anxiety Disorder
293.84 Anxiety Disorder Due to ... *[Indicate the General
       Medical Condition]*
       *Specify if:* With Generalized Anxiety/With Panic
       Attacks/With Obsessive-Compulsive Symptoms

\_\_\_.\_\_   Substance-Induced Anxiety Disorder *(refer to Sub-stance-Related Disorders for substance-specific codes)*
*Specify if:* With Generalized Anxiety/With Panic Attacks/With Obsessive-Compulsive Symptoms/With Phobic Symptoms
*Specify if:* With Onset During Intoxication/With Onset During Withdrawal

300.00   Anxiety Disorder NOS

# SOMATOFORM DISORDERS

300.81   Somatization Disorder
300.82   Undifferentiated Somatoform Disorder
300.11   Conversion Disorder
*Specify type:* With Motor Symptom or Deficit/With Sensory Symptom or Deficit/With Seizures or Convulsions/With Mixed Presentation
307.xx   Pain Disorder
   .80   Associated With Psychologic Factors
   .89   Associated With Both Psychologic Factors and a General Medical Condition
*Specify if:* Acute/Chronic
300.7   Hypochondriasis
*Specify if:* With Poor Insight
300.7   Body Dysmorphic Disorder
300.82   Somatoform Disorder NOS

# FACTITIOUS DISORDERS

300.xx   Factitious Disorder
   .16   With Predominantly Psychologic Signs and Symptoms
   .19   With Predominantly Physical Signs and Symptoms
   .19   With Combined Psychologic and Physical Signs and Symptoms
300.19   Factitious Disorder NOS

# DISSOCIATIVE DISORDERS

300.12   Dissociative Amnesia
300.13   Dissociative Fugue
300.14   Dissociative Identity Disorder
300.6   Depersonalization Disorder
300.15   Dissociative Disorder NOS

# SEXUAL AND GENDER IDENTITY DISORDERS

## Sexual Dysfunctions

*The following specifiers apply to all primary Sexual Dysfunctions:*
Lifelong Type/Acquired Type
Generalized Type/Situational Type
Due to Psychologic Factors/Due to Combined Factors

### Sexual Desire Disorders

302.71  Hypoactive Sexual Desire Disorder
302.79  Sexual Aversion Disorder

### Sexual Arousal Disorders

302.72  Female Sexual Arousal Disorder
302.72  Male Erectile Disorder

### Orgasmic Disorders

302.73  Female Orgasmic Disorder
302.74  Male Orgasmic Disorder
302.75  Premature Ejaculation

### Sexual Pain Disorders

302.76  Dyspareunia (Not Due to a General Medical Condition)
306.51  Vaginismus (Not Due to a General Medical Condition)

### Sexual Dysfunction Due to a General Medical Condition

625.8  Female Hypoactive Sexual Desire Disorder Due to ... *[Indicate the General Medical Condition]*
608.89  Male Hypoactive Sexual Desire Disorder Due to ... *[Indicate the General Medical Condition]*
607.84  Male Erectile Disorder Due to ... *[Indicate the General Medical Condition]*

625.0    Female Dyspareunia Due to ... *[Indicate the General Medical Condition]*

608.89   Male Dyspareunia Due to ... *[Indicate the General Medical Condition]*

625.8    Other Female Sexual Dysfunction Due to ... *[Indicate the General Medical Condition]*

608.89   Other Male Sexual Dysfunction Due to ... *[Indicate the General Medical Condition]*

___.__   Substance-Induced Sexual Dysfunction *(refer to Substance-Related Disorders for substance-specific codes)*
         *Specify if:* With Impaired Desire/With Impaired Arousal/With Impaired Orgasm/With Sexual Pain
         *Specify if:* With Onset During Intoxication

302.70   Sexual Dysfunction NOS


## Paraphilias

302.4    Exhibitionism
302.81   Fetishism
302.89   Frotteurism
302.2    Pedophilia
         *Specify if:* Sexually Attracted to Males/Sexually Attracted to Females/Sexually Attracted to Both
         *Specify if:* Limited to Incest
         *Specify type:* Exclusive Type/Nonexclusive Type
302.83   Sexual Masochism
302.84   Sexual Sadism
302.3    Transvestic Fetishism
         *Specify if:* With Gender Dysphoria
302.82   Voyeurism
302.9    Paraphilia NOS


## Gender Identity Disorders

302.xx   Gender Identity Disorder
    .6   In Children
    .85  In Adolescents or Adults
         *Specify if:* Sexually Attracted to Males/Sexually Attracted to Females/Sexually Attracted to Both/Sexually Attracted to Neither
302.6    Gender Identity Disorder NOS
302.9    Sexual Disorder NOS

# EATING DISORDERS

307.1    Anorexia Nervosa
         *Specify type:* Restricting Type; Binge-Eating/
         Purging Type
307.51   Bulimia Nervosa
         *Specify type:* Purging Type/Nonpurging Type
307.50   Eating Disorder NOS

# SLEEP DISORDERS

## Primary Sleep Disorders

### *Dyssomnias*

307.42   Primary Insomnia
307.44   Primary Hypersomnia
         *Specify if:* Recurrent
347      Narcolepsy
780.59   Breathing-Related Sleep Disorder
307.45   Circadian Rhythm Sleep Disorder
         *Specify type:* Delayed Sleep Phase Type/Jet Lag
         Type/Shift Work Type/Unspecified Type
307.47   Dyssomnia NOS

### *Parasomnias*

307.47   Nightmare Disorder
307.46   Sleep Terror Disorder
307.46   Sleepwalking Disorder
307.47   Parasomnia NOS

## Sleep Disorders Related to Another Mental Disorder

307.42   Insomnia Related to ... *[Indicate the Axis I or
         Axis II Disorder]*
307.44   Hypersomnia Related to ... *[Indicate the Axis I or
         Axis II Disorder]*

## Other Sleep Disorders

780.xx   Sleep Disorder Due to ... *[Indicate the General
         Medical Condition]*

.52   Insomnia Type
.54   Hypersomnia Type
.59   Parasomnia Type
.59   Mixed Type
___.___   Substance-Induced Sleep Disorder *(refer to Substance-Related Disorders for substance-specific codes)*
*Specify type*: Insomnia Type/Hypersomnia Type/ Parasomnia Type/Mixed Type
*Specify if*: With Onset During Intoxication/With Onset During Withdrawal

# IMPULSE-CONTROL DISORDERS NOT ELSEWHERE CLASSIFIED

312.34   Intermittent Explosive Disorder
312.32   Kleptomania
312.33   Pyromania
312.31   Pathologic Gambling
312.39   Trichotillomania
312.30   Impulse-Control Disorder NOS

# ADJUSTMENT DISORDERS

309.xx   Adjustment Disorder
.0   With Depressed Mood
.24   With Anxiety
.28   With Mixed Anxiety and Depressed Mood
.3   With Disturbance of Conduct
.4   With Mixed Disturbance of Emotions and Conduct
.9   Unspecified
*Specify if*: Acute/Chronic

# PERSONALITY DISORDERS

*NOTE: These are coded on Axis II.*
301.0    Paranoid Personality Disorder
301.20   Schizoid Personality Disorder
301.22   Schizotypal Personality Disorder
301.7    Antisocial Personality Disorder
301.83   Borderline Personality Disorder
301.50   Histrionic Personality Disorder
301.81   Narcissistic Personality Disorder

301.82 Avoidant Personality Disorder
301.6 Dependent Personality Disorder
301.4 Obsessive-Compulsive Personality Disorder
301.9 Personality Disorder NOS

# OTHER CONDITIONS THAT MAY BE A FOCUS OF CLINICAL ATTENTION

## Psychologic Factors Affecting Medical Condition

316 ... *[Specified Psychologic Factor]* Affecting ... *[Indicate the General Medical Condition]*
*Choose name based on nature of factors:*
Mental Disorder Affecting Medical Condition
Psychological Symptoms Affecting Medical Condition
Personality Traits or Coping Style Affecting Medical Condition
Maladaptive Health Behaviors Affecting Medical Condition
Stress-Related Physiological Response Affecting Medical Condition
Other or Unspecified Psychological Factors Affecting Medical Condition

## Medication-Induced Movement Disorders

332.1 Neuroleptic-Induced Parkinsonism
333.92 Neuroleptic Malignant Syndrome
333.7 Neuroleptic-Induced Acute Dystonia
333.99 Neuroleptic-Induced Acute Akathisia
333.82 Neuroleptic-Induced Tardive Dyskinesia
333.1 Medication-Induced Postural Tremor
333.90 Medication-Induced Movement Disorder NOS

## Other Medication-Induced Disorder

995.2 Adverse Effects of Medication NOS

## Relational Problems

V61.9 Relational Problem Related to a Mental Disorder or General Medical Condition

V61.20   Parent-Child Relational Problem
V61.10   Partner Relational Problem
V61.8    Sibling Relational Problem
V62.81   Relational Problem NOS

## Problems Related to Abuse or Neglect

V61.21   Physical Abuse of Child (code 995.5 if focus of attention is on victim)
V61.21   Sexual Abuse of Child (code 995.5 if focus of attention is on victim)
V61.21   Neglect of Child (code 995.5 if focus of attention is on victim)
___.___   Physical Abuse of Adult
V61.12   (if by partner)
V62.83   (if by person other than partner) (code 995.81 if focus of attention is on victim)
___.___   Sexual Abuse of Adult
V61.12   (if by partner)
V62.83   (if by person other than partner) (code 995.83 if focus of attention is on victim)

## Additional Conditions That May Be a Focus of Clinical Attention

V15.81   Noncompliance With Treatment
V65.2    Malingering
V71.01   Adult Antisocial Behavior
V71.02   Child or Adolescent Antisocial Behavior
V62.89   Borderline Intellectual Functioning
*NOTE: This is coded on Axis II.*
780.9    Age-Related Cognitive Decline
V62.82   Bereavement
V62.3    Academic Problem
V62.2    Occupational Problem
313.82   Identity Problem
V62.89   Religious or Spiritual Problem
V62.4    Acculturation Problem
V62.89   Phase of Life Problem

# ADDITIONAL CODES

| | |
|---|---|
| 300.9 | Unspecified Mental Disorder (nonpsychotic) |
| V71.09 | No Diagnosis or Condition on Axis I |
| 799.9 | Diagnosis or Condition Deferred on Axis I |
| V71.09 | No Diagnosis on Axis II |
| 799.9 | Diagnosis Deferred on Axis II |

From American Psychiatric Association. (2000). *Diagnostic and statistical manual of mental disorders* (4th ed., text rev.) *(DSM-IV-TR)*. Washington, DC: Author.

# APPENDIX C

# Assessment Tools for Children and Adolescents

## APPENDIX C-1: STAGES OF DEVELOPMENT (ACCORDING TO FREUD, SULLIVAN, AND ERIKSON)

| Freud | Sullivan | Erikson |
|---|---|---|
| **Oral**—birth to 1½ years<br>**Pleasure-pain principle**<br>**Id,** the instinctive and primitive mind, is dominant<br>Demanding, impulsive, irrational, asocial, selfish, trustful, omnipotent, and dependent<br>Primary thought processes<br>Unconscious instincts—source-energy-aim-object<br>Mouth—Primary source of pleasure<br>Immediate release of tension/anxiety and immediate gratification through oral gratification<br>Task—Develop a sense of trust that needs will be met | **Infancy**—birth to 1½ years<br>Mothering object relieves tension through empathetic intervention and tenderness, leading to decreased anxiety and increased satisfaction and security. Mother becomes symbolized as "good mother."<br>Goal is biological satisfaction and psychological security.<br>Denial of tension relief creates anxiety, and mother becomes symbolized as "bad mother." Anxiety in mother yields anxiety and fear in child via empathy.<br>These states are experienced by the child in diffuse undifferentiated manner<br>Task—Learn to count on others for satisfaction and security to trust. | **Infancy**—birth to 1½ years<br>**Trust vs. Mistrust**<br>Egocentric<br>Danger: During second half of first year, an abrupt and prolonged separation may intensify the natural sense of loss and may lead to a sense of mistrust that may last through life.<br>Task—Develop a basic sense of trust that leads to hope. Trust requires a feeling of physical comfort and a minimal experience of fear or uncertainty. If this occurs, the child will extend trust to the world and self. |

**Anal**—1½ to 3 years
**Reality principle**—Postpone immediate discharge of energy and seek actual object to satisfy needs
Learning to defer pleasure
Gaining satisfaction from tolerating some tension-mastering impulses
Focus on toilet training—retaining/letting go; power struggle
**Ego development**—Functions of the ego include problem-solving skills, perception, ability to mediate id impulses.
Task—Delay immediate gratification
**Phallic**—3 to 7 years
**Superego develops** via incorporating moral values, ideals, and judgments of right and wrong that are held by parents. Superego is primarily

**Childhood**—1½ to 6 years
Muscular maturation and learning to communicate verbally
Learning social skills through consensual validation
Beginning to develop self system via reflected appraisals:
 Good me
 Bad me
 Not me
Levels of awareness
 Aware
 Selective inattention
 Dissociation
Task—Learn to delay satisfaction of wishes with relative comfort.

**Early Childhood**—1½ to 3 years
**Autonomy vs. Shame/Doubt**
Develop confidence in physical and mental abilities that leads to the development an autonomous will.
Danger: Development of a deep sense of shame/doubt if child is deprived of the opportunity to rebel. Learns to expect defeat in any battle of wills with those who are bigger and stronger.
Task—Gain self-control of and independence within the environment.

**Play**—3 to 6 years
**Initiative vs. Guilt**
Interest in socially appropriate goals leads to a sense of purpose.

*Continued*

| Freud | Sullivan | Erikson |
|---|---|---|
| unconscious and functions on the **reward and punishment principle** (sexual identity attained via resolving oedipal conflict). Conflict differs for boy and girl masturbatory activity. Task—Develop sexual identity through identification with same-sex parent. | | Imagination is greatly expanded because of increased ability to move around freely and increased ability to communicate. Intrusive activity and curiosity and consuming fantasies, which lead to feelings of guilt and anxiety Establishment of conscience Danger: May develop a deep-seated conviction that he or she is essentially bad, with a resultant stifling of initiative or a conversion of moralism to vindictiveness Task—Achieve a sense of purpose and develop a sense of mastery over tasks. |
| | | **School age**—6 to 12 years **Industry vs. Inferiority** Develops a healthy competitive drive that leads to confidence In learning to accept instruction and to win recognition by producing |
| **Latency**—7 to 12 years De-sexualization; libido diffused Involved in learning social skills, exploring, building, collecting, accomplishing, and hero worship Peer group loyalty begins Gang and scout behavior | **Juvenile**—6 to 9 years Absorbed in learning to deal with ever-widening outside world, peers, and other adults; reflections and revisions of self-image and parental images | |

| | | |
|---|---|---|
| Growing independence from family Task—Sexuality is repressed during this time; learn to form close relationship(s) with same sex peers. | Task—Develop satisfying interpersonal relationships with peers that involve competition and compromise. | "things," the child opens the way for the capacity of work enjoyment. Danger: The development of a sense of inadequacy and inferiority in a child who does not receive recognition Task—Gain a sense of self-confidence and recognition through learning, competing, and performing successfully. |
| | **Preadolescence**—9 to 12 years Develops intimate interpersonal relationship with person of same sex who is perceived to be much like oneself in interests, feelings, and mutual collaboration Task—Learn to care for others of same sex who are outside the family. Sullivan called this the "normal homosexual phase." | |
| **Genital phase** (Adolescence)— 13 to 20 years | **Adolescence—12 to 20 years** *Early adolescence—12-14 years* | **Adolescence—12 to 20 years Identity vs. Identity** |

*Continued*

| Freud | Sullivan | Erikson |
|-------|----------|---------|
| Fluctuation regarding emotion stability and physical maturation. Very ambivalent and labile, seeking life goals and emancipation from parents | Establishing satisfying relationships with opposite sex | **Diffusion** Differentiation from parents leads to fidelity (sense of self) |
| Dependence *vs.* independence reappraisal of parents and self; intense peer loyalty | *Late adolescence—14 to 20 years* Interdependent and establishing durable sexual relations with a select member of the opposite sex | The physiological revolution that comes with puberty (rapid body growth and sexual maturity) forces the young person to question beliefs and to re-fight many of the earlier battles |
| Task—Form close relationships and with members of the opposite sex based on genuine caring and pleasure in the interaction. | Task—Form intimate and long-lasting relationships with the opposite sex and develop a sense of identity. | Danger: Temporary identity diffusion (instability) may result in a permanent inability to integrate a personal identity. |
| | | Task—Integrate all the tasks previously mastered into a secure sense of self. |
| | | **Young adulthood**—20 to 30 years **Intimacy vs. Isolation** Maturity and social responsibility results in the ability to love and be loved. |

As people feel more secure in their identity, they are able to establish intimacy with themselves (their inner life) and with others, eventually in a love-based satisfying sexual relationship with a member of the opposite sex.

Danger: Fear of losing identity may prevent intimate relationship and result in a deep sense of isolation.

Task—Form intense long-term relationships and commit to another person, cause, institution, or creative effort.

**Adulthood**—30 to 65 years

**Generativity vs. Self-absorption**

Interest in nurturing subsequent generations creates a sense of caring, contributing, and generativity.

Danger: Lack of generativity results in self-absorption and stagnation.

Task—Achieve life goals and obtain concern and awareness of future generations.

*Continued*

| Freud | Sullivan | Erikson |
|-------|----------|---------|
|       |          | **Senescence**—65 years to death **Integrity vs. Despair** Acceptance of mortality and satisfaction with life leads to wisdom. Satisfying intimacy with other human beings and adaptive response to triumphs and disappointments Marked by a sense of what life is, was, and its place in the flow of history Danger—Without this "accrued ego integration," there is despair, usually marked by a display of displeasure and distrust. Task—Derive meaning from one's whole life and obtain/maintain a sense of self-worth. |

Developed from original sources by Freud, Sullivan, and Erikson.

# APPENDIX C-2: DEVELOPMENTAL ASSESSMENT TOOL

## HISTORY OF PRESENT ILLNESS

- Chief complaint
- Development and duration of problems
- Help sought and tried
- Effect of problem on child's life at home and school
- Effect of problem on family and sibling's life

## DEVELOPMENTAL HISTORY

- Pregnancy, birth, neonatal data
- Developmental milestones
- Description of eating, sleeping, elimination habits, and routines
- Attachment behaviors
- Types of play
- Social skills and friendships
- Sexual activity

## DEVELOPMENT ASSESSMENT

- Psychomotor
- Language
- Cognitive
- Interpersonal-social
- Academic achievement
- Behavior (response to stress, changes in the environment)
- Problem solving and coping skills (impulse control, delay of gratification)
- Energy level and motivation

## NEUROLOGIC ASSESSMENT

- Cerebral functions
- Cerebellar functions
- Sensory functions
- Reflexes
- Cranial nerves

- Functions can be observed in developmental assessment and while playing games involving a specific ability (e.g., "Simon Says, touch your nose.")

# MEDICAL HISTORY

- Review of body systems
- Trauma, hospitalization, operations, and child's response
- Illnesses or injuries affecting the central nervous system
- Medications (past and current)
- Allergies

# FAMILY HISTORY

- Illnesses in related family members (e.g., seizures, mental disorders, mental retardation, hyperactivity, drug and alcohol abuse, diabetes, cancer)
- Background of family members (occupation, education, social, activities, religion)
- Family relationships (separation, divorce, deaths, contact with extended family, support system)

# MENTAL STATUS ASSESSMENT

- General appearance
- Activity level
- Coordination/motor function
- Affect
- Speech
- Manner of relating
- Intellectual functions
- Thought processes and content
- Characteristics of child's play

# APPENDIX C-3: CHILD AND ADOLESCENT MENTAL STATUS EXAM

## GENERAL APPEARANCE

- Size—height and weight
- General health and nutrition
- Dress and grooming
- Distinguishing characteristics
- Gestures and mannerisms
- Looks/acts younger or older than chronological age

## SPEECH

- Rate, rhythm, intonation
- Pitch and modulation
- Vocabulary and grammar appropriate to age
- Mute, hesitant, talkative
- Articulation problems
- Other expressive problems
- Unusual characteristics (pronoun reversal, echolalia, gender confusion, neologisms)

## INTELLECTUAL FUNCTIONS

- Fund of general information
- Ability to communicate (follow directions, answer questions)
- Memory
- Creativity
- Sense of humor
- Social awareness
- Learning and problem solving
- Conscience (sense of right and wrong, accepts guilt and limits)

## CHARACTERISTICS OF CHILD'S PLAY

- Age appropriate use of toys
- Themes of play
- Imagination and pretend play
- Role and gender play
- Age-appropriate play with peers

- Relationship with peers (empathy, sharing, waiting for turns, best friends)

## ACTIVITY LEVEL

- Hyperactivity/hypoactivity
- Tics, other body movements
- Autoerotic and self-comforting movements (thumb sucking, ear/hair pulling, masturbation)

## COORDINATION/MOTOR FUNCTION

- Posture
- Gait
- Balance
- Gross motor movement
- Fine motor movement
- Writing and drawing skills
- Unusual characteristics (bizarre postures, tiptoe walking, hand flapping, head banging, hand biting)

## MANNER OF RELATING

- Eye contact
- Ability to separate from caregiver, be independent
- Attitude toward interviewer
- Behavior during interview (ability to have fun/play, low frustration tolerance, impulsive, aggressive)

## THOUGHT PROCESSES AND CONTENT

- Orientation
- Attention span
- Self-concept and body image
- Sex role, gender identity
- Ego-defense mechanisms
- Perceptual distortions (hallucinations, illusions)
- Preoccupations, concerns, and unusual ideas
- Fantasies and dreams

Adapted from Goodman, J.D., & Sours, J. (1987). *The child mental status examination* (2nd ed.). New York: Basic Books.

# APPENDIX D

# Assessment Guides

## APPENDIX D-1: DEFENSE MECHANISMS

| Mild use | Extreme example |
|---|---|
| **Repression** | |
| Man forgets wife's birthday after a marital fight. | Woman is unable to enjoy sex after having pushed out of awareness a traumatic sexual incident from childhood. |
| **Sublimation** | |
| Woman who is angry with her boss writes a short story about a heroic woman. By definition, use of sublimation is always constructive. | None. |
| **Regression** | |
| Four-year-old with a new baby brother starts sucking his thumb and wanting a bottle. | Man who loses a promotion starts complaining to others, hands in sloppy work, misses appointments, and comes in late for meetings. |
| **Displacement** | |
| Patient criticizes a nurse after his family fails to visit. | Child who is unable to acknowledge fear of his father becomes fearful of animals. |

*Continued*

| Mild use | Extreme example |
|---|---|
| **Projection** | |
| Man who is unconsciously attracted to other women teases his wife about flirting. | Woman who has repressed an attraction toward other women refuses to socialize. She fears another woman will make homosexual advances toward her. |
| **Compensation** | |
| Short man becomes assertively verbal and excels in business. | Individual drinks when self-esteem is low to diffuse discomfort temporarily. |
| **Reaction-Formation** | |
| Recovering alcoholic constantly preaches about the evils of drink. | Mother who has an unconscious hostility toward her daughter is overprotective and hovers over her to protect her from harm, interfering with her normal growth and development. |
| **Denial** | |
| Man reacts to news of the death of a loved one by saying, "No, I don't believe you. The doctor said he was fine." | Woman whose husband died 3 years ago still keeps his clothes in the closet and talks about him in the present tense. |
| **Conversion** | |
| Student is unable to take a final examination because of a terrible headache. | Man becomes blind after seeing his wife flirt with other men. |
| **Undoing** | |
| After flirting with her male secretary, a woman brings her husband tickets to a show. | Man with rigid and moralistic beliefs and repressed sexuality is driven to wash his hands when around attractive women to gain composure. |
| **Rationalization** | |
| "I didn't get the raise because the boss doesn't like me." | Father who thinks his son was fathered by another man excuses his malicious treatment of the boy by saying, "He is lazy and disobedient," when that is not the case. |

| Mild use | Extreme example |
|---|---|
| **Identification** | |
| Five-year-old girl dresses in her mother's shoes and dress and meets her father at the door. | Young boy thinks a neighborhood pimp with money and drugs is someone to look up to. |
| **Introjection** | |
| After his wife's death, husband has transient complaints of chest pains and difficulty breathing—the symptoms his wife had before she died. | Young girl whose parents were overcritical and belittling grows up thinking that she is not any good. She has taken on her parent's evaluation of her as part of her self-image. |
| **Suppression** | |
| Businessman who is preparing to make an important speech that day is told by his wife that morning that she wants a divorce. Although visibly upset, he puts the incident aside until after his speech, when he can give the matter his total concentration. | A woman who feels a lump in her breast shortly before leaving for a 3-week vacation puts the information in the back of her mind until after returning from her vacation. |

From Varcarolis, E.M. (2002). *Foundations of psychiatric mental health nursing* (4th ed.). Philadelphia: Saunders.

# APPENDIX D-2: HAMILTON RATING SCALE FOR ANXIETY

Max Hamilton designed this scale to help clinicians gather information about anxiety states. The symptom inventory provides scaled information that classifies anxiety behaviors and assists the clinician in targeting behaviors and achieving outcome measures. Provide a rating for each indicator based on the following scale:

    0 = None
    1 = Mild
    2 = Moderate
    3 = Disabling
    4 = Severe, Grossly Disabling

| Item | Symptoms | Rating |
|------|----------|--------|
| Anxious mood | Worries, anticipation of the worst, fearful anticipation, irritability | _____ |
| Tension | Feelings of tension, fatigability, startle response, moved to tears easily, trembling, feelings of restlessness, inability to relax | _____ |
| Fear | Of dark, of strangers, of being left alone, of animals, of traffic, of crowds | _____ |
| Insomnia | Difficulty in falling asleep, broken sleep, unsatisfying sleep and fatigue on waking, dreams, nightmares, night terrors | _____ |
| Intellectual (cognitive) | Difficulty in concentration, poor memory | _____ |
| Depressed mood | Loss of interest, lack of pleasure in hobbies, depression, early waking, diurnal swings | _____ |
| Somatic (sensory) | Tinnitus, blurring of vision, hot and cold flushes, feelings of weakness, prickling sensation | _____ |
| Somatic (muscular) | Pains and aches, twitches, stiffness, myoclonic jerks, grinding of teeth, unsteady voice, increased muscular tone | _____ |
| Cardiovascular symptoms | Tachycardia, palpitations, pain in chest, throbbing of vessels, fainting feelings, missing beat | _____ |
| Respiratory symptoms | Pressure of constriction in chest, choking feelings, sighing, dyspnea | _____ |
| Gastrointestinal symptoms | Difficulty in swallowing, wind, abdominal pain, burning sensations, abdominal fullness, nausea, vomiting, borborygmi, looseness of bowels, loss of weight, constipation | _____ |
| Genitourinary symptoms | Frequency of micturition, urgency of micturition, amenorrhea, menorrhagia, development of frigidity, premature ejaculation, loss of libido, impotence | _____ |

| Item | Symptoms | Rating |
|------|----------|--------|
| Autonomic symptoms | Dry mouth, flushing, pallor, tendency to sweat, giddiness, tension headache, raising of hair | _____ |
| Behavior at interview | Fidgeting, restlessness or pacing, tremor of hands, furrowed brow, strained face, sighing or rapid respiration, facial pallor, swallowing, belching, brisk tendon jerks, dilated pupils, exophthalmos | _____ |

Adapted from Hamilton, M. (1959). The assessment of anxiety states by rating. *British Journal of Medical Psychology, 32,* 50–55; reprinted with permission.

## APPENDIX D-3: HAMILTON DEPRESSION RATING SCALE (HDRS)

### PLEASE COMPLETE THE SCALE BASED ON A STRUCTURED INTERVIEW

Instructions: for each item select the one "cue" which best characterizes the patient. Be sure to record the answers in the appropriate spaces (positions 0 through 4).

---

1 **DEPRESSED MOOD** (*sadness,    hopeless,    helpless, worthless*)

   0 ☐ Absent.
   1 ☐ These feeling states indicated only on questioning.
   2 ☐ These feeling states spontaneously reported verbally.
   3 ☐ Communicates feeling states non-verbally, i.e. through facial expression, posture,voice and tendency to weep.
   4 ☐ Patient reports virtually only these feeling states in his/her spontaneous verbal and non-verbal communication.

2 **FEELINGS OF GUILT**

   0 ☐ Absent.
   1 ☐ Self reproach, feels he/she has let people down.
   2 ☐ Ideas of guilt or rumination over past errors or sinful deeds.
   3 ☐ Present illness is a punishment. Delusions of guilt.
   4 ☐ Hears accusatory or denunciatory voices and/or experiences threatening visual hallucinations.

### 3 SUICIDE
0 □ Absent.
1 □ Feels life is not worth living.
2 □ Wishes he/she were dead or any thoughts of possible death to self.
3 □ Ideas or gestures of suicide.
4 □ Attempts at suicide (any serious attempt rate 4).

### 4 INSOMNIA: EARLY IN THE NIGHT
0 □ No difficulty falling asleep.
1 □ Complains of occasional difficulty falling asleep, i.e. more than ½ hour.
2 □ Complains of nightly difficulty falling asleep.

### 5 INSOMNIA: MIDDLE OF THE NIGHT
0 □ No difficulty.
1 □ Patient complains of being restless and disturbed during the night.
2 □ Waking during the night – any getting out of bed rates 2 (except for purposes of voiding).

### 6 INSOMNIA: EARLY HOURS OF THE MORNING
0 □ No difficulty.
1 □ Waking in early hours of the morning but goes back to sleep.
2 □ Unable to fall asleep again if he/she gets out of bed.

### 7 WORK AND ACTIVITIES
0 □ No difficulty.
1 □ Thoughts and feelings of incapacity, fatigue or weakness related to activities, work or hobbies.
2 □ Loss of interest in activity, hobbies or work – either directly reported by the patient or indirect in listlessness, indecision and vacillation (feels he/she has to push self to work or activities).
3 □ Decrease in actual time spent in activities or decrease in productivity. Rate 3 if the patient does not spend at least three hours a day in activities (job or hobbies) excluding routine chores.
4 □ Stopped working because of present illness. Rate 4 if patient engages in no activities except routine chores, or if patient fails to perform routine chores unassisted.

8 **RETARDATION** (slowness of thought and speech, impaired ability to concentrate, decreased motor activity)
   0 ☐ Normal speech and thought.
   1 ☐ Slight retardation during the interview.
   2 ☐ Obvious retardation during the interview.
   3 ☐ Interview difficult.
   4 ☐ Complete stupor.

9 **AGITATION**
   0 ☐ None.
   1 ☐ Fidgetiness.
   2 ☐ Playing with hands, hair, etc.
   3 ☐ Moving about, can't sit still.
   4 ☐ Hand wringing, nail biting, hair-pulling, biting of lips.

10 **ANXIETY PSYCHIC**
   0 ☐ No difficulty.
   1 ☐ Subjective tension and irritability.
   2 ☐ Worrying about minor matters.
   3 ☐ Apprehensive attitude apparent in face or speech.
   4 ☐ Fears expressed without questioning.

11 **ANXIETY SOMATIC** (physiological concomitants of anxiety) such as:
   gastro-intestinal – dry mouth, wind, indigestion, diarrhea, cramps, belching
   cardio-vascular – palpitations, headaches
   respiratory – hyperventilation, sighing
   urinary frequency
   sweating
   0 ☐ Absent.
   1 ☐ Mild.
   2 ☐ Moderate.
   3 ☐ Severe.
   4 ☐ Incapacitating.

12 **SOMATIC SYMPTOMS GASTRO-INTESTINAL**
   0 ☐ None.
   1 ☐ Loss of appetite but eating without staff encouragement. Heavy feelings in abdomen.
   2 ☐ Difficulty eating without staff urging. Requests or requires laxatives or medication for bowels or medication for gastro-intestinal symptoms.

## 13 GENERAL SOMATIC SYMPTOMS
0 ☐ None.
1 ☐ Heaviness in limbs, back or head. Backaches, headaches, muscle aches. Loss of energy and fatigability.
2 ☐ Any clear-cut symptom rates 2.

## 14 GENITAL SYMPTOMS (symptoms such as loss of libido, menstrual disturbances)
0 ☐ Absent.
1 ☐ Mild.
2 ☐ Severe.

## 15 HYPOCHONDRIASIS
0 ☐ Not present.
1 ☐ Self-absorption (bodily).
2 ☐ Preoccupation with health.
3 ☐ Frequent complaints, requests for help, etc.
4 ☐ Hypochondriacal delusions.

## 16 LOSS OF WEIGHT (*RATE EITHER a OR b*)
a) **According to the patient:**
   0 ☐ No weight loss.
   1 ☐ Probable weight loss associated with present illness.
   2 ☐ Definite (according 2 to patient) weight loss.
   3 ☐ Not assessed.

b) **According to weekly measurements:**
   0 ☐ Less than 1 lb weight loss in week.
   1 ☐ Greater than 1 lb weight loss in week.
   2 ☐ Greater than 2 lb weight loss in week.
   3 ☐ Not assessed.

## 17 INSIGHT
0 ☐ Acknowledges being depressed and ill.
1 ☐ Acknowledges illness but attributes cause to bad food, climate, overwork, virus, need for rest, etc.
2 ☐ Denies being ill at all.

Total score: ☐☐

---

This scale is in the public domain.

# APPENDIX D-4: MANIA QUESTIONNAIRE

Use this questionnaire to help determine if you need to see a mental health professional for diagnosis and treatment of mania or manic-depression or bipolar disorder.

**Instructions:** You might reproduce this scale and use it on a weekly basis to track your moods. It also might be used to show your doctor how your symptoms have changed from one visit to the next. Changes of 5 or more points are significant. This scale is not designed to make a diagnosis of mania or take the place of a professional diagnosis. If you suspect you are manic, please consult with a mental health professional as soon as possible.

The 18 items below refer to how you have felt and behaved DURING THE PAST WEEK. For each item, indicate the extent to which it is true by circling the appropriate number next to the item.

Key:

| | |
|---|---|
| 0 = Not at all | 3 = Moderately |
| 1 = A little | 4 = Quite a lot |
| 2 = Somewhat | 5 = Very much |

| | | | | | | | |
|---|---|---|---|---|---|---|---|
| 1. My mind has never been sharper. | 0 | 1 | 2 | 3 | 4 | 5 |
| 2. I need less sleep than usual. | 0 | 1 | 2 | 3 | 4 | 5 |
| 3. I have so many plans and new ideas that it is hard for me to work. | 0 | 1 | 2 | 3 | 4 | 5 |
| 4. I feel a pressure to talk and talk. | 0 | 1 | 2 | 3 | 4 | 5 |
| 5. I have been particularly happy. | 0 | 1 | 2 | 3 | 4 | 5 |
| 6. I have been more active than usual. | 0 | 1 | 2 | 3 | 4 | 5 |
| 7. I talk so fast that people have a hard time keeping up with me. | 0 | 1 | 2 | 3 | 4 | 5 |
| 8. I have more new ideas than I can handle. | 0 | 1 | 2 | 3 | 4 | 5 |
| 9. I have been irritable. | 0 | 1 | 2 | 3 | 4 | 5 |
| 10. It's easy for me to think of jokes and funny stories. | 0 | 1 | 2 | 3 | 4 | 5 |
| 11. I have been feeling like "the life of the party." | 0 | 1 | 2 | 3 | 4 | 5 |

*Continued*

| | | |
|---|---|---|
| 12. I have been full of energy. | 0 1 2 3 4 5 |
| 13. I have been thinking about sex. | 0 1 2 3 4 5 |
| 14. I have been feeling particularly playful. | 0 1 2 3 4 5 |
| 15. I have special plans for the world. | 0 1 2 3 4 5 |
| 16. I have been spending too much money. | 0 1 2 3 4 5 |
| 17. My attention keeps jumping from one idea to another. | 0 1 2 3 4 5 |
| 18. I find it hard to slow down and stay in one place. | 0 1 2 3 4 5 |

# APPENDIX D-5: BRIEF PSYCHIATRIC RATING SCALE

DIRECTIONS: Place an X in the appropriate box to represent level of severity of each symptom.

Patient Name _____ Physician _____
Patient SS# ____ UT# ____ HH# _____ Date _____

| | Not Present | Very Mild | Mild | Moderate | Mod. Severe | Severe | Extremely Severe |
|---|---|---|---|---|---|---|---|
| SOMATIC CONCERN—preoccupation with physical health, fear of physical illness, hypochondriasis | ☐ | ☐ | ☐ | ☐ | ☐ | ☐ | ☐ |
| ANXIETY—worry, fear, over-concern for present or future, uneasiness | ☐ | ☐ | ☐ | ☐ | ☐ | ☐ | ☐ |
| EMOTIONAL WITHDRAWAL—lack of spontaneous interaction, isolation deficiency in relating to others | ☐ | ☐ | ☐ | ☐ | ☐ | ☐ | ☐ |

| | □ | □ | □ | □ | □ | □ | □ |
|---|---|---|---|---|---|---|---|
| CONCEPTUAL DISORGANIZATION— thought processes confused, disconnected, disorganized, disrupted | | | | | | | |
| GUILT FEELINGS—self-blame, shame, remorse for past behavior | □ | □ | □ | □ | □ | □ | □ |
| TENSION—physical and motor manifestations of nervousness, overactivation | □ | □ | □ | □ | □ | □ | □ |
| MANNERISMS AND POSTURING—peculiar, bizarre, unnatural motor behavior (not including tic) | □ | □ | □ | □ | □ | □ | □ |
| GRANDIOSITY— exaggerated self-opinion, arrogance, conviction of unusual power or abilities | □ | □ | □ | □ | □ | □ | □ |
| DEPRESSIVE MOOD— sorrow, sadness, despondency, pessimism | □ | □ | □ | □ | □ | □ | □ |
| HOSTILITY—animosity, contempt, belligerence, disdain for others | □ | □ | □ | □ | □ | □ | □ |
| SUSPICIOUSNESS— mistrust, belief others harbor malicious or discriminatory intent | □ | □ | □ | □ | □ | □ | □ |
| HALLUCINATORY BEHAVIOR—perceptions without normal stimulus correspondence | □ | □ | □ | □ | □ | □ | □ |
| MOTOR RETARDATION— slowed, weakened movements or speech, reduced body tone | □ | □ | □ | □ | □ | □ | □ |
| UNCOOPERATIVENESS— resistance, guardedness, rejection of authority | □ | □ | □ | □ | □ | □ | □ |
| UNUSUAL THOUGHT CONTENT—unusual, odd, strange, bizarre thought content | □ | □ | □ | □ | □ | □ | □ |

*Continued*

| BLUNTED AFFECT— reduced emotional tone, reduction in formal intensity of feelings, flatness | ☐ | ☐ | ☐ | ☐ | ☐ | ☐ | ☐ |
| EXCITEMENT—emotional tone, agitation, increased reactivity | ☐ | ☐ | ☐ | ☐ | ☐ | ☐ | ☐ |
| DISORIENTATION— confusion or lack of proper association for person, place, or time | ☐ | ☐ | ☐ | ☐ | ☐ | ☐ | ☐ |

**Global Assessment Scale (Range 0–100)** _____

From Overall, J.E., & Gorham, D.R. (1962). The Brief Psychiatric Rating Scale. *Psychological Reports, 10,* 799–812; reprinted by permission. Copyright Southern Universities Press, 1962.

# APPENDIX D-6: SAMPLE QUESTIONS TO IDENTIFY PERSONALITY DISORDERS

The nurse uses a variety of therapeutic techniques to obtain the answers to the following questions. Use your discretion and decide which questions are appropriate to complete your assessment.

**The following questions are NOT meant to be used in a checklist fashion. They should be woven into the assessment, with only a few of the questions used for each diagnosis. Often the answer to one can eliminate certain diagnoses.**

## OBSESSIVE-COMPULSIVE PERSONALITY

1. Do you tend to drive yourself pretty hard, frequently feeling like you need to do just a little more? (yes)
2. Do you think that most people would view you as witty and light-hearted? (no)
3. Do you tend toward being a perfectionist? (yes)
4. Do you tend to keep lists or sometimes feel a need to keep checking things, like is the door locked? (yes)

# DEPENDENT PERSONALITY

1. Is it sort of hard for you to argue with your spouse, because you're worried that he or she will really get mad at you and start to dislike you? (yes)
2. When you wake up in the morning, do you need to plan your day around the activities of your husband or wife? (yes)
3. Do you enjoy making most decisions in your house, or would you prefer that others make the most important decisions? (prefers others to make decision)
4. When you were younger, did you often dream of finding someone who would take care of you and guide you? (yes)

# AVOIDANT PERSONALITY

1. Throughout most of your life, have you found yourself being worried that people won't like you? (yes)
2. Do you often find yourself sort of feeling inadequate and not up to new challenges and tasks? (yes)
3. Do you tend to be very careful about selecting friends, perhaps only having one or two close friends in your whole life? (yes)
4. Have you often felt hurt by others, so that you are pretty wary of opening yourself to other people? (yes)

# SCHIZOID PERSONALITY

1. Do you tend to really enjoy being around people, or do you much prefer being alone? (much prefers being alone)
2. Do you care a lot about what people think about you as a person? (tends not to care)
3. Are you a real emotional person? (no, feels strongly that he or she is not emotional)
4. During the course of your life, have you had only about one or two friends? (yes)

# ANTISOCIAL PERSONALITY

1. If you felt like the situation really warranted it, do you think that you would find it pretty easy to lie? (yes)
2. Have you ever been arrested or pulled over by the police? (yes)

3. Over the years have you found yourself able to take care of yourself in a physical fight? (yes)
4. Do you sometimes find yourself resenting people who give you orders? (yes)

# HISTRIONIC PERSONALITY

1. Do people of the opposite sex frequently find you attractive? (answered with an unabashed "yes")
2. Do you frequently find yourself being the center of attention, even if you don't want to be? (yes)
3. Do you view yourself as being a powerfully emotional person? (yes)
4. Do you think that you'd make a reasonably good actor or actress? (yes)

# NARCISSISTIC PERSONALITY

1. Do you find that when you get really down to it, most people aren't quite up to your standards? (yes)
2. If people give you a hard time, do you tend to put them in their place quickly? (yes)
3. If someone criticizes you, do you find yourself getting angry pretty quickly? (yes)
4. Do you think that compared with other people, you are a very special person? (answered with a self-assured "yes")

# BORDERLINE PERSONALITY

1. Do you frequently feel let down by people? (yes)
2. If a friend or family member hurts you, do you sometimes feel like hurting yourself, perhaps by cutting at yourself and burning yourself? (yes)
3. Do you find that other people cause you to feel angry a couple of times per week? (yes)
4. Do you think that your friends would view you as sort of moody? (yes)
5. Does anxiety make you want to self-mutilate? (yes)

# SCHIZOTYPAL PERSONALITY

1. Do you tend to stay by yourself, even though you would like to be with others? (yes)

2. Do you sometimes feel like other people are watching you or have some sort of special interest in you? (yes)
3. Have you ever felt like you had some special powers like ESP or some sort of magical influence over others? (yes)
4. Do you feel that people often want to reject you or that they find you odd? (yes)

## PARANOID PERSONALITY

1. Do you find that people often have a tendency to be disloyal or dishonest? (yes)
2. Is it fairly easy for you to get jealous, especially if some one is making eyes at your spouse? (yes)
3. Do you tend to keep things to yourself just to make sure the wrong people don't get the right information? (yes)
4. Do you feel that other people take advantage of you? (yes)

---

Adapted from Roberts, J.K.A. (1984). Differential diagnoses in neuropsychiatry. Chichester: John Wiley & Sons Limited, p. 26; and Shea, S.C. (1998). Psychiatric interviewing: The art of understanding. Philadelphia: Saunders, pp. 420–422; with permission.

# APPENDIX D-7: ASSESSMENTS FOR SUBSTANCE ABUSE

## APPENDIX D-7A: EMERGENCY DEPARTMENT BRIEF ASSESSMENT FOR SUBSTANCE ABUSE

The nurse uses a variety of therapeutic techniques to obtain the answers to the following questions. Use your discretion and decide which questions are appropriate to complete your assessment.

**If the client is impaired or unable to focus, friends and family members may be able to answer for the client.**

1. What drug(s) did you take before coming to the emergency department/hospital/clinic/session?

2. How did you take the drug(s) (e.g., intravenously, intramuscularly, orally, subcutaneously, smoking, intranasally)?
3. How much did you take (e.g., glasses of beer/wine/whisky)?
4. When was the last dose taken?
5. How long have you been using the substance? When did you start this last episode of use?
6. How often and how much do you usually use?
7. What kinds of problems have substance use caused for you? With your family/friends? Job? Health? Finances? The law?

## APPENDIX D-7B: BRIEF MICHIGAN ALCOHOL SCREENING TEST (MAST)

*Scoring Yes to 3 or more indicates alcoholism.*
1. Do you feel you are a normal drinker?
2. Do friends or relatives think you are a normal drinker?
3. Have you ever attended a meeting of Alcoholics Anonymous?
4. Have you ever gotten in trouble at work because of drinking?
5. Have you ever lost friends or girlfriends/boyfriends because of drinking?
6. Have you ever neglected your obligations, your family, or your work for 2 or more days in a row because of your drinking?
7. Have you ever had delirium tremens (DTs), severe shaking, or heard voices or seen things that were not there after heavy drinking?
8. Have you ever gone to anyone for help about your drinking?
9. Have you ever been in a hospital because of your drinking?
10. Have you ever been arrested for drunken driving or other drunken behavior?

From Pokorny, A.D., Miller, B.A., & Kaplan, H.B. (1972). The brief MAST: A shortened version of the Michigan Alcohol Screening Test. *American Journal of Psychiatry, 129,* 342–345; reprinted by permission. Copyright © 1972 by American Psychiatric Association. Available at <http://ajp.psychiatryonline.org>

# APPENDIX D-7C: DRUG ABUSE SCREEN TEST (DAST)

The following questions concern information about your involvement with drugs, not including alcoholic beverages, during the past 12 months.

In the statements, "drug abuse" refers (1) to the use of prescribed or OTC drugs in excess of the directions and (2) any nonmedical use of drugs. The various classes of drugs may include cannabis, solvents, antianxiety drugs, sedative-hypnotics, cocaine, stimulants, hallucinogens, and narcotics. Remember that the questions do not include alcoholic beverages.

*These questions refer to the past 12 months.*

| | |
|---|---|
| Have you used drugs other than those required for medical purposes? | Yes _____ No _____ |
| Do you abuse more than one drug at a time? | Yes _____ No _____ |
| Are you always able to stop using drugs when you want to? | Yes _____ No _____ |
| Have you had "blackouts" or "flashbacks" as a result of drug use? | Yes _____ No _____ |
| Do you ever feel bad about your drug abuse? | Yes _____ No _____ |
| Does your spouse (or parents) ever complain about your involvement with drugs? | Yes _____ No _____ |
| Have you neglected your family because of your use of drugs? | Yes _____ No _____ |
| Have you engaged in illegal activities to obtain drugs? | Yes _____ No _____ |
| Have you ever experienced withdrawal symptoms (felt sick) when you stopped taking drugs? | Yes _____ No _____ |
| Have you had medical problems as a result of your drug use (e.g., memory loss, hepatitis, convulsions, bleeding, etc.)? | Yes _____ No _____ |
| **Scoring**: 1 positive response warrants further evaluation. | Yes _____ No _____ |

From Skinner, H.A. (1982). *Drug Abuse Screening Test (DAST)* Langford Lance, England: Elsevier Science, p. 363; reprinted with permission.

# APPENDIX D-8: CRITERIA FOR HOSPITALIZATION FOR EATING DISORDERS

## PHYSICAL CRITERIA

1. Weight loss over 30% over 6 months
2. Rapid decline in weight
3. Severe hypothermia as a result of loss of subcutaneous tissue or dehydration (temperature less than 36 °C or 96.8 °F)
4. Inability to gain weight repeatedly with outpatient treatment
5. Heart rate less than 40 beats/minute
6. Systolic blood pressure less than 70 mm Hg
7. Hypokalemia (potassium under 3 mEq/L) or other electrolyte disturbances not corrected by oral supplementation
8. Electrocardiograph changes (especially arrhythmias)

## PSYCHIATRIC CRITERIA

1. Suicidal or severely out-of-control self-mutilating behaviors
2. Out-of-control use of laxatives, emetics, diuretics, or street drugs
3. Failure to comply with treatment contract
4. Severe depression
5. Psychosis
6. Family crisis/dysfunction

# APPENDIX D-9: FUNCTIONAL DEMENTIA SCALE

Circle one rating for each item:
1. None or little of the time
2. Some of the time
3. Good part of the time
4. Most or all of the time

Client_____
Observer_____
Position or relation to
  patient_____
Facility_____
Date_____

| 1 | 2 | 3 | 4 | (1) Has difficulty in completing simple tasks on own (e.g., dressing, bathing, doing arithmetic). |
| 1 | 2 | 3 | 4 | (2) Spends time either sitting or in apparently purposeless activity. |
| 1 | 2 | 3 | 4 | (3) Wanders at night or needs to be restrained to prevent wandering. |
| 1 | 2 | 3 | 4 | (4) Hears things that are not there. |
| 1 | 2 | 3 | 4 | (5) Requires supervision or assistance in eating. |
| 1 | 2 | 3 | 4 | (6) Loses things. |
| 1 | 2 | 3 | 4 | (7) Appearance is disorderly if left to own devices. |
| 1 | 2 | 3 | 4 | (8) Moans. |
| 1 | 2 | 3 | 4 | (9) Cannot control bowel function. |
| 1 | 2 | 3 | 4 | (10) Threatens to harm others. |
| 1 | 2 | 3 | 4 | (11) Cannot control bladder function. |
| 1 | 2 | 3 | 4 | (12) Needs to be watched so doesn't injure self (e.g., by careless smoking, leaving the stove on, falling). |
| 1 | 2 | 3 | 4 | (13) Destructs materials around him/her (e.g., breaks furniture, throws food trays, tears up magazines). |
| 1 | 2 | 3 | 4 | (14) Shouts or yells. |
| 1 | 2 | 3 | 4 | (15) Accuses others of doing him bodily harm or stealing his/her possessions—when you are sure the accusations are not true. |
| 1 | 2 | 3 | 4 | (16) Is unaware of limitations imposed by illness. |
| 1 | 2 | 3 | 4 | (17) Becomes confused and does not know where he/she is. |
| 1 | 2 | 3 | 4 | (18) Has trouble remembering. |
| 1 | 2 | 3 | 4 | (19) Has sudden changes of mood (e.g., gets upset, angered, or cries easily). |
| 1 | 2 | 3 | 4 | (20) If left alone, wanders aimlessly during the day or needs to be restrained to prevent wandering. |

# APPENDIX D-10: LIFE CHANGE EVENTS

| Life Change | Life-Changing Event Unit (LCU) |
|---|---|
| **Health** | |
| An injury or illness that: | 74 |
| Kept you in bed a week or more, or sent you to the hospital | 44 |
| Was less serious than above | |
| Major dental work | 26 |
| Major change in eating habits | 27 |
| Major change in sleep habits | 26 |
| Major change in your usual type and/or amount of recreation | 28 |
| | |
| **Work** | |
| Change to a new type of work | 51 |
| Change in your work hours or conditions | 35 |
| Change in your responsibilities at work: | |
| More responsibilities | 29 |
| Fewer responsibilities | 21 |
| Promotion | 31 |
| Demotion | 42 |
| Transfer | 32 |
| Troubles at work: | |
| With your boss | 29 |
| With coworkers | 35 |
| With persons under your supervision | 35 |
| Other work troubles | 28 |
| Major business adjustment | 60 |
| Retirement | 52 |
| Loss of job: | |
| Laid off from work | 68 |
| Fired from work | 79 |
| Correspondence course to help you in your work | 18 |
| | |
| **Home and Family** | |
| Major change in living conditions | 42 |
| Change in residence: | |
| Move within the same town or city | 25 |
| Move to a different town, city, or state | 47 |
| Change in family get-togethers | 25 |

| Life Change | Life-Changing Event Unit (LCU) |
|---|---|
| Major change in health or behavior of family member | 55 |
| Marriage | 50 |
| Pregnancy | 67 |
| Miscarriage or abortion | 65 |
| Gain of a new family member: | |
| Birth of a child | 66 |
| Adoption of a child | 65 |
| A relative moving in with you | 59 |
| Spouse beginning or ending work | 46 |
| Child leaving home: | |
| To attend college | 41 |
| Due to marriage | 41 |
| For other reasons | 45 |
| Change in arguments with spouse | 50 |
| In-law problems | 38 |
| Change in the marital status of your parents: | |
| Divorce | 59 |
| Remarriage | 50 |
| Separation from spouse: | |
| Due to work | 53 |
| Due to marital problems | 76 |
| Divorce | 96 |
| Birth of a grandchild | 43 |
| Death of spouse | 119 |
| Death of other family member: | |
| Child | 123 |
| Brother or sister | 102 |
| Parent | 100 |
| **Personal and Social** | |
| Change in personal habits | 26 |
| Beginning or ending school or college | 38 |
| Change of school or college | 35 |
| Change in political beliefs | 24 |
| Change in religious beliefs | 29 |
| Change in social activities | 27 |
| Vacation | 24 |
| New close personal relationship | 37 |
| Engagement to marry | 45 |
| Girlfriend or boyfriend problems | 39 |
| Sexual differences | 44 |

*Continued*

| Life Change | Life-Changing Event Unit (LCU) |
|---|---|
| "Falling out" of a close personal relationship | 47 |
| An accident | 48 |
| Minor violation of the law | 20 |
| Being held in jail | 75 |
| Death of a close friend | 70 |
| Major decision regarding your immediate future | 51 |
| Major personal achievement | 36 |
| **Financial** | |
| Major change in finances: | |
|   Increase in income | 38 |
|   Decrease in income | 60 |
|   Investment and/or credit difficulties | 56 |
| Loss or damage of personal property | 43 |
| Moderate purchase | 20 |
| Major purchase | 37 |
| Foreclosure on a mortgage or loan | 58 |

Six-month totals ≥300 LCUs or 1-year totals ≥500 LCUs are considered indications of high recent life stress.
From Miller, M.A., & Rahe, R.H. (1997). Life changes scaling for the 1990s. *Journal of Psychosomatic Research, 43*(3), 279–292.

# APPENDIX D-11: ABUSE ASSESSMENT SCREEN

1. Have you ever been emotionally or physically abused by your partner or someone important to you?
   Yes _____    No _____
   If yes, by whom?  _____
   Number of times  _____
2. Within the past year, have you been hit, slapped, kicked, or otherwise physically hurt by someone?
   Yes _____    No _____
   If yes, by whom?  _____
   Number of times  _____

3. Since you have been pregnant, have you been hit, slapped, kicked, or otherwise physically hurt by someone?
   Yes _____  No _____
   If yes, by whom?  _____
   Number of times  _____
4. Within the past year, has anyone forced you to have sexual activities?
   Yes _____  No _____
   If yes, by whom?  _____
   Number of times  _____
5. Are you afraid of your partner or anyone listed above?
   Yes _____  No _____

---

The Abuse Assessment Screen was developed by the Nursing Research Consortium on Violence and Abuse (1989). Its reproduction and use is encouraged. Used with permission of Peace at Home, Boston, Massachusetts.

# APPENDIX D-12: SAD PERSON'S SCALE

| | | |
|---|---|---|
| S | Sex | Men are three times more likely to kill themselves than women, although women make attempts three times more often than men. |
| A | Age | High-risk groups: 19 years or younger; 45 years or older, especially the elderly (65 years or older). |
| D | Depression | Studies report that 35% to 79% of those who attempt suicide manifested a depressive syndrome. |
| P | Previous attempts | Of those who commit suicide, 65% to 70% have made previous attempts. |
| E | ETOH | ETOH (alcohol) is associated with up to 65% of successful suicides. Estimates are that 15% of alcoholics commit suicide. Heavy drug use is considered to be in this group and is given the same weight as alcohol. |
| R | Rational thinking loss | People with functional or organic psychoses (schizophrenia, dementia) are more apt to commit suicide than those in the general population. |

*Continued*

| S | Social supports lacking | A suicidal person often lacks significant others (friends, relatives), meaningful employment, and religious or spiritual supports. All three of these areas need to be assessed. |
| O | Organized plan | The presence of a specific plan for suicide (date, place, means) signifies a person at high risk. |
| N | No spouse | Repeated studies indicate that people who are widowed, separated, divorced, or single are at greater risk than those who are married. |
| S | Sickness | Chronic, debilitating, and severe illness is a risk factor. Suicide risk is two times higher among people with cancer and is high among AIDS clients; clients on hemodialysis or with DTs and respiratory diseases are all at high risk. |

| **Points** | **Guidelines for Points Intervention** |
| --- | --- |
| 0–2 | Treat at home with follow-up care. |
| 3–4 | Closely follow up and consider possible hospitalization. |
| 5–6 | Strongly consider hospitalization. |
| 7–10 | Hospitalize. |

Adapted from Patterson, W., et al. (1983). Evaluation of suicidal patients: The SAD PERSONS Scale. *Psychosomatics, 24*(4), 343; reprinted with permission.

# APPENDIX D-13: OVERT AGGRESSION SCALE

## VERBAL AGGRESSION

_____ Makes loud noises, shouts angrily
_____ Yells mild personal insults (e.g., "You're stupid.")
_____ Curses viciously, uses foul language in anger, makes moderate threats to others or self
_____ Makes clear threats of violence towards others or self ("I'm gonna kill you.") or requests help to control self

# PHYSICAL AGGRESSION AGAINST OBJECTS

_____ Slams doors, scatters clothing, makes a mess
_____ Throws objects down, kicks furniture without breaking it, marks the wall
_____ Breaks objects, smashes window
_____ Sets fires, throws objects dangerously

# PHYSICAL AGGRESSION AGAINST SELF

_____ Picks or scratches skin, hits self, pulls hair (with no or minor injury only)
_____ Bangs head, hits fist into objects, throws self onto floor or onto objects (hurts self without serious injury)
_____ Small cuts or bruises, minor burns
_____ Mutilates self; causes deep cuts, bites that bleed, internal injury, fracture, loss of consciousness, loss of teeth

# PHYSICAL AGGRESSION AGAINST OTHER PEOPLE

_____ Makes threatening gesture, swings at people, grabs at clothes
_____ Strikes, kicks, pushes, pulls hair (without injury to them)
_____ Attacks others, causing mild to moderate physical injury (bruises, sprain, welts)
_____ Attacks others, causing severe physical injury (broken bones, deep lacerations, internal injury)

From Yudofsky, S.C., Silver, J.M., Jackson, W., et al. (1986). The Overt Aggression Scale for the objective rating of verbal and physical aggression. _American Journal of Psychiatry, 143_, 35–39; reprinted with permission. Copyright © 1986 by the American Psychiatric Association; http://ajp.psychiatry online.org.

# APPENDIX E

# Abnormal Involuntary Movement Scale (AIMS)

NAME: _____

DATE: _____

Prescribing Practitioner: _____

Public Health Service

Alcohol, Drug Abuse, and

Mental Health Administration

National Institute of Mental Health

CODE: 0 = None

1 = Minimal, may be extreme normal

2 = Mild

3 = Moderate

4 = Severe

INSTRUCTIONS:

Complete examination procedure before making ratings

MOVEMENT RATINGS:

Rate highest severity observed.

Rate movements that occur upon

activation one less than those

observed spontaneously.

Circle movement as well as code

number that applies.

Facial and Oral Movements

| | Rater | Rater |
|---|---|---|
| | Date | Date |
| 1. Muscles of facial expression (e.g., movements of forehead, eyebrows periorbital area, cheeks, including frowning, blinking, smiling, grimacing) | 0 1 2 3 4 | 0 1 2 3 4 |

*Continued*

| | | |
|---|---|---|
| 2. Lips and perioral area (e.g., puckering, pouting, smacking) | 0 1 2 3 4 | 0 1 2 3 4 |
| 3. Jaw (e.g., biting, clenching, chewing, mouth opening, lateral movement) | 0 1 2 3 4 | 0 1 2 3 4 |
| 4. Tongue: Rate only increases in movement both in and out of mouth, not inability to sustain movement. Darting in and out of mouth. | 0 1 2 3 4 | 0 1 2 3 4 |

**Extremity Movements**

| | | |
|---|---|---|
| 5. Upper (arms, wrists, hands, fingers): Include choreic movements (i.e., rapid, objectively purposeless, irregular, spontaneous) and athetoid movements (i.e., slow, irregular, complex, serpentine). Do not include tremor (i.e., repetitive, regular, rhythmic). | 0 1 2 3 4 | 0 1 2 3 4 |
| 6. Lower (legs, knees, ankles, toes) (e.g., lateral knee movement, foot tapping, heel dropping, foot squirming, inversion and eversion of foot) | 0 1 2 3 4 | 0 1 2 3 4 |

**Trunk Movements**

| | | |
|---|---|---|
| 7. Neck, shoulders, hips (e.g., rocking, twisting, squirming, pelvic gyrations) | 0 1 2 3 4 | 0 1 2 3 4 |

| Global Judgments | 8. Severity of abnormal movements overall | 0 1 2 3 4 | 0 1 2 3 4 |
| | 9. Incapacitation due to abnormal movements | 0 1 2 3 4 | 0 1 2 3 4 |
| | 10. Patient's awareness of abnormal movements. Rate only patient's report.<br>No awareness<br>Aware, no distress<br>Aware, mild distress<br>Aware, moderate distress<br>Aware, severe distress | 0 1 2 3 4 | 0 1 2 3 4 |
| Dental Status | 11. Current problems with teeth and/or dentures | No Yes | No Yes |
| | 12. Are dentures usually worn? | No Yes | No Yes |
| | 13. Edentia? | No Yes | No Yes |
| | 14. Do movements disappear in sleep? | No Yes | No Yes |

## AIMS EXAMINATION PROCEDURE

Either before or after completing the Examination Procedure, observe the patient unobtrusively, at rest (e.g., in waiting room).

The chair to be used in this examination should be a hard, firm one without arms.

1. Ask patient whether there is anything in his/her mouth (i.e., gum, candy) and if there is, to remove it.
2. Ask patient about the current condition of his/her teeth. Ask patient if he/she wears dentures. Do teeth or denture bother patient now?
3. Ask patient whether he/she notices any movements in mouth, face, hands, or feet. If yes, ask to describe and to what extent they currently bother patient or interfere with his/her activities.
4. Have patient sit in chair with hands on knees, legs slightly apart, and feet flat on floor. (Look at entire body for movements while in this position.)
5. Ask patient to sit with hands hanging unsupported. If male, between legs; if female and wearing a dress, hanging over knees. (Observe hands and other body areas.)
6. Ask patient to open mouth. (Observe tongue at rest within mouth.) Do this twice.
7. Ask patient to protrude tongue. (Observe abnormalities of tongue movement.) Do this twice.
8. *Ask patient to tap thumb with each finger as rapidly as possible for 10 to 15 seconds; separately with right hand, then with left hand. (Observe facial and leg movement.)
9. Flex and extend patient's left and right arms (one at a time). (Note any rigidity.)
10. Ask patient to stand up. (Observe in profile. Observe all body areas again, hips included.)
11. *Ask patient to extend both arms outstretched in front with palms down. (Observe trunk, legs, and mouth.)
12. *Have patient walk a few paces, turn, and walk back to chair. (Observe hands and gait.) Do this twice.

---

*Activated movements.

# APPENDIX F

# Nursing Care in Electroconvulsive Therapy

| 1. Emotional and educational support to the client and family | 1a. Encourage the client to discuss feelings, including myths regarding ECT.<br>1b. Teach the client and the family what to expect with ECT. |
|---|---|
| 2. Pretreatment protocol | 2a. Ascertain if the client and the family have received a full explanation, including the option to withdraw the consent at any time.<br>2b. Pretreatment care:<br>&bull; Withhold food and fluids for 6 to 8 hours before treatment. (Cardiac medication is given with sips of water.)<br>&bull; Remove dentures, glasses, hearing aids, contact lenses, hairpins, and so on.<br>&bull; Have client void before treatment. |

| | |
|---|---|
| | 2c. Preoperative medications (if ordered):<br>• Give either glycopyrrolate (Robinul) or atropine to prevent potential for aspiration and to help minimize bradyarrhythmias in response to electrical stimulants. |
| 3. Nursing care during the procedure | 3a. Place a blood pressure cuff on one of the client's arms.<br>3b. As the intravenous line is inserted and EEG and ECG electrodes are attached, give a brief explanation to the client.<br>3c. Clip the pulse oximeter to the client's finger.<br>3d. Monitor blood pressure throughout treatment.<br>3e. Medications given:<br>• Short-acting anesthetic (methohexital sodium [Brevital], thiopental [Pentothal])<br>• Muscle relaxant (succinylcholine [Anectine])<br>• 100% oxygen by mask via positive pressure throughout<br>3f. Check that the bite block is in place to prevent biting of the tongue.<br>3g. Electrical stimulus given (seizure should last 30 to 60 seconds). |

*Continued*

| 4. Posttreatment nursing care | 4a. Have the client go to a properly staffed recovery room (with blood pressure cuff and oximeter in place) where oxygen, suction, and other emergency equipment is available. |
| --- | --- |
| | 4b. Once the client is awake, talk to the client and check vital signs. |
| | 4c. Often the client is confused, so give frequent orientation reassurance. Orientation statements are brief, distinct, and simple. |
| | 4d. Return the client to the unit after he or she has maintained a 90% oxygen saturation level, vital signs are stable, and mental status is satisfactory. |
| | 4e. Check the gag reflex before giving the client fluids, medicine, or breakfast. |

*ECG,* Electrocardiographic; *ECT,* electroconvulsive therapy; *EEG,* electroencephalographic.
Data from Burns, C.M., & Stuart, G.W. (1991). Nursing care in electroconvulsive therapy. *Psychiatric Clinics of North America, 14*(4), 971.

# Index

Note: Page numbers followed by *f* indicates figures, *b* indicates boxes and *t* indicates tables.

715

## O

# NURSING CARE PLANS